Periodic Table of the Elements

Main groups

1 1A	2 2A		3 3B	4 4B	5 5B	6 6B	7 7B	8	9 8B	10	11 1B	12 2B	13 3A	14 4A	15 5A	16 6A	17 7A	18 8A
1 H 1.00794																		2 He 4.002602
3 Li 6.941	4 Be 9.012182												5 B 10.811	6 C 12.0107	7 N 14.0067	8 O 15.9994	9 F 18.998403	10 Ne 20.1797
11 Na 22.989770	12 Mg 24.3050												13 Al 26.981538	14 Si 28.0855	15 P 30.973761	16 S 32.065	17 Cl 35.453	18 Ar 39.948
19 K 39.0983	20 Ca 40.078		21 Sc 44.955910	22 Ti 47.867	23 V 50.9415	24 Cr 51.9961	25 Mn 54.938049	26 Fe 55.845	27 Co 58.933200	28 Ni 58.6934	29 Cu 63.546	30 Zn 65.38	31 Ga 69.723	32 Ge 72.64	33 As 74.92160	34 Se 78.96	35 Br 79.904	36 Kr 83.798
37 Rb 85.4678	38 Sr 87.62		39 Y 88.90585	40 Zr 91.224	41 Nb 92.90638	42 Mo 95.94	43 Tc (98)	44 Ru 101.07	45 Rh 102.90550	46 Pd 106.42	47 Ag 107.8582	48 Cd 112.411	49 In 114.818	50 Sn 118.710	51 Sb 121.760	52 Te 127.60	53 I 126.90447	54 Xe 131.293
55 Cs 132.90545	56 Ba 137.327		71 Lu 174.9668	72 Hf 178.49	73 Ta 180.9479	74 W 183.84	75 Re 186.207	76 Os 190.23	77 Ir 192.217	78 Pt 195.078	79 Au 196.96655	80 Hg 200.59	81 Tl 204.3833	82 Pb 207.2	83 Bi 208.98038	84 Po (209)	85 At (210)	86 Rn (222)
87 Fr (223)	88 Ra (226)		103 Lr (262)	104 Rf (267)	105 Db (268)	106 Sg (271)	107 Bh (272)	108 Hs (277)	109 Mt (276)	110 Ds (281)	111 Rg (280)	112 Cn (285)	113 (284)	114 (289)	115 (288)	116 (293)	117 (293)	118 (294)

Transition metals

*Lanthanide series

57 *La 138.9055	58 Ce 140.116	59 Pr 140.90765	60 Nd 144.24	61 Pm (145)	62 Sm 150.36	63 Eu 151.964	64 Gd 157.25	65 Tb 158.92534	66 Dy 162.500	67 Ho 164.93032	68 Er 167.259	69 Tm 168.93421	70 Yb 173.054

†Actinide series

89 †Ac (227)	90 Th 232.0381	91 Pa 231.03588	92 U 238.02891	93 Np (237)	94 Pu (244)	95 Am (243)	96 Cm (247)	97 Bk (247)	98 Cf (251)	99 Es (252)	100 Fm (257)	101 Md (258)	102 No (259)

Mastering CHEMISTRY®

Dear Student:

In this course you will be using MasteringChemistry®, an online tutorial and homework program that accompanies your textbook. *If you have joined a MasteringChemistry course before and can still log in*: Save time by following the guide for joining another course (available from www.masteringchemistry.com > Tours & Training > Getting Started) instead of this page.

What You Need:

- ✓ **A valid email address**
- ✓ **A student access code**
  (Comes in the Student Access Code Card/Kit that may have been packaged with your new textbook or that may be available separately in your school's bookstore. Otherwise, you can purchase access online at www.masteringchemistry.com.)
- ✓ **The ZIP or other postal code for your school: 95929**
- ✓ **A Course ID:** _____ (Provided by your instructor)

1. Register

- Go to www.masteringchemistry.com and click **Students** under **Register**.
- To register using the student access code inside the MasteringChemistry Student Access Code Card/Kit, select **Yes, I have an access code**. Click **Continue**.

  –OR– *Purchase access online*: Select **No, I need to purchase access online now**. Select your textbook, whether you want access to the eText, and click **Continue**. Follow the on-screen instructions to purchase access using a credit card. The purchase path includes registration, but the process is a bit different from the steps printed here.

- **License Agreement and Privacy Policy:** Click **I Accept** to indicate that you have read and agree to the license agreement and privacy policy.
- Select the appropriate option under "Do you have a Pearson Education account?" Continue to give the requested information until you complete the process. The **Confirmation & Summary** page confirms your registration. This information will also be emailed to you for your records. You can either click **Log In Now** or return to www.masteringchemistry.com later.

2. Log In

- Go to www.masteringchemistry.com.
- Enter your Login Name and Password that you specified during registration and click **Log In**.

3. Join Your Instructor's Online Course and/or Open Self-Study Resources

Upon first login, you'll be asked to do one or more of the following:

- **Join a Course** by entering the **MasteringChemistry Course ID** provided by your instructor. If you don't have a Course ID now, you can return to join the MasteringChemistry course later. When you join a course, you may also be asked for a Student ID (follow on-screen instructions).
- **Explore the Study Area** or **Launch Your eText**, if these resources are available for your textbook.

To Access MasteringChemistry Again Later

Simply go to www.masteringchemistry.com, enter your Login Name and Password, and click **Log In**.

After you have joined a course: You can open any assignments from the **Assignments Due Soon** area or from the **Assignments** page. For self-study, click **eText** or **Study Area**, if these options are available.

Support

Access Customer Support at http://www.masteringchemistry.com/support, where you will find:

- System Requirements
- Answers to Frequently Asked Questions
- Registration Tips & Tricks video
- Additional contact information for Customer Support, including Live Chat

ALWAYS LEARNING   PEARSON

John E. McMurry • Robert C. Fay

With Contributions by Jordan Fantini

Chemistry

Custom Edition for California State University at Chico

Taken from:
Chemistry, Sixth Edition
by John E. McMurry and Robert C. Fay

Cover Art: Courtesy of PhotoDisc/Getty Images.

Taken from:

Chemistry, Sixth Edition
by John E. McMurry and Robert C. Fay
Copyright © 2012, 2008, 2004, 2001 by Pearson Education, Inc.
Published by Prentice Hall
Upper Saddle River, New Jersey 07458

This special edition published in cooperation with Pearson Learning Solutions.

Pearson Learning Solutions, 501 Boylston Street, Suite 900, Boston, MA 02116
A Pearson Education Company
www.pearsoned.com

Printed in the United States of America

10 11 12 13 V0CR 16 15 14

000200010270762521

MP

ISBN 10: 1-256-16087-3
ISBN 13: 978-1-256-16087-8

Brief Contents

Contents

8   Thermochemistry: Chemical Energy   266

9   Gases: Their Properties and Behavior   308

10   Liquids, Solids, and Phase Changes   346

11 Solutions and Their Properties   392

12 Chemical Kinetics   432

13 Chemical Equilibrium   492

22 Nuclear Chemistry   888

Inquiries

Applications

Preface

Francie came away from her first chemistry lecture in a glow. In one hour she found out that everything was made up of atoms which were in continual motion. She grasped the idea that nothing was ever lost or destroyed. Even if something was burned up or rotted away, it did not disappear from the face of the earth; it changed into something else—gases, liquids, and powders. Everything, decided Francie after that first lecture, was vibrant with life and there was no death in chemistry. She was puzzled as to why learned people didn't adopt chemistry as a religion.

—Betty Smith, *A Tree Grows in Brooklyn*

OK, not everyone has such a breathless response to their chemistry lectures, and few would mistake chemistry for a religion, yet chemistry *is* a subject with great logical beauty. Moreover, chemistry is the fundamental, enabling science that underlies many of the great advances of the last century that have so lengthened and enriched our lives. It's study truly can be a fascinating experience.

ABOUT THIS BOOK

Our primary purpose in writing this book has been to fashion a clear and cohesive introduction to chemistry, covering both important principles and important facts. We write to explain chemistry to students today the way we wish it had been explained to us years ago when we were students ourselves. We can't claim that learning chemistry will always be easy, but we *can* promise that we have done our best in planning, writing, and illustrating this book to make the learning process as smooth as possible.

Beginning with atomic structure, the book proceeds to bonding, molecules, and bulk physical properties of substances, and then continues with all the topics necessary for a study of chemical transformations—kinetics, equilibrium, thermodynamics, and electrochemistry. The concepts described in earlier chapters are then applied to discussing more specialized topics, including the chemistry of main-group and transition elements, metals, and modern solid-state materials. Finally, the book concludes with a brief look at organic and biological chemistry.

To help students succeed in learning chemistry, we have put extraordinary effort into this book. Transitions between topics are smooth, explanations are lucid, and reminders of earlier material are frequent. Insofar as possible, distractions within the text are minimized. Each chapter is broken into numerous sections to provide frequent breathers, and each section has a consistent format. Sections generally begin with an explanation of their subject, move to a Worked Example that shows how to solve problems, and end with one or more Problems for the reader to work through. Each chapter concludes with a brief Inquiry that describes an interesting application or extension of the chapter topic. Throughout the book, every attempt has been made to explain chemistry in a visual, intuitive way so that it can be understood by all who give it an honest effort.

NEW TO THE 6th EDITION

In preparing this 6th edition, we have reworked the entire book at the sentence level and made many hundreds of alterations, updates, and small reorganizations to make it as easy as possible for our readers to understand and learn chemistry. In addition, a number of more substantial changes, reorganizations, and rewrites have been made. Among them are the following:

- The text is now shorter than the previous edition by 60 pages.

- Chapter 18 (*Hydrogen, Oxygen and Water*) has been streamlined throughout, and the former Section 18.14 on reactivity of water has been deleted.

- Chapter 19 (*Main-Group Elements*) has been shortened by removing the former Section 19.8 on germanium, tin, and lead, eliminating the coverage of polyphosphoric acids, and integrating the former material on the Haber ammonia synthesis into earlier chapters. Brief discussions of aluminum (Section 19.5) and graphene (Section 19.7) have been added.

- Chapter 22 (*Nuclear Chemistry*) has been shortened and reorganized to focus on the energy changes that take place during nuclear reactions and on fission, fusion, nuclear transmutation, and applications of nuclear chemistry. The former introductory material on nuclear reactions has been moved into Chapter 2 (*Atoms, Molecules, and Ions*), and the coverage of radioactive decay rates has been moved into Chapter 12 (*Chemical Kinetics*).

- The former Chapters 23 and 24 (*Organic Chemistry* and *Biochemistry*) have been shortened and integrated into a new Chapter 23 (*Organic and Biological Chemistry.*)

- Energy and its measurement have moved from Chapter 8 to Chapter 1, and the mole concept has moved from Chapter 3 to Chapter 2 to introduce these important topics earlier.

- Problems and problem solving have also received attention, and more than 300 new problems have been added. The 1st edition of this book pioneered the use of visual, non-numerical, Conceptual Problems, which test the understanding of principles rather than the ability to put numbers into a formula. Every subsequent edition has expanded their use. Don't make the mistake of thinking that these Conceptual Problems are simple just because they don't have numbers. Many are real challenges that will test the ability of any student.

- The art in this new edition has been improved in many ways to make the numbered figures more self-contained, informative, and easily read:
  - The boundaries of numbered figures are more clearly distinguished.
  - The figure numbers are called out in bold red print in the text so that it's easy to find the text corresponding to a given figure.
  - Internal art captions are set off in a different font from art labels so that students can more readily grasp the main points of each illustration.
  - Numerous small explanations are placed directly on the relevant parts of the figures themselves instead of having long captions beneath figures. The effect is to make the text flow naturally into the figures and thereby entice readers to spend more time understanding those figures.
  - Important text within the illustrations is color-coded to focus attention on it.

- The best features of previous editions have been retained:
  - The design remains spacious, readable, and unintimidating.
  - The writing style remains clear and concise.
  - Remember... notes to help students connect concepts from previous chapters to new contexts in subsequent chapters.
  - Worked problems are identified by subject and are immediately followed by a similar problem for students to solve.
  - Each chapter ends with a summary, a list of key words with accompanying page references, and a large set of end-of-chapter problems.
  - Most end-of-chapter problems are classified by text section and paired by topic. These are followed by a group of unclassified Chapter Problems and a final set of Multiconcept Problems, which draw on and connect concepts from several chapters.

We sincerely hope that this new edition will meet the goals we have set for it and that both students and faculty will find it to be friendly, accessible, and above all effective in teaching chemistry.

ACKNOWLEDGEMENTS

Our thanks go to our families and to the many talented people who helped bring this new edition into being. Foremost is Jordan Fantini of Denison University, who joined us as a contributing author for this edition. Jordan offered valuable input on every chapter, wrote many new end-of chapter problems, and wrote several new *INQUIRY* essays. In addition, we are grateful to Terry Haugen, Acquisitions Editor, and Carol DuPont, Assistant Editor, for their insights and suggestions that improved the book, to Erin Gardner, Marketing Manager, who brought new energy to marketing the sixth edition, to Carol Pritchard-Martinez for her work in improving the art program and manuscript development, to Wendy Perez and Gina Cheselka for their production efforts, and to Eric Schrader for his photo research.

We are particularly pleased to acknowledge the outstanding contributions of several colleagues who created the many important supplements that turn a textbook into a complete package:

- Robert Pribush at Butler University, who prepared the accompanying Test Bank and created the Instructor Resource Manual.
- Joseph Topich at Virginia Commonwealth University, who prepared both the full and partial solutions manuals
- Alan Earhart at Southeast Community College and Bradley J. Sieve at Northern Kentucky University, who contributed valuable content for the Instructor Resource DVD.
- Julie Klare at Gwinnett Technical College, who prepared the Student Study Guide to accompany this sixth edition.

In addition, we are grateful to Mingming Xu of West Virginia University and Matt Wise of the University of Colorado at Boulder for error checking the entire text.

Finally, we want to thank our colleagues at so many other institutions who read, criticized, and improved our work.

John McMurry
Robert C. Fay

REVIEWERS OF THE SIXTH EDITION OF *CHEMISTRY*

Tabitha Ruvarashe Chigwada, *West Virginia University*
Claire Cohen-Schmidt, *University of Toledo*
Kyle Wesley Felling, *University of Central Arkansas*
Milton D. Johnston, Jr., *University of South Florida*
Jerome B. Keister, *State University of New York–Buffalo*

Angela J. Nealy, M.S., *MedTech College*
Jennifer Robertson-Honecker, *West Virginia University*
Robert L. Swofford, *Wake Forest University*
Mingming Xu, *West Virginia University*
James Zubricky, *University of Toledo*

REVIEWERS OF THE PREVIOUS EDITIONS OF *CHEMISTRY*

Laura Andersson, *Big Bend Community College*
David Atwood, *University of Kentucky*
Mufeed Basti, *North Carolina A&T State University*
David S. Ballantine, *Northern Illinois University*
Debbie Beard, *Mississippi State University*
Ronald Bost, *North Central Texas University*
Danielle Brabazon, *Loyola College*
Robert Burk, *Carleton University*
Myron Cherry, *Northeastern State University*
Allen Clabo, *Francis Marion University*
Paul Cohen, *University of New Jersey*
Katherine Covert, *West Virginia University*
David De Haan, *University of San Diego*
Nordulf W. G. Debye, *Towson University*
Dean Dickerhoof, *Colorado School of Mines*
Kenneth Dorris, *Lamar University*
Jon A. Draeger, *University of Pittsburgh at Bradford*
Brian Earle, *Cedar Valley College*
Amina El- Ashmawy, *Collin County Community College*
Joseph W. Ellison, *United States Military Academy at West Point*
Erik Eriksson, *College of the Canyons*
Peter M. Fichte, *Coker College*
Kathy Flynn, *College of the Canyons*
Joanne Follweiler, *Lafayette College*
Ted Foster, *Folsom Lake College*
Cheryl Frech, *University of Central Oklahoma*
Mark Freilich, *University of Memphis*
Mark Freitag, *Creighton University*
Travis Fridgen, *Memorial University of Newfoundland*
Jack Goldsmith, *University of South Carolina Aiken*
Thomas Grow, *Pensacola Junior College*
Katherine Geiser-Bush, *Durham Technical Community College*
Mildred Hall, *Clark State University*
Tracy A. Halmi, *Pennsylvania State University Erie*
Keith Hansen, *Lamar University*
Lois Hansen-Polcar, *Cuyahoga Community College*
Wesley Hanson, *John Brown University*
Michael Hauser, *St. Louis Community College–Meramec*
M. Dale Hawley, *Kansas State University*
Patricia Heiden, *Michigan Tech University*
Thomas Hermann, *University of California–San Diego*
Thomas Herrington, *University of San Diego*
Margaret E. Holzer, *California State University–Northridge*
Todd Hopkins, *Baylor University*
Narayan S. Hosmane, *Northern Illinois University*
Jeff Joens, *Florida International University*
Jerry Keister, *University of Buffalo*
Chulsung Kim, *University of Dubuque*
Ranjit Koodali, *University of South Dakota*

Valerie Land, *University of Arkansas Community College*
John Landrum, *Florida International University*
Leroy Laverman, *University of California–Santa Barbara*
Celestia Lau, *Lorain County Community College*
Stephen S. Lawrence, *Saginaw Valley State University*
David Leddy, *Michigan Technological University*
Shannon Lieb, *Butler University*
Karen Linscott, *Tri-County Technical College*
Irving Lipschitz, *University of Massachusetts–Lowell*
Rudy Luck, *Michigan Technological University*
Ashley Mahoney, *Bethel College*
Jack F. McKenna, *St. Cloud State University*
Iain McNab, *University of Toronto*
Christina Mewhinney, *Eastfield College*
David Miller, *California State University–Northridge*
Rebecca S. Miller, *Texas Tech University*
Abdul Mohammed, *North Carolina A&T State University*
Linda Mona, *United States Naval Academy*
Edward Mottell, *Rose-Hulman Institute*
Gayle Nicoll, *Texas Technological University*
Allyn Ontko, *University of Wyoming*
Robert H. Paine, *Rochester Institute of Technology*
Cynthia N. Peck, *Delta College*
Eileen Pérez, *University of South Florida*
Michael R. Ross, *College of St. Benedict/St. John's University*
Lev Ryzhkov, *Towson University*
Svein Saebo, *Mississippi State University*
John Schreifels, *George Mason University*
Patricia Schroeder, *Johnson County Community College*
David Shoop, *John Brown University*
Penny Snetsinger, *Sacred Heart University*
Robert L. Snipp, *Creighton University*
Steven M. Socol, *McHenry County College*
Thomas E. Sorensen, *University of Wisconsin–Milwaukee*
L. Sreerama, *St. Cloud State University*
Keith Stein, *University of Missouri–St. Louis*
Beth Steiner, *University of Akron*
Kelly Sullivan, *Creighton University*
Susan Sutheimer, *Green Mountain College*
Andrew Sykes, *University of South Dakota*
Erach Talaty, *Wichita State University*
Edwin Thall, *Florida Community College at Jacksonville*
Donald Van Derveer, *Georgia Institute of Technology*
John B. Vincent, *University of Alabama*
Steve Watton, *Virginia Commonwealth University*
Marcy Whitney, *University of Alabama*
James Wu, *Tarrant County Community College*
Crystal Lin Yau, *Towson University*

Supplements

FOR THE STUDENT

MasteringChemistry® (http://www.masteringchemistry.com) is the most effective, widely used online tutorial, homework and assessment system for chemistry. It helps instructors maximize class time with customizable, easy-to-assign, and automatically graded assessments that motivate students to learn outside of class and arrive prepared for lecture. These assessments can easily be customized and personalized by instructors to suit their individual teaching style. The powerful gradebook provides unique insight into student and class performance even before the first test. As a result, instructors can spend class time where students need it most.

Pearson eText. Pearson eText gives students access to the text whenever and wherever they have access to the Internet. The Pearson eText pages look exactly like the printed text, and include powerful interactive and customization functions. Users can create notes, highlight text, create book marks, zoom, view in single-page or two-page format, and so forth.

Selected Solutions Manual (0-321-72726-6) by Joseph Topich, Virginia Commonwealth University. This manual contains solutions to all in-chapter problems and even-numbered end-of-chapter problems.

Study Guide (0-321-72724-X) by Julie Klare at Gwinnett Technical College. For each chapter, the Study Guide includes learning goals, an overview, progressive review section with worked examples, and self-tests with answers.

Laboratory Manual (0-321-72720-7) by Stephanie Dillon at Florida State University. This manual contains 27 experiments. that focus on real-world applications. Each experiment is specifically referenced to the sixth edition of Chemistry and corresponds with one or more topics covered in each chapter.

FOR THE INSTRUCTOR

Instructor Resource Center on DVD (0-321-72341-4) This DVD provides an integrated collection of resources designed to enhance your classroom lectures. This DVD features all art from the sixth edition in JPG and PDF format for high resolution printing as well as four pre-built PowerPoint presentations. The first presentation contains all images, figures and tables; the second includes a completely modifiable lecture outline; the third contains worked in chapter sample exercises; and the fourth contains "Clicker" questions to be used with the Classroom Response System. Also included are movies and animations, which can be easily inserted into your lecture presentations. For test preparation, this DVD also contains both the Word and TestGen versions of the Printed Test Bank designed to accompany the sixth edition which allows you to create and tailor exams to your students' needs. Finally, the Instructor Resource Manual is also included.

Solutions Manual (0-321-72336-8) by Joseph Topich, Virginia Commonwealth University. This solutions manual provides worked-out solutions to all in-chapter, conceptual, and end-of-chapter questions and problems. With instructor's permission, this manual may be made available to students.

Printed Test Bank (0-321-72723-1) by Robert A. Pribush, Butler University. The printed Test Bank contains nearly 4,400 multiple-choice questions.

Instructor Resource Manual (0-321-72339-2) by Robert A. Pribush, Butler University. This manual contains teaching tips, common misconceptions, lecture outlines, and suggested chapter learning goals for students, as well as lecture/laboratory demonstrations and literature references. It also describes the various resources, such as printed test bank questions, animations, and movies that are available to instructors.

BlackBoard Test Bank (0-321-72721-5) Available for download on the Instructor Resource Center.

WebCT Test Bank (0-321-72340-6) Available for download on the Instructor Resource Center.

About the Authors

John McMurry (*left*), educated at Harvard and Columbia, has taught more than 20,000 students in general and organic chemistry over a 40-year period. An emeritus Professor of Chemistry at Cornell University, Dr. McMurry previously spent 13 years on the faculty at the University of California at Santa Cruz. He has received numerous awards, including the Alfred P. Sloan Fellowship (1969–71), the National Institute of Health Career Development Award (1975–80), the Alexander von Humboldt Senior Scientist Award (1986–87), and the Max Planck Research Award (1991). With the publication of this new edition, he has now authored or coauthored 34 textbooks in various fields of chemistry.

Robert C. Fay (*right*), Professor Emeritus at Cornell University, taught general and inorganic chemistry at Cornell for 45 years beginning in 1962. Known for his clear, well-organized lectures, Dr. Fay was the 1980 recipient of the Clark Distinguished Teaching Award. He has also taught as a visiting professor at Harvard University and the University of Bologna (Italy). A Phi Beta Kappa graduate of Oberlin College, Dr. Fay received his Ph.D. from the University of Illinois. He has been an NSF Science Faculty Fellow at the University of East Anglia and the University of Sussex (England) and a NATO/Heineman Senior Fellow at Oxford University.

CHAPTER 1

Chemistry: Matter and Measurement

Instruments for scientific measurements have changed greatly over the centuries. In the 18th century, latitude was determined using this astrolabe.

CONTENTS

Life has changed more in the past two centuries than in all the previously recorded span of human history. Earth's population has increased more than fivefold since 1800 and life expectancy has nearly doubled because of our ability to synthesize medicines, control diseases, and increase crop yields. Methods of transportation have changed from horses and buggies to automobiles and airplanes because of our ability to harness the energy in petroleum. Many goods are now made of polymers and ceramics instead of wood and metal because of our ability to manufacture materials with properties unlike any found in nature.

In one way or another, all these changes involve **chemistry**, the study of the composition, properties, and transformations of matter. Chemistry is deeply involved in both the changes that take place in nature and the profound social changes of the past two centuries. In addition, chemistry is central to the current revolution in molecular biology that is revealing the details of how life is genetically controlled. No educated person today can understand the modern world without a basic knowledge of chemistry.

▲ The sequence of the approximately 5.8 billion nucleic acid units, or *nucleotides*, present in the human genome has been determined using instruments like this.

1.1 APPROACHING CHEMISTRY: EXPERIMENTATION

By opening this book, you have already decided that you need to know more about chemistry. Perhaps you want to learn how medicines are made, how genes can be sequenced and manipulated, how fertilizers and pesticides work, how living organisms function, how new high-temperature ceramics are used in space vehicles, or how microelectronic circuits are etched onto silicon chips. How do you approach chemistry?

One way to approach chemistry or any other science is to look around you and try to think of logical explanations for what you see. You would certainly observe, for instance, that different substances have different forms and appearances. Some substances are gases, some are liquids, and some are solids; some are hard and shiny, but others are soft and dull. You'd also observe that different substances behave differently. Iron rusts but gold does not; copper conducts electricity but sulfur doesn't. How can these and a vast number of other observations be explained?

▲ Gold, one of the most valuable of elements, has been prized since antiquity for its beauty and resistance to corrosion.

▲ Iron, although widely used as a structural and building material, corrodes easily.

In fact, the natural world is far too complex to be understood by looking and thinking alone, so a more active approach is needed. Specific questions must be asked, and experiments must be carried out to find their answers. Only when the results of many experiments are known can we devise an interpretation, or *hypothesis*, that explains the results. The hypothesis, in turn, can be used to make more predictions and to suggest more experiments until a consistent explanation, or **theory**, is finally arrived at.

It's important to keep in mind as you study chemistry or any other science that scientific theories are not laws of nature and can never be absolutely proven. There's always the chance that a new experiment might give results that can't be explained by present theory. All a theory can do is to represent the best explanation that we can come up with at the present time. If new experiments uncover results that present theories can't explain, the theories will have to be modified or perhaps even replaced.

1.2 CHEMISTRY AND THE ELEMENTS

Everything you see around you is formed from one or more of 118 presently known *elements*. An **element** is a fundamental substance that can't be chemically changed or broken down into anything simpler. Mercury, silver, and sulfur are common examples, as listed in Table 1.1.

▲ Samples of mercury, silver, and sulfur (clockwise from top left).

TABLE 1.1	**Names and Symbols of Some Common Elements.** Latin names from which the symbols of some elements are derived are shown in parentheses.						
Aluminum	**Al**	Chlorine	**Cl**	Manganese	**Mn**	Copper (*cuprum*)	**Cu**
Argon	**Ar**	Fluorine	**F**	Nitrogen	**N**	Iron (*ferrum*)	**Fe**
Barium	**Ba**	Helium	**He**	Oxygen	**O**	Lead (*plumbum*)	**Pb**
Boron	**B**	Hydrogen	**H**	Phosphorus	**P**	Mercury (*hydrargyrum*)	**Hg**
Bromine	**Br**	Iodine	**I**	Silicon	**Si**	Potassium (*kalium*)	**K**
Calcium	**Ca**	Lithium	**Li**	Sulfur	**S**	Silver (*argentum*)	**Ag**
Carbon	**C**	Magnesium	**Mg**	Zinc	**Zn**	Sodium (*natrium*)	**Na**

Actually, the previous statement about everything being made of one or more of 118 elements is an exaggeration because only about 90 of the 118 occur naturally. The remaining 28 have been produced artificially by nuclear chemists using high-energy particle accelerators.

Furthermore, only 83 of the 90 or so naturally occurring elements are found in any appreciable abundance. Hydrogen is thought to account for approximately 75% of the observed mass in the universe; oxygen and silicon together account for 75% of the mass of the Earth's crust; and oxygen, carbon, and hydrogen make up more than 90% of the mass of the human body (**Figure 1.1**). By contrast, there is probably less than 20 grams of the element francium (Fr) dispersed over the entire Earth at any one time. Francium is an unstable radioactive element, atoms of which are continually being formed and destroyed. We'll discuss radioactivity in Chapter 2.

For simplicity, chemists refer to specific elements using one- or two-letter symbols. As shown by the examples in Table 1.1, the first letter of an element's symbol is always capitalized and the second letter, if any, is lowercase. Many of the symbols are just the first one or two letters of the element's English name: H = hydrogen, C = carbon, Al = aluminum, and so forth. Other symbols derive from Latin or other languages: Na = sodium (Latin, *natrium*), Pb = lead (Latin, *plumbum*), W = tungsten (German, *wolfram*). The names, symbols, and other information about all 118 known elements are given inside the front cover of this book, organized in a format you've undoubtedly seen before called the **periodic table**.

(a) Relative abundance on Earth

Oxygen is the most abundant element in both the Earth's crust and the human body.

(b) Relative abundance in the human body

Figure 1.1
Estimated elemental composition by mass percent of (a) the Earth's crust and (b) the human body. Only the major constituents are shown in each case; small amounts of many other elements are also present.

▶ **PROBLEM 1.1** Look at the alphabetical list of elements inside the front cover, and find the symbols for the following elements:

(a) Cadmium (used in batteries)

(b) Antimony (used in alloys with other metals)

(c) Americium (used in smoke detectors)

▶ **PROBLEM 1.2** Look at the alphabetical list of elements inside the front cover, and tell what elements the following symbols represent:

(a) Ag (b) Rh (c) Re (d) Cs (e) Ar (f) As

1.3 ELEMENTS AND THE PERIODIC TABLE

Ten elements have been known since the beginning of recorded history: antimony (Sb), carbon (C), copper (Cu), gold (Au), iron (Fe), lead (Pb), mercury (Hg), silver (Ag), sulfur (S), and tin (Sn). The first "new" element to be found in several thousand years was arsenic (As), discovered in about 1250. In fact, only 24 elements were known when the United States was founded in 1776.

▲ Left to right, samples of chlorine, bromine, and iodine, one of Döbereiner's triads of elements with similar chemical properties.

As the pace of scientific discovery quickened in the late 1700s and early 1800s, chemists began to look for similarities among elements that might allow general conclusions to be drawn. Particularly important among the early successes was Johann Döbereiner's observation in 1829 that there were several *triads*, or groups of three elements, that appeared to behave similarly. Calcium (Ca), strontium (Sr), and barium (Ba) form one such triad; chlorine (Cl), bromine (Br), and iodine (I) form another; and lithium (Li), sodium (Na), and potassium (K) form a third. By 1843, 16 such triads were known and chemists were searching for an explanation.

Numerous attempts were made in the mid-1800s to account for the similarities among groups of elements, but the breakthrough came in 1869 when the Russian chemist Dmitri Mendeleev created the forerunner of the modern periodic table. Mendeleev's creation is an ideal example of how a scientific theory develops. At first there is only disconnected information—a large number of elements and many observations about their properties and behavior. As more and more facts become known, people try to organize the data in ways that make sense until ultimately a consistent hypothesis emerges.

A good hypothesis must do two things: It must explain known facts, and it must make predictions about phenomena yet unknown. If the predictions are tested and found true, then the hypothesis is a good one and will stand until additional facts are discovered that require it to be modified or discarded. Mendeleev's hypothesis about how known chemical information could be organized passed all tests. Not only did the periodic table arrange data in a useful and consistent way to explain known facts about chemical reactivity, it also led to several remarkable predictions that were later found to be accurate.

Using the experimentally observed chemistry of the elements as his primary organizing principle, Mendeleev arranged the known elements in order of the relative masses of their atoms with hydrogen = 1 (called their *atomic masses*, Section 2.6) and then grouped them according to their chemical reactivity. On so doing, he realized that there were several "holes" in the table, some of which are shown in **Figure 1.2**. The chemical behavior of aluminum (relative mass ≈ 27.3) is similar to that of boron (relative mass ≈ 11), but there was no element known at the time that fit into the slot below aluminum. In the same way, silicon (relative mass ≈ 28) is similar in many respects to carbon (relative mass ≈ 12), but there was no element known that fit below silicon.

There is an unknown element, which turns out to be gallium (Ga), beneath aluminum (Al)…

…and another unknown element, which turns out to be germanium (Ge), beneath silicon (Si).

Figure 1.2
A portion of Mendeleev's periodic table. The table shows the relative masses of atoms as known at the time and some of the holes representing unknown elements.

Looking at the holes in the table, Mendeleev predicted that two then-unknown elements existed and might be found at some future time. Furthermore, he predicted with remarkable accuracy what the properties of these unknown elements would be. The element immediately below aluminum, which he called *eka*-aluminum from a Sanskrit word meaning "first," should have a relative mass near 68 and should have a low melting point. Gallium, discovered in 1875, has exactly these properties. The

▲ Gallium is a shiny, low-melting metal.

▲ Germanium is a hard, gray semimetal.

element below silicon, which Mendeleev called *eka*-silicon, should have a relative mass near 72 and should be dark gray in color. Germanium, discovered in 1886, fits the description perfectly (Table 1.2).

TABLE 1.2 A Comparison of Predicted and Observed Properties for Gallium (*eka*-Aluminum) and Germanium (*eka*-Silicon)

Element	Property	Mendeleev's Prediction	Observed Property
Gallium	Relative mass	68	69.7
	Density	5.9 g/cm^3	5.91 g/cm^3
	Melting point	Low	29.8 °C
Germanium	Relative mass	72	72.6
	Density	5.5 g/cm^3	5.35 g/cm^3
	Color	Dark gray	Light gray

In the modern periodic table, shown in Figure 1.3, elements are placed on a grid with 7 horizontal rows, called **periods**, and 18 vertical columns, called **groups**. When organized in this way, *the elements in a given group have similar chemical properties.* Lithium, sodium, potassium, and the other metallic elements in group 1A behave similarly. Beryllium, magnesium, calcium, and the other elements in group 2A behave similarly. Fluorine, chlorine, bromine, and the other elements in group 7A behave similarly, and so on throughout the table. (Mendeleev, by the way, was completely unaware of the existence of the group 8A elements—He, Ne, Ar, Kr, Xe, and Rn—because none were known when he constructed his table. All are colorless, odorless gases with little or no chemical reactivity, and none were discovered until 1894, when argon was first isolated.)

The overall form of the periodic table is well accepted, but chemists in different countries have historically used different conventions for labeling the groups. To resolve these difficulties, an international standard calls for numbering the groups from 1 to 18 going left to right. This standard has not yet found complete acceptance, however, and we'll continue to use the U.S. system of numbers and capital letters—group 3B instead of group 3 and group 7A instead of group 17, for example. Labels for the newer system are also shown in Figure 1.3.

One further note: There are actually 32 groups in the periodic table rather than 18, but to make the table fit manageably on a page, the 14 elements beginning with lanthanum (the *lanthanides*) and the 14 beginning with actinium (the *actinides*) are pulled out and shown below the others. These groups are not numbered.

We'll see repeatedly throughout this book that the periodic table of the elements is the most important organizing principle in chemistry. The time you take now to

Atomic Number
Chemical symbol

1																	2
H																	He

3	4											5	6	7	8	9	10
Li	Be											B	C	N	O	F	Ne

| 11 | 12 | | | | | | | | | | | 13 | 14 | 15 | 16 | 17 | 18 |
| Na | Mg | | | | | | | | | | | Al | Si | P | S | Cl | Ar |

| 19 | 20 | 21 | 22 | 23 | 24 | 25 | 26 | 27 | 28 | 29 | 30 | 31 | 32 | 33 | 34 | 35 | 36 |
| K | Ca | Sc | Ti | V | Cr | Mn | Fe | Co | Ni | Cu | Zn | Ga | Ge | As | Se | Br | Kr |

| 37 | 38 | 39 | 40 | 41 | 42 | 43 | 44 | 45 | 46 | 47 | 48 | 49 | 50 | 51 | 52 | 53 | 54 |
| Rb | Sr | Y | Zr | Nb | Mo | Tc | Ru | Rh | Pd | Ag | Cd | In | Sn | Sb | Te | I | Xe |

| 55 | 56 | 71 | 72 | 73 | 74 | 75 | 76 | 77 | 78 | 79 | 80 | 81 | 82 | 83 | 84 | 85 | 86 |
| Cs | Ba | Lu | Hf | Ta | W | Re | Os | Ir | Pt | Au | Hg | Tl | Pb | Bi | Po | At | Rn |

| 87 | 88 | 103 | 104 | 105 | 106 | 107 | 108 | 109 | 110 | 111 | 112 | 113 | 114 | 115 | 116 | 117 | 118 |
| Fr | Ra | Lr | Rf | Db | Sg | Bh | Hs | Mt | Ds | Rg | Cn | | | | | | |

57	58	59	60	61	62	63	64	65	66	67	68	69	70
La	Ce	Pr	Nd	Pm	Sm	Eu	Gd	Tb	Dy	Ho	Er	Tm	Yb
89	90	91	92	93	94	95	96	97	98	99	100	101	102
Ac	Th	Pa	U	Np	Pu	Am	Cm	Bk	Cf	Es	Fm	Md	No

Figure 1.3

The periodic table. Each element is identified by a one- or two-letter symbol and is characterized by an atomic number. The table begins with hydrogen (H, atomic number 1) in the upper left-hand corner and continues to the yet unnamed element with atomic number 118. The 14 elements beginning with lanthanum (La, atomic number 57) and the 14 elements beginning with actinium (Ac, atomic number 89) are pulled out and shown below the others.

Main groups

Periods

1 1A Atomic Number 2
   Chemical symbol 2A

Transition metal groups

Main groups

13 14 15 16 17 18
3A 4A 5A 6A 7A 8A

Period	1A/1	2A/2	3B/3	4B/4	5B/5	6B/6	7B/7	8B/8	8B/9	8B/10	1B/11	2B/12	3A/13	4A/14	5A/15	6A/16	7A/17	8A/18
1	1 H																	2 He
2	3 Li	4 Be											5 B	6 C	7 N	8 O	9 F	10 Ne
3	11 Na	12 Mg											13 Al	14 Si	15 P	16 S	17 Cl	18 Ar
4	19 K	20 Ca	21 Sc	22 Ti	23 V	24 Cr	25 Mn	26 Fe	27 Co	28 Ni	29 Cu	30 Zn	31 Ga	32 Ge	33 As	34 Se	35 Br	36 Kr
5	37 Rb	38 Sr	39 Y	40 Zr	41 Nb	42 Mo	43 Tc	44 Ru	45 Rh	46 Pd	47 Ag	48 Cd	49 In	50 Sn	51 Sb	52 Te	53 I	54 Xe
6	55 Cs	56 Ba	71 Lu	72 Hf	73 Ta	74 W	75 Re	76 Os	77 Ir	78 Pt	79 Au	80 Hg	81 Tl	82 Pb	83 Bi	84 Po	85 At	86 Rn
7	87 Fr	88 Ra	103 Lr	104 Rf	105 Db	106 Sg	107 Bh	108 Hs	109 Mt	110 Ds	111 Rg	112 Cn	113	114	115	116	117	118

Lanthanides

57 La	58 Ce	59 Pr	60 Nd	61 Pm	62 Sm	63 Eu	64 Gd	65 Tb	66 Dy	67 Ho	68 Er	69 Tm	70 Yb

Actinides

89 Ac	90 Th	91 Pa	92 U	93 Np	94 Pu	95 Am	96 Cm	97 Bk	98 Cf	99 Es	100 Fm	101 Md	102 No

Figure 1.3

The periodic table. Each element is identified by a one- or two-letter symbol and is characterized by an atomic number. The table begins with hydrogen (H, atomic number 1) in the upper left-hand corner and continues to the yet unnamed element with atomic number 118. The 14 elements beginning with lanthanum (La, atomic number 57) and the 14 elements beginning with actinium (Ac, atomic number 89) are pulled out and shown below the others.

Elements are organized into 18 vertical columns, or *groups*, and 7 horizontal rows, or *periods*. The two groups on the left and the six on the right are the *main groups*; the ten in the middle are the *transition metal groups*. The 14 elements beginning with lanthanum are the *lanthanides*, and the 14 elements beginning with actinium are the *actinides*. Together, the lanthanides and actinides are known as the *inner transition metal groups*. Two systems for numbering the groups are shown above the top row and are explained in the text.

Figure 1.3

The periodic table.

Main groups / Atomic Number / Chemical symbol / Periods / Transition metal groups / Main groups

Period	1 (1A)	2 (2A)	3 (3B)	4 (4B)	5 (5B)	6 (6B)	7 (7B)	8 (8B)	9 (8B)	10 (8B)	11 (1B)	12 (2B)	13 (3A)	14 (4A)	15 (5A)	16 (6A)	17 (7A)	18 (8A)
1	1 H																	2 He
2	3 Li	4 Be											5 B	6 C	7 N	8 O	9 F	10 Ne
3	11 Na	12 Mg											13 Al	14 Si	15 P	16 S	17 Cl	18 Ar
4	19 K	20 Ca	21 Sc	22 Ti	23 V	24 Cr	25 Mn	26 Fe	27 Co	28 Ni	29 Cu	30 Zn	31 Ga	32 Ge	33 As	34 Se	35 Br	36 Kr
5	37 Rb	38 Sr	39 Y	40 Zr	41 Nb	42 Mo	43 Tc	44 Ru	45 Rh	46 Pd	47 Ag	48 Cd	49 In	50 Sn	51 Sb	52 Te	53 I	54 Xe
6	55 Cs	56 Ba	71 Lu	72 Hf	73 Ta	74 W	75 Re	76 Os	77 Ir	78 Pt	79 Au	80 Hg	81 Tl	82 Pb	83 Bi	84 Po	85 At	86 Rn
7	87 Fr	88 Ra	103 Lr	104 Rf	105 Db	106 Sg	107 Bh	108 Hs	109 Mt	110 Ds	111 Rg	112 Cn	113	114	115	116	117	118

Lanthanides:

57 La	58 Ce	59 Pr	60 Nd	61 Pm	62 Sm	63 Eu	64 Gd	65 Tb	66 Dy	67 Ho	68 Er	69 Tm	70 Yb

Actinides:

89 Ac	90 Th	91 Pa	92 U	93 Np	94 Pu	95 Am	96 Cm	97 Bk	98 Cf	99 Es	100 Fm	101 Md	102 No

The periodic table. Each element is identified by a one- or two-letter symbol and is characterized by an atomic number. The table begins with hydrogen (H, atomic number 1) in the upper left-hand corner and continues to the yet unnamed element with atomic number 118. The 14 elements beginning with lanthanum (La, atomic number 57) and the 14 elements beginning with actinium (Ac, atomic number 89) are pulled out and shown below the others.

Elements are organized into 18 vertical columns, or *groups*, and 7 horizontal rows, or *periods*. The two groups on the left and the six on the right are the *main groups*; the ten in the middle are the *transition metal groups*. The 14 elements beginning with lanthanum are the *lanthanides*, and the 14 elements beginning with actinium are the *actinides*. Together, the lanthanides and actinides are known as the *inner transition metal groups*. Two systems for numbering the groups are shown above the top row and are explained in the text.

Those elements (except hydrogen) on the left side of the zigzag line running from boron (B) to astatine (At) are metals; those elements (plus hydrogen) to the right of the line are **nonmetals**; and seven of the nine elements abutting the line are metalloids, or semimetals.

Metals

Semimetals

Nonmetals

familiarize yourself with the layout and organization of the periodic table will pay off later on. Notice in Figure 1.3, for instance, that there is a regular progression in the size of the seven periods (rows). The first period has only 2 elements, hydrogen (H) and helium (He); the second and third periods have 8 elements each; the fourth and fifth periods have 18 elements each; and the sixth and seventh periods, which include the lanthanides and actinides, have 32 elements each. We'll see in Chapter 5 that this regular progression in the periodic table reflects a similar regularity in the structure of atoms.

Notice also that not all groups in the periodic table have the same number of elements. The two larger groups on the left and the six larger groups on the right are called the **main groups**. Most of the elements on which life is based—carbon, hydrogen, nitrogen, oxygen, and phosphorus, for instance—are main-group elements. The 10 smaller groups in the middle of the table are called the **transition metal groups**. Most of the metals you're probably familiar with—iron, copper, zinc, and gold, for instance—are transition metals. And the 14 groups shown separately at the bottom of the table are called the **inner transition metal groups**.

1.4 SOME CHEMICAL PROPERTIES OF THE ELEMENTS

Any characteristic that can be used to describe or identify matter is called a **property**. Examples include volume, amount, odor, color, and temperature. Still other properties include such characteristics as melting point, solubility, and chemical behavior. For example, we might list some properties of sodium chloride (table salt) by saying that it melts at 1474 °F (or 801 °C), dissolves in water, and undergoes a chemical reaction when it comes into contact with a silver nitrate solution.

Properties can be classified as either *intensive* or *extensive*, depending on whether the value of the property changes with the amount of the sample. **Intensive properties**, like temperature and melting point, have values that do not depend on the amount of sample: a small ice cube might have the same temperature as a massive iceberg. **Extensive properties**, like length and volume, have values that *do* depend on the sample size: an ice cube is much smaller than an iceberg.

Properties can also be classified as either *physical* or *chemical*, depending on whether the property involves a change in the chemical makeup of a substance. **Physical properties** are characteristics that do not involve a change in a sample's chemical makeup, whereas **chemical properties** are characteristics that *do* involve a change in chemical makeup. The melting point of ice, for instance, is a physical property because melting causes the water to change only in form, from solid to liquid, but not in chemical makeup. The rusting of an iron bicycle left in the rain is a chemical property, however, because iron combines with oxygen and moisture from the air to give the new substance, rust. Table 1.3 lists other examples of both physical and chemical properties.

▲ Addition of a solution of silver nitrate to a solution of sodium chloride yields a white precipitate of solid silver chloride.

TABLE 1.3   Some Examples of Physical and Chemical Properties

Physical Properties		Chemical Properties
Temperature	Amount	Rusting (of iron)
Color	Odor	Combustion (of gasoline)
Melting point	Solubility	Tarnishing (of silver)
Electrical conductivity	Hardness	Hardening (of cement)

As noted previously, the elements in a group of the periodic table often show remarkable similarities in their chemical properties. Look at the following groups, for instance, to see some examples:

- **Group 1A—Alkali metals** Lithium (Li), sodium (Na), potassium (K), rubidium (Rb), and cesium (Cs) are soft, silvery metals. All react rapidly, often violently, with water to form products that are highly alkaline, or basic—hence the name *alkali metals*. Because of their high reactivity, the alkali metals are never found in nature in the pure state but only in combination with other elements. Francium (Fr) is also an alkali metal but, as noted previously, it is so rare that little is known about it.

    Note that group 1A also contains hydrogen (H) even though, as a colorless gas, it is completely different in appearance and behavior from the alkali metals. We'll see the reason for this classification in Section 5.13.

- **Group 2A—Alkaline earth metals** Beryllium (Be), magnesium (Mg), calcium (Ca), strontium (Sr), barium (Ba), and radium (Ra) are also lustrous, silvery metals but are less reactive than their neighbors in group 1A. Like the alkali metals, the alkaline earths are never found in nature in the pure state.

▲ Sodium, one of the alkali metals, reacts violently with water to yield hydrogen gas and an alkaline (basic) solution.

▲ Magnesium, one of the alkaline earth metals, burns in air.

- **Group 7A—Halogens** Fluorine (F), chlorine (Cl), bromine (Br), and iodine (I), are colorful, corrosive nonmetals. They are found in nature only in combination with other elements, such as with sodium in table salt (sodium chloride, NaCl). In fact, the group name *halogen* is taken from the Greek word *hals*, meaning "salt." Astatine (At) is also a halogen, but it exists in such tiny amounts that little is known about it.

- **Group 8A—Noble gases** Helium (He), neon (Ne), argon (Ar), krypton (Kr), xenon (Xe), and radon (Rn) are colorless gases with very low chemical reactivity. Helium and neon don't combine with any other element; argon, krypton, and xenon combine with very few.

As indicated in Figure 1.3, the elements of the periodic table are often divided into three major categories: metals, nonmetals, and semimetals.

◀ Bromine, a halogen, is a corrosive dark red liquid at room temperature.

◀ Neon, one of the noble gases, is used in neon lights and signs.

- **Metals** Metals, the largest category of elements, are found on the left side of the periodic table, bounded on the right by a zigzag line running from boron (B) at the top to astatine (At) at the bottom. The metals are easy to characterize by their appearance. All except mercury are solid at room temperature, and most have the silvery shine we normally associate with metals. In addition, metals are generally malleable rather than brittle, can be twisted and drawn into wires without breaking, and are good conductors of heat and electricity.

- **Nonmetals** Except for hydrogen, nonmetals are found on the right side of the periodic table and, like metals, are easy to characterize by their appearance. Eleven of the seventeen nonmetals are gases, one is a liquid (bromine), and only five are solids at room temperature (carbon, phosphorus, sulfur, selenium, and iodine). None are silvery in appearance, and several are brightly colored. The solid nonmetals are brittle rather than malleable and are poor conductors of heat and electricity.

▲ Lead, aluminum, copper, gold, iron, and silver (clockwise from left) are typical metals. All conduct electricity and can be drawn into wires.

▲ Bromine, carbon, phosphorus, and sulfur (clockwise from top left) are typical nonmetals. None conduct electricity or can be made into wires.

- **Semimetals** Seven of the nine elements adjacent to the zigzag boundary between metals and nonmetals—boron, silicon, germanium, arsenic, antimony, tellurium, and astatine—are called semimetals because their properties are intermediate between those of their metallic and nonmetallic neighbors. Although most are silvery in appearance and all are solid at room temperature, semimetals are brittle rather than malleable and tend to be poor conductors of heat and electricity. Silicon, for example, is a widely used *semiconductor*, a substance whose electrical conductivity is intermediate between that of a metal and an insulator.

▶ **PROBLEM 1.3**   Identify the following elements as metals, nonmetals, or semimetals:

(a) Ti   **(b)** Te   **(c)** Se   **(d)** Sc   **(e)** At   **(f)** Ar

CONCEPTUAL PROBLEM 1.4   The three so-called coinage metals are located near the middle of the periodic table. Identify them.

1.5 EXPERIMENTATION AND MEASUREMENT

Chemistry is an experimental science. But if our experiments are to be reproducible, we must be able to describe fully the substances we're working with—their amounts, volumes, temperatures, and so forth. Thus, one of the most important requirements in chemistry is that we have a way to measure things.

Under an international agreement concluded in 1960, scientists throughout the world now use the International System of Units for measurement, abbreviated **SI** for the French *Système Internationale d'Unités*. Based on the metric system, which is used in all industrialized countries of the world except the United States, the SI system has seven fundamental units (Table 1.4). These seven fundamental units, along with others derived from them, suffice for all scientific measurements. We'll look at three of the most common units in this chapter—those for mass, length, and temperature—and will discuss others as the need arises in later chapters.

TABLE 1.4   The Seven Fundamental SI Units of Measure

Physical Quantity	Name of Unit	Abbreviation
Mass	kilogram	kg
Length	meter	m
Temperature	kelvin	K
Amount of substance	mole	mol
Time	second	s
Electric current	ampere	A
Luminous intensity	candela	cd

One problem with any system of measurement is that the sizes of the units often turn out to be inconveniently large or small. For example, a chemist describing the diameter of a sodium atom (0.000 000 000 372 m) would find the meter (m) to be inconveniently large, but an astronomer describing the average distance from the Earth to the Sun (150,000,000,000 m) would find the meter to be inconveniently small. For this reason, SI units are modified through the use of prefixes when they refer to either smaller or larger quantities. Thus, the prefix *milli-* means one-thousandth, and a *milli*meter (mm) is 1/1000 of 1 meter. Similarly, the prefix *kilo-* means one thousand, and a *kilo*meter (km) is 1000 meters. [Note that the SI unit for mass (kilogram) already contains the *kilo-* prefix.] A list of prefixes is shown in Table 1.5, with the most commonly used ones in red.

Notice how numbers that are either very large or very small are indicated in Table 1.5 using an exponential format called **scientific notation**. For example, the

TABLE 1.5   Some Prefixes for Multiples of SI Units.
The most commonly used prefixes are shown in red.

Factor	Prefix	Symbol	Example
$1,000,000,000,000 = 10^{12}$	tera	T	1 teragram (Tg) $= 10^{12}$ g
$1,000,000,000 = 10^9$	giga	G	1 gigameter (Gm) $= 10^9$ m
$1,000,000 = 10^6$	mega	M	1 megameter (Mm) $= 10^6$ m
$1000 = 10^3$	kilo	k	1 kilogram (kg) $= 10^3$ g
$100 = 10^2$	hecto	h	1 hectogram (hg) $= 100$ g
$10 = 10^1$	deka	da	1 dekagram (dag) $= 10$ g
$0.1 = 10^{-1}$	deci	d	1 decimeter (dm) $= 0.1$ m
$0.01 = 10^{-2}$	centi	c	1 centimeter (cm) $= 0.01$ m
$0.001 = 10^{-3}$	milli	m	1 milligram (mg) $= 0.001$ g
*$0.000\ 001 = 10^{-6}$	micro	μ	1 micrometer (μm) $= 10^{-6}$ m
*$0.000\ 000\ 001 = 10^{-9}$	nano	n	1 nanosecond (ns) $= 10^{-9}$ s
*$0.000\ 000\ 000\ 001 = 10^{-12}$	pico	p	1 picosecond (ps) $= 10^{-12}$ s
*$0.000\ 000\ 000\ 000\ 001 = 10^{-15}$	femto	f	1 femtomole (fmol) $= 10^{-15}$ mol

*For very small numbers, it is becoming common in scientific work to leave a thin space every three digits to the right of the decimal point, analogous to the comma placed every three digits to the left of the decimal point in large numbers.

number 55,000 is written in scientific notation as 5.5×10^4, and the number 0.003 20 as 3.20×10^{-3}. Review Appendix A if you are uncomfortable with scientific notation or if you need to brush up on how to do mathematical manipulations on numbers with exponents.

Notice also that all measurements contain both a number and a unit label. A number alone is not much good without a unit to define it. If you asked a friend how far it was to the nearest tennis court, the answer "3" alone wouldn't tell you much. 3 blocks? 3 kilometers? 3 miles?

▸ **PROBLEM 1.5**   Express the following quantities in scientific notation:
  (a) The diameter of a sodium atom, 0.000 000 000 372 m
  (b) The distance from the Earth to the Sun, 150,000,000,000 m

▸ **PROBLEM 1.6**   What units do the following abbreviations represent?
  (a) μg   **(b)** dm   **(c)** ps   **(d)** kA   **(e)** mmol

1.6 MASS AND ITS MEASUREMENT

Mass is defined as the amount of *matter* in an object. **Matter**, in turn, is a catchall term used to describe anything with a physical presence—anything you can touch, taste, or smell. (Stated more scientifically, matter is anything that has mass.) Mass is measured in SI units by the **kilogram** (kg; 1 kg = 2.205 U.S. lb). Because the kilogram is too large for many purposes in chemistry, the metric **gram** (g; 1 g = 0.001 kg), the **milligram** (mg; 1 mg = 0.001 g = 10^{-6} kg), and the **microgram** (μg; 1 μg = 0.001 mg = 10^{-6} g = 10^{-9} kg) are more commonly used. (The symbol μ is the lowercase Greek letter mu.) One gram is a bit less than half the mass of a new U.S. dime.

$$1 \text{ kg} = 1000 \text{ g} = 1,000,000 \text{ mg} = 1,000,000,000 \text{ } \mu\text{g}   (2.205 \text{ lb})$$
$$1 \text{ g} = 1000 \text{ mg} = 1,000,000 \text{ } \mu\text{g}   (0.035\ 27 \text{ oz})$$
$$1 \text{ mg} = 1000 \text{ } \mu\text{g}$$

▲ The mass of a U.S. dime is approximately 2.27 g.

The standard kilogram is set as the mass of a cylindrical bar of platinum–iridium alloy stored in a vault in a suburb of Paris, France. There are 40 copies of this bar distributed throughout the world, with two (Numbers 4 and 20) stored at the U.S. National Institute of Standards and Technology near Washington, D.C.

The terms "mass" and "weight," although often used interchangeably, have quite different meanings. *Mass* is a physical property that measures the amount of matter in an object, whereas *weight* measures the force with which gravity pulls on an object. Mass is independent of an object's location: your body has the same amount of matter whether you're on Earth or on the moon. Weight, however, *does* depend on an object's location. If you weigh 140 lb on Earth, you would weigh only about 23 lb on the moon, which has a lower gravity than the Earth.

At the same location on Earth, two objects with identical masses experience an identical pull of the Earth's gravity and have identical weights. Thus, the mass of an object can be measured by comparing its weight to the weight of a reference standard of known mass. Much of the confusion between mass and weight is simply due to a language problem. We speak of "weighing" when we really mean that we are measuring mass by comparing two weights. **Figure 1.4** shows balances typically used for measuring mass in the laboratory.

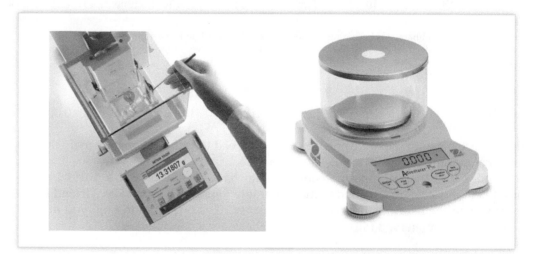

Figure 1.4
Some balances used for measuring mass in the laboratory.

1.7 LENGTH AND ITS MEASUREMENT

The **meter (m)** is the standard unit of length in the SI system. Although originally defined in 1790 as being 1 ten-millionth of the distance from the equator to the North Pole, the meter was redefined in 1889 as the distance between two thin lines on a bar of platinum–iridium alloy stored near Paris, France. To accommodate an increasing need for precision, the meter was redefined again in 1983 as equal to the distance traveled by light through a vacuum in 1/299,792,458 second. Although this new definition isn't as easy to grasp as the distance between two scratches on a bar, it has the great advantage that it can't be lost or damaged.

One meter is 39.37 inches, about 10% longer than an English yard and much too large for most measurements in chemistry. Other more commonly used measures of length are the **centimeter (cm;** 1 cm = 0.01 m, a bit less than half an inch), the **millimeter (mm;** 1 mm = 0.001 m, about the thickness of a U.S. dime), the **micrometer (μm;** 1 μm = 10^{-6} m), the **nanometer (nm;** 1 nm = 10^{-9} m), and the **picometer (pm;** 1 pm = 10^{-12} m). Thus, a chemist might refer to the diameter of a sodium atom as 372 pm (3.72×10^{-10} m).

1 m = 100 cm = 1000 mm = 1,000,000 μm = 1,000,000,000 nm   (1.0936 yd)

1 cm = 10 mm = 10,000 μm = 10,000,000 nm   (0.3937 in.)

1 mm = 1000 μm = 1,000,000 nm

▲ The length of the bacteria on the tip of this pin is about 5×10^{-7} m

1.8 TEMPERATURE AND ITS MEASUREMENT

Just as the kilogram and the meter are slowly replacing the pound and the yard as common units for mass and length measurement in the United States, the **degree Celsius (°C)** is slowly replacing the degree Fahrenheit (°F) as the common unit for temperature measurement. In scientific work, however, the **kelvin (K)** has replaced both. (Note that we say only "kelvin," not "kelvin degree.")

For all practical purposes, the kelvin and the degree Celsius are the same—both are one-hundredth of the interval between the freezing point of water and the boiling point of water at standard atmospheric pressure. The only real difference between the two units is that the numbers assigned to various points on the scales differ. Whereas the Celsius scale assigns a value of 0 °C to the freezing point of water and 100 °C to the boiling point of water, the Kelvin scale assigns a value of 0 K to the coldest possible temperature, −273.15 °C, sometimes called *absolute zero*. Thus, 0 K = −273.15 °C and 273.15 K = 0 °C. For example, a warm spring day with a Celsius temperature of 25 °C has a Kelvin temperature of 25 + 273.15 = 298 K.

$$\text{Temperature in K} = \text{Temperature in °C} + 273.15$$

$$\text{Temperature in °C} = \text{Temperature in K} - 273.15$$

In contrast to the Kelvin and Celsius scales, the common Fahrenheit scale specifies an interval of 180° between the freezing point (32 °F) and the boiling point (212 °F) of water. Thus, it takes 180 degrees Fahrenheit to cover the same range as 100 degrees Celsius (or kelvins), and a degree Fahrenheit is therefore only 100/180 = 5/9 as large as a degree Celsius. **Figure 1.5** compares the Fahrenheit, Celsius, and Kelvin scales.

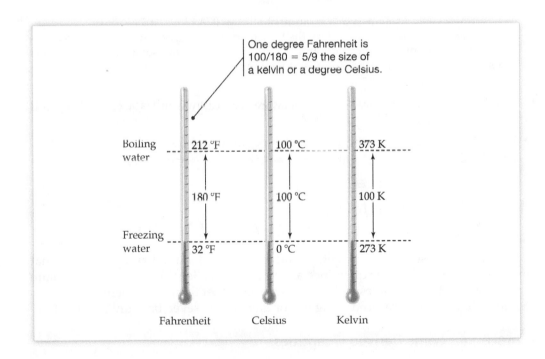

Figure 1.5
A comparison of the Fahrenheit, Celsius, and Kelvin temperature scales.

Two adjustments are needed to convert between Fahrenheit and Celsius scales—one to adjust for the difference in degree size and one to adjust for the difference in zero points. The size adjustment is made using the relationships 1 °C = (9/5) °F and 1 °F = (5/9) °C. The zero-point adjustment is made by remembering that the freezing point of water is higher by 32 on the Fahrenheit scale than on the Celsius scale. Thus, if you want to convert from Celsius to Fahrenheit, you do a size adjustment (multiply °C by 9/5) and then a zero-point adjustment (add 32). If you want to convert from Fahrenheit to Celsius, you find out how many Fahrenheit degrees there are above freezing (by subtracting 32) and then do a size adjustment (multiply by 5/9). The following formulas describe the conversions, and Worked Example 1.1 shows how to do a calculation.

CELSIUS TO FAHRENHEIT

$$^\circ F = \left(\frac{9\,^\circ F}{5\,^\circ C} \times\,^\circ C\right) + 32\,^\circ F$$

FAHRENHEIT TO CELSIUS

$$^\circ C = \frac{5\,^\circ C}{9\,^\circ F} \times (^\circ F - 32\,^\circ F)$$

WORKED EXAMPLE 1.1

CONVERTING FROM FAHRENHEIT TO CELSIUS

The melting point of table salt is 1474 °F. What temperature is this on the Celsius and Kelvin scales?

SOLUTION

There are two ways to do this and every other problem in chemistry. One is to think things through to be sure you understand what's going on; the other is to plug numbers into a formula and hope for the best. The thinking approach always works; the formula approach works only if you use the right equation. Let's try both ways.

The thinking approach: We're given a temperature in degrees Fahrenheit, and we need to convert to degrees Celsius. A temperature of 1474 °F corresponds to 1474 °F − 32 °F = 1442 °F above the freezing point of water. Because a degree Fahrenheit is only 5/9 as large as a degree Celsius, 1442 degrees Fahrenheit above freezing equals 1442 × 5/9 = 801 degrees Celsius above freezing (0 °C), or 801 °C. The same number of degrees above freezing on the Kelvin scale (273.15 K) corresponds to a temperature of 273.15 + 801 = 1074 K.

The formula approach: Set up an equation using the temperature conversion formula for changing from Fahrenheit to Celsius:

$$^\circ C = \left(\frac{5\,^\circ C}{9\,^\circ F}\right)(1474\,^\circ F - 32\,^\circ F) = 801\,^\circ C$$

Converting to kelvins gives a temperature of 801° + 273.15° = 1074 K.

Because the answers obtained by the two approaches agree, we can feel fairly confident that our thinking is on track and that we understand the subject. (If the answers did *not* agree, we'd be alerted to a misunderstanding somewhere.)

▲ The melting point of sodium chloride is 1474 °F, or 801 °C.

▶ **PROBLEM 1.7**   The normal body temperature of a healthy adult is 98.6 °F. What is this value on both Celsius and Kelvin scales?

▶ **PROBLEM 1.8**   Carry out the indicated temperature conversions.
(a) −78 °C = ? K   (b) 158 °C = ? °F   (c) 375 K = ? °F

1.9 DERIVED UNITS: VOLUME AND ITS MEASUREMENT

Look back at the seven fundamental SI units given in Table 1.4 and you'll find that measures for such familiar quantities as area, volume, density, speed, and pressure are missing. All are examples of *derived* quantities rather than fundamental quantities because they can be expressed using one or more of the seven base units (Table 1.6).

TABLE 1.6   Some Derived Quantities

Quantity	Definition	Derived Unit (Name)
Area	Length times length	m^2
Volume	Area times length	m^3
Density	Mass per unit volume	kg/m^3
Speed	Distance per unit time	m/s
Acceleration	Change in speed per unit time	m/s^2
Force	Mass times acceleration	$(kg \cdot m)/s^2$ (newton, N)
Pressure	Force per unit area	$kg/(m \cdot s^2)$ (pascal, Pa)
Energy	Force times distance	$(kg \cdot m^2)/s^2$ (joule, J)

Volume, the amount of space occupied by an object, is measured in SI units by the **cubic meter (m^3)**, defined as the amount of space occupied by a cube 1 meter on edge (Figure 1.6).

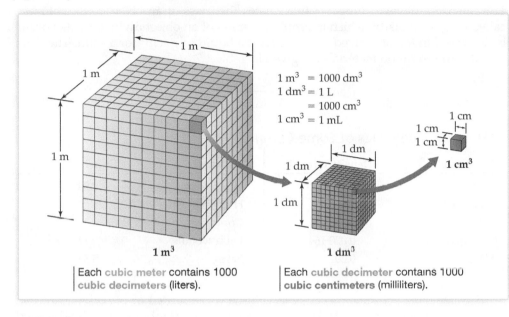

$$1\ m^3 = 1000\ dm^3$$
$$1\ dm^3 = 1\ L$$
$$= 1000\ cm^3$$
$$1\ cm^3 = 1\ mL$$

1 m^3

Each cubic meter contains 1000 cubic decimeters (liters).

1 dm^3

Each cubic decimeter contains 1000 cubic centimeters (milliliters).

1 cm^3

Figure 1.6
Units for measuring volume. A cubic meter is the volume of a cube 1 meter along each edge.

A cubic meter equals 264.2 U.S. gallons, much too large a quantity for normal use in chemistry. As a result, smaller, more convenient measures are commonly employed. Both the **cubic decimeter** (1 dm^3 = 0.001 m^3), equal in size to the more familiar metric **liter (L)**, and the **cubic centimeter** (1 cm^3 = 0.001 dm^3 = 10^{-6} m^3), equal in size to the metric **milliliter (mL)**, are particularly convenient. Slightly larger than 1 U.S. quart, a liter has the volume of a cube 1 dm on edge. Similarly, a milliliter has the volume of a cube 1 cm on edge (Figure 1.6).

$$1\ m^3 = 1000\ dm^3 = 1{,}000{,}000\ cm^3 \qquad (264.2\ gal)$$

$$1\ dm^3 = 1L = 1000\ mL \qquad (1.057\ qt)$$

Figure 1.7 shows some of the equipment frequently used in the laboratory for measuring liquid volume.

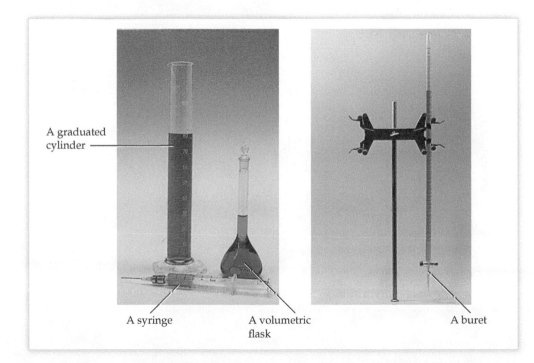

A graduated cylinder

A syringe

A volumetric flask

A buret

Figure 1.7
Common items of laboratory equipment used for measuring liquid volume.

▲ Which weighs more, the brass weight or the pillow? Actually, both have identical masses and weights, but the brass has a higher density because its volume is smaller.

1.10 DERIVED UNITS: DENSITY AND ITS MEASUREMENT

The intensive physical property that relates the mass of an object to its volume is called *density*. **Density**, which is simply the mass of an object divided by its volume, is expressed in the SI derived unit g/mL for a liquid or g/cm^3 for a solid. The densities of some common materials are given in Table 1.7.

$$\text{Density} = \frac{\text{Mass (g)}}{\text{Volume (mL or cm}^3\text{)}}$$

TABLE 1.7 Densities of Some Common Materials

Substance	Density (g/cm³)	Substance	Density (g/cm³)
Ice (0 °C)	0.917	Human fat	0.94
Water (3.98 °C)	1.0000	Human muscle	1.06
Gold	19.31	Cork	0.22–0.26
Helium (25 °C)	0.000 164	Balsa wood	0.12
Air (25 °C)	0.001 185	Earth	5.54

Because most substances change in volume when heated or cooled, densities are temperature-dependent. At 3.98 °C, for example, a 1.0000 mL container holds exactly 1.0000 g of water (density = 1.0000 g/mL). As the temperature is raised, however, the volume occupied by the water expands so that only 0.9584 g fits in the 1.0000 mL container at 100 °C (density = 0.9584 g/mL). When reporting a density, the temperature must also be specified.

Although most substances expand when heated and contract when cooled, water behaves differently. Water contracts when cooled from 100 °C to 3.98 °C, but below this temperature it begins to expand again. Thus, the density of liquid water is at its maximum of 1.0000 g/mL at 3.98 °C but decreases to 0.999 87 g/mL at 0 °C (Figure 1.8). When freezing occurs, the density drops still further to a value of 0.917 g/cm^3 for ice at 0 °C. Ice and any other substance with a density less than that of water will float, but any substance with a density greater than that of water will sink.

Figure 1.8
The density of water at different temperatures.

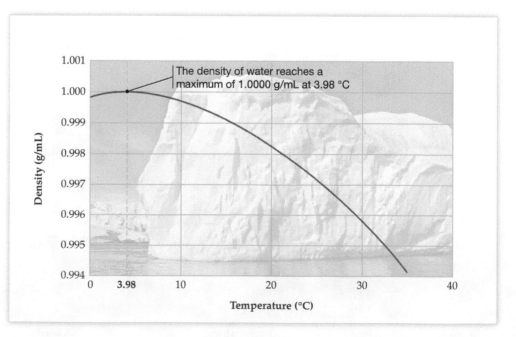

The density of water reaches a maximum of 1.0000 g/mL at 3.98 °C

Knowing the density of a substance, particularly a liquid, can be very **useful** because it's often easier to measure a liquid by volume than by mass. Suppose, for example, that you needed 1.55 g of ethyl alcohol. Rather than trying to weigh exactly the right amount, it would be much easier to look up the density of ethyl alcohol (0.7893 g/mL at 20 °C) and measure the correct volume with a syringe.

$$\text{Density} = \frac{\text{Mass}}{\text{Volume}} \quad \text{so} \quad \text{Volume} = \frac{\text{Mass}}{\text{Density}}$$

$$\text{Volume} = \frac{1.55 \text{ g ethyl alcohol}}{0.7893 \frac{\text{g}}{\text{mL}}} = 1.96 \text{ mL ethyl alcohol}$$

▲ The precise mass of a liquid is easily measured with a syringe if the density of the liquid is known.

CALCULATING A DENSITY

What is the density of the element copper in g/cm^3 if a sample weighing 324.5 g has a volume of 36.2 cm^3?

SOLUTION

Density is mass divided by volume:

$$\text{Density} = \frac{\text{Mass}}{\text{Volume}} = \frac{324.5 \text{ g}}{36.2 \text{ cm}^3} = 8.96 \text{ g/cm}^3$$

WORKED EXAMPLE 1.3

USING DENSITY TO CALCULATE A VOLUME

What is the volume in cm^3 of 454 g of gold? (See Table 1.7.)

SOLUTION

Because density is defined as mass divided by volume, volume is mass divided by density:

$$\text{Volume} = \frac{454 \text{ g gold}}{19.31 \text{ g/cm}^3} = 23.5 \text{ cm}^3 \text{ gold}$$

▶ **PROBLEM 1.9** What is the density of glass in g/cm^3 if a sample weighing 27.43 g has a volume of 12.40 cm^3?

▶ **PROBLEM 1.10** Chloroform, a substance once used as an anesthetic, has a density of 1.483 g/mL at 20 °C. How many milliliters would you use if you needed 9.37 g?

1.11 DERIVED UNITS: ENERGY AND ITS MEASUREMENT

The word *energy* is familiar to everyone but is surprisingly hard to define in simple, nontechnical terms. A good working definition, however, is to say that **energy** is the capacity to supply heat or do work. The water falling over a dam, for instance, contains energy that can be used to turn a turbine and generate electricity. A tank of propane gas contains energy that, when released in the chemical process of combustion, can heat a house or barbecue a hamburger.

Energy is classified as either *kinetic* or *potential*. **Kinetic energy (E_K)** is the energy of motion. The amount of kinetic energy in a moving object with mass m and velocity v is given by the equation

$$E_K = \frac{1}{2}mv^2$$

The larger the mass of an object and the larger its velocity, the larger the amount of kinetic energy. Thus, water that has fallen over a dam from a great height has a greater velocity and more kinetic energy than the same amount of water that has fallen only a short distance.

Potential energy (E_p), by contrast, is stored energy—perhaps stored in an object because of its height or in a molecule because of chemical reactions it can undergo. The water sitting in a reservoir behind the dam contains potential energy because of its height above the stream at the bottom of the dam. When the water is allowed to fall, its potential energy is converted into kinetic energy. Propane and other substances used as fuels contain potential energy because they can undergo a combustion reaction with oxygen that releases heat. (We'll look at energy in more detail in Chapter 8.)

The units for energy, $(kg \cdot m^2)/s^2$, follow from the expression for kinetic energy, $E_K = 1/2\, mv^2$. If, for instance, your body has a mass of 50.0 kg (about 110 lb) and you are riding on a bicycle at a velocity of 10.0 m/s (about 22 mi/h), your kinetic energy is 2500 $(kg \cdot m^2)/s^2$.

$$E_K = \frac{1}{2} mv^2 = \frac{1}{2} (50.0 \text{ kg})\left(10.0 \frac{m}{s}\right)^2 = 2500 \frac{kg \cdot m^2}{s^2} = 2500 \text{ J}$$

The SI derived unit for energy $(kg \cdot m^2)/s^2$ is given the name **joule (J)** after the English physicist James Prescott Joule (1818–1889). The joule is a fairly small amount of energy—it takes roughly 100,000 J to heat a coffee cup full of water from room temperature to boiling—so kilojoules (kJ) are more frequently used in chemistry.

In addition to the SI energy unit joule, some chemists and biochemists still use the unit calorie (cal, with a lowercase c). Originally defined as the amount of energy necessary to raise the temperature of 1 g of water by 1 °C (specifically, from 14.5 °C to 15.5 °C), one calorie is now defined as exactly 4.184 J.

$$1 \text{ cal} = 4.184 \text{ J (exactly)}$$

Nutritionists use the somewhat confusing unit Calorie (Cal, with a capital C), which is equal to 1000 calories, or 1 kilocalorie (kcal).

$$1 \text{ Cal} = 1000 \text{ cal} = 1 \text{ kcal} = 4.184 \text{ kJ}$$

The energy value, or caloric content, of food is measured in Calories. Thus, the statement that a banana contains 70 Calories means that 70 Cal (70 kcal, or 290 kJ) of energy is released when the banana is used by the body for fuel.

▶ **PROBLEM 1.11**   What is the kinetic energy in kilojoules of a 2360 lb (1070 kg) car moving at 63.3 mi/h (28.3 m/s)?

▶ **PROBLEM 1.12**   A Big Mac hamburger from McDonald's contains 540 Calories.
(a) How many kilojoules does a Big Mac contain?
(b) For how many hours could the amount of energy in a Big Mac light a 100 watt lightbulb? (1 watt = 1 J/s)

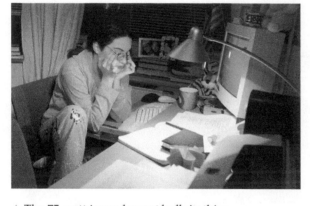

▲ The 75 watt incandescent bulb in this lamp uses energy at the rate of 75 J/s. Only about 5% of that energy appears as light, however; the remaining 95% is given off as heat.

1.12 ACCURACY, PRECISION, AND SIGNIFICANT FIGURES IN MEASUREMENT

Measuring things, whether in cooking, construction, or chemistry, is something that most of us do every day. But how good are those measurements? Any measurement is only as good as the skill of the person doing the work and the reliability of the equipment being used. You've probably noticed, for instance, that you often get slightly different readings when you weigh yourself on a bathroom scale and on a scale at the doctor's office, so there's always some uncertainty about your real weight. The same is true in chemistry—there is always some uncertainty in the value of a measurement.

In talking about the degree of uncertainty in a measurement, we use the words *accuracy* and *precision*. Although most of us use the words interchangeably in daily life, there's actually an important distinction between them. **Accuracy** refers to how close to the true value a given measurement is, whereas **precision** refers to how well a number of independent measurements agree with one another. To see the difference, imagine that you weigh a tennis ball whose true mass is 54.441 778 g. Assume that you take three independent measurements on each of three different types of balance to obtain the data shown in the following table.

Measurement #	Bathroom Scale	Lab Balance	Analytical Balance
1	0.1 kg	54.4 g	54.4418 g
2	0.0 kg	54.5 g	54.4417 g
3	0.1 kg	54.3 g	54.4418 g
(average)	(0.07 kg)	(54.4 g)	(54.4418 g)

▲ This tennis ball has a mass of about 54 g.

If you use a bathroom scale, your measurement (average = 0.07 kg) is neither accurate nor precise. Its accuracy is poor because it measures to only one digit that is far from the true value, and its precision is poor because any two measurements may differ substantially. If you now weigh the ball on an inexpensive laboratory balance, the value you get (average = 54.4 g) has three digits and is fairly accurate, but it is still not very precise because the three readings vary from 54.3 g to 54.5 g, perhaps due to air movements in the room or to a sticky mechanism. Finally, if you weigh the ball on an expensive analytical balance like those found in research laboratories, your measurement (average = 54.4418 g) is both precise and accurate. It's accurate because the measurement is very close to the true value, and it's precise because it has six digits that vary little from one reading to another.

To indicate the uncertainty in a measurement, the value you record should use all the digits you are sure of plus one additional digit that you estimate. In reading a thermometer that has a mark for each degree, for example, you could be certain about the digits of the nearest mark—say 25 °C—but you would have to estimate between two marks—say between 25 °C and 26 °C—to obtain a value of 25.3 °C.

The total number of digits recorded for a measurement is called the measurement's number of **significant figures**. For example, the mass of the tennis ball as determined on the single-pan balance (54.4 g) has three significant figures, whereas the mass determined on the analytical balance (54.4418 g) has six significant figures. All digits but the last are certain; the final digit is an estimate, which we generally assume to have an error of plus or minus one (±1).

Finding the number of significant figures in a measurement is usually easy but can be troublesome if zeros are present. Look at the following four quantities:

4.803 cm	Four significant figures: 4, 8, 0, 3
0.006 61 g	Three significant figures: 6, 6, 1
55.220 K	Five significant figures: 5, 5, 2, 2, 0
34,200 m	Anywhere from three (3, 4, 2) to five (3, 4, 2, 0, 0) significant figures

The following rules cover the different situations that arise:

1. *Zeros in the middle of a number are like any other digit; they are always significant.* Thus, 4.803 cm has four significant figures.

2. *Zeros at the beginning of a number are not significant*; they act only to locate the decimal point. Thus, 0.006 61 g has three significant figures. (Note that 0.006 61 g can be rewritten as 6.61×10^{-3} g or as 6.61 mg.)

3. *Zeros at the end of a number and after the decimal point are always significant.* The assumption is that these zeros would not be shown unless they were significant.

Thus, 55.220 K has five significant figures. (If the value were known to only four significant figures, we would write 55.22 K.)

4. *Zeros at the end of a number and before the decimal point may or may not be significant.* We can't tell whether they are part of the measurement or whether they just locate the decimal point. Thus, 34,200 m may have three, four, or five significant figures. Often, however, a little common sense is helpful. A temperature reading of 20 °C probably has two significant figures rather than one, since one significant figure would imply a temperature anywhere from 10 °C to 30 °C and would be of little use. Similarly, a volume given as 300 mL probably has three significant figures. On the other hand, a figure of 93,000,000 mi for the distance between the Earth and the Sun probably has only two or three significant figures.

The fourth rule shows why it's helpful to write numbers in scientific notation rather than ordinary notation. Doing so makes it possible to indicate the number of significant figures. Thus, writing the number 34,200 as 3.42×10^4 indicates three significant figures but writing it as 3.4200×10^4 indicates five significant figures.

One further point about significant figures: certain numbers, such as those obtained when counting objects, are exact and have an effectively infinite number of significant figures. A week has exactly 7 days, for instance, not 6.9 or 7.0 or 7.1, and a foot has exactly 12 inches, not 11.9 or 12.0 or 12.1. In addition, the power of 10 used in scientific notation is an exact number. That is, the number 10^3 is exactly 1000, but the number 1×10^3 has one significant figure.

WORKED EXAMPLE 1.4

SIGNIFICANT FIGURES

How many significant figures does each of the following measurements have?

(a) 0.036 653 m   (b) 7.2100×10^{-3} g   (c) 72,100 km   (d) $25.03

SOLUTION

(a) 5 (by rule 2)   (b) 5 (by rule 3)
(c) 3, 4, or 5 (by rule 4)   (d) $25.03 is an exact number

▶ PROBLEM 1.13   A 1.000 mL sample of acetone, a common solvent used as a paint remover, was placed in a small bottle whose mass was known to be 38.0015 g. The following values were obtained when the acetone-filled bottle was weighed: 38.7798 g, 38.7795 g, and 38.7801 g. How would you characterize the precision and accuracy of these measurements if the true mass of the acetone was 0.7791 g?

▶ PROBLEM 1.14   How many significant figures does each of the following quantities have? Explain your answers.

(a) 76.600 kJ   (b) $4.502\,00 \times 10^3$ g   (c) 3000 nm   (d) 0.003 00 mL
(e) 18 students   (f) 3×10^{-5} g   (g) 47.60 mL   (h) 2070 mi

1.13 ROUNDING NUMBERS

It often happens, particularly when doing arithmetic on a calculator, that a quantity appears to have more significant figures than are really justified. You might calculate the gas mileage of your car, for instance, by finding that it takes 11.70 gallons of gasoline to drive 278 miles:

$$\text{Mileage} = \frac{\text{Miles}}{\text{Gallons}} = \frac{278 \text{ mi}}{11.70 \text{ gal}} = 23.760\,684 \text{ mi/gal (mpg)}$$

Although the answer on the calculator has eight digits, your measurement is really not as precise as it appears. In fact, your answer is precise to only three significant figures and should be **rounded off** to 23.8 mi/gal by removing all nonsignificant figures.

How do you decide how many figures to keep and how many to ignore? For most purposes, a simple procedure using just two rules is sufficient.

1. *In carrying out a multiplication or division, the answer can't have more significant figures than either of the original numbers.* If you think about it, this rule is just common sense. If you don't know the number of miles you drove to better than three significant figures (278 could mean 277, 278, or 279), you certainly can't calculate your mileage to more than the same number of significant figures.

▲ Calculators often display more figures than are justified by the precision of the data.

Three significant figures Three significant figures

$$\frac{278 \text{ mi}}{11.70 \text{ gal}} = 23.8 \text{ mi/gal}$$

Four significant figures

2. *In carrying out an addition or subtraction, the answer can't have more digits to the right of the decimal point than either of the original numbers.* For example, if you have 3.18 L of water and you add 0.013 15 L more, you now have 3.19 L. Again, this rule is just common sense. If you don't know the volume you started with past the second decimal place (it could be 3.17, 3.18, or 3.19), you can't know the total of the combined volumes past the same decimal place.

Ends two places past decimal point
3.18? ??
+ 0.013 15   Ends five places past decimal point
3.19? ??
Ends two places past decimal point

Once you decide how many digits to retain for your answer, the rules for rounding off numbers are as follows:

1. *If the first digit you remove is less than 5, round down by dropping it and all following digits.* Thus, 5.664 525 becomes 5.66 when rounded to three significant figures because the first of the dropped digits (4) is less than 5.

2. *If the first digit you remove is 6 or greater, round up by adding 1 to the digit on the left.* Thus, 5.664 525 becomes 5.7 when rounded to two significant figures because the first of the dropped digits (6) is greater than 5.

3. *If the first digit you remove is 5 and there are more nonzero digits following, round up.* Thus, 5.664 525 becomes 5.665 when rounded to four significant figures because there are nonzero digits (2, 5) after the 5.

4. *If the digit you remove is a 5 with nothing following, round down.* Thus, 5.664 525 becomes 5.664 52 when rounded to six significant figures because there is nothing after the 5.

WORKED EXAMPLE 1.5

A CALCULATION USING SIGNIFICANT FIGURES

It takes 9.25 hours to fly from London, England, to Chicago, Illinois, a distance of 3952 miles. What is the average speed of the airplane in miles per hour?

SOLUTION

First, set up an equation dividing the number of miles flown by the number of hours:

$$\text{Average speed} = \frac{3952 \text{ mi}}{9.25 \text{ h}} = 427.243\,24 \text{ mi/h}$$

continued on next page

Next, decide how many significant figures should be in your answer. Because the problem involves a division, and because one of the quantities you started with (9.25 h) has only three significant figures, the answer must also have three significant figures. Finally, round off your answer. The first digit to be dropped (2) is less than 5, so the answer 427.243 24 must be rounded off to 427 mi/h.

In doing this or any other problem, use all figures, significant or not, for the calculation and then round off the final answer. Don't round off at any intermediate step.

▶ **PROBLEM 1.15**   Round off each of the following quantities to the number of significant figures indicated in parentheses:

(a) 3.774 499 L (4)   **(b)** 255.0974 K (3)   **(c)** 55.265 kg (4)   **(d)** 906.401 kJ (5)

▶ **PROBLEM 1.16**   Carry out the following calculations, expressing each result with the correct number of significant figures:

(a) 24.567 g + 0.044 78 g = ? g
(b) 4.6742 g ÷ 0.003 71 L = ? g/L
(c) 0.378 mL + 42.3 mL − 1.5833 mL = ? mL

CONCEPTUAL PROBLEM 1.17   What is the temperature reading on the following Celsius thermometer? How many significant figures do you have in your answer?

1.14 CALCULATIONS: CONVERTING
FROM ONE UNIT TO ANOTHER

Because so many scientific activities involve numerical calculations—measuring, weighing, preparing solutions, and so forth—it's often necessary to convert a quantity from one unit to another. Converting between units isn't difficult; we all do it every day. If you run 7.5 laps around a 200 meter track, for instance, you have to convert between the distance unit *lap* and the distance unit *meter* to find that you have run 1500 m (7.5 laps times 200 meters/lap). Converting from one scientific unit to another is just as easy.

$$7.5 \; \cancel{laps} \times \frac{200 \; meters}{1 \; \cancel{lap}} = 1500 \; meters$$

The simplest way to carry out calculations that involve different units is to use the **dimensional-analysis method**. In this method, a quantity described in one unit is converted into an equivalent quantity with a different unit by multiplying with a **conversion factor** that expresses the relationship between units.

Original quantity × Conversion factor = Equivalent quantity

As an example, we know from Section 1.7 that 1 meter equals 39.37 inches. Writing this relationship as a ratio restates it in the form of a conversion factor, either meters per inch or inches per meter.

Conversion factors between meters and inches $\dfrac{1 \; m}{39.37 \; in.}$ equals $\dfrac{39.37 \; in.}{1 \; m}$ equals   1

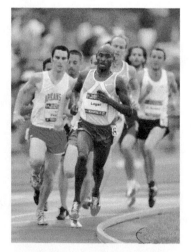

▲ Runners have to convert from laps to meters to find out how far they have run.

Note that this and all other conversion factors are effectively equal to 1 because the quantity above the division line (the numerator) is equal in value to the quantity below the division line (the denominator). Thus, multiplying by a conversion factor is equivalent to multiplying by 1 and so does not change the value of the quantity.

The key to the dimensional-analysis method of problem solving is that units are treated like numbers and can thus be multiplied and divided just as numbers can. The idea when solving a problem is to set up an equation so that unwanted units cancel, leaving only the desired units. Usually it's best to start by writing what you know and then manipulating that known quantity. For example, say you know your height is 69.5 inches and you want to find it in meters. Begin by writing your height in inches and then set up an equation multiplying your height by the conversion factor meters per inch:

$$69.5 \ \text{in.} \ \times \ \frac{1 \ \text{m}}{39.37 \ \text{in.}} \ = \ 1.77 \ \text{m}$$

Starting quantity   Conversion factor   Equivalent quantity

The unit "in." cancels because it appears both above and below the division line, so the only unit that remains is "m."

The dimensional-analysis method gives the right answer only if the conversion factor is arranged so that the unwanted units cancel. If the equation is set up in any other way, the units won't cancel properly and you won't get the right answer. Thus, if you were to multiply your height in inches by an inverted conversion factor of inches per meter rather than meters per inch, you would end up with an incorrect answer expressed in meaningless units.

$$69.5 \ \text{in} \ \times \ \frac{39.37 \ \text{in.}}{1 \ \text{m}} \ = \ 2740 \ \text{in.}^2/\text{m} \quad ??$$

The main drawback to using the dimensional-analysis method is that it's easy to get the right answer without really understanding what you're doing. It's therefore best after solving a problem to think through a rough estimate, or "ballpark" solution, as a check on your work. If your ballpark check isn't close to the answer you get from the detailed solution, there's a misunderstanding somewhere and you should think through the problem again.

Even if you don't make an estimate, it's important to be sure that your calculated answer makes sense. If, for example, you were trying to calculate the volume of a human cell and you came up with the answer 5.3 cm^3, you should realize that such an answer couldn't possibly be right. Cells are too tiny to be distinguished with the naked eye, but a volume of 5.3 cm^3 is about the size of a walnut.

The dimensional-analysis method and the use of ballpark checks are techniques that will help you solve problems of many kinds, not just unit conversions. Problems sometimes seem complicated, but you can usually sort out the complications by analyzing the problem properly.

▲ What is the volume of a red blood cell?

- Identify the information given, including units.
- Identify the information needed in the answer, including units.
- Find a relationship between the known information and unknown answer, and plan a strategy for getting from one to the other.
- Solve the problem.
- Make a rough estimate to be sure your calculated answer is reasonable.

Examples 1.6–1.8 show how to devise strategies and estimate answers. To conserve space, we'll use this approach routinely in only the next few chapters, but you should make it a standard part of your problem solving.

▲ This Koenigsegg CCXR has a top speed of 265 mph.

UNIT CONVERSION USING SIGNIFICANT FIGURES

The Koenigsegg CCXR is the fastest sports car in the world, with a top speed of 265 miles per hour. What is this speed in kilometers per hour?

STRATEGY

The known information is the speed in mi/h; the unknown is the speed in km/h. Find the appropriate conversion factor inside the back cover of this book, and use the dimensional-analysis method to set up an equation so the "mi" units cancel.

SOLUTION

$$\frac{265 \text{ mi}}{1 \text{ h}} \times \frac{1.609 \text{ km}}{1 \text{ mi}} = 426 \frac{\text{km}}{\text{h}}$$

A very fast car!

BALLPARK CHECK

The answer is certainly large, perhaps several hundred km/h. A better estimate is to realize that, because 1 mi = 1.609 km, it takes about 1 1/2 times as many kilometers as miles to measure the same distance. Thus, 265 mi is about 400 km, and 265 mi/h is about 400 km/h. The estimate agrees with the detailed solution.

COMPLEX UNIT CONVERSIONS AND SIGNIFICANT FIGURES

A large sport utility vehicle moving at a speed of 125 km/h might use gasoline at a rate of 16 L per 100 km. What does this correspond to in mi/gal?

STRATEGY

We are given a gasoline mileage in L/km (or km/L), and we need to find the mileage in mi/gal. Thus, two conversions are necessary, one from kilometers to miles and one from liters to gallons. It's best to do multiple conversions one step at a time until you get used to them. First, convert the distance from kilometers to miles and the amount of fuel from liters to gallons, and then divide the distance by the amount of fuel to find the mileage.

SOLUTION

$$100 \text{ km} \times \frac{0.6214 \text{ mi}}{1 \text{ km}} = 62.14 \text{ mi} \qquad 16 \text{ L} \times \frac{1 \text{ gal}}{3.79 \text{ L}} = 4.22 \text{ gal}$$

$$\frac{62.14 \text{ mi}}{4.22 \text{ gal}} = 14.73 \frac{\text{mi}}{\text{gal}} \qquad \text{Round off to 15 mi/gal}$$

Note that extra digits are carried through the intermediate calculations and only the final answer is rounded off.

   When you become more confident in working multiple conversion problems, you can set up one large equation in which all unwanted units cancel.

$$\frac{100 \text{ km}}{16 \text{ L}} \times \frac{3.79 \text{ L}}{1 \text{ gal}} \times \frac{0.6214 \text{ mi}}{1 \text{ km}} = 14.73 \frac{\text{mi}}{\text{gal}} \qquad \text{Round off to 15 mi/gal}$$

BALLPARK CHECK

The mileage is probably low, perhaps in the range of 10 to 15 mi/gal. This is a difficult problem to estimate, however, because it requires several different conversions. It's therefore best to think the problem through one step at a time, writing down the intermediate estimates:

- A distance of 100 km per 16 L is approximately 6 km/L.
- Because 1 km is about 0.6 mi, 6 km/L is about 4 mi/L.
- Because 1 L is approximately 1 qt, or 1/4 gal, 4 mi/L is about 16 mi/gal.

This estimate agrees with the detailed solution.

WORKED EXAMPLE 1.8

COMPLEX UNIT CONVERSIONS AND SIGNIFICANT FIGURES

The volcanic explosion that destroyed the Indonesian island of Krakatau on August 27, 1883, released an estimated 4.3 cubic miles (mi^3) of debris into the atmosphere and affected global weather for years. In SI units, how many cubic meters (m^3) of debris were released?

STRATEGY

We are given a volume in cubic miles and need to convert to cubic meters. It's probably simplest to convert first from mi^3 to km^3 and then convert km^3 to m^3.

SOLUTION

$$4.3 \; mi^3 \times \left(\frac{1 \; km}{0.6214 \; mi} \right)^3 = 17.92 \; km^3$$

$$17.92 \; km^3 \times \left(\frac{1000 \; m}{1 \; km} \right)^3 = 1.792 \times 10^{10} \; m^3$$

$$= 1.8 \times 10^{10} \; m^3 \quad \text{Rounded off}$$

BALLPARK CHECK

One meter is much less than 1 mile, so it takes a large number of cubic meters to equal 1 mi^3, and the answer is going to be very large. Because 1 km is about 0.6 mi, 1 km^3 is about $(0.6)^3 = 0.2$ times as large as 1 mi^3. Thus, each mi^3 contains about 5 km^3, and 4.3 mi^3 contains about 20 km^3. Each km^3, in turn, contains $(1000 \; m)^3 = 10^9 \; m^3$. Thus, the volume of debris from the Krakatau explosion was about $20 \times 10^9 \; m^3$, or $2 \times 10^{10} \; m^3$. The estimate agrees with the detailed solution.

▶ **PROBLEM 1.18** Calculate answers to the following problems, and check your solutions by making ballpark estimates.

(a) The melting point of gold is 1064 °C. What is this temperature in degrees Fahrenheit?

(b) How large, in cubic centimeters, is the volume of a red blood cell if the cell has a cylindrical shape with a diameter of 6×10^{-6} m and a height of 2×10^{-6} m?

▶ **PROBLEM 1.19** Gemstones are weighed in *carats*, with 1 carat = 200 mg (exactly). What is the mass in grams of the Hope Diamond, the world's largest blue diamond at 44.4 carats? What is this mass in ounces?

▶ **PROBLEM 1.20** A pure diamond with a mass of 0.1000 g contains 5.014×10^{21} carbon atoms and has a density of 3.52 g/cm^3. What is the volume of the Hope Diamond (Problem 1.19), and how many carbon atoms does it contain?

INQUIRY WHAT ARE THE RISKS AND BENEFITS OF CHEMICALS?

▲ Is this a poison or a treatment for leukemia?

Life is not risk-free—we all take many risks each day, often without even thinking about it. We may decide to ride a bike rather than drive, even though the likelihood per mile of being killed on a bicycle is 10 times greater than in a car. We may decide to smoke cigarettes, even though smoking kills more than 170,000 people each year in the United States.

What about risks from "chemicals"? News reports sometimes make it seem that our food is covered with pesticides and filled with dangerous additives, that our land is polluted by toxic waste dumps, and that our medicines are unsafe. How bad are the risks from chemicals, and how are the risks evaluated?

First, it's important to realize that *everything*, including your own body, is made of chemicals—that's what matter is. There is no such thing as a "chemical-free" food, cosmetic, cleanser, or anything else. Second, there is no meaningful distinction between a "natural" substance and a "synthetic" one; a chemical is a chemical. Many naturally occurring substances—snake venom, for example—are extraordinarily toxic, and many synthetic substances—polyethylene, for example—are harmless.

Risk evaluation of chemicals is carried out by exposing test animals, usually mice or rats, to a chemical and then monitoring for signs of harm. To limit the expense and time needed for testing, the amounts administered are often hundreds or thousands of times larger than those a person might normally encounter. The *acute chemical toxicity* (as opposed to chronic toxicity) observed in animal tests is reported as an LD_{50} *value*, the amount of a substance per kilogram of body weight that is a lethal dose for 50% of the test animals. Some LD_{50} values of different substances are shown in Table 1.8. The lower the value, the more toxic the substance.

TABLE 1.8   Some LD_{50} Values in Rats

Substance	LD_{50} (g/kg)	Substance	LD_{50} (g/kg)
Strychnine	0.005	Chloroform	1.2
Arsenic trioxide	0.015	Iron(II) sulfate	1.5
DDT	0.115	Ethyl alcohol	7.1
Aspirin	1.1	Sodium cyclamate	12.8

Even with an LD_{50} value established in test animals, the risk of human exposure to a given substance is still hard to assess. If a substance is harmful to rats, is it necessarily harmful to humans? How can a large dose for a small animal be translated into a small dose for a large human? All substances are toxic to some organisms to some extent, and the difference between help and harm is often a matter of degree. Vitamin A, for example, is necessary for vision, yet it can promote cancer at high doses. Arsenic trioxide is the most classic of poisons, yet it induces remissions in some types of leukemia and is sold for drug use under the name Trisenox. Even water can be toxic if drunk in large amounts because it dilutes the salt in body fluids and causes a potentially life-threatening condition called *hyponatremia* that has resulted in the death of several marathon runners. Furthermore, how we evaluate risk is strongly influenced by familiarity. Many foods contain natural ingredients far more toxic than synthetic additives or pesticide residues, but the ingredients are ignored because the foods are familiar.

All decisions involve trade-offs. Does the benefit of a pesticide that increases food production outweigh a possible health risk to 1 person in 1 million? Do the beneficial effects of a new drug outweigh a potentially dangerous side effect in a small number of users? Different people will have different opinions, but an honest evaluation of the facts is surely better than a purely emotional response.

▶ **PROBLEM 1.21**   Table salt (sodium chloride) has an LD_{50} of 4 g/kg in rats. Assuming that rats and humans have the same LD_{50}, how much salt would a 155 lb person have to consume to have a 50% chance of dying?

SUMMARY

Chemistry is the study of the composition, properties, and transformations of **matter**. It is best approached by posing questions, conducting experiments, and devising **theories** to interpret the experimental results.

All matter is formed from one or more of 118 presently known **elements**—fundamental substances that can't be chemically broken down. Elements are symbolized by one- or two-letter abbreviations and can be organized into a **periodic table** with **groups** (columns) and **periods** (rows). Elements in the same group of the periodic table show similar chemical behavior. The two larger groups on the left and the six larger groups on the right of the table are called the **main groups**, the 10 smaller ones in the middle of the table are called the **transition metal groups**, and the 14 shown separately at the bottom of the table are called the **inner transition metal groups**. Elements are classified as **metals**, **nonmetals**, or **semimetals**.

The characteristics, or **properties**, that are used to describe matter can be classified in several ways. **Physical properties** are those that can be determined without changing the chemical composition of the sample, whereas **chemical properties** are those that do involve a chemical change in the sample. **Intensive properties** are those whose values do not depend on the size of the sample, whereas **extensive properties** are those whose values do depend on sample size.

Accurate measurement is crucial to scientific experimentation. The units used are those of the Système Internationale (**SI units**). There are seven fundamental SI units, together with other derived units. **Mass**, the amount of matter in an object, is measured in **kilograms (kg)**; **length** is measured in **meters (m)**; **temperature** is measured in **kelvin (K)**; and **volume** is measured in **cubic meters** (m^3). The more familiar metric **liter (L)** and **milliliter (mL)** are also still used for measuring volume, and the **Celsius degree (°C)** is still used for measuring temperature. **Density** is an intensive physical property that relates mass to volume and is measured in the derived SI unit g/cm^3 or g/mL. **Energy** is the capacity to supply heat or do work and is measured in the derived SI unit ($kg \cdot m^2/s^2$), or **joule (J)**. Energy is of two kinds, potential and kinetic. **Kinetic energy (E_K)** is the energy of motion, and **potential energy (E_P)** is stored energy.

Because many experiments involve numerical calculations, it's often necessary to manipulate and convert different units of measure. The simplest way to carry out such conversions is to use the **dimensional-analysis method**, in which an equation is set up so that unwanted units cancel and only the desired units remain. It's also important when measuring physical quantities or carrying out calculations to indicate the precision of the measurement by **rounding off** the result to the correct number of **significant figures**.

KEY WORDS

accuracy   *19*
alkali metal   *8*
alkaline earth metal   *8*
Celsius degree (°C)   *13*
centimeter (cm)   *12*
chemical property   *7*
chemistry   *1*
conversion factor   *22*
cubic centimeter (cm³)   *15*
cubic decimeter (dm³)   *15*
cubic meter (m³)   *15*
density   *16*
dimensional-analysis
  method   *22*

element   *2*
energy   *17*
extensive property   *7*
gram (g)   *11*
group (periodic table)   *5*
halogen   *8*
inner transition metal
  group   *7*
intensive property   *7*
joule (J)   *18*
kelvin (K)   *13*
kilogram (kg)   *11*
kinetic energy (E_K)   *17*
liter (L)   *15*

main group   *7*
mass   *11*
matter   *11*
metal   *9*
meter (m)   *12*
microgram (μg)   *11*
micrometer (μm)   *12*
milligram (mg)   *11*
milliliter (mL)   *15*
millimeter (mm)   *12*
nanometer (nm)   *12*
noble gas   *8*
nonmetal   *9*
period (periodic table)   *5*

periodic table   *2*
physical property   *7*
picometer (pm)   *12*
potential energy (E_P)   *18*
precision   *19*
property   *7*
rounding off   *21*
scientific notation   *10*
semimetal   *9*
SI unit   *10*
significant figure   *19*
theory   *2*
transition metal group   *7*

CONCEPTUAL PROBLEMS

Problems at the end of each chapter begin with a section called "Conceptual Problems." The problems in this section are visual rather than numerical and are intended to probe your understanding rather than your facility with numbers and formulas. Answers to even-numbered problems (in color) can be found at the end of the book following the appendixes. Problems 1.1–1.21 appear within the chapter.

1.22 Where on the following outline of a periodic table are the indicated elements or groups of elements?

(a) Alkali metals

(b) Halogens

(c) Alkaline earth metals

(d) Transition metals

(e) Hydrogen

(f) Helium

1.23 Where on the following outline of a periodic table does the dividing line between metals and nonmetals fall?

1.24 Is the red element on the following periodic table likely to be a gas, a liquid, or a solid? What is the atomic number of the blue element? Name at least one other element that is chemically similar to the green element.

1.25 The radioactive element indicated on the following periodic table is used in smoke detectors. Identify it, give its atomic number, and tell what kind of group it's in.

1.26 Characterize each of the following dartboards according to the accuracy and precision of the results.

1.27 How many milliliters of water does the graduated cylinder in **(a)** contain, and how tall in centimeters is the paper clip in **(b)**? How many significant figures do you have in each answer?

(a)   **(b)**

1.28 Assume that you have two graduated cylinders, one with a capacity of 5 mL **(a)** and the other with a capacity of 50 mL **(b)**. Draw a line in each, showing how much liquid you would add if you needed to measure 2.64 mL of water. Which cylinder will give the more accurate measurement? Explain.

(a)   **(b)**

1.29 The following cylinder contains three liquids that do not mix with one another: water (density = 1.0 g/mL), vegetable oil (density = 0.93 g/mL), and mercury (density = 13.5 g/mL). Which liquid is which?

SECTION PROBLEMS

SECTION PROBLEMS

The Section Problems at the end of each chapter cover specific topics from the various sections of the chapter. These problems are presented in pairs, with each even-numbered problem followed by an odd-numbered one requiring similar skills. These paired problems are followed by unpaired Chapter Problems that draw on various parts of the chapter. Even-numbered problems (in color) are answered at the end of the book following the appendixes.

Elements and the Periodic Table (Sections 1.2–1.4)

1.30 How many elements are presently known? About how many occur naturally?

1.31 What are the rows called and what are the columns called in the periodic table?

1.32 How many groups are there in the periodic table? How are they labeled?

1.33 What common characteristics do elements within a group of the periodic table have?

1.34 Where in the periodic table are the main-group elements found? Where are the transition metal groups found?

1.35 Where in the periodic table are the metallic elements found? Where are the nonmetallic elements found?

1.36 What is a semimetal, and where in the periodic table are semimetals found?

1.37 List several general properties of the following:
(a) Alkali metals   (b) Noble gases   (c) Halogens

1.38 Without looking at a periodic table, list as many alkali metals as you can. (There are five common ones.)

1.39 Without looking at a periodic table, list as many alkaline earth metals as you can. (There are five common ones.)

1.40 Without looking at a periodic table, list as many halogens as you can. (There are four common ones.)

1.41 Without looking at a periodic table, list as many noble gases as you can. (There are six common ones.)

1.42 At room temperature, a certain element is found to be a soft, silver-colored solid that reacts violently with water and is a good conductor of electricity. Is the element likely to be a metal, a nonmetal, or a semimetal?

1.43 At room temperature, a certain element is found to be shiny, silver-colored solid that is a poor conductor of electricity. When a sample of the element is hit with a hammer, it shatters. Is the element likely to be a metal, a nonmetal, or a semimetal?

1.44 In which of the periodic groups 1A, 2A, 5A, and 7A is the first letter of all elements' symbol the same as the first letter of their name?

1.45 For which elements in groups 1A, 2A, 5A, and 7A of the periodic table does the first letter of their symbol differ from the first letter of their name?

1.46 What are the symbols for the following elements?
(a) Gadolinium (used in color TV screens)
(b) Germanium (used in semiconductors)
(c) Technetium (used in biomedical imaging)
(d) Arsenic (used in pesticides)

1.47 What are the symbols for the following elements?
(a) Cadmium (used in rechargeable ni-cad batteries)
(b) Iridium (used for hardening alloys)

(c) Beryllium (used in the space shuttle)
(d) Tungsten (used in lightbulbs)

1.48 Give the names corresponding to the following symbols:
(a) Te   (b) Re   (c) Be
(d) Ar   (e) Pu

1.49 Give the names corresponding to the following symbols:
(a) B   (b) Rh   (c) Cf
(d) Os   (e) Ga

1.50 What is wrong with each of the following statements?
(a) The symbol for tin is Ti.
(b) The symbol for manganese is Mg.
(c) The symbol for potassium is Po.
(d) The symbol for helium is HE.

1.51 What is wrong with each of the following statements?
(a) The symbol for carbon is ca.
(b) The symbol for sodium is So.
(c) The symbol for nitrogen is Ni.
(d) The symbol for chlorine is Cr.

Units and Significant Figures (Sections 1.5–1.13)

1.52 What is the difference between mass and weight?

1.53 What is the difference between a derived SI unit and a fundamental SI unit? Give an example of each.

1.54 What SI units are used for measuring the following quantities? For derived units, express your answers in terms of the six fundamental units.
(a) Mass   (b) Length   (c) Temperature
(d) Volume   (e) Energy   (f) Density

1.55 What SI prefixes correspond to the following multipliers?
(a) 10^3 (b) 10^{-6} (c) 10^9
(d) 10^{-12} (e) 10^{-2}

1.56 Which is larger, a Fahrenheit degree or a Celsius degree? By how much?

1.57 What is the difference between a kelvin and a Celsius degree?

1.58 What is the difference between a cubic decimeter (SI) and a liter (metric)?

1.59 What is the difference between a cubic centimeter (SI) and a milliliter (metric)?

1.60 Which of the following statements use exact numbers?
(a) 1 ft = 12 in.
(b) 1 cal = 4.184 J
(c) The height of Mt. Everest is 29,035 ft.
(d) The world record for the 1 mile run, set by Morocco's Hicham el Guerrouj in July, 1999, is 3 minutes, 43.13 seconds.

1.61 What is the difference in mass between a nickel that weighs 4.8 g and a nickel that weighs 4.8673 g?

1.62 Bottles of wine sometimes carry the notation "Volume = 75 cL." What does the unit cL mean?

1.63 What do the following abbreviations stand for?
(a) dL   (b) dm   (c) μm
(d) nL   (e) MJ

1.64 Which quantity in each of the following pairs is larger?

(a) 5.63×10^6 cm or 6.02×10^1 km

(b) 46 μs or 3.2×10^{-2} ms

(c) 200,098 g or 17×10^1 kg

1.65 Which quantity in each of the following pairs is smaller?

(a) 154 pm or 7.7×10^{-9} cm

(b) 1.86×10^{11} μm or 2.02×10^2 km

(c) 2.9 GA or 3.1×10^{15} μA

1.66 How many picograms are in 1 mg? In 35 ng?

1.67 How many microliters are in 1 L? In 20 mL?

1.68 Carry out the following conversions:

(a) 5 pm = ____ cm = ____ nm

(b) 8.5 cm^3 = ____ m^3 = ____ mm^3

(c) 65.2 mg = ____ g = ____ pg

1.69 Which is larger, and by approximately how much?

(a) A liter or a quart   (b) A mile or a kilometer

(c) A gram or an ounce   (d) A centimeter or an inch

1.70 How many significant figures are in each of the following measurements?

(a) 35.0445 g   (b) 59.0001 cm   (c) 0.030 03 kg

(d) 0.004 50 m   (e) 67,000 m^2 (f) 3.8200×10^3 L

1.71 How many significant figures are in each of the following measurements?

(a) \$130.95   (b) 2000.003 g   (c) 5 ft 3 in.

(d) 510 J   (e) 5.10×10^2 J   (f) 10 students

1.72 The Vehicle Assembly Building at the John F. Kennedy Space Center in Cape Canaveral, Florida, is the largest building in the world, with a volume of 3,666,500 m^3. Express this volume in scientific notation.

1.73 The diameter of the Earth at the equator is 7926.381 mi. Round off this quantity to four significant figures; to two significant figures. Express the answers in scientific notation.

1.74 Express the following measurements in scientific notation:

(a) 453.32 mg   (b) 0.000 042 1 mL   (c) 667,000 g

1.75 Convert the following measurements from scientific notation to standard notation:

(a) 3.221×10^{-3} mm   (b) 8.940×10^5 m

(c) $1.350\ 82 \times 10^{-12}$ m^3 (d) 6.4100×10^2 km

1.76 Round off the following quantities to the number of significant figures indicated in parentheses:

(a) 35,670.06 m (4, 6)   (b) 68.507 g (2, 3)

(c) 4.995×10^3 cm (3)   (d) $2.309\ 85 \times 10^{-4}$ kg (5)

1.77 Round off the following quantities to the number of significant figures indicated in parentheses:

(a) 7.0001 kg (4)   (b) 1.605 km (3)

(c) 13.2151 g/cm^3 (3)   (d) 2,300,000.1 (7)

1.78 Express the results of the following calculations with the correct number of significant figures:

(a) 4.884×2.05 (b) $94.61 \div 3.7$

(c) $3.7 \div 94.61$ (d) $5502.3 + 24 + 0.01$

(e) $86.3 + 1.42 - 0.09$ (f) 5.7×2.31

1.79 Express the results of the following calculations with the correct number of significant figures:

(a) $\dfrac{3.41 - 0.23}{5.233} \times 0.205$ (b) $\dfrac{5.556 \times 2.3}{4.223 - 0.08}$

1.80 The world record for the women's outdoor 20,000 meter run, set in 2000 by Tegla Loroupe, is 1:05:26.6 (seconds are given to the nearest tenth). What was her average speed, expressed in miles per hour with the correct number of significant figures? (Assume that the race distance is accurate to 5 significant figures.)

1.81 In the U.S., the emissions limit for carbon monoxide in motorcycle engine exhaust is 12.0 g of carbon monoxide per kilometer driven. What is this limit expressed in mg per mile with the correct number of significant figures?

Unit Conversions (Section 1.14)

1.82 Carry out the following conversions:

(a) How many grams of meat are in a quarter-pound hamburger (0.25 lb)?

(b) How tall in meters is the Willis Tower, formerly called the Sears Tower, in Chicago (1454 ft)?

(c) How large in square meters is the land area of Australia (2,941,526 mi^2)?

1.83 Convert the following quantities into SI units with the correct number of significant figures:

(a) 5.4 in.   (b) 66.31 lb   (c) 0.5521 gal

(d) 65 mi/h   (e) 978.3 yd^3 (f) 2.380 mi^2

1.84 The volume of water used for crop irrigation is measured in acre-feet, where 1 acre-foot is the amount of water needed to cover 1 acre of land to a depth of 1 ft.

(a) If there are 640 acres per square mile, how many cubic feet of water are in 1 acre-foot?

(b) How many acre-feet are in Lake Erie (total volume = 116 mi^3)?

1.85 The height of a horse is usually measured in *hands* instead of in feet, where 1 hand equals 1/3 ft (exactly).

(a) How tall in centimeters is a horse of 18.6 hands?

(b) What is the volume in cubic meters of a box measuring $6 \times 2.5 \times 15$ hands?

1.86 Concentrations of substances dissolved in solution are often expressed as mass per unit volume. For example, normal human blood has a cholesterol concentration of about 200 mg/100 mL. Express this concentration in the following units:

(a) mg/L   (b) μg/mL   (c) g/L   (d) ng/μL

(e) How much total blood cholesterol in grams does a person have if the normal blood volume in the body is 5 L?

1.87 Weights in England are commonly measured in *stones*, where 1 stone = 14 lb. What is the weight in pounds of a person who weighs 8.65 stones?

1.88 Among many alternative units that might be considered as a measure of time is the *shake* rather than the second. Based on the expression "faster than a shake of a lamb's tail," we'll define 1 shake as equal to 2.5×10^{-4} s. If a car is traveling at 55 mi/h, what is its speed in cm/shake?

1.89 Administration of digitalis, a drug used to control atrial fibrillation in heart patients, must be carefully controlled because even a modest overdosage can be fatal. To take differences between patients into account, drug dosages are prescribed in terms of mg/kg body weight. Thus, a child and an adult differ greatly in weight, but both receive the same dosage per kilogram of body weight. At a dosage of 20 μg/kg body weight, how many milligrams of digitalis should a 160 lb patient receive?

Temperature (Section 1.8)

1.90 The normal body temperature of a goat is 39.9 °C, and that of an Australian spiny anteater is 22.2 °C. Express these temperatures in degrees Fahrenheit.

1.91 Of the 90 or so naturally occurring elements, only four are liquid near room temperature: mercury (melting point = −38.87 °C), bromine (melting point = −7.2 °C), cesium (melting point = 28.40 °C), and gallium (melting point = 29.78 °C). Convert these melting points to degrees Fahrenheit.

1.92 Tungsten, the element used to make filaments in lightbulbs, has a melting point of 6192 °F. Convert this temperature to degrees Celsius and to kelvin.

1.93 Suppose that your oven is calibrated in degrees Fahrenheit but a recipe calls for you to bake at 175 °C. What oven setting should you use?

1.94 Suppose you were dissatisfied with both Celsius and Fahrenheit units and wanted to design your own temperature scale based on ethyl alcohol (ethanol). On the Celsius scale, ethanol has a melting point of −117.3 °C and a boiling point of 78.5 °C, but on your new scale calibrated in units of degrees ethanol, °E, you define ethanol to melt at 0 °E and boil at 200 °E.
 (a) How does your ethanol degree compare in size with a Celsius degree?
 (b) How does an ethanol degree compare in size with a Fahrenheit degree?
 (c) What are the melting and boiling points of water on the ethanol scale?
 (d) What is normal human body temperature (98.6 °F) on the ethanol scale?
 (e) If the outside thermometer reads 130 °E, how would you dress to go out?

1.95 Answer parts (a)–(d) of Problem 1.94 assuming that your new temperature scale is based on ammonia, NH_3. On the

Celsius scale, ammonia has a melting point of −77.7 °C and a boiling point of −33.4 °C, but on your new scale calibrated in units of degrees ammonia, °A, you define ammonia to melt at 0 °A and boil at 100 °A.

Density (Section 1.10)

1.96 The density of silver is 10.5 g/cm³. What is the mass (in kilograms) of a cube of silver that measures 0.62 m on each side?

1.97 A vessel contains 4.67 L of bromine, whose density is 3.10 g/cm³. What is the mass of the bromine in the vessel (in kilograms)?

1.98 Aspirin has a density of 1.40 g/cm³. What is the volume in cubic centimeters of an aspirin tablet weighing 250 mg? Of a tablet weighing 500 lb?

1.99 Gaseous hydrogen has a density of 0.0899 g/L at 0 °C, and gaseous chlorine has a density of 3.214 g/L at the same temperature. How many liters of each would you need if you wanted 1.0078 g of hydrogen and 35.45 g of chlorine?

1.100 What is the density of lead in g/cm³ if a rectangular bar measuring 0.50 cm in height, 1.55 cm in width, and 25.00 cm in length has a mass of 220.9 g?

1.101 What is the density of lithium metal in g/cm³ if a cylindrical wire with a diameter of 2.40 mm and a length of 15.0 cm has a mass of 0.3624 g?

Energy (Section 1.11)

1.102 Which has more kinetic energy, a 1400 kg car moving at 115 km/h or a 12,000 kg truck moving at 38 km/h?

1.103 Assume that the kinetic energy of a 1400 kg car moving at 115 km/h (Problem 1.102) is converted entirely into heat. How many calories of heat are released, and what amount of water in liters could be heated from 20.0 °C to 50.0 °C by the car's energy? (One calorie raises the temperature of 1 mL of water by 1 °C.)

1.104 The combustion of 45.0 g of methane (natural gas) releases 2498 kJ of heat energy. How much energy in kilocalories (kcal) would combustion of 0.450 ounces of methane release?

1.105 Sodium (Na) metal undergoes a chemical reaction with chlorine (Cl) gas to yield sodium chloride, or common table salt. If 1.00 g of sodium reacts with 1.54 g of chlorine, 2.54 g of sodium chloride is formed and 17.9 kJ of heat is released. How much sodium and how much chlorine in grams would have to react to release 171 kcal of heat?

CHAPTER PROBLEMS

1.106 When an irregularly shaped chunk of silicon weighing 8.763 g was placed in a graduated cylinder containing 25.00 mL of water, the water level in the cylinder rose to 28.76 mL. What is the density of silicon in g/cm³?

1.107 Lignum vitae is a hard, durable, and extremely dense wood used to make ship bearings. A sphere of this wood with a diameter of 7.60 cm has a mass of 313 g.

 (a) What is the density of the lignum vitae sphere?
 (b) Will the sphere float or sink in water?
 (c) Will the sphere float or sink in chloroform? (The density of chloroform is 1.48 g/mL).

1.108 Sodium chloride has a melting point of 1074 K and a boiling point of 1686 K. Convert these temperatures to degrees Celsius and to degrees Fahrenheit.

1.109 A large tanker truck for carrying gasoline has a capacity of 3.4×10^4 L.

(a) What is the tanker's capacity in gallons?

(b) If the retail price of gasoline is $3.00 per gallon, what is the value of the truck's full load of gasoline?

1.110 The density of chloroform, a widely used organic solvent, is 1.4832 g/mL at 20 °C. How many milliliters would you use if you wanted 112.5 g of chloroform?

1.111 More sulfuric acid (density = 1.8302 g/cm^3) is produced than any other chemical—approximately 3.6×10^{11} lb/yr worldwide. What is the volume of this amount in liters?

1.112 Answer the following questions:

(a) An old rule of thumb in cooking says: "A pint's a pound the world around." What is the density in g/mL of a substance for which 1 pt = 1 lb exactly?

(b) There are exactly 640 acres in 1 square mile. How many square meters are in 1 acre?

(c) A certain type of wood has a density of 0.40 g/cm^3. What is the mass of 1.0 cord of this wood in kg, where 1 cord is 128 cubic feet of wood?

(d) A particular sample of crude oil has a density of 0.85 g/mL. What is the mass of 1.00 barrel of this crude oil in kg, where a barrel of oil is exactly 42 gallons?

(e) A gallon of ice cream contains exactly 32 servings, and each serving has 165 Calories, of which 30.0% are derived from fat. How many Calories derived from fat would you consume if you ate one half-gallon of ice cream?

1.113 A 1.0 ounce piece of chocolate contains 15 mg of caffeine, and a 6.0 ounce cup of regular coffee contains 105 mg of caffeine. How much chocolate would you have to consume to get as much caffeine as you would from 2.0 cups of coffee?

1.114 A bag of Hershey's Kisses contains the following information:

Serving size: 9 pieces = 41 grams

Calories per serving: 230

Total fat per serving: 13 g

(a) The bag contains 2.0 lbs of Hershey's Kisses. How many Kisses are in the bag?

(b) The density of a Hershey's Kiss is 1.4 g/mL. What is the volume of a single Hershey's Kiss?

(c) How many Calories are in one Hershey's Kiss?

(d) Each gram of fat yields 9 Calories when metabolized. What percent of the calories in Hershey's Kisses are derived from fat?

1.115 Vinaigrette salad dressing consists mainly of oil and vinegar. The density of olive oil is 0.918 g/cm^3, the density of vinegar is 1.006 g/cm^3, and the two do not mix. If a certain mixture of olive oil and vinegar has a total mass of 397.8 g and a total volume of 422.8 cm^3, what is the volume of oil and what is the volume of vinegar in the mixture?

1.116 At a certain point, the Celsius and Fahrenheit scales "cross," giving the same numerical value on both. At what temperature does this crossover occur?

1.117 Imagine that you place a cork measuring 1.30 cm × 5.50 cm × 3.00 cm in a pan of water and that on top of the cork you place a small cube of lead measuring 1.15 cm on each edge. The density of cork is 0.235 g/cm^3, and the density of lead is 11.35 g/cm^3. Will the combination of cork plus lead float or sink?

1.118 The LD_{50} of aspirin in rats is given in the *Inquiry* at the end of the chapter. If a baby aspirin tablet contains 81 mg of aspirin, how many whole tablets would a 0.75 lb rat have to consume to have at least a 50% chance of dying from the dose?

1.119 An Eastern diamondback rattlesnake was milked until 0.134 g of venom was obtained. The venom was then administered subcutaneously in equal portions to 550 mice with an average weight of 0.70 oz, and exactly half the mice died. What is the LD_{50} (in g/kg) for the snake venom in mice? See the *Inquiry* at the end of this chapter.

1.120 A 125 mL sample of water at 293.2 K was heated for 8 min, 25 s so as to give a constant temperature increase of 3.0 °F/min. What is the final temperature of the water in degrees Celsius?

1.121 A calibrated flask was filled to the 25.00 mL mark with ethyl alcohol. By weighing the flask before and after adding the alcohol, it was determined that the flask contained 19.7325 g of alcohol. In a second experiment, 25.0920 g of metal beads were added to the flask, and the flask was again filled to the 25.00 mL mark with ethyl alcohol. The total mass of the metal plus alcohol in the flask was determined to be 38.4704 g. What is the density of the metal in g/mL?

1.122 Brass is a copper–zinc alloy. What is the mass in grams of a brass cylinder having a length of 1.62 in. and a diameter of 0.514 in. if the composition of the brass is 67.0% copper and 33.0% zinc by mass? The density of copper is 8.92 g/cm^3, and the density of zinc is 7.14 g/cm^3. Assume that the density of the brass varies linearly with composition.

1.123 Ocean currents are measured in *Sverdrups* (sv) where $1 \text{ sv} = 10^9 \text{ m}^3/\text{s}$. The Gulf Stream off the tip of Florida, for instance, has a flow of 35 sv.

(a) What is the flow of the Gulf Stream in milliliters per minute?

(b) What mass of water in the Gulf Stream flows past a given point in 24 hours? The density of seawater is 1.025 g/mL.

(c) How much time is required for 1 petaliter (PL; $1 \text{ PL} = 10^{15}$ L) of seawater to flow past a given point?

1.124 The element gallium (Ga) has the second largest liquid range of any element, melting at 29.78 °C and boiling at 2204 °C at atmospheric pressure.

(a) Is gallium a metal, a nonmetal, or a semimetal?

(b) Name another element whose chemical properties might be similar to those of gallium.

(c) What is the density of gallium in g/cm^3 at 25 °C if a 1 in. cube has a mass of 0.2133 lb?

(d) Assume that you construct a thermometer using gallium as the fluid instead of mercury, and that you define the melting point of gallium as 0 °G and the boiling point of gallium as 1000 °G. What is the melting point of sodium chloride (801 °C) on the gallium scale?

1.125 Distances over land are measured in *statute miles* (5280 ft), but distances over water are measured in *nautical miles*, where 1 nautical mile was originally defined as 1 minute of arc along an Earth meridian, or 1/21,600 of the Earth's circumference through the poles. A ship's speed through the water is measured in *knots*, where 1 knot = 1 nautical mile per hour. Historically, the unit *knot* derived from the practice of measuring a ship's speed by throwing a log tied to a knotted line over the side. The line had a knot tied in it at intervals of 47 ft. 3 in., and the number of knots run out in 28 seconds was counted to determine speed.

(a) How many feet are in a nautical mile? How many meters?

(b) The northern bluefin tuna can weigh up to 1500 pounds and can swim at speeds up to 48 miles per hour. How fast is this in knots?

(c) A *league* is defined as 3 nautical miles. The Mariana Trench, with a depth of 35,798 feet, is the deepest point in the ocean. How many leagues deep is this?

(d) By international agreement, the nautical mile is now defined as exactly 1852 meters. By what percentage does this current definition differ from the original definition, and by what percentage does it differ from a statute mile?

CHAPTER 2

Atoms, Molecules, and Ions

If you could take a large piece of pure gold and cut it into ever smaller and smaller pieces, you would find that it is made of a vast number of tiny fundamental units that we call *atoms*. In fact, one pound of gold contains 1.387×10^{24} atoms!

CONTENTS

Further investigations in the decades following Lavoisier led the Fren[ch]
Joseph Proust (1754–1826) to formulate a second fundamental chemica[l law]
that we now call the **law of definite proportions**:

> **Law of Definite Proportions** Different samples of a pure
> compound always contain the
> portion of elements by mass.

Every sample of water (H_2O) contains 1 part hydrogen and 8 parts
mass; every sample of carbon dioxide (CO_2) contains 3 parts carbon and 8 pa[rts]
by mass; and so on. *Elements combine in specific proportions, not in random prop*[ortions.]

2.2 THE LAW OF MULTIPLE PROPORTIONS DALTON'S ATOMIC THEORY

At the same time that Proust was formulating the law of definite proportion
lish schoolteacher John Dalton (1766–1844) was exploring along similar lines
led him to propose what has come to be called the **law of multiple proporti**[ons]

> **Law of Multiple Proportions** Elements can combine in differe
> form different chemical compo[unds]
> mass ratios that are small who[le]
> multiples of each other.

The key to Dalton's proposition was his realization that the *same* eleme[nts]
times combine in different ratios to give *different* chemical compounds. Fo[r example,]
nitrogen and oxygen can combine either in a 7:8 mass ratio to make the c[ompound]
we know today as nitric oxide (NO) or in a 7:16 mass ratio to make the c[ompound]
we know as nitrogen dioxide (NO_2). The second compound contains exact[ly twice as]
much oxygen as the first.

| NO: | 7 g nitrogen per 8 g oxygen | N:O mass ratio = 7:8 |
| NO$_2$: | 7 g nitrogen per 16 g oxygen | N:O mass ratio = 7:1[6] |

Comparison of N:O ratios
in NO and NO$_2$

$$\frac{\text{N:O mass ratio in NO}}{\text{N:O mass ratio in NO}_2} = \frac{(7\text{ g N})/(8\text{ }}{(7\text{ g N})/(16}$$

This result makes sense only if we assume that matter is composed
atoms that have characteristic masses and combine with one another in sp[ecific,]
well-defined ways (**Figure 2.2**).

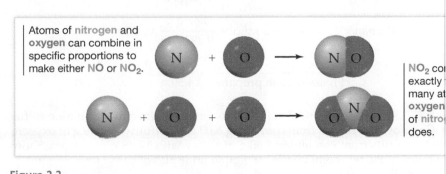

Atoms of nitrogen and oxygen can combine in specific proportions to make either NO or NO$_2$.

NO$_2$ co[ntains]
exactly
many at
oxygen
of nitro[gen]
does.

Figure 2.2
An illustration of Dalton's law of multiple proportions.

People have always been fascinated by changes, particularly by changes that are dramatic or useful. In the ancient world, the change that occurred when a stick of wood burned, gave off heat, and turned into a small pile of ash was especially important. Similarly, the change that occurred when a reddish lump of rock (iron ore) was heated with charcoal and produced a gray metal (iron) useful for making weapons, tools, and other implements was of enormous value. Observing such changes eventually caused philosophers to think about what different materials might be composed of and led to the idea of fundamental substances that we today call elements.

At the same time philosophers were pondering the question of elements, they were also thinking about related matters: What is an element made of? Is matter continuously divisible into ever smaller and smaller pieces, or is there an ultimate limit? Can you cut a piece of gold in two, take one of the pieces and cut *it* in two, and so on infinitely, or is there a point at which you must stop? Most thinkers, including Plato and Aristotle, believed that matter is continuously divisible, but the Greek philosopher Democritus (460–370 B.C.) disagreed. Democritus proposed that matter is composed of tiny, discrete particles, which we now call *atoms*, from the Greek word *atomos*, meaning "indivisible." Little else was learned about elements and atoms until the birth of modern experimental science some 2000 years later.

2.1 THE CONSERVATION OF MASS AND THE LAW OF DEFINITE PROPORTIONS

The Englishman Robert Boyle (1627–1691) is generally credited with being the first to study chemistry as a separate intellectual discipline and the first to carry out rigorous chemical experiments. Through a careful series of researches into the nature and behavior of gases, Boyle provided clear evidence for the atomic makeup of matter. In addition, Boyle was the first to clearly define an element as a substance that cannot be chemically broken down further and to suggest that a substantial number of different elements might exist. Atoms of these different elements, in turn, can join together in different ways to yield a vast number of different substances we call **chemical compounds**.

Progress in chemistry was slow in the decades following Boyle, and it was not until the work of Joseph Priestley (1733–1804) that the next great leap was made. Priestley prepared and isolated the gas oxygen in 1774 by heating the compound mercury oxide (HgO) according to the chemical equation we would now write as
$2\,HgO \rightarrow 2\,Hg + O_2$.

◄ Heating the red powder HgO causes it
to decompose into the silvery liquid
mercury and the colorless gas oxygen.

In this standard format for w
described by its **chemical formu**
ments and uses subscripts to indi
given, the number 1 is understor
NaCl, water as H_2O, and sucrose
written in a standard format call
stances undergoing change are
formed are written on the right, a
direction of the chemical transfor

Soon after Priestley's discov
oxygen is the key substance invol
strated with careful measuremer
container, the mass of the combu
ing reactants. When hydrogen ga
(H_2O), for instance, the mass of t
gen and oxygen consumed. Calle
cornerstone of chemical science.

Law of Mass Conserva

It's easy to demonstrate the la
ment like that shown in **Figure 2.1.**
potassium iodide (KI) are each c
immediate chemical reaction occu
mercury iodide (HgI_2). Filtering t
and evaporation of the water fror
nitrate (KNO_3). Thus, the combine
exactly equal to the combined mas

The combined mass
these two reactants

$$Hg(NO_3)_2 + 2$$

Mercury   Potas
nitrate   iodid

Known amounts of solid KI and solid $Hg(NO_3)_2$ are weighed and then dissolved in water.

The solutions are mixed to giv solid HgI_2, which is removed by filtration.

Figure 2.1
An illustration of the law of mass conservation. In any chemical reaction, the mass of the final products equals the combined mass of the starting reactants.

▲ These samples of sulfur and carbon have different masses but contain the same number of atoms.

▲ Sulfur burns with a bluish flame to yield colorless SO_2 gas.

Taking all three laws together—the law of mass conservation, the law of definite proportions, and the law of multiple proportions—ultimately led Dalton to propose a new theory of matter. He reasoned as follows:

- *Elements are made up of tiny particles called* **atoms**. Although Dalton didn't know what atoms were like, he nevertheless felt they were necessary to explain why there were so many different elements.

- *Each element is characterized by the mass of its atoms. Atoms of the same element have the same mass, but atoms of different elements have different masses.* Dalton realized that there must be some feature that distinguishes the atoms of one element from those of another. Because Proust's law of definite proportions showed that elements always combine in specific mass ratios, Dalton reasoned that the distinguishing feature among atoms of different elements must be mass.

- *The chemical combination of elements to make different chemical compounds occurs when atoms join in small whole-number ratios.* Only if whole numbers of atoms combine will different samples of a pure chemical compound always contain the same proportion of elements by mass (the law of definite proportions and the law of multiple proportions). Fractional parts of atoms are never involved in chemical reactions.

- *Chemical reactions only rearrange how atoms are combined in chemical compounds; the atoms themselves don't change.* Dalton realized that atoms must be chemically indestructible for the law of mass conservation to be valid. If the same numbers and kinds of atoms are present in both reactants and products, then the masses of reactants and products must also be the same.

Not everything that Dalton proposed was correct. He thought, for instance, that water had the formula HO rather than H_2O. Nevertheless, his atomic theory of matter was ultimately accepted and came to form a cornerstone of modern chemical science.

WORKED EXAMPLE 2.1

USING THE LAW OF MULTIPLE PROPORTIONS

Methane and propane are both constituents of natural gas. A sample of methane contains 5.70 g of carbon atoms and 1.90 g of hydrogen atoms combined in a certain way, whereas a sample of propane contains 4.47 g of carbon atoms and 0.993 g of hydrogen atoms combined in a different way. Show that the two compounds obey the law of multiple proportions.

STRATEGY

Find the C:H mass ratio in each compound, and then compare the ratios to see whether they are small whole-number multiples of each other.

SOLUTION

$$\text{Methane:} \quad \text{C:H mass ratio} = \frac{5.70 \text{ g C}}{1.90 \text{ g H}} = 3.00$$

$$\text{Propane:} \quad \text{C:H mass ratio} = \frac{4.47 \text{ g C}}{0.993 \text{ g H}} = 4.50$$

$$\frac{\text{C:H mass ratio in methane}}{\text{C:H mass ratio in propane}} = \frac{3.00}{4.50} = \frac{2}{3}$$

▶ **PROBLEM 2.1** Compounds A and B are colorless gases obtained by combining sulfur with oxygen. Compound A results from combining 6.00 g of sulfur with 5.99 g of oxygen, and compound B results from combining 8.60 g of sulfur with 12.88 g of oxygen. Show that the mass ratios in the two compounds are simple multiples of each other.

2.3 ATOMIC STRUCTURE: ELECTRONS

Dalton's atomic theory is fine as far as it goes, but it leaves unanswered the obvious question: What is an atom made of? Dalton himself had no way of answering this question, and it was not until nearly a century later that experiments by the English physicist J. J. Thomson (1856–1940) provided some clues. Thomson's experiments involved the use of *cathode-ray tubes* (CRTs), early predecessors of the tubes found in older televisions and computer displays.

As shown in **Figure 2.3a**, a cathode-ray tube is a sealed glass vessel from which the air has been removed and in which two thin pieces of metal, called *electrodes*, have been sealed. When a sufficiently high voltage is applied across the electrodes, an electric current flows through the tube from the negatively charged electrode (the *cathode*) to the positively charged electrode (the *anode*). If the tube is not fully evacuated but still contains a small amount of air or other gas, the flowing current is visible as a glow called a *cathode ray*. Furthermore, if the anode has a hole in it and the end of the tube is coated with a phosphorescent substance such as zinc sulfide, some of the rays pass through the hole and strike the end of the tube, where they are visible as a bright spot of light— exactly what happens in a CRT television screen or computer monitor.

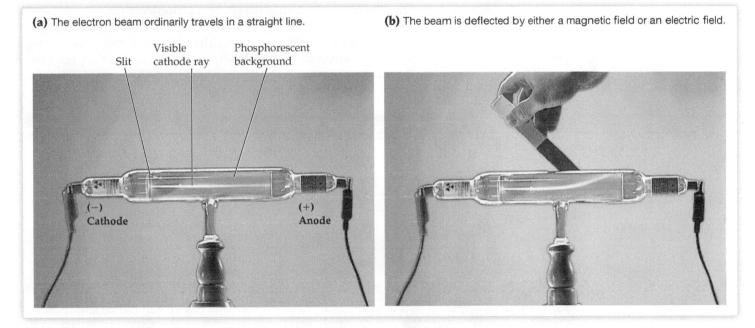

(a) The electron beam ordinarily travels in a straight line.

(b) The beam is deflected by either a magnetic field or an electric field.

Slit   Visible
        cathode ray   Phosphorescent
                       background

(−)
Cathode

(+)
Anode

Figure 2.3
A cathode-ray tube. In a cathode-ray tube, a stream of electrons emitted from the negatively charged cathode passes through a slit, moves toward the positively charged anode, and is detected by a phosphorescent strip.

Experiments by a number of physicists in the 1890s had shown that cathode rays can be deflected by bringing either a magnet or an electrically charged plate near the tube (**Figure 2.3b**). Because the beam is produced at a negative electrode and is deflected toward a positive plate, Thomson proposed that cathode rays must consist of tiny, negatively charged particles, which we now call **electrons**. Furthermore, because electrons are emitted from electrodes made of many different metals, all these different metals must contain electrons.

Thomson reasoned that the amount of deflection of the electron beam in a cathode-ray tube due to a nearby magnetic or electric field should depend on three factors:

1. *The strength of the deflecting magnetic or electric field.* The stronger the magnet or the higher the voltage on the charged plate, the greater the deflection.

2. *The size of the negative charge on the electron.* The larger the charge on the particle, the greater its interaction with the magnetic or electric field and the greater the deflection.

3. *The mass of the electron.* The lighter the particle, the greater its deflection (just as a Ping-Pong ball is more easily deflected than a bowling ball).

By carefully measuring the amount of deflection caused by electric and magnetic fields of known strength, Thomson was able to calculate the ratio of the electron's electric charge to its mass: its *charge-to-mass ratio, e/m*. The modern value is

$$\frac{e}{m} = 1.758\ 820 \times 10^8\ \text{C/g}$$

where e is the magnitude of the charge on the electron in coulombs (C) and m is the mass of the electron in grams. (We'll say more about coulombs and electrical charge in Chapter 17.) Note that because e is defined as a positive quantity, the actual (negative) charge on the electron is $-e$.

Thomson was able to measure only the ratio of charge to mass, not charge or mass itself, and it was left to the American R. A. Millikan (1868–1953) to devise a method for measuring the mass of an electron (**Figure 2.4**). In Millikan's experiment, a fine mist of oil was sprayed into a chamber, and the tiny droplets were allowed to fall between two horizontal plates. Observing the spherical droplets through a telescopic eyepiece made it possible to determine how rapidly they fell through the air, which in turn allowed their masses to be calculated. The droplets were then given a negative charge by irradiating them with X rays. By applying a voltage to the plates, with the upper plate positive, it was possible to counteract the downward fall of the charged droplets and keep them suspended.

Figure 2.4
Millikan's oil drop experiment.

With the voltage on the plates and the mass of the droplets known, Millikan was able to show that the charge on a given droplet was always a small whole-number multiple of e, whose modern value is $1.602\ 176 \times 10^{-19}$ C. Substituting the value of e into Thomson's charge-to-mass ratio then gives the mass m of the electron as $9.109\,382 \times 10^{-28}$ g:

$$\text{Because} \quad \frac{e}{m} = 1.758\,820 \times 10^8 \text{ C/g}$$

$$\text{then} \quad m = \frac{e}{1.758\,820 \times 10^8 \text{ C/g}} = \frac{1.602\,176 \times 10^{-19} \text{ C}}{1.758\,820 \times 10^8 \text{ C/g}}$$

$$= 9.109\,382 \times 10^{-28} \text{ g}$$

2.4 ATOMIC STRUCTURE: PROTONS AND NEUTRONS

Think about the consequences of Thomson's cathode-ray experiments. Because matter is electrically neutral overall, the fact that the atoms in an electrode can give off negatively charged particles (electrons) must mean that those same atoms also contain positively charged particles for electrical balance. The search for those positively charged particles and for an overall picture of atomic structure led to a landmark experiment published in 1911 by the New Zealand physicist Ernest Rutherford (1871–1937).

Rutherford's work involved the use of *alpha (α) particles*, a type of emission previously found to be given off by a number of naturally occurring radioactive elements, including radium, polonium, and radon. Rutherford knew that alpha particles are about 7000 times more massive than electrons and that they have a positive charge that is twice the magnitude of the charge on an electron, but opposite in sign.

When Rutherford directed a beam of alpha particles at a thin gold foil, he found that almost all the particles passed through the foil undeflected. A very small number, however (about 1 of every 20,000), were deflected at an angle, and a few actually bounced back toward the particle source (Figure 2.5).

An alpha particle
(relative mass = 7000;
charge = +2e)

An electron
(relative mass = 1;
charge = −1e)

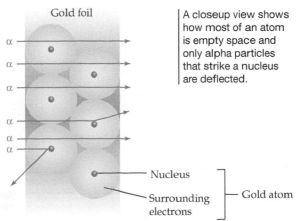

Experiment

Radioactive sample emits beam of **alpha particles**

Zinc sulfide screen

Lead block shield

Gold foil

Some alpha particles are deflected

Most alpha particles hit here

Results

When a beam of **alpha particles** is directed at a thin gold foil, most particles pass through undeflected, but some are deflected at large angles and a few bounce back toward the particle source.

Conclusion

Because the majority of particles are not deflected, the gold atoms must be almost entirely empty space. The atom's mass is concentrated in a tiny dense core, which deflects the occasional alpha particle.

Gold foil

α

A closeup view shows how most of an atom is empty space and only alpha particles that strike a nucleus are deflected.

Nucleus

Surrounding electrons

Gold atom

Figure 2.5
Rutherford's scattering experiment.

▲ The relative size of the nucleus in an atom is roughly the same as that of a pea in the middle of this huge stadium.

Rutherford explained his results by proposing that a metal atom must be almost entirely empty space and have its mass concentrated in a tiny central core that he called the **nucleus**. If the nucleus contains the atom's positive charges and most of its mass, and if the electrons are a relatively large distance away, then it is clear why the observed scattering results are obtained: most alpha particles encounter empty space as they fly through the foil. Only when a positive alpha particle chances to come near a small but massive positive nucleus is it repelled strongly enough to make it bounce backward.

Modern measurements show that an atom has a diameter of roughly 10^{-10} m and that a nucleus has a diameter of about 10^{-15} m. It's difficult to imagine from these numbers alone, though, just how small a nucleus really is. For comparison purposes, if an atom were the size of a large domed stadium, the nucleus would be approximately the size of a small pea in the center of the playing field.

Further experiments by Rutherford and others between 1910 and 1930 showed that a nucleus is composed of two kinds of particles, called *protons* and *neutrons*. **Protons** have a mass of $1.672\,622 \times 10^{-24}$ g (about 1836 times that of an electron) and are positively charged. Because the charge on a proton is opposite in sign but equal in size to that on an electron, the numbers of protons and electrons in a neutral atom are equal. **Neutrons** ($1.674\,927 \times 10^{-24}$ g) are almost identical in mass to protons but carry no charge, and the number of neutrons in a nucleus is not directly related to the numbers of protons and electrons. Table 2.1 compares the three fundamental subatomic particles, and **Figure 2.6** gives an overall view of the atom.

TABLE 2.1   A Comparison of Subatomic Particles

Particle	Mass		Charge	
	grams	amu*	coulombs	e
Electron	$9.109\,382 \times 10^{-28}$	$5.485\,799 \times 10^{-4}$	$-1.602\,176 \times 10^{-19}$	-1
Proton	$1.672\,622 \times 10^{-24}$	$1.007\,276$	$+1.602\,176 \times 10^{-19}$	$+1$
Neutron	$1.674\,927 \times 10^{-24}$	$1.008\,665$	0	0

* The atomic mass unit (amu) is defined in Section 2.6.

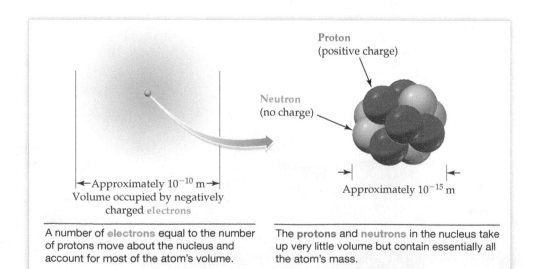

Figure 2.6
A view of the atom.

WORKED EXAMPLE 2.2

CALCULATIONS USING ATOMIC SIZE

Ordinary "lead" pencils actually are made of a form of carbon called graphite. If a pencil line is 0.35 mm wide and the diameter of a carbon atom is 1.5×10^{-10} m, how many atoms wide is the line?

STRATEGY

Begin with the known information, and set up an equation using appropriate conversion factors so that the unwanted units cancel. In this example, let's begin with the width of the pencil line in millimeters, then convert to meters, and then divide the line width in meters by the diameter of a single atom in meters.

SOLUTION

$$\text{Atoms} = 0.35 \ \cancel{mm} \ \times \ \frac{1 \ \cancel{m}}{1000 \ \cancel{mm}} \ \times \ \frac{1 \ \text{atom}}{1.5 \times 10^{-10} \ \cancel{m}} = 2.3 \times 10^{6} \ \text{atoms}$$

BALLPARK CHECK

A single carbon atom is about 10^{-10} m across, so it takes 10^{10} carbon atoms placed side by side to stretch 1 m, 10^{7} carbon atoms to stretch 1 mm, and about 0.3×10^{7} (or 3×10^{6}; 3 *million*) carbon atoms to stretch 0.35 mm. The estimate agrees with the solution.

▶ **PROBLEM 2.2**   The gold foil Rutherford used in his scattering experiment had a thickness of approximately 0.005 mm. If a single gold atom has a diameter of 2.9×10^{-8} cm, how many atoms thick was Rutherford's foil?

▶ **PROBLEM 2.3**   A small speck of carbon the size of a pinhead contains about 10^{19} atoms, the diameter of a carbon atom is 1.5×10^{-10} m, and the circumference of the Earth at the equator is 40,075 km. How many times around the Earth would the atoms from this speck of carbon extend if they were laid side by side?

2.5 ATOMIC NUMBERS

Thus far, we've described atoms only in general terms and have not yet answered the most important question: What is it that makes one atom different from another? How, for example, does an atom of gold differ from an atom of carbon? The answer turns out to be quite simple. *Elements differ from one another according to the number of protons in their atoms' nuclei*, a value called the element's **atomic number (Z)**. That is, all atoms of a given element contain the same number of protons in their nuclei. All hydrogen atoms, atomic number 1, have 1 proton; all helium atoms, atomic number 2, have 2 protons; all carbon atoms, atomic number 6, have 6 protons; and so on. In addition, every neutral atom contains a number of electrons equal to its number of protons.

Atomic Number (Z) = Number of protons in an atom's nucleus
= Number of electrons around an atom's nucleus

A hydrogen atom   A carbon atom   A gold atom
(1 proton; 1 electron) (6 protons; 6 electrons) (79 protons; 79 electrons)

In addition to protons, the nuclei of all atoms (other than hydrogen) also contain neutrons. The sum of the numbers of protons (Z) and neutrons (N) in an atom is called the atom's **mass number (A)**. That is, $A = Z + N$.

Mass Number (A) = Number of protons (Z) + number of neutrons (N)

Most hydrogen atoms have 1 proton and no neutrons, so their mass number is $A = 1 + 0 = 1$. Most helium atoms have 2 protons and 2 neutrons, so their mass number is $A = 2 + 2 = 4$. Most carbon atoms have 6 protons and 6 neutrons, so their mass number is $A = 6 + 6 = 12$; and so on. Except for hydrogen, stable atoms always contain at least as many neutrons as protons, although there is no simple way to predict how many neutrons a given atom will have.

Notice that we said *most* hydrogen atoms have mass number 1, *most* helium atoms have mass number 4, and *most* carbon atoms have mass number 12. In fact, different atoms of the same element can have different mass numbers depending on how many neutrons they have. Atoms with identical atomic numbers but different mass numbers are called **isotopes**. Hydrogen, for example, has three isotopes.

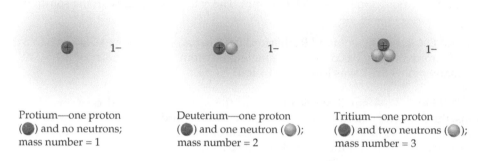

Protium—one proton
(⬤) and no neutrons;
mass number = 1

Deuterium—one proton
(⬤) and one neutron (◯);
mass number = 2

Tritium—one proton
(⬤) and two neutrons (◯);
mass number = 3

All hydrogen atoms have 1 proton in their nucleus (otherwise they wouldn't be hydrogen), but 99.985% of them have no neutrons. These hydrogen atoms, called *protium*, have mass number 1. In addition, 0.015% of hydrogen atoms, called *deuterium*, have 1 neutron and mass number 2. Still other hydrogen atoms, called *tritium*, have 2 neutrons and mass number 3. An unstable, radioactive isotope, tritium occurs only in trace amounts on Earth but is made artificially in nuclear reactors. As other examples, there are 15 known isotopes of nitrogen, only 2 of which occur naturally on Earth, and 25 known isotopes of uranium, only 3 of which occur naturally. In total, more than 3600 isotopes of the 118 known elements have been identified.

A specific isotope is represented by showing its element symbol, along with its mass number as a left superscript and its atomic number as a left subscript. Thus, protium is represented as ^1_1H, deuterium as ^2_1H, and tritium as ^3_1H. Similarly, the two naturally occurring isotopes of nitrogen are represented as $^{14}_7\text{N}$ (spoken as "nitrogen-14") and $^{15}_7\text{N}$ (nitrogen-15). The number of neutrons in an isotope is not given explicitly but can be calculated by subtracting the atomic number (subscript) from the mass number (superscript). For example, subtracting the atomic number 7 from the mass number 14 indicates that a $^{14}_7\text{N}$ atom has 7 neutrons.

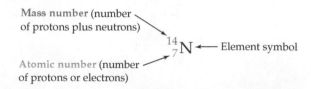

Mass number (number
of protons plus neutrons)

$^{14}_7\text{N}$ ◀— Element symbol

Atomic number (number
of protons or electrons)

The number of neutrons in an atom has relatively little effect on the atom's chemical properties. The chemical behavior of an element is determined almost entirely by the number of electrons it has, which in turn is determined by the number of protons in its nucleus. All three isotopes of hydrogen therefore behave similarly (although not identically) in their chemical reactions.

▲ Uranium-235 is used as fuel in this nuclear-powered icebreaker.

WORKED EXAMPLE 2.3

INTERPRETING AN ISOTOPE SYMBOL

The isotope of uranium used to generate nuclear power is $^{235}_{92}U$. How many protons, neutrons, and electrons does an atom of $^{235}_{92}U$ have?

STRATEGY

The atomic number (subscript 92) in the symbol $^{235}_{92}U$ indicates the number of protons and electrons in the atom. The number of neutrons is the difference between the mass number (superscript 235) and the atomic number (92).

SOLUTION

An atom of $^{235}_{92}U$ has 92 protons, 92 electrons, and $235 - 92 = 143$ neutrons.

WORKED EXAMPLE 2.4

WRITING AN ISOTOPE SYMBOL

Element X is toxic to humans in high concentration but is essential to life in low concentrations. Identify element X, whose atoms contain 24 protons, and write the symbol for the isotope of X that has 28 neutrons.

STRATEGY

The number of protons in an atom's nucleus is the element's atomic number. The mass number is the sum of the atomic number and the number of neutrons.

SOLUTION

According to the periodic table, the element with atomic number 24 is chromium (Cr). The particular isotope of chromium in this instance has a mass number of $24 + 28 = 52$ and is written $^{52}_{24}Cr$.

▶ **PROBLEM 2.4** The isotope $^{75}_{34}Se$ is used medically for the diagnosis of pancreatic disorders. How many protons, neutrons, and electrons does an atom of $^{75}_{34}Se$ have?

▶ **PROBLEM 2.5** Chlorine, one of the elements in common table salt (sodium chloride), has two main isotopes, with mass numbers 35 and 37. Look up the atomic number of chlorine, tell how many neutrons each isotope contains, and give the standard symbol for each.

▶ **PROBLEM 2.6** An atom of element X contains 47 protons and 62 neutrons. Identify the element, and write the symbol for the isotope in the standard format.

2.6 ATOMIC MASSES AND THE MOLE

Pick up a pencil, and look at the small amount of tip visible. How many atoms (pencil lead is made of carbon) do you think are in the tip? One thing is certain: atoms are so tiny that the number needed to make a visible sample is enormous. In fact, even the smallest speck of dust visible to the naked eye contains at least 10^{17} atoms. Thus, the mass in grams of a single atom is much too small a number for convenience so chemists use a unit called an **atomic mass unit (amu)**, also called a *dalton* (Da) in biological work. One amu is defined as exactly 1/12 the mass of an atom of $^{12}_{6}C$ and is equal to $1.660\,539 \times 10^{-24}$ g.

$$\text{Mass of one } ^{12}_{6}C \text{ atom} = 12 \text{ amu (exactly)}$$

$$1 \text{ amu} = \frac{\text{Mass of one } ^{12}_{6}C \text{ atom}}{12} = 1.660\,539 \times 10^{-24} \text{ g}$$

Because the mass of an atom's electrons is negligible compared to the mass of its protons and neutrons, defining 1 amu as 1/12 the mass of a $^{12}_{6}C$ atom means that protons and neutrons both have a mass of almost exactly 1 amu (Table 2.1 on page 42).

Thus, the mass of a specific atom in atomic mass units—called the atom's *isotopic mass*—is numerically close to the atom's mass number. A $_1^1$H atom, for instance, has a mass of 1.007 825 amu; a $_{92}^{235}$U atom has a mass of 235.043 930 amu; and so forth.

Most elements occur naturally as a mixture of different isotopes. Thus, if you look at the periodic table inside the front cover, you'll see listed below the symbol for each element a value called the element's *atomic mass*, or *atomic weight*. The unit amu is understood but not specified.

An element's **atomic mass** is the weighted average of the isotopic masses of the element's naturally occurring isotopes. Carbon, for example, occurs on Earth as a mixture of two major isotopes, $_6^{12}$C (98.89% natural abundance) and $_6^{13}$C (1.11% natural abundance). Although the isotopic mass of any individual carbon atom is either 12 amu (a carbon-12 atom) or 13.0034 amu (a carbon-13 atom), the average isotopic mass—that is, the atomic mass—of a large collection of carbon atoms is 12.011 amu. A third carbon isotope, $_6^{14}$C, also exists, but its natural abundance is so small that it can be ignored when calculating atomic mass.

$$\text{Atomic mass of C} = (\text{Mass of } _6^{12}\text{C})(\text{Abundance of } _6^{12}\text{C}) + (\text{Mass of } _6^{13}\text{C})(\text{Abundance of } _6^{13}\text{C})$$

$$= (12 \text{ amu})(0.9889) + (13.0034 \text{ amu})(0.0111)$$

$$= 11.867 \text{ amu} + 0.144 \text{ amu} = 12.011 \text{ amu}$$

A particularly useful point about atomic masses is that they act as conversion factors between numbers of atoms and masses; that is, they allow us to *count* a large number of atoms by *weighing* a sample of the substance. For instance, knowing that carbon has an atomic mass of 12.011 amu lets us calculate that a small pencil tip made of carbon and weighing 15 mg (1.5×10^{-2} g) contains 7.5×10^{20} atoms:

$$(1.5 \times 10^{-2} \, g)\left(\frac{1 \text{ amu}}{1.6605 \times 10^{-24} \, g}\right)\left(\frac{1 \text{ C atom}}{12.011 \text{ amu}}\right) = 7.5 \times 10^{20} \text{ C atoms}$$

As another example, the fact that the atomic mass of silver is 107.868 amu means that a silver ring weighing 1.872 g contains 1.045×10^{22} silver atoms:

$$(1.872 \, g)\left(\frac{1 \text{ amu}}{1.6605 \times 10^{-24} \, g}\right)\left(\frac{1 \text{ Ag atom}}{107.868 \text{ amu}}\right) = 1.045 \times 10^{22} \text{ Ag atoms}$$

Let's think some more about what it means to be able to count atoms using atomic masses. As we've just seen, the total mass of a given number of atoms is the atom's atomic mass times the number of atoms. Thus, if you have two samples of different elements that both contain the same number of atoms, then the ratio of masses of the two samples is the same as the ratio of their atomic masses. Take carbon and silver, for instance. The average mass ratio of one carbon atom (12.011 amu) to one silver atom (107.868 amu) is 12.011 : 107.868, so the mass ratio of any given number of C atoms to the same number of Ag atoms is always 12.011 : 107.868. Furthermore, the numerical value of the ratio is the same regardless of the mass units used. That is, 12.011 *amu* of carbon contains exactly the same number of atoms as 107.868 *amu* of silver, and 12.011 *grams* of carbon contains exactly the same number of atoms as 107.868 *grams* of silver.

$$\frac{12.011 \text{ amu}}{107.868 \text{ amu}} = \frac{12.011 \text{ mg}}{107.868 \text{ mg}} = \frac{12.011 \, g}{107.868 \, g} = \frac{12.011 \text{ kg}}{107.868 \text{ kg}} = 0.111 \, 35$$

When referring to the enormous numbers of atoms that make up the visible amounts we typically deal with, chemists use the fundamental SI unit for amount called a *mole*, abbreviated *mol*. One **mole** of any element is the amount whose mass in grams, called its **molar mass**, is numerically equal to its atomic mass. One mole of carbon atoms has a mass of 12.011 g, one mole of silver atoms has a mass of 107.868 g, and so on. Molar mass thus acts as a conversion factor that lets you convert between mass in grams and number of atoms. Whenever you have the same number of moles of different elements, you also have the same number of atoms.

How many atoms are there in a mole? Experiments show that one mole of any element contains $6.022\ 141 \times 10^{23}$ atoms, a value called **Avogadro's number**, abbreviated N_A, after the Italian scientist who first recognized the importance of the mass/number relationship. Avogadro's number of atoms of any element—that is, one mole—has a mass in grams equal to the element's atomic mass.

It's hard to grasp the magnitude of a quantity as large as Avogadro's number, but some comparisons might give you a sense of scale: The age of the universe in seconds (13.7 billion years, or 4.32×10^{17} s) is less than a millionth the size of Avogadro's number. The number of milliliters of water in the world's oceans (1.3×10^{24} mL) is only twice the size of Avogadro's number. The mass of the Earth in kilograms (5.98×10^{24} kg) is only ten times Avogadro's number, and so on.

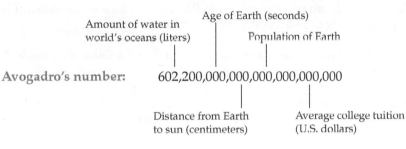

We'll return to the mole and see its uses in Section 3.3.

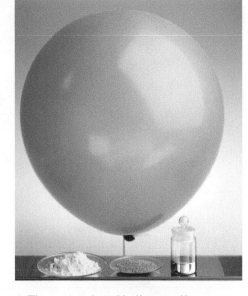

▲ These samples of helium, sulfur, copper, and mercury each contain 1 mole. Do they have the same mass?

WORKED EXAMPLE 2.5

CALCULATING AN ATOMIC MASS

Chlorine has two naturally occurring isotopes: $^{35}_{17}$Cl, with a natural abundance of 75.76% and an isotopic mass of 34.969 amu, and $^{37}_{17}$Cl, with a natural abundance of 24.24% and an isotopic mass of 36.966 amu. What is the atomic mass of chlorine?

STRATEGY

The atomic mass of an element is the weighted average of the isotopic masses, which equals the sum of the masses of each isotope times the natural abundance of that isotope:

Atomic mass $= \left(\text{Mass of } ^{35}_{17}\text{Cl}\right)\left(\text{Abundance of } ^{35}_{17}\text{Cl}\right)$

$$+ \left(\text{Mass of } ^{37}_{17}\text{Cl}\right)\left(\text{Abundance of } ^{37}_{17}\text{Cl}\right)$$

SOLUTION

Atomic mass $=$ (34.969 amu)(0.7576) + (36.966 amu)(0.2424) $=$ 35.45 amu

BALLPARK CHECK

The atomic mass is somewhere between 35 amu and 37 amu, the masses of the two individual isotopes, and is closer to 35 amu, the mass of the more abundant isotope—perhaps about 35.5 amu.

WORKED EXAMPLE 2.6

CONVERTING FROM MASS TO NUMBERS OF MOLES AND ATOMS

How many moles and how many atoms of silicon are in a sample weighing 10.53 g? The atomic mass of silicon is 28.0855 amu.

STRATEGY

The fact that the atomic mass of silicon is 28.0855 amu means that 1 mol of silicon has a mass of 28.0855 g. Use this molar mass to convert between mass and number of moles, and then use Avogadro's number to find the number of atoms.

continued on the next page

SOLUTION

$$(10.53 \text{ g Si}) \left(\frac{1 \text{ mol Si}}{28.0855 \text{ g Si}} \right) = 0.3749 \text{ mol Si}$$

$$(0.3749 \text{ mol Si}) \left(\frac{6.022 \times 10^{23} \text{ atoms Si}}{1 \text{ mol Si}} \right) = 2.258 \times 10^{23} \text{ atoms Si}$$

BALLPARK CHECK

A mass of 10.53 g of silicon is a bit more than 1/3 the molar mass of silicon (28.0855 g/mol), so the sample contains a bit more than 0.33 mol. This number of moles, in turns, contains a bit more than 1/3 of Avogadro's number of atoms, or about 2×10^{23} atoms.

▶ **PROBLEM 2.7** Copper metal has two naturally occurring isotopes: copper-63 (69.15%; isotopic mass = 62.93 amu) and copper-65 (30.85%; isotopic mass = 64.93 amu). Calculate the atomic mass of copper, and check your answer in a periodic table.

▶ **PROBLEM 2.8** Based on your answer to Problem 2.7, how many atoms of copper are in an old penny made of pure copper and weighing 2.15 g?

▶ **PROBLEM 2.9** What is the mass in grams of each of the following samples?
  (a) 1.505 mol of Ti   **(b)** 0.337 mol of Na   **(c)** 2.583 mol of U

▶ **PROBLEM 2.10** How many moles are in each of the following samples?
  (a) 11.51 g of Ti   **(b)** 29.127 g of Na   **(c)** 1.477 kg of U

2.7 NUCLEAR CHEMISTRY: THE CHANGE OF ONE ELEMENT INTO ANOTHER

We saw at the beginning of this chapter, and we'll see repeatedly throughout the book, that the identities of atoms don't change when different chemical substances react with one another to give products. When natural gas (methane; CH_4) burns in oxygen, for instance, the C, H, and O atoms combine in a different way to yield carbon dioxide (CO_2) and water (H_2O), but they still remain C, H, and O atoms. When metallic sodium (Na) reacts with gaseous chlorine atoms (Cl), solid sodium chloride (NaCl) forms but the Na and Cl atoms remain the same. Yet anyone who reads a newspaper or watches television knows that atoms *can* change identity, resulting in the conversion of one element into another. Atomic weapons, nuclear energy, and radioactive radon gas in our homes are all topics of societal importance, and all involve **nuclear chemistry**—the study of the properties and changes of atomic nuclei.

Take the element carbon, for example. There are 15 known isotopes of carbon, two of which occur commonly (^{12}C and ^{13}C) and one of which (^{14}C) is produced in small amounts in the upper atmosphere by the action of cosmic rays on ^{14}N atoms. The remaining 12 carbon isotopes have been produced artificially. Only the two commonly occurring isotopes are stable; the other 13 undergo spontaneous changes to their nuclei. Carbon-14, for instance, slowly decays to give nitrogen-14 plus an electron, a process we can write as the following *nuclear equation* (as opposed to a chemical equation, described previously in Section 2.1).

$$^{14}_{6}\text{C} \rightarrow {}^{14}_{7}\text{N} + {}^{0}_{-1}\text{e}$$

In a **nuclear equation**, the element symbols represent only the *nuclei* of atoms rather than the entire neutral atoms, so the subscript represents only the number of nuclear charges (protons). An emitted electron is written as $^{0}_{-1}\text{e}$, where the superscript 0 indicates that the mass of an electron is essentially zero when compared to that of a proton or neutron, and the subscript indicates that the charge is −1.

Nuclear reactions, such as the spontaneous change of ^{14}C to ^{14}N, are distinguished from chemical reactions, such as that of sodium with chlorine, in several ways:

• A nuclear reaction involves a change in an atom's nucleus, usually producing a different element. A chemical reaction, by contrast, involves only a change in the way that different atoms are combined. A chemical reaction never changes the nuclei themselves or produces a different element.

• Different isotopes of an element have essentially the same behavior in chemical reactions but often have completely different behavior in nuclear reactions.

• The energy change accompanying a nuclear reaction is far greater than that accompanying a chemical reaction. The nuclear transformation of 1.0 g of uranium-235 ($^{235}_{92}U$) releases more than one *million* times as much energy as the chemical combustion of 1.0 g of methane.

2.8 RADIOACTIVITY

Scientists have known since 1896 that many nuclei are **radioactive**—they undergo a spontaneous decay and emit some form of *radiation*. Early studies of radioactive isotopes, or **radioisotopes**, by Ernest Rutherford in 1897 showed that there are three common types of radiation with markedly different properties: *alpha* (α), *beta* (β), and *gamma* (γ) *radiation*, named after the first three letters of the Greek alphabet.

Alpha (α) Radiation

Using the simple experiment shown in **Figure 2.7**, Rutherford found that α **radiation** consists of a stream of particles that are repelled by a positively charged electrode, attracted by a negatively charged electrode, and have a mass-to-charge ratio identifying them as helium nuclei, $^{4}_{2}He^{2+}$. Alpha particles thus consist of two protons and two neutrons.

The radioactive source in the shielded box emits radiation, which passes between two electrodes.

Beta radiation is strongly deflected toward the positive electrode.

β rays

Gamma radiation is undeflected.

γ rays

α rays

Alpha radiation is deflected toward the negative electrode.

Figure 2.7
The effect of an electric field on α, β, and γ radiation.

Because the emission of an α particle from a nucleus results in a loss of two protons and two neutrons, it reduces the mass number of the nucleus by 4 and reduces the atomic number by 2. Alpha emission is particularly common for heavy radioactive isotopes. Uranium-238, for example, spontaneously emits an α particle and forms thorium-234.

92 protons
146 neutrons
238 nucleons

2 protons
2 neutrons
4 nucleons

90 protons
144 neutrons
234 nucleons

$$^{238}_{92}U \longrightarrow\ ^{4}_{2}He\ +\ ^{234}_{90}Th$$

Note how the nuclear equation for the radioactive decay of uranium-238 is written. The equation is said to be *balanced* because the total number of neutrons and protons, collectively called **nucleons**, or nuclear particles, is the same on both sides of the equation and the number of charges on the nuclei and on any elementary particles (protons and electrons) is the same on both sides. In the decay of $^{238}_{92}U$ to give $^{4}_{2}He$ and $^{234}_{90}Th$, for instance, there are 238 nucleons and 92 nuclear charges on both sides of the equation.

Beta (β) Radiation

Further work by Rutherford in the late 1800s showed that **β radiation** consists of a stream of particles that are attracted to a positive electrode (Figure 2.7), repelled by a negative electrode, and have a mass-to-charge ratio identifying them as electrons, $^{0}_{-1}e$ or β^-. Beta emission occurs when a neutron in the nucleus spontaneously decays into a proton plus an electron, which is then ejected. The product nucleus has the same mass number as the starting nucleus because a neutron has turned into a proton, but it has a higher atomic number because it has the newly created proton. The reaction of ^{131}I to give ^{131}Xe is an example:

Writing the emitted β particle as $^{0}_{-1}e$ in the nuclear equation makes clear the charge balance of the nuclear reaction. The subscript in the $^{131}_{53}I$ nucleus on the left (53) is balanced by the sum of the two subscripts on the right ($54 - 1 = 53$).

Gamma (γ) Radiation

Gamma (γ) radiation is unaffected by either electric or magnetic fields (Figure 2.7) and has no mass. Like visible light, ultraviolet rays, and X rays, γ radiation is simply electromagnetic radiation of very high energy, which we'll discuss in more detail in Section 5.1. Gamma radiation almost always accompanies α and β emission as a mechanism for the release of energy, but it is often not shown when writing nuclear equations because it changes neither the mass number nor the atomic number of the product nucleus.

Positron Emission and Electron Capture

In addition to α, β, and γ radiation, two other types of radioactive decay processes also occur commonly: *positron emission* and *electron capture*. **Positron emission** occurs when a proton in the nucleus changes into a neutron plus an ejected *positron* ($^{0}_{+1}e$ or β^+), a particle that can be thought of as a positive electron. A positron has the same mass as an electron but an opposite charge.

The result of positron emission is a decrease in the atomic number of the product nucleus but no change in the mass number. Potassium-40, for example, undergoes positron emission to yield argon-40, a nuclear reaction important in geology for dating rocks. Note once again that the sum of the two subscripts on the right of the nuclear equation ($18 + 1 = 19$) is equal to the subscript in the $^{40}_{19}K$ nucleus on the left.

You might already know that the acronym PET used in medical imaging stands for *positron emission tomography*. A chemical compound containing a positron-emitting isotope, usually ^{18}F, is injected into the body and accumulates at a certain site, such as in a tumor. When decay occurs, the emitted positron reacts with a nearby electron and is instantly annihilated, releasing gamma rays whose position in the body can be detected.

Electron capture is a process in which the nucleus captures one of the surrounding electrons in an atom, thereby converting a proton into a neutron. The mass number of the product nucleus is unchanged, but the atomic number decreases by 1, just as in positron emission. The conversion of mercury-197 into gold-197 is an example:

$$^{197}_{80}\text{Hg} + ^{0}_{-1}\text{e} \longrightarrow ^{197}_{79}\text{Au}$$

Characteristics of the different kinds of radioactive decay processes are summarized in Table 2.2.

▲ A PET scan of a 62 year old man with a brain tumor, as indicated by the yellow and orange area in the lower left portion of the brain.

TABLE 2.2 A Summary of Radioactive Decay Processes

Process	Symbol	Change in Atomic Number	Change in Mass Number	Change in Neutron Number
Alpha emission	$^4_2$He or α	−2	−4	−2
Beta emission	$^0_{-1}$e or β^-	+1	0	−1
Gamma emission	$^0_0\gamma$ or γ	0	0	0
Positron emission	$^0_1$e or β^+	−1	0	+1
Electron capture	E. C.	−1	0	+1

WORKED EXAMPLE 2.7

BALANCING NUCLEAR EQUATIONS

Write a balanced nuclear equation for each of the following processes:

(a) Alpha emission from curium-242: $^{242}_{96}\text{Cm} \longrightarrow ^4_2\text{He} + ?$

(b) Beta emission from magnesium-28: $^{28}_{12}\text{Mg} \longrightarrow ^0_{-1}\text{e} + ?$

(c) Positron emission from xenon-118: $^{118}_{54}\text{Xe} \longrightarrow ^0_1\text{e} + ?$

STRATEGY

The key to writing nuclear equations is to make sure that the number of nucleons is the same on both sides of the equation and that the number of nuclear charges plus electron or positron charges is the same.

SOLUTION

(a) In α emission, the mass number decreases by 4 and the atomic number decreases by 2, giving plutonium-238: $^{242}_{96}\text{Cm} \longrightarrow ^4_2\text{He} + ^{238}_{94}\text{Pu}$

(b) In β emission, the mass number is unchanged and the atomic number increases by 1, giving aluminum-28: $^{28}_{12}\text{Mg} \longrightarrow ^0_{-1}\text{e} + ^{28}_{13}\text{Al}$

(c) In positron emission, the mass number is unchanged and the atomic number decreases by 1, giving iodine-118: $^{118}_{54}\text{Xe} \longrightarrow ^0_1\text{e} + ^{118}_{53}\text{I}$

▶ **PROBLEM 2.11**   Write a balanced nuclear equation for each of the following processes:

(a) Beta emission from ruthenium-106: $^{106}_{44}\text{Ru} \rightarrow {}^{0}_{-1}e + ?$

(b) Alpha emission from bismuth-189: $^{189}_{83}\text{Bi} \rightarrow {}^{4}_{2}\text{He} + ?$

(c) Electron capture by polonium-204: $^{204}_{84}\text{Po} + {}^{0}_{-1}e \rightarrow ?$

▶ **PROBLEM 2.12**   What particle is produced by decay of thorium-214 to radium-210?

$$^{214}_{90}\text{Th} \rightarrow {}^{210}_{88}\text{Ra} + ?$$

CONCEPTUAL PROBLEM 2.13   Identify the isotopes involved, and tell what type of decay process is occurring in the following nuclear reaction:

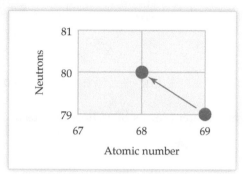

2.9 NUCLEAR STABILITY

Why do some nuclei undergo spontaneous radioactive decay while others do not? Why, for instance, does a carbon-*14* nucleus, with 6 protons and *8* neutrons, spontaneously emit a *β* particle, whereas a carbon-*13* nucleus, with 6 protons and 7 neutrons, is nonradioactive?

The answer has to do with the neutron/proton ratio in the nucleus and with the forces holding the nucleus together. To see the effect of the neutron/proton ratio on nuclear stability, look at the grid in **Figure 2.8**. Numbers on the side of the grid give the number of neutrons in different nuclei, and numbers along the bottom give the

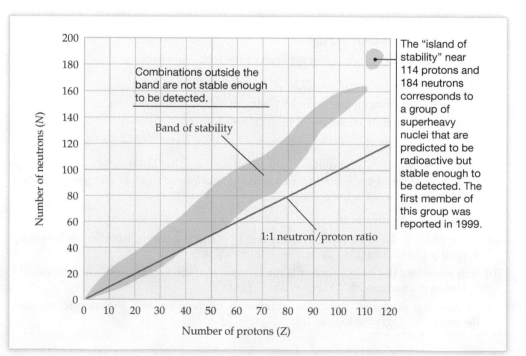

Figure 2.8

The band of nuclear stability. The band indicates various neutron/proton combinations that give rise to nuclei that are either nonradioactive or that are radioactive but decay slowly enough to exist for a measurable time.

number of protons. The first 92 elements are naturally occurring, while the remainder are the artificially produced **transuranium elements**. (Actually, only 90 of the first 92 elements occur naturally. Technetium and promethium do not occur naturally because all their isotopes are radioactive and have very short lifetimes. Francium and astatine occur on Earth only in very tiny amounts.)

When the more than 3600 known isotopes are plotted on the neutron/proton grid in Figure 2.8, they fall in a curved band sometimes called the *band of nuclear stability*. Even within the band, only 264 of the isotopes are nonradioactive. The others decay spontaneously, although their rates of decay vary enormously. On either side of the band is a so-called sea of instability representing the large number of unstable neutron–proton combinations that have never been detected. Particularly interesting is the island of stability predicted to exist for a few superheavy isotopes near 114 protons and 184 neutrons. The first members of this group—$^{287}114$, $^{288}114$, and $^{289}114$—were prepared in 1999 and do indeed seem to be stable enough to live for several seconds before they decay.

Several generalizations can be made about nuclear stability:

• Every element in the periodic table has at least one radioactive isotope.

• Hydrogen is the only element whose most abundant isotope ($^{1}_{1}H$) contains more protons (1) than neutrons (0).

• The ratio of neutrons to protons gradually increases, giving a curved appearance to the band of stability.

• All isotopes heavier than bismuth-209 are radioactive, even though they may decay slowly and be stable enough to occur naturally.

A close-up look at a segment of the band of nuclear stability (**Figure 2.9**) shows the interesting trend that radioactive nuclei with higher neutron/proton ratios (top side

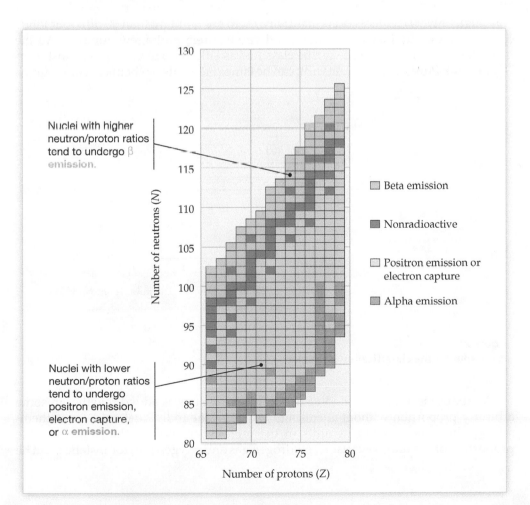

Figure 2.9

A close-up look at the band of nuclear stability. This look at the region from $Z = 66$ (dysprosium) through $Z = 79$ (gold) shows the types of radioactive processes that various radioisotopes undergo.

of the band) tend to emit β particles while nuclei with lower neutron/proton ratios (bottom side of the band) tend to undergo nuclear decay by positron emission, electron capture, or α emission.

The trend shown in Figure 2.9 makes sense if you think about it: The nuclei on the top side of the band are neutron-rich and therefore undergo a process—β emission—that *decreases* the neutron/proton ratio by converting a neutron into a proton. The nuclei on the bottom side of the band, by contrast, are neutron-poor and therefore undergo processes that *increase* the neutron/proton ratio. Take a minute to convince yourself that α emission does, in fact, increase the neutron/proton ratio for heavy nuclei in which n > p.

This process decreases the neutron/proton ratio:
$$\begin{cases} \text{Beta emission:} & \text{Neutron} \rightarrow \text{Proton} + \beta^- \end{cases}$$

These processes increase the neutron/proton ratio:
$$\begin{cases} \text{Positron emission:} & \text{Proton} \rightarrow \text{Neutron} + \beta^+ \\ \text{Electron capture:} & \text{Proton} + \text{Electron} \rightarrow \text{Neutron} \\ \text{Alpha emission:} & {}^{A}_{Z}X \rightarrow {}^{A-4}_{Z-2}Y + {}^{4}_{2}He \end{cases}$$

▶ **PROBLEM 2.14**

(a) Of the two isotopes ^{173}Au and ^{199}Au, one decays by β emission and one decays by α emission. Which does which?

(b) Of the two isotopes ^{196}Pb and ^{206}Pb, one is nonradioactive and one decays by positron emission. Which is which?

2.10   MIXTURES AND CHEMICAL COMPOUNDS; MOLECULES AND COVALENT BONDS

Although only 90 elements occur naturally, there are far more than 90 different kinds of matter on Earth. Just look around, and you'll surely find a few hundred. All the many kinds of matter you see can be classified as either mixtures or pure substances (**Figure 2.10**). Pure substances, in turn, can be either elements or chemical compounds.

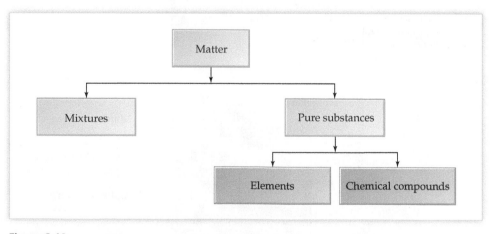

Figure 2.10
A scheme for the classification of matter.

A **mixture** is simply a blend of two or more substances added together in some arbitrary proportion without chemically changing the individual substances themselves. Thus, the constituent units in the mixture are not all the same, and the proportion of the units is variable. Hydrogen gas and oxygen gas, for instance, can be mixed in any ratio without changing them (as long as there is no flame nearby to initiate reaction), just as a spoonful of sugar and a spoonful of salt can be mixed.

A chemical compound, in contrast to a mixture, is a pure substance that is formed when atoms of different elements combine in a specific way to create a new material with properties completely unlike those of its constituent elements. A chemical compound has a constant composition throughout, and its constituent units are all identical. For example, when atoms of sodium (a soft, silvery metal) combine with atoms of chlorine (a toxic, yellow-green gas), the familiar white solid called sodium chloride (table salt) is formed. Similarly, when two atoms of hydrogen combine with one atom of oxygen, water is formed.

To see how a chemical compound is formed, imagine what must happen when two atoms approach each other at the beginning of a chemical reaction. Because the electrons of an atom occupy a much greater volume than the nucleus, it's the electrons that actually make the contact when atoms collide. Thus, it's the electrons that form the connections, or **chemical bonds**, that join atoms together in compounds. Chemical bonds between atoms are usually classified as either *covalent* or *ionic*. As a general rule, covalent bonds occur primarily between nonmetal atoms, while ionic bonds occur primarily between metal and nonmetal atoms. Let's look briefly at both kinds, beginning with covalent bonds.

A **covalent bond**, the most common kind of chemical bond, results when two atoms *share* several (usually two) electrons. A simple way to think about a covalent bond is to imagine it as a tug-of-war. If two people pull on the same rope, they are effectively joined together. Neither person can escape from the other as long as both hold on. Similarly with atoms: when two atoms both hold on to some shared electrons, the atoms are bonded together (**Figure 2.11**).

▲ The crystalline quartz sand on this beach is a pure compound (SiO_2), but the seawater is a liquid mixture of many compounds dissolved in water.

The two teams are joined together because both are tugging on the same rope.

Similarly, two atoms are joined together when both **nuclei** (+) tug on the same **electrons (dots)**.

Figure 2.11
A covalent bond between atoms is analogous to a tug-of-war.

The unit of matter that results when two or more atoms are joined by covalent bonds is called a **molecule**. A hydrogen chloride molecule (HCl) results when a hydrogen atom and a chlorine atom share two electrons. A water molecule (H_2O) results when each of two hydrogen atoms shares two electrons with a single oxygen atom. An ammonia molecule (NH_3) results when each of three hydrogen atoms shares two electrons with a nitrogen atom, and so on. To visualize these and other molecules, it helps to imagine the individual atoms as spheres joined together to form molecules with specific three-dimensional shapes, as shown in **Figure 2.12**. *Ball-and-stick* models specifically indicate the covalent bonds between atoms, while *space-filling* models accurately portray overall molecular shape but don't explicitly show covalent bonds.

Figure 2.12
Molecular models. Drawings such as these help in visualizing molecules.

Ball-and-stick models show atoms (spheres) joined together by covalent bonds (sticks).

Space-filling models portray the overall molecular shape but don't explicitly show covalent bonds.

Hydrogen chloride (HCl)   Water (H₂O)   Ammonia (NH₃)   Methane (CH₄)

Chemists normally represent a molecule by giving its **structural formula**, which shows the specific connections between atoms and therefore gives much more information than the chemical formula alone. Ethyl alcohol, for example, has the chemical formula C_2H_6O and the following structural formula:

C_2H_6O

Chemical formula   Structural formula   Molecular model

Ethyl alcohol

A structural formula uses lines between atoms to indicate the covalent bonds. Thus, the two carbon atoms in ethyl alcohol are covalently bonded to each other, the oxygen atom is bonded to one of the carbon atoms, and the six hydrogen atoms are distributed three to one carbon, two to the other carbon, and one to the oxygen.

Structural formulas are particularly important in *organic chemistry*—the chemistry of carbon compounds—where the behavior of large, complex molecules is almost entirely governed by their structure. Take even a relatively simple substance like glucose, for instance. The molecular formula of glucose, $C_6H_{12}O_6$, tells nothing about how the atoms are connected. In fact, you could probably imagine a great many different ways in which the 24 atoms might be connected. The structural formula for glucose, however, shows that 5 carbons and 1 oxygen form a ring of atoms, with the remaining 5 oxygens each bonded to 1 hydrogen and distributed on different carbons.

Glucose—$C_6H_{12}O_6$ [Red = O, gray = C, ivory = H]

Even some elements exist as molecules rather than as individual atoms. Hydrogen, nitrogen, oxygen, fluorine, chlorine, bromine, and iodine all exist as diatomic (two-atom) molecules whose two atoms are held together by covalent bonds. We therefore have to write them as such—H_2, N_2, O_2, F_2, Cl_2, Br_2, and I_2—when using any of these elements in a chemical equation. Notice that all these diatomic elements except hydrogen cluster toward the far right side of the periodic table.

WORKED EXAMPLE 2.8

DRAWING A STRUCTURAL FORMULA

Propane, C_3H_8, has a structure in which the three carbon atoms are bonded in a row, each end carbon is bonded to three hydrogens, and the middle carbon is bonded to two hydrogens. Draw the structural formula, using lines between atoms to represent covalent bonds.

SOLUTION

Propane

WORKED CONCEPTUAL EXAMPLE 2.9

VISUAL REPRESENTATIONS OF MIXTURES AND COMPOUNDS

Which of the following drawings represents a mixture, which a pure compound, and which an element?

(a)   **(b)**   **(c)**

STRATEGY

Most people (professional chemists included) find chemistry easier to grasp when they can visualize the behavior of atoms, thereby turning symbols into pictures. The Conceptual Problems in this text are intended to help you do that, frequently representing atoms and molecules as collections of spheres. Don't take the pictures literally; focus instead on interpreting what they represent.

continued on the next page

SOLUTION

Drawing **(a)** represents a mixture of two diatomic elements, one composed of two red atoms and one composed of two blue atoms. Drawing **(b)** represents molecules of a pure diatomic element because all atoms are identical. Drawing **(c)** represents molecules of a pure compound composed of one red and one blue atom.

▶ **PROBLEM 2.15** Draw the structural formula of methylamine, CH_5N, a substance responsible for the odor of rotting fish. The carbon atom is bonded to the nitrogen atom and to three hydrogens. The nitrogen atom is bonded to the carbon and two hydrogens.

▶ **PROBLEM 2.16** Methionine, one of the 20 amino acid building blocks from which proteins are made, has the following structure. What is the chemical formula of methionine? In writing the formula, list the element symbols in alphabetical order and give the number of each element as a subscript.

Methionine
(an amino acid)

CONCEPTUAL PROBLEM 2.17 Which of the following drawings represents a collection of hydrogen peroxide (H_2O_2) molecules? The red spheres represent oxygen atoms and the ivory spheres represent hydrogen.

(a)   **(b)**   **(c)**   **(d)**

CONCEPTUAL PROBLEM 2.18 Adrenaline, the so-called "flight or fight" hormone, can be represented by the following ball-and-stick model. What is the chemical formula of adrenaline? (Gray = C, ivory = H, red = O, blue = N)

2.11 IONS AND IONIC BONDS

In contrast to a covalent bond, an **ionic bond** results not from a sharing of electrons but from a transfer of one or more electrons from one atom to another. As noted previously, ionic bonds generally form between a metal and a nonmetal. Metals, such as sodium, magnesium, and zinc, tend to give up electrons, whereas nonmetals, such as oxygen, nitrogen, and chlorine, tend to accept electrons.

For example, when sodium metal comes in contact with chlorine gas, a sodium atom gives an electron to a chlorine atom, resulting in the formation of two charged particles, called **ions**. Because a sodium atom loses one electron, it loses one negative charge and becomes an Na^+ ion with a charge of +1. Such positive ions are called **cations** (pronounced **cat**-ions). Conversely, because a chlorine atom gains an electron, it gains a negative charge and becomes a Cl^- ion with a charge of −1. Such negative ions are called **anions** (**an**-ions).

A similar reaction takes place when magnesium and chlorine molecules (Cl_2) come in contact to form $MgCl_2$. A magnesium atom transfers an electron to each of two chlorine atoms, yielding the doubly charged Mg^{2+} cation and two Cl^- anions.

$$Mg + Cl_2 \rightarrow Mg^{2+} + Cl^- + Cl^- (MgCl_2)$$

Because opposite charges attract, positively charged cations like Na^+ and Mg^{2+} experience a strong electrical attraction to negatively charged anions like Cl^-, an attraction that we call an ionic bond. Unlike what happens when covalent bonds are formed, though, we can't really talk about discrete Na^+Cl^- *molecules* under normal conditions. We can speak only of an **ionic solid**, in which equal numbers of Na^+ and Cl^- ions are packed together in a regular way (**Figure 2.13**). In a crystal of table salt, for instance, each Na^+ ion is surrounded by six nearby Cl^- ions, and each Cl^- ion is surrounded by six nearby Na^+ ions, but we can't specify what pairs of ions "belong" to each other as we can with atoms in covalent molecules.

▲ Chlorine is a toxic green gas, sodium is a reactive metal, and sodium chloride is a harmless white solid.

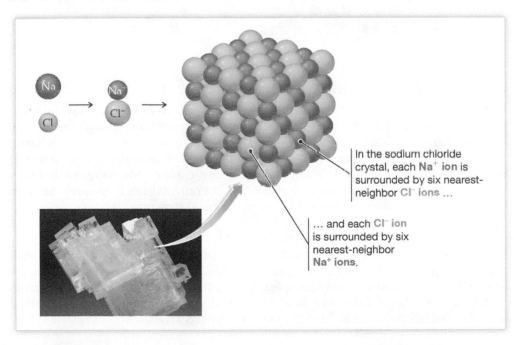

In the sodium chloride crystal, each **Na^+ ion** is surrounded by six nearest-neighbor Cl^- ions …

… and each Cl^- ion is surrounded by six nearest-neighbor Na^+ ions.

Figure 2.13
The arrangement of Na^+ ions and Cl^- ions in a crystal of sodium chloride. There is no discrete "molecule" of NaCl. Instead, the entire crystal is an ionic solid.

Charged, covalently bonded groups of atoms, called **polyatomic ions**, are also common—ammonium ion (NH_4^+), hydroxide ion (OH^-), nitrate ion (NO_3^-), and the doubly charged sulfate ion (SO_4^{2-}) are examples. You can think of these polyatomic ions as charged molecules because they consist of specific numbers and kinds of atoms joined together by covalent bonds, with the overall unit having a positive or negative charge. When writing the formulas of substances that contain more than one of these ions, parentheses are placed around the entire polyatomic unit. The formula $Ba(NO_3)_2$, for instance, indicates a substance made of Ba^{2+} cations and NO_3^- polyatomic anions in a 1:2 ratio. We'll say more about these ions in Section 2.12.

WORKED EXAMPLE 2.10

IDENTIFYING IONIC AND MOLECULAR COMPOUNDS

Which of the following compounds would you expect to be ionic and which molecular (covalent)?

(a) BaF_2 (b) SF_4 (c) PH_3 (d) CH_3OH

STRATEGY

Remember that covalent bonds generally form between nonmetal atoms, while ionic bonds form between metal and nonmetal atoms.

SOLUTION

Compound (a) is composed of a metal (barium) and a nonmetal (fluorine) and is likely to be ionic. Compounds (b)–(d) are composed entirely of nonmetals and therefore are probably molecular.

▸ **PROBLEM 2.19** Which of the following compounds would you expect to be ionic and which molecular (covalent)?

(a) LiBr   (b) $SiCl_4$ (c) BF_3 (d) CaO

CONCEPTUAL PROBLEM 2.20 Which of the following drawings is most likely to represent an ionic compound and which a molecular (covalent) compound? Explain.

(a)   (b)

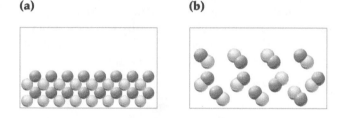

2.12 NAMING CHEMICAL COMPOUNDS

In the early days of chemistry, when few pure substances were known, newly discovered compounds were often given fanciful names—morphine, quicklime, potash, and barbituric acid (said to be named by its discoverer in honor of his friend Barbara) to cite a few. Today, with more than 40 million pure compounds known, there would be chaos unless a systematic method for naming compounds were used. Every chemical compound must be given a name that not only defines it uniquely but also allows chemists (and computers) to know its chemical structure.

Different kinds of compounds are named by different rules. Ordinary table salt, for instance, is named *sodium chloride* because of its formula NaCl, but common table sugar ($C_{12}H_{22}O_{11}$) is named *β-D-fructofuranosyl-α-D-glucopyranoside* because of special rules for carbohydrates. (Organic compounds often have quite complex structures and correspondingly complex names, though we'll not discuss them in this text.) We'll begin by seeing how to name simple ionic compounds and then introduce additional rules in later chapters as the need arises.

▲ Morphine, a pain-killing agent found in the opium poppy, was named after Morpheus, the Greek god of dreams.

Naming Binary Ionic Compounds

Binary ionic compounds—those made of only two elements—are named by identifying first the positive ion and then the negative ion. The positive ion takes the same name as the element, while the negative ion takes the first part of its name from the element and then adds the ending *-ide*. For example, KBr is named potassium bromide: *potassium* for the K^+ ion, and *bromide* for the negative Br^- ion derived from the element *brom*ine. **Figure 2.14** shows some common main-group ions, and **Figure 2.15** shows some common transition-metal ions.

LiF	$CaBr_2$	$AlCl_3$
Lithium fluoride	Calcium bromide	Aluminum chloride

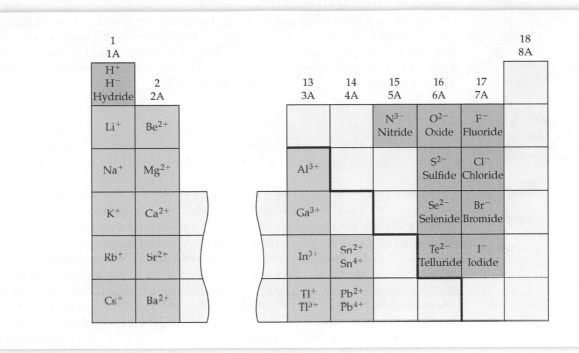

Figure 2.14

Main-group cations (blue) and anions (purple). A **cation** bears the same name as the element it is derived from; an **anion** name has an *-ide* ending.

Figure 2.14 illustrates several interesting points. Note, for instance, that metals tend to form cations and nonmetals tend to form anions, as mentioned previously in Section 2.11. Note also that elements within a given group of the periodic table form similar kinds of ions and that the charge on the ion is related to the group number. Main-group metals usually form cations whose charge is equal to the group number. Group 1A elements form singly positive ions (M^+, where M is a metal), group 2A elements form doubly positive ions (M^{2+}), and group 3A elements form triply positive ions (M^{3+}). Main-group nonmetals usually form anions whose charge is equal to the group number in the U.S. system minus eight. Thus, group 6A elements form doubly negative ions ($6 - 8 = -2$), group 7A elements form singly negative ions ($7 - 8 = -1$), and group 8A elements form no ions at all ($8 - 8 = 0$). We'll see the reason for this behavior in Chapter 6.

3 3B	4 4B	5 5B	6 6B	7 7B	8	9 8B	10	11 1B	12 2B
Sc^{3+}	Ti^{3+}	V^{3+}	Cr^{2+} Cr^{3+}	Mn^{2+}	Fe^{2+} Fe^{3+}	Co^{2+}	Ni^{2+}	Cu^+ Cu^{2+}	Zn^{2+}
Y^{3+}					Ru^{3+}	Rh^{3+}	Pd^{2+}	Ag^+	Cd^{2+}
									Hg^{2+}

Figure 2.15

Common transition metal ions. Only ions that exist in aqueous solution are shown.

Notice also, in both Figures 2.14 and 2.15, that some metals form more than one kind of cation. Iron, for instance, forms both the doubly charged Fe^{2+} ion and the triply charged Fe^{3+} ion. In naming these ions, we distinguish between them by using a Roman numeral in parentheses to indicate the number of charges. Thus, $FeCl_2$ is

▲ Crystals of iron(II) chloride tetrahydrate are greenish, and crystals of iron(III) chloride hexahydrate are brownish yellow.

named iron(II) chloride and $FeCl_3$ is iron(III) chloride. Alternatively, an older method distinguishes between the ions by using the Latin name of the element (*ferrum* in the case of iron) together with the ending *-ous* for the ion with lower charge and *-ic* for the ion with higher charge. Thus, $FeCl_2$ is sometimes called ferrous chloride and $FeCl_3$ is called ferric chloride. Although still in use, this older naming system is being phased out and we'll rarely use it in this book.

Fe^{2+}	Fe^{3+}	Sn^{2+}	Sn^{4+}
Iron(II) ion	Iron(III) ion	Tin(II) ion	Tin(IV) ion
Ferrous ion	Ferric ion	Stannous ion	Stannic ion
(From the Latin *ferrum* = iron)		(From the Latin *stannum* = tin)	

In any neutral compound, the total number of positive charges must equal the total number of negative charges. Thus, you can always figure out the number of positive charges on a metal cation by counting the number of negative charges on the associated anion(s). In $FeCl_2$, for example, the iron ion must be Fe(II) because there are two Cl^- ions associated with it. Similarly, in $TiCl_3$ the titanium ion is Ti(III) because there are three Cl^- anions associated with it. As a general rule, a Roman numeral is needed for transition-metal compounds to avoid ambiguity. In addition, the main-group metals tin (Sn), thallium (Tl), and lead (Pb) can form more than one kind of ion and need Roman numerals for naming their compounds. Metals in group 1A and group 2A form only one cation, however, so Roman numerals are not needed.

WORKED EXAMPLE 2.11

NAMING BINARY IONIC COMPOUNDS

Give systematic names for the following compounds:

(a) $BaCl_2$ (b) $CrCl_3$ (c) PbS   (d) Fe_2O_3

STRATEGY

Try to figure out the number of positive charges on each cation by counting the number of negative charges on the associated anion(s). Refer to Figures 2.14 and 2.15 as necessary.

SOLUTION

(a) Barium chloride	No Roman numeral is necessary because barium, a group 2A element, forms only Ba^{2+}.
(b) Chromium(III) chloride	The Roman numeral III is necessary to specify the +3 charge on chromium (a transition metal).
(c) Lead(II) sulfide	The sulfide anion (S^{2-}) has a double negative charge, so the lead cation must be doubly positive.
(d) Iron(III) oxide	The three oxide anions (O^{2-}) have a total negative charge of −6, so the two iron cations must have a total charge of +6. Thus, each is Fe(III).

WORKED EXAMPLE 2.12

CONVERTING NAMES INTO FORMULAS

Write formulas for the following compounds:

(a) Magnesium fluoride   (b) Tin(IV) oxide   (c) Iron(III) sulfide

STRATEGY

For transition metal compounds, the charge on the cation is indicated by the Roman numeral in the name. Knowing the number of positive charges, you can then figure out the number of necessary negative charges for the associated anions.

SOLUTION

(a) MgF_2 Magnesium (group 2A) forms only a 2+ cation, so there must be two fluoride ions (F^-) to balance the charge.

(b) SnO_2 Tin(IV) has a +4 charge, so there must be two oxide ions (O^{2-}) to balance the charge.

(c) Fe_2S_3 Iron(III) has a +3 charge and sulfide ion a −2 charge (S^{2-}), so there must be two irons and three sulfurs.

▶ **PROBLEM 2.21**   Give systematic names for the following compounds:

(a) CsF   **(b)** K_2O **(c)** CuO   **(d)** BaS   **(e)** $BeBr_2$

▶ **PROBLEM 2.22**   Write formulas for the following compounds:

(a) Vanadium(III) chloride   **(b)** Manganese(IV) oxide

(c) Copper(II) sulfide   **(d)** Aluminum oxide

CONCEPTUAL PROBLEM 2.23 Three binary ionic compounds are represented on the following periodic table: red with red, green with green, and blue with blue. Name each, and tell its likely formula.

Naming Binary Molecular Compounds

Binary molecular compounds with covalent bonds are named in much the same way as binary ionic compounds by assuming that one of the elements in the compound is more cationlike and the other element is more anionlike. As with ionic compounds, the cationlike element takes the name of the element itself, and the anionlike element takes an -*ide* ending. The compound HF, for example, is called *hydrogen fluoride*.

HF   Hydrogen is more cationlike because it is farther left in the periodic table, and fluoride is more anionlike because it is farther right. The compound is therefore named *hydrogen fluoride*.

We'll see a quantitative way to decide which element is more cationlike and which is more anionlike in Section 7.4 but you might note for now that it's usually possible to decide by looking at the relative positions of the elements in the periodic table. The farther left and toward the bottom of the periodic table an element occurs, the more likely it is to be cationlike; the farther right and toward the top an element occurs (except for the noble gases), the more likely it is to be anionlike.

The following examples show how this generalization applies:

CO   Carbon monoxide (C is in group 4A; O is in group 6A)

CO_2 Carbon dioxide

PCl_3 Phosphorus trichloride (P is in group 5A; Cl is in group 7A)

SF_4 Sulfur tetrafluoride (S is in group 6A; F is in group 7A)

N_2O_4 Dinitrogen tetroxide (N is in group 5A; O is in group 6A)

TABLE 2.3 Numerical Prefixes for Naming Compounds	
Prefix	**Meaning**
mono-	1
di-	2
tri-	3
tetra-	4
penta-	5
hexa-	6
hepta-	7
octa-	8
nona-	9
deca-	10

Because nonmetals often combine with one another in different proportions to form different compounds, numerical prefixes are usually included in the names of binary molecular compounds to specify the numbers of each kind of atom present. The compound CO, for example, is called carbon *mono*xide, and CO_2 is called carbon *di*oxide. Table 2.3 lists the most common numerical prefixes. Note that when the prefix ends in *a* or *o* (but not *i*) and the anion name begins with a vowel (*oxide*, for instance), the *a* or *o* on the prefix is dropped to avoid having two vowels together in the name. Thus, we write carbon *mono*xide rather than carbon *mono*oxide for CO and dinitrogen *tetr*oxide rather than dinitrogen *tetra*oxide for N_2O_4. A *mono-* prefix is not used for the atom named first: CO_2 is called carbon dioxide rather than monocarbon dioxide.

WORKED EXAMPLE 2.13

NAMING BINARY MOLECULAR COMPOUNDS

Give systematic names for the following compounds:

(a) PCl_3 (b) N_2O_3 (c) P_4O_7 (d) BrF_3

STRATEGY

Look at a periodic table to see which element in each compound is more cationlike (farther to the left or lower) and which is more anionlike (farther to the right or higher). Then name the compound using the appropriate numerical prefix.

SOLUTION

(a) Phosphorus trichloride   (b) Dinitrogen trioxide
(c) Tetraphosphorus heptoxide   (d) Bromine trifluoride

▶ **PROBLEM 2.24**   Give systematic names for the following compounds:

(a) NCl_3 (b) P_4O_6 (c) S_2F_2 (d) SeO_2

▶ **PROBLEM 2.25**   Write formulas for compounds with the following names:

(a) Disulfur dichloride   (b) Iodine monochloride

(c) Nitrogen triiodide

CONCEPTUAL PROBLEM 2.26   Give systematic names for the following compounds:

(a)   (b)

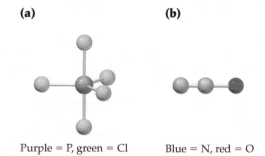

Purple = P, green = Cl   Blue = N, red = O

Naming Compounds with Polyatomic Ions

Ionic compounds that contain polyatomic ions (Section 2.11) are named in the same way as binary ionic compounds: First the cation is identified and then the anion. For example, $Ba(NO_3)_2$ is called *barium nitrate* because Ba^{2+} is the cation and the NO_3^- polyatomic anion has the name *nitrate*. Unfortunately, there is no simple systematic way of naming the polyatomic ions themselves, so it's necessary to memorize the names, formulas, and charges of the most common ones, listed in Table 2.4. The ammonium ion (NH_4^+) is the only cation on the list; all the others are anions.

TABLE 2.4   Some Common Polyatomic Ions

Formula	Name	Formula	Name
Cation		**Singly charged anions (continued)**	
NH_4^+	Ammonium	NO_2^-	Nitrite
		NO_3^-	Nitrate
Singly charged anions			
$CH_3CO_2^-$	Acetate	**Doubly charged anions**	
CN^-	Cyanide	CO_3^{2-}	Carbonate
ClO^-	Hypochlorite	CrO_4^{2-}	Chromate
ClO_2^-	Chlorite	$Cr_2O_7^{2-}$	Dichromate
ClO_3^-	Chlorate	O_2^{2-}	Peroxide
ClO_4^-	Perchlorate	HPO_4^{2-}	Hydrogen phosphate
$H_2PO_4^-$	Dihydrogen phosphate	SO_3^{2-}	Sulfite
HCO_3^-	Hydrogen carbonate (or bicarbonate)	SO_4^{2-}	Sulfate
		$S_2O_3^{2-}$	Thiosulfate
HSO_4^-	Hydrogen sulfate (or bisulfate)		
		Triply charged anion	
OH^-	Hydroxide	PO_4^{3-}	Phosphate
MnO_4^-	Permanganate		

Several points about the ions in Table 2.4 need special mention. First, note that the names of most polyatomic anions end in *-ite* or *-ate*. Only hydroxide (OH^-), cyanide (CN^-), and peroxide (O_2^{2-}) have the *-ide* ending. Second, note that several of the ions form a series of **oxoanions**, binary polyatomic anions in which an atom of a given element is combined with different numbers of oxygen atoms—hypochlorite (ClO^-), chlorite (ClO_2^-), chlorate (ClO_3^-), and perchlorate (ClO_4^-), for example. When there are only two oxoanions in a series, as with sulfite (SO_3^{2-}) and sulfate (SO_4^{2-}), the ion with fewer oxygens takes the *-ite* ending and the ion with more oxygens takes the *-ate* ending.

SO_3^{2-}	Sulf*ite* ion (fewer oxygens)	SO_4^{2-}	Sulf*ate* ion (more oxygens)
NO_2^-	Nitr*ite* ion (fewer oxygens)	NO_3^-	Nitr*ate* ion (more oxygens)

When there are more than two oxoanions in a series, the prefix *hypo-* (meaning "less than") is used for the ion with the fewest oxygens, and the prefix *per-* (meaning "more than") is used for the ion with the most oxygens.

ClO^-	*Hypo*chlorite ion (less oxygen than chlorite)
ClO_2^-	Chlorite ion
ClO_3^-	Chlorate ion
ClO_4^-	*Per*chlorate ion (more oxygen than chlorate)

Third, note that several pairs of ions are related by the presence or absence of a hydrogen. The hydrogen carbonate anion (HCO_3^-) differs from the carbonate anion (CO_3^{2-}) by the presence of H^+, and the hydrogen sulfate anion (HSO_4^-) differs from the sulfate anion (SO_4^{2-}) by the presence of H^+. The ion that has the additional hydrogen is sometimes referred to using the prefix *bi-*, although this usage is now discouraged; for example, $NaHCO_3$ is sometimes called sodium bicarbonate.

HCO_3^-	Hydrogen carbonate (*bi*carbonate) ion	CO_3^{2-}	Carbonate ion
HSO_4^-	Hydrogen sulfate (*bi*sulfate) ion	SO_4^{2-}	Sulfate ion

WORKED EXAMPLE 2.14

NAMING COMPOUNDS WITH POLYATOMIC IONS

Give systematic names for the following compounds:

(a) $LiNO_3$ (b) $KHSO_4$ (c) $CuCO_3$ (d) $Fe(ClO_4)_3$

STRATEGY

Unfortunately, there is no alternative: The names and charges of the common polyatomic ions must be memorized. Refer to Table 2.4 if you need help.

SOLUTION

(a) Lithium nitrate	Lithium (group 1A) forms only the Li^+ ion and does not need a Roman numeral.
(b) Potassium hydrogen sulfate	Potassium (group 1A) forms only the K^+ ion.
(c) Copper(II) carbonate	The carbonate ion has a −2 charge, so copper must be +2. A Roman numeral is needed because copper, a transition metal, can form more than one ion.
(d) Iron(III) perchlorate	There are three perchlorate ions, each with a −1 charge, so the iron must have a +3 charge.

WORKED EXAMPLE 2.15

WRITING FORMULAS OF COMPOUNDS WITH POLYATOMIC IONS

Write formulas for the following compounds:

(a) Potassium hypochlorite   (b) Silver(I) chromate
(c) Iron(III) carbonate

SOLUTION

(a) KClO	Potassium forms only the K^+ ion, so only one ClO^- is needed.
(b) Ag_2CrO_4	The polyatomic chromate ion has a −2 charge, so two Ag^+ ions are needed.
(c) $Fe_2(CO_3)_3$	Iron(III) has a +3 charge and the polyatomic carbonate ion has a −2 charge, so there must be two iron ions and three carbonate ions. The polyatomic carbonate ion is set off in parentheses to indicate that there are three of them.

▶ **PROBLEM 2.27** Give systematic names for the following compounds:
(a) $Ca(ClO)_2$ (b) $Ag_2S_2O_3$ (c) NaH_2PO_4
(d) $Sn(NO_3)_2$ (e) $Pb(CH_3CO_2)_4$ (f) $(NH_4)_2SO_4$

▶ **PROBLEM 2.28** Write formulas for the following compounds:
(a) Lithium phosphate   (b) Magnesium hydrogen sulfate
(c) Manganese(II) nitrate   (d) Chromium(III) sulfate

CONCEPTUAL PROBLEM 2.29 The following drawings are those of solid ionic compounds, with red spheres representing the cations and blue spheres representing the anions in each.

    (1)   **(2)**

Which of the following formulas are consistent with each drawing?
(a) LiBr   (b) $NaNO_2$ (c) $CaCl_2$
(d) K_2CO_3 (e) $Fe_2(SO_4)_3$

INQUIRY WHERE DO CHEMICAL ELEMENTS COME FROM?

Cosmologists theorize that the universe began some 13.7 billion years ago in an extraordinary event they call the big bang. Initially, the temperature must have been inconceivably high, but after 1 second, the temperature had dropped to about 10^{10} K and elementary particles began to form: protons, neutrons, and electrons, as well as positrons and *neutrinos*—neutral particles with a mass much less than that of an electron. After 3 minutes, the temperature had dropped to 10^9 K, and protons began fusing with neutrons to form helium nuclei ($^4_2\text{He}^{2+}$). Matter remained in this form for many millions of years until the expanding universe had cooled to about 10,000 K. Electrons were then able to bind to protons and to helium nuclei, forming stable hydrogen and helium atoms.

The attractive force of gravity acting on regions of higher-than-average density slowly produced massive local concentrations of matter and ultimately formed billions of galaxies, each with many billions of stars. As the gas clouds of hydrogen and helium condensed under gravitational attraction and stars formed, their temperatures reached 10^7 K and their densities reached 100 g/cm^3. Protons and neutrons again fused to yield helium nuclei, generating vast amounts of heat and light.

Most of these early stars probably burned out after a few billion years, but a few were so massive that, as their nuclear fuel diminished, gravitational attraction caused a rapid contraction leading to still higher core temperatures and higher densities—up to 5×10^8 K and 5×10^5 g/cm^3. Much larger nuclei were now formed, including carbon, oxygen, silicon, magnesium, and iron. Ultimately, these massive stars underwent gravitational collapse, resulting in the synthesis of still heavier elements and explosions visible throughout the universe as *supernovas*.

Matter from exploding supernovas was blown throughout the galaxy, forming a new generation of stars and planets. Our own sun and solar system formed only about 4.5 billion years ago from matter released by former supernovas. Except for hydrogen and helium, all the atoms in our bodies, our planet, and our solar system were created more than 5 billion years ago in exploding stars. We are made of stardust.

▶ **PROBLEM 2.30** What two elements are thought to be the first ones formed in the big bang?

▲ The stars in the Milky Way galaxy condensed from gas clouds under gravitational attraction.

▲ In 1667, the instantaneous gravitational collapse of the massive star Cassiopeia A resulted in a supernova explosion, whose remnants are still visible.

SUMMARY

Elements are made of tiny particles called **atoms**, which can combine in simple numerical ratios according to the **law of multiple proportions**. Atoms are composed of three fundamental particles: **protons** are positively charged, **electrons** are negatively charged, and **neutrons** are neutral. According to the nuclear model of an atom proposed by Ernest Rutherford, protons and neutrons are clustered into a dense core called the **nucleus**, while electrons move around the nucleus at a relatively great distance.

Elements differ from one another according to how many protons their atoms contain, a value called the **atomic number (Z)** of the element. The sum of an atom's protons and neutrons is its **mass number (A)**. Although all atoms of a specific element have the same atomic number, different atoms of an element can have different mass numbers, depending on how many neutrons they have. Atoms with identical atomic numbers but different mass numbers are called **isotopes**. Atomic masses are measured using the **atomic mass unit (amu)**, defined as 1/12 the mass of a ^{12}C atom. Because both protons and neutrons have a mass of approximately 1 amu, the mass of an atom in atomic mass units (the isotopic mass) is numerically close to the atom's mass number. The element's **atomic mass** is a weighted mass average of its naturally occurring isotopes.

When referring to the enormous numbers of atoms that make up visible amounts of matter, the fundamental SI unit called a *mole* is used. One **mole** is the amount whose mass in grams, called its **molar mass**, is numerically equal to the atomic mass. Numerically, one mole of any element contains 6.022×10^{23} atoms, a value called **Avogadro's number (N_A)**.

Nuclear chemistry is the study of the properties and reactions of atomic nuclei. Nuclear reactions differ from chemical reactions in that they involve a change in an atom's nucleus, producing a different element. Nuclear reactions are written using balanced **nuclear equations**, in which the element symbols represent only the nuclei rather than neutral atoms.

Radioactivity is the spontaneous emission of radiation from an unstable nucleus. **Alpha (α) radiation** consists of helium nuclei, small particles containing two protons and two neutrons ($^4_2He^{2+}$). **Beta (β) radiation** consists of electrons ($^0_{-1}e$), and **gamma (γ) radiation** consists of high-energy electromagnetic radiation that has no mass. **Positron emission** is the conversion of a proton in the nucleus into a neutron plus an ejected *positron* (^0_1e or β^+), a particle that has the same mass as an electron but a positive charge. **Electron capture** is the capture of a surrounding electron by a proton in the nucleus. The process is accompanied by the emission of γ rays and results in the conversion of a proton in the nucleus into a neutron.

Most substances are **chemical compounds**, formed when atoms of two or more elements combine in a **chemical reaction**. The atoms in a compound are held together by one of two kinds of **chemical bonds**. **Covalent bonds** form when two atoms share electrons to give a new unit of matter called a **molecule**. **Ionic bonds** form when one atom completely transfers one or more electrons to another atom, resulting in the formation of **ions**. Positively charged ions (**cations**) are strongly attracted to negatively charged ions (**anions**) by electrical forces.

Chemical compounds are named systematically by following a series of rules. Binary ionic compounds are named by identifying first the positive ion and then the negative ion. Binary molecular compounds are similarly named by identifying the cationlike and anionlike elements. Naming compounds with **polyatomic ions** involves memorizing the names and formulas of the most common ones.

KEY WORDS

alpha (α) radiation *49*	**chemical equation** *36*	**law of mass**	**nucleon** *50*
anion *59*	**chemical formula** *36*	**conservation** *36*	**nucleus** *42*
atom *38*	**covalent bond** *55*	**law of multiple**	**oxoanion** *65*
atomic mass *46*	**electron** *39*	**proportions** *37*	**polyatomic ion** *59*
atomic mass unit (amu) *45*	**electron capture** *51*	**mass number (A)** *44*	**positron emission** *50*
atomic number (Z) *43*	**gamma (γ) radiation** *50*	**mixture** *54*	**proton** *42*
Avogadro's number (N_A) *47*	**ion** *59*	**molar mass** *47*	**radioactive** *49*
	ionic bond *58*	**mole** *46*	**radioisotope** *49*
beta (β) radiation *50*	**ionic solid** *59*	**molecule** *55*	**structural formula** *56*
cation *59*	**isotope** *44*	**neutron** *42*	**transuranium element** *53*
chemical bond *55*	**law of definite**	**nuclear chemistry** *48*	
chemical compound *35*	**proportions** *37*	**nuclear equation** *48*	

CONCEPTUAL PROBLEMS

Problems 2.1–2.30 appear within the chapter.

2.31 In the following drawings, red spheres represent cations and blue spheres represent anions. Match each of the drawings **(a)–(d)** with the following ionic compounds:

(i) $Ca_3(PO_4)_2$ (ii) Li_2CO_3
(iii) $FeCl_2$ (iv) $MgSO_4$

(a)   **(b)**

(c)   **(d)**

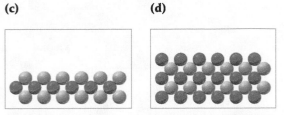

2.32 If yellow spheres represent sulfur atoms and red spheres represent oxygen atoms, which of the following drawings shows a collection of sulfur dioxide (SO_2) units?

(a)   **(b)**

(c)   **(d)**

2.33 Assume that the mixture of substances in drawing **(a)** undergoes a reaction. Which of the drawings **(b)–(d)** represents a product mixture consistent with the law of mass conservation?

(a)

(b)   **(c)**   **(d)**

2.34 If red and blue spheres represent atoms of different elements, which two of the following drawings illustrate the law of multiple proportions?

(a)   **(b)**

(c)   **(d)**

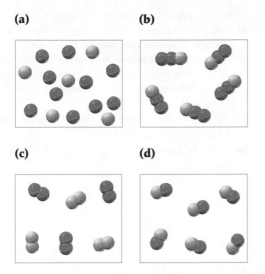

2.35 Which of the following three drawings represents a neutral Na atom, which represents a Ca atom with two positive electrical charges (Ca^{2+}), and which represents an F atom with one minus charge (F^-)?

(a)   **(b)**   **(c)**

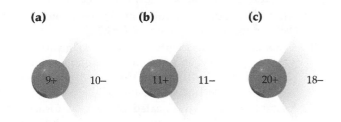

9+   10–   11+   11–   20+   18–

2.36 Give molecular formulas corresponding to each of the following ball-and-stick molecular representations (red = O, gray = C, blue = N, ivory = H). In writing the formula, list the elements in alphabetical order.

(a) Alanine (an amino acid)

(b) Ethylene glycol (automobile antifreeze)

(c) Acetic acid (vinegar)

2.37 Isotope A decays to isotope E through the following series of steps, in which the products of the individual decay events are themselves radioactive and undergo further decay until a stable nucleus is ultimately reached. Two kinds of processes are represented, one by the shorter arrows pointing right and the other by the longer arrows pointing left.

(a) To what kind of nuclear decay process does each kind of arrow correspond?

(b) Identify and write the symbol $_Z^A X$ for each isotope in the series:

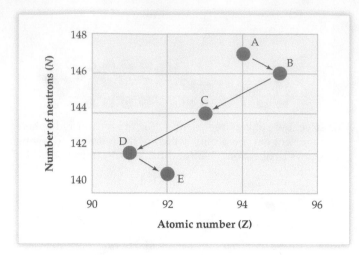

SECTION PROBLEMS

Atomic Theory (Sections 2.1 and 2.2)

2.38 How does Dalton's atomic theory account for the law of mass conservation and the law of definite proportions?

2.39 What is the law of multiple proportions, and how does Dalton's atomic theory account for it?

2.40 A sample of mercury with a mass of 114.0 g was combined with 12.8 g of oxygen gas, and the resulting reaction gave 123.1 g of mercury(II) oxide. How much oxygen was left over after the reaction was complete?

2.41 A sample of $CaCO_3$ was heated, causing it to form CaO and CO_2 gas. Solid CaO remained behind, while the CO_2 escaped to the atmosphere. If the $CaCO_3$ weighed 612 g and the CaO weighed 343 g, how many grams of CO_2 were formed in the reaction?

2.42 Benzene, ethane, and ethylene are just three of a large number of *hydrocarbons*—compounds that contain only carbon and hydrogen. Show how the following data are consistent with the law of multiple proportions.

Compound	Mass of carbon in 5.00 g sample	Mass of hydrogen in 5.00 g sample
Benzene	4.61 g	0.39 g
Ethane	4.00 g	1.00 g
Ethylene	4.29 g	0.71 g

2.43 In addition to carbon monoxide (CO) and carbon dioxide (CO_2), there is a third compound of carbon and oxygen called *carbon suboxide*. If a 2.500 g sample of carbon suboxide contains 1.32 g of C and 1.18 g of O, show that the law of multiple proportions is followed.

2.44 The atomic mass of carbon (12.011 amu) is approximately 12 times that of hydrogen (1.008 amu).

(a) Show how you can use this knowledge to calculate possible formulas for benzene, ethane, and ethylene (Problem 2.42).

(b) Show how your answer to part (a) is consistent with the actual formulas for benzene (C_6H_6), ethane (C_2H_6), and ethylene (C_2H_4).

2.45 What is a possible formula for carbon suboxide (Problem 2.43)?

2.46 If the atomic mass of an element is x, what is the mass in grams of 6.02×10^{23} atoms of the element?

2.47 If 6.02×10^{23} atoms of element Y have a mass of 83.80 g, what is the identity of Y?

2.48 If the atomic mass of an element is x, what is the mass in grams of 3.17×10^{20} atoms of the element?

2.49 If 4.61×10^{21} atoms of element Z have a mass of 0.815 g, what is the identity of Z?

2.50 A compound of zinc and sulfur contains 67.1% zinc by mass. What is the ratio of zinc and sulfur atoms in the compound?

2.51 There are two compounds of titanium and chlorine. One compound contains 31.04% titanium by mass, and the other contains 74.76% chlorine by mass. What are the ratios of titanium and chlorine atoms in the two compounds?

2.52 In methane, one part hydrogen combines with three parts carbon by mass. If a sample of a compound containing only carbon and hydrogen contains 32.0 g of carbon and 8.0 g of hydrogen, could the sample be methane? If the sample is not methane, show that the law of multiple proportions is followed for methane and this other substance.

2.53 In borane, one part hydrogen combines with 3.6 parts boron by mass. A compound containing only hydrogen and boron contains 6.0 g of hydrogen and 43.2 g of boron. Could this compound be borane? If it is not borane, show that the law of multiple proportions is followed for borane and this other substance.

Elements and Atoms (Sections 2.3–2.6)

2.54 What is the difference between an atom's atomic number and its mass number?

2.55 What is the difference between an element's atomic number and its atomic mass?

2.56 The subscript giving the atomic number of an atom is often left off when writing an isotope symbol. For example, $_6^{13}C$ is often written simply as ^{13}C. Why is this allowable?

2.57 Iodine has a *lower* atomic mass than tellurium (126.90 for iodine, 127.60 for tellurium) even though it has a *higher* atomic number (53 for iodine, 52 for tellurium). Explain.

2.58 Copper has two naturally occurring isotopes, including ^{65}Cu. Look at the periodic table and tell whether the second isotope is ^{63}Cu or ^{66}Cu.

2.59 Sulfur has four naturally occurring isotopes, including ^{33}S, ^{34}S, and ^{36}S. Look at the periodic table and tell whether the fourth isotope is ^{32}S or ^{35}S.

2.60 Give the names and symbols for the following elements:
(a) An element with atomic number 6
(b) An element with 18 protons in its nucleus
(c) An element with 23 electrons

2.61 The radioactive isotope cesium-137 was produced in large amounts in fallout from the 1985 nuclear power plant disaster at Chernobyl, Ukraine. Write the symbol for this isotope in standard format.

2.62 Write symbols for the following isotopes:
(a) Radon-220
(b) Polonium-210
(c) Gold-197

2.63 Write symbols for the following isotopes:
(a) $Z = 58$ and $A = 140$
(b) $Z = 27$ and $A = 60$

2.64 How many protons, neutrons, and electrons are in each of the following atoms?
(a) $^{15}_{7}$N   (b) $^{60}_{27}$Co   (c) $^{131}_{53}$I
(d) $^{142}_{58}$Ce

2.65 How many protons and neutrons are in the nucleus of the following atoms?
(a) ^{27}Al   (b) ^{32}S   (c) ^{64}Zn
(d) ^{207}Pb

2.66 Identify the following elements:
(a) $^{24}_{12}$X   (b) $^{58}_{28}$X   (c) $^{104}_{46}$X
(d) $^{183}_{74}$X

2.67 Identify the following elements:
(a) $^{202}_{80}$X   (b) $^{195}_{78}$X   (c) $^{184}_{76}$X
(d) $^{209}_{83}$X

2.68 Which of the following isotope symbols can't be correct?
$^{18}_{9}$F $^{12}_{5}$C $^{33}_{35}$Br $^{18}_{8}$O $^{11}_{5}$Bo

2.69 Which of the following isotope symbols can't be correct?
$^{14}_{7}$Ni $^{131}_{54}$Xe $^{54}_{26}$Fe $^{73}_{23}$Ge $^{1}_{2}$He

2.70 Naturally occurring boron consists of two isotopes: ^{10}B (19.9%) with an isotopic mass of 10.0129 amu and ^{11}B (80.1%) with an isotopic mass of 11.009 31 amu. What is the atomic mass of boron? Check your answer by looking at a periodic table.

2.71 Naturally occurring silver consists of two isotopes: ^{107}Ag (51.84%) with an isotopic mass of 106.9051 amu and ^{109}Ag (48.16%) with an isotopic mass of 108.9048 amu. What is the atomic mass of silver? Check your answer in a periodic table.

2.72 Magnesium has three naturally occurring isotopes: ^{24}Mg (23.985 amu) with 78.99% abundance, ^{25}Mg (24.986 amu) with 10.00% abundance, and a third with 11.01% abundance. Look up the atomic mass of magnesium, and then calculate the mass of the third isotope.

2.73 A sample of naturally occurring silicon consists of ^{28}Si (27.9769 amu), ^{29}Si (28.9765 amu), and ^{30}Si (29.9738 amu). If the atomic mass of silicon is 28.0855 amu and the natural abundance of ^{29}Si is 4.68%, what are the natural abundances of ^{28}Si and ^{30}Si?

Nuclear Reactions and Radioactivity (Sections 2.7–2.9)

2.74 Positron emission and electron capture both give a product nucleus whose atomic number is 1 less than the starting nucleus. Explain.

2.75 What is the difference between an α particle and a helium atom?

2.76 Why does beta emission *raise* the atomic number of the product while positron emission *lowers* the atomic number?

2.77 Why do nuclei that are neutron rich emit β particles, but nuclei that are neutron poor emit α particles or positrons or undergo electron capture?

2.78 Complete and balance the following nuclear equations:
(a) $^{126}_{50}$Sn $\rightarrow$ $^{0}_{-1}$e + ?   (b) $^{210}_{88}$Ra $\rightarrow$ $^{4}_{2}$He + ?
(c) $^{77}_{37}$Rb $\rightarrow$ $^{0}_{1}$e + ?   (d) $^{76}_{36}$Kr + $^{0}_{-1}$e $\rightarrow$?

2.79 Complete and balance the following nuclear equations:
(a) $^{90}_{38}$Sr $\rightarrow$ $^{0}_{-1}$e + ?   (b) $^{247}_{100}$Fm $\rightarrow$ $^{4}_{2}$He + ?
(c) $^{49}_{25}$Mn $\rightarrow$ $^{0}_{1}$e + ?   (d) $^{37}_{18}$Ar + $^{0}_{-1}$e $\rightarrow$?

2.80 What particle is produced in each of the following decay reactions?
(a) $^{188}_{80}$Hg $\rightarrow$ $^{188}_{79}$Au + ?
(b) $^{218}_{85}$At $\rightarrow$ $^{214}_{83}$Bi + ?
(c) $^{234}_{90}$Th $\rightarrow$ $^{234}_{91}$Pa + ?

2.81 What particle is produced in each of the following decay reactions?
(a) $^{24}_{11}$Na $\rightarrow$ $^{24}_{12}$Mg + ?
(b) $^{135}_{60}$Nd $\rightarrow$ $^{135}_{59}$Pr + ?
(c) $^{170}_{78}$Pt $\rightarrow$ $^{166}_{76}$Os + ?

2.82 Write balanced nuclear equations for the following processes:
(a) Alpha emission of ^{162}Re
(b) Electron capture of ^{138}Sm
(c) Beta emission of ^{188}W
(d) Positron emission of ^{165}Ta

2.83 Write balanced nuclear equations for the following processes:
(a) Beta emission of ^{157}Eu
(b) Electron capture of ^{126}Ba
(c) Alpha emission of ^{146}Sm
(d) Positron emission of ^{125}Ba

2.84 Of the two isotopes of tungsten, ^{160}W and ^{185}W, one decays by β emission and one decays by α emission. Which does which? Explain.

2.85 Of the two isotopes of iodine, ^{136}I and ^{122}I, one decays by β emission and one decays by positron emission. Which does which? Explain.

2.86 Americium-241, a radioisotope used in smoke detectors, decays by a series of 12 reactions involving sequential loss of α, α, β, α, α, β, α, α, α, β, α, and β particles. Identify each intermediate nucleus and the final stable product nucleus.

2.87 Radon-222 decays by a series of three α emissions and two β emissions. What is the final stable nucleus?

2.88 Thorium-232 decays by a 10-step series, ultimately yielding lead-208. How many α particles and how many β particles are emitted?

2.89 How many α particles and how many β particles are emitted in the 11-step decay of ^{235}U into ^{207}Pb?

Chemical Compounds (Sections 2.10 and 2.11)

2.90 What is the difference between a covalent bond and an ionic bond? Give an example of each.

2.91 Which of the following bonds are likely to be covalent and which ionic? Explain:
  (a) B···Br   **(b)** Na···Br   **(c)** Br···Cl   **(d)** O···Br

2.92 The symbol CO stands for carbon monoxide, but the symbol Co stands for the element cobalt. Explain.

2.93 Correct the error in each of the following statements:
  (a) The formula of ammonia is NH3.
  (b) Molecules of potassium chloride have the formula KCl.
  (c) Cl^- is a cation.
  (d) CH_4 is a polyatomic ion.

2.94 How many protons and electrons are in each of the following ions?
  (a) Be^{2+} **(b)** Rb^+ **(c)** Se^{2-} **(d)** Au^{3+}

2.95 What is the identity of the element X in the following ions?
  (a) X^{2+}, a cation that has 36 electrons
  (b) X^-, an anion that has 36 electrons

2.96 The structural formula of isopropyl alcohol, better known as "rubbing alcohol," is shown. What is the chemical formula of isopropyl alcohol?

Isopropyl alcohol

2.97 Lactic acid, a compound found both in sour milk and in tired muscles, has the structure shown. What is its chemical formula?

Lactic acid

2.98 Butane, the fuel used in disposable lighters, has the formula C_4H_{10}. The carbon atoms are connected in the sequence C—C—C—C, and each carbon has four covalent bonds. Draw the structural formula of butane.

2.99 Cyclohexane, C_6H_{12}, is an important starting material used in the industrial synthesis of nylon. Each carbon has four covalent bonds, two to hydrogen and two to other carbons. Draw the structural formula of cyclohexane.

2.100 Isooctane, the substance in gasoline from which the term *octane rating* derives, has the formula C_8H_{18}. Each carbon has four covalent bonds, and the atoms are connected in the sequence shown. Draw the complete structural formula of isooctane.

2.101 Fructose, $C_6H_{12}O_6$, is the sweetest naturally occurring sugar and is found in many fruits and berries. Each carbon has four covalent bonds, each oxygen has two covalent bonds, each hydrogen has one covalent bond, and the atoms are connected in the sequence shown. Draw the complete structural formula of fructose.

Naming Compounds (Section 2.12)

2.102 Write formulas for the following binary compounds:
  (a) Potassium chloride   **(b)** Tin(II) bromide
  (c) Calcium oxide   **(d)** Barium chloride
  (e) Aluminum hydride

2.103 Write formulas for the following compounds:
  (a) Calcium acetate   **(b)** Iron(II) cyanide
  (c) Sodium dichromate   **(d)** Chromium(III) sulfate
  (e) Mercury(II) perchlorate

2.104 Name the following ions:
  (a) Ba^{2+} **(b)** Cs^+ **(c)** V^{3+}
  (d) HCO_3^- **(e)** NH_4^+ **(f)** Ni^{2+}
  (g) NO_2^- **(h)** ClO_2^- **(i)** Mn^{2+}
  (j) ClO_4^-

2.105 Name the following binary molecular compounds:
  (a) CCl_4 **(b)** ClO_2
  (c) N_2O **(d)** N_2O_3

2.106 What are the formulas of the compounds formed from the following ions:
  (a) Ca^{2+} and Br^-
  (b) Ca^{2+} and SO_4^{2-}
  (c) Al^{3+} and SO_4^{2-}

2.107 What are the formulas of the compounds formed from the following ions:
  (a) Na^+ and NO_3^- **(b)** K^+ and SO_4^{2-} **(c)** Sr^{2+} and Cl^-

2.108 Write formulas for compounds of calcium with each of the following:
  (a) chlorine   **(b)** oxygen   **(c)** sulfur

2.109 Write formulas for compounds of rubidium with each of the following:
  (a) bromine   **(b)** nitrogen   **(c)** selenium

2.110 Give the formulas and charges of the following ions:
  (a) Sulfite ion   **(b)** Phosphate ion
  (c) Zirconium(IV) ion   **(d)** Chromate ion
  (e) Acetate ion   **(f)** Thiosulfate ion

2.111 What are the charges on the positive ions in the following compounds?
  (a) $Zn(CN)_2$ **(b)** $Fe(NO_2)_3$
  (c) $Ti(SO_4)_2$ **(d)** $Sn_3(PO_4)_2$
  (e) Hg_2S **(f)** MnO_2
  (g) KIO_4 **(h)** $Cu(CH_3CO_2)_2$

2.112 Name the following binary compounds of nitrogen and oxygen:

(a) NO   **(b)** N_2O **(c)** NO_2

(d) N_2O_4 **(e)** N_2O_5

2.113 Name the following binary compounds of sulfur and oxygen:

(a) SO   **(b)** S_2O_2 **(c)** S_5O

(d) S_7O_2 **(e)** SO_3

2.114 Fill in the missing information to give formulas for the following compounds:

(a) $Na_?SO_4$ **(b)** $Ba_?(PO_4)_2$ **(c)** $Ga_?(SO_4)_?$

2.115 Write formulas for each of the following compounds:

(a) Sodium peroxide

(b) Aluminum bromide

(c) Chromium(III) sulfate

CHAPTER PROBLEMS

2.116 Germanium has five naturally occurring isotopes: ^{70}Ge, 20.5%, 69.924 amu; ^{72}Ge, 27.4%, 71.922 amu; ^{73}Ge, 7.8%, 72.923 amu; ^{74}Ge, 36.5%, 73.921 amu; and ^{76}Ge, 7.8%, 75.921 amu. What is the atomic mass of germanium?

2.117 Fluorine occurs naturally as a single isotope. How many protons, neutrons, and electrons are present in deuterium fluoride (^2HF)? (Deuterium is ^2H.)

2.118 Ammonia (NH_3) and hydrazine (N_2H_4) are both compounds of nitrogen and hydrogen. Based on the law of multiple proportions, how many grams of hydrogen would you expect 2.34 g of nitrogen to combine with to yield ammonia? To yield hydrazine?

2.119 If 3.670 g of nitrogen combines with 0.5275 g of hydrogen to yield compound X, how many grams of nitrogen would combine with 1.575 g of hydrogen to make the same compound? Is X ammonia or hydrazine (Problem 2.118)?

2.120 Identify the following atoms:

(a) A halogen with 53 electrons

(b) A noble gas with $A = 84$

2.121 Hydrogen has three isotopes (^1H, ^2H, and ^3H), and chlorine has two isotopes (^{35}Cl and ^{37}Cl). How many isotopic kinds of HCl are there? Write the formula for each, and tell how many protons, neutrons, and electrons each contains.

2.122 Prior to 1961, the atomic mass unit was defined as 1/16 the mass of the atomic mass of oxygen; that is, the atomic mass of oxygen was defined as exactly 16 amu. What was the mass of a ^{12}C atom prior to 1961 if the atomic mass of oxygen on today's scale is 15.9994 amu?

2.123 What was the mass in atomic mass units of a ^{40}Ca atom prior to 1961 if its mass on today's scale is 39.9626 amu? (See Problem 2.122)

2.124 The *molecular mass* of a compound is the sum of the atomic masses of all atoms in the molecule. What is the molecular mass of acetaminophen ($C_8H_9NO_2$), the active ingredient in Tylenol?

2.125 The *mass percent* of an element in a compound is the mass of the element (total mass of the element's atoms in the compound) divided by the mass of the compound (total mass of all atoms in the compound) times 100%. What is the mass percent of each element in acetaminophen? (See Problem 2.124.)

Acetaminophen

2.126 Radioactive ^{100}Tc decays to form ^{100}Mo. There are two possible pathways for this decay. Write balanced equations for both.

2.127 ^{226}Ac can decay by any of three different nuclear processes: α emission, β emission, or electron capture. Write a balanced nuclear equation for the decay of ^{226}Ac by each process.

2.128 Tetrahydrofuran, an organic substance used as a solvent in many pharmaceutical processes, has the formula C_4H_8O. In tetrahydrofuran, the four C atoms are bonded in a row, each C atom is bonded to two H atoms, each H atom is bonded to one C atom, and the O atom is bonded to two C atoms. Write a structural formula for tetrahydrofuran.

2.129 In an alternate universe, the smallest negatively charged particle, analogous to our electron, is called a blorvek. To determine the charge on a single blorvek, an experiment like Millikan's with charged oil droplets was carried out and the following results were recorded:

Droplet Number	Charge (C)
1	7.74×10^{-16}
2	4.42×10^{-16}
3	2.21×10^{-16}
4	4.98×10^{-16}
5	6.64×10^{-16}

(a) Based on these observations, what is the largest possible value for the charge on a blorvek?

(b) Further experiments found a droplet with a charge of 5.81×10^{-16} C. Does this new result change your answer to part **(a)**? If so, what is the new largest value for the blorvek's charge?

CHAPTER 3

Mass Relationships in Chemical Reactions

All chemical reactions, including those responsible for the spectacular displays of exploding fireworks, require specific mass relationships between reactants.

CONTENTS

It's sometimes easy when beginning the study of chemistry to forget that *reactions* are at the heart of the science. New words, ideas, and principles are introduced so quickly that the central concern of chemistry—the change of one substance into another—can get lost in the rush.

In this chapter, we'll begin learning about how to describe chemical reactions, starting with a look at the conventions for writing chemical equations and at the mass relationships between reactants and products. Because most chemical reactions are carried out using solutions rather than pure substances, we'll also discuss units for describing the concentration of a substance in solution. Finally, we'll see how chemical formulas are determined and how molecular masses are measured.

3.1 BALANCING CHEMICAL EQUATIONS

The previous chapters have provided several examples of reactions: hydrogen reacting with oxygen to yield water, sodium reacting with chlorine to yield sodium chloride, mercury(II) nitrate reacting with potassium iodide to yield mercury(II) iodide, and so forth.

Look carefully at how these equations are written. Because hydrogen, oxygen, and chlorine exist as covalent H_2, O_2, and Cl_2 diatomic molecules rather than as isolated atoms (Section 2.10), we must write them as such in chemical equations. Now look at the atoms on each side of the reaction arrow. Although we haven't explicitly stated it yet, chemical equations are always written so that they are **balanced**; that is, so that the numbers and kinds of atoms on both sides of the reaction arrow are the same. This requirement is just a consequence of the **mass conservation law** (Section 2.1). Because atoms are neither created nor destroyed in chemical reactions, their numbers and kinds must remain the same in both products and reactants.

Balancing a chemical equation involves finding out how many *formula units* of each different substance take part in the reaction. A **formula unit**, as its name implies, is one unit—whether atom, ion, or molecule—corresponding to a given formula. One formula unit of NaCl is one Na^+ ion and one Cl^- ion, one formula unit of $MgBr_2$ is one Mg^{2+} ion and two Br^- ions, and one formula unit of H_2O is one H_2O molecule.

Complicated equations generally need to be balanced using a systematic method, such as we'll discuss in the next chapter, but simpler equations can often be balanced using a mixture of common sense and trial-and-error:

1. Write the unbalanced equation using the correct chemical formula for each reactant and product. In the combustion reaction of methane (CH_4; natural gas) with oxygen to yield carbon dioxide and water, for example, we begin by writing:

$$CH_4 + O_2 \longrightarrow CO_2 + H_2O \quad \text{Unbalanced}$$

2. Find suitable **coefficients**—the numbers placed before formulas to indicate how many formula units of each substance are required to balance the equation. Only these coefficients can be changed when balancing an equation; the formulas

Remember...

According to the **law of mass conservation**, mass is neither created nor destroyed in chemical reactions. (Section 2.1)

themselves can't be changed. Again using the reaction of methane with oxygen as an example, we can balance the equation by adding a coefficient of 2 to both O_2 and H_2O. By so doing, we now have 1 carbon atom, 4 hydrogen atoms, and 4 oxygen atoms on both sides of the equation:

Add these coefficients to balance the equation.

$$CH_4 + 2\,O_2 \longrightarrow CO_2 + 2\,H_2O$$

3. Reduce the coefficients to their smallest whole-number values, if necessary, by dividing them all by a common divisor.

4. Check your answer by making sure that the numbers and kinds of atoms are the same on both sides of the equation.

Let's work through some additional examples:

WORKED EXAMPLE 3.1

BALANCING A CHEMICAL EQUATION

Propane, C_3H_8, is a colorless, odorless gas often used as a heating and cooking fuel in campers and rural homes. Write a balanced equation for the combustion reaction of propane with oxygen to yield carbon dioxide and water.

STRATEGY AND SOLUTION

Follow the four steps described in the text:

Step 1. Write the unbalanced equation using correct chemical formulas for all substances:

$$C_3H_8 + O_2 \longrightarrow CO_2 + H_2O \qquad \text{Unbalanced}$$

Step 2. Find coefficients to balance the equation. It's usually best to begin with the most complex substance—in this case C_3H_8—and to deal with one element at a time. Look at the unbalanced equation, and note that there are 3 carbon atoms on the left side of the equation but only 1 on the right side. If we add a coefficient of 3 to CO_2 on the right, the carbons balance:

$$C_3H_8 + O_2 \longrightarrow 3\,CO_2 + H_2O \qquad \text{Balanced for C}$$

Next, look at the number of hydrogen atoms. There are 8 hydrogens on the left but only 2 (in H_2O) on the right. By adding a coefficient of 4 to the H_2O on the right, the hydrogens balance:

$$C_3H_8 + O_2 \longrightarrow 3\,CO_2 + 4\,H_2O \qquad \text{Balanced for C and H}$$

Finally, look at the number of oxygen atoms. There are 2 on the left but 10 on the right. By adding a coefficient of 5 to the O_2 on the left, the oxygens balance:

$$C_3H_8 + 5\,O_2 \longrightarrow 3\,CO_2 + 4\,H_2O \qquad \text{Balanced for C, H, and O}$$

Step 3. Make sure the coefficients are reduced to their smallest whole-number values. In fact, our answer is already correct, but we might have arrived at a different answer through trial and error:

$$2\,C_3H_8 + 10\,O_2 \longrightarrow 6\,CO_2 + 8\,H_2O$$

Although the preceding equation is balanced, the coefficients are not the smallest whole numbers. It would be necessary to divide all coefficients by 2 to reach the final equation.

Step 4. Check your answer. Count the numbers and kinds of atoms on both sides of the equation to make sure they're the same:

3 C, 8 H, and 10 O atoms on this side   3 C, 8 H, and 10 O atoms on this side

$$C_3H_8 + 5\,O_2 \longrightarrow 3\,CO_2 + 4\,H_2O$$

CO_2

H_2O

Propane (C_3H_8)

O_2

▲ Propane is used as a fuel in camp stoves and in rural homes.

BALANCING A CHEMICAL EQUATION

The major ingredient in ordinary safety matches is potassium chlorate, $KClO_3$, a substance that can act as a source of oxygen in combustion reactions. Its reaction with ordinary table sugar (sucrose, $C_{12}H_{22}O_{11}$), for example, occurs violently to yield potassium chloride, carbon dioxide, and water. Write a balanced equation for the reaction.

STRATEGY AND SOLUTION

Step 1. Write the unbalanced equation, making sure the formulas for all substances are correct:

$$KClO_3 + C_{12}H_{22}O_{11} \longrightarrow KCl + CO_2 + H_2O \qquad \text{Unbalanced}$$

Step 2. Find coefficients to balance the equation by starting with the most complex substance (sucrose) and considering one element at a time. Since there are 12 C atoms on the left and only 1 on the right, we can balance for carbon by adding a coefficient of 12 to CO_2 on the right:

$$KClO_3 + C_{12}H_{22}O_{11} \longrightarrow KCl + 12\,CO_2 + H_2O \qquad \text{Balanced for C}$$

Since there are 22 H atoms on the left and only 2 on the right, we can balance for hydrogen by adding a coefficient of 11 to H_2O on the right:

$$KClO_3 + C_{12}H_{22}O_{11} \longrightarrow KCl + 12\,CO_2 + 11\,H_2O \qquad \text{Balanced for C and H}$$

There are now 35 O atoms on the right but only 14 on the left (11 in sucrose and 3 in $KClO_3$). Thus, 21 oxygens must be added on the left. We can do this without disturbing the C and H balance by adding 7 more $KClO_3$, giving a coefficient of 8 for $KClO_3$ on the left:

$$8\,KClO_3 + C_{12}H_{22}O_{11} \longrightarrow KCl + 12\,CO_2 + 11\,H_2O \qquad \text{Balanced for C, H, and O}$$

Potassium and chlorine can both be balanced by adding a coefficient of 8 to KCl on the right:

$$8\,KClO_3 + C_{12}H_{22}O_{11} \longrightarrow 8\,KCl + 12\,CO_2 + 11\,H_2O \qquad \text{Balanced for C, H, O, K, and Cl}$$

Step 3 and 4. The coefficients in the balanced equation are already reduced to their smallest whole-number values, and a check shows that the numbers and kinds of atoms are the same on both sides of the equation.

8 K, 8 Cl, 12 C, 22 H, and 35 O atoms | 8 K, 8 Cl, 12 C, 22 H, and 35 O atoms

$$8\,KClO_3 + C_{12}H_{22}O_{11} \longrightarrow 8\,KCl + 12\,CO_2 + 11\,H_2O$$

▲ Safety matches contain potassium chlorate, which acts as a source of oxygen for ignition.

BALANCING A CHEMICAL EQUATION

Write a balanced equation for the reaction of element A (red spheres) with element B (blue spheres) as represented below:

STRATEGY

Balancing the reactions shown in graphic representations of this sort is just a matter of counting the numbers of reactant and product formula units. In this example, the reactant box contains three red A_2 molecules and nine blue B_2 molecules, while the product box contains six AB_3 molecules with no reactant left over.

SOLUTION

$$3\,A_2 + 9\,B_2 \longrightarrow 6\,AB_3 \quad \text{or} \quad A_2 + 3\,B_2 \longrightarrow 2\,AB_3$$

▶ **PROBLEM 3.1**   Sodium chlorate, $NaClO_3$, decomposes when heated to yield sodium chloride and oxygen, a reaction used to provide oxygen for the emergency breathing masks in many airliners. Balance the equation.

▶ **PROBLEM 3.2**   Balance the following equations:
   (a) $C_6H_{12}O_6 \longrightarrow C_2H_6O + CO_2$ (fermentation of sugar to yield ethyl alcohol)
   (b) $CO_2 + H_2O \longrightarrow C_6H_{12}O_6 + O_2$ (photosynthesis reaction in green plants)
   (c) $NH_3 + Cl_2 \longrightarrow N_2H_4 + NH_4Cl$ (synthesis of hydrazine for rocket fuel)

CONCEPTUAL PROBLEM 3.3   Write a balanced equation for the reaction of element A (red spheres) with element B (green spheres) as represented below:

3.2   REPRESENTING CHEMISTRY ON DIFFERENT LEVELS

What does it mean when we write a chemical formula or equation? Answering this question isn't as easy as it sounds because a chemical symbol can have different meanings under different circumstances. Chemists use the same symbols to represent chemistry on both a small-scale, microscopic level and a large-scale, macroscopic level, and they tend to slip back and forth between the two levels without realizing the confusion this can cause for newcomers to the field.

On the microscopic level, chemical symbols represent the behavior of individual atoms and molecules. Atoms and molecules are much too small to be seen, but we can nevertheless describe their microscopic behavior if we read the equation $2 H_2 + O_2 \longrightarrow 2 H_2O$ to mean "Two molecules of hydrogen react with one molecule of oxygen to yield two molecules of water." It's this microscopic world that we deal with when trying to understand how reactions occur, and it's often helpful to visualize a molecule as a collection of spheres stuck together. In trying to understand how H_2 reacts with O_2, for example, you might picture H_2 and O_2 molecules as made of two spheres pressed together and a water molecule as made of three spheres.

On the macroscopic level, formulas and equations represent the large-scale behaviors of atoms and molecules that give rise to visible properties. In other words, the symbols H_2, O_2, and H_2O represent not just single molecules but vast numbers of molecules that together have a set of measurable physical properties. A *single* isolated H_2O molecule is neither solid nor liquid nor gas, but a huge collection of H_2O molecules appears to us as a colorless liquid that freezes at 0 °C and boils at 100 °C. Clearly, it's this macroscopic behavior we deal with in the laboratory when we weigh specific amounts of reactants, place them in a flask, and observe visible changes.

In the same way, a single atom of copper is neither solid, liquid, nor gas, does not conduct electricity, and has no color on a microscopic level. On a macroscopic level, however, a large collection of copper atoms appears to us as a shiny, reddish-brown metal that can be drawn into electrical wires or made into coins.

What does a chemical formula or equation mean? It means different things depending on the context. The symbol H_2O can mean either one tiny, invisible molecule or a vast collection of molecules large enough to swim in.

3.3 CHEMICAL ARITHMETIC: STOICHIOMETRY

Imagine a laboratory experiment—perhaps the reaction of ethylene, C_2H_4, with hydrogen chloride, HCl, to prepare ethyl chloride, C_2H_5Cl, a colorless, low-boiling liquid that doctors and athletic trainers use as a spray-on anesthetic for minor injuries. You might note that in writing this and other equations, the designations (*g*) for gas, (*l*) for liquid, (*s*) for solid, and (*aq*) for aqueous solutions are often appended to the symbols of reactants and products to show their physical state. We'll do this frequently from now on.

$C_2H_4(g)$ + $HCl(g)$ ⟶ $C_2H_5Cl(l)$
Ethylene   Hydrogen chloride   Ethyl chloride
                                            (an anesthetic)

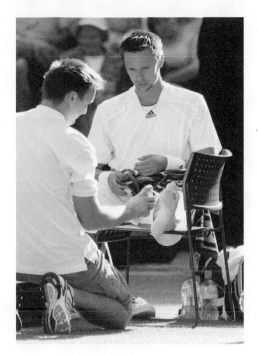

▲ Ethyl chloride is often used as a spray-on anesthetic for athletic injuries.

How much ethylene and how much hydrogen chloride should you use for your experiment? According to the coefficients of the balanced equation, a 1 : 1 numerical ratio of the two reactants is needed. But because you can't count the reactant molecules, you have to weigh them. That is, you must convert a *number* ratio of reactant molecules, as given by coefficients in the balanced equation, into a *mass* ratio to be sure you are using the right amounts.

Mass ratios are determined by using the *molecular masses* (also called *molecular weights*) of the substances involved in a reaction. Just as the atomic mass of an element is the average mass of the element's *atoms* (Section 2.6), the **molecular mass** of a substance is the average mass of the substance's *molecules*. Numerically, molecular mass (or, more generally, **formula mass** to include both ionic and molecular substances) equals the sum of the atomic masses of all atoms in the molecule.

◀◾ **Molecular Mass**   Sum of atomic masses of all atoms in a molecule.

◀◾ **Formula Mass**   Sum of atomic masses of all atoms in a formula unit of any compound, molecular or ionic.

As examples, the molecular mass of ethylene is 28.0 amu, the molecular mass of hydrogen chloride is 36.5 amu, and the molecular mass of ethyl chloride is 64.5 amu. (These numbers are rounded off to one decimal place for convenience; the actual values are known more precisely.)

For ethylene, C_2H_4:

atomic mass of 2 C = (2)(12.0 amu)	=	24.0 amu
atomic mass of 4 H = (4)(1.0 amu)	=	4.0 amu
Molecular mass of C_2H_4	=	28.0 amu

For hydrogen chloride, HCl:

atomic mass of H	=	1.0 amu
atomic mass of Cl	=	35.5 amu
Molecular mass of HCl = 36.5 amu		

For ethyl chloride, C_2H_5Cl:

atomic mass of 2 C = (2)(12.0 amu)	=	24.0 amu
atomic mass of 5 H = (5)(1.0 amu)	=	5.0 amu
atomic mass of Cl	=	35.5 amu
Molecular mass of C_2H_5Cl	=	64.5 amu

How do we use molecular masses? We saw in Section 2.6 that one **mole** of any element is the amount whose mass, or *molar mass*, is numerically equal to the element's atomic mass in grams. In the same way, one mole of any chemical compound is numerically equal to the compound's molecular mass (or formula mass) in grams and contains **Avogadro's number** of formula units (6.022×10^{23}). Thus, 1 mol of ethylene has a mass of 28.0 g, 1 mol of HCl has a mass of 36.5 g, 1 mol of C_2H_5Cl has a mass of 64.5 g, and so on.

Molec. mass of HCl = 36.5 amu	Molar mass of HCl = 36.5 g	1 mol of HCl = 6.022×10^{23} HCl molecules
Molec. mass of C_2H_4 = 28.0 amu	Molar mass of C_2H_4 = 28.0 g	1 mol of C_2H_4 = 6.022×10^{23} C_2H_4 molecules
Molec. mass of C_2H_5Cl = 64.5 amu	Molar mass of C_2H_5Cl = 64.5 g	1 mol of C_2H_5Cl = 6.022×10^{23} C_2H_5Cl molecules

Remember...

The **mole** is the fundamental SI unit for measuring amount of matter. One mole of any substance—atom, ion, or molecule—is the amount whose mass in grams is numerically equal to the substance's atomic or formula mass. One mole contains **Avogadro's number** (6.022×10^{23}) of formula units. (Section 2.6)

In any balanced chemical equation, the coefficients tell the number of formula units, and thus the number of moles, of each substance in the reaction. You can then use molar masses as conversion factors to calculate reactant masses. If you saw the following balanced equation for the industrial synthesis of ammonia, for instance, you would know that 3 mol of $H_2(g)$ (3 mol $\times$ 2.0 g/mol = 6.0 g) is needed for reaction with 1 mol of $N_2(g)$ (28.0 g) to yield 2 mol of $NH_3(g)$ (2 mol $\times$ 17.0 g/mol = 34.0 g).

This number of moles of hydrogen... ...reacts with this number of moles of nitrogen... ...to yield this number of moles of ammonia.

$$3 \, H_2(g) + 1 \, N_2(g) \longrightarrow 2 \, NH_3(g)$$

In referring to the chemical arithmetic needed for mole–mass conversions, we use the word **stoichiometry** (stoy-key-**ahm**-uh-tree; from the Greek *stoicheion*, "element, " and *metron*, "measure"). Let's look again at the reaction of ethylene with HCl and assume that we have 15.0 g of ethylene and need to know how many grams of HCl to use in the reaction.

$$C_2H_4(g) + HCl(g) \longrightarrow C_2H_5Cl(l)$$

According to the coefficients in the balanced equation, 1 molecule of HCl reacts with 1 molecule of ethylene, so 1 mol of HCl is needed for reaction with each mole of ethylene. To find out how many grams of HCl are needed to react with 15.0 g of ethylene, we first have to find out how many moles of ethylene are in 15.0 g. We do this gram-to-mole conversion by calculating the molar mass of ethylene and using that value as a conversion factor:

Molecular mass of C_2H_4 = (2 $\times$ 12.0 amu) + (4 $\times$ 1.0 amu) = 28.0 amu

Molar mass of C_2H_4 = 28.0 g/mol

$$\text{Moles of } C_2H_4 = 15.0 \, \text{g ethylene} \times \frac{1 \, \text{mol ethylene}}{28.0 \, \text{g ethylene}} = 0.536 \, \text{mol ethylene}$$

Now that we know how many moles of ethylene we have (0.536 mol), we also know from the balanced equation how many moles of HCl we need (0.536 mol), and we have to do a mole-to-gram conversion to find the mass of HCl required. Once again, the conversion is done by calculating the molar mass of HCl and using that value as a conversion factor:

Molecular mass of HCl = 1.0 amu + 35.5 amu = 36.5 amu

Molar mass of HCl = 36.5 g/mol

$$\text{Grams of HCl} = 0.536 \, \text{mol } C_2H_4 \times \frac{1 \, \text{mol HCl}}{1 \, \text{mol } C_2H_4} \times \frac{36.5 \, \text{g HCl}}{1 \, \text{mol HCl}} = 19.6 \, \text{g HCl}$$

Thus, 19.6 g of HCl is needed to react with 15.0 g of ethylene.

Look carefully at the sequence of steps in the calculation just completed. *Moles* (numbers of molecules) are given by the coefficients in the balanced equation but *grams* are used to weigh reactants in the laboratory. Moles tell us *how many molecules* of each reactant are needed, while grams tell us *how much mass* of each reactant is needed.

Moles $\longrightarrow$ Numbers of molecules or formula units
Grams $\longrightarrow$ Mass

The flow diagram in **Figure 3.1** illustrates the necessary conversions. Note again that you can't go directly from the number of grams of one reactant to the number of grams of another reactant. You *must* first convert to moles.

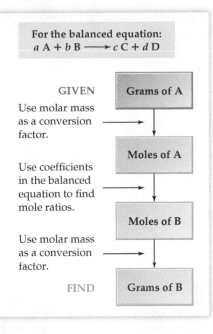

For the balanced equation:
$a\,A + b\,B \longrightarrow c\,C + d\,D$

GIVEN — Grams of A
Use molar mass as a conversion factor.
Moles of A
Use coefficients in the balanced equation to find mole ratios.
Moles of B
Use molar mass as a conversion factor.
FIND — Grams of B

Figure 3.1
Conversions between moles and grams for a chemical reaction. The numbers of moles tell how many molecules of each reactant are needed, as given by the coefficients of the balanced equation; the numbers of grams tell what mass of each reactant is needed.

WORKED EXAMPLE 3.4

CALCULATING A MOLECULAR MASS
What is the molecular mass of table sugar (sucrose, $C_{12}H_{22}O_{11}$), and what is its molar mass in g/mol?

STRATEGY
The molecular mass of a substance is the sum of the atomic masses of the constituent atoms. List the elements present in the molecule, and look up the atomic mass of each (we'll round off to one decimal place for convenience):

C (12.0 amu); H (1.0 amu); O (16.0 amu)

Then, multiply the atomic mass of each element by the number of times that element appears in the chemical formula, and total the results.

SOLUTION

C_{12} (12 × 12.0 amu) = 144.0 amu
H_{22} (22 × 1.0 amu) = 22.0 amu
O_{11} (11 × 16.0 amu) = 176.0 amu
_____
Molecular mass of $C_{12}H_{22}O_{11}$ = 342.0 amu

Because one molecule of sucrose has a mass of 342.0 amu, 1 mol of sucrose has a mass of 342.0 g. Thus, the molar mass of sucrose is 342.0 g/mol.

WORKED EXAMPLE 3.5

CONVERTING MASS TO MOLES
How many moles of sucrose are in a tablespoon of sugar containing 2.85 g? (The molar mass of sucrose, $C_{12}H_{22}O_{11}$, was calculated in Worked Example 3.4.)

STRATEGY
The problem gives the mass of sucrose and asks for a mass-to-mole conversion. Use the molar mass of sucrose as a conversion factor, and set up an equation so that the unwanted unit cancels.

SOLUTION

$$2.85 \text{ g sucrose} \times \frac{1 \text{ mol sucrose}}{342.0 \text{ g sucrose}} = 0.008\,33 \text{ mol sucrose}$$

$$= 8.33 \times 10^{-3} \text{ mol sucrose}$$

Sucrose

BALLPARK CHECK
Because the molecular mass of sucrose is 342.0 amu, 1 mol of sucrose has a mass of 342.0 g. Thus, 2.85 g of sucrose is a bit less than one-hundredth of a mole, or 0.01 mol. The estimate agrees with the detailed solution.

WORKED EXAMPLE 3.6

CONVERTING MOLES TO MASS

How many grams are in 0.0626 mol of $NaHCO_3$, the main ingredient in Alka-Seltzer tablets?

STRATEGY

The problem gives the number of moles of $NaHCO_3$ and asks for a mole-to-mass conversion. First, calculate the molar mass of $NaHCO_3$. Then use molar mass as a conversion factor, and set up an equation so that the unwanted unit cancels.

SOLUTION

Formula mass of $NaHCO_3$ = 23.0 amu + 1.0 amu + 12.0 amu + (3 × 16.0 amu)

$$= 84.0 \text{ amu}$$

Molar mass of $NaHCO_3$ = 84.0 g/mol

$$0.0626 \text{ mol NaHCO}_3 \times \frac{84.0 \text{ g NaHCO}_3}{1 \text{ mol NaHCO}_3} = 5.26 \text{ g NaHCO}_3$$

WORKED EXAMPLE 3.7

FINDING THE MASS OF ONE REACTANT, GIVEN THE MASS OF ANOTHER

Aqueous solutions of sodium hypochlorite (NaOCl), best known as household bleach, are prepared by reaction of sodium hydroxide with chlorine. How many grams of NaOH are needed to react with 25.0 g of Cl_2?

$$2 \text{ NaOH}(aq) + Cl_2(g) \longrightarrow \text{NaOCl}(aq) + \text{NaCl}(aq) + H_2O(l)$$

STRATEGY

Finding the relationship between numbers of reactant formula units always requires working in moles, using the general strategy outlined in Figure 3.1.

SOLUTION

First, find out how many moles of Cl_2 are in 25.0 g of Cl_2. This gram-to-mole conversion is done in the usual way, using the molar mass of Cl_2 (70.9 g/mol) as the conversion factor:

$$25.0 \text{ g Cl}_2 \times \frac{1 \text{ mol Cl}_2}{70.9 \text{ g Cl}_2} = 0.353 \text{ mol Cl}_2$$

Next, look at the coefficients in the balanced equation. Each mole of Cl_2 reacts with 2 mol of NaOH, so 0.353 mol of Cl_2 reacts with 2 × 0.353 = 0.706 mol of NaOH. With the number of moles of NaOH known, carry out a mole-to-gram conversion using the molar mass of NaOH (40.0 g/mol) as a conversion factor to find that 28.2 g of NaOH is required for the reaction:

$$\text{Grams of NaOH} = 0.353 \text{ mol Cl}_2 \times \frac{2 \text{ mol NaOH}}{1 \text{ mol Cl}_2} \times \frac{40.0 \text{ g NaOH}}{1 \text{ mol NaOH}}$$

$$= 28.2 \text{ g NaOH}$$

The problem can also be worked by combining the steps and setting up one large equation:

$$\text{Grams of NaOH} = 25.0 \text{ g Cl}_2 \times \frac{1 \text{ mol Cl}_2}{70.9 \text{ g Cl}_2} \times \frac{2 \text{ mol NaOH}}{1 \text{ mol Cl}_2} \times \frac{40.0 \text{ g NaOH}}{1 \text{ mol NaOH}}$$

$$= 28.2 \text{ g NaOH}$$

BALLPARK CHECK

The molar mass of NaOH is about half that of Cl_2, and 2 mol of NaOH is needed per 1 mol of Cl_2. Thus, the needed mass of NaOH will be similar to that of Cl_2, or about 25 g.

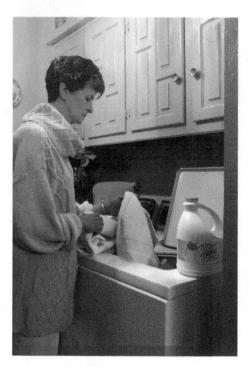

▲ Household bleach is an aqueous solution of NaOCl, made by reaction of NaOH with Cl_2.

▶ **PROBLEM 3.4** Calculate the formula mass or molecular mass of the following substances:

(a) Fe_2O_3 (rust)

(b) H_2SO_4 (sulfuric acid)

(c) $C_6H_8O_7$ (citric acid)

(d) $C_{16}H_{18}N_2O_4S$ (penicillin G)

CONCEPTUAL PROBLEM 3.5 Aspirin can be represented by the adjacent ball-and-stick molecular model. Give the formula for aspirin, and calculate its molecular mass (red = O, gray = C, ivory = H). How many moles of aspirin are in a tablet weighing 500 mg? How many molecules?

Aspirin

▶ **PROBLEM 3.6** Aspirin is prepared by reaction of salicylic acid ($C_7H_6O_3$) with acetic anhydride ($C_4H_6O_3$) according to the following equation:

$$C_7H_6O_3 + C_4H_6O_3 \longrightarrow C_9H_8O_4 + CH_3CO_2H$$

Salicylic acid   Acetic anhydride   Aspirin   Acetic acid

(a) How many grams of acetic anhydride are needed to react with 4.50 g of salicylic acid?

(b) How many grams of aspirin will result?

(c) How many grams of acetic acid are formed as a byproduct?

3.4 YIELDS OF CHEMICAL REACTIONS

In the stoichiometry examples worked out in the preceding section, we made the unstated assumption that all reactions "go to completion." That is, we assumed that all reactant molecules are converted to products. In fact, few reactions behave so nicely. More often, a large majority of molecules react as expected, but other processes, or *side reactions*, also occur. Thus, the amount of product actually formed, called the **yield** of the reaction, is usually less than the amount predicted by calculations.

The amount of product actually formed in a reaction divided by the amount theoretically possible and multiplied by 100% is the reaction's **percent yield**. For example, if a given reaction *could* provide 6.9 g of a product according to its stoichiometry, but actually provides only 4.7 g, then its percent yield is 4.7/6.9 × 100% = 68%.

$$\text{Percent yield} = \frac{\text{Actual yield of product}}{\text{Theoretical yield of product}} \times 100\%$$

Worked Examples 3.8 and 3.9 show how to calculate and use percent yield.

WORKED EXAMPLE 3.8

CALCULATING A PERCENT YIELD

Methyl *tert*-butyl ether (MTBE, $C_5H_{12}O$), a gasoline additive now being phased out in many places because of health concerns, can be made by reaction of isobutylene (C_4H_8) with methanol (CH_4O). What is the percent yield of the reaction if 32.8 g of methyl *tert*-butyl ether is obtained from reaction of 26.3 g of isobutylene with sufficient methanol?

$$C_4H_8(g) + CH_4O(l) \longrightarrow C_5H_{12}O(l)$$

Isobutylene   Methyl *tert*-butyl ether (MTBE)

Methyl *tert*-butyl ether

STRATEGY

We need to calculate the amount of methyl *tert*-butyl ether that could be produced theoretically from 26.3 g of isobutylene and compare that theoretical amount to the

continued on next page

actual amount (32.8 g). As always, stoichiometry problems begin by calculating the molar masses of reactants and products. Coefficients of the balanced equation then tell mole ratios, and molar masses act as conversion factors between moles and masses.

SOLUTION

Isobutylene, C_4H_8: Molec. mass = $(4 \times 12.0 \text{ amu}) + (8 \times 1.0 \text{ amu}) = 56.0 \text{ amu}$

Molar mass of isobutylene = 56.0 g/mol

MTBE, $C_5H_{12}O$:   Molec. mass = $(5 \times 12.0 \text{ amu}) + (12 \times 1.0 \text{ amu}) + 16.0 \text{ amu}$

= 88.0 amu

Molar mass of MTBE = 88.0 g/mol

To calculate the amount of MTBE that could theoretically be produced from 26.3 g of isobutylene, we first have to find the number of moles of reactant, using molar mass as the conversion factor:

$$26.3 \text{ g isobutylene} \times \frac{1 \text{ mol isobutylene}}{56.0 \text{ g isobutylene}} = 0.470 \text{ mol isobutylene}$$

According to the balanced equation, 1 mol of product is produced per mol of reactant, so we know that 0.470 mol of isobutylene can theoretically yield 0.470 mol of MTBE. Finding the mass of this MTBE requires a mole-to-mass conversion:

$$0.470 \text{ mol isobutylene} \times \frac{1 \text{ mol MTBE}}{1 \text{ mol isobutylene}} \times \frac{88.0 \text{ g MTBE}}{1 \text{ mol MTBE}} = 41.4 \text{ g MTBE}$$

Dividing the actual amount by the theoretical amount and multiplying by 100% gives the percent yield:

$$\frac{32.8 \text{ g MTBE}}{41.4 \text{ g MTBE}} \times 100\% = 79.2\%$$

WORKED EXAMPLE 3.9

CALCULATING A YIELD IN GRAMS, GIVEN A PERCENT YIELD

Diethyl ether ($C_4H_{10}O$), the "ether" used medically as an anesthetic, is prepared commercially by treatment of ethyl alcohol (C_2H_6O) with an acid. How many grams of diethyl ether would you obtain from 40.0 g of ethyl alcohol if the percent yield of the reaction is 87%?

Diethyl ether

$$2\,C_2H_6O(l) \xrightarrow{\text{Acid}} C_4H_{10}O(l) + H_2O(l)$$

$\quad$ Ethyl alcohol $\qquad$ Diethyl ether

STRATEGY

Treat this as a typical stoichiometry problem to find the amount of diethyl ether that can theoretically be formed from 40.0 g of ethyl alcohol, and then multiply the answer by 87% to find the amount actually formed.

SOLUTION

First, calculate the molar masses of the reactant and product:

Ethyl alcohol, C_2H_6O: Molec. mass = $(2 \times 12.0 \text{ amu}) + (6 \times 1.0 \text{ amu}) + 16.0 \text{ amu}$

= 46.0 amu

Molar mass of ethyl alcohol = 46.0 g/mol

Diethyl ether, $C_4H_{10}O$: Molec. mass = $(4 \times 12.0 \text{ amu}) + (10 \times 1.0 \text{ amu}) + 16.0 \text{ amu}$

= 74.0 amu

Molar mass of diethyl ether = 74.0 g/mol

Next, find how many moles of ethyl alcohol are in 40.0 g by using molar mass as a conversion factor:

$$40.0 \text{ g ethyl alcohol} \times \frac{1 \text{ mol ethyl alcohol}}{46.0 \text{ g ethyl alcohol}} = 0.870 \text{ mol ethyl alcohol}$$

Because we started with 0.870 mol of ethyl alcohol, and because the balanced equation indicates that 2 mol of ethyl alcohol yield 1 mol of diethyl ether, we can theoretically obtain 0.435 mol of product:

$$0.870 \; \text{mol ethyl alcohol} \times \frac{1 \, \text{mol diethyl ether}}{2 \, \text{mol ethyl alcohol}} = 0.435 \text{ mol diethyl ether}$$

We therefore need to find how many grams of diethyl ether are in 0.435 mol, using molar mass as the conversion factor:

$$0.435 \; \text{mol diethyl ether} \times \frac{74.0 \, \text{g diethyl ether}}{1 \, \text{mol diethyl ether}} = 32.2 \text{ g diethyl ether}$$

Finally, we have to multiply the theoretical amount of product by the observed yield (87% = 0.87) to find how much diethyl ether is actually formed:

$$32.2 \text{ g diethyl ether} \times 0.87 = 28 \text{ g diethyl ether}$$

▶ **PROBLEM 3.7**   Ethyl alcohol is prepared industrially by the reaction of ethylene, C_2H_4, with water. What is the percent yield of the reaction if 4.6 g of ethylene gives 4.7 g of ethyl alcohol?

$$C_2H_4(g) + H_2O(l) \longrightarrow C_2H_6O(l)$$

Ethylene   Ethyl alcohol

Ethyl alcohol

▶ **PROBLEM 3.8**   Dichloromethane (CH_2Cl_2), used as a solvent in the decaffeination of coffee beans, is prepared by reaction of methane (CH_4) with chlorine. How many grams of dichloromethane result from reaction of 1.85 kg of methane if the yield is 43.1%?

$$CH_4(g) + 2 Cl_2(g) \longrightarrow CH_2Cl_2(l) + 2 HCl(g)$$

Methane   Chlorine   Dichloromethane

Dichloromethane

3.5 REACTIONS WITH LIMITING AMOUNTS OF REACTANTS

Because chemists usually write balanced equations, it's easy to get the impression that reactions are always carried out using exactly the right proportions of reactants. In fact, this is often not the case. Many reactions are carried out using an excess amount of one reactant—more than is actually needed according to stoichiometry. Look, for instance, at the industrial synthesis of ethylene glycol, $C_2H_6O_2$, a substance used both as automobile antifreeze and as a starting material for the preparation of polyester polymers. Approximately 18 million metric tons of ethylene glycol are prepared each year worldwide by reaction of ethylene oxide, C_2H_4O, with water at high temperature (1 metric ton = 1000 kg = 2205 lb).

C_2H_4O + H_2O $\xrightarrow{\text{Heat}}$ $C_2H_6O_2$
Ethylene oxide   Water   Ethylene glycol

Because water is so cheap and so abundant, it doesn't make sense to worry about using exactly 1 mol of water for each mole of ethylene oxide. Rather, it's much easier to use an excess of water to be certain that enough is present to consume entirely the more valuable ethylene oxide reactant. Of course, when an excess of water is present, only the amount required by stoichiometry undergoes reaction. The excess water does not react and remains unchanged.

Whenever the ratios of reactant molecules used in an experiment are different from those given by the coefficients of the balanced equation, a surplus of one reactant is left over after the reaction is finished. Thus, the extent to which a chemical reaction takes place depends on the reactant that is present in limiting amount—the **limiting reactant**. The other reactant is said to be the *excess reactant*.

The situation with excess reactants and limiting reactants is analogous to what sometimes happens with people and chairs. If there are five people in a room but only three chairs, then only three people can sit while the other two stand because the number of people sitting is limited by the number of available chairs. In the same way, if 5 moles of water come in contact with 3 moles of ethylene oxide, only 3 moles of water can undergo a reaction while the other 2 moles of water are unchanged.

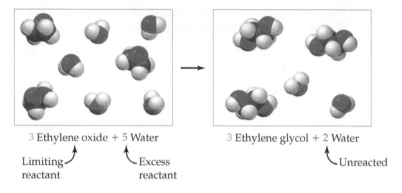

3 Ethylene oxide + 5 Water   3 Ethylene glycol + 2 Water

Limiting ⟋   ⟍ Excess   ⟍ Unreacted
reactant   reactant

Worked Example 3.10 shows how to tell whether a limiting amount of one reactant is present and how to calculate the amounts of the excess reactant consumed and remaining.

CALCULATING THE AMOUNT OF AN EXCESS REACTANT

Cisplatin, an anticancer agent used for the treatment of solid tumors, is prepared by the reaction of ammonia with potassium tetrachloroplatinate. Assume that 10.0 g of K_2PtCl_4 and 10.0 g of NH_3 are allowed to react.

$$K_2PtCl_4(aq) + 2\,NH_3(aq) \longrightarrow Pt(NH_3)_2Cl_2(s) + 2\,KCl(aq)$$

Potassium   Cisplatin
tetrachloroplatinate

Cisplatin

(a) Which reactant is limiting, and which is in excess?
(b) How many grams of the excess reactant are consumed, and how many grams remain?
(c) How many grams of cisplatin are formed?

STRATEGY

When solving a problem that deals with limiting reactants, the idea is to find how many moles of all reactants are actually present and compare the mole ratios of those actual amounts to the mole ratios required by the balanced equation. That comparison will identify the reactant there is too much of (the excess reactant) and the reactant there is too little of (the limiting reactant).

SOLUTION

(a) Finding the molar amounts of reactants always begins by calculating formula masses and using molar masses as conversion factors:

Form. mass of $K_2PtCl_4 = (2 \times 39.1\ \text{amu}) + 195.1\ \text{amu} + (4 \times 35.5\ \text{amu}) = 415.3\ \text{amu}$

Molar mass of $K_2PtCl_4 = 415.3\ \text{g/mol}$

Moles of $K_2PtCl_4 = 10.0\ \text{g}\ \cancel{K_2PtCl_4} \times \dfrac{1\ \text{mol}\ K_2PtCl_4}{415.3\ \cancel{\text{g}\ K_2PtCl_4}} = 0.0241\ \text{mol}\ K_2PtCl_4$

Molec. mass of $NH_3 = 14.0\ \text{amu} + (3 \times 1.0\ \text{amu}) = 17.0\ \text{amu}$

Molar mass of $NH_3 = 17.0\ \text{g/mol}$

Moles of $NH_3 = 10.0\ \text{g}\ \cancel{NH_3} \times \dfrac{1\ \text{mol}\ NH_3}{17.0\ \cancel{\text{g}\ NH_3}} = 0.588\ \text{mol}\ NH_3$

These calculations tell us that we have 0.588 mol of ammonia and 0.0241 mol of K_2PtCl_4, or $0.588/0.0241 = 24.4$ times as much ammonia as K_2PtCl_4. The coefficients in the balanced equation, however, say that only *two* times as much ammonia as K_2PtCl_4 is needed. Thus, a large excess of NH_3 is present, and K_2PtCl_4 is the limiting reactant.

(b) With the identities of the excess reactant and limiting reactant known, we now have to find how many moles of each undergo reaction and then carry out mole-to-gram conversions to find the mass of each reactant consumed. The entire amount of the limiting reactant (K_2PtCl_4) is used up, but only the amount of the excess reactant (NH_3) required by stoichiometry undergoes reaction:

Moles of K_2PtCl_4 consumed $= 0.0241\ \text{mol}\ K_2PtCl_4$

Moles of NH_3 consumed $= 0.0241\ \cancel{\text{mol}\ K_2PtCl_4} \times \dfrac{2\ \text{mol}\ NH_3}{1\ \cancel{\text{mol}\ K_2PtCl_4}} = 0.0482\ \text{mol}\ NH_3$

Grams of NH_3 consumed $= 0.0482\ \cancel{\text{mol}\ NH_3} \times \dfrac{17.0\ \text{g}\ NH_3}{1\ \cancel{\text{mol}\ NH_3}} = 0.819\ \text{g}\ NH_3$

Grams of NH_3 not consumed $= (10.0\ \text{g} - 0.819\ \text{g})\ NH_3 = 9.2\ \text{g}\ NH_3$

(c) The balanced equation shows that 1 mol of cisplatin is formed for each mole of K_2PtCl_4 consumed. Thus, 0.0241 mol of cisplatin is formed from 0.0241 mol of K_2PtCl_4. To determine the mass of cisplatin produced, we must calculate its molar mass and then carry out a mole-to-gram conversion:

Molec. mass of $Pt(NH_3)_2Cl_2 = 195.1\ \text{amu} + (2 \times 17.0\ \text{amu}) + (2 \times 35.5\ \text{amu}) = 300.1\ \text{amu}$

Molar mass of $Pt(NH_3)_2Cl_2 = 300.1\ \text{g/mol}$

Grams of $Pt(NH_3)_2Cl_2 = 0.0241\ \cancel{\text{mol}\ Pt(NH_3)_2Cl_2} \times \dfrac{300.1\ \text{g}\ Pt(NH_3)_2Cl_2}{1\ \cancel{\text{mol}\ Pt(NH_3)_2Cl_2}} = 7.23\ \text{g}\ Pt(NH_3)_2Cl_2$

▶ **PROBLEM 3.9**   Lithium oxide is used aboard the space shuttle to remove water from the air supply. If 80.0 kg of water is to be removed and 65 kg of Li_2O is available, which reactant is limiting? How many kilograms of the excess reactant remain?

$$Li_2O(s) + H_2O(g) \longrightarrow 2\ LiOH(s)$$

▶ **PROBLEM 3.10**   After lithium hydroxide is produced aboard the space shuttle by reaction of Li_2O with H_2O (Problem 3.9), it is used to remove exhaled carbon dioxide from the air supply. How many grams of CO_2 can 500.0 g of LiOH absorb?

$$LiOH(s) + CO_2(g) \longrightarrow LiHCO_3(s)$$

CONCEPTUAL PROBLEM 3.11   The following diagram represents the reaction of A (red spheres) with B_2 (blue spheres):

(a) Write a balanced equation for the reaction, and identify the limiting reactant.
(b) How many moles of product can be made from 1.0 mol of A and 1.0 mol of B_2?

3.6 CONCENTRATIONS OF REACTANTS IN SOLUTION: MOLARITY

For a chemical reaction to occur, the reacting molecules or ions must come into contact. This means that the reactants must be mobile, which in turn means that most chemical reactions are carried out in the liquid state or in solution rather than in the solid state. It's therefore necessary to have a standard means to describe exact quantities of substances in solution.

As we've seen, stoichiometry calculations for chemical reactions always require working in moles. Thus, the most generally useful means of expressing a solution's concentration is **molarity (M)**, the number of moles of a substance, or **solute**, dissolved in enough solvent to make one liter of solution. For example, a solution made by dissolving 1.00 mol (58.5 g) of NaCl in enough water to give 1.00 L of solution has a concentration of 1.00 mol/L, or 1.00 M. The molarity of any solution is found by dividing the number of moles of solute by the number of liters of solution:

$$\text{Molarity (M)} = \frac{\text{Moles of solute}}{\text{Liters of solution}}$$

Note that it's the final volume of the *solution* that's important, not the starting volume of the *solvent* used. The final volume of the solution might be a bit larger than the volume of the solvent because of the additional volume of the solute. In practice, a solution of known molarity is prepared by weighing an appropriate amount of solute and placing it in a container called a *volumetric flask*, as shown in **Figure 3.2**. Enough solvent is added to dissolve the solute, and further solvent is added until an accurately calibrated final volume is reached. The solution is then shaken until it's uniformly mixed.

Molarity can be used as a conversion factor to relate a solution's volume to the number of moles of solute. If we know the molarity and volume of a solution, we can

A measured number of moles of solute is placed in a volumetric flask.

Enough solvent is added to dissolve the solute by swirling.

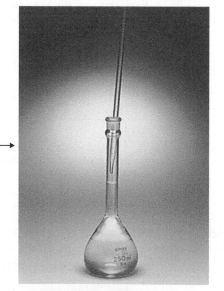

Further solvent is added to reach the calibration mark on the neck of the flask, and the solution is shaken until uniform.

Figure 3.2
Preparing a solution of known molarity.

calculate the number of moles of solute. If we know the number of moles of solute and the molarity of the solution, we can find the solution's volume. Worked Examples 3.11 and 3.12 show how the calculations are done.

$$\text{Molarity} = \frac{\text{Moles of solute}}{\text{Volume of solution (L)}}$$

$$\text{Moles of solute} = \text{Molarity} \times \text{Volume of solution} \qquad \text{Volume of solution} = \frac{\text{Moles of solute}}{\text{Molarity}}$$

WORKED EXAMPLE 3.11

CALCULATING THE MOLARITY OF A SOLUTION

What is the molarity of a solution made by dissolving 2.355 g of sulfuric acid (H_2SO_4) in water and diluting to a final volume of 50.0 mL?

STRATEGY

Molarity is the number of moles of solute per liter of solution. Thus, it's necessary to find the number of moles of sulfuric acid in 2.355 g and then divide by the volume of the solution.

SOLUTION

Molec. mass of H_2SO_4 = (2 × 1.0 amu) + 32.1 amu + (4 × 16.0 amu) = 98.1 amu

Molar mass of H_2SO_4 = 98.1 g/mol

$$2.355 \text{ g } H_2SO_4 \times \frac{1 \text{ mol } H_2SO_4}{98.1 \text{ g } H_2SO_4} = 0.0240 \text{ mol } H_2SO_4$$

$$\frac{0.0240 \text{ mol } H_2SO_4}{0.0500 \text{ L}} = 0.480 \text{ M}$$

The solution has a sulfuric acid concentration of 0.480 M.

WORKED EXAMPLE 3.12

CALCULATING THE NUMBER OF MOLES OF SOLUTE IN A SOLUTION

Hydrochloric acid is sold commercially as a 12.0 M aqueous solution. How many moles of HCl are in 300.0 mL of 12.0 M solution?

STRATEGY

The number of moles of solute is calculated by multiplying the molarity of the solution by its volume.

SOLUTION

$$\text{Moles of HCl} = (\text{Molarity of solution}) \times (\text{Volume of solution})$$

$$= \frac{12.0 \text{ mol HCl}}{1 \text{ L}} \times 0.3000 \text{ L} = 3.60 \text{ mol HCl}$$

There are 3.60 mol of HCl in 300.0 mL of 12.0 M solution.

BALLPARK CHECK

One liter of 12.0 M HCl solution contains 12 mol of HCl, so 300 mL (0.3 L) of solution contains 0.3 × 12 = 3.6 mol.

▶ **PROBLEM 3.12** How many moles of solute are present in the following solutions?
(a) 125 mL of 0.20 M $NaHCO_3$ **(b)** 650.0 mL of 2.50 M H_2SO_4

▶ **PROBLEM 3.13** How many grams of solute would you use to prepare the following solutions?
(a) 500.0 mL of 1.25 M NaOH   **(b)** 1.50 L of 0.250 M glucose ($C_6H_{12}O_6$)

▶ **PROBLEM 3.14** How many milliliters of a 0.20 M glucose ($C_6H_{12}O_6$) solution are needed to provide a total of 25.0 g of glucose?

▶ **PROBLEM 3.15** The concentration of cholesterol ($C_{27}H_{46}O$) in normal blood is approximately 0.005 M. How many grams of cholesterol are in 750 mL of blood?

Cholesterol

3.7 DILUTING CONCENTRATED SOLUTIONS

▲ Just as frozen orange juice concentrate must be diluted before use by adding water, many chemical solutions must also be diluted.

For convenience, chemicals are sometimes bought and stored as concentrated solutions, which are then diluted before use. Aqueous hydrochloric acid, for example, is sold commercially as a 12.0 M solution, yet it is most commonly used in the laboratory after dilution with water to a final concentration of either 6.0 M or 1.0 M.

$$\text{Concentrated solution} + \text{Solvent} \longrightarrow \text{Dilute solution}$$

The main thing to remember when diluting a concentrated solution is that the number of moles of solute is constant; only the volume of the solution is changed by adding more solvent. Because the number of moles of solute can be calculated by multiplying molarity times volume, we can set up the following equation:

$$\text{Moles of solute (constant)} = \text{Molarity} \times \text{Volume}$$
$$= M_i \times V_i = M_f \times V_f$$

where M_i is the initial molarity, V_i is the initial volume, M_f is the final molarity, and V_f is the final volume after dilution. Rearranging this equation into a more useful form shows that the molar concentration after dilution (M_f) can be found by multiplying the initial concentration (M_i) by the ratio of initial and final volumes (V_i/V_f):

$$M_f = M_i \times \frac{V_i}{V_f}$$

Suppose, for example, that we dilute 50.0 mL of a solution of 2.00 M H_2SO_4 to a volume of 200.0 mL. The solution volume *increases* by a factor of four (from 50 mL to 200 mL), so the concentration of the solution must *decrease* by a factor of four (from 2.00 M to 0.500 M):

$$M_f = 2.00 \text{ M} \times \frac{50.0 \text{ mL}}{200.0 \text{ mL}} = 0.500 \text{ M}$$

In practice, dilutions are usually carried out as shown in **Figure 3.3**. The volume to be diluted is withdrawn using a calibrated tube called a *pipet*, placed in an empty volumetric flask of the chosen volume, and diluted to the calibration mark on the flask. The one common exception to this order of steps is when diluting a strong acid such as H_2SO_4, where a large amount of heat is released. In such instances, it is much safer to add the acid slowly to the water rather than adding water to the acid.

WORKED EXAMPLE 3.13

DILUTING A SOLUTION

How would you prepare 500.0 mL of 0.2500 M NaOH solution starting from a concentration of 1.000 M?

STRATEGY

The problem gives initial and final concentrations (M_i and M_f) and final volume (V_f) and asks for the initial volume (V_i) that we need to dilute. Rewriting the equation $M_i \times V_i = M_f \times V_f$ as $V_i = (M_f/M_i) \times V_f$ gives the answer.

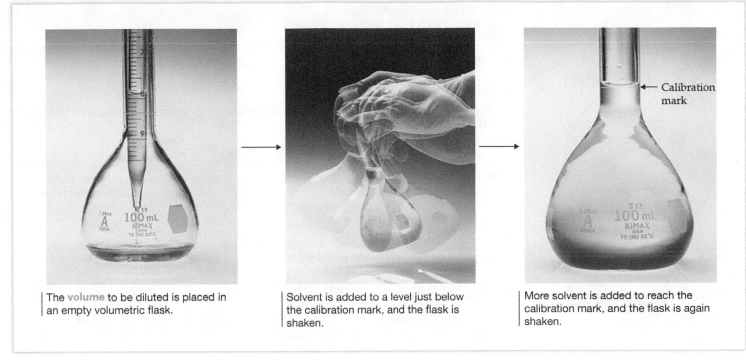

| The volume to be diluted is placed in an empty volumetric flask. | Solvent is added to a level just below the calibration mark, and the flask is shaken. | More solvent is added to reach the calibration mark, and the flask is again shaken. |

Figure 3.3
The procedure for diluting a concentrated solution.

SOLUTION

$$V_i = \frac{M_f}{M_i} \times V_f = \frac{0.2500\ M}{1.000\ M} \times 500.0\ \text{mL} = 125.0\ \text{mL}$$

We need to place 125.0 mL of 1.000 M NaOH solution in a 500.0 mL volumetric flask and fill to the calibration mark with water.

BALLPARK CHECK

Because the concentration decreases by a factor of four after dilution (from 1.000 M to 0.2500 M), the volume must increase by a factor of four. Thus, to prepare 500.0 mL of solution, we should start with $500.0/4 = 125.0$ mL.

▶ **PROBLEM 3.16**   What is the final concentration if 75.0 mL of a 3.50 M glucose solution is diluted to a volume of 400.0 mL?

▶ **PROBLEM 3.17**   Sulfuric acid is normally purchased at a concentration of 18.0 M. How would you prepare 250.0 mL of 0.500 M aqueous H_2SO_4? (Remember to add the acid to water rather than water to the acid.)

3.8 SOLUTION STOICHIOMETRY

We remarked in Section 3.6 that molarity is a conversion factor between numbers of moles of solute and the volume of a solution. Thus, if we know the volume and molarity of a solution, we can calculate the number of moles of solute. If we know the number of moles of solute and molarity, we can find the volume.

As indicated by the flow diagram in **Figure 3.4**, using molarity is critical for carrying out stoichiometry calculations on substances in solution. Molarity makes it possible to calculate the volume of one solution needed to react with a given volume of another solution. This sort of calculation is particularly important in the chemistry of acids and bases, as shown in Worked Example 3.14.

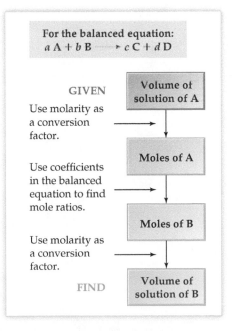

For the balanced equation:
$$a\,A + b\,B \longrightarrow c\,C + d\,D$$

GIVEN → **Volume of solution of A**

Use molarity as a conversion factor. →

Moles of A

Use coefficients in the balanced equation to find mole ratios. →

Moles of B

Use molarity as a conversion factor. →

FIND → **Volume of solution of B**

Figure 3.4
Using molarity as a conversion factor between moles and volume in stoichiometry calculations.

▲ Neutralization of sodium hydrogen carbonate with acid leads to release of CO_2 gas, visible in this fizzing solution.

WORKED EXAMPLE 3.14

REACTION STOICHIOMETRY IN SOLUTION

Stomach acid, a dilute solution of HCl in water, can be neutralized by reaction with sodium hydrogen carbonate, $NaHCO_3$, according to the equation

$$HCl(aq) + NaHCO_3(aq) \longrightarrow NaCl(aq) + H_2O(l) + CO_2(g)$$

How many milliliters of 0.125 M $NaHCO_3$ solution are needed to neutralize 18.0 mL of 0.100 M HCl?

STRATEGY

Solving stoichiometry problems always requires finding the number of moles of one reactant, using the coefficients of the balanced equation to find the number of moles of the other reactant, and then finding the amount of the other reactant. The flow diagram summarizing the situation was shown in Figure 3.4.

SOLUTION

We first have to find how many moles of HCl are in 18.0 mL of a 0.100 M solution by multiplying volume times molarity:

$$\text{Moles of HCl} = 18.0 \text{ mL} \times \frac{1 \text{ L}}{1000 \text{ mL}} \times \frac{0.100 \text{ mol}}{1 \text{ L}} = 1.80 \times 10^{-3} \text{ mol HCl}$$

Next, check the coefficients of the balanced equation to find that 1 mol of HCl reacts with 1 mol of $NaHCO_3$, and then calculate how many milliliters of a 0.125 M $NaHCO_3$ solution contains 1.80×10^{-3} mol:

$$1.80 \times 10^{-3} \text{ mol HCl} \times \frac{1 \text{ mol NaHCO}_3}{1 \text{ mol HCl}} \times \frac{1 \text{ L solution}}{0.125 \text{ mol NaHCO}_3} = 0.0144 \text{ L solution}$$

Thus, 14.4 mL of the 0.125 M $NaHCO_3$ solution is needed to neutralize 18.0 mL of the 0.100 M HCl solution.

BALLPARK CHECK

The balanced equation shows that HCl and $NaHCO_3$ react in a 1 : 1 molar ratio, and we are told that the concentrations of the two solutions are about the same. Thus, the volume of the $NaHCO_3$ solution must be about the same as that of the HCl solution.

▶ **PROBLEM 3.18** What volume of 0.250 M H_2SO_4 is needed to react with 50.0 mL of 0.100 M NaOH? The equation is

$$H_2SO_4(aq) + 2\,NaOH(aq) \longrightarrow Na_2SO_4(aq) + 2\,H_2O(l)$$

▶ **PROBLEM 3.19** What is the molarity of an HNO_3 solution if 68.5 mL is needed to react with 25.0 mL of 0.150 M KOH solution? The equation is

$$HNO_3(aq) + KOH(aq) \longrightarrow KNO_3(aq) + H_2O(l)$$

3.9 TITRATION

There are two ways to make a solution of known molarity. One way is to use the method described in Section 3.6; that is, to dissolve an accurately weighed amount of solute in enough solvent to reach an accurately calibrated volume. Often though, it's more convenient to make up a solution quickly, using an estimated amount of solute and an estimated amount of solvent, and then determine the solution's exact molarity by *titration*.

Titration is a procedure for determining the concentration of a solution by allowing a measured volume of that solution to react with a second solution of another substance (the *standard solution*) whose concentration is known. By finding the volume of the standard solution that reacts with the measured volume of the first solution, the concentration of the first solution can be calculated. (It's necessary, though, that the reaction go to completion and have a yield of 100%.)

To see how titration works, let's imagine that we have an HCl solution (an acid) whose concentration we want to find by allowing it to react with NaOH (a base) in what is called an acid–base neutralization reaction. (We'll learn more about acid–base neutralizations in the next chapter.) The balanced equation is

$$NaOH(aq) + HCl(aq) \longrightarrow NaCl(aq) + H_2O(l)$$

We'll begin the titration by measuring out a known volume of the HCl solution and adding a small amount of an *indicator*, a compound that undergoes a color change during the course of the reaction. The compound phenolphthalein, for instance, is colorless in acid solution but turns red in base solution. Next, we fill a calibrated glass tube called a *buret* with an NaOH standard solution of known concentration and slowly add the NaOH to the HCl. When the phenolphthalein just begins to turn pink, all the HCl has completely reacted and the solution now has a tiny amount of excess NaOH. By then reading from the buret to find the volume of the NaOH standard solution that has been added to react with the known volume of HCl solution, we can calculate the concentration of the HCl. The strategy is summarized in **Figure 3.5**, and the procedure is shown in **Figure 3.6**.

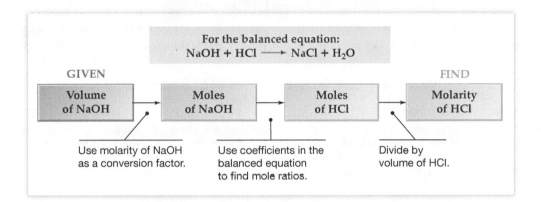

Figure 3.5
A flow diagram for an acid–base titration. The calculations needed to determine the concentration of an HCl solution by titration with an NaOH standard solution are summarized.

A measured volume of acid solution is placed in a flask, and phenolphthalein indicator is added.

Base solution of known concentration is added from a buret until the indicator changes **color**. Reading the volume of base from the buret allows calculation of the acid concentration.

Figure 3.6
Titration of an acid solution of unknown concentration with a base solution of known concentration.

Let's assume that we take 20.0 mL of the HCl solution and find that we have to add 48.6 mL of 0.100 M NaOH from a buret to obtain complete reaction. Using the molarity of the NaOH standard solution as a conversion factor, we can calculate the number of moles of NaOH undergoing reaction:

$$\text{Moles of NaOH} = 0.0486 \text{ L NaOH} \times \frac{0.100 \text{ mol NaOH}}{1 \text{ L NaOH}}$$

$$= 0.004\,86 \text{ mol NaOH}$$

According to the balanced equation, the number of moles of HCl is the same as that of NaOH:

$$\text{Moles of HCl} = 0.004\,86 \text{ mol NaOH} \times \frac{1 \text{ mol HCl}}{1 \text{ mol NaOH}} = 0.004\,86 \text{ mol HCl}$$

Dividing the number of moles of HCl by the volume then gives the molarity of the HCl:

$$\text{HCl molarity} = \frac{0.004\,86 \text{ mol HCl}}{0.0200 \text{ L HCl}} = 0.243 \text{ M HCl}$$

▶ **PROBLEM 3.20**   A 25.0 mL sample of vinegar (dilute acetic acid, CH_3CO_2H) is titrated and found to react with 94.7 mL of 0.200 M NaOH. What is the molarity of the acetic acid solution? The reaction is

$$\text{NaOH}(aq) + CH_3CO_2H(aq) \longrightarrow CH_3CO_2Na(aq) + H_2O(l)$$

CONCEPTUAL PROBLEM 3.21   Assume that the buret contains H^+ ions, the flask contains OH^- ions, the volumes in the buret and the flask are identical, and the concentration of the acid in the buret is 1.00 M. If the entire volume of the buret is required for titration of the base in the flask, what is the concentration of base? The equation is $H^+(aq) + OH^-(aq) \longrightarrow H_2O(l)$.

3.10 PERCENT COMPOSITION AND EMPIRICAL FORMULAS

All the substances we've dealt with thus far have had known formulas. When, however, a new compound is made in the laboratory or found in nature, its formula must be experimentally determined.

Determining the formula of a new compound begins with analyzing the substance to find what elements it contains and how much of each element is present—that is, to find its *composition*. The **percent composition** of a compound is expressed by identifying the elements present and giving the mass percent of each.

For example, we might express the percent composition of a certain colorless liquid found in gasoline by saying that it contains 84.1% carbon and 15.9% hydrogen by mass. In other words, a 100.0 g sample of the compound contains 84.1 g of carbon atoms and 15.9 g of hydrogen atoms.

Knowing a compound's percent composition makes it possible to calculate the compound's chemical formula. As shown in **Figure 3.7**, the strategy is to find the relative number of moles of each element in the compound and then use those numbers to establish the mole ratios of the elements. The mole ratios, in turn, correspond to the subscripts in the chemical formula.

Let's use for our example the colorless liquid whose composition is 84.1% carbon and 15.9% hydrogen by mass. Arbitrarily taking 100 g of the substance to make the calculation easier, we find by using molar masses as conversion factors that the 100 g contains:

$$84.1 \ \cancel{g \ C} \times \frac{1 \ \text{mol C}}{12.01 \ \cancel{g \ C}} = 7.00 \ \text{mol C}$$

$$15.9 \ \cancel{g \ H} \times \frac{1 \ \text{mol H}}{1.008 \ \cancel{g \ H}} = 15.8 \ \text{mol H}$$

With the relative numbers of moles of C and H known, we find the mole ratio by dividing both by the smaller number (7.00):

$$C_{\left(\frac{7.00}{7.00}\right)}H_{\left(\frac{15.8}{7.00}\right)} = C_1H_{2.26}$$

The C:H mole ratio of 1:2.26 means that we can write $C_1H_{2.26}$ as a temporary formula for the liquid. Multiplying the subscripts by small integers in a trial-and-error procedure until whole numbers are found then gives the **empirical formula**, which tells the smallest whole-number ratios of atoms in the compound. In the present instance, multiplication of the subscripts by 4 is needed to give the empirical formula C_4H_9. (The subscripts may not always be *exact* integers because of small errors in the data, but the discrepancies should be small.)

$$C_{(1\times4)}H_{(2.26\times4)} = C_4H_{9.04} = C_4H_9$$

An empirical formula determined from percent composition tells only the ratios of atoms in a compound. The **molecular formula**, which tells the actual numbers of atoms in a molecule, can be either the same as the empirical formula or a multiple of it. To determine the molecular formula, it's necessary to know the molecular mass of the substance. In the present instance, the molecular mass of our compound (a substance called octane) is 114.2 amu, which is a simple multiple of the empirical molecular mass for C_4H_9 (57.1 amu).

To find the multiple, divide the molecular mass by the empirical formula mass:

$$\text{Multiple} = \frac{\text{Molecular mass}}{\text{Empirical formula mass}} = \frac{114.2}{57.1} = 2.00$$

Then multiply the subscripts in the empirical formula by this multiple to obtain the molecular formula. In our example, the molecular formula of octane is $C_{(4\times2)}H_{(9\times2)}$, or C_8H_{18}.

Just as we can find the empirical formula of a substance from its percent composition, we can also find the percent composition of a substance from its empirical (or molecular) formula. The strategies for the two kinds of calculations are exactly opposite. Aspirin, for example, has the molecular formula $C_9H_8O_4$ and thus has a C:H:O mole ratio of 9:8:4. We can convert this mole ratio into a mass ratio, and thus into percent composition, by carrying out mole-to-gram conversions.

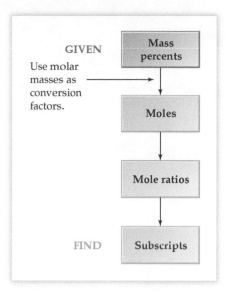

Figure 3.7
Calculating the formula of a compound from its percent composition.

Let's assume we start with 1 mol of compound to simplify the calculation:

$$1 \text{ mol aspirin} \times \frac{9 \text{ mol C}}{1 \text{ mol aspirin}} \times \frac{12.0 \text{ g C}}{1 \text{ mol C}} = 108 \text{ g C}$$

$$1 \text{ mol aspirin} \times \frac{8 \text{ mol H}}{1 \text{ mol aspirin}} \times \frac{1.01 \text{ g H}}{1 \text{ mol H}} = 8.08 \text{ g H}$$

$$1 \text{ mol aspirin} \times \frac{4 \text{ mol O}}{1 \text{ mol aspirin}} \times \frac{16.0 \text{ g O}}{1 \text{ mol O}} = 64.0 \text{ g O}$$

Dividing the mass of each element by the total mass and multiplying by 100% then gives the percent composition:

$$\text{Total mass of 1 mol aspirin} = 108 \text{ g} + 8.08 \text{ g} + 64.0 \text{ g} = 180 \text{ g}$$

$$\% \text{ C} = \frac{108 \text{ g C}}{180 \text{ g}} \times 100\% = 60.0\%$$

$$\% \text{ H} = \frac{8.08 \text{ g H}}{180 \text{ g}} \times 100\% = 4.49\%$$

$$\% \text{ O} = \frac{64.0 \text{ g O}}{180 \text{ g}} \times 100\% = 35.6\%$$

The answer can be checked by confirming that the sum of the mass percentages is within a rounding error of 100%: 60.0% + 4.49% + 35.6% = 100.1%.

Worked Examples 3.15 and 3.16 show further conversions between percent composition and empirical formulas.

Ascorbic acid

WORKED EXAMPLE 3.15

CALCULATING AN EMPIRICAL FORMULA FROM A PERCENT COMPOSITION

Vitamin C (ascorbic acid) contains 40.92% C, 4.58% H, and 54.50% O by mass. What is the empirical formula of ascorbic acid?

STRATEGY

Assume that you have 100.00 g of ascorbic acid, and then carry out the procedure outlined in Figure 3.7.

SOLUTION

First, find the number of moles of each element in the sample:

$$40.92 \text{ g C} \times \frac{1 \text{ mol C}}{12.0 \text{ g C}} = 3.41 \text{ mol C}$$

$$4.58 \text{ g H} \times \frac{1 \text{ mol H}}{1.01 \text{ g H}} = 4.53 \text{ mol H}$$

$$54.50 \text{ g O} \times \frac{1 \text{ mol O}}{16.0 \text{ g O}} = 3.41 \text{ mol O}$$

Dividing each of the three numbers by the smallest (3.41 mol) gives a C:H:O mole ratio of 1:1.33:1 and a temporary formula of $C_1H_{1.33}O_1$. Multiplying the subscripts by small integers in a trial-and-error procedure until whole numbers are found then gives the empirical formula: $C_{(3 \times 1)}H_{(3 \times 1.33)}O_{(3 \times 1)} = C_3H_4O_3$.

WORKED EXAMPLE 3.16

CALCULATING A PERCENT COMPOSITION FROM A FORMULA

Glucose, or blood sugar, has the molecular formula $C_6H_{12}O_6$. What is the empirical formula, and what is the percent composition of glucose?

STRATEGY AND SOLUTION

The empirical formula is found by reducing the subscripts in the molecular formula to their smallest whole-number values. In this case, dividing the subscripts by 6 reduces $C_6H_{12}O_6$ to CH_2O.

The percent composition of glucose can be calculated either from the molecular formula or from the empirical formula. Using the molecular formula, for instance, the C:H:O mole ratio of 6:12:6 can be converted into a mass ratio by assuming that we have 1 mol of compound and carrying out mole-to-gram conversions:

$$1 \text{ mol glucose} \times \frac{6 \text{ mol C}}{1 \text{ mol glucose}} \times \frac{12.0 \text{ g C}}{1 \text{ mol C}} = 72.0 \text{ g C}$$

$$1 \text{ mol glucose} \times \frac{12 \text{ mol H}}{1 \text{ mol glucose}} \times \frac{1.01 \text{ g H}}{1 \text{ mol H}} = 12.1 \text{ g H}$$

$$1 \text{ mol glucose} \times \frac{6 \text{ mol O}}{1 \text{ mol glucose}} \times \frac{16.0 \text{ g O}}{1 \text{ mol O}} = 96.0 \text{ g O}$$

Dividing the mass of each element by the total mass, and multiplying by 100%, gives the percent composition. Note that the sum of the mass percentages is 100%.

Total mass of 1 mol glucose = 72.0 g + 12.1 g + 96.0 g = 180.1 g

$$\% \text{ C} = \frac{72.0 \text{ g C}}{180.1 \text{ g}} \times 100\% = 40.0\%$$

$$\% \text{ H} = \frac{12.1 \text{ g H}}{180.1 \text{ g}} \times 100\% = 6.72\%$$

$$\% \text{ O} = \frac{96.0 \text{ g O}}{180.1 \text{ g}} \times 100\% = 53.3\%$$

Glucose

▶ **PROBLEM 3.22** What is the empirical formula, and what is the percent composition of dimethylhydrazine, $C_2H_8N_2$, a colorless liquid used as a rocket fuel?

▶ **PROBLEM 3.23** What is the empirical formula of the ingredient in Bufferin tablets that has the percent composition C 14.25%, O 56.93%, Mg 28.83% by mass?

▶ **PROBLEM 3.24** What is the percent composition of citric acid, an organic acid, commonly found in citrus fruits, whose structure is shown in the nearby margin? (Gray = C, red = O, H = ivory.)

Citric acid

3.11 DETERMINING EMPIRICAL FORMULAS: ELEMENTAL ANALYSIS

One of the most common methods used to determine percent composition and empirical formulas, particularly for organic compounds containing carbon and hydrogen, is *combustion analysis*. In this method, a compound of unknown composition is burned with oxygen to produce the volatile combustion products CO_2 and H_2O, which are separated and have their amounts determined by an automated instrument. Methane (CH_4), for instance, burns according to the balanced equation

$$CH_4(g) + 2 O_2(g) \longrightarrow CO_2(g) + 2 H_2O(g)$$

With the amounts of the carbon-containing product (CO_2) and hydrogen-containing product (H_2O) established, the strategy is to calculate the number of moles of carbon and hydrogen in the products, from which we can find the C:H mole ratio of the starting compound. This information, in turn, provides the chemical formula, as outlined by the flow diagram in Figure 3.8.

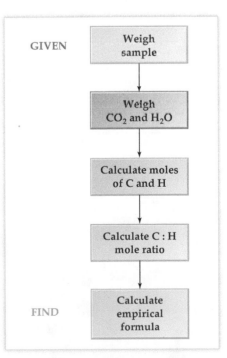

Figure 3.8
Determining an empirical formula from combustion analysis of a compound containing C and H.

As an example of how combustion analysis works, imagine that we have a sample of a pure substance—say, naphthalene, which is often used for household moth balls. We weigh a known amount of the sample, burn it in pure oxygen, and then analyze the products. Let's say that 0.330 g of naphthalene reacts with O_2 and that 1.133 g of CO_2 and 0.185 g of H_2O are formed. The first thing to find out is the number of moles of carbon and hydrogen in the CO_2 and H_2O products so that we can calculate the number of moles of each element originally present in the naphthalene sample.

$$\text{Moles of C in 1.133 g } CO_2 = 1.133 \text{ g } CO_2 \times \frac{1 \text{ mol } CO_2}{44.01 \text{ g } CO_2} \times \frac{1 \text{ mol C}}{1 \text{ mol } CO_2}$$

$$= 0.02574 \text{ mol C}$$

$$\text{Moles of H in 0.185 g } H_2O = 0.185 \text{ g } H_2O \times \frac{1 \text{ mol } H_2O}{18.02 \text{ g } H_2O} \times \frac{2 \text{ mol H}}{1 \text{ mol } H_2O}$$

$$= 0.0205 \text{ mol H}$$

Although it's not necessary in this instance since naphthalene contains only carbon and hydrogen, we can make sure that all the mass is accounted for and that no other elements are present. To do so, we carry out mole-to-gram conversions to find the number of grams of C and H in the starting sample:

$$\text{Mass of C} = 0.02574 \text{ mol C} \times \frac{12.01 \text{ g C}}{1 \text{ mol C}} = 0.3091 \text{ g C}$$

$$\text{Mass of H} = 0.0205 \text{ mol H} \times \frac{1.01 \text{ g H}}{1 \text{ mol H}} = 0.0207 \text{ g H}$$

$$\text{Total mass of C and H} = 0.3091 \text{ g} + 0.0207 \text{ g} = 0.3298 \text{ g}$$

Because the total mass of the C and H in the products (0.3298 g) is the same as the mass of the starting sample (0.330 g), we know that no other elements are present in naphthalene.

With the relative number of moles of C and H in naphthalene known, divide the larger number of moles by the smaller number to get the formula $C_{1.26}H_1$.

$$C_{\left(\frac{0.02574}{0.0205}\right)}H_{\left(\frac{0.0205}{0.0205}\right)} = C_{1.26}H_1$$

Then multiply the subscripts by small integers in a trial-and-error procedure until whole numbers are found to obtain the whole-number formula C_5H_4:

Multiply subscripts by 2: $C_{(1.26 \times 2)}H_{(1 \times 2)} = C_{2.52}H_2$

Multiply subscripts by 3: $C_{(1.26 \times 3)}H_{(1 \times 3)} = C_{3.78}H_3$

Multiply subscripts by 4: $C_{(1.26 \times 4)}H_{(1 \times 4)} = C_{5.04}H_4 = C_5H_4$ (Both subscripts are integers)

Elemental analysis provides only an empirical formula. To determine the molecular formula, it's also necessary to know the substance's molecular mass. In the present problem, the molecular mass of naphthalene is 128.2 amu, or twice the empirical formula mass of C_5H_4 (64.1 amu). Thus, the molecular formula of naphthalene is $C_{(2 \times 5)}H_{(2 \times 4)} = C_{10}H_8$.

Worked Example 3.17 shows a combustion analysis when the sample contains oxygen in addition to carbon and hydrogen. Because oxygen yields no combustion products, its presence in a molecule can't be directly detected by this method. Rather, the presence of oxygen must be inferred by subtracting the calculated masses of C and H from the total mass of the sample.

Naphthalene

WORKED EXAMPLE 3.17

CALCULATING AN EMPIRICAL FORMULA AND A MOLECULAR FORMULA FROM A COMBUSTION ANALYSIS

Caproic acid, the substance responsible for the aroma of goats, dirty socks, and old shoes, contains carbon, hydrogen, and oxygen. On combustion analysis, a 0.450 g sample of caproic acid gives 0.418 g of H_2O and 1.023 g of CO_2. What is the empirical formula of caproic acid? If the molecular mass of caproic acid is 116.2 amu, what is the molecular formula?

STRATEGY

Use the steps outlined in Figure 3.8 to find the empirical formula of caproic acid. Then calculate a formula mass and compare it to the known molecular mass.

SOLUTION

First, find the molar amounts of C and H in the sample:

$$\text{Moles of C} = 1.023 \text{ g CO}_2 \times \frac{1 \text{ mol CO}_2}{44.01 \text{ g CO}_2} \times \frac{1 \text{ mol C}}{1 \text{ mol CO}_2} = 0.023\,24 \text{ mol C}$$

$$\text{Moles of H} = 0.418 \text{ g H}_2\text{O} \times \frac{1 \text{ mol H}_2\text{O}}{18.02 \text{ g H}_2\text{O}} \times \frac{2 \text{ mol H}}{1 \text{ mol H}_2\text{O}} = 0.0464 \text{ mol H}$$

Next, find the number of grams of C and H in the sample:

$$\text{Mass of C} = 0.023\,24 \text{ mol C} \times \frac{12.01 \text{ g C}}{1 \text{ mol C}} = 0.2791 \text{ g C}$$

$$\text{Mass of H} = 0.0464 \text{ mol H} \times \frac{1.01 \text{ g H}}{1 \text{ mol H}} = 0.0469 \text{ g H}$$

Subtracting the masses of C and H from the mass of the starting sample indicates that 0.124 g is unaccounted for:

$$0.450 \text{ g} - (0.2791 \text{ g} + 0.0469 \text{ g}) = 0.124 \text{ g}$$

Because we are told that oxygen is also present in the sample, the "missing" mass must be due to oxygen, which can't be detected by combustion. We therefore need to find the number of moles of oxygen in the sample:

$$\text{Moles of O} = 0.124 \text{ g O} \times \frac{1 \text{ mol O}}{16.00 \text{ g O}} = 0.007\,75 \text{ mol O}$$

Knowing the relative numbers of moles of all three elements, C, H, and O, we divide the three numbers of moles by the smallest number (0.007 75 mol of oxygen) to arrive at a C:H:O ratio of 3:6:1.

$$C_{\left(\frac{0.02324}{0.00775}\right)} H_{\left(\frac{0.0464}{0.00775}\right)} O_{\left(\frac{0.00775}{0.00775}\right)} = C_3H_6O$$

The empirical formula of caproic acid is therefore C_3H_6O, and the empirical formula mass is 58.1 amu. Because the molecular mass of caproic acid is 116.2, or twice the empirical formula mass, the molecular formula of caproic acid must be $C_{(2\times3)}H_{(2\times6)}O_{(2\times1)} = C_6H_{12}O_2$.

Caproic acid

▶ **PROBLEM 3.25** Menthol, a flavoring agent obtained from peppermint oil, contains carbon, hydrogen, and oxygen. On combustion analysis, 1.00 g of menthol yields 1.161 g of H_2O and 2.818 g of CO_2. What is the empirical formula of menthol?

▶ **PROBLEM 3.26** Ribose, a sugar present in the cells of all living organisms, has a molecular mass of 150 amu and the empirical formula CH_2O. What is the molecular formula of ribose?

▶ **PROBLEM 3.27** Convert the following percent compositions into molecular formulas:
  (a) Diborane: H 21.86%, B 78.14%; Molec. mass = 27.7 amu
  (b) Trioxan: C 40.00%, H 6.71%, O 53.28%; Molec. mass = 90.08 amu

Menthol

Ribose

3.12 DETERMINING MOLECULAR MASSES: MASS SPECTROMETRY

As we saw in the previous section, determining a compound's molecular formula requires a knowledge of its molecular mass. But how is molecular mass determined?

The most common method of determining both atomic and molecular masses is with an instrument called a *mass spectrometer*. More than 20 different kinds of mass spectrometer are commercially available, depending on the intended application, but the electron-impact, magnetic-sector instrument shown in **Figure 3.9a** is particularly common. In this instrument, the sample is vaporized and injected as a dilute gas into an evacuated chamber, where it is bombarded with a beam of high-energy electrons. The electron beam knocks other electrons from the sample molecules, which become positively charged ions. Some of these ionized molecules survive, and others fragment into smaller ions. The various ions of different masses are then accelerated by an electric field and passed between the poles of a strong magnet, which deflects them through a curved, evacuated pipe.

(a) A mass spectrometer

The resulting ions are passed between the poles of a magnet and are deflected according to their mass-to-charge ratio.

Magnet

Slits

Accelerating grid

Heated filament

The deflected ions pass through a slit into a detector assembly.

Slit

Detector

Molecules are **ionized** by collision with a high-energy electron beam.

Sample inlet

Electron beam

To vacuum pump

(b) A mass spectrum for naphthalene

Mass = 128

Intensity

Mass

20   40   60   80   100   120

Figure 3.9

Mass spectrometry. (a) Schematic illustration of an electron-impact, magnetic-sector mass spectrometer. **(b)** A mass spectrum of naphthalene, molec. mass = 128, showing peaks of different masses on the horizontal axis.

The radius of deflection of a charged ion M^+ as it passes between the magnet poles depends on its mass, with lighter ions deflected more strongly than heavier ones. By varying the strength of the magnetic field, it's possible to focus ions of different masses through a slit at the end of the curved pipe and onto a detector assembly. The mass spectrum that results is plotted as a graph of ion mass versus intensity—that is, as the molecular masses of the various ions versus the relative number of those ions produced in the instrument.

Although a typical mass spectrum contains ions of many different masses, the heaviest ion is generally due to the ionized molecule itself, the so-called molecular ion. By measuring the mass of this molecular ion, the molecular mass of the molecule can be determined. The naphthalene sample discussed in the previous section, for example, gives rise to an intense peak at mass 128 amu in its spectrum, consistent with a molecular formula of $C_{10}H_8$ (**Figure 3.9b**).

Modern mass spectrometers are so precise that molecular masses can often be measured to seven significant figures. A $^{12}C_{10}{}^1H_8$ molecule of naphthalene, for example, has a molecular mass of 128.0626 amu as measured by mass spectrometry.

▲ What did these two have in common?

INQUIRY DID BEN FRANKLIN HAVE AVOGADRO'S NUMBER?

At length being at Clapham, where there is on the common a large pond ... I fetched out a cruet of oil and dropped a little of it on the water. I saw it spread itself with surprising swiftness upon the surface. The oil, although not more than a teaspoonful, produced an instant calm over a space several yards square which spread amazingly and extended itself gradually ... making all that quarter of the pond, perhaps half an acre, as smooth as a looking glass.

Excerpt from a letter of Benjamin Franklin to William Brownrigg, 1773.

Benjamin Franklin, author and renowned statesman, was also an inventor and a scientist. Every schoolchild knows of Franklin's experiment with a kite and a key, demonstrating that lightning is electricity. Less well-known is that his measurement of the extent to which oil spreads on water makes possible a simple estimate of molecular size and Avogadro's number.

The calculation goes like this: Avogadro's number is the number of molecules in a mole. So, if we can estimate both the number of molecules and the number of moles in Franklin's teaspoon of oil, we can calculate Avogadro's number. Let's start by calculating the number of molecules in the oil.

1. The volume (V) of oil Franklin used was 1 tsp = 4.9 cm^3, and the area (A) covered by the oil was 1/2 acre = 2.0×10^7 cm^2. Let's assume that the oil molecules are tiny cubes that pack closely together and form a layer only one molecule thick. As shown in the accompanying figure, the volume of the oil equals the surface area of the layer times the length (l) of the side of one molecule: $V = A \times l$. Rearranging this equation to find the length then gives us an estimate of molecular size:

Area = A

2. The area of the oil layer is the area of the side of one molecule (l^2) times the number of molecules (N) of oil: $A = l^2 \times N$. Rearranging this equation gives the number of molecules:

$$N = \frac{A}{l^2} = \frac{2.0 \times 10^7 \text{ cm}^2}{(2.4 \times 10^{-7} \text{ cm})^2} = 3.5 \times 10^{20} \text{ molecules}$$

3. To calculate the number of moles, we first need to know the mass (m) of the oil. This could have been determined by weighing, but Franklin neglected to do so. Let's therefore estimate the mass by multiplying the volume (V) of the oil by the density (D) of a typical oil, 0.95 g/cm^3. [Since oil floats on water, the density of oil must be a bit less than the density of water (1.00 g/cm^3).]

$$m = V \times D = 4.9 \text{ cm}^3 \times 0.95 \frac{\text{g}}{\text{cm}^3} = 4.7 \text{ g}$$

4. We now have to make one final assumption about the molecular mass of the oil before completing the calculation. Assuming that a typical oil has molec. mass = 900 amu, then the mass of 1 mol of oil is 900 g. Dividing the mass of the oil by the mass of one mole gives the number of moles of oil:

$$\text{Moles of oil} = \frac{4.7 \text{ g}}{900 \text{ g/mol}} = 0.0052 \text{ mol}$$

5. Finally, the number of molecules per mole—Avogadro's number—can be obtained:

$$\text{Avogadro's number} = \frac{3.5 \times 10^{20} \text{ molecules}}{0.0052 \text{ mol}} = 6.7 \times 10^{22}$$

The calculation is not very accurate, but Franklin wasn't really intending for us to calculate Avogadro's number when he made a rough estimate of how much his oil spread out. Nevertheless, the result isn't too bad for such a simple experiment.

▶ **PROBLEM 3.28** What do you think are the main sources of error in calculating Avogadro's number by spreading oil on a pond?

▶ **PROBLEM 3.29** Recalculate Avogadro's number assuming that the oil molecules are shaped like tall rectangular boxes rather than cubes, with two edges of equal length and the third edge four times the length of the other two. Assume also that the molecules stand on end in the water.

SUMMARY

Because mass is neither created nor destroyed in chemical reactions, all chemical equations must be **balanced**—that is, the numbers and kinds of atoms on both sides of the reaction arrow must be the same. A balanced equation tells the number ratio of reactant and product **formula units** in a reaction.

Just as atomic mass is the mass of an atom, **molecular mass** is the mass of a molecule. The analogous term **formula mass** is used for ionic and other nonmolecular substances. Molecular mass is the sum of the atomic masses of all atoms in the molecule. One mole of a substance is the amount whose mass in grams is numerically equal to the substance's molecular or formula mass. Carrying out chemical calculations using mass–mole relationships is called **stoichiometry** and is done using molar masses as conversion factors.

The amount of product actually formed in a reaction—the reaction's **yield**—is often less than the amount theoretically possible. Dividing the actual amount by the theoretical amount and multiplying by 100% gives the reaction's **percent yield**. Often, reactions are carried out with an excess of one reactant beyond that called for by the balanced equation. In such cases, the extent to which the reaction takes place depends on the reactant present in limiting amount, the **limiting reactant**.

The concentration of a substance in solution is usually expressed as **molarity (M)**, defined as the number of moles of a substance (the **solute**) dissolved per liter of solution. A solution's molarity acts as a conversion factor between solution volume and number of moles of solute, making it possible to carry out stoichiometry calculations on solutions. Often, chemicals are stored as concentrated aqueous solutions that are diluted before use. When carrying out a dilution, only the volume is changed by adding solvent; the amount of solute is unchanged. A solution's exact concentration can often be determined by **titration**.

The chemical makeup of a substance is described by its **percent composition**—the percentage of the substance's mass due to each of its constituent elements. Elemental analysis is used to calculate a substance's **empirical formula**, which gives the smallest whole-number ratio of atoms of the elements in the compound. To determine the **molecular formula**, which may be a simple multiple of the empirical formula, it's also necessary to know the substance's molecular mass. Molecular masses are usually determined by mass spectrometry.

KEY WORDS

balanced equation *75*	**formula unit** *75*	**molecular mass** *79*	**stoichiometry** *80*
coefficient *75*	**limiting reactant** *86*	**percent composition** *94*	**titration** *92*
empirical formula *95*	**molarity (M)** *88*	**percent yield** *83*	**yield** *83*
formula mass *79*	**molecular formula** *95*	**solute** *88*	

CONCEPTUAL PROBLEMS

Problems 3.1–3.29 appear within the chapter.

3.30 Box **(a)** represents 1.0 mL of a solution of particles at a given concentration. Which of the boxes **(b)**–**(d)** represents 1.0 mL of the solution that results after **(a)** has been diluted by doubling the volume of its solvent?

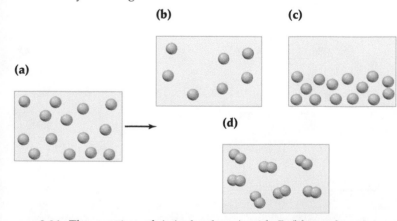

(b)   **(c)**

(a)

(d)

3.31 The reaction of A (red spheres) with B (blue spheres) is shown in the following diagram:

Which equation best describes the stoichiometry of the reaction?

(a) $A_2 + 2 B \longrightarrow A_2B_2$

(b) $10 A + 5 B_2 \longrightarrow 5 A_2B_2$

(c) $2 A + B_2 \longrightarrow A_2B_2$

(d) $5 A + 5 B_2 \longrightarrow 5 A_2B_2$

3.32 Cytosine, a constituent of deoxyribonucleic acid (DNA) can be represented by the following molecular model. If 0.001 mol of cytosine is submitted to combustion analysis, how many moles of CO_2 and how many moles of H_2O would be formed? (Gray = C, red = O, blue = N, ivory = H.)

3.33 If blue spheres represent nitrogen atoms and red spheres represent oxygen atoms, which box represents reactants and which represents products for the reaction $2\,NO(g) + O_2(g) \longrightarrow 2\,NO_2(g)$?

(a)   **(b)**

(c)   **(d)**

3.34 Fluoxetine, marketed as an antidepressant under the name *Prozac*, can be represented by the following ball and stick molecular model. Write the molecular formula for fluoxetine, and calculate its molecular mass (red = O, gray = C, blue = N, yellow-green = F, ivory = H).

Fluoxetine

3.35 What is the percent composition of cysteine, one of the 20 amino acids commonly found in proteins? (Gray = C, red = O, blue = N, yellow = S, ivory = H.)

Cysteine

3.36 The following diagram represents the reaction of A_2 (red spheres) with B_2 (blue spheres):

(a) Write a balanced equation for the reaction, and identify the limiting reactant.

(b) How many moles of product can be made from 1.0 mol of A_2 and 1.0 mol of B_2?

3.37 A hydrocarbon of unknown formula C_xH_y was submitted to combustion analysis with the following results. What is the empirical formula of the hydrocarbon?

$$C_xH_y \xrightarrow{\;O_2\;}$$

⬤ – H_2O ⬤ – CO_2

SECTION PROBLEMS

Balancing Equations (Section 3.1)

3.38 Which of the following equations are balanced?

(a) The development reaction in silver-halide photography:

$$2\,AgBr + 2\,NaOH + C_6H_6O_2 \longrightarrow \\ 2\,Ag + H_2O + 2\,NaBr + C_6H_4O_2$$

(b) The preparation of household bleach:

$$2\,NaOH + Cl_2 \longrightarrow NaOCl + NaCl + H_2O$$

3.39 Which of the following equations are balanced? Balance any that need it.

(a) The thermite reaction, used in welding:

$$Al + Fe_2O_3 \longrightarrow Al_2O_3 + Fe$$

(b) The photosynthesis of glucose from CO_2:

$$6\,CO_2 + 6\,H_2O \longrightarrow C_6H_{12}O_6 + 6\,O_2$$

(c) The separation of gold from its ore:

$$Au + 2\,NaCN + O_2 + H_2O \longrightarrow \\ NaAu(CN)_2 + 3\,NaOH$$

3.40 Balance the following equations:

(a) $Mg + HNO_3 \longrightarrow H_2 + Mg(NO_3)_2$

(b) $CaC_2 + H_2O \longrightarrow Ca(OH)_2 + C_2H_2$

(c) $S + O_2 \longrightarrow SO_3$

(d) $UO_2 + HF \longrightarrow UF_4 + H_2O$

3.41 Balance the following equations:

(a) The explosion of ammonium nitrate:

$$NH_4NO_3 \longrightarrow N_2 + O_2 + H_2O$$

(b) The spoilage of wine into vinegar:

$$C_2H_6O + O_2 \longrightarrow C_2H_4O_2 + H_2O$$

(c) The burning of rocket fuel:

$$C_2H_8N_2 + N_2O_4 \longrightarrow N_2 + CO_2 + H_2O$$

3.42 Balance the following equations:

(a) $SiCl_4 + H_2O \longrightarrow SiO_2 + HCl$

(b) $P_4O_{10} + H_2O \longrightarrow H_3PO_4$

(c) $CaCN_2 + H_2O \longrightarrow CaCO_3 + NH_3$

(d) $NO_2 + H_2O \longrightarrow HNO_3 + NO$

3.43 Balance the following equations:

(a) $VCl_3 + Na + CO \longrightarrow V(CO)_6 + NaCl$

(b) $RuI_3 + CO + Ag \longrightarrow Ru(CO)_5 + AgI$

(c) $CoS + CO + Cu \longrightarrow Co_2(CO)_8 + Cu_2S$

Molecular Masses and Stoichiometry (Section 3.3)

3.44 What are the molecular (formula) masses of the following substances?

(a) Hg_2Cl_2 (calomel, used at one time as a bowel purgative)

(b) $C_4H_8O_2$ (butyric acid, responsible for the odor of rancid butter)

(c) CF_2Cl_2 (a chlorofluorocarbon that destroys the stratospheric ozone layer)

3.45 What are the formulas of the following substances?

(a) $PCl_?$; Molec. mass = 137.3 amu

(b) Nicotine, $C_{10}H_{14}N_?$; Molec. mass = 162.2 amu

3.46 What are the molecular masses of the following pharmaceuticals?

(a) $C_{33}H_{35}FN_2O_5$ (atorvastatin, lowers blood cholesterol)

(b) $C_{22}H_{27}F_3O_4S$ (fluticasone, anti-inflammatory)

(c) $C_{16}H_{16}ClNO_2S$ (clopidogrel, inhibits blood clots)

3.47 What are the molecular masses of the following herbicides?

(a) $C_6H_6Cl_2O_3$ (2, 4-dichlorophenoxyacetic acid, effective on broadleaf plants)

(b) $C_{15}H_{22}ClNO_2$ (metolachlor, pre-emergent herbicide)

(c) $C_8H_6Cl_2O_3$ (dicamba, effective on broadleaf plants)

3.48 How many grams are in a mole of each of the following substances?

(a) Ti   (b) Br_2 (c) Hg   (d) H_2O

3.49 How many moles are in a gram of each of the following substances?

(a) Cr   (b) Cl_2 (c) Au   (d) NH_3

3.50 How many moles of ions are in 27.5 g of $MgCl_2$?

3.51 How many moles of anions are in 35.6 g of AlF_3?

3.52 What is the molecular mass of chloroform if 0.0275 mol weighs 3.28 g?

3.53 What is the molecular mass of cholesterol if 0.5731 mol weighs 221.6 g?

3.54 Iron(II) sulfate, $FeSO_4$, is prescribed for the treatment of anemia. How many moles of $FeSO_4$ are present in a standard 300 mg tablet? How many iron(II) ions?

3.55 The "lead" in lead pencils is actually almost pure carbon, and the mass of a period mark made by a lead pencil is about 0.0001 g. How many carbon atoms are in the period?

3.56 An average cup of coffee contains about 125 mg of caffeine, $C_8H_{10}N_4O_2$. How many moles of caffeine are in a cup? How many molecules of caffeine?

Caffeine

3.57 What is the mass in grams of each of the following samples?

(a) 0.0015 mol of sodium

(b) 0.0015 mol of lead

(c) 0.0015 mol of diazepam (Valium), $C_{16}H_{13}ClN_2O$

3.58 A sample that weighs 25.12 g contains 6.022×10^{23} particles. If 25.00% of the total number of particles are argon atoms and 75.00% are another element, what is the chemical identity of the other constituent?

3.59 A sample that weighs 107.75 g is a mixture of 30% helium atoms and 70% krypton atoms. How many particles are present in the sample?

3.60 Titanium metal is obtained from the mineral rutile, TiO_2. How many kilograms of rutile are needed to produce 100.0 kg of Ti?

3.61 Iron metal can be produced from the mineral hematite, Fe_2O_3, by reaction with carbon. How many kilograms of iron are present in 105 kg of hematite?

3.62 In the preparation of iron from hematite (Problem 3.61), Fe_2O_3 reacts with carbon:

$$Fe_2O_3 + C \longrightarrow Fe + CO_2 \quad \text{Unbalanced}$$

(a) Balance the equation.

(b) How many moles of carbon are needed to react with 525 g of hematite?

(c) How many grams of carbon are needed to react with 525 g of hematite?

3.63 An alternative method for preparing pure iron from Fe_2O_3 (Problem 3.61) is by reaction with carbon monoxide:

$$Fe_2O_3 + CO \longrightarrow Fe + CO_2 \quad \text{Unbalanced}$$

(a) Balance the equation.

(b) How many grams of CO are needed to react with 3.02 g of Fe_2O_3?

(c) How many grams of CO are needed to react with 1.68 mol of Fe_2O_3?

3.64 Magnesium metal burns in oxygen to form magnesium oxide, MgO.

(a) Write a balanced equation for the reaction.

(b) How many grams of oxygen are needed to react with 25.0 g of Mg? How many grams of MgO will result?

(c) How many grams of Mg are needed to react with 25.0 g of O_2? How many grams of MgO will result?

3.65 Ethylene gas, C_2H_4, reacts with water at high temperature to yield ethyl alcohol, C_2H_6O.

(a) How many grams of ethylene are needed to react with 0.133 mol of H_2O? How many grams of ethyl alcohol will result?

(b) How many grams of water are needed to react with 0.371 mol of ethylene? How many grams of ethyl alcohol will result?

3.66 Pure oxygen was first made by heating mercury(II) oxide:

$$HgO \xrightarrow{\text{Heat}} Hg + O_2 \quad \text{Unbalanced}$$

(a) Balance the equation.

(b) How many grams of mercury and how many grams of oxygen are formed from 45.5 g of HgO?

(c) How many grams of HgO would you need to obtain 33.3 g of O_2?

3.67 Titanium dioxide (TiO_2), the substance used as the pigment in white paint, is prepared industrially by reaction of $TiCl_4$ with O_2 at high temperature.

$$TiCl_4 + O_2 \xrightarrow{\text{Heat}} TiO_2 + 2\,Cl_2$$

How many kilograms of TiO_2 can be prepared from 5.60 kg of $TiCl_4$?

3.68 Silver metal reacts with chlorine (Cl_2) to yield silver chloride. If 2.00 g of Ag reacts with 0.657 g of Cl_2, what is the empirical formula of silver chloride?

3.69 Aluminum reacts with oxygen to yield aluminum oxide. If 5.0 g of Al reacts with 4.45 g of O_2, what is the empirical formula of aluminum oxide?

3.70 The industrial production of hydriodic acid takes place by treatment of iodine with hydrazine (N_2H_4):

$$2\,I_2 + N_2H_4 \longrightarrow 4\,HI + N_2$$

(a) How many grams of I_2 are needed to react with 36.7 g of N_2H_4?

(b) How many grams of HI are produced from the reaction of 115.7 g of N_2H_4 with excess iodine?

3.71 An alternative method for producing hydriodic acid (Problem 3.70) is the reaction of iodine with hydrogen sulfide:

$$H_2S + I_2 \longrightarrow 2\,HI + S$$

(a) How many grams of I_2 are needed to react with 49.2 g of H_2S?

(b) How many grams of HI are produced from the reaction of 95.4 g of H_2S with excess I_2?

Limiting Reactants and Reaction Yield
(Sections 3.4 and 3.5)

3.72 Assume that you have 1.39 mol of H_2 and 3.44 mol of N_2. How many grams of ammonia (NH_3) can you make, and how many grams of which reactant will be left over?

$$3\,H_2 + N_2 \longrightarrow 2\,NH_3$$

3.73 Hydrogen and chlorine react to yield hydrogen chloride: $H_2 + Cl_2 \rightarrow 2\,HCl$. How many grams of HCl are formed from reaction of 3.56 g of H_2 with 8.94 g of Cl_2? Which reactant is limiting?

3.74 How many grams of the dry-cleaning solvent 1,2-dichloroethane (also called ethylene chloride), $C_2H_4Cl_2$, can be prepared by reaction of 15.4 g of ethylene, C_2H_4, with 3.74 g of Cl_2?

$$C_2H_4 + Cl_2 \longrightarrow C_2H_4Cl_2$$

1,2-Dichloroethane
(ethylene chloride)

3.75 How many grams of each product result from the following reactions, and how many grams of which reactant is left over?

(a) $(1.3\ \text{g NaCl}) + (3.5\ \text{g AgNO}_3) \longrightarrow$
$$(x\ \text{g AgCl}) + (y\ \text{g NaNO}_3)$$

(b) $(2.65\ \text{g BaCl}_2) + (6.78\ \text{g H}_2\text{SO}_4) \longrightarrow$
$$(x\ \text{g BaSO}_4) + (y\ \text{g HCl})$$

3.76 Nickel(II) sulfate, used for nickel plating, is prepared by treatment of nickel(II) carbonate with sulfuric acid:

$$NiCO_3 + H_2SO_4 \longrightarrow NiSO_4 + CO_2 + H_2O$$

(a) How many grams of H_2SO_4 are needed to react with 14.5 g of $NiCO_3$?

(b) How many grams of $NiSO_4$ are obtained if the yield is 78.9%?

3.77 Hydrazine, N_2H_4, once used as a rocket propellant, reacts with oxygen:

$$N_2H_4 + O_2 \longrightarrow N_2 + 2\,H_2O$$

(a) How many grams of O_2 are needed to react with 50.0 g of N_2H_4?

(b) How many grams of N_2 are obtained if the yield is 85.5%?

3.78 Limestone ($CaCO_3$) reacts with hydrochloric acid according to the equation $CaCO_3 + 2\,HCl \rightarrow CaCl_2 + H_2O + CO_2$. If 1.00 mol of CO_2 has a volume of 22.4 L under the reaction conditions, how many liters of gas can be formed by reaction of 2.35 g of $CaCO_3$ with 2.35 g of HCl? Which reactant is limiting?

3.79 Sodium azide (NaN_3) yields N_2 gas when heated to 300 °C, a reaction used in automobile air bags. If 1.00 mol of N_2 has a volume of 47.0 L under the reaction conditions, how many liters of gas can be formed by heating 38.5 g of NaN_3? The reaction is

$$2\,NaN_3 \longrightarrow 3\,N_2(g) + 2\,Na$$

3.80 Acetic acid (CH_3CO_2H) reacts with isopentyl alcohol ($C_5H_{12}O$) to yield isopentyl acetate ($C_7H_{14}O_2$), a fragrant substance with the odor of bananas. If the yield from the reaction of acetic acid with isopentyl alcohol is 45%, how many grams of isopentyl acetate are formed from 3.58 g of acetic acid and 4.75 g of isopentyl alcohol? The reaction is

$$CH_3CO_2H + C_5H_{12}O \longrightarrow C_7H_{14}O_2 + H_2O$$

Isopentyl acetate

3.81 Cisplatin [$Pt(NH_3)_2Cl_2$], a compound used in cancer treatment, is prepared by reaction of ammonia with potassium tetrachloroplatinate:

$$K_2PtCl_4 + 2 NH_3 \longrightarrow 2 KCl + Pt(NH_3)_2Cl_2$$

How many grams of cisplatin are formed from 55.8 g of K_2PtCl_4 and 35.6 g of NH_3 if the reaction takes place in 95% yield based on the limiting reactant?

3.82 If 1.87 g of acetic acid reacts with 2.31 g of isopentyl alcohol to give 2.96 g of isopentyl acetate (Problem 3.80), what is the percent yield of the reaction?

3.83 If 3.42 g of K_2PtCl_4 and 1.61 g of NH_3 give 2.08 g of cisplatin (Problem 3.81), what is the percent yield of the reaction?

Molarity, Solution Stoichiometry, Dilution, and Titration (Sections 3.6–3.9)

3.84 How many moles of solute are present in each of the following solutions?
(a) 35.0 mL of 1.200 M HNO_3
(b) 175 mL of 0.67 M glucose ($C_6H_{12}O_6$)

3.85 How many grams of solute would you use to prepare each of the following solutions?
(a) 250.0 mL of 0.600 M ethyl alcohol (C_2H_6O)
(b) 167 mL of 0.200 M boric acid (H_3BO_3)

3.86 How many milliliters of a 0.45 M $BaCl_2$ solution contain 15.0 g of $BaCl_2$?

3.87 How many milliliters of a 0.350 M KOH solution contain 0.0171 mol of KOH?

3.88 The sterile saline solution used to rinse contact lenses can be made by dissolving 400 mg of NaCl in sterile water and diluting to 100 mL. What is the molarity of the solution?

3.89 The concentration of glucose ($C_6H_{12}O_6$) in normal blood is approximately 90 mg per 100 mL. What is the molarity of the glucose?

3.90 Copper reacts with dilute nitric acid according to the following equation:

$$3 Cu(s) + 8 HNO_3(aq) \longrightarrow$$
$$3 Cu(NO_3)_2(aq) + 2 NO(g) + 4 H_2O(l)$$

If a copper penny weighing 3.045 g is dissolved in a small amount of nitric acid and the resultant solution is diluted to 50.0 mL with water, what is the molarity of the $Cu(NO_3)_2$?

3.91 Pennies minted after 1982 are mostly zinc (97.5%) with a copper cover. If a post-1982 penny is dissolved in a small amount of nitric acid, the copper coating reacts as in Problem 3.90 and the exposed zinc reacts according to the following equation:

$$Zn(s) + 2 HNO_3(aq) \longrightarrow Zn(NO_3)_2(aq) + H_2(g)$$

For a penny that weighs 2.482 g, what is the molarity of the $Zn(NO_3)_2$ if the resultant solution is diluted to 250.0 mL with water?

3.92 A bottle of 12.0 M hydrochloric acid has only 35.7 mL left in it. What will the HCl concentration be if the solution is diluted to 250.0 mL?

3.93 What is the volume of the solution that would result by diluting 70.00 mL of 0.0913 M NaOH to a concentration of 0.0150 M?

3.94 A flask containing 450 mL of 0.500 M HBr was accidentally knocked to the floor. How many grams of K_2CO_3 would you need to put on the spill to neutralize the acid according to the following equation?

$$2 HBr(aq) + K_2CO_3(aq) \longrightarrow 2 KBr(aq) + CO_2(g) + H_2O(l)$$

3.95 The odor of skunks is caused by chemical compounds called *thiols*. These compounds, of which butanethiol ($C_4H_{10}S$) is a representative example, can be deodorized by reaction with household bleach (NaOCl) according to the following equation:

$$2 C_4H_{10}S + NaOCl(aq) \longrightarrow C_8H_{18}S_2 + NaCl + H_2O(aq)$$

Butanethiol

How many grams of butanethiol can be deodorized by reaction with 5.00 mL of 0.0985 M NaOCl?

3.96 Potassium permanganate ($KMnO_4$) reacts with oxalic acid ($H_2C_2O_4$) in aqueous sulfuric acid according to the following equation:

$$2 KMnO_4 + 5 H_2C_2O_4 + 3 H_2SO_4 \longrightarrow$$
$$2 MnSO_4 + 10 CO_2 + 8 H_2O + K_2SO_4$$

How many milliliters of a 0.250 M $KMnO_4$ solution are needed to react completely with 3.225 g of oxalic acid?

3.97 Oxalic acid, $H_2C_2O_4$, is a toxic substance found in spinach leaves. What is the molarity of a solution made by dissolving 12.0 g of oxalic acid in enough water to give 400.0 mL of solution? How many milliliters of 0.100 M KOH would you need to titrate 25.0 mL of the oxalic acid solution according to the following equation?

$$H_2C_2O_4(aq) + 2 KOH(aq) \longrightarrow K_2C_2O_4(aq) + 2 H_2O(l)$$

Oxalic acid

Formulas and Elemental Analysis (Sections 3.10 and 3.11)

3.98 Urea, a substance commonly used as a fertilizer, has the formula CH_4N_2O. What is its percent composition by mass?

Urea

3.99 Calculate the mass percent composition of each of the following substances:
(a) Malachite, a copper-containing mineral: $Cu_2(OH)_2CO_3$
(b) Acetaminophen, a headache remedy: $C_8H_9NO_2$
(c) Prussian blue, an ink pigment: $Fe_4[Fe(CN)_6]_3$

3.100 An unknown liquid is composed of 5.57% H, 28.01% Cl, and 66.42% C. The molecular mass found by mass spectrometry is 126.58 amu. What is the molecular formula of the compound?

3.101 An unknown liquid is composed of 34.31% C, 5.28% H, and 60.41% I. The molecular mass found by mass spectrometry is 210.06 amu. What is the molecular formula of the compound?

3.102 What is the empirical formula of stannous fluoride, the first fluoride compound added to toothpaste to protect teeth against decay? Its mass percent composition is 24.25% F, 75.75% Sn.

3.103 What are the empirical formulas of each of the following substances?

(a) Ibuprofen, a headache remedy: 75.69% C, 15.51% O, 8.80% H

(b) Magnetite, a naturally occurring magnetic mineral: 72.36% Fe, 27.64% O

(c) Zircon, a mineral from which cubic zirconia is made: 34.91% O, 15.32% Si, 49.77% Zr

3.104 Combustion analysis of 45.62 mg of toluene, a commonly used solvent, gives 35.67 mg of H_2O and 152.5 mg of CO_2. What is the empirical formula of toluene?

3.105 Coniine, a toxic substance isolated from poison hemlock, contains only carbon, hydrogen, and nitrogen. Combustion analysis of a 5.024 mg sample yields 13.90 mg of CO_2 and 6.048 mg of H_2O. What is the empirical formula of coniine?

3.106 Cytochrome c is an iron-containing enzyme found in the cells of all aerobic organisms. If cytochrome c is 0.43% Fe by mass, what is its minimum molecular mass?

3.107 Nitrogen fixation in the root nodules of peas and other leguminous plants is carried out by the molybdenum-containing enzyme *nitrogenase*. What is the molecular mass of nitrogenase if the enzyme contains two molybdenum atoms and is 0.0872% Mo by mass?

3.108 Disilane, Si_2H_x, is analyzed and found to contain 90.28% silicon by mass. What is the value of x?

3.109 A certain metal sulfide, MS_2, is used extensively as a high-temperature lubricant. If MS_2 is 40.06% sulfur by mass, what is the identity of the metal M?

3.110 The mass of an organic compound was found by mass spectrometry to be 70.042 11 amu. Is the sample C_5H_{10}, C_4H_6O, or $C_3H_6N_2$? Exact masses of elements are: 1.007 825 (^1H); 12.000 00 (^{12}C); 14.003 074 (^{14}N); 15.994 915 (^{16}O).

3.111 The mass of an organic compound was found by mass spectrometry to be 58.077 46 amu. Is the sample C_4H_{10}, C_3H_6O, or $C_2H_6N_2$? Exact masses of elements are: 1.007 825 (^1H); 12.000 00 (^{12}C); 14.003 074 (^{14}N); 15.994 915 (^{16}O).

3.112 Combustion analysis of a 31.472 mg sample of the widely used flame retardant Decabrom gave 1.444 mg of CO_2. Is the molecular formula of Decabrom $C_{12}Br_{10}$ or $C_{12}Br_{10}O$?

3.113 The stimulant amphetamine contains only carbon, hydrogen, and nitrogen. Combustion analysis of a 42.92 mg sample of amphetamine gives 37.187 mg of H_2O and 125.75 mg of CO_2. If the molar mass of amphetamine is less than 160 g/mol, what is its molecular formula?

Amphetamine

CHAPTER PROBLEMS

3.114 *Ringer's solution*, used in the treatment of burns and wounds, is prepared by dissolving 4.30 g of NaCl, 0.150 g of KCl, and 0.165 g of $CaCl_2$ in water and diluting to a volume of 500.0 mL. What is the molarity of each of the component ions in the solution?

3.115 Balance the following equations:

(a) $C_6H_5NO_2 + O_2 \longrightarrow CO_2 + H_2O + NO_2$

(b) $Au + H_2SeO_4 \longrightarrow Au_2(SeO_4)_3 + H_2SeO_3 + H_2O$

(c) $NH_4ClO_4 + Al \longrightarrow Al_2O_3 + N_2 + Cl_2 + H_2O$

3.116 The estimated concentration of gold in the oceans is 1.0×10^{-11} g/mL.

(a) Express the concentration in mol/L.

(b) Assuming that the volume of the oceans is 1.3×10^{21} L, estimate the amount of dissolved gold in grams in the oceans.

3.117 Silver sulfide, the tarnish on silverware, comes from reaction of silver metal with hydrogen sulfide (H_2S):

$$Ag + H_2S + O_2 \longrightarrow Ag_2S + H_2O \quad \text{Unbalanced}$$

(a) Balance the equation.

(b) If the reaction were used intentionally to prepare Ag_2S, how many grams would be formed from 496 g of Ag, 80.0 g of H_2S, and 40.0 g of O_2 if the reaction takes place in 95% yield based on the limiting reactant?

3.118 Give the percent composition of each of the following substances:

(a) Glucose, $C_6H_{12}O_6$

(b) Sulfuric acid, H_2SO_4

(c) Potassium permanganate, $KMnO_4$

(d) Saccharin, $C_7H_5NO_3S$

3.119 What are the empirical formulas of substances with the following mass percent compositions?

(a) Aspirin: 4.48% H, 60.00% C, 35.52% O

(b) Ilmenite (a titanium-containing ore): 31.63% O, 31.56% Ti, 36.81% Fe

(c) Sodium thiosulfate (photographic "fixer"): 30.36% O, 29.08% Na, 40.56% S

3.120 The reaction of tungsten hexachloride (WCl_6) with bismuth gives hexatungsten dodecachloride (W_6Cl_{12}).

$$WCl_6 + Bi \longrightarrow W_6Cl_{12} + BiCl_3 \quad \text{Unbalanced}$$

(a) Balance the equation.

(b) How many grams of bismuth react with 150.0 g of WCl_6?

(c) When 228 g of WCl_6 react with 175 g of Bi, how much W_6Cl_{12} is formed based on the limiting reactant?

3.121 Sodium borohydride, $NaBH_4$, a substance used in the synthesis of many pharmaceutical agents, can be prepared by reaction of NaH with B_2H_6 according to the equation $2\,NaH + B_2H_6 \rightarrow 2\,NaBH_4$.

(a) How many grams of $NaBH_4$ can be prepared by reaction between 8.55 g of NaH and 6.75 g of B_2H_6?

(b) Which reactant is limiting, and how many grams of the excess reactant will be left over?

3.122 Ferrocene, a substance proposed for use as a gasoline additive, has the percent composition 5.42% H, 64.56% C, and 30.02% Fe. What is the empirical formula of ferrocene?

3.123 The molar mass of HCl is 36.5 g/mol, and the average mass per HCl molecule is 36.5 amu. Use the fact that 1 amu = 1.6605×10^{-24} g to calculate Avogadro's number.

3.124 What is the molarity of each ion in a solution prepared by dissolving 0.550 g of Na_2SO_4, 1.188 g of Na_3PO_4, and 0.223 g of Li_2SO_4 in water and diluting to a volume of 100.00 mL?

3.125 Ethylene glycol, commonly used as automobile antifreeze, contains only carbon, hydrogen, and oxygen. Combustion analysis of a 23.46 mg sample yields 20.42 mg of H_2O and 33.27 mg of CO_2. What is the empirical formula of ethylene glycol? What is its molecular formula if it has a molecular mass of 62.0 amu?

3.126 The molecular mass of ethylene glycol (Problem 3.125) is 62.0689 amu when calculated using the atomic masses found in a standard periodic table, yet the molecular mass determined experimentally by high-resolution mass spectrometry is 62.0368 amu. Explain the discrepancy.

3.127 Balance the following equations:

(a) $CO(NH_2)_2(aq) + HOCl(aq) \longrightarrow$
$$NCl_3(aq) + CO_2(aq) + H_2O(l)$$

(b) $Ca_3(PO_4)_2(s) + SiO_2(s) + C(s) \longrightarrow$
$$P_4(g) + CaSiO_3(l) + CO(g)$$

3.128 Assume that gasoline has the formula C_8H_{18} and has a density of 0.703 g/mL. How many pounds of CO_2 are produced from the complete combustion of 1.00 gal of gasoline?

3.129 A sample of $CaCO_3$ with a mass of 6.35 g is placed in 500.0 mL of 0.31 M HCl, forming $CaCl_2$, H_2O, and CO_2. What mass in grams of CO_2 is produced?

3.130 Compound X contains only carbon, hydrogen, nitrogen, and chlorine. When 1.00 g of X is dissolved in water and allowed to react with excess silver nitrate, $AgNO_3$, all the chlorine in X reacts and 1.95 g of solid AgCl is formed. When 1.00 g of X undergoes complete combustion, 0.900 g of CO_2 and 0.735 g of H_2O are formed. What is the empirical formula of X?

3.131 A pulverized rock sample believed to be pure calcium carbonate, $CaCO_3$, is subjected to chemical analysis and found to contain 51.3% Ca, 7.7% C, and 41.0% O by mass. Why can't this rock sample be pure $CaCO_3$?

3.132 Salicylic acid, used in the manufacture of aspirin, contains only the elements C, H, and O and has only one acidic hydrogen that reacts with NaOH. When 1.00 g of salicylic acid undergoes complete combustion, 2.23 g CO_2 and 0.39 g H_2O are obtained. When 1.00 g of salicylic acid is titrated with 0.100 M NaOH, 72.4 mL of base is needed for complete reaction. What are the empirical and molecular formulas of salicylic acid?

3.133 Compound X contains only the elements C, H, O, and S. A 5.00 g sample undergoes complete combustion to give 4.83 g of CO_2, 1.48 g of H_2O, and a certain amount of SO_2 that is further oxidized to SO_3 and dissolved in water to form sulfuric acid, H_2SO_4. On titration of the H_2SO_4, 109.8 mL of 1.00 M NaOH is needed for complete reaction. (Both H atoms in sulfuric acid are acidic and react with NaOH.)

(a) What is the empirical formula of X?

(b) When 5.00 g of X is titrated with NaOH, it is found that X has two acidic hydrogens that react with NaOH and that 54.9 mL of 1.00 M NaOH is required to completely neutralize the sample. What is the molecular formula of X?

3.134 Assume that you have 1.00 g of a mixture of benzoic acid (molec. mass = 122 amu) and gallic acid (molec. mass = 170 amu), both of which contain one acidic hydrogen that reacts with NaOH. On titrating the mixture with 0.500 M NaOH, 14.7 mL of base is needed to completely react with both acids. What mass in grams of each acid is present in the original mixture?

3.135 A certain alcoholic beverage contains only ethanol (C_2H_6O) and water. When a sample of this beverage undergoes combustion, the ethanol burns but the water simply evaporates and is collected along with the water produced by combustion. The combustion reaction is

$$C_2H_6O(l) + 3\,O_2(g) \longrightarrow 2\,CO_2(g) + 3\,H_2O(g)$$

When a 10.00 g sample of this beverage is burned, 11.27 g of water is collected. What is the mass in grams of ethanol, and what is the mass of water in the original sample?

3.136 A mixture of FeO and Fe_2O_3 with a mass of 10.0 g is converted to 7.43 g of pure Fe metal. What are the amounts in grams of FeO and Fe_2O_3 in the original sample?

3.137 A compound of formula XCl_3 reacts with aqueous $AgNO_3$ to yield solid AgCl according to the following equation:

$$XCl_3(aq) + 3\,AgNO_3(aq) \longrightarrow X(NO_3)_3(aq) + 3\,AgCl(s)$$

When a solution containing 0.634 g of XCl_3 was allowed to react with an excess of aqueous $AgNO_3$, 1.68 g of solid AgCl was formed. What is the identity of the atom X?

3.138 When eaten, dietary carbohydrates are digested to yield glucose ($C_6H_{12}O_6$), which is then metabolized to yield carbon dioxide and water:

$$C_6H_{12}O_6 + O_2 \longrightarrow CO_2 + H_2O \quad \text{Unbalanced}$$

Balance the equation, and calculate both the mass in grams and the volume in liters of the CO_2 produced from 66.3 g of glucose, assuming that 1 mol of CO_2 has a volume of 25.4 L at normal body temperature.

3.139 Other kinds of titrations are possible in addition to acid–base titrations. For example, the concentration of a solution of potassium permanganate, $KMnO_4$, can be determined by titration against a known amount of oxalic acid, $H_2C_2O_4$, according to the following equation:

$$5\,H_2C_2O_4(aq) + 2\,KMnO_4(aq) + 3\,H_2SO_4(aq) \longrightarrow$$
$$10\,CO_2(g) + 2\,MnSO_4(aq) + K_2SO_4(aq) + 8\,H_2O(l)$$

What is the concentration of a $KMnO_4$ solution if 22.35 mL reacts with 0.5170 g of oxalic acid?

3.140 A copper wire having a mass of 2.196 g was allowed to react with an excess of sulfur. The excess sulfur was then burned, yielding SO_2 gas. The mass of the copper sulfide produced was 2.748 g.

(a) What is the percent composition of copper sulfide?

(b) What is its empirical formula?

(c) Calculate the number of copper ions per cubic centimeter if the density of the copper sulfide is 5.6 g/cm^3.

3.141 Element X, a member of group 5A, forms two chlorides, XCl_3 and XCl_5. Reaction of an excess of Cl_2 with 8.729 g of XCl_3 yields 13.233 g of XCl_5. What is the atomic mass and the identity of the element X?

3.142 A mixture of XCl_3 and XCl_5 (see Problem 3.141) weighing 10.00 g contains 81.04% Cl by mass. How many grams of XCl_3 and how many grams of XCl_5 are present in the mixture?

3.143 A 1.268 g sample of a metal carbonate (MCO_3) was treated with 100.00 mL of 0.1083 M sulfuric acid (H_2SO_4), yielding CO_2 gas and an aqueous solution of the metal sulfate (MSO_4). The solution was boiled to remove all the dissolved CO_2 and was then titrated with 0.1241 M NaOH. A 71.02 mL volume of NaOH was required to neutralize the excess H_2SO_4.

(a) What is the identity of the metal M?

(b) How many liters of CO_2 gas were produced if the density of CO_2 is 1.799 g/L?

3.144 Ammonium nitrate, a potential ingredient of terrorist bombs, can be made nonexplosive by addition of diammonium hydrogen phosphate, $(NH_4)_2HPO_4$. Analysis of such a $NH_4NO_3-(NH_4)_2HPO_4$ mixture showed the mass percent of nitrogen to be 30.43%. What is the mass ratio of the two components in the mixture?

3.145 Window glass is typically made by mixing soda ash (Na_2CO_3), limestone ($CaCO_3$), and silica sand (SiO_2) and then heating to 1500 °C to drive off CO_2 from the Na_2CO_3 and $CaCO_3$. The resultant glass consists of about 12% Na_2O by mass, 13% CaO by mass, and 75% SiO_2 by mass. How much of each reactant would you start with to prepare 0.35 kg of glass?

3.146 An unidentified metal M reacts with an unidentified halogen X to form a compound MX_2. When heated, the compound decomposes by the reaction:

$$2\,MX_2(s) \longrightarrow 2\,MX(s) + X_2(g)$$

When 1.12 g of MX_2 is heated, 0.720 g of MX is obtained, along with 56.0 mL of X_2 gas. Under the conditions used, 1.00 mol of the gas has a volume of 22.41 L.

(a) What is the atomic mass and identity of the halogen X?

(b) What is the atomic mass and identity of the metal M?

3.147 A compound with the formula $XOCl_2$ reacts with water, yielding HCl and another acid H_2XO_3, which has two acidic hydrogens that react with NaOH. When 0.350 g of $XOCl_2$ was added to 50.0 mL of water and the resultant solution was titrated, 96.1 mL of 0.1225 M NaOH was required to react with all the acid.

(a) Write a balanced equation for the reaction of $XOCl_2$ with H_2O.

(b) What are the atomic mass and identity of element X?

3.148 Element M is prepared industrially by a two-step procedure according to the following (unbalanced) equations:

(1) $M_2O_3(s) + C(s) + Cl_2(g) \longrightarrow MCl_3(l) + CO(g)$

(2) $MCl_3(l) + H_2(g) \longrightarrow M(s) + HCl(g)$

Assume that 0.855 g of M_2O_3 is submitted to the reaction sequence. When the HCl produced in step (2) is dissolved in water and titrated with 0.511 M NaOH, 144.2 mL of the NaOH solution is required to neutralize the HCl.

(a) Balance both equations.

(b) What is the atomic mass of element M, and what is its identity?

(c) What mass of M in grams is produced in the reaction?

CHAPTER 4

Reactions in Aqueous Solution

The corrosion evident on this sunken boat occurs by a typical oxidation–reduction reaction of the kind discussed in this chapter.

CONTENTS

Ours is a world based on water. Approximately 71% of the Earth's surface is covered by water, and another 3% is covered by ice; 66% of the mass of an adult human body is water, and water is needed to sustain all living organisms. It's therefore not surprising that a large amount of important chemistry takes place in water—that is, in *aqueous solution*.

We saw in the previous chapter how chemical reactions are described and how specific mass relationships among reactant and product substances must be obeyed when reactions occur. In this chapter, we'll continue our study of chemical reactions by seeing how different reactions can be classified and by learning some of the general ways reactions take place.

4.1 SOME WAYS THAT CHEMICAL REACTIONS OCCUR

In beginning a study of chemical reactions in aqueous solution, it's useful to classify them into three general categories: *precipitation reactions*, *acid–base neutralization reactions*, and *oxidation–reduction reactions*. Let's look briefly at an example of each before studying them in more detail in subsequent sections.

▲ Reaction of aqueous $Pb(NO_3)_2$ with aqueous KI gives a yellow precipitate of PbI_2.

- **Precipitation reactions** are processes in which soluble ionic reactants yield an insoluble solid product that drops out of the solution, thereby removing some of the dissolved ions. Most precipitations take place when the anions and cations of two ionic compounds change partners. For example, an aqueous solution of lead(II) nitrate reacts with an aqueous solution of potassium iodide to yield an aqueous solution of potassium nitrate plus an insoluble yellow precipitate of lead iodide:

$$Pb(NO_3)_2(aq) + 2\,KI(aq) \longrightarrow 2\,KNO_3(aq) + PbI_2(s)$$

- **Acid–base neutralization reactions** are processes in which an acid reacts with a base to yield water plus an ionic compound called a *salt*. Acids, as we'll see shortly, are compounds that produce H^+ ions when dissolved in water, and bases are compounds that produce OH^- ions when dissolved in water. Thus, a neutralization reaction removes H^+ and OH^- ions from solution, just as a precipitation reaction removes metal and nonmetal ions. The reaction between hydrochloric acid and aqueous sodium hydroxide to yield water plus aqueous sodium chloride is a typical example:

$$HCl(aq) + NaOH(aq) \longrightarrow H_2O(l) + NaCl(aq)$$

- **Oxidation–reduction reactions**, or **redox reactions**, are processes in which one or more electrons are transferred between reaction partners (atoms, molecules, or ions). As a result of this electron transfer, the charges on atoms in the various reactants change. When metallic magnesium reacts with aqueous hydrochloric acid, for instance, a magnesium atom gives an electron to each of two H^+ ions, forming an Mg^{2+} ion and an H_2 molecule. The charge on the magnesium changes from 0 to +2, and the charge on each hydrogen changes from +1 to 0:

$$Mg(s) + 2\,HCl(aq) \longrightarrow MgCl_2(aq) + H_2(g)$$

▸ **PROBLEM 4.1** Classify each of the following processes as a precipitation, acid–base neutralization, or redox reaction:
(a) $AgNO_3(aq) + KCl(aq) \longrightarrow AgCl(s) + KNO_3(aq)$
(b) $Cl_2(g) + 2\,NaBr(aq) \longrightarrow Br_2(aq) + 2\,NaCl(aq)$
(c) $Ca(OH)_2(aq) + 2\,HNO_3(aq) \longrightarrow 2\,H_2O(l) + Ca(NO_3)_2(aq)$

4.2 ELECTROLYTES IN AQUEOUS SOLUTION

We all know from experience that both sugar (sucrose) and table salt (NaCl) dissolve in water. The solutions that result, though, are quite different. When sucrose, a molecular substance, dissolves in water, the resulting solution contains neutral sucrose *molecules* surrounded by water. When NaCl, an ionic substance, dissolves in water, the solution contains separate Na^+ and Cl^- *ions* surrounded by water. Because of the presence of the charged ions, the NaCl solution conducts an electric current, but the sucrose solution does not.

$$C_{12}H_{22}O_{11}(s) \xrightarrow{H_2O} C_{12}H_{22}O_{11}(aq)$$
Sucrose

$$NaCl(s) \xrightarrow{H_2O} Na^+(aq) + Cl^-(aq)$$

The electrical conductivity of an aqueous NaCl solution is easy to demonstrate using a battery, a lightbulb, and several pieces of wire, connected as shown in **Figure 4.1**. When the wires are dipped into an aqueous NaCl solution, the positively charged Na^+ ions move through the solution toward the wire connected to the negatively charged terminal of the battery and the negatively charged Cl^- ions move toward the wire connected to the positively charged terminal of the battery. The resulting movement of electrical charges allows a current to flow, so the bulb lights. When the wires are dipped into an aqueous sucrose solution, however, there are no ions to carry the current, so the bulb remains dark.

A solution of NaCl conducts electricity because of the movement of charged particles (ions), thereby completing the circuit and allowing the bulb to light.

A solution of sucrose does not conduct electricity or complete the circuit because it contains no charged particles. The bulb therefore remains dark.

Figure 4.1

Testing the conductivity of aqueous solutions.

Substances such as NaCl or KBr, which dissolve in water to produce conducting solutions of ions, are called **electrolytes**. Substances such as sucrose or ethyl alcohol, which do not produce ions in aqueous solution, are **nonelectrolytes**. Most electrolytes are ionic compounds, but some are molecular. Hydrogen chloride, for instance, is a gaseous molecular compound when pure but **dissociates**, or splits apart to give H^+ and Cl^- ions, when it dissolves in water.

$$HCl(g) \xrightarrow{\text{H}_2\text{O}} H^+(aq) + Cl^-(aq)$$

Compounds that dissociate to a large extent (70–100%) into ions when dissolved in water are said to be **strong electrolytes**, while compounds that dissociate to only a small extent are **weak electrolytes**. Potassium chloride and most other ionic compounds, for instance, are largely dissociated in dilute solution and are thus strong electrolytes. Acetic acid (CH_3CO_2H), by contrast, dissociates only to the extent of about 1.3% in a 0.10 M solution and is a weak electrolyte. As a result, a 0.10 M solution of acetic acid is only weakly conducting.

For 0.10 M solutions:

$$KCl(aq) \rightleftharpoons K^+(aq) + Cl^-(aq) \quad \dashv \; \text{Strong electrolyte}$$
$$(2\%) \qquad\qquad (98\%)$$

$$CH_3CO_2H(aq) \rightleftharpoons H^+(aq) + CH_3CO_2^-(aq) \quad \dashv \; \text{Weak electrolyte}$$
$$(99\%) \qquad\qquad (1\%)$$

Note that when we write a dissociation equation, we often use a forward-and-backward double arrow ($\rightleftharpoons$) to indicate that the reaction takes place in both directions. That is, dissociation is a dynamic process in which an *equilibrium* is established between the forward and reverse reactions. The balance between the two opposing reactions defines the exact concentrations of the various species in solution. We'll learn much more about chemical equilibria in Chapters 13 and 14.

A brief list of some common substances classified according to their electrolyte strength is given in Table 4.1. Note that pure water is a nonelectrolyte because it does not dissociate appreciably into H^+ and OH^- ions. We'll explore the dissociation of water in more detail in Section 14.4.

TABLE 4.1   Electrolyte Classification of Some Common Substances

Strong Electrolytes	Weak Electrolytes	Nonelectrolytes
HCl, HBr, HI	CH_3CO_2H	H_2O
$HClO_4$	HF	CH_3OH (methyl alcohol)
HNO_3	HCN	C_2H_5OH (ethyl alcohol)
H_2SO_4		$C_{12}H_{22}O_{11}$ (sucrose)
KBr		Most compounds of carbon
NaCl		(organic compounds)
NaOH, KOH		
Other soluble ionic compounds		

WORKED EXAMPLE 4.1

CALCULATING THE CONCENTRATION OF IONS IN A SOLUTION

What is the total molar concentration of ions in a 0.350 M solution of the strong electrolyte Na_2SO_4, assuming complete dissociation?

STRATEGY

First, we need to know how many ions are produced by dissociation of Na_2SO_4. Writing the equation for dissolving Na_2SO_4 in water shows that 3 mol of ions are formed: 2 mol of Na^+ and 1 mol of SO_4^{2-}.

$$Na_2SO_4(s) \xrightarrow{\text{H}_2\text{O}} 2\,Na^+(aq) + SO_4^{2-}(aq)$$

continued on next page

SOLUTION

Assuming complete dissociation, the total molar concentration of ions is three times the molarity of Na_2SO_4, or 1.05 M:

$$\frac{0.350 \; \cancel{\text{mol } Na_2SO_4}}{1 \; L} \times \frac{3 \; \text{mol ions}}{1 \; \cancel{\text{mol } Na_2SO_4}} = 1.05 \; M$$

▶ **PROBLEM 4.2** What is the molar concentration of Br^- ions in a 0.225 M aqueous solution of $FeBr_3$, assuming complete dissociation?

CONCEPTUAL PROBLEM 4.3 Three different substances A_2X, A_2Y, and A_2Z are dissolved in water, with the following results. (Water molecules are omitted for clarity.) Which of the substances is the strongest electrolyte, and which is the weakest? Explain.

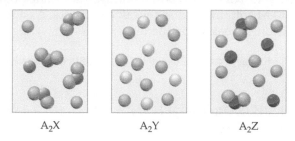

A_2X A_2Y A_2Z

4.3 AQUEOUS REACTIONS AND NET IONIC EQUATIONS

The equations we've been writing up to this point have all been **molecular equations**. That is, all the substances involved in the reactions have been written using their complete formulas as if they were *molecules*. In Section 4.1, for instance, we wrote the precipitation reaction of lead(II) nitrate with potassium iodide to yield solid PbI_2 using only the parenthetical (*aq*) to indicate that the substances are dissolved in aqueous solution. Nowhere in the equation was it indicated that ions are involved.

A molecular equation

$$Pb(NO_3)_2(aq) + 2 \, KI(aq) \longrightarrow 2 \, KNO_3(aq) + PbI_2(s)$$

In fact, lead nitrate, potassium iodide, and potassium nitrate are strong electrolytes that dissolve in water to yield solutions of ions. Thus, it's more accurate to write the precipitation reaction as an **ionic equation**, in which all the ions are explicitly shown.

An ionic equation

$$Pb^{2+}(aq) + 2 \, NO_3^-(aq) + 2 \, K^+(aq) + 2 \, I^-(aq) \longrightarrow 2 \, K^+(aq) + 2 \, NO_3^-(aq) + PbI_2(s)$$

A look at this ionic equation shows that the NO_3^- and K^+ ions undergo no change during the reaction. Instead, they appear on both sides of the reaction arrow and act merely as **spectator ions**, whose only role is to balance the charge. The actual reaction, when stripped to its essentials, can be described more simply by writing a **net ionic equation**, in which only the ions undergoing change are shown—the Pb^{2+} and I^- ions in this instance. The spectator ions are not shown in a net ionic equation.

An ionic equation

$$Pb^{2+}(aq) + 2 \, \cancel{NO_3^-}(aq) + 2 \, \cancel{K^+}(aq) + 2 \, I^-(aq) \longrightarrow 2 \, \cancel{K^+}(aq) + 2 \, \cancel{NO_3^-}(aq) + PbI_2(s)$$

A net ionic equation

$$Pb^{2+}(aq) + 2 \, I^-(aq) \longrightarrow PbI_2(s)$$

Leaving the spectator ions out of a net ionic equation doesn't imply that their presence is irrelevant. If a reaction occurs by mixing a solution of Pb^{2+} ions with a solution of I^- ions, then those solutions must also contain additional ions to balance the charge in each. The Pb^{2+} solution must also contain an anion, and the I^- solution must also contain a cation. Leaving these other ions out of the net ionic equation only implies that their specific identity is not important. Any nonreactive spectator ions could fill the same role.

WORKED EXAMPLE 4.2

WRITING A NET IONIC EQUATION

Aqueous hydrochloric acid reacts with zinc metal to yield hydrogen gas and aqueous zinc chloride. Write a net ionic equation for the process.

$$2\,HCl(aq) + Zn(s) \longrightarrow H_2(g) + ZnCl_2(aq)$$

STRATEGY

First, write the ionic equation, listing all the species present in solution. Both HCl (a molecular compound; Table 4.1) and $ZnCl_2$ (an ionic compound) are strong electrolytes that exist as ions in solution. Then find the ions that are present on both sides of the reaction arrow—the spectator ions—and cancel them, leaving the net ionic equation.

SOLUTION

Ionic equation

$$2\,H^+(aq) + \cancel{2\,Cl^-(aq)} + Zn(s) \longrightarrow H_2(g) + Zn^{2+}(aq) + \cancel{2\,Cl^-(aq)}$$

Net ionic equation

$$2\,H^+(aq) + Zn(s) \longrightarrow H_2(g) + Zn^{2+}(aq)$$

▶ **PROBLEM 4.4** Write net ionic equations for the following reactions:

(a) $2\,AgNO_3(aq) + Na_2CrO_4(aq) \longrightarrow Ag_2CrO_4(s) + 2\,NaNO_3(aq)$

(b) $H_2SO_4(aq) + MgCO_3(s) \longrightarrow H_2O(l) + CO_2(g) + MgSO_4(aq)$

(c) $Hg(NO_3)_2(aq) + 2\,NH_4I(aq) \longrightarrow HgI_2(s) + 2\,NH_4NO_3(aq)$

▲ Zinc metal reacts with aqueous hydrochloric acid to give hydrogen gas and aqueous Zn^{2+} ions.

4.4 PRECIPITATION REACTIONS AND SOLUBILITY GUIDELINES

To predict whether a precipitation reaction will occur on mixing aqueous solutions of two substances, you must know the **solubility** of each potential product—how much of each compound will dissolve in a given amount of solvent at a given temperature. If a substance has a low solubility in water, it's likely to precipitate from an aqueous solution. If a substance has a high solubility in water, no precipitate will form.

Solubility is a complex matter, and it's not always possible to make correct predictions about a substance. In addition, solubilities depend on the concentrations of the reactant ions, and the very words *soluble* and *insoluble* are imprecise. Using a concentration of 0.01 M as the lower limit a substance can have to be considered soluble, a compound is probably soluble if it meets either (or both) of the following criteria:

1. **A compound is probably soluble if it contains one of the following cations:**
   • Li^+, Na^+, K^+, Rb^+, Cs^+ (group 1A cations)
   • NH_4^+ (ammonium ion)

   That is, essentially all ionic compounds containing an alkali metal or ammonium cation are soluble in water and will not precipitate, regardless of the anions present.

2. **A compound is probably soluble if it contains one of the following anions:**
   • Cl^-, Br^-, I^- (halide)
       except: Ag^+, Hg_2^{2+}, and Pb^{2+} halides
   • NO_3^- (nitrate), ClO_4^- (perchlorate), $CH_3CO_2^-$ (acetate), and SO_4^{2-} (sulfate)
       except: Sr^{2+}, Ba^{2+}, Hg_2^{2+}, and Pb^{2+} sulfates

   That is, most ionic compounds containing a halide, nitrate, perchlorate, acetate, or sulfate anion are soluble in water and will not precipitate regardless of the cations present. The exceptions that *will* precipitate are silver (I), mercury(I), and Pb(II) halides, and strontium, barium, mercury(I), and lead(II) sulfates.

Looked at from the other side, a compound that does *not* contain one of the cations or anions listed above is probably *not* soluble. Thus, carbonates (CO_3^{2-}), sulfides (S^{2-}), phosphates (PO_4^{3-}), and hydroxides (OH^-) are generally not soluble unless they contain an alkali metal or ammonium cation. The main exceptions are the sulfides and hydroxides of Ca^{2+}, Sr^{2+}, Ba^{2+}. These guidelines are summarized in Table 4.2.

TABLE 4.2   Solubility Guidelines for Ionic Compounds in Water

Soluble Compounds	Common Exceptions
Li^+, Na^+, K^+, Rb^+, Cs^+ (group 1A cations)	None
NH_4^+ (ammonium ion)	None
Cl^-, Br^-, I^- (halide)	Halides of Ag^+, Hg_2^{2+}, Pb^{2+}
NO_3^- (nitrate)	None
ClO_4^- (perchlorate)	None
$CH_3CO_2^-$ (acetate)	None
SO_4^{2-} (sulfate)	Sulfates of Sr^{2+}, Ba^{2+}, Hg_2^{2+}, Pb^{2+}
Insoluble Compounds	**Common Exceptions**
CO_3^{2-} (carbonate)	Carbonates of group 1A cations, NH_4^+
S^{2-} (sulfide)	Sulfides of group 1A cations, NH_4^+, Ca^{2+}, Sr^{2+}, and Ba^{2+}
PO_4^{3-} (phosphate)	Phosphates of group 1A cations, NH_4^+
OH^- (hydroxide)	Hydroxides of group 1A cations, NH_4^+, Ca^{2+}, Sr^{2+}, and Ba^{2+}

You might notice that most of the ions that impart solubility to compounds are singly charged—either singly positive (Li^+, Na^+, K^+, Rb^+, Cs^+, NH_4^+) or singly negative (Cl^-, Br^-, I^-, NO_3^-, ClO_4^-, $CH_3CO_2^-$). Very few doubly charged ions or triply charged ions form soluble compounds. This solubility behavior arises because of the relatively strong ionic bonds in compounds containing ions with multiple charges. The greater the strength of the ionic bonds holding ions together in a crystal, the more difficult it is to break those bonds apart during the solution process. We'll return to this topic in Section 6.8.

The solubility guidelines not only let us predict whether a precipitate will form when solutions of two ionic compounds are mixed but also let us prepare a specific compound by purposefully carrying out a precipitation. If, for example, you wanted to prepare a sample of solid silver carbonate, Ag_2CO_3, you could mix a solution of $AgNO_3$ with a solution of Na_2CO_3. Both starting compounds are soluble in water, as is $NaNO_3$. Silver carbonate is the only insoluble combination of ions and will therefore precipitate from solution.

▲ Reaction of aqueous $AgNO_3$ with aqueous Na_2CO_3 gives a white precipitate of Ag_2CO_3.

$$2\,AgNO_3(aq) + Na_2CO_3(aq) \longrightarrow Ag_2CO_3(s) + 2\,NaNO_3(aq)$$

WORKED EXAMPLE 4.3

PREDICTING THE PRODUCT OF A PRECIPITATION REACTION

Will a precipitation reaction occur when aqueous solutions of $CdCl_2$ and $(NH_4)_2S$ are mixed? If so, write the net ionic equation.

STRATEGY

Write the possible reaction, identify the two potential products, and predict the solubility of each. In the present instance, $CdCl_2$ and $(NH_4)_2S$ might give CdS and NH_4Cl:

$$??\quad CdCl_2(aq) + (NH_4)_2S(aq) \longrightarrow CdS + 2\,NH_4Cl \quad ??$$

SOLUTION

Of the two possible products, the solubility guidelines predict that CdS, a sulfide, is insoluble and that NH_4Cl, an ammonium compound and a halide, is soluble. Thus, a precipitation reaction will likely occur:

$$Cd^{2+}(aq) + S^{2-}(aq) \longrightarrow CdS(s)$$

WORKED EXAMPLE 4.4

USING A PRECIPITATION REACTION TO PREPARE A SUBSTANCE

How might you use a precipitation reaction to prepare a sample of $CuCO_3$? Write the net ionic equation.

STRATEGY

To prepare a precipitate of $CuCO_3$, a soluble Cu^{2+} compound must react with a soluble CO_3^{2-} compound.

SOLUTION

A look at the solubility guidelines suggests that a soluble copper compound, such as $Cu(NO_3)_2$, and a soluble carbonate, such as Na_2CO_3, might work. (There are many other possibilities.)

$$Cu(NO_3)_2(aq) + Na_2CO_3(aq) \longrightarrow 2\,NaNO_3(aq) + CuCO_3(s)$$
$$Cu^{2+}(aq) + CO_3^{2-}(aq) \longrightarrow CuCO_3(s)$$

WORKED CONCEPTUAL EXAMPLE 4.5

IDENTIFYING PRECIPITATION REACTIONS

When aqueous solutions of two ionic compounds are mixed, the following results are obtained. (Only the anion of the first compound, represented by blue spheres, and the cation of the second compound, represented by red spheres, are shown.) Which cations and anions, chosen from the following lists, are compatible with the observed results?

Anion

$$\begin{bmatrix} NO_3^-,\ Cl^-, \\ CO_3^{2-},\ PO_4^{3-} \end{bmatrix}$$

Cation

$$\begin{bmatrix} Ca^{2+},\ Ag^+, \\ K^+,\ Cd^{2+} \end{bmatrix}$$

STRATEGY

The process represented in the drawing is a precipitation reaction because ions in solution drop to the bottom of the container in an ordered arrangement. Counting the spheres shows that the cation and anion react in equal numbers (8 of each), so they must have the same number of charges—either both singly charged or both doubly charged. (There is no triply charged cation in the list.) Look at all the possible combinations, and decide which would precipitate.

SOLUTION

Possible combinations of singly charged ions: $AgNO_3$, KNO_3, $AgCl$, KCl
Possible combinations of doubly charged ions: $CaCO_3$, $CdCO_3$

Of the possible combinations, $AgCl$, $CaCO_3$, and $CdCO_3$ are insoluble, so the anion might be Cl^- or CO_3^{2-} and the cation might be Ag^+, Ca^{2+}, or Cd^{2+}.

▶ **PROBLEM 4.5** Predict whether each of the following compounds is likely to be soluble in water:

(a) $CdCO_3$ (b) MgO (c) Na_2S
(d) $PbSO_4$ (e) $(NH_4)_3PO_4$ (f) $HgCl_2$

▶ **PROBLEM 4.6** Predict whether a precipitation reaction will occur in each of the following situations. Write a net ionic equation for each reaction that occurs.

(a) $NiCl_2(aq) + (NH_4)_2S(aq) \longrightarrow ?$ (b) $Na_2CrO_4(aq) + Pb(NO_3)_2(aq) \longrightarrow ?$
(c) $AgClO_4(aq) + CaBr_2(aq) \longrightarrow ?$ (d) $ZnCl_2(aq) + K_2CO_3(aq) \longrightarrow ?$

▶ **PROBLEM 4.7**   How might you use a precipitation reaction to prepare a sample of $Ca_3(PO_4)_2$? Write the net ionic equation.

CONCEPTUAL PROBLEM 4.8   An aqueous solution containing an anion, represented by blue spheres, is added to another solution containing a cation, represented by red spheres, and the following result is obtained. Which cations and anions, chosen from the following lists, are compatible with the observed results?

Anion   Cation

Anions: S^{2-}, PO_4^{3-}, SO_4^{2-}, ClO_4^-

Cations: Mg^{2+}, Fe^{3+}, NH_4^+, Zn^{2+}

4.5   ACIDS, BASES, AND NEUTRALIZATION REACTIONS

We've mentioned acids and bases briefly on several previous occasions, but now let's look more carefully at both. In 1777, the French chemist Antoine Lavoisier proposed that all acids contain a common element: oxygen. In fact, the word *oxygen* is derived from a Greek phrase meaning "acid former." Lavoisier's idea had to be modified, however, when the English chemist Sir Humphrey Davy (1778–1829) showed in 1810 that muriatic acid (now called hydrochloric acid) contains only hydrogen and chlorine but no oxygen. Davy's studies thus suggested that the common element in acids is *hydrogen*, not oxygen.

The relationship between acidic behavior and the presence of hydrogen in a compound was clarified in 1887 by the Swedish chemist Svante Arrhenius (1859–1927). Arrhenius proposed that an **acid** is a substance that dissociates in water to give hydrogen ions (H^+) and a **base** is a substance that dissociates in water to give hydroxide ions (OH^-):

An acid $HA(aq) \longrightarrow H^+(aq) + A^-(aq)$

A base $MOH(aq) \longrightarrow M^+(aq) + OH^-(aq)$

In these equations, HA is a general formula for an acid—for example, HCl or HNO_3—and MOH is a general formula for a metal hydroxide—for example, NaOH or KOH.

Although convenient to use in equations, the symbol $H^+(aq)$ does not really represent the structure of the ion present in aqueous solution. As a bare hydrogen nucleus (a proton) with no electron nearby, H^+ is much too reactive to exist by itself. Rather, the H^+ bonds to the oxygen atom of a water molecule, giving the more stable **hydronium ion, H_3O^+**. We'll sometimes write $H^+(aq)$ for convenience, particularly when balancing equations, but will more often write $H_3O^+(aq)$ to represent an aqueous acid solution. Hydrogen chloride, for instance, gives $Cl^-(aq)$ and $H_3O^+(aq)$ when it dissolves in water.

HCl H_2O H_3O^+ Cl^-

Different acids dissociate to different extents in aqueous solution. Acids that dissociate to a large extent are strong electrolytes and **strong acids**, whereas acids that dissociate to only a small extent are weak electrolytes and **weak acids**. We've already seen in Table 4.1, for instance, that HCl, $HClO_4$, HNO_3, and H_2SO_4 are strong electrolytes and therefore strong acids, while CH_3CO_2H and HF are weak electrolytes and therefore weak acids. You might note that acetic acid actually contains four hydrogens, but only the one bonded to the oxygen atom dissociates.

Acetic Acid

Nonacidic

Acidic

Different acids can have different numbers of acidic hydrogens and yield different numbers of H_3O^+ ions in solution. Hydrochloric acid (HCl) is said to be a **monoprotic acid** because it provides only one H^+ ion, but sulfuric acid (H_2SO_4) is a **diprotic acid** because it can provide two H^+ ions. Phosphoric acid (H_3PO_4) is a **triprotic acid** and can provide three H^+ ions. With sulfuric acid, the first dissociation of an H^+ is complete—all H_2SO_4 molecules lose one H^+—but the second dissociation is incomplete, as indicated by the double arrow in the following equation:

Sulfuric acid:
$$H_2SO_4(aq) + H_2O(l) \longrightarrow HSO_4^-(aq) + H_3O^+(aq)$$
$$HSO_4^-(aq) + H_2O(l) \rightleftharpoons SO_4^{2}{}^-(aq) + H_3O^+(aq)$$

With phosphoric acid, none of the three dissociations is complete:

Phosphoric acid:
$$H_3PO_4(aq) + H_2O(l) \rightleftharpoons H_2PO_4^-(aq) + H_3O^+(aq)$$
$$H_2PO_4^-(aq) + H_2O(l) \rightleftharpoons HPO_4^{2-}(aq) + H_3O^+(aq)$$
$$HPO_4^{2-}(aq) + H_2O(l) \rightleftharpoons PO_4^{3-}(aq) + H_3O^+(aq)$$

Bases, like acids, can also be either strong or weak, depending on the extent to which they dissociate and produce OH^- ions in aqueous solution. Most metal hydroxides, such as $NaOH$ and $Ba(OH)_2$, are strong electrolytes and **strong bases**, but ammonia (NH_3) is a weak electrolyte and a **weak base**. Ammonia is weakly basic, not because it contains OH^- ions in its formula, but because it reacts to a small extent with water to yield NH_4^+ and OH^- ions. In fact, aqueous solutions of ammonia are often called *ammonium hydroxide*, although this is really a misnomer because the concentrations of NH_4^+ and OH^- ions are low.

$$NH_3(g) + H_2O(l) \rightleftharpoons NH_4^+(aq) + OH^-(aq)$$

As with the dissociation of acetic acid, discussed in Section 4.2, the reaction of ammonia with water takes place only to a small extent (about 1%). Most of the ammonia remains unreacted, and we therefore write the reaction with a double arrow to show that a dynamic equilibrium exists between the forward and reverse reactions.

Table 4.3 summarizes the names, formulas, and classification of some common acids and bases.

▲ Shouldn't this bottle be labeled "Aqueous Ammonia" rather than "Ammonium Hydroxide"?

TABLE 4.3   Some Common Acids and Bases

Strong acid	$HClO_4$	Perchloric acid	$NaOH$	Sodium hydroxide	Strong base
	H_2SO_4	Sulfuric acid	KOH	Potassium hydroxide	
	HBr	Hydrobromic acid	$Ba(OH)_2$	Barium hydroxide	
	HCl	Hydrochloric acid	$Ca(OH)_2$	Calcium hydroxide	
	HNO_3	Nitric acid			
	H_3PO_4	Phosphoric acid	NH_3	Ammonia	
	HF	Hydrofluoric acid			
Weak acid	HNO_2	Nitrous acid			Weak base
	CH_3CO_2H	Acetic acid			

Remember...

Oxoanions are binary polyatomic anions in which an atom of a given element is combined with different numbers of oxygen atoms. (Section 2.12)

Naming Acids

Most acids are **oxoacids**, meaning that they contain oxygen in addition to hydrogen and another element. When dissolved in water, an oxoacid yields one or more H^+ ions and an **oxoanion** like those we saw in Section 2.12 (Table 2.4).

TABLE 4.4   Common Oxoacids and Their Anions

Oxoacid		Oxoanion	
HNO_2	Nit*rous* acid	NO_2^-	Nit*rite* ion
HNO_3	Nit*ric* acid	NO_3^-	Nit*rate* ion
H_3PO_4	Phosphor*ic* acid	PO_4^{3-}	Phosph*ate* ion
H_2SO_3	Sulfur*ous* acid	SO_3^{2-}	Sulf*ite* ion
H_2SO_4	Sulfur*ic* acid	SO_4^{2-}	Sulf*ate* ion
$HClO$	*Hypo*chlor*ous* acid	ClO^-	*Hypo*chlor*ite* ion
$HClO_2$	Chlor*ous* acid	ClO_2^-	Chlor*ite* ion
$HClO_3$	Chlor*ic* acid	ClO_3^-	Chlor*ate* ion
$HClO_4$	*Per*chlor*ic* acid	ClO_4^-	*Per*chlor*ate* ion

The names of oxoacids are related to the names of the corresponding oxoanions, with the *-ite* or *-ate* ending of the anion name replaced by *-ous acid* or *-ic acid*, respectively. In other words, the acid with fewer oxygens has an *-ous* ending, and the acid with more oxygens has an *-ic* ending. The compound HNO_2, for example, is called *nitrous acid* because it has fewer oxygens and yields the nit*rite* ion (NO_2^-) when dissolved in water, while HNO_3 is called *nitric acid* because it has more oxygens and yields the nit*rate* ion (NO_3^-) when dissolved in water.

Nit*rous* acid gives nit*rite* ion

$$HNO_2(aq) + H_2O(l) \rightleftharpoons H_3O^+(aq) + NO_2^-(aq)$$

Nit*ric* acid gives nit*rate* ion

$$HNO_3(aq) + H_2O(l) \longrightarrow H_3O^+(aq) + NO_3^-(aq)$$

In a similar way, hypochlor*ous* acid yields the hypochlor*ite* ion, chlor*ous* acid yields the chlor*ite* ion, chlor*ic* acid yields the chlor*ate* ion, and perchlor*ic* acid yields the perchlor*ate* ion (Table 4.4).

In addition to the oxoacids, there are a small number of other common acids, such as HCl, that do not contain oxygen. For such compounds, the prefix *hydro-* and the suffix *-ic acid* are used for the aqueous solution.

Hydrogen chloride gives *hydro*chlor*ic acid*

$$HCl(g) + H_2O(l) \xrightarrow{\text{Dissolve in water}} H_3O^+(aq) + Cl^-(aq)$$

Hydrogen cyanide gives *hydro*cyan*ic acid*

$$HCN(g) + H_2O(l) \underset{\text{Dissolve in water}}{\rightleftharpoons} H_3O^+(aq) + CN^-(aq)$$

WORKED EXAMPLE 4.6

NAMING ACIDS

Name the following acids:

(a) $HBrO(aq)$ **(b)** $H_2S(aq)$

STRATEGY

To name an acid, look at the formula and decide whether the compound is an oxoacid. If so, the name must reflect the number of oxygen atoms, according to Table 4.4. If the compound is not an oxoacid, it is named using the prefix *hydro-* and the suffix *-ic acid*.

SOLUTION

(a) This compound is an oxoacid that yields hypobromite ion (BrO^-) when dissolved in water. Its name is hypobromous acid.

(b) This compound is not an oxoacid but yields sulfide ion when dissolved in water. As a pure gas, H_2S is named hydrogen sulfide. In water solution, it is called hydrosulfuric acid.

▶ **PROBLEM 4.9**   Name the following acids:

(a) HIO_4 (b) $HBrO_2$ (c) H_2CrO_4

▶ **PROBLEM 4.10**   Give likely chemical formulas corresponding to the following names:

(a) Phosphorous acid   (b) Hydroselenic acid

Neutralization Reactions

When an acid and a base are mixed in the right stoichiometric proportion, both acidic and basic properties disappear because of a neutralization reaction that produces water and an ionic **salt**. The anion of the salt (A^-) comes from the acid, and the cation of the salt (M^+) comes from the base:

A neutralization reaction

$$\underset{\text{Acid}}{HA(aq)} + \underset{\text{Base}}{MOH(aq)} \longrightarrow \underset{\text{Water}}{H_2O(l)} + \underset{\text{A salt}}{MA(aq)}$$

Because salts are generally strong electrolytes in aqueous solution, we can write the neutralization reaction of a strong acid with a strong base as an ionic equation:

$$H^+(aq) + A^-(aq) + M^+(aq) + OH^-(aq) \longrightarrow H_2O(l) + M^+(aq) + A^-(aq)$$

Canceling the ions that appear on both sides of the ionic equation gives the net ionic equation, which describes the reaction of any strong acid with any strong base in water:

$$H^+(aq) + \cancel{A^-(aq)} + \cancel{M^+(aq)} + OH^-(aq) \longrightarrow H_2O(l) + \cancel{M^+(aq)} + \cancel{A^-(aq)}$$
$$H^+(aq) + OH^-(aq) \longrightarrow H_2O(l)$$
$$\text{or}\quad H_3O^+(aq) + OH^-(aq) \longrightarrow 2\,H_2O(l)$$

For the reaction of a weak acid with a strong base, a similar neutralization occurs, but we must write the molecular formula of the acid rather than simply $H^+(aq)$, because the dissociation of the acid in water is incomplete. Instead, the acid exists primarily as the neutral molecule. In the reaction of the weak acid HF with the strong base KOH, for example, we write the net ionic equation as

$$HF(aq) + OH^-(aq) \longrightarrow H_2O(l) + F^-(aq)$$

WORKED EXAMPLE 4.7

WRITING IONIC AND NET IONIC EQUATIONS FOR AN ACID–BASE REACTION

Write both an ionic equation and a net ionic equation for the neutralization reaction of aqueous HBr and aqueous $Ba(OH)_2$.

STRATEGY

Hydrogen bromide is a strong acid whose aqueous solution contains H^+ ions and Br^- ions. Barium hydroxide is a strong base whose aqueous solution contains Ba^{2+} and OH^- ions. Thus, we have a mixture of four different ions on the reactant side. Write the neutralization reaction as an ionic equation, and then cancel spectator ions to give the net ionic equation.

SOLUTION

Ionic equation

$$2\,H^+(aq) + 2\,Br^-(aq) + Ba^{2+}(aq) + 2\,OH^-(aq) \longrightarrow 2\,H_2O(l) + 2\,Br^-(aq) + Ba^{2+}(aq)$$

Net ionic equation

$$2\,H^+(aq) + 2\,OH^-(aq) \longrightarrow 2\,H_2O(l)$$
$$\text{or}\quad H^+(aq) + OH^-(aq) \longrightarrow H_2O(l)$$

The reaction of HBr with $Ba(OH)_2$ involves the combination of a proton (H^+) from the acid with OH^- from the base to yield water and an aqueous salt ($BaBr_2$).

▶ **PROBLEM 4.11** Write a balanced ionic equation and net ionic equation for each of the following acid–base reactions:

(a) $2\,CsOH(aq) + H_2SO_4(aq) \longrightarrow$ (b) $Ca(OH)_2(aq) + 2\,CH_3CO_2H(aq) \longrightarrow$

CONCEPTUAL PROBLEM 4.12 The following pictures represent aqueous solutions of three acids HA (A = X, Y, or Z), with water molecules omitted for clarity. Which of the three is the strongest acid, and which is the weakest?

= HA   = H_3O^+ = A^-

HX   HY   HZ

4.6 OXIDATION–REDUCTION (REDOX) REACTIONS

Purple aqueous permanganate ion, $MnO_4{}^-$, reacts with aqueous Fe^{2+} ion to yield Fe^{3+} and pale pink Mn^{2+}. Magnesium metal burns in air with an intense white light to form solid magnesium oxide. Red phosphorus reacts with liquid bromine to form liquid phosphorus tribromide. Although these and many thousands of other reactions appear unrelated, and many don't even take place in aqueous solution, all are *oxidation–reduction (redox)* reactions.

$$MnO_4{}^-(aq) + 5\,Fe^{2+}(aq) + 8\,H^+(aq) \longrightarrow Mn^{2+}(aq) + 5\,Fe^{3+}(aq) + 4\,H_2O(l)$$

$$2\,Mg(s) + O_2(g) \longrightarrow 2\,MgO(s)$$

$$2\,P(s) + 3\,Br_2(l) \longrightarrow 2\,PBr_3(l)$$

▲ Aqueous potassium permanganate, deep purple in color, is frequently used as an *oxidizing agent*, as described in the text.

▲ Magnesium metal burns in air to give MgO.

▲ Elemental phosphorus reacts spectacularly with bromine to give PBr_3.

Historically, the word *oxidation* referred to the combination of an element with oxygen to yield an oxide, and the word *reduction* referred to the removal of oxygen from an oxide to yield the element. Such oxidation–reduction processes have been crucial to the development of human civilization and still have enormous commercial value. The oxidation (rusting) of iron metal by reaction with moist air has been known for millennia and is still a serious problem that causes enormous structural damage to buildings, boats, and bridges. The reduction of iron ore (Fe_2O_3) with charcoal (C) to make iron metal has been carried out since prehistoric times and is still used today in the initial stages of steelmaking.

$$4\,Fe(s) + 3\,O_2(g) \longrightarrow 2\,Fe_2O_3(s) \qquad \text{Rusting of iron: an \textbf{oxidation} of Fe}$$

$$2\,Fe_2O_3(s) + 3\,C(s) \longrightarrow 4\,Fe(s) + 3\,CO_2(g) \qquad \text{Manufacture of iron: a \textbf{reduction} of } Fe_2O_3$$

Today, the words oxidation and reduction have taken on a much broader meaning. An **oxidation** is now defined as the loss of one or more electrons by a substance, whether element, compound, or ion, and a **reduction** is the gain of one or more electrons by a substance. Thus, an **oxidation–reduction**, or **redox**, **reaction** is any process in which electrons are transferred from one substance to another.

$$\text{Oxidation} \longrightarrow$$

$$A^{2-} \longrightarrow A^- + \text{electron}$$
$$A^- \longrightarrow A + \text{electron}$$
$$A \longrightarrow A^+ + \text{electron}$$
$$A^+ \longrightarrow A^{2+} + \text{electron}$$

Reactant A might be:
a neutral atom,
a monatomic ion,
a polyatomic ion,
or a molecule.

$$\longleftarrow \text{Reduction}$$

How can you tell when a redox reaction takes place? The answer is that we can assign to each atom in a compound a value called an **oxidation number** (or *oxidation state*), which indicates whether the atom is neutral, electron-rich, or electron-poor. By comparing the oxidation number of an atom before and after reaction, we can tell whether the atom has gained or lost electrons. Note that oxidation numbers don't necessarily imply ionic charges; they are just a convenient device to help keep track of electrons during redox reactions.

The rules for assigning oxidation numbers are as follows:

1. **An atom in its elemental state has an oxidation number of 0.** For example:

Na   H$_2$ Br$_2$ S   Ne

Oxidation number 0

2. **An atom in a monatomic ion has an oxidation number identical to its charge.** Review Section 2.12 to see the charges on some common ions. For example:

Na^+ Ca^{2+} Al^{3+} Cl^- O^{2-}
+1   +2   +3   −1   −2

3. **An atom in a polyatomic ion or in a molecular compound usually has the same oxidation number it would have if it were a monatomic ion.** In the hydroxide ion (OH^-), for instance, the hydrogen atom has an oxidation number of +1, as if it were H^+, and the oxygen atom has an oxidation number of −2, as if it were a monatomic O^{2-} ion.

In general, the farther left an element is in the periodic table, the more probable that it will be "cationlike." Metals, therefore, usually have positive oxidation numbers. The farther right an element is in the periodic table, the more probable that it will be "anionlike." Nonmetals, such as O, N, and the halogens, usually have negative oxidation numbers. We'll see the reasons for these trends in Sections 6.3–6.5.

(a) **Hydrogen can be either +1 or −1.** When bonded to a metal, such as Na or Ca, hydrogen has an oxidation number of −1. When bonded to a nonmetal, such as C, N, O, or Cl, hydrogen has an oxidation number of +1.

$$Na{-}H \qquad H{-}Ca{-}H \qquad H{-}Cl \qquad H{-}S{-}H$$
$$\;+1 \quad -1 \qquad -1 \quad +2 \quad -1 \qquad +1 \quad -1 \qquad +1 \quad -2 \quad +1$$

(b) **Oxygen usually has an oxidation number of −2.** The major exception is in compounds called *peroxides*, which contain either the O_2^{2-} ion or an O—O covalent bond in a molecule. Both oxygen atoms in a peroxide have an oxidation number of −1.

$$H{-}O{-}H \qquad H{-}O{-}O{-}H \qquad [O{-}O]^{2-}$$
$$+1 \quad -2 \quad +1 \qquad +1 \quad -1 \quad -1 \quad +1 \qquad -1 \quad -1$$

(c) **Halogens usually have an oxidation number of −1.** The major exception is in compounds of chlorine, bromine, or iodine in which the halogen atom is bonded to oxygen. In such cases, the oxygen has an oxidation number of −2, and the halogen has a positive oxidation number. In Cl_2O, for instance, the O atom has an oxidation number of −2 and each Cl atom has an oxidation number of +1.

$$Cl{-}O{-}Cl \qquad H{-}O{-}Br$$
$$+1 \quad -2 \quad +1 \qquad +1 \quad -2 \quad +1$$

4. **The sum of the oxidation numbers is 0 for a neutral compound and is equal to the net charge for a polyatomic ion.** This rule is particularly useful for finding the oxidation number of an atom in difficult cases. The general idea is to assign oxidation numbers to the "easy" atoms first and then find the oxidation number of the "difficult" atom by subtraction. For example, suppose we need to know the oxidation number of the sulfur atom in sulfuric acid (H_2SO_4). Since each H atom is +1 and each O atom is −2, the S atom must have an oxidation number of +6 for the compound to have no net charge:

$$H_2SO_4 \qquad 2(+1) + (?) + 4(-2) = 0 \text{ net charge}$$
$$+1 \quad ? \quad -2 \qquad ? = 0 - 2(+1) - 4(-2) = +6$$

To find the oxidation number of the chlorine atom in the perchlorate anion (ClO_4^-), we know that each oxygen is −2, so the Cl atom must have an oxidation number of +7 for there to be a net charge of −1 on the ion:

$$ClO_4^- \qquad ? + 4(-2) = -1 \text{ net charge}$$
$$? \quad -2 \qquad ? = -1 - 4(-2) = +7$$

To find the oxidation number of the nitrogen atom in the ammonium cation (NH_4^+), we know that each H atom is +1, so the N atom must have an oxidation number of −3 for the ion to have a net charge of +1:

$$NH_4^+ \qquad ? + 4(+1) = +1 \text{ net charge}$$
$$? \quad +1 \qquad ? = +1 - 4(+1) = -3$$

WORKED EXAMPLE 4.8

ASSIGNING OXIDATION NUMBERS

Assign oxidation numbers to each atom in the following substances:

(a) CdS (b) AlH_3 (c) $S_2O_3^{2-}$ (d) $Na_2Cr_2O_7$

STRATEGY
(a) The sulfur atom in S^{2-} has an oxidation number of -2, so Cd must be $+2$.
(b) H bonded to a metal has the oxidation number -1, so Al must be $+3$.
(c) O usually has the oxidation number -2, so S must be $+2$ for the anion to have a net charge of -2: for $(2\,S^{+2})(3\,O^{-2})$, $2(+2) + 3(-2) = -2$ net charge.
(d) Na is always $+1$, and oxygen is -2, so Cr must be $+6$ for the compound to be neutral: for $(2\,Na^{+})(2\,Cr^{+6})(7\,O^{-2})$, $2(+1) + 2(+6) + 7(-2) = 0$ net charge.

SOLUTION

(a) CdS (b) AlH₃ (c) S₂O₃²⁻ (d) Na₂Cr₂O₇
   +2 −2   +3 −1   +2 −2   +1 +6 −2

▸ **PROBLEM 4.13** Assign an oxidation number to each atom in the following compounds:
(a) $SnCl_4$ (b) CrO_3 (c) $VOCl_3$
(d) V_2O_3 (e) HNO_3 (f) $FeSO_4$

4.7 IDENTIFYING REDOX REACTIONS

Once oxidation numbers are assigned, it's clear why all the reactions mentioned in the previous section are redox processes. Take the rusting of iron, for example. Two of the reactants, Fe and O_2, are elements, and both therefore have an oxidation number of 0. In the product, however, the oxygen atoms have an oxidation number of -2 and the iron atoms have an oxidation number of $+3$. Thus, Fe has undergone a change from 0 to $+3$ (a loss of electrons, or oxidation), and O has undergone a change from 0 to -2 (a gain of electrons, or reduction). Note that the total number of electrons given up by the atoms being oxidized (4 Fe × 3 electrons/Fe = 12 electrons) is the same as the number gained by the atoms being reduced (6 O × 2 electrons/O = 12 electrons).

A similar analysis can be carried out for the production of iron metal from its ore. The iron atom is reduced because it goes from an oxidation number of $+3$ in the reactant (Fe_2O_3) to 0 in the product (Fe). At the same time, the carbon atom is oxidized because it goes from an oxidation number of 0 in the reactant (C) to $+4$ in the product (CO_2).

The oxygen atoms undergo no change because they have an oxidation number of -2 in both reactant and product. The total number of electrons given up by the atoms being oxidized (3 C × 4 electrons/C = 12 electrons) is the same as the number gained by the atoms being reduced (4 Fe × 3 electrons/Fe = 12 electrons).

As these examples show, oxidations and reductions always occur together. Whenever one atom loses one or more electrons, another atom must gain those

▲ The iron used in this prehistoric dagger handle was made by the reduction of iron ore with charcoal.

electrons. The substance that *causes* a reduction by giving up electrons—the iron atom in the reaction of Fe with O_2 and the carbon atom in the reaction of C with Fe_2O_3—is called a **reducing agent**. The substance that causes an oxidation by accepting electrons—the oxygen atom in the reaction of Fe with O_2 and the iron atom in the reaction of C with Fe_2O_3—is called an **oxidizing agent**. The reducing agent is itself oxidized when it gives up electrons, and the oxidizing agent is itself reduced when it accepts electrons.

Reducing agent:	Oxidizing agent:
• Causes reduction	• Causes oxidation
• Loses one or more electrons	• Gains one or more electrons
• Undergoes oxidation	• Undergoes reduction
• Oxidation number of atom increases	• Oxidation number of atom decreases

We'll see in later chapters that redox reactions are common for almost every element in the periodic table except for the noble gas elements of group 8A. In general, metals give up electrons and act as reducing agents, while reactive nonmetals such as O_2 and the halogens accept electrons and act as oxidizing agents.

Oxidizing agents; gain e⁻

Reducing agents; lose e⁻

Different metals can give up different numbers of electrons in redox reactions. Lithium, sodium, and the other group 1A elements give up only one electron and become monopositive ions with oxidation numbers of +1. Beryllium, magnesium, and the other group 2A elements, however, typically give up two electrons and become dipositive ions. The transition metals in the middle of the periodic table can give up a variable number of electrons to yield more than one kind of ion depending on the exact reaction. Titanium, for example, can react with chlorine to yield either $TiCl_3$ or $TiCl_4$. Because a chloride ion has a −1 oxidation number, the titanium atom in $TiCl_3$ must have a +3 oxidation number and the titanium atom in $TiCl_4$ must be +4.

WORKED EXAMPLE 4.9

IDENTIFYING OXIDIZING AND REDUCING AGENTS

Assign oxidation numbers to all atoms, tell in each case which substance is undergoing oxidation and which reduction, and identify the oxidizing and reducing agents.

(a) $Ca(s) + 2 H^+(aq) \longrightarrow Ca^{2+}(aq) + H_2(g)$

(b) $2 Fe^{2+}(aq) + Cl_2(aq) \longrightarrow 2 Fe^{3+}(aq) + 2 Cl^-(aq)$

STRATEGY AND SOLUTION

(a) The elements Ca and H_2 have oxidation numbers of 0; Ca^{2+} is +2 and H^+ is +1:

$$\underset{0}{Ca(s)} + \underset{+1}{2 H^+(aq)} \longrightarrow \underset{+2}{Ca^{2+}(aq)} + \underset{0}{H_2(g)}$$

Ca is oxidized because its oxidation number increases from 0 to +2, and H^+ is reduced because its oxidation number decreases from +1 to 0. The reducing agent is the substance that gives away electrons, thereby going to a higher oxidation number, and the oxidizing agent is the substance that accepts electrons, thereby going to a lower oxidation number. In the present case, calcium is the reducing agent and H^+ is the oxidizing agent.

(b) Atoms of the neutral element Cl_2 have an oxidation number of 0; the monatomic ions have oxidation numbers equal to their charge:

$$2\,Fe^{2+}(aq) \ + \ Cl_2(aq) \longrightarrow 2\,Fe^{3+}(aq) \ + \ 2\,Cl^-(aq)$$
$$\quad\;\uparrow\qquad\qquad\uparrow\qquad\qquad\uparrow\qquad\qquad\uparrow$$
$$\quad\;+2\qquad\qquad0\qquad\qquad+3\qquad\qquad-1$$

Fe^{2+} is oxidized because its oxidation number increases from +2 to +3, and Cl_2 is reduced because its oxidation number decreases from 0 to -1. Fe^{2+} is the reducing agent, and Cl_2 is the oxidizing agent.

▶ **PROBLEM 4.14** Aqueous copper(II) ion reacts with aqueous iodide ion to yield solid copper(I) iodide and aqueous iodine. Write the balanced net ionic equation, assign oxidation numbers to all species present, and identify the oxidizing and reducing agents.

▶ **PROBLEM 4.15** In each of the following reactions, tell which substance is undergoing an oxidation and which a reduction, and identify the oxidizing and reducing agents.

(a) $SnO_2(s) + 2\,C(s) \longrightarrow Sn(s) + 2\,CO(g)$

(b) $Sn^{2+}(aq) + 2\,Fe^{3+}(aq) \longrightarrow Sn^{4+}(aq) + 2\,Fe^{2+}(aq)$

(c) $4\,NH_3(g) + 5\,O_2(g) \longrightarrow 4\,NO(g) + 6\,H_2O(l)$

4.8 THE ACTIVITY SERIES OF THE ELEMENTS

The reaction of an aqueous cation, usually a metal ion, with a free element to give a different cation and a different element is among the simplest of all redox processes. Aqueous copper(II) ion reacts with iron metal, for example, to give iron(II) ion and copper metal (**Figure 4.2**):

$$Fe(s) + Cu^{2+}(aq) \longrightarrow Fe^{2+}(aq) + Cu(s)$$

Figure 4.2
The redox reaction of iron with aqueous copper(II) ion.

Similarly, aqueous acid reacts with magnesium metal to yield magnesium ion and hydrogen gas:

$$Mg(s) + 2\,H^+(aq) \longrightarrow Mg^{2+}(aq) + H_2(g)$$

Whether a reaction occurs between a given ion and a given element depends on the relative ease with which the various substances gain or lose electrons—that is, on how easily each substance is reduced or oxidized. By noting the results from a succession of different reactions, it's possible to construct an **activity series**, which ranks the elements in order of their reducing ability in aqueous solution (Table 4.5).

TABLE 4.5　A Partial Activity Series of the Elements

Oxidation Reaction

Strongly reducing	These elements react rapidly with aqueous H^+ ions (acid) or with liquid H_2O to release H_2 gas.	$Li \longrightarrow Li^+ + e^-$ $K \longrightarrow K^+ + e^-$ $Ba \longrightarrow Ba^{2+} + 2\,e^-$ $Ca \longrightarrow Ca^{2+} + 2\,e^-$ $Na \longrightarrow Na^+ + e^-$
	These elements react with aqueous H^+ ions or with steam to release H_2 gas.	$Mg \longrightarrow Mg^{2+} + 2\,e^-$ $Al \longrightarrow Al^{3+} + 3\,e^-$ $Mn \longrightarrow Mn^{2+} + 2\,e^-$ $Zn \longrightarrow Zn^{2+} + 2\,e^-$ $Cr \longrightarrow Cr^{3+} + 3\,e^-$ $Fe \longrightarrow Fe^{2+} + 2\,e^-$
	These elements react with aqueous H^+ ions to release H_2 gas.	$Co \longrightarrow Co^{2+} + 2\,e^-$ $Ni \longrightarrow Ni^{2+} + 2\,e^-$ $Sn \longrightarrow Sn^{2+} + 2\,e^-$
		$H_2 \longrightarrow 2\,H^+ + 2\,e^-$
Weakly reducing	These elements do not react with aqueous H^+ ions to release H_2.	$Cu \longrightarrow Cu^{2+} + 2\,e^-$ $Ag \longrightarrow Ag^+ + e^-$ $Hg \longrightarrow Hg^{2+} + 2\,e^-$ $Pt \longrightarrow Pt^{2+} + 2\,e^-$ $Au \longrightarrow Au^{3+} + 3\,e^-$

Elements at the top of Table 4.5 give up electrons readily and are stronger reducing agents, whereas elements at the bottom give up electrons less readily and are weaker reducing agents. As a result, any element higher in the activity series will reduce the ion of any element lower in the activity series. Because copper is above silver, for example, copper metal gives electrons to Ag^+ ions (**Figure 4.3**).

$$Cu(s) + 2\,Ag^+(aq) \longrightarrow Cu^{2+}(aq) + 2\,Ag(s)$$

Conversely, because gold is below silver in the activity series, gold metal does not give electrons to Ag^+ ions.

$$Au(s) + 3\,Ag^+(aq) \not\longrightarrow Au^{3+}(aq) + 3\,Ag(s) \quad \textit{Does not occur}$$

The position of hydrogen in the activity series is particularly important because it indicates which metals react with aqueous acid (H^+) to release H_2 gas. The metals at the top of the series—the alkali metals of group 1A and alkaline earth metals of

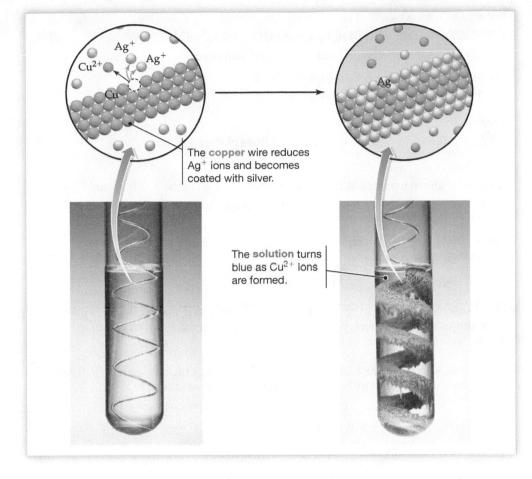

Figure 4.3
The redox reaction of copper with aqueous Ag^+ ion.

The **copper** wire reduces Ag^+ ions and becomes coated with silver.

The **solution** turns blue as Cu^{2+} ions are formed.

group 2A—are such powerful reducing agents that they react even with pure water, in which the concentration of H^+ is very low:

Oxidized   Reduced   Unchanged

$$2\,Na(s) \; + \; 2\,H_2O(l) \longrightarrow 2\,Na^+(aq) \; + \; 2\,OH^-(aq) \; + \; H_2(g)$$

$$\begin{array}{ccccc} 0 & +1\;-2 & +1 & -2\;+1 & 0 \end{array}$$

In contrast, the metals in the middle of the series react with aqueous acid but not with water, and the metals at the bottom of the series react with neither aqueous acid nor water:

$$Fe(s) \; + \; 2\,H^+(aq) \longrightarrow Fe^{2+}(aq) \; + \; H_2(g)$$

$$Ag(s) \; + \; H^+(aq) \longrightarrow \text{No reaction}$$

Notice that the most easily oxidized metals—those at the top of the activity series—are on the left of the periodic table, whereas the least easily oxidized metals—those at the bottom of the activity series—are in the transition metal groups closer to the right side of the table. We'll see the reasons for this behavior in Chapter 6.

More active metals   Less active metals

WORKED EXAMPLE 4.10

PREDICTING THE PRODUCTS OF REDOX REACTIONS

Predict whether the following redox reactions will occur:

(a) $Hg^{2+}(aq) + Zn(s) \longrightarrow Hg(l) + Zn^{2+}(aq)$

(b) $2 H^+(aq) + Cu(s) \longrightarrow H_2(g) + Cu^{2+}(aq)$

STRATEGY

Look at Table 4.5 to find the relative reactivities of the elements.

SOLUTION

(a) Zinc is above mercury in the activity series, so this reaction will occur.

(b) Copper is below hydrogen in the activity series, so this reaction will not occur.

▶ **PROBLEM 4.16**   Predict whether the following reactions will occur:

(a) $2 H^+(aq) + Pt(s) \longrightarrow H_2(g) + Pt^{2+}(aq)$

(b) $Ca^{2+}(aq) + Mg(s) \longrightarrow Ca(s) + Mg^{2+}(aq)$

▶ **PROBLEM 4.17**   Element B will reduce the cation of element A (A^+) but will not reduce the cation of element C (C^+). Will element C reduce the cation of element A? Explain.

▶ **PROBLEM 4.18**   Use the following reactions to arrange the elements A, B, C, and D in order of their redox reactivity from most reactive to least reactive.

$$A + D^+ \longrightarrow A^+ + D \qquad\qquad C^+ + D \longrightarrow C + D^+$$
$$B^+ + D \longrightarrow B + D^+ \qquad\qquad B + C^+ \longrightarrow B^+ + C$$

4.9 BALANCING REDOX REACTIONS: THE HALF-REACTION METHOD

Simple redox reactions can often be balanced by the trial-and-error method described in Section 3.1, but many reactions are so complex that a more systematic approach is needed. A number of different methods are available, but we'll look only at the **half-reaction method**, which focuses on the transfer of electrons, a subject of particular interest when discussing batteries and other aspects of electrochemistry (Chapter 17).

The key to the half-reaction method is to realize that a redox reaction can be broken into two parts, or **half-reactions**. One half-reaction describes the oxidation part of the process, and the other describes the reduction part. Each half is balanced separately, and the two halves are then added to obtain the final equation. As an example, let's look at the reaction of aqueous potassium dichromate ($K_2Cr_2O_7$) with aqueous NaCl. The reaction occurs in acidic solution according to the unbalanced net ionic equation

$$Cr_2O_7{}^{2-}(aq) + Cl^-(aq) \longrightarrow Cr^{3+}(aq) + Cl_2(aq) \quad \text{Unbalanced}$$

The first step is to decide which atoms have been oxidized and which have been reduced. In the present case, the chloride ion is oxidized from -1 to 0, and the chromium atom is reduced from $+6$ to $+3$. Thus, we can write two unbalanced half-reactions that show the separate parts:

$$\text{Oxidation half-reaction:} \quad Cl^-(aq) \longrightarrow Cl_2(aq)$$

$$\text{Reduction half-reaction:} \quad Cr_2O_7{}^{2-}(aq) \longrightarrow Cr^{3+}(aq)$$

With the two half-reactions identified, each is balanced separately. Begin by balancing for all atoms other than H and O. The oxidation half-reaction needs a

◀ The orange **dichromate ion** is reduced by addition of Cl^- to give the green Cr^{3+} ion.

coefficient of 2 before the Cl^-, and the reduction half-reaction needs a coefficient of 2 before the Cr^{3+}.

Oxidation   Add this coefficient to balance for Cl.
$$2\,Cl^-(aq) \longrightarrow Cl_2(aq)$$

Reduction   Add this coefficient to balance for Cr.
$$Cr_2O_7^{2-}(aq) \longrightarrow 2\,Cr^{3+}(aq)$$

Next, balance both half-reactions for oxygen by adding H_2O to the side with less O, and then balance for hydrogen by adding H^+ to the side with less H. The oxidation half-reaction has no O or H, but the reduction half-reaction needs 7 H_2O on the product side to balance for O, and then 14 H^+ on the reactant side to balance for H:

Oxidation $$2\,Cl^-(aq) \longrightarrow Cl_2(aq)$$

Reduction   Then, add 14 H^+ to balance for H.   First, add 7 H_2O to balance for O.
$$Cr_2O_7^{2-}(aq) + 14\,H^+(aq) \longrightarrow 2\,Cr^{3+}(aq) + 7\,H_2O(l)$$

Now, balance both half-reactions for charge by adding electrons (e^-) to the side with the greater positive charge. The oxidation half-reaction has 2 minus charges on the reactant side (2 Cl^-) and must therefore have 2 e^- added to the product side. The reduction half-reaction has a net of 12 positive charges on the reactant side and 6 positive charges on the product side and so must have 6 e^- added to the reactant side:

Oxidation   Add these electrons to balance for charge.
$$2\,Cl^-(aq) \longrightarrow Cl_2(aq) + 2\,e^-$$

Reduction   Add these electrons to balance for charge.
$$Cr_2O_7^{2-}(aq) + 14\,H^+(aq) + 6\,e^- \longrightarrow 2\,Cr^{3+}(aq) + 7\,H_2O(l)$$

With both half-reactions now balanced, we need to multiply the equations by suitable coefficients so that the number of electrons is the same in both. That is, the number of electrons released in the oxidation half-reaction must be the same as the number consumed in the reduction half-reaction. Because the reduction half-reaction has $6\,e^-$ but the oxidation half-reaction has only $2\,e^-$, the oxidation half-reaction must be multiplied by 3:

Multiply by this coefficient to equalize the numbers of electrons in the two half-reactions.

Oxidation $3 \times [2\,Cl^-(aq) \longrightarrow Cl_2(aq) + 2\,e^-]$

or $6\,Cl^-(aq) \longrightarrow 3\,Cl_2(aq) + 6\,e^-$

Reduction $Cr_2O_7^{2-}(aq) + 14\,H^+(aq) + 6\,e^- \longrightarrow 2\,Cr^{3+}(aq) + 7\,H_2O(l)$

Adding the two half-reactions together and canceling the species that occur on both sides (only the electrons in this example) then gives the final balanced equation. Check the answer to make sure it is balanced both for atoms and for charge.

$$6\,Cl^-(aq) \longrightarrow 3\,Cl_2(aq) + \cancel{6\,e^-}$$

$$Cr_2O_7^{2-}(aq) + 14\,H^+(aq) + \cancel{6\,e^-} \longrightarrow 2\,Cr^{3+}(aq) + 7\,H_2O(l)$$

$$Cr_2O_7^{2-}(aq) + 14\,H^+(aq) + 6\,Cl^-(aq) \longrightarrow 3\,Cl_2(aq) + 2\,Cr^{3+}(aq) + 7\,H_2O(l)$$

Charge: $(-2) + (+14) + (6 \times -1) = +6$ Charge: $(2 \times +3) = +6$

To summarize, balancing a redox reaction in acidic solution by the half-reaction method is a six-step process, followed by a check of the answer (**Figure 4.4.**)

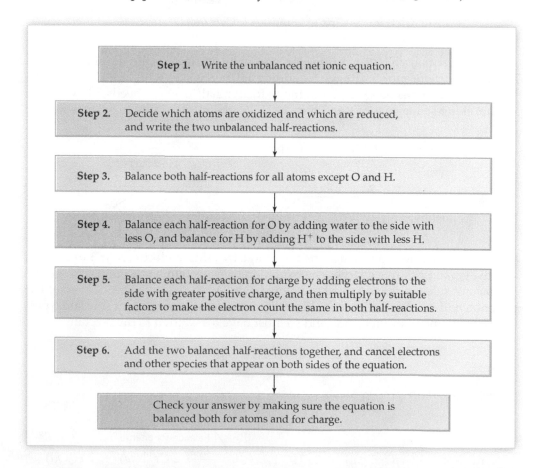

Step 1.   Write the unbalanced net ionic equation.

Step 2.   Decide which atoms are oxidized and which are reduced, and write the two unbalanced half-reactions.

Step 3.   Balance both half-reactions for all atoms except O and H.

Step 4.   Balance each half-reaction for O by adding water to the side with less O, and balance for H by adding H^+ to the side with less H.

Step 5.   Balance each half-reaction for charge by adding electrons to the side with greater positive charge, and then multiply by suitable factors to make the electron count the same in both half-reactions.

Step 6.   Add the two balanced half-reactions together, and cancel electrons and other species that appear on both sides of the equation.

Check your answer by making sure the equation is balanced both for atoms and for charge.

Figure 4.4
Using the half-reaction method to balance redox equations for reactions in acidic solution.

Worked Example 4.12 shows how to use the method for balancing an equation for a reaction that takes place in basic solution. The procedure is the same as that used for balancing a reaction in acidic solution, but OH^- ions are added as a final step to neutralize any H^+ ions that appear in the equation. This simply reflects the fact that basic solutions contain negligibly small amounts of H^+ but relatively large amounts of OH^-.

WORKED EXAMPLE 4.11

WRITING HALF-REACTIONS

Write unbalanced half-reactions for the following net ionic equations:

(a) $Mn^{2+}(aq) + ClO_3^-(aq) \longrightarrow MnO_2(s) + ClO_2(aq)$

(b) $Cr_2O_7^{2-}(aq) + Fe^{2+}(aq) \longrightarrow Cr^{3+}(aq) + Fe^{3+}(aq)$

STRATEGY

Look at each equation to see which atoms are being oxidized (increasing in oxidation number) and which are being reduced (decreasing in oxidation number).

SOLUTION

(a) Oxidation: $Mn^{2+}(aq) \longrightarrow MnO_2(s)$ Mn goes from +2 to +4

  Reduction: $ClO_3^-(aq) \longrightarrow ClO_2(aq)$ Cl goes from +5 to +4

(b) Oxidation: $Fe^{2+}(aq) \longrightarrow Fe^{3+}(aq)$ Fe goes from +2 to +3

  Reduction: $Cr_2O_7^{2-}(aq) \longrightarrow Cr^{3+}(aq)$ Cr goes from +6 to +3

WORKED EXAMPLE 4.12

BALANCING AN EQUATION FOR A REACTION IN BASE

Aqueous sodium hypochlorite (NaOCl; household bleach) is a strong oxidizing agent that reacts with chromite ion $[Cr(OH)_4^-]$ in basic solution to yield chromate ion (CrO_4^{2-}) and chloride ion. The net ionic equation is

$$ClO^-(aq) + Cr(OH)_4^-(aq) \longrightarrow CrO_4^{2-}(aq) + Cl^-(aq) \quad \text{Unbalanced}$$

Balance the equation using the half-reaction method.

STRATEGY

Follow the steps outlined in Figure 4.4.

SOLUTION

Steps 1 and 2. The unbalanced net ionic equation shows that chromium is oxidized (from +3 to +6) and chlorine is reduced (from +1 to −1). Thus, we can write the following half-reactions:

Oxidation half-reaction: $Cr(OH)_4^-(aq) \longrightarrow CrO_4^{2-}(aq)$

Reduction half-reaction: $ClO^-(aq) \longrightarrow Cl^-(aq)$

Step 3. The half-reactions are already balanced for atoms other than O and H.

Step 4. Balance both half-reactions for O by adding H_2O to the sides with less O, and then balance both for H by adding H^+ to the sides with less H:

Oxidation: $Cr(OH)_4^-(aq) \longrightarrow CrO_4^{2-}(aq) + 4\,H^+(aq)$

Reduction: $ClO^-(aq) + 2\,H^+(aq) \longrightarrow Cl^-(aq) + H_2O(l)$

Step 5. Balance both half-reactions for charge by adding electrons to the sides with the greater positive charge:

Oxidation: $Cr(OH)_4^-(aq) \longrightarrow CrO_4^{2-}(aq) + 4\,H^+(aq) + 3\,e^-$

Reduction: $ClO^-(aq) + 2\,H^+(aq) + 2\,e^- \longrightarrow Cl^-(aq) + H_2O(l)$

   Next, multiply the half-reactions by factors that make the electron count in each the same. The oxidation half-reaction must be multiplied by 2, and the reduction half-reaction must be multiplied by 3 to give 6 e^- in both:

Oxidation: $2 \times [Cr(OH)_4^-(aq) \longrightarrow CrO_4^{2-}(aq) + 4\,H^+(aq) + 3\,e^-]$

  or $2\,Cr(OH)_4^-(aq) \longrightarrow 2\,CrO_4^{2-}(aq) + 8\,H^+(aq) + 6\,e^-$

Reduction: $3 \times [ClO^-(aq) + 2\,H^+(aq) + 2\,e^- \longrightarrow Cl^-(aq) + H_2O(l)]$

  or $3\,ClO^-(aq) + 6\,H^+(aq) + 6\,e^- \longrightarrow 3\,Cl^-(aq) + 3\,H_2O(l)$

continued on next page

Step 6. Add the balanced half-reactions:

$$2\,Cr(OH)_4^-(aq) \longrightarrow 2\,CrO_4^{2-}(aq) + 8\,H^+(aq) + 6\,e^-$$

$$3\,ClO^-(aq) + 6\,H^+(aq) + 6\,e^- \longrightarrow 3\,Cl^-(aq) + 3\,H_2O(l)$$

$$2\,Cr(OH)_4^-(aq) + 3\,ClO^-(aq) + 6\,H^+(aq) + 6\,e^- \longrightarrow$$
$$2\,CrO_4^{2-}(aq) + 3\,Cl^-(aq) + 3\,H_2O(l) + 8\,H^+(aq) + 6\,e^-$$

Now, cancel the species that appear on both sides of the equation:

$$2\,Cr(OH)_4^-(aq) + 3\,ClO^-(aq) \longrightarrow 2\,CrO_4^{2-}(aq) + 3\,Cl^-(aq) + 3\,H_2O(l) + 2\,H^+(aq)$$

Finally, since we know that the reaction takes place in basic solution, we must add 2 OH^- ions to both sides of the equation to neutralize the 2 H^+ ions on the right, giving 2 additional H_2O. The final net ionic equation, balanced for both atoms and charge, is

$$2\,Cr(OH)_4^-(aq) + 3\,ClO^-(aq) + 2\,OH^-(aq) \longrightarrow 2\,CrO_4^{2-}(aq) + 3\,Cl^-(aq) + 5\,H_2O(l)$$

Charge: $(2 \times -1) + (3 \times -1) + (2 \times -1) = -7$ Charge: $(2 \times -2) + (3 \times -1) = -7$

▶ **PROBLEM 4.19** Write unbalanced half-reactions for the following net ionic equations:

(a) $MnO_4^-(aq) + IO_3^-(aq) \longrightarrow MnO_2(s) + IO_4^-(aq)$

(b) $NO_3^-(aq) + SO_2(aq) \longrightarrow SO_4^{2-}(aq) + NO_2(g)$

▶ **PROBLEM 4.20** Balance the following net ionic equation by the half-reaction method. The reaction takes place in acidic solution.

$$NO_3^-(aq) + Cu(s) \longrightarrow NO(g) + Cu^{2+}(aq) \quad \text{Unbalanced}$$

▶ **PROBLEM 4.21** Balance the following equation by the half-reaction method. The reaction takes place in basic solution.

$$Fe(OH)_2(s) + O_2(g) \longrightarrow Fe(OH)_3(s) \quad \text{Unbalanced}$$

4.10 REDOX STOICHIOMETRY

Remember...

The reaction used for a **titration** must go to completion and have a yield of 100%. (Section 3.9)

We saw in Section 3.9 that the concentration of an acid or base solution can be determined by **titration**. A measured volume of the acid or base solution of unknown concentration is placed in a flask, and a base or acid solution of known concentration is slowly added from a buret. By measuring the volume of the added solution necessary for a complete reaction, as signaled by the color change of an indicator, the unknown concentration can be calculated.

A similar procedure can be carried out to determine the concentration of many oxidizing or reducing agents using a *redox titration*. All that's necessary is that the substance whose concentration you want to determine undergo an oxidation or reduction reaction in 100% yield and that there be some means, such as a color change, to indicate when the reaction is complete. The color change might be due to one of the substances undergoing reaction or to some added indicator.

Let's imagine that we have a potassium permanganate solution whose concentration we want to find. Aqueous $KMnO_4$ reacts with oxalic acid, $H_2C_2O_4$, in acidic solution according to the net ionic equation

$$5\,H_2C_2O_4(aq) + 2\,MnO_4^-(aq) + 6\,H^+(aq) \longrightarrow 10\,CO_2(g) + 2\,Mn^{2+}(aq) + 8\,H_2O(l)$$

The reaction takes place in 100% yield and is accompanied by a sharp color change when the intense purple color of the MnO_4^- ion disappears.

The strategy used is outlined in **Figure 4.5**. As with acid–base titrations, the general idea is to measure a known amount of one substance—in this case, $H_2C_2O_4$—and use mole ratios from the balanced equation to find the number of moles of the second substance—in this case, $KMnO_4$—necessary for complete reaction. With the molar

For the balanced equation:

$$5\, H_2C_2O_4 + 2\, MnO_4^- + 6\, H^+ \longrightarrow 10\, CO_2 + 2\, Mn^{2+} + 8\, H_2O$$

GIVEN   FIND

| Mass of $H_2C_2O_4$ | Moles of $H_2C_2O_4$ | Moles of $KMnO_4$ | Molarity of $KMnO_4$ |

Use molar mass as a conversion factor.   Use coefficients in the balanced equation to find mole ratios.   Divide by volume of $KMnO_4$ solution.

Figure 4.5
A summary of calculations for determining the concentration of a $KMnO_4$ solution by redox titration of $H_2C_2O_4$.

amount of $KMnO_4$ thus known, titration gives the volume of solution containing that amount. Dividing the number of moles by the volume gives the concentration.

As an example of how the procedure works, let's carefully weigh some amount of $H_2C_2O_4$—say, 0.2585 g—and dissolve it in approximately 100 mL of 0.5 M H_2SO_4. The exact volume isn't important because we're concerned only with the amount of dissolved $H_2C_2O_4$, not with its concentration. Next, we place an aqueous $KMnO_4$ solution of unknown concentration in a buret and slowly add it to the $H_2C_2O_4$ solution. The purple color of MnO_4^- initially disappears as reaction occurs, but we continue the addition until a faint color persists, indicating that all the $H_2C_2O_4$ has reacted and that MnO_4^- ion is no longer being reduced. At this equivalence point, or *end point*, of the titration, we might find that 22.35 mL of the $KMnO_4$ solution has been added (**Figure 4.6**).

A precise amount of oxalic acid is weighed and dissolved in aqueous H_2SO_4.

Aqueous KMnO₄ of unknown concentration is added from a buret until …

… the purple color persists, indicating that all of the oxalic acid has reacted.

Figure 4.6
The redox titration of oxalic acid, $H_2C_2O_4$, with $KMnO_4$.

To calculate the molarity of the $KMnO_4$ solution, we need to find the number of moles of $KMnO_4$ present in the 22.35 mL of solution used for titration. We do this by first calculating the number of moles of oxalic acid that react with the permanganate ion, using a gram-to-mole conversion with the molar mass of $H_2C_2O_4$ as the conversion factor:

$$\text{Moles of } H_2C_2O_4 = 0.2585 \text{ g } \cancel{H_2C_2O_4} \times \frac{1 \text{ mol } H_2C_2O_4}{90.04 \text{ g } \cancel{H_2C_2O_4}}$$

$$= 2.871 \times 10^{-3} \text{ mol } H_2C_2O_4$$

According to the balanced equation, 5 mol of oxalic acid react with 2 mol of permanganate ion. Thus, we can calculate the number of moles of $KMnO_4$ that react with 2.871×10^{-3} mol of $H_2C_2O_4$:

$$\text{Moles of } KMnO_4 = 2.871 \times 10^{-3} \text{ mol } \cancel{H_2C_2O_4} \times \frac{2 \text{ mol } KMnO_4}{5 \text{ mol } \cancel{H_2C_2O_4}}$$

$$= 1.148 \times 10^{-3} \text{ mol } KMnO_4$$

Knowing both the number of moles of $KMnO_4$ that react (1.148×10^{-3} mol) and the volume of the $KMnO_4$ solution (22.35 mL), we can calculate the molarity:

$$\text{Molarity} = \frac{1.148 \times 10^{-3} \text{ mol } KMnO_4}{22.35 \text{ mL}} \times \frac{1000 \text{ mL}}{1 \text{ L}} = 0.051\ 36 \text{ M}$$

The molarity of the $KMnO_4$ solution is 0.051 36 M.

WORKED EXAMPLE 4.13

USING A REDOX REACTION TO DETERMINE A SOLUTION'S CONCENTRATION

The concentration of an aqueous I_3^- solution can be determined by titration with aqueous sodium thiosulfate, $Na_2S_2O_3$, in the presence of a starch indicator, which turns from deep blue to colorless when all the I_3^- has reacted. What is the molar concentration of I_3^- in an aqueous solution if 24.55 mL of 0.102 M $Na_2S_2O_3$ is needed for complete reaction with 10.00 mL of the I_3^- solution? The net ionic equation is

$$2\,S_2O_3^{2-}(aq) + I_3^-(aq) \longrightarrow S_4O_6^{2-}(aq) + 3\,I^-(aq)$$

STRATEGY AND SOLUTION

The procedure is similar to that outlined in Figure 4.5. We first need to find the number of moles of thiosulfate ion used for the titration:

$$24.55 \text{ mL} \times \frac{1 \text{ L}}{1000 \text{ mL}} \times \frac{0.102 \text{ mol } S_2O_3^{2-}}{1 \text{ L}} = 2.50 \times 10^{-3} \text{ mol } S_2O_3^{2-}$$

According to the balanced equation, 2 mol of $S_2O_3^{2-}$ ion react with 1 mol of I_3^- ion. Thus, we can find the number of moles of I_3^- ion:

$$2.50 \times 10^{-3} \text{ mol } \cancel{S_2O_3^{2-}} \times \frac{1 \text{ mol } I_3^-}{2 \text{ mol } \cancel{S_2O_3^{2-}}} = 1.25 \times 10^{-3} \text{ mol } I_3^-$$

Knowing both the number of moles of I_3^- (1.25×10^{-3} mol) and the volume of the I_3^- solution (10.00 mL) then lets us calculate molarity:

$$\frac{1.25 \times 10^{-3} \text{ mol } I_3^-}{10.00 \text{ mL}} \times \frac{10^3 \text{ mL}}{1 \text{ L}} = 0.125 \text{ M}$$

The molarity of the I_3^- solution is 0.125 M.

BALLPARK CHECK

According to the balanced equation, the amount of $S_2O_3^{2-}$ needed for the reaction (2 mol) is twice the amount of I_3^- (1 mol). The titration results indicate that the volume of the $S_2O_3^{2-}$ solution (24.55 mL) is a little over twice the volume of the I_3^- solution (10.00 mL). Thus, the concentrations of the two solutions must be about the same—approximately 0.1 M.

▲ The reddish I_3^- solution turns a deep blue color when it is added to a solution containing a small amount of starch.

▶ **PROBLEM 4.22** What is the molar concentration of Fe^{2+} ion in an aqueous solution if 31.50 mL of 0.105 M $KBrO_3$ is required for complete reaction with 10.00 mL of the Fe^{2+} solution? The net ionic equation is:

$$6\,Fe^{2+}(aq) + BrO_3^-(aq) + 6\,H^+(aq) \longrightarrow 6\,Fe^{3+}(aq) + Br^-(aq) + 3\,H_2O(l)$$

4.11 SOME APPLICATIONS OF REDOX REACTIONS

Redox reactions take place with almost every element in the periodic table except the noble gases and occur in a vast number of processes throughout nature, biology, and industry. Here are just a few examples:

- **Combustion** is the burning of a fuel by oxidation with oxygen in air. Gasoline, fuel oil, natural gas, wood, paper, and other organic substances of carbon and hydrogen are the most common fuels. Even some metals, such as magnesium and calcium, will burn in air.

$$CH_4(g) + 2\,O_2(g) \longrightarrow CO_2(g) + 2\,H_2O(l)$$
  Methane
  (natural gas)

- **Bleaching** uses redox reactions to decolorize or lighten colored materials. Dark hair is bleached to turn it blond, clothes are bleached to remove stains, wood pulp is bleached to make white paper, and so on. The exact oxidizing agent used depends on the situation—hydrogen peroxide (H_2O_2) is used for hair, sodium hypochlorite (NaOCl) is used for clothes, and elemental chlorine is used for wood pulp—but the principle is always the same. In all cases, colored impurities are destroyed by reaction with a strong oxidizing agent.

- **Batteries**, although they come in many types and sizes, are all based on redox reactions. In a typical redox reaction carried out in the laboratory—say, the reaction of zinc metal with Ag^+ to yield Zn^{2+} and silver metal—the reactants are simply mixed in a flask and electrons are transferred by direct contact between them. In a battery, however, the two reactants are kept in separate compartments and the electrons are transferred through a wire running between them.

  The inexpensive alkaline battery commonly used in flashlights and other small household items uses a thin steel can containing zinc powder and a paste of potassium hydroxide as one reactant, separated by paper from a paste of powdered carbon and manganese dioxide as the other reactant. A graphite rod with a metal cap sticks into the MnO_2 to provide electrical contact. When the can and the graphite rod are connected by a wire, zinc sends electrons flowing through the wire toward the MnO_2 in a redox reaction. The resultant electrical current can be used to light a bulb or power a small electronic device. The reaction is

▲ Dark hair can be bleached by a redox reaction with hydrogen peroxide.

$$Zn(s) + 2\,MnO_2(s) \longrightarrow ZnO(s) + Mn_2O_3(s)$$

  We'll look at the chemistry of batteries in more detail in Section 17.9.

- **Metallurgy**, the extraction and purification of metals from their ores, makes use of numerous redox processes. We'll see in Section 21.2, for example, that metallic zinc is prepared by reduction of ZnO with *coke*, a form of carbon:

$$ZnO(s) + C(s) \longrightarrow Zn(s) + CO(g)$$

- **Corrosion** is the deterioration of a metal by oxidation, such as the rusting of iron in moist air. The economic consequences of rusting are enormous: It has been estimated that up to one-fourth of the iron produced in the United States is used to replace bridges, buildings, and other structures that have been destroyed by corrosion. (The raised dot in the formula $Fe_2O_3 \cdot H_2O$ for rust indicates that one water molecule is associated with each Fe_2O_3 in an unspecified way.)

$$4\,Fe(s) + 3\,O_2(g) \xrightarrow{\text{H}_2\text{O}} 2\,Fe_2O_3 \cdot H_2O(s)$$

$$\text{Rust}$$

- **Respiration** is the process of breathing and using oxygen for the many biological redox reactions that provide the energy needed by living organisms. The energy is released from food molecules slowly and in complex, multistep pathways, but the overall result of respiration is similar to that of a combustion reaction. For example, the simple sugar glucose ($C_6H_{12}O_6$) reacts with O_2 to give CO_2 and H_2O according to the following equation:

$$C_6H_{12}O_6 + 6\,O_2 \longrightarrow 6\,CO_2 + 6\,H_2O + \text{energy}$$

Glucose
(a carbohydrate)

▸ **PROBLEM 4.23**   In the common lead storage battery used in automobiles, the following two half-reactions occur in acid solution:

Oxidation $Pb(s) + HSO_4^-(aq) \longrightarrow PbSO_4(s)$

Reduction $PbO_2(s) + HSO_4^-(aq) \longrightarrow PbSO_4(s)$

Write a balanced equation for the overall battery reaction.

INQUIRY HOW CAN CHEMISTRY BE GREEN?

Chemistry has made our lives longer, safer, and far more comfortable than they would otherwise be. The medicines, fertilizers, insecticides, adhesives, textiles, dyes, building materials, and polymers that we take for granted are all products of the chemical industry. But these benefits have not come without a price. Many chemical processes produce hazardous wastes that must be dealt with—reaction solvents and byproducts that might evaporate into the air or leach into groundwater if not disposed of properly.

▲ Green chemistry can help prevent this kind of problem in the future.

It's unlikely that all chemical processes will ever be completely benign, but awareness of the environmental problems caused by chemistry has grown dramatically in recent years, giving rise to a movement called *green chemistry*. Green chemistry is the design and implementation of chemical processes that reduce waste and minimize or eliminate the generation of hazardous substances. Twelve principles form the foundation of green chemistry:

Prevent waste—Waste should be prevented rather than cleaned up after it has been created.

Maximize atom economy—Processes should maximize the incorporation of all reactant atoms into the final product to minimize leftover waste.

Use less-hazardous processes—Methods of chemical synthesis should use nontoxic reactants and generate nontoxic wastes.

Design safer chemicals—Chemical products should be designed from the beginning to have minimal toxicity.

Use safer solvents—Solvents and other auxiliary substances used in reactions should be safe and used sparingly.

Design for energy efficiency—Energy usage in chemical processes should be minimized, with reactions carried out at room temperature if possible.

Use renewable feedstocks—Raw materials should come from renewable sources when feasible.

Minimize derivatives—Syntheses should be designed with minimal use of protecting groups to avoid extra steps and reduce waste.

Use catalysis—Reactions should be catalytic rather than stoichiometric.

Design for degradation—Products should be designed to be biodegradable at the end of their useful lifetimes.

Monitor pollution in real time—Processes should be monitored in real time for the formation of hazardous substances.

Prevent accidents—Chemical substances and processes should minimize the potential for fires, explosions, or other accidents.

The 12 principles of green chemistry won't all be met in most applications, but they provide goals to aim for and they can make chemists think more carefully about the environmental implications of their work. Among the successes already recorded is a new process for converting glycerin, a by-product of producing biodiesel fuel from vegetable oil, into propylene glycol, which is used in automobile antifreeze. The process occurs in a single step and gives only water as the by-product.

Glycerin   Propylene glycol

▶ **PROBLEM 4.24** Many dozens of different solvents are used in various chemical processes. If you were designing a green process that required a solvent, what properties would you look for, and what solvent might you choose?

SUMMARY

Many reactions, particularly those that involve ionic compounds, take place in aqueous solution. Substances whose aqueous solutions contain ions conduct electricity and are called **electrolytes**. Ionic compounds, such as NaCl, and molecular compounds that **dissociate** substantially into ions when dissolved in water are **strong electrolytes**. Substances that dissociate to only a small extent are **weak electrolytes**, and substances that do not produce ions in aqueous solution are **nonelectrolytes**.

Acids are compounds that dissociate in aqueous solutions to yield an anion and a **hydronium ion, H₃O⁺**. Acids that dissociate to a large extent are **strong acids**; acids that dissociate to a small extent are **weak acids**. Similarly, **bases** are compounds that dissociate in aqueous solution to yield a cation and hydroxide ion, OH⁻.

There are three important classes of aqueous reactions. **Precipitation reactions** occur when solutions of two ionic substances are mixed and a precipitate falls from solution. To predict whether a precipitate will form, you must know the **solubility** of each potential product. **Acid–base neutralization reactions** occur when an acid is mixed with a base, yielding water and an ionic **salt**. The neutralization of a strong acid with a strong base can be written as a **net ionic equation**, in which nonparticipating, **spectator ions** are not specified:

$$H^+(aq) + OH^-(aq) \longrightarrow H_2O(l)$$

Oxidation–reduction reactions, or **redox reactions**, are processes in which one or more electrons are transferred between reaction partners. An **oxidation** is the loss of one or more electrons; a **reduction** is the gain of one or more electrons. Redox reactions can be identified by assigning to each atom in a substance an **oxidation number**, which provides a measure of whether the atom is neutral, electron rich, or electron poor. Comparing the oxidation numbers of an atom before and after reaction shows whether the atom has gained or lost electrons.

Oxidations and reductions must occur together. Whenever one substance loses one or more electrons (is oxidized), another substance gains the electrons (is reduced). The substance that causes a reduction by giving up electrons is called a **reducing agent**. The substance that causes an oxidation by accepting electrons is called an **oxidizing agent**. The reducing agent is itself oxidized when it gives up electrons, and the oxidizing agent is itself reduced when it accepts electrons.

Among the simplest of redox processes is the reaction of an aqueous cation, usually a metal ion, with a free element to give a different ion and a different element. Noting the results from a succession of different reactions makes it possible to organize an **activity series**, which ranks the elements in order of their reducing ability in aqueous solution.

Redox reactions can be balanced using the **half-reaction method**, which divides a reaction into oxidation and reduction parts and focuses on equalizing the transfer of electrons between the parts. The concentration of an oxidizing agent or a reducing agent in solution can be determined by a redox titration.

KEY WORDS

acid *120*	half-reaction method *132*	oxidation–reduction	solubility *117*
acid–base neutralization	hydronium ion, H₃O⁺ *120*	reaction *125*	spectator ion *116*
reaction *113*	ionic equation *116*	oxidizing agent *128*	strong acid *120*
activity series *130*	molecular equation *116*	oxoacid *122*	strong base *121*
base *120*	monoprotic acid *121*	precipitation reaction *113*	strong electrolyte *115*
diprotic acid *121*	net ionic equation *116*	redox reaction *125*	triprotic acid *121*
dissociate *115*	nonelectrolyte *115*	reducing agent *128*	weak acid *121*
electrolyte *115*	oxidation *125*	reduction *125*	weak base *121*
half-reaction *132*	oxidation number *125*	salt *123*	weak electrolyte *115*

CONCEPTUAL PROBLEMS

Problems 4.1–4.24 appear within the chapter.

4.25 Assume that an aqueous solution of a cation, represented as a red sphere, is allowed to mix with a solution of an anion, represented as a yellow sphere. Three possible outcomes are represented by boxes (1)–(3):

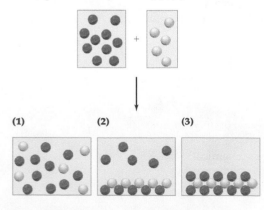

Which outcome corresponds to each of the following reactions?

(a) $2\,Na^+(aq) + CO_3^{2-}(aq) \longrightarrow$

(b) $Ba^{2+}(aq) + CrO_4^{2-}(aq) \longrightarrow$

(c) $2\,Ag^+(aq) + SO_3^{2-}(aq) \longrightarrow$

4.26 Assume that an aqueous solution of a cation, represented as a blue sphere, is allowed to mix with a solution of an anion, represented as a red sphere, and that the following result is obtained:

Which combinations of cation and anion, chosen from the following lists, are compatible with the observed results? Explain.

Cations: Na^+, Ca^{2+}, Ag^+, Ni^{2+}

Anions: Cl^-, CO_3^{2-}, CrO_4^{2-}, NO_3^-

4.27 Assume that an aqueous solution of OH^-, represented as a blue sphere, is allowed to mix with a solution of an acid H_nA, represented as a red sphere. Three possible outcomes are depicted by boxes (1)–(3), where the green spheres represent A^{n-}, the anion of the acid:

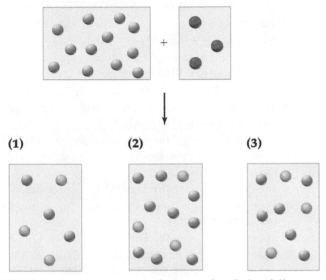

Which outcome corresponds to each of the following reactions?

(a) $HF + OH^- \longrightarrow H_2O + F^-$

(b) $H_2SO_3 + 2\,OH^- \longrightarrow 2\,H_2O + SO_3^{2-}$

(c) $H_3PO_4 + 3\,OH^- \longrightarrow 3\,H_2O + PO_4^{3-}$

4.28 The concentration of an aqueous solution of NaOCl (sodium hypochlorite; the active ingredient in household bleach) can be determined by a redox titration with iodide ion in acidic solution:

$$OCl^-(aq) + 2\,I^-(aq) + 2\,H^+(aq) \longrightarrow$$
$$Cl^-(aq) + I_2(aq) + H_2O(l)$$

Assume that the blue spheres in the buret represent I^- ions, the red spheres in the flask represent OCl^- ions, the concentration of the I^- ions in the buret is 0.120 M, and the volumes in the buret and the flask are identical. What is the concentration of NaOCl in the flask? What percentage of the I^- solution in the buret must be added to the flask to react with all the OCl^- ions?

4.29 Assume that the electrical conductivity of a solution depends on the total concentration of dissolved ions and that you measure the conductivity of three different solutions while carrying out titration procedures:

(a) Begin with 1.00 L of 0.100 M KCl, and titrate by adding 0.100 M $AgNO_3$.

(b) Begin with 1.00 L of 0.100 M HF, and titrate by adding 0.100 M KOH.

(c) Begin with 1.00 L of 0.100 M $BaCl_2$, and titrate by adding 0.100 M Na_2SO_4.

Which of the following graphs corresponds to which titration?

4.30 Based on the positions in the periodic table, which of the following reactions would you expect to occur?

(a) $Red^+ + Green \longrightarrow Red + Green^+$

(b) $Blue + Green^+ \longrightarrow Blue^+ + Green$

(c) $Red + Blue^+ \longrightarrow Red^+ + Blue$

4.31 The following two redox reactions occur between aqueous cations and solid metals. Will a solution of green cations react with solid blue metal? Explain.

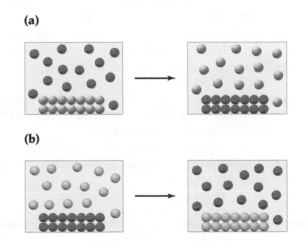

SECTION PROBLEMS

Aqueous Reactions, Net Ionic Equations, and Electrolytes (Sections 4.2 and 4.3)

4.32 Classify each of the following reactions as a precipitation, acid–base neutralization, or oxidation–reduction:

(a) $Hg(NO_3)_2(aq) + 2\,NaI(aq) \longrightarrow 2\,NaNO_3(aq) + HgI_2(s)$

(b) $2\,HgO(s) \xrightarrow{\text{heat}} 2\,Hg(l) + O_2(g)$

(c) $H_3PO_4(aq) + 3\,KOH(aq) \longrightarrow K_3PO_4(aq) + 3\,H_2O(l)$

4.33 Classify each of the following reactions as a precipitation, acid–base neutralization, or oxidation–reduction:

(a) $S_8(s) + 8\,O_2(g) \longrightarrow 8\,SO_2(g)$

(b) $NiCl_2(aq) + Na_2S(aq) \longrightarrow NiS(s) + 2\,NaCl(aq)$

(c) $2\,CH_3CO_2H(aq) + Ba(OH)_2(aq) \longrightarrow$
$(CH_3CO_2)_2Ba(aq) + 2\,H_2O(l)$

4.34 Write net ionic equations for the reactions listed in Problem 4.32.

4.35 Write net ionic equations for the reactions listed in Problem 4.33.

4.36 The following aqueous solutions were tested with a light-bulb conductivity apparatus, as shown in Figure 4.1. What result—dark, dim, or bright—do you expect from each?

(a) 0.10 M potassium chloride   (b) 0.10 M methanol

(c) 0.10 M acetic acid

4.37 The following aqueous solutions were tested with a light-bulb conductivity apparatus, as shown in Figure 4.1. What result—dark, dim, or bright—do you expect from each?

(a) 0.10 M hydrofluoric acid

(b) 0.10 M sodium chloride

(c) 0.10 M glucose ($C_6H_{12}O_6$)

4.38 Individual solutions of $Ba(OH)_2$ and H_2SO_4 both conduct electricity, but the conductivity disappears when equal molar amounts of the solutions are mixed. Explain.

4.39 A solution of HCl in water conducts electricity, but a solution of HCl in chloroform, $CHCl_3$, does not. What does this observation tell you about how HCl exists in water and how it exists in chloroform?

4.40 Classify each of the following substances as either a strong electrolyte, weak electrolyte, or nonelectrolyte:

(a) HBr   (b) HF   (c) $NaClO_4$

(d) $(NH_4)_2CO_3$ (e) NH_3 (f) Ethyl alcohol

4.41 Is it possible for a molecular substance to be a strong electrolyte? Explain.

4.42 What is the total molar concentration of ions in each of the following solutions, assuming complete dissociation?

(a) A 0.750 M solution of K_2CO_3

(b) A 0.355 M solution of $AlCl_3$

4.43 What is the total molar concentration of ions in each of the following solutions?

(a) A 1.250 M solution of CH_3OH

(b) A 0.225 M solution of $HClO_4$

Precipitation Reactions and Solubility Guidelines (Section 4.4)

4.44 Which of the following substances are likely to be soluble in water?

(a) Ag_2O (b) $Ba(NO_3)_2$ (c) $SnCO_3$ (d) Fe_2O_3

4.45 Which of the following substances are likely to be soluble in water?

(a) ZnS   (b) $Au_2(CO_3)_3$ (c) $PbCl_2$ (d) MnO_2

4.46 Predict whether a precipitation reaction will occur when aqueous solutions of the following substances are mixed:

(a) $NaOH + HClO_4$ (b) $FeCl_2 + KOH$

(c) $(NH_4)_2SO_4 + NiCl_2$ (d) $CH_3CO_2Na + HCl$

4.47 Predict whether a precipitation reaction will occur when aqueous solutions of the following substances are mixed:

(a) $MnCl_2 + Na_2S$ (b) $HNO_3 + CuSO_4$

(c) $Hg(NO_3)_2 + Na_3PO_4$ (d) $Ba(NO_3)_2 + KOH$

4.48 Which of the following solutions will not form a precipitate when added to 0.10 M $BaCl_2$?

(a) 0.10 M $LiNO_3$ (b) 0.10 M K_2SO_4 (c) 0.10 M $AgNO_3$

4.49 Which of the following solutions will not form a precipitate when added to 0.10 M NaOH?

(a) 0.10 M $MgBr_2$ (b) 0.10 M NH_4Br (c) 0.10 M $FeCl_2$

4.50 How would you prepare the following substances by a precipitation reaction?

(a) $PbSO_4$ (b) $Mg_3(PO_4)_2$ (c) $ZnCrO_4$

4.51 How would you prepare the following substances by a precipitation reaction?

(a) $Al(OH)_3$ (b) FeS   (c) $CoCO_3$

4.52 Assume that you have an aqueous mixture of $NaNO_3$ and $AgNO_3$. How could you use a precipitation reaction to separate the two metal ions?

4.53 Assume that you have an aqueous mixture of $BaCl_2$ and $CuCl_2$. How could you use a precipitation reaction to separate the two metal ions?

4.54 Assume that you have an aqueous solution of an unknown salt. Treatment of the solution with dilute NaOH, Na_2SO_4, and KCl produces no precipitate. Which of the following cations might the solution contain?

(a) Ag^+ (b) Cs^+ (c) Ba^{2+} (d) NH_4^+

4.55 Assume that you have an aqueous solution of an unknown salt. Treatment of the solution with dilute $BaCl_2$, $AgNO_3$, and $Cu(NO_3)_2$ produces no precipitate. Which of the following anions might the solution contain?

(a) Cl^- (b) NO_3^- (c) OH^- (d) SO_4^{2-}

Acids, Bases, and Neutralization Reactions (Section 4.5)

4.56 Assume that you are given a solution of an unknown acid or base. How can you tell whether the unknown substance is acidic or basic?

4.57 Why do we use a double arrow ($\rightleftharpoons$) to show the dissociation of a weak acid or weak base in aqueous solution?

4.58 Write balanced ionic equations for the following reactions:

(a) Aqueous perchloric acid is neutralized by aqueous calcium hydroxide.

(b) Aqueous sodium hydroxide is neutralized by aqueous acetic acid.

4.59 Write balanced ionic equations for the following reactions:

(a) Aqueous hydrobromic acid is neutralized by aqueous calcium hydroxide.

(b) Aqueous barium hydroxide is neutralized by aqueous nitric acid.

4.60 Write balanced net ionic equations for the following reactions:

(a) $LiOH(aq) + HI(aq) \longrightarrow$?

(b) $HBr(aq) + Ca(OH)_2(aq) \longrightarrow$?

4.61 Write balanced net ionic equations for the following reactions. Note that $HClO_3$ is a strong acid.

(a) $Fe(OH)_3(s) + H_2SO_4(aq) \longrightarrow$?

(b) $HClO_3(aq) + NaOH(aq) \longrightarrow$?

4.62 If the following solutions are mixed, is the resulting solution acidic, basic, or neutral?

(a) 50.0 mL of 0.100 M HBr and 30.0 mL of 0.200 M KOH

(b) 100.0 mL of 0.0750 M HCl and 75.0 mL of 0.100 M $Ba(OH)_2$

4.63 If the following solutions are mixed, is the resulting solution acidic, basic, or neutral?

(a) 65.0 mL of 0.0500 M $HClO_4$ and 40.0 mL of 0.0750 M NaOH

(b) 125.0 mL of 0.100 M HNO_3 and 90.0 mL of 0.0750 M $Ca(OH)_2$

4.64 How many milliliters of 1.00 M KOH must be added to neutralize the following solutions?

(a) a mixture of 0.240 M LiOH (25.0 mL) and 0.200 M HBr (75.0 mL)

(b) a mixture of 0.300 M HCl (45.0 mL) and 0.250 M NaOH (10.0 mL)

4.65 How many milliliters of 2.00 M HCl must be added to neutralize the following solutions?

(a) a mixture of 0.160 M HNO_3 (100.0 mL) and 0.100 M KOH (400.0 mL)

(b) a mixture of 0.120 M NaOH (350.0 mL) and 0.190 M HBr (150.0 mL)

Redox Reactions and Oxidation Numbers (Sections 4.6–4.8)

4.66 Where in the periodic table are the best reducing agents found? The best oxidizing agents?

4.67 Where in the periodic table are the most easily reduced elements found? The most easily oxidized?

4.68 In each of the following instances, tell whether the substance gains electrons or loses electrons in a redox reaction:

(a) An oxidizing agent

(b) A reducing agent

(c) A substance undergoing oxidation

(d) A substance undergoing reduction

4.69 Tell for each of the following substances whether the oxidation number increases or decreases in a redox reaction:

(a) An oxidizing agent

(b) A reducing agent

(c) A substance undergoing oxidation

(d) A substance undergoing reduction

4.70 Assign oxidation numbers to each element in the following compounds:

(a) NO_2 (b) SO_3 (c) $COCl_2$

(d) CH_2Cl_2 (e) $KClO_3$ (f) HNO_3

4.71 Assign oxidation numbers to each element in the following compounds:

(a) $VOCl_3$ (b) $CuSO_4$ (c) CH_2O

(d) Mn_2O_7 (e) OsO_4 (f) H_2PtCl_6

4.72 Assign oxidation numbers to each element in the following ions:

(a) ClO_3^- (b) SO_3^{2-} (c) $C_2O_4^{2-}$

(d) NO_2^- (e) BrO^- (f) AsO_4^{3-}

4.73 Assign oxidation numbers to each element in the following ions:

(a) $Cr(OH)_4^-$ (b) $S_2O_3^{2-}$ (c) NO_3^-

(d) MnO_4^{2-} (e) HPO_4^{2-} (f) $V_2O_7^{4-}$

4.74 Which element is oxidized and which is reduced in each of the following reactions?

(a) $Ca(s) + Sn^{2+}(aq) \longrightarrow Ca^{2+}(aq) + Sn(s)$

(b) $ICl(s) + H_2O(l) \longrightarrow HCl(aq) + HOI(aq)$

4.75 Which element is oxidized and which is reduced in each of the following reactions?

(a) $Si(s) + 2\,Cl_2(g) \longrightarrow SiCl_4(l)$

(b) $Cl_2(g) + 2\,NaBr(aq) \longrightarrow Br_2(aq) + 2\,NaCl(aq)$

4.76 Use the activity series of metals (Table 4.5; page 130) to predict the outcome of each of the following reactions. If no reaction occurs, write N.R.

(a) $Na^+(aq) + Zn(s) \longrightarrow$? (b) $HCl(aq) + Pt(s) \longrightarrow$?

(c) $Ag^+(aq) + Au(s) \longrightarrow$? (d) $Au^{3+}(aq) + Ag(s) \longrightarrow$?

4.77 Neither strontium (Sr) nor antimony (Sb) is shown in the activity series of Table 4.5. Based on their positions in the periodic table, which would you expect to be the better reducing agent? Will the following reaction occur? Explain.

$$2\,Sb^{3+}(aq) + 3\,Sr(s) \longrightarrow 2\,Sb(s) + 3\,Sr^{2+}(aq)$$

4.78 (a) Use the following reactions to arrange the elements A, B, C, and D in order of their decreasing ability as reducing agents:

$A + B^+ \longrightarrow A^+ + B \qquad C^+ + D \longrightarrow$ no reaction

$B + D^+ \longrightarrow B^+ + D \qquad B + C^+ \longrightarrow B^+ + C$

(b) Which of the following reactions would you expect to occur according to the activity series you established in part (a)?

(1) $A^+ + C \longrightarrow A + C^+$ (2) $A^+ + D \longrightarrow A + D^+$

4.79 (a) Use the following reactions to arrange the elements A, B, C, and D in order of their decreasing ability as reducing agents:

$2\,A + B^{2+} \longrightarrow 2\,A^+ + B \qquad B + D^{2+} \longrightarrow B^{2+} + D$

$A^+ + C \longrightarrow$ no reaction $\qquad 2\,C + B^{2+} \longrightarrow 2\,C^+ + B$

(b) Which of the following reactions would you expect to occur according to the activity series you established in part (a)?

(1) $2\,A^+ + D \longrightarrow 2\,A + D^{2+}$

(2) $D^{2+} + 2\,C \longrightarrow D + 2\,C^+$

Balancing Redox Reactions (Section 4.9)

4.80 Classify each of the following unbalanced half-reactions as either an oxidation or a reduction:

(a) $NO_3^-(aq) \longrightarrow NO(g)$ (b) $Zn(s) \longrightarrow Zn^{2+}(aq)$

(c) $Ti^{3+}(aq) \longrightarrow TiO_2(s)$ (d) $Sn^{4+}(aq) \longrightarrow Sn^{2+}(aq)$

4.81 Classify each of the following unbalanced half-reactions as either an oxidation or a reduction:

(a) $O_2(g) \longrightarrow OH^-(aq)$ (b) $H_2O_2(aq) \longrightarrow O_2(g)$

(c) $MnO_4^-(aq) \longrightarrow MnO_4^{2-}(aq)$

(d) $CH_3OH(aq) \longrightarrow CH_2O(aq)$

4.82 Balance the half-reactions in Problem 4.80, assuming that they occur in acidic solution.

4.83 Balance the half-reactions in Problem 4.81, assuming that they occur in basic solution.

4.84 Write unbalanced oxidation and reduction half-reactions for the following processes:

(a) $Te(s) + NO_3^-(aq) \longrightarrow TeO_2(s) + NO(g)$

(b) $H_2O_2(aq) + Fe^{2+}(aq) \longrightarrow Fe^{3+}(aq) + H_2O(l)$

4.85 Write unbalanced oxidation and reduction half-reactions for the following processes:

(a) $Mn(s) + NO_3^-(aq) \longrightarrow Mn^{2+}(aq) + NO_2(g)$

(b) $Mn^{3+}(aq) \longrightarrow MnO_2(s) + Mn^{2+}(aq)$

4.86 Balance the following half-reactions:

(a) (acidic) $Cr_2O_7^{2-}(aq) \longrightarrow Cr^{3+}(aq)$

(b) (basic) $CrO_4^{2-}(aq) \longrightarrow Cr(OH)_4^-(aq)$

(c) (basic) $Bi^{3+}(aq) \longrightarrow BiO_3^-(aq)$

(d) (basic) $ClO^-(aq) \longrightarrow Cl^-(aq)$

4.87 Balance the following half-reactions:

(a) (acidic) $VO^{2+}(aq) \longrightarrow V^{3+}(aq)$

(b) (basic) $Ni(OH)_2(s) \longrightarrow Ni_2O_3(s)$

(c) (acidic) $NO_3^-(aq) \longrightarrow NO_2(aq)$

(d) (basic) $Br_2(aq) \longrightarrow BrO_3^-(aq)$

4.88 Write balanced net ionic equations for the following reactions in basic solution:

(a) $MnO_4^-(aq) + IO_3^-(aq) \longrightarrow MnO_2(s) + IO_4^-(aq)$

(b) $Cu(OH)_2(s) + N_2H_4(aq) \longrightarrow Cu(s) + N_2(g)$

(c) $Fe(OH)_2(s) + CrO_4^{2-}(aq) \longrightarrow$
$$Fe(OH)_3(s) + Cr(OH)_4^-(aq)$$

(d) $H_2O_2(aq) + ClO_4^-(aq) \longrightarrow ClO_2^-(aq) + O_2(g)$

4.89 Write balanced net ionic equations for the following reactions in basic solution:

(a) $S_2O_3^{2-}(aq) + I_2(aq) \longrightarrow S_4O_6^{2-}(aq) + I^-(aq)$

(b) $Mn^{2+}(aq) + H_2O_2(aq) \longrightarrow MnO_2(s) + H_2O(l)$

(c) $Zn(s) + NO_3^-(aq) \longrightarrow NH_3(aq) + Zn(OH)_4^{2-}(aq)$

(d) $Bi(OH)_3(s) + Sn(OH)_3^-(aq) \longrightarrow Bi(s) + Sn(OH)_6^{2-}(aq)$

4.90 Write balanced net ionic equations for the following reactions in acidic solution:

(a) $Zn(s) + VO^{2+}(aq) \longrightarrow Zn^{2+}(aq) + V^{3+}(aq)$

(b) $Ag(s) + NO_3^-(aq) \longrightarrow Ag^+(aq) + NO_2(g)$

(c) $Mg(s) + VO_4^{3-}(aq) \longrightarrow Mg^{2+}(aq) + V^{2+}(aq)$

(d) $I^-(aq) + IO_3^-(aq) \longrightarrow I_3^-(aq)$

4.91 Write balanced net ionic equations for the following reactions in acidic solution:

(a) $MnO_4^-(aq) + C_2H_5OH(aq) \longrightarrow$
$$Mn^{2+}(aq) + CH_3CO_2H(aq)$$

(b) $H_2O_2(aq) + Cr_2O_7^{2-}(aq) \longrightarrow O_2(g) + Cr^{3+}(aq)$

(c) $Sn^{2+}(aq) + IO_4^-(aq) \longrightarrow Sn^{4+}(aq) + I^-(aq)$

(d) $PbO_2(s) + Cl^-(aq) \longrightarrow PbCl_2(s) + O_2(g)$

Redox Titrations (Section 4.10)

4.92 Iodine, I_2, reacts with aqueous thiosulfate ion in neutral solution according to the balanced equation

$$I_2(aq) + 2 S_2O_3^{2-}(aq) \longrightarrow S_4O_6^{2-}(aq) + 2 I^-(aq)$$

How many grams of I_2 are present in a solution if 35.20 mL of 0.150 M $Na_2S_2O_3$ solution is needed to titrate the I_2 solution?

4.93 How many milliliters of 0.250 M $Na_2S_2O_3$ solution is needed for complete reaction with 2.486 g of I_2 according to the equation in Problem 4.92?

4.94 Dichromate ion, $Cr_2O_7^{2-}$, reacts with aqueous iron(II) ion in acidic solution according to the balanced equation

$$Cr_2O_7^{2-}(aq) + 6 Fe^{2+}(aq) + 14 H^+(aq) \longrightarrow$$
$$2 Cr^{3+}(aq) + 6 Fe^{3+}(aq) + 7 H_2O(l)$$

What is the concentration of Fe^{2+} if 46.99 mL of 0.2004 M $K_2Cr_2O_7$ is needed to titrate 50.00 mL of the Fe^{2+} solution?

4.95 A volume of 18.72 mL of 0.1500 M $K_2Cr_2O_7$ solution was required to titrate a sample of $FeSO_4$ according to the equation in Problem 4.94. What is the mass of the sample?

4.96 What is the molar concentration of As(III) in a solution if 22.35 mL of 0.100 M $KBrO_3$ is needed for complete reaction with 50.00 mL of the As(III) solution? The balanced equation is:

$$3 H_3AsO_3(aq) + BrO_3^-(aq) \longrightarrow Br^-(aq) + 3 H_3AsO_4(aq)$$

4.97 Standardized solutions of $KBrO_3$ are frequently used in redox titrations. The necessary solution can be made by dissolving $KBrO_3$ in water and then titrating it with an As(III) solution. What is the molar concentration of a $KBrO_3$ solution if 28.55 mL of the solution is needed to titrate 1.550 g of As_2O_3? See Problem 4.96 for the balanced equation. (As_2O_3 dissolves in aqueous acid solution to yield H_3AsO_3: $As_2O_3 + 3 H_2O \longrightarrow 2 H_3AsO_3$.)

4.98 The metal content of iron in ores can be determined by a redox procedure in which the sample is first oxidized with Br_2 to convert all the iron to Fe^{3+} and then titrated with Sn^{2+} to reduce the Fe^{3+} to Fe^{2+}. The balanced equation is:

$$2 Fe^{3+}(aq) + Sn^{2+}(aq) \longrightarrow 2 Fe^{2+}(aq) + Sn^{4+}(aq)$$

What is the mass percent Fe in a 0.1875 g sample of ore if 13.28 mL of a 0.1015 M Sn^{2+} solution is needed to titrate the Fe^{3+}?

4.99 The concentration of the Sn^{2+} solution used in Problem 4.98 can be found by letting it react with a known amount of Fe^{3+}. What is the molar concentration of an Sn^{2+} solution if 23.84 mL is required for complete reaction with 1.4855 g of Fe_2O_3?

4.100 Alcohol levels in blood can be determined by a redox reaction with potassium dichromate according to the balanced equation

$$C_2H_5OH(aq) + 2 Cr_2O_7^{2-}(aq) + 16 H^+(aq) \longrightarrow$$
$$2 CO_2(g) + 4 Cr^{3+}(aq) + 11 H_2O(l)$$

What is the blood alcohol level in mass percent if 8.76 mL of 0.049 88 M $K_2Cr_2O_7$ is required for complete reaction with a 10.002 g sample of blood?

4.101 Calcium levels in blood can be determined by adding oxalate ion to precipitate calcium oxalate, CaC_2O_4, followed by dissolving the precipitate in aqueous acid and titrating the resulting oxalic acid ($H_2C_2O_4$) with $KMnO_4$:

$$5 H_2C_2O_4(aq) + 2 MnO_4^-(aq) + 6 H^+(aq) \longrightarrow$$
$$10 CO_2(g) + 2 Mn^{2+}(aq) + 8 H_2O(l)$$

How many milligrams of Ca^{2+} are present in 10.0 mL of blood if 21.08 mL of 0.000 988 M $KMnO_4$ solution is needed for the titration?

CHAPTER PROBLEMS

4.102 Balance the equations for the following reactions in basic solution:

(a) $[Fe(CN)_6]^{3-}(aq) + N_2H_4(aq) \longrightarrow [Fe(CN)_6]^{4-}(aq) + N_2(g)$

(b) $SeO_3^{2-}(aq) + Cl_2(g) \longrightarrow SeO_4^{2-}(aq) + Cl^-(aq)$

(c) $Co^{2+}(aq) + HO_2^-(aq) \longrightarrow Co(OH)_3(s)$

4.103 An alternative procedure to that given in Problem 4.98 for determining the amount of iron in a sample is to convert the iron to Fe^{2+} and then titrate it with a solution of $Ce(NH_4)_2(NO_3)_6$:

$$Fe^{2+}(aq) + Ce^{4+}(aq) \longrightarrow Fe^{3+}(aq) + Ce^{3+}(aq)$$

What is the mass percent of iron in a sample if 1.2284 g of the sample requires 57.91 mL of 0.1018 M $Ce(NH_4)_2(NO_3)_6$ for complete reaction?

4.104 Assign oxidation numbers to each atom in the following substances:

(a) Ethane, C_2H_6, a constituent of natural gas

(b) Borax, $Na_2B_4O_7$, a mineral used in laundry detergents

(c) $Mg_2Si_2O_6$, a silicate mineral

4.105 Balance the equations for the following reactions in acidic solution:

(a) $PbO_2(s) + Mn^{2+}(aq) \longrightarrow Pb^{2+}(aq) + MnO_4^-(aq)$

(b) $As_2O_3(s) + NO_3^-(aq) \longrightarrow H_3AsO_4(aq) + HNO_2(aq)$

(c) $Br_2(aq) + SO_2(g) \longrightarrow Br^-(aq) + HSO_4^-(aq)$

(d) $NO_2^-(aq) + I^-(aq) \longrightarrow I_2(s) + NO(g)$

4.106 (a) Use the following reactions to arrange the elements A, B, C, and D in order of their decreasing ability as reducing agents:

$C + B^+ \longrightarrow C^+ + B$ $\qquad$ $A^+ + D \longrightarrow$ No reaction

$C^+ + A \longrightarrow$ No reaction $\qquad$ $D + B^+ \longrightarrow D^+ + B$

(b) Which of the following reactions would you expect to occur according to the activity series you established in part (a)?

(1) $A^+ + C \longrightarrow A + C^+$

(2) $A^+ + B \longrightarrow A + B^+$

4.107 Some metals occur naturally in their elemental state while others occur as compounds in ores. Gold, for instance, is found as the free metal; mercury is obtained by heating mercury(II) sulfide ore in oxygen; and zinc is obtained by heating zinc(II) oxide ore with coke (carbon). Judging from their positions in the activity series, which of the metals silver, platinum, and chromium would probably be obtained by

(a) finding it in its elemental state

(b) heating its sulfide with oxygen

(c) heating its oxide with coke

4.108 A sample weighing 14.98 g and containing a small amount of copper was treated to give a solution containing aqueous Cu^{2+} ions. Sodium iodide was then added to yield solid copper(I) iodide plus I_3^- ion, and the I_3^- was titrated with thiosulfate, $S_2O_3^{2-}$. The titration required 10.49 mL of 0.100 M $Na_2S_2O_3$ for complete reaction. What is the mass percent copper in the sample? The balanced equations are

$$2 Cu^{2+}(aq) + 5 I^-(aq) \longrightarrow 2 CuI(s) + I_3^-(aq)$$

$$I_3^-(aq) + 2 S_2O_3^{2-}(aq) \longrightarrow 3 I^-(aq) + S_4O_6^{2-}(aq)$$

4.109 The solubility of an ionic compound can be described quantitatively by a value called the *solubility product constant*, K_{sp}. For the general process $A_aB_b \rightleftharpoons a\,A^{n+} + b\,B^{m-}$, $K_{sp} = [A^{n+}]^a\,[B^{m-}]^b$. The brackets refer to concentrations in moles per liter.

(a) Write the expression for the solubility product constant of Ag_2CrO_4.

(b) If $K_{sp} = 1.1 \times 10^{-12}$ for Ag_2CrO_4, what are the molar concentrations of Ag^+ and CrO_4^{2-} in a saturated solution?

4.110 Write the expression for the solubility product constant of MgF_2 (see Problem 4.109). If $[Mg^{2+}] = 2.6 \times 10^{-4}$ mol/L in a saturated solution, what is the value of K_{sp}?

4.111 Succinic acid, an intermediate in the metabolism of food molecules, has molecular mass = 118.1 amu. When 1.926 g of succinic acid was dissolved in water and titrated, 65.20 mL of 0.5000 M NaOH solution was required to neutralize the acid. How many acidic hydrogens are there in a molecule of succinic acid?

Succinic acid

4.112 How could you use a precipitation reaction to separate each of the following pairs of cations? Write the formula for each reactant you would add, and write a balanced net ionic equation for each reaction.

(a) K^+ and Hg_2^{2+} $\qquad$ (b) Pb^{2+} and Ni^{2+}

(c) Ca^{2+} and NH_4^+ $\qquad$ (d) Fe^{2+} and Ba^{2+}

4.113 How could you use a precipitation reaction to separate each of the following pairs of anions? Write the formula for each reactant you would add, and write a balanced net ionic equation for each reaction.

(a) Cl^- and NO_3^- $\qquad$ (b) S^{2-} and SO_4^{2-}

(c) SO_4^{2-} and CO_3^{2-} $\qquad$ (d) OH^- and ClO_4^-

4.114 Write a balanced net ionic equation for each of the following reactions:

(a) $Mn(OH)_2(s) + H_2O_2(aq) \xrightarrow{\text{Base}} Mn(OH)_3(s)$

(b) $MnO_4^{2-}(aq) \xrightarrow{\text{Acid}} MnO_2(s) + MnO_4^-(aq)$

(c) $IO_3^-(aq) + I^-(aq) \xrightarrow{\text{Acid}} I_3^-(aq)$

(d) $P(s) + PO_4^{3-}(aq) \xrightarrow{\text{Base}} HPO_3^{2-}(aq)$

4.115 A 100.0 mL solution containing aqueous HCl and HBr was titrated with 0.1235 M NaOH. The volume of base required to neutralize the acid was 47.14 mL. Aqueous $AgNO_3$ was then added to precipitate the Cl^- and Br^- ions as AgCl and AgBr. The mass of the silver halides obtained was 0.9974 g. What are the molarities of the HCl and HBr in the original solution?

4.116 Write balanced net ionic equations for the following reactions in acidic solution:

(a) $S_4O_6^{2-}(aq) + Al(s) \longrightarrow H_2S(aq) + Al^{3+}(aq)$

(b) $S_2O_3^{2-}(aq) + Cr_2O_7^{2-}(aq) \longrightarrow S_4O_6^{2-}(aq) + Cr^{3+}(aq)$

(c) $ClO_3^-(aq) + As_2S_3(s) \longrightarrow$
$$Cl^-(aq) + H_2AsO_4^-(aq) + HSO_4^-(aq)$$

(d) $IO_3^-(aq) + Re(s) \longrightarrow ReO_4^-(aq) + I^-(aq)$

(e) $HSO_4^-(aq) + As_4(s) + Pb_3O_4(s) \longrightarrow$
$$PbSO_4(s) + H_2AsO_4^-(aq)$$

(f) $HNO_2(aq) \longrightarrow NO_3^-(aq) + NO(g)$

4.117 Write balanced net ionic equations for the following reactions in basic solution:

(a) $C_4H_4O_6^{2-}(aq) + ClO_3^-(aq) \longrightarrow CO_3^{2-}(aq) + Cl^-(aq)$

(b) $Al(s) + BiONO_3(s) \longrightarrow$
$$Bi(s) + NH_3(aq) + Al(OH)_4^-(aq)$$

(c) $H_2O_2(aq) + Cl_2O_7(aq) \longrightarrow ClO_2^-(aq) + O_2(g)$

(d) $Tl_2O_3(s) + NH_2OH(aq) \longrightarrow TlOH(s) + N_2(g)$

(e) $Cu(NH_3)_4^{2+}(aq) + S_2O_4^{2-}(aq) \longrightarrow$
$$SO_3^{2-}(aq) + Cu(s) + NH_3(aq)$$

(f) $Mn(OH)_2(s) + MnO_4^-(aq) \longrightarrow MnO_2(s)$

4.118 A mixture of CuO and Cu_2O with a mass of 10.50 g is reduced to give 8.66 g of pure Cu metal. What are the amounts in grams of CuO and Cu_2O in the original mixture?

4.119 When 75.0 mL of a 0.100 M lead(II) nitrate solution is mixed with 100.0 mL of a 0.190 M potassium iodide solution, a yellow-orange precipitate of lead(II) iodide is formed.

(a) What mass in grams of lead(II) iodide is formed, assuming the reaction goes to completion?

(b) What is the molarity of each of the ions Pb^{2+}, K^+, NO_3^-, and I^- in the resulting solution?

4.120 A sample of metal (M) reacted with both steam and aqueous HCl to release H_2, but did not react with water at room temperature. When 1.000 g of the metal was burned in oxygen, it formed 1.890 g of a metal oxide, M_2O_3. What is the identity of the metal?

4.121 An unknown metal (M) was found not to react with either water or steam, but its reactivity with aqueous acid was not investigated. When a 1.000 g sample of the metal was burned in oxygen and the resulting metal oxide converted to a metal sulfide, 1.504 g of sulfide was obtained. What is the identity of the metal?

4.122 Hydrogen peroxide can be either an oxidizing or reducing agent depending on the circumstances. Write balanced net ionic equations for each of the following reactions, and determine in each case whether hydrogen peroxide is oxidized (acts as a reducing agent) or reduced (acts as an oxidizing agent).

(a) $HCl(aq) + H_2O_2(aq) \longrightarrow Cl_2(aq) + H_2O(l)$

(b) (acidic) $MnO_4^-(aq) + H_2O_2(aq) \longrightarrow Mn^{2+}(aq) + O_2(g)$

(c) $H_2O_2(aq) + Cl_2(aq) \longrightarrow HCl(aq) + O_2(g)$

4.123 A mixture of acetic acid (CH_3CO_2H; monoprotic) and oxalic acid ($H_2C_2O_4$; diprotic) requires 27.15 mL of 0.100 M NaOH to neutralize it. When an identical amount of the mixture is titrated, 15.05 mL of 0.0247 M $KMnO_4$ is needed for complete reaction. What is the mass percent of each acid in the mixture? (Acetic acid does not react with MnO_4^-. The equation for the reaction of oxalic acid with MnO_4^- was given in Problem 4.101.)

4.124 Iron content in ores can be determined by a redox procedure in which the sample is first reduced with Sn^{2+}, as in Problem 4.98, and then titrated with $KMnO_4$ to oxidize the Fe^{2+} to Fe^{3+}. The balanced equation is

$$MnO_4^-(aq) + 5\,Fe^{2+}(aq) + 8\,H^+(aq) \longrightarrow$$
$$Mn^{2+}(aq) + 5\,Fe^{3+}(aq) + 4\,H_2O(l)$$

What is the mass percent Fe in a 2.368 g sample if 48.39 mL of a 0.1116 M $KMnO_4$ solution is needed to titrate the Fe^{3+}?

4.125 A mixture of $FeCl_2$ and NaCl is dissolved in water, and addition of aqueous silver nitrate then yields 7.0149 g of a precipitate. When an identical amount of the mixture is titrated with MnO_4^-, 14.28 mL of 0.198 M $KMnO_4$ is needed for complete reaction. What are the mass percents of the two compounds in the mixture? Na^+ and Cl^- do not react with MnO_4^-. The equation for the reaction of Fe^{2+} with MnO_4^- was given in Problem 4.124.

MULTICONCEPT PROBLEMS

4.126 Assume that you dissolve 10.0 g of a mixture of NaOH and $Ba(OH)_2$ in 250.0 mL of water and titrate with 1.50 M hydrochloric acid. The titration is complete after 108.9 mL of the acid has been added. What is the mass in grams of each substance in the mixture?

4.127 The following three solutions are mixed: 100.0 mL of 0.100 M Na_2SO_4, 50.0 mL of 0.300 M $ZnCl_2$, and 100.0 mL of 0.200 M $Ba(CN)_2$.

(a) What ionic compounds will precipitate out of solution?

(b) What is the molarity of each ion remaining in the solution assuming complete precipitation of all insoluble compounds?

4.128 A 250.0 g sample of a white solid is known to be a mixture of KNO_3, $BaCl_2$, and NaCl. When 100.0 g of this mixture is dissolved in water and allowed to react with excess H_2SO_4, 67.3 g of a white precipitate is collected. When the remaining 150.0 g of the mixture is dissolved in water and allowed to react with excess $AgNO_3$, 197.6 g of a second precipitate is collected.

(a) What are the formulas of the two precipitates?

(b) What is the mass of each substance in the original 250 g mixture?

4.129 Four solutions are prepared and mixed in the following order:

(1) Start with 100.0 mL of 0.100 M $BaCl_2$

(2) Add 50.0 mL of 0.100 M $AgNO_3$

(3) Add 50.0 mL of 0.100 M H_2SO_4

(4) Add 250.0 mL of 0.100 M NH_3

Write an equation for any reaction that occurs after each step, and calculate the concentrations of Ba^{2+}, Cl^-, NO_3^-, NH_3, and NH_4^+ in the final solution, assuming that all reactions go to completion.

4.130 To 100.0 mL of a solution that contains 0.120 M $Cr(NO_3)_2$ and 0.500 M HNO_3 is added 20.0 mL of 0.250 M $K_2Cr_2O_7$. The dichromate and chromium(II) ions react to give chromium(III) ions.

(a) Write a balanced net ionic equation for the reaction.

(b) Calculate the concentrations of all ions in the solution after reaction. Check your concentrations to make sure that the solution is electrically neutral.

4.131 Sodium nitrite, $NaNO_2$, is frequently added to processed meats as a preservative. The amount of nitrite ion in a sample can be determined by acidifying to form nitrous acid (HNO_2), letting the nitrous acid react with an excess of iodide ion, and then titrating the I_3^- ion that results with thiosulfate solution in the presence of a starch indicator. The unbalanced equations are

(1) $HNO_2 + I^- \longrightarrow NO + I_3^-$ (in acidic solution)

(2) $I_3^- + S_2O_3^{2-} \longrightarrow I^- + S_4O_6^{2-}$

(a) Balance the two redox equations.

(b) When a nitrite-containing sample with a mass of 2.935 g was analyzed, 18.77 mL of 0.1500 M $Na_2S_2O_3$ solution was needed for the reaction. What is the mass percent of NO_2^- ion in the sample?

4.132 Brass is an approximately 4:1 alloy of copper and zinc, along with small amounts of tin, lead, and iron. The mass percents of copper and zinc can be determined by a procedure that begins with dissolving the brass in hot nitric acid. The resulting solution of Cu^{2+} and Zn^{2+} ions is then treated with aqueous ammonia to lower its acidity, followed by addition of sodium thiocyanate (NaSCN) and sulfurous acid (H_2SO_3) to precipitate copper(I) thiocyanate (CuSCN). The solid CuSCN is collected, dissolved in aqueous acid, and treated with potassium iodate (KIO_3) to give iodine, which is then titrated with aqueous sodium thiosulfate ($Na_2S_2O_3$). The filtrate remaining after CuSCN has been removed is neutralized by addition of aqueous ammonia, and a solution of diammonium hydrogen phosphate [$(NH_4)_2HPO_4$] is added to yield a precipitate of zinc ammonium phosphate ($ZnNH_4PO_4$). Heating the precipitate to 900 °C converts it to zinc pyrophosphate ($Zn_2P_2O_7$), which is weighed. The equations are

(1) $Cu(s) + NO_3^-(aq) \longrightarrow Cu^{2+}(aq) + NO(g)$ (in acid)

(2) $Cu^{2+}(aq) + SCN^-(aq) + HSO_3^-(aq) \longrightarrow$
    $CuSCN(s) + HSO_4^-(aq)$ (in acid)

(3) $Cu^+(aq) + IO_3^-(aq) \longrightarrow Cu^{2+}(aq) + I_2(aq)$ (in acid)

(4) $I_2(aq) + S_2O_3^{2-}(aq) \longrightarrow I^-(aq) + S_4O_6^{2-}(aq)$ (in acid)

(5) $ZnNH_4PO_4(s) \longrightarrow Zn_2P_2O_7(s) + H_2O(g) + NH_3(g)$

(a) Balance all equations.

(b) When a brass sample with a mass of 0.544 g was subjected to the preceding analysis, 10.82 mL of 0.1220 M sodium thiosulfate was required for the reaction with iodine. What is the mass percent copper in the brass?

(c) The brass sample in part (b) yielded 0.246 g of $Zn_2P_2O_7$. What is the mass percent zinc in the brass?

4.133 A certain metal sulfide, MS_n (where n is a small integer), is widely used as a high-temperature lubricant. The substance is prepared by reaction of the metal pentachloride (MCl_5) with sodium sulfide (Na_2S). Heating the metal sulfide to 700 °C in air gives the metal trioxide (MO_3) and sulfur dioxide (SO_2), which reacts with Fe^{3+} ion under aqueous acidic conditions to give sulfate ion (SO_4^{2-}). Addition of aqueous $BaCl_2$ then forms a precipitate of $BaSO_4$. The unbalanced equations are:

(1) $MCl_5(s) + Na_2S(s) \longrightarrow MS_n(s) + S(l) + NaCl(s)$

(2) $MS_n(s) + O_2(g) \longrightarrow MO_3(s) + SO_2(g)$

(3) $SO_2(g) + Fe^{3+}(aq) \longrightarrow Fe^{2+}(aq) + SO_4^{2-}(aq)$ (in acid)

(4) $SO_4^{2-}(aq) + Ba^{2+}(aq) \longrightarrow BaSO_4(s)$

Assume that you begin with 4.61 g of MCl_5 and that reaction (1) proceeds in 91.3% yield. After oxidation of the MS_n product, oxidation of SO_2, and precipitation of sulfate ion, 7.19 g of $BaSO_4(s)$ is obtained.

(a) How many moles of sulfur are present in the MS_n sample?

(b) Assuming several possible values for n ($n = 1, 2, 3 \ldots$), what is the atomic mass of M in each case?

(c) What is the likely identity of the metal M, and what is the formula of the metal sulfide MS_n?

(d) Balance all equations.

4.134 On heating a 0.200 g sample of a certain semimetal in air, the corresponding oxide M_2O_3 was obtained. When the oxide was dissolved in aqueous acid and titrated with $KMnO_4$, 10.7 mL of 0.100 M MnO_4^- was required for complete reaction. The unbalanced equation is

$$H_3MO_3(aq) + MnO_4^-(aq) \longrightarrow$$
$$H_3MO_4(aq) + Mn^{2+} \text{ (in acid)}$$

(a) Balance the equation.

(b) How many moles of oxide were formed, and how many moles of semimetal were in the initial 0.200 g sample?

(c) What is the identity of the semimetal M?

CHAPTER 5

Periodicity and the Electronic Structure of Atoms

Periodicity, the presence of repeating patterns, is common throughout nature, as seen here in these basalt columns at the biosphere reserve, Gangolfsberg, Bavaria.

CONTENTS

The periodic table, introduced in Section 1.3, is the most important organizing principle in chemistry. If you know the properties of any one element in a group, or column, of the periodic table, you can make a good guess at the properties of every other element in the same group and even of the elements in neighboring groups. Although the periodic table was originally constructed from empirical observations, its scientific underpinnings have long been established and are well understood.

To see why it's called the *periodic* table, look at the graph of atomic radius versus atomic number in **Figure 5.1**, which shows a periodic rise-and-fall pattern. Beginning on the left with atomic number 1 (hydrogen), the size of the atoms increases to a maximum at atomic number 3 (lithium), then decreases to a minimum, then increases again to a maximum at atomic number 11 (sodium), then decreases, and so on. It turns out that all the maxima occur for atoms of group 1A elements—Li, Na, K, Rb, Cs, and Fr—and that the minima occur for atoms of the group 7A elements—F, Cl, Br, and I.

Figure 5.1
A graph of atomic radius in picometers (pm) versus atomic number. A clear rise-and-fall pattern of periodicity is evident. (Accurate data are not available for the group 8A elements.)

There's nothing unique about the periodicity of atomic radii shown in Figure 5.1. Any of several dozen other physical or chemical properties could be plotted in a similar way with similar results. We'll look at several examples of such periodicity in this chapter and the next.

5.1 LIGHT AND THE ELECTROMAGNETIC SPECTRUM

What fundamental property of atoms is responsible for the periodic variations we observe in atomic radii and in so many other characteristics of the elements? This question occupied the thoughts of chemists for more than 50 years after Mendeleev, and it was not until well into the 1920s that the answer was established. To understand how the answer slowly emerged, it's necessary to look first at the nature of visible light and other forms of radiant energy. Historically, studies of the interaction of radiant energy with matter have provided immense insight into atomic structure.

Although they appear quite different to our senses, visible light, infrared radiation, microwaves, radio waves, X rays, and other forms of radiant energy are all different kinds of **electromagnetic energy**. Collectively, they make up the **electromagnetic spectrum**, shown in **Figure 5.2**.

Figure 5.2
The electromagnetic spectrum. The spectrum consists of a continuous range of wavelengths and frequencies, from radio waves at the low-frequency end to gamma rays at the high-frequency end.

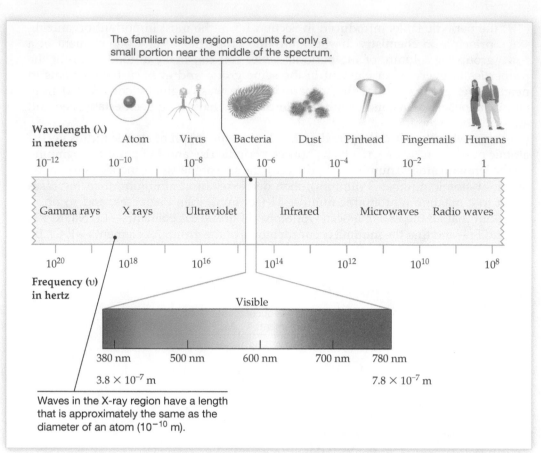

The familiar visible region accounts for only a small portion near the middle of the spectrum.

Wavelength (λ) in meters

| Atom | Virus | Bacteria | Dust | Pinhead | Fingernails | Humans |

| 10^{-12} | 10^{-10} | 10^{-8} | 10^{-6} | 10^{-4} | 10^{-2} | 1 |

Gamma rays   X rays   Ultraviolet   Infrared   Microwaves   Radio waves

| 10^{20} | 10^{18} | 10^{16} | 10^{14} | 10^{12} | 10^{10} | 10^{8} |

Frequency (υ) in hertz

Visible

380 nm   500 nm   600 nm   700 nm   780 nm

3.8×10^{-7} m 7.8×10^{-7} m

Waves in the X-ray region have a length that is approximately the same as the diameter of an atom (10^{-10} m).

Electromagnetic energy traveling through a vacuum behaves in some ways like ocean waves traveling through water. Like ocean waves, electromagnetic energy is characterized by a *frequency*, a *wavelength*, and an *amplitude*. If you could stand in one place and look at a sideways, cutaway view of an ocean wave moving through the water, you would see a regular rise-and-fall pattern like that in **Figure 5.3**.

▲ Ocean waves, like electromagnetic waves, are characterized by a wavelength, a frequency, and an amplitude.

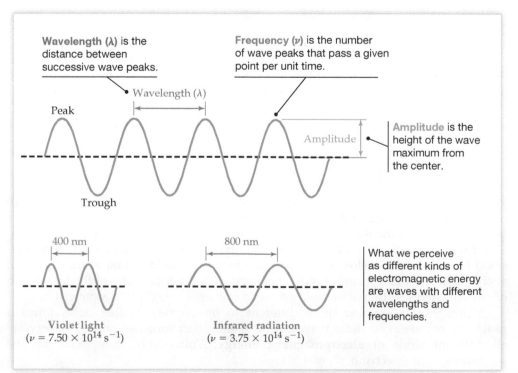

Wavelength (λ) is the distance between successive wave peaks.

Frequency (ν) is the number of wave peaks that pass a given point per unit time.

Peak

Wavelength (λ)

Amplitude is the height of the wave maximum from the center.

Amplitude

Trough

400 nm

800 nm

Violet light
($\nu = 7.50 \times 10^{14}\,\mathrm{s}^{-1}$)

Infrared radiation
($\nu = 3.75 \times 10^{14}\,\mathrm{s}^{-1}$)

What we perceive as different kinds of electromagnetic energy are waves with different wavelengths and frequencies.

Figure 5.3
The nature of electromagnetic waves. The waves are characterized by a wavelength, a frequency, and an amplitude.

The **frequency** (ν, Greek nu) of a wave is simply the number of wave peaks that pass by a given point per unit time, usually expressed in units of reciprocal seconds, or **hertz** (**Hz**; $1\ Hz = 1\ s^{-1}$). The **wavelength** (λ, Greek lambda) of the wave is the distance from one wave peak to the next, and the **amplitude** of the wave is the height of the wave, measured from the center line between peak and trough. Physically, what we perceive as the intensity of electromagnetic energy is proportional to the square of the wave amplitude. A feeble beam and a blinding glare of light may have the same wavelength and frequency, but they differ greatly in amplitude.

Multiplying the wavelength of a wave in meters (m) by its frequency in reciprocal seconds (s^{-1}) gives the speed of the wave in meters per second (m/s). The rate of travel of all electromagnetic energy in a vacuum is a constant value, commonly called the speed of light and abbreviated c. Its numerical value is defined as exactly $2.997\ 924\ 58 \times 10^8$ m/s, usually rounded off to 3.00×10^8 m/s:

$$\text{Wavelength} \times \text{Frequency} = \text{Speed}$$

$$\lambda\ (\text{m}) \times \nu\ (\text{s}^{-1}) = c\ (\text{m/s})$$

which can be rewritten as:

$$\lambda = \frac{c}{\nu} \quad \text{or} \quad \nu = \frac{c}{\lambda}$$

This equation says that frequency and wavelength are inversely related: Electromagnetic energy with a longer wavelength has a lower frequency, and energy with a shorter wavelength has a higher frequency.

WORKED EXAMPLE 5.1

CALCULATING A FREQUENCY FROM A WAVELENGTH

The light blue glow given off by mercury streetlamps has a wavelength of 436 nm. What is its frequency in hertz?

STRATEGY

We are given a wavelength and need to find the corresponding frequency. Wavelength and frequency are inversely related by the equation $\lambda\nu = c$, which can be solved for ν. Don't forget to convert from nanometers to meters.

SOLUTION

$$\nu = \frac{c}{\lambda} = \frac{\left(3.00 \times 10^8\ \frac{\text{m}}{\text{s}}\right)}{(436\ \text{nm})\left(\frac{1\ \text{m}}{10^9\ \text{nm}}\right)}$$

$$= 6.88 \times 10^{14}\ \text{s}^{-1} = 6.88 \times 10^{14}\ \text{Hz}$$

The frequency of the light is $6.88 \times 10^{14}\ \text{s}^{-1}$, or 6.88×10^{14} Hz.

▲ Does the blue glow from this mercury lamp correspond to a longer or shorter wavelength than the yellow glow from a sodium lamp?

▶ **PROBLEM 5.1** What is the frequency of a gamma ray with $\lambda = 3.56 \times 10^{-11}$ m? Of a radar wave with $\lambda = 10.3$ cm?

▶ **PROBLEM 5.2** What is the wavelength in meters of an FM radio wave with frequency $\nu = 102.5$ MHz? Of a medical X ray with $\nu = 9.55 \times 10^{17}$ Hz?

CONCEPTUAL PROBLEM 5.3 Two electromagnetic waves are represented to the right.

(a) Which wave has the higher frequency?

(b) Which wave represents a more intense beam of light?

(c) Which wave represents blue light, and which represents red light?

(a)

(b)

5.2   ELECTROMAGNETIC ENERGY AND ATOMIC LINE SPECTRA

The light that we see from the sun or from a typical lightbulb is "white" light, meaning that it consists of an essentially continuous distribution of wavelengths spanning the entire visible region of the electromagnetic spectrum. When a narrow beam of white light is passed through a glass prism, the different wavelengths travel through the glass at different rates. As a result, the white light is separated into its component colors, ranging from red at the long-wavelength end of the spectrum (780 nm) to violet at the short-wavelength end (380 nm) (**Figure 5.4a**). This separation into colors also occurs when light travels through water droplets in the air, forming a rainbow, or through oriented ice crystals in clouds, causing a *parhelion*, or sundog (**Figure 5.4b**).

(a)   **(b)**

Figure 5.4
Separation of white light into its constituent colors. **(a)** When a narrow beam of ordinary white light is passed through a glass prism, different wavelengths travel through the glass at different rates and appear as different colors. A similar effect occurs when light passes through water droplets in the air, forming a rainbow, or **(b)** through ice crystals in clouds, causing an unusual weather phenomenon called a parhelion, or sundog.

What do visible light and other kinds of electromagnetic energy have to do with atomic structure? It turns out that atoms give off light when heated or otherwise energetically excited, thereby providing a clue to their atomic makeup. Unlike the white light from the sun, though, the light given off by an energetically excited atom is not a continuous distribution of wavelengths. When passed first through a narrow slit and then through a prism, the light emitted by an excited atom is found to consist of only a few wavelengths rather than a full rainbow of colors, giving a series of discrete lines on an otherwise dark background—a so-called **line spectrum** that is unique for each element. Excited sodium atoms, produced by heating NaCl or some other sodium salt in the flame of a Bunsen burner, give off yellow light; hydrogen atoms give off a red light made of several different colors (**Figure 5.5**); and so on. In fact, the brilliant colors of fireworks are produced by mixtures of metal atoms that have been heated by explosive powder.

Soon after the discovery that energetic atoms emit light of specific wavelengths, chemists began cataloging the line spectra of various elements. They rapidly found that each element has its own unique spectral "signature, " and they began using the results to identify the elements present in minerals and other substances. Not until the work of the Swiss schoolteacher Johann Balmer in 1885, though, was a pattern discovered in atomic line spectra. It was known at the time that hydrogen produced a spectrum with four lines, as shown in Figure 5.5. The wavelengths of the four lines are 656.3 nm (red), 486.1 nm (blue-green), 434.0 nm (blue), and 410.1 nm (indigo).

Thinking about the hydrogen spectrum and trying by trial-and-error to organize the data in various ways, Balmer discovered that the wavelengths of the four lines in

▲ Excited hydrogen atoms give off a red light, and excited neon atoms emit orange light.

The visible line spectrum of energetically excited sodium atoms consists of a closely spaced pair of yellow lines.

The visible line spectrum of excited hydrogen atoms consists of four lines, from indigo at 410 nm to red at 656 nm.

Figure 5.5
Atomic line spectra.

the hydrogen spectrum can be expressed by the equation

$$\frac{1}{\lambda} = R_\infty \left[\frac{1}{2^2} - \frac{1}{n^2} \right] \qquad \text{or} \qquad \nu = R_\infty \cdot c \left[\frac{1}{2^2} - \frac{1}{n^2} \right]$$

where R_∞ is a constant (now called the *Rydberg constant*) equal to 1.097×10^{-2} nm^{-1} and n is an integer greater than 2. The red spectral line at 656.3 nm, for example, results from Balmer's equation when $n = 3$:

$$\frac{1}{\lambda} = [1.097 \times 10^{-2}\,\text{nm}^{-1}] \left[\frac{1}{2^2} - \frac{1}{3^2} \right] = 1.524 \times 10^{-3}\,\text{nm}^{-1}$$

$$\lambda = \frac{1}{1.524 \times 10^{-3}\,\text{nm}^{-1}} = 656.3\,\text{nm}$$

Similarly, a value of $n = 4$ gives the blue-green line at 486.1 nm, a value of $n = 5$ gives the blue line at 434.0 nm, and so on. Solve Balmer's equation yourself to make sure.

Subsequent to the discovery of the Balmer series of lines in the visible region of the electromagnetic spectrum, it was found that many other spectral lines are also present in nonvisible regions of the spectrum. Hydrogen, for instance, shows a series of spectral lines in the ultraviolet region and several other series in the infrared region.

By adapting Balmer's equation, the Swedish physicist Johannes Rydberg was able to show that every line in the entire spectrum of hydrogen can be fit by a generalized **Balmer–Rydberg equation**:

Balmer–Rydberg equation
$$\frac{1}{\lambda} = R_\infty \left[\frac{1}{m^2} - \frac{1}{n^2} \right] \qquad \text{or} \qquad \nu = R_\infty \cdot c \left[\frac{1}{m^2} - \frac{1}{n^2} \right]$$

where m and n represent integers with $n > m$. If $m = 1$, then the ultraviolet series of lines results. If $m = 2$, then Balmer's series of visible lines results. If $m = 3$, an infrared series is described, and so forth for still larger values of m. Some of these other spectral lines are calculated in Worked Example 5.2.

We'll look further at the Balmer–Rydberg equation and ultimately see what the integers m and n represent in Section 5.8.

WORKED EXAMPLE 5.2

USING THE BALMER–RYDBERG EQUATION

What are the two longest-wavelength lines in nanometers in the series of the hydrogen spectrum when $m = 1$ and $n > 1$?

STRATEGY

The wavelength λ is greatest when n is smallest; that is, when $n = 2$ and $n = 3$.

$$\frac{1}{\lambda} = R_\infty \left[\frac{1}{m^2} - \frac{1}{n^2} \right] \quad \text{where } m = 1$$

SOLUTION

Solving the equation first for $n = 2$ gives

$$\frac{1}{\lambda} = R_\infty \left[\frac{1}{1^2} - \frac{1}{2^2} \right] = \left(1.097 \times 10^{-2} \, \text{nm}^{-1} \right) \left(1 - \frac{1}{4} \right) = 8.228 \times 10^{-3} \, \text{nm}^{-1}$$

or $\quad \lambda = \dfrac{1}{8.228 \times 10^{-3} \, \text{nm}^{-1}} = 121.5 \, \text{nm}$

Solving the equation next for $n = 3$ gives

$$\frac{1}{\lambda} = R_\infty \left[\frac{1}{1^2} - \frac{1}{3^2} \right] = \left(1.097 \times 10^{-2} \, \text{nm}^{-1} \right)\left(1 - \frac{1}{9} \right) = 9.751 \times 10^{-3} \, \text{nm}^{-1}$$

$$\lambda = \frac{1}{9.751 \times 10^{-3} \, \text{nm}^{-1}} = 102.6 \, \text{nm}$$

The two longest-wavelength lines are at 121.5 nm and 102.6 nm.

WORKED EXAMPLE 5.3

USING THE BALMER–RYDBERG EQUATION

What is the shortest-wavelength line in nanometers in the series of the hydrogen spectrum when $m = 1$ and $n > 1$?

STRATEGY

The shortest-wavelength line occurs when n is infinitely large so that $1/n^2$ is zero. That is, if $n = \infty$, then $1/n^2 = 0$.

SOLUTION

$$\frac{1}{\lambda} = R_\infty \left[\frac{1}{1^2} - \frac{1}{\infty^2} \right] = \left(1.097 \times 10^{-2} \, \text{nm}^{-1} \right)(1 - 0) = 1.097 \times 10^{-2} \, \text{nm}^{-1}$$

or $\quad \lambda = \dfrac{1}{1.097 \times 10^{-2} \, \text{nm}^{-1}} = 91.16 \, \text{nm}$

The shortest-wavelength line is at 91.16 nm.

▶ **PROBLEM 5.4**   The Balmer equation can be extended beyond the visible portion of the electromagnetic spectrum to include lines in the ultraviolet. What is the wavelength in nanometers of ultraviolet light in the Balmer series corresponding to a value of $n = 7$?

▶ **PROBLEM 5.5**   What is the longest-wavelength line in nanometers in the infrared series for hydrogen where $m = 3$?

▶ **PROBLEM 5.6**   What is the shortest-wavelength line in nanometers in the infrared series for hydrogen where $m = 3$?

5.3 PARTICLELIKE PROPERTIES OF ELECTROMAGNETIC ENERGY

The existence of atomic line spectra and the fit of the visible hydrogen spectrum to the Balmer–Rydberg equation imply the existence of a general underlying principle about atomic structure, but it was years before that principle was found.

One important step toward developing a model of atomic structure came in 1905, when Albert Einstein (1879–1955) proposed an explanation of the *photoelectric effect*. Scientists had known since the late 1800s that irradiating a clean metal surface with light causes electrons to be ejected from the metal. Furthermore, the frequency of the light used for the irradiation must be above some threshold value, which is different for every metal. Blue light ($\nu \approx 6.5 \times 10^{14}$ Hz) causes metallic sodium to emit electrons, for example, but red light ($\nu \approx 4.5 \times 10^{14}$ Hz) has no effect on sodium.

Einstein explained the photoelectric effect by assuming that a beam of light behaves as if it were a stream of small particles, called **photons**, whose energy (E) is related to their frequency, ν, (or wavelength, λ) by the equation, $E = h\nu = hc/\lambda$. The proportionality constant h represents a fundamental physical constant that we now call Planck's constant and that has the value $h = 6.626 \times 10^{-34}$ J·s. For example, one photon of red light with a frequency $\nu = 4.62 \times 10^{14}$ s^{-1} (wavelength $\lambda = 649$ nm) has an energy of 3.06×10^{-19} J. [Recall from Section 1.11 that the SI unit for energy is the *joule* (J), where 1 J = 1 (kg·m^2)/s^2.]

$$E = h\nu = (6.626 \times 10^{-34}\,\text{J·s})\,(4.62 \times 10^{14}\,\text{s}^{-1}) = 3.06 \times 10^{-19}\,\text{J}$$

You might also recall from Section 2.6 that 1 *mole* (mol) of anything is the amount that contains Avogadro's number (6.022×10^{23}) of entities. Thus, it's often convenient to express electromagnetic energy on a per-mole basis rather than a per-photon basis. Multiplying the per-photon energy of 3.06×10^{-19} J by Avogadro's number gives an energy of 184 kJ/mol.

$$\left(3.06 \times 10^{-19}\,\frac{\text{J}}{\text{photon}}\right)\left(6.022 \times 10^{23}\,\frac{\text{photon}}{\text{mol}}\right) = 1.84 \times 10^{5}\,\frac{\text{J}}{\text{mol}}$$

$$\left(1.84 \times 10^{5}\,\frac{\text{J}}{\text{mol}}\right)\left(\frac{1\,\text{kJ}}{1000\,\text{J}}\right) = 184\,\text{kJ/mol}$$

Higher frequencies and shorter wavelengths correspond to higher energy radiation, while lower frequencies and longer wavelengths correspond to lower energy. Blue light ($\lambda \approx 450$ nm), for instance, has a shorter wavelength and is more energetic than red light ($\lambda \approx 650$ nm). Similarly, an X ray ($\lambda \approx 1$ nm) has a shorter wavelength and is more energetic than an FM radio wave ($\lambda \approx 10^{10}$ nm, or 10 m).

If the frequency (or energy) of the photon striking a metal is below a minimum value, no electron is ejected. Above the threshold level, however, sufficient energy is transferred from the photon to an electron to overcome the attractive forces holding the electron to the metal (**Figure 5.6**).

Note again that the energy of an individual photon depends only on its frequency (or wavelength), not on the intensity of the light beam. The intensity of a light beam is a measure of the *number* of photons in the beam, whereas frequency is a measure of the *energies* of those photons. A low-intensity beam of high-energy photons might easily knock a few electrons loose from a metal, but a high-intensity beam of low-energy photons might not be able to knock loose a single electron.

As a rough analogy, think of throwing balls of different masses at a glass window. A thousand Ping-Pong balls (lower energy) would only bounce off the window, but a single baseball (higher energy) would break the glass. In the same way, low-energy photons bounce off the metal surface, but a single photon at or above a certain threshold energy can "break" the metal and dislodge an electron.

▲ A glass window can be broken by a single baseball, but a thousand Ping-Pong balls would only bounce off.

Figure 5.6
The photoelectric effect.

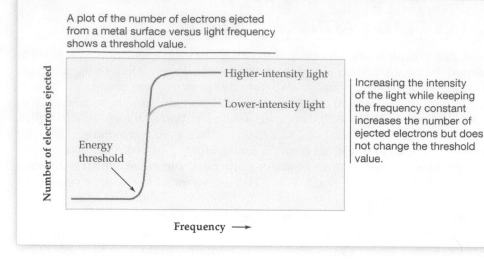

A plot of the number of electrons ejected from a metal surface versus light frequency shows a threshold value.

Higher-intensity light

Lower-intensity light

Energy threshold

Number of electrons ejected

Frequency →

Increasing the intensity of the light while keeping the frequency constant increases the number of ejected electrons but does not change the threshold value.

The main conclusion from Einstein's work was that the behavior of light and other forms of electromagnetic energy is more complex than had been formerly believed. In addition to behaving as waves, light energy can also behave as small particles. The idea might seem strange at first but becomes less so if you think of light as analogous to matter. Both are said to be *quantized*, meaning that both matter and electromagnetic energy occur only in discrete amounts. Just as there can be either 1 or 2 hydrogen atoms but not 1.5 or 1.8, there can be 1 or 2 photons of light but not 1.5 or 1.8. The amount, or **quantum**, of energy corresponding to one photon of light is almost inconceivably small, just as the amount of matter in one atom is inconceivably small, but the idea is the same.

An analogy of quantization from daily life is that of stairs versus a ramp. A ramp changes height continuously, but stairs change height only in discrete amounts and are thus quantized.

Understanding of the particlelike nature of electromagnetic energy explains in part the puzzle of atomic line spectra. Energetically excited atoms are unable to emit light of continuously varying wavelengths and therefore don't give a continuous spectrum. Instead, the atoms are constrained to emit quanta of only a few specific energies, and they therefore give a line spectrum.

Based on this insight, the Danish physicist Niels Bohr (1885–1962) proposed in 1914 a model of the hydrogen atom as a nucleus with an electron circling around it, much as a planet orbits the sun. According to Bohr, the energy levels of the orbits are quantized so that only certain specific orbits corresponding to certain specific energies for the electron are available. The observed spectral emission lines result when an electron falls from a higher-energy outer orbit to a lower-energy inner orbit, emitting a quantum of energy corresponding to the energy difference between the two allowed orbits (**Figure 5.7**).

▲ A ramp changes height continuously, but stairs are quantized, changing height only in discrete amounts. In the same way, electromagnetic energy is not continuous but is emitted only in discrete amounts.

Only specific orbits (paths) with specific energies are allowable for electrons.

When an **electron** falls from a higher-energy outer orbit to a lower-energy inner orbit, it emits a specific amount of electromagnetic energy, whose frequency corresponds to the energy difference between the two orbits.

Figure 5.7
The Bohr model of the hydrogen atom. In this model, an electron travels in a circular orbit around the nucleus.

WORKED EXAMPLE 5.4

CALCULATING THE ENERGY OF A PHOTON FROM ITS FREQUENCY

What is the energy in kilojoules per mole of radar waves with $\nu = 3.35 \times 10^8$ Hz?

STRATEGY

The energy of a photon with frequency ν can be calculated with the equation $E = h\nu$. To find the energy per mole of photons, the energy of one photon must be multiplied by Avogadro's number (Section 2.6).

SOLUTION

$$E = h\nu = (6.626 \times 10^{-34} \text{ J} \cdot \text{s})(3.35 \times 10^8 \text{ s}^{-1}) \quad = 2.22 \times 10^{-25} \text{ J}$$

$$\left(2.22 \times 10^{-25} \frac{\text{J}}{\text{photon}}\right)\left(6.022 \times 10^{23} \frac{\text{photon}}{\text{mol}}\right) = 0.134 \text{ J/mol}$$

$$= 1.34 \times 10^{-4} \text{ kJ/mol}$$

▶ **PROBLEM 5.7**   What is the energy in kilojoules per mole of photons corresponding to the shortest-wavelength line in the series of the hydrogen spectrum when $m = 1$ and $n > 1$? (Worked Example 5.3)?

▶ **PROBLEM 5.8**   The biological effects of a given dose of electromagnetic energy generally become more serious as the energy of the radiation increases: Infrared radiation has a pleasant warming effect; ultraviolet radiation causes tanning and burning; and X rays can cause considerable tissue damage. What energies in kilojoules per mole are associated with the following wavelengths: infrared radiation with $\lambda = 1.55 \times 10^{-6}$ m, ultraviolet light with $\lambda = 250$ nm, and X rays with $\lambda = 5.49$ nm?

5.4 WAVELIKE PROPERTIES OF MATTER

The analogy between matter and radiant energy developed in the early 1900s was further extended in 1924 by the French physicist Louis de Broglie (1892–1987). de Broglie suggested that, if *light* can behave in some respects like *matter*, then perhaps *matter* can behave in some respects like *light*. That is, perhaps matter is wavelike as well as particlelike.

In developing his theory about the wavelike behavior of matter, de Broglie focused on the inverse relationship between energy and wavelength for photons:

$$\text{Since} \quad E = \frac{hc}{\lambda} \quad \text{then} \quad \lambda = \frac{hc}{E}$$

Using the famous equation $E = mc^2$ proposed in 1905 by Einstein as part of his special theory of relativity, and substituting for E, then gives

$$\lambda = \frac{hc}{E} = \frac{hc}{mc^2} = \frac{h}{mc}$$

de Broglie suggested that a similar equation might be applied to moving particles like electrons by replacing the speed of light, c, by the speed of the particle, v. The resultant **de Broglie equation** thus allows calculation of a "wavelength" of an electron or of any other particle or object of mass m moving at velocity v:

de Broglie equation $\lambda = \dfrac{h}{mv}$

To see how the de Broglie equation can be used, look at the electron in a hydrogen atom. The mass of an electron is 9.11×10^{-31} kg, and the velocity v of an electron in a hydrogen atom is 2.2×10^6 m/s (about 1% of the speed of light). Thus, the de Broglie wavelength of an electron in a hydrogen atom is 3.3×10^{-10} m, or 330 pm. Note that

Planck's constant, which is usually expressed in units of joule seconds (J·s), is expressed for the present purposes in units of $(kg·m^2)/s$ [1 J = 1 $(kg·m^2)/s^2$].

$$\lambda = \frac{h}{mv} = \frac{6.626 \times 10^{-34} \frac{kg·m^2}{s}}{(9.11 \times 10^{-31}\, kg)\left(2.2 \times 10^6\, \frac{m}{s}\right)} = 3.3 \times 10^{-10}\, m$$

What does it mean to say that light and matter act both as waves and as particles? The answer is "not much," at least not on the everyday human scale, because dual wave/particle description of light and matter is really just a mathematical *model*. Since we can't see atoms and observe their behavior directly, the best we can do is to construct a set of mathematical equations that correctly account for atomic properties and behavior.

The problem in trying to understand the dual wave/particle description of light and matter is that our common sense isn't up to the task. Our intuition has been developed from personal experiences, using our eyes and other senses to tell us how light and matter are "supposed" to behave. We have no personal experience on the atomic scale, though, and thus have no common-sense way of dealing with the behavior of light and matter at that level. On the atomic scale, where distances and masses are so tiny, light and matter behave in a manner different from what we're used to.

▶ **PROBLEM 5.9**   What is the de Broglie wavelength in meters of a small car with a mass of 1150 kg traveling at a velocity of 55.0 mi/h (24.6 m/s)? Is this wavelength longer or shorter than the diameter of an atom (approximately 200 pm)?

5.5   QUANTUM MECHANICS AND THE HEISENBERG UNCERTAINTY PRINCIPLE

With the particlelike nature of energy and the wavelike nature of matter established, let's return to the problem of atomic structure. Several models of atomic structure were proposed in the late nineteenth and early twentieth centuries, such as the Bohr model described in Section 5.3. The Bohr model was important historically because of its conclusion that electrons have only specific energy levels available to them, but the model fails for atoms with more than one electron.

The breakthrough in understanding atomic structure came in 1926, when the Austrian physicist Erwin Schrödinger (1887–1961) proposed what has come to be called the **quantum mechanical model** of the atom. The fundamental idea behind the model is that it's best to abandon the notion of an electron as a small particle moving around the nucleus in a defined path and to concentrate instead on the electron's wavelike properties. In fact, it was shown in 1927 by Werner Heisenberg (1901–1976) that it is *impossible* to know precisely where an electron is and what path it follows—a statement called the **Heisenberg uncertainty principle**.

The Heisenberg uncertainty principle can be understood by imagining what would happen if we tried to determine the position of an electron at a given moment. For us to "see" the electron, light photons of an appropriate frequency would have to interact with and bounce off the electron. But such an interaction would transfer energy from the photon to the electron, thereby increasing the energy of the electron and making it move faster. Thus, the very act of determining the electron's position would make that position change.

In mathematical terms, Heisenberg's principle states that the uncertainty in the electron's position, Δx, times the uncertainty in its momentum, Δmv, is equal to or greater than the quantity $h/4\pi$:

◀▬ **Heisenberg uncertainty principle** $(\Delta x)(\Delta mv) \geq \dfrac{h}{4\pi}$

According to this equation, we can never know both the position and the velocity of an electron (or of any other object) beyond a certain level of precision. If we know the *velocity* with a high degree of certainty (Δmv is small), then the *position* of the electron must be uncertain (Δx must be large). Conversely, if we know the position of the electron exactly (Δx is small), then we can't know its velocity (Δmv must be large). As a result, an electron will always appear as something of a blur whenever we attempt to make any physical measurements of its position and velocity.

A brief calculation can help make the conclusions of the uncertainty principle clearer. As mentioned in the previous section, the mass m of an electron is 9.11×10^{-31} kg and the velocity v of an electron in a hydrogen atom is 2.2×10^6 m/s. If we assume that the velocity is known to within 10%, or 0.2×10^6 m/s, then the uncertainty in the electron's position in a hydrogen atom is greater than 3×10^{-10} m, or 300 pm. But since the diameter of a hydrogen atom is only 240 pm, *the uncertainty in the electron's position is similar in size to the atom itself!*

$$\text{If } (\Delta x)(\Delta mv) \geq \frac{h}{4\pi} \quad \text{then } (\Delta x) \geq \frac{h}{(4\pi)(\Delta mv)}$$

$$\Delta x \geq \frac{6.626 \times 10^{-34} \frac{\text{kg} \cdot \text{m}^2}{\text{s}}}{(4)(3.1416)(9.11 \times 10^{-31} \text{ kg})\left(0.2 \times 10^6 \frac{\text{m}}{\text{s}}\right)}$$

$$\Delta x \geq 3 \times 10^{-10} \text{ m} \quad \text{or} \quad 300 \text{ pm}$$

When the mass m of an object is relatively large, as in daily life, then both Δx and Δv in the Heisenberg relationship are very small, so we have no problem in measuring both position and velocity for visible objects. The problem arises only on the atomic scale.

▲ Even the motion of very fast objects such as bullets can be captured in daily life. On the atomic scale, however, velocity and position can't both be known precisely.

5.6 WAVE FUNCTIONS AND QUANTUM NUMBERS

Schrödinger's quantum mechanical model of atomic structure is framed in the form of a mathematical expression called a *wave equation* because it is similar in form to the equation used to describe the motion of ordinary waves in fluids. The solutions to the wave equation are called **wave functions**, or **orbitals**, and are represented by the symbol ψ (Greek psi). The best way to think about an electron's wave function is to regard it as an expression whose square, ψ^2, defines the probability of finding the electron within a given volume of space around the nucleus. As Heisenberg showed, we can never be completely certain about an electron's position. A wave function, however, tells where the electron will most probably be found.

$$\begin{array}{ccc} \text{Wave} \\ \text{equation} \end{array} \xrightarrow{\text{Solve}} \begin{array}{c} \text{Wave function} \\ \text{or orbital } (\psi) \end{array} \longrightarrow \begin{array}{c} \text{Probability of finding} \\ \text{electron in a region} \\ \text{of space } (\psi^2) \end{array}$$

A wave function is characterized by three parameters called **quantum numbers**, represented as n, l, and m_l, which describe the energy level of the orbital and the three-dimensional shape of the region in space occupied by a given electron.

- **The principal quantum number (n)** is a positive integer ($n = 1, 2, 3, 4, \ldots$) on which the size and energy level of the orbital primarily depend. For hydrogen and other one-electron atoms, such as He^+, the energy of an orbital depends only on n. For atoms with more than one electron, the energy level of an orbital depends both on n and on the l quantum number.

  As the value of n increases, the number of allowed orbitals increases and the size of those orbitals becomes larger, thus allowing an electron to be farther from the nucleus. Because it takes energy to separate a negative charge from a positive charge, this increased distance between the electron and the nucleus means that the energy of the electron in the orbital increases as the quantum number n increases.

  We often speak of orbitals as being grouped according to the principal quantum number n into successive layers, or **shells**, around the nucleus. Those orbitals with $n = 3$, for example, are said to be in the third shell.

• **The angular-momentum quantum number (l)** defines the three-dimensional shape of the orbital. For an orbital whose principal quantum number is n, the angular-momentum quantum number l can have any integral value from 0 to $n - 1$. Thus, within each shell, there are n different shapes for orbitals.

If $n = 1$, then $l = 0$

If $n = 2$, then $l = 0$ or 1

If $n = 3$, then $l = 0, 1,$ or 2

...and so forth

Just as it's convenient to think of orbitals as being grouped into shells according to the principal quantum number n, we often speak of orbitals within a shell as being further grouped into **subshells** according to the angular-momentum quantum number l. Different subshells are usually designated by letters rather than by numbers, following the order s, p, d, f, g. (Historically, the letters $s, p, d,$ and f arose from the use of the words *sharp, principal, diffuse,* and *fundamental* to describe various lines in atomic spectra.) After f, successive subshells are designated alphabetically: $g, h,$ and so on.

Quantum number l:	0	1	2	3	4	...
Subshell notation:	s	p	d	f	g	...

As an example, an orbital with $n = 3$ and $l = 2$ is a $3d$ orbital: 3 to represent the third shell and d to represent the $l = 2$ subshell.

• **The magnetic quantum number (m_l)** defines the spatial orientation of the orbital with respect to a standard set of coordinate axes. For an orbital whose angular-momentum quantum number is l, the magnetic quantum number m_l can have any integral value from $-l$ to $+l$. Thus, within each subshell—orbitals with the same shape, or value of l—there are $2l + 1$ different spatial orientations for those orbitals. We'll explore this point further in the next section.

If $l = 0$, then $m_l = 0$

If $l = 1$, then $m_l = -1, 0,$ or $+1$

If $l = 2$, then $m_l = -2, -1, 0, +1,$ or $+2$

...and so forth

A summary of the allowed combinations of quantum numbers for the first four shells is given in Table 5.1.

TABLE 5.1 Allowed Combinations of Quantum Numbers n, l, and m_l for the First Four Shells

n	l	m_l	Orbital Notation	Number of Orbitals in Subshell	Number of Orbitals in Shell
1	0	0	$1s$	1	1
2	0	0	$2s$	1	4
	1	$-1, 0, +1$	$2p$	3	
3	0	0	$3s$	1	9
	1	$-1, 0, +1$	$3p$	3	
	2	$-2, -1, 0, +1, +2$	$3d$	5	
4	0	0	$4s$	1	16
	1	$-1, 0, +1$	$4p$	3	
	2	$-2, -1, 0, +1, +2$	$4d$	5	
	3	$-3, -2, -1, 0, +1, +2, +3$	$4f$	7	

The energy levels of various orbitals are shown in **Figure 5.8**. As noted earlier in this section, the energy levels of different orbitals in a hydrogen atom depend only on the principal quantum number n, but the energy levels of orbitals in multielectron atoms depend on both n and l. In other words, the orbitals in a given shell all have the same energy for hydrogen but have slightly different energies for other atoms, depending on their subshell. In fact, there is even some crossover of energies between one shell and another. A $3d$ orbital in some multielectron atoms has a higher energy than a $4s$ orbital, for instance.

Figure 5.8

Energy levels of atomic orbitals: (a) hydrogen and (b) a typical multielectron atom. The differences between energies of various subshells in **(b)** are exaggerated for clarity.

WORKED EXAMPLE 5.5

USING QUANTUM NUMBERS TO IDENTIFY AN ORBITAL

Identify the shell and subshell of an orbital with the quantum numbers $n = 3$, $l = 1$, $m_l = 1$.

STRATEGY

The principal quantum number n gives the shell number, and the angular-momentum quantum number l gives the subshell designation. The magnetic quantum number m_l is related to the spatial orientation of the orbital.

SOLUTION

A value of $n = 3$ indicates that the orbital is in the third shell, and a value of $l = 1$ indicates that the orbital is of the p type. Thus, the orbital has the designation $3p$.

WORKED EXAMPLE 5.6

ASSIGNING QUANTUM NUMBERS TO AN ORBITAL

Give the possible combinations of quantum numbers for a $4p$ orbital.

STRATEGY

The designation $4p$ indicates that the orbital has a principal quantum number $n = 4$ and an angular-momentum quantum number $l = 1$. The magnetic quantum number m_l can have any of the three values $-1, 0,$ or $+1$.

SOLUTION

The allowable combinations are

$$n = 4, l = 1, m_l = -1 \qquad n = 4, l = 1, m_l = 0 \qquad n = 4, l = 1, m_l = +1$$

▸ **PROBLEM 5.10**   Extend Table 5.1 to show allowed combinations of quantum numbers when $n = 5$. How many orbitals are in the fifth shell?

▸ **PROBLEM 5.11**   Give orbital notations for electrons in orbitals with the following quantum numbers:

(a) $n = 2, l = 1, m_l = 1$ (b) $n = 4, l = 3, m_l = -2$ (c) $n = 3, l = 2, m_l = -1$

▸ **PROBLEM 5.12**   Give the allowed combinations of quantum numbers for the following orbitals:

(a) A $3s$ orbital   (b) A $2p$ orbital   (c) A $4d$ orbital

5.7   THE SHAPES OF ORBITALS

We said in the previous section that the square of a wave function, or orbital, describes the probability of finding the electron within a specific region of space. The shape of that spatial region is defined by the angular-momentum quantum number l, with $l = 0$ called an s orbital, $l = 1$ a p orbital, $l = 2$ a d orbital, and so forth. Of the various possibilities, s, p, d, and f orbitals are the most important because these are the only ones actually occupied in known elements. Let's look at each of the four individually.

s Orbitals

All s orbitals are spherical, meaning that the probability of finding an s electron depends only on distance from the nucleus, not on direction. Furthermore, because there is only one possible orientation of a sphere in space, an s orbital has $m_l = 0$ and there is only one s orbital per shell.

As shown in **Figure 5.9**, the value of ψ^2 for an s orbital is greatest near the nucleus and then drops off rapidly as distance from the nucleus increases, although it never

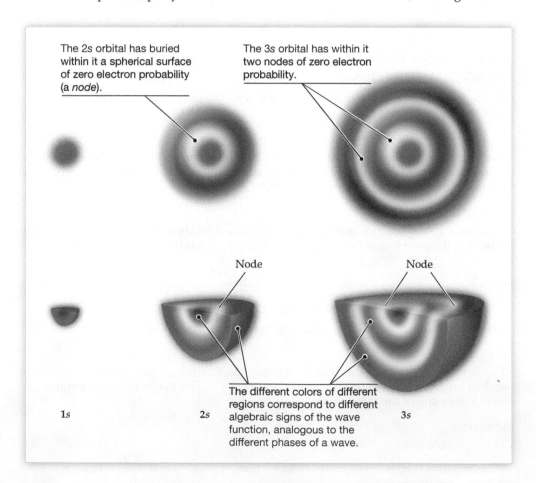

The 2s orbital has buried within it a spherical surface of zero electron probability (a *node*).

The 3s orbital has within it two nodes of zero electron probability.

Node

Node

1s   2s

The different colors of different regions correspond to different algebraic signs of the wave function, analogous to the different phases of a wave.

3s

Figure 5.9

Representations of 1s, 2s, and 3s orbitals. Slices through these spherical orbitals are shown on the top and cutaway views on the bottom, with the probability of finding an electron represented by the density of the shading.

goes all the way to zero, even at a large distance. As a result, there is no definite boundary to the atom and no definite size. For purposes like that of Figure 5.9, however, we usually imagine a boundary surface enclosing the volume where an electron spends most (say, 95%) of its time.

Although all s orbitals are spherical, there are significant differences among the s orbitals in different shells. For one thing, the size of the s orbital increases in successively higher shells, implying that an electron in an outer-shell s orbital is farther from the nucleus on average than an electron in an inner-shell s orbital. For another thing, the electron distribution in an outer-shell s orbital has more than one region of high probability. As shown in Figure 5.9, a $2s$ orbital is essentially a sphere within a sphere and has two regions of high probability, separated by a surface of zero probability called a **node**. Similarly, a $3s$ orbital has three regions of high probability and two spherical nodes.

The concept of an orbital node—a surface of zero electron probability separating regions of nonzero probability—is difficult to grasp because it raises the question "How does an electron get from one region of the orbital to another if it's not allowed to be at the node?" The question is misleading, though, because it assumes particle-like behavior for the electron rather than wavelike behavior.

In fact, nodes are an intrinsic property of waves, from moving waves of water in the ocean to the stationary, or standing, wave generated by vibrating a rope or guitar string (**Figure 5.10**). A node simply corresponds to the zero-amplitude part of the wave. On either side of the node is a nonzero wave amplitude. Note that a wave has two **phases**—peaks above the zero line and troughs below—corresponding to different algebraic signs, $+$ and $-$. Similarly, the different regions of $2s$ and $3s$ orbitals have different phases, $+$ and $-$, as indicated in Figure 5.9 by different colors.

When a rope is fixed at one end and vibrated rapidly at the other, a standing wave is generated.

The wave has two phases with different algebraic signs, $+$ and $-$, separated by zero-amplitude regions, called *nodes*.

Figure 5.10
A standing wave in a vibrating rope.

p Orbitals

The *p* orbitals are dumbbell-shaped rather than spherical, with their electron distribution concentrated in identical lobes on either side of the nucleus and separated by a planar node cutting through the nucleus. As a result, the probability of finding a *p* electron near the nucleus is zero. The two lobes of a *p* orbital have different phases, as indicated in **Figure 5.11** by different colors. We'll see in Chapter 7 that these phases are crucial for bonding because only lobes of the same phase can interact in forming covalent chemical bonds.

Figure 5.11

Representations of the three 2*p* orbitals. Each orbital is dumbbell-shaped and oriented in space along one of the three coordinate axes *x*, *y*, or *z*.

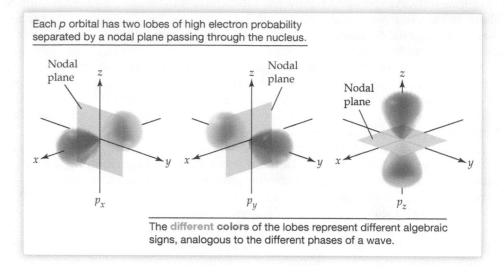

Each *p* orbital has two lobes of high electron probability separated by a nodal plane passing through the nucleus.

The **different colors** of the lobes represent different algebraic signs, analogous to the different phases of a wave.

There are three allowable values of m_l when $l = 1$, so each shell beginning with the second has three *p* orbitals, which are oriented in space at 90° angles to one another along the three coordinate axes *x*, *y*, and *z*. The three *p* orbitals in the second shell, for example, are designated $2p_x$, $2p_y$, and $2p_z$. As you might expect, *p* orbitals in the third and higher shells are larger than those in the second shell and extend farther from the nucleus. Their shape is roughly the same, however.

d and f Orbitals

The third and higher shells each contain five *d* orbitals, which differ from their *s* and *p* counterparts because they have two different shapes. Four of the five *d* orbitals are cloverleaf-shaped and have four lobes of maximum electron probability separated by two nodal planes through the nucleus (**Figure 5.12a–d**). The fifth *d* orbital is similar in shape to a p_z orbital but has an additional donut-shaped region of electron probability centered in the *xy* plane (**Figure 5.12e**). In spite of their different shapes, all five *d* orbitals in a given shell have the same energy. As with *p* orbitals, alternating lobes of the *d* orbitals have different phases.

You've probably noticed that both the number of nodal planes through the nucleus and the overall geometric complexity of the orbitals increases with the *l* quantum number of the subshell: An *s* orbital has one lobe and no nodal plane through the nucleus; a *p* orbital has two lobes and one nodal plane; and a *d* orbital has four lobes and two nodal planes. The seven *f* orbitals are more complex still, having eight lobes of maximum electron probability separated by three nodal planes through the nucleus. (Figure 5.12f shows one of the seven 4*f* orbitals.) Most of the elements we'll deal with in the following chapters don't use *f* orbitals in bonding, however, so we won't spend time on them.

▶ **PROBLEM 5.13**   How many nodal planes through the nucleus do you think a *g* orbital has?

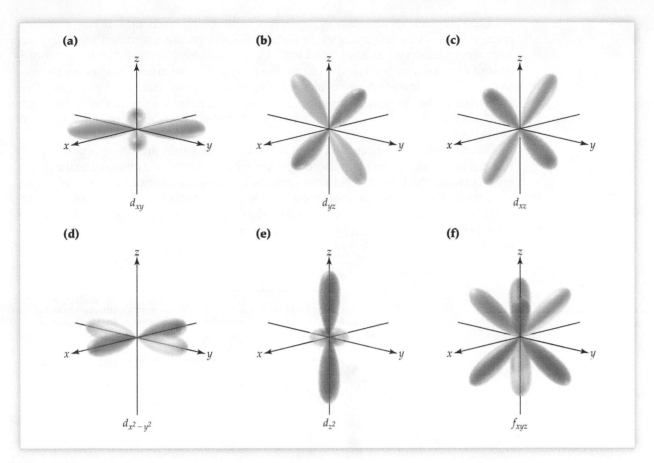

Figure 5.12
Representations of the five 3d orbitals. Four of the orbitals are shaped like a
cloverleaf (**a–d**), and the fifth is shaped like an elongated dumbbell inside a
donut (**e**). Also shown is one of the seven 4f orbitals (**f**). As with p orbitals in
Figure 5.11, the different colors of the lobes reflect different phases.

CONCEPTUAL PROBLEM 5.14   Give a possible combination of n and l quantum numbers for the following fourth-shell orbital:

5.8 QUANTUM MECHANICS
AND ATOMIC LINE SPECTRA

Now that we've seen how atomic structure is described according to the quantum mechanical model, let's return briefly to the subject of atomic line spectra first mentioned in Section 5.2. How does the quantum mechanical model account for the discrete wavelengths of light found in a line spectrum and for the Balmer–Rydberg equation that gives the values of those wavelengths?

Each electron in an atom occupies an orbital, and each orbital has a specific energy level. Thus, the energies available to electrons are quantized and can have only the specific values associated with the orbitals they occupy. When an atom is heated in a flame or electric discharge, the added thermal energy causes an electron to jump from a lower-energy orbital to a higher-energy orbital. In a hydrogen atom, for instance, the electron might jump from the 1s orbital to a second-shell orbital, to a third-shell orbital, or to an orbital in any higher shell, depending on the amount of energy added.

But the energetically excited atom is relatively unstable, and the electron rapidly returns to a lower-energy level accompanied by *emission* of energy equal to the difference between the higher and lower orbitals. Because the energies of the orbitals are quantized, the amount of energy emitted is also quantized. Thus, we observe the emission of only specific frequencies of radiation (Figure 5.13). By measuring the frequencies emitted by excited hydrogen atoms, we can calculate the energy differences between orbitals.

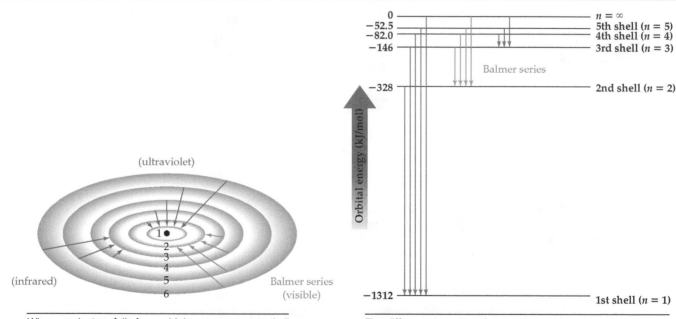

When an electron falls from a higher-energy outer-shell orbital to a lower-energy inner-shell orbital, it emits electromagnetic energy whose frequency corresponds to the energy difference between the orbitals.

The different spectral series correspond to electronic transitions from outer-shell orbitals to different inner-shell orbitals.

Figure 5.13
The origin of atomic line spectra.

The variables m and n in the Balmer–Rydberg equation for hydrogen (Section 5.2) represent the principal quantum numbers of the two orbitals involved in the electronic transition. The variable n corresponds to the principal quantum number of the higher-energy, outer-shell orbital that the transition is *from*, and the variable m corresponds to the principal quantum number of the lower-energy, inner-shell orbital that the transition is *to*. When $m = 1$, for example, the frequencies of emitted light correspond to energy differences between various outer-shell orbitals and the first-shell orbital. When $m = 2$ (now called the Balmer series), the frequencies correspond to energy differences between outer-shell orbitals and the second-shell orbitals.

$$\frac{1}{\lambda} = R_\infty \left(\frac{1}{m^2} - \frac{1}{n^2} \right)$$

Shell the transition is *to*
(inner-shell)

Shell the transition is *from*
(outer-shell)

Notice in Figure 5.13 that as n becomes larger and approaches infinity, the energy difference between the n shell and the first shell converges to a value of 1312 kJ/mol. That is, 1312 kJ is released when electrons come from a great distance (the "infinite" shell) and add to H^+ to give a mole of hydrogen atoms, each with an electron in its first shell:

$$H^+ + e^- \longrightarrow H + \text{Energy} \qquad (1312 \text{ kJ/mol})$$

Because the energy released on adding an electron to H^+ is equal to the energy absorbed on removing an electron from a hydrogen atom, we can also say that 1312 kJ/mol is required to remove the electron from a hydrogen atom. We'll see in the next chapter that the amount of energy necessary to remove an electron from a given atom provides an important clue about that element's chemical reactivity.

What is true for hydrogen is also true for all other atoms: All atoms show atomic line spectra when energetically excited electrons fall from higher-energy orbitals in outer shells to lower-energy orbitals in inner shells. As you might expect, though, these spectra become very complex for multielectron atoms in which different orbitals within a shell no longer have identical energies and in which a large number of electronic transitions are possible.

WORKED EXAMPLE 5.7

CALCULATING THE ENERGY DIFFERENCE BETWEEN TWO ORBITALS

What is the energy difference in kilojoules per mole between the first and second shells of the hydrogen atom if the lowest-energy emission in the spectral series with $m = 1$ and $n = 2$ occurs at $\lambda = 121.5$ nm?

STRATEGY

The lowest-energy emission line in the spectral series with $m = 1$ and $n = 2$ corresponds to the emission of light as an electron falls from the second shell to the first shell, with the energy of that light equal to the energy difference between shells. Knowing the wavelength of the light, we can calculate the energy of one photon using the equation, $E = hc/\lambda$, and then multiply by Avogadro's number to find the answer in joules (or kilojoules) per mole:

SOLUTION

$$E = \frac{hcN_A}{\lambda} = \frac{(6.626 \times 10^{-34} \text{ J} \cdot \text{s})\left(3.00 \times 10^8 \frac{m}{s}\right)\left(10^9 \frac{nm}{m}\right)(6.022 \times 10^{23} \text{ mol}^{-1})}{121.5 \text{ nm}}$$

$$= 9.85 \times 10^5 \text{ J/mol} = 985 \text{ kJ/mol}$$

The energy difference between the first and second shells of the hydrogen atom is 985 kJ/mol.

▶ **PROBLEM 5.15** Calculate in kilojoules per mole the energy necessary to completely remove an electron from the first shell of a hydrogen atom ($R_\infty = 1.097 \times 10^{-2} \text{ nm}^{-1}$).

5.9 ELECTRON SPIN AND THE PAULI EXCLUSION PRINCIPLE

The three quantum numbers n, l, and m_l discussed in Section 5.6 define the energy, shape, and spatial orientation of orbitals, but they don't quite tell the whole story. When the line spectra of many multielectron atoms are studied in detail, it turns out that some lines actually occur as very closely spaced pairs. (You can see this pairing if you look closely at the visible spectrum of sodium in Figure 5.5.) Thus, there are more energy levels than simple quantum mechanics predicts, and a fourth quantum number is required. Denoted m_s, this fourth quantum number is related to a property called *electron spin*.

Figure 5.14
Electron spin. Electrons behave in some ways as if they were tiny charged spheres spinning around an axis. This **spin** (blue arrow) gives rise to a tiny magnetic field (green arrow) and to a fourth quantum number, m_s, which can have a value of either $+1/2$ or $-1/2$.

In some ways, electrons behave as if they were spinning around an axis, somewhat as the Earth spins daily. This spinning charge gives rise to a tiny magnetic field and to a **spin quantum number (m_s)**, which can have either of two values, $+1/2$ or $-1/2$ (**Figure 5.14**). A spin of $+1/2$ is usually represented by an up arrow ($\uparrow$), and a spin of $-1/2$ by a down arrow ($\downarrow$). Note that the value of m_s is independent of the other three quantum numbers, unlike the values of n, l, and m_l, which are interrelated.

The importance of the spin quantum number comes when electrons occupy specific orbitals in multielectron atoms. According to the **Pauli exclusion principle**, proposed in 1925 by the Austrian physicist Wolfgang Pauli (1900–1958), no two electrons in an atom can have the same four quantum numbers. In other words, the set of four quantum numbers associated with an electron acts as a unique "address" for that electron in an atom, and no two electrons can have the same address.

◀▬▶ **Pauli exclusion principle**   No two electrons in an atom can have the same four quantum numbers.

Think about the consequences of the Pauli exclusion principle. Electrons that occupy the same orbital have the same three quantum numbers, n, l, and m_l. But if they have the same values for n, l, and m_l, they must have different values for the fourth quantum number: either $m_s = +1/2$ or $m_s = -1/2$. Thus, an orbital can hold only two electrons, which must have opposite spins. An atom with x number of electrons therefore has at least $x/2$ occupied orbitals (although it might have more if some of its orbitals are only half-filled).

5.10 ORBITAL ENERGY LEVELS IN MULTIELECTRON ATOMS

As we said in Section 5.6, the energy level of an orbital in a hydrogen atom, which has only one electron, is determined by its principal quantum number n. Within a shell, all hydrogen orbitals have the same energy, independent of their other quantum numbers. The situation is different in multielectron atoms, however, where the energy level of a given orbital depends not only on the shell but also on the subshell. The s, p, d, and f orbitals within a given shell have slightly different energies in a multielectron atom, as shown previously in Figure 5.8, and there is even some crossover of energies between orbitals in different shells.

The difference in energy between subshells in multielectron atoms results from electron–electron repulsions. In hydrogen, the only electrical interaction is the attraction of the positive nucleus for the negative electron, but in multielectron atoms there are many different interactions. Not only are there the attractions of the nucleus for each electron, there are also the repulsions between every electron and each of its neighbors.

The repulsion of outer-shell electrons by inner-shell electrons is particularly important because the outer-shell electrons are pushed farther away from the nucleus and are thus held less tightly. Part of the attraction of the nucleus for an outer electron is thereby canceled, an effect we describe by saying that the outer electrons are *shielded* from the nucleus by the inner electrons (**Figure 5.15**). The nuclear charge actually felt by an electron, called the **effective nuclear charge**, Z_{eff}, is often substantially lower than the actual nuclear charge Z.

◀▬▶ **Effective nuclear charge** $Z_{eff} = Z_{actual} -$ Electron shielding

How does electron shielding lead to energy differences among orbitals within a shell? The answer is a consequence of the differences in orbital shapes. Compare a $2s$ orbital with a $2p$ orbital, for instance. The $2s$ orbital is spherical and has a large probability density near the nucleus, while the $2p$ orbitals are dumbbell-shaped and have a node at the nucleus (Section 5.7). An electron in a $2s$ orbital therefore spends more time closer to the nucleus than an electron in a $2p$ orbital does and is less

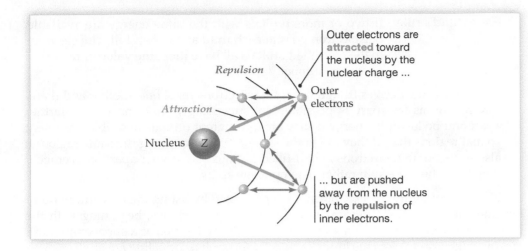

shielded. A $2s$ electron thus feels a higher Z_{eff}, is more tightly held by the nucleus, and is lower in energy than a $2p$ electron. In the same way, a $3p$ electron spends more time closer to the nucleus, feels a higher Z_{eff}, and has a lower energy than a $3d$ electron. More generally, within any given shell, a lower value of the angular-momentum quantum number l corresponds to a higher Z_{eff} and to a lower energy for the electron.

The idea that electrons in different orbitals are shielded differently and feel different values of Z_{eff} is a very useful one that we'll return to on several occasions to explain various chemical phenomena.

5.11 ELECTRON CONFIGURATIONS OF MULTIELECTRON ATOMS

All the parts are now in place to provide an electronic description for every element. Knowing the relative energies of the various orbitals, we can predict for each element which orbitals are occupied by electrons—the element's **electron configuration**.

A set of three rules called the **aufbau principle**, from the German word for "building up," guides the filling order of orbitals. In general, each successive electron added to an atom occupies the lowest-energy orbital available. The resultant lowest-energy configuration is called the **ground-state electron configuration** of the atom. Often, several orbitals will have the same energy level—for example, the three p orbitals or the five d orbitals in a given subshell. Orbitals that have the same energy level are said to be **degenerate**.

Rules of the aufbau principle:

1. **Lower-energy orbitals fill before higher-energy orbitals.** The ordering of energy levels for orbitals was shown in Figure 5.8 on page 163.

2. **An orbital can hold only two electrons, which must have opposite spins.** This is just a restatement of the Pauli exclusion principle (Section 5.9), emphasizing that no two electrons in an atom can have the same four quantum numbers.

3. **If two or more degenerate orbitals are available, one electron goes into each until all are half-full**, a statement called **Hund's rule**. Only then does a second electron fill one of the orbitals. Furthermore, the electrons in each of the singly occupied orbitals must have the same value for their spin quantum number.

▷▶ **Hund's rule** If two or more orbitals with the same energy are available, one electron goes in each until all are half full. The electrons in the half-filled orbitals all have the same value of their spin quantum number.

Hund's rule derives from the fact that electrons repel one another and therefore remain as far apart as possible. Not surprisingly, they can remain farther apart and be lower in energy if they are in different orbitals describing different spatial regions than if they are in the same orbital occupying the same region. It also turns out that electrons in half-filled orbitals stay farther apart on average if they have the same spin rather than opposite spins.

Electron configurations are normally represented by listing the n quantum number and the s, p, d, or f designation of the occupied orbitals, beginning with the lowest energy one, and showing the occupancy of each orbital as a superscript. Let's look at some examples to see how the rules of the aufbau principle are applied.

- **Hydrogen:** Hydrogen has only one electron, which must go into the lowest-energy, $1s$ orbital. Thus, the ground-state electron configuration of hydrogen is $1s^1$.

$$\text{H: } 1s^1$$

- **Helium:** Helium has two electrons, both of which fit into the lowest-energy, $1s$ orbital. The two electrons have opposite spins.

$$\text{He: } 1s^2$$

- **Lithium and beryllium:** With the $1s$ orbital full, both the third and fourth electrons go into the next available orbital, $2s$.

$$\text{Li: } 1s^2 2s^1 \qquad \text{Be: } 1s^2 2s^2$$

- **Boron through neon:** The six elements from boron through neon have their three $2p$ orbitals filled successively. Because these three $2p$ orbitals have the same energy, they are degenerate and are filled according to Hund's rule. In carbon, for instance, the two $2p$ electrons are in different orbitals, which can be arbitrarily specified as $2p_x$, $2p_y$, or $2p_z$ when writing the electron configuration. The same is true of nitrogen, whose three $2p$ electrons must be in three different orbitals. Although not usually noted in the written electron configuration, the electrons in each of the singly occupied carbon and nitrogen $2p$ orbitals must have the same value of the spin quantum number—either $+1/2$ or $-1/2$.

For clarity, we sometimes specify electron configurations using orbital-filling diagrams, in which electrons are represented by arrows. The two values of the spin quantum numbers are indicated by having the arrow point either up or down. An up–down pair indicates that an orbital is filled, while a single up (or down) arrow indicates that an orbital is half filled. Note in the diagrams for carbon and nitrogen that the degenerate $2p$ orbitals are half filled rather than filled, according to Hund's rule, and that the electron spin is the same in each.

B: $1s^2 2s^2 2p^1$ or $\underset{1s}{\uparrow\downarrow}$ $\underset{2s}{\uparrow\downarrow}$ $\underset{\hspace{2em}2p}{\uparrow \quad \underline{} \quad \underline{}}$

C: $1s^2 2s^2 2p_x{}^1 2p_y{}^1$ or $\underset{1s}{\uparrow\downarrow}$ $\underset{2s}{\uparrow\downarrow}$ $\underset{\hspace{2em}2p}{\uparrow \quad \uparrow \quad \underline{}}$

N: $1s^2 2s^2 2p_x{}^1 2p_y{}^1 2p_z{}^1$ or $\underset{1s}{\uparrow\downarrow}$ $\underset{2s}{\uparrow\downarrow}$ $\underset{\hspace{2em}2p}{\uparrow \quad \uparrow \quad \uparrow}$

From oxygen through neon, the three $2p$ orbitals are successively filled. For fluorine and neon, it's no longer necessary to distinguish among the different $2p$ orbitals, so we can simply write $2p^5$ and $2p^6$.

O: $1s^2\,2s^2\,2p_x^2\,2p_y^{\,1}\,2p_z^{\,1}$ or $\underset{1s}{\uparrow\downarrow}\quad\underset{2s}{\uparrow\downarrow}\quad\underset{2p}{\uparrow\downarrow\ \uparrow\ \uparrow}$

F: $1s^2\,2s^2\,2p^5$ or $\underset{1s}{\uparrow\downarrow}\quad\underset{2s}{\uparrow\downarrow}\quad\underset{2p}{\uparrow\downarrow\ \uparrow\downarrow\ \uparrow}$

Ne: $1s^2\,2s^2\,2p^6$ or $\underset{1s}{\uparrow\downarrow}\quad\underset{2s}{\uparrow\downarrow}\quad\underset{2p}{\uparrow\downarrow\ \uparrow\downarrow\ \uparrow\downarrow}$

- **Sodium and magnesium:** The $3s$ orbital is filled next, giving sodium and magnesium the ground-state electron configurations shown. Note that we often write the configurations in a shorthand version by giving the symbol of the noble gas in the previous row to indicate electrons in filled shells and then specifying only those electrons in partially filled shells.

Neon configuration

Na: $1s^2\,2s^2\,2p^6\,3s^1$ or $[\text{Ne}]\,3s^1$

Mg: $1s^2\,2s^2\,2p^6\,3s^2$ or $[\text{Ne}]\,3s^2$

- **Aluminum through argon:** The $3p$ orbitals are now filled according to the same rules used previously for filling the $2p$ orbitals of boron through neon. Rather than explicitly identify which of the degenerate $3p$ orbitals are occupied in Si, P, and S, we'll simplify the writing by giving just the total number of electrons in the subshell. For example, we'll write $3p^2$ for silicon rather than $3p_x^{\,1}\,3p_y^{\,1}$.

Al: $[\text{Ne}]\,3s^2\,3p^1$ **Si:** $[\text{Ne}]\,3s^2\,3p^2$ **P:** $[\text{Ne}]\,3s^2\,3p^3$

S: $[\text{Ne}]\,3s^2\,3p^4$ **Cl:** $[\text{Ne}]\,3s^2\,3p^5$ **Ar:** $[\text{Ne}]\,3s^2\,3p^6$

- **Elements past argon:** Following the filling of the $3p$ subshell in argon, the first crossover in the orbital filling order is encountered. Rather than continue filling the third shell by populating the $3d$ orbitals, the next two electrons in potassium and calcium go into the $4s$ subshell. Only then does filling of the $3d$ subshell occur to give the first transition metal series from scandium through zinc.

K: $[\text{Ar}]\,4s^1$ **Ca:** $[\text{Ar}]\,4s^2$ **Sc:** $[\text{Ar}]\,4s^2\,3d^1$ $\longrightarrow$ **Zn:** $[\text{Ar}]\,4s^2\,3d^{10}$

The experimentally determined ground-state electron configurations of the elements are shown in **Figure 5.16.**

5.12 SOME ANOMALOUS ELECTRON CONFIGURATIONS

The guidelines discussed in the previous section for determining ground-state electron configurations work well but are not completely accurate. A careful look at Figure 5.16 shows that 90 electron configurations are correctly accounted for by the rules but that 21 of the predicted configurations are incorrect.

The reasons for the anomalies often have to do with the unusual stability of both half-filled and fully filled subshells. Chromium, for example, which we would predict to have the configuration $[\text{Ar}]\,4s^2\,3d^4$, actually has the configuration $[\text{Ar}]\,4s^1\,3d^5$. By moving an electron from the $4s$ orbital to an energetically similar $3d$ orbital, chromium trades one filled subshell ($4s^2$) for two half-filled subshells ($4s^1\,3d^5$), thereby allowing the two electrons to be farther apart. In the same way, copper, which we would predict to have the configuration $[\text{Ar}]\,4s^2\,3d^9$, actually has the configuration $[\text{Ar}]\,4s^1\,3d^{10}$. By transferring an electron from the $4s$ orbital to a $3d$ orbital, copper trades one filled subshell ($4s^2$) for a different filled subshell ($3d^{10}$) and gains a half-filled subshell ($4s^1$).

1 1A	2 2A	3 3B	4 4B	5 5B	6 6B	7 7B	8 8B	9 8B	10	11 1B	12 2B	13 3A	14 4A	15 5A	16 6A	17 7A	18 8A
1 H $1s^1$																	2 He $1s^2$
3 Li $2s^1$	4 Be $2s^2$											5 B $2s^22p^1$	6 C $2s^22p^2$	7 N $2s^22p^3$	8 O $2s^22p^4$	9 F $2s^22p^5$	10 Ne $2s^22p^6$
11 Na $3s^1$	12 Mg $3s^2$											13 Al $3s^23p^1$	14 Si $3s^23p^2$	15 P $3s^23p^3$	16 S $3s^23p^4$	17 Cl $3s^23p^5$	18 Ar $3s^23p^6$
19 K $4s^1$	20 Ca $4s^2$	21 Sc $4s^23d^1$	22 Ti $4s^23d^2$	23 V $4s^23d^3$	24 Cr $4s^13d^5$	25 Mn $4s^23d^5$	26 Fe $4s^23d^6$	27 Co $4s^23d^7$	28 Ni $4s^23d^8$	29 Cu $4s^13d^{10}$	30 Zn $4s^23d^{10}$	31 Ga $4s^23d^{10}4p^1$	32 Ge $4s^23d^{10}4p^2$	33 As $4s^23d^{10}4p^3$	34 Se $4s^23d^{10}4p^4$	35 Br $4s^23d^{10}4p^5$	36 Kr $4s^23d^{10}4p^6$
37 Rb $5s^1$	38 Sr $5s^2$	39 Y $5s^24d^1$	40 Zr $5s^24d^2$	41 Nb $5s^14d^4$	42 Mo $5s^14d^5$	43 Tc $5s^24d^5$	44 Ru $5s^14d^7$	45 Rh $5s^14d^8$	46 Pd $4d^{10}$	47 Ag $5s^14d^{10}$	48 Cd $5s^24d^{10}$	49 In $5s^24d^{10}5p^1$	50 Sn $5s^24d^{10}5p^2$	51 Sb $5s^24d^{10}5p^3$	52 Te $5s^24d^{10}5p^4$	53 I $5s^24d^{10}5p^5$	54 Xe $5s^24d^{10}5p^6$
55 Cs $6s^1$	56 Ba $6s^2$	71 Lu $6s^24f^{14}5d^1$	72 Hf $6s^24f^{14}5d^2$	73 Ta $6s^24f^{14}5d^3$	74 W $6s^24f^{14}5d^4$	75 Re $6s^24f^{14}5d^5$	76 Os $6s^24f^{14}5d^6$	77 Ir $6s^24f^{14}5d^7$	78 Pt $6s^14f^{14}5d^9$	79 Au $6s^14f^{14}5d^{10}$	80 Hg $6s^24f^{14}5d^{10}$	81 Tl $6s^24f^{14}5d^{10}6p^1$	82 Pb $6s^24f^{14}5d^{10}6p^2$	83 Bi $6s^24f^{14}5d^{10}6p^3$	84 Po $6s^24f^{14}5d^{10}6p^4$	85 At $6s^24f^{14}5d^{10}6p^5$	86 Rn $6s^24f^{14}5d^{10}6p^6$
87 Fr $7s^1$	88 Ra $7s^2$	103 Lr $7s^25f^{14}6d^1$	104 Rf $7s^25f^{14}6d^2$	105 Db $7s^25f^{14}6d^3$	106 Sg $7s^25f^{14}6d^4$	107 Bh $7s^25f^{14}6d^5$	108 Hs $7s^25f^{14}6d^6$	109 Mt $7s^25f^{14}6d^7$	110 Ds $7s^15f^{14}6d^9$	111 Rg $7s^15f^{14}6d^{10}$	112 Cn $7s^25f^{14}6d^{10}$	113 —	114 —	115 —	116 —	117 —	118 —

57 La $6s^25d^1$	58 Ce $6s^24f^15d^1$	59 Pr $6s^24f^3$	60 Nd $6s^24f^4$	61 Pm $6s^24f^5$	62 Sm $6s^24f^6$	63 Eu $6s^24f^7$	64 Gd $6s^24f^75d^1$	65 Tb $6s^24f^9$	66 Dy $6s^24f^{10}$	67 Ho $6s^24f^{11}$	68 Er $6s^24f^{12}$	69 Tm $6s^24f^{13}$	70 Yb $6s^24f^{14}$
89 Ac $7s^26d^1$	90 Th $7s^26d^2$	91 Pa $7s^25f^26d^1$	92 U $7s^25f^36d^1$	93 Np $7s^25f^46d^1$	94 Pu $7s^25f^6$	95 Am $7s^25f^7$	96 Cm $7s^25f^76d^1$	97 Bk $7s^25f^9$	98 Cf $7s^25f^{10}$	99 Es $7s^25f^{11}$	100 Fm $7s^25f^{12}$	101 Md $7s^25f^{13}$	102 No $7s^25f^{14}$

Figure 5.16
Outer-shell, ground-state electron configurations of the elements.

Most of the anomalous electron configurations shown in Figure 5.16 occur in elements with atomic numbers greater than $Z = 40$, where the energy differences between subshells are small. In all cases, the transfer of an electron from one subshell to another lowers the total energy of the atom because of a decrease in electron–electron repulsions.

▶ **PROBLEM 5.16** Look at the electron configurations in Figure 5.16, and identify the 21 anomalous ones.

5.13 ELECTRON CONFIGURATIONS AND THE PERIODIC TABLE

Why are electron configurations so important, and what do they have to do with the periodic table? The answers emerge when you look closely at Figure 5.16. Focusing only on the electrons in the outermost shell, called the **valence shell**, all the elements in a given group of the periodic table have similar valence-shell electron configurations (Table 5.2). The group 1A elements, for example, all have an s^1 valence-shell configuration; the group 2A elements have an s^2 valence-shell configuration; the group 3A elements have an $s^2 p^1$ valence-shell configuration; and so on across every group of the periodic table (except for the small number of anomalies). Furthermore, because the valence-shell electrons are outermost and least tightly held, they are the most important for determining an element's properties, thus explaining why the elements in a given group of the periodic table have similar chemical behavior.

The periodic table can be divided into four regions, or blocks, of elements according to the orbitals being filled (**Figure 5.17**). The group 1A and 2A elements on the left side of the table are called the **s-block elements** because they result from the filling of an s orbital; the group 3A–8A elements on the right side of the table are the **p-block elements** because they result from the filling of p orbitals; the transition metal **d-block elements** in the middle of the table result from the filling of d orbitals; and the lanthanide/actinide **f-block elements** detached at the bottom of the table result from the filling of f orbitals.

TABLE 5.2 Valence-Shell Electron Configurations of Main-Group Elements

Group	Valence-Shell Electron Configuration	
1A	ns^1	(1 total)
2A	ns^2	(2 total)
3A	$ns^2 np^1$	(3 total)
4A	$ns^2 np^2$	(4 total)
5A	$ns^2 np^3$	(5 total)
6A	$ns^2 np^4$	(6 total)
7A	$ns^2 np^5$	(7 total)
8A	$ns^2 np^6$	(8 total)

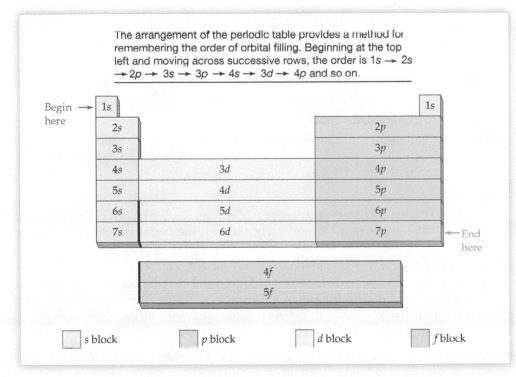

Figure 5.17
Blocks of the periodic table. Each block corresponds to the filling of a different kind of orbital.

Thinking of the periodic table as outlined in Figure 5.17 provides a useful way to remember the order of orbital filling. Beginning at the top left corner of the periodic table and going across successive rows gives the correct orbital-filling order. The first row of the periodic table, for instance, contains only the two s-block elements H and He, so the first available s orbital ($1s$) is filled first. The second row begins with two s-block elements (Li and Be) and continues with six p-block elements (B through Ne), so the next available s orbital ($2s$) and then the first available p orbitals ($2p$) are filled. Moving similarly across the third row, the $3s$ and $3p$ orbitals are filled. The fourth row again starts with two s-block elements (K and Ca) but is then followed by 10 d-block elements (Sc through Zn) and six p-block elements (Ga through Kr). Thus, the order of orbital filling is $4s$ followed by the first available d orbitals ($3d$) followed by $4p$. Continuing through successive rows of the periodic table gives the entire filling order:

$$1s \rightarrow 2s \rightarrow 2p \rightarrow 3s \rightarrow 3p \rightarrow 4s \rightarrow 3d \rightarrow 4p \rightarrow 5s \rightarrow 4d \rightarrow$$
$$5p \rightarrow 6s \rightarrow 4f \rightarrow 5d \rightarrow 6p \rightarrow 7s \rightarrow 5f \rightarrow 6d \rightarrow 7p$$

WORKED EXAMPLE 5.8

ASSIGNING A GROUND-STATE ELECTRON CONFIGURATION TO AN ATOM

Give the ground-state electron configuration of arsenic, $Z = 33$, and draw an orbital-filling diagram, indicating the electrons as up or down arrows.

STRATEGY

Think of the periodic table as having s, p, d, and f blocks of elements, as shown in Figure 5.17. Start with hydrogen at the upper left, and fill orbitals until 33 electrons have been added. Remember that only 2 electrons can go into an orbital and that each one of a set of degenerate orbitals must be half filled before any one can be completely filled.

SOLUTION

As: $1s^2\, 2s^2\, 2p^6\, 3s^2\, 3p^6\, 4s^2\, 3d^{10}\, 4p^3$ or $[Ar]\, 4s^2\, 3d^{10}\, 4p^3$

An orbital-filling diagram indicates the electrons in each orbital as arrows. Note that the three $4p$ electrons all have the same spin:

As: [Ar] $\underset{4s}{\uparrow\downarrow}$ $\underset{3d}{\uparrow\downarrow\ \uparrow\downarrow\ \uparrow\downarrow\ \uparrow\downarrow\ \uparrow\downarrow}$ $\underset{4p}{\uparrow\ \uparrow\ \uparrow}$

WORKED CONCEPTUAL EXAMPLE 5.9

IDENTIFYING AN ATOM FROM ITS GROUND-STATE ELECTRON CONFIGURATION

Identify the atom with the following ground-state electron configuration:

[Kr] $\uparrow\downarrow$ $\uparrow\ \uparrow\ \uparrow\ \uparrow\ \uparrow$ $\_\ \_\ \_$

STRATEGY

One way to do this problem is to identify the electron configuration and decide which atom has that configuration. Alternatively, you can just count the electrons, thereby finding the atomic number of the atom.

SOLUTION

The atom whose ground-state electron configuration is depicted is in the fifth row because it follows krypton. It has the configuration $5s^2\, 4d^5$, which identifies it as technetium. Alternatively, it has $36 + 7 = 43$ electrons and is the element with $Z = 43$.

▶ **PROBLEM 5.17**   Give expected ground-state electron configurations for the following atoms, and draw orbital-filling diagrams for parts **(a)**–**(c)**.

(a) Ti ($Z = 22$)   **(b)** Zn ($Z = 30$)   **(c)** Sn ($Z = 50$)   **(d)** Pb ($Z = 82$)

▶ **PROBLEM 5.18**   Take a guess. What do you think is a likely ground-state electron configuration for the sodium *ion*, Na^+, formed by loss of an electron from a neutral sodium atom? What is a likely ground-state electron configuration for the chloride ion, Cl^-, formed by adding an electron to a neutral chlorine atom?

CONCEPTUAL PROBLEM 5.19   Identify the atom with the following ground-state electron configuration:

[Ar] ↕ ↕ ↕ ↕ ↑ ↑ _ _ _

5.14 ELECTRON CONFIGURATIONS AND PERIODIC PROPERTIES: ATOMIC RADII

We began this chapter by saying that atomic radius is one of many elemental properties to show periodic behavior. You might wonder, though, how we can talk about a definite size for an atom, having said in Section 5.7 that the electron clouds around atoms have no specific boundaries. What's usually done is to define an atom's radius as being half the distance between the nuclei of two identical atoms when they are bonded together. In Cl_2, for example, the distance between the two chlorine nuclei is 198 pm; in diamond (elemental carbon), the distance between two carbon nuclei is 154 pm. Thus, we say that the atomic radius of chlorine is half the Cl—Cl distance, or 99 pm, and the atomic radius of carbon is half the C—C distance, or 77 pm.

It's possible to check the accuracy of atomic radii by making sure that the assigned values are additive. For instance, since the atomic radius of Cl is 99 pm and the atomic radius of C is 77 pm, the distance between Cl and C nuclei when those two atoms are bonded together ought to be roughly 99 pm + 77 pm, or 176 pm. In fact, the measured distance between chlorine and carbon in chloromethane (CH_3Cl) is 178 pm, remarkably close to the expected value.

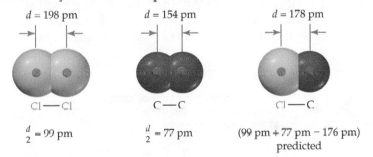

$d = 198$ pm	$d = 154$ pm	$d = 178$ pm
Cl—Cl	C—C	Cl—C
$\frac{d}{2} = 99$ pm	$\frac{d}{2} = 77$ pm	(99 pm + 77 pm – 176 pm) predicted

As shown pictorially in **Figure 5.18** and graphically in Figure 5.1 at the beginning of this chapter, a comparison of atomic radius versus atomic number shows a

Figure 5.18
Atomic radii of the elements in picometers.

Radius increases ↓	Radius decreases →																Radius increases ↓
H 37																	He
Li 152	Be 112											B 83	C 77	N 75	O 73	F 72	Ne
Na 186	Mg 160											Al 143	Si 117	P 110	S 104	Cl 99	Ar
K 227	Ca 197	Sc 162	Ti 147	V 134	Cr 128	Mn 127	Fe 126	Co 125	Ni 124	Cu 128	Zn 134	Ga 135	Ge 122	As 120	Se 116	Br 114	Kr
Rb 248	Sr 215	Y 180	Zr 160	Nb 146	Mo 139	Tc 136	Ru 134	Rh 134	Pd 137	Ag 144	Cd 151	In 167	Sn 140	Sb 140	Te ·143	I 133	Xe
Cs 265	Ba 222	Lu 173	Hf 159	Ta 146	W 139	Re 137	Os 135	Ir 136	Pt 138	Au 144	Hg 151	Tl 170	Pb 175	Bi 150	Po 167	At	Rn

periodic rise-and-fall pattern. Atomic radii increase going down a group of the periodic table (Li < Na < K < Rb < Cs, for instance) but decrease going across a row from left to right (Na > Mg > Al > Si > P > S > Cl, for instance). How can this behavior be explained?

The increase in radius going down a group of the periodic table occurs because successively larger valence-shell orbitals are occupied. In Li, for example, the outermost occupied shell is the second one ($2s^1$); in Na it's the third one ($3s^1$); in K it's the fourth one ($4s^1$); and so on through Rb ($5s^1$), Cs ($6s^1$), and Fr ($7s^1$). Because larger shells are occupied, the atomic radii are also larger.

The decrease in radius from left to right across the periodic table occurs because of an increase in effective nuclear charge caused by the increasing number of protons in the nucleus. As we saw in Section 5.10, Z_{eff}, the effective nuclear charge actually felt by an electron, is lower than the true nuclear charge Z because of shielding by other electrons in the atom. The amount of shielding felt by an electron depends on both the shell and subshell of the other electrons with which it is interacting.

As a general rule, a valence-shell electron is . . .

- . . . strongly shielded by electrons in inner shells, which are closer to the nucleus.
- . . . less strongly shielded by other electrons in the same shell, according to the order $s > p > d > f$.
- . . . only weakly shielded by other electrons in the same subshell, which are at the same distance from the nucleus.

Going across the third period from Na to Ar, for example, each additional electron adds to the same shell (from $3s^1$ for Na to $3s^2 3p^6$ for Ar). Because electrons in the same shell are at approximately the same distance from the nucleus, they are relatively ineffective at shielding one another. At the same time, though, the nuclear charge Z increases from +11 for Na to +18 for Ar. Thus, the *effective* nuclear charge for the valence-shell electrons increases across the period, drawing all the valence-shell electrons closer to the nucleus and progressively shrinking the atomic radii (**Figure 5.19**).

Figure 5.19
Plots of atomic radius and calculated Z_{eff} for the highest-energy electron versus atomic number.

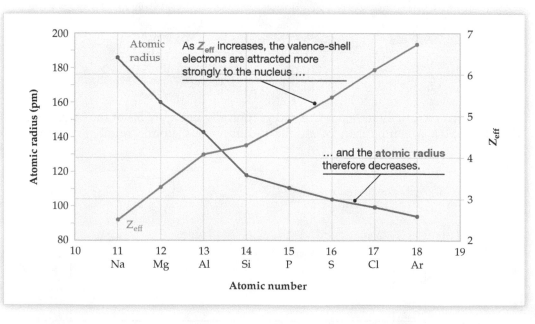

What is true of atomic radius is also true of other atomic properties, whose periodicity can be explained by electron configurations. We'll continue the subject in the next chapter.

▶ **PROBLEM 5.20** Which atom in each of the following pairs would you expect to be larger? Explain.

(a) Mg or Ba   (b) W or Hf   (c) Si or Sn   (d) Os or Lu

INQUIRY WHAT DO COMPACT FLUORESCENT LIGHTS HAVE TO DO WITH ATOMIC LINE SPECTRA?

In the standard incandescent lightbulb that has been used for more than a century, an electrical current passes through a thin tungsten filament, which is thereby heated and begins to glow. The wavelengths and intensity of the light emitted depend on the temperature of the glowing filament—typically about 2500 °C—and cover the range from ultraviolet (200–400 nm, through the visible (400–800 nm), to the infrared 800–2000 nm. The ultraviolet frequencies are blocked by the glass of the bulb, the visible frequencies pass through (the whole point of the lightbulb, after all), and the infrared frequencies warm the bulb and its surroundings.

Despite its long history, an incandescent bulb is actually an extremely inefficient device. In fact, only about 5% of the electrical energy consumed by the bulb is converted into visible light, with most of the remaining 95% converted into heat. Thus, many households and businesses are replacing their incandescent lightbulbs with modern compact fluorescent bulbs in an effort to use less energy. (Not that fluorescent bulbs are terribly efficient themselves—only about 20% of the energy they consume is converted into light—but that still makes them about four times better than incandescents.)

A fluorescent bulb is, in essence, a variation of the cathode-ray tube described in Section 2.3. The bulb has two main parts, an argon-filled glass tube (either straight or coiled) containing a small amount of mercury vapor, and electronic circuitry that provides a controlled high-voltage current. The current passes through a filament, which heats up and emits a flow of electrons through the tube. In the tube, some of the flowing electrons collide with mercury atoms, transferring their kinetic energy and exciting mercury electrons to higher-energy orbitals. Photons are then released when the excited mercury electrons fall back to the ground state, generating an atomic line spectrum.

Some photons emitted by the excited mercury atoms are in the visible range and contribute to the light we observe, but most are in the ultraviolet range at 185 nm and 254 nm and are invisible to our eyes. To capture this ultraviolet energy, fluorescent bulbs are coated on the inside with a *phosphor*, a substance that absorbs the ultraviolet light and re-emits the energy as visible light. As a result, fluorescent lights waste much less energy than incandescent bulbs.

Many different phosphors are used in fluorescent lights, each emitting its own line spectrum with visible light of various colors. Typically, a so-called *triphosphor* mixture is used, consisting of several complex metal oxides and rare-earth ions: $Y_2O_3:Eu^{3+}$ (red emitting), $CeMgAl_{11}O_{19}:Tb^{3+}$ (green emitting), and $BaMgAl_{10}O_{17}:Eu^{2+}$ (blue emitting). The final color that results can be tuned as desired by the manufacturer, but typically the three emissions together are distributed fairly evenly over the visible spectrum and provide a color reproduction that our eyes perceive as natural white light (Figure 5.20).

▲ Compact fluorescent bulbs like those shown here are a much more energy-efficient way to light a home than typical incandescent lightbulbs.

Figure 5.20

The triphosphor spectrum emitted from a typical fluorescent bulb. The triphosphor spectrum is distributed over the visible spectrum and is perceived by our eyes as white light.

▶ **PROBLEM 5.21** How do atomic line spectra give rise to the light emitted from fluorescent bulbs?

SUMMARY

Understanding the nature of atoms and molecules begins with an understanding of light and other kinds of **electromagnetic energy** that make up the **electromagnetic spectrum**. An electromagnetic wave travels through a vacuum at the speed of light (c) and is characterized by its **frequency (ν)**, **wavelength (λ)**, and **amplitude**. Unlike the white light of the sun, which consists of a nearly continuous distribution of wavelengths, the light emitted by an excited atom consists of only a few discrete wavelengths, a so-called **line spectrum**. The observed wavelengths correspond to the specific energy differences between energies of different orbitals.

Atomic line spectra arise because electromagnetic energy occurs only in discrete amounts, or **quanta**. Just as light behaves in some respects like a stream of small particles (**photons**), so electrons and other tiny units of matter behave in some respects like waves. The wavelength of a particle of mass m traveling at a velocity v is given by the **de Broglie equation**, $\lambda = h/mv$, where h is Planck's constant.

The **quantum mechanical model** proposed in 1926 by Erwin Schrödinger describes an atom by a mathematical equation similar to that used to describe wave motion. The behavior of each electron in an atom is characterized by a **wave function**, or **orbital**, whose square defines the probability of finding the electron in a given volume of space. Each wave function has a set of three parameters called **quantum numbers**. The **principal quantum number n** defines the size of the orbital; the **angular-momentum quantum number l** defines the shape of the orbital; and the **magnetic quantum number m_l** defines the spatial orientation of the orbital. In a hydrogen atom, which contains only one electron, the energy of an orbital depends only on n. In a multielectron

atom, the energy of an orbital depends on both n and l. In addition, the **spin quantum number m_s** specifies the electron spin as either $+1/2$ or $-1/2$.

Orbitals can be grouped into successive layers, or **shells**, according to their principal quantum number n. Within a shell, orbitals are grouped into s, p, d, and f **subshells** according to their angular-momentum quantum numbers l. An orbital in an s subshell is spherical, an orbital in a p subshell is dumbbell-shaped, and four of the five orbitals in a d subshell are cloverleaf-shaped.

The **ground-state electron configuration** of a multielectron atom is arrived at by following a series of rules called the **aufbau principle**.

1. The lowest-energy orbitals fill first.
2. Only two electrons of opposite spin go into any one orbital (the **Pauli exclusion principle**).
3. If two or more orbitals are equal in energy (**degenerate**), each is half filled before any one of them is completely filled (**Hund's rule**).

The periodic table is the most important organizing principle of chemistry. It is successful because elements in each group of the periodic table have similar **valence-shell electron configurations** and therefore have similar properties. For example, atomic radii of elements show a periodic rise-and-fall pattern according to the positions of the elements in the table. Atomic radii increase going down a group because n increases, and they decrease from left to right across a period because the **effective nuclear charge (Z_{eff})** increases.

KEY WORDS

amplitude 153
angular-momentum
    quantum number (*l*) 162
aufbau principle 171
Balmer–Rydberg
    equation 155
d-block element 175
de Broglie equation 159
degenerate 171
effective nuclear
    charge (Z_eff) 170
electromagnetic energy 151

electromagnetic
    spectrum 151
electron configuration 171
f-block element 175
frequency (*ν*) 153
ground-state electron
    configuration 171
Heisenberg uncertainty
    principle 160
hertz (Hz) 153
Hund's rule 171
line spectrum 154

magnetic quantum
    number (*m_l*) 162
node 165
orbital 161
p-block element 175
Pauli exclusion
    principle 170
phase 165
photon 157
principal quantum
    number (*n*) 161
quantum 158

quantum mechanical
    model 160
quantum number 161
s-block element 175
shell 161
spin quantum
    number (*m_s*) 170
subshell 162
valence shell 175
wave function 161
wavelength (λ) 153

CONCEPTUAL PROBLEMS

Problems 5.1–5.21 appear within the chapter.

5.22 Where on the blank outline of the periodic table do elements that meet the following descriptions appear?

   (a) Elements with the valence-shell ground-state electron configuration $ns^2\,np^5$

   (b) An element whose fourth shell contains two p electrons

   (c) An element with the ground-state electron configuration $[Ar]\,4s^2 3d^{10} 4p^5$

5.23 Where on the periodic table do elements that meet the following descriptions appear?

    (a) Elements with electrons whose largest principal quantum number is $n = 4$

    (b) Elements with the valence-shell ground-state electron configuration $ns^2\,np^3$

    (c) Elements that have only one unpaired p electron

    (d) The d-block elements

    (e) The p-block elements

5.24 One of the elements shown on the following periodic table has an anomalous ground-state electron configuration. Which is it —red, blue, or green—and why?

5.25 Two electromagnetic waves are represented below.

    (a) Which wave has the greater intensity?

    (b) Which wave corresponds to higher-energy radiation?

    (c) Which wave represents yellow light, and which represents infrared radiation?

5.26 What atom has the following orbital-filling diagram?

5.27 The following orbital-filling diagram represents an excited state rather than the ground state of an atom. Identify the atom, and give its ground-state electron configuration.

$$[\text{Ar}] \quad \frac{\downarrow\uparrow}{4s} \quad \frac{\downarrow\uparrow}{}\,\frac{\downarrow\uparrow}{}\,\frac{\downarrow\uparrow}{}\,\frac{\downarrow\uparrow}{}\,\frac{\downarrow\uparrow}{3d} \quad \frac{\downarrow\uparrow}{}\,\frac{\downarrow\uparrow}{}\,\frac{}{4p}$$

5.28 Which of the following three spheres represents a Ca atom, which an Sr atom, and which a Br atom?

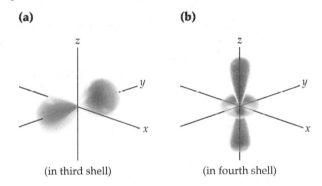

5.29 Identify each of the following orbitals, and give n and l quantum numbers for each.

SECTION PROBLEMS

Electromagnetic Energy and Atomic Spectra (Sections 5.1–5.3)

5.30 Which has the higher frequency, red light or violet light? Which has the longer wavelength? Which has the greater energy?

5.31 Which has the higher frequency, infrared light or ultraviolet light? Which has the longer wavelength? Which has the greater energy?

5.32 The Hubble Space Telescope detects electromagnetic energy in the wavelength range 1.15×10^{-7} m to 2.0×10^{-6} m. What region of the electromagnetic spectrum is found completely within this range? What regions fall partially in this range?

5.33 The Green Bank Telescope in West Virginia—the world's largest steerable radio telescope—detects frequencies from 290 MHz to 90 GHz. What region or regions of the electromagnetic spectrum are found completely or partially within its detection range?

5.34 What is the wavelength in meters of ultraviolet light with $\nu = 5.5 \times 10^{15}\ \text{s}^{-1}$?

5.35 What is the frequency of a microwave with $\lambda = 4.33 \times 10^{-3}$ m?

5.36 Calculate the energies of the following waves in kilojoules per mole, and tell which member of each pair has the higher value.

(a) An FM radio wave at 99.5 MHz and an AM radio wave at 1150 kHz

(b) An X ray with $\lambda = 3.44 \times 10^{-9}$ m and a microwave with $\lambda = 6.71 \times 10^{-2}$ m

5.37 The MRI (magnetic resonance imaging) body scanners used in hospitals operate with 400 MHz radiofrequency energy. How much energy does this correspond to in kilojoules per mole?

5.38 A certain cellular telephone transmits at a frequency of 825 MHz and receives at a frequency of 875 MHz.

(a) What is the wavelength of the transmitted signal in cm?

(b) What is the wavelength of the received signal in cm?

5.39 Optical fibers allow the fast transmission of vast amounts of data. In one type of fiber, the wavelength of transmitted light is 1.3×10^3 nm.

(a) What is the frequency of the light?

(b) Fiber optic cable is available in 12 km lengths. How long will it take for a signal to travel that distance assuming that the speed of light in the cable is the same as in a vacuum?

5.40 What is the wavelength in meters of photons with the following energies? In what region of the electromagnetic spectrum does each appear?

(a) 90.5 kJ/mol   (b) 8.05×10^{-4} kJ/mol

(c) 1.83×10^3 kJ/mol

5.41 What is the energy of each of the following photons in kilojoules per mole?

(a) $\nu = 5.97 \times 10^{19}$ s^{-1} (b) $\nu = 1.26 \times 10^6$ s^{-1}

(c) $\lambda = 2.57 \times 10^2$ m

5.42 The data encoded on CDs, DVDs, and Blu-ray discs is read by lasers. What is the wavelength in nanometers and the energy in joules of the following lasers?

(a) CD laser, $\nu = 3.85 \times 10^{14}$ s^{-1}

(b) DVD laser, $\nu = 4.62 \times 10^{14}$ s^{-1}

(c) Blu-ray laser, $\nu = 7.41 \times 10^{14}$ s^{-1}

5.43 The semimetal germanium is used as a component in photodetectors, which generate electric current when exposed to light. If a germanium photodetector responds to photons in the range $\lambda = 400-1700$ nm, will the following light sources be detected?

(a) a laser with $\nu = 4.35 \times 10^{14}$ s^{-1}

(b) photons with $E = 43$ kJ/mol

(c) electromagnetic radiation with $\nu = 706$ THz

5.44 According to the equation for the Balmer line spectrum of hydrogen, a value of $n = 3$ gives a red spectral line at 656.3 nm, a value of $n = 4$ gives a green line at 486.1 nm, and a value of $n = 5$ gives a blue line at 434.0 nm. Calculate the energy in kilojoules per mole of the radiation corresponding to each of these spectral lines.

5.45 According to the values cited in Problem 5.44, the wavelength differences between lines in the Balmer series become smaller as n becomes larger. In other words, the wavelengths converge toward a minimum value as n becomes very large. At what wavelength in nanometers do the lines converge?

Particles and Waves (Section 5.4–5.5)

5.46 Protons and electrons can be given very high energies in particle accelerators. What is the wavelength in meters of an electron (mass = 9.11×10^{-31} kg) that has been accelerated to 99% of the speed of light? In what region of the electromagnetic spectrum is this wavelength?

5.47 What is the wavelength in meters of a proton (mass = 1.673×10^{-24} g) that has been accelerated to 25% of the speed of light? In what region of the electromagnetic spectrum is this wavelength?

5.48 What is the de Broglie wavelength in meters of a baseball weighing 145 g and traveling at 156 km/h?

5.49 What is the de Broglie wavelength in meters of a mosquito weighing 1.55 mg and flying at 1.38 m/s?

5.50 At what speed in meters per second must a 145 g baseball be traveling to have a de Broglie wavelength of 0.500 nm?

5.51 What velocity would an electron (mass = 9.11×10^{-31} kg) need for its de Broglie wavelength to be that of red light (750 nm)?

5.52 Use the Heisenberg uncertainty principle to calculate the uncertainty in meters in the position of a honeybee weighing 0.68 g and traveling at a velocity of 0.85 m/s. Assume that the uncertainty in the velocity is 0.1 m/s.

5.53 The mass of a helium atom is 4.0026 amu, and its average velocity at 25 °C is 1.36×10^3 m/s. What is the uncertainty in meters in the position of a helium atom if the uncertainty in its velocity is 1%?

Orbitals and Quantum Mechanics (Sections 5.6–5.9)

5.54 What are the four quantum numbers, and what does each specify?

5.55 What is the Heisenberg uncertainty principle, and how does it affect our description of atomic structure?

5.56 Why do we have to use an arbitrary value such as 95% to determine the spatial limitations of an orbital?

5.57 How many nodal surfaces does a 4s orbital have? Draw a cutaway representation of a 4s orbital showing the nodes and the regions of maximum electron probability.

5.58 What is meant by the term effective nuclear charge, Z_{eff}, and what causes it?

5.59 How does electron shielding in multielectron atoms give rise to energy differences among 3s, 3p, and 3d orbitals?

5.60 Give the allowable combinations of quantum numbers for each of the following electrons:

(a) A 4s electron   (b) A 3p electron

(c) A 5f electron   (d) A 5d electron

5.61 Give the orbital designations of electrons with the following quantum numbers:

(a) $n = 3, l = 0, m_l = 0$ (b) $n = 2,\ l = 1,\ m_l = -1$

(c) $n = 4, l = 3, m_l = -2$ (d) $n = 4,\ l = 2,\ m_l = 0$

5.62 Tell which of the following combinations of quantum numbers are not allowed. Explain your answers.

(a) $n = 3, l = 0, m_l = -1$

(b) $n = 3, l = 1, m_l = 1$

(c) $n = 4, l = 4, m_l = 0$

5.63 Which of the following combinations of quantum numbers can refer to an electron in a ground-state cobalt atom ($Z = 27$)?

(a) $n = 3, l = 0, m_l = 2$

(b) $n = 4, l = 2, m_l = -2$

(c) $n = 3, l = 1, m_l = 0$

5.64 What is the maximum number of electrons in an atom whose highest-energy electrons have the principal quantum number $n = 5$?

5.65 What is the maximum number of electrons in an atom whose highest-energy electrons have the principal quantum number $n = 4$ and the angular-momentum quantum number $l = 0$?

5.66 The wavelength of light at which the Balmer series converges (Problem 5.45) corresponds to the amount of energy required to completely remove an electron from the second shell of a hydrogen atom. Calculate this energy in kilojoules per mole.

5.67 One series of lines of the hydrogen spectrum is caused by emission of energy accompanying the fall of an electron from outer shells to the fourth shell. The lines can be calculated using the Balmer–Rydberg equation:

$$\frac{1}{\lambda} = R_\infty \left[\frac{1}{m^2} - \frac{1}{n^2} \right]$$

where $m = 4$, $R_\infty = 1.097 \times 10^{-2}$ nm^{-1}, and n is an integer greater than 4. Calculate the wavelengths in nanometers and energies in kilojoules per mole of the first two lines in the series. In what region of the electromagnetic spectrum do they fall?

5.68 Sodium atoms emit light with a wavelength of 330 nm when an electron moves from a $4p$ orbital to a $3s$ orbital. What is the energy difference between the orbitals in kilojoules per mole?

5.69 Excited rubidium atoms emit red light with $\lambda = 795$ nm. What is the energy difference in kilojoules per mole between orbitals that give rise to this emission?

Electron Configurations (Sections 5.10–5.13)

5.70 Why does the number of elements in successive periods of the periodic table increase by the progression 2, 8, 18, 32?

5.71 Which two of the four quantum numbers determine the energy level of an orbital in a multielectron atom?

5.72 Which orbital in each of the following pairs is higher in energy?

(a) $5p$ or $5d$ (b) $4s$ or $3p$ (c) $6s$ or $4d$

5.73 Order the orbitals for a multielectron atom in each of the following lists according to increasing energy:

(a) $4d, 3p, 2p, 5s$ (b) $2s, 4s, 3d, 4p$ (c) $6s, 5p, 3d, 4p$

5.74 According to the aufbau principle, which orbital is filled immediately *after* each of the following in a multielectron atom?

(a) $4s$ (b) $3d$ (c) $5f$ (d) $5p$

5.75 According to the aufbau principle, which orbital is filled immediately *before* each of the following?

(a) $3p$ (b) $4p$ (c) $4f$ (d) $5d$

5.76 Give the expected ground-state electron configurations for the following elements:

(a) Ti   (b) Ru   (c) Sn   (d) Sr   (e) Se

5.77 Give the expected ground-state electron configurations for atoms with the following atomic numbers:

(a) $Z = 55$ (b) $Z = 40$ (c) $Z = 80$ (d) $Z = 62$

5.78 Draw orbital-filling diagrams for the following atoms. Show each electron as an up or down arrow, and use the abbreviation of the preceding noble gas to represent inner-shell electrons.

(a) Rb   (b) W   (c) Ge   (d) Zr

5.79 Draw orbital-filling diagrams for atoms with the following atomic numbers. Show each electron as an up or down arrow, and use the abbreviation of the preceding noble gas to represent inner-shell electrons.

(a) $Z = 25$ (b) $Z = 56$ (c) $Z = 28$ (d) $Z = 47$

5.80 Order the electrons in the following orbitals according to their shielding ability: $4s, 4d, 4f$.

5.81 Order the following elements according to increasing Z_{eff}: Ca, Se, Kr, K.

5.82 How many unpaired electrons are present in each of the following ground-state atoms?

(a) O   (b) Si   (c) K   (d) As

5.83 Identify the following atoms:

(a) It has the ground-state electron configuration [Ar] $4s^2 3d^{10} 4p^1$.

(b) It has the ground-state electron configuration [Kr] $4d^{10}$.

5.84 At what atomic number is the filling of a g orbital likely to begin?

5.85 Assuming that g orbitals fill according to Hund's rule, what is the atomic number of the first element to have a filled g orbital?

Electron Configurations and Periodic Properties (Section 5.14)

5.86 Why do atomic radii increase going down a group of the periodic table?

5.87 Why do atomic radii decrease from left to right across a period of the periodic table?

5.88 Order the following atoms according to increasing atomic radius: S, F, O.

5.89 Which atom in each of the following pairs has a larger radius?

(a) Na or K   (b) V or Ta

(c) V or Zn   (d) Li or Ba

5.90 The amount of energy that must be added to remove an electron from a neutral atom to give a positive ion is called the atom's *ionization energy*. Which would you expect to have the larger ionization energy, Na or Mg? Explain.

5.91 The amount of energy released when an electron adds to a neutral atom to give a negative ion is called the atom's *electron affinity*. Which would you expect to have the larger electron affinity, C or F? Explain.

5.92 What is the expected ground-state electron configuration of the recently discovered element with $Z = 116$?

5.93 What is the atomic number and expected ground-state electron configuration of the yet undiscovered element directly below Fr in the periodic table?

CHAPTER PROBLEMS

5.94 Orbital energies in single-electron atoms or ions, such as He^+, can be described with an equation similar to the Balmer–Rydberg equation:

$$\frac{1}{\lambda} = Z^2 R \left[\frac{1}{m^2} - \frac{1}{n^2} \right]$$

where Z is the atomic number. What wavelength of light in nm is emitted when the electron in He^+ falls from $n = 3$ to $n = 2$?

5.95 Like He^+, the Li^{2+} ion is a single-electron system (Problem 5.94). What wavelength of light in nm must be absorbed to promote the electron in Li^{2+} from $n = 1$ to $n = 4$?

5.96 Use the Balmer equation to calculate the wavelength in nanometers of the spectral line for hydrogen when $n = 6$. What is the energy in kilojoules per mole of the radiation corresponding to this line?

5.97 Lines in a certain series of the hydrogen spectrum are caused by emission of energy accompanying the fall of an electron from outer shells to the fifth shell. Use the Balmer–Rydberg equation to calculate the wavelengths in nanometers and energies in kilojoules per mole of the two longest-wavelength lines in the series. In what region of the electromagnetic spectrum do they fall?

5.98 What is the shortest wavelength in nanometers in the series you calculated in Problem 5.97?

5.99 What is the wavelength in meters of photons with the following energies? In what region of the electromagnetic spectrum does each appear?
(a) 142 kJ/mol   (b) 4.55×10^{-2} kJ/mol
(c) 4.81×10^4 kJ/mol

5.100 What is the energy of each of the following photons in kilojoules per mole?
(a) $\nu = 3.79 \times 10^{11}\ s^{-1}$ (b) $\nu = 5.45 \times 10^4\ s^{-1}$
(c) $\lambda = 4.11 \times 10^{-5}$ m

5.101 The *second* in the SI system is defined as the duration of 9,192,631,770 periods of radiation corresponding to the transition between two energy levels of a cesium-133 atom. What is the energy difference between the two levels in kilojoules per mole?

5.102 Write the symbol, give the ground-state electron configuration, and draw an orbital-filling diagram for each of the following atoms. Use the abbreviation of the preceding noble gas to represent the inner-shell electrons.
(a) The heaviest alkaline earth metal
(b) The lightest transition metal
(c) The heaviest actinide metal
(d) The lightest semimetal
(e) The group 6A element in the fifth period

5.103 Imagine a universe in which the four quantum numbers can have the same possible values as in our universe except that the angular-momentum quantum number l can have integral values of $0, 1, 2, \ldots, n + 1$ (instead of $0, 1, 2, \ldots, n - 1$).
(a) How many elements would be in the first two rows of the periodic table in this universe?
(b) What would be the atomic number of the element in the second row and fifth column?

(c) Draw an orbital-filling diagram for the element with atomic number 12.

5.104 Cesium metal is frequently used in photoelectric cells because the amount of energy necessary to eject electrons from a cesium surface is relatively small—only 206.5 kJ/mol. What wavelength of light in nanometers does this correspond to?

5.105 The laser light used in compact disc players has $\lambda = 780$ nm. In what region of the electromagnetic spectrum does this light appear? What is the energy of this light in kilojoules per mole?

5.106 Draw orbital-filling diagrams for the following atoms. Show each electron as an up or down arrow, and use the abbreviation of the preceding noble gas to represent inner-shell electrons.
(a) Sr   (b) Cd   (c) has $Z = 22$ (d) has $Z = 34$

5.107 The atomic radii of Y (180 pm) and La (187 pm) are significantly different, but the radii of Zr (160 pm) and Hf (159 pm) are essentially identical. Explain.

5.108 You're probably familiar with using Scotch Tape for wrapping presents but may not know that it can also generate electromagnetic radiation. When Scotch Tape is unrolled in a vacuum (but not in air), photons with a range of frequencies around $\nu = 2.9 \times 10^{18}\ s^{-1}$ are emitted in nanosecond bursts.
(a) What is the wavelength in meters of photons with $\nu = 2.9 \times 10^{18}\ s^{-1}$?
(b) What is the energy in kJ/mol of photons with $\nu = 2.9 \times 10^{18}\ s^{-1}$?
(c) What type of electromagnetic radiation are these photons?

5.109 Hard wintergreen-flavored candies are *triboluminescent*, meaning that they emit flashes of light when crushed. (You can see it for yourself if you look in a mirror while crunching a wintergreen Life Saver in your mouth in a dark room.) The strongest emission is around $\lambda = 450$ nm.
(a) What is the frequency in s^{-1} of photons with $\lambda = 450$ nm?
(b) What is the energy in kJ/mol of photons with $\lambda = 450$ nm?
(c) What is the color of the light with $\lambda = 450$ nm?

5.110 One method for calculating Z_{eff} is to use the equation

$$Z_{eff} = \sqrt{\frac{(E)(n^2)}{1312\ kJ/mol}}$$

where E is the energy necessary to remove an electron from an atom and n is the principal quantum number of the electron. Use this equation to calculate Z_{eff} values for the highest-energy electrons in potassium ($E = 418.8$ kJ/mol) and krypton ($E = 1350.7$ kJ/mol).

5.111 One watt (W) is equal to 1 J/s. Assuming that 5.0% of the energy output of a 75 W lightbulb is visible light and that the average wavelength of the light is 550 nm, how many photons are emitted by the lightbulb each second?

5.112 Microwave ovens work by irradiating food with microwave radiation, which is absorbed and converted into heat. Assuming that radiation with $\lambda = 15.0$ cm is used, that all the energy is converted to heat, and that

4.184 J is needed to raise the temperature of 1.00 g of water by 1.00 °C, how many photons are necessary to raise the temperature of a 350 mL cup of water from 20 °C to 95 °C?

5.113 Photochromic sunglasses, which darken when exposed to light, contain a small amount of colorless AgCl embedded in the glass. When irradiated with light, metallic silver atoms are produced and the glass darkens: $AgCl \longrightarrow Ag + Cl$. Escape of the chlorine atoms is prevented by the rigid structure of the glass, and the reaction therefore reverses as soon as the light is removed. If 310 kJ/mol of energy is required to make the reaction proceed, what wavelength of light is necessary?

5.114 The amount of energy necessary to remove an electron from an atom is a quantity called the *ionization energy*, E_i. This energy can be measured by a technique called *photoelectron spectroscopy*, in which light of wavelength λ is directed at an atom, causing an electron to be ejected. The kinetic energy of the ejected electron (E_k) is measured by determining its velocity, v ($E_k = mv^2/2$), and E_i is then calculated using the conservation of energy principle. That is, the energy of the incident light equals E_i plus E_k. What is the ionization energy of selenium atoms in kilojoules per mole if light with $\lambda = 48.2$ nm produces electrons with a velocity of 2.371×10^6 m/s? The mass, m, of an electron is 9.109×10^{-31} kg.

5.115 X rays with a wavelength of 1.54×10^{-10} m are produced when a copper metal target is bombarded with high-energy electrons that have been accelerated by a voltage difference of 30,000 V. The kinetic energy of the electrons equals the product of the voltage difference and the electronic charge in coulombs, where 1 volt-coulomb = 1 J.

(a) What is the kinetic energy in joules and the de Broglie wavelength in meters of an electron that has been accelerated by a voltage difference of 30,000 V?

(b) What is the energy in joules of the X rays emitted by the copper target?

5.116 In the Bohr model of atomic structure, electrons are constrained to orbit a nucleus at specific distances, given by the equation

$$r = \frac{n^2 a_0}{Z}$$

where r is the radius of the orbit, Z is the charge on the nucleus, a_0 is the *Bohr radius* and has a value of 5.292×10^{-11} m, and n is a positive integer ($n = 1, 2, 3, \ldots$)

like a principal quantum number. Furthermore, Bohr concluded that the energy level E of an electron in a given orbit is

$$E = \frac{-Ze^2}{2r}$$

where e is the charge on an electron. Derive an equation that will let you calculate the difference ΔE between any two energy levels. What relation does your equation have to the Balmer–Rydberg equation?

5.117 Assume that the rules for quantum numbers are different and that the spin quantum number m_s can have any of three values, $m_s = -1/2, 0, +1/2$, while all other rules remain the same.

(a) Draw an orbital-filling diagram for the element with $Z = 25$, showing the individual electrons in the outermost subshell as up arrows, down arrows, or 0. How many partially filled orbitals does the element have?

(b) What is the atomic number of the element in the 3rd column of the 4th row under these new rules? What block does it belong to ($s, p, d,$ or f)?

5.118 Given the subshells $1s, 2s, 2p, 3s, 3p,$ and $3d$, identify those that meet the following descriptions:

(a) Has $l = 2$

(b) Can have $m_l = -1$

(c) Is empty in a nitrogen atom

(d) Is full in a carbon atom

(e) Contains the outermost electrons in a beryllium atom

(f) Can contain two electrons, both with spin $m_s = +1/2$

5.119 A hydrogen atom with an electron in the first shell ($n = 1$) absorbs ultraviolet light with a wavelength of 1.03×10^{-7} m. To what shell does the electron jump?

5.120 A minimum energy of 7.21×10^{-19} J is required to produce the photoelectric effect in chromium metal.

(a) What is the minimum frequency of light needed to remove an electron from chromium?

(b) Light with a wavelength of 2.50×10^{-7} m falls on a piece of chromium in an evacuated glass tube. What is the minimum de Broglie wavelength of the emitted electrons? (Note that the energy of the incident light must be conserved; that is, the photon's energy must equal the sum of the energy needed to eject the electron plus the kinetic energy of the electron.)

MULTICONCEPT PROBLEMS

5.121 A photon produced by an X-ray machine has an energy of 4.70×10^{-16} J.

(a) What is the frequency of the photon?

(b) What is the wavelength of radiation of frequency (a)?

(c) What is the velocity of an electron with a de Broglie wavelength equal to (b)?

(d) What is the kinetic energy of an electron traveling at velocity (c)?

5.122 An energetically excited hydrogen atom has its electron in a $5f$ subshell. The electron drops down to the $3d$ subshell, releasing a photon in the process.

(a) Give the n and l quantum numbers for both subshells, and give the range of possible m_l quantum numbers.

(b) What wavelength of light is emitted by the process?

(c) The hydrogen atom now has a single electron in the $3d$ subshell. What is the energy in kJ/mol required to remove this electron?

5.123 Consider the noble gas xenon.

(a) Write the electron configuration of xenon using the abbreviation of the previous noble gas.

(b) When xenon absorbs 801 kJ/mol of energy, it is excited into a higher-energy state in which the outermost electron has been promoted to the next available subshell. Write the electron configuration for this excited xenon.

(c) The energy required to completely remove the outermost electron from the excited xenon atom is 369 kJ/mol, almost identical to that of cesium (376 kJ/mol). Explain.

6

Ionic Bonds and Some Main-Group Chemistry

This statue at the 700 year old Wieliczka salt mine in Poland was carved entirely out of salt.

CONTENTS

Now that we have a description of the electronic structure of isolated atoms, let's extend that description to atoms in chemical compounds. What is the force that holds atoms together in chemical compounds? Certainly there must be *some* force holding atoms together; otherwise, they would simply fly apart and no chemical compounds could exist. As we saw in Section 2.10, the forces that hold atoms together are called chemical bonds and are of two types: covalent bonds and ionic bonds. In this and the next chapter, we'll look at the nature of chemical bonds and at the energy changes that accompany their formation and breakage. We'll begin in the present chapter with a look at ions and at the ionic bonds formed between halogens and main-group metals.

6.1   ELECTRON CONFIGURATIONS OF IONS

We've seen on several occasions, particularly during the discussion of redox reactions in Sections 4.7 and 4.8, that metals (left side of the periodic table) tend to give up electrons in their chemical reactions and form cations. Conversely, halogens and some other nonmetals (right side of the table) tend to accept electrons in their chemical reactions and form anions. What are the ground-state electron configurations of the resultant ions?

For main-group elements, the electrons given up by a metal in forming a cation come from the highest-energy occupied orbital, while the electrons that are accepted by a nonmetal in forming an anion go into the lowest-energy unoccupied orbital according to the aufbau principle (Section 5.11). When a sodium atom ($1s^2 2s^2 2p^6 3s^1$) reacts with a chlorine atom and gives up an electron, for example, the valence-shell $3s$ electron of sodium is lost, giving an Na^+ ion with the noble-gas electron configuration of neon ($1s^2 2s^2 2p^6$). At the same time, when the chlorine atom ($1s^2 2s^2 2p^6 3s^2 3p^5$) accepts an electron from sodium, the electron fills the remaining vacancy in the $3p$ subshell to give a Cl^- ion with the noble-gas electron configuration of argon ($1s^2 2s^2 2p^6 3s^2 3p^6$).

$$\textbf{Na: } 1s^2 2s^2 2p^6 3s^1 \xrightarrow{-e} \textbf{Na}^+\textbf{: } 1s^2 2s^2 2p^6$$

$$\textbf{Cl: } 1s^2 2s^2 2p^6 3s^2 3p^5 \xrightarrow{+e^-} \textbf{Cl}^-\textbf{: } 1s^2 2s^2 2p^6 3s^2 3p^6$$

What is true for sodium is also true for the other elements in group 1A: All form positive ions by losing their valence-shell s electron when they undergo reaction, and all the resultant ions have noble-gas electron configurations. Similarly for the elements in group 2A: All form a doubly positive ion when they react, losing both their valence-shell s electrons. An Mg atom ($1s^2 2s^2 2p^6 3s^2$), for example, goes to an Mg^{2+} ion with the neon configuration $1s^2 2s^2 2p^6$ by loss of its two $3s$ electrons.

$$\textbf{Group 1A atom: } [\text{Noble gas}]\, ns^1 \xrightarrow{-e^-} \textbf{Group 1A ion}^+\textbf{: } [\text{Noble gas}]$$

$$\textbf{Group 2A atom: } [\text{Noble gas}]\, ns^2 \xrightarrow{-2\,e^-} \textbf{Group 2A ion}^{2+}\textbf{: } [\text{Noble gas}]$$

Just as the group 1A and 2A metals *lose* the appropriate number of electrons to yield ions with noble-gas configurations, the group 6A and group 7A nonmetals *gain* the appropriate number of electrons when they react with metals. The halogens in group 7A gain one electron to form singly charged anions with noble-gas configurations, and the elements in group 6A gain two electrons to form doubly charged anions with noble-gas configurations. Oxygen ($1s^2 2s^2 2p^4$), for example, becomes the O^{2-} ion with the neon configuration ($1s^2 2s^2 2p^6$) when it reacts with a metal:

$$\textbf{Group 6A atom: } [\text{Noble gas}]\, ns^2\, np^4 \xrightarrow{+2\,e^-} \textbf{Group 6A ion}^{2-}\textbf{: } [\text{Noble gas}]\, ns^2\, np^6$$

$$\textbf{Group 7A atom: } [\text{Noble gas}]\, ns^2\, np^5 \xrightarrow{+e^-} \textbf{Group 7A ion}^-\textbf{: } [\text{Noble gas}]\, ns^2\, np^6$$

The formulas and electron configurations of the most common main-group ions are listed in Table 6.1.

Remember...

The **ground-state electron configuration** of an atom or ion is a description of the atomic orbitals that are occupied in the lowest-energy state of the atom or ion. (Section 5.11)

Remember...

According to the **aufbau principle**, lower-energy orbitals fill before higher-energy ones and an orbital can hold only two electrons, which have opposite spins.   (Section 5.11)

TABLE 6.1   Some Common Main-Group Ions and Their Noble-Gas Electron Configurations

Group 1A	Group 2A	Group 3A	Group 6A	Group 7A	Electron Configuration
H^+					[None]
H^-					[He]
Li^+	Be^{2+}				[He]
Na^+	Mg^{2+}	Al^{3+}	O^{2-}	F^-	[Ne]
K^+	Ca^{2+}	$*Ga^{3+}$	S^{2-}	Cl^-	[Ar]
Rb^+	Sr^{2+}	$*In^{3+}$	Se^{2-}	Br^-	[Kr]
Cs^+	Ba^{2+}	$*Tl^{3+}$	Te^{2-}	I^-	[Xe]

* These ions don't have a true noble-gas electron configuration because they have an additional filled d subshell.

The situation is a bit different for ion formation from the transition-metal elements than it is for the main-group elements. Transition metals react with nonmetals to form cations by first losing their valence-shell s electrons and then losing one or more d electrons. As a result, all the remaining valence electrons in transition-metal cations occupy d orbitals. Iron, for instance, forms the Fe^{2+} ion by losing its two $4s$ electrons and forms the Fe^{3+} ion by losing two $4s$ electrons and one $3d$ electron:

$$\textbf{Fe: } [Ar]\, 4s^2\, 3d^6 \xrightarrow{-2\,e^-} \textbf{Fe}^{2+}\textbf{: } [Ar]\, 3d^6$$

$$\textbf{Fe: } [Ar]\, 4s^2\, 3d^6 \xrightarrow{-3\,e^-} \textbf{Fe}^{3+}\textbf{: } [Ar]\, 3d^5$$

It may seem strange that building up the periodic table adds the $3d$ electrons *after* the $4s$ electrons, whereas ion formation from a transition metal removes the $4s$ electrons *before* the $3d$ electrons. Note, though, that the two processes are not the reverse of one another, so they can't be compared directly. Building up the periodic table adds one electron to the valence shell and also adds one positive charge to the nucleus, but ion formation removes an electron from the valence shell without altering the nucleus.

▶ **PROBLEM 6.1**   Predict the ground-state electron configuration for each of the following ions, and explain your answers.

(a) Ra^{2+} (b) Y^{3+} (c) Ti^{4+} (d) N^{3-}

▶ **PROBLEM 6.2**   What doubly positive ion has the following ground-state electron configuration? $1s^2\, 2s^2\, 2p^6\, 3s^2\, 3p^6\, 3d^{10}$

6.2 IONIC RADII

Remember...

Atomic radii increase down a column of the periodic table because successively larger valence-shell orbitals are occupied, and radii decrease from left to right across a row of the periodic table because the effective nuclear charge increases across the row. (Section 5.14)

Just as there are systematic differences in the radii of atoms (Section 5.14), there are also systematic differences in the radii of ions. As shown in **Figure 6.1** for the elements of groups 1A and 2A, atoms shrink dramatically when an electron is removed to form a cation. The radius of an Na atom, for example, is 186 pm, but that of an Na^+ cation is 102 pm. Similarly, the radius of an Mg atom is 160 pm and that of an Mg^{2+} cation is 72 pm.

The cation that results when an electron is removed from a neutral atom is smaller than the original atom both because the electron is removed from a large,

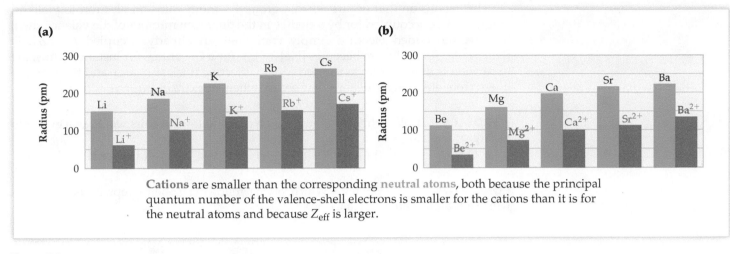

Cautions are smaller than the corresponding neutral atoms, both because the principal quantum number of the valence-shell electrons is smaller for the cations than it is for the neutral atoms and because Z_{eff} is larger.

Figure 6.1
Radii of (a) group 1A atoms and their cations; (b) group 2A atoms and their cations.

valence-shell orbital and because there is an increase in the effective nuclear charge, Z_{eff} for the remaining electrons (Section 5.10). On going from a neutral Na atom to a charged Na^+ cation, for example, the electron configuration changes from $1s^2 2s^2 2p^6 3s^1$ to $1s^2 2s^2 2p^6$. The valence shell of the Na *atom* is the *third* shell, but the valence shell of the Na^+ *cation* is the *second* shell. Thus, the Na^+ ion has a smaller valence shell than the Na atom and therefore a smaller size. In addition, the effective nuclear charge felt by the valence-shell electrons is greater in the Na^+ cation than in the neutral atom. The Na atom has 11 protons and 11 electrons, but the Na^+ cation has 11 protons and only 10 electrons. The smaller number of electrons in the cation means that they shield one another to a lesser extent and therefore are pulled in more strongly toward the nucleus.

The same effects felt by the group 1A elements when a single electron is lost are felt by the group 2A elements when two electrons are lost. For example, loss of two valence-shell electrons from an Mg atom ($1s^2 2s^2 2p^6 3s^2$) gives the Mg^{2+} cation ($1s^2 2s^2 2p^6$). The smaller valence shell of the Mg^{2+} cation and the increase in effective nuclear charge combine to cause a dramatic shrinkage. A similar shrinkage occurs whenever any of the metal atoms on the left-hand two-thirds of the periodic table is converted into a cation.

Just as neutral atoms shrink when converted to cations by loss of one or more electrons, they expand when converted to anions by gain of one or more electrons. As shown in Figure 6.2 for the group 7A elements (halogens), the expansion is dramatic. Chlorine, for example, nearly doubles in radius, from 99 pm for the neutral atom to 184 pm for the chloride anion.

Remember...

The effective nuclear charge (Z_{eff}) felt by an electron is due to electron shielding of outer electrons by inner electrons and may be substantially lower than the actual nuclear charge:

$$Z_{eff} = Z_{actual} - \text{electron shielding.}$$
(Section 5.10)

Anions are larger than their neutral atoms because of additional electron–electron repulsions and a decrease in Z_{eff}.

Figure 6.2
Radii of the group 7A atoms (halogens) and their anions.

The expansion that occurs when a group 7A atom gains an electron to yield an anion can't be accounted for by a change in the quantum number of the valence shell, because the added electron simply completes an already occupied p subshell: [Ne] $3s^2 3p^5$ for a Cl atom becomes [Ne] $3s^2 3p^6$ for a Cl$^-$ anion, for instance. Thus, the expansion is due entirely to the decrease in effective nuclear charge and the increase in electron–electron repulsions that occurs when an extra electron is added.

▶ **PROBLEM 6.3** Which atom or ion in each of the following pairs would you expect to be larger? Explain.

(a) O or O^{2-} (b) O or S   (c) Fe or Fe^{3+} (d) H or H$^-$

CONCEPTUAL PROBLEM 6.4 Which of the following spheres represents a K$^+$ ion, which a K atom, and which a Cl$^-$ ion?

$r = 227$ pm $r = 184$ pm $r = 133$ pm

6.3 IONIZATION ENERGY

We saw in the previous chapter that the absorption of electromagnetic energy by an atom leads to a change in electron configuration. When energy is added, a valence-shell electron is promoted from a lower-energy orbital to a higher-energy one with a larger principal quantum number n. If enough energy is absorbed, the electron can even be removed completely from the atom, leaving behind a cation. The amount of energy necessary to remove the highest-energy electron from an isolated neutral atom in the gaseous state is called the atom's **ionization energy**, abbreviated E_i. For hydrogen, $E_i = 1312.0$ kJ/mol.

1312.0 kJ/mol

H   H$^+$ +   e$^-$

As shown by the plot in **Figure 6.3**, ionization energies differ widely, from a low of 375.7 kJ/mol for cesium to a high of 2372.3 kJ/mol for helium. Furthermore, the data show a clear periodicity. The minimum E_i values correspond to the group 1A elements (alkali metals), the maximum E_i values correspond to the group 8A elements (noble gases), and a gradual increase in E_i occurs from left to right across a row of the periodic table—from Na to Ar, for example. Note that all the values are positive, meaning that energy must always be added to remove an electron from an atom.

The periodicity evident in Figure 6.3 can be explained by looking at electron configurations. Atoms of the group 8A elements have filled valence subshells, either s for helium or both s and p for the other noble gases. As we saw in Section 5.14, an electron in a filled valence subshell feels a relatively high Z_{eff} because electrons in the same subshell don't **shield** one another very strongly. As a result, the electrons are held tightly to the nucleus, the radius of the atom is small, and the energy necessary to remove an electron is relatively large. Atoms of group 1A elements, by contrast,

Remember...

Valence electrons are strongly **shielded** by inner-shell (core) electrons, are less strongly shielded by other electrons in the same shell according to the order $s > p > d > f$, and are only weakly shielded by other electrons in the same subshell. (Section 5.14)

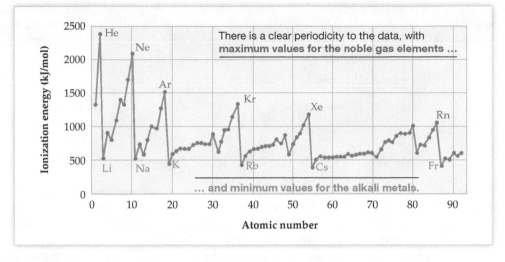

Figure 6.3
Ionization energies of the first 92 elements.

have only a single *s* electron in their valence shell. This single valence electron is shielded from the nucleus by all the inner-shell electrons, called the **core electrons**, resulting in a low Z_{eff}. The valence electron is thus held loosely, and the energy necessary to remove it is relatively small.

The plot of ionization energies in Figure 6.3 also shows other trends in the data beyond the obvious periodicity. One such trend is that ionization energies gradually decrease going down a group in the periodic table, from He to Rn and from Li to Fr, for instance. As the atomic number increases going down a group, both the principal quantum number of the valence-shell electrons and their average distance from the nucleus also increase. As a result, the valence-shell electrons are less tightly held and E_i is smaller.

Yet another point about the E_i data is that minor irregularities occur across a row of the periodic table. A close look at E_i values of the first 20 elements (**Figure 6.4**) shows that the E_i of beryllium is larger than that of its neighbor boron and the E_i of nitrogen is larger than that of its neighbor oxygen. Similarly, magnesium has a larger E_i than aluminum and phosphorus has a slightly larger E_i than sulfur.

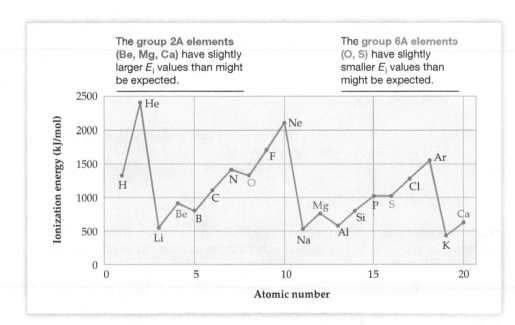

Figure 6.4
Ionization energies of the first 20 elements.

The slightly enlarged E_i values for the group 2A elements Be, Mg, and others can be explained by their electron configurations. Compare beryllium with boron, for instance. A $2s$ electron is removed on ionization of beryllium, but a $2p$ electron is removed on ionization of boron:

$$\text{Be } (1s^2\, 2s^2) \longrightarrow \text{Be}^+ (1s^2\, 2s^1) + \text{e}^- \qquad E_i = 899.4 \text{ kJ/mol}$$

s electron removed

$$\text{B } (1s^2\, 2s^2\, 2p^1) \longrightarrow \text{B}^+ (1s^2\, 2s^2) + \text{e}^- \qquad E_i = 800.6 \text{ kJ/mol}$$

p electron removed

Because a $2s$ electron spends more time closer to the nucleus than a $2p$ electron, it is held more tightly and is harder to remove. Thus, the E_i of beryllium is larger than that of boron. Put another way, the $2p$ electron of boron is shielded somewhat by the $2s$ electrons and is thus more easily removed than a $2s$ electron of beryllium.

The lowered E_i values for atoms of group 6A elements can be explained by their electron configurations as well. Comparing nitrogen with oxygen, for instance, the nitrogen electron is removed from a half-filled orbital, whereas the oxygen electron is removed from a filled orbital:

Half-filled orbital

$$\text{N } (1s^2\, 2s^2\, 2p_x^{\,1}\, 2p_y^{\,1}\, 2p_z^{\,1}) \longrightarrow \text{N}^+ (1s^2\, 2s^2\, 2p_x^{\,1}\, 2p_y^{\,1}) + \text{e}^- \qquad E_i = 1402.3 \text{ kJ/mol}$$

Filled orbital

$$\text{O } (1s^2\, 2s^2\, 2p_x^{\,2}\, 2p_y^{\,1}\, 2p_z^{\,1}) \longrightarrow \text{O}^+ (1s^2\, 2s^2\, 2p_x^{\,1}\, 2p_y^{\,1}\, 2p_z^{\,1}) + \text{e}^- \quad E_i = 1313.9 \text{ kJ/mol}$$

Because electrons repel one another and tend to stay as far apart as possible, electrons that are forced together in a filled orbital are slightly higher in energy than those in a half-filled orbital, so removing one is slightly easier. Thus, oxygen has a smaller E_i than nitrogen.

WORKED EXAMPLE 6.1

IONIZATION ENERGIES

Arrange the elements Se, Cl, and S in order of increasing ionization energy.

STRATEGY

Ionization energy generally increases from left to right across a row of the periodic table and decreases from top to bottom down a group. Chlorine should have a larger E_i than its neighbor sulfur, and selenium should have a smaller E_i than sulfur.

SOLUTION

The order is Se < S < Cl.

▶ **PROBLEM 6.5**   Using the periodic table as your guide, predict which element in each of the following pairs has the larger ionization energy:

(a) K or Br   (b) S or Te   (c) Ga or Se   (d) Ne or Sr

6.4   HIGHER IONIZATION ENERGIES

Ionization is not limited to the loss of a single electron from an atom. Two, three, or even more electrons can be lost sequentially from an atom, and the amount of energy associated with each step can be measured.

$$\text{M} + \text{Energy} \longrightarrow \text{M}^+ + \text{e}^- \qquad \text{First ionization energy } (E_{i1})$$
$$\text{M}^+ + \text{Energy} \longrightarrow \text{M}^{2+} + \text{e}^- \qquad \text{Second ionization energy } (E_{i2})$$
$$\text{M}^{2+} + \text{Energy} \longrightarrow \text{M}^{3+} + \text{e}^- \qquad \text{Third ionization energy } (E_{i3})$$
$$\ldots \text{ and so forth}$$

Successively larger amounts of energy are required for each ionization step because it is much harder to pull a negatively charged electron away from a positively charged ion than from a neutral atom. Interestingly, though, the energy differences between successive steps vary dramatically from one element to another. Removing the second electron from sodium takes nearly 10 times as much energy as removing the first one (4562 versus 496 kJ/mol), but removing the second electron from magnesium takes only twice as much energy as removing the first one (1451 versus 738 kJ/mol).

Large jumps in successive ionization energies are also found for other elements, as can be seen by following the zigzag line in Table 6.2. Magnesium has a large jump between its second and third ionization energies, aluminum has a large jump between its third and fourth ionization energies, silicon has a large jump between its fourth and fifth ionization energies, and so on.

TABLE 6.2   Higher Ionization Energies (kJ/mol) for Main-Group Third-Row Elements

Group	1A	2A	3A	4A	5A	6A	7A	8A
E_i Number	Na	Mg	Al	Si	P	S	Cl	Ar
E_{i1}	496	738	578	787	1,012	1,000	1,251	1,520
E_{i2}	4,562	1,451	1,817	1,577	1,903	2,251	2,297	2,665
E_{i3}	6,912	7,733	2,745	3,231	2,912	3,361	3,822	3,931
E_{i4}	9,543	10,540	11,575	4,356	4,956	4,564	5,158	5,770
E_{i5}	13,353	13,630	14,830	16,091	6,273	7,013	6,540	7,238
E_{i6}	16,610	17,995	18,376	19,784	22,233	8,495	9,458	8,781
E_{i7}	20,114	21,703	23,293	23,783	25,397	27,106	11,020	11,995

The large increases in ionization energies highlighted by the zigzag line in Table 6.2 are yet another consequence of electron configurations. It's relatively easier to remove an electron from a *partially* filled valence shell because Z_{eff} is lower, but it's relatively harder to remove an electron from a *filled* valence shell because Z_{eff} is higher. In other words, ions formed by reaction of main-group elements usually have filled s and p subshells (a noble-gas electron configuration), which corresponds to having eight electrons (an *octet*) in the valence shell of an atom or ion. Sodium ([Ne] $3s^1$) loses only one electron easily, magnesium ([Ne] $3s^2$) loses only two electrons easily, aluminum ([Ne] $3s^2 3p^1$) loses only three electrons easily, and so on across the row. We'll further explore the stability of valence-shell electron octets in Section 6.6.

8 electrons in
outer (2nd) shell

$$\text{Na } (1s^2\,2s^2\,2p^6\,3s^1) \longrightarrow \text{Na}^+ (1s^2\,2s^2\,2p^6) + \text{e}^-$$

$$\text{Mg } (1s^2\,2s^2\,2p^6\,3s^2) \longrightarrow \text{Mg}^{2+} (1s^2\,2s^2\,2p^6) + 2\,\text{e}^-$$

$$\text{Al } (1s^2\,2s^2\,2p^6\,3s^2\,3p^1) \longrightarrow \text{Al}^{3+} (1s^2\,2s^2\,2p^6) + 3\,\text{e}^-$$

$$\vdots \qquad\qquad\qquad \vdots$$

$$\text{Cl } (1s^2\,2s^2\,2p^6\,3s^2\,3p^5) \longrightarrow \text{Cl}^{7+} (1s^2\,2s^2\,2p^6) + 7\,\text{e}^-$$

> **WORKED EXAMPLE 6.2**
>
> ## HIGHER IONIZATION ENERGIES
>
> Which has the larger fifth ionization energy, Ge or As?
>
> **STRATEGY**
>
> Look at their positions in the periodic table. The group 4A element germanium has four valence-shell electrons and thus has four relatively low ionization energies, whereas the group 5A element arsenic has five valence-shell electrons and has five low ionization energies.
>
> **SOLUTION**
>
> Germanium has a larger E_{i5} than arsenic.

▸ **PROBLEM 6.6**

(a) Which has the larger third ionization energy, Be or N?

(b) Which has the larger fourth ionization energy, Ga or Ge?

▸ **PROBLEM 6.7**   Three atoms have the following electron configurations:

(a) $1s^2\,2s^2\,2p^6\,3s^2\,3p^1$

(b) $1s^2\,2s^2\,2p^6\,3s^2\,3p^5$

(c) $1s^2\,2s^2\,2p^6\,3s^2\,3p^6\,4s^1$

Which of the three has the largest E_{i1}? Which has the smallest E_{i4}?

CONCEPTUAL PROBLEM 6.8   Order the indicated three elements according to the ease with which each is likely to lose its third electron:

6.5   ELECTRON AFFINITY

Just as it's possible to measure the energy change on *removing* an electron from an atom to form a *cation*, it's also possible to measure the energy change on *adding* an electron to an atom to form an *anion*. An element's **electron affinity**, abbreviated E_{ea}, is the energy change that occurs when an electron is added to an isolated atom in the gaseous state.

Ionization energies (Section 6.3) are always positive because energy must always be added to separate a negatively charged electron from the resultant positively charged cation. Electron affinities, however, are generally negative because energy is usually released when a neutral atom adds an additional electron.* We'll see in Chapter 8 that this same convention is used throughout chemistry: A positive energy change means that energy is added, and a negative energy change means that energy is released.

---

*We have defined E_{ea} as the energy *released* when a neutral atom *gains* an electron to form an anion and have given it a negative sign. Some books and reference sources adopt the opposite point of view, defining E_{ea} as the energy *gained* when an anion *loses* an electron to form a neutral atom and giving it a positive value. The two definitions are simply the reverse of one another, so the sign of the energy change is also reversed.

The more negative the E_{ea}, the greater the tendency of the atom to accept an electron and the more stable the anion that results. In contrast, an atom that forms an unstable anion by addition of an electron has, in principle, a positive value of E_{ea}, but no experimental measurement can be made because the process does not take place. All we can say is that the E_{ea} for such an atom is greater than zero. The E_{ea} of hydrogen, for instance, is -72.8 kJ/mol, meaning that energy is released and the H⁻ anion is stable. The E_{ea} of neon, however, is greater than 0 kJ/mol, meaning that Ne does not add an electron and the Ne⁻ anion is not stable.

$$\text{H}\,(1s^1) + \text{e}^- \longrightarrow \text{H}^-\,(1s^2) + 72.8\text{ kJ/mol} \qquad E_{ea} = -72.8\text{ kJ/mol}$$

$$\text{Ne}\,(1s^2\,2s^2\,2p^6) + \text{e}^- + \text{Energy} \longrightarrow \text{Ne}^-\,(1s^2\,2s^2\,2p^6\,3s^1) \qquad E_{ea} > 0\text{ kJ/mol}$$

As with ionization energies, electron affinities show a periodicity that is related to the electron configurations of the elements. The data in **Figure 6.5** indicate that group 7A elements have the most negative electron affinities, corresponding to the largest release of energy, while group 2A and group 8A elements have near-zero or positive electron affinities, corresponding to a small release or even an absorption of energy.

A negative value for E_{ea}, such as those for the group 7A elements (halogens), means that energy is released when an electron adds to an atom.

A value of zero, such as those for the group 2A elements (alkaline earths) and group 8A elements (noble gases), means that energy is absorbed but the exact amount can't be measured.

Figure 6.5
Electron affinities for elements 1–57 and 72–86.

The value of an element's electron affinity is due to an interplay of several offsetting factors. Attraction between the additional electron and the nucleus favors a negative E_{ea}, but the increase in electron–electron repulsions that results from addition of the extra electron favors a positive E_{ea}.

Large negative E_{ea}'s are found for the halogens (F, Cl, Br, I) because each of these elements has both a high Z_{eff} and room in its valence shell for an additional electron. Halide anions have a noble-gas electron configuration with filled s and p sublevels, and the attraction between the additional electron and the atomic nucleus is high. Positive E_{ea}'s are found for the noble-gas elements (He, Ne, Ar, Kr, Xe), however, because the s and p sublevels in these elements are already full, so the additional electron must go into the next higher shell, where it is shielded from the nucleus and feels a relatively low Z_{eff}. The attraction of the nucleus for the added electron is therefore small and is outweighed by the additional electron–electron repulsions.

A halogen: $\quad \text{Cl}\,(\ldots 3s^2\,3p^5) + \text{e}^- \longrightarrow \text{Cl}^-\,(\ldots 3s^2\,3p^6) \qquad E_{ea} = -348.6\text{ kJ/mol}$

A noble gas: $\text{Ar}\,(\ldots 3s^2\,3p^6) + \text{e}^- \longrightarrow \text{Ar}^-\,(\ldots 3s^2\,3p^6\,4s^1) \quad E_{ea} > 0\text{ kJ/mol}$

In looking for other trends in the data of Figure 6.5, the near-zero E_{ea}'s of the alkaline-earth metals (Be, Mg, Ca, Sr, Ba) are particularly striking. Atoms of these elements have filled s subshells, which means that the additional electron must go into a p subshell. The higher energy of the p subshell, together with a relatively low Z_{eff} for elements on the left side of the periodic table, means that alkaline-earth atoms accept an electron reluctantly and have E_{ea} values near zero.

An alkaline earth: $Mg\,(\ldots 3s^2) + e^- \longrightarrow Mg^-\,(\ldots 3s^2\,3p^1)$ $E_{ea} \approx 0\ kJ/mol$

WORKED EXAMPLE 6.3

ELECTRON AFFINITIES

Why does nitrogen have a less favorable (more positive) E_{ea} than its neighbors on either side, C and O?

STRATEGY AND SOLUTION

The magnitude of an element's E_{ea} depends on the element's valence-shell electron configuration. The electron configurations of C, N, and O are

> Carbon: $1s^2\,2s^2\,2p_x{}^1\,2p_y{}^1$ Nitrogen: $1s^2\,2s^2\,2p_x{}^1\,2p_y{}^1\,2p_z{}^1$
>
> Oxygen: $1s^2\,2s^2\,2p_x{}^2\,2p_y{}^1\,2p_z{}^1$

Carbon has only two electrons in its $2p$ subshell and can readily accept another in its vacant $2p_z$ orbital. Nitrogen, however, has a half-filled $2p$ subshell, so the additional electron must pair up in a $2p$ orbital where it feels a repulsion from the electron already present. Thus, the E_{ea} of nitrogen is less favorable than that of carbon. Oxygen also must add an electron to an orbital that already has one electron, but the additional stabilizing effect of increased Z_{eff} across the periodic table counteracts the effect of electron repulsion, resulting in a more favorable E_{ea} for O than for N.

▶ **PROBLEM 6.9**   Why does manganese, atomic number 25, have a less favorable E_{ea} than its neighbors on either side?

CONCEPTUAL PROBLEM 6.10   Which of the indicated three elements has the least favorable E_{ea}, and which has the most favorable E_{ea}?

6.6 THE OCTET RULE

Let's list the important points discussed in the previous four sections and see if we can draw some general conclusions:

- **Group 1A elements** have a relatively low E_{i1}, so they tend to lose their ns^1 valence-shell electron easily when they react, thereby adopting the electron configuration of the noble gas in the previous row of the periodic table.
- **Group 2A elements** have relatively low E_{i1} and E_{i2}, so they tend to lose both their ns^2 valence-shell electrons easily when they react and adopt a noble-gas electron configuration.

- **Group 7A elements** have a relatively large negative E_{ea}, so they tend to gain one electron easily when they react, changing from ns^2np^5 to ns^2np^6 and thereby adopting the configuration of the neighboring noble gas in the same row.
- **Group 8A (noble gas) elements** are essentially inert and undergo very few reactions. They neither gain nor lose electrons easily.

All these observations can be gathered into a single statement called the **octet rule**:

> **Octet rule** Main-group elements tend to undergo reactions that leave them with eight outer-shell electrons. That is, main-group elements react so that they attain a noble-gas electron configuration with filled s and p sublevels in their valence electron shell.

As we'll see in the next chapter, there are exceptions to the octet rule, particularly for elements in the third and lower rows of the periodic table. Nevertheless, the rule is useful for making predictions and for providing insights about chemical bonding.

Why does the octet rule work? What factors determine how many electrons an atom is likely to gain or lose? Clearly, electrons are most likely to be lost if they are held loosely in the first place—that is, if they feel a relatively low effective nuclear charge, Z_{eff}, and have lower ionization energies. Valence-shell electrons in the group 1A, 2A, and 3A metals, for instance, are shielded from the nucleus by core electrons, feel a low Z_{eff}, and are therefore lost relatively easily. Once the next lower noble-gas configuration is reached, though, loss of an additional electron suddenly becomes much more difficult because it must come from an inner shell, where it feels a much higher Z_{eff}.

Conversely, electrons are most likely to be gained if they can be held tightly by a high Z_{eff}. Valence-shell electrons in the group 6A and 7A elements, for example, are poorly shielded, feel high values of Z_{eff}, and aren't lost easily. The high Z_{eff} thus makes possible the gain of one or more additional electrons into vacant valence-shell orbitals. Once the noble-gas configuration is reached, though, lower-energy orbitals are no longer available. An additional electron would have to be placed in a higher-energy orbital, where it would feel only a low Z_{eff}.

Eight is therefore the magic number for valence-shell electrons. Taking electrons *from* a filled octet is difficult because they are tightly held by a high Z_{eff}; adding more electrons *to* a filled octet is difficult because, with s and p sublevels full, no low-energy orbital is available.

WORKED EXAMPLE 6.4

CHEMICAL REACTIONS AND THE OCTET RULE

Lithium metal reacts with nitrogen to yield Li_3N. What noble-gas configuration does the nitrogen atom in Li_3N have?

STRATEGY AND SOLUTION

The compound Li_3N contains three Li^+ ions, each formed by loss of a $2s$ electron from lithium metal (group 1A). The nitrogen atom in Li_3N must therefore gain three electrons over the neutral atom, making it triply negative (N^{3-}) and giving it a valence-shell octet with the neon configuration:

$$\text{N configuration: } (1s^2\,2s^2\,2p^3) \qquad N^{3-} \text{ configuration: } (1s^2\,2s^2\,2p^6)$$

▶ **PROBLEM 6.11**   What noble-gas configurations are the following elements likely to adopt in reactions when they form ions?

(a) Rb   (b) Ba   (c) Ga   (d) F

▶ **PROBLEM 6.12**   What are group 6A elements likely to do when they form ions—gain electrons or lose them? How many?

6.7 IONIC BONDS AND THE FORMATION OF IONIC SOLIDS

When an element that gives up an electron relatively easily (that is, has a small positive ionization energy) comes in contact with an element that accepts an electron easily (that is, has a large negative electron affinity), the element with the small E_i can transfer an electron to the element with the negative E_{ea}, yielding a cation and an anion. Sodium, for example, reacts with chlorine to give Na^+ ions and Cl^- ions:

$$Na + Cl \longrightarrow Na^+ Cl^-$$

$$1s^2\,2s^2\,2p^6\,3s^1 \quad 1s^2\,2s^2\,2p^6\,3s^2\,3p^5 \qquad 1s^2\,2s^2\,2p^6 \quad 1s^2\,2s^2\,2p^6\,3s^2\,3p^6$$

What about the overall energy change, ΔE, for the reaction of sodium with chlorine to yield Na^+ and Cl^- ions? (The Greek capital letter delta, Δ, is used to represent a change in the value of the indicated quantity, in this case an energy change ΔE.) It's apparent from E_i and E_{ea} values that the amount of energy released when a chlorine atom accepts an electron ($E_{ea} = -348.6$ kJ/mol) is insufficient to offset the amount absorbed when a sodium atom loses an electron ($E_i = +495.8$ kJ/mol):

E_i for Na	$= +495.8$ kJ/mol	(Unfavorable)
E_{ea} for Cl	$= -348.6$ kJ/mol	(Favorable)
ΔE	$= +147.2$ kJ/mol	(Unfavorable)

Remember...

In an **ionic solid**, oppositely charged ions are attracted to one another by ionic bonds and are packed together in a regular way. We can't specify which ions "belong" to each other, however, as we can with atoms in covalent molecules.   (Section 2.11)

The net ΔE for the reaction of sodium and chlorine atoms would be unfavorable by $+147.2$ kJ/mol, and no reaction would occur, unless some other factor were involved. This additional factor, which is more than enough to overcome the unfavorable energy change of electron transfer, is the large gain in stability due to the electrostatic attractions between product anions and cations and the formation of an **ionic solid**.

The actual reaction of solid sodium metal with gaseous chlorine molecules to form solid sodium chloride occurs all at once rather than in a stepwise manner, but it's easier to make an energy calculation if we imagine a series of hypothetical steps for which exact energy changes can be measured experimentally. There are five steps to take into account to calculate the overall energy change.

Step 1. Solid Na metal is first converted into isolated, gaseous Na atoms, a process called *sublimation*. Because energy must be added to disrupt the forces holding atoms together in a solid, the heat of sublimation has a positive value: +107.3 kJ/mol for Na.

$$Na(s) \longrightarrow Na(g)$$
+107.3 kJ/mol

Step 2. Gaseous Cl_2 molecules are split into individual Cl atoms. Energy must be added to break molecules apart, and the energy required for bond breaking therefore has a positive value: +243 kJ/mol for Cl_2 (or 122 kJ/mol for 1/2 Cl_2). We'll look further into bond dissociation energies in Section 7.2.

$$1/2\ Cl_2(g) \longrightarrow Cl(g)$$
+122 kJ/mol

Step 3. Isolated Na atoms are ionized into Na^+ ions plus electrons. The energy required is the first ionization energy of sodium (E_{i1}) and has a positive value: +495.8 kJ/mol.

$$Na(g) \longrightarrow Na^+(g) + e^-$$
+495.8 kJ/mol

Step 4. Cl^- ions are formed from Cl atoms by addition of an electron. The energy released is the electron affinity of chlorine (E_{ea}) and has a negative value: −348.6 kJ/mol.

$$Cl(g) + e^- \longrightarrow Cl^-(g)$$
−348.6 kJ/mol

Step 5. Lastly, solid NaCl is formed from isolated Na^+ and Cl^- ions. The energy change is a measure of the overall electrostatic interactions between ions in the solid. It is the amount of energy released when isolated ions condense to form a solid, and it has a negative value: −787 kJ/mol for NaCl.

$$Na^+(g) + Cl^-(g) \longrightarrow NaCl(s)$$
−787 kJ/mol

Net reaction: $Na(s) + 1/2\ Cl_2(g) \longrightarrow NaCl(s)$

Net energy change: −411 kJ/mol

The five hypothetical steps in the reaction between sodium metal and gaseous chlorine are depicted in **Figure 6.6** in a pictorial format called a **Born–Haber cycle**, which shows how each step contributes to the overall energy change and how the

(3) $Na(g) \rightarrow Na^+(g) + e^-$
495.8 kJ/mol

(4) $Cl(g) + e^- \rightarrow Cl^-(g)$
−348.6 kJ/mol

(2) $\frac{1}{2} Cl_2(g) \rightarrow Cl(g)$ 122 kJ/mol

(1) $Na(s) \rightarrow Na(g)$ 107.3 kJ/mol

(5) $Na^+(g) + Cl^-(g) \rightarrow NaCl(s)$
−787 kJ/mol

Net reaction
$Na(s) + \frac{1}{2} Cl_2(g) \rightarrow NaCl(s)$
−411 kJ/mol

The **sum of the energy changes for the five steps** equals the net energy change for the overall reaction.

The **most favorable step** is the formation of solid NaCl from gaseous Na^+ and Cl^- ions

Figure 6.6
A Born–Haber cycle for the formation of NaCl(s) from Na(s) and $Cl_2(g)$.

net process is the sum of the individual steps. As indicated in the diagram, steps 1, 2, and 3 have positive values and absorb energy, while steps 4 and 5 have negative values and release energy. The largest contribution is step 5, which measures the electrostatic forces between ions in the solid product—that is, the strength of the ionic bonding. Were it not for this large amount of stabilization of the solid due to ionic bonding, no reaction would take place.

A similar Born–Haber cycle for the reaction of magnesium with chlorine shows the energy changes involved in the reaction of an alkaline-earth element (Figure 6.7). As in the reaction of sodium and chlorine to form NaCl, there are five contributions to the overall energy change. First, solid magnesium metal must be converted into isolated gaseous magnesium atoms (sublimation). Second, the bond in Cl_2 molecules must be broken to yield chlorine atoms. Third, the magnesium atoms must lose two electrons to form the dipositive Mg^{2+} ions. Fourth, the chlorine atoms formed in step 2 must accept electrons to form Cl^- ions. Fifth, the gaseous ions must combine to form the ionic solid, $MgCl_2$. As the Born–Haber cycle indicates, it is the large contribution from ionic bonding that releases enough energy to drive the entire process.

Figure 6.7
A Born–Haber cycle for the formation of $MgCl_2$ from the elements.

(4) $2 Cl(g) + 2 e^- \rightarrow 2 Cl^-(g)$
−697.2 kJ/mol

(3b) $Mg^+(g) \rightarrow Mg^{2+}(g) + e^-$
1450.7 kJ/mol

(3a) $Mg(g) \rightarrow Mg^+(g) + e^-$
737.7 kJ/mol

(5) $Mg^{2+}(g) + 2 Cl^-(g) \rightarrow MgCl_2(s)$
−2524 kJ/mol

(2) $Cl_2(g) \rightarrow 2 Cl(g)$ 243 kJ/mol
(1) $Mg(s) \rightarrow Mg(g)$ 147.7 kJ/mol

Net reaction
$Mg(s) + Cl_2(g) \rightarrow MgCl_2(s)$
−642 kJ/mol

The large **contribution from ionic bonding** in the solid provides more than enough energy to remove two electrons from magnesium in **steps 3a and 3b.**

▶ **PROBLEM 6.13**   Calculate the net energy change in kilojoules per mole that takes place on formation of KF(s) from the elements: $K(s) + 1/2 F_2(g) \longrightarrow KF(s)$. The following information is needed:

Heat of sublimation for $K(s) = 89.2$ kJ/mol E_{ea} for $F(g) = -328$ kJ/mol

Bond dissociation energy for $F_2(g) = 158$ kJ/mol E_i for $K(g) = 418.8$ kJ/mol

Electrostatic interactions in KF(s) $= -821$ kJ/mol

6.8   LATTICE ENERGIES IN IONIC SOLIDS

The measure of the electrostatic interaction energies between ions in a solid—and thus the measure of the strength of the solid's ionic bonds—is called the **lattice energy (U).** By convention, lattice energy is defined as the amount of energy that must be added to break up an ionic solid into its individual gaseous ions, so it has a

positive value. The formation of a solid from ions is the reverse of the breakup, however, and step 5 in the Born–Haber cycle of Figure 6.6 therefore has a negative value,
$-U$.

$$NaCl(s) \longrightarrow Na^+(g) + Cl^-(g) \qquad U = +787 \text{ kJ/mol} \quad \text{(Energy absorbed)}$$

$$Na^+(g) + Cl^-(g) \longrightarrow NaCl(s) \qquad -U = -787 \text{ kJ/mol} \quad \text{(Energy released)}$$

The force F that results from the interaction of electric charges is described by
Coulomb's law and is equal to a constant k times the product of the charges on the
ions, z_1 and z_2, divided by the square of the distance d between their centers (nuclei):

Coulomb's Law $\quad F = k \times \dfrac{z_1 z_2}{d^2}$

Because energy is equal to force times distance, the negative of the lattice energy is

$$-U = F \times d = k \times \frac{z_1 z_2}{d}$$

The value of the constant k depends on the arrangement of the ions in the specific
compound and is different for different substances.

Lattice energies are large when the distance d between ions is small and when the
charges z_1 and z_2 are large. A small distance d means that the ions are close together,
which implies that they have small ionic radii. Thus, if z_1 and z_2 are held constant,
the largest lattice energies belong to compounds formed from the smallest ions, as
listed in Table 6.3.

Within a series of compounds that have the same anion but different cations, lattice energy increases as the cation becomes smaller. Comparing LiF, NaF, and KF, for
example, cation size follows the order $K^+ > Na^+ > Li^+$, so lattice energies follow
the order LiF > NaF > KF. Similarly, within a series of compounds that have the
same cation but different anions, lattice energy increases as anion size decreases.
Comparing LiF, LiCl, LiBr, and LiI, for example, anion size follows the order
$I^- > Br^- > Cl^- > F^-$, so lattice energies follow the reverse order
LiF > LiCl > LiBr > LiI.

TABLE 6.3 Lattice Energies of Some Ionic Solids (kJ/mol)

Cation	F⁻	Cl⁻	Br⁻	I⁻	O²⁻
Li^+	1036	853	807	757	2925
Na^+	923	787	747	704	2695
K^+	821	715	682	649	2360
Be^{2+}	3505	3020	2914	2800	4443
Mg^{2+}	2957	2524	2440	2327	3791
Ca^{2+}	2630	2258	2176	2074	3401
Al^{3+}	5215	5492	5361	5218	15,916

Table 6.3 also shows that compounds of ions with higher charges have larger lattice energies than compounds of ions with lower charges. In comparing NaI, MgI_2,
and AlI_3, for example, the order of charges on the cations is $Al^{3+} > Mg^{2+} > Na^+$,
and the order of lattice energies is $AlI_3 > MgI_2 > NaI$.

WORKED EXAMPLE 6.5

LATTICE ENERGIES

Which has the larger lattice energy, NaCl or CsI?

STRATEGY

The magnitude of a substance's lattice energy is affected both by the charges on its constituent ions and by the sizes of those ions. The higher the charges on the ions and the smaller the sizes of the ions, the larger the lattice energy. In this case, all four ions— Na^+, Cs^+, Cl^-, and I^-—are singly charged, so they differ only in size.

SOLUTION

Because Na^+ is smaller than Cs^+ and Cl^- is smaller than I^-, the distance between ions is smaller in NaCl than in CsI. Thus, NaCl has the larger lattice energy.

WORKED CONCEPTUAL EXAMPLE 6.6

LATTICE ENERGIES

Which of the following alkali metal halides has the larger lattice energy, and which has the smaller lattice energy? Explain.

(a)　　　　　　　　　　　　**(b)**

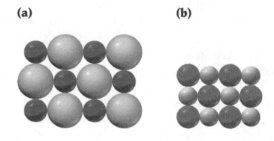

STRATEGY

The magnitude of a lattice energy depends directly on the charge on the ions and inversely on the distance between ions (that is, on the radii of the ions). In this instance, all the ions in both drawings are singly charged, so only the size of the ions is important.

SOLUTION

The ions in drawing **(b)** are smaller than those in drawing **(a)**, so **(b)** has the larger lattice energy.

▶ **PROBLEM 6.14**　Which substance in each of the following pairs has the larger lattice energy?

　(a) KCl or RbCl　　　**(b)** CaF_2 or BaF_2　　　**(c)** CaO or KI

CONCEPTUAL PROBLEM 6.15　One of the following pictures represents NaCl and one represents MgO. Which is which, and which has the larger lattice energy?

(a)　　　　　　　　　　　　**(b)**

6.9 SOME CHEMISTRY OF THE ALKALI METALS

Now that we know something about ionization energies, electron affinities, lattice energies, and the octet rule, let's look briefly at the chemistry of some elements that form ionic bonds. The alkali metals of group 1A—Li, Na, K, Rb, Cs, and Fr—have the smallest ionization energies of all the elements because of their valence-shell ns^1 electron configurations (Figure 6.3). They therefore lose this ns^1 electron easily in chemical reactions to yield 1+ ions and are thus among the most powerful **reducing agents** in the periodic table (Sections 4.6–4.8). In fact, the chemistry of the alkali metals is dominated by their ability to donate an electron to another element or compound.

As their group name implies, the alkali metals are *metallic*. They have a bright, silvery appearance, are malleable, and are good conductors of electricity. Unlike the more common metals such as iron, though, the alkali metals are all soft enough to cut with a dull knife, have low melting points and densities, and are so reactive that they must be stored under oil to prevent their instantaneous reaction with oxygen and moisture. None are found in the elemental state in nature; they occur only in salts. Their properties are summarized in Table 6.4.

Remember...

A **reducing agent** is a substance that loses one or more electrons and is itself oxidized. An oxidizing agent is a substance that gains one or more electrons and is itself reduced. (Sections 4.6–4.8)

TABLE 6.4 Properties of Alkali Metals

Name	Melting Point (°C)	Boiling Point (°C)	Density (g/cm³)	First Ionization Energy (kJ/mol)	Abundance on Earth (%)	Atomic Radius (pm)	Ionic (M⁺) Radius (pm)
Lithium	180.5	1342	0.534	520.2	0.0020	152	68
Sodium	97.7	883	0.971	495.8	2.36	186	102
Potassium	63.3	759	0.862	418.8	2.09	227	138
Rubidium	39.3	688	1.532	403.0	0.009 0	248	152
Cesium	28.4	671	1.873	375.7	0.000 10	265	167
Francium	—	—	—	~400	Trace	—	—

Production of Alkali Metals

Alkali metals are produced commercially by reduction of their chloride salts, although the exact procedure differs for each element. Both lithium metal and sodium metal are produced by *electrolysis*, a process in which an electric current is passed through the molten salt. The details of the process won't be discussed until Sections 17.12 and 17.13, but the fundamental idea is to use electrical energy to break down an ionic compound into its elements. A high reaction temperature is necessary to keep the salt liquid.

$$2\ LiCl(l) \xrightarrow[\text{450 °C}]{\text{Electrolysis in KCl}} 2\ Li(l) + Cl_2(g)$$

$$2\ NaCl(l) \xrightarrow[\text{580 °C}]{\text{Electrolysis in CaCl}_2} 2\ Na(l) + Cl_2(g)$$

Potassium, rubidium, and cesium metals are produced by chemical reduction rather than by electrolysis. Sodium is the reducing agent used in potassium production, and calcium is the reducing agent used for preparing rubidium and cesium.

$$KCl(l) + Na(l) \underset{}{\overset{\text{850 °C}}{\rightleftharpoons}} K(g) + NaCl(l)$$

$$2\ RbCl(l) + Ca(l) \underset{}{\overset{\text{750 °C}}{\rightleftharpoons}} 2\ Rb(g) + CaCl_2(l)$$

$$2\ CsCl(l) + Ca(l) \underset{}{\overset{\text{750 °C}}{\rightleftharpoons}} 2\ Cs(g) + CaCl_2(l)$$

All three of the above reductions appear contrary to the **activity series**, described in Section 4.8, according to which sodium is not a strong enough reducing agent to react with K^+ and calcium is not a strong enough reducing agent to react with either Rb^+ or Cs^+. At high reaction temperatures, however, equilibria are established in which

▲ A sample of sodium metal.

Remember...

The **activity series**, shown in Table 4.5 on page 130, ranks the elements in order of their reducing ability. Elements at the top of the activity series, such as Li and Na, are stronger reducing agents, while elements at the bottom, such as Au and Hg, are weaker reducing agents. (Section 4.8)

small amounts of the products are formed. These products are then removed from the reaction mixture by distillation, thereby driving the reactions toward more product formation. We'll explore the general nature of such chemical equilibria in Chapter 13.

Reactions of Alkali Metals

Alkali metals react rapidly with group 7A elements (halogens) to yield colorless, crystalline ionic salts called *halides*. The reactivity of an alkali metal increases as its ionization energy decreases, giving a reactivity order Cs > Rb > K > Na > Li. Cesium is the most reactive, combining almost explosively with the halogens.

$$2\,M(s) + X_2 \longrightarrow 2\,MX(s)$$
A metal halide

where   M = Alkali metal (Li, Na, K, Rb, or Cs)

X = Halogen (F, Cl, Br, or I)

All the alkali metals also react rapidly with oxygen, but different metals give different kinds of products. Lithium reacts with O_2 to yield the *oxide*, Li_2O; sodium reacts to yield the *peroxide*, Na_2O_2; and the remaining alkali metals, K, Rb, and Cs, form either peroxides or *superoxides*, MO_2, depending on the reaction conditions and on how much oxygen is present. The reasons for the differences have to do largely with the differences in stability of the various products and with how the ions pack together in crystals. The alkali metal cations have a +1 charge in all cases, but the oxygen anions might be either O^{2-}, O_2^{2-}, or O_2^{-}.

$$4\,Li(s) + O_2(g) \longrightarrow 2\,Li_2O(s) \qquad \text{An \emph{oxide}; the anion is } O^{2-}$$
$$2\,Na(s) + O_2(g) \longrightarrow Na_2O_2(s) \qquad \text{A \emph{peroxide}; the anion is } O_2^{2-}$$
$$K(s) + O_2(g) \longrightarrow KO_2(s) \qquad \text{A \emph{superoxide}; the anion is } O_2^{-}$$

Potassium superoxide, KO_2, is a particularly valuable compound because of its use in spacecraft and in self-contained breathing devices to remove moisture and CO_2 from exhaled air, generating oxygen in the process:

$$2\,KO_2(s) + H_2O(g) \longrightarrow KOH(s) + KO_2H(s) + O_2(g)$$
$$4\,KO_2(s) + 2\,CO_2(g) \longrightarrow 2\,K_2CO_3(s) + 3\,O_2(g)$$

Perhaps the most well-known and dramatic reaction of the alkali metals is with water to yield hydrogen gas and an alkali metal hydroxide, MOH. In fact, it's this reaction that gives the elements their group name because the solution of metal hydroxide that results from adding an alkali metal to water is *alkaline*, or basic. Lithium undergoes the reaction with vigorous bubbling as hydrogen is released, sodium reacts rapidly with evolution of heat, and potassium reacts so violently that

Lithium reacts vigorously, with bubbling.   Sodium reacts violently.   Potassium reacts almost explosively.

▲ All the alkali metals react with water to generate H_2 gas.

the hydrogen produced bursts instantly into flame. Rubidium and cesium react almost explosively.

$$2\,M(s) + 2\,H_2O(l) \longrightarrow 2\,M^+(aq) + 2\,OH^-(aq) + H_2(g)$$

where   M = Li, Na, K, Rb, or Cs

Finally, the alkali metals also react with ammonia to yield H_2 gas plus a metal *amide*, MNH_2, a reaction analogous to that between an alkali metal and water.

$$2\,M(s) + 2\,NH_3(l) \longrightarrow 2\,M^+(soln) + 2\,NH_2^-(soln) + H_2(g)$$

where   M = Li, Na, K, Rb, or Cs

The reaction is sufficiently slow at lower temperatures that it's possible for the alkali metals to dissolve in liquid ammonia at $-33\,°C$, forming deep blue solutions of metal cations and dissolved electrons. These solutions are extremely powerful reducing agents.

$$M(s) \xrightarrow[\text{solvent}]{\text{Liquid } NH_3} M^+(soln) + e^-(soln)$$

where   M = Li, Na, K, Rb, or Cs

▲ Sodium metal dissolves in liquid ammonia at low temperature to yield a blue solution of Na^+ ions and solvent-surrounded electrons.

▶ **PROBLEM 6.16**   Assign charges to the oxygen-containing anions in the following compounds:

(a) Li_2O (b) K_2O_2 (c) CsO_2

▶ **PROBLEM 6.17**   Complete the following equations so that the same numbers and kinds of atoms appear on both sides of the reaction arrow. If no reaction takes place, write N.R.

(a) $Cs(s) + H_2O(l) \longrightarrow$?   (b) $Rb(s) + O_2(g) \longrightarrow$?   (c) $K(s) + NH_3(g) \longrightarrow$?

6.10 SOME CHEMISTRY OF THE ALKALINE-EARTH METALS

The alkaline-earth elements of group 2A—Be, Mg, Ca, Sr, Ba, and Ra—are similar to the alkali metals in many respects. They differ, however, in that they have ns^2 valence-shell electron configurations and can therefore lose two electrons in forming doubly positive ions, M^{2+}. Because their first ionization energy is larger than that of alkali metals (Figure 6.3), the group 2A metals are somewhat less reactive than alkali metals. The general reactivity trend is Ba > Sr > Ca > Mg > Be.

Although harder than their neighbors in group 1A, the alkaline-earth elements are still relatively soft, silvery metals. They tend, however, to have higher melting points and densities than alkali metals, as listed in Table 6.5. Alkaline-earth elements are less reactive toward oxygen and water than alkali metals but are nevertheless found in nature only in salts, not in the elemental state.

TABLE 6.5   Properties of Alkaline-Earth Metals

Name	Melting Point (°C)	Boiling Point (°C)	Density (g/cm³)	First Ionization Energy (kJ/mol)	Abundance on Earth (%)	Atomic Radius (pm)	Ionic (M^{2+}) Radius (pm)
Beryllium	1287	2471	1.848	899.4	0.000 28	112	44
Magnesium	650	1090	1.738	737.7	2.33	160	66
Calcium	842	1484	1.55	589.8	4.15	197	99
Strontium	777	1382	2.54	549.5	0.038	215	112
Barium	727	1897	3.62	502.9	0.042	222	134
Radium	700	1140	~5.0	509.3	Trace	223	143

Production of Alkaline-Earth Metals

Pure alkaline-earth metals, like alkali metals, are produced commercially by reduction of their salts, either chemically or through electrolysis. Beryllium is prepared by reduction of BeF_2 with magnesium, and magnesium is prepared by electrolysis of its molten chloride.

$$BeF_2(l) + Mg(l) \xrightarrow{1300\ °C} Be(l) + MgF_2(l)$$

$$MgCl_2(l) \xrightarrow[750\ °C]{Electrolysis} Mg(l) + Cl_2(g)$$

Calcium, strontium, and barium are all made by high-temperature reduction of their oxides with aluminum metal.

$$3\ MO(l) + 2\ Al(l) \xrightarrow{High\ temp} 3\ M(l) + Al_2O_3(s)$$

$$\text{where} \quad M = Ca,\ Sr,\ or\ Ba$$

Reactions of Alkaline-Earth Metals

Alkaline-earth metals react with halogens to yield ionic halide salts, MX_2, and with oxygen to form oxides, MO:

$$M + X_2 \longrightarrow MX_2 \quad \text{where} \quad M = Be,\ Mg,\ Ca,\ Sr,\ or\ Ba$$

$$2\ M + O_2 \longrightarrow 2\ MO \quad\quad\quad\quad X = F,\ Cl,\ Br,\ or\ I$$

▲ Calcium metal reacts very slowly with water at room temperature.

Beryllium and magnesium are relatively unreactive toward oxygen at room temperature, but both burn with a brilliant white glare when ignited by a flame. Calcium, strontium, and barium are so reactive that they are best stored under oil to keep them from contact with air. Like the heavier alkali metals, strontium and barium form peroxides, MO_2.

With the exception of beryllium, the alkaline-earth elements react with water to yield metal hydroxides, $M(OH)_2$. Magnesium undergoes reaction only at temperatures above 100 °C, while calcium and strontium react slowly with liquid water at room temperature. Only barium reacts vigorously at room temperature.

$$M(s) + 2\ H_2O(l) \longrightarrow M(OH)_2 + H_2(g)$$

$$\text{where} \quad M = Mg,\ Ca,\ Sr,\ or\ Ba$$

▶ **PROBLEM 6.18**   Predict the products of the following reactions, and balance the equations so that the numbers and kinds of atoms are the same on both sides of the reaction arrows:

(a) $Be(s) + Br_2(l) \longrightarrow$?   (b) $Sr(s) + H_2O(l) \longrightarrow$?   (c) $Mg(s) + O_2(g) \longrightarrow$?

▶ **PROBLEM 6.19**   What product do you think is formed by reaction of magnesium with sulfur, a group 6A element? What is the charge on the sulfide ion in the product?

6.11 SOME CHEMISTRY OF THE HALOGENS

The halogens of group 7A—F, Cl, Br, I, and At—are completely different from the main-group metals we've been discussing up to this point. The halogens are nonmetals rather than metals, they exist as diatomic molecules rather than as individual atoms, and they tend to gain rather than lose electrons when they enter into reactions because of their ns^2np^5 electron configurations. In other words, the halogens are characterized by large negative electron affinities and large positive ionization energies. Some of their properties are listed in Table 6.6.

TABLE 6.6   Properties of Halogens

Name	Melting Point (°C)	Boiling Point (°C)	Density (g/cm³)	Electron Affinity (kJ/mol)	Abundance on Earth (%)	Atomic Radius (pm)	Ionic (X⁻) Radius (pm)
Fluorine	−220	−188	1.50 (*l*)	−328	0.062	72	133
Chlorine	−101	−34	2.03 (*l*)	−349	0.013	99	181
Bromine	−7	59	3.12 (*l*)	−325	0.000 3	114	196
Iodine	114	184	4.930(*s*)	−295	0.000 05	133	220
Astatine	—	—	—	−270	Trace	—	—

Halogens are too reactive to occur in nature as free elements. Instead, they are found only as their anions in various salts and minerals. Even the name *halogen* implies reactivity, since it comes from the Greek words *hals* (salt) and *gennan* (to form). Thus, a halogen is literally a salt former.

Production of Halogens

All the free halogens are produced commercially by oxidation of their anions. Fluorine and chlorine are both produced by electrolysis: fluorine from a molten 1:2 molar mixture of KF and HF, and chlorine from molten NaCl.

$$2\,HF(l) \xrightarrow[100\,°C]{\text{Electrolysis}} H_2(g) + F_2(g)$$

$$2\,NaCl(l) \xrightarrow[580\,°C]{\text{Electrolysis}} 2\,Na(l) + Cl_2(g)$$

Bromine and iodine are both prepared by oxidation of the corresponding halide ion with chlorine. Naturally occurring aqueous solutions of bromide ion with concentrations of up to 5000 ppm are found in Arkansas and in the Dead Sea in Israel. Iodide ion solutions of up to 100 ppm concentration are found in Oklahoma and Michigan.

$$2\,Br^-(aq) + Cl_2(g) \longrightarrow Br_2(l) + 2\,Cl^-(aq)$$
$$2\,I^-(aq) + Cl_2(g) \longrightarrow I_2(s) + 2\,Cl^-(aq)$$

▲ The Dead Sea in Israel has a particularly high concentration of bromide ion.

Reactions of Halogens

Halogens are among the most reactive elements in the periodic table. Fluorine, in fact, forms compounds with every other element except the three noble gases He, Ne, and Ar. As noted previously, their large negative electron affinities allow halogens to accept electrons from other atoms to yield halide anions, X^-.

Halogens react with every metal in the periodic table to yield metal halides. With alkali and alkaline-earth metals, the formula of the halide product is easily predictable. With transition metals, though, more than one product can sometimes form depending on the reaction conditions and the amounts of reactants present. Iron, for instance, can react with Cl_2 to form either $FeCl_2$ or $FeCl_3$. Without knowing a good deal more about transition-metal chemistry, it's not possible to make predictions at this point. The reaction can be generalized as

$$2\,M + n\,X_2 \longrightarrow 2\,MX_n \quad \text{where} \quad M = \text{Metal}$$
$$X = F,\,Cl,\,Br,\,\text{or}\,I$$

▲ This beautiful piece of glass was etched with gaseous HF, one of the few substances that reacts with and etches glass (SiO_2), according to the equation $SiO_2(s) + 4\,HF(g) \rightarrow SiF_4(g) + 2\,H_2O(l)$.

Remember...

An **acid** is a substance that dissociates in water to give hydrogen ions (H^+), and a base is a substance that dissociates in water to give hydroxide ions (OH^-).   (Section 4.5)

XeF$_2$

XeF$_4$

XeF$_6$

Unlike the metallic elements, halogens become less rather than more reactive going down the periodic table because of their generally decreasing electron affinity. Thus, their reactivity order is $F_2 > Cl_2 > Br_2 > I_2$. Fluorine often reacts violently, chlorine and bromine somewhat less so, and iodine often sluggishly.

In addition to their reaction with metals, halogens also react with hydrogen gas to yield hydrogen halides, HX. Fluorine reacts explosively with hydrogen as soon as the two gases come in contact. Chlorine also reacts explosively once the reaction is initiated by a spark or by ultraviolet light, but the mixture of gases is stable in the dark. Bromine and iodine react more slowly.

$$H_2(g) + X_2 \longrightarrow 2\,HX(g) \qquad \text{where} \qquad X = F, Cl, Br, \text{ or } I$$

Hydrogen halides are useful because they are **acids**—compounds that produce H^+ ions when dissolved in water. An aqueous solution of HCl, for instance, is used throughout the chemical industry in a vast number of processes, from pickling steel (removing its iron oxide coating) to dissolving animal bones for producing gelatin.

$$HX \xrightarrow[\text{in } H_2O]{\text{Dissolve}} H^+(aq) + X^-(aq)$$

Hydrogen fluoride (HF) is used frequently for etching glass because it is one of the few substances that reacts with glass.

6.12 SOME CHEMISTRY OF THE NOBLE GASES

The noble gases of group 8A—He, Ne, Ar, Kr, Xe, and Rn—are neither metals nor reactive nonmetals. Rather, they are colorless, odorless, unreactive gases. The $1s^2$ valence-shell electron configuration for He and ns^2np^6 for the others already contain octets and thus make it difficult for the noble gases to either gain or lose electrons.

Although sometimes referred to as rare gases or inert gases, these older names are not really accurate because the group 8A elements are neither rare nor completely inert. Argon, for instance, makes up nearly 1% by volume of dry air, and there are several dozen known compounds of krypton and xenon, although none occur naturally. Some properties of the noble gases are listed in Table 6.7.

TABLE 6.7   Properties of Noble Gases

Name	Melting Point (°C)	Boiling Point (°C)	First Ionization Energy (kJ/mol)	Abundance in Dry Air (vol %)
Helium	−272.2	−268.9	2372.3	5.2×10^{-4}
Neon	−248.6	−246.1	2080.6	1.8×10^{-3}
Argon	−189.3	−185.9	1520.4	0.93
Krypton	−157.4	−153.2	1350.7	1.1×10^{-4}
Xenon	−111.8	−108.0	1170.4	9×10^{-6}
Radon	−71	−61.7	1037	Trace

Helium and neon undergo no chemical reactions and form no known compounds. Argon forms only HArF, and krypton and xenon react only with fluorine. Depending on the reaction conditions and on the amounts of reactants present, xenon can form three different fluorides: XeF_2, XeF_4, and XeF_6.

$$Xe(g) + F_2(g) \longrightarrow XeF_2(s)$$
$$Xe(g) + 2\,F_2(g) \longrightarrow XeF_4(s)$$
$$Xe(g) + 3\,F_2(g) \longrightarrow XeF_6(s)$$

The lack of reactivity of the noble gases is a consequence of their unusually large ionization energies (Figure 6.3) and their unusually small electron affinities (Figure 6.5), which result from their valence-shell electron configurations.

INQUIRY IS EATING SALT UNHEALTHY?

If you're like most people, you probably feel a little guilty about reaching for the salt-shaker at mealtime. The notion that high salt intake and high blood pressure go hand in hand is surely among the most highly publicized pieces of nutritional advice to appear in recent decades.

▲ Harvesting salt.

Salt has not always been held in such disrepute. Historically, salt has been prized since the earliest recorded times as a seasoning and a food preservative. Words and phrases in many languages reflect the importance of salt as a life-giving and life-sustaining substance. We refer to a kind and generous person as "the salt of the earth," for instance, and we speak of being "worth one's salt." In Roman times, soldiers were paid in salt; the English word salary is derived from the Latin word for paying salt wages (*salarium*).

Salt is perhaps the easiest of all minerals to obtain and purify. The simplest method, used for thousands of years throughout the world in coastal climates where sunshine is abundant and rainfall is scarce, is to evaporate seawater. Although the exact amount varies depending on the source, seawater contains an average of about 3.5% by mass of dissolved substances, most of which is sodium chloride. It has been estimated that evaporation of all the world's oceans would yield approximately *4.5 million cubic miles* of NaCl.

Only about 10% of current world salt production comes from evaporation of seawater. Most salt is obtained by mining the vast deposits of halite, or rock salt, formed by evaporation of ancient inland seas. These salt beds vary in thickness up to hundreds of meters and vary in depth from a few meters to thousands of meters below the Earth's surface. Salt mining has gone on for at least 3400 years, and the Wieliczka mine in Galicia, Poland (shown on the chapter-opening page), was worked continuously for more than 700 years until its closure in 1996.

Let's get back now to the dinner table. What about the link between dietary salt intake and high blood pressure? There's no doubt that most people in industrialized nations have a relatively high salt intake, and there's no doubt that high blood pressure among industrialized populations is on the rise. What's not so clear is exactly how the two observations are related.

The case against salt has been made largely by comparing widely diverse populations with different dietary salt intakes—by comparing the health of modern Americans with that of inhabitants of the Amazon rain forest, for example. Obviously, though, industrialization brings with it far more changes than simply an increase in dietary salt intake, and many of these other changes may be much more important than salt in contributing to hypertension.

In a study called the DASH-Sodium study, published in 2001, a strong correlation was found between a change in salt intake and a change in blood pressure. When volunteers cut back their salt intake from 8.3 g per day—roughly what Americans typically consume—to 3.8 g per day, significant drops in blood pressure were found. The largest reduction in blood pressure was seen in people already diagnosed with hypertension, but even subjects with normal blood pressure lowered their readings by several percentage points.

What should an individual do? The best answer, as in so many things, is to use moderation and common sense. People with hypertension should make a strong effort to lower their sodium intake; others might be well advised to choose unsalted snacks, use less salt in preparing food, and read nutrition labels for sodium content.

But one further point: Nutritional advice is never one-size-fits-all. Atheletes, construction workers, farm workers, and others who sweat profusely, may well need to *increase* their salt intake to avoid problems with low sodium and potassium levels.

▶ **PROBLEM 6.20** How is salt obtained commercially?

SUMMARY

Metallic elements, on the left side of the periodic table, tend to give up electrons to form cations, while the halogens and a few other nonmetallic elements, on the right side of the table, tend to accept electrons to form anions. The electrons given up by a main-group metal in forming a cation come from the highest-energy occupied orbital, while the electrons that are accepted by a nonmetal in forming an anion go into the lowest-energy unoccupied orbital. Sodium metal, for instance, loses its valence-shell $3s$ electron to form an Na^+ ion with the electron configuration of neon, while chlorine gains a $3p$ electron to form a Cl^- anion with the electron configuration of argon.

The amount of energy necessary to remove a valence electron from an isolated neutral atom is called the atom's **ionization energy (E_i)**. Ionization energies are smallest for metallic elements on the left side of the periodic table and largest for nonmetallic elements on the right side. As a result, metals usually give up electrons and act as reducing agents in chemical reactions.

Ionization is not limited to the removal of a single electron from an atom. Two, three, or even more electrons can be removed sequentially from an atom, although larger amounts of energy are required for each successive ionization step. In general, valence-shell electrons are much more easily removed than **core electrons**.

The amount of energy released or absorbed when an electron adds to an isolated neutral atom is called the atom's **electron affinity (E_{ea})**. By convention, a negative E_{ea} corresponds to a release of energy and a positive E_{ea} corresponds to an absorption of energy. Electron affinities are most negative for group 7A elements and most positive for group 2A and 8A elements. As a result, the group 7A elements usually accept electrons and act as oxidizing agents in chemical reactions.

In general, reactions of main-group elements can be described by the **octet rule**, which states that these elements tend to undergo reactions so as to attain a noble-gas electron configuration with filled s and p sublevels in their valence shell. Elements on the left side of the periodic table tend to give up electrons until a noble-gas configuration is reached; elements on the right side of the table tend to accept electrons until a noble-gas configuration is reached; and the noble gases themselves are essentially unreactive.

Main-group metals in groups 1A and 2A react with halogens in group 7A, during which the metal loses one or more electrons to the halogen. The product, a metal halide such as NaCl, is an ionic solid that consists of metal cations and halide anions electrostatically attracted to one another by ionic bonds. The sum of the interaction energies among all ions in a crystal is called the crystal's **lattice energy (U)**.

KEY WORDS

Born–Haber cycle   *199*
core electron   *191*

Coulomb's law   *201*
electron affinity (E_{ea})   *194*

ionization energy (E_i)   *190*
lattice energy (U)   *200*

octet rule   *197*

CONCEPTUAL PROBLEMS

Problems 6.1–6.20 appear within the chapter.

6.21 In the following drawings, red spheres represent cations and blue spheres represent anions. Match each of the drawings **(a)**–**(d)** with the following ionic compounds:

   (i) $Ca_3(PO_4)_2$ **(ii)** Li_2CO_3 **(iii)** $FeCl_2$ **(iv)** $MgSO_4$

(a)   **(b)**

(c)   **(d)**

6.22 Which of the following drawings is more likely to represent an ionic compound, and which a covalent compound?

  (a)   **(b)**

6.23 Circle the approximate part or parts of the periodic table where the following elements appear:

  (a) Elements with the smallest values of E_{i1}

  (b) Elements with the largest atomic radii

  (c) Elements with the most negative values of E_{ea}

6.24 Where on the periodic table would you find the element that has an ion with each of the following electron configurations? Identify each ion.

(a) 3+ ion: $1s^2 2s^2 2p^6$ (b) 3+ ion: $[Ar] 3d^3$

(c) 2+ ion: $[Kr] 5s^2 4d^{10}$ (d) 1+ ion: $[Kr] 4d^{10}$

6.25 Which of the following spheres is likely to represent a metal atom, and which a nonmetal atom? Which sphere in the products represents a cation, and which an anion?

6.26 Each of the pictures (a)–(d) represents one of the following substances at 25 °C: sodium, chlorine, iodine, sodium chloride. Which picture corresponds to which substance?

(a)   (b)   (c)   (d)

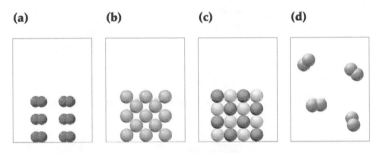

6.27 Which of the following alkali metal halides has the largest lattice energy, and which has the smallest lattice energy? Explain.

(a)   (b)   (c)

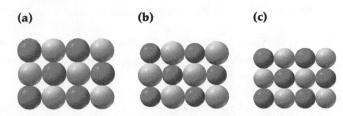

6.28 Three binary compounds are represented on the following drawing: red with red, blue with blue, and green with green. Give a likely formula for each compound.

6.29 Given the following values for the formation of LiCl(s) from its elements, draw a Born–Haber cycle similar to that shown in Figure 6.6 on page 199.

E_{ea} for Cl(g) = −348.6 kJ/mol

Heat of sublimation for Li(s) = +159.4 kJ/mol

E_{i1} for Li(g) = +520 kJ/mol

Bond dissociation energy for $Cl_2(g)$ = +243 kJ/mol

Lattice energy for LiCl(s) = +853 kJ/mol

SECTION PROBLEMS

Ions, Ionization Energy, and Electron Affinity
(Sections 6.1–6.5)

6.30 What is the difference between a covalent bond and an ionic bond? Give an example of each.

6.31 What is the difference between a molecule and an ion? Give an example of each.

6.32 How many protons and electrons are in each of the following ions?

(a) Be^{2+} (b) Rb^+ (c) Se^{2-} (d) Au^{3+}

6.33 What is the identity of the element X in the following ions?

(a) X^{2+}, a cation that has 36 electrons

(b) X^-, an anion that has 36 electrons

6.34 What are the likely ground-state electron configurations of the following cations?

(a) La^{3+} (b) Ag^+ (c) Sn^{2+}

6.35 What are the likely ground-state electron configurations of the following anions?

(a) Se^{2-} (b) N^{3-}

6.36 What is the electron configuration of Ca^{2+}? What is the electron configuration of Ti^{2+}?

6.37 What tripositive ion has the electron configuration $[Kr] 4d^3$? What neutral atom has the electron configuration $[Kr] 5s^2 4d^2$?

6.38 There are two elements in the transition-metal series Sc through Zn that have four unpaired electrons in their 2+ ions. Identify them.

6.39 Identify the element whose 2+ ion has the ground-state electron configuration $[Ar] 3d^{10}$.

6.40 Which group of elements in the periodic table has the largest E_{i1}, and which group has the smallest? Explain.

6.41 Which element in the periodic table has the smallest ionization energy? Which has the largest?

6.42 **(a)** Which has the smaller second ionization energy, K or Ca?

(b) Which has the larger third ionization energy, Ga or Ca?

6.43 **(a)** Which has the smaller fourth ionization energy, Sn or Sb?

(b) Which has the larger sixth ionization energy, Se or Br?

6.44 Three atoms have the following electron configurations:

(a) $1s^2\,2s^2\,2p^6\,3s^2\,3p^3$

(b) $1s^2\,2s^2\,2p^6\,3s^2\,3p^6$

(c) $1s^2\,2s^2\,2p^6\,3s^2\,3p^6\,4s^2$

Which of the three has the largest E_{i2}? Which has the smallest E_{i7}?

6.45 Write the electron configuration of the atom in the third row of the periodic table that has the smallest E_{i4}.

6.46 The first four ionization energies in kJ/mol of a certain second-row element are 801, 2427, 3660, and 25,025. What is the likely identity of the element?

6.47 The first four ionization energies in kJ/mol of a certain second-row element are 900, 1757, 14,849, and 21,007. What is the likely identity of the element?

6.48 Which element in each of the following sets has the smallest first ionization energy, and which has the largest?

(a) Li, Ba, K   **(b)** B, Be, Cl   **(c)** Ca, C, Cl

6.49 What elements meet the following descriptions?

(a) Has largest E_{i3} **(b)** Has largest E_{i7}

6.50 What is the relationship between the electron affinity of a singly charged cation such as Na^+ and the ionization energy of the neutral atom?

6.51 What is the relationship between the ionization energy of a singly charged anion such as Cl^- and the electron affinity of the neutral atom?

6.52 Which has the more negative electron affinity, Na^+ or Na? Na^+ or Cl?

6.53 Which has the more negative electron affinity, Br or Br^-?

6.54 Why is energy usually released when an electron is added to a neutral atom but absorbed when an electron is removed from a neutral atom?

6.55 Why does ionization energy increase regularly across the periodic table from group 1A to group 8A, whereas electron affinity increases irregularly from group 1A to group 7A and then falls dramatically for group 8A?

6.56 No element has a negative second electron affinity. That is, the process $A^-(g) + e^- \longrightarrow A^{2-}(g)$ is unfavorable for every element. Suggest a reason.

6.57 Why does phosphorus have a less-negative electron affinity than its neighbors silicon and sulfur?

Ionic Bonds and Lattice Energy (Sections 6.7 and 6.8)

6.58 Order the following compounds according to their expected lattice energies: LiCl, KCl, KBr, $MgCl_2$.

6.59 Order the following compounds according to their expected lattice energies: $AlBr_3$, $MgBr_2$, LiBr, CaO.

6.60 Calculate the energy change in kilojoules per mole when lithium atoms lose an electron to bromine atoms to form isolated Li^+ and Br^- ions. [The E_i for Li(g) is 520 kJ/mol; the E_{ea} for Br(g) is −325 kJ/mol.]

6.61 Cesium has the smallest ionization energy of all elements (376 kJ/mol), and chlorine has the most negative electron affinity (−349 kJ/mol). Will a cesium atom transfer an electron to a chlorine atom to form isolated $Cs^+(g)$ and $Cl^-(g)$ ions? Explain.

6.62 Find the lattice energy of LiBr(s) in Table 6.3, and calculate the energy change in kilojoules per mole for the formation of solid LiBr from the elements. [The sublimation energy for Li(s) is +159.4 kJ/mol, the bond dissociation energy of $Br_2(g)$ is +224 kJ/mol, and the energy necessary to convert $Br_2(l)$ to $Br_2(g)$ is 30.9 kJ/mol.]

6.63 Look up the lattice energies in Table 6.3, and calculate the energy change in kilojoules per mole for the formation of the following substances from their elements:

(a) LiF(s) [The sublimation energy for Li(s) is +159.4 kJ/mol, the E_i for Li(g) is 520 kJ/mol, the E_{ea} for F(g) is −328 kJ/mol, and the bond dissociation energy of $F_2(g)$ is +158 kJ/mol.]

(b) $CaF_2(s)$ [The sublimation energy for Ca(s) is +178.2 kJ/mol, $E_{i1} = +589.8$ kJ/mol,   and $E_{i2} = +1145$ kJ/mol.]

6.64 Born–Haber cycles, such as those shown in Figures 6.6 and 6.7, are called *cycles* because they form closed loops. If any five of the six energy changes in the cycle are known, the value of the sixth can be calculated. Use the following five values to calculate the lattice energy in kilojoules per mole for sodium hydride, NaH(s):

E_{ea} for H(g) = −72.8 kJ/mol

E_{i1} for Na(g) = +495.8 kJ/mol

Heat of sublimation for Na(s) = +107.3 kJ/mol

Bond dissociation energy for $H_2(g)$ = +435.9 kJ/mol

Net energy change for the formation of NaH(s) from its elements = −60 kJ/mol

6.65 Calculate a lattice energy for $CaH_2(s)$ in kilojoules per mole using the following information:

E_{ea} for H(g) = −72.8 kJ/mol

E_{i1} for Ca(g) = +589.8 kJ/mol

E_{i2} for Ca(g) = +1145 kJ/mol

Heat of sublimation for Ca(s) = +178.2 kJ/mol

Bond dissociation energy for $H_2(g)$ = +435.9 kJ/mol

Net energy change for the formation of $CaH_2(s)$ from its elements = −186.2 kJ/mol

6.66 Calculate the overall energy change in kilojoules per mole for the formation of CsF(s) from its elements using the following data:

E_{ea} for F(g) = −328 kJ/mol

E_{i1} for Cs(g) = +375.7 kJ/mol

E_{i2} for Cs(g) = +2422 kJ/mol

Heat of sublimation for Cs(s) = +76.1 kJ/mol

Bond dissociation energy for $F_2(g)$ = +158 kJ/mol

Lattice energy for CsF(s) = +740 kJ/mol

6.67 The estimated lattice energy for $CsF_2(s)$ is +2347 kJ/mol. Use the data given in Problem 6.66 to calculate an overall energy change in kilojoules per mole for the formation of $CsF_2(s)$ from its elements. Does the overall reaction absorb energy or release it? In light of your answer to Problem 6.66, which compound is more likely to form in the reaction of cesium with fluorine, CsF or CsF_2?

6.68 Calculate the overall energy change in kilojoules per mole for the formation of CaCl(s) from the elements. The following data are needed:

E_{ea} for Cl(g) = −348.6 kJ/mol

E_{i1} for Ca(g) = +589.8 kJ/mol

E_{i2} for Ca(g) = +1145 kJ/mol

Heat of sublimation for Ca(s) = +178.2 kJ/mol

Bond dissociation energy for $Cl_2(g)$ = +243 kJ/mol

Lattice energy for $CaCl_2(s)$ = +2258 kJ/mol

Lattice energy for CaCl(s) = +717 kJ/mol (estimated)

6.69 Use the data in Problem 6.68 to calculate an overall energy change for the formation of $CaCl_2(s)$ from the elements. Which is more likely to form, CaCl or $CaCl_2$?

6.70 Use the data and the result in Problem 6.64 to draw a Born–Haber cycle for the formation of NaH(s) from its elements.

6.71 Use the data and the result in Problem 6.63(a) to draw a Born–Haber cycle for the formation of LiF(s) from its elements.

Main-Group Chemistry (Sections 6.9–6.12)

6.72 Little is known about the chemistry of astatine (At) from direct observation, but reasonable predictions can be made.

(a) Is astatine likely to be a gas, a liquid, or a solid?

(b) Is astatine likely to react with sodium? If so, what is the formula of the product?

6.73 Look at the properties of the alkali metals summarized in Table 6.4, and predict reasonable values for the melting point, boiling point, density, and atomic radius of francium.

6.74 Why does chemical reactivity increase from top to bottom in groups 1A and 2A?

6.75 Why does chemical reactivity decrease from top to bottom in group 7A?

6.76 Write chemical equations for the reaction of potassium with the following substances, making sure that the numbers and kinds of atoms are the same on both sides of the equations. If no reaction occurs, write N.R.

(a) H_2O (b) NH_3 (c) Br_2 (d) O_2

6.77 Write chemical equations for the reaction of calcium with the following substances, making sure that the numbers and kinds of atoms are the same on both sides of the equations. If no reaction occurs, write N.R.

(a) H_2O (b) He   (c) Br_2 (d) O_2

6.78 Write chemical equations for the reaction of chlorine with the following substances, making sure that the numbers and kinds of atoms are the same on both sides of the equations. If no reaction occurs, write N.R.

(a) H_2 (b) Ar   (c) Rb

6.79 Milk of magnesia, a widely used antacid, is an aqueous suspension of $Mg(OH)_2$. How would you prepare $Mg(OH)_2$ from magnesium metal?

6.80 The element bromine was first prepared by oxidation of aqueous potassium bromide with solid manganese(IV) oxide. Write a balanced net ionic equation for the reaction in aqueous acidic solution. (Mn^{2+} is also formed.)

6.81 The first preparation of chlorine was similar to the synthesis of elemental bromine (Problem 6.80). A later method entailed the reaction of hydrogen chloride and oxygen at 400 °C. Write a balanced equation for the reaction. (Water is also formed.)

6.82 Passing an electric current (*electrolysis*) through a solution of Al_2O_3 in molten cryolite (Na_3AlF_6) around 1000 °C produces aluminum metal, which separates from the solution as a liquid. Write a balanced equation for the reaction. (Oxygen is also formed.)

6.83 Barium metal can be prepared from its oxide by heating with aluminum at 1200 °C. (Aluminum oxide is also formed.) At the reaction temperature, the oxides are solids, aluminum is a liquid, and barium is a gas. Write a balanced equation for the reaction.

6.84 Reaction of titanium and chlorine at 300 °C yields a metal halide that is 25.25% Ti by mass. The melting point (−24 °C) and boiling point (136 °C) of the halide suggest it is a molecular compound rather than an ionic one.

(a) What are the formula and name of the compound, assuming the molecular formula is the same as the empirical formula?

(b) Write the balanced equation for the reaction.

(c) When treated with magnesium, the compound yields high-purity titanium metal. Write a balanced equation for the reaction.

6.85 Niobium reacts with fluorine at room temperature to give a solid binary compound that is 49.44% Nb by mass.

(a) What is the empirical formula of the compound?

(b) Write a balanced equation for the reaction.

(c) The compound reacts with hydrogen to regenerate metallic niobium. Write a balanced equation for the reaction.

CHAPTER PROBLEMS

6.86 Cu^+ has an ionic radius of 77 pm, but Cu^{2+} has an ionic radius of 73 pm. Explain.

6.87 The following ions all have the same number of electrons: Ti^{4+}, Sc^{3+}, Ca^{2+}, S^{2-}. Order them according to their expected sizes, and explain your answer.

6.88 Calculate overall energy changes in kilojoules per mole for the formation of MgF(s) and $MgF_2(s)$ from their elements. In light of your answers, which compound is more likely to form in the reaction of magnesium with fluorine, MgF or MgF_2? The following data are needed:

E_{ea} for F(g) = −328 kJ/mol

E_{i1} for Mg(g) = +737.7 kJ/mol

E_{i2} for Mg(g) = +1450.7 kJ/mol

Heat of sublimation for Mg(s) = +147.7 kJ/mol

Bond dissociation energy for $F_2(g)$ = +158 kJ/mol

Lattice energy for $MgF_2(s)$ = +2952 kJ/mol

Lattice energy for MgF(s) = 930 kJ/mol (estimated)

6.89 Draw Born–Haber cycles for the formation of both MgF and MgF_2 (Problem 6.88).

6.90 We saw in Section 6.7 that the reaction of solid sodium with gaseous chlorine to yield solid sodium chloride (Na^+Cl^-) is favorable by 411 kJ/mol. Calculate the energy change for the alternative reaction that yields chlorine sodide (Cl^+Na^-), and then explain why sodium chloride formation is preferred.

$$2\,Na(s) + Cl_2(g) \longrightarrow 2\,Cl^+Na^-(s)$$

Assume that the lattice energy for Cl^+Na^- is the same as that for Na^+Cl^-. The following data are needed in addition to that found in Section 6.7:

E_{ea} for Na(g) = -52.9 kJ/mol

E_{i1} for Cl(g) = $+1251$ kJ/mol

6.91 Draw a Born–Haber cycle for the reaction of sodium with chlorine to yield chlorine sodide (Problem 6.90).

6.92 Write chemical equations for the reaction of lithium with the following substances, making sure that the numbers and kinds of atoms are the same on both sides of the equations. If no reaction occurs, write N.R.

(a) H_2O (b) NH_3 (c) Br_2

(d) N_2 (e) O_2

6.93 Write chemical equations for the reaction of fluorine with the following substances, making sure that the numbers and kinds of atoms are the same on both sides of the equations. If no reaction occurs, write N.R.

(a) H_2 (b) Na   (c) Sr

6.94 Each of the following pairs of elements will react to form a binary ionic compound. Write the formula of each compound formed, and give its name.

(a) Magnesium and chlorine

(b) Calcium and oxygen

(c) Lithium and nitrogen

(d) Aluminum and oxygen

6.95 Element X reacts with element Y to give a product containing X^{3+} ions and Y^{2-} ions.

(a) Is element X likely to be a metal or a nonmetal? Explain.

(b) Is element Y likely to be a metal or a nonmetal? Explain.

(c) What is the formula of the product?

(d) In what groups of the periodic table are elements X and Y likely to be found?

6.96 Many early chemists noted a diagonal relationship among elements in the periodic table, whereby a given element is sometimes more similar to the element below and to the right than it is to the element directly below. Lithium is more similar to magnesium than to sodium, for example, and boron is more similar to silicon than to aluminum. Use your knowledge about the periodic trends of such properties as atomic radii and Z_{eff} to explain the existence of diagonal relationships.

6.97 Heating elemental cesium and platinum together for two days at 973 K gives a dark red ionic compound that is 57.67% Cs and 42.33% Pt.

(a) What is the empirical formula of the compound?

(b) What are the charge and electron configuration of the cesium ion?

(c) What are the charge and electron configuration of the platinum ion?

6.98 Use the following information plus the data given in Tables 6.2 and 6.3 to calculate the second electron affinity, E_{ea2}, of oxygen. Is the O^{2-} ion stable in the gas phase? Why is it stable in solid MgO?

Heat of sublimation for Mg(s) = $+147.7$ kJ/mol

Bond dissociation energy for $O_2(g)$ = $+498.4$ kJ/mol

E_{ea1} for O(g) = -141.0 kJ/mol

Net energy change for formation of MgO(s) from its elements = -601.7 kJ/mol

6.99 (a) Which element from each set has the largest atomic radius? Explain.

(i) Ba, Ti, Ra, Li   (ii) F, Al, In, As

(b) Which element from each set has the smallest ionization energy? Explain.

(i) Tl, Po, Se, Ga   (ii) Cs, Ga, Bi, Se

6.100 (a) Which of the elements Be, N, O, and F has the most negative electron affinity? Explain.

(b) Which of the ions Se^{2-}, F^-, O^{2-}, and Rb^+ has the largest radius? Explain.

6.101 Given the following information, construct a Born–Haber cycle to calculate the lattice energy of $CaC_2(s)$:

Net energy change for the formation of $CaC_2(s)$ = -60 kJ/mol

Heat of sublimation for Ca(s) = $+178$ kJ/mol

E_{i1} for Ca(g) = $+590$ kJ/mol

E_{i2} for Ca(g) = $+1145$ kJ/mol

Heat of sublimation for C(s) = $+717$ kJ/mol

Bond dissociation energy for $C_2(g)$ = $+614$ kJ/mol

E_{ea1} for $C_2(g)$ = -315 kJ/mol

E_{ea2} for $C_2(g)$ = $+410$ kJ/mol

6.102 Given the following information, construct a Born–Haber cycle to calculate the lattice energy of $CrCl_2I(s)$:

Net energy change for the formation of $CrCl_2I(s)$ = -420 kJ/mol

Bond dissociation energy for $Cl_2(g)$ = $+243$ kJ/mol

Bond dissociation energy for $I_2(s)$ = $+151$ kJ/mol

Heat of sublimation for $I_2(s)$ = $+62$ kJ/mol

Heat of sublimation for Cr(s) = $+397$ kJ/mol

E_{i1} for Cr(g) = 652 kJ/mol

E_{i2} for Cr(g) = 1588 kJ/mol

E_{i3} for Cr(g) = 2882 kJ/mol

E_{ea} for Cl(g) = -349 kJ/mol

E_{ea} for I(g) = -295 kJ/mol

MULTICONCEPT PROBLEMS

6.103 Consider the electronic structure of the element bismuth.

    (a) The first ionization energy of bismuth is $E_{i1} = +703$ kJ/mol. What is the longest possible wavelength of light that could ionize an atom of bismuth?

    (b) Write the electron configurations of neutral Bi and the Bi^+ cation.

    (c) What are the n and l quantum numbers of the electron removed when Bi is ionized to Bi^+?

    (d) Would you expect element 115 to have an ionization energy greater than, equal to, or less than that of bismuth? Explain.

6.104 Iron is commonly found as Fe, Fe^{2+}, and Fe^{3+}.

    (a) Write electron configurations for each of the three.

    (b) What are the n and l quantum numbers of the electron removed on going from Fe^{2+} to Fe^{3+}?

    (c) The third ionization energy of Fe is $E_{i3} = +2952$ kJ/mol. What is the longest wavelength of light that could ionize $Fe^{2+}(g)$ to $Fe^{3+}(g)$?

    (d) The third ionization energy of Ru is less than the third ionization energy of Fe. Explain.

6.105 The ionization energy of an atom can be measured by photoelectron spectroscopy, in which light of wavelength λ is directed at an atom, causing an electron to be ejected. The kinetic energy of the ejected electron (E_K) is measured by determining its velocity, v, since $E_K = 1/2\ mv^2$. The E_i is then calculated using the relationship that the energy of the incident light equals the sum of E_i plus E_K.

    (a) What is the ionization energy of rubidium atoms in kilojoules per mole if light with $\lambda = 58.4$ nm produces electrons with a velocity of 2.450×10^6 m/s? (The mass of an electron is 9.109×10^{-31} kg.)

    (b) What is the ionization energy of potassium in kilojoules per mole if light with $\lambda = 142$ nm produces electrons with a velocity of 1.240×10^6 m/s?

Covalent Bonds and Molecular Structure

Shape is important, both in architecture and in chemistry.

CONTENTS

W e saw in the previous chapter that a bond between a metal and a reactive nonmetal is typically formed by the transfer of electrons between atoms. The metal atom loses one or more electrons and becomes a cation, while the reactive nonmetal atom gains one or more electrons and becomes an anion. The oppositely charged ions are held together by the electrostatic attractions that we call ionic bonds.

How, though, do bonds form between atoms of the same or similar elements? How can we describe the bonds in such substances as H_2, Cl_2, CO_2, and the tens of millions of other nonionic compounds? Simply put, the answer is that the bonds in such compounds are formed by the *sharing* of electrons between atoms rather than by the transfer of electrons from one atom to another. As we saw in Section 2.10, a bond formed by the sharing of electrons is called a *covalent bond*, and the unit of matter held together by one or more covalent bonds is called a *molecule*. We'll explore the nature of covalent bonding in this chapter.

7.1   COVALENT BONDING IN MOLECULES

To see how the formation of a covalent, shared-electron bond between atoms can be described, let's look at the H—H bond in the H_2 molecule as the simplest example. When two hydrogen atoms come close together, electrostatic interactions begin to develop between them. The two positively charged nuclei repel each other, and the two negatively charged electrons repel each other, but each nucleus attracts both electrons (Figure 7.1). If the attractive forces are stronger than the repulsive forces, a covalent bond is formed, with the two atoms held together and the two shared electrons occupying the region between the nuclei.

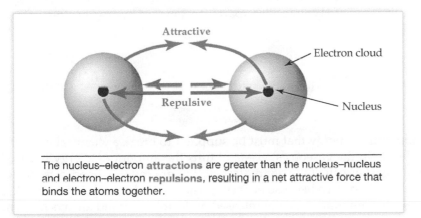

Attractive

Electron cloud

Repulsive

Nucleus

The nucleus–electron **attractions** are greater than the nucleus–nucleus and electron–electron **repulsions**, resulting in a net attractive force that binds the atoms together.

Figure 7.1
A covalent H—H bond. The bond is the net result of attractive and repulsive electrostatic forces.

In essence, the shared electrons act as a kind of "glue" to bind the two atoms into an H_2 molecule. Both nuclei are simultaneously attracted to the same electrons and are therefore held together, much as two tug-of-war teams pulling on the same rope are held together.

The magnitudes of the various attractive and repulsive forces between nuclei and electrons in a covalent bond depend on how close the atoms are. If the hydrogen atoms are too far apart, the attractive forces are small and no bond exists. If the hydrogen atoms are too close together, the repulsive interaction between the nuclei becomes so strong that it pushes the atoms apart. Thus, there is an optimum distance between nuclei called the **bond length** where net attractive forces are maximized and the H—H molecule is most stable. In the H_2 molecule, the bond length is 74 pm. On a graph of energy versus internuclear distance, the bond length is the H—H distance in the minimum-energy, most stable arrangement (Figure 7.2).

Every covalent bond has its own characteristic length that leads to maximum stability and that is roughly predictable from a knowledge of atomic radii (Section 5.14). For example, because the atomic radius of hydrogen is 37 pm and the atomic radius of chlorine is 99 pm, the H—Cl bond length in a hydrogen chloride molecule should be approximately 37 pm + 99 pm = 136 pm. The actual value is 127 pm.

Figure 7.2
A graph of potential energy versus internuclear distance for the H_2 molecule.

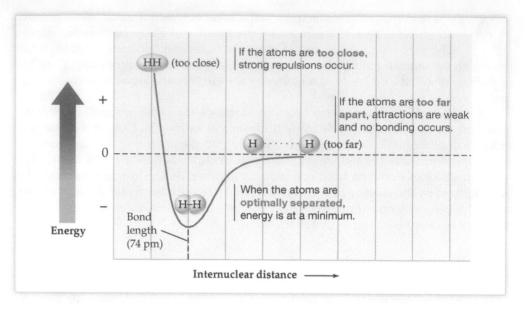

7.2 STRENGTHS OF COVALENT BONDS

Look again at Figure 7.2, the graph of energy versus internuclear distance for the H_2 molecule, and note how the H_2 molecule is lower in energy than two separate hydrogen atoms. When pairs of hydrogen atoms bond together, they form lower-energy H_2 molecules and release 436 kJ/mol. Looked at from the other direction, 436 kJ must be *added* to split 1 mol of H_2 molecules apart into 2 mol of hydrogen atoms.

The amount of energy that must be supplied to break a chemical bond in an isolated molecule in the gaseous state—and thus the amount of energy released when the bond forms—is called the **bond dissociation energy (D).** Bond dissociation energies are always positive because energy must always be supplied to break a bond. Conversely, the amount of energy released on forming a bond always has a negative value.

Every bond in every molecule has its own specific bond dissociation energy. Not surprisingly, though, bonds between the same pairs of atoms usually have similar dissociation energies. For example, carbon–carbon bonds usually have D values of approximately 350–380 kJ/mol regardless of the exact structure of the molecule. Note in the following examples that covalent bonds are indicated by lines between atoms, as described in Section 2.10.

Remember...

The structural formula of a molecule uses **lines between the atoms** to indicate the shared electrons in covalent bonds. (Section 2.10)

Because similar bonds have similar bond dissociation energies, it's possible to construct a table of average values to compare different kinds of bonds (Table 7.1). Keep in mind, though, that the actual value in a specific molecule might vary by ±10% from the average.

TABLE 7.1 Average Bond Dissociation Energies, D (kJ/mol)

H—H	436[a]	C—H	410	N—H	390	O—F	180	I—I	151[a]
H—C	410	C—C	350	N—C	300	O—Cl	200	S—F	310
H—F	570[a]	C—F	450	N—F	270	O—Br	210	S—Cl	250
H—Cl	432[a]	C—Cl	330	N—Cl	200	O—I	220	S—Br	210
H—Br	366[a]	C—Br	270	N—Br	240	O—N	200	S—S	225
H—I	298[a]	C—I	240	N—N	240	O—O	180		
H—N	390	C—N	300	N—O	200	F—F	159a		
H—O	460	C—O	350	O—H	460	Cl—Cl	243[a]		
H—S	340	C—S	260	O—C	350	Br—Br	193[a]		

Multiple covalent bonds[b]

C=C	728	C≡C	965	C=O	732	O=O	498[a]	N≡N	945[a]

[a] Exact value

[b] We'll discuss multiple covalent bonds in Section 7.5.

The bond dissociation energies listed in Table 7.1 cover a wide range, from a low of 151 kJ/mol for the I—I bond to a high of 570 kJ/mol for the H—F bond. As a rule of thumb, though, most of the bonds commonly encountered in naturally occurring molecules (C—H, C—C, C—O) have values in the range 350–400 kJ/mol.

7.3 A COMPARISON OF IONIC AND COVALENT COMPOUNDS

Look at the comparison between NaCl and HCl in Table 7.2 to get an idea of the difference between ionic and covalent compounds. Sodium chloride, an ionic compound, is a white solid with a melting point of 801 °C and a boiling point of 1465 °C. Hydrogen chloride, a covalent compound, is a colorless gas with a melting point of −115 °C and a boiling point of −84.9 °C. What accounts for such large differences in properties between ionic compounds and covalent compounds?

TABLE 7.2 Some Physical Properties of NaCl and HCl

Property	NaCl	HCl
Formula mass	58.44 amu	36.46 amu
Physical appearance	White solid	Colorless gas
Type of bond	Ionic	Covalent
Melting point	801 °C	−115 °C
Boiling point	1465 °C	−84.9 °C

▲ Sodium chloride, an ionic compound, is a white, crystalline solid that melts at 801 °C. Hydrogen chloride, a molecular compound, is a gas at room temperature.

Ionic compounds are high-melting solids because of their ionic bonds. As discussed previously in Section 2.11, a visible sample of sodium chloride consists not of NaCl molecules but of a vast three-dimensional network of ions in which each Na$^+$ cation is attracted to many surrounding Cl$^-$ anions and each Cl$^-$ ion is attracted to many surrounding Na$^+$ ions. For sodium chloride to melt or boil so that the ions break free of one another, every ionic attraction in the entire crystal—the lattice energy—must be overcome, a process that requires a large amount of energy.

Covalent compounds, by contrast, are low-melting solids, liquids, or even gases. A sample of a covalent compound, such as hydrogen chloride, consists of discrete HCl molecules. The covalent bond within an individual molecule may be very strong, but the attractive forces between the different molecules are fairly weak. As a

Remember...

Lattice energy (U) is the amount of energy that must be supplied to break an ionic solid into its individual gaseous ions and is thus a measure of the strength of the crystal's ionic bonds. (Section 6.8)

result, relatively little energy is required to overcome the forces between molecules and cause a covalent compound to melt or boil. We'll look at the nature of intermolecular forces and the boiling process in Chapter 10.

7.4 POLAR COVALENT BONDS: ELECTRONEGATIVITY

We've given the impression up to this point that a given bond is either purely ionic, with electrons completely transferred, or purely covalent, with electrons shared equally. In fact, though, ionic and covalent bonds represent only the two extremes of a continuous range of possibilities. Between these two extremes are the large majority of bonds in which the bonding electrons are shared unequally between two atoms but are not completely transferred. Such bonds are said to be **polar covalent bonds** (**Figure 7.3**). The lowercase Greek letter delta (δ) is used to symbolize the resultant *partial* charges on the atoms, either partial positive ($\delta+$) for the atom that has a smaller share of the bonding electrons or partial negative ($\delta-$) for the atom that has a larger share.

Figure 7.3
The bonding continuum from nonpolar covalent to ionic. [The symbol δ (Greek delta) means partial charge, either partial positive ($\delta+$) or partial negative ($\delta-$)].

Nonpolar covalent (electronically symmetrical)   Polar covalent (partial charges)   Ionic (full charges)

Polar covalent bonds have an unsymmetrical electron distribution in which the bonding electrons are attracted more strongly by one atom than the other.

The extent of electron transfer in a compound is most easily visualized with what are called *electrostatic potential maps*, which use color to portray the calculated electron distribution in an isolated, gas-phase molecule. Yellow–green represents a neutral, nonpolar atom; blue represents a deficiency of electrons on an atom (partial positive charge), and red represents a surplus of electrons on an atom (partial negative charge). As examples of different points along the bonding spectrum, look at the three substances Cl_2, HCl, and NaCl.

- Cl_2 The bond in a chlorine molecule is nonpolar covalent, with the bonding electrons attracted equally to the two identical chlorine atoms. A similar situation exists in all such molecules that contain a covalent bond between two identical atoms. Thus, both chlorine atoms in Cl_2 are nonpolar, as shown by their identical yellow–green coloration in an electrostatic potential map.

A nonpolar covalent bond. Yellow-green represents a neutral, nonpolar atom.

- HCl The bond in a hydrogen chloride molecule is polar covalent. The chlorine atom attracts the bonding electron pair more strongly than hydrogen does, resulting in an unsymmetrical distribution of electrons. Chlorine thus has a partial negative charge (orange in the electrostatic potential map), and hydrogen has a partial positive charge (blue in the electrostatic potential map). Experimentally, the H—Cl, bond has been found to be about 83% covalent and 17% ionic.

$$\delta^+ H - Cl^{\delta^-}$$

$$[H : Cl]$$

| **A polar covalent bond.**
The bonding electrons are attracted more strongly by Cl than by H.

- **NaCl** The bond in solid sodium chloride is a largely ionic one between Na$^+$ and Cl$^-$. In spite of what we've said previously, though, experiments show that the NaCl bond is only about 80% ionic and that the electron transferred from Na to Cl still spends some of its time near sodium. Thus, the electron-poor sodium atom is blue in an electrostatic potential map, while the electron-rich chlorine is red.

Na$^+$Cl$^-$ **An ionic bond.** Blue indicates a partial positive charge; red indicates a partial negative charge.

Bond polarity is due to differences in **electronegativity (EN)**, defined as the ability of an atom in a molecule to attract the shared electrons in a covalent bond. As shown in **Figure 7.4**, electronegativities are expressed on a unitless scale, with fluorine, the most highly electronegative element, assigned a value of 4.0. Metallic elements on the left of the periodic table attract electrons only weakly and are the least electronegative elements. Halogens and other reactive nonmetals in the upper right of the table attract electrons strongly and are the most electronegative. Figure 7.4 also shows that electronegativity generally decreases down the periodic table within a group.

Figure 7.4
Electronegativity values and trends in the periodic table.

H 2.1																	He
Li 1.0	Be 1.5			Electronegativity increases from left to right.								B 2.0	C 2.5	N 3.0	O 3.5	F 4.0	Ne
Na 0.9	Mg 1.2											Al 1.5	Si 1.8	P 2.1	S 2.5	Cl 3.0	Ar
K 0.8	Ca 1.0	Sc 1.3	Ti 1.5	V 1.6	Cr 1.6	Mn 1.5	Fe 1.8	Co 1.9	Ni 1.9	Cu 1.9	Zn 1.6	Ga 1.6	Ge 1.8	As 2.0	Se 2.4	Br 2.8	Kr
Rb 0.8	Sr 1.0	Y 1.2	Zr 1.4	Nb 1.6	Mo 1.8	Tc 1.9	Ru 2.2	Rh 2.2	Pd 2.2	Ag 1.9	Cd 1.7	In 1.7	Sn 1.8	Sb 1.9	Te 2.1	I 2.5	Xe
Cs 0.7	Ba 0.9	Lu 1.1	Hf 1.3	Ta 1.5	W 1.7	Re 1.9	Os 2.2	Ir 2.2	Pt 2.2	Au 2.4	Hg 1.9	Tl 1.8	Pb 1.9	Bi 1.9	Po 2.0	At 2.1	Rn

Electronegativity decreases from top to bottom.

Because electronegativity measures the ability of an atom in a molecule to attract shared electrons, it seems reasonable that it should be related to **electron affinity** (E_{ea}, Section 6.5) and **ionization energy** (E_i, Section 6.3). Electron affinity, after all, is a measure of the tendency of an isolated atom to gain an electron, and ionization energy is a measure of the tendency of an isolated atom to lose an electron. In fact, one of the ways in which electronegativities were first calculated was by taking the average of the absolute values of E_{ea} and E_i and setting up a scale with fluorine assigned a value of 4.0.

Remember...
Electron affinity (E_{ea}) is defined as the energy change that occurs when an electron is added to an isolated gaseous atom. (Section 6.5)
Ionization energy (E_i), in contrast, is the amount of energy needed to remove the highest-energy electron from an isolated neutral atom in the gaseous state.   (Section 6.3)

How can we use electronegativity to predict bond polarity? A general but somewhat arbitrary guideline is that bonds between atoms with the same or similar
electronegativities are nonpolar covalent, bonds between atoms whose electronegativities differ by more than about 2 units are substantially ionic, and bonds between
atoms whose electronegativities differ by less than 2 units are polar covalent. Thus,
we can be reasonably sure that a C—Cl, bond in chloroform, $CHCl_3$, is polar covalent, while an Na^+Cl^- bond in sodium chloride is largely ionic.

Chlorine:	EN = 3.0	Chlorine:	EN = 3.0
Carbon:	EN = 2.5	Sodium:	EN = 0.9
Difference = 0.5		Difference = 2.1	

▶ **PROBLEM 7.1**   Use the electronegativity values in Figure 7.4 to predict whether the
bonds in the following compounds are polar covalent or ionic:

(a) $SiCl_4$ **(b)** CsBr   **(c)** $FeBr_3$ **(d)** CH_4

▶ **PROBLEM 7.2**   Order the following compounds according to the increasing ionic
character of their bonds: CCl_4, $BaCl_2$, $TiCl_3$, Cl_2O.

CONCEPTUAL PROBLEM 7.3   An electrostatic potential map of water is shown below.
Which atom, H or O, is positively polarized (electron-poor) and which is negatively
polarized (electron-rich)? Is this polarity pattern consistent with the electronegativity values of O and H given in Figure 7.4?

Water

7.5   ELECTRON-DOT STRUCTURES

One way to picture the sharing of electrons between atoms in covalent or polar covalent bonds is to use **electron-dot structures**, or *Lewis structures,* named after G. N.
Lewis of the University of California at Berkeley. An electron-dot structure represents an atom's valence electrons by dots and indicates by the placement of the dots
how the valence electrons are distributed in a molecule. A hydrogen molecule, for
instance, is written showing a pair of dots between the hydrogen atoms, indicating
that the hydrogens share the pair of electrons in a covalent bond:

By sharing two electrons in a covalent bond, each hydrogen effectively has one
electron pair and the stable, $1s^2$ electron configuration of helium.

Atoms other than hydrogen also form covalent bonds by sharing electron pairs, and the electron-dot structures of the resultant molecules are drawn by assigning the correct number of valence electrons to each atom. Group 3A atoms, such as boron, have three valence electrons; group 4A atoms, such as carbon, have four valence electrons; and so on across the periodic table. The group 7A element fluorine has seven valence electrons, and an electron-dot structure for the F_2 molecule shows how a covalent bond can form:

$$:\ddot{F}\cdot \qquad \cdot\ddot{F}: \qquad \longrightarrow \qquad :\ddot{F}:\ddot{F}:$$

A bonding pair
A lone pair

Two F atoms
(seven valence electrons
per atom)

An F_2 molecule
(each F is surrounded
by eight valence electrons)

Six of the seven valence electrons in a fluorine atom are already paired in three filled atomic orbitals and thus are not shared in bonding. The seventh fluorine valence electron, however, is unpaired and can be shared in a covalent bond with another fluorine. Each atom in the resultant F_2 molecule thereby gains a noble-gas configuration with eight valence-shell electrons and thus obeys the octet rule, discussed in Section 6.6. The three pairs of nonbonding electrons on each fluorine atom are called **lone pairs**, or *nonbonding pairs*, and the shared electrons are called a **bonding pair**.

The tendency of main-group atoms to fill their s and p subshells and thereby achieve a noble-gas configuration when they form bonds is an important guiding principle that makes it possible to predict the formulas and electron-dot structures of a great many molecules. As a general rule, a main-group atom shares as many of its valence-shell electrons as possible, either until it has no more to share or until it reaches an octet configuration. The following guidelines apply:

- **Group 3A elements**, such as boron, have three valence electrons and can therefore form three electron-pair bonds in neutral molecules such as borane, BH_3. The boron atom in the resultant molecule has only three bonding pairs of electrons, however, and can't reach an electron octet. (The bonding situation in BH_3 is actually more complicated than suggested here; we'll deal with it in Section 19.4.)

$$\cdot\dot{B}\cdot + 3\,H\cdot \longrightarrow H:\ddot{B}:H$$

Only six electrons around boron
Borane

- **Group 4A elements**, such as carbon, have four valence electrons and form four bonds, as in methane, CH_4. The carbon atom in the resultant molecule has four bonding pairs of electrons.

$$\cdot\dot{C}\cdot + 4\,H\cdot \longrightarrow H:\ddot{C}:H$$

Methane

- **Group 5A elements**, such as nitrogen, have five valence electrons and form three bonds, as in ammonia, NH_3. The nitrogen atom in the resultant molecule has three bonding pairs of electrons and one lone pair.

$$\cdot\dot{N}\cdot + 3\,H\cdot \longrightarrow H:\ddot{N}:H$$

Ammonia

Remember...
According to the **octet rule**, main-group elements tend to undergo reactions that give them a noble-gas electron configuration with filled s and p sublevels in their valence electron shell.   (Section 6.6).

- **Group 6A elements**, such as oxygen, have six valence electrons and form two bonds, as in water, H_2O. The oxygen atom in the resultant molecule has two bonding pairs of electrons and two lone pairs.

$$\cdot \ddot{O} \cdot \; + \; 2\,H\cdot \; \longrightarrow \; H\!:\!\ddot{O}\!:\!H$$

Water

- **Group 7A elements** (halogens), such as fluorine, have seven valence electrons and form one bond, as in hydrogen fluoride, HF. The fluorine atom in the resultant molecule has one bonding pair of electrons and three lone pairs.

$$:\ddot{F}\cdot \; + \; H\cdot \; \longrightarrow \; H\!:\!\ddot{F}\!:$$

Hydrogen
fluoride

- **Group 8A elements** (noble gases), such as neon, rarely form covalent bonds because they already have valence-shell octets.

$$:\ddot{Ne}: \quad | \text{ Does not form covalent bonds}$$

These conclusions are summarized in Table 7.3.

TABLE 7.3   Covalent Bonding for Second-Row Elements

Group	Number of Valence Electrons	Number of Bonds	Example
3A	3	3	BH_3
4A	4	4	CH_4
5A	5	3	NH_3
6A	6	2	H_2O
7A	7	1	HF
8A	8	0	Ne

Not all covalent bonds contain just one shared electron pair, or **single bond**, like those just discussed. In molecules such as O_2, N_2, and many others, the atoms share more than one pair of electrons, leading to the formation of *multiple* covalent bonds. The oxygen atoms in the O_2 molecule, for example, reach valence-shell octets by sharing two pairs, or four electrons, in a **double bond**. Similarly, the nitrogen atoms in the N_2 molecule share three pairs, or six electrons, in a **triple bond**. (Although the O_2 molecule does have a double bond, the following electron-dot structure is incorrect in some respects, as we'll see in Section 7.14.)

In speaking of molecules with multiple bonds, we often use the term **bond order** to refer to the number of electron pairs shared between atoms. Thus, the F—F, bond in the F_2 molecule has a bond order of 1, the O=O, bond in the O_2 molecule has a bond order of 2, and the N≡N, bond in the N_2 molecule has a bond order of 3.

Multiple bonds are both shorter and stronger than their corresponding single-bond counterparts because there are more shared electrons holding the atoms together. Compare, for example, the O=O double bond in O_2 with the O—O single bond in H_2O_2 (hydrogen peroxide), and compare the N≡N triple bond in N_2 with the N—N single bond in N_2H_4 (hydrazine):

Bond length:	121 pm	148 pm	110 pm	145 pm
Bond strength:	498 kJ/mol	213 kJ/mol	945 kJ/mol	275 kJ/mol

One final point about covalent bonds involves the origin of the bonding electrons. Although most covalent bonds form when two atoms each contribute one electron, bonds can also form when one atom donates both electrons (a lone pair) to another atom that has a vacant valence orbital. The ammonium ion (NH_4^+), for instance, forms when the two lone-pair electrons from the nitrogen atom of ammonia, $:NH_3$, bond to H^+. Such bonds are sometimes called **coordinate covalent bonds**.

An ordinary covalent bond—each atom donates one electron.

$$H\cdot + \cdot H \longrightarrow H:H$$

A coordinate covalent bond—the nitrogen atom donates both electrons.

$$H^+ + \begin{matrix} H \\ :N:H \\ H \end{matrix} \longrightarrow \begin{bmatrix} H \\ H:N:H \\ H \end{bmatrix}^+$$

Note that the nitrogen atom in the ammonium ion (NH_4^+) has more than the usual number of bonds—four instead of three—but that it still has an octet of valence electrons. Nitrogen, oxygen, phosphorus, and sulfur form coordinate covalent bonds frequently.

WORKED EXAMPLE 7.1

DRAWING AN ELECTRON-DOT STRUCTURE

Draw an electron-dot structure for phosphine, PH_3.

STRATEGY

The number of covalent bonds formed by a main-group element depends on the element's group number. Phosphorus, a group 5A element, has five valence electrons and can achieve a valence-shell octet by forming three bonds and leaving one lone pair. Each hydrogen supplies one electron.

SOLUTION

$$\begin{matrix} H \\ H:P:H \end{matrix} \quad \text{Phosphine}$$

▶ **PROBLEM 7.4**   Draw electron-dot structures for the following molecules:
(a) H_2S, a poisonous gas produced by rotten eggs
(b) $CHCl_3$, chloroform

▶ **PROBLEM 7.5**   Draw an electron-dot structure for the hydronium ion, H_3O^+, and show how a coordinate covalent bond is formed by the reaction of H_2O with H^+.

7.6 ELECTRON-DOT STRUCTURES OF POLYATOMIC MOLECULES

Compounds Containing Only Hydrogen and Second-Row Elements

Many of the naturally occurring compounds on which life is based—proteins, fats, carbohydrates, and numerous others—contain only hydrogen and one or more of the second-row elements carbon, nitrogen, and oxygen. Electron-dot structures are relatively easy to draw for such compounds because the octet rule is almost always followed and the number of bonds formed by each element is predictable (Table 7.3).

For relatively small molecules that contain only a few second-row atoms in addition to hydrogen, the second-row atoms are bonded to one another in a central core, with hydrogens on the periphery. In ethane (C_2H_6), for instance, two carbon atoms, each of which forms four bonds, combine with six hydrogens, each of which forms one bond. Joining the two carbon atoms and adding the appropriate number of hydrogens to each yields only one possible structure:

Ethane, C_2H_6

For larger molecules that contain numerous second-row atoms, there is usually more than one possible electron-dot structure. In such cases, some additional knowledge about the order of connections among atoms is necessary before a structure can be drawn. In drawing structures, we'll follow the usual convention of indicating a two-electron covalent bond by a line. Similarly, we'll use two lines between atoms to represent four shared electrons (two pairs) in a double bond, and three lines to represent six shared electrons (three pairs) in a triple bond. Worked Examples 7.2–7.5 and Problems 7.6–7.8 will give you more practice with electron-dot structures.

WORKED EXAMPLE 7.2

DRAWING AN ELECTRON-DOT STRUCTURE

Draw an electron-dot structure for hydrazine, N_2H_4.

STRATEGY

Nitrogen, a group 5A element, has five valence electrons and forms three bonds. Join the two nitrogen atoms, and add two hydrogen atoms to each.

SOLUTION

Hydrazine, N_2H_4

WORKED EXAMPLE 7.3

DRAWING AN ELECTRON-DOT STRUCTURE

Draw an electron-dot structure for carbon dioxide, CO_2.

STRATEGY

Connect the atoms so that carbon forms four bonds and each oxygen forms two bonds. The only possible structure contains two carbon–oxygen double bonds.

SOLUTION

Carbon dioxide, CO_2

WORKED EXAMPLE 7.4

DRAWING AN ELECTRON-DOT STRUCTURE

Draw an electron-dot structure for the deadly gas hydrogen cyanide, HCN.

STRATEGY

First, connect the carbon and nitrogen atoms. The only way the carbon can form four bonds and the nitrogen can form three bonds is if there is a carbon–nitrogen triple bond.

SOLUTION

Hydrogen cyanide, HCN

WORKED CONCEPTUAL EXAMPLE 7.5

IDENTIFYING MULTIPLE BONDS IN MOLECULES

The following structure is a representation of histidine, an amino acid constituent of proteins. Only the connections between atoms are shown; multiple bonds are not indicated. Give the chemical formula of histidine, and complete the structure by showing where the multiple bonds and lone pairs are located (red = O, gray = C, blue = N, ivory = H).

Histidine

STRATEGY

Count the atoms of each element to find the formula. Then look at each atom in the structure to find what is needed for completion. Each carbon (gray) should have four bonds, each oxygen (red) should have two bonds and two lone pairs, and each nitrogen (blue) should have three bonds and one lone pair.

continued on next page

SOLUTION

Histidine has the formula $C_6H_9N_3O_2$.

▶ **PROBLEM 7.6**   Draw electron-dot structures for the following molecules:

(a) Propane, C_3H_8

(b) Hydrogen peroxide, H_2O_2

(c) Methylamine, CH_5N

(d) Ethylene, C_2H_4

(e) Acetylene, C_2H_2

(f) Phosgene, Cl_2CO

▶ **PROBLEM 7.7**   There are two molecules with the formula C_2H_6O. Draw electron-dot structures for both.

CONCEPTUAL PROBLEM 7.8   The following structure is a representation of cytosine, a constituent of the DNA found in all living cells. Only the connections between atoms are shown; multiple bonds are not indicated. Give the formula of cytosine, and complete the structure by showing where the multiple bonds and lone pairs are located (red = O, gray = C, blue = N, ivory = H).

Compounds Containing Elements below the Second Row

The simple method for drawing electron-dot structures that works so well for compounds of second-row elements occasionally breaks down for compounds that contain elements below the second row of the periodic table where, as noted in Section 6.6, the octet rule sometimes fails. In sulfur tetrafluoride, for instance, the sulfur atom forms four bonds rather than two and has ten electrons in its valence shell rather than eight:

Sulfur tetrafluoride, SF_4

When the octet rule fails, it often does so for elements toward the right side of the periodic table (groups 3A–8A) that are in the third row and lower (**Figure 7.5**). Atoms of these elements are larger than their second-row counterparts, can accommodate more than four atoms close around them, and therefore form more than four bonds. The second-row element nitrogen, for instance, bonds to only three chlorine atoms in forming NCl_3 and thus obeys the octet rule, while the third-row element phosphorus bonds to five chlorine atoms in forming PCl_5 and thus does not follow the octet rule.

Figure 7.5
The octet rule occasionally fails for the main-group elements shown in blue.

1 1A																		18 8A
H	2 2A											13 3A	14 4A	15 5A	16 6A	17 7A		He
Li	Be											B	C	N	O	F		Ne
Na	Mg	3 3B	4 4B	5 5B	6 6B	7 7B	— 8B —	9	10	11 1B	12 2B	Al	Si	P	S	Cl		Ar
K	Ca	Sc	Ti	V	Cr	Mn	Fe	Co	Ni	Cu	Zn	Ga	Ge	As	Se	Br		Kr
Rb	Sr	Y	Zr	Nb	Mo	Tc	Ru	Rh	Pd	Ag	Cd	In	Sn	Sb	Te	I		Xe
Cs	Ba	Lu	Hf	Ta	W	Re	Os	Ir	Pt	Au	Hg	Tl	Pb	Bi	Po	At		Rn
Fr	Ra	Lr	Rf	Db	Sg	Bh	Hs	Mt	Ds	Rg	Cn							

Atoms of these elements, all of which are in the third row or lower, are larger than their second-row counterparts and can therefore accommodate more bonded atoms.

A general method of drawing electron-dot structures that works for any compound is to use the following steps:

▷ Drawing Electron-Dot Structures

Step 1. Find the total number of valence electrons for all atoms in the molecule. Add one additional electron for each negative charge in an anion, and subtract one electron for each positive charge in a cation. In SF_4, for example, the total is 34—6 from sulfur and 7 from each of 4 fluorines. In OH^-, the total is 8—6 from oxygen, 1 from hydrogen, and 1 for the negative charge. In NH_4^+, the total is 8—5 from nitrogen, 1 from each of 4 hydrogens, minus 1 for the positive charge.

$$SF_4 \qquad\qquad OH^- \qquad\qquad NH_4^+$$

$$6e + (4 \times 7e) \qquad 6e + 1e + 1e \qquad 5e + (4 \times 1e) - 1e$$
$$= 34e \qquad\qquad = 8e \qquad\qquad = 8e$$

Step 2. Decide what the connections are between atoms, and draw lines to represent the bonds. Often, you'll be told the connections; other times you'll have to guess. Remember that

• Hydrogen and the halogens usually form only one bond.

• Elements in the second row usually form the number of bonds given in Table 7.3.

• Elements in the third row and lower are often a central atom around which other atoms are grouped and form more bonds than predicted by the octet rule.

Also, it's usually the case that the central atom is the least electronegative one (except H). If, for example, you were asked to predict the connections in SF_4, a good guess would be that each fluorine forms one bond to sulfur, which occurs as the central atom and forms more bonds than are predicted by its group number.

Sulfur tetrafluoride, SF_4

Step 3. Subtract the number of valence electrons used for bonding from the total number calculated in step 1 to find the number that remain. Assign as many of these remaining electrons as necessary to the terminal atoms (other than hydrogen) so that each has an octet. In SF_4, 8 of the 34 total valence electrons are used in covalent bonding, leaving $34 - 8 = 26$. Twenty-four of the 26 are assigned to the four terminal fluorine atoms to reach an octet configuration for each:

$8 + 24 = 32$ electrons distributed

Step 4. If unassigned electrons remain after step 3, place them on the central atom. In SF_4, 32 of the 34 electrons have been assigned, leaving the final 2 to be placed on the central S atom:

34 electrons distributed

Step 5. If no unassigned electrons remain after step 3 but the central atom does not yet have an octet, use one or more lone pairs of electrons from a neighboring atom to form a multiple bond (either double or triple). Oxygen, carbon, nitrogen, and sulfur often form multiple bonds. Worked Example 7.7 shows how to deal with such a case.

WORKED EXAMPLE 7.6

DRAWING AN ELECTRON-DOT STRUCTURE

Draw an electron-dot structure for phosphorus pentachloride, PCl_5.

STRATEGY

Follow the steps outlined in the text. First, count the total number of valence electrons. Phosphorus has 5, and each chlorine has 7, for a total of 40. Next, decide on the connections between atoms, and draw lines to indicate the bonds. Because chlorine normally forms only one bond, it's likely in the case of PCl_5 that all five chlorines are bonded to a central phosphorus atom:

$$
\begin{array}{ccc}
 & Cl & \\
Cl & | & Cl \\
 & \diagdown P \diagup & \\
Cl & & Cl
\end{array}
$$

Ten of the 40 valence electrons are necessary for the five P—Cl bonds, leaving 30 to be distributed so that each chlorine has an octet. All 30 remaining valence electrons are used in this step.

SOLUTION

Phosphorus pentachloride, PCl_5

WORKED EXAMPLE 7.7

DRAWING AN ELECTRON-DOT STRUCTURE

Draw an electron-dot structure for formaldehyde, CH_2O, a compound used in manufacturing the adhesives for making plywood and particle board.

STRATEGY

First, count the total number of valence electrons. Carbon has 4, each hydrogen has 1, and the oxygen has 6, for a total of 12. Next, decide on the probable connections between atoms, and draw a line to indicate each bond. In the case of formaldehyde, the less electronegative atom (carbon) is the central atom, and both hydrogens and the oxygen are bonded to carbon:

Six of the 12 valence electrons are used for bonds, leaving 6 for assignment to the terminal oxygen atom.

At this point, all the valence electrons are assigned, but the central carbon atom still does not have an octet. We therefore move two of the oxygen electrons from a lone pair into a bonding pair, generating a carbon–oxygen double bond and satisfying the octet rule for both oxygen and carbon.

SOLUTION

Formaldehyde, CH_2O

WORKED EXAMPLE 7.8

DRAWING AN ELECTRON-DOT STRUCTURE

Draw an electron-dot structure for XeF_5^+, one of the very few noble-gas ions.

STRATEGY

Count the total number of valence electrons. Xenon has 8, each fluorine has 7, and 1 is subtracted to account for the positive charge, giving a total of 42. Then, decide on the probable connections between atoms, and draw a line for each bond. In the case of XeF_5^+, it's likely that the five fluorines are bonded to xenon, a fifth-row atom.

With 10 of the 42 valence electrons used in bonds, distribute as many of the remaining 32 electrons as necessary so that each of the terminal fluorine atoms has an octet. Two electrons still remain, so we assign them to xenon to give the final structure, which has a positive charge.

SOLUTION

▶ **PROBLEM 7.9**   Carbon monoxide, CO, is a deadly gas produced by incomplete combustion of fuels. Draw an electron-dot structure for CO.

▶ **PROBLEM 7.10**   Draw an electron-dot structure for each of the following molecules:
(a) $AlCl_3$ (b) ICl_3 (c) $XeOF_4$ (d) HOBr

▶ **PROBLEM 7.11**   Draw an electron-dot structure for each of the following ions:
(a) OH^- (b) H_3S^+ (c) HCO_3^- (d) ClO_4^-

7.7 ELECTRON-DOT STRUCTURES AND RESONANCE

The stepwise procedure given in the previous section for drawing electron-dot structures sometimes leads to an interesting problem. Look at ozone, O_3, for instance. Step 1 says that there are 18 valence electrons in the molecule, and steps 2–4 let us draw the following structure:

$$:\ddot{O}-\ddot{O}-\ddot{O}:$$

We find at this point that the central atom does not yet have an octet, and we therefore have to move one of the lone pairs of electrons on a terminal oxygen to become a bonding pair and give the central oxygen an octet. But do we take a lone pair from the "right-hand" oxygen or the "left-hand" one? Both possibilities lead to acceptable structures:

Which of the two structures for O_3 is correct? In fact, neither is correct by itself. Whenever it's possible to write more than one valid electron-dot structure for a molecule, the actual electronic structure is an *average* of the different possibilities, called a **resonance hybrid**. Note that the two resonance forms differ only in the placement of the valence-shell electrons (both bonding and nonbonding). The total number of valence electrons remains the same in both structures, the connections between atoms remain the same, and the relative positions of the atoms remain the same.

Ozone doesn't have one O=O double bond and one O—O single bond as the individual structures imply. Rather, ozone has two equivalent O—O bonds that we can think of as having a bond order of 1.5, midway between pure single bonds and pure double bonds. Both bonds have an identical length of 128 pm.

We can't draw a single electron-dot structure that indicates the equivalence of the two O—O bonds in O_3 because the conventions we use in drawings to indicate electron placement aren't good enough. Instead, the idea of resonance is indicated by drawing the two (or more) individual electron-dot structures and using a double-headed *resonance arrow* (↔) to show that both contribute to the resonance hybrid. A straight, double-headed arrow always indicates resonance; it is never used for any other purpose.

This double-headed arrow means that the structures on either side are contributors to a resonance hybrid.

$$:\ddot{O}-\ddot{O}=\ddot{O} \longleftrightarrow \ddot{O}=\ddot{O}-\ddot{O}:$$

The fact that single electron-dot structures can't be written for all molecules indicates that such structures are oversimplified and don't always give an accurate representation of the electron distribution in a molecule. There's a more accurate way of describing electron distributions called *molecular orbital theory*, which we'll look into shortly. This theory is more complex, however, so chemists still make routine use of simple resonance electron-dot structures.

WORKED EXAMPLE 7.9

DRAWING RESONANCE STRUCTURES

The nitrate ion, NO_3^-, has three equivalent oxygen atoms, and its electronic structure is a resonance hybrid of three electron-dot structures. Draw them.

STRATEGY

Begin as you would for drawing any electron-dot structure. There are 24 valence electrons in the nitrate ion: 5 from nitrogen, 6 from each of 3 oxygens, and 1 for the negative charge. The three equivalent oxygens are all bonded to nitrogen, the less electronegative central atom:

6 of 24 valence electrons assigned

Distributing the remaining 18 valence electrons among the three terminal oxygen atoms completes the octet of each oxygen but leaves nitrogen with only 6 electrons.

To give nitrogen an octet, one of the oxygen atoms must use a lone pair to form an N—O double bond. But which one? There are three possibilities, and thus three electron-dot structures for the nitrate ion, which differ only in the placement of bonding and lone-pair electrons. The connections between atoms are the same in all three structures, and the atoms have the same positions in all structures.

SOLUTION

▶ **PROBLEM 7.12** Called "laughing gas," nitrous oxide (N_2O) is sometimes used by dentists as an anesthetic. Given the connections N—N—O draw two resonance structures for N_2O.

▶ **PROBLEM 7.13** Draw as many resonance structures as possible for each of the following molecules or ions, giving all atoms (except H) octets:
  (a) SO_2 **(b)** CO_3^{2-} **(c)** HCO_2^- **(d)** BF_3

CONCEPTUAL PROBLEM 7.14 The following structure shows the connections between atoms for anisole, a compound used in perfumery. Draw two resonance structures for anisole, showing the positions of the multiple bonds in each (red = O, gray = C, ivory = H).

7.8 FORMAL CHARGES

Closely related to the ideas of electronegativity and polar covalent bonds discussed in Section 7.4 is the concept of **formal charges** on specific atoms in electron-dot structures. Formal charges result from a kind of electron "bookkeeping" and can be calculated in the following way: Find the number of valence electrons around an atom in a given electron-dot structure, and compare that value with the number of valence electrons in the isolated atom. If the numbers aren't the same, then the atom in the molecule has either gained or lost electrons and thus has a formal charge. If the atom in a molecule has more electrons than the isolated atom, it has a negative formal charge; if it has fewer electrons, it has a positive formal charge.

$$\text{Formal charge} = \begin{pmatrix} \text{Number of} \\ \text{valence electrons} \\ \text{in free atom} \end{pmatrix} - \begin{pmatrix} \text{Number of} \\ \text{valence electrons} \\ \text{in bonded atom} \end{pmatrix}$$

In counting the number of valence electrons in a bonded atom, it's necessary to make a distinction between unshared, nonbonding electrons and shared, bonding electrons. For bookkeeping purposes, an atom can be thought of as "owning" all its nonbonding electrons but only half of its bonding electrons, because the bonding electrons are shared with another atom. Thus, we can rewrite the definition of formal charge as

$$\text{Formal charge} = \begin{pmatrix} \text{Number of} \\ \text{valence electrons} \\ \text{in free atom} \end{pmatrix} - \frac{1}{2} \begin{pmatrix} \text{Number of} \\ \text{bonding} \\ \text{electrons} \end{pmatrix} - \begin{pmatrix} \text{Number of} \\ \text{nonbonding} \\ \text{electrons} \end{pmatrix}$$

In the ammonium ion (NH_4^+), for instance, each of the four equivalent hydrogen atoms has 2 valence electrons in its covalent bond to nitrogen and the nitrogen atom has 8 valence electrons, 2 from each of its four N—H bonds:

$$\left[\begin{array}{c} H \\ H : \ddot{N} : H \\ H \end{array} \right]^+ \quad \begin{array}{l} \text{Ammonium ion} \\ \text{8 valence electrons around nitrogen} \\ \text{2 valence electrons around each hydrogen} \end{array}$$

For bookkeeping purposes, each hydrogen owns half of its 2 shared bonding electrons, or 1, while the nitrogen atom owns half of its 8 shared bonding electrons, or 4. Because an isolated hydrogen atom has 1 electron and the hydrogens in the ammonium ion each still own 1 electron, they have neither gained nor lost electrons and thus have no formal charge. An isolated nitrogen atom, however, has 5 valence electrons, while the nitrogen atom in NH_4^+ owns only 4 and thus has a formal charge of +1. The sum of the formal charges on all the atoms (+1 in this example) must equal the overall charge on the ion.

$$\left[\begin{array}{c} H \\ H : \ddot{N} : H \\ H \end{array} \right]^+$$

For hydrogen:	Isolated hydrogen valence electrons	1
	Bound hydrogen bonding electrons	2
	Bound hydrogen nonbonding electrons	0

$$\text{Formal charge} = 1 - \frac{1}{2}(2) - 0 = 0$$

For nitrogen:	Isolated nitrogen valence electrons	5
	Bound nitrogen bonding electrons	8
	Bound nitrogen nonbonding electrons	0

$$\text{Formal charge} = 5 - \frac{1}{2}(8) - 0 = +1$$

The value of formal charge calculations comes from their application to the resonance structures described in the previous section. It often happens that the resonance structures of a given substance are not equivalent. One of the structures may be "better" than the others, meaning that it approximates the actual electronic structure of the substance more closely. The resonance hybrid in such cases is thus weighted more strongly toward the more favorable structure.

Take the organic substance called acetamide, for instance, a compound related to proteins. We can write two valid resonance structures for acetamide, both of which fulfill the octet rule for the C, N, and O atoms. One of the two structures has no formal charges, while the other has formal charges on the O and N atoms. (Check for yourself that the formal charges are correct.)

This structure is lower in energy.

This structure is higher in energy.

Acetamide

Which of the two structures gives a more accurate representation of the molecule? Because energy is required to separate + and − charges, the structure without formal charges is probably lower in energy than the structure with formal charges. Thus, the actual electronic structure of acetamide is closer to that of the more favorable, lower-energy structure.

As another example, the resonance structure for N_2O that places the formal negative charge on the more electronegative oxygen atom rather than on the less electronegative nitrogen atom is probably a more accurate representation of the molecule.

$$:N\equiv\overset{+}{N}-\overset{..}{\underset{..}{O}}:^{-} \longleftrightarrow {}^{-}\overset{..}{\underset{..}{N}}=\overset{+}{N}=\overset{..}{\underset{..}{O}}$$

This electron-dot structure . . . is more favorable than . . . this one.

WORKED EXAMPLE 7.10

CALCULATING FORMAL CHARGES

Calculate the formal charge on each atom in the following electron-dot structure for SO_2:

$$:\overset{..}{\underset{..}{O}}-\overset{..}{S}=\overset{..}{\underset{..}{O}}$$

STRATEGY

Find the number of valence electrons on each atom (its periodic group number). Then subtract half the number of the atom's bonding electrons and all of its nonbonding electrons.

SOLUTION

For sulfur:	Isolated sulfur valence electrons	6
	Bound sulfur bonding electrons	6
	Bound sulfur nonbonding electrons	2

Formal charge = $6 - \frac{1}{2}(6) - 2 = +1$

For singly bonded oxygen:	Isolated oxygen valence electrons	6
	Bound oxygen bonding electrons	2
	Bound oxygen nonbonding electrons	6

Formal charge = $6 - \frac{1}{2}(2) - 6 = -1$

For doubly bonded oxygen:	Isolated oxygen valence electrons	6
	Bound oxygen bonding electrons	4
	Bound oxygen nonbonding electrons	4

Formal charge = $6 - \frac{1}{2}(4) - 4 = 0$

The sulfur atom of SO_2 has a formal charge of +1, and the singly bonded oxygen atom has a formal charge of −1. We might therefore write the structure for SO_2 as

$$^{-}:\overset{..}{\underset{..}{O}}-\overset{+}{\overset{..}{S}}=\overset{..}{\underset{..}{O}}$$

▶ **PROBLEM 7.15**   Calculate the formal charge on each atom in the three resonance structures for the nitrate ion in Worked Example 7.9.

▶ **PROBLEM 7.16**   Calculate the formal charge on each atom in the following electron-dot structures:

(a) Cyanate ion: $\left[\ddot{N}{=}C{=}\ddot{O} \right]^{-}$ **(b)** Ozone: $\ddot{O}{-}\ddot{O}{=}\ddot{O}$

7.9   MOLECULAR SHAPES: THE VSEPR MODEL

Look at the following ball-and-stick models of water, ammonia, and methane. Each of these molecules—and every other molecule as well—has a specific three-dimensional shape. Often, particularly for biologically important molecules, three-dimensional shape plays a crucial part in determining the molecule's chemistry.

Water, H_2O Ammonia, NH_3 Methane, CH_4

Like so many other properties, the shape of a molecule is determined by the electronic structure of its atoms. That shape can often be predicted using what is called the **valence-shell electron-pair repulsion (VSEPR) model.** Electrons in bonds and in lone pairs can be thought of as "charge clouds" that repel one another and stay as far apart as possible, thus causing molecules to assume specific shapes. There are only two steps to remember in applying the VSEPR model:

⊣▬▬ **Applying the VSEPR Model**

Step 1.   Write an electron-dot structure for the molecule, as described in Section 7.6, and count the number of electron charge clouds surrounding the atom of interest. A charge cloud is simply a group of electrons, either in a bond or in a lone pair. Thus, the number of charge clouds is the total number of bonds and lone pairs. Multiple bonds count the same as single bonds because it doesn't matter how many electrons occupy each cloud.

Step 2.   Predict the geometric arrangement of charge clouds around each atom by assuming that the clouds are oriented in space as far away from one another as possible. How they achieve this orientation depends on their number. Let's look at the possibilities.

Two Charge Clouds

When there are only two charge clouds on an atom, as occurs on the carbon atoms of CO_2 (two double bonds) and HCN (one single bond and one triple bond), the clouds are farthest apart when they point in opposite directions. Thus, CO_2 and HCN are linear molecules with **bond angles** of 180°.

A CO_2 molecule is linear, with a bond angle of 180°.

$$\ddot{O}{=}C{=}\ddot{O}$$

An HCN molecule is linear, with a bond angle of 180°.

$$H{-}C{\equiv}N:$$

Three Charge Clouds

When there are three charge clouds on an atom, as occurs on the carbon atom of formaldehyde (two single bonds and one double bond) and the sulfur atom of SO_2 (one single bond, one double bond, and one lone pair), the clouds are farthest apart when they lie in the same plane and point to the corners of an equilateral triangle. Thus, a formaldehyde molecule has a *trigonal planar* shape, with H—C—H and H—C=O bond angles near 120°. Similarly, an SO_2 molecule has a trigonal planar arrangement of its three charge clouds on sulfur, but one corner of the triangle is occupied by a lone pair and two corners by oxygen atoms. The molecule therefore has a *bent* shape, with an O—S=O bond angle of approximately 120° rather than 180°. (For consistency, we'll use the word *shape* to refer to the overall arrangement of atoms in a molecule, not to the geometric arrangement of charge clouds around a specific atom.)

A formaldehyde molecule is trigonal planar, with bond angles of roughly 120°.

Top view

Side view

An SO_2 molecule is bent, with a bond angle of approximately 120°.

Top view

Side view

Four Charge Clouds

When there are four charge clouds on an atom, as occurs on the central atoms in CH_4 (four single bonds), NH_3 (three single bonds and one lone pair), and H_2O (two single bonds and two lone pairs), the clouds are farthest apart if they extend toward the corners of a regular tetrahedron. As illustrated in **Figure 7.6**, a regular tetrahedron is a geometric solid whose four identical faces are equilateral triangles. The central atom lies in the center of the tetrahedron, the charge clouds point toward the four corners, and the angle between two lines drawn from the center to any two corners is 109.5°.

A regular tetrahedron

A tetrahedral molecule

| The atom is located in the **center** of a regular tetrahedron. | The four charge clouds point to the **four corners** of the tetrahedron. | The angle between any two bonds is 109.5°. |

Figure 7.6
The tetrahedral geometry of an atom with four charge clouds.

Because valence electron octets are so common, particularly for second-row elements, the atoms in a great many molecules have geometries based on the tetrahedron. Methane, for example, has a tetrahedral shape, with H—C—H bond angles of 109.5°. In NH_3, the nitrogen atom has a tetrahedral arrangement of its four charge clouds, but one corner of the tetrahedron is occupied by a lone pair, resulting in a *trigonal pyramidal* shape for the molecule. Similarly, H_2O has two corners of the tetrahedron occupied by lone pairs and thus has a *bent* shape.

A methane molecule is tetrahedral, with bond angles of 109.5°.

An ammonia molecule is trigonal pyramidal, with bond angles of 107°.

A water molecule is bent, with a bond angle of 104.5°.

Note how the three-dimensional shapes of the molecules in the preceding three structures are drawn. Solid lines are assumed to be in the plane of the paper, dashed lines recede behind the plane of the paper away from the viewer, and heavy, wedged lines protrude out of the paper toward the viewer. Note also that the H—N—H bond angles in ammonia (107°) and the H—O—H bond angle in water (104.5°) are less than the ideal 109.5° tetrahedral value. The angles are diminished somewhat from the tetrahedral value because of the presence of lone pairs. Charge clouds of lone-pair electrons spread out more than charge clouds of bonding electrons because they aren't confined to the space between two nuclei. As a result, the somewhat enlarged lone-pair charge clouds tend to compress the bond angles in the rest of the molecule.

Five Charge Clouds

Five charge clouds, such as are found on the central atoms in PCl_5, SF_4, ClF_3, and I_3^-, are oriented toward the corners of a geometric figure called a *trigonal bipyramid*. Three clouds lie in a plane and point toward the corners of an equilateral triangle, the fourth cloud points directly up, and the fifth cloud points down:

A trigonal bipyramid   Side view   Top view

Trigonal bipyramidal geometry differs from the linear, trigonal planar, and tetrahedral geometries discussed previously because it has two kinds of positions—three *equatorial* positions (around the "equator" of the bipyramid) and two *axial* positions (along the "axis" of the bipyramid). The three equatorial positions are at angles of 120° to one another and at an angle of 90° to the axial positions. The two axial positions are at angles of 180° to each other and at an angle of 90° to the equatorial positions.

Different substances containing a trigonal bipyramidal arrangement of charge clouds on an atom adopt different shapes, depending on whether the five charge clouds contain bonding or nonbonding electrons. Phosphorus pentachloride, for instance, has all five positions around phosphorus occupied by chlorine atoms and thus has a trigonal bipyramidal shape:

A PCl_5 molecule is trigonal bipyramidal.

The sulfur atom in SF_4 is bonded to four other atoms and has one nonbonding electron lone pair. Because an electron lone pair spreads out and occupies more space than a bonding pair, the nonbonding electrons in SF_4 occupy an equatorial position where they are close to (90° away from) only two charge clouds. Were they instead to occupy an axial position, they would be close to three charge clouds. As a result, SF_4 has a shape often described as that of a seesaw. The two axial bonds form the board, and the two equatorial bonds form the legs of the seesaw. (You have to tilt your head 90° to see it in the following image.)

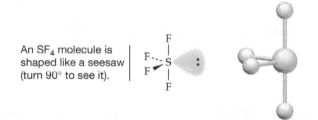

An SF_4 molecule is shaped like a seesaw (turn 90° to see it).

The chlorine atom in ClF_3 is bonded to three other atoms and has two nonbonding electron lone pairs. Both lone pairs occupy equatorial positions, resulting in a T shape for the ClF_3 molecule. (As with the seesaw, you have to tilt your head 90° to see the T in the image below.)

A ClF_3 molecule is T-shaped.

The central iodine atom in the I_3^- ion is bonded to two other atoms and has three lone pairs. All three lone pairs occupy equatorial positions, resulting in a linear shape for I_3^-.

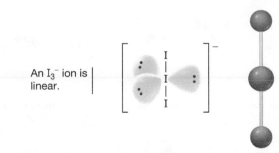

An I_3^- ion is linear.

Six Charge Clouds

Six charge clouds around an atom orient toward the six corners of a regular octahedron, a geometric solid whose eight faces are equilateral triangles. All six positions are equivalent, and the angle between any two adjacent positions is 90°.

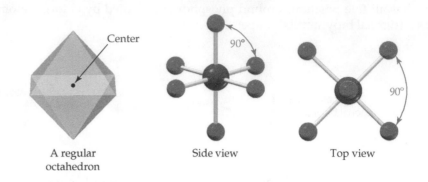

A regular   Side view   Top view
octahedron

As was true in the case of five charge clouds, different shapes are possible for molecules having atoms with six charge clouds, depending on whether the clouds are of bonding or nonbonding electrons. In sulfur hexafluoride, for instance, all six positions around sulfur are occupied by fluorine atoms:

An SF_6 molecule is octahedral.

The antimony atom in the $SbCl_5{}^{2-}$ ion also has six charge clouds but is bonded to only five atoms and has one nonbonding electron lone pair. As a result, the ion has a *square pyramidal* shape—a pyramid with a square base:

An $SbCl_5{}^{2-}$ ion has a square pyramidal shape.

The xenon atom in XeF_4 is bonded to four atoms and has two lone pairs. The lone pairs orient as far away from each other as possible to minimize electronic repulsions, giving the molecule a *square planar* shape:

An XeF_4 molecule has a square planar shape.

All the geometries for two to six charge clouds are summarized in Table 7.4.

TABLE 7.4   Geometry around Atoms with 2, 3, 4, 5, and 6 Charge Clouds

Number of Bonds	Number of Lone Pairs	Number of Charge Clouds		Geometry	Example

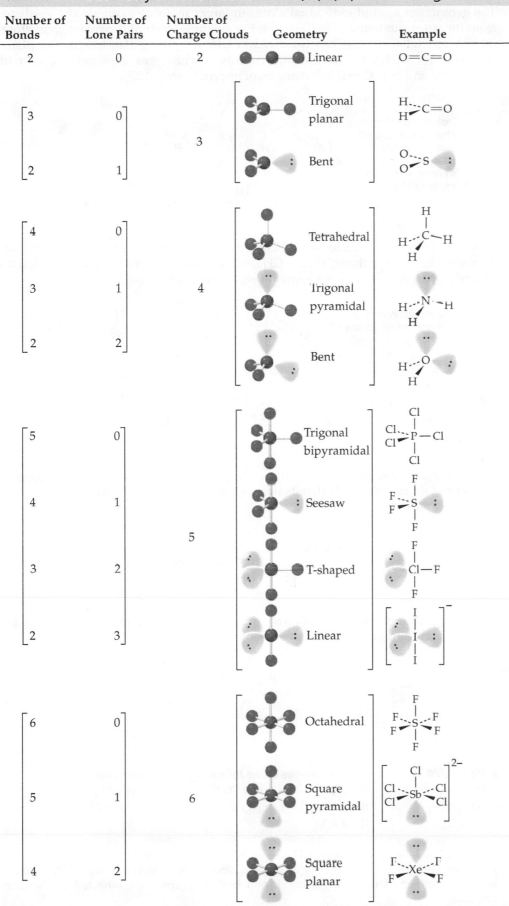

Shapes of Larger Molecules

The geometries around individual atoms in larger molecules can also be predicted from the rules summarized in Table 7.4. For example, each of the two carbon atoms in ethylene ($H_2C=CH_2$) has three charge clouds, giving rise to trigonal planar geometry for each carbon. The molecule as a whole has a planar shape, with H—C—C and H—C—H bond angles of approximately 120°.

Each carbon atom in ethylene has trigonal planar geometry. As a result, the entire molecule is planar, with bond angles of 120°.

Top view

Side view

Carbon atoms bonded to four other atoms are each at the center of a tetrahedron. As shown below for ethane, $H_3C—CH_3$, the two tetrahedrons are joined so that the central carbon atom of one is a corner atom of the other.

Each carbon atom in ethane has tetrahedral geometry, with bond angles of 109.5°.

WORKED EXAMPLE 7.11

USING THE VSEPR MODEL TO PREDICT A SHAPE

Predict the shape of BrF_5.

STRATEGY

First, draw an electron-dot structure for BrF_5 to determine that the central bromine atom has six charge clouds (five bonds and one lone pair). Then predict how the six charge clouds are arranged.

Bromine pentafluoride

SOLUTION

Six charge clouds imply an octahedral arrangement. The five attached atoms and one lone pair give BrF_5 a square pyramidal shape:

▶ **PROBLEM 7.17**   Predict the shapes of the following molecules or ions:
- **(a)** O_3
- **(b)** H_3O^+
- **(c)** XeF_2
- **(d)** PF_6^-
- **(e)** $XeOF_4$
- **(f)** AlH_4^-
- **(g)** BF_4^-
- **(h)** $SiCl_4$
- **(i)** ICl_4^-
- **(j)** $AlCl_3$

▶ **PROBLEM 7.18**   Acetic acid, CH_3CO_2H, is the main organic constituent of vinegar. Draw an electron-dot structure for acetic acid, and show its overall shape. (The two carbons are connected by a single bond, and both oxygens are connected to the same carbon.)

CONCEPTUAL PROBLEM 7.19   What is the geometry around the central atom in each of the following molecular models?

(a)   **(b)**

7.10   VALENCE BOND THEORY

The electron-dot structures described in Sections 7.5 and 7.6 provide a simple way to predict the distribution of valence electrons in a molecule, and the VSEPR model discussed in Section 7.9 provides a simple way to predict molecular shapes. Neither model, however, says anything about the electronic nature of covalent bonds. To describe bonding, a quantum mechanical model called **valence bond theory** has been developed.

Valence bond theory provides an easily visualized orbital picture of how electron pairs are shared in a covalent bond. In essence, a covalent bond results when two atoms approach each other closely enough so that a singly occupied valence orbital on one atom spatially *overlaps* a singly occupied valence orbital on the other atom. The now-paired electrons in the overlapping orbitals are attracted to the nuclei of both atoms and thus bond the two atoms together. In the H_2 molecule, for instance, the H—H bond results from the overlap of two singly occupied hydrogen $1s$ orbitals.

$1s$ $1s$ H_2 molecule

Recall that atomic orbitals arise from the Schrödinger wave equation and that the two lobes of a p atomic orbital have different phases, as represented by different colors. In the valence bond model, the two overlapping lobes must be of the same phase, and the strength of the covalent bond that forms depends on the amount of orbital overlap: the greater the overlap, the stronger the bond. This, in turn, means that bonds formed by overlap of other than s orbitals have a directionality to them. In the F_2 molecule, for instance, each fluorine atom has the electron configuration [He] $2s^2\, 2p_x^2\, 2p_y^2\, 2p_z^1$ and the F—F bond results from the overlap of two singly occupied $2p$ orbitals. The two $2p$ orbitals must point directly at each other for optimum overlap to occur, and the F—F bond forms along the orbital axis. Such bonds that result from head-on orbital overlap are called **sigma (σ) bonds.**

Remember...
The **Schrödinger wave equation** focuses on the wavelike properties of atoms to describe the quantum mechanical model of atomic structure. The solutions to the wave equation are called wave functions, or orbitals.   (Section 5.6)

The two lobes of a p orbital have different mathematical signs in the wave function, corresponding to the different **phases** of a wave.   (Section 5.7)

Bonds form between two   A sigma (σ) bond forms from
lobes of the same phase.   head-on orbital overlap.

$2p$ $2p$ F_2 molecule

In HCl, the covalent bond involves overlap of a hydrogen $1s$ orbital with a chlorine $3p$ orbital and forms along the p-orbital axis:

$1s$ $3p$ HCl molecule

The key ideas of valence bond theory can be summarized as follows:

Principles of Valence Bond Theory

- Covalent bonds are formed by overlap of atomic orbitals, each of which contains one electron of opposite spin. The two overlapping lobes must be of the same phase.
- Each of the bonded atoms maintains its own atomic orbitals, but the electron pair in the overlapping orbitals is shared by both atoms.
- The greater the amount of orbital overlap, the stronger the bond. This leads to a directional character for the bond when other than *s* orbitals are involved.

7.11 HYBRIDIZATION AND sp^3 HYBRID ORBITALS

How does valence bond theory describe the electronic structure of complex polyatomic molecules, and how does it account for the observed geometries around atoms in molecules? Let's look first at a simple tetrahedral molecule such as methane, CH_4. There are several problems to be dealt with.

Carbon has the ground-state electron configuration $[He]\ 2s^2\ 2p_x^1\ 2p_y^1$. It thus has four valence electrons, two of which are paired in a $2s$ orbital and two of which are unpaired in different $2p$ orbitals that we'll arbitrarily designate as $2p_x$ and $2p_y$. But how can carbon form four bonds if two of its valence electrons are already paired and only two unpaired electrons remain for sharing? The answer is that an electron must be promoted from the lower-energy $2s$ orbital to the vacant, higher-energy $2p_z$ orbital, giving an *excited-state configuration* $[He]\ 2s^1\ 2p_x^1\ 2p_y^1\ 2p_z^1$ that has *four* unpaired electrons and can thus form four bonds.

Energy

Carbon:
ground-state electron
configuration

Carbon:
excited-state electron
configuration

A second problem is more difficult to resolve: If excited-state carbon uses two kinds of orbitals for bonding, $2s$ and $2p$, how can it form four *equivalent* bonds? Furthermore, if the three $2p$ orbitals in carbon are at angles of 90° to one another, and if the $2s$ orbital has no directionality, how can carbon form bonds with angles of 109.5° directed to the corners of a regular tetrahedron? The answers to these questions were provided in 1931 by Linus Pauling, who introduced the idea of *hybrid orbitals*.

Pauling showed how the quantum mechanical wave functions for *s* and *p* atomic orbitals derived from the Schrödinger wave equation can be mathematically combined to form a new set of equivalent wave functions called **hybrid atomic orbitals.** When one *s* orbital combines with three *p* orbitals, as occurs in an excited-state carbon atom, four equivalent hybrid orbitals, called sp^3 **hybrids**, result. (The superscript 3 in the name sp^3 tells how many *p* atomic orbitals are combined to construct the hybrid orbitals, not how many electrons occupy the orbital.)

Energy

Carbon:
excited-state electron
configuration

Carbon:
sp^3-hybridized
configuration

Each of the four equivalent sp^3 hybrid orbitals has two lobes of different phase like an atomic p orbital (Section 5.7) but one of the lobes is larger than the other, giving the orbital a directionality. The four large lobes are oriented toward the four corners of a tetrahedron at angles of 109.5°, as shown in **Figure 7.7**. For consistency in the use of colors, we'll routinely show the different phases of orbitals in red and blue and will show the large lobes of the resultant hybrid orbitals in green.

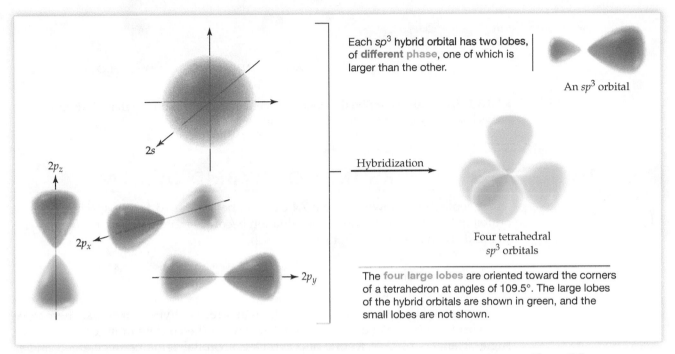

Each sp^3 hybrid orbital has two lobes, of **different phase**, one of which is larger than the other.

An sp^3 orbital

Hybridization

Four tetrahedral sp^3 orbitals

The **four large lobes** are oriented toward the corners of a tetrahedron at angles of 109.5°. The large lobes of the hybrid orbitals are shown in green, and the small lobes are not shown.

Figure 7.7
The formation of four sp^3 hybrid orbitals by combination of an atomic s orbital with three atomic p orbitals.

The shared electrons in a covalent bond made with a spatially directed hybrid orbital spend most of their time in the region between the two bonded nuclei. As a result, covalent bonds made with sp^3 hybrid orbitals are often strong ones. In fact, the energy released on forming the four strong C—H bonds in CH_4 more than compensates for the energy required to form the excited state of carbon. **Figure 7.8** shows how the four C—H sigma bonds in methane can form by head-on overlap of carbon sp^3 hybrid orbitals with hydrogen $1s$ orbitals.

Four carbon sp^3 hybrid orbitals

Four hydrogen 1s atomic orbitals

Methane

Each of the four C–H bonds results from head-on overlap of a singly occupied **carbon sp^3 hybrid orbital** with a singly occupied **hydrogen 1s orbital**.

Figure 7.8
The bonding in methane (CH_4).

The same kind of sp^3 hybridization that describes the bonds to carbon in the tetrahedral methane molecule can also be used to describe bonds to nitrogen in the trigonal pyramidal ammonia molecule, to oxygen in the bent water molecule, and to all other atoms that the VSEPR model predicts to have a tetrahedral arrangement of four charge clouds.

Methane, CH$_4$ Ammonia, NH$_3$ Water, H$_2$O

▸ **PROBLEM 7.20**   Describe the bonding in ethane, C$_2$H$_6$, and tell what kinds of orbitals on each atom overlap to form the C—C and C—H bonds.

7.12   OTHER KINDS OF HYBRID ORBITALS

Other geometries shown in Table 7.4 can also be accounted for by specific kinds of orbital hybridization, although the situation becomes more complex for atoms with five and six charge clouds. Let's look at each.

sp^2 Hybridization

Atoms with three charge clouds undergo hybridization by combination of one atomic s orbital with two p orbitals, resulting in three sp^2 **hybrid orbitals.** These three sp^2 hybrids lie in a plane and are oriented toward the corners of an equilateral triangle at angles of 120° to one another. One p orbital remains unchanged and is oriented at a 90° angle to the plane of the sp^2 hybrids, as shown in **Figure 7.9.**

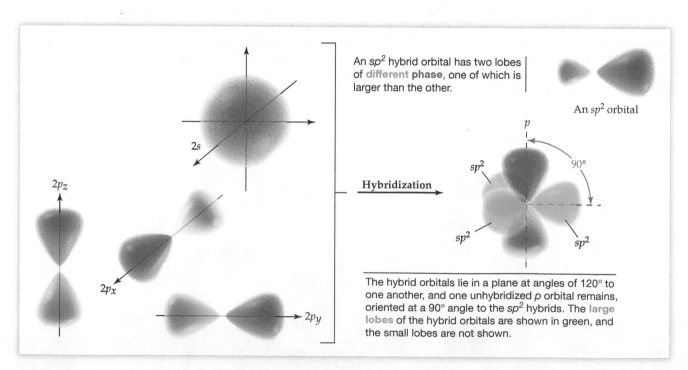

An sp^2 hybrid orbital has two lobes of different phase, one of which is larger than the other.

An sp^2 orbital

The hybrid orbitals lie in a plane at angles of 120° to one another, and one unhybridized p orbital remains, oriented at a 90° angle to the sp^2 hybrids. The large lobes of the hybrid orbitals are shown in green, and the small lobes are not shown.

Figure 7.9
The formation of sp^2 hybrid orbitals by combination of one s orbital and two p orbitals.

The presence of the unhybridized p orbital on an sp^2-hybridized atom has some interesting consequences. Look, for example, at ethylene, $H_2C=CH_2$, a colorless gas used as starting material for the industrial preparation of polyethylene. Each carbon atom in ethylene has three charge clouds and is sp^2-hybridized. When two sp^2-hybridized carbon atoms approach each other with sp^2 orbitals aligned head-on for σ bonding, the unhybridized p orbitals on the carbons also approach each other and form a bond, but in a parallel, sideways manner rather than head-on. Such a sideways bond, in which the shared electrons occupy regions above and below a line connecting the nuclei rather than directly between the nuclei, is called a **pi (π) bond** (**Figure 7.10**). In addition, four C—H bonds form in ethylene by overlap of the remaining four sp^2 orbitals with hydrogen 1s orbitals.

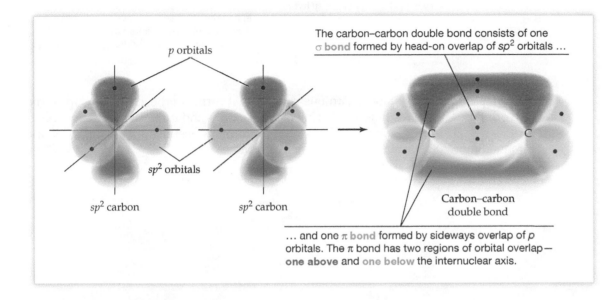

The carbon–carbon double bond consists of one σ bond formed by head-on overlap of sp^2 orbitals …

p orbitals

sp^2 orbitals

sp^2 carbon sp^2 carbon

Carbon–carbon
double bond

… and one π bond formed by sideways overlap of p orbitals. The π bond has two regions of orbital overlap— one above and one below the internuclear axis.

Figure 7.10
The structure of a carbon–carbon double bond.

The π bond has two regions of orbital overlap, one above and one below a line drawn between the nuclei, the *internuclear axis*. Both regions are part of the same bond, and the two shared electrons are spread over both regions. As always, the p lobes must be of the same phase for overlap leading to bond formation. The net result of both σ and π overlap is the sharing of four electrons and the formation of a carbon–carbon double bond.

▶ **PROBLEM 7.21** Describe the hybridization of the carbon atom in formaldehyde, $H_2C=O$, and make a rough sketch of the molecule showing the orbitals involved in bonding.

sp Hybridization

Atoms with two charge clouds undergo hybridization by combination of one atomic s orbital with one p orbital, resulting in two ***sp* hybrid orbitals** that are oriented 180° from each other. Since only one p orbital is involved when an atom undergoes sp hybridization, the other two p orbitals are unchanged and are oriented at 90° angles to the sp hybrids, as shown in **Figure 7.11**.

One of the simplest examples of sp hybridization occurs in acetylene, H—C≡C—H, a colorless gas used in welding. Both carbon atoms in the acetylene molecule have linear geometry and are sp-hybridized. When the two sp-hybridized carbon atoms approach each other with their sp orbitals aligned head-on for σ bonding, the unhybridized p orbitals on each carbon are aligned for π bonding. Two p orbitals are aligned in an up/down position, and two are aligned in an in/out position. Thus, there are two mutually perpendicular π bonds that form by sideways

Figure 7.11
sp Hybridization.

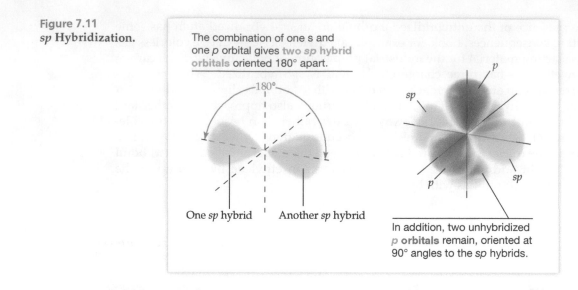

The combination of one s and one p orbital gives **two sp hybrid orbitals** oriented 180° apart.

180°

One *sp* hybrid   Another *sp* hybrid

In addition, two unhybridized *p* **orbitals** remain, oriented at 90° angles to the *sp* hybrids.

overlap of *p* orbitals, along with one σ bond that forms by head-on overlap of the *sp* orbitals. The net result is the sharing of six electrons and formation of a triple bond (**Figure 7.12**). In addition, two C—H bonds form in acetylene by overlap of the remaining two *sp* orbitals with hydrogen 1*s* orbitals.

Figure 7.12
Formation of a triple bond by two sp-hybridized atoms.

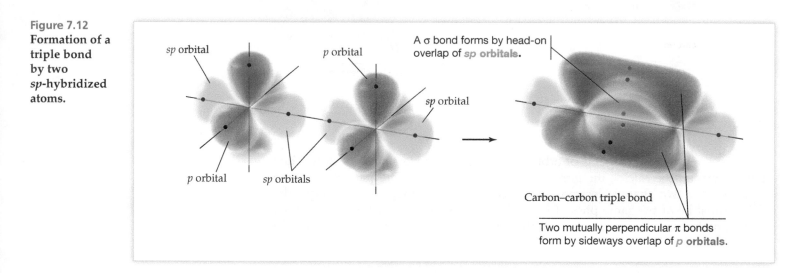

sp orbital

p orbital

A σ bond forms by head-on overlap of *sp* **orbitals.**

sp orbital

p orbital   *sp* orbitals

Carbon–carbon triple bond

Two mutually perpendicular π bonds form by sideways overlap of *p* **orbitals.**

▶ **PROBLEM 7.22** Describe the hybridization of the carbon atom in the hydrogen cyanide molecule, H—C≡N, and make a rough sketch to show the hybrid orbitals it uses for bonding.

Atoms with Five and Six Charge Clouds

Main-group atoms with five or six charge clouds, such as the phosphorus in PCl_5 and the sulfur in SF_6, were at one time thought to undergo hybridization by combination of five and six atomic orbitals, respectively. Because a given shell has a total of only four *s* and *p* orbitals, however, the need to use five or six orbitals implies that *d* orbitals are involved. As we'll see in Section 20.11, hybridization involving *d* orbitals is indeed involved for many compounds of transition metals. Recent quantum mechanical calculations indicate, however, that main-group compounds do not use *d* orbitals in hybridization but instead use a more complex bonding pattern that is not easily explained by valence bond theory.

A summary of the three common kinds of hybridization for main-group elements and the geometry that each corresponds to is given in Table 7.5.

TABLE 7.5 Hybrid Orbitals and Their Geometry

Number of Charge Clouds	Arrangement of Charge Clouds	Hybridization
2	Linear	sp
3	Trigonal planar	sp^2
4	Tetrahedral	sp^3

WORKED EXAMPLE 7.12

PREDICTING THE HYBRIDIZATION OF AN ATOM

Describe the hybridization of the carbon atoms in allene, $H_2C{=}C{=}CH_2$, and make a rough sketch of the molecule showing its hybrid orbitals.

STRATEGY

Draw an electron-dot structure to find the number of charge clouds on each atom.

Then predict the geometry around each atom using the VSEPR model (Table 7.5).

SOLUTION

Because the central carbon atom in allene has two charge clouds (two double bonds), it has a linear geometry and is sp-hybridized. Because the two terminal carbon atoms have three charge clouds each (one double bond and two C—H bonds), they have trigonal planar geometry and are sp^2-hybridized. The central carbon uses its sp orbitals to form two σ bonds at 180° angles and uses its two unhybridized p orbitals to form π bonds, one to each of the terminal carbons. Each terminal carbon atom uses an sp^2 orbital for σ bonding to carbon, a p orbital for π bonding, and its two remaining sp^2 orbitals for C—H bonds. Note that the mutually perpendicular arrangement of the two π bonds results in a similar perpendicular arrangement of the two CH_2 groups.

$H_2C{=}C{=}CH_2$

▶ **PROBLEM 7.23** Describe the hybridization of the carbon atom in carbon dioxide, and make a rough sketch of the molecule showing its hybrid orbitals and π bonds.

▶ **PROBLEM 7.24** Describe the hybridization of the carbon atom in the poisonous gas phosgene, Cl_2CO, and make a rough sketch of the molecule showing its hybrid orbitals and π bonds.

CONCEPTUAL PROBLEM 7.25 Identify each of the following sets of hybrid orbitals:

   (a)   **(b)**   **(c)**

7.13   MOLECULAR ORBITAL THEORY: THE HYDROGEN MOLECULE

The valence bond model that describes covalent bonding through orbital overlap is easy to visualize and leads to a satisfactory description for most molecules. It does, however, have some problems. Perhaps the most serious flaw in the valence bond model is that it sometimes leads to an incorrect electronic description. For this reason, another bonding description called **molecular orbital (MO) theory** is often used. The molecular orbital model is more complex and less easily visualized than the valence bond model, particularly for larger molecules, but it sometimes gives a more satisfactory accounting of chemical and physical properties.

To introduce some of the basic ideas of molecular orbital theory, let's look again at orbitals. The concept of an orbital derives from the quantum mechanical wave equation, in which the square of the wave function gives the probability of finding an electron within a given region of space. The kinds of orbitals that we've been concerned with up to this point are called *atomic orbitals* because they are characteristic of individual atoms. Atomic orbitals on the same atom can combine to form hybrids, and atomic orbitals on different atoms can overlap to form covalent bonds, but the orbitals and the electrons in them remain localized on specific atoms.

> **Atomic orbital**   A wave function whose square gives the probability of finding an electron within a given region of space *in an atom.*

Molecular orbital theory takes a different approach to bonding by considering the molecule as a whole rather than concentrating on individual atoms. A **molecular orbital** is to a molecule what an atomic orbital is to an atom.

> **Molecular orbital**   A wave function whose square gives the probability of finding an electron within a given region of space *in a molecule.*

Like atomic orbitals, molecular orbitals have specific energy levels and specific shapes, and they can be occupied by a maximum of two electrons with opposite spins. The energy and shape of a molecular orbital depend on the size and complexity of the molecule and can thus be fairly complicated, but the fundamental analogy between atomic and molecular orbitals remains. Let's look at the molecular orbital description of the simple diatomic molecule H_2 to see some general features of MO theory.

Imagine what might happen when two isolated hydrogen atoms approach each other and begin to interact. The $1s$ orbitals begin to blend together, and the electrons spread out over both atoms. Molecular orbital theory says that there are two ways for the orbital interaction to occur—an additive way and a subtractive way. The additive interaction leads to formation of a molecular orbital that is roughly egg-shaped, whereas the subtractive interaction leads to formation of a molecular orbital that contains a **node** between atoms (**Figure 7.13**).

Remember...

A **node** is a surface of zero electron probability separating regions of nonzero probability within an orbital.   (Section 5.7)

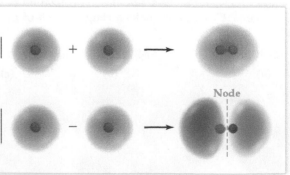

The additive combination of atomic $1s$ orbitals forms a lower-energy, bonding molecular orbital.

The subtractive combination of atomic $1s$ orbitals forms a higher-energy, antibonding molecular orbital that has a **node** between the nuclei.

Node

Figure 7.13
Formation of molecular orbitals in the H_2 molecule.

The additive combination, denoted σ, is lower in energy than the two isolated 1s orbitals and is called a **bonding molecular orbital** because any electrons it contains spend most of their time in the region between the two nuclei, bonding the atoms together. The subtractive combination, denoted σ* and spoken as "sigma star," is higher in energy than the two isolated 1s orbitals and is called an **antibonding molecular orbital.** Any electrons it contains can't occupy the central region between the nuclei and can't contribute to bonding.

Diagrams of the sort shown in **Figure 7.14** are used to show the energy relationships of the various orbitals. The two isolated H atomic orbitals are shown on either side, and the two H_2 molecular orbitals are shown in the middle. Each of the starting hydrogen atomic orbitals has one electron, which pair up and occupy the lower-energy bonding MO after covalent bond formation.

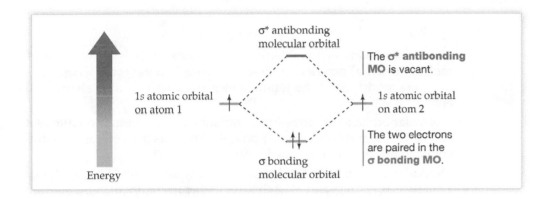

Figure 7.14
Energy levels of molecular orbitals for the H_2 molecule.

Similar MO diagrams can be drawn, and predictions about stability can be made, for related diatomic species such as H_2^- and He_2. For example, we might imagine constructing the H_2^- ion by bringing together a neutral H· atom with one electron and an H:⁻ anion with two electrons. Since the resultant H_2^- ion has three electrons, two of them will occupy the lower-energy bonding σ MO and one will occupy the higher-energy antibonding σ* MO as shown in **Figure 7.15a**. Two electrons are lowered in energy while only one electron is raised in energy, so a net gain in stability results. We therefore predict (and find experimentally) that the H_2^- ion is stable.

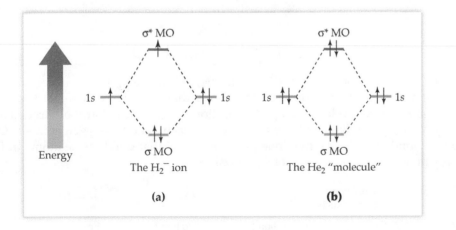

Figure 7.15
Energy levels of molecular orbitals for (a) the stable H_2^- ion and (b) the unstable He_2 molecule.

What about He_2? A hypothetical He_2 molecule has four electrons, two of which occupy the lower-energy bonding orbital and two of which occupy the higher-energy antibonding orbital, as shown in **Figure 7.15b**. Since the decrease in energy for the two bonding electrons is counteracted by the increase in energy for the two antibonding electrons, the He_2 molecule has no net bonding energy and is not stable.

Bond orders—the number of electron pairs shared between atoms (Section 7.5)—can be calculated from MO diagrams by subtracting the number of antibonding electrons from the number of bonding electrons and dividing the difference by 2:

$$\text{Bond order} = \frac{\left(\begin{array}{c}\text{Number of} \\ \text{bonding electrons}\end{array}\right) - \left(\begin{array}{c}\text{Number of} \\ \text{antibonding electrons}\end{array}\right)}{2}$$

The H_2 molecule, for instance, has a bond order of 1 because it has two bonding electrons and no antibonding electrons. In the same way, the H_2^- ion has a bond order of 1/2, and the hypothetical He_2 molecule has a bond order of 0, which accounts for the instability of He_2.

The key ideas of the molecular orbital theory of bonding can be summarized as follows:

Key Ideas of Molecular Orbital Theory

- Molecular orbitals are to molecules what atomic orbitals are to atoms. A molecular orbital describes a region of space in a molecule where electrons are most likely to be found, and it has a specific size, shape, and energy level.

- Molecular orbitals are formed by combining atomic orbitals on different atoms. The number of molecular orbitals formed is the same as the number of atomic orbitals combined.

- Molecular orbitals that are lower in energy than the starting atomic orbitals are bonding, and MOs that are higher in energy than the starting atomic orbitals are antibonding.

- Electrons occupy molecular orbitals beginning with the MO of lowest energy. A maximum of two electrons can occupy each orbital, and their spins are paired.

- Bond order can be calculated by subtracting the number of electrons in antibonding MOs from the number in bonding MOs and dividing the difference by 2.

▶ **PROBLEM 7.26** Construct an MO diagram for the He_2^+ ion. Is this ion likely to be stable? What is its bond order?

7.14 MOLECULAR ORBITAL THEORY: OTHER DIATOMIC MOLECULES

Having looked at bonding in the H_2 molecule, let's move up a level in complexity by looking at the bonding in several second-row diatomic molecules—N_2, O_2, and F_2. The valence bond model developed in Section 7.10 predicts that the nitrogen atoms in N_2 are triply bonded and have one lone pair each, that the oxygen atoms in O_2 are doubly bonded and have two lone pairs each, and that the fluorine atoms in F_2 are singly bonded and have three lone pairs each:

Valence bond theory predicts:	:N≡N:	Ö=Ö	:F—F:
	1 σ bond and 2 π bonds	1 σ bond and 1 π bond	1 σ bond

Unfortunately, this simple valence bond picture can't be right because it predicts that the electrons in all three molecules are *spin-paired*. In other words, the electron-dot structures indicate that the occupied atomic orbitals in all three molecules contain two electrons each. It can be demonstrated experimentally, however, that the O_2 molecule has two electrons that are not spin-paired and that these electrons therefore must be in different, singly occupied orbitals.

Experimental evidence for the electronic structure of O_2 rests on the observation that substances with unpaired electrons are attracted by magnetic fields and are thus said to be **paramagnetic.** The more unpaired electrons a substance has, the stronger the paramagnetic attraction. Substances whose electrons are all spin-paired, by contrast, are weakly repelled by magnetic fields and are said to be **diamagnetic.** Both N_2 and F_2 are diamagnetic, just as predicted by their electron-dot structures, but O_2 is paramagnetic. When liquid O_2 is poured over the poles of a strong magnet, the O_2 sticks to the poles, as shown in Figure 7.16.

Why is O_2 paramagnetic? Although electron-dot structures and valence bond theory fail in their descriptions, MO theory explains the experimental results nicely. In a molecular orbital description of N_2, O_2, and F_2, two atoms come together and their valence-shell atomic orbitals interact to form molecular orbitals. Four orbital interactions occur, leading to the formation of four bonding MOs and four antibonding MOs, whose relative energies are shown in Figure 7.17. (Note that the relative energies of the σ_{2p} and π_{2p} orbitals in N_2 are different from those in O_2 and F_2.)

Figure 7.16

Paramagnetism. Why does liquid O_2 stick to the poles of a magnet?

Figure 7.17
Energy levels of molecular orbitals for (a) N_2 and (b) O_2 and F_2.

The diagrams in Figure 7.17 show the following orbital interactions:

- The 2s orbitals interact to give σ_{2s} and σ^*_{2s} MOs.
- The two 2p orbitals that lie on the internuclear axis interact head-on to give σ_{2p} and σ^*_{2p} MOs.
- The two remaining pairs of 2p orbitals that are perpendicular to the internuclear axis interact in a sideways manner to give two degenerate π_{2p} and two degenerate π^*_{2p} MOs oriented 90° apart.

Remember...

Degenerate orbitals are those that have the same energy. (Section 5.11)

The shapes of the σ_{2p}, σ^*_{2p}, π_{2p}, and π^*_{2p} MOs are shown in Figure 7.18.

When appropriate numbers of valence electrons are added to occupy the molecular orbitals, the results shown in Figure 7.19 are obtained. Both N_2 and F_2 have all their electrons spin-paired, but O_2 has two unpaired electrons in the degenerate π^*_{2p} orbitals. Both N_2 and F_2 are therefore diamagnetic, whereas O_2 is paramagnetic.

We should also point out that MO diagrams like those in Figure 7.19 are usually obtained from mathematical calculations and can't necessarily be predicted. MO theory is therefore less easy to visualize and understand on an intuitive level than valence bond theory.

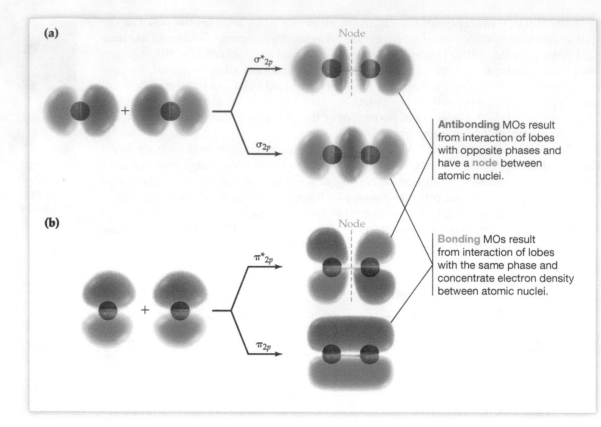

Figure 7.18

Formation of (a) σ_{2p} and σ^*_{2p} MOs by head-on interaction of two p atomic orbitals, and (b) π_{2p} and π^*_{2p} MOs by sideways interaction.

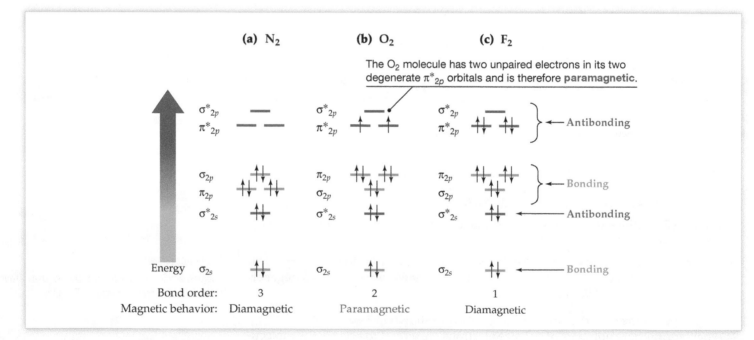

Figure 7.19

Energy levels of molecular orbitals for the second-row diatomic molecules (a) N_2, (b) O_2, and (c) F_2.

▶ **PROBLEM 7.27** The B_2 and C_2 molecules have MO diagrams similar to that of N_2 in Figure 7.17a. What MOs are occupied in B_2 and C_2, and what is the bond order in each? Would you expect either of these substances to be paramagnetic?

7.15 COMBINING VALENCE BOND THEORY AND MOLECULAR ORBITAL THEORY

Whenever two different theories explain the same concept, the question comes up: Which theory is better? The question isn't easy to answer, though, because it depends on what is meant by "better." Valence bond theory is better because of its simplicity and ease of visualization, but MO theory is better because of its accuracy. Best of all, though, is a joint use of the two theories that combines the strengths of both.

Valence bond theory has two main problems: (1) For molecules such as O_2, valence bond theory makes an incorrect prediction about electronic structure. (2) For molecules such as O_3, no single structure is adequate and the concept of resonance involving two or more structures must be added (Section 7.7). The first problem occurs infrequently, but the second is much more common. To better deal with resonance, chemists often use a combination of bonding theories in which the σ bonds in a given molecule are described by valence bond theory and π bonds in the same molecule are described by MO theory.

Take O_3, for instance. Valence bond theory says that ozone is a resonance hybrid of two equivalent structures, both of which have two O—O σ bonds and one O=O π bond (Section 7.7). One structure has a lone pair of electrons in the *p* orbital on the left-hand oxygen atom and a π bond to the right-hand oxygen. The other structure has a lone pair of electrons in the *p* orbital on the right-hand oxygen and a π bond to the left-hand oxygen. The actual structure of O_3 is an average of the two resonance forms in which four electrons occupy the entire region encompassed by the overlapping set of three *p* orbitals. The only difference between the resonance structures is in the placement of *p* electrons. The atoms themselves are in the same positions in both, and the geometries are the same in both (Figure 7.20).

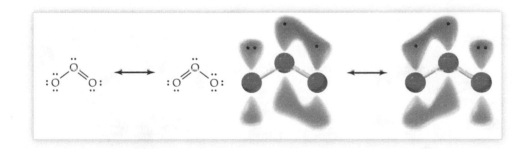

Figure 7.20
The structure of ozone.

Valence bond theory thus gives a good description of the ozone O—O σ bonds, whose electrons are localized between specific pairs of atoms, but a poor description of the π bonds among *p* atomic orbitals, whose four electrons are spread out, or *delocalized*, over the molecule. Yet this is exactly what MO theory does best—describe bonds in which electrons are delocalized throughout a molecule. Thus, a combination of valence bond theory and MO theory is used. The σ bonds are best described in valence bond terminology as being localized between pairs of atoms, and the π electrons are best described by MO theory as being delocalized over the entire molecule.

Lowest-energy π molecular orbital

▶ **PROBLEM 7.28** Draw two resonance structures for the formate ion, HCO_2^-, and sketch a π molecular orbital showing how the π electrons are delocalized over both oxygen atoms.

▲ A right hand fits only into a right-handed glove with a complementary shape, not into a left-handed glove.

INQUIRY HOW DOES MOLECULAR SHAPE LEAD TO HANDEDNESS IN MOLECULES?

Why does a right-handed glove fit only on your right hand and not on your left hand? Why do the threads on a lightbulb twist only in one direction so that you have to turn the bulb clockwise to screw it in? The reason has to do with the shapes of the glove and the lightbulb threads and the fact that both have a *handedness* to them. When the right-handed glove is held up to a mirror, the reflected image looks like a left-handed glove. (Try it.) When the lightbulb with clockwise threads is reflected in a mirror, the threads in the mirror image twist in a counterclockwise direction.

Molecules too can have shapes that give them a handedness and can thus exist in mirror-image forms, one right-handed and one left-handed. Take, for example, the main classes of biomolecules found in living organisms: carbohydrates (sugars), proteins, fats, and nucleic acids. These and most other biomolecules are handed, and usually only one of the two possible mirror-image forms occurs naturally in a given organism. The other form can often be made in the laboratory but does not occur naturally.

The biological consequences of molecular shape can be dramatic. Look at the structures of dextromethorphan and levomethorphan, for instance. (The Latin prefixes *dextro-* and *levo-* mean "right" and "left," respectively.) Dextromethorphan is a common cough suppressant found in many over-the-counter cold medicines, but its mirror-image, levomethorphan, is a powerful narcotic pain-reliever similar in its effects to morphine. The two substances are chemically identical except for their handedness, yet their biological properties are very different.

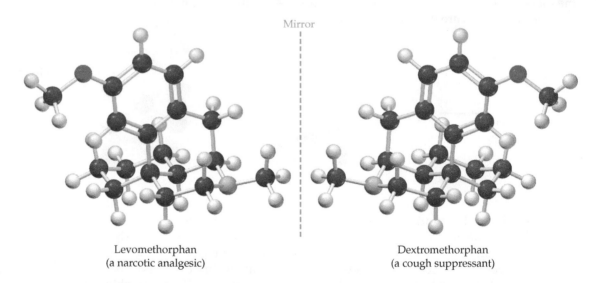

Levomethorphan
(a narcotic analgesic)

Dextromethorphan
(a cough suppressant)

▲ The gray spheres in these structures represent carbon atoms, the ivory spheres represent hydrogen, the red spheres represent oxygen, and the blue spheres represent nitrogen.

As another example of the effects of shape and molecular handedness, look at the substance called *carvone*. Left-handed carvone occurs in mint plants and has the characteristic odor of spearmint, while right-handed carvone occurs in several herbs and has the odor of caraway seeds. Again, the two structures are the same except for their handedness, yet they have entirely different odors.

Why do different mirror-image forms of molecules have different biological properties? The answer goes back to the question about why a right-handed glove fits only the right hand. A right hand in a right-handed glove is a perfect match because the two shapes are complementary. Putting the right hand into a left-handed glove produces a mismatch because the two shapes are *not* complementary. In the same way, handed molecules such as dextromethorphan and carvone have specific shapes that match only complementary-shaped receptor sites in the body. The

◀ Two plants both produce carvone, but the mint leaves yield the "left-handed" form, while the caraway seeds yield the "right-handed" form.

"Left-handed" carvone
(odor of spearmint)

"Right-handed" carvone
(odor of caraway)

mirror-image forms of the molecules can't fit into the receptor sites and thus don't elicit the same biological response.

Precise molecular shape is critically important to every living organism. Almost every chemical interaction in living systems is governed by complementarity between handed molecules and their glovelike receptors.

▶ **PROBLEM 7.29** Why is molecular shape so important in biological chemistry?

CONCEPTUAL PROBLEM 7.30 One of the following two molecules has a handedness to it and can exist in two mirror-image forms; the other does not. Which is which? Why?

(a)   **(b)**

SUMMARY

A **covalent bond** results from the sharing of electrons between atoms. Every covalent bond has a specific **bond length** that leads to optimum stability and a specific **bond dissociation energy** that describes the strength of the bond. Energy is released when a bond is formed, and energy is absorbed when a bond is broken. As a general rule, a main-group atom shares as many of its valence-shell electrons as possible, either until it has no more to share or until it reaches an octet. Atoms in the third and lower rows of the periodic table can accommodate more than the number of bonds predicted by the octet rule.

An **electron-dot structure** represents an atom's valence electrons by dots and shows the two electrons in a **single bond** as a pair of dots shared between atoms. In the same way, a **double bond** is represented as four dots or two lines between atoms, and a **triple bond** is represented as six dots or three lines between atoms. Occasionally, a molecule can be represented by more than one electron-dot structure. In such cases, no single structure is adequate by itself. The actual electronic structure of the molecule is a **resonance hybrid** of the different individual structures.

In a bond between dissimilar atoms, such as that in HCl, one atom often attracts the bonding electrons more strongly than the other, giving rise to a **polar covalent bond**. Bond polarity is due to differences in **electronegativity**, the ability of an atom in a molecule to attract shared electrons. Electronegativity increases from left to right across a row and generally decreases from top to bottom in a group of the periodic table.

Molecular shape can often be predicted using the **valence-shell electron-pair repulsion (VSEPR) model,** which treats the electrons around atoms as charge clouds that repel one another and therefore orient themselves as far away from one another as possible. Atoms with two charge clouds adopt a linear arrangement of the clouds, atoms with three charge clouds adopt a trigonal planar arrangement, and atoms with four charge clouds adopt a tetrahedral arrangement. Similarly, atoms with five charge clouds are trigonal bipyramidal and atoms with six charge clouds are octahedral.

According to **valence bond theory,** covalent bond formation occurs by the overlap of two singly occupied atomic orbital lobes of the same phase, either head-on along the internuclear axis to form a **σ bond** or sideways above and below the internuclear axis to form a **π bond.** The observed geometry of covalent bonding in main-group compounds is described by assuming that *s* and *p* atomic orbitals combine to generate **hybrid orbitals,** which are strongly oriented in specific directions: *sp* hybrid orbitals have linear geometry, *sp*² hybrid orbitals have trigonal planar geometry, and *sp*³ hybrid orbitals have tetrahedral geometry. The bonding of main-group atoms with five and six charge clouds is more complex.

Molecular orbital theory sometimes gives a more accurate picture of electronic structure than the valence bond model. A **molecular orbital** is a wave function whose square gives the probability of finding an electron in a given region of space in a molecule. Combination of two atomic orbitals gives two molecular orbitals, a **bonding MO** that is lower in energy than the starting atomic orbitals and an **antibonding MO** that is higher in energy than the starting atomic orbitals. Molecular orbital theory is particularly useful for describing delocalized π bonding in molecules.

KEY WORDS

antibonding molecular orbital 251
bond angle 236
bond dissociation energy (D) 218
bond length 217
bond order 224
bonding molecular orbital 251
bonding pair 223
coordinate covalent bond 225
diamagnetic 253
double bond 224
electron-dot structure 222
electronegativity (EN) 221
formal charge 234
hybrid atomic orbital 244
lone pair 223
molecular orbital 250
molecular orbital (MO) theory 250
paramagnetic 253
pi (π) bond 247
polar covalent bond 220
resonance hybrid 232
sigma (σ) bond 243
single bond 224
sp hybrid orbital 247
*sp*² hybrid orbital 246
*sp*³ hybrid orbital 244
triple bond 224
valence bond theory 243
valence-shell electron-pair repulsion (VSEPR) model 236

CONCEPTUAL PROBLEMS

Problems 7.1–7.30 appear within the chapter.

7.31 Two electrostatic potential maps are shown, one of methyllithium (CH₃Li) and the other of chloromethane (CH₃Cl). Based on their polarity patterns, which do you think is which?

(a)   **(b)**

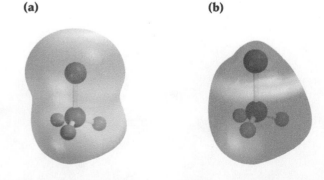

7.32 What is the geometry around the central atom in each of the following molecular models?

(a)   **(b)**   **(c)**   **(d)**

7.33 What is the geometry around the central atom in each of the following molecular models? (There may be a "hidden" atom directly behind a visible atom in some cases.)

(a)   **(b)**   **(c)**

7.34 Three of the following molecular models have a tetrahedral central atom, and one does not. Which is the odd one? (There may be a "hidden" atom directly behind a visible atom in some cases.)

(a)   **(b)**   **(c)**   **(d)**

7.35 The VSEPR model is a simple predictive tool that is usually, but not always, correct. Take urea, for instance, a waste product excreted in animal urine:

Urea

What hybridization would you expect for the C and N atoms in urea according to the VSEPR model, and what approximate values would you expect for the various bond angles? What are the actual hybridizations and bond angles based on the molecular model shown? (Red = O, gray = C, blue = N, ivory = H):

7.36 The following ball-and-stick molecular model is a representation of acetaminophen, the active ingredient in such over-the-counter headache remedies as Tylenol (red = O, gray = C, blue = N, ivory = H):

(a) What is the formula of acetaminophen?

(b) Indicate the positions of the multiple bonds in acetaminophen.

(c) What is the geometry around each carbon?

(d) What is the hybridization of each carbon?

Acetaminophen

7.37 The following ball-and-stick molecular model is a representation of thalidomide, a drug that causes birth defects when taken by expectant mothers but is valuable for its use against leprosy. The lines indicate only the connections between atoms, not whether the bonds are single, double, or triple (red = O, gray = C, blue = N, ivory = H).

(a) What is the formula of thalidomide?

(b) Indicate the positions of the multiple bonds in thalidomide.

(c) What is the geometry around each carbon?

(d) What is the hybridization of each carbon?

Thalidomide

SECTION PROBLEMS

Electronegativity and Polar Covalent Bonds (Section 7.4)

7.38 What general trends in electronegativity occur in the periodic table?

7.39 Predict the electronegativity of the undiscovered element with $Z = 119$.

7.40 Order the following elements according to increasing electronegativity: Li, Br, Pb, K, Mg, C.

7.41 Order the following elements according to decreasing electronegativity: C, Ca, Cs, Cl, Cu.

7.42 Which of the following substances are largely ionic, and which are covalent?

    (a) HF   **(b)** HI   **(c)** $PdCl_2$

    (d) BBr_3 **(e)** NaOH   **(f)** CH_3Li

7.43 Use the electronegativity data in Figure 7.4 to predict which bond in each of the following pairs is more polar:

    (a) C—H or C—Cl   **(b)** Si—Li or Si—Cl

    (c) N—Cl or N—Mg

7.44 Show the direction of polarity for each of the bonds in Problem 7.43, using the δ+/δ− notation.

7.45 Show the direction of polarity for each of the covalent bonds in Problem 7.42, using the δ+/δ− notation.

7.46 Which of the substances $CdBr_2$, P_4, BrF_3, MgO, NF_3, $BaCl_2$, $POCl_3$, and LiBr are:

    (a) largely ionic?   **(b)** nonpolar covalent?

    (c) polar covalent?

7.47 Which of the substances S_8, $CaCl_2$, $SOCl_2$, NaF, CBr_4, BrCl, LiF, and AsI_3 are:

    (a) largely ionic?   **(b)** nonpolar covalent?

    (c) polar covalent?

7.48 Using only the elements P, Br, and Mg, give formulas for the following:

(a) an ionic compound

(b) a molecular compound with polar covalent bonds that obeys the octet rule and has no formal charges

7.49 Using only the elements Ca, Cl, Si, give formulas for the following:

(a) an ionic compound

(b) a molecular compound with polar covalent bonds that obeys the octet rule and has no formal charges

7.50 Which compound do you expect to have the stronger N—N bond, N_2H_2 or N_2H_4? Explain.

7.51 Which compound do you expect to have the stronger N—O bond, NO or NO_2? Explain.

7.52 Name the following molecular compounds:

(a) PCl_3 (b) N_2O_3 (c) P_4O_7

(d) BrF_3 (e) NCl_3 (f) P_4O_6

(g) S_2F_2 (h) SeO_2

7.53 Write formulas for the following molecular compounds:

(a) Disulfur dichloride

(b) Iodine monochloride

(c) Nitrogen triiodide

(d) Dichlorine monoxide

(e) Chlorine trioxide

(f) Tetrasulfur tetranitride

Electron-Dot Structures and Resonance (Sections 7.5–7.7)

7.54 Why does the octet rule apply primarily to main-group elements, not to transition metals?

7.55 Which of the following substances contains an atom that does not follow the octet rule?

(a) $AlCl_3$ (b) PCl_3 (c) PCl_5 (d) $SiCl_4$

7.56 Draw electron-dot structures for the following molecules or ions:

(a) CBr_4 (b) NCl_3 (c) C_2H_5Cl

(d) BF_4^- (e) O_2^{2-} (f) NO^+

7.57 Draw electron-dot structures for the following molecules, which contain atoms from the third row or lower:

(a) $SbCl_3$ (b) KrF_2 (c) ClO_2

(d) PF_5 (e) H_3PO_4 (f) $SeOCl_2$

7.58 Draw as many resonance structures as you can that obey the octet rule for each of the following molecules or ions:

(a) HN_3 (b) SO_3 (c) SCN^-

7.59 Draw as many resonance structures as you can for the following nitrogen-containing compounds. Not all will obey the octet rule.

(a) N_2O (b) NO   (c) NO_2 (d) N_2O_3 ($ONNO_2$)

7.60 Oxalic acid, $H_2C_2O_4$, is a mildly poisonous substance found in the leaves of rhubarb, spinach, and many other plants. (You'd have to eat about 15 lb or so of spinach leaves to ingest a lethal amount.) If oxalic acid has a C—C single bond and no C—H bond, draw its electron-dot structure showing lone pairs and identifying any multiple bonds.

7.61 Draw an electron-dot structure for carbon disulfide, CS_2, showing lone pairs and identifying any multiple bonds.

7.62 Which of the following pairs of structures represent resonance forms, and which do not?

7.63 Which of the following pairs of structures represent resonance forms, and which do not?

7.64 Identify the third-row elements, X, that form the following ions:

7.65 Identify the fourth-row elements, X, that form the following compounds:

(a)   (b)

7.66 Write electron-dot structures for molecules with the following connections, showing lone pairs and identifying any multiple bonds:

(a)   (b)

7.67 Write electron-dot structures for molecules with the following connections, showing lone pairs and identifying any multiple bonds:

(a)   (b)

Formal Charges (Section 7.8)

7.68 Draw an electron-dot structure for carbon monoxide, CO, and assign formal charges to both atoms.

7.69 Assign formal charges to the atoms in the following structures:

(a)   (b)

(c)

7.70 Assign formal charges to the atoms in the following resonance forms of ClO_2^-:

7.71 Assign formal charges to the atoms in the following resonance forms of H_2SO_3:

7.72 Assign formal charges to the atoms in the following structures. Which of the two do you think is the more important contributor to the resonance hybrid?

(a)   (b)

7.73 Calculate formal charges for the C and O atoms in the following two resonance structures. Which structure do you think is the more important contributor to the resonance hybrid? Explain.

7.74 Draw two electron-dot resonance structures that obey the octet rule for trichloronitromethane, CCl_3NO_2, and show the formal charges on N and O in both structures. (Carbon is connected to the chlorines and to nitrogen; nitrogen is also connected to both oxygens.)

7.75 Draw two electron-dot resonance structures that obey the octet rule for nitrosyl chloride, NOCl (nitrogen is the central atom). Show formal charges, if present, and predict which of the two structures is a more accurate representation of the molecule.

The VSEPR Model (Section 7.9)

7.76 What geometric arrangement of charge clouds do you expect for atoms that have the following number of charge clouds?
(a) 3   (b) 5   (c) 2   (d) 6

7.77 What shape do you expect for molecules that meet the following descriptions?
(a) A central atom with two lone pairs and three bonds to other atoms
(b) A central atom with two lone pairs and two bonds to other atoms
(c) A central atom with two lone pairs and four bonds to other atoms

7.78 How many charge clouds are there around the central atom in molecules that have the following geometry?
(a) Tetrahedral   (b) Octahedral
(c) Bent   (d) Linear
(e) Square pyramidal   (f) Trigonal pyramidal

7.79 How many charge clouds are there around the central atom in molecules that have the following geometry?
(a) Seesaw   (b) Square planar
(c) Trigonal bipyramidal (d) T-shaped
(e) Trigonal planar   (f) Linear

7.80 What shape do you expect for each of the following molecules?
(a) H_2Se (b) $TiCl_4$ (c) O_3 (d) GaH_3

7.81 What shape do you expect for each of the following molecules?
(a) XeO_4 (b) SO_2Cl_2 (c) OsO_4 (d) SeO_2

7.82 What shape do you expect for each of the following molecules or ions?
(a) SbF_5 (b) IF_4^+ (c) SeO_3^{2-} (d) CrO_4^{2-}

7.83 Predict the shape of each of the following ions:
(a) NO_3^- (b) NO_2^+ (c) NO_2^-

7.84 What shape do you expect for each of the following anions?
(a) PO_4^{3-} (b) MnO_4^- (c) SO_4^{2-}
(d) SO_3^{2-} (e) ClO_4^- (f) SCN^-

7.85 What shape do you expect for each of the following cations?
(a) XeF_3^+ (b) SF_3^+ (c) ClF_2^+ (d) CH_3^+

7.86 What bond angles do you expect for each of the following?
(a) The F—S—F angle in SF_2
(b) The H—N—N angle in N_2H_2
(c) The F—Kr—F angle in KrF_4
(d) The Cl—N—O angle in NOCl

7.87 What bond angles do you expect for each of the following?
(a) The Cl—P—Cl angle in PCl_6^-
(b) The Cl—I—Cl angle in ICl_2^-
(c) The O—S—O angle in SO_4^{2-}
(d) The O—B—O angle in BO_3^{3-}

7.88 Acrylonitrile is used as the starting material for manufacturing acrylic fibers. Predict values for all bond angles in acrylonitrile.

$$H_2C=C-C\equiv N\colon \quad \text{Acrylonitrile}$$

7.89 Predict values for all bond angles in dimethyl sulfoxide, a powerful solvent used in veterinary medicine to treat inflammation.

$$H_3C-S-CH_3 \quad \text{Dimethyl sulfoxide}$$

7.90 Oceanographers study the mixing of water masses by releasing tracer molecules at a site and then detecting their presence at other places. The molecule trifluoromethyl-sulfur pentafluoride is one such tracer. Draw an electron-dot structure for CF_3SF_5, and predict the bond angles around both carbon and sulfur.

7.91 A potential replacement for the chlorofluorocarbon refrigerants that harm the Earth's protective ozone layer is a compound called E143a, or trifluoromethyl methyl ether, F_3COCH_3. Draw an electron-dot structure for F_3COCH_3, and predict the geometry around both the carbons and the oxygen.

7.92 Explain why cyclohexane, a substance that contains a six-membered ring of carbon atoms, is not flat but instead has a puckered, nonplanar shape. Predict the values of the C—C—C bond angles.

Cyclohexane   Side view

7.93 Like cyclohexane (Problem 7.92), benzene also contains a six-membered ring of carbon atoms, but it is flat rather than puckered. Explain, and predict the values of the C—C—C bond angles.

Benzene

Valence Bond Theory and Molecular Orbital Theory (Sections 7.10–7.15)

7.94 What is the difference in spatial distribution between electrons in a π bond and electrons in a σ bond?

7.95 What is the difference in spatial distribution between electrons in a bonding MO and electrons in an antibonding MO?

7.96 What hybridization do you expect for atoms that have the following numbers of charge clouds?
(a) 2 (b) 3 (c) 4

7.97 What spatial arrangement of charge clouds corresponds to each of the following kinds of hybridization?
(a) sp^3 (b) sp^2 (c) sp

7.98 What hybridization would you expect for the indicated atom in each of the following molecules?
(a) $H_2C=O$ (b) BH_3 (c) CH_3SH (d) $H_2C=NH$

7.99 What hybridization would you expect for the indicated atom in each of the following ions?
(a) BH_4^- (b) HCO_2^- (c) CH_3^+ (d) CH_3^-

7.100 Oxaloacetic acid is an intermediate involved in the citric acid cycle of food metabolism. What are the hybridizations of the various carbon atoms in oxaloacetic acid, and what are the approximate values of the various bond angles?

$$H-O-C-C-C-C-O-H \quad \text{Oxaloacetic acid}$$

7.101 The atoms in the amino acid glycine are connected as shown:

$$H-N-C-C-O-H$$

(a) Draw an electron-dot structure for glycine, showing lone pairs and identifying any multiple bonds.
(b) Predict approximate values for the H—C—H, O—C—O, and H—N—H bond angles.
(c) Which hybrid orbitals are used by the C and N atoms?

7.102 Use the MO energy diagram in Figure 7.17b to describe the bonding in O_2^+, O_2, and O_2^-. Which of the three is likely to be stable? What is the bond order of each? Which contain unpaired electrons?

7.103 Use the MO energy diagram in Figure 7.17a to describe the bonding in N_2^+, N_2, and N_2^-. Which of the three is likely to be stable? What is the bond order of each? Which contain unpaired electrons?

7.104 The C_2 molecule can be represented by an MO diagram similar to that in Figure 7.17a.
(a) What is the bond order of C_2?
(b) To increase the bond order of C_2, should you add or remove an electron?
(c) Give the charge and the bond order of the new species made in part (b).

7.105 Look at the molecular orbital diagram for O_2 in Figure 7.19 and answer the following questions:
(a) What is the bond order of O_2?
(b) To increase the bond order of O_2, should you add or remove an electron?
(c) Give the charge and the bond order of the new species made in part (b).

7.106 Look at the MO diagrams of corresponding neutral diatomic species in Figure 7.19, and predict whether each of the following ions is diamagnetic or paramagnetic. Diagrams for Li_2 and C_2 are similar to N_2; Cl_2 is similar to F_2.

(a) C_2^{2-} **(b)** C_2^{2+} **(c)** F_2^- **(d)** Cl_2 **(e)** Li_2^+

7.107 Look at the MO diagrams of corresponding neutral diatomic species in Figure 7.19, and predict whether each of the following ions is diamagnetic or paramagnetic. MO diagrams for Li_2 and C_2 are similar to N_2; Cl_2 is similar to F_2.

(a) O_2^{2+} **(b)** N_2^{2+} **(c)** C_2^+ **(d)** F_2^{2+} **(e)** Cl_2^+

7.108 Make a sketch showing the location and geometry of the p orbitals in the allyl cation. Describe the bonding in this cation using a localized valence bond model for σ bonding and a delocalized MO model for π bonding.

Allyl cation

7.109 Make a sketch showing the location and geometry of the p orbitals in the nitrite ion, NO_2^-. Describe the bonding in this ion using a localized valence bond model for σ bonding and a delocalized MO model for π bonding.

CHAPTER PROBLEMS

7.110 Vitamin C (ascorbic acid) has the following connections among atoms. Complete the following electron-dot structure for vitamin C, showing lone pairs and identifying any multiple bonds:

Vitamin C

7.111 Tell the hybridization of each carbon atom in ascorbic acid (Problem 7.110).

7.112 Sinapaldehyde, a compound present in the toasted wood used for aging wine, has the following connections among atoms. Complete the electron-dot structure for sinapaldehyde, identify any multiple bonds in the molecule, and tell the hybridization of each carbon atom.

Sinapaldehyde

7.113 Thiofulminic acid, $H-C{\equiv}N-S$ has recently been detected at very low temperatures.
   (a) Draw an electron-dot structure for thiofulminic acid, and assign formal charges.
   (b) A related compound with the same formula and the connection $H-N-C-S$ is also known. Draw an electron-dot structure for this related compound and assign formal charges.
   (c) Which of the two molecules is likely to be more stable? Explain.

7.114 The odor of cinnamon oil is due to cinnamaldehyde, C_9H_8O. What is the hybridization of each carbon atom in cinnamaldehyde? How many σ bonds and how many π bonds does cinnamaldehyde have?

Cinnamaldehyde

7.115 Draw three resonance structures for sulfur tetroxide, SO_4, whose connections are shown below. (This is a neutral molecule; it is not sulfate ion.) Assign formal charges to the atoms in each structure.

Sulfur tetroxide

7.116 Draw two resonance structures for methyl isocyanate, CH_3NCO, a toxic gas that was responsible for the deaths of at least 3000 people when it was accidentally released into the atmosphere in December 1984 in Bhopal, India. Assign formal charges to the atoms in each resonance structure.

7.117 There are two possible shapes for diimide, $H-N{=}N-H$ Draw both, and tell whether they are resonance forms.

7.118 Boron trifluoride reacts with dimethyl ether to form a compound with a coordinate covalent bond:

$$\underset{\substack{\text{Boron} \\ \text{trifluoride}}}{F-\overset{\displaystyle F}{\underset{\displaystyle F}{B}}} + \underset{\substack{\text{Dimethyl} \\ \text{ether}}}{:\overset{\displaystyle CH_3}{\underset{\displaystyle CH_3}{O}}} \longrightarrow F-\overset{\displaystyle F}{\underset{\displaystyle F}{B}}-\overset{\displaystyle CH_3}{\underset{\displaystyle CH_3}{O}}:$$

   (a) Assign formal charges to the B and O atoms in both the reactants and product.
   (b) Describe the geometry and hybridization of the B and O atoms in both reactants and product.

7.119 What is the hybridization of the B and N atoms in borazine, what are the values of the B—N—B and N—B—N bond angles, and what is the overall shape of the molecule?

Borazine

7.120 Benzyne, C_6H_4, is a highly energetic and reactive molecule. What hybridization do you expect for the two triply bonded carbon atoms? What are the "theoretical" values for the C—C≡C bond angles? Why do you suppose benzyne is so reactive?

Benzyne

7.121 Propose structures for molecules that meet the following descriptions:
(a) Contains a C atom that has two π bonds and two σ bonds
(b) Contains an N atom that has one π bond and two σ bonds
(c) Contains an S atom that has a coordinate covalent bond

7.122 Write an electron-dot structure for chloral hydrate, also known in old detective novels as "knockout drops."

$$Cl-\overset{\overset{\displaystyle Cl}{|}}{\underset{\underset{\displaystyle Cl}{|}}{C}}-\overset{\overset{\displaystyle O-H}{|}}{\underset{\underset{\displaystyle H}{|}}{C}}-O-H$$ Chloral hydrate

7.123 Draw a molecular orbital energy diagram for Li_2. What is the bond order? Is the molecule likely to be stable? Explain.

7.124 Calcium carbide, CaC_2, reacts with water to produce acetylene, C_2H_2, and is sometimes used as a convenient source of that substance. Use the MO energy diagram in Figure 7.17a to describe the bonding in the carbide anion, C_2^{2-}. What is its bond order?

7.125 Use VSEPR theory to answer the following questions:
(a) Which molecule, BF_3 or PF_3, has the smaller F—X—F angles?
(b) Which ion, PCl_4^+ or ICl_2^-, has the smaller Cl—X—Cl angles?
(c) Which ion, CCl_3^- or PCl_6^-, has the smaller Cl—X—Cl angles?

7.126 The overall energy change during a chemical reaction can be calculated from a knowledge of bond dissociation energies using the following relationship:

Energy change = D(Bonds broken) − D(Bonds formed)

Use the data in Table 7.1 to calculate an energy change for the reaction of methane with chlorine.

$$CH_4(g) + Cl_2(g) \longrightarrow CH_3Cl(g) + HCl(g)$$

7.127 The following molecular model is that of aspartame, $C_{14}H_{18}N_2O_5$, known commercially as NutraSweet. Only the connections between atoms are shown; multiple bonds are not indicated. Complete the structure by indicating the positions of the multiple bonds and lone pairs.

Aspartame

7.128 The N_2O_5 molecule has six N—O σ bonds and two N—O π bonds, but has no N—N bonds and no O—O bonds. Draw eight resonance structures for N_2O_5, and assign formal charges to the atoms in each. Which resonance structures make the more important contributions to the resonance hybrid?

7.129 In the cyanate ion, OCN^-, carbon is the central atom.
(a) Draw as many resonance structures as you can for OCN^-, and assign formal charges to the atoms in each.
(b) Which resonance structure makes the greatest contribution to the resonance hybrid? Which makes the least contribution? Explain.
(c) Is OCN^- linear or bent? Explain.
(d) Which hybrid orbitals are used by the C atom, and how many π bonds does the C atom form?

7.130 Aspirin has the following connections among atoms. Complete the electron-dot structure for aspirin, tell how many σ bonds and how many π bonds the molecule contains, and tell the hybridization of each carbon atom.

Aspirin

7.131 The cation $[H-C-N-Xe-F]^+$ is entirely linear. Draw an electron-dot structure consistent with that geometry, and tell the hybridization of the C and N atoms.

7.132 At high temperatures, sulfur vapor is predominantly in the form of $S_2(g)$ molecules.
(a) Assuming that the molecular orbitals for third-row diatomic molecules are analogous to those for second-row molecules, construct an MO diagram for the valence orbitals of $S_2(g)$.
(b) Is S_2 likely to be paramagnetic or diamagnetic?
(c) What is the bond order of $S_2(g)$?

(d) When two electrons are added to S_2, the disulfide ion S_2^{2-} is formed. Is the bond length in S_2^{2-} likely to be shorter or longer than the bond length in S_2? Explain.

7.133 Carbon monoxide is produced by incomplete combustion of fossil fuels.

(a) Give the electron configuration for the valence molecular orbitals of CO. The orbitals have the same energy order as those of the N_2 molecule.

(b) Do you expect CO to be paramagnetic or diamagnetic?

(c) What is the bond order of CO? Does this match the bond order predicted by the electron-dot structure?

(d) CO can react with OH^- to form the formate ion, HCO_2^-. Draw an electron-dot structure for the formate ion, and give any resonance structures if appropriate.

7.134 Draw an electron-dot structure for each of the following substances, and predict the molecular geometry of every nonterminal atom.

(a) F_3S-S-F **(b)** $CH_3-C\equiv C-CO_2^-$

7.135 The ion I_5^- is shaped like a big "V." Draw an electron-dot structure consistent with this overall geometry.

MULTICONCEPT PROBLEMS

7.136 The neutral OH molecule has been implicated in certain ozone-destroying processes that take place in the upper atmosphere.

(a) Draw electron-dot structures for the OH molecule and the OH^- ion.

(b) Electron affinity can be defined for molecules just as it is defined for single atoms. Assuming that the electron added to OH is localized in a single atomic orbital on one atom, identify which atom is accepting the electron, and give the n and l quantum numbers of the atomic orbital.

(c) The electron affinity of OH is similar to but slightly more negative than that of O atoms. Explain.

7.137 Suppose that the Pauli exclusion principle were somehow changed to allow three electrons per orbital rather than two.

(a) Instead of an octet, how many outer-shell electrons would be needed for a noble-gas electron configuration?

(b) How many electrons would be shared in a covalent bond?

(c) Give the electron configuration, and draw an electron-dot structure for element X with $Z = 12$.

(d) Draw an electron-dot structure for the molecule X_2.

(e) Assuming that the molecular orbital energy diagram in Figure 7.17b is valid, tell the bond order for the X_2 molecule.

7.138 The dichromate ion, $Cr_2O_7^{2-}$, has neither Cr—Cr nor O—O bonds.

(a) Taking both $4s$ and $3d$ electrons into account, draw an electron-dot structure that minimizes the formal charges on the atoms.

(b) How many outer-shell electrons does each Cr atom have in your electron-dot structure? What is the likely geometry around the Cr atoms?

7.139 Just as individual bonds in a molecule are often polar, molecules as a whole are also often polar because of the net sum of individual bond polarities. There are three possible structures for substances with the formula $C_2H_2Cl_2$, two of which are polar overall and one of which is not.

(a) Draw the three possible structures for $C_2H_2Cl_2$, predict an overall shape for each, and explain how they differ.

(b) Which of the three structures is nonpolar, and which two are polar? Explain.

(c) Two of the three structures can be interconverted by a process called cis–trans isomerization, in which

rotation around the central carbon–carbon bond takes place when the molecules are irradiated with ultraviolet light. If light with a wavelength of approximately 200 nm is required for isomerization, how much energy in kJ/mol is involved?

(d) Sketch the orbitals involved in the central carbon–carbon bond, and explain why so much energy is necessary for bond rotation to occur.

7.140 Cyclooctatetraene dianion, $C_8H_8^{2-}$, is an organic ion with the structure shown. Considering only the π bonds and not the σ bonds, cyclooctatetraene dianion can be described by the following energy diagram of its π molecular orbitals:

Cyclooctatetraene dianion

Cyclooctatetraene dianion
pi (π) molecular orbitals

(a) What is the hybridization of the 8 carbon atoms?

(b) Three of the π molecular orbitals are bonding, three are antibonding, and two are *nonbonding*, meaning that they have the same energy level as isolated p orbitals. Which is which?

(c) Complete the MO energy diagram by assigning the appropriate numbers of p electrons to the various molecular orbitals, indicating the electrons using up/down arrows ($\uparrow\downarrow$).

(d) Based on your MO energy diagram, is the dianion paramagnetic or diamagnetic?

CHAPTER 8

Thermochemistry: Chemical Energy

Many chemical reactions occur for the same reason that water goes down this falls rather than up. Potential energy is lowered in both cases.

CONTENTS

Why do chemical reactions occur? Stated simply, the answer involves *stability*. For a reaction to take place spontaneously, the final products of the reaction must be more stable than the starting reactants.

But what is "stability," and what does it mean to say that one substance is more stable than another? The key factor in determining the stability of a substance is energy. Less stable substances have higher energy and are generally converted into more stable substances with lower energy. But what, in turn, does it mean for a substance to have higher or lower energy? We'll explore some different forms of energy in this chapter and look at the subject of **thermochemistry**, the absorption or release of heat energy that accompanies chemical reactions.

8.1   ENERGY AND ITS CONSERVATION

You might recall from Section 1.11 that energy is defined as the capacity to supply heat or do work. The fuel in your car, for instance, contains energy that is released on combustion and propels the car forward. You might also recall that energy is described as either *kinetic* or *potential*. Kinetic energy (E_K) is the energy of motion and is given by the equation

$$E_K = \frac{1}{2}mv^2 \quad \text{where } m = \text{mass and } v = \text{velocity}$$

Potential energy (E_P), by contrast, is stored energy—perhaps stored in a molecule because of reactions it can undergo.

Let's pursue the relationship between potential energy and kinetic energy a bit further. According to the **conservation of energy law**, energy can be neither created nor destroyed; it can only be converted from one form into another.

Conservation of Energy Law   Energy cannot be created or destroyed; it can only be converted from one form into another.

To take an example, think about a hydroelectric dam. The water sitting motionless in the reservoir behind the dam has potential energy because of its height above the outlet stream, but it has no kinetic energy because it isn't moving ($v = 0$). When the water falls through the penstocks of the dam, however, its height and potential energy decrease while its velocity and kinetic energy increase. The moving water then spins the turbine of a generator, converting its kinetic energy into electrical energy (**Figure 8.1**).

Remember...

Energy is the capacity to supply heat or do work and is classified as either **kinetic energy**—the energy of motion—or **potential energy**—stored energy not yet released. (Section 1.11)

At the top of the dam, the energy is potential (E_P).

As the **water falls through the penstock**, its velocity increases and its potential energy is converted into kinetic energy (E_K) that is used to spin a turbine and generate electricity.

Reservoir

Dam

Powerhouse
Generator

Inlet

Penstock

Turbine

Outlet

Figure 8.1
Conservation of energy. The total amount of energy contained by the water in the reservoir is constant.

The conversion of the kinetic energy in falling water into electricity illustrates several other important points about energy. One is that energy has many forms. Thermal energy, for example, seems different from the kinetic energy of falling water, yet is really quite similar. *Thermal energy* is just the kinetic energy of molecular motion, which we measure by finding the **temperature** of an object. An object has a low temperature and we perceive it as cold if its atoms or molecules are moving slowly. Conversely, an object has a high temperature and we perceive it as hot if its atoms or molecules are moving rapidly and are colliding forcefully with a thermometer or other measuring device.

Heat, in turn, is the amount of thermal energy transferred from one object to another as the result of a temperature difference between the two. Rapidly moving molecules in a hotter object collide with more slowly moving molecules in a colder object, transferring kinetic energy and causing the slower moving molecules to speed up.

Chemical energy is another kind of energy that seems different from that of the water in a reservoir, yet again is really quite similar. Chemical energy is a kind of potential energy in which chemical bonds act as the storage medium. Just as water releases its potential energy when it falls to a more stable position, chemicals can release their potential energy in the form of heat or light when they undergo reactions and form more stable products. We'll explore this topic shortly.

A second point illustrated by falling water involves the conservation of energy law. To keep track of all the energy involved, it's necessary to take into account the entire chain of events that ensue from the falling water: the sound of the crashing water, the heating of the rocks at the bottom of the dam, the driving of turbines and electrical generators, the transmission of electrical power, the appliances powered by the electricity, and so on. Carrying the process to its logical extreme, it's necessary to take the entire universe into account when keeping track of all the energy in the water because the energy lost in one form *always* shows up elsewhere in another form. So important is the conservation of energy law that it's also known as the **first law of thermodynamics**.

> **First Law of Thermodynamics**   Energy cannot be created or destroyed; it can only be converted from one form into another.

8.2   INTERNAL ENERGY AND STATE FUNCTIONS

When keeping track of the energy changes in a chemical reaction, it's often helpful to think of the reaction as being isolated from the world around it. The substances we focus on in an experiment—the starting reactants and the final products—are collectively called the **system**, while everything else—the reaction flask, the solvent, the room, the building, and so on—is called the **surroundings**. If the system could be truly isolated from its surroundings so that no energy transfer could occur between them, then the total **internal energy (E)** of the system, defined as the sum of all the kinetic and potential energies for every molecule or ion in the system, would be conserved and remain constant throughout the reaction. In fact, this assertion is just a restatement of the first law of thermodynamics:

> **First Law of Thermodynamics (Restated)**   The total internal energy E of an isolated system is constant.

In practice, of course, it's not possible to truly isolate a chemical reaction from its surroundings. In any real situation, the chemicals are in physical contact with the walls of a flask or container, and the container itself is in contact with the surrounding air or laboratory bench. What's important, however, is not that the system be isolated but that we be able to measure accurately any energy that enters the system from the surroundings or leaves the system and flows to the surroundings (**Figure 8.2**). That is, we must be able to measure any *change* in the internal energy of the

Figure 8.2
Energy changes in a chemical reaction.

The energy change is the difference between final and initial states.

$$\Delta E = E_{final} - E_{initial}$$

Surroundings

Energy flowing out of the system to the surroundings has a negative sign because $E_{final} < E_{initial}$.

The **system** is the mixture of reactants, and the *surroundings* are the flask, the solvent, the room, and the rest of the universe.

Energy flowing into the system from the surroundings has a positive sign because $E_{final} > E_{initial}$.

System

system, ΔE. The energy change ΔE represents the difference in internal energy between the final state of the system after reaction and the initial state of the system before reaction:

$$\Delta E = E_{final} - E_{initial}$$

By convention, energy changes are measured from the point of view of the system. Any energy that flows *from* the system *to* the surroundings has a negative sign because the system has lost it (that is, E_{final} is smaller than $E_{initial}$). Any energy that flows *to* the system *from* the surroundings has a positive sign because the system has gained it (E_{final} is larger than $E_{initial}$). If, for instance, we were to burn 1.00 mol of methane in the presence of 2.00 mol of oxygen, 802 kJ would be released as heat and transferred from the system to the surroundings. The system has 802 kJ less energy, so $\Delta E = -802$ kJ. This energy flow can be detected and measured by placing the reaction vessel in a water bath and noting the temperature rise of the bath during the reaction.

$$CH_4(g) + 2\,O_2(g) \longrightarrow CO_2(g) + 2\,H_2O(g) + 802\ kJ\ energy \qquad \Delta E = -802\ kJ$$

The methane combustion experiment tells us that the products of the reaction, $CO_2(g)$ and $2\,H_2O(g)$, have 802 kJ less internal energy than the reactants, $CH_4(g)$ and $2\,O_2(g)$, even though we don't know the exact values at the beginning ($E_{initial}$) and end (E_{final}) of the reaction. Note that the value $\Delta E = -802$ kJ for the reaction refers to the energy released when reactants are converted to products *in the molar amounts represented by coefficients in the balanced equation.* That is, 802 kJ is released when 1 mol of gaseous methane reacts with 2 mol of gaseous oxygen to give 1 mol of gaseous carbon dioxide and 2 mol of gaseous water vapor.

The internal energy of a system depends on many things: chemical identity, sample size, temperature, pressure, physical state (gas, liquid, or solid), and so forth. What the internal energy does not depend on is the system's past history. It doesn't matter what the system's temperature or physical state was an hour ago, and it doesn't matter how the chemicals were obtained. All that matters is the present condition of the system. Thus, internal energy is said to be a **state function**, one whose value depends only on the present state of the system. Pressure, volume, and temperature are other examples of state functions, but work and heat are not.

State Function   A function or property whose value depends only on the present state, or condition, of the system, not on the path used to arrive at that state.

We can illustrate the idea of a state function by imagining a cross-country trip, say from the Artichoke Capitol of the World (Castroville, California), to the Hub of the Universe (Boston, Massachusetts). You are the system, and your position is a state function because how you got to wherever you are is irrelevant. Because your position is a state function, the *change* in your position after you complete your travel (Castroville and Boston are about 2720 miles apart) is independent of the path you take, whether through North Dakota or Louisiana (**Figure 8.3**).

Figure 8.3
State functions. Because your position is a state function, the change in your position on going from Castroville, California, to Boston, Massachusetts, is independent of the path you take.

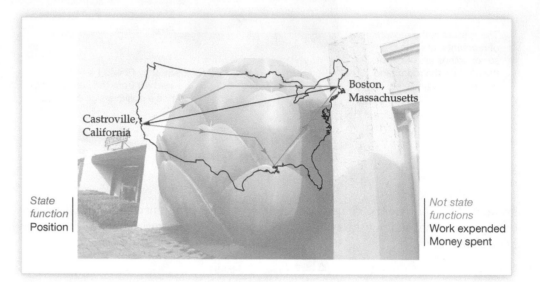

The cross-country trip shown in Figure 8.3 illustrates an important point about state functions: their reversibility. Imagine that, after traveling from Castroville to Boston, you turn around and go back. Because your final position is now identical to your initial position, the change in your position is zero. The overall change in any state function is zero when the system returns to its original condition. For a nonstate function, however, the overall change is not zero when the system returns to its original condition. Any work you do in making the trip, for instance, is not recovered when you return to your initial position, and any money or time you spend does not reappear.

▶ **PROBLEM 8.1** Which of the following are state functions, and which are not?
(a) The temperature of an ice cube
(b) The volume of an aerosol can
(c) The amount of time required for Paula Radcliffe to run her world-record marathon: 2:15:25

8.3 EXPANSION WORK

Just as energy comes in many forms, so too does *work*. In physics, **work (w)** is defined as the force (F) that produces the movement of an object times the distance moved (d):

$$\text{Work} = \text{Force} \times \text{Distance}$$
$$w = F \times d$$

When you run up stairs, for instance, your leg muscles provide a force sufficient to overcome gravity and lift you higher. When you swim, you provide a force sufficient to push water out of the way and pull yourself forward.

The most common type of work encountered in chemical systems is the *expansion work* (also called *pressure–volume*, or *PV, work*) done as the result of a volume change in the system. In the combustion reaction of propane (C_3H_8) with oxygen, for instance, the balanced equation says that 7 moles of products come from 6 moles of reactants:

▲ This runner going uphill is doing a lot of work to overcome gravity.

$$\underbrace{C_3H_8(g) \ + \ 5\,O_2(g)}_{\text{6 mol of gas}} \longrightarrow \underbrace{3\,CO_2(g) \ + \ 4\,H_2O(g)}_{\text{7 mol of gas}}$$

If the reaction takes place inside a container outfitted with a movable piston, the greater volume of gas in the product will force the piston outward against the pressure of the atmosphere (P), moving air molecules aside and thereby doing work (**Figure 8.4**).

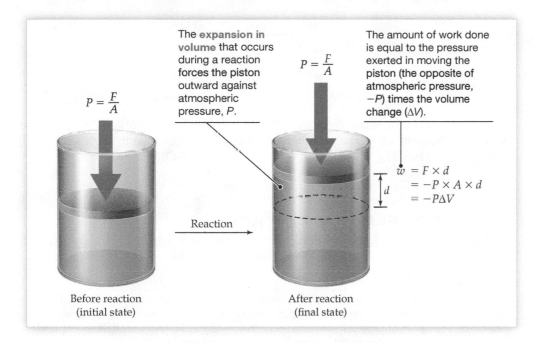

The **expansion in volume** that occurs during a reaction forces the piston outward against atmospheric pressure, P.

$P = \dfrac{F}{A}$

The amount of work done is equal to the pressure exerted in moving the piston (the opposite of atmospheric pressure, $-P$) times the volume change (ΔV).

$P = \dfrac{F}{A}$

$\begin{aligned} w &= F \times d \\ &= -P \times A \times d \\ &= -P\Delta V \end{aligned}$

Before reaction
(initial state)

Reaction

After reaction
(final state)

Figure 8.4
Expansion work in a chemical reaction.

A short calculation gives the exact amount of work done during the expansion. We know from physics that force (F) is area (A) times pressure (P). In Figure 8.4, the force that the expanding gas exerts is the area of the piston times the pressure that the gas exerts against the piston. This pressure is equal in magnitude but opposite in sign to the external atmospheric pressure that opposes the movement, so it has the value $-P$.

$$F = -P \times A \qquad \text{where } P \text{ is the external atmospheric pressure}$$

If the piston is pushed out a distance d, then the amount of work done is equal to force times distance, or pressure times area times distance:

$$w = F \times d = -P \times A \times d$$

This equation can be simplified by noticing that the area of the piston times the distance the piston moves is just the volume change in the system: $\Delta V = A \times d$. Thus, the amount of work done is equal to the pressure the gas exerts against the piston times the volume change, hence the name PV work:

A negative value ↘   ↙ A positive value

$$w \ = \ -P\Delta V \qquad\qquad \text{Work done during expansion}$$

What about the sign of the work done during the expansion? Because the work is done by the system to move air molecules aside as the piston rises, work energy must be leaving the system. Thus, the negative sign of the work in the preceding equation is consistent with the convention previously established for ΔE (Section 8.2), whereby we always adopt the point of view of the system. Any energy that flows out of the system has a negative sign because the system has lost it ($E_{\text{final}} < E_{\text{initial}}$).

If the pressure is given in the unit atmospheres (atm) and the volume change is given in liters, then the amount of work done has the unit liter atmosphere (L·atm), where 1 atm = 101×10^3 kg/(m·s^2). Thus, 1 L·atm = 101 J:

$$1\,\text{L}\cdot\text{atm} = (1\,\text{L})\left(\frac{10^{-3}\,\text{m}^3}{1\,\text{L}}\right)\left(101 \times 10^3\,\frac{\text{kg}}{\text{m}\cdot\text{s}^2}\right) = 101\,\frac{\text{kg}\cdot\text{m}^2}{\text{s}^2} = 101\,\text{J}$$

When a reaction takes place with a contraction in volume rather than an expansion, the ΔV term has a negative sign and the work has a positive sign. This is again consistent with adopting the point of view of the system because the system has now gained work energy $(E_{final} > E_{initial})$. An example is the industrial synthesis of ammonia by reaction of hydrogen with nitrogen. Four moles of gaseous reactants yield only 2 mol of gaseous products, so the volume of the system contracts and work is gained by the system.

$$3\,H_2(g) \;+\; N_2(g) \longrightarrow 2\,NH_3(g)$$

4 mol of gas   2 mol of gas

A positive value   A negative value

$$w = -P\Delta V \qquad\qquad \text{Work gained during contraction}$$

If there is no volume change, then $\Delta V = 0$ and there is no work. Such is the case for the combustion of methane, where 3 mol of gaseous reactants give 3 mol of gaseous products: $CH_4(g) + 2\,O_2(g) \longrightarrow CO_2(g) + 2\,H_2O(g)$

WORKED EXAMPLE 8.1

CALCULATING THE AMOUNT OF *PV* WORK

Calculate the work in kilojoules done during a reaction in which the volume expands from 12.0 L to 14.5 L against an external pressure of 5.0 atm.

STRATEGY

Expansion work done during a chemical reaction is calculated with the formula $w = -P\Delta V$, where P is the external pressure opposing the change in volume. In this instance, $P = 5.0$ atm and $\Delta V = (14.5 - 12.0)\,L = 2.5\,L$. Remember that an expanding system loses work energy, which thus has a negative sign.

SOLUTION

$$w = -(5.0\,\text{atm})(2.5\,\text{L}) = -12.5\,\text{L}\cdot\text{atm}$$

$$(-12.5\,\text{L}\cdot\text{atm})\left(101\,\frac{\text{J}}{\text{L}\cdot\text{atm}}\right) = -1.3 \times 10^3\,\text{J} = -1.3\,\text{kJ}$$

▶ **PROBLEM 8.2**   Calculate the work in kilojoules done during a synthesis of ammonia in which the volume contracts from 8.6 L to 4.3 L at a constant external pressure of 44 atm. In which direction does the work energy flow? What is the sign of the energy change?

CONCEPTUAL PROBLEM 8.3   How much work is done in kilojoules, and in which direction, as a result of the following reaction?

2.5 atm

2.5 atm

V = 2.0 L

V = 3.0 L

Reaction

8.4 ENERGY AND ENTHALPY

We've seen up to this point that a system can exchange energy with its surroundings either by transferring heat or by doing work. Using the symbol q to represent transferred heat and the formula $w = -P\Delta V$, we can represent the total change in internal energy of a system, ΔE, as

$$\Delta E = q + w = q - P\Delta V$$

where q has a positive sign if the system gains heat and a negative sign if the system loses heat. Rearranging the equation to solve for q gives the amount of heat transferred:

$$q = \Delta E + P\Delta V$$

Let's look at two ways in which a chemical reaction might be carried out. On the one hand, a reaction might be carried out in a closed container with a constant volume, so that $\Delta V = 0$. In such a case, no PV work can be done so the energy change in the system is due entirely to heat transfer. We indicate this heat transfer at constant volume by the symbol q_v.

$$q_v = \Delta E \qquad \text{At constant volume; } \Delta V = 0$$

▲ Chemical reactions are often carried out in open vessels at constant atmospheric pressure.

Alternatively, a reaction might be carried out in an open flask or other apparatus that keeps the pressure constant and allows the volume of the system to change freely. In such a case, $\Delta V \neq 0$ and the energy change in the system is due to both heat transfer and PV work. We indicate the heat transfer at constant pressure by the symbol q_p:

$$q_p = \Delta E + P\Delta V \qquad \text{At constant pressure}$$

Because reactions carried out at constant pressure in open containers are so common in chemistry, the heat change q_p for such a process is given a special symbol and is called the **heat of reaction**, or **enthalpy change (ΔH)**. The **enthalpy (H)** of a system is the name given to the quantity $E + PV$.

$$q_p = \Delta E + P\Delta V = \overset{\text{Enthalpy change}}{\Delta H}$$

Note that only the enthalpy *change* during a reaction is important. As with internal energy, enthalpy is a state function whose value depends only on the current state of the system, not on the path taken to arrive at that state. Thus, we don't need to know the exact value of the system's enthalpy before and after a reaction. We need to know only the difference between final and initial states:

$$\Delta H = H_{\text{final}} - H_{\text{initial}}$$
$$= H_{\text{products}} - H_{\text{reactants}}$$

How big a difference is there between $q_v = \Delta E$, the heat flow at constant volume, and $q_p = \Delta H$, the heat flow at constant pressure? Let's look again at the combustion reaction of propane, C_3H_8, with oxygen as an example. When the reaction is carried out in a closed container at constant volume, no PV work is possible so all the energy released is released as heat: $\Delta E = -2046$ kJ. When the same reaction is carried out in an open container at constant pressure, however, only 2044 kJ of heat is released ($\Delta H = -2044$ kJ). The difference, 2 kJ, is due to the small amount of expansion work done against the atmosphere as 6 mol of gaseous reactants are converted into 7 mol of gaseous products.

$$\underset{\text{Propane}}{C_3H_8(g)} + 5\,O_2(g) \longrightarrow 3\,CO_2(g) + 4\,H_2O(g) \qquad \begin{aligned} \Delta E &= -2046 \text{ kJ} \\ \Delta H &= -2044 \text{ kJ} \\ P\Delta V &= +2 \text{ kJ} \end{aligned}$$

That is:

$$\begin{bmatrix} q_v = & q_p & + & w \\ \Delta E = & \Delta H & - & P\Delta V \\ -2046 \text{ kJ} = & -2044 \text{ kJ} & - & (+2 \text{ kJ}) \end{bmatrix}$$

What is true of the propane + oxygen reaction is also true of most other reactions: The difference between ΔH and ΔE is usually small, so the two quantities are nearly equal. Of course, if no volume change occurs and no work is done, such as in the combustion of methane in which 3 mol of gaseous reactants give 3 mol of gaseous products, then ΔH and ΔE are the same:

$$CH_4(g) + 2\,O_2(g) \longrightarrow CO_2(g) + 2\,H_2O(g) \qquad \Delta E = \Delta H = -802 \text{ kJ}$$

CONCEPTUAL PROBLEM 8.4 The following reaction has $\Delta E = -186$ kJ/mol.

(a) Is the sign of $P\Delta V$ positive or negative? Explain.
(b) What is the sign and approximate magnitude of ΔH? Explain.

8.5 THE THERMODYNAMIC STANDARD STATE

The value of the enthalpy change ΔH reported for a reaction is the amount of heat released or absorbed when reactants are converted to products at the same temperature and pressure and in the molar amounts represented by coefficients in the balanced chemical equation. In the combustion reaction of propane discussed in the previous section, for instance, the reaction of 1 mol of propane gas with 5 mol of oxygen gas to give 3 mol of CO_2 gas and 4 mol of water vapor releases 2044 kJ. The actual amount of heat released in a specific reaction, however, depends on the actual amounts of reactants. Thus, reaction of 0.5000 mol of propane with 2.500 mol of O_2 releases 0.5000×2044 kJ = 1022 kJ.

Note that the physical states of reactants and products must be specified as solid (s), liquid (l), gaseous (g), or aqueous (aq) when enthalpy changes are reported. The enthalpy change for the reaction of propane with oxygen is $\Delta H = -2044$ kJ if water is produced as a gas but $\Delta H = -2220$ kJ if water is produced as a liquid.

$$C_3H_8(g) + 5\,O_2(g) \longrightarrow 3\,CO_2(g) + 4\,H_2O(g) \qquad \Delta H = -2044 \text{ kJ}$$
$$C_3H_8(g) + 5\,O_2(g) \longrightarrow 3\,CO_2(g) + 4\,H_2O(l) \qquad \Delta H = -2220 \text{ kJ}$$

The difference of 176 kJ between the values of ΔH for the two reactions arises because the conversion of liquid water to gaseous water requires energy. If liquid water is produced, ΔH is larger (more negative), but if gaseous water is produced, ΔH is smaller (less negative) because 44.0 kJ/mol is needed for the vaporization.

$$H_2O(l) \longrightarrow H_2O(g) \qquad \Delta H = 44.0 \text{ kJ}$$
$$\text{or} \quad 4\,H_2O(l) \longrightarrow 4\,H_2O(g) \qquad \Delta H = 176 \text{ kJ}$$

In addition to specifying the physical state of reactants and products when reporting an enthalpy change, it's also necessary to specify the pressure and temperature. To ensure that all measurements are reported in the same way so that different reactions can be compared, a set of conditions called the **thermodynamic standard state** has been defined.

Thermodynamic Standard State Most stable form of a substance at 1 atm pressure* and at a specified temperature, usually 25 °C; 1 M concentration for all substances in solution.

Measurements made under these standard conditions are indicated by addition of the superscript ° to the symbol of the quantity reported. Thus, an enthalpy change measured under standard conditions is called a **standard enthalpy of reaction** and is indicated by the symbol $\Delta H°$. The reaction of propane with oxygen, for example, might be written

$$C_3H_8(g) + 5\,O_2(g) \longrightarrow 3\,CO_2(g) + 4\,H_2O(g) \qquad \Delta H° = -2044 \text{ kJ}$$

WORKED EXAMPLE 8.2

CALCULATING ΔE FOR A REACTION

The reaction of nitrogen with hydrogen to make ammonia has $\Delta H° = -92.2$ kJ. What is the value of ΔE in kilojoules if the reaction is carried out at a constant pressure of 40.0 atm and the volume change is -1.12 L?

$$N_2(g) + 3\,H_2(g) \longrightarrow 2\,NH_3(g) \qquad \Delta H° = -92.2 \text{ kJ}$$

STRATEGY

We are given an enthalpy change ΔH, a volume change ΔV, and a pressure P and asked to find an energy change ΔE. Rearrange the equation $\Delta H = \Delta E + P\Delta V$ to the form $\Delta E = \Delta H - P\Delta V$ and substitute the appropriate values for ΔH, P, and ΔV:

SOLUTION

$$\Delta E = \Delta H - P\Delta V$$
$$\text{where} \quad \Delta H = -92.2 \text{ kJ}$$
$$P\Delta V = (40.0 \text{ atm})(-1.12 \text{ L}) = -44.8 \text{ L} \cdot \text{atm}$$
$$= (-44.8 \text{ L} \cdot \text{atm})\left(101 \frac{\text{J}}{\text{L} \cdot \text{atm}}\right) = -4520 \text{ J} = -4.52 \text{ kJ}$$
$$\Delta E = (-92.2 \text{ kJ}) - (-4.52 \text{ kJ}) = -87.7 \text{ kJ}$$

Note that ΔE is smaller (less negative) than ΔH for this reaction because the volume change is negative. The products have less volume than the reactants so a contraction occurs and a small amount of PV work is gained by the system.

▶ **PROBLEM 8.5** The reaction between hydrogen and oxygen to yield water vapor has $\Delta H° = -484$ kJ. How much PV work is done, and what is the value of ΔE in kilojoules for the reaction of 0.50 mol of H_2 with 0.25 mol of O_2 at atmospheric pressure if the volume change is -5.6 L?

$$2\,H_2(g) + O_2(g) \longrightarrow 2\,H_2O(g) \qquad \Delta H° = -484 \text{ kJ}$$

*The standard pressure, listed here and in most other books as 1 atmosphere (atm), has been redefined to be 1 *bar*, which is equal to 0.986 923 atm. The difference is small, however.

Trinitrotoluene

▶ **PROBLEM 8.6** The explosion of 2.00 mol of solid trinitrotoluene (TNT; $C_7H_5N_3O_6$) with a volume of approximately 274 mL produces gases with a volume of 448 L at room temperature and 1.0 atm pressure. How much *PV* work in kilojoules is done during the explosion?

$$2\,C_7H_5N_3O_6(s) \longrightarrow 12\,CO(g) + 5\,H_2(g) + 3\,N_2(g) + 2\,C(s)$$

8.6 ENTHALPIES OF PHYSICAL AND CHEMICAL CHANGE

Almost every change in a system involves either a gain or a loss of enthalpy. The change can be either physical, such as the melting of a solid to a liquid, or chemical, such as the burning of propane. Let's look at examples of both kinds.

Enthalpies of Physical Change

What would happen if you started with a block of ice at a low temperature, say −10 °C, and slowly increased its enthalpy by adding heat? The initial input of heat would cause the temperature of the ice to rise until it reached 0 °C. Additional heat would then cause the ice to melt without raising its temperature as the added energy is expended in overcoming the forces that hold H_2O molecules together in the ice crystal. The amount of heat necessary to melt a substance without changing its temperature is called the *enthalpy of fusion*, or *heat of fusion* (ΔH_{fusion}). For H_2O, $\Delta H_{fusion} = 6.01$ kJ/mol at 0 °C.

Once the ice has melted, further input of heat raises the temperature of the liquid water until it reaches 100 °C, and adding still more heat then causes the water to boil. Once again, energy is necessary to overcome the forces holding molecules together in the liquid, so the temperature does not rise again until all the liquid has been converted into vapor. The amount of heat required to vaporize a substance without changing its temperature is called the *enthalpy of vaporization*, or *heat of vaporization* (ΔH_{vap}). For H_2O, $\Delta H_{vap} = 40.7$ kJ/mol at 100 °C.

Another kind of physical change in addition to melting and boiling is **sublimation**, the direct conversion of a solid to a vapor without going through a liquid state. Solid CO_2 (dry ice), for example, changes directly from solid to vapor at atmospheric pressure without first melting to a liquid. Since enthalpy is a state function, the enthalpy change on going from solid to vapor must be constant regardless of the path taken. Thus, at a given temperature, a substance's *enthalpy of sublimation*, or *heat of sublimation* (ΔH_{subl}), equals the sum of the heat of fusion and heat of vaporization (**Figure 8.5**).

Figure 8.5

Enthalpy as a state function. Because enthalpy is a state function, the value of the enthalpy change from solid to vapor does not depend on the path taken between the two states.

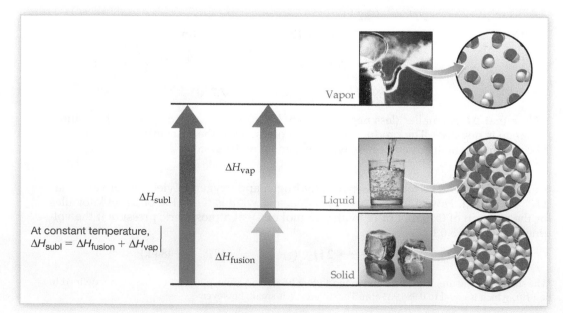

At constant temperature,
$\Delta H_{subl} = \Delta H_{fusion} + \Delta H_{vap}$

ΔH_{vap}

ΔH_{subl}

ΔH_{fusion}

Vapor

Liquid

Solid

Enthalpies of Chemical Change

We saw in Section 8.4 that an enthalpy change is often called a *heat of reaction* because it is a measure of the heat flow into or out of a system at constant pressure. If the products of a reaction have more enthalpy than the reactants, then heat has flowed into the system from the surroundings and ΔH has a positive sign. Such reactions are said to be **endothermic** (*endo* means "within," so heat flows in). The reaction of 1 mol of barium hydroxide octahydrate* with ammonium chloride, for example, absorbs 80.3 kJ from the surroundings ($\Delta H° = +80.3$ kJ). The surroundings, having lost heat, become cold—so cold, in fact, that the temperature drops below freezing (**Figure 8.6**).

$$Ba(OH)_2 \cdot 8\, H_2O(s) + 2\, NH_4Cl(s) \longrightarrow$$
$$BaCl_2(aq) + 2\, NH_3(aq) + 10\, H_2O(l) \qquad \Delta H° = +80.3 \text{ kJ}$$

If the products of a reaction have less enthalpy than the reactants, then heat has flowed out of the system to the surroundings and ΔH has a negative sign. Such reactions are said to be **exothermic** (*exo* means "out," so heat flows out). The so-called thermite reaction of aluminum with iron(III) oxide, for instance, releases so much heat ($\Delta H° = -852$ kJ), and the surroundings get so hot, that the reaction is used in construction work to weld iron.

$$2\, Al(s) + Fe_2O_3(s) \longrightarrow 2\, Fe(s) + Al_2O_3(s) \qquad \Delta H° = -852 \text{ kJ}$$

As noted previously, the value of $\Delta H°$ given for an equation assumes that the equation is balanced to represent the numbers of moles of reactants and products, that all substances are in their standard states, and that the physical state of each substance is as specified. The actual amount of heat released in a specific reaction depends on the amounts of reactants, as illustrated in Worked Example 8.3.

It should also be emphasized that $\Delta H°$ values refer to the reaction going in the direction written. For the reverse reaction, the sign of $\Delta H°$ must be changed. Because of the reversibility of state functions (Section 8.2), the enthalpy change for a reverse reaction is equal in magnitude but opposite in sign to that for the corresponding forward reaction. For example, the reaction of iron with aluminum oxide to yield aluminum and iron oxide (the reverse of the thermite reaction) would be endothermic and have $\Delta H° = +852$ kJ:

$$2\, Fe(s) + Al_2O_3(s) \longrightarrow 2\, Al(s) + Fe_2O_3(s) \qquad \Delta H° = +852 \text{ kJ}$$
$$2\, Al(s) + Fe_2O_3(s) \longrightarrow 2\, Fe(s) + Al_2O_3(s) \qquad \Delta H° = 852 \text{ kJ}$$

Figure 8.6
The endothermic reaction of barium hydroxide octahydrate with ammonium chloride. The reaction draws so much heat from the surroundings that the temperature falls below 0 °C.

WORKED EXAMPLE 8.3

CALCULATING THE AMOUNT OF HEAT RELEASED IN A REACTION

How much heat in kilojoules is evolved when 5.00 g of aluminum reacts with a stoichiometric amount of Fe_2O_3?

$$2\, Al(s) + Fe_2O_3(s) \longrightarrow 2\, Fe(s) + Al_2O_3(s) \qquad \Delta H° = -852 \text{ kJ}$$

STRATEGY

According to the balanced equation, 852 kJ of heat is evolved from the reaction of 2 mol of Al. To find out how much heat is evolved from the reaction of 5.00 g of Al, we have to find out how many moles of aluminum are in 5.00 g.

SOLUTION

The molar mass of Al is 26.98 g/mol, so 5.00 g of Al equals 0.185 mol:

$$5.00 \text{ g Al} \times \frac{1 \text{ mol Al}}{26.98 \text{ g Al}} = 0.185 \text{ mol Al}$$

continued on next page

---

*Barium hydroxide octahydrate, $Ba(OH)_2 \cdot 8\, H_2O$, is a crystalline compound that contains eight water molecules clustered around the barium ion. We'll learn more about hydrates in Section 18.14.

Because 2 mol of Al releases 852 kJ of heat, 0.185 mol of Al releases 78.8 kJ of heat:

$$0.185 \text{ mol Al} \times \frac{852 \text{ kJ}}{2 \text{ mol Al}} = 78.8 \text{ kJ}$$

BALLPARK CHECK

Since the molar mass of Al is about 27 g, 5 g of aluminum is roughly 0.2 mol, and the heat evolved is about (852 kJ/2 mol)(0.2 mol), or approximately 85 kJ.

▶ **PROBLEM 8.7** How much heat in kilojoules is evolved or absorbed in each of the following reactions?

   (a) Burning of 15.5 g of propane:

$$C_3H_8(g) + 5 O_2(g) \longrightarrow 3 CO_2(g) + 4 H_2O(l) \qquad \Delta H° = -2220 \text{ kJ}$$

   (b) Reaction of 4.88 g of barium hydroxide octahydrate with ammonium chloride:

$$Ba(OH)_2 \cdot 8 H_2O(s) + 2 NH_4Cl(s) \longrightarrow$$
$$BaCl_2(aq) + 2 NH_3(aq) + 10 H_2O(l) \qquad \Delta H° = +80.3 \text{ kJ}$$

▶ **PROBLEM 8.8** Nitromethane (CH_3NO_2), sometimes used as a fuel in drag racers, burns according to the following equation. How much heat is released by burning 100.0 g of nitromethane?

$$4 CH_3NO_2(l) + 7 O_2(g) \longrightarrow 4 CO_2(g) + 6 H_2O(g) + 4 NO_2(g) \qquad \Delta H° = -2441.6 \text{ kJ}$$

8.7 CALORIMETRY AND HEAT CAPACITY

The amount of heat transferred during a reaction can be measured with a device called a *calorimeter*, shown schematically in **Figure 8.7**. At its simplest, a calorimeter is just an insulated vessel with a stirrer, a thermometer, and a loose-fitting lid to keep the contents at atmospheric pressure. The reaction is carried out inside the vessel, and the heat evolved or absorbed is calculated from the temperature change. Because the pressure inside the calorimeter is constant (atmospheric pressure), the temperature measurement makes it possible to calculate the enthalpy change ΔH during a reaction.

Figure 8.7

A calorimeter for measuring the heat flow in a reaction at constant pressure (ΔH).

Thermometer

The reaction takes place inside an insulated vessel outfitted with a loose-fitting top, a thermometer, and a stirrer.

Stirrer

Insulated vessel

Reaction mixture

Measuring the **temperature change** that accompanies the reaction makes it possible to calculate ΔH.

A somewhat more complicated device called a *bomb calorimeter* is used to measure the heat released during a combustion reaction, or burning of a flammable substance. (More generally, a *combustion* reaction is any reaction that produces a flame.) The sample is placed in a small cup and sealed in an oxygen atmosphere inside a steel bomb that is itself placed in an insulated, water-filled container (**Figure 8.8**). The reactants are ignited electrically, and the evolved heat is calculated from the temperature change of the surrounding water. Since the reaction takes place at constant volume rather than constant pressure, the measurement provides a value for ΔE rather than ΔH.

The reaction is carried out inside a steel bomb, and the heat evolved is transferred to the surrounding water, where the **temperature rise** is measured.

Figure 8.8
A bomb calorimeter for measuring the heat evolved at constant volume (ΔE) in a combustion reaction.

How can the temperature change inside a calorimeter be used to calculate ΔH (or ΔE) for a reaction? When a calorimeter and its contents absorb a given amount of heat, the temperature rise that results depends on the calorimeter's *heat capacity*. **Heat capacity (C)** is the amount of heat required to raise the temperature of an object or substance by a given amount, a relationship that can be expressed by the equation

$$C = \frac{q}{\Delta T}$$

where q is the quantity of heat transferred and ΔT is the temperature change that results ($\Delta T = T_{final} - T_{initial}$).

The greater the heat capacity, the greater the amount of heat needed to produce a given temperature change. A bathtub full of water, for instance, has a greater heat capacity than a coffee cup full, and it therefore takes far more heat to warm the tubful than the cupful. The exact amount of heat absorbed is equal to the heat capacity times the temperature rise:

$$q = C \times \Delta T$$

Heat capacity is an **extensive property**, so its value depends on both the size of an object and its composition. To compare different substances, it's useful to define a quantity called the *specific heat capacity*, or simply **specific heat**, the amount of heat necessary to raise the temperature of 1 g of a substance by 1 °C. The amount of heat necessary to raise the temperature of a given object, then, is the specific heat times the mass of the object times the rise in temperature:

$$q = \text{Specific heat} \times \text{Mass of substance} \times \Delta T$$

Worked Example 8.5 shows how specific heats are used in calorimetry calculations.

Closely related to specific heat is the **molar heat capacity (C_m)**, defined as the amount of heat necessary to raise the temperature of 1 mol of a substance by 1 °C.

Remember...

Extensive properties, such as length and volume, have values that depend on the sample size. Intensive properties, such as temperature and melting point, have values that do not depend on the amount of the sample. (Section 1.4)

The amount of heat necessary to raise the temperature of a given number of moles of a substance is thus

$$q = C_m \times \text{Moles of substance} \times \Delta T$$

Values of specific heats and molar heat capacities for some common substances are given in Table 8.1. The values are temperature dependent, so the temperatures at which the measurements are taken must be specified.

TABLE 8.1   Specific Heats and Molar Heat Capacities for Some Common Substances at 25 °C

Substance	Specific Heat J/(g · °C)	Molar Heat Capacity J/(mol · °C)
Air (dry)	1.01	29.1
Aluminum	0.897	24.2
Copper	0.385	24.4
Gold	0.129	25.4
Iron	0.449	25.1
Mercury	0.140	28.0
NaCl	0.859	50.2
Water(s)*	2.03	36.6
Water(l)	4.179	75.3

*At −11 °C

As indicated in Table 8.1, the specific heat of liquid water is considerably higher than that of most other substances, so a large transfer of heat is necessary to either cool or warm a given amount of water. One consequence is that large lakes or other bodies of water tend to moderate the air temperature in surrounding areas. Another consequence is that the human body, which is about 60% water, is able to maintain a relatively steady internal temperature under changing outside conditions.

▲ Lake Chelan in the North Cascades of Washington State is the third deepest freshwater lake in the United States at 1486 ft. Such large masses of water moderate the temperature of the surroundings because of their high heat capacity.

WORKED EXAMPLE 8.4

CALCULATING A SPECIFIC HEAT

What is the specific heat of silicon if it takes 192 J to raise the temperature of 45.0 g of Si by 6.0 °C?

STRATEGY

To find a specific heat of a substance, calculate the amount of energy necessary to raise the temperature of 1 g of the substance by 1 °C.

SOLUTION

$$\text{Specific heat of Si} = \frac{192\,\text{J}}{(45.0\,\text{g})(6.0\,°\text{C})} = 0.71\,\text{J}/(\text{g} \cdot °\text{C})$$

WORKED EXAMPLE 8.5

CALCULATING ΔH IN A CALORIMETRY EXPERIMENT

Aqueous silver ion reacts with aqueous chloride ion to yield a white precipitate of solid silver chloride:

$$\text{Ag}^+(aq) + \text{Cl}^-(aq) \longrightarrow \text{AgCl}(s)$$

When 10.0 mL of 1.00 M $AgNO_3$ solution is added to 10.0 mL of 1.00 M NaCl solution at 25.0 °C in a calorimeter, a white precipitate of AgCl forms and the temperature of the aqueous mixture increases to 32.6 °C. Assuming that the specific heat of the aqueous mixture is 4.18 J/(g·°C), that the density of the mixture is 1.00 g/mL, and that the calorimeter itself absorbs a negligible amount of heat, calculate ΔH in kilojoules for the reaction.

STRATEGY

Because the temperature rises during the reaction, heat must be released and ΔH must be negative. The amount of heat evolved during the reaction is equal to the amount of heat absorbed by the mixture:

Heat evolved = Specific heat × Mass of mixture × Temperature change

Calculating the heat evolved on a per-mole basis then gives the enthalpy change ΔH.

SOLUTION

$$\text{Specific heat} = 4.18 \text{ J/(g·°C)}$$

$$\text{Mass} = (20.0 \text{ mL})\left(1.00 \frac{\text{g}}{\text{mL}}\right) = 20.0 \text{ g}$$

$$\text{Temperature change} = 32.6 \text{ °C} - 25.0 \text{ °C} = 7.6 \text{ °C}$$

$$\text{Heat evolved} = \left(4.18 \frac{\text{J}}{\text{g·°C}}\right)(20.0 \text{ g})(7.6 \text{ °C}) = 6.4 \times 10^2 \text{ J}$$

According to the balanced equation, the number of moles of AgCl produced equals the number of moles of Ag^+ (or Cl^-) reacted:

$$\text{Moles of } Ag^+ = (10.0 \text{ mL})\left(\frac{1.00 \text{ mol } Ag^+}{1000 \text{ mL}}\right) = 1.00 \times 10^{-2} \text{ mol } Ag^+$$

$$\text{Moles of AgCl} = 1.00 \times 10^{-2} \text{ mol AgCl}$$

$$\text{Heat evolved per mole of AgCl} = \frac{6.4 \times 10^2 \text{ J}}{1.00 \times 10^{-2} \text{ mol AgCl}} = 64 \text{ kJ/mol AgCl}$$

Therefore, $\Delta H = -64 \text{ kJ}$ (negative because heat is released)

▲ The reaction of aqueous $AgNO_3$ with aqueous NaCl to yield solid AgCl is an exothermic process.

▸ **PROBLEM 8.9**   Assuming that Coca Cola has the same specific heat as water [4.18 J/(g·°C)], calculate the amount of heat in kilojoules transferred when one can (about 350 g) is cooled from 25 °C to 3 °C.

▸ **PROBLEM 8.10**   What is the specific heat of lead if it takes 97.2 J to raise the temperature of a 75.0 g block by 10.0 °C?

▸ **PROBLEM 8.11**   When 25.0 mL of 1.0 M H_2SO_4 is added to 50.0 mL of 1.0 M NaOH at 25.0 °C in a calorimeter, the temperature of the aqueous solution increases to 33.9 °C. Assuming that the specific heat of the solution is 4.18 J/(g·°C), that its density is 1.00 g/mL, and that the calorimeter itself absorbs a negligible amount of heat, calculate ΔH in kilojoules for the reaction.

$$H_2SO_4(aq) + 2\,NaOH(aq) \longrightarrow 2\,H_2O(l) + Na_2SO_4(aq)$$

8.8   HESS'S LAW

Now that we've discussed in general terms the energy changes that occur during chemical reactions, let's look at a specific example in detail. In particular, let's look at the *Haber process*, the industrial method by which more than 120 million metric tons of ammonia is produced each year worldwide, primarily for use as fertilizer (1 metric ton = 1000 kg). The reaction of hydrogen with nitrogen to make ammonia is exothermic, with $\Delta H° = -92.2$ kJ.

$$3\,H_2(g) + N_2(g) \longrightarrow 2\,NH_3(g) \qquad \Delta H° = -92.2 \text{ kJ}$$

If we dig into the details of the reaction, we find that it's not as simple as it looks. In fact, the overall reaction occurs in a series of steps, with hydrazine (N_2H_4) produced at an intermediate stage:

$$2\,H_2(g) + N_2(g) \longrightarrow N_2H_4(g) \xrightarrow{\;H_2\;} 2\,NH_3(g)$$
$$\text{Hydrazine} \qquad\qquad \text{Ammonia}$$

The enthalpy change for the conversion of hydrazine to ammonia can be measured as $\Delta H° = -187.6$ kJ, but if we wanted to measure $\Delta H°$ for the formation of hydrazine from hydrogen and nitrogen, we would have difficulty because the reaction doesn't go cleanly. Some of the hydrazine is converted into ammonia and some of the starting nitrogen remains.

Fortunately, there's a way around the difficulty—a way that makes it possible to measure an energy change indirectly when a direct measurement can't be made. The trick is to realize that, because enthalpy is a state function, ΔH is the same no matter what path is taken between two states. Thus, the sum of the enthalpy changes for the individual steps in a sequence must equal the enthalpy change for the overall reaction, a statement known as **Hess's law**:

Hess's law   The overall enthalpy change for a reaction is equal to the sum the enthalpy changes for the individual steps in the reaction.

Reactants and products in the individual steps can be added and subtracted like algebraic quantities in determining the overall equation. In the synthesis of ammonia, for example, the sum of steps 1 and 2 is equal to the overall reaction. Thus, the sum of the enthalpy changes for steps 1 and 2 is equal to the enthalpy change for the overall reaction. With this knowledge, we can calculate the enthalpy change for step 1. **Figure 8.9** shows the situation pictorially, and Worked Examples 8.6 and 8.7 give additional examples of Hess's law calculations.

Step 1.	$2\,H_2(g) + N_2(g) \longrightarrow \cancel{N_2H_4(g)}$	$\Delta H°_1 = \;?$
Step 2.	$\cancel{N_2H_4(g)} + H_2(g) \longrightarrow 2\,NH_3(g)$	$\Delta H°_2 = -187.6$ kJ
Overall reaction	$3\,H_2(g) + N_2(g) \longrightarrow 2\,NH_3(g)$	$\Delta H°_{\text{reaction}} = \;-92.2$ kJ

Since $\Delta H°_1 + \Delta H°_2 = \Delta H°_{\text{reaction}}$

then $\Delta H°_1 = \Delta H°_{\text{reaction}} - \Delta H°_2$

$$= (-92.2 \text{ kJ}) - (-187.6 \text{ kJ}) = +95.4 \textbf{ kJ}$$

Figure 8.9
Enthalpy changes for steps in the synthesis of ammonia from nitrogen and hydrogen. If $\Delta H°$ values for step 2 and for the overall reaction are known, then $\Delta H°$ for step 1 can be calculated.

Intermediates $H_2 + N_2H_4$

(Step 1)
$\Delta H° = 95.4$ kJ

(Step 2)
$\Delta H° = -187.6$ kJ

Reactants $3\,H_2 + N_2$

(Overall)
$\Delta H° = -92.2$ kJ

Product $2\,NH_3$

The enthalpy change for the overall reaction equals the sum of the enthalpy changes for the individual steps 1 and 2, a statement known as Hess's law.

WORKED EXAMPLE 8.6

USING HESS'S LAW TO CALCULATE $\Delta H°$

Methane, the main constituent of natural gas, burns in oxygen to yield carbon dioxide and water:

$$CH_4(g) + 2\,O_2(g) \longrightarrow CO_2(g) + 2\,H_2O(l)$$

Use the following information to calculate $\Delta H°$ in kilojoules for the combustion of methane:

$$CH_4(g) + O_2(g) \longrightarrow CH_2O(g) + H_2O(g) \qquad \Delta H° = -275.6\ kJ$$
$$CH_2O(g) + O_2(g) \longrightarrow CO_2(g) + H_2O(g) \qquad \Delta H° = -526.7\ kJ$$
$$H_2O(l) \longrightarrow H_2O(g) \qquad\qquad\quad \Delta H° = \quad 44.0\ kJ$$

STRATEGY

It often takes some trial and error, but the idea is to combine the individual reactions so that their sum is the desired reaction. The important points are that:

- All the reactants [$CH_4(g)$ and $O_2(g)$] must appear on the left.
- All the products [$CO_2(g)$ and $H_2O(l)$] must appear on the right.
- All intermediate products [$CH_2O(g)$ and $H_2O(g)$] must occur on *both* the left and the right so that they cancel.
- A reaction written in the reverse of the direction given [$H_2O(g) \longrightarrow H_2O(l)$] must have the sign of its $\Delta H°$ reversed (Section 8.6).
- If a reaction is multiplied by a coefficient [$H_2O(g) \longrightarrow H_2O(l)$ is multiplied by 2], then $\Delta H°$ for the reaction must be multiplied by that same coefficient.

SOLUTION

$$CH_4(g) + O_2(g) \longrightarrow \cancel{CH_2O(g)} + \cancel{H_2O(g)} \qquad\qquad \Delta H° = -275.6\ kJ$$
$$\cancel{CH_2O(g)} + O_2(g) \longrightarrow CO_2(g) + \cancel{H_2O(g)} \qquad\qquad \Delta H° = -526.7\ kJ$$
$$2\,[\cancel{H_2O(g)} \longrightarrow H_2O(l)] \qquad 2\,[\Delta H° = -44.0\ kJ] = \quad -88.0\ kJ$$
$$\overline{CH_4(g) \longrightarrow 2\,O_2(g) \longrightarrow CO_2(g) + 2\,H_2O(l) \qquad\qquad\qquad \Delta H° = -890.3\ kJ}$$

WORKED EXAMPLE 8.7

USING HESS'S LAW TO CALCULATE $\Delta H°$

Water gas is the name for the mixture of CO and H_2 prepared by reaction of steam with carbon at 1000 °C:

$$C(s) + H_2O(g) \longrightarrow CO(g) + H_2(g)$$
$$\text{"Water gas"}$$

The hydrogen is then purified and used as a starting material for preparing ammonia. Use the following information to calculate $\Delta H°$ in kilojoules for the water-gas reaction:

$$C(s) + O_2(g) \longrightarrow CO_2(g) \qquad \Delta H° = -393.5\ kJ$$
$$2\,CO(g) + O_2(g) \longrightarrow 2\,CO_2(g) \qquad \Delta H° = -566.0\ kJ$$
$$2\,H_2(g) + O_2(g) \longrightarrow 2\,H_2O(g) \qquad \Delta H° = -483.6\ kJ$$

STRATEGY

As in Worked Example 8.6, the idea is to find a combination of the individual reactions whose sum is the desired reaction. In this instance, it's necessary to reverse the second and third steps and to multiply both by 1/2 to make the overall equation balance. In so doing, the signs of the enthalpy changes for those steps must be changed and multiplied by 1/2. Note that $CO_2(g)$ and $O_2(g)$ cancel because they appear on both the right and left sides of equations.

continued on next page

Methylene chloride

SOLUTION

$$C(s) + \cancel{O_2(g)} \longrightarrow \cancel{CO_2(g)} \qquad\qquad\qquad \Delta H° = -393.5 \text{ kJ}$$
$$1/2 \, [\cancel{2 CO_2(g)} \longrightarrow 2 CO(g) + \cancel{O_2(g)}] \qquad 1/2 \, [\Delta H° = 566.0 \text{ kJ}] = \quad 283.0 \text{ kJ}$$
$$1/2 \, [2 H_2O(g) \longrightarrow 2 H_2(g) + \cancel{O_2(g)}] \qquad 1/2 \, [\Delta H° = 483.6 \text{ kJ}] = \quad 241.8 \text{ kJ}$$

$$C(s) + H_2O(g) \longrightarrow CO(g) + H_2(g) \qquad\qquad \Delta H° = \quad 131.3 \text{ kJ}$$

The water-gas reaction is endothermic by 131.3 kJ.

▶ **PROBLEM 8.12**   The industrial degreasing solvent methylene chloride, CH_2Cl_2, is prepared from methane by reaction with chlorine:

$$CH_4(g) + 2 Cl_2(g) \longrightarrow CH_2Cl_2(g) + 2 HCl(g)$$

Use the following data to calculate $\Delta H°$ in kilojoules for the reaction:

$$CH_4(g) + Cl_2(g) \longrightarrow CH_3Cl(g) + HCl(g) \qquad \Delta H° = \; -98.3 \text{ kJ}$$
$$CH_3Cl(g) + Cl_2(g) \longrightarrow CH_2Cl_2(g) + HCl(g) \qquad \Delta H° = -104 \text{ kJ}$$

CONCEPTUAL PROBLEM 8.13   The reaction of A with B to give D proceeds in two steps and can be represented by the following Hess's law diagram.

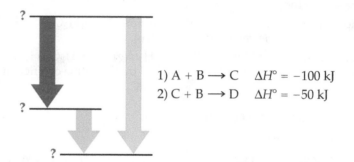

1) $A + B \longrightarrow C \quad \Delta H° = -100 \text{ kJ}$
2) $C + B \longrightarrow D \quad \Delta H° = -50 \text{ kJ}$

(a) What is the equation and $\Delta H°$ for the net reaction?
(b) Which arrow on the diagram corresponds to which step, and which arrow corresponds to the net reaction?
(c) The diagram shows three energy levels. The energies of which substances are represented by each?

CONCEPTUAL PROBLEM 8.14   Draw a Hess's law diagram similar to that in Problem 8.13 depicting the energy changes for the reaction in Problem 8.12.

8.9   STANDARD HEATS OF FORMATION

Where do the $\Delta H°$ values we've been using in previous sections come from? There are so many chemical reactions—hundreds of millions are known—that it's impossible to measure $\Delta H°$ for all of them. A better way is needed.

The most efficient way to manage with the smallest number of experimental measurements is to use what are called **standard heats of formation ($\Delta H°_f$)**.

⊲▭▭ **Standard Heat of Formation**   The enthalpy change $\Delta H°_f$ for the formation of 1 mol of a substance in its standard state from its constituent elements in their standard states.

Note several points about this definition. First, the "reaction" to form a substance from its constituent elements can be (and often is) hypothetical. We can't combine carbon and hydrogen in the laboratory to make methane, for instance, yet the heat of formation for methane is $\Delta H°_f = -74.8$ kJ/mol, which corresponds to the standard enthalpy change for the hypothetical reaction

$$C(s) + 2\,H_2(g) \longrightarrow CH_4(g) \qquad \Delta H° = -74.8 \text{ kJ}$$

Second, each substance in the reaction must be in its most stable, standard form at 1 atm pressure and the specified temperature (usually 25 °C). Carbon, for instance, is most stable as solid graphite rather than as diamond under these conditions, and hydrogen is most stable as gaseous H_2 molecules rather than as H atoms. Table 8.2 gives standard heats of formation for some common substances, and Appendix B gives a more detailed list.

TABLE 8.2 Standard Heats of Formation for Some Common Substances at 25 °C

Substance	Formula	$\Delta H°_f$ (kJ/mol)	Substance	Formula	$\Delta H°_f$ (kJ/mol)
Acetylene	$C_2H_2(g)$	227.4	Hydrogen chloride	$HCl(g)$	−92.3
Ammonia	$NH_3(g)$	−46.1	Iron(III) oxide	$Fe_2O_3(s)$	−824.2
Carbon dioxide	$CO_2(g)$	−393.5	Magnesium carbonate	$MgCO_3(s)$	−1095.8
Carbon monoxide	$CO(g)$	−110.5	Methane	$CH_4(g)$	−74.8
Ethanol	$C_2H_5OH(l)$	−277.7	Nitric oxide	$NO(g)$	91.3
Ethylene	$C_2H_4(g)$	52.3	Water (g)	$H_2O(g)$	−241.8
Glucose	$C_6H_{12}O_6(s)$	−1273.3	Water (l)	$H_2O(l)$	−285.8

No elements are listed in Table 8.2 because, by definition, the most stable form of any element in its standard state has $\Delta H°_f = 0$ kJ; that is, the enthalpy change for the formation of an element from itself is zero. Defining $\Delta H°_f$ as zero for all elements thus establishes a thermochemical "sea level," or reference point, from which other enthalpy changes are measured.

How can standard heats of formation be used for thermochemical calculations? The standard enthalpy change for any chemical reaction is found by subtracting the sum of the heats of formation of all reactants from the sum of the heats of formation of all products, with each heat of formation multiplied by the coefficient of that substance in the balanced equation.

$$\Delta H°_{\text{reaction}} = \Delta H°_f \,(\text{Products}) - \Delta H°_f \,(\text{Reactants})$$

To find $\Delta H°$ for the reaction

$$a\,A + b\,B + \cdots \longrightarrow c\,C + d\,D + \cdots$$

Subtract the sum of the heats of formation for these reactants . . .	. . . from the sum of the heats of formation for these products.

$$\Delta H°_{\text{reaction}} = [c\,\Delta H°_f(C) + d\,\Delta H°_f(D) + \cdots] - [a\,\Delta H°_f(A) + b\,\Delta H°_f(B) + \cdots]$$

As an example, let's calculate $\Delta H°$ for the fermentation of glucose to make ethyl alcohol (ethanol), the reaction that occurs during the production of alcoholic beverages:

$$C_6H_{12}O_6(s) \longrightarrow 2\,C_2H_5OH(l) + 2\,CO_2(g) \qquad \Delta H° = ?$$

Using the data in Table 8.2 gives the following answer:

$\Delta H° = [2\,\Delta H°_f\,(\text{Ethanol}) + 2\,\Delta H°_f\,(CO_2)] - [\Delta H°_f\,(\text{Glucose})]$

$\quad = (2\text{ mol})(-277.7\text{ kJ/mol}) + (2\text{ mol})(-393.5\text{ kJ/mol}) - (1\text{ mol})(-1273.3\text{ kJ/mol})$

$\quad = -69.1$ kJ

The fermentation reaction is exothermic by 69.1 kJ.

▲ Fermentation of the sugar from grapes yields the ethyl alcohol in wine.

Why does this calculation "work"? It works because enthalpy is a state function and the calculation is really just an application of Hess's law. That is, the sum of the individual equations corresponding to the heat of formation for each substance in the reaction equals the enthalpy change for the overall reaction:

(1) $C_6H_{12}O_6(s) \longrightarrow 6\,\cancel{C}(s) + 6\,\cancel{H_2}(g) + 3\,\cancel{O_2}(g)$ $\hspace{2cm} -\Delta H°_f = +1273.3 \text{ kJ}$

(2) $2\,[2\,\cancel{C}(s) + 3\,\cancel{H_2}(g) + 1/2\,\cancel{O_2}(g) \longrightarrow C_2H_5OH(l)]$ $\hspace{0.3cm} 2\,[\Delta H°_f = -277.7 \text{ kJ}] = -555.4 \text{ kJ}$

(3) $2\,[\cancel{C}(s) + \cancel{O_2}(g) \longrightarrow CO_2(g)]$ $\hspace{2.2cm} 2\,[\Delta H°_f = -393.5 \text{ kJ}] = -787.0 \text{ kJ}$

Net $C_6H_{12}O_6(s) \longrightarrow 2\,C_2H_5OH(l) + 2\,CO_2(g)$ $\hspace{2cm} \Delta H° = -69.1 \text{ kJ}$

Note that reaction (1) represents the formation of glucose from its elements written in reverse, so the sign of $\Delta H°_f$ is reversed. Note also that reactions (2) and (3), which represent the formation of ethyl alcohol and carbon dioxide, respectively, are multiplied by 2 to arrive at the balanced equation for the overall reaction.

When we use heats of formation to calculate standard reaction enthalpies, what we're really doing is referencing the enthalpies of both products and reactants to the same point: their constituent elements. By thus referencing product and reactant enthalpies to the same point, they are referenced to each other and the difference between them is the reaction enthalpy (**Figure 8.10**). Worked Examples 8.8 and 8.9 further illustrate how to use standard heats of formation.

Figure 8.10

The standard reaction enthalpy, $\Delta H°$, for the generalized reaction A → B. The value of $\Delta H°$ for the reaction is the difference between the standard heats of formation of product B and reactant A.

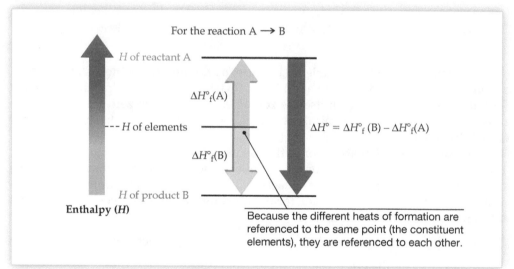

For the reaction A → B

H of reactant A

$\Delta H°_f(A)$

H of elements

$\Delta H° = \Delta H°_f(B) - \Delta H°_f(A)$

$\Delta H°_f(B)$

H of product B

Enthalpy (H)

Because the different heats of formation are referenced to the same point (the constituent elements), they are referenced to each other.

WORKED EXAMPLE 8.8

USING STANDARD HEATS OF FORMATION TO CALCULATE $\Delta H°$

Calculate $\Delta H°$ in kilojoules for the synthesis of lime (CaO) from limestone ($CaCO_3$), the key step in the manufacture of cement.

$$CaCO_3(s) \longrightarrow CaO(s) + CO_2(g) \quad \Delta H°_f[CaCO_3(s)] = -1207.6 \text{ kJ/mol}$$
$$\Delta H°_f[CaO(s)] = -634.9 \text{ kJ/mol}$$
$$\Delta H°_f[CO_2(g)] = -393.5 \text{ kJ/mol}$$

STRATEGY

Subtract the heat of formation of the reactant from the sum of the heats of formation of the products.

SOLUTION

$$\Delta H° = [\Delta H°_f(CaO) + \Delta H°_f(CO_2)] - [\Delta H°_f(CaCO_3)]$$
$$= (1 \text{ mol})(-634.9 \text{ kJ/mol}) + (1 \text{ mol})(-393.5 \text{ kJ/mol}) - (1 \text{ mol})(-1207.6 \text{ kJ/mol})$$
$$= 179.2 \text{ kJ}$$

The reaction is endothermic by 179.2 kJ.

WORKED EXAMPLE 8.9

USING STANDARD HEATS OF FORMATION TO CALCULATE $\Delta H°$

Oxyacetylene welding torches burn acetylene gas, $C_2H_2(g)$. Use the information in Table 8.2 to calculate $\Delta H°$ in kilojoules for the combustion reaction of acetylene to yield $CO_2(g)$ and $H_2O(g)$.

STRATEGY

Write the balanced equation, look up the appropriate heats of formation for each reactant and product in Table 8.2, and then carry out the calculation, making sure to multiply each $\Delta H°_f$ by the coefficient given in the balanced equation. Remember also that $\Delta H°_f (O_2) = 0$ kJ/mol.

SOLUTION

The balanced equation is

$$2\,C_2H_2(g) + 5\,O_2(g) \longrightarrow 4\,CO_2(g) + 2\,H_2O(g)$$

The necessary heats of formation are

$$\Delta H°_f\,[C_2H_2(g)] = 227.4\text{ kJ/mol} \qquad \Delta H°_f\,[H_2O(g)] = -241.8\text{ kJ/mol}$$

$$\Delta H°_f\,[CO_2(g)] = -393.5\text{ kJ/mol}$$

The standard enthalpy change for the reaction is

$$\Delta H° = [4\,\Delta H°_f\,(CO_2)] + 2\,\Delta H°_f\,(H_2O)] - [2\,\Delta H°_f\,(C_2H_2)]$$

$$= (4\text{ mol})(-393.5\text{ kJ/mol}) + (2\text{ mol})(-241.8\text{ kJ/mol}) - (2\text{ mol})(227.4\text{ kJ/mol})$$

$$= -2512.4\text{ kJ}$$

▲ Acetylene burns at a high temperature, making the reaction useful for cutting and welding iron.

▶ **PROBLEM 8.15** Use the information in Table 8.2 to calculate $\Delta H°$ in kilojoules for the reaction of ammonia with O_2 to yield nitric oxide (NO) and $H_2O(g)$, a step in the Ostwald process for the commercial production of nitric acid.

▶ **PROBLEM 8.16** Use the information in Table 8.2 to calculate $\Delta H°$ in kilojoules for the photosynthesis of glucose ($C_6H_{12}O_6$) and O_2 from CO_2 and liquid H_2O, a reaction carried out by all green plants.

8.10 BOND DISSOCIATION ENERGIES

The procedure described in the previous section for determining heats of reaction from heats of formation is extremely useful, but it still presents a problem. To use the method, it's necessary to know $\Delta H°_f$ for every substance in a reaction. This implies, in turn, that vast numbers of measurements are needed because there are over 40 million known chemical compounds. In practice, though, only a few thousand $\Delta H°_f$ values have been determined.

For those reactions where insufficient $\Delta H°_f$ data are available to allow an exact calculation of $\Delta H°$, it's often possible to estimate $\Delta H°$ by using the average **bond dissociation energies (D)** discussed previously in Section 7.2. Although we didn't identify it as such at the time, a bond dissociation energy is really just a standard enthalpy change for the corresponding bond-breaking reaction.

For the reaction $X-Y \longrightarrow X + Y$ $\Delta H° = D = $ Bond dissociation energy

When we say, for example, that the bond dissociation energy of Cl_2 is 243 kJ/mol, we mean that the standard enthalpy change for the reaction $Cl_2(g) \longrightarrow 2\,Cl(g)$ is $\Delta H° = 243$ kJ. Bond dissociation energies are always positive because energy must always be put into bonds to break them.

Remember...

Bond dissociation energy is the amount of energy that must be supplied to break a chemical bond in an isolated molecule in the gaseous state and is thus the amount of energy released when the bond forms. (Section 7.2)

Applying Hess's law, we can calculate an approximate enthalpy change for any reaction by subtracting the sum of the bond dissociation energies in the products from the sum of the bond dissociation energies in the reactants:

$$\Delta H° = D(\text{Reactant bonds}) - D(\text{Product bonds})$$

In the reaction of H_2 with Cl_2 to yield HCl, for example, the reactants have one Cl—Cl bond and one H—H bond, while the product has two H—Cl bonds.

$$H_2(g) + Cl_2(g) \longrightarrow 2\,HCl(g)$$

According to the data in Table 7.1 on page 219, the bond dissociation energy of Cl_2 is 243 kJ/mol, that of H_2 is 436 kJ/mol, and that of HCl is 432 kJ/mol. We can thus calculate an approximate standard enthalpy change for the reaction.

$$\begin{aligned}
\Delta H° &= D(\text{Reactant bonds}) - D(\text{Product bonds}) \\
&= (D_{\text{Cl—Cl}} + D_{\text{H—H}}) - (2\,D_{\text{H—Cl}}) \\
&= [(1\text{ mol})(243\text{ kJ/mol}) + (1\text{ mol})(436\text{ kJ/mol})] - (2\text{ mol})(432\text{ kJ/mol}) \\
&= -185\text{ kJ}
\end{aligned}$$

The reaction is exothermic by approximately 185 kJ.

WORKED EXAMPLE 8.10

USING BOND DISSOCIATION ENERGIES TO CALCULATE $\Delta H°$

Use the data in Table 7.1 on page 219 to find an approximate $\Delta H°$ in kilojoules for the industrial synthesis of chloroform by reaction of methane with Cl_2.

$$CH_4(g) + 3\,Cl_2(g) \longrightarrow CHCl_3(g) + 3\,HCl(g)$$

STRATEGY

Identify all the bonds in the reactants and products, and look up the appropriate bond dissociation energies in Table 7.1. Then subtract the sum of the bond dissociation energies in the products from the sum of the bond dissociation energies in the reactants to find the enthalpy change for the reaction.

SOLUTION

The reactants have four C—H bonds and three Cl—Cl bonds; the products have one C—H bond, three C—Cl bonds, and three H—Cl bonds. The bond dissociation energies from Table 7.1 are:

C—H	D = 410 kJ/mol	Cl—Cl	D = 243 kJ/mol
C—Cl	D = 330 kJ/mol	H—Cl	D = 432 kJ/mol

Subtracting the product bond dissociation energies from the reactant bond dissociation energies gives the enthalpy change for the reaction:

$$\begin{aligned}
\Delta H° &= [3\,D_{\text{Cl—Cl}} + 4\,D_{\text{C—H}}] - [D_{\text{C—H}} + 3\,D_{\text{H—Cl}} + 3\,D_{\text{C—Cl}}] \\
&= [(3\text{ mol})(243\text{ kJ/mol}) + (4\text{ mol})(410\text{ kJ/mol})] - [(1\text{ mol})(410\text{ kJ/mol}) \\
&\qquad\qquad\qquad\qquad\qquad + (3\text{ mol})(432\text{ kJ/mol}) + (3\text{ mol})(330\text{ kJ/mol})] \\
&= -327\text{ kJ}
\end{aligned}$$

The reaction is exothermic by approximately 330 kJ.

▶ **PROBLEM 8.17** Use the data in Table 7.1 on page 219 to calculate an approximate $\Delta H°$ in kilojoules for the industrial synthesis of ethyl alcohol from ethylene: $C_2H_4(g) + H_2O(g) \longrightarrow C_2H_5OH(g)$.

▶ **PROBLEM 8.18** Use the data in Table 7.1 to calculate an approximate $\Delta H°$ in kilojoules for the synthesis of hydrazine from ammonia: $2\,NH_3(g) + Cl_2(g) \longrightarrow N_2H_4(g) + 2\,HCl(g)$.

Ethyl alcohol

8.11 FOSSIL FUELS, FUEL EFFICIENCY, AND HEATS OF COMBUSTION

Surely the most familiar of all exothermic reactions is the one that takes place every time you turn up a thermostat, drive a car, or light a match: the burning of a carbon-based fuel by reaction with oxygen to yield H_2O, CO_2, and heat. The amount of energy released on burning a substance is called its **heat of combustion**, or *combustion enthalpy*, $\Delta H°_c$, and is simply the standard enthalpy change for the reaction of 1 mol of the substance with oxygen. Hydrogen, for instance, has $\Delta H°_c = -285.8$ kJ/mol, and methane has $\Delta H°_c = -890.3$ kJ/mol. Note that the H_2O product in giving heats of combustion is $H_2O(l)$ rather than $H_2O(g)$.

$$H_2(g) + 1/2\,O_2(g) \longrightarrow H_2O(l) \qquad\qquad \Delta H°_c = -285.8 \text{ kJ/mol}$$
$$CH_4(g) + 2\,O_2(g) \longrightarrow CO_2(g) + 2\,H_2O(l) \quad \Delta H°_c = -890.3 \text{ kJ/mol}$$

To compare the efficiency of different fuels, it's more useful to calculate combustion enthalpies per gram or per milliliter of substance rather than per mole (Table 8.3). For applications where weight is important, as in rocket engines, hydrogen is ideal because its combustion enthalpy per gram is the highest of any known fuel. For applications where volume is important, as in automobiles, a mixture of *hydrocarbons*—compounds of carbon and hydrogen—such as those in gasoline is most efficient because hydrocarbon combustion enthalpies per milliliter are relatively high. Octane and toluene are representative examples.

TABLE 8.3 Thermochemical Properties of Some Fuels

Fuel	Combustion Enthalpy		
	kJ/mol	kJ/g	kJ/mL
Hydrogen, $H_2(l)$	−285.8	−141.8	−9.9*
Ethanol, $C_2H_5OH(l)$	−1366.8	−29.7	−23.4
Graphite, $C(s)$	−393.5	−32.8	−73.8
Methane, $CH_4(g)$	−890.3	−55.5	−30.8*
Methanol, $CH_3OH(l)$	−725.9	−22.7	−17.9
Octane, $C_8H_{18}(l)$	−5470	−47.9	−33.6
Toluene, $C_7H_8(l)$	−3910	−42.3	−36.7

*Calculated for the compressed liquid at 0 °C

With the exception of hydrogen, all common fuels are organic compounds, whose energy is derived ultimately from the sun through the photosynthesis of carbohydrates in green plants. Although the details are complex, the net result of the photosynthesis reaction is the conversion of carbon dioxide and water into glucose, $C_6H_{12}O_6$, plus oxygen. Glucose, once formed, is converted into cellulose and starch, which in turn act as structural materials for plants and as food sources for animals. The conversion is highly endothermic and therefore requires a large input of solar energy. It has been estimated that the total annual amount of solar energy absorbed by the Earth's vegetation is approximately 10^{19} kJ, an amount sufficient to synthesize 5×10^{14} kg of glucose per year.

$$6\,CO_2(g) + 6\,H_2O(l) \longrightarrow C_6H_{12}O_6(s) + 6\,O_2(g) \qquad \Delta H° = 2803 \text{ kJ}$$

The fossil fuels we use most—coal, petroleum, and natural gas—are derived from the decayed remains of organisms from previous geologic eras. Both coal and petroleum are enormously complex mixtures of compounds. Coal is primarily of vegetable origin, and many of the compounds it contains are structurally similar to graphite (pure carbon). Petroleum is a viscous liquid mixture of hydrocarbons that are primarily of marine origin, and natural gas is primarily methane, CH_4.

▲ Much coal lies near the surface of the Earth and is obtained by strip mining.

Coal is burned just as it comes from the mine, but petroleum must be *refined* before use. Refining begins with *distillation*, the separation of crude liquid oil into fractions on the basis of their boiling points (bp). So-called straight-run gasoline (bp 30–200 °C) consists of compounds with 5–11 carbon atoms per molecule; kerosene (bp 175–300 °C) contains compounds in the C_{11}–C_{14} range; gas oil (bp 275–400 °C) contains C_{14}–C_{25} substances; and lubricating oils contain whatever remaining compounds will distill. Left over is a tarry residue of asphalt (**Figure 8.11**).

Figure 8.11
The products of petroleum refining.

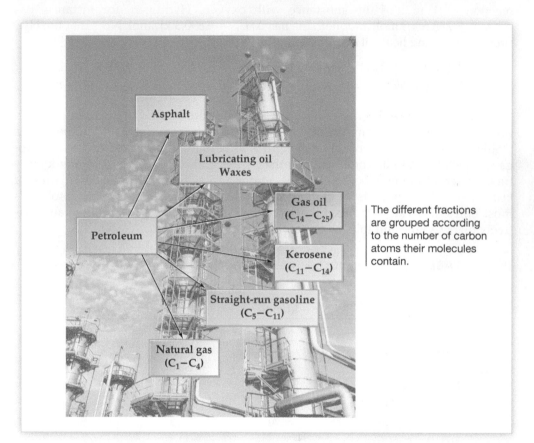

The different fractions are grouped according to the number of carbon atoms their molecules contain.

As the world's petroleum deposits become more scarce, other sources of energy will have to be found to replace them. Hydrogen, although it burns cleanly and is relatively nonpolluting, has numerous drawbacks: low availability, difficulty in transport and storage, and low combustion enthalpy per milliliter, to name a few. Ethanol and methanol look like potential choices for alternative fuels because both can be produced relatively cheaply and have reasonable combustion enthalpies. At present, ethanol is produced largely by fermentation of corn or cane sugar, but methods are being developed to produce it from waste wood by the breakdown of cellulose to glucose and subsequent fermentation. Methanol is produced directly from natural gas in a two-step process:

$$CH_4(g) + H_2O(g) \longrightarrow CO(g) + 3\,H_2(g)$$
$$CO(g) + 2\,H_2(g) \longrightarrow CH_3OH(l)$$

Butane

▶ **PROBLEM 8.19**   Liquid butane (C_4H_{10}), the fuel used in many disposable lighters, has $\Delta H°_f = -147.5$ kJ/mol and a density of 0.579 g/mL. Write a balanced equation for the combustion of butane, and use Hess's law to calculate the enthalpy of combustion in kJ/mol, kJ/g, and kJ/mL.

8.12   AN INTRODUCTION TO ENTROPY

We said in the introduction to this chapter that chemical reactions (and physical processes) occur when the final state is more stable than the initial state. Because less stable substances generally have higher internal energy and are converted into more stable substances with lower internal energy, energy is generally released in chemical reactions. At the same time, though, we've seen that some reactions and processes occur even though they absorb rather than release energy. The endothermic reaction of barium hydroxide octahydrate with ammonium chloride shown previously in Figure 8.6, for example, absorbs 80.3 kJ of heat ($\Delta H° = +80.3$ kJ) and leaves the surroundings so cold that the temperature drops below 0 °C.

$$Ba(OH)_2 \cdot 8\,H_2O(s) + 2\,NH_4Cl(s) \longrightarrow BaCl_2(aq) + 2\,NH_3(aq) + 10\,H_2O(l)$$
$$\Delta H° = +80.3 \text{ kJ}$$

An example of a physical process that takes place spontaneously yet absorbs energy takes place every time an ice cube melts. At a temperature of 0 °C, ice spontaneously absorbs heat from the surroundings to turn from solid into liquid water.

What's going on? Because the reaction of barium hydroxide octahydrate with ammonium chloride and the melting ice cube absorb heat yet still take place spontaneously, there must be some other factor in addition to energy that determines whether a reaction or process will occur. We'll take only a brief look at this additional factor now and return for a more in-depth study in Chapter 16.

Before exploring the situation further, it's important to understand what the word *spontaneous* means in chemistry, for it's not quite the same as in everyday language. In chemistry, a **spontaneous process** is one that, once started, proceeds on its own without a continuous external influence. The change need not happen quickly, like a spring uncoiling or a sled going downhill. It can also happen slowly, like the gradual rusting away of an iron bridge or abandoned car. A *nonspontaneous* process, by contrast, takes place only in the presence of a continuous external influence. Energy must be continuously expended to re-coil a spring or to push a sled uphill. When the external influence stops, the process also stops.

What do the reaction of barium hydroxide octahydrate and the melting of an ice cube have in common that allows the two processes to take place spontaneously even though they absorb heat? The common feature of these and all other processes that absorb heat yet occur spontaneously is an increase in the amount of molecular randomness of the system. The eight water molecules rigidly held in the $Ba(OH)_2 \cdot 8\,H_2O$ crystal break loose and become free to move about randomly in the aqueous liquid product. Similarly, the rigidly held H_2O molecules in the ice lose their crystalline ordering and move around freely in liquid water.

The amount of molecular randomness in a system is called the system's **entropy (S)**. Entropy has the units J/K (not kJ/K) and is a quantity that can be determined for pure substances, as we'll see in Section 16.5. The larger the value of S, the greater the molecular randomness of the particles in the system. Gases, for example, have more randomness and higher entropy than liquids, and liquids have more randomness and higher entropy than solids (**Figure 8.12**).

A change in entropy is represented as $\Delta S = S_{\text{final}} - S_{\text{initial}}$. When randomness increases, as it does when barium hydroxide octahydrate reacts or ice melts, ΔS has a positive value because $S_{\text{final}} > S_{\text{initial}}$. The reaction of $Ba(OH)_2 \cdot 8\,H_2O(s)$ with $NH_4Cl(s)$ has $\Delta S° = +428$ J/K, and the melting of ice has $\Delta S° = +22.0$ J/(K·mol). When randomness decreases, ΔS is negative because $S_{\text{final}} < S_{\text{initial}}$. The freezing of water, for example, has $\Delta S° = -22.0$ J/(K·mol). (As with $\Delta H°$, the superscript ° is used in $\Delta S°$ to refer to the standard entropy change in a reaction where products and reactants are in their standard states.)

Thus, two factors determine the spontaneity of a chemical or physical change in a system: a release or absorption of heat (ΔH) and an increase or decrease in molecular

▲ Sledding downhill is a spontaneous process that, once started, continues on its own. Dragging the sled back uphill is a nonspontaneous process that requires a continuous input of energy.

Figure 8.12
Entropy is a measure of molecular randomness.

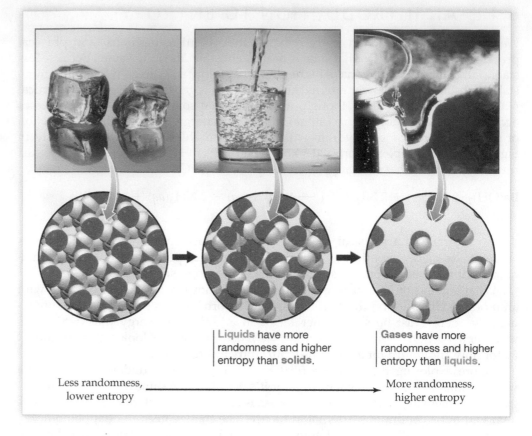

Liquids have more randomness and higher entropy than **solids**.

Gases have more randomness and higher entropy than **liquids**.

Less randomness, lower entropy ⟶ More randomness, higher entropy

randomness (ΔS). To decide whether a process is spontaneous, both enthalpy and entropy changes must be taken into account:

Spontaneous process: Favored by decrease in H (negative ΔH)
                               Favored by increase in S (positive ΔS)

Nonspontaneous process: Favored by increase in H (positive ΔH)
                               Favored by decrease in S (negative ΔS)

Note that the two factors don't have to operate in the same direction. Thus, it's possible for a process to be *disfavored* by enthalpy (endothermic, positive ΔH) yet still be spontaneous because it is strongly *favored* by entropy (positive ΔS). The melting of ice [$\Delta H° = +6.01$ kJ/mol; $\Delta S° = +22.0$ J/(K·mol)] is just such a process, as is the reaction of barium hydroxide octahydrate with ammonium chloride ($\Delta H° = +80.3$ kJ; $\Delta S° = +428$ J/K). In the latter case, 3 mol of solid reactants produce 10 mol of liquid water, 2 mol of dissolved ammonia, and 3 mol of dissolved ions (1 mol of Ba^{2+} and 2 mol of Cl^-), with a consequent large increase in molecular randomness:

$$\underbrace{Ba(OH)_2 \cdot 8\,H_2O(s) \; + \; 2\,NH_4Cl(s)}_{\text{3 mol solid reactants}} \longrightarrow BaCl_2(aq) \; + \; 2\,NH_3(aq) \; + \; 10\,H_2O(l)$$

3 mol dissolved ions   2 mol dissolved molecules   10 mol liquid water molecules

$$\Delta H° \; = \; +80.3 \text{ kJ} \longleftarrow \text{Unfavorable}$$

$$\Delta S° \; = \; +428 \text{ J/K} \longleftarrow \text{Favorable}$$

Conversely, it's also possible for a process to be favored by enthalpy (exothermic, negative ΔH) yet be nonspontaneous because it is strongly disfavored by entropy (negative ΔS). The conversion of liquid water to ice is nonspontaneous above 0 °C, for example, because the process is disfavored by entropy [$\Delta S° = -22.0 \, J/(K \cdot mol)$] even though it is favored by enthalpy ($\Delta H° = -6.01 \, kJ/mol$).

WORKED EXAMPLE 8.11

PREDICTING THE SIGN OF ΔS FOR A REACTION

Predict whether $\Delta S°$ is likely to be positive or negative for each of the following reactions:

(a) $H_2C{=}CH_2(g) + Br_2(g) \longrightarrow BrCH_2CH_2Br(l)$
(b) $2 \, C_2H_6(g) + 7 \, O_2(g) \longrightarrow 4 \, CO_2(g) + 6 \, H_2O(g)$

STRATEGY

Look at each reaction, and try to decide whether molecular randomness increases or decreases. Reactions that increase the number of gaseous molecules generally have a positive ΔS, while reactions that decrease the number of gaseous molecules have a negative ΔS.

SOLUTION

(a) The amount of molecular randomness in the system decreases when 2 mol of gaseous reactants combine to give 1 mol of liquid product, so the reaction has a negative $\Delta S°$.

(b) The amount of molecular randomness in the system increases when 9 mol of gaseous reactants give 10 mol of gaseous products, so the reaction has a positive $\Delta S°$.

▶ **PROBLEM 8.20** Ethane, C_2H_6, can be prepared by the reaction of acetylene, C_2H_2, with hydrogen. Is $\Delta S°$ for the reaction likely to be positive or negative? Explain.

$$C_2H_2(g) + 2 \, H_2(g) \longrightarrow C_2H_6(g)$$

CONCEPTUAL PROBLEM 8.21 Is the reaction represented in the following drawing likely to have a positive or a negative value of $\Delta S°$? Explain.

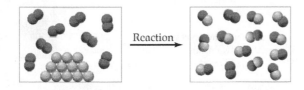

8.13 AN INTRODUCTION TO FREE ENERGY

How do we weigh the relative contributions of enthalpy changes (ΔH) and entropy changes (ΔS) to the overall spontaneity of a process? To take both factors into account when deciding the spontaneity of a chemical reaction or other process, we define a quantity called the **Gibbs free-energy change (ΔG)**, which is related to ΔH and ΔS by the equation $\Delta G = \Delta H - T\Delta S$.

The value of the free-energy change ΔG determines whether a chemical or physical process will occur spontaneously. If ΔG has a negative value, free energy is released and the process is spontaneous. If ΔG has a value of 0, the process is neither spontaneous nor nonspontaneous but is instead at an equilibrium. And if ΔG has a positive value, free energy is absorbed and the process is nonspontaneous.

$\Delta G < 0$ Process is spontaneous
$\Delta G = 0$ Process is at equilibrium—neither spontaneous nor nonspontaneous
$\Delta G > 0$ Process is nonspontaneous

The fact that the $T\Delta S$ term in the free-energy equation is temperature dependent implies that some processes might be either spontaneous or nonspontaneous, depending on the temperature. At low temperature, for instance, an unfavorable (positive) ΔH term might be larger than a favorable (positive) $T\Delta S$ term, but at higher temperature, the $T\Delta S$ term might be larger. Thus, an endothermic process that is nonspontaneous at low temperature can become spontaneous at higher temperature. This, in fact, is exactly what happens in the ice/water transition. At a temperature below 0 °C, the melting of ice is nonspontaneous because the unfavorable ΔH term outweighs the favorable $T\Delta S$ term. At a temperature above 0 °C, however, the melting of ice is spontaneous because the favorable $T\Delta S$ term outweighs the unfavorable ΔH term (**Figure 8.13**). At exactly 0 °C, the two terms are balanced.

$$\Delta G° = \Delta H° - T\Delta S°$$

At $-10\,°C$ (263 K): $\Delta G° = 6.01\ \dfrac{kJ}{mol} - (263\ K)\left(0.0220\ \dfrac{kJ}{K \cdot mol}\right) = +0.22\ kJ/mol$

At $0\,°C$ (273 K): $\Delta G° = 6.01\ \dfrac{kJ}{mol} - (273\ K)\left(0.0220\ \dfrac{kJ}{K \cdot mol}\right) = 0.00\ kJ/mol$

At $+10\,°C$ (283 K): $\Delta G° = 6.01\ \dfrac{kJ}{mol} - (283\ K)\left(0.0220\ \dfrac{kJ}{K \cdot mol}\right) = -0.22\ kJ/mol$

Figure 8.13
Melting and freezing. The melting of ice is disfavored by enthalpy ($\Delta H > 0$) but favored by entropy ($\Delta S > 0$). The freezing of water is favored by enthalpy ($\Delta H < 0$) but disfavored by entropy ($\Delta S < 0$).

$\Delta S° = +22.0\ J/(K \cdot mol)$ (Entropy increases)
$\Delta H° = +6.01\ kJ/mol$ (Endothermic)
Spontaneous above 0 °C

Spontaneous below 0 °C
$\Delta S° = -22.0\ J/(K \cdot mol)$ (Entropy decreases)
$\Delta H° = -6.01\ kJ/mol$ (Exothermic)

Solid water

Liquid water

Below 0 °C, the enthalpy term ΔH dominates the entropy term $T\Delta S$ in the Gibbs free-energy equation, so freezing is spontaneous.

At 0 °C the entropy and enthalpy terms are exactly balanced.

Above 0 °C, the entropy term dominates the enthalpy term, so melting is spontaneous.

An example of a chemical reaction in which temperature controls spontaneity is that of carbon with water to yield carbon monoxide and hydrogen. The reaction has an unfavorable ΔH term (positive) but a favorable $T\Delta S$ term (positive) because randomness increases when a solid and 1 mol of gas are converted into 2 mol of gas:

$$C(s) + H_2O(g) \longrightarrow CO(g) + H_2(g) \qquad \Delta H° = +131\ kJ \qquad \text{Unfavorable}$$
$$\Delta S° = +134\ J/K \qquad \text{Favorable}$$

No reaction occurs if carbon and water are mixed at room temperature because the unfavorable ΔH term outweighs the favorable $T\Delta S$ term. At approximately 978 K (705 °C), however, the reaction becomes spontaneous because the favorable $T\Delta S$ term becomes larger than the unfavorable ΔH term. Below 978 K, ΔG has a positive value; at 978 K, $\Delta G = 0$; and above 978 K, ΔG has a negative value. (The calculation is not exact because values of ΔH and ΔS themselves vary somewhat with temperature.)

$$\Delta G° = \Delta H° - T\Delta S°$$

At 695 °C (968 K): $\Delta G° = 131 \text{ kJ} - (968 \text{ K})\left(0.134 \dfrac{\text{kJ}}{\text{K}}\right) = +1 \text{ kJ}$

At 705 °C (978 K): $\Delta G° = 131 \text{ kJ} - (978 \text{ K})\left(0.134 \dfrac{\text{kJ}}{\text{K}}\right) = 0 \text{ kJ}$

At 715 °C (988 K): $\Delta G° = 131 \text{ kJ} - (988 \text{ K})\left(0.134 \dfrac{\text{kJ}}{\text{K}}\right) = -1 \text{ kJ}$

The reaction of carbon with water is, in fact, the first step of an industrial process for manufacturing methanol (CH_3OH). As supplies of natural gas and oil diminish, this reaction may become important for the manufacture of synthetic fuels.

A process is at equilibrium when it is balanced between spontaneous and non-spontaneous—that is, when $\Delta G = 0$ and it is energetically unfavorable to go either from reactants to products or from products to reactants. Thus, at the equilibrium point, we can set up the equation

$$\Delta G = \Delta H - T\Delta S = 0 \quad \text{At equilibrium}$$

Solving this equation for T gives

$$T = \frac{\Delta H}{\Delta S}$$

which makes it possible to calculate the temperature at which a changeover in behavior between spontaneous and nonspontaneous occurs. Using the known values of $\Delta H°$ and $\Delta S°$ for the melting of ice, for instance, we find that the point at which liquid water and solid ice are in equilibrium is

$$T = \frac{\Delta H°}{\Delta S°} = \frac{6.01 \text{ kJ}}{0.0220 \dfrac{\text{kJ}}{\text{K}}} = 273 \text{ K} = 0 \text{ °C}$$

Not surprisingly, the ice/water equilibrium point is 273 K, or 0 °C, the melting point of ice.

In the same way, the temperature at which the reaction of carbon with water changes between spontaneous and nonspontaneous is 978 K, or 705 °C:

$$T = \frac{\Delta H°}{\Delta S°} = \frac{131 \text{ kJ}}{0.134 \dfrac{\text{kJ}}{\text{K}}} = 978 \text{ K}$$

This section and the preceding one serve only as an introduction to entropy and free energy. We'll return in Chapter 16 for a more in-depth look at these two important topics.

WORKED EXAMPLE 8.12

USING THE FREE-ENERGY EQUATION TO CALCULATE EQUILIBRIUM TEMPERATURE

Lime (CaO) is produced by heating limestone ($CaCO_3$) to drive off CO_2 gas, a reaction used to make Portland cement. Is the reaction spontaneous under standard conditions at 25 °C? Calculate the temperature at which the reaction becomes spontaneous.

$$CaCO_3(s) \longrightarrow CaO(s) + CO_2(g) \quad \Delta H° = 179.2 \text{ kJ}; \ \Delta S° = 160.0 \text{ J/K}$$

STRATEGY

The spontaneity of the reaction at a given temperature can be found by determining whether ΔG is positive or negative at that temperature. The changeover point between spontaneous and nonspontaneous can be found by setting $\Delta G = 0$ and solving for T.

SOLUTION

At 25 °C (298 K), we have

$$\Delta G = \Delta H - T\Delta S = 179.2 \text{ kJ} - (298 \text{ K})\left(0.1600 \dfrac{\text{kJ}}{\text{K}}\right) = +131.5 \text{ kJ}$$

Because ΔG is positive at this temperature, the reaction is nonspontaneous.

continued on next page

The changeover point between spontaneous and nonspontaneous is approximately

$$T = \frac{\Delta H}{\Delta S} = \frac{179.2\ kJ}{0.1600\ \dfrac{kJ}{K}} = 1120\ K$$

The reaction becomes spontaneous above approximately 1120 K (847 °C).

WORKED CONCEPTUAL EXAMPLE 8.13

PREDICTING THE SIGNS OF ΔH, ΔS, AND ΔG FOR A REACTION

What are the signs of ΔH, ΔS, and ΔG for the following nonspontaneous transformation?

STRATEGY

First, decide what kind of process is represented in the drawing. Then decide whether the process increases or decreases the entropy of the system and whether it is exothermic or endothermic.

SOLUTION

The drawing shows ordered particles in a solid subliming to give a gas. Formation of a gas from a solid increases molecular randomness, so ΔS is positive. Furthermore, because we're told that the process is nonspontaneous, ΔG is also positive. Because the process is favored by ΔS (positive) yet still nonspontaneous, ΔH must be unfavorable (positive). This makes sense, because conversion of a solid to a liquid or gas requires energy and is always endothermic.

▶ **PROBLEM 8.22** Which of the following reactions are spontaneous under standard conditions at 25 °C, and which are nonspontaneous?

(a) $AgNO_3(aq) + NaCl(aq) \longrightarrow AgCl(s) + NaNO_3(aq)$ $\Delta G° = -55.7\ kJ$

(b) $2\ C(s) + 2\ H_2(g) \longrightarrow C_2H_4(g)$ $\Delta G° = 68.1\ kJ$

▶ **PROBLEM 8.23** Is the Haber process for the industrial synthesis of ammonia spontaneous or nonspontaneous under standard conditions at 25 °C? At what temperature (°C) does the changeover occur?

$$N_2(g) + 3\ H_2(g) \longrightarrow 2\ NH_3(g) \quad \Delta H° = -92.2\ kJ;\ \Delta S° = -199\ J/K$$

CONCEPTUAL PROBLEM 8.24 The following reaction is exothermic:

(a) Write a balanced equation for the reaction.

(b) What are the signs of ΔH and ΔS for the reaction?

(c) Is the reaction likely to be spontaneous at low temperatures only, at high temperatures only, or at all temperatures? Explain.

INQUIRY WHAT ARE BIOFUELS?

The petroleum era began in August 1859, when the world's first oil well was drilled near Titusville, Pennsylvania. Since that time, approximately 1.2×10^{12} barrels of petroleum have been used throughout the world, primarily as fuel for automobiles (1 barrel = 42 gallons).

No one really knows how much petroleum remains on Earth. Current world consumption is approximately 3.1×10^{10} barrels per year, and currently known recoverable reserves are estimated at 1.1×10^{12} barrels. Thus, the world's known petroleum reserves will be exhausted in approximately 35 years at the current rate of consumption. Additional petroleum reserves will surely be found, but consumption is also increasing, making any prediction of the amount of time remaining highly inaccurate. Only two things are certain: The amount of petroleum remaining *is* finite, and we *will* run out at some point, whenever that might be. Thus, alternative energy sources are needed.

Of the various alternative energy sources now being explored, *biofuels*—fuels derived from recently living organisms such as trees, corn, sugar cane, and rapeseed—look promising because they are renewable and because they are more nearly *carbon neutral* than fossil fuels, meaning that the amount of CO_2 released to the environment during the manufacture and burning of a biofuel is similar to the amount of CO_2 removed from the environment by photosynthesis during the plant's growth. Note that the phrase *carbon neutral* doesn't mean that biofuels don't release CO_2 when burned; they release just as much CO_2 as any other fuel.

The two biofuels receiving the most attention at present are ethanol and biodiesel. Ethanol, sometimes called bioethanol to make it sound more attractive, is simply ethyl alcohol, the same substance found in alcoholic drinks and produced in the same way: by yeast-catalyzed fermentation of carbohydrate.

▲ Vegetable oil from the bright yellow rapeseed plant is a leading candidate for large-scale production of biodiesel fuel.

Glucose
($C_6H_{12}O_6$)

Ethanol
(C_2H_5OH)

The only difference between beverage ethanol and fuel ethanol is the source of the sugar. Beverage ethanol comes primarily from fermentation of sugar in grapes (for wine) or grains (for distilled liquors), while fuel ethanol comes primarily from fermentation of cane sugar or corn. Much current work is being done, however, on developing economical methods of converting cheap cellulose-based agricultural and logging wastes into fermentable sugars.

Biodiesel consists primarily of organic compounds called *long-chain methyl esters*, which are produced by reaction of common vegetable oils with methyl alcohol in the presence of an acid catalyst. Any vegetable oil can be used, but rapeseed oil and soybean oil are the most common. (*Canola* oil, of which you may have heard, is a specific cultivar of generic rapeseed.) Once formed, the biodiesel is typically mixed in up to 30% concentration with petroleum-based diesel fuel for use in automobiles and trucks.

A typical long-chain methyl ester in biodiesel

▶ **PROBLEM 8.25** Write balanced equations for the combustion reactions of ethanol (C_2H_6O) and biodiesel ($C_{19}H_{38}O_2$) with oxygen to give CO_2 and H_2O.

▶ **PROBLEM 8.26** Biodiesel has a more favorable (more negative) combustion enthalpy per gram than ethanol. Explain, in light of your answer to Problem 8.25.

SUMMARY

Energy is either *kinetic* or *potential*. Kinetic energy (E_K) is the energy of motion. Its value depends on both the mass m and velocity v of an object according to the equation $E_K = (1/2)mv^2$. Potential energy (E_P) is the energy stored in an object because of its position or in a chemical substance because of its composition. **Heat** is the thermal energy transferred between two objects as the result of a temperature difference, whereas **temperature** is a measure of the kinetic energy of molecular motion.

According to the **conservation of energy law**, also known as the **first law of thermodynamics**, energy can be neither created nor destroyed. Thus, the total energy of an isolated system is constant. The total **internal energy (E)** of a system—the sum of all kinetic and potential energies for each particle in the system—is a **state function** because its value depends only on the present condition of the system, not on how that condition was reached.

Work (w) is defined as the distance moved times the force that produces the motion. In chemistry, most work is expansion work (*PV* work) done as the result of a volume change during a reaction when air molecules are pushed aside. The amount of work done by an expanding gas is given by the equation $w = -P\Delta V$, where P is the pressure against which the system must push and ΔV is the change in volume of the system.

The total internal energy change that takes place during a reaction is the sum of the heat transferred (q) and the work done ($-P\Delta V$). The equation

$$\Delta E = q + (-P\Delta V) \quad \text{or} \quad q = \Delta E + P\Delta V = \Delta H$$

where ΔH is the **enthalpy change** of the system, is a fundamental equation of thermochemistry. In general, the $P\Delta V$ term is much smaller than the ΔE term, so that the total internal energy change of a reacting system is approximately equal to ΔH, also called the **heat of reaction**. Reactions that have a negative ΔH are **exothermic** because heat is lost by the system, and reactions that have a positive ΔH are **endothermic** because heat is absorbed by the system.

Because enthalpy is a state function, ΔH is the same regardless of the path taken between reactants and products. Thus, the sum of the enthalpy changes for the individual steps in a reaction is equal to the overall enthalpy change for the entire reaction, a relationship known as **Hess's law**. Using this law, it is possible to calculate overall enthalpy changes for individual steps that can't be measured directly. Hess's law also makes it possible to calculate the enthalpy change of any reaction if the standard heats of formation ($\Delta H°_f$) are known for the reactants and products. The **standard heat of formation** is the enthalpy change for the hypothetical formation of 1 mol of a substance in its **thermodynamic standard state** from the most stable forms of the constituent elements in their standard states (1 atm pressure and a specified temperature, usually 25 °C).

In addition to enthalpy, **entropy (S)**—a measure of the amount of molecular randomness in a system—is also important in determining whether a process will occur spontaneously. Together, changes in enthalpy and entropy define a quantity called the **Gibbs free-energy change (ΔG)** according to the equation $\Delta G = \Delta H - T\Delta S$. If ΔG is negative, the reaction is **spontaneous**; if ΔG is positive, the reaction is nonspontaneous.

KEY WORDS

conservation of energy
   law   267
endothermic   277
enthalpy (H)   273
enthalpy change (ΔH)   273
entropy (S)   291
exothermic   277
first law of
   thermodynamics   268

Gibbs free-energy change
   (ΔG)   293
heat   268
heat capacity (C)   279
heat of combustion
   ($\Delta H°_c$)   289
heat of reaction (ΔH)   273
Hess's law   282
internal energy (E)   268

molar heat capacity
   (C_m)   279
specific heat   279
spontaneous process   291
standard enthalpy of
   reaction ($\Delta H°$)   275
standard heat of formation
   ($\Delta H°_f$)   284
state function   269

sublimation   276
system, surroundings   268
temperature   268
thermochemistry   267
thermodynamic standard
   state   275
work (w)   270

CONCEPTUAL PROBLEMS

Problems 8.1–8.26 appear within the chapter.

8.27 The following reaction is exothermic:

(a) Write a balanced equation for the reaction (red spheres represent A atoms and ivory spheres represent B atoms).

(b) What are the signs (+ or −) of ΔH and ΔS for the reaction?

(c) Is the reaction likely to be spontaneous at lower temperatures only, at higher temperatures only, or at all temperatures?

8.28 Imagine a reaction that results in a change in both volume and temperature:

(a) Has any work been done? If so, is its sign positive or negative?

(b) Has there been an enthalpy change? If so, what is the sign of ΔH? Is the reaction exothermic or endothermic?

8.29 Redraw the following diagram to represent the situation (a) when work has been gained by the system and (b) when work has been lost by the system:

8.30 Acetylene, C_2H_2, reacts with H_2 in two steps to yield ethane, CH_3CH_3:

(1) $HC\equiv CH + H_2 \longrightarrow H_2C=CH_2$ $\Delta H° = -175.1$ kJ
(2) $H_2C=CH_2 + H_2 \longrightarrow CH_3CH_3$ $\Delta H° = -136.3$ kJ
Net $HC\equiv CH + 2\,H_2 \longrightarrow CH_3CH_3$ $\Delta H° = -311.4$ kJ

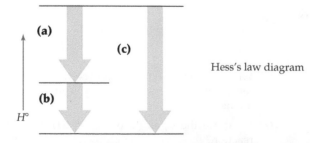

Hess's law diagram

Which arrow (a, b, c) in the Hess's law diagram corresponds to which step, and which arrow corresponds to the net reaction? Where are the reactants located on the diagram, and where are the products located?

8.31 Draw a Hess's law diagram similar to the one in Problem 8.30 for the reaction of ethyl alcohol (CH_3CH_2OH) with oxygen to yield acetic acid (CH_3CO_2H).

(1) $CH_3CH_2OH(l) + 1/2\,O_2(g) \longrightarrow$
$CH_3CHO(g) + H_2O(l)$ $\Delta H° = -174.2$ kJ

(2) $CH_3CHO(g) + 1/2\,O_2(g) \longrightarrow$
$CH_3CO_2H(l)$ $\Delta H° = -318.4$ kJ

Net $CH_3CH_2OH(l) + O_2(g) \longrightarrow$
$CH_3CO_2H(l) + H_2O(l)$ $\Delta H° = -492.6$ kJ

8.32 A reaction is carried out in a cylinder fitted with a movable piston. The starting volume is $V = 5.00$ L, and the apparatus is held at constant temperature and pressure. Assuming that $\Delta H = -35.0$ kJ and $\Delta E = -34.8$ kJ, redraw the piston to show its position after reaction. Does V increase, decrease, or remain the same?

8.33 The following drawing portrays a reaction of the type A $\longrightarrow$ B + C, where the different colored spheres represent different molecular structures. Assume that the reaction has $\Delta H° = +55$ kJ. Is the reaction likely to be spontaneous at all temperatures, nonspontaneous at all temperatures, or spontaneous at some but nonspontaneous at others? Explain.

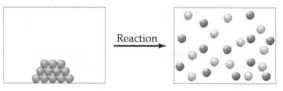

8.34 What are the signs of ΔH, ΔS, and ΔG for the following spontaneous change? Explain.

8.35 The following reaction of A_3 molecules is spontaneous:

(a) Write a balanced equation for the reaction.

(b) What are the signs of ΔH, ΔS, and ΔG for the reaction? Explain.

SECTION PROBLEMS

Heat, Work, and Energy (Sections 8.1–8.3)

8.36 What is the difference between heat and temperature? Between work and energy? Between kinetic energy and potential energy?

8.37 What is internal energy?

8.38 Which has more kinetic energy, a 1400 kg car moving at 115 km/h or a 12,000 kg truck moving at 38 km/h?

8.39 Assume that the kinetic energy of a 1400 kg car moving at 115 km/h (Problem 8.38) could be converted entirely into heat. What amount of water could be heated from 20 °C to 50 °C by the car's energy?

8.40 Calculate the work done in joules by a chemical reaction if the volume increases from 3.2 L to 3.4 L against a constant external pressure of 3.6 atm. What is the sign of the energy change?

8.41 The addition of H_2 to C=C double bonds is an important reaction used in the preparation of margarine from vegetable oils. If 50.0 mL of H_2 and 50.0 mL of ethylene (C_2H_4) are allowed to react at 1.5 atm, the product ethane (C_2H_6) has a volume of 50.0 mL. Calculate the amount of PV work done, and tell the direction of the energy flow.

$$C_2H_4(g) + H_2(g) \longrightarrow C_2H_6(g)$$

8.42 Assume that the nutritional content of an apple—say 50 Cal (1 Cal = 1000 cal)—could be used to light a lightbulb. For how many minutes would there be light from each of the following?
(a) a 100 watt incandescent bulb (1 W = 1 J/s)
(b) a 23 watt compact fluorescent bulb, which provides a similar amount of light

8.43 A double cheeseburger has a caloric content of 440 Cal (1 Cal = 1000 cal). If this energy could be used to operate a television set, for how many hours would the following sets run?
(a) a 275 watt 46 in. plasma TV (1 W = 1 J/s)
(b) a 175 watt 46 in. LCD TV

8.44 A reaction inside a cylindrical container with a movable piston causes the volume to change from 12.0 L to 18.0 L while the pressure outside the container remains constant at 0.975 atm. (The volume of a cylinder is $V = \pi r^2 h$, where h is the height; 1 L·atm = 101.325 J.)
(a) What is the value in joules of the work w done during the reaction?
(b) The diameter of the piston is 17.0 cm. How far does the piston move?

8.45 At a constant pressure of 0.905 atm, a chemical reaction takes place in a cylindrical container with a movable piston having a diameter of 40.0 cm. During the reaction, the height of the piston drops by 65.0 cm. (The volume of a cylinder is $V = \pi r^2 h$, where h is the height; 1 L·atm = 101.325 J.)
(a) What is the change in volume in liters during the reaction?
(b) What is the value in joules of the work w done during the reaction?

Energy and Enthalpy (Sections 8.4–8.6)

8.46 What is the difference between the internal energy change ΔE and the enthalpy change ΔH? Which of the two is measured at constant pressure, and which at constant volume?

8.47 What is the sign of ΔH for an exothermic reaction? For an endothermic reaction?

8.48 Under what circumstances are ΔE and ΔH essentially equal?

8.49 Which of the following has the highest enthalpy content, and which the lowest at a given temperature: $H_2O(s)$, $H_2O(l)$, or $H_2O(g)$? Explain.

8.50 The enthalpy change for the reaction of 50.0 mL of ethylene with 50.0 mL of H_2 at 1.5 atm pressure (Problem 8.41) is $\Delta H = -0.31$ kJ. What is the value of ΔE?

8.51 Assume that a particular reaction evolves 244 kJ of heat and that 35 kJ of PV work is gained by the system. What are the values of ΔE and ΔH for the system? For the surroundings?

8.52 What is the enthalpy change (ΔH) for a reaction at a constant pressure of 1.00 atm if the internal energy change (ΔE) is 44.0 kJ and the volume increase is 14.0 L? (1 L·atm = 101.325 J.)

8.53 A reaction takes place at a constant pressure of 1.10 atm with an internal energy change (ΔE) of 71.5 kJ and a volume decrease of 13.6 L. What is the enthalpy change (ΔH) for the reaction? (1 L·atm = 101.325 J.)

8.54 Used in welding metals, the reaction of acetylene with oxygen has $\Delta H° = -1256.2$ kJ:

$$C_2H_2(g) + 5/2\ O_2(g) \longrightarrow H_2O(g) + 2\ CO_2(g)$$
$$\Delta H° = -1256.2 \text{ kJ}$$

How much PV work is done in kilojoules and what is the value of ΔE in kilojoules for the reaction of 6.50 g of acetylene at atmospheric pressure if the volume change is -2.80 L?

8.55 Ethyl chloride (C_2H_5Cl), a substance used as a topical anesthetic, is prepared by reaction of ethylene with hydrogen chloride:

$$C_2H_4(g) + HCl(g) \longrightarrow C_2H_5Cl(g) \quad \Delta H° = -72.3 \text{ kJ}$$

Ethyl chloride

How much PV work is done in kilojoules, and what is the value of ΔE in kilojoules if 89.5 g of ethylene and 125 g of HCl are allowed to react at atmospheric pressure and the volume change is -71.5 L?

8.56 The familiar "ether" used as an anesthetic agent is diethyl ether, $C_4H_{10}O$. Its heat of vaporization is +26.5 kJ/mol at its boiling point. How much energy in kilojoules is required to convert 100 mL of diethyl ether at its boiling point from liquid to vapor if its density is 0.7138 g/mL?

Diethyl ether

8.57 How much energy in kilojoules is required to convert 100 mL of water at its boiling point from liquid to vapor, and how does this compare with the result calculated in Problem 8.56 for diethyl ether? [$\Delta H_{vap}(H_2O) = +40.7$ kJ/mol]

8.58 Aluminum metal reacts with chlorine with a spectacular display of sparks:

$$2\,Al(s) + 3\,Cl_2(g) \longrightarrow 2\,AlCl_3(s) \quad \Delta H° = -1408.4 \text{ kJ}$$

How much heat in kilojoules is released on reaction of 5.00 g of Al?

8.59 How much heat in kilojoules is evolved or absorbed in the reaction of 1.00 g of Na with H_2O? Is the reaction exothermic or endothermic?

$$2\,Na(s) + 2\,H_2O(l) \longrightarrow 2\,NaOH(aq) + H_2(g)$$
$$\Delta H° = -368.4 \text{ kJ}$$

8.60 How much heat in kilojoules is evolved or absorbed in the reaction of 2.50 g of Fe_2O_3 with enough carbon monoxide to produce iron metal? Is the process exothermic or endothermic?

$$Fe_2O_3(s) + 3\,CO(g) \longrightarrow 2\,Fe(s) + 3\,CO_2(g)$$
$$\Delta H° = -24.8 \text{ kJ}$$

8.61 How much heat in kilojoules is evolved or absorbed in the reaction of 233.0 g of calcium oxide with enough carbon to produce calcium carbide? Is the process exothermic or endothermic?

$$CaO(s) + 3\,C(s) \longrightarrow CaC_2(s) + CO(g) \quad \Delta H° = 464.6 \text{ kJ}$$

Calorimetry and Heat Capacity (Section 8.7)

8.62 What is the difference between heat capacity and specific heat?

8.63 Does a measurement carried out in a bomb calorimeter give a value for ΔH or ΔE? Explain.

8.64 Sodium metal is sometimes used as a cooling agent in heat-exchange units because of its relatively high molar heat capacity of 28.2 J/(mol·°C). What is the specific heat of sodium in J/(g·°C)?

8.65 Titanium metal is used as a structural material in many high-tech applications, such as in jet engines. What is the specific heat of titanium in J/(g·°C) if it takes 89.7 J to raise the temperature of a 33.0 g block by 5.20 °C? What is the molar heat capacity of titanium in J/(mol·°C)?

8.66 When 1.045 g of CaO is added to 50.0 mL of water at 25.0 °C in a calorimeter, the temperature of the water increases to 32.3 °C. Assuming that the specific heat of the solution is

4.18 J/(g·°C) and that the calorimeter itself absorbs a negligible amount of heat, calculate ΔH in kilojoules for the reaction

$$CaO(s) + H_2O(l) \longrightarrow Ca(OH)_2(aq)$$

8.67 When 0.187 g of benzene, C_6H_6, is burned in a bomb calorimeter, the surrounding water bath rises in temperature by 7.48 °C. Assuming that the bath contains 250.0 g of water and that the calorimeter itself absorbs a negligible amount of heat, calculate combustion energies (ΔE) for benzene in both kJ/g and kJ/mol.

Benzene

8.68 When a solution containing 8.00 g of NaOH in 50.0 g of water at 25.0 °C is added to a solution of 8.00 g of HCl in 250.0 g of water at 25.0 °C in a calorimeter, the temperature of the solution increases to 33.5 °C. Assuming that the specific heat of the solution is 4.18 J/(g·°C) and that the calorimeter absorbs a negligible amount of heat, calculate ΔH in kilojoules for the reaction

$$NaOH(aq) + HCl(aq) \longrightarrow NaCl(aq) + H_2O(l)$$

When the experiment is repeated using a solution of 10.00 g of HCl in 248.0 g of water, the same temperature increase is observed. Explain.

8.69 Instant cold packs used to treat athletic injuries contain solid NH_4NO_3 and a pouch of water. When the pack is squeezed, the pouch breaks and the solid dissolves, lowering the temperature because of the endothermic reaction

$$NH_4NO_3(s) \xrightarrow{H_2O} NH_4NO_3(aq) \quad \Delta H = +25.7 \text{ kJ}$$

What is the final temperature in a squeezed cold pack that contains 50.0 g of NH_4NO_3 dissolved in 125 mL of water? Assume a specific heat of 4.18 J/(g·°C) for the solution, an initial temperature of 25.0 °C, and no heat transfer between the cold pack and the environment.

Hess's Law and Heats of Formation (Sections 8.8 and 8.9)

8.70 How is the standard state of an element defined?

8.71 What is a compound's standard heat of formation?

8.72 What is Hess's law, and why does it "work"?

8.73 Why do elements always have $\Delta H°_f = 0$?

8.74 What phase of matter is associated with the standard states of the following elements and compounds?

(a) Cl_2 **(b)** Hg **(c)** CO_2 **(d)** Ga

8.75 What is the phase of the standard states of the following elements and compounds?

(a) NH_3 **(b)** Fe **(c)** N_2 **(d)** Br_2

8.76 Write balanced equations for the formation of the following compounds from their elements:

(a) iron(III) oxide

(b) sucrose (table sugar, $C_{12}H_{22}O_{11}$)

(c) uranium hexafluoride (a solid at 25 °C)

8.77 Write balanced equations for the formation of the following compounds from their elements:

(a) ethanol (C_2H_6O)

(b) sodium sulfate

(c) dichloromethane (a liquid, CH_2Cl_2)

8.78 Sulfuric acid (H_2SO_4), the most widely produced chemical in the world, is made by a two-step oxidation of sulfur to sulfur trioxide, SO_3, followed by reaction with water. Calculate $\Delta H°_f$ for SO_3 in kJ/mol, given the following data:

$$S(s) + O_2(g) \longrightarrow SO_2(g) \qquad \Delta H° = -296.8 \text{ kJ}$$
$$SO_2(g) + 1/2\, O_2(g) \longrightarrow SO_3(g) \quad \Delta H° = -98.9 \text{ kJ}$$

8.79 Calculate $\Delta H°_f$ in kJ/mol for benzene, C_6H_6, from the following data:

$$2\, C_6H_6(l) + 15\, O_2(g) \longrightarrow 12\, CO_2(g) + 6\, H_2O(l)$$
$$\Delta H° = -6534 \text{ kJ}$$
$$\Delta H°_f\, (CO_2) = -393.5 \text{ kJ/mol}$$
$$\Delta H°_f\, (H_2O) - -285.8 \text{ kJ/mol}$$

8.80 The standard enthalpy change for the reaction of $SO_3(g)$ with $H_2O(l)$ to yield $H_2SO_4(aq)$ is $\Delta H° = -227.8$ kJ. Use the information in Problem 8.78 to calculate $\Delta H°_f$ for $H_2SO_4(aq)$ in kJ/mol. [For $H_2O(l)$, $\Delta H°_f = -285.8$ kJ/mol.]

8.81 Acetic acid (CH_3CO_2H), whose aqueous solutions are known as *vinegar*, is prepared by reaction of ethyl alcohol (CH_3CH_2OH) with oxygen:

$$CH_3CH_2OH(l) + O_2(g) \longrightarrow CH_3CO_2H(l) + H_2O(l)$$

Use the following data to calculate $\Delta H°$ in kilojoules for the reaction:

$$\Delta H°_f\, [CH_3CH_2OH(l)] = -277.7 \text{ kJ/mol}$$
$$\Delta H°_f\, [CH_3CO_2H(l)] = -484.5 \text{ kJ/mol}$$
$$\Delta H°_f\, [H_2O(l)] = -285.8 \text{ kJ/mol}$$

8.82 Styrene (C_8H_8), the precursor of polystyrene polymers, has a standard heat of combustion of -4395 kJ/mol. Write a balanced equation for the combustion reaction, and calculate $\Delta H°_f$ for styrene in kJ/mol.

$$\Delta H°_f\, [CO_2(g)] = -393.5 \text{ kJ/mol};$$
$$\Delta H°_f\, [H_2O(l)] = -285.8 \text{ kJ/mol}$$

Styrene

8.83 Methyl *tert*-butyl ether (MTBE), $C_5H_{12}O$, a gasoline additive used to boost octane ratings, has $\Delta H°_f = -313.6$ kJ/mol. Write a balanced equation for its combustion reaction, and calculate its standard heat of combustion in kilojoules.

8.84 Methyl *tert*-butyl ether (Problem 8.83) is prepared by reaction of methanol(l) ($\Delta H°_f = -239.2$ kJ/mol) with 2-methyl-propene(g), according to the equation

$$\begin{array}{c} CH_3 \\ | \\ CH_3-C=CH_2 \end{array} + CH_3OH \longrightarrow$$

2-Methylpropene

$$\begin{array}{c} CH_3 \\ | \\ CH_3-C-O-CH_3 \quad \Delta H° = -57.5 \text{ kJ} \\ | \\ CH_3 \end{array}$$

Methyl *tert*-butyl ether

Calculate $\Delta H°_f$ in kJ/mol for 2-methylpropene.

8.85 One possible use for the cooking fat left over after making french fries is to burn it as fuel. Write a balanced equation, and use the following data to calculate the amount of energy released in kJ/mL from the combustion of cooking fat:

$$\text{Formula} = C_{51}H_{88}O_6 \qquad \Delta H°_f = -1310 \text{ kJ/mol}$$
$$\text{Density} = 0.94 \text{ g/ml}$$

8.86 Given the standard heats of formation shown in Appendix B, what is $\Delta H°$ in kilojoules for the reaction $CaCO_3(s) \longrightarrow CaO(s) + CO_2(g)$?

8.87 Given the standard heats of formation shown in Appendix B, what is $\Delta H°$ in kilojoules for the reaction $3\, N_2O_4(g) + 2\, H_2O(l) \longrightarrow 4\, HNO_3(aq) + 2\, NO(g)$.

Bond Dissociation Energies (Section 8.10)

8.88 Use the bond dissociation energies in Table 7.1 on page 219 to calculate an approximate $\Delta H°$ in kilojoules for the reaction of ethylene with hydrogen to yield ethane.

$$H_2C=CH_2(g) + H_2(g) \longrightarrow CH_3CH_3(g)$$

8.89 Use the bond dissociation energies in Table 7.1 to calculate an approximate $\Delta H°$ in kilojoules for the industrial synthesis of isopropyl alcohol (rubbing alcohol) by reaction of water with propene.

$$CH_3CH=CH_2 + H_2O \longrightarrow \begin{array}{c} OH \\ | \\ CH_3CHCH_3 \end{array}$$

Propene   Isopropyl alcohol

8.90 Calculate an approximate heat of combustion for butane in kilojoules by using the bond dissociation energies in Table 7.1. (The strength of the $O=O$ bond is 498 kJ/mol, and that of a $C=O$ bond in CO_2 is 804 kJ/mol.)

Butane

8.91 Use the bond dissociation energies in Table 7.1 to calculate an approximate heat of reaction, $\Delta H°$ in kilojoules, for the industrial reaction of ethanol with acetic acid to yield ethyl acetate (used as nail-polish remover) and water.

Acetic acid   Ethanol

Ethyl acetate

Free Energy and Entropy (Sections 8.12 and 8.13)

8.92 What does entropy measure?

8.93 What are the two terms that make up the free-energy change for a reaction, ΔG, and which of the two is usually more important?

8.94 How is it possible for a reaction to be spontaneous yet endothermic?

8.95 Is it possible for a reaction to be nonspontaneous yet exothermic? Explain.

8.96 Tell whether the entropy changes for the following processes are likely to be positive or negative:
   (a) The fizzing of a newly opened can of soda
   (b) The growth of a plant from seed

8.97 Tell whether the entropy changes, ΔS, for the following processes are likely to be positive or negative:
   (a) The conversion of liquid water to water vapor at 100 °C
   (b) The freezing of liquid water to ice at 0 °C
   (c) The eroding of a mountain by a glacier

8.98 Tell whether the free-energy changes, ΔG, for the processes listed in Problem 8.97 are likely to be positive, negative, or zero.

8.99 When a bottle of perfume is opened, odorous molecules mix with air and slowly diffuse throughout the entire room. Is ΔG for the diffusion process positive, negative, or zero? What about ΔH and ΔS for the diffusion?

8.100 One of the steps in the cracking of petroleum into gasoline involves the thermal breakdown of large hydrocarbon molecules into smaller ones. For example, the following reaction might occur:

$$C_{11}H_{24} \longrightarrow C_4H_{10} + C_4H_8 + C_3H_6$$

Is ΔS for this reaction likely to be positive or negative? Explain.

8.101 The commercial production of 1,2-dichloroethane, a solvent used in dry cleaning, involves the reaction of ethylene with chlorine:

$$C_2H_4(g) + Cl_2(g) \longrightarrow C_2H_4Cl_2(l)$$

Is ΔS for this reaction likely to be positive or negative? Explain.

8.102 Tell whether reactions with the following values of ΔH and ΔS are spontaneous or nonspontaneous and whether they are exothermic or endothermic:
   (a) $\Delta H = -48$ kJ; $\Delta S = +135$ J/K at 400 K
   (b) $\Delta H = -48$ kJ; $\Delta S = -135$ J/K at 400 K
   (c) $\Delta H = +48$ kJ; $\Delta S = +135$ J/K at 400 K
   (d) $\Delta H = +48$ kJ; $\Delta S = -135$ J/K at 400 K

8.103 Tell whether reactions with the following values of ΔH and ΔS are spontaneous or nonspontaneous and whether they are exothermic or endothermic:
   (a) $\Delta H = -128$ kJ; $\Delta S = 35$ J/K at 500 K
   (b) $\Delta H = +67$ kJ; $\Delta S = -140$ J/K at 250 K
   (c) $\Delta H = +75$ kJ; $\Delta S = 95$ J/K at 800 K

8.104 Suppose that a reaction has $\Delta H = -33$ kJ and $\Delta S = -58$ J/K. At what temperature will it change from spontaneous to nonspontaneous?

8.105 Suppose that a reaction has $\Delta H = +41$ kJ and $\Delta S = -27$ J/K. At what temperature, if any, will it change between spontaneous and nonspontaneous?

8.106 Which of the reactions (a)–(d) in Problem 8.102 are spontaneous at all temperatures, which are nonspontaneous at all temperatures, and which have an equilibrium temperature?

8.107 Vinyl chloride ($H_2C=CHCl$), the starting material used in the industrial preparation of poly(vinyl chloride), is prepared by a two-step process that begins with the reaction of Cl_2 with ethylene to yield 1,2-dichloroethane:

$$Cl_2(g) + H_2C=CH_2(g) \longrightarrow ClCH_2CH_2Cl(l)$$

$$\Delta H° = -217.5 \text{ kJ}$$
$$\Delta S° = -233.9 \text{ J/K}$$

Vinyl chloride

   (a) Tell whether the reaction is favored by entropy, by enthalpy, by both, or by neither, and then calculate $\Delta G°$ at 298 K.
   (b) Tell whether the reaction has an equilibrium temperature between spontaneous and nonspontaneous. If yes, calculate the equilibrium temperature.

8.108 Ethyl alcohol has $\Delta H_{fusion} = 5.02$ kJ/mol and melts at -114.1 °C. What is the value of ΔS_{fusion} for ethyl alcohol?

8.109 Chloroform has $\Delta H_{vaporization} = 29.2$ kJ/mol and boils at 61.2 °C. What is the value of $\Delta S_{vaporization}$ for chloroform?

CHAPTER PROBLEMS

8.110 When 1.50 g of magnesium metal is allowed to react with 200 mL of 6.00 M aqueous HCl, the temperature rises from 25.0 °C to 42.9 °C. Calculate ΔH in kilojoules for the reaction, assuming that the heat capacity of the calorimeter is 776 J/°C, that the specific heat of the final solution is the same as that of water $[(4.18 \text{ J}/(g \cdot °C)]$, and that the density of the solution is 1.00 g/mL.

8.111 Use the data in Appendix B to find standard enthalpies of reaction in kilojoules for the following processes:

(a) $C(s) + CO_2(g) \longrightarrow 2\,CO(g)$

(b) $2\,H_2O_2(aq) \longrightarrow 2\,H_2O(l) + O_2(g)$

(c) $Fe_2O_3(s) + 3\,CO(g) \longrightarrow 2\,Fe(s) + 3\,CO_2(g)$

8.112 Find $\Delta H°$ in kilojoules for the reaction of nitric oxide with oxygen, $2\,NO(g) + O_2(g) \longrightarrow N_2O_4(g)$, given the following data:

$$N_2O_4(g) \longrightarrow 2\,NO_2(g) \qquad \Delta H° = 55.3 \text{ kJ}$$
$$NO(g) + 1/2\,O_2(g) \longrightarrow NO_2(g) \quad \Delta H° = -58.1 \text{ kJ}$$

8.113 The boiling point of a substance is defined as the temperature at which liquid and vapor coexist in equilibrium. Use the heat of vaporization ($\Delta H_{vap} = 30.91$ kJ/mol) and the entropy of vaporization $[\Delta S_{vap} = 93.2 \text{ J}/(K \cdot mol)]$ to calculate the boiling point (°C) of liquid bromine.

8.114 What is the melting point of benzene in kelvin if $\Delta H_{fusion} = 9.95$ kJ/mol and $\Delta S_{fusion} = 35.7 \text{ J}/(K \cdot mol)$?

8.115 Metallic mercury is obtained by heating the mineral cinnabar (HgS) in air:

$$HgS(s) + O_2(g) \longrightarrow Hg(l) + SO_2(g)$$

(a) Use the data in Appendix B to calculate $\Delta H°$ in kilojoules for the reaction.

(b) The entropy change for the reaction is $\Delta S° = +36.7$ J/K. Is the reaction spontaneous at 25 °C?

(c) Under what conditions, if any, is the reaction nonspontaneous? Explain.

8.116 Use the average bond dissociation energies in Table 7.1 to calculate approximate reaction enthalpies in kilojoules for the following processes:

(a) $2\,CH_4(g) \longrightarrow C_2H_6(g) + H_2(g)$

(b) $C_2H_6(g) + F_2(g) \longrightarrow C_2H_5F(g) + HF(g)$

(c) $N_2(g) + 3\,H_2(g) \longrightarrow 2\,NH_3(g)$

8.117 Methanol (CH_3OH) is made industrially in two steps from CO and H_2. It is so cheap to make that it is being considered for use as a precursor to hydrocarbon fuels, such as methane (CH_4):

Step 1. $CO(g) + 2\,H_2(g) \longrightarrow CH_3OH(l)$
$$\Delta S° = -332 \text{ J/K}$$

Step 2. $CH_3OH(l) \longrightarrow CH_4(g) + 1/2\,O_2(g)$
$$\Delta S° = 162 \text{ J/K}$$

(a) Calculate $\Delta H°$ in kilojoules for step 1.

(b) Calculate $\Delta G°$ in kilojoules for step 1.

(c) Is step 1 spontaneous at 298 K?

(d) Which term is more important, $\Delta H°$ or $\Delta S°$?

(e) In what temperature range is step 1 spontaneous?

(f) Calculate $\Delta H°$ for step 2.

(g) Calculate $\Delta G°$ for step 2.

(h) Is step 2 spontaneous at 298 K?

(i) Which term is more important, $\Delta H°$ or $\Delta S°$?

(j) In what temperature range is step 2 spontaneous?

(k) Calculate an overall $\Delta G°$, $\Delta H°$, and $\Delta S°$ for the formation of CH_4 from CO and H_2.

(l) Is the overall reaction spontaneous at 298 K?

(m)If you were designing a production facility, would you plan on carrying out the reactions in separate steps or together? Explain.

8.118 Isooctane, C_8H_{18}, is the component of gasoline from which the term *octane rating* derives.

Isooctane

(a) Write a balanced equation for the combustion of isooctane(*l*) with O_2 to yield $CO_2(g)$ and $H_2O(l)$.

(b) The standard molar heat of combustion for isooctane(*l*) is −5461 kJ/mol. Calculate $\Delta H°_f$ for isooctane(*l*).

8.119 We said in Section 8.1 that the potential energy of water at the top of a dam or waterfall is converted into heat when the water dashes against rocks at the bottom. The potential energy of the water at the top is equal to $E_P = mgh$, where m is the mass of the water, g is the acceleration of the falling water due to gravity ($g = 9.81 \text{ m/s}^2$), and h is the height of the water. Assuming that all the energy is converted to heat, calculate the temperature rise of the water in degrees Celsius after falling over California's Yosemite Falls, a distance of 739 m. The specific heat of water is $4.18 \text{ J}/(g \cdot K)$.

8.120 For a process to be spontaneous, the total entropy of the system *and its surroundings* must increase; that is

$$\Delta S_{total} = \Delta S_{system} + \Delta S_{surr} > 0 \quad \text{For a spontaneous process}$$

Furthermore, the entropy change in the surroundings, ΔS_{surr}, is related to the enthalpy change for the process by the equation $\Delta S_{surr} = -\Delta H/T$.

(a) Since both ΔG and ΔS_{total} offer criteria for spontaneity, they must be related. Derive a relationship between them.

(b) What is the value of ΔS_{surr} for the photosynthesis of glucose from CO_2 at 298 K?

$$6\,CO_2(g) + 6\,H_2O(l) \longrightarrow C_6H_{12}O_6(s) + 6\,O_2(g)$$
$$\Delta G° = 2879 \text{ kJ}$$
$$\Delta S° = -262 \text{ J/K}$$

8.121 Set up a Hess's law cycle, and use the following information to calculate $\Delta H°_f$ for aqueous nitric acid, $HNO_3(aq)$. You will need to use fractional coefficients for some equations.

$$3\ NO_2(g) + H_2O(l) \longrightarrow 2\ HNO_3(aq) + NO(g)$$
$$\Delta H° = -137.3\ kJ$$

$$2\ NO(g) + O_2(g) \longrightarrow 2\ NO_2(g) \qquad \Delta H° = -116.2\ kJ$$

$$4\ NH_3(g) + 5\ O_2(g) \longrightarrow 4\ NO(g) + 6\ H_2O(l)$$
$$\Delta H° = -1165.2\ kJ$$

$$NH_3(g) \qquad \Delta H°_f = -46.1\ kJ/mol$$
$$H_2O(l) \qquad \Delta H°_f = -285.8\ kJ/mol$$

8.122 Hess's law can be used to calculate reaction enthalpies for hypothetical processes that can't be carried out in the laboratory. Set up a Hess's law cycle that will let you calculate $\Delta H°$ for the conversion of methane to ethylene:

$$2\ CH_4(g) \longrightarrow C_2H_4(g) + 2\ H_2(g)$$

You can use the following information:

$$2\ C_2H_6(g) + 7\ O_2(g) \longrightarrow 4\ CO_2(g) + 6\ H_2O(l)$$
$$\Delta H° = -3120.8\ kJ$$

$$CH_4(g) + 2\ O_2(g) \longrightarrow CO_2(g) + 2\ H_2O(l)$$
$$\Delta H° = -890.3\ kJ$$

$$C_2H_4(g) + H_2(g) \longrightarrow C_2H_6(g) \qquad \Delta H° = -136.3\ kJ$$

$$H_2O(l) \qquad \Delta H°_f = -285.8\ kJ/mol$$

8.123 A 110.0 g piece of molybdenum metal is heated to 100.0 °C and placed in a calorimeter that contains 150.0 g of water at 24.6 °C. The system reaches equilibrium at a final temperature of 28.0 °C. Calculate the specific heat of molybdenum metal in $J/(g \cdot °C)$. The specific heat of water is $4.184\ J/(g \cdot °C)$.

8.124 Given 400.0 g of hot tea at 80.0 °C, what mass of ice at 0 °C must be added to obtain iced tea at 10.0 °C? The specific heat of the tea is $4.18\ J/(g \cdot °C)$, and ΔH_{fusion} for ice is $+6.01\ kJ/mol$.

8.125 Citric acid has three dissociable hydrogens. When 5.00 mL of 0.64 M citric acid and 45.00 mL of 0.77 M NaOH are mixed at an initial temperature of 26.0 °C, the temperature rises to 27.9 °C as the citric acid is neutralized. The combined mixture has a

mass of 51.6 g and a specific heat of $4.0\ J/(g \cdot °C)$. Assuming that no heat is transferred to the surroundings, calculate the enthalpy change for the reaction of 1.00 mol of citric acid in kJ. Is the reaction exothermic or endothermic?

Citric acid

8.126 Assume that 100.0 mL of 0.200 M CsOH and 50.0 mL of 0.400 M HCl are mixed in a calorimeter. The solutions start out at 22.50 °C, and the final temperature after reaction is 24.28 °C. The densities of the solutions are all 1.00 g/mL, and the specific heat of the mixture is $4.2\ J/(g \cdot °C)$. What is the enthalpy change for the neutralization reaction of 1.00 mol of CsOH in kJ?

8.127 Imagine that you dissolve 10.0 g of a mixture of $NaNO_3$ and KF in 100.0 g of water and find that the temperature rises by 2.22 °C. Using the following data, calculate the mass of each compound in the original mixture. Assume that the specific heat of the solution is $4.18\ J/(g \cdot °C)$.

$$NaNO_3(s) \longrightarrow NaNO_3(aq) \quad \Delta H = +20.4\ kJ/mol$$
$$KF(s) \longrightarrow KF(aq) \qquad \Delta H = -17.7\ kJ/mol$$

8.128 Consider the reaction: $4\ CO(g) + 2\ NO_2(g) \longrightarrow 4\ CO_2(g) + N_2(g)$. Using the following information, determine $\Delta H°$ for the reaction at 25 °C.

$NO(g)$	$\Delta H°_f = +91.3\ kJ/mol$
$CO_2(g)$	$\Delta H°_f = -393.5\ kJ/mol$
$2\ NO(g) + O_2(g) \longrightarrow 2\ NO_2(g)$	$\Delta H° = -116.2\ kJ$
$2\ CO(g) + O_2(g) \longrightarrow 2\ CO_2(g)$	$\Delta H° = -566.0\ kJ$

MULTICONCEPT PROBLEMS

8.129 The reaction $S_8(g) \longrightarrow 4\ S_2(g)$ has $\Delta H° = +237\ kJ$

(a) The S_8 molecule has eight sulfur atoms arranged in a ring. What is the hybridization and geometry around each sulfur atom in S_8?

(b) The average S—S bond dissociation energy is 225 kJ/mol. Using the value of $\Delta H°$ given above, what is the S=S double bond energy in $S_2(g)$?

(c) Assuming that the bonding in S_2 is similar to the bonding in O_2, give a molecular orbital description of the bonding in S_2. Is S_2 likely to be paramagnetic or diamagnetic?

8.130 Phosgene, $COCl_2(g)$, is a toxic gas used as an agent of warfare in World War I.

(a) Draw an electron-dot structure for phosgene.

(b) Using the table of bond dissociation energies (Table 7.1) and the value $\Delta H°_f = 716.7\ kJ/mol$ for $C(g)$, estimate $\Delta H°_f$ for $COCl_2(g)$ at 25 °C. Compare your answer to

the actual $\Delta H°_f$ given in Appendix B, and explain why your calculation is only an estimate.

8.131 Acid spills are often neutralized with sodium carbonate or sodium hydrogen carbonate. For neutralization of acetic acid, the unbalanced equations are

(1) $CH_3CO_2H(l) + Na_2CO_3(s) \longrightarrow$
$$CH_3CO_2Na(aq) + CO_2(g) + H_2O(l)$$

(2) $CH_3CO_2H(l) + NaHCO_3(s) \longrightarrow$
$$CH_3CO_2Na(aq) + CO_2(g) + H_2O(l)$$

(a) Balance both equations.

(b) How many kilograms of each substance is needed to neutralize a 1.000 gallon spill of pure acetic acid (density = 1.049 g/mL)?

(c) How much heat in kilojoules is absorbed or liberated in each reaction? See Appendix B for standard heats of formation; $\Delta H°_f = -726.1\ kJ/mol$ for $CH_3CO_2Na(aq)$.

8.132 (a) Write a balanced equation for the reaction of potassium metal with water.

(b) Use the data in Appendix B to calculate $\Delta H°$ for the reaction of potassium metal with water.

(c) Assume that a chunk of potassium weighing 7.55 g is dropped into 400.0 g of water at 25.0 °C. What is the final temperature of the water if all the heat released is used to warm the water?

(d) What is the molarity of the KOH solution prepared in part **(c)**, and how many milliliters of 0.554 M H_2SO_4 are required to neutralize it?

8.133 Hydrazine, a component of rocket fuel, undergoes combustion to yield N_2 and H_2O:

$$N_2H_4(l) + O_2(g) \longrightarrow N_2(g) + 2\,H_2O(l)$$

(a) Draw an electron-dot structure for hydrazine, predict the geometry about each nitrogen atom, and tell the hybridization of each nitrogen.

(b) Use the following information to set up a Hess's law cycle, and then calculate $\Delta H°$ for the combustion reaction. You will need to use fractional coefficients for some equations.

$$2\,NH_3(g) + 3\,N_2O(g) \longrightarrow 4\,N_2(g) + 3\,H_2O(l)$$
$$\Delta H° = -1011.2\ kJ$$

$$N_2O(g) + 3\,H_2(g) \longrightarrow N_2H_4(l) + H_2O(l)$$
$$\Delta H° = -317.2\ kJ$$

$$4\,NH_3(g) + O_2(g) \longrightarrow 2\,N_2H_4(l) + 2\,H_2O(l)$$
$$\Delta H° = -286.0\ kJ$$

$$H_2O(l)\qquad \Delta H°_f = -285.8\ kJ/mol$$

(c) How much heat is released on combustion of 100.0 g of hydrazine?

8.134 Reaction of gaseous fluorine with compound **X** yields a single product **Y**, whose mass percent composition is 61.7% F and 38.3% Cl.

(a) What is a probable molecular formula for product **Y**, and what is a probable formula for **X**?

(b) Draw an electron-dot structure for **Y**, and predict the geometry around the central atom.

(c) Calculate $\Delta H°$ for the synthesis of **Y** using the following information:

$$2\,ClF(g) + O_2(g) \longrightarrow Cl_2O(g) + OF_2(g)$$
$$\Delta H° = +205.4\ kJ$$

$$2\,ClF_3(l) + 2\,O_2(g) \longrightarrow Cl_2O(g) + 3\,OF_2(g)$$
$$\Delta H° = +532.8\ kJ$$

$$OF_2(g)\qquad \Delta H°_f = +24.5\ kJ/mol$$

(d) How much heat in kilojoules is released or absorbed in the reaction of 25.0 g of **X** with a stoichiometric amount of F_2, assuming 87.5% yield for the reaction?

CHAPTER 9

Gases: Their Properties and Behavior

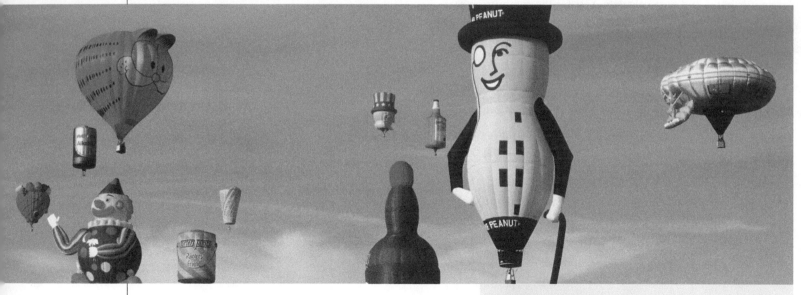

Without the invisible blanket of air surrounding us, balloons like Mr. Peanut couldn't float.

CONTENTS

A quick look around tells you that matter takes many forms. Most of the things around you are *solids*, substances whose constituent atoms, molecules, or ions are held rigidly together in a definite way, giving the solid a definite volume and shape. Other substances are *liquids*, whose constituent atoms or molecules are held together less strongly, giving the liquid a definite volume but a changeable and indefinite shape. Still other substances are *gases*, whose constituent atoms or molecules have little attraction for one another and are therefore free to move about in whatever volume is available.

Although gases are few in number—only about a hundred substances are gases at room temperature—their study was enormously important in the historical development of chemical theories. We'll look briefly at this historical development in the present chapter, and we'll see how the behavior of gases can be described.

9.1 GASES AND GAS PRESSURE

We live surrounded by a blanket of air—the mixture of gases that make up the Earth's atmosphere. As shown in Table 9.1, nitrogen and oxygen account for more than 99% by volume of dry air. The remaining 1% is largely argon, with trace amounts of several other substances also present. Carbon dioxide, about which there is so much current concern because of its relationship to global warming, is present in air only to the extent of about 0.0385%, or 385 parts per million (ppm). Although small, this value has risen in the past 160 years from an estimated 290 ppm in 1850, as the burning of fossil fuels and the deforestation of tropical rain forests have increased.

TABLE 9.1 Composition of Dry Air at Sea Level

Constituent	% Volume	% Mass
N_2	78.08	75.52
O_2	20.95	23.14
Ar	0.93	1.29
CO_2	0.0385	0.059
Ne	1.82×10^{-3}	1.27×10^{-3}
He	5.24×10^{-4}	7.24×10^{-5}
CH_4	1.7×10^{-4}	9.4×10^{-5}
Kr	1.14×10^{-4}	3.3×10^{-4}

Air is typical of gases in many respects, and its behavior illustrates several important points about gases. For instance, gas mixtures are always *homogeneous*, meaning that they are uniform in composition. Unlike liquids, which often fail to mix with one another and which may separate into distinct layers—oil and water, for example—gases always mix completely. Furthermore, gases are *compressible*. When pressure is applied, the volume of a gas contracts proportionately. Solids and liquids, however, are nearly incompressible, and even the application of great pressure changes their volume only slightly.

Homogeneous mixing and compressibility both occur because the molecules in gases are far apart (Figure 9.1). Mixing occurs because individual gas molecules have little interaction with their neighbors and the chemical identities of those neighbors are therefore irrelevant. In solids and liquids, by contrast, molecules are packed closely together, where they are affected by various attractive and repulsive forces that can inhibit their mixing. Compressibility is possible in gases because less than 0.1% of the volume of a typical gas is taken up by the molecules themselves under normal circumstances; the remaining 99.9% is empty space. By contrast, approximately 70% of a solid's or liquid's volume is taken up by the molecules.

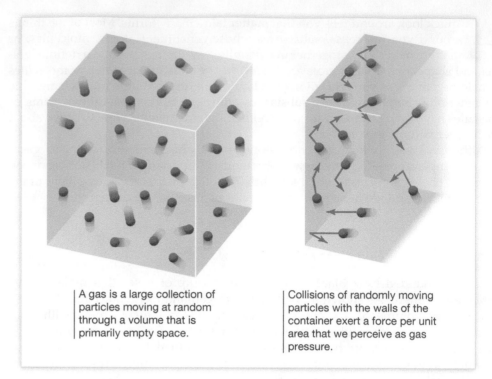

A gas is a large collection of particles moving at random through a volume that is primarily empty space.

Collisions of randomly moving particles with the walls of the container exert a force per unit area that we perceive as gas pressure.

Figure 9.1
Molecular view of a gas.

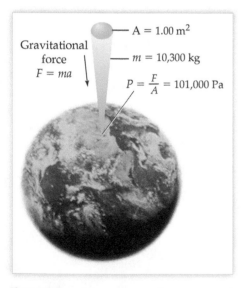

$A = 1.00 \text{ m}^2$

Gravitational force
$F = ma$

$m = 10,300 \text{ kg}$

$P = \dfrac{F}{A} = 101,000 \text{ Pa}$

Figure 9.2
Atmospheric pressure. A column of air 1 m^2 in cross-sectional area extending from the Earth's surface through the upper atmosphere has a mass of about 10,300 kg, producing an atmospheric pressure of approximately 101,000 Pa.

One of the most obvious characteristics of gases is that they exert a measurable *pressure* on the walls of their container (Figure 9.1). We're all familiar with inflating a balloon or pumping up a bicycle tire and feeling the hardness that results from the pressure inside. In scientific terms, **pressure (P)** is defined as a force (F) exerted per unit area (A). Force, in turn, is defined as mass (m) times acceleration (a), which, on Earth, is usually the acceleration due to gravity, $a = 9.81 \text{ m/s}^2$.

$$\text{Pressure } (P) = \frac{F}{A} = \frac{m \times a}{A}$$

The SI unit for force is the **newton (N)**, where $1 \text{ N} = 1 \text{ (kg} \cdot \text{m)/s}^2$, and the SI unit for pressure is the **pascal (Pa)**, where $1 \text{ Pa} = 1 \text{ N/m}^2 = 1 \text{ kg/(m} \cdot \text{s}^2)$. Expressed in more familiar units, a pascal is actually a very small amount—the pressure exerted by a mass of 10.2 mg resting on an area of 1.00 cm^2. In rough terms, a penny sitting on the tip of your finger exerts a pressure of about 250 Pa.

$$P = \frac{m \times a}{A} = \frac{(10.2 \text{ mg})\left(\dfrac{1 \text{ kg}}{10^6 \text{ mg}}\right)\left(9.81 \dfrac{\text{m}}{\text{s}^2}\right)}{(1.00 \text{ cm}^2)\left(\dfrac{1 \text{ m}^2}{10^4 \text{ cm}^2}\right)} = \frac{1.00 \times 10^{-4} \dfrac{\text{kg} \cdot \text{m}}{\text{s}^2}}{1.00 \times 10^{-4} \text{ m}^2} = 1.00 \text{ Pa}$$

Just as the air in a tire and a penny on your finger exert pressure, the mass of air in the atmosphere pressing down on the Earth's surface exerts what we call *atmospheric pressure*. In fact, a 1 m^2 column of air extending from the Earth's surface through the upper atmosphere has a mass of about 10,300 kg, producing an atmospheric pressure of approximately 101,000 Pa, or 101 kPa (**Figure 9.2**).

$$P = \frac{m \times a}{A} = \frac{10,300 \text{ kg} \times 9.81 \dfrac{\text{m}}{\text{s}^2}}{1.00 \text{ m}^2} = 101,000 \text{ Pa} = 101 \text{ kPa}$$

As is frequently the case with SI units, which must serve many disciplines, the pascal is an inconvenient size for most chemical measurements. Thus, the alternative pressure units *millimeter of mercury (mm Hg)*, *atmosphere (atm)*, and *bar* are more often used.

The **millimeter of mercury**, also called a *torr* after the 17th-century Italian scientist Evangelista Torricelli (1608–1647), is based on atmospheric pressure measurements using a mercury *barometer*. As shown in **Figure 9.3**, a barometer consists of a long, thin tube that is sealed at one end, filled with mercury, and then inverted into a dish of mercury. Some mercury runs from the tube into the dish until the downward pressure of the mercury inside the column is exactly balanced by the outside atmospheric pressure, which presses on the mercury in the dish and pushes it up the column. The height of the mercury column varies slightly from day to day depending on the altitude and weather conditions, but atmospheric pressure at sea level was originally defined as exactly 760 mm Hg.

The empty space above the mercury in the sealed end of the tube is a vacuum.

The downward pressure of the mercury in the column is exactly balanced by the outside **atmospheric pressure** that presses down on the mercury in the dish and pushes it up the column.

Atmospheric pressure

760 mm

Mercury-filled dish

Figure 9.3
A mercury barometer. The barometer measures atmospheric pressure by determining the height of a mercury column supported in a sealed glass tube.

Knowing the density of mercury ($1.359\ 51 \times 10^4\ \text{kg/m}^3$ at 0 °C) and the acceleration due to gravity ($9.806\ 65\ \text{m/s}^2$), it's possible to calculate the pressure exerted by the column of mercury 760 mm (0.760 m) in height. Thus, 1 standard **atmosphere** of pressure (1 atm) is now defined as exactly 101,325 Pa:

$$P = (0.760\ \text{m})\left(1.359\ 51 \times 10^4\ \frac{\text{kg}}{\text{m}^3}\right)\left(9.806\ 65\ \frac{\text{m}}{\text{s}^2}\right) = 101{,}325\ \text{Pa}$$

1 atm = 760 mm Hg = 101,325 Pa

Although not strictly an SI unit, the **bar** is quickly gaining popularity as a unit of pressure because it is a particularly convenient power of 10 of the SI unit pascal and because it differs from 1 atm by only about 1%:

$$1\ \text{bar} = 100{,}000\ \text{Pa} = 100\ \text{kPa} = 0.986\ 923\ \text{atm}$$

Gas pressure inside a container is often measured using an open-end **manometer**, a simple instrument similar in principle to the mercury barometer. As shown in **Figure 9.4**, an open-end manometer consists of a U tube filled with mercury, with one end connected to a gas-filled container and the other end open to the atmosphere. The difference between the pressure of the gas in the container and the pressure

Figure 9.4
Open-end manometers for measuring pressure in a gas-filled bulb.

(a) The mercury level is higher in the arm open to the bulb because the pressure in the bulb is lower than atmospheric.

(b) The mercury level is higher in the arm open to the atmosphere because the pressure in the bulb is higher than atmospheric.

of the atmosphere is equal to the difference between the heights of the mercury levels in the two arms of the U-tube. If the gas pressure inside the container is less than atmospheric, the mercury level is higher in the arm connected to the container (Figure 9.4a). If the gas pressure inside the container is greater than atmospheric, the mercury level is higher in the arm open to the atmosphere (Figure 9.4b).

WORKED EXAMPLE 9.1

CONVERTING BETWEEN DIFFERENT UNITS OF PRESSURE

Typical atmospheric pressure on top of Mt. Everest (29,035 ft) is 265 mm Hg. Convert this value to pascals, atmospheres, and bars.

STRATEGY

Use the conversion factors 101,325 Pa/760 mm Hg, 1 atm/760 mm Hg, and 1 bar/10^5 Pa to carry out the necessary calculations.

SOLUTION

$$(265 \text{ mm Hg})\left(\frac{101{,}325 \text{ Pa}}{760 \text{ mm Hg}}\right) = 3.53 \times 10^4 \text{ Pa}$$

$$(265 \text{ mm Hg})\left(\frac{1 \text{ atm}}{760 \text{ mm Hg}}\right) = 0.349 \text{ atm}$$

$$(3.53 \times 10^4 \text{ Pa})\left(\frac{1 \text{ bar}}{10^5 \text{ Pa}}\right) = 0.353 \text{ bar}$$

BALLPARK CHECK

One atmosphere equals 760 mm Hg pressure. Since 265 mm Hg is about 1/3 of 760 mm Hg, the air pressure on Mt. Everest is about 1/3 of standard atmospheric pressure—approximately 30,000 Pa, 0.3 atm, or 0.3 bar.

▲ Atmospheric pressure decreases as altitude increases. On the top of Mt. Everest, typical atmospheric pressure is 265 mm Hg.

WORKED EXAMPLE 9.2

USING AN OPEN-END MANOMETER

Assume that you are using an open-end manometer (Figure 9.4) filled with mineral oil rather than mercury. What is the gas pressure in the bulb in millimeters of mercury if the level of mineral oil in the arm connected to the bulb is 237 mm higher than the level in the arm connected to the atmosphere and atmospheric pressure is 746 mm Hg? The density of mercury is 13.6 g/mL, and the density of mineral oil is 0.822 g/mL.

STRATEGY

The gas pressure in the bulb equals the difference between the outside pressure and the manometer reading. The manometer reading indicates that the pressure of the gas in the bulb is less than atmospheric because the liquid level is higher on the side connected to the sample. Because mercury is more dense than mineral oil by a factor of 13.6/0.822, or 16.5, a given pressure will hold a column of mercury only 1/16.5 times the height of a column of mineral oil.

SOLUTION

$$P_{manometer} = 237 \text{ mm mineral oil} \times \frac{0.822 \text{ mm Hg}}{13.6 \text{ mm mineral oil}} = 14.3 \text{ mm Hg}$$

$$P_{bulb} = P_{outside} - P_{manometer} = 746 \text{ mm Hg} - 14.3 \text{ mm Hg} = 732 \text{ mm Hg}$$

▶ **PROBLEM 9.1** Yet another common measure of pressure is the unit pounds per square inch (psi). How many pounds per square inch correspond to 1.00 atm? To 1.00 mm Hg?

▶ **PROBLEM 9.2** If the density of water is 1.00 g/mL and the density of mercury is 13.6 g/mL, how high a column of water in meters can be supported by standard atmospheric pressure? By 1 bar?

▶ **PROBLEM 9.3** What is the pressure in atmospheres in a container of gas connected to a mercury-filled, open-end manometer if the level in the arm connected to the container is 24.7 cm higher than in the arm open to the atmosphere and atmospheric pressure is 0.975 atm?

CONCEPTUAL PROBLEM 9.4 What is the pressure of the gas inside the apparatus shown on the right in mm Hg if the outside pressure is 750 mm Hg?

9.2 THE GAS LAWS

Unlike solids and liquids, different gases show remarkably similar physical behavior regardless of their chemical makeup. Helium and fluorine, for example, are vastly different in their chemical properties yet are almost identical in much of their physical behavior. Numerous observations made in the late 1600s showed that the physical properties of any gas can be defined by four variables: pressure (P), temperature (T), volume (V), and amount, or number of moles (n). The specific relationships among these four variables are called the **gas laws**, and a gas whose behavior follows the laws exactly is called an **ideal gas**.

Boyle's Law: The Relationship between Gas Volume and Pressure

Imagine that you have a sample of gas inside a cylinder with a movable piston at one end (**Figure 9.5**). What would happen if you were to increase the pressure on the gas by pushing down on the piston? Experience probably tells you that the volume of gas in the cylinder would decrease as you increase the pressure. According to **Boyle's law**, the volume of a fixed amount of gas at a constant temperature varies inversely with its pressure. If the gas pressure is doubled, the volume is halved; if the pressure is halved, the gas volume doubles.

🔑 **Boyle's law** $V \propto 1/P$ or $PV = k$ at constant n and T

The volume of an ideal gas varies inversely with pressure. That is, P times V is constant when n and T are kept constant. (The symbol $\propto$ means "is proportional to," and k denotes a constant.)

Figure 9.5
Boyle's law.

At constant n and T, the volume of an ideal gas decreases proportionately as its pressure increases. **If the pressure is doubled, the volume is halved.**

$P = 1.0$ atm
$V = 1.0$ L

Increase pressure

Decrease pressure

$P = 2.0$ atm
$V = 0.5$ L

If the pressure is halved, the volume is doubled.

The validity of Boyle's law can be demonstrated by making a simple series of pressure–volume measurements on a gas sample (Table 9.2) and plotting them as in Figure 9.6. When V is plotted versus P, the result is a curve in the form of a hyperbola. When V is plotted versus $1/P$, however, the result is a straight line. Such graphical behavior is characteristic of mathematical equations of the form $y = mx + b$. In this case, $y = V$, $m =$ the slope of the line (the constant k in the present instance), $x = 1/P$, and $b =$ the y-intercept (a constant; 0 in the present instance). (See Appendix A.3 for a review of linear equations.)

$$V = k\left(\frac{1}{P}\right) + 0 \quad \text{(or } PV = k)$$
$$\uparrow \quad \uparrow \; \uparrow \qquad \uparrow$$
$$y = m \; x \; + b$$

TABLE 9.2   Pressure–Volume Measurements on a Gas Sample at Constant n, T

Pressure (mm Hg)	Volume (L)
760	1
380	2
253	3
190	4
152	5
127	6
109	7
95	8
84	9
76	10

A plot of V versus P for a gas sample is a **hyperbola**.

A plot of V versus $1/P$ is a **straight line**. Such a graph is characteristic of equations having the form $y = mx + b$.

Figure 9.6
Boyle's law plot.

Charles's Law: The Relationship between Gas Volume and Temperature

Imagine that you again have a gas sample inside a cylinder with a movable piston at one end (Figure 9.7). What would happen if you were to raise the temperature of the sample while letting the piston move freely to keep the pressure constant? Experience tells you that the piston would move up because the volume of the gas in the cylinder would expand. According to **Charles's law**, the volume of a fixed amount of an ideal gas at a constant pressure varies directly with its absolute temperature. If the gas temperature in kelvin is doubled, the volume is doubled; if the gas temperature is halved, the volume is halved.

Charles's law $V \propto T$ or $V/T = k$ at constant n and P

The volume of an ideal gas varies directly with absolute temperature. That is, V divided by T is constant when n and P are held constant.

At constant n and P, the volume of an ideal gas changes proportionately as its absolute temperature changes. If the absolute **temperature doubles**, the **volume doubles.**

1 atm

1 atm

Heat

Cool

$V = 0.5$ L

$V = 1.0$ L

$T = 200$ K

$T = 400$ K

If the absolute **temperature** is halved, the **volume is halved.**

Figure 9.7
Charles's law.

The validity of Charles's law can be demonstrated by making a series of temperature–volume measurements on a gas sample, giving the results listed in Table 9.3. Like Boyle's law, Charles's law takes the mathematical form $y = mx + b$, where $y = V$, $m = $ the slope of the line (the constant k in the present instance), $x = T$, and $b = $ the y-intercept (0 in the present instance). A plot of V versus T is therefore a straight line whose slope is the constant k (Figure 9.8).

$$V = kT + 0 \quad \left(\text{or } \frac{V}{T} = k\right)$$
$$\uparrow \quad \uparrow\uparrow \quad \uparrow$$
$$y = mx + b$$

The plots of volume versus temperature demonstrate an interesting point. When temperature is plotted on the Celsius scale, the straight line can be extrapolated to $V = 0$ at $T = -273$ °C (Figure 9.8a). But because matter can't have a negative volume, this extrapolation suggests that -273 °C must be the lowest possible temperature, or *absolute zero* on the Kelvin scale (Figure 9.8b). In fact, the approximate value of absolute zero was first determined using this simple method.

TABLE 9.3	Temperature–Volume Measurements on a Gas Sample at Constant n and P

Temperature (K)	Volume (L)
123	0.45
173	0.63
223	0.82
273	1.00
323	1.18
373	1.37

(a)   (b)

A plot of V versus T for a gas sample is a straight line that can be extrapolated to absolute zero, $0 \text{ K} = -273 \,°\text{C}$.

Figure 9.8
Charles's law plot.

Avogadro's Law: The Relationship between Volume and Amount

Imagine that you have two more gas samples inside cylinders with movable pistons (**Figure 9.9**). One cylinder contains 1 mol of a gas and the other contains 2 mol of gas at the same temperature and pressure as the first. Common sense says that the gas in the second cylinder will have twice the volume of the gas in the first cylinder because there is twice as much of it. According to **Avogadro's law**, the volume of an ideal gas at a fixed pressure and temperature depends on its molar amount. If the amount of the gas is doubled, the gas volume is doubled; if the amount is halved, the volume is halved.

 Avogadro's law $V \propto n$ or $V/n = k$ at constant T and P

The volume of an ideal gas varies directly with its molar amount. That is, V divided by n is constant when T and P are held constant.

At constant T and P, the volume of an ideal gas changes proportionately with its molar amount. If the **molar amount doubles**, the **volume doubles**.

1 atm

1 atm

$V = 44.8$ L

Add gas

Remove gas

$V = 22.4$ L

$n = 1$ mol

$n = 2$ mol

If the **molar amount is halved**, the **volume is halved**.

Figure 9.9
Avogadro's law.

Put another way, Avogadro's law also says that equal volumes of different gases at the same temperature and pressure contain the same molar amounts. A 1 L container of oxygen contains the same number of moles as a 1 L container of helium, fluorine, argon, or any other gas at the same T and P. Furthermore, 1 mol of an ideal gas occupies a volume, called the **standard molar volume**, of 22.414 L at 0 °C and exactly 1 atm pressure. For comparison, the standard molar volume is nearly identical to the volume of three basketballs.

WORKED CONCEPTUAL EXAMPLE 9.3

VISUAL REPRESENTATIONS OF GAS LAWS

Show the approximate level of the movable piston in drawings **(a)** and **(b)** after the indicated changes have been made to the initial gas sample.

(initial)	(a)	(b)
$T = 250$ K	$T = 375$ K	$T = 250$ K
$n = 0.140$ mol	$n = 0.140$ mol	$n = 0.070$ mol
$P = 1.0$ atm	$P = 1.0$ atm	$P = 0.50$ atm

STRATEGY

Identify which of the variables P, n, and T have changed, and calculate the effect of each change on the volume according to the appropriate gas law.

SOLUTION

(a) The temperature T has increased by a factor of $375/250 = 1.5$, while the molar amount n and the pressure P are unchanged. According to Charles's law, the volume will increase by a factor of 1.5.

(b) The temperature T is unchanged, while both the molar amount n and the pressure P are halved. According to Avogadro's law, halving the molar amount will halve the volume, and according to Boyle's law, halving the pressure will double the volume. The two changes cancel, so the volume is unchanged.

(initial)	(a)	(b)
$T = 250$ K	$T = 375$ K	$T = 250$ K
$n = 0.140$ mol	$n = 0.140$ mol	$n = 0.070$ mol
$P = 1.0$ atm	$P = 1.0$ atm	$P = 0.50$ atm

CONCEPTUAL PROBLEM 9.5   Show the approximate level of the movable piston in drawings **(a)** and **(b)** after the indicated changes have been made to the initial gas sample at a constant pressure of 1.0 atm.

1 atm	**(a)**	**(b)**
(initial) $T = 300$ K $n = 0.3$ mol	$T = 400$ K $n = 0.225$ mol	$T = 200$ K $n = 0.225$ mol

9.3 THE IDEAL GAS LAW

All three gas laws discussed in the previous section can be combined into a single statement called the **ideal gas law**, which describes how the volume of a gas is affected by changes in pressure, temperature, and amount. When the values of any three of the variables P, V, T, and n are known, the value of the fourth can be calculated using the ideal gas law. The proportionality constant R in the equation is called the **gas constant** and has the same value for all gases.

Ideal gas law $V = \dfrac{nRT}{P}$ or $PV = nRT$

The ideal gas law can be rearranged in different ways to take the form of Boyle's law, Charles's law, or Avogadro's law.

Boyle's law: $PV = nRT = k$ (When n and T are constant)

Charles's law: $\dfrac{V}{T} = \dfrac{nR}{P} = k$ (When n and P are constant)

Avogadro's law: $\dfrac{V}{n} = \dfrac{RT}{P} = k$ (When T and P are constant)

The value of the gas constant R can be calculated from knowledge of the standard molar volume of a gas. Since 1 mol of a gas occupies a volume of 22.414 L at 0 °C (273.15 K) and 1 atm pressure, the gas constant R is equal to 0.082 058 (L · atm)/(K · mol), or 8.3145 J/(K · mol) in SI units:

$$R = \frac{P \cdot V}{n \cdot T} = \frac{(1\ \text{atm})(22.414\ \text{L})}{(1\ \text{mol})(273.15\ \text{K})} = 0.082\ 058\ \frac{\text{L} \cdot \text{atm}}{\text{K} \cdot \text{mol}}$$

$$= 8.3145\ \text{J}/(\text{K} \cdot \text{mol})\qquad (\text{When } P \text{ is in pascals and } V \text{ is in cubic meters})$$

The specific conditions used in the calculation—0 °C (273.15 K) and 1 atm pressure—are said to represent **standard temperature and pressure**, abbreviated **STP**. These standard conditions are generally used when reporting measurements on gases. Note that the standard temperature for gas measurements (0 °C, or

273.15 K) is different from that usually assumed for thermodynamic measurements (25 °C, or 298.15 K; Section 8.5).

➡ **Standard Temperature and Pressure (STP) for Gases** $T = 0\,°C$ $P = 1\,atm$

We should also point out that the standard pressure for gas measurements, still listed here and in most other books as 1 atm (101,325 Pa), has actually been redefined to be 1 bar, or 100,000 Pa. This new standard pressure is now 0.986 923 atm, making the newly defined standard molar volume 22.711 L rather than 22.414 L. Like most other books, we'll continue for the present using 1 atm as the standard pressure.

The name *ideal* gas law implies that there must be some gases whose behavior is *nonideal*. In fact, there is no such thing as an ideal gas that obeys the equation perfectly under all circumstances. All real gases are nonideal to some extent and deviate slightly from the behavior predicted by the gas laws. As Table 9.4 shows, for example, the actual molar volume of a real gas often differs slightly from the 22.414 L ideal value. Under most conditions, though, the deviations from ideal behavior are so slight as to make little difference. We'll discuss circumstances in Section 9.8 where the deviations are greater.

TABLE 9.4 Molar Volumes of Some Real Gases at 0 °C and 1 atm

WORKED EXAMPLE 9.4

GAS LAW CALCULATIONS

How many moles of gas (air) are in the lungs of an average adult with a lung capacity of 3.8 L? Assume that the lungs are at 1.00 atm pressure and a normal body temperature of 37 °C.

STRATEGY

This problem asks for a value of n when V, P, and T are given. Rearrange the ideal gas law to the form $n = PV/RT$, convert the temperature from degrees Celsius to kelvin, and substitute the given values of P, V, and T into the equation.

SOLUTION

$$n = \frac{PV}{RT} = \frac{(1.00\ \text{atm})(3.8\ \text{L})}{\left(0.082\ 06\ \dfrac{\text{L} \cdot \text{atm}}{\text{K} \cdot \text{mol}}\right)(310\ \text{K})} = 0.15\ \text{mol}$$

The lungs of an average adult hold 0.15 mol of air.

BALLPARK CHECK

A lung volume of 4 L is about 1/6 of 22.4 L, the standard molar volume of an ideal gas. Thus, the lungs have a capacity of about 1/6 mol, or 0.17 mol.

▲ How many moles of methane are in these tanks?

WORKED EXAMPLE 9.5

GAS LAW CALCULATIONS

In a typical automobile engine, the mixture of gasoline and air in a cylinder is compressed from 1.0 atm to 9.5 atm prior to ignition. If the uncompressed volume of the cylinder is 410 mL, what is the volume in milliliters when the mixture is fully compressed?

STRATEGY

This is a Boyle's law problem because only P and V are changing, while n and T remain fixed. We can therefore set up the following equation and solve for V_{final}.

$$(PV)_{initial} = (PV)_{final} = nRT$$

SOLUTION

$$V_{final} = \frac{(PV)_{initial}}{P_{final}} = \frac{(1.0 \text{ atm})(410 \text{ mL})}{9.5 \text{ atm}} = 43 \text{ mL}$$

BALLPARK CHECK

Because the pressure in the cylinder increases about 10-fold, the volume must decrease about 10-fold according to Boyle's law, from approximately 400 mL to 40 mL.

▸ **PROBLEM 9.6**   How many moles of methane gas, CH_4, are in a storage tank with a volume of 1.000×10^5 L at STP? How many grams?

▸ **PROBLEM 9.7**   An aerosol spray can with a volume of 350 mL contains 3.2 g of propane gas (C_3H_8) as propellant. What is the pressure in atmospheres of gas in the can at 20 °C?

▸ **PROBLEM 9.8**   A helium gas cylinder of the sort used to fill balloons has a volume of 43.8 L and a pressure of 1.51×10^4 kPa at 25.0 °C. How many moles of helium are in the tank?

▸ **PROBLEM 9.9**   What final temperature (°C) is required for the pressure inside an automobile tire to increase from 2.15 atm at 0 °C to 2.37 atm, assuming the volume remains constant?

CONCEPTUAL PROBLEM 9.10   Show the approximate level of the movable piston in drawings **(a)**, **(b)**, and **(c)** after the indicated changes have been made to the gas.

(initial)
$T = 25$ °C
$n = 0.075$ mol
$P = 0.92$ atm

(a)
$T = 50$ °C
$n = 0.075$ mol
$P = 0.92$ atm

(b)
$T = 175$ °C
$n = 0.075$ mol
$P = 2.7$ atm

(c)
$T = 25$ °C
$n = 0.22$ mol
$P = 2.7$ atm

9.4 STOICHIOMETRIC RELATIONSHIPS WITH GASES

Many chemical reactions, including some of the most important processes in the chemical industry, involve gases. Approximately 120 million metric tons of ammonia, for instance, is manufactured each year worldwide by the reaction of hydrogen with nitrogen according to the equation $3\,H_2 + N_2 \rightarrow 2\,NH_3$. Thus, it's necessary to be able to calculate amounts of gaseous reactants just as it's necessary to calculate amounts of solids, liquids, and solutions (Sections 3.3–3.8).

Most gas calculations are just applications of the ideal gas law in which three of the variables P, V, T, and n are known and the fourth variable must be calculated. The reaction used in the deployment of automobile air bags, for instance, is the high-temperature decomposition of sodium azide, NaN_3, to produce N_2 gas. (The sodium is then removed by a subsequent reaction.) How many liters of N_2 gas at 1.15 atm and 30 °C are produced by decomposition of 45.0 g of NaN_3?

$$2\,NaN_3(s) \longrightarrow 2\,Na(s) + 3\,N_2(g)$$

▲ Automobile air bags are inflated with N_2 gas produced by decomposition of sodium azide.

Values for P and T are given, the value of n can be calculated, and the ideal gas law will then let us find V. To find n, the number of moles of N_2 gas produced, we first need to find how many moles of NaN_3 are in 45.0 g:

Molar mass of NaN_3 = 65.0 g/mol

$$\text{Moles of } NaN_3 = (45.0 \text{ g } NaN_3)\left(\frac{1 \text{ mol } NaN_3}{65.0 \text{ g } NaN_3}\right) = 0.692 \text{ mol } NaN_3$$

Next, find how many moles of N_2 are produced in the decomposition reaction. According to the balanced equation, 2 mol of NaN_3 yields 3 mol of N_2, so 0.692 mol of NaN_3 yields 1.04 mol of N_2:

$$\text{Moles of } N_2 = (0.692 \text{ mol } NaN_3)\left(\frac{3 \text{ mol } N_2}{2 \text{ mol } NaN_3}\right) = 1.04 \text{ mol } N_2$$

Finally, use the ideal gas law to calculate the volume of N_2. Remember to use the Kelvin temperature (303 K) rather than the Celsius temperature (30 °C) in the calculation.

$$V = \frac{nRT}{P} = \frac{(1.04 \text{ mol } N_2)\left(0.082\,06\,\dfrac{L \cdot atm}{K \cdot mol}\right)(303 \text{ K})}{1.15 \text{ atm}} = 22.5 \text{ L}$$

Worked Example 9.6 illustrates another gas stoichiometry calculation.

Still other applications of the ideal gas law make it possible to calculate such properties as density and molar mass. Densities are calculated by weighing a known volume of a gas at a known temperature and pressure, as shown in **Figure 9.10**. Using the ideal gas law to find the volume at STP and then dividing the measured mass by the volume gives the density at STP. Worked Example 9.7 gives a sample calculation.

A bulb of known volume is evacuated and weighed when empty.

The bulb is then filled with gas at a known pressure and temperature, and weighed again. Dividing the mass by the volume gives the density.

Vacuum

Fill and weigh

Known volume

Figure 9.10
Determining the density of an unknown gas.

Molar masses, and therefore molecular masses, can also be calculated using the ideal gas law. Imagine, for instance, that an unknown gas found bubbling up in a swamp is collected, placed in a glass bulb, and found to have a density of 0.714 g/L at STP. What is the molecular mass of the gas?

Let's assume that we have 1.00 L of sample, which has a mass of 0.714 g. Since the density is measured at STP, we know T, P, and V, and we need to find n, the molar amount of gas that has a mass of 0.714 g:

$$n = \frac{PV}{RT} = \frac{(1.00 \text{ atm})(1.00 \text{ L})}{\left(0.082\,06\,\dfrac{\text{L} \cdot \text{atm}}{\text{K} \cdot \text{mol}}\right)(273 \text{ K})} = 0.0446 \text{ mol}$$

Dividing the mass of the sample by the number of moles then gives the molar mass:

$$\text{Molar mass} = \frac{0.714 \text{ g}}{0.0446 \text{ mol}} = 16.0 \text{ g/mol}$$

Thus, the molar mass of the unknown gas (actually methane, CH_4) is 16.0 g/mol, and the molecular mass is 16.0 amu.

It's often true in chemistry, particularly in gas-law calculations, that a problem can be solved in more than one way. As an alternative method for calculating the molar mass of the unknown swamp gas, you might recognize that 1 mol of an ideal gas has a volume of 22.4 L at STP. Since 1.00 L of the unknown gas has a mass of 0.714 g, 22.4 L of the gas (1 mol) has a mass of 16.0 g:

$$\text{Molar mass} = \left(0.714\,\frac{\text{g}}{\text{L}}\right)\left(22.4\,\frac{\text{L}}{\text{mol}}\right) = 16.0 \text{ g/mol}$$

Worked Example 9.8 illustrates another calculation of the molar mass of an unknown gas.

WORKED EXAMPLE 9.6

FINDING A MASS USING GAS LAW CALCULATIONS

A typical high-pressure tire on a bicycle might have a volume of 365 mL and a pressure of 7.80 atm at 25 °C. Suppose the rider filled the tire with helium to minimize weight. What is the mass of the helium in the tire?

STRATEGY

We are given V, P, and T, and we need to use the ideal gas law to calculate n, the number of moles of helium in the tire. With n known, we then do a mole-to-mass conversion.

SOLUTION

$$n = \frac{PV}{RT} = \frac{(7.80 \text{ atm})(0.365 \text{ L})}{\left(0.082\,06\,\dfrac{\text{L} \cdot \text{atm}}{\text{K} \cdot \text{mol}}\right)(298 \text{ K})} = 0.116 \text{ mol}$$

$$\text{Grams of helium} = 0.116 \text{ mol He} \times \frac{4.00 \text{ g He}}{1 \text{ mol He}} = 0.464 \text{ g}$$

WORKED EXAMPLE 9.7

FINDING A DENSITY USING GAS LAW CALCULATIONS

What is the density in g/L of ammonia at STP if the gas in a 1.000 L bulb weighs 0.672 g at 25 °C and 733.4 mm Hg pressure?

STRATEGY

The density of any substance is mass divided by volume. For the ammonia sample, the mass is 0.672 g but the volume of the gas is given under nonstandard conditions and must first be converted to STP. Because the amount of sample n is constant, we can set the quantity PV/RT measured under nonstandard conditions equal to PV/RT at STP and then solve for V at STP.

SOLUTION

$$n = \left(\frac{PV}{RT}\right)_{measured} = \left(\frac{PV}{RT}\right)_{STP} \quad \text{or} \quad V_{STP} = \left(\frac{PV}{RT}\right)_{measured}\left(\frac{RT}{P}\right)_{STP}$$

$$V_{STP} = \left(\frac{733.4 \text{ mm Hg} \times 1.000 \text{ L}}{298 \text{ K}}\right)\left(\frac{273 \text{ K}}{760 \text{ mm Hg}}\right) = 0.884 \text{ L}$$

The amount of gas in the 1.000 L bulb under the measured nonstandard conditions would have a volume of only 0.884 L at STP. Dividing the given mass by this volume gives the density of ammonia at STP:

$$\text{Density} = \frac{\text{Mass}}{\text{Volume}} = \frac{0.672 \text{ g}}{0.884 \text{ L}} = 0.760 \text{ g/L}$$

WORKED EXAMPLE 9.8

IDENTIFYING AN UNKNOWN USING GAS LAW CALCULATIONS

To identify the contents of an unlabeled cylinder of gas, a sample was collected and found to have a density of 5.380 g/L at 15 °C and 736 mm Hg pressure. What is the molar mass of the gas?

STRATEGY

Let's assume we have a 1.000 L sample of the gas, which weighs 5.380 g. We know the temperature, volume, and pressure of the gas and can therefore use the ideal gas law to find n, the number of moles in the sample. Dividing the mass by the number of moles then gives the molar mass.

SOLUTION

$$PV = nRT \quad \text{or} \quad n = \frac{PV}{RT}$$

$$n = \frac{\left(736 \text{ mm Hg} \times \dfrac{1 \text{ atm}}{760 \text{ mm Hg}}\right)(1.000 \text{ L})}{\left(0.082\,06\,\dfrac{\text{L} \cdot \text{atm}}{\text{K} \cdot \text{mol}}\right)(288 \text{ K})} = 0.0410 \text{ mol}$$

$$\text{Molar mass} = \frac{5.380 \text{ g}}{0.0410 \text{ mol}} = 131 \text{ g/mol}$$

The gas is probably xenon (atomic mass = 131.3 amu).

▶ **PROBLEM 9.11** Carbonate-bearing rocks like limestone ($CaCO_3$) react with dilute acids such as HCl to produce carbon dioxide, according to the equation

$$CaCO_3(s) + 2\,HCl(aq) \longrightarrow CaCl_2(aq) + CO_2(g) + H_2O(l)$$

How many grams of CO_2 are formed by complete reaction of 33.7 g of limestone? What is the volume in liters of this CO_2 at STP?

▶ **PROBLEM 9.12** Propane gas (C_3H_8) is used as a fuel in rural areas. How many liters of CO_2 are formed at STP by the complete combustion of the propane in a container with a volume of 15.0 L and a pressure of 4.5 atm at 25 °C? The unbalanced equation is

$$C_3H_8(g) + O_2(g) \longrightarrow CO_2(g) + H_2O(l)$$

▶ **PROBLEM 9.13** A foul-smelling gas produced by the reaction of HCl with Na_2S was collected, and a 1.00 L sample was found to have a mass of 1.52 g at STP. What is the molecular mass of the gas? What is its likely formula and name?

▲ Carbonate-bearing rocks like limestone ($CaCO_3$) react with dilute acids such as HCl to produce bubbles of carbon dioxide.

9.5 PARTIAL PRESSURE AND DALTON'S LAW

Just as the gas laws apply to all pure gases, regardless of chemical identity, they also apply to *mixtures* of gases, such as air. The pressure, volume, temperature, and amount of a gas mixture are all related by the ideal gas law.

What is responsible for the pressure in a gas mixture? Because the pressure of a pure gas at constant temperature and volume is proportional to its amount ($P = nRT/V$), the pressure contribution from each individual gas in a mixture is also proportional to *its* amount in the mixture. In other words, the total pressure exerted by a mixture of gases in a container at constant V and T is equal to the sum of the pressures of each individual gas in the container, a statement known as **Dalton's law of partial pressures**.

▸ Dalton's law of partial pressures $P_{total} = P_1 + P_2 + P_3 + \dots$ at constant V and T, where P_1, $P_2, \dots$ refer to the pressures each individual gas would have if it were alone.

The individual pressure contributions of the various gases in the mixture, P_1, P_2, and so forth, are called *partial pressures* and refer to the pressure each individual gas would exert if it were alone in the container. That is,

$$P_1 = n_1\left(\frac{RT}{V}\right) \qquad P_2 = n_2\left(\frac{RT}{V}\right) \qquad P_3 = n_3\left(\frac{RT}{V}\right) \qquad \dots \text{ and so forth}$$

But because all the gases in the mixture have the same temperature and volume, we can rewrite Dalton's law to indicate that the total pressure depends only on the total molar amount of gas present and not on the chemical identities of the individual gases:

$$P_{total} = (n_1 + n_2 + n_3 + \dots)\left(\frac{RT}{V}\right)$$

The concentration of any individual component in a gas mixture is usually expressed as a **mole fraction (X)**, which is defined simply as the number of moles of the component divided by the total number of moles in the mixture:

▸ Mole fraction $(X) = \dfrac{\text{Moles of component}}{\text{Total moles in mixture}}$

The mole fraction of component 1, for example, is

$$X_1 = \frac{n_1}{n_1 + n_2 + n_3 + \dots} = \frac{n_1}{n_{total}}$$

But because $n = PV/RT$, we can also write

$$X_1 = \frac{P_1\left(\dfrac{V}{RT}\right)}{P_{total}\left(\dfrac{V}{RT}\right)} = \frac{P_1}{P_{total}}$$

which can be rearranged to solve for P_1, the partial pressure of component 1:

$$P_1 = X_1 \cdot P_{total}$$

This equation says that the partial pressure exerted by each component in a gas mixture is equal to the mole fraction of that component times the total pressure. In air, for example, the mole fractions of N_2, O_2, Ar, and CO_2 are 0.7808, 0.2095, 0.0093, and 0.000 38, respectively (Table 9.1), and the total pressure of the air is the sum of the individual partial pressures:

$$P_{air} = P_{N_2} + P_{O_2} + P_{Ar} + P_{CO_2} + \cdots$$

Thus, at a total air pressure of 1 atm (760 mm Hg), the partial pressures of the individual components are

$$P_{N_2} = 0.780\ 8 \text{ atm } N_2 = 593.4 \text{ mm Hg}$$
$$P_{O_2} = 0.209\ 5 \text{ atm } O_2 = 159.2 \text{ mm Hg}$$
$$P_{Ar} = 0.009\ 3 \text{ atm Ar} = 7.1 \text{ mm Hg}$$
$$P_{CO_2} = 0.000\ 38 \text{ atm } CO_2 = 0.3 \text{ mm Hg}$$
$$\overline{P_{air} = 1.000\ 0 \text{ atm air} = 760.0 \text{ mm Hg}}$$

There are numerous practical applications of Dalton's law, ranging from the use of anesthetic agents in hospital operating rooms, where partial pressures of both oxygen and anesthetic in the patient's lungs must be constantly monitored, to the composition of diving gases used for underwater exploration. Worked Example 9.9 gives an illustration.

WORKED EXAMPLE 9.9

USING PARTIAL PRESSURES AND MOLE FRACTIONS

At an underwater depth of 250 ft, the pressure is 8.38 atm. What should the mole percent of oxygen in the diving gas be for the partial pressure of oxygen in the gas to be 0.21 atm, the same as in air at 1.0 atm?

STRATEGY

The partial pressure of a gas in a mixture is equal to the mole fraction of the gas times the total pressure. Rearranging this equation lets us solve for mole fraction of O_2.

SOLUTION

$$\text{Since } P_{O_2} = X_{O_2} \cdot P_{total}, \text{ then } X_{O_2} = \frac{P_{O_2}}{P_{total}}$$

$$X_{O_2} = \frac{0.21 \text{ atm}}{8.38 \text{ atm}} = 0.025$$

$$\text{Percent } O_2 = 0.025 \times 100\% = 2.5\% \ O_2$$

▲ The partial pressure of oxygen in the scuba tanks must be the same underwater as in air at atmospheric pressure.

The diving gas should contain 2.5% O_2 for the partial pressure of O_2 to be the same at 8.38 atm as it is in air at 1.0 atm.

BALLPARK CHECK

Because the pressure underwater is about 8 times atmospheric pressure, the percentage of O_2 in the diving gas should be about 1/8 times the percentage of O_2 in air (20%), or about 2.5%.

▶ **PROBLEM 9.14** What is the mole fraction of each component in a mixture of 12.45 g of H_2, 60.67 g of N_2, and 2.38 g of NH_3?

▶ **PROBLEM 9.15** What is the total pressure in atmospheres and what is the partial pressure of each component if the gas mixture in Problem 9.14 is in a 10.00 L steel container at 90 °C?

▶ **PROBLEM 9.16** On a humid day in summer, the mole fraction of gaseous H_2O (water vapor) in the air at 25 °C can be as high as 0.0287. Assuming a total pressure of 0.977 atm, what is the partial pressure in atmospheres of H_2O in the air?

CONCEPTUAL PROBLEM 9.17 What is the partial pressure of each gas—red, yellow, and green—if the total pressure inside the following container is 600 mm Hg?

9.6 THE KINETIC–MOLECULAR THEORY OF GASES

Thus far, we've concentrated on just describing the behavior of gases rather than on understanding the reasons for that behavior. Actually, the reasons are straightforward and were explained more than a century ago using a model called the **kinetic–molecular theory**. The kinetic–molecular theory is based on the following assumptions:

1. A gas consists of tiny particles, either atoms or molecules, moving about at random.

2. The volume of the particles themselves is negligible compared with the total volume of the gas. Most of the volume of a gas is empty space.

3. The gas particles act independently of one another; there are no attractive or repulsive forces between particles.

4. Collisions of the gas particles, either with other particles or with the walls of a container, are elastic. That is, the total kinetic energy of the gas particles is constant at constant T.

5. The average kinetic energy of the gas particles is proportional to the Kelvin temperature of the sample.

Beginning with these assumptions, it's possible not only to understand the behavior of gases but also to derive quantitatively the ideal gas law (though we'll not do so here). For example, let's look at how the individual gas laws follow from the five postulates of kinetic–molecular theory:

- **Boyle's law ($P \propto 1/V$):** Gas pressure is a measure of the number and forcefulness of collisions between gas particles and the walls of their container. The smaller the volume at constant n and T, the more crowded together the particles are and the greater the frequency of collisions. Thus, pressure increases as volume decreases (**Figure 9.11a**).

- **Charles's law ($V \propto T$):** Temperature is a measure of the average kinetic energy of the gas particles. The higher the temperature at constant n and P, the faster the gas particles move and the more room they need to move around in to avoid increasing their collisions with the walls of the container. Thus, volume increases as temperature increases (**Figure 9.11b**).

- **Avogadro's law ($V \propto n$):** The more particles there are in a gas sample, the more volume the particles need at constant P and T to avoid increasing their collisions with the walls of the container. Thus, volume increases as amount increases (**Figure 9.11c**).

- **Dalton's law ($P_{total} = P_1 + P_2 + \cdots$):** The chemical identity of the particles in a gas is irrelevant. Total pressure of a fixed volume of gas depends only on the temperature T and the total number of moles of gas n. The pressure exerted by a specific kind of particle thus depends on the mole fraction of that kind of particle in the mixture (**Figure 9.11d**).

One of the more important conclusions from kinetic–molecular theory comes from assumption 5—the relationship between temperature and E_K, the kinetic energy of molecular motion. It can be shown that the total kinetic energy of a mole of

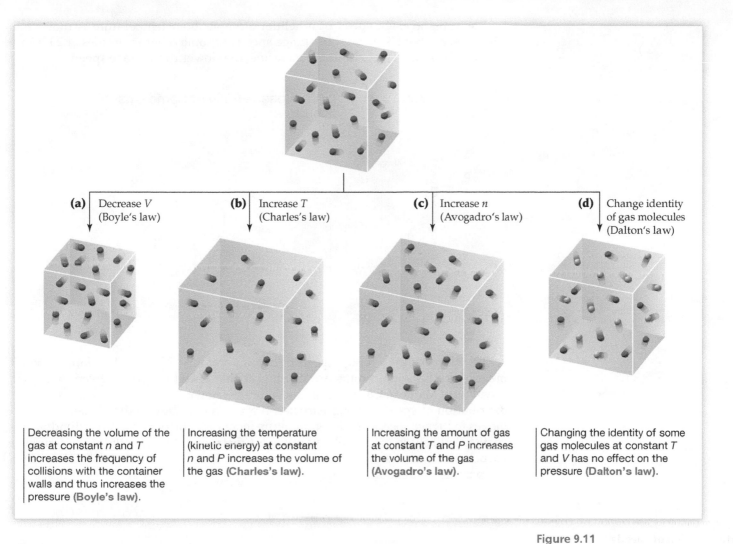

(a) Decrease V (Boyle's law)

(b) Increase T (Charles's law)

(c) Increase n (Avogadro's law)

(d) Change identity of gas molecules (Dalton's law)

Decreasing the volume of the gas at constant n and T increases the frequency of collisions with the container walls and thus increases the pressure **(Boyle's law)**.	Increasing the temperature (kinetic energy) at constant n and P increases the volume of the gas **(Charles's law)**.	Increasing the amount of gas at constant T and P increases the volume of the gas **(Avogadro's law)**.	Changing the identity of some gas molecules at constant T and V has no effect on the pressure **(Dalton's law)**.

Figure 9.11
A kinetic–molecular view of the gas laws.

gas particles equals $3RT/2$ and that the average kinetic energy per particle is thus $3RT/2N_A$ where N_A is Avogadro's number. Knowing this relationship makes it possible to calculate the average speed u of a gas particle at a given temperature. To take a helium atom at room temperature (298 K), for instance, we can write

$$E_K = \frac{3}{2}\frac{RT}{N_A} = \frac{1}{2}mu^2$$

which can be rearranged to give

$$u^2 = \frac{3RT}{mN_A}$$

$$\text{or}\quad u = \sqrt{\frac{3RT}{mN_A}} = \sqrt{\frac{3RT}{M}}\qquad \text{where } M \text{ is the molar mass}$$

Substituting appropriate values for R [8.314 J/(K · mol)] and for M, the molar mass of helium (4.00×10^{-3} kg/mol), we have

$$u = \sqrt{\frac{(3)\left(8.314\,\dfrac{J}{K\cdot mol}\right)(298\ K)}{4.00 \times 10^{-3}\,\dfrac{kg}{mol}}} = \sqrt{1.86 \times 10^6\,\frac{J}{kg}}$$

$$= \sqrt{1.86 \times 10^6\,\frac{\dfrac{kg\cdot m^2}{s^2}}{kg}} = 1.36 \times 10^3\ \text{m/s}$$

Thus, the average speed of a helium atom at room temperature is more than 1.3 km/s, or about 3000 mi/h! Average speeds of some other molecules at 25 °C are given in Table 9.5. The heavier the molecule, the slower the average speed.

TABLE 9.5   Average Speeds (m/s) of Some Gas Molecules at 25 °C

Just because the average speed of helium atoms at 298 K is 1.36 km/s doesn't mean that all helium atoms are moving at that speed or that a given atom will travel from Maine to California in one hour. As shown in **Figure 9.12**, there is a broad distribution of speeds among particles in a gas, a distribution that flattens out and moves to higher speeds as the temperature increases. Furthermore, an individual gas particle is likely to travel only a very short distance before it collides with another particle and bounces off in a different direction. Thus, the actual path followed by a gas particle is a random zigzag.

Figure 9.12
The distribution of speeds for helium atoms at different temperatures.

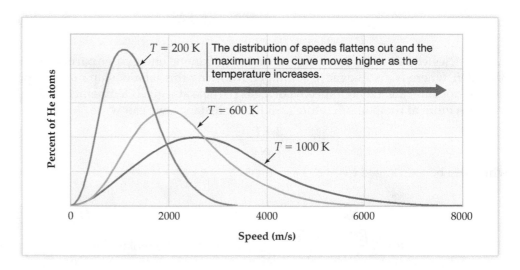

For helium at room temperature and 1 atm pressure, the average distance between collisions, called the *mean free path*, is only about 2×10^{-7} m, or 1000 atomic diameters, and there are approximately 10^{10} collisions per second. For a larger O_2 molecule, the mean free path is about 6×10^{-8} m.

▶ **PROBLEM 9.18**   Calculate the average speed of a nitrogen molecule in m/s on a hot day in summer ($T = 37 \,°C$) and on a cold day in winter ($T = -25\,°C$).

▶ **PROBLEM 9.19**   At what temperature does the average speed of an oxygen molecule equal that of an airplane moving at 580 mph?

9.7 GRAHAM'S LAW: DIFFUSION AND EFFUSION OF GASES

The constant motion and high velocities of gas particles have some important practical consequences. One such consequence is that gases mix rapidly when they come in contact. Take the stopper off a bottle of perfume, for instance, and the odor will spread rapidly through a room as perfume molecules mix with the molecules in the air. This mixing of different molecules by random molecular motion with frequent collisions is called **diffusion**. A similar process in which gas molecules escape without collisions through a tiny hole into a vacuum is called **effusion** (Figure 9.13).

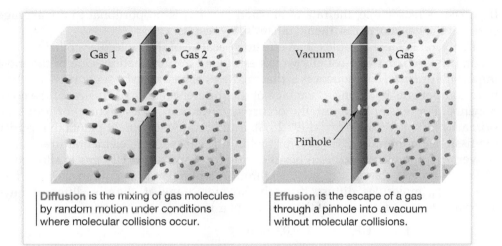

Diffusion is the mixing of gas molecules by random motion under conditions where molecular collisions occur.

Effusion is the escape of a gas through a pinhole into a vacuum without molecular collisions.

Figure 9.13
Diffusion and effusion of gases.

According to **Graham's law**, formulated in the mid-1800s by the Scottish chemist Thomas Graham (1805–1869), the rate of effusion of a gas is inversely proportional to the square root of its mass. In other words, the lighter the molecule, the more rapidly it effuses.

 Graham's law Rate of effusion $\propto \dfrac{1}{\sqrt{m}}$

The rate of effusion of a gas is inversely proportional to the square root of its mass, m.

In comparing two gases at the same temperature and pressure, we can set up an equation showing that the ratio of the effusion rates of the two gases is inversely proportional to the ratio of the square roots of their masses:

$$\frac{\text{Rate}_1}{\text{Rate}_2} = \frac{\sqrt{m_2}}{\sqrt{m_1}} = \sqrt{\frac{m_2}{m_1}}$$

The inverse relationship between the rate of effusion and the square root of the mass follows directly from the connection between temperature and kinetic energy described in the previous section. Because temperature is a measure of average kinetic energy and is independent of the gas's chemical identity, different gases at the same temperature have the same average kinetic energy:

Since $\dfrac{1}{2}mu^2 = \dfrac{3\,RT}{2\,N_A}$ for any gas

then $\left(\dfrac{1}{2}mu^2\right)_{\text{gas 1}} = \left(\dfrac{1}{2}mu^2\right)_{\text{gas 2}}$ at the same T

Canceling the factor of 1/2 from both sides and rearranging, we find that the average speeds of the molecules in two gases vary as the inverse ratio of the square roots of their masses:

$$\text{Since} \quad \left(\frac{1}{2}mu^2\right)_{\text{gas 1}} = \left(\frac{1}{2}mu^2\right)_{\text{gas 2}}$$

$$\text{then} \quad (mu^2)_{\text{gas 1}} = (mu^2)_{\text{gas 2}} \quad \text{and} \quad \frac{(u_{\text{gas 1}})^2}{(u_{\text{gas 2}})^2} = \frac{m_2}{m_1}$$

$$\text{so} \quad \frac{u_{\text{gas 1}}}{u_{\text{gas 2}}} = \frac{\sqrt{m_2}}{\sqrt{m_1}} = \sqrt{\frac{m_2}{m_1}}$$

If, as seems reasonable, the rate of effusion of a gas is proportional to the average speed of the gas molecules, then Graham's law results.

Diffusion is more complex than effusion because of the molecular collisions that occur, but Graham's law usually works as a good approximation. One of the most important practical consequences is that mixtures of gases can be separated into their pure components by taking advantage of the different rates of diffusion of the components. For example, naturally occurring uranium is a mixture of isotopes, primarily ^{235}U (0.72%) and ^{238}U (99.28%). In uranium enrichment plants that purify the fissionable uranium-235 used for fuel in nuclear reactors, elemental uranium is converted into volatile uranium hexafluoride (bp 56 °C), and UF_6 gas is allowed to diffuse from one chamber to another through a permeable membrane. The $^{235}UF_6$ and $^{238}UF_6$ molecules diffuse through the membrane at slightly different rates according to the square root of the ratio of their masses:

$$\text{For } ^{235}UF_6, m = 349.03 \text{ amu}$$

$$\text{For } ^{238}UF_6, m = 352.04 \text{ amu}$$

$$\text{so} \quad \frac{\text{Rate of } ^{235}UF_6 \text{ diffusion}}{\text{Rate of } ^{238}UF_6 \text{ diffusion}} = \sqrt{\frac{352.04 \text{ amu}}{349.03 \text{ amu}}} = 1.0043$$

The UF_6 gas that passes through the membrane is thus very slightly enriched in the lighter, faster-moving isotope. After repeating the process many thousands of times, a separation of isotopes can be achieved. Approximately 35% of the Western world's nuclear fuel supply—some 5000 tons per year—is produced by this gas diffusion method, although the percentage is dropping because better methods are now available.

▲ Much of the uranium-235 used as a fuel in nuclear reactors is obtained by gas diffusion of UF_6 in these cylinders.

WORKED EXAMPLE 9.10

USING GRAHAM'S LAW TO CALCULATE DIFFUSION RATES

Assume that you have a sample of hydrogen gas containing H_2, HD, and D_2 that you want to separate into pure components (H = ^{1}H and D = ^{2}H). What are the relative rates of diffusion of the three molecules according to Graham's law?

STRATEGY

First, find the masses of the three molecules: for H_2, m = 2.016 amu; for HD, m = 3.022 amu; for D_2, m = 4.028 amu. Then apply Graham's law to different pairs of gas molecules.

SOLUTION

Because D_2 is the heaviest of the three molecules, it will diffuse most slowly. If we call its relative rate 1.000, we can then compare HD and H_2 with D_2:

Comparing HD with D_2, we have

$$\frac{\text{Rate of HD diffusion}}{\text{Rate of } D_2 \text{ diffusion}} = \sqrt{\frac{\text{mass of } D_2}{\text{mass of HD}}} = \sqrt{\frac{4.028 \text{ amu}}{3.022 \text{ amu}}} = 1.155$$

Comparing H_2 with D_2, we have

$$\frac{\text{Rate of } H_2 \text{ diffusion}}{\text{Rate of } D_2 \text{ diffusion}} = \sqrt{\frac{\text{mass of } D_2}{\text{mass of } H_2}} = \sqrt{\frac{4.028 \text{ amu}}{2.016 \text{ amu}}} = 1.414$$

Thus, the relative rates of diffusion are H_2 (1.414) > HD (1.154) > D_2 (1.000).

▶ **PROBLEM 9.20**   Which gas in each of the following pairs diffuses more rapidly, and what are the relative rates of diffusion?

   (a) Kr and O_2 **(b)** N_2 and acetylene (C_2H_2)

▶ **PROBLEM 9.21**   What are the relative rates of diffusion of the three naturally occurring isotopes of neon, ^{20}Ne, ^{21}Ne, and ^{22}Ne?

9.8 THE BEHAVIOR OF REAL GASES

Before ending this discussion of gases, it's worthwhile expanding on a point made earlier: The behavior of a real gas is often a bit different from that of an ideal gas. For instance, kinetic–molecular theory assumes that the volume of the gas particles themselves is negligible compared with the total gas volume. The assumption is valid at STP, where the volume taken up by molecules of a typical gas is only about 0.05% of the total volume, but the assumption is not valid at 500 atm and 0 °C, where the volume of the molecules is about 20% of the total volume (**Figure 9.14**). As a result, the volume of a real gas at high pressure is larger than predicted by the ideal gas law.

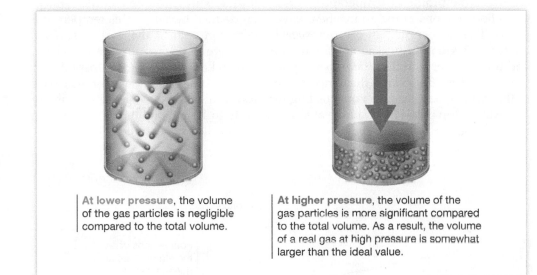

Figure 9.14
The volume of a real gas.

At lower pressure, the volume of the gas particles is negligible compared to the total volume.

At higher pressure, the volume of the gas particles is more significant compared to the total volume. As a result, the volume of a real gas at high pressure is somewhat larger than the ideal value.

A second issue arising with real gases is the assumption that there are no attractive forces between particles. At lower pressures, this assumption is reasonable because the gas particles are so far apart. At higher pressures, however, the particles are much closer together and the attractive forces between them become more important. In general, intermolecular attractions become significant at a distance of about 10 molecular diameters and increase rapidly as the distance diminishes (**Figure 9.15**). The result is to draw the molecules of real gases together slightly, decreasing the volume at a given pressure (or decreasing the pressure for a given volume).

Note that the effect of molecular volume—to increase V—is opposite that of intermolecular attractions—to decrease V. The two factors therefore tend to cancel at intermediate pressures, but the effect of molecular volume dominates above about 350 atm.

Both ways in which the behavior of real gases deviates from the ideal gas law can be dealt with mathematically by a modification of the ideal gas law called the **van der Waals equation**, which uses two correction factors, called a and b. The increase in V, caused by the effect of molecular volume, is corrected by subtracting an amount nb from the observed volume. The decrease in V (or, equivalently, the decrease in P),

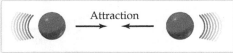

Figure 9.15
Molecules attract one another at distances up to about 10 molecular diameters. The result is a decrease in the actual volume of most real gases when compared with ideal gases at pressures up to 300 atm.

caused by the effect of intermolecular attractions, is best corrected by adding an amount an^2/V^2 to the pressure.

Correction for
intermolecular attractions

Correction for
molecular volume

van der Waals equation: $\left(P + \dfrac{an^2}{V^2}\right)(V - nb) = nRT$

or $P = \dfrac{nRT}{V - nb} - \dfrac{an^2}{V^2}$

▶ **PROBLEM 9.22** Assume that you have 0.500 mol of N_2 in a volume of 0.600 L at 300 K. Calculate the pressure in atmospheres using both the ideal gas law and the van der Waals equation. For N_2, $a = 1.35$ $(L^2 \cdot atm)/mol^2$, and $b = 0.0387$ L/mol.

9.9 THE EARTH'S ATMOSPHERE

The mantle of gases surrounding the Earth is far from the uniform mixture you might expect. Although atmospheric pressure decreases in a regular way at higher altitudes, the profile of temperature versus altitude is much more complex (**Figure 9.16**). Four regions of the atmosphere have been defined based on this temperature curve. The temperature in the *troposphere*, the region nearest the Earth's surface, decreases regularly up to about 12 km altitude, where it reaches a minimum value, and then increases in the *stratosphere*, up to about 50 km. Above the stratosphere, in the *mesosphere*, (50–85 km), the temperature again decreases but then again increases in the *thermosphere*. To give you a feeling for these altitudes, passenger jets normally fly near the top of the troposphere at altitudes of 10 to 12 km, and the world altitude record for jet aircraft is 37.65 km—roughly in the middle of the stratosphere.

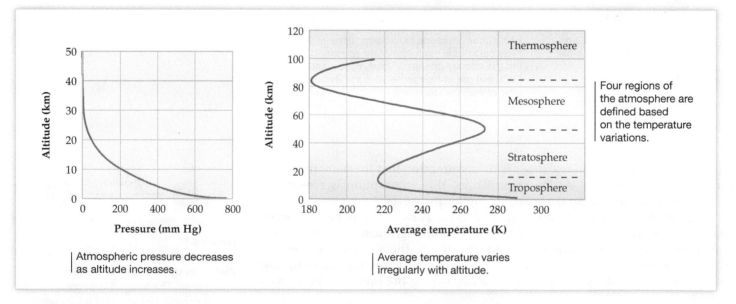

Atmospheric pressure decreases as altitude increases.

Average temperature varies irregularly with altitude.

Figure 9.16
Variations of atmospheric pressure and average temperature with altitude.

Chemistry of the Troposphere

Not surprisingly, it's the layer nearest the Earth's surface—the troposphere—that is the most easily disturbed by human activities and has the greatest effect on the Earth's surface conditions. Among those effects, air pollution, acid rain, and global warming are particularly important.

Air Pollution Air pollution has appeared in the last two centuries as an unwanted by-product of industrialized societies. Its causes are relatively straightforward; its control is difficult. The main causes of air pollution are the release of unburned hydrocarbon molecules and the production of nitric oxide, NO, during combustion of petroleum products in older industrial plants and the approximately 750 million automobile and truck engines presently in use worldwide. The NO is further oxidized by reaction with air to yield nitrogen dioxide, NO_2, which splits into NO plus free oxygen atoms in the presence of sunlight (symbolized by $h\nu$). Reaction of the oxygen atoms with O_2 molecules then yields ozone, O_3, a highly reactive substance that can further combine with unburned hydrocarbons in the air. The end result is the production of so-called photochemical smog, the hazy, brownish layer lying over many cities.

$$NO_2(g) + h\nu \longrightarrow NO(g) + O(g)$$
$$O(g) + O_2(g) \longrightarrow O_3(g)$$

Acid Rain Acid rain, a second major environmental problem, results primarily from the production of sulfur dioxide, SO_2, that accompanies the burning of sulfur-containing coal in power generating plants. Sulfur dioxide is slowly converted to SO_3 by reaction with oxygen in air, and SO_3 dissolves in rainwater to yield dilute sulfuric acid, H_2SO_4.

$$S(\text{in coal}) + O_2(g) \longrightarrow SO_2(g)$$
$$2\,SO_2(g) + O_2(g) \longrightarrow 2\,SO_3(g)$$
$$SO_3(g) + H_2O(l) \longrightarrow H_2SO_4(aq)$$

Among the many dramatic effects of acid rain are the extinction of fish in acidic lakes throughout parts of the northeastern United States, Canada, and Scandinavia, the damage to forests throughout much of central and eastern Europe, and the deterioration everywhere of marble buildings and statuary. Marble is a form of calcium carbonate, $CaCO_3$, and, like all metal carbonates, reacts with acid to produce CO_2. The result is a slow eating away of the stone.

$$CaCO_3(s) + H_2SO_4(aq) \longrightarrow CaSO_4(aq) + H_2O(l) + CO_2(g)$$

Global Warming The third major atmospheric problem, global warming, is more complicated and less well understood than either air pollution or acid rain. The fundamental cause of the problem is that human activities over the past century appear to have disturbed the Earth's delicate thermal balance. One component of that balance is the radiant energy the Earth's surface receives from the sun, some of which is radiated back into space as infrared energy. Although much of this radiation passes out through the atmosphere, some is absorbed by atmospheric gases, particularly water vapor, carbon dioxide, and methane. This absorbed radiation warms the atmosphere and acts to maintain a relatively stable temperature at the Earth's surface. Should increasing amounts of radiation be absorbed, however, increased atmospheric heating would result and global temperatures would rise.

Careful measurements show that concentrations of atmospheric carbon dioxide have been rising in the last 160 years, largely because of the increased use of fossil fuels, from an estimated 290 parts per million (ppm) in 1850 to 385 ppm in 2009 (**Figure 9.17**). Thus, there is concern among atmospheric scientists that increased absorption of infrared radiation and widespread global warming will follow. Most atmospheric scientists believe, in fact, that global warming has begun, with current measurements showing a warming of the mid-troposphere by about 0.4 °C in the last 25 yrs. In addition, some computer models predict a potential warming of as much as 3 °C by the year 2050. Should this occur, the result would be a significant increase in melting of glacial ice and a consequent rise in ocean levels.

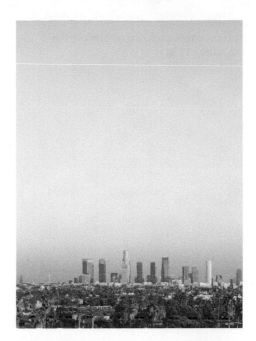

▲ The photochemical smog over many cities is the end result of pollution from automobile exhausts.

▲ The details on this marble statue have been eaten away over the years by acid rain.

Figure 9.17
Annual concentration of atmospheric CO_2 since 1850.

Year

The concentration of atmospheric CO_2 has increased in the last 160 years, from 290 ppm in 1850 to a current level of 385 ppm.

Many atmospheric scientists worry that global atmospheric warming is occurring as a result.

Chemistry of the Upper Atmosphere

Relatively little of the atmosphere's mass is located above the troposphere, but the chemistry that occurs there is nonetheless crucial to maintaining life on Earth. Particularly important is what takes place in the *ozone layer*, an atmospheric band stretching from about 20–40 km above the Earth's surface. Ozone (O_3) is a severe pollutant at low altitudes but is critically important in the upper atmosphere because it absorbs intense ultraviolet radiation from the sun. Even though it is present in very small amounts in the stratosphere, ozone acts as a shield to prevent high-energy solar radiation from reaching the Earth's surface, where it can cause such health problems as eye cataracts and skin cancer.

Around 1976, a disturbing decrease in the amount of ozone present over the South Pole began showing up (**Figure 9.18**), and more recently a similar phenomenon has been found over the North Pole. Ozone levels drop to below 50% of normal in the polar spring before returning to near normal in the autumn.

Figure 9.18
A false-color satellite image of the ozone hole over Antarctica on September 24, 2009.

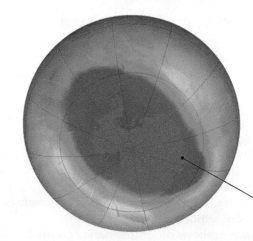

The **lowest ozone concentrations** are represented by the purple and violet regions, where ozone levels are up to 50% lower than normal.

The principal cause of ozone depletion is the presence in the stratosphere of *chlorofluorocarbons* (CFCs), such as CF_2Cl_2 and $CFCl_3$. Because they are inexpensive and stable, yet not toxic, flammable, or corrosive, CFCs are ideal as propellants in aerosol cans, as refrigerants, as solvents, and as fire-extinguishing agents. In addition, they are used for blowing bubbles into foamed plastic insulation. Unfortunately, the chemical stability that makes CFCs so useful also causes them to persist in the environment. Molecules released at ground level slowly diffuse into the stratosphere, where they undergo a complex series of reactions that ultimately result in ozone destruction.

Several different mechanisms of ozone destruction predominate under different stratospheric conditions. All are multistep processes that begin when ultraviolet light ($h\nu$) strikes a CFC molecule, breaking a carbon–chlorine bond and generating a chlorine atom:

$$CFCl_3 + h\nu \longrightarrow CFCl_2 + Cl$$

The resultant chlorine atom reacts with ozone to yield O_2 and ClO, and two ClO molecules then give Cl_2O_2. Further reaction occurs when Cl_2O_2 is struck by more ultraviolet light to generate O_2 and two more chlorine atoms.

(1) $2\,[Cl + O_3 \longrightarrow O_2 + ClO]$

(2) $2\,ClO \longrightarrow Cl_2O_2$

(3) $Cl_2O_2 + h\nu \longrightarrow 2\,Cl + O_2$

Net: $2\,O_3 + h\nu \longrightarrow 3\,O_2$

Look at the overall result of the above reaction sequence. Chlorine atoms are used up in the first step but are regenerated in the third step, so they don't appear in the net equation. Thus, the net sequence is a never-ending *chain reaction*, in which the generation of just a few chlorine atoms from a few CFC molecules leads to the continuing destruction of a great many ozone molecules.

Recognition of the problem led the U.S. government in 1980 to ban the use of CFCs for aerosol propellants and, more recently, for refrigerants. Worldwide action to reduce CFC use began in September 1987, and an international ban on the industrial production and release of CFCs took effect in 1996. The ban has not been wholly successful, however, because of a substantial black market that has developed, particularly in Russia and China, where up to $300 million per year of illegal CFCs are thought to be manufactured. Even with these stringent efforts, amounts of CFCs in the stratosphere won't return to pre-1980 levels until the middle of this century.

▶ **PROBLEM 9.23**   The ozone layer is about 20 km thick, has an average total pressure of 10 mm Hg (1.3×10^{-2} atm), and has an average temperature of 230 K. The partial pressure of ozone in the layer is only about 1.2×10^{-6} mm Hg (1.6×10^{-9} atm). How many meters thick would the layer be if all the ozone contained in it were compressed into a thin layer of pure O_3 at STP?

INQUIRY HOW DO INHALED ANESTHETICS WORK?

William Morton's demonstration in 1846 of ether-induced anesthesia during dental surgery ranks as one of the most important medical breakthroughs of all time. Before then, all surgery had been carried out with the patient conscious. Use of chloroform as an anesthetic quickly followed Morton's work, made popular by Queen Victoria of England, who in 1853 gave birth to a child while anesthetized by chloroform.

Literally hundreds of substances in addition to ether and chloroform have subsequently been shown to act as inhaled anesthetics. Halothane, isoflurane, sevoflurane, and desflurane are among the most commonly used agents at present. All four are nontoxic, nonflammable, and potent at relatively low doses.

Despite their importance, surprisingly little is known about how inhaled anesthetics work in the body. Even the definition of anesthesia as a behavioral state is imprecise, and the nature of the changes in brain function leading to anesthesia are unknown. Remarkably, the potency of different inhaled anesthetics correlates well with their solubility in olive oil: the more soluble in olive oil, the more potent as an anesthetic. This unusual observation has led many scientists to believe that anesthetics act by dissolving in the fatty membranes surrounding nerve cells. The resultant changes in the fluidity and shape of the membranes apparently decrease the ability of sodium ions to pass into the nerve cells, thereby blocking the firing of nerve impulses.

▲ On April 7, 1853, Queen Victoria of England gave birth to her eighth child, while anesthetized by chloroform, changing forever the practice of obstetrics.

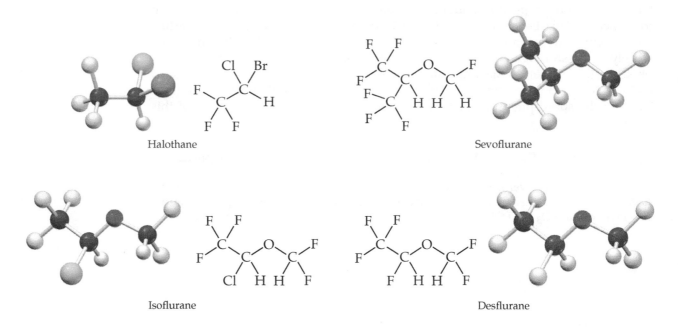

Halothane

Sevoflurane

Isoflurane

Desflurane

Depth of anesthesia is determined by the concentration of anesthetic agent that reaches the brain. Brain concentration, in turn, depends on the solubility and transport of the anesthetic agent in the bloodstream and on its partial pressure in inhaled air. Anesthetic potency is usually expressed as a *minimum alveolar concentration (MAC)*, defined as the percent concentration of anesthetic in inhaled air that results in anesthesia in 50% of patients. As shown in Table 9.6, nitrous oxide, N_2O, is the least potent of the common anesthetics. Fewer than 50% of patients are immobilized by breathing an 80:20 mix of nitrous oxide and oxygen. Halothane is the most potent agent; a partial pressure of only 5.7 mm Hg is sufficient to anesthetize 50% of patients.

TABLE 9.6   Relative Potency of Inhaled Anesthetics

Anesthetic	MAC (%)	MAC (partial pressure, mm Hg)
Nitrous oxide	—	>760
Desflurane	6.2	47
Sevoflurane	2.5	19
Isoflurane	1.4	11
Halothane	0.75	5.7

▶ **PROBLEM 9.24**   For ether, a partial pressure of 15 mm Hg results in anesthesia in 50% of patients. What is the MAC for ether?

▶ **PROBLEM 9.25**   Chloroform has an MAC of 0.77%.

(a) What partial pressure of chloroform is required to anesthetize 50% of patients?

(b) What mass of chloroform in 10.0 L of air at STP will produce the appropriate MAC?

SUMMARY

A gas is a collection of atoms or molecules moving independently through a volume that is largely empty space. Collisions of the randomly moving particles with the walls of their container exert a force per unit area that we perceive as **pressure**. The SI unit for pressure is the **pascal**, but the **atmosphere**, the **millimeter of mercury**, and the **bar** are more commonly used.

The physical condition of any gas is defined by four variables: pressure (P), temperature (T), volume (V), and molar amount (n). The specific relationships among these variables are called the **gas laws**:

Boyle's law:
: The volume of a gas varies inversely with its pressure. That is, $V \propto 1/P$ or $PV = k$ at constant n, T.

Charles's law:
: The volume of a gas varies directly with its Kelvin temperature. That is, $V \propto T$ or $V/T = k$ at constant n, P.

Avogadro's law:
: The volume of a gas varies directly with its molar amount. That is, $V \propto n$ or $V/n = k$ at constant T, P.

The three individual gas laws can be combined into a single **ideal gas law**, $PV = nRT$. If any three of the four variables P, V, T, and n are known, the fourth can be calculated. The constant R in the equation is called the **gas constant** and has the same value for all gases. At **standard temperature and pressure** (**STP**; 1 atm and 0 °C), the **standard molar volume** of an ideal gas is 22.414 L.

The gas laws apply to mixtures of gases as well as to pure gases. According to **Dalton's law of partial pressures**, the total pressure exerted by a mixture of gases in a container is equal to the sum of the pressures each individual gas would exert alone.

The behavior of gases can be accounted for using a model called the **kinetic–molecular theory**, a group of five postulates:

1. A gas consists of tiny particles moving at random.
2. The volume of the gas particles is negligible compared with the total volume.
3. There are no forces between particles, either attractive or repulsive.
4. Collisions of gas particles are elastic.
5. The average kinetic energy of gas particles is proportional to their absolute temperature.

The connection between temperature and kinetic energy obtained from the kinetic–molecular theory makes it possible to calculate the average speed of a gas particle at any temperature. An important practical consequence of this relationship is **Graham's law**, which states that the rate of a gas's **effusion**, or spontaneous passage through a pinhole in a membrane, depends inversely on the square root of the gas's mass.

Real gases differ in their behavior from that predicted by the ideal gas law, particularly at high pressure, where gas particles are forced close together and intermolecular attractions become significant. The deviations from ideal behavior can be dealt with mathematically by the **van der Waals equation**.

KEY WORDS

atmosphere (atm)   *311*
Avogadro's law   *316*
bar   *311*
Boyle's law   *313*
Charles's law   *315*
Dalton's law of partial
   pressures   *324*

diffusion   *329*
effusion   *329*
gas constant (R)   *318*
gas laws   *313*
Graham's law   *329*
ideal gas   *313*
ideal gas law   *318*

kinetic–molecular
   theory   *326*
manometer   *311*
millimeter of
   mercury (mm Hg)   *311*
mole fraction (X)   *324*
newton (N)   *310*

pascal (Pa)   *310*
pressure (P)   *310*
standard molar volume   *317*
standard temperature and
   pressure (STP)   *318*
van der Waals equation   *331*

CONCEPTUAL PROBLEMS

Problems 9.1–9.25 appear within the chapter.

9.26 A 1:1 mixture of helium (red) and argon (blue) at 300 K is portrayed below on the left. Draw the same mixture when the temperature is lowered to 150 K.

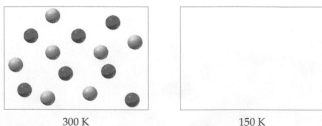

300 K   150 K

9.27 The following drawing represents a container holding a mixture of four gases, red, blue, green, and black. If the total pressure inside the container is 420 mm Hg, what is the partial pressure of each individual component?

9.28 Assume that you have a sample of gas in a cylinder with a movable piston, as shown in the following drawing:

Redraw the apparatus to show what the sample will look like after **(a)** the temperature is increased from 300 K to 450 K at constant pressure, **(b)** the pressure is increased from 1 atm to 2 atm at constant temperature, and **(c)** the temperature is decreased from 300 K to 200 K and the pressure is decreased from 3 atm to 2 atm.

9.29 Assume that you have a sample of gas at 350 K in a sealed container, as represented in **(a)**. Which of the drawings **(b)–(d)** represents the gas after the temperature is lowered from 350 K to 150 K?

(a)

(b)   **(c)**   **(d)**

9.30 Assume that you have a mixture of He (atomic mass = 4 amu) and Xe (atomic mass = 131 amu) at 300 K. Which of the drawings best represents the mixture (blue = He; red = Xe)?

(a)   **(b)**   **(c)**

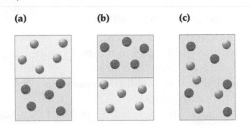

9.31 Three bulbs, two of which contain different gases and one of which is empty, are connected as shown in the following drawing. Redraw the apparatus to represent the gases after the stopcocks are opened and the system is allowed to come to equilibrium.

9.32 The apparatus shown is called a *closed-end* manometer because the arm not connected to the gas sample is closed to the atmosphere and is under vacuum. Explain how you can read the gas pressure in the bulb.

9.33 Redraw the following open-end manometer to show what it would look like when stopcock A is opened.

9.34 Effusion of a 1:1 mixture of two gases through a small pinhole produces the results shown below.
   (a) Which gas molecules—yellow or blue—have a higher average speed?
   (b) If the yellow molecules have a molecular mass of 25 amu, what is the molecular mass of the blue molecules?

9.35 A glass tube has one end in a dish of mercury and the other end closed by a stopcock. The distance from the surface of the mercury to the bottom of the stopcock is 850 mm. The apparatus is at 25 °C, and the mercury level in the tube is the same as that in the dish.

(1)   (2)   (3)

(a) Show on drawing (1) what the approximate level of mercury in the tube will be when the temperature of the entire apparatus is lowered from +25 °C to −25 °C.

(b) Show on drawing (2) what the approximate level of mercury in the tube will be when a vacuum pump is connected to the top of the tube, the stopcock is opened, the tube is evacuated, the stopcock is closed, and the pump is removed.

(c) Show on drawing (3) what the approximate level of mercury in the tube will be when the stopcock in drawing (2) is opened.

SECTION PROBLEMS

Gases and Gas Pressure (Section 9.1)

9.36 What is temperature a measure of?

9.37 Why are gases so much more compressible than solids or liquids?

9.38 Atmospheric pressure at the top of Pikes Peak in Colorado is approximately 480 mm Hg. Convert this value to atmospheres and to pascals.

9.39 Carry out the following conversions:
   (a) 352 torr to kPa
   (b) 0.255 atm to mm Hg
   (c) 0.0382 mm Hg to Pa

9.40 What is the pressure in millimeters of mercury inside a container of gas connected to a mercury-filled open-end manometer of the sort shown in Figure 9.4 when the level in the arm connected to the container is 17.6 cm lower than the level in the arm open to the atmosphere and the atmospheric pressure reading outside the apparatus is 754.3 mm Hg?

9.41 What is the pressure in atmospheres inside a container of gas connected to a mercury-filled open-end manometer when the level in the arm connected to the container is 28.3 cm higher than the level in the arm open to the atmosphere and the atmospheric pressure reading outside the apparatus is 1.021 atm?

9.42 Assume that you have an open-end manometer filled with ethyl alcohol (density = 0.7893 g/mL at 20 °C) rather than mercury (density = 13.546 g/mL at 20 °C). What is the pressure in pascals if the level in the arm open to the atmosphere is 55.1 cm higher than the level in the arm connected to the gas sample and the atmospheric pressure reading is 752.3 mm Hg?

Ethyl alcohol

9.43 Assume that you have an open-end manometer filled with chloroform (density = 1.4832 g/mL at 20 °C) rather than mercury (density = 13.546 g/mL at 20 °C). What is the difference in height between the liquid in the two arms if the pressure in the arm connected to the gas sample is 0.788 atm and the atmospheric pressure reading is 0.849 atm? In which arm is the chloroform level higher?

Chloroform

9.44 Calculate the average molecular mass of air from the data given in Table 9.1.

9.45 What is the average molecular mass of a diving-gas mixture that contains 2.0% by volume O_2 and 98.0% by volume He?

The Gas Laws (Sections 9.2 and 9.3)

9.46 Assume that you have a cylinder with a movable piston. What would happen to the gas pressure inside the cylinder if you were to do the following?
   (a) Triple the Kelvin temperature while holding the volume constant
   (b) Reduce the amount of gas by 1/3 while holding the temperature and volume constant
   (c) Decrease the volume by 45% at constant T
   (d) Halve the Kelvin temperature, and triple the volume

9.47 Assume that you have a cylinder with a movable piston. What would happen to the gas volume of the cylinder if you were to do the following?
   (a) Halve the Kelvin temperature while holding the pressure constant
   (b) Increase the amount of gas by 1/4 while holding the temperature and pressure constant
   (c) Decrease the pressure by 75% at constant T
   (d) Double the Kelvin temperature, and double the pressure

9.48 Which sample contains more molecules: 1.00 L of O_2 at STP, 1.00 L of air at STP or 1.00 L of H_2 at STP?

9.49 Which sample contains more molecules: 2.50 L of air at 50 °C and 750 mm Hg pressure or 2.16 L of CO_2 at −10 °C and 765 mm Hg pressure?

9.50 Oxygen gas is commonly sold in 49.0 L steel containers at a pressure of 150 atm. What volume in liters would the gas occupy at a pressure of 1.02 atm if its temperature remained unchanged? If its temperature was raised from 20.0 °C to 35.0 °C at constant $P = 150$ atm?

9.51 A compressed air tank carried by scuba divers has a volume of 8.0 L and a pressure of 140 atm at 20 °C. What is the volume of air in the tank in liters at STP?

9.52 If 15.0 g of CO_2 gas has a volume of 0.30 L at 300 K, what is its pressure in millimeters of mercury?

9.53 If 2.00 g of N_2 gas has a volume of 0.40 L and a pressure of 6.0 atm, what is its Kelvin temperature?

9.54 The matter in interstellar space consists almost entirely of hydrogen atoms at a temperature of 100 K and a density of approximately 1 atom/cm^3. What is the gas pressure in millimeters of mercury?

9.55 Methane gas, CH_4, is sold in a 43.8 L cylinder containing 5.54 kg. What is the pressure inside the cylinder in kilopascals at 20 °C?

9.56 Many laboratory gases are sold in steel cylinders with a volume of 43.8 L. What mass in grams of argon is inside a cylinder whose pressure is 17,180 kPa at 20 °C?

9.57 A small cylinder of helium gas used for filling balloons has a volume of 2.30 L and a pressure of 13,800 kPa at 25 °C. How many balloons can you fill if each one has a volume of 1.5 L and a pressure of 1.25 atm at 25 °C?

Gas Stoichiometry (Section 9.4)

9.58 Which sample contains more molecules, 15.0 L of steam (gaseous H_2O) at 123.0 °C and 0.93 atm pressure or a 10.5 g ice cube at −5.0 °C?

9.59 Which sample contains more molecules, 3.14 L of Ar at 85.0 °C and 1111 mm Hg pressure or 11.07 g of Cl_2?

9.60 Imagine that you have two identical flasks, one containing hydrogen at STP and the other containing oxygen at STP. How can you tell which is which without opening them?

9.61 Imagine that you have two identical flasks, one containing chlorine gas and the other containing argon at the same temperature and pressure. How can you tell which is which without opening them?

9.62 What is the total mass in grams of oxygen in a room measuring 4.0 m by 5.0 m by 2.5 m? Assume that the gas is at STP and that air contains 20.95% oxygen by volume.

9.63 The average oxygen content of arterial blood is approximately 0.25 g of O_2 per liter. Assuming a body temperature of 37 °C, how many moles of oxygen are transported by each liter of arterial blood? How many milliliters?

9.64 One mole of an ideal gas has a volume of 22.414 L at STP. Assuming ideal behavior, what are the densities of the following gases in g/L at STP?

(a) CH_4 **(b)** CO_2 **(c)** O_2

9.65 What is the density in g/L of a gas mixture that contains 27.0% F_2 and 73.0% He by volume at 714 mm Hg and 27.5 °C?

9.66 An unknown gas is placed in a 1.500 L bulb at a pressure of 356 mm Hg and a temperature of 22.5 °C, and is found to weigh 0.9847 g. What is the molecular mass of the gas?

9.67 What are the molecular masses of the gases with the following densities:
(a) 1.342 g/L at STP
(b) 1.053 g/L at 25 °C and 752 mm Hg

9.68 Pure oxygen gas was first prepared by heating mercury(II) oxide, HgO:

$$2\,HgO(s) \longrightarrow 2\,Hg(l) + O_2(g)$$

What volume in liters of oxygen at STP is released by heating 10.57 g of HgO?

9.69 How many grams of HgO would you need to heat if you wanted to prepare 0.0155 mol of O_2 according to the equation in Problem 9.68?

9.70 Hydrogen gas can be prepared by reaction of zinc metal with aqueous HCl:

$$Zn(s) + 2\,HCl(aq) \longrightarrow ZnCl_2(aq) + H_2(g)$$

(a) How many liters of H_2 would be formed at 742 mm Hg and 15 °C if 25.5 g of zinc was allowed to react?
(b) How many grams of zinc would you start with if you wanted to prepare 5.00 L of H_2 at 350 mm Hg and 30.0 °C?

9.71 Ammonium nitrate can decompose explosively when heated according to the equation

$$2\,NH_4NO_3(s) \longrightarrow 2\,N_2(g) + 4\,H_2O(g) + O_2(g)$$

How many liters of gas would be formed at 450 °C and 1.00 atm pressure by explosion of 450 g of NH_4NO_3?

9.72 The reaction of sodium peroxide (Na_2O_2) with CO_2 is used in space vehicles to remove CO_2 from the air and generate O_2 for breathing:

$$2\,Na_2O_2(s) + 2\,CO_2(g) \longrightarrow 2\,Na_2CO_3(s) + O_2(g)$$

(a) Assuming that air is breathed at an average rate of 4.50 L/min (25 °C; 735 mm Hg) and that the concentration of CO_2 in expelled air is 3.4% by volume, how many grams of CO_2 are produced in 24 h?
(b) How many days would a 3.65 kg supply of Na_2O_2 last?

9.73 Titanium(III) chloride, a substance used in catalysts for preparing polyethylene, is made by high-temperature reaction of $TiCl_4$ vapor with H_2:

$$2\,TiCl_4(g) + H_2(g) \longrightarrow 2\,TiCl_3(s) + 2\,HCl(g)$$

(a) How many grams of $TiCl_4$ are needed for complete reaction with 155 L of H_2 at 435 °C and 795 mm Hg pressure?
(b) How many liters of HCl gas at STP will result from the reaction described in part **(a)**?

Dalton's Law and Mole Fraction (Section 9.5)

9.74 Use the information in Table 9.1 to calculate the partial pressure in atmospheres of each gas in dry air at STP.

9.75 Natural gas is a mixture of many substances, primarily CH_4, C_2H_6, C_3H_8, and C_4H_{10}. Assuming that the total pressure of the gases is 1.48 atm and that their mole ratio is 94 : 4.0 : 1.5 : 0.50, calculate the partial pressure in atmospheres of each gas.

9.76 A special gas mixture used in bacterial growth chambers contains 1.00% by weight CO_2 and 99.0% O_2. What is the partial pressure in atmospheres of each gas at a total pressure of 0.977 atm?

9.77 A gas mixture for use in some lasers contains 5.00% by weight HCl, 1.00% H_2, and 94% Ne. The mixture is sold in cylinders that have a volume of 49.0 L and a pressure of 13,800 kPa at 21.0 °C. What is the partial pressure in kilopascals of each gas in the mixture?

9.78 What is the mole fraction of each gas in the mixture described in Problem 9.77?

9.79 A mixture of Ar and N_2 gases has a density of 1.413 g/L at STP. What is the mole fraction of each gas?

9.80 A mixture of 14.2 g of H_2 and 36.7 g of Ar is placed in a 100.0 L container at 290 K.

(a) What is the partial pressure of H_2 in atmospheres?

(b) What is the partial pressure of Ar in atmospheres?

9.81 A 20.0 L flask contains 0.776 g of He and 3.61 g of CO_2 at 300 K.

(a) What is the partial pressure of He in mm Hg?

(b) What is the partial pressure of CO_2 in mm Hg?

9.82 A sample of magnesium metal reacts with aqueous HCl to yield H_2 gas:

$$Mg(s) + 2\,HCl(aq) \longrightarrow MgCl_2(aq) + H_2(g)$$

The gas that forms is found to have a volume of 3.557 L at 25 °C and a pressure of 747 mm Hg. Assuming that the gas is saturated with water vapor at a partial pressure of 23.8 mm Hg, what is the partial pressure in millimeters of mercury of the H_2? How many grams of magnesium metal were used in the reaction?

9.83 Chlorine gas was first prepared in 1774 by the oxidation of NaCl with MnO_2:

$$2\,NaCl(s) + 2\,H_2SO_4(l) + MnO_2(s) \longrightarrow$$
$$Na_2SO_4(s) + MnSO_4(s) + 2\,H_2O(g) + Cl_2(g)$$

Assume that the gas produced is saturated with water vapor at a partial pressure of 28.7 mm Hg and that it has a volume of 0.597 L at 27 °C and 755 mm Hg pressure.

(a) What is the mole fraction of Cl_2 in the gas?

(b) How many grams of NaCl were used in the experiment, assuming complete reaction?

Kinetic–Molecular Theory and Graham's Law (Sections 9.6 and 9.7)

9.84 What are the basic assumptions of the kinetic–molecular theory?

9.85 What is the difference between effusion and diffusion?

9.86 What is the difference between heat and temperature?

9.87 Why does a helium-filled balloon lose pressure faster than an air-filled balloon?

9.88 The average temperature at an altitude of 20 km is 220 K. What is the average speed in m/s of an N_2 molecule at this altitude?

9.89 At what temperature (°C) will xenon atoms have the same average speed that Br_2 molecules have at 20 °C?

9.90 Which has a higher average speed, H_2 at 150 K or He at 375 °C?

9.91 Which has a higher average speed, a Ferrari at 145 mph or a gaseous UF_6 molecule at 145 °C?

9.92 An unknown gas is found to diffuse through a porous membrane 2.92 times more slowly than H_2. What is the molecular mass of the gas?

9.93 What is the molecular mass of a gas that diffuses through a porous membrane 1.86 times faster than Xe? What might the gas be?

9.94 Rank the following gases in order of their speed of diffusion through a membrane, and calculate the ratio of their diffusion rates: HCl, F_2, Ar.

9.95 Which will diffuse through a membrane more rapidly, CO or N_2? Assume that the samples contain only the most abundant isotopes of each element, ^{12}C, ^{16}O, and ^{14}N.

9.96 A big-league fastball travels at about 45 m/s. At what temperature (°C) do helium atoms have this same average speed?

9.97 Traffic on the German autobahns reaches speeds of up to 230 km/h. At what temperature (°C) do oxygen molecules have this same average speed?

CHAPTER PROBLEMS

9.98 What is the greatest atmospheric concern—air pollution, acid rain, global warming, or ozone depletion—for each of the following?
(a) $CFCl_3$ **(b)** S (in coal) **(c)** CO_2 **(d)** NO

9.99 What is the role or effect of ozone in the troposphere and in the stratosphere?

9.100 Chlorine occurs as a mixture of two isotopes, ^{35}Cl and ^{37}Cl. What is the ratio of the diffusion rates of the three species $(^{35}Cl)_2$, $^{35}Cl^{37}Cl$, and $(^{37}Cl)_2$?

9.101 What would the atmospheric pressure be in millimeters of mercury if our atmosphere were composed of pure CO_2 gas?

9.102 The surface temperature of Venus is about 1050 K, and the pressure is about 75 Earth atmospheres. Assuming that these conditions represent a Venusian "STP," what is the standard molar volume in liters of a gas on Venus?

9.103 When you look directly up at the sky, you are actually looking through a very tall, transparent column of air that extends from the surface of the Earth thousands of kilometers into space. If the air in this column were liquefied, how tall would it be? The density of liquid air is 0.89 g/mL.

9.104 Uranium hexafluoride, a molecular solid used for purification of the uranium isotope needed to fuel nuclear power plants, sublimes at 56.5 °C. Assume that you have a 22.9 L vessel that contains 512.9 g of UF_6 at 70.0 °C.

(a) What is the pressure in the vessel calculated using the ideal gas law?

(b) What is the pressure in the vessel calculated using the van der Waals equation? (For UF_6, $a = 15.80$ $(L^2 \cdot atm)/mol^2$; $b = 0.1128$ L/mol.)

9.105 A driver with a nearly empty fuel tank may say she is "running on fumes." If a 15.0 gallon automobile gas tank had only gasoline vapor remaining in it, what is the farthest the vehicle could travel if it gets 20.0 miles per gallon on liquid gasoline? Assume the average molar mass of molecules in gasoline is 105 g/mol, the density of liquid gasoline is 0.75 g/mL, the pressure is 743 mm Hg, and the temperature is 25 °C.

9.106 Two 112 L tanks are filled with gas at 330 K. One contains 5.00 mol of Kr, and the other contains 5.00 mol of O_2. Considering the assumptions of kinetic–molecular theory, rank the gases from low to high for each of the following properties:

(a) collision frequency   (b) density (g/L)

(c) average speed   (d) pressure

9.107 Two identical 732.0 L tanks each contain 212.0 g of gas at 293 K, with neon in one tank and nitrogen in the other. Based on the assumptions of kinetic–molecular theory, rank the gases from low to high for each of the following properties:

(a) average speed   (b) pressure

(c) collision frequency   (d) density (g/L)

9.108 Pakistan's K2 is the world's second tallest mountain, with an altitude of 28,251 ft. Its base camp, where climbers stop to acclimate, is located about 16,400 ft above sea level.

(a) Approximate atmospheric pressure P at different altitudes is given by the equation $P = e^{-h/7000}$, where P is in atmospheres and h is the altitude in meters. What is the approximate atmospheric pressure in mm Hg at K2 base camp?

(b) What is the atmospheric pressure in mm Hg at the summit of K2?

(c) Assuming the mole fraction of oxygen in air is 0.2095, what is the partial pressure of oxygen in mm Hg at the summit of K2?

9.109 When a 10.00 L vessel containing 42.189 g of I_2 is heated to 1173 K, some I_2 dissociates: $I_2(g) \rightarrow 2\,I(g)$. If the final pressure in the vessel is 1.733 atm, what are the mole fractions of the two components $I_2(g)$ and $I(g)$ after the reaction?

9.110 Assume that you take a flask, evacuate it to remove all the air, and find its mass to be 478.1 g. You then fill the flask with argon to a pressure of 2.15 atm and reweigh it. What would the balance read in grams if the flask has a volume of 7.35 L and the temperature is 20.0 °C?

9.111 The apparatus shown consists of three bulbs connected by stopcocks. What is the pressure inside the system when the stopcocks are opened? Assume that the lines connecting the bulbs have zero volume and that the temperature remains constant.

$CO_2(g)$	$H_2(g)$	$Ar(g)$
$P = 2.13$ atm	$P = 0.861$ atm	$P = 1.15$ atm
$V = 1.50$ L	$V = 1.00$ L	$V = 2.00$ L

9.112 The apparatus shown consists of three temperature-jacketed 1.000 L bulbs connected by stopcocks. Bulb **A** contains a mixture of $H_2O(g)$, $CO_2(g)$, and $N_2(g)$ at 25 °C and a total

pressure of 564 mm Hg. Bulb **B** is empty and is held at a temperature of −70 °C. Bulb **C** is also empty and is held at a temperature of −190 °C. The stopcocks are closed, and the volume of the lines connecting the bulbs is zero. CO_2 sublimes at −78 °C, and N_2 boils at −196 °C.

(a) The stopcock between **A** and **B** is opened, and the system is allowed to come to equilibrium. The pressure in **A** and **B** is now 219 mm Hg. What do bulbs **A** and **B** contain?

(b) How many moles of H_2O are in the system?

(c) Both stopcocks are opened, and the system is again allowed to come to equilibrium. The pressure throughout the system is 33.5 mm Hg. What do bulbs **A**, **B**, and **C** contain?

(d) How many moles of N_2 are in the system?

(e) How many moles of CO_2 are in the system?

9.113 Assume that you have 1.00 g of nitroglycerin in a 500.0 mL steel container at 20.0 °C and 1.00 atm pressure. An explosion occurs, raising the temperature of the container and its contents to 425 °C. The balanced equation is

$$4\,C_3H_5N_3O_9(l) \longrightarrow$$
$$12\,CO_2(g) + 10\,H_2O(g) + 6\,N_2(g) + O_2(g)$$

Nitroglycerin

(a) How many moles of nitroglycerin and how many moles of gas (air) were in the container originally?

(b) How many moles of gas are in the container after the explosion?

(c) What is the pressure in atmospheres inside the container after the explosion according to the ideal gas law?

9.114 Use both the ideal gas law and the van der Waals equation to calculate the pressure in atmospheres of 45.0 g of NH_3 gas in a 1.000 L container at 0 °C, 50 °C, and 100 °C. For NH_3, $a = 4.17\ (L^2 \cdot atm)/mol^2$ and $b = 0.0371$ L/mol.

9.115 When solid mercury(I) carbonate, Hg_2CO_3, is added to nitric acid, HNO_3, a reaction occurs to give mercury(II) nitrate, $Hg(NO_3)_2$, water, and two gases **A** and **B**:

$$Hg_2CO_3(s) + HNO_3(aq) \longrightarrow$$
$$Hg(NO_3)_2(aq) + H_2O(l) + A(g) + B(g)$$

(a) When the gases are placed in a 500.0 mL bulb at 20 °C, the pressure is 258 mm Hg. How many moles of gas are present?

(b) When the gas mixture is passed over CaO(s), gas **A** reacts, forming $CaCO_3(s)$:

$$CaO(s) + A(g) + B(g) \longrightarrow CaCO_3(s) + B(g)$$

The remaining gas **B** is collected in a 250.0 mL container at 20 °C and found to have a pressure of 344 mm Hg. How many moles of **B** are present?

(c) The mass of gas **B** collected in part **(b)** was found to be 0.218 g. What is the density of **B** in g/L?

(d) What is the molecular mass of **B**, and what is its formula?

(e) Write a balanced equation for the reaction of mercury(I) carbonate with nitric acid.

9.116 Dry ice (solid CO_2) has occasionally been used as an "explosive" in mining. A hole is drilled, dry ice and a small amount of gunpowder are placed in the hole, a fuse is added, and the hole is plugged. When lit, the exploding gunpowder rapidly vaporizes the dry ice, building up an immense pressure. Assume that 500.0 g of dry ice is placed in a cavity with a volume of 0.800 L and the ignited gunpowder heats the CO_2 to 700 K. What is the final pressure inside the hole?

9.117 Consider the combustion reaction of 0.148 g of a hydrocarbon having formula C_nH_{2n+2} with an excess of O_2 in a 400.0 mL steel container. Before reaction, the gaseous mixture had a temperature of 25.0 °C and a pressure of 2.000 atm. After complete combustion and loss of considerable heat, the mixture of products and excess O_2 had a temperature of 125.0 °C and a pressure of 2.983 atm.

(a) What is the formula and molar mass of the hydrocarbon?

(b) What are the partial pressures in atmospheres of the reactants?

(c) What are the partial pressures in atmospheres of the products and the excess O_2?

9.118 Natural gas is a mixture of hydrocarbons, primarily methane (CH_4) and ethane (C_2H_6). A typical mixture might have $X_{methane} = 0.915$ and $X_{ethane} = 0.085$. Let's assume that we have a 15.50 g sample of natural gas in a volume of 15.00 L at a temperature of 20.00 °C.

(a) How many total moles of gas are in the sample?

(b) What is the pressure of the sample in atmospheres?

(c) What is the partial pressure of each component in the sample in atmospheres?

(d) When the sample is burned in an excess of oxygen, how much heat in kilojoules is liberated?

9.119 A mixture of $CS_2(g)$ and excess $O_2(g)$ is placed in a 10.0 L reaction vessel at 100.0 °C and a pressure of 3.00 atm. A spark causes the CS_2 to ignite, burning it completely, according to the equation

$$CS_2(g) + 3 O_2(g) \longrightarrow CO_2(g) + 2 SO_2(g)$$

After reaction, the temperature returns to 100.0 °C, and the mixture of product gases (CO_2, SO_2, and unreacted O_2) is found to have a pressure of 2.40 atm. What is the partial pressure of each gas in the product mixture?

9.120 Gaseous compound **Q** contains only xenon and oxygen. When 0.100 g of **Q** is placed in a 50.0 mL steel vessel at 0 °C, the pressure is 0.229 atm.

(a) What is the molar mass of **Q**, and what is a likely formula?

(b) When the vessel and its contents are warmed to 100 °C, **Q** decomposes into its constituent elements. What is the total pressure, and what are the partial pressures of xenon and oxygen in the container?

9.121 When 10.0 g of a mixture of $Ca(ClO_3)_2$ and $Ca(ClO)_2$ is heated to 700 °C in a 10.0 L vessel, both compounds decompose, forming $O_2(g)$ and $CaCl_2(s)$. The final pressure inside the vessel is 1.00 atm.

(a) Write balanced equations for the decomposition reactions.

(b) What is the mass of each compound in the original mixture?

9.122 A 5.00 L vessel contains 25.0 g of PCl_3 and 3.00 g of O_2 at 15 °C. The vessel is heated to 200.0 °C, and the contents react to give $POCl_3$. What is the final pressure in the vessel, assuming that the reaction goes to completion and that all reactants and products are in the gas phase?

9.123 When 2.00 mol of $NOCl(g)$ was heated to 225 °C in a 400.0 L steel reaction vessel, the NOCl partially decomposed according to the equation $2 NOCl(g) \rightarrow 2 NO(g) + Cl_2(g)$. The pressure in the vessel after reaction is 0.246 atm.

(a) What is the partial pressure of each gas in the vessel after reaction?

(b) What percent of the NOCl decomposed?

9.124 Ozone (O_3) can be prepared in the laboratory by passing an electrical discharge through oxygen gas: $3 O_2(g) \rightarrow 2 O_3(g)$. Assume that an evacuated steel vessel with a volume of 10.00 L is filled with 32.00 atm of O_2 at 25 °C and an electric discharge is passed through the vessel, causing some of the oxygen to be converted into ozone. As a result, the pressure inside the vessel drops to 30.64 atm at 25.0 °C. What is the final mass percent of ozone in the vessel?

9.125 A steel container with a volume of 500.0 mL is evacuated, and 25.0 g of $CaCO_3$ is added. The container and contents are then heated to 1500 K, causing the $CaCO_3$ to decompose completely, according to the equation $CaCO_3(s) \rightarrow CaO(s) + CO_2(g)$.

(a) Using the ideal gas law and ignoring the volume of any solids remaining in the container, calculate the pressure inside the container at 1500 K.

(b) Now make a more accurate calculation of the pressure inside the container. Take into account the volume of solid CaO (density = 3.34 g/mL) in the container, and use the van der Waals equation to calculate the pressure. The van der Waals constants for $CO_2(g)$ are: $a = 3.59$ ($L^2 \cdot atm$)/mol^2, and $b = 0.0427$ L/mol.

9.126 Nitrogen dioxide dimerizes to give dinitrogen tetroxide: $2 NO_2(g) \rightarrow N_2O_4(g)$. At 298 K, 9.66 g of an NO_2/N_2O_4 mixture exerts a pressure of 0.487 atm in a volume of 6.51 L. What are the mole fractions of the two gases in the mixture?

9.127 A certain nonmetal reacts with hydrogen at 440 °C to form a poisonous, foul-smelling gas. The density of the gas at 25 °C and 1.00 atm is 3.309 g/L. What is the formula of the gas?

MULTICONCEPT PROBLEMS

9.128 An empty 4.00 L steel vessel is filled with 1.00 atm of $CH_4(g)$ and 4.00 atm of $O_2(g)$ at 300 °C. A spark causes the CH_4 to burn completely, according to the equation:

$$CH_4(g) + 2\,O_2(g) \longrightarrow CO_2(g) + 2\,H_2O(g) \qquad \Delta H° = -802 \text{ kJ}$$

(a) What mass of $CO_2(g)$ is produced in the reaction?

(b) What is the final temperature inside the vessel after combustion, assuming that the steel vessel has a mass of 14.500 kg, the mixture of gases has an average molar heat capacity of 21 J/(mol · °C), and the heat capacity of steel is 0.449 J/(g · °C)?

(c) What is the partial pressure of $CO_2(g)$ in the vessel after combustion?

9.129 When a gaseous compound **X** containing only C, H, and O is burned in O_2, 1 volume of the unknown gas reacts with 3 volumes of O_2 to give 2 volumes of CO_2 and 3 volumes of gaseous H_2O. Assume all volumes are measured at the same temperature and pressure.

(a) Calculate a formula for the unknown gas, and write a balanced equation for the combustion reaction.

(b) Is the formula you calculated an empirical formula or a molecular formula? Explain.

(c) Draw two different possible electron-dot structures for the compound **X**.

(d) Combustion of 5.000 g of **X** releases 144.2 kJ heat. Look up $\Delta H°_f$ values for $CO_2(g)$ and $H_2O(g)$ in Appendix B, and calculate $\Delta H°_f$ for compound **X**.

9.130 Isooctane, C_8H_{18}, is the component of gasoline from which the term *octane rating* derives.

(a) Write a balanced equation for the combustion of isooctane to yield CO_2 and H_2O.

(b) Assuming that gasoline is 100% isooctane, that isooctane burns to produce only CO_2 and H_2O, and that the density of isooctane is 0.792 g/mL, what mass of CO_2 in kilograms is produced each year by the annual U.S. gasoline consumption of 4.6×10^{10} L?

(c) What is the volume in liters of this CO_2 at STP?

(d) How many moles of air are necessary for the combustion of 1 mol of isooctane, assuming that air is 21.0% O_2 by volume? What is the volume in liters of this air at STP?

9.131 The *Rankine* temperature scale used in engineering is to the Fahrenheit scale as the Kelvin scale is to the Celsius scale. That is, 1 Rankine degree is the same size as 1 Fahrenheit degree, and 0 °R = absolute zero.

(a) What temperature corresponds to the freezing point of water on the Rankine scale?

(b) What is the value of the gas constant R on the Rankine scale in $(L \cdot atm)/(°R \cdot mol)$?

(c) Use the van der Waals equation to determine the pressure inside a 400.0 mL vessel that contains 2.50 mol of CH_4 at a temperature of 525 °R. For CH_4, $a = 2.253$ $(L^2 \cdot atm)/mol^2$; $b = 0.04278$ L/mol.

9.132 Chemical explosions are characterized by the instantaneous release of large quantities of hot gases, which set up a shock wave of enormous pressure (up to 700,000 atm)

and velocity (up to 20,000 mi/h). For example, explosion of nitroglycerin ($C_3H_5N_3O_9$) releases four gases, **A**, **B**, **C**, and **D**:

$$n\ C_3H_5N_3O_9(l) \longrightarrow a\ A(g) + b\ B(g) + c\ C(g) + d\ D(g)$$

Assume that the explosion of 1 mol (227 g) of nitroglycerin releases gases with a temperature of 1950 °C and a volume of 1323 L at 1.00 atm pressure.

(a) How many moles of hot gas are released by the explosion of 0.004 00 mol of nitroglycerin?

(b) When the products released by explosion of 0.004 00 mol of nitroglycerin were placed in a 500.0 mL flask and the flask was cooled to −10 °C, product **A** solidified, and the pressure inside the flask was 623 mm Hg. How many moles of **A** were present, and what is its likely identity?

(c) When gases **B**, **C**, and **D** were passed through a tube of powdered Li_2O, gas **B** reacted to form Li_2CO_3. The remaining gases, **C** and **D**, were collected in another 500.0 mL flask and found to have a pressure of 260 mm Hg at 25 °C. How many moles of **B** were present, and what is its likely identity?

(d) When gases **C** and **D** were passed through a hot tube of powdered copper, gas **C** reacted to form CuO. The remaining gas, **D**, was collected in a third 500.0 mL flask and found to have a mass of 0.168 g and a pressure of 223 mm Hg at 25 °C. How many moles each of **C** and **D** were present, and what are their likely identities?

(e) Write a balanced equation for the explosion of nitroglycerin.

9.133 Combustion analysis of 0.1500 g of methyl *tert*-butyl ether, an octane booster used in gasoline, gave 0.3744 g of CO_2 and 0.1838 g of H_2O. When a flask having a volume of 1.00 L was evacuated and then filled with methyl *tert*-butyl ether vapor at a pressure of 100.0 kPa and a temperature of 54.8 °C, the mass of the flask increased by 3.233 g.

Methyl *tert*-butyl ether

(a) What is the empirical formula of methyl *tert*-butyl ether?

(b) What is the molecular mass and molecular formula of methyl *tert*-butyl ether?

(c) Write a balanced equation for the combustion reaction.

(d) The enthalpy of combustion for methyl *tert*-butyl ether is $\Delta H°_{combustion} = -3368.7$ kJ/mol. What is its standard enthalpy of formation, $\Delta H°_f$?

CHAPTER 10

Liquids, Solids, and Phase Changes

The three phases of water—solid, liquid, and vapor—are all present in winter at this hot spring in Yellowstone National Park

CONTENTS

The kinetic–molecular theory developed in the previous chapter accounts for the properties of gases by assuming that gas particles act independently of one another. Because the attractive forces between them are so weak, the particles in gases are free to move about at random and occupy whatever volume is available. The same is not true in liquids and solids, however. Liquids and solids are distinguished from gases by the presence of substantial attractive forces between particles. In liquids, these attractive forces are strong enough to hold the particles in close contact while still letting them slip and slide over one another. In solids, the forces are so strong that they hold the particles in place and prevent their movement (**Figure 10.1**).

In **gases**, the particles feel little attraction for one another and are free to move about randomly.

In **liquids**, the particles are held close together by attractive forces but are free to move around one another.

In **solids**, the particles are held in an ordered arrangement.

Figure 10.1
A molecular comparison of gases, liquids, and solids.

In this chapter, we'll examine the nature of the forces responsible for the properties of liquids and solids, paying particular attention to the ordering of particles in solids and to the different kinds of solids that result. In addition, we'll look at what happens during transitions between solid, liquid, and gaseous states and at the effects of temperature and pressure on these transitions.

10.1 POLAR COVALENT BONDS AND DIPOLE MOMENTS

Before looking at the forces between molecules, it's first necessary to develop the ideas of *bond dipoles* and *dipole moments*. We saw in Section 7.4 that **polar covalent bonds** form between atoms of different electronegativity. Chlorine is more electronegative than carbon, for instance, so the chlorine atom in chloromethane (CH_3Cl) attracts the electrons in the C—Cl bond. The C—Cl bond is therefore polarized so that the chlorine atom is slightly electron-rich ($\delta-$) and the carbon atom is slightly electron-poor ($\delta+$).

Because the polar C—Cl bond in chloromethane has two polar ends—a positive end and a negative end—we describe it as being a bond **dipole**, and we often represent the dipole using an arrow with a cross at one end (↦) to indicate the direction of electron displacement. The point of the arrow represents the negative end of the dipole ($\delta-$), and the crossed end (which looks like a plus sign) represents the positive end ($\delta+$). This polarity is clearly visible in an **electrostatic potential map** (Section 7.4), which shows the electron-rich chlorine atom as red and the electron-poor remainder of the molecule as blue-green.

Remember...
Polar covalent bonds are those in which the bonding electrons are shared unequally between two atoms but are not completely transferred. Thus, they are intermediate between nonpolar covalent bonds and ionic bonds. (Section 7.4)

Remember...
An **electrostatic potential map** uses color to portray the calculated electron distribution in a molecule. Electron-rich regions are red, and electron-poor regions are blue. (Section 7.4)

Chlorine is at the negative end of the bond dipole.
Carbon is at the positive end of the bond dipole.

Chloromethane, CH_3Cl

Just as individual bonds in molecules are often polar, molecules as a whole are also often polar because of the net sum of individual bond polarities and lone-pair contributions. The resultant *molecular dipoles* can be looked at in the following way: Assume that there is a center of mass of all positive charges (nuclei) in a molecule and a center of mass of all negative charges (electrons). If these two centers don't coincide, the molecule has a net polarity.

The measure of net molecular polarity is a quantity called the **dipole moment, μ** (Greek mu), which is defined as the magnitude of the charge Q at either end of the molecular dipole times the distance r between the charges: $\mu = Q \times r$. Dipole moments are expressed in *debyes* (D), where $1\,D = 3.336 \times 10^{-30}$ coulomb meters (C·m) in SI units. To calibrate your thinking, the charge on an electron is 1.60×10^{-19} C. Thus, if one proton and one electron were separated by 100 pm (a bit less than the length of a typical covalent bond), then the dipole moment would be 1.60×10^{-29} C·m, or 4.80 D:

$$\mu = Q \times r$$

$$\mu = (1.60 \times 10^{-19}\,\text{C})(100 \times 10^{-12}\,\text{m})\left(\frac{1\,D}{3.336 \times 10^{-30}\,\text{C·m}}\right) = 4.80\,D$$

It's relatively easy to measure dipole moments experimentally, and values for some common substances are given in Table 10.1. Once the dipole moment is known, it's then possible to get an idea of the amount of charge separation in a molecule. In chloromethane, for example, the experimentally measured dipole moment is $\mu = 1.90$ D. If we assume that the contributions of the nonpolar C—H bonds are small, then most of the chloromethane dipole moment is due to the C—Cl bond. Since the C—Cl bond distance is 179 pm, we can calculate that the dipole moment of chloromethane would be 1.79×4.80 D = 8.59 D if the C—Cl bond were ionic—that is, if a full negative charge on chlorine were separated from a full positive charge on carbon by a distance of 179 pm. But because the measured dipole moment of chloromethane is only 1.90 D, we can conclude that the C—Cl bond is only about $(1.90/8.59)(100\%) = 22\%$ ionic. Thus, the chlorine atom in chloromethane has an excess of about 0.2 electron, and the carbon atom has a deficiency of about 0.2 electron.

Not surprisingly, the largest dipole moment listed in Table 10.1 belongs to the ionic compound NaCl. Water and ammonia also have substantial dipole moments because both oxygen and nitrogen are electronegative relative to hydrogen and because both O and N have lone pairs of electrons that make substantial contributions to net molecular polarity:

TABLE 10.1	Dipole Moments of Some Common Compounds
Compound	**Dipole Moment (D)**
NaCl*	9.0
CH_3Cl	1.90
H_2O	1.85
NH_3	1.47
HCl	1.11
CO_2	0
CCl_4	0

* Measured in the gas phase

Ammonia ($\mu = 1.47$ D)   Water ($\mu = 1.85$ D)

In contrast with water and ammonia, carbon dioxide and tetrachloromethane (CCl_4) have zero dipole moments. Molecules of both substances contain *individual* polar covalent bonds, but because of the symmetry of their structures, the individual bond polarities exactly cancel.

O=C=O

Carbon dioxide ($\mu = 0$)

Tetrachloromethane ($\mu = 0$)

WORKED EXAMPLE 10.1

CALCULATING PERCENT IONIC CHARACTER FROM A DIPOLE MOMENT

The dipole moment of HCl is 1.11 D, and the distance between atoms is 127 pm. What is the percent ionic character of the HCl bond?

STRATEGY

If HCl were 100% ionic, a negative charge (Cl⁻) would be separated from a positive charge (H⁺) by 127 pm. Calculate the expected dipole moment, and compare that calculated value to the actual value.

SOLUTION

The calculated dipole moment is

$$\mu = Q \times r$$

$$\mu = (1.60 \times 10^{-19}\,C)(127 \times 10^{-12}\,m)\left(\frac{1\,D}{3.336 \times 10^{-30}\,C \cdot m}\right) = 6.09\,D$$

The observed dipole moment of 1.11 D for HCl implies that the H—Cl bond is only about 18% ionic:

$$\frac{1.11\,D}{6.09\,D} \times 100\% = 18.2\%$$

WORKED EXAMPLE 10.2

PREDICTING THE PRESENCE OF A DIPOLE MOMENT

Would you expect vinyl chloride (H_2C—$CHCl$), the starting material used for preparation of poly(vinyl chloride) polymer, to have a dipole moment? If so, indicate the direction.

STRATEGY

First, use the VSEPR model described in Section 7.9 to predict the molecular shape of vinyl chloride. Then, assign polarities to the individual bonds according to the differences in electronegativity of the bonded atoms (Figure 7.4 on page 221), and make a reasonable guess about the overall polarity that would result by summing the individual contributions.

SOLUTION

Because both carbon atoms have three charge clouds, each has trigonal planar geometry and the molecule as a whole is planar:

Only the C—Cl bond has a substantial polarity, giving the molecule a net polarity:

▶ **PROBLEM 10.1** The dipole moment of HF is $\mu = 1.83$ D, and the bond length is 92 pm. Calculate the percent ionic character of the H—F bond. Is HF more ionic or less ionic than HCl (Worked Example 10.1)?

▶ **PROBLEM 10.2** Tell which of the following compounds is likely to have a dipole moment, and show the direction of each.

   (a) SF_6 **(b)** $H_2C{=}CH_2$ **(c)** $CHCl_3$ **(d)** CH_2Cl_2

CONCEPTUAL PROBLEM 10.3 The dipole moment of methanol is $\mu = 1.70$ D. Use arrows to indicate the direction in which electrons are displaced.

CONCEPTUAL PROBLEM 10.4 Methylamine, CH_3NH_2, is responsible for the odor of rotting fish. Look at the following electrostatic potential map of methylamine, and explain the observed polarity.

10.2 INTERMOLECULAR FORCES

Now that we know a bit about molecular polarities, let's see how they give rise to some of the forces that occur between molecules. The existence of such forces is easy to show. Take H_2O, for example. An individual H_2O molecule consists of two hydrogen atoms and one oxygen atom joined together in a specific way by the *intra*molecular forces that we call covalent bonds. But a visible sample of H_2O exists either as solid ice, liquid water, or gaseous vapor, depending on its temperature. Thus, there must also be some ***inter*molecular forces** that act between molecules to hold them close together at certain temperatures (**Figure 10.2**). (Strictly speaking, the term *intermolecular* refers only to molecular substances, but we'll use it generally to refer to interactions among all kinds of particles, including molecules, ions, and atoms.)

Intermolecular forces as a whole are usually called **van der Waals forces** after the Dutch scientist Johannes van der Waals (1837–1923). These forces are of several different types, including *dipole–dipole forces*, *London dispersion forces*, and *hydrogen bonds*. In addition, *ion–dipole forces* operate between ions and molecules. All these intermolecular forces are electrostatic in origin and result from the mutual attraction of unlike charges or the mutual repulsion of like charges. If the particles are ions, then full charges are present and the ion–ion attractions are so strong (energies on the order of 500–1000 kJ/mol) that they give rise to what we call **ionic bonds** (Section 6.7). If the particles are neutral, then only partial charges are present at best, but even so, the attractive forces can be substantial.

Ion–Dipole Forces

We saw in the previous section that a molecule has a net polarity and an overall dipole moment if the sum of its individual bond dipoles is nonzero. One side of the molecule has a net excess of electrons and a partial negative charge ($\delta-$), while the

Remember...

Ionic bonds generally form between the cation of a metal and the anion of a reactive nonmetal. (Section 6.7)

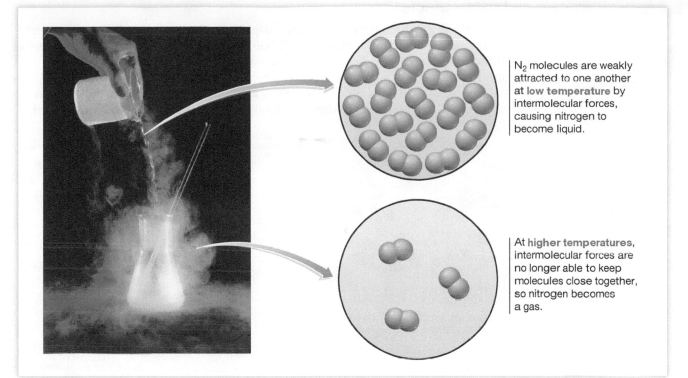

Figure 10.2
Intermolecular forces.

other side has a net deficiency of electrons and a partial positive charge ($\delta+$). An **ion–dipole force** is the result of electrical interactions between an ion and the partial charges on a polar molecule (**Figure 10.3**).

Figure 10.3
Ion–dipole forces.

As you might expect, the favored orientation of a polar molecule in the presence of ions is one where the positive end of the dipole is near an anion and the negative end of the dipole is near a cation. The magnitude of the interaction energy E depends on the charge on the ion z, on the strength of the dipole as measured by its dipole moment μ, and on the inverse square of the distance r from the ion to the dipole: $E \propto z\mu/r^2$. Ion–dipole forces are particularly important in aqueous solutions of ionic substances such as NaCl, in which polar water molecules surround the ions. We'll explore this point in more detail in the next chapter.

Dipole–Dipole Forces

Neutral but polar molecules experience **dipole–dipole forces** as the result of electrical interactions among dipoles on neighboring molecules. The forces can be either attractive or repulsive, depending on the orientation of the molecules (**Figure 10.4**), and the net force in a large collection of molecules is a summation of many individual interactions of both types. The forces are generally weak, with energies on the order of 3–4 kJ/mol, and are significant only when molecules are in close contact.

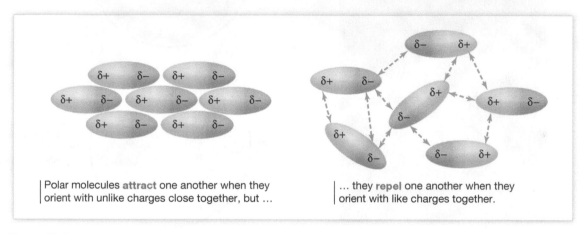

Polar molecules **attract** one another when they orient with unlike charges close together, but ...

... they **repel** one another when they orient with like charges together.

Figure 10.4
Dipole–dipole forces.

Not surprisingly, the strength of a given dipole–dipole interaction depends on the sizes of the dipole moments involved. The more polar the substance, the greater the strength of its dipole–dipole interactions. Butane, for instance, is a nonpolar molecule with a molecular mass of 58 amu and a boiling point of −0.5 °C, while acetone has the same molecular mass yet boils 57 °C higher because it is polar.

Butane (C_4H_{10})
Mol mass = 58 amu
bp = −0.5 °C

Acetone (C_3H_6O)
Mol mass = 58 amu
bp = 56.1 °C

Table 10.2 lists several substances with similar molecular masses but different dipole moments and indicates that there is a rough correlation between dipole moment and boiling point. The larger the dipole moment, the stronger the intermolecular forces and the greater the amount of heat that must be added to overcome those forces. Thus, substances with higher dipole moments generally have higher boiling points.

TABLE 10.2	Comparison of Molecular Masses, Dipole Moments, and Boiling Points		
Substance	Mol Mass (amu)	Dipole Moment (D)	bp (K)
$CH_3CH_2CH_3$	44.10	0.08	231
CH_3OCH_3	46.07	1.30	248
CH_3Cl	50.49	1.90	249
CH_3CN	41.05	3.93	355

London Dispersion Forces

The causes of intermolecular forces among charged and polar particles are easy to understand, but it's less obvious how attractive forces arise among nonpolar molecules or among the individual atoms of a noble gas. Benzene (C_6H_6), for instance, has zero dipole moment and therefore experiences no dipole–dipole forces. Nevertheless, there must be *some* intermolecular forces present among benzene molecules because the substance is a liquid rather than a gas at room temperature, with a melting point of 5.5 °C and a boiling point of 80.1 °C.

Benzene
$\mu = 0$
mp = 5.5 °C
bp = 80.1 °C

All atoms and molecules, regardless of structure, experience **London dispersion forces**, which result from the motion of electrons. Take even a simple nonpolar molecule like Br_2, for instance. Averaged over time, the distribution of electrons throughout the molecule is symmetrical, but at any given instant there may be more electrons at one end of the molecule than at the other, giving the molecule a short-lived dipole moment. This instantaneous dipole on one molecule can affect the electron distributions in neighboring molecules and *induce* temporary dipoles in those neighbors (Figure 10.5). As a result, weak attractive forces develop and Br_2 is a liquid at room temperature rather than a gas.

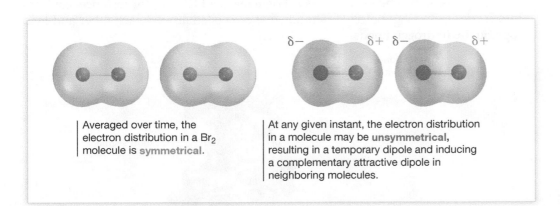

Averaged over time, the electron distribution in a Br_2 molecule is **symmetrical**.

At any given instant, the electron distribution in a molecule may be **unsymmetrical**, resulting in a temporary dipole and inducing a complementary attractive dipole in neighboring molecules.

Figure 10.5
London dispersion forces.

Dispersion forces are generally small, with energies in the range 1–10 kJ/mol, and their exact magnitude depends on the ease with which a molecule's electron cloud can be distorted by a nearby electric field, a property referred to as

TABLE 10.3	Melting Points and Boiling Points of the Halogens	
Halogen	**mp (K)**	**bp (K)**
F_2	53.5	85.0
Cl_2	171.6	239.1
Br_2	265.9	331.9
I_2	386.8	457.5

polarizability. A smaller molecule or lighter atom is less polarizable and has smaller dispersion forces because it has only a few, tightly held electrons. A larger molecule or heavier atom, however, is more polarizable and has larger dispersion forces because it has many electrons, some of which are less tightly held and are farther from the nucleus. Among the halogens, for instance, the F_2 molecule is small and less polarizable, while I_2 is larger and more polarizable. As a result, F_2 has smaller dispersion forces and is a gas at room temperature, while I_2 has larger dispersion forces and is a solid (Table 10.3).

Shape is also important in determining the magnitude of the dispersion forces affecting a molecule. More spread-out shapes, which maximize molecular surface area, allow greater contact between molecules and give rise to higher dispersion forces than do more compact shapes, which minimize molecular contact. Pentane, for example, boils at 309.2 K, whereas 2,2-dimethylpropane boils at 282.6 K. Both substances have the same molecular formula, C_5H_{12}, but pentane is longer and somewhat spread out, whereas 2,2-dimethylpropane is more spherical and compact (**Figure 10.6**).

Figure 10.6
The effect of molecular shape on London dispersion forces.

Pentane (bp = 309.2 K)

2,2-Dimethylpropane (bp = 282.6 K)

Longer, **less compact molecules** like pentane feel stronger dispersion forces and consequently have higher boiling points.

More compact molecules like 2,2-dimethylpropane feel weaker dispersion forces and have lower boiling points.

Hydrogen Bonds

In many ways, *hydrogen bonds* are responsible for life on Earth. They cause water to be a liquid rather than a gas at ordinary temperatures, and they are the primary intermolecular force that holds huge biomolecules in the shapes needed to play their essential roles in biochemistry. Deoxyribonucleic acid (DNA), for instance, contains two enormously long molecular strands that are coiled around each other and held together by hydrogen bonds.

Hydrogen bond between chains

A short segment of DNA

A **hydrogen bond** is an attractive interaction between a hydrogen atom bonded to a very electronegative atom (O, N, or F) and an unshared electron pair on another electronegative atom. For example, hydrogen bonds occur in both water and ammonia:

Water   Ammonia

Hydrogen bonds arise because O—H, N—H, and F—H bonds are highly polar, with a partial positive charge on the hydrogen and a partial negative charge on the electronegative atom. In addition, the hydrogen atom has no core electrons to shield its nucleus, and it has a small size so it can be approached closely by other molecules. As a result, the dipole–dipole attraction between the hydrogen and an unshared electron pair on a nearby atom is unusually strong, giving rise to a hydrogen bond. Water, in particular, is able to form a vast three-dimensional network of hydrogen bonds because each H_2O molecule has two hydrogens and two electron pairs (**Figure 10.7**).

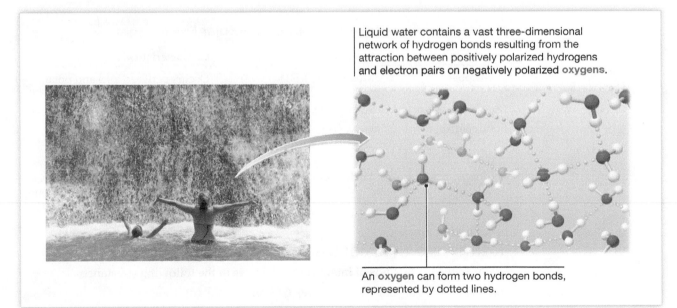

Liquid water contains a vast three-dimensional network of hydrogen bonds resulting from the attraction between positively polarized hydrogens and electron pairs on negatively polarized **oxygens**.

An **oxygen** can form two hydrogen bonds, represented by dotted lines.

Figure 10.7
Hydrogen-bonding in water.

Hydrogen bonds can be quite strong, with energies up to 40 kJ/mol. To see one effect of hydrogen-bonding, look at Table 10.4, which plots the boiling points of the covalent binary hydrides for the group 4A–7A elements. As you might expect, the boiling points generally increase with molecular mass down a group of the periodic table as a result of increased London dispersion forces—for example, $CH_4 < SiH_4 < GeH_4 < SnH_4$. Three substances, however, are clearly anomalous: NH_3, H_2O, and HF. All three have higher boiling points than might be expected because of the hydrogen bonds they contain.

TABLE 10.4 Boiling Points of the Covalent Binary Hydrides of Groups 4A, 5A, 6A, and 7A

The boiling points generally increase with increasing molecular mass down a group of the periodic table, but the hydrides of nitrogen (NH_3), oxygen (H_2O), and fluorine (HF) have abnormally high boiling points because these molecules form hydrogen bonds.

A comparison of the various kinds of intermolecular forces is shown in Table 10.5.

TABLE 10.5 A Comparison of Intermolecular Forces

Force	Strength	Characteristics
Ion–dipole	Moderate (10–50 kJ/mol)	Occurs between ions and polar solvents
Dipole–dipole	Weak (3–4 kJ/mol)	Occurs between polar molecules
London dispersion	Weak (1–10 kJ/mol)	Occurs between all molecules; strength depends on size, polarizability
Hydrogen bond	Moderate (10–40 kJ/mol)	Occurs between molecules with O—H, N—H, and F—H bonds

WORKED EXAMPLE 10.3

IDENTIFYING INTERMOLECULAR FORCES

Identify the likely kinds of intermolecular forces in the following substances:

(a) HCl   (b) CH_3CH_3 (c) CH_3NH_2 (d) Kr

STRATEGY

Look at the structure of each substance, and decide what intermolecular forces are present. All molecules have dispersion forces; polar molecules have dipole–dipole forces; and molecules with O—H, N—H, or F—H bonds have hydrogen bonds.

SOLUTION

(a) HCl is a polar molecule but can't form hydrogen bonds. It has dipole–dipole forces and dispersion forces.

(b) CH_3CH_3 is a nonpolar molecule and has only dispersion forces.

(c) CH_3NH_2 is a polar molecule that can form hydrogen bonds. In addition, it has dipole–dipole forces and dispersion forces.

(d) Kr is nonpolar and has only dispersion forces.

▸ **PROBLEM 10.5**   Of the substances Ar, Cl$_2$, CCl$_4$, and HNO$_3$, which has:

(a) The largest dipole–dipole forces?

(b) The largest hydrogen-bond forces?

(c) The smallest dispersion forces?

▸ **PROBLEM 10.6**   Consider the kinds of intermolecular forces present in the following compounds, and rank the substances in likely order of increasing boiling point: H$_2$S (34 amu), CH$_3$OH (32 amu), C$_2$H$_6$ (30 amu), Ar (40 amu).

10.3 SOME PROPERTIES OF LIQUIDS

Many familiar and observable properties of liquids can be explained by the intermolecular forces just discussed. We all know, for instance, that some liquids, such as water or gasoline, flow easily when poured, whereas others, such as motor oil or maple syrup, flow sluggishly.

The measure of a liquid's resistance to flow is called its **viscosity**. Not surprisingly, viscosity is related to the ease with which individual molecules move around in the liquid and thus to the intermolecular forces present. Substances with small, nonpolar molecules, such as pentane and benzene, experience only weak intermolecular forces and have relatively low viscosities, whereas larger, more polar substances, such as glycerol [C$_3$H$_5$(OH)$_3$], experience stronger intermolecular forces and so have higher viscosities.

Another familiar property of liquids is **surface tension**, the resistance of a liquid to spread out and increase its surface area. Surface tension is caused by the difference in intermolecular forces experienced by molecules at the surface of a liquid and those experienced by molecules in the interior. Molecules at the surface feel attractive forces on only one side and are thus pulled in toward the liquid, while molecules in the interior are surrounded and are pulled equally in all directions (**Figure 10.8**). The ability of a water strider to walk on water and the beading up of water on a newly waxed car are both due to surface tension.

▲ Surface tension allows a water strider to walk on a pond without penetrating the surface.

Surface tension causes these drops of liquid mercury to form beads.

Molecules or atoms on the **surface** feel attractive forces on only one side and are thus drawn in toward the liquid.

Molecules or atoms in the **middle** of a liquid are attracted equally in all directions.

Figure 10.8

Surface tension. Surface tension is the resistance of a liquid to spread out and increase its surface area.

Surface tension, like viscosity, is generally higher in liquids that have stronger intermolecular forces. Both properties are also temperature-dependent because molecules at higher temperatures have more kinetic energy to counteract the attractive forces holding them together. Data for some common substances are given in Table 10.6. Note that mercury has a particularly large surface tension, causing droplets to form beads (Figure 10.8) and giving the top of the mercury column in a barometer a rounded shape called a *meniscus*.

TABLE 10.6   Viscosities and Surface Tensions of Some Common Substances at 20 °C

Name	Formula	Viscosity $(N \cdot s/m^2)$	Surface Tension (J/m^2)
Pentane	C_5H_{12}	2.4×10^{-4}	1.61×10^{-2}
Benzene	C_6H_6	6.5×10^{-4}	2.89×10^{-2}
Water	H_2O	1.00×10^{-3}	7.29×10^{-2}
Ethanol	C_2H_5OH	1.20×10^{-3}	2.23×10^{-2}
Mercury	Hg	1.55×10^{-3}	4.6×10^{-1}
Glycerol	$C_3H_5(OH)_3$	1.49	6.34×10^{-2}

10.4   PHASE CHANGES

Solid ice melts to liquid water, liquid water freezes to solid ice or evaporates to gaseous steam, and gaseous steam condenses to liquid water. Such processes, in which the physical form but not the chemical identity of a substance changes, are called **phase changes**, or *changes of state*. Matter in any one state, or **phase**, can change into either of the other two. Solids can even change directly into gases, as occurs when dry ice (solid CO_2) sublimes. The names of the various phase changes are:

Fusion (melting)	solid → liquid
Freezing	liquid → solid
Vaporization	liquid → gas
Condensation	gas → liquid
Sublimation	solid → gas
Deposition	gas → solid

Remember...

The value of the **free-energy change** ΔG is a general criterion for the spontaneity of a chemical or physical process. If $\Delta G < 0$, the process is spontaneous; if $\Delta G = 0$, the process is at equilibrium; and if $\Delta G > 0$, the process is nonspontaneous. (Section 8.13)

Like all naturally occurring processes, every phase change has associated with it a **free-energy change,** ΔG. As we saw in Section 8.13, ΔG is made up of two contributions, an enthalpy part (ΔH) and a temperature-dependent entropy part ($T\Delta S$), according to the equation $\Delta G = \Delta H - T\Delta S$. The enthalpy part is the heat flow associated with making or breaking the intermolecular attractions that hold liquids and solids together, while the entropy part is associated with the difference in molecular randomness between the various phases. Gases are more random and have more entropy than liquids, which in turn are more random and have more entropy than solids.

The melting of a solid to a liquid, the sublimation of a solid to a gas, and the vaporization of a liquid to a gas all involve a change from a less random phase to a more random one, and all absorb heat energy to overcome the intermolecular forces holding particles together. Thus, both ΔS and ΔH are positive for these phase changes. By contrast, the freezing of a liquid to a solid, the deposition of a gas to a solid, and the condensation of a gas to a liquid all involve a change from a more random phase to a less random one, and all release heat energy as intermolecular attractions increase to hold particles more tightly together. Thus, both ΔS and ΔH have negative values for these phase changes. The situations are summarized in Figure 10.9.

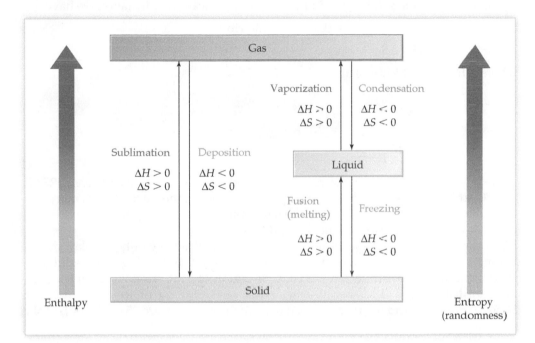

Figure 10.9
Phase changes and randomness. Changes from a less random phase to a more random one (up arrows) have positive values of ΔH and ΔS. Changes from a more random phase to a less random one (down arrows) have negative values of ΔH and ΔS.

▲ Evaporation of perspiration carries away heat and cools the body after exertion.

Let's look at the transitions of solid ice to liquid water and liquid water to gaseous steam to see examples of energy relationships during phase changes. For the melting, or fusion, of ice to water, $\Delta H = +6.01$ kJ/mol and $\Delta S = +22.0$ J/(K·mol); for the vaporization of water to steam, $\Delta H = +40.67$ kJ/mol and $\Delta S = +109$ J/(K·mol). Both ΔH and ΔS are larger for the liquid $\rightarrow$ vapor change than for the solid $\rightarrow$ liquid change because many more intermolecular attractions need to be overcome and much more randomness is gained in the change of liquid to vapor. This highly endothermic conversion of liquid water to gaseous water vapor is used by many organisms as a cooling mechanism. When our bodies perspire on a warm day, evaporation of the perspiration absorbs heat and leaves the skin feeling cooler.

▲ Why do citrus growers spray their trees with water on cold nights?

For phase changes in the opposite direction, the numbers have the same absolute values but opposite signs. That is, $\Delta H = -6.01$ kJ/mol and $\Delta S = -22.0$ J/(K·mol) for the freezing of liquid water to ice, and $\Delta H = -40.67$ kJ/mol and $\Delta S = -109$ J/(K·mol) for the condensation of water vapor to liquid water. Citrus growers take advantage of the exothermic freezing of water when they spray their trees with water on cold nights to prevent frost damage. As water freezes on the leaves, it releases heat that protects the tree.

Knowing the values of ΔH and ΔS for a phase transition makes it possible to calculate the temperature at which the change occurs. Recall from Section 8.13 that ΔG is negative for a spontaneous process, positive for a nonspontaneous process, and zero for a process at equilibrium. Thus, by setting $\Delta G = 0$ and solving for T in the free-energy equation, we can calculate the temperature at which two phases are in equilibrium. For the solid → liquid phase change in water, for instance, we have

$$\Delta G = \Delta H - T\Delta S = 0 \qquad \text{at equilibrium}$$

$$\text{or} \qquad T = \Delta H / \Delta S$$

where $\Delta H = +6.01$ kJ/mol and $\Delta S = +22.0$ J/(K·mol)

$$\text{so} \qquad T = \frac{6.01\ \dfrac{kJ}{mol}}{0.0220\ \dfrac{kJ}{K \cdot mol}} = 273\ K$$

In other words, ice turns into liquid water, and liquid water turns into ice, at 273 K, or 0 °C, at 1 atm pressure—hardly a surprise. In practice, the calculation is more useful in the opposite direction. That is, the temperature at which a phase change occurs is measured and then used to calculate $\Delta S\ (= \Delta H / T)$.

The results of continuously adding heat to a substance can be displayed on a *heating curve* like that shown in **Figure 10.10** for H_2O. Beginning with solid H_2O at an arbitrary temperature, say −25.0 °C, addition of heat raises the ice's temperature until it reaches 0 °C. Because the molar heat capacity of ice (Section 8.7) is 36.57 J/(mol·°C), and because we need to raise the temperature 25.0 °C, 914 J/mol is required:

Energy to heat ice from −25 °C to 0 °C = $\left(36.57\ \dfrac{J}{mol \cdot °C}\right)(25.0\ °C) = 914\ J/mol$

Remember...

The **molar heat capacity (C_m)** of a substance is the amount of heat necessary to raise the temperature of 1 mol of the substance by 1 °C. (Section 8.7)

Figure 10.10
A heating curve for 1 mol of H_2O, showing the temperature changes and phase transitions that occur when heat is added.

Once the temperature of the ice reaches 0 °C, addition of further heat goes into disrupting hydrogen bonds and other intermolecular forces rather than into increasing the temperature, as indicated by the plateau at 0 °C on the heating curve in Figure 10.10. At this temperature—the melting point—solid and liquid coexist in equilibrium as molecules break free from their positions in the ice crystals and enter the liquid phase. Not until the solid turns completely to liquid does the temperature again rise. The amount of energy required to overcome enough intermolecular forces to convert a solid into a liquid is the *enthalpy of fusion*, or **heat of fusion**, ΔH_{fusion}. For ice, $\Delta H_{fusion} = +6.01$ kJ/mol.

Continued addition of heat to liquid water raises the temperature until it reaches 100 °C. Because the molar heat capacity of liquid water is 75.4 J/(mol·°C), 7.54 kJ/mol is required:

$$\text{Energy to heat water from } 0\,°C \text{ to } 100\,°C = \left(75.4 \frac{J}{mol \cdot °C}\right)(100\,°C) = 7.54 \times 10^3 \text{ J/mol}$$

Once the temperature of the water reaches 100 °C, addition of further heat again goes into overcoming intermolecular forces rather than into increasing the temperature, as indicated by the second plateau at 100 °C on the heating curve. At this temperature—the boiling point—liquid and vapor coexist in equilibrium as molecules break free from the surface of the liquid and enter the gas phase. The amount of energy necessary to convert a liquid into a gas is called the *enthalpy of vaporization*, or **heat of vaporization**, ΔH_{vap}. For water, $\Delta H_{vap} = +40.67$ kJ/mol. Only after the liquid has been completely vaporized does the temperature again rise.

Notice that the largest part (40.67 kJ/mol) of the 56.05 kJ/mol required to convert solid ice at −25 °C to gaseous steam at 125 °C is used for vaporization. The heat of vaporization for water is large because of the vast number of hydrogen bonds that must all be broken before molecules can escape from the liquid.

Table 10.7 gives further data on both heat of fusion and heat of vaporization for some common compounds. What is true for water is also true for other compounds: The heat of vaporization of a compound is always larger than its heat of fusion because all intermolecular forces must be overcome before vaporization can occur, but relatively fewer intermolecular forces must be overcome for a solid to change to a liquid.

TABLE 10.7   Heats of Fusion and Heats of Vaporization for Some Common Compounds

Name	Formula	ΔH_{fusion} (kJ/mol)	ΔH_{vap} (kJ/mol)
Ammonia	NH_3	5.66	23.33
Benzene	C_6H_6	9.87	30.72
Ethanol	C_2H_5OH	4.93	38.56
Helium	He	0.02	0.08
Mercury	Hg	2.30	59.11
Water	H_2O	6.01	40.67

WORKED EXAMPLE 10.4

CALCULATING AN ENTROPY OF VAPORIZATION

The boiling point of water is 100 °C, and the enthalpy change for the conversion of water to steam is $\Delta H_{vap} = 40.67$ kJ/mol. What is the entropy change for vaporization, ΔS_{vap}, in J/(K·mol)?

STRATEGY

At the temperature where a phase change occurs, the two phases coexist in equilibrium and ΔG, the free-energy difference between the phases, is zero: $\Delta G = \Delta H - T\Delta S = 0$.

continued on next page

Rearranging this equation gives $\Delta S = \Delta H/T$, where both ΔH and T are known. Remember that T must be expressed in kelvin.

SOLUTION

$$\Delta S_{vap} = \frac{\Delta H_{vap}}{T} = \frac{40.67 \frac{kJ}{mol}}{373.15 \text{ K}} = 0.1090 \text{ kJ/(K} \cdot \text{mol)} = 109.0 \text{ J/(K} \cdot \text{mol)}$$

As you might expect, there is a large positive entropy change, corresponding to a large increase in randomness, on converting water from a liquid to a gas.

▶ **PROBLEM 10.7** Which of the following processes would you expect to have a positive value of ΔS, and which a negative value?

(a) Sublimation of dry ice

(b) Formation of dew on a cold morning

(c) Mixing of cigarette smoke with air in a closed room

▶ **PROBLEM 10.8** Chloroform ($CHCl_3$) has $\Delta H_{vap} = 29.2 \text{ kJ/mol}$ and $\Delta S_{vap} = 87.5 \text{ J/(K} \cdot \text{mol)}$. What is the boiling point of chloroform in kelvin?

10.5 EVAPORATION, VAPOR PRESSURE, AND BOILING POINT

Remember...

The gas pressure inside a container can be measured using an open-end **manometer**, which consists of a U-tube filled with mercury. The difference between the pressure of the gas and the pressure of the atmosphere is equal to the difference between the heights of the mercury levels in the two arms of the U-tube.   (Section 9.1)

The conversion of a liquid to a vapor is visible when the liquid boils, but it occurs under other conditions as well. Let's imagine the two experiments illustrated in Figure 10.11. In one experiment, we place a liquid in an open container; in the other experiment, we place the liquid in a closed container connected to a mercury **manometer** (Section 9.1). After a certain amount of time has passed, the liquid in the first container has evaporated, while the liquid in the second container remains but the pressure has risen. At equilibrium and at a constant temperature, the pressure increase has a constant value called the **vapor pressure** of the liquid.

▲ Because bromine is colored, it's possible to see its reddish vapor above the liquid.

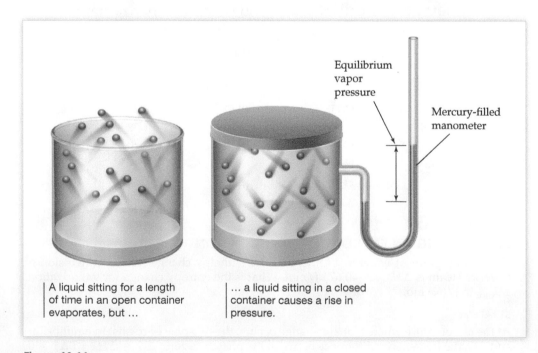

A liquid sitting for a length of time in an open container evaporates, but ...

... a liquid sitting in a closed container causes a rise in pressure.

Figure 10.11
The origin of vapor pressure.

Evaporation and vapor pressure are both explained on a molecular level by the kinetic–molecular theory, developed in Section 9.6 to account for the behavior of gases. The molecules in a liquid are in constant motion but at a variety of speeds depending on the amount of kinetic energy they have. In considering a large sample, molecular kinetic energies follow a distribution curve like that shown in Figure 10.12, with the exact shape of the curve dependent on the temperature. The higher the temperature and the lower the boiling point of the substance, the greater the fraction of molecules in the sample that have sufficient kinetic energy to break free from the surface of the liquid and escape into the vapor.

Remember...
The kinetic–molecular theory is a group of five postulates that can be used to account for the behavior of gases and to derive the ideal gas law. Temperature and kinetic energy are related according to the equation $E_k = (3/2)RT$. (Section 9.6)

Figure 10.12
The distribution of molecular kinetic energies in a liquid.

Molecules that enter the vapor phase in an open container can escape from the liquid and drift away until the liquid evaporates entirely, but molecules in a closed container are trapped. As more and more molecules pass from the liquid to the vapor, the chances increase that random motion will cause some of them to return occasionally to the liquid. Ultimately, the number of molecules returning to the liquid and the number escaping become equal, at which point a dynamic equilibrium exists. Although *individual* molecules are constantly passing back and forth from one phase to the other, the *total numbers* of molecules in both liquid and vapor phases remain constant.

The numerical value of a liquid's vapor pressure depends on the magnitude of the intermolecular forces present and on the temperature. The smaller the intermolecular forces, the higher the vapor pressure, because loosely held molecules escape more easily. The higher the temperature, the higher the vapor pressure, because a larger fraction of molecules have sufficient kinetic energy to escape.

The Clausius–Clapeyron Equation

As indicated in Figure 10.13, the vapor pressure of a liquid rises with temperature in a nonlinear way. A linear relationship *is* found, however, when the natural logarithm of the vapor pressure, $\ln P_{vap}$, is plotted against the inverse of the Kelvin temperature, $1/T$. Table 10.8 gives the appropriate data for water, and Figure 10.13 shows the plot. As noted in Section 9.2, a linear graph is characteristic of mathematical equations of the form $y = mx + b$. In the present instance, $y = \ln P_{vap}$, $x = 1/T$, m is the slope of the line $(-\Delta H_{vap}/R)$, and b is the y-intercept (a constant, C). Thus, the data fit an expression known as the **Clausius–Clapeyron equation:**

Clausius–Clapeyron equation
$$\ln P_{vap} = \left(-\frac{\Delta H_{vap}}{R}\right)\frac{1}{T} + C$$

where ΔH_{vap} is the heat of vaporization of the liquid, R is the gas constant (Section 9.3), and C is a constant characteristic of each specific substance.

TABLE 10.8   Vapor Pressure of Water at Various Temperatures

Temp (K)	P_{vap} (mm Hg)	$\ln P_{vap}$	$1/T$	Temp (K)	P_{vap} (mm Hg)	$\ln P_{vap}$	$1/T$
273	4.58	1.522	0.003 66	333	149.4	5.007	0.003 00
283	9.21	2.220	0.003 53	343	233.7	5.454	0.002 92
293	17.5	2.862	0.003 41	353	355.1	5.872	0.002 83
303	31.8	3.459	0.003 30	363	525.9	6.265	0.002 75
313	55.3	4.013	0.003 19	373	760.0	6.633	0.002 68
323	92.5	4.527	0.003 10	378	906.0	6.809	0.002 65

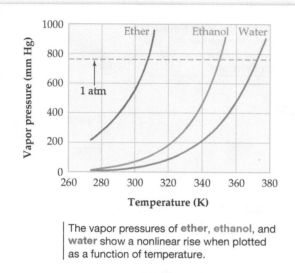

The vapor pressures of **ether**, **ethanol**, and **water** show a nonlinear rise when plotted as a function of temperature.

A plot of $\ln P_{vap}$ versus $1/T$ (Kelvin) for water, prepared from the data in Table 10.8, shows a linear relationship.

Figure 10.13
Vapor pressure of liquids at different temperatures.

▲ What is the vapor pressure of the liquid at its boiling point?

The Clausius–Clapeyron equation makes it possible to calculate the heat of vaporization of a liquid by measuring its vapor pressure at several temperatures and then plotting the results to obtain the slope of the line. Alternatively, once the heat of vaporization and the vapor pressure at one temperature are known, the vapor pressure of the liquid at any other temperature can be calculated, as shown in Worked Example 10.5.

When the vapor pressure of a liquid rises to the point where it becomes equal to the external pressure, the liquid boils and changes into vapor. On a molecular level, you might picture boiling in the following way: Imagine that a few molecules in the interior of the liquid momentarily break free from their neighbors and form a microscopic bubble. If the external pressure from the atmosphere is greater than the vapor pressure inside the bubble, the bubble is immediately crushed. At the temperature where the external pressure and the vapor pressure in the bubble are the same, however, the bubble is not crushed. Instead, it rises through the denser liquid, grows larger as more molecules join it, and appears as part of the vigorous action we associate with boiling.

The temperature at which a liquid boils when the external pressure is exactly 1 atm is called the **normal boiling point**. On the plots in Figure 10.13, the normal boiling points of the three liquids are reached when the curves cross the dashed line representing 760 mm Hg—for ether, 34.6 °C (307.8 K); for ethanol, 78.3 °C (351.5 K); and for water, 100.0 °C (373.15 K).

If the external pressure is less than 1 atm, then the vapor pressure necessary for boiling is reached earlier than 1 atm and the liquid boils at a lower than normal temperature. On top of Mt. Everest, for example, where the atmospheric pressure is only about 260 mm Hg, water boils at approximately 71 °C rather than 100 °C. Conversely, if the external pressure on a liquid is greater than 1 atm, the vapor pressure necessary for boiling is reached later and the liquid boils at a greater than normal temperature. Pressure cookers take advantage of this effect by causing water to boil at a higher temperature, thereby allowing food to cook more rapidly.

WORKED EXAMPLE 10.5

CALCULATING A VAPOR PRESSURE USING THE CLAUSIUS–CLAPEYRON EQUATION

The vapor pressure of ethanol at 34.7 °C is 100.0 mm Hg, and the heat of vaporization of ethanol is 38.6 kJ/mol. What is the vapor pressure of ethanol in millimeters of mercury at 65.0 °C?

STRATEGY

There are several ways to do this problem. One way is to use the vapor pressure at $T = 307.9$ K (34.7 °C) to find a value for C in the Clausius–Clapeyron equation. You could then use that value to solve for $\ln P_{vap}$ at $T = 338.2$ K (65.0 °C).

Alternatively, because C is a constant, its value is the same at any two pressures and temperatures. That is:

$$C = \ln P_1 + \frac{\Delta H_{vap}}{RT_1} = \ln P_2 + \frac{\Delta H_{vap}}{RT_2}$$

This equation can be rearranged to solve for the desired quantity, $\ln P_2$:

$$\ln P_2 = \ln P_1 + \left(\frac{\Delta H_{vap}}{R}\right)\left(\frac{1}{T_1} - \frac{1}{T_2}\right)$$

where $P_1 = 100.0$ mm Hg and $\ln P_1 = 4.6052$, $\Delta H_{vap} = 38.6$ kJ/mol, $R = 8.3145$ J/(K · mol), $T_2 = 338.2$ K (65.0 °C), and $T_1 = 307.9$ K (34.7 °C).

SOLUTION

$$\ln P_2 = 4.6052 + \left(\frac{38,600 \dfrac{J}{mol}}{8.3145 \dfrac{J}{K \cdot mol}}\right)\left(\frac{1}{307.9 \text{ K}} - \frac{1}{338.2 \text{ K}}\right)$$

$$\ln P_2 = 4.6052 + 1.3509 = 5.9561$$

$$P_2 = \text{antiln} (5.9561) = 386.1 \text{ mm Hg}$$

Antilogarithms are reviewed in Appendix A.2.

WORKED EXAMPLE 10.6

CALCULATING A HEAT OF VAPORIZATION USING THE CLAUSIUS–CLAPEYRON EQUATION

Ether has $P_{vap} = 400$ mm Hg at 17.9 °C and a normal boiling point of 34.6 °C. What is the heat of vaporization, ΔH_{vap}, for ether in kJ/mol?

STRATEGY

The heat of vaporization, ΔH_{vap}, of a liquid can be obtained either graphically from the slope of a plot of $\ln P_{vap}$ versus $1/T$ or algebraically from the Clausius–Clapeyron equation. As derived in Worked Example 10.5,

$$\ln P_2 = \ln P_1 + \left(\frac{\Delta H_{vap}}{R}\right)\left(\frac{1}{T_1} - \frac{1}{T_2}\right)$$

continued on next page

which can be solved for ΔH_{vap}:

$$\Delta H_{vap} = \frac{(\ln P_2 - \ln P_1)(R)}{\left(\dfrac{1}{T_1} - \dfrac{1}{T_2}\right)}$$

where $P_1 = 400$ mm Hg and $\ln P_1 = 5.991$, $P_2 = 760$ mm Hg at the normal boiling point and $\ln P_2 = 6.633$, $R = 8.3145$ J/(K·mol), $T_1 = 291.1$ K (17.9 °C), and $T_2 = 307.8$ K (34.6 °C).

SOLUTION

$$\Delta H_{vap} = \frac{(6.633 - 5.991)\left(8.3145\ \dfrac{J}{K \cdot mol}\right)}{\dfrac{1}{291.1\ K} - \dfrac{1}{307.8\ K}} = 28{,}600\ J/mol = 28.6\ kJ/mol$$

▶ **PROBLEM 10.9** The normal boiling point of benzene is 80.1 °C, and the heat of vaporization is $\Delta H_{vap} = 30.7$ kJ/mol. What is the boiling point of benzene in °C on top of Mt. Everest, where $P = 260$ mm Hg?

▶ **PROBLEM 10.10** Bromine has $P_{vap} = 400$ mm Hg at 41.0 °C and a normal boiling point of 331.9 K. What is the heat of vaporization, ΔH_{vap}, of bromine in kJ/mol?

10.6 KINDS OF SOLIDS

It's clear from a brief look around that most substances are solids rather than liquids or gases at room temperature. It's also clear that there are many different kinds of solids. Some solids, such as iron and aluminum, are hard and metallic. Others, such as sugar and table salt, are crystalline and easily broken. And still others, such as rubber and many plastics, are soft and amorphous.

The most fundamental distinction between kinds of solids is that some are crystalline and others are amorphous. **Crystalline solids** are those whose constituent particles—atoms, ions, or molecules—have an ordered arrangement extending over a long range. This order on the atomic level is also seen on the visible level because crystalline solids usually have flat faces and distinct angles (**Figure 10.14a**). **Amorphous solids**, by contrast, are those whose constituent particles are randomly arranged and have no ordered long-range structure (**Figure 10.14b**). Rubber is an example.

(a) A crystalline solid, such as this amethyst, has flat faces and distinct angles. These regular macroscopic features reflect a similarly ordered arrangement of particles at the atomic level.

(b) An amorphous solid like rubber has a disordered arrangement of its constituent particles.

Figure 10.14
Some different kinds of solids.

Crystalline solids can be further categorized as *ionic, molecular, covalent network,* or *metallic.*

Ionic solids are those like sodium chloride, whose constituent particles are ions. A crystal of sodium chloride is composed of alternating Na^+ and Cl^- ions ordered in a regular three-dimensional arrangement and held together by ionic bonds, as discussed in Sections 2.11 and 6.7.

Molecular solids are those like sucrose or ice, whose constituent particles are molecules held together by the intermolecular forces discussed in Section 10.2. A crystal of ice, for example, is composed of H_2O molecules held together in a regular way by hydrogen bonding (**Figure 10.15a**).

Covalent network solids are those like quartz (**Figure 10.15b**) or diamond, whose atoms are linked together by covalent bonds into a giant three-dimensional array. In effect, a covalent network solid is one *very* large molecule.

Metallic solids, such as silver or iron, also consist of large arrays of atoms, but their crystals have metallic properties such as electrical conductivity. We'll discuss metals in Chapter 21.

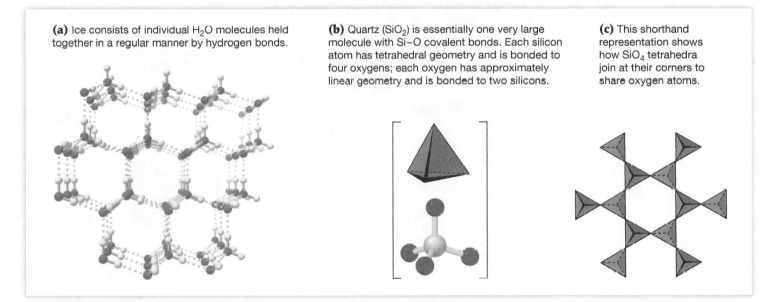

(a) Ice consists of individual H_2O molecules held together in a regular manner by hydrogen bonds.

(b) Quartz (SiO_2) is essentially one very large molecule with Si–O covalent bonds. Each silicon atom has tetrahedral geometry and is bonded to four oxygens; each oxygen has approximately linear geometry and is bonded to two silicons.

(c) This shorthand representation shows how SiO_4 tetrahedra join at their corners to share oxygen atoms.

Figure 10.15
Crystal structures of ice, a molecular solid, and quartz, a covalent network solid.

A summary of the different types of crystalline solids and their characteristics is given in Table 10.9.

TABLE 10.9   Types of Crystalline Solids and Their Characteristics

Type of Solid	Intermolecular Forces	Properties	Examples
Ionic	Ion–ion forces	Brittle, hard, high-melting	$NaCl$, KBr, $MgCl_2$
Molecular	Dispersion forces, dipole–dipole forces, hydrogen bonds	Soft, low-melting, nonconducting	H_2O, Br_2, CO_2, CH_4
Covalent network	Covalent bonds	Hard, high-melting	C (diamond), SiO_2
Metallic	Metallic bonds	Variable hardness and melting point, conducting	Na, Zn, Cu, Fe

10.7 PROBING THE STRUCTURE OF SOLIDS: X-RAY CRYSTALLOGRAPHY

How can the structure of a solid be found experimentally? According to a principle of optics, the wavelength of light used to observe an object must be less than twice the length of the object itself. Since atoms have diameters of around 2×10^{-10} m and the visible light detected by our eyes has wavelengths of $4-7 \times 10^{-7}$ m, it's impossible to see atoms using even the finest optical microscope. To "see" atoms, we must use "light" with a wavelength of approximately 10^{-10} m, which is in the X-ray region of the electromagnetic spectrum (Section 5.1).

The origins of X-ray crystallography go back to the work of Max von Laue in 1912. On passing X rays through a crystal of sodium chloride and letting them strike a photographic plate, Laue noticed that a pattern of spots was produced on the plate, indicating that the X rays were being *diffracted* by the atoms in the crystal. A typical diffraction pattern is shown in **Figure 10.16**.

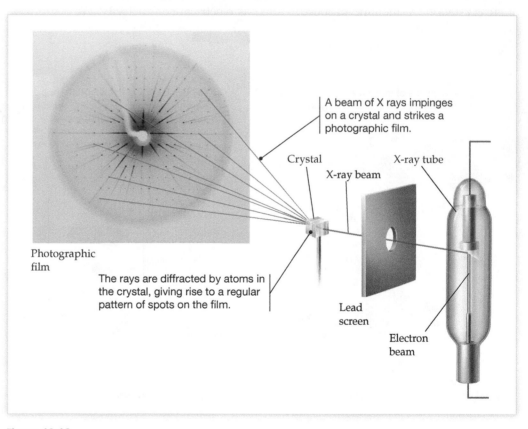

Photographic film

A beam of X rays impinges on a crystal and strikes a photographic film.

Crystal

X-ray beam

X-ray tube

The rays are diffracted by atoms in the crystal, giving rise to a regular pattern of spots on the film.

Lead screen

Electron beam

Figure 10.16
An X-ray diffraction experiment.

Diffraction of electromagnetic radiation occurs when a beam is scattered by an object containing regularly spaced lines (such as those in a diffraction grating) or points (such as the atoms in a crystal). This scattering can happen only if the spacing between the lines or points is comparable to the wavelength of the radiation.

As shown schematically in **Figure 10.17**, diffraction is due to *interference* between two waves passing through the same region of space at the same time. If the waves are in-phase, peak to peak and trough to trough, the interference is constructive and the combined wave is increased in intensity. If the waves are out-of-phase, however, the interference is destructive and the wave is canceled. Constructive interference gives rise to the intense spots observed on Laue's photographic plate, while destructive interference causes the surrounding light areas.

Constructive interference occurs if the waves are in-phase, producing a wave with increased intensity.

Destructive interference occurs if the waves are out-of phase, resulting in cancellation.

Figure 10.17
Interference of electromagnetic waves.

How does the diffraction of X rays by atoms in a crystal give rise to the observed pattern of spots on a photographic plate? According to an explanation advanced in 1913 by the English physicist William H. Bragg and his 22-year-old son, William L. Bragg, the X rays are diffracted by different layers of atoms in the crystal, leading to constructive interference in some instances but destructive interference in others.

To understand the Bragg analysis, imagine that incoming X rays with wavelength λ strike a crystal face at an angle θ and then bounce off at the same angle, just as light bounces off a mirror (**Figure 10.18**). Those rays that strike an atom in the top layer are all reflected at the same angle θ, and those rays that strike an atom in the second layer are also reflected at the angle θ. But because the second layer of atoms is farther from the X-ray source, the distance that the X rays have to travel to reach the second layer is farther than the distance they have to travel to reach the first layer by an amount indicated as BC in Figure 10.18. Using trigonometry, you can show that the extra distance BC is equal to the distance between atomic layers d (= AC) times the sine of the angle θ:

$$\sin \theta = \frac{BC}{d} \quad \text{so} \quad BC = d \sin \theta$$

The extra distance $BC = CB'$ must also be traveled again by the *reflected* rays as they exit the crystal, making the total extra distance traveled equal to $2d \sin \theta$.

$$BC + CB' = 2d \sin \theta$$

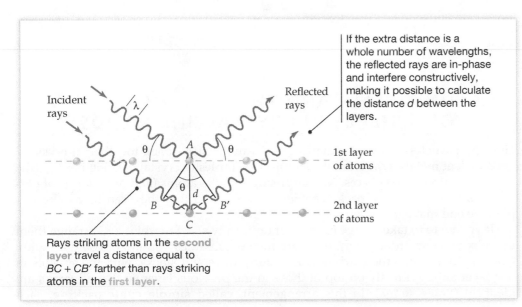

If the extra distance is a whole number of wavelengths, the reflected rays are in-phase and interfere constructively, making it possible to calculate the distance d between the layers.

Incident rays

Reflected rays

1st layer of atoms

2nd layer of atoms

Rays striking atoms in the second layer travel a distance equal to $BC + CB'$ farther than rays striking atoms in the first layer.

Figure 10.18
Diffraction of X rays of wavelength λ from atoms in the top two layers of a crystal.

The key to the Bragg analysis is the realization that the different rays striking the two layers of atoms are in-phase initially but can be in-phase after reflection only if the extra distance $BC + CB'$ is equal to a whole number of wavelengths $n\lambda$, where n is an integer (1, 2, 3, ...). If the extra distance is not a whole number of wavelengths, then the reflected rays will be out-of-phase and will cancel. Setting the extra distance $2d \sin \theta = n\lambda$ and rearranging to solve for d gives the **Bragg equation**:

$$BC + CB' = 2d \sin \theta = n\lambda$$

◀■▶ **Bragg equation** $d = \dfrac{n\lambda}{2 \sin \theta}$

Of the variables in the Bragg equation, the value of the wavelength λ is known, the value of $\sin \theta$ can be measured, and the value of n is a small integer, usually 1. Thus, the distance d between layers of atoms in a crystal can be calculated. For their work, the Braggs shared the 1915 Nobel Prize in Physics. The younger Bragg was 25 years old at the time.

Computer-controlled X-ray diffractometers are now available that automatically rotate a crystal and measure the diffraction from all angles. Analysis of the X-ray diffraction pattern then makes it possible to measure the interatomic distance between any two nearby atoms in a crystal. For molecular substances, this knowledge of interatomic distances indicates which atoms are close enough to form a bond. X-ray analysis thus provides a means for determining the structures of molecules (**Figure 10.19**).

Figure 10.19

A computer-generated structure of adenosine triphosphate (ATP) as determined by X-ray crystallography. ATP has been called "the energy currency of the living cell" because it fuels many metabolic processes.

10.8   UNIT CELLS AND THE PACKING OF SPHERES IN CRYSTALLINE SOLIDS

How do particles—whether atoms, ions, or molecules—pack together in crystals? Let's look at metals, which are the simplest examples of crystal packing because the individual atoms are spheres. Not surprisingly, metal atoms (and other kinds of particles as well) generally pack together in crystals so that they can be as close as possible and maximize intermolecular attractions.

If you were to take a large number of uniformly sized marbles and arrange them in a box in some orderly way, there are four possibilities you might come up with. One way to arrange the marbles is in orderly rows and stacks, with the spheres in one layer sitting directly on top of those in the previous layer so that all layers are identical (**Figure 10.20a**). In this arrangement, called **simple cubic packing**, each sphere is touched by six neighbors—four in its own layer, one above, and one below—and is thus said to have a **coordination number** of 6. Only 52% of the available volume is occupied by the spheres in simple cubic packing, making inefficient use of space and minimizing attractive forces. Of all the metals in the periodic table, only polonium crystallizes in this way.

Alternatively, space could be used more efficiently if, instead of stacking the spheres directly on top of one another, you slightly separate the spheres in a given layer and offset alternating layers in an *a-b-a-b* arrangement so that the spheres in the *b* layers fit into the depressions between spheres in the *a* layers, and vice versa (**Figure 10.20b**). In this arrangement, called **body-centered cubic packing**, each sphere has a coordination number of 8—four neighbors above and four below—and space is used quite efficiently: 68% of the available volume is occupied. Iron, sodium, and 14 other metals crystallize in this way.

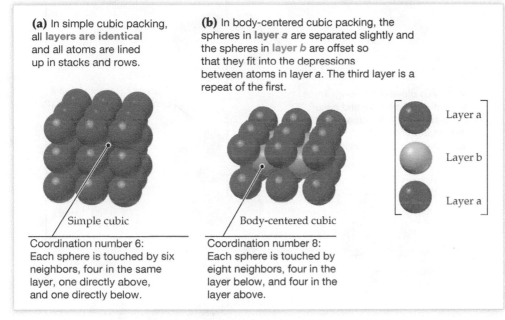

(a) In simple cubic packing, all **layers are identical** and all atoms are lined up in stacks and rows.

Simple cubic

Coordination number 6:
Each sphere is touched by six neighbors, four in the same layer, one directly above, and one directly below.

(b) In body-centered cubic packing, the spheres in **layer a** are separated slightly and the spheres in **layer b** are offset so that they fit into the depressions between atoms in layer *a*. The third layer is a repeat of the first.

Body-centered cubic

Coordination number 8:
Each sphere is touched by eight neighbors, four in the layer below, and four in the layer above.

Layer a

Layer b

Layer a

Figure 10.20
Simple cubic packing and body-centered cubic packing.

The remaining two packing arrangements of spheres are both said to be *closest-packed*. The **hexagonal closest-packed** arrangement (**Figure 10.21a**) has two alternating layers, *a-b-a-b*. Each layer has a hexagonal arrangement of touching spheres, which are offset so that spheres in a *b* layer fit into the small triangular depressions between spheres in an *a* layer. Zinc, magnesium, and 19 other metals crystallize in this way.

The **cubic closest-packed** arrangement (**Figure 10.21b**) has *three* alternating layers, *a-b-c-a-b-c*. The *a-b* layers are identical to those in the hexagonal closest-packed arrangement, but the third layer is offset from both *a* and *b* layers. Silver, copper, and 16 other metals crystallize with this arrangement.

In both kinds of closest-packed arrangements, each sphere has a coordination number of 12—six neighbors in the same layer, three above, and three below—and 74% of the available volume is filled. The next time you're in a grocery store, look to see how the oranges or apples are stacked in their display box. They'll almost certainly have a closest-packed arrangement.

◀ What kind of packing arrangement do these oranges have?

Figure 10.21

Hexagonal closest-packing and cubic closest-packing. In both kinds of packing, each sphere is touched by 12 neighbors, 6 in the same layer, 3 in the layer above, and 3 in the layer below.

(a) Hexagonal closest-packing: Two alternating hexagonal layers *a* and *b* are offset so that the spheres in one layer sit in the small triangular depressionsof neighboring layers.

Top view

(b) Cubic closest-packing: Three alternating layers *a*, *b*, and *c* are offset so that the spheres in one layer sit in the small triangular depressions of neighboring layers.

Top view

Layer *a*

Layer *b*

Layer *a*

Both arragements have a coordination number of 12.

Layer *a*

Layer *c*

Layer *b*

Layer *a*

▲ Just as these bricks are stacked together in a regular way on the pallet, a crystal is made of many small repeating units called unit cells that stack together in a regular way.

Unit Cells

Having taken a bulk view of how spheres can pack in a crystal, let's now take a close-up view. Just as a large brick wall is made up of many identical bricks stacked together in a repeating pattern, a crystal is made up of many small repeat units called **unit cells** stacked together in three dimensions.

Fourteen different unit-cell geometries occur in crystalline solids. All are parallelepipeds—six-sided geometric solids whose faces are parallelograms. We'll be concerned here only with those unit cells that have cubic symmetry; that is, cells whose edges are equal in length and whose angles are 90°.

There are three kinds of cubic unit cells: *primitive-cubic*, *body-centered cubic*, and *face-centered cubic*. As shown in **Figure 10.22a**, a **primitive-cubic unit cell** for a metal has an atom at each of its eight corners, where it is shared with seven neighboring cubes that come together at the same point. As a result, only 1/8 of each corner atom "belongs" to a given cubic unit. This primitive-cubic unit cell, with all atoms arranged in orderly rows and stacks, is the repeat unit found in simple cubic packing.

A **body-centered cubic unit cell** has eight corner atoms plus an additional atom in the center of the cube (**Figure 10.22b**). This body-centered cubic unit cell, with two repeating offset layers and with the spheres in a given layer slightly separated, is the repeat unit found in body-centered cubic packing.

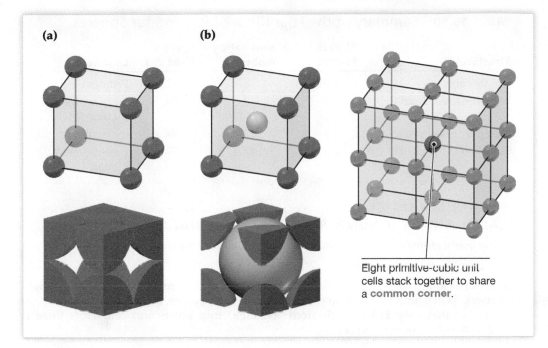

Figure 10.22
Geometries of (a) primitive-cubic and (b) body-centered cubic unit cells. Both skeletal (top) and space-filling views (bottom) are shown.

A **face-centered cubic unit cell** has eight corner atoms plus an additional atom in the center of each of its six faces, where it is shared with one other neighboring cube (**Figure 10.23a**). Thus, 1/2 of each face atom belongs to a given unit cell. This face-centered cubic unit cell is the repeat unit found in cubic closest-packing, as can be seen by looking down the body diagonal of a unit cell (**Figure 10.23b**). The faces of the unit-cell cube are at 54.7° angles to the layers of the atoms.

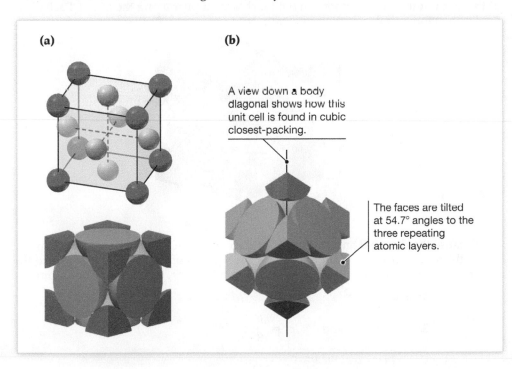

Figure 10.23
Geometry of a face-centered cubic unit cell.

A summary of stacking patterns, coordination numbers, amount of space used, and unit cells for the four kinds of packing of spheres is given in Table 10.10. Hexagonal closest-packing is the only one of the four that has a noncubic unit cell.

TABLE 10.10 Summary of the Four Kinds of Packing for Spheres

Structure	Stacking Pattern	Coordination Number	Space Used (%)	Unit Cell
Simple cubic	a-a-a-a-	6	52	Primitive cubic
Body-centered cubic	a-b-a-b-	8	68	Body-centered cubic
Hexagonal closest-packed	a-b-a-b-	12	74	(Noncubic)
Cubic closest-packed	a-b-c-a-b-c-	12	74	Face-centered cubic

WORKED EXAMPLE 10.7

CALCULATING THE NUMBER OF ATOMS IN A UNIT CELL

How many atoms are in one primitive-cubic unit cell of a metal?

STRATEGY AND SOLUTION

As shown in Figure 10.22a, a primitive-cubic unit cell has an atom at each of its eight corners. When unit cells are stacked together, each corner atom is shared by eight cubes, so that only 1/8 of each atom "belongs" to a given unit cell. Thus there is $1/8 \times 8 = 1$ atom per unit cell.

WORKED EXAMPLE 10.8

USING UNIT-CELL DIMENSIONS TO CALCULATE THE RADIUS OF AN ATOM

Silver metal crystallizes in a cubic closest-packed arrangement with the edge of the unit cell having a length $d = 407$ pm. What is the radius in picometers of a silver atom?

STRATEGY AND SOLUTION

Cubic closest-packing uses a face-centered cubic unit cell. Looking at any one face of the cube head-on shows that the face atoms touch the corner atoms along the diagonal of the face but that corner atoms do not touch one another along the edges. Each diagonal is therefore equal to four atomic radii, $4r$:

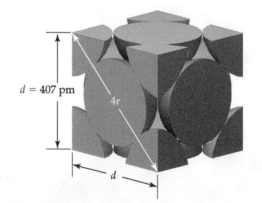

Because the diagonal and two edges of the cube form a right triangle, we can use the Pythagorean theorem to set the sum of the squares of the two edges equal to the square of the diagonal, $d^2 + d^2 = (4r)^2$ and then solve for r, the radius of one atom:

$$d^2 + d^2 = (4r)^2$$

$$2d^2 = 16r^2 \quad \text{and} \quad r^2 = \frac{d^2}{8}$$

thus $\quad r = \sqrt{\frac{d^2}{8}} = \sqrt{\frac{(407 \text{ pm})^2}{8}} = 144 \text{ pm}$

The radius of a silver atom is 144 pm.

WORKED EXAMPLE 10.9

USING UNIT-CELL DIMENSIONS TO CALCULATE THE DENSITY OF A METAL

Nickel has a face-centered cubic unit cell with a length of 352.4 pm along an edge. What is the density of nickel in g/cm^3?

STRATEGY

Density is mass divided by volume. The mass of a single unit cell can be calculated by counting the number of atoms in the cell and multiplying by the mass of a single atom. The volume of a single cubic unit cell with edge d is $d^3 = (3.524 \times 10^{-8} cm)^3 = 4.376 \times 10^{-23} cm^3$.

SOLUTION

Each of the eight corner atoms in a face-centered cubic unit cell is shared by eight unit cells, so that only $1/8 \times 8 = 1$ atom belongs to a single cell. In addition, each of the six face atoms is shared by two unit cells, so that $1/2 \times 6 = 3$ atoms belong to a single cell. Thus, a single cell has 1 corner atom and 3 face atoms, for a total of 4, and each atom has a mass equal to the molar mass of nickel (58.69 g/mol) divided by Avogadro's number (6.022×10^{23} atoms/mol). We can now calculate the density:

$$\text{Density} = \frac{\text{Mass}}{\text{Volume}} = \frac{(4 \text{ atoms}) \left(\dfrac{58.69 \, \frac{g}{\text{mol}}}{6.022 \times 10^{23} \, \frac{\text{atoms}}{\text{mol}}} \right)}{4.376 \times 10^{-23} \, cm^3} = 8.909 \, g/cm^3$$

The calculated density of nickel is $8.909 \, g/cm^3$. (The measured value is $8.90 \, g/cm^3$.)

WORKED CONCEPTUAL EXAMPLE 10.10

IDENTIFYING A UNIT CELL

Imagine a tiled floor in the following pattern. Identify the smallest repeating rectangular unit, analogous to a two-dimensional unit cell.

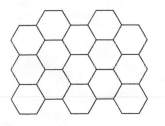

STRATEGY

Using trial and error, the idea is to draw two perpendicular sets of parallel lines that define a repeating rectangular unit. There may be more than one possibility.

SOLUTION

or

▶ **PROBLEM 10.11** How many atoms are in the following:

(a) One body-centered cubic unit cell of a metal

(b) One face-centered cubic unit cell of a metal

▶ **PROBLEM 10.12** Polonium metal crystallizes in a simple cubic arrangement, with the edge of a unit cell having a length $d = 334$ pm. What is the radius in picometers of a polonium atom?

▶ **PROBLEM 10.13** What is the density of polonium (Problem 10.12) in g/cm^3?

CONCEPTUAL PROBLEM 10.14 Imagine a tiled floor in the following pattern. Identify the smallest repeating unit, analogous to a two-dimensional unit cell.

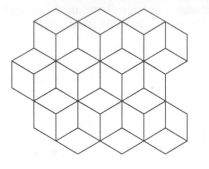

10.9 STRUCTURES OF SOME IONIC SOLIDS

Remember...

Atomic radius decreases when an atom is converted to a cation by loss of an electron and increases when the atom is converted to an anion by gain of an electron. (Section 6.2)

Simple ionic solids such as NaCl and KBr are like metals in that the individual ions are spheres that pack together in a regular way. They differ from metals, however, in that the spheres are not all the same size—anions generally have larger radii than cations (Section 6.2). As a result, ionic solids adopt a variety of different unit cells, depending on the size and charge of the ions. NaCl, KCl, and a number of other salts have a face-centered cubic unit cell in which the larger Cl⁻ anions occupy corners and faces while the smaller Na⁺ cations fit into the holes between adjacent anions (Figure 10.24).

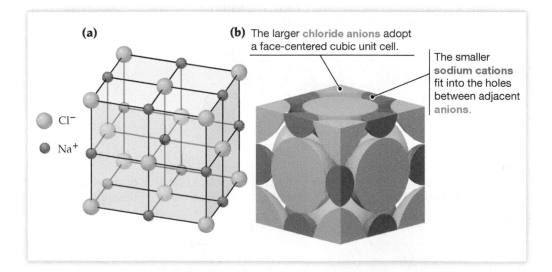

Figure 10.24
The unit cell of NaCl. Both a skeletal view **(a)** and a space-filling view **(b)** in which the unit cell is viewed edge-on are shown.

It's necessary, of course, that the unit cell of an ionic substance be electrically neutral, with equal numbers of positive and negative charges. In the NaCl unit cell, for instance, there are four Cl⁻ anions ($1/8 \times 8 = 1$ corner atom, plus $1/2 \times 6 = 3$ face atoms) and also four Na⁺ cations ($1/4 \times 12 = 3$ edge atoms, plus 1 center atom). (Remember that each corner atom in a cubic unit cell is shared by eight cells, each face atom is shared by two cells, and each edge atom is shared by four cells.)

Two other common ionic unit cells are shown in Figure 10.25. Copper(I) chloride has a face-centered cubic arrangement of the larger Cl⁻ anions, with the smaller Cu⁺ cations in holes so that each is surrounded by a tetrahedron of four anions. Barium

Figure 10.25
Unit cells of (a) CuCl and (b) BaCl$_2$.

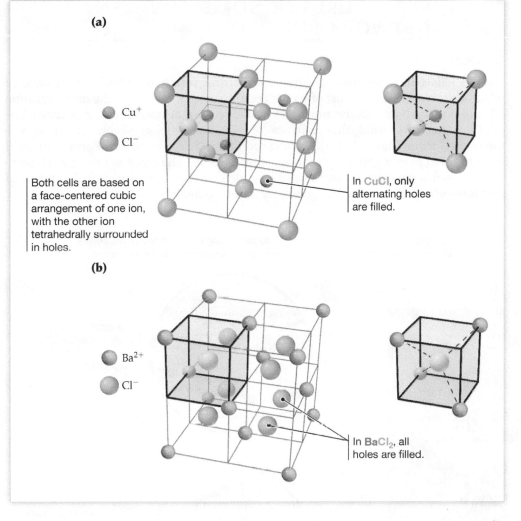

(a)

Cu$^+$

Cl$^-$

Both cells are based on a face-centered cubic arrangement of one ion, with the other ion tetrahedrally surrounded in holes.

In CuCl, only alternating holes are filled.

(b)

Ba^{2+}

Cl$^-$

In BaCl$_2$, all holes are filled.

chloride, by contrast, has a face-centered cubic arrangement of the smaller Ba^{2+} *cations*, with the larger Cl$^-$ anions surrounded tetrahedrally. As required for charge neutrality, there are twice as many Cl$^-$ anions as Ba^{2+} cations.

▶ **PROBLEM 10.15** Count the numbers of + and − charges in the CuCl and BaCl$_2$ unit cells (Figure 10.25), and show that both cells are electrically neutral.

CONCEPTUAL PROBLEM 10.16 Rhenium oxide crystallizes in the following cubic unit cell:

Oxygen

Rhenium

(a) How many rhenium atoms and how many oxygen atoms are in each unit cell?
(b) What is the formula of rhenium oxide?
(c) What is the oxidation state of rhenium?
(d) What is the geometry around each oxygen atom?
(e) What is the geometry around each rhenium atom?

10.10 STRUCTURES OF SOME COVALENT NETWORK SOLIDS

Carbon

Carbon exists in more than 40 known structural forms, or **allotropes,** several of which are crystalline but most of which are amorphous. Graphite, the most common allotrope of carbon and the most stable under normal conditions, is a crystalline covalent network solid that consists of two-dimensional sheets of fused six-membered rings (**Figure 10.26a**). Each carbon atom is sp^2-hybridized and is bonded with trigonal planar geometry to three other carbons. The diamond form of elemental carbon is a covalent network solid in which each carbon atom is sp^3-hybridized and is bonded with tetrahedral geometry to four other carbons (**Figure 10.26b**).

(a) Graphite is a covalent network solid consisting of two-dimensional sheets of sp^2-hybridized carbon atoms organized into six-membered rings.

The atoms in each sheet are offset slightly from the atoms in neighboring sheets.

(b) Diamond is a vast, three-dimensional array of sp^3-hybridized carbon atoms, each of which is bonded with tetrahedral geometry to four other carbons.

Figure 10.26
Two crystalline allotropes of carbon, (a) graphite and (b) diamond.

In addition to graphite and diamond, a third crystalline allotrope of carbon called *fullerene* was discovered in 1985 as a constituent of soot. Fullerene consists of spherical C_{60} molecules with the extraordinary shape of a soccer ball. The C_{60} ball has 12 pentagonal and 20 hexagonal faces, with each atom sp^2-hybridized and bonded to three other atoms (**Figure 10.27a**). Closely related to both graphite and fullerene are a group of carbon allotropes called *nanotubes*—tubular structures made of repeating six-membered carbon rings, as if a sheet of graphite were rolled up (**Figure 10.27b**). Typically, the tubes have a diameter of about 2–30 nm and a length of up to 1 mm.

The different structures of the carbon allotropes lead to widely different properties. Because of its three-dimensional network of strong single bonds that tie all atoms in a crystal together, diamond is the hardest known substance. In addition to its use in jewelry, diamond is widely used industrially for the tips of saw blades and drilling bits. It is an electrical insulator and has a melting point of about 8700 °C at a

Figure 10.27
Fullerene, C_{60}, and carbon nanotubes.

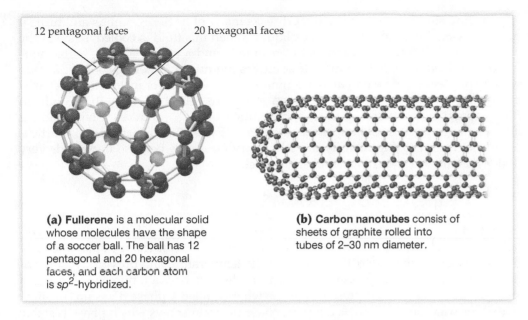

12 pentagonal faces   20 hexagonal faces

(a) Fullerene is a molecular solid whose molecules have the shape of a soccer ball. The ball has 12 pentagonal and 20 hexagonal faces, and each carbon atom is sp^2-hybridized.

(b) Carbon nanotubes consist of sheets of graphite rolled into tubes of 2–30 nm diameter.

pressure of 6–10 million atm. Clear, colorless, and highly crystalline, diamonds are very rare and are found in only a few places in the world, particularly in central and southern Africa.

Graphite is the black, slippery substance used as the "lead" in pencils, as an electrode material in batteries, and as a lubricant in locks. All these properties result from its sheetlike structure. Air and water molecules can adsorb onto the flat faces of the sheets, allowing the sheets to slide over one another and giving graphite its greasy feeling and lubricating properties. Graphite is more stable than diamond at normal pressures but can be converted into diamond at very high pressure and temperature. In fact, approximately 120,000 kg of industrial diamonds is synthesized annually by applying 150,000 atm pressure to graphite at high temperature.

Fullerene, black and shiny like graphite, is the subject of much current research because of its interesting electronic properties. When fullerene is allowed to react with rubidium metal, a superconducting material called rubidium fulleride, Rb_3C_{60}, is formed. (We'll discuss superconductors in more detail in Section 21.7.) Carbon nanotubes are being studied for use as fibers in the structural composites used to make golf clubs, bicycle frames, boats, and airplanes. Their tensile strength is approximately 50–60 times greater than that of steel.

Silica

Just as living organisms are based on carbon compounds, most rocks and minerals are based on silicon compounds. Quartz and much sand, for instance, are nearly pure *silica*, SiO_2. Silicon and oxygen together, in fact, make up nearly 75% of the mass of the Earth's crust. Considering that silicon and carbon are both in group 4A of the periodic table, you might expect SiO_2 to be similar in its properties to CO_2. In fact, though, CO_2 is a molecular substance and a gas at room temperature, whereas SiO_2 (Figure 10.15b on page 367) is a covalent network solid with a melting point over 1600 °C.

The dramatic difference in properties between CO_2 and SiO_2 is due primarily to the difference in electronic structure between carbon and silicon. The π part of a *carbon*–oxygen **double bond** is formed by sideways overlap of a carbon $2p$ orbital with an oxygen $2p$ orbital (Section 7.12). If a similar *silicon*–oxygen double bond were to form, it would require overlap of an oxygen $2p$ orbital and a silicon $3p$ orbital. But because the Si—O bond distance is longer than the C—O distance and a $3p$ orbital is larger than a $2p$ orbital, overlap between the two is not as favorable. As a result, silicon forms four single bonds to four oxygens in a covalent network structure rather than two double bonds to two oxygens in a molecular structure.

Remember...

Two atoms form a **double bond** when they approach each other with their hybrid orbitals aligned head-on for σ bonding and with their unhybridized p orbitals aligned in a parallel, sideways manner to form a π bond. (Section 7.12)

▲ Colored glasses contain transition metal ions.

Heating silica above about 1600 °C breaks many of its Si—O bonds and turns it from a crystalline solid into a viscous liquid. When this fluid is cooled, some of the Si—O bonds re-form in a random arrangement, and a noncrystalline, amorphous solid called *quartz glass* is formed. If additives are mixed in before cooling, a wide variety of glasses can be prepared. Common window glass, for instance, is prepared by adding $CaCO_3$ and Na_2CO_3. Addition of various transition metal ions results in the preparation of colored glasses, and addition of B_2O_3 produces a high-melting *borosilicate glass* that is sold under the trade name Pyrex. Borosilicate glass is particularly useful for cooking utensils and laboratory glassware because it expands very little when heated and is thus unlikely to crack.

10.11 PHASE DIAGRAMS

Now that we've looked at the three phases of matter individually, let's take an overall view. As noted previously, any one phase of matter can change spontaneously into either of the other two, depending on the temperature and pressure. A convenient way to picture this pressure–temperature dependency of a pure substance in a closed system without air present is to use what is called a **phase diagram**. As illustrated for water in **Figure 10.28**, a typical phase diagram shows which phase is stable at different combinations of pressure and temperature. When a boundary line between phases is crossed by changing either the temperature or the pressure, a phase change occurs.

Figure 10.28

A phase diagram for H_2O. Various features of the diagram are discussed in the text. Note that the pressure and temperature axes are not drawn to scale.

▲ At the triple point, solid exists in the boiling liquid. That is, solid, liquid, and gas coexist in equilibrium.

The simplest way to understand a phase diagram is to begin at the origin in the lower left corner of Figure 10.28 and travel up and right along the boundary line between solid on the left and gas on the right. Points on this line represent pressure/temperature combinations at which the two phases are in equilibrium in a closed system and a direct phase transition between solid ice and gaseous water vapor occurs. At some point along the solid/gas line, an intersection is reached where two lines diverge to form the bounds of the liquid region. The solid/liquid boundary for H_2O goes up and slightly left, while the liquid/gas boundary continues curving up and to the right. Called the **triple point**, this three-way intersection represents a unique combination of pressure and temperature at which all three phases coexist in equilibrium. For water, the triple-point temperature T_t is 0.0098 °C, and the triple-point pressure P_t is 6.0×10^{-3} atm.

Continuing up and slightly left from the triple point, the solid/liquid boundary line represents the melting point of solid ice (or the freezing point of liquid water) at various pressures. When the pressure is 1 atm, the melting point—called the **normal melting point**—is exactly 0 °C. There is a slight negative slope to the line, indicating that the melting point of ice decreases as pressure increases. Water is unusual in this respect, because most substances have a positive slope to their solid/liquid line, indicating that their melting points *increase* with pressure. We'll say more about this behavior shortly.

Continuing up and right from the triple point, the liquid/gas boundary line represents the pressure/temperature combinations at which liquid and gas coexist and water vaporizes (or steam condenses). In fact, the part of the curve up to 1 atm pressure is simply the vapor pressure curve we saw previously in Figure 10.13. When the pressure is 1 atm, water is at its normal boiling point of 100 °C. Continuing along the liquid/gas boundary line, we suddenly reach the **critical point**, where the line abruptly ends. The critical temperature T_c is the temperature beyond which a gas cannot be liquefied, no matter how great the pressure, and the critical pressure P_c is the pressure beyond which a liquid cannot be vaporized, no matter how high the temperature. For water, $T_c = 374.4$ °C and $P_c = 217.7$ atm.

We're all used to seeing solid/liquid and liquid/gas phase transitions, but behavior at the critical point lies so far outside our normal experiences that it's hard to imagine. Think of it this way: A *gas* at the critical point is under such high pressure, and its molecules are so close together, that it becomes indistinguishable from a liquid. A *liquid* at the critical point is at such a high temperature, and its molecules are so relatively far apart, that it becomes indistinguishable from a gas. Thus, the two phases simply become one and form a **supercritical fluid** that is neither true liquid nor true gas. No distinct physical phase change occurs on going beyond the critical point. Rather, a whitish, pearly sheen momentarily appears, and the visible boundary between liquid and gas suddenly vanishes. Frankly, you have to see it to believe it.

The phase diagram of CO_2 shown in **Figure 10.29** has many of the same features as that of water but differs in several interesting respects. First, the triple point is at $P_t = 5.11$ atm, meaning that CO_2 can't be a liquid below this pressure, no matter what the temperature. At 1 atm pressure, CO_2 is a solid below −78.5 °C but a gas above this temperature. Second, the slope of the solid/liquid boundary is positive, meaning that the solid phase is favored as the pressure rises and that the melting point of solid CO_2 therefore increases with pressure.

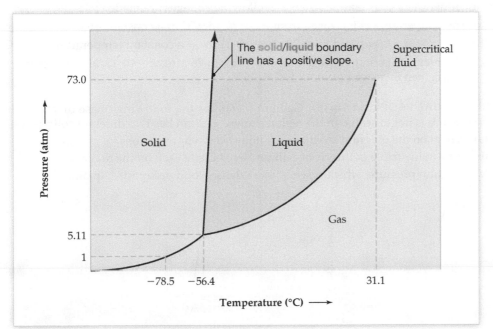

Figure 10.29

A phase diagram for CO_2. The pressure and temperature axes are not to scale.

Figure 10.30
Pressure and melting point. Why does the weighted wire cut through this block of ice?

The effect of pressure on the slope of the solid/liquid boundary line—negative for H_2O but positive for CO_2 and most other substances—depends on the relative densities of the solid and liquid phases. For CO_2 and most other substances, the solid phase is denser than the liquid because particles are packed closer together in the solid. Increasing the pressure pushes the molecules even closer together, thereby favoring the solid phase even more and giving the solid/liquid boundary line a positive slope. Water, however, becomes less dense when it freezes to a solid because large empty spaces are left between molecules due to the ordered three-dimensional network of hydrogen bonds in ice (Figure 10.15a). As a result, increasing the pressure favors the liquid phase, giving the solid/liquid boundary a negative slope.

Figure 10.30 shows a simple demonstration of the effect of pressure on melting point. If a thin wire with heavy weights at each end is draped over a block of ice near 0 °C, the wire rapidly cuts through the block because the increased pressure lowers the melting point of the ice under the wire, causing the ice to liquefy. If the same experiment is tried with a block of dry ice (solid CO_2), however, nothing happens. The dry ice is unaffected because the increased pressure under the wire makes melting more difficult rather than less difficult.

WORKED EXAMPLE 10.11

INTERPRETING A PHASE DIAGRAM

Freeze-dried foods are prepared by freezing the food and removing water by subliming the ice at low pressure. Look at the phase diagram of water in Figure 10.28, and tell the maximum pressure in mm Hg at which ice and water vapor are in equilibrium.

STRATEGY

Solid and vapor are in equilibrium only below the triple-point pressure, $P_t = 6.0 \times 10^{-3}$ atm, which needs to be converted to millimeters of mercury.

SOLUTION

$$6.0 \times 10^{-3} \text{ atm} \times \frac{760 \text{ mm Hg}}{1 \text{ atm}} = 4.6 \text{ mm Hg}$$

▶ **PROBLEM 10.17** Look at the phase diagram of CO_2 in Figure 10.29, and tell the minimum pressure in atmospheres at which liquid CO_2 can exist.

▶ **PROBLEM 10.18** Look at the phase diagram of CO_2 in Figure 10.29, and describe what happens to a CO_2 sample when the following changes are made:

(a) The temperature is increased from −100 °C to 0 °C at a constant pressure of 2 atm.

(b) The pressure is reduced from 72 atm to 5.0 atm at a constant temperature of 30 °C.

(c) The pressure is first increased from 3.5 atm to 76 atm at −10 °C, and the temperature is then increased from −10 °C to 45 °C.

CONCEPTUAL PROBLEM 10.19 Gallium metal has the following phase diagram (the pressure axis is not to scale). In the region shown, gallium has two different solid phases.

(a) Where on the diagram are the solid, liquid, and vapor regions?

(b) How many triple points does gallium have? Circle each on the diagram.

(c) At 1 atm pressure, which phase is more dense, solid or liquid? Explain.

INQUIRY LIQUIDS MADE OF IONS?

When you think of ionic compounds, you probably think of crystalline, high-melting solids: sodium chloride (mp = 801 °C), magnesium oxide (mp = 2825 °C), lithium carbonate (mp = 732 °C), and so on. It's certainly true that many ionic compounds fit that description, but not all. Some ionic compounds are actually liquid at room temperature. Ionic liquids, in fact, have been known for nearly a century—the first such compound to be discovered was ethylammonium nitrate, $CH_3CH_2NH_3^+ NO_3^-$, with a melting point of just 12 °C.

Generally speaking, the ionic liquids used today are salts in which the cation has an irregular shape and in which one or both of the ions are large and bulky so that the charges are dispersed over a large volume. Both factors minimize the crystal lattice energy, thereby making the solid less stable and favoring the liquid. Typical cations are derived from nitrogen-containing organic compounds called *amines*, either 1,3-dialkylimidazolium ions or *N*-alkylpyridinium ions.

▲ As surprising as it sounds, the bottom liquid in this reactor is composed of ions.

A 1,3-dialkylimidazolium ion   An *N*-alkylpyridium ion

Anions are just as varied as the cations, and more than 500 different ionic liquids with different anion/cation combinations are commercially available. Hexafluorophosphate, tetrafluoroborate, alkyl sulfates, trifluoromethanesulfonate, and halides are typical anions.

Hexafluoro-phosphate   Tetrafluoro-borate

Methyl sulfate   Trifluoromethane-sulfonate   Halide

For many years, ionic liquids were just laboratory curiosities. More recently, though, they have been found to be excellent solvents, particularly for use in green chemistry processes like those described in the Chapter 4 *Inquiry*. Among the properties of ionic liquids:

- They dissolve both polar and nonpolar compounds, giving highly concentrated solutions and thereby minimizing the amount of liquid needed.
- They can be fine-tuned for use in specific reactions by varying cation and anion structures.
- They are nonflammable.
- They are stable at high temperatures.
- They have negligible vapor pressures and don't evaporate.
- They are generally recoverable and can be reused many times.

Among their potential applications, ionic liquids are now being explored for use as electrolytes in high-temperature batteries, as solvents for the extraction of heavy organic materials from oil shale, and as replacements for toxic or flammable organic solvents in many industrial processes. We'll be hearing much more about ionic liquids in the coming years.

▶ **PROBLEM 10.20** How does an ionic liquid differ from a typical molecular liquid, such as water?

▶ **PROBLEM 10.21** What structural features do ionic liquids have that prevent them from forming solids easily?

SUMMARY

The presence of polar covalent bonds in a molecule can cause the molecule to have a net polarity, a property measured by the **dipole moment**.

Intermolecular forces, known collectively as **van der Waals forces**, are the attractions responsible for holding particles together in the liquid and solid phases. There are several kinds of intermolecular forces, all of which arise from electrical attractions. **Dipole–dipole forces** occur between two polar molecules. **London dispersion forces** are characteristic of all molecules and result from the presence of temporary dipole moments caused by momentarily unsymmetrical electron distributions. A **hydrogen bond** is the attraction between a positively polarized hydrogen atom bonded to O, N, or F and a lone pair of electrons on an O, N, or F atom of another molecule. In addition, **ion–dipole forces** occur between an ion and a polar molecule.

Matter in any one **phase**—solid, liquid, or gas—can undergo a **phase change** to either of the other two phases. Like all naturally occurring processes, a phase change has associated with it a free-energy change, $\Delta G = \Delta H - T\Delta S$. The enthalpy component, ΔH, is a measure of the change in intermolecular forces; the entropy component, ΔS, is a measure of the change in molecular randomness accompanying the phase transition. The enthalpy change for the solid–liquid transition is called the **heat of fusion**, and the enthalpy change for the liquid–vapor transition is the **heat of vaporization**.

The effects of temperature and pressure on phase changes can be displayed graphically on a **phase diagram**. A typical phase diagram has three regions—solid, liquid, and gas—separated by three boundary lines that represent pressure/temperature combinations at which two phases are in equilibrium and phase changes occur. At exactly 1 atm pressure, the temperature at the solid/liquid boundary corresponds to the **normal melting point** of the substance, and the temperature at the liquid/gas boundary corresponds to the **normal boiling point**. The three lines meet at the **triple point**, a unique combination of temperature and pressure at which all three phases coexist in equilibrium. The liquid/gas line runs from the triple point to the **critical point**, a pressure/temperature combination beyond which liquid and gas phases become a **supercritical fluid** that is neither a true liquid nor a true gas.

Solids can be characterized as **amorphous** if their particles are randomly arranged or **crystalline** if their particles are ordered. Crystalline solids can be further characterized as **ionic solids** if their particles are ions, **molecular solids** if their particles are molecules, **covalent network solids** if they consist of a covalently bonded array of atoms without discrete molecules, or **metallic solids** if their particles are metal atoms.

The regular three-dimensional network of particles in a crystal is made up of small repeating units called **unit cells**. There are 14 kinds of unit cells, 3 of which have cubic symmetry. **Simple cubic packing** uses a **primitive-cubic** unit cell, with an atom at each corner of the cube. **Body-centered cubic packing** uses a **body-centered cubic** unit cell, with an atom at the center and at each corner of the cube. **Cubic closest-packing** uses a **face-centered cubic** unit cell, with an atom at the center of each face and at each corner of the cube. A fourth kind of packing, called **hexagonal closest-packing**, uses a noncubic unit cell.

KEY WORDS

allotrope *378*
amorphous solid *366*
body-centered cubic
   packing *371*
body-centered cubic
   unit cell *372*
Bragg equation *370*
Clausius–Clapeyron
   equation *363*
coordination number *370*
covalent network solid *367*
critical point *381*

crystalline solid *366*
cubic closest-packing *371*
diffraction *368*
dipole *347*
dipole moment (μ) *348*
dipole–dipole force *352*
face-centered cubic
   unit cell *373*
heat of fusion
   (ΔH_{fusion}) *361*
heat of vaporization
   (ΔH_{vap}) *361*

hexagonal closest-
   packing *371*
hydrogen bond *355*
intermolecular force *350*
ion–dipole force *351*
ionic solid *367*
London dispersion force *353*
metallic solid *367*
molecular solid *367*
normal boiling point *364*
normal melting point *381*
phase *358*

phase change *358*
phase diagram *380*
primitive-cubic
   unit cell *372*
simple cubic packing *370*
supercritical fluid *381*
surface tension *357*
triple point *380*
unit cell *372*
van der Waals forces *350*
vapor pressure *362*
viscosity *357*

CONCEPTUAL PROBLEMS

Problems 10.1–10.21 appear within the chapter.

10.22 Ethyl acetate, $CH_3CO_2CH_2CH_3$, is commonly used as a solvent and nail-polish remover. Look at the following electrostatic potential map of ethyl acetate, and explain the observed polarity.

10.23 Identify each of the following kinds of packing:

(a)   **(b)**   **(c)**   **(d)**

10.24 Zinc sulfide, or sphalerite, crystallizes in the following cubic unit cell:

S²⁻

Zn²⁺

(a) What kind of packing do the sulfide ions adopt?

(b) How many S^{2-} ions and how many Zn^{2+} ions are in the unit cell?

10.25 Perovskite, a mineral containing calcium, oxygen, and titanium, crystallizes in the following cubic unit cell:

Calcium

Oxygen

Titanium

(a) What is the formula of perovskite?

(b) What is the oxidation number of the titanium atom in perovskite?

10.26 The phase diagram of a substance is shown below.

(a) Approximately what is the normal boiling point and what is the normal melting point of the substance?

(b) What is the physical state of the substance under the following conditions?

(i) $T = 150$ K, $P = 0.5$ atm

(ii) $T = 325$ K, $P = 0.9$ atm

(iii) $T = 450$ K, $P = 265$ atm

10.27 Boron nitride, BN, is a covalent network solid with a structure similar to that of graphite. Sketch a small portion of the boron nitride structure.

10.28 Imagine a tiled floor made of square and octagonal tiles in the following pattern. Identify the smallest repeating unit, analogous to a unit cell.

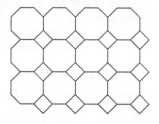

10.29 The following phase diagram of elemental carbon has three different solid phases in the region shown.

(a) Show where the solid, liquid, and vapor regions are on the diagram.

(b) How many triple points does carbon have? Circle each on the diagram.

(c) Graphite is the most stable solid phase under normal conditions. Identify the graphite phase on the diagram.

(d) On heating graphite to 2500 K at a pressure of 100,000 atm, it can be converted into diamond. Identify the diamond phase on the graph.

(e) Which phase is more dense, graphite or diamond? Explain.

10.30 Acetic acid, the principal nonaqueous constituent of vinegar, exists as a *dimer* in the liquid phase, with two acetic acid molecules joined together by two hydrogen bonds. Sketch the structure you would expect this dimer to have.

Acetic acid

10.31 Assume that you have a liquid in a cylinder equipped with a movable piston. There is no air in the cylinder, the volume of space above the liquid is 200 mL, and the equilibrium vapor pressure above the liquid is 28.0 mm Hg. What is the equilibrium pressure above the liquid when the volume of space is decreased from 200 mL to 100 mL at constant temperature?

$V = 200$ mL
$P = 28.0$ mm Hg

Lower piston

$V = 100$ mL
$P = ?$

SECTION PROBLEMS

Dipole Moments and Intermolecular Forces (Sections 10.1 – 10.3)

10.32 Why don't all molecules with polar covalent bonds have dipole moments?

10.33 What is the difference between London dispersion forces and dipole–dipole forces?

10.34 What are the most important kinds of intermolecular forces present in each of the following substances?
(a) Chloroform, $CHCl_3$
(b) Oxygen, O_2
(c) Polyethylene, C_nH_{2n+2}
(d) Methanol, CH_3OH

10.35 Of the substances Xe, CH_3Cl, HF, which has:
(a) The smallest dipole–dipole forces?
(b) The largest hydrogen bond forces?
(c) The largest dispersion forces?

10.36 Methanol (CH_3OH; bp = 65 °C) boils nearly 230 °C higher than methane (CH_4; bp = −164 °C), but 1-decanol ($C_{10}H_{21}OH$; bp = 231 °C) boils only 57 °C higher than decane ($C_{10}H_{22}$; bp = 174 °C). Explain.

Methanol

1-Decanol

10.37 Which substance in each of the following pairs would you expect to have larger dispersion forces?
(a) Ethane, C_2H_6, or octane, C_8H_{18}
(b) HCl or HI
(c) H_2O or H_2Se

10.38 Which of the following substances would you expect to have a nonzero dipole moment? Explain, and show the direction of each.
(a) Cl_2O
(b) XeF_4
(c) Chloroethane, CH_3CH_2Cl
(d) BF_3

10.39 Which of the following substances would you expect to have a nonzero dipole moment? Explain, and show the direction of each.
(a) NF_3
(b) CH_3NH_2
(c) XeF_2
(d) PCl_5

10.40 The dipole moment of BrCl is 0.518 D and the distance between atoms is 213.9 pm. What is the percent ionic character of the BrCl bond?

10.41 The dipole moment of ClF is 0.887 D and the distance between atoms is 162.8 pm. What is the percent ionic character of the ClF bond?

10.42 Why is the dipole moment of SO_2 1.63 D, but that of CO_2 is zero?

10.43 Draw three-dimensional structures of PCl_3 and PCl_5, and then explain why one of the molecules has a dipole moment and one does not.

10.44 The class of ions PtX_4^{2-}, where X is a halogen, has a square planar geometry.
(a) Draw a structure for a $PtBr_2Cl_2^{2-}$ ion that has no dipole moment.
(b) Draw a structure for a $PtBr_2Cl_2^{2-}$ ion that has a dipole moment.

10.45 Of the two compounds SiF_4 and SF_4, which is polar and which is nonpolar?

10.46 Draw a picture showing how hydrogen bonding takes place between two ammonia molecules.

10.47 1,3-Propanediol can form *intra*molecular as well as intermolecular hydrogen bonds. Draw a structure of 1,3-propanediol showing an intramolecular hydrogen bond.

HO — C — C — C — OH

1,3-Propanediol

10.48 A magnetized needle gently placed on the surface of a glass of water acts like a makeshift compass. Is it water's viscosity or its surface tension that keeps the needle on top?

10.49 Water flows quickly through the narrow neck of a bottle, but maple syrup flows sluggishly. Is this different behavior due to a difference in viscosity or in surface tension for the liquids?

Vapor Pressure and Phase Changes (Sections 10.4 and 10.5)

10.50 Why is ΔH_{vap} usually larger than ΔH_{fusion}?

10.51 Why is the heat of sublimation, ΔH_{subl}, equal to the sum of ΔH_{vap} and ΔH_{fusion} at the same temperature?

10.52 Mercury has mp = −38.8 °C and bp = 356.6 °C. What, if any, phase changes take place under the following conditions at 1.0 atm pressure?
(a) The temperature of a sample is raised from −30 °C to 365 °C.
(b) The temperature of a sample is lowered from 291 K to 238 K.
(c) The temperature of a sample is lowered from 638 K to 231 K.

10.53 Iodine has mp = 113.7 °C and bp = 184.4 °C. What, if any, phase changes take place under the following conditions at 1.0 atm pressure?

(a) The temperature of a solid sample is held at 113.7 °C while heat is added.

(b) The temperature of a sample is lowered from 452 K to 389 K.

10.54 Water at room temperature is placed in a flask connected by rubber tubing to a vacuum pump, and the pump is turned on. After several minutes, the volume of the water has decreased and what remains has turned to ice. Explain.

10.55 Ether at room temperature is placed in a flask connected by a rubber tube to a vacuum pump, the pump is turned on, and the ether begins boiling. Explain.

10.56 How much energy in kilojoules is needed to heat 5.00 g of ice from −10.0 °C to 30.0 °C? The heat of fusion of water is 6.01 kJ/mol, and the molar heat capacity is 36.6 J/(K·mol) for ice and 75.3 J/(K·mol) for liquid water.

10.57 How much energy in kilojoules is released when 15.3 g of steam at 115.0 °C is condensed to give liquid water at 75.0 °C? The heat of vaporization of liquid water is 40.67 kJ/mol, and the molar heat capacity is 75.3 J/(K·mol) for the liquid and 33.6 J/(K·mol) for the vapor.

10.58 How much energy in kilojoules is released when 7.55 g of water at 33.5 °C is cooled to −10.0 °C? (See Problem 10.56 for the necessary data.)

10.59 How much energy in kilojoules is released when 25.0 g of ethanol vapor at 93.0 °C is cooled to −10.0 °C? Ethanol has mp = −114.1 °C, bp = 78.3 °C, ΔH_{vap} = 38.56 kJ/mol, and ΔH_{fusion} = 4.93 kJ/mol. The molar heat capacity is 112.3 J/(K·mol) for the liquid and 65.6 J/(K·mol) for the vapor.

10.60 Draw a molar heating curve for ethanol, C_2H_5OH, similar to that shown for water in Figure 10.10 on page 360. Begin with solid ethanol at its melting point, and raise the temperature to 100 °C. The necessary data are given in Problem 10.59.

10.61 Draw a molar heating curve for sodium similar to that shown for water in Figure 10.10. Begin with solid sodium at its melting point, and raise the temperature to 1000 °C. The necessary data are mp = 97.8 °C, bp = 883 °C, ΔH_{vap} = 89.6 kJ/mol, and ΔH_{fusion} = 2.64 kJ/mol. Assume that the molar heat capacity is 20.8 J/(K·mol) for both liquid and vapor phases and does not change with temperature.

10.62 Naphthalene, better known as "mothballs," has bp = 218 °C and ΔH_{vap} = 43.3 kJ/mol. What is the entropy of vaporization, ΔS_{vap} in J/(K·mol) for naphthalene?

10.63 What is the entropy of fusion, ΔS_{fusion} in J/(K·mol) for sodium? The necessary data are given in Problem 10.61.

10.64 Carbon disulfide, CS_2, has P_{vap} = 100 mm Hg at −5.1 °C and a normal boiling point of 46.5 °C. What is ΔH_{vap} for carbon disulfide in kJ/mol?

Carbon disulfide

10.65 The vapor pressure of $SiCl_4$ is 100 mm Hg at 5.4 °C, and the normal boiling point is 57.7 °C. What is ΔH_{vap} for $SiCl_4$ in kJ/mol?

Silicon tetrachloride

10.66 What is the vapor pressure of CS_2 in mm Hg at 20.0 °C? (See Problem 10.64.)

10.67 What is the vapor pressure of $SiCl_4$ in mm Hg at 30.0 °C? (See Problem 10.65.)

10.68 Dichloromethane, CH_2Cl_2, is an organic solvent used for removing caffeine from coffee beans. The following table gives the vapor pressure of dichloromethane at various temperatures. Fill in the rest of the table, and use the data to plot curves of P_{vap} versus T and ln P_{vap} versus $1/T$.

Temp (K)	P_{vap} (mm Hg)	ln P_{vap}	$1/T$
263	80.1	?	?
273	133.6	?	?
283	213.3	?	?
293	329.6	?	?
303	495.4	?	?
313	724.4	?	?

10.69 The following table gives the vapor pressure of mercury at various temperatures. Fill in the rest of the table, and use the data to plot curves of P_{vap} versus T and ln P_{vap} versus $1/T$.

Temp (K)	P_{vap} (mm Hg)	ln P_{vap}	$1/T$
500	39.3	?	?
520	68.5	?	?
540	114.4	?	?
560	191.6	?	?
580	286.4	?	?
600	432.3	?	?

10.70 Use the plot you made in Problem 10.68 to find a value in kJ/mol for ΔH_{vap} for dichloromethane.

10.71 Use the plot you made in Problem 10.69 to find a value in kJ/mol for ΔH_{vap} for mercury. The normal boiling point of mercury is 630 K.

10.72 Choose any two temperatures and corresponding vapor pressures in the table given in Problem 10.68, and use those values to calculate ΔH_{vap} for dichloromethane in kJ/mol. How does the value you calculated compare to the value you read from your plot in Problem 10.70?

10.73 Choose any two temperatures and corresponding vapor pressures in the table given in Problem 10.69, and use those values to calculate ΔH_{vap} for mercury in kJ/mol. How does the value you calculated compare to the value you read from your plot in Problem 10.71?

Kinds and Structures of Solids (Sections 10.6 – 10.9)

10.74 List the four main classes of crystalline solids, and give a specific example of each.

10.75 What kinds of particles are present in each of the four main classes of crystalline solids?

10.76 Which of the substances Na_3PO_4, CBr_4, rubber, Au, and quartz best fits each of the following descriptions?
(a) amorphous solid   (b) ionic solid
(c) molecular solid   (d) covalent network solid
(e) metallic solid

10.77 Which of the substances diamond, Hg, Cl_2, glass, and KCl best fits each of the following descriptions?
(a) amorphous solid   (b) ionic solid
(c) molecular solid   (d) covalent network solid
(e) metallic solid

10.78 Silicon carbide is very hard, has no known melting point, and diffracts X rays. What type of solid is it: amorphous, ionic, molecular, covalent network, or metallic?

10.79 Arsenic tribromide melts at 31.1 °C, diffracts X rays, and does not conduct electricity in either the solid or liquid phase. What type of solid is it: amorphous, ionic, molecular, covalent network, or metallic?

10.80 Diffraction of X rays with $\lambda = 154.2$ pm occurred at an angle $\theta = 22.5°$ from a metal surface. What is the spacing (in pm) between the layers of atoms that diffracted the X rays?

10.81 Diffraction of X rays with $\lambda = 154.2$ pm occurred at an angle $\theta = 76.84°$ from a metal surface. What is the spacing (in pm) between layers of atoms that diffracted the X rays?

10.82 What is a unit cell?

10.83 Which of the four kinds of packing used by metals makes the most efficient use of space, and which makes the least efficient use?

10.84 Copper crystallizes in a face-centered cubic unit cell with an edge length of 362 pm. What is the radius of a copper atom in picometers? What is the density of copper in g/cm^3?

10.85 Lead crystallizes in a face-centered cubic unit cell with an edge length of 495 pm. What is the radius of a lead atom in picometers? What is the density of lead in g/cm^3?

10.86 Aluminum has a density of 2.699 g/cm^3 and crystallizes with a face-centered cubic unit cell. What is the edge length of a unit cell in picometers?

10.87 Tungsten crystallizes in a body-centered cubic unit cell with an edge length of 317 pm. What is the length in picometers of a unit-cell diagonal that passes through the center atom?

10.88 In light of your answer to Problem 10.87, what is the radius in picometers of a tungsten atom?

10.89 Sodium has a density of 0.971 g/cm^3 and crystallizes with a body-centered cubic unit cell. What is the radius of a sodium atom, and what is the edge length of the cell in picometers?

10.90 Titanium metal has a density of 4.506 g/cm^3 and an atomic radius of 144.8 pm. In what cubic unit cell does titanium crystallize?

10.91 Calcium metal has a density of 1.55 g/cm^3 and crystallizes in a cubic unit cell with an edge length of 558.2 pm.
(a) How many Ca atoms are in one unit cell?
(b) In which of the three cubic unit cells does calcium crystallize?

10.92 Sodium hydride, NaH, crystallizes in a face-centered cubic unit cell similar to that of NaCl (Figure 10.24; page 376). How many Na^+ ions touch each H^- ion, and how many H^- ions touch each Na^+ ion?

10.93 Cesium chloride crystallizes in a cubic unit cell with Cl^- ions at the corners and a Cs^+ ion in the center. Count the numbers of + and − charges, and show that the unit cell is electrically neutral.

10.94 If the edge length of an NaH unit cell is 488 pm, what is the length in picometers of an Na—H bond? (See Problem 10.92.)

10.95 The edge length of a CsCl unit cell (Problem 10.93) is 412.3 pm. What is the length in picometers of the Cs—Cl bond? If the ionic radius of a Cl^- ion is 181 pm, what is the ionic radius in picometers of a Cs^+ ion?

Phase Diagrams (Section 10.11)

10.96 Look at the phase diagram of CO_2 in Figure 10.29, and tell what phases are present under the following conditions:
(a) $T = -60$ °C, $P = 0.75$ atm
(b) $T = -35$ °C, $P = 18.6$ atm
(c) $T = -80$ °C, $P = 5.42$ atm

10.97 Look at the phase diagram of H_2O in Figure 10.28, and tell what happens to an H_2O sample when the following changes are made:
(a) The temperature is reduced from 48 °C to −4.4 °C at a constant pressure of 6.5 atm.
(b) The pressure is increased from 85 atm to 226 atm at a constant temperature of 380 °C.

10.98 Bromine has $T_t = -7.3$ °C, $P_t = 44$ mm Hg, $T_c = 315$ °C, and $P_c = 102$ atm. The density of the liquid is 3.1 g/cm^3, and the density of the solid is 3.4 g/cm^3. Sketch a phase diagram for bromine, and label all points of interest.

10.99 Oxygen has $T_t = 54.3$ K, $P_t = 1.14$ mm Hg, $T_c = 154.6$ K, and $P_c = 49.77$ atm. The density of the liquid is 1.14 g/cm^3, and the density of the solid is 1.33 g/cm^3. Sketch a phase diagram for oxygen, and label all points of interest.

10.100 Refer to the bromine phase diagram you sketched in Problem 10.98, and tell what phases are present under the following conditions:
(a) $T = -10$ °C, $P = 0.0075$ atm
(b) $T = 25$ °C, $P = 16$ atm

10.101 Refer to the oxygen phase diagram you sketched in Problem 10.99, and tell what phases are present under the following conditions:
(a) $T = -210$ °C, $P = 1.5$ atm
(b) $T = -100$ °C, $P = 66$ atm

10.102 Does solid oxygen (Problem 10.99) melt when pressure is applied, as water does? Explain.

10.103 Assume that you have samples of the following three gases at 25 °C. Which of the three can be liquefied by applying pressure, and which cannot? Explain.
Ammonia: $T_c = 132.5$ °C and $P_c = 112.5$ atm
Methane: $T_c = -82.1$ °C and $P_c = 45.8$ atm
Sulfur dioxide: $T_c = 157.8$ °C and $P_c = 77.7$ atm

10.104 Benzene has a melting point of 5.53 °C and a boiling point of 80.09 °C at atmospheric pressure. Its density is 0.8787 g/cm^3 when liquid and 0.899 g/cm^3 when solid; it has $T_c = 289.01$ °C, $P_c = 48.34$ atm, $T_t = 5.52$ °C, and $P_t = 0.0473$ atm. Starting from a point at 200 K and 66.5 atm, trace the following path on a phase diagram:
(1) First, increase T to 585 K while keeping P constant.
(2) Next, decrease P to 38.5 atm while keeping T constant.
(3) Then, decrease T to 278.66 K while keeping P constant.
(4) Finally, decrease P to 0.0025 atm while keeping T constant.
What is your starting phase, and what is your final phase?

10.105 Refer to the oxygen phase diagram you drew in Problem 10.99, and trace the following path starting from a point at 0.0011 atm and −225 °C:

(1) First, increase P to 35 atm while keeping T constant.

(2) Next, increase T to −150 °C while keeping P constant.

(3) Then, decrease P to 1.0 atm while keeping T constant.

(4) Finally, decrease T to −215 °C while keeping P constant.

What is your starting phase, and what is your final phase?

10.106 How many phase transitions did you pass through in Problem 10.104, and what are they?

10.107 What phase transitions did you pass through in Problem 10.105?

CHAPTER PROBLEMS

10.108 Fluorine is more electronegative than chlorine (Figure 7.4), yet fluoromethane (CH_3F; $\mu = 1.86$ D) has a smaller dipole moment than chloromethane (CH_3Cl; $\mu = 1.90$ D). Explain.

10.109 What is the atomic radius in picometers of an argon atom if solid argon has a density of 1.623 g/cm^3 and crystallizes at low temperature in a face-centered cubic unit cell?

10.110 Mercury has mp = −38.8 °C, a molar heat capacity of 27.9 J/(K·mol) for the liquid and 28.2 J/(K·mol) for the solid, and ΔH_{fusion} = 2.33 kJ/mol. Assuming that the heat capacities don't change with temperature, how much energy in kilojoules is needed to heat 7.50 g of Hg from a temperature of −50.0 °C to +50.0 °C?

10.111 Silicon carbide, SiC, is a covalent network solid with a structure similar to that of diamond. Sketch a small portion of the SiC structure.

10.112 In Denver, the Mile-High City, water boils at 95 °C. What is atmospheric pressure in atmospheres in Denver? ΔH_{vap} for H_2O is 40.67 kJ/mol.

10.113 There are three compounds with the formula $C_2H_2Br_2$. Two of the three have dipole moments, and one does not. Draw the structures of all three compounds, and tell which has no dipole moment.

10.114 If a protein can be induced to crystallize, its molecular structure can be determined by X-ray crystallography. Protein crystals, though solid, contain a large amount of water molecules along with the protein. The protein chicken egg-white lysozyme, for instance, crystallizes with a unit cell having angles of 90° and with edge lengths of 7.9×10^3 pm, 7.9×10^3 pm, and 3.8×10^3 pm. There are eight molecules in the unit cell. If the lysozyme molecule has a molecular mass of 1.44×10^4 amu and a density of 1.35 g/cm^3, what percent of the unit cell is occupied by the protein?

10.115 The molecular structure of a scorpion toxin, a small protein, was determined by X-ray crystallography. The unit cell has angles of 90°, contains 16 molecules, and has a volume of 1.019×10^2 nm^3. If the molecular mass of the toxin is 3336 amu and the density is about 1.35 g/cm^3, what percent of the unit cell is occupied by protein?

10.116 Magnesium metal has ΔH_{fusion} = 9.037 kJ/mol and ΔS_{fusion} = 9.79 J/(K·mol). What is the melting point in °C of magnesium?

10.117 Titanium tetrachloride, $TiCl_4$, has a melting point of −23.2 °C and has ΔH_{fusion} = 9.37 kJ/mol. What is the entropy of fusion, ΔS_{fusion} in J/(K·mol), for $TiCl_4$?

10.118 Dichlorodifluoromethane, CCl_2F_2, one of the chlorofluorocarbon refrigerants responsible for destroying part of the Earth's ozone layer, has P_{vap} = 40.0 mm Hg at −81.6 °C

and P_{vap} = 400 mm Hg at −43.9 °C. What is the normal boiling point of CCl_2F_2 in °C?

Dichlorodifluoromethane

10.119 The chlorofluorocarbon refrigerant trichlorofluoromethane, CCl_3F, has P_{vap} = 100.0 mm Hg at −23 °C and ΔH_{vap} = 24.77 kJ/mol.

(a) What is the normal boiling point of trichlorofluoromethane in °C?

(b) What is ΔS_{vap} for trichlorofluoromethane?

10.120 Nitrous oxide, N_2O, occasionally used as an anesthetic by dentists under the name "laughing gas," has P_{vap} = 100 mm Hg at −110.3 °C and a normal boiling point of −88.5 °C. What is the heat of vaporization of nitrous oxide in kJ/mol?

10.121 Acetone, a common laboratory solvent, has ΔH_{vap} = 29.1 kJ/mol and a normal boiling point of 56.1 °C. At what temperature in °C does acetone have P_{vap} = 105 mm Hg?

Acetone

10.122 Use the following data to sketch a phase diagram for krypton: T_t = −169 °C, P_t = 133 mm Hg, T_c = −63 °C, P_c = 54 atm, mp = −156.6 °C, bp = −152.3 °C. The density of solid krypton is 2.8 g/cm^3, and the density of the liquid is 2.4 g/cm^3. Can a sample of gaseous krypton at room temperature be liquefied by raising the pressure?

10.123 What is the physical phase of krypton (Problem 10.122) under the following conditions:

(a) P = 5.3 atm, T = −153 °C

(b) P = 65 atm, T = 250 K

10.124 Calculate the percent volume occupied by the spheres in a body-centered cubic unit cell.

10.125 Iron crystallizes in a body-centered cubic unit cell with an edge length of 287 pm. What is the radius of an iron atom in picometers?

10.126 Iron metal has a density of 7.86 g/cm^3 and a molar mass of 55.85 g. Use this information together with the data in Problem 10.125 to calculate a value for Avogadro's number.

10.127 Silver metal crystallizes in a face-centered cubic unit cell with an edge length of 408 pm. The molar mass of silver is 107.9 g/mol, and its density is 10.50 g/cm^3. Use these data to calculate a value for Avogadro's number.

10.128 A drawing of the NaCl unit cell is shown in Figure 10.24.

    (a) What is the edge length in picometers of the NaCl unit cell? The ionic radius of Na^+ is 97 pm, and the ionic radius of Cl^- is 181 pm.

    (b) What is the density of NaCl in g/cm^3?

10.129 Niobium oxide crystallizes in the following cubic unit cell:

    (a) How many niobium atoms and how many oxygen atoms are in each unit cell?

    (b) What is the formula of niobium oxide?

    (c) What is the oxidation state of niobium?

10.130 For each of the following substances, identify the intermolecular force or forces that predominate. Using your knowledge of the relative strengths of the various forces, rank the substances in order of their normal boiling points.

$$Al_2O_3, \; F_2, \; H_2O, \; Br_2, \; ICl, \; NaCl$$

10.131 One form of silver telluride (Ag_2Te) crystallizes with a cubic unit cell and a density of 7.70 g/cm^3. X-ray crystal-lography shows that the edge of the cubic unit cell has a length of 529 pm. How many Ag atoms are in the unit cell?

10.132 Substance **X** has a vapor pressure of 100 mm Hg at its triple point (48 °C). When 1 mol of **X** is heated at 1 atm pressure with a constant rate of heat input, the following heating curve is obtained:

    (a) Sketch the phase diagram for **X**, including labels for different phases, triple point, melting point, and boiling point.

    (b) For each of the following, choose which phase of **X** (solid, liquid, or gas) fits the description:

        (i) Is the most dense at 50 °C

        (ii) Is the least dense at 50 °C

        (iii) Has the greatest specific heat

        (iv) Predominates at 80 °C and 1 atm

        (v) Can have a vapor pressure of 20 mm Hg

MULTICONCEPT PROBLEMS

10.133 Look up thermodynamic data for ethanol (C_2H_5OH) in Appendix B, estimate the normal boiling point of ethanol, and calculate the vapor pressure of ethanol at 25 °C.

10.134 The mineral *magnetite* is an iron oxide ore that has a density of 5.20 g/cm^3. At high temperature, magnetite reacts with carbon monoxide to yield iron metal and carbon dioxide. When 2.660 g of magnetite is allowed to react with sufficient carbon monoxide, the CO_2 product is found to have a volume of 1.136 L at 298 K and 751 mm Hg pressure.

    (a) What mass of iron in grams is formed in the reaction?

    (b) What is the formula of magnetite?

    (c) Magnetite has a somewhat complicated cubic unit cell with an edge length of 839 pm. How many Fe and O atoms are present in each unit cell?

10.135 A group 3A metal has a density of 2.70 g/cm^3 and a cubic unit cell with an edge length of 404 pm. Reaction of a 1.07 cm^3 chunk of the metal with an excess of hydrochloric acid gives a colorless gas that occupies 4.00 L at 23.0 °C and a pressure of 740 mm Hg.

    (a) Identify the metal.

    (b) Is the unit cell primitive, body-centered, or face-centered?

    (c) What is the atomic radius of the metal atom in picometers?

10.136 A cube-shaped crystal of an alkali metal, 1.62 mm on an edge, was vaporized in a 500.0 mL evacuated flask. The resulting vapor pressure was 12.5 mm Hg at 802 °C. The structure of the solid metal is known to be body-centered cubic.

    (a) What is the atomic radius of the metal atom in picometers?

    (b) Use the data in Figure 5.18 on page 177 to identify the alkali metal.

    (c) What are the densities of the solid and the vapor in g/cm^3?

10.137 Assume that 1.588 g of an alkali metal undergoes complete reaction with the amount of gaseous halogen contained in a 0.500 L flask at 298 K and 755 mm Hg pressure. In the reaction, 22.83 kJ is released ($\Delta H = -22.83$ kJ). The product, a binary ionic compound, crystallizes in a unit cell with anions in a face-centered cubic arrangement and with cations centered along each edge between anions. In addition, there is a cation in the center of the cube.

    (a) What is the identity of the alkali metal?

    (b) The edge length of the unit cell is 535 pm. Find the radius of the alkali metal cation from the data in Figure 6.1 on page 189, and then calculate the radius of the halide anion. Identify the anion from the data in Figure 6.2 on page 189.

    (c) Sketch a space-filling, head-on view of the unit cell, labeling the ions. Are the anions in contact with one another?

    (d) What is the density of the compound in g/cm^3?

    (e) What is the standard heat of formation for the compound?

CHAPTER 11

Solutions and Their Properties

Coastal California redwoods are the tallest trees in the world, with heights of up to 379 ft. The rise of sap in these massive redwoods is due to osmotic pressure, one of the unique properties of solutions that we'll discuss in this chapter.

CONTENTS

Thus far, we've been concerned only with pure substances, both elements and compounds. If you look around, though, most of the substances you see in day-to-day life are *mixtures*. Air is a gaseous mixture of (primarily) oxygen and nitrogen, gasoline is a liquid mixture of many different components, and rocks are solid mixtures of different minerals.

A mixture, as we saw in Section 2.10, is any combination of two or more pure substances blended together in some arbitrary proportion without chemically changing the individual substances themselves. Mixtures can be classified as either *heterogeneous* or *homogeneous*, depending on their appearance. A heterogeneous mixture is one in which the mixing of components is visually nonuniform and that therefore has regions of different composition. Sugar with salt and oil with water are examples. A homogeneous mixture is one in which the mixing *is* uniform, at least to the naked eye, and that therefore has a constant composition throughout. Seawater (sodium chloride with water) and brass (copper with zinc) are examples. We'll explore the properties of some homogeneous mixtures in this chapter, with particular emphasis on the mixtures we call *solutions*.

11.1 SOLUTIONS

Homogeneous mixtures can be classified according to the size of their constituent particles as either *solutions* or *colloids*. **Solutions**, the most common class of homogeneous mixtures, contain particles with diameters in the range 0.1–2 nm, the size of a typical ion or small molecule. They are transparent, although they may be colored, and they don't separate on standing. **Colloids**, such as milk and fog, contain larger particles, with diameters in the range 2–500 nm. Although they are often murky or opaque to light, colloids don't separate on standing. Mixtures called *suspensions* also exist, having even larger particles than colloids. These are not truly homogeneous, however, because their particles separate out on standing and are visible with a low-power microscope. Blood, paint, and aerosol sprays are examples.

We usually think of a solution as a solid dissolved in a liquid or as a mixture of liquids, but there are many other kinds of solutions as well. In fact, any one state of matter can form a solution with any other state, and seven different kinds of solutions are possible (Table 11.1). Even solutions of one solid with another and solutions of a gas in a solid are well-known. Metal alloys, such as stainless steel (4–30% chromium in iron) and brass (10–40% zinc in copper), are solid/solid solutions, and hydrogen in palladium is a gas/solid solution. Metallic palladium, in fact, is able to absorb up to 935 times its own volume of H_2 gas.

TABLE 11.1   Some Different Kinds of Solutions

Kind of Solution	Example
Gas in gas	Air (O_2, N_2, Ar, and other gases)
Gas in liquid	Carbonated water (CO_2 in water)
Gas in solid	H_2 in palladium metal
Liquid in liquid	Gasoline (mixture of hydrocarbons)
Liquid in solid	Dental amalgam (mercury in silver)
Solid in liquid	Seawater (NaCl and other salts in water)
Solid in solid	Metal alloys, such as sterling silver (92.5% Ag, 7.5% Cu)

▲ The pewter in this 200 year old jug is a solid/solid solution of approximately 96% tin and 4% copper.

For solutions in which a gas or solid is dissolved in a liquid, the dissolved substance is called the **solute** and the liquid is called the **solvent**. When one liquid is dissolved in another, the minor component is usually considered the solute and the major component is the solvent. Thus, ethyl alcohol is the solute and water the solvent in a mixture of 10% ethyl alcohol and 90% water, but water is the solute and ethyl alcohol the solvent in a mixture of 90% ethyl alcohol and 10% water.

11.2 ENERGY CHANGES AND THE SOLUTION PROCESS

With the exception of gas/gas mixtures, such as air, the different kinds of solutions listed in Table 11.1 involve *condensed phases*, either liquid or solid. Thus, all the intermolecular forces described in Chapter 10 to explain the properties of pure liquids and solids are also important for explaining the properties of solutions. The situation is more complex for solutions than for pure substances, though, because there are three types of interactions among particles that have to be taken into account: solvent–solvent interactions, solvent–solute interactions, and solute–solute interactions.

A good rule of thumb, often summarized in the phrase "like dissolves like," is that solutions will form when the three types of intermolecular interactions are similar in kind and in magnitude. Thus, ionic solids like NaCl dissolve in polar solvents like water because the strong ion–dipole attractions between Na^+ and Cl^- ions and polar H_2O molecules are similar in magnitude to the strong hydrogen bonding attractions between water molecules and to the strong ion–ion attractions between Na^+ and Cl^- ions. In the same way, nonpolar organic substances like cholesterol, $C_{27}H_{46}O$, dissolve in nonpolar organic solvents like benzene, C_6H_6, because of the similar London dispersion forces present among both kinds of molecules. Oil, however, does not dissolve appreciably in water because the two liquids have different kinds of intermolecular forces.

▲ Why don't oil and water mix?

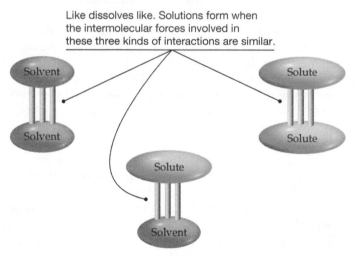

Like dissolves like. Solutions form when the intermolecular forces involved in these three kinds of interactions are similar.

The dissolution of a solid in a liquid can be visualized as shown in **Figure 11.1** for NaCl. When solid NaCl is placed in water, those ions that are less tightly held because of their position at a corner or an edge of the crystal are exposed to water molecules, which collide with them until an ion happens to break free. More water molecules then cluster around the ion, stabilizing it by means of ion–dipole attractions. A new edge or corner is thereby exposed on the crystal, and the process continues until the entire crystal has dissolved. The ions in solution are said to be *solvated*—more specifically, *hydrated*, when water is the solvent—meaning that they are surrounded and stabilized by an ordered shell of solvent molecules.

Like all chemical and physical processes, the dissolution of a solute in a solvent has associated with it a free-energy change, $\Delta G = \Delta H - T\Delta S$, whose value describes its spontaneity (Section 8.13). If ΔG is negative, the process is spontaneous and the substance dissolves; if ΔG is positive, the process is nonspontaneous and the substance does not dissolve. The enthalpy term ΔH measures the heat flow into or out of the system during dissolution, and the temperature-dependent entropy term $T\Delta S$ measures the change in the amount of molecular randomness in the system. The enthalpy change is called the *heat of solution*, or **enthalpy of solution (ΔH_{soln})**, and the entropy change is called the **entropy of solution (ΔS_{soln})**.

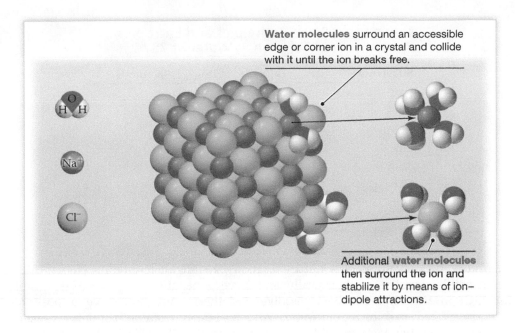

Figure 11.1
Dissolution of NaCl crystals in water.

Water molecules surround an accessible edge or corner ion in a crystal and collide with it until the ion breaks free.

Additional water molecules then surround the ion and stabilize it by means of ion–dipole attractions.

What values might we expect for ΔH_{soln} and ΔS_{soln}? Let's take the entropy change first. Entropies of solution are usually positive because molecular randomness usually increases during dissolution: $+43.4\ \text{J/(K} \cdot \text{mol)}$ for NaCl in water, for example. When a solid dissolves in a liquid, randomness increases on going from a well-ordered crystal to a less-ordered state in which solvated ions or molecules are able to move freely in solution. When one liquid dissolves in another, randomness increases as the different molecules intermingle (**Figure 11.2**). Table 11.2 lists values of ΔS_{soln} for some common ionic substances.

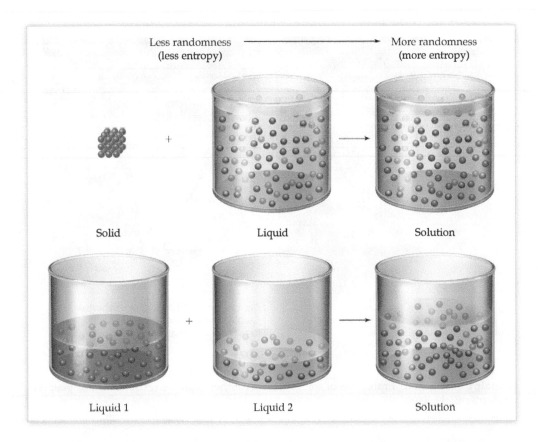

Less randomness (less entropy)   More randomness (more entropy)

Solid   +   Liquid   →   Solution

Liquid 1   +   Liquid 2   →   Solution

Figure 11.2
Entropy of solution. Entropies of solution are usually positive because molecular randomness usually increases when a solid dissolves in a liquid or one liquid dissolves in another.

TABLE 11.2   Some Enthalpies and Entropies of Solution in Water at 25 °C

Substance	ΔH_{soln} (kJ/mol)	ΔS_{soln} [J/(K · mol)]
LiCl	−37.0	10.5
NaCl	3.9	43.4
KCl	17.2	75.0
LiBr	−48.8	21.5
NaBr	−0.6	54.6
KBr	19.9	89.0
KOH	−57.6	12.9

Values for enthalpies of solution, ΔH_{soln}, are difficult to predict (Table 11.2). Some solids dissolve exothermically and have a negative ΔH_{soln} (−37.0 kJ/mol for LiCl in water), but others dissolve endothermically and have a positive ΔH_{soln} (+17.2 kJ/mol for KCl in water). Athletes benefit from both situations when they use instant hot packs or cold packs to treat injuries. Both kinds of instant packs consist of a pouch of water and a dry chemical, either $CaCl_2$ or $MgSO_4$ for hot packs, and NH_4NO_3 for cold packs. When the pack is squeezed, the pouch breaks and the solid dissolves, either raising or lowering the temperature (Figure 11.3).

Hot packs: $CaCl_2(s)$ $\Delta H_{soln} = -81.3 \text{ kJ/mol}$

                     $MgSO_4(s)$ $\Delta H_{soln} = -91.2 \text{ kJ/mol}$

Cold pack: $NH_4NO_3(s)$ $\Delta H_{soln} = +25.7 \text{ kJ/mol}$

Dissolution of $CaCl_2$ in water is **exothermic**, causing the temperature of the water to rise from its initial 25 °C value.

Dissolution of NH_4NO_3 is **endothermic**, causing the temperature of the water to fall from its initial 25 °C value.

Figure 11.3
Enthalpy of solution. Enthalpies of solution can be either negative (exothermic) or positive (endothermic).

The exact value of ΔH_{soln} for a given substance results from an interplay of the three kinds of interactions mentioned earlier:

- **Solvent–solvent interactions:** Energy is absorbed (positive ΔH) to overcome intermolecular forces between solvent molecules because the molecules must be separated and pushed apart to make room for solute particles.

- **Solute–solute interactions:** Energy is absorbed (positive ΔH) to overcome intermolecular forces holding solute particles together in a crystal. For an ionic solid, this is the **lattice energy**. As a result, substances with higher lattice energies tend to be less soluble than substances with lower lattice energies. Compounds with singly charged ions are thus more soluble than compounds with doubly or triply charged ions, as we saw when discussing solubility guidelines in Section 4.4.

- **Solvent–solute interactions:** Energy is released (negative ΔH) when solvent molecules cluster around solute particles and solvate them. For ionic substances in water, the amount of hydration energy released is generally greater for smaller cations than for larger ones because water molecules can approach the positive nuclei of smaller ions more closely and thus bind more tightly. In addition, hydration energy generally increases as the charge on the ion increases.

The first two kinds of interactions are endothermic, requiring an input of energy to spread apart solvent molecules and to break apart crystals. Only the third interaction is exothermic, as attractive intermolecular forces develop between solvent and solute particles. The sum of the three interactions determines whether ΔH_{soln} is endothermic or exothermic. For some substances, the one exothermic interaction is sufficiently large to outweigh the two endothermic interactions, but for other substances, the opposite is true (**Figure 11.4**).

Remember...

Lattice energy *(U)* is the sum of the electrostatic interaction energies between ions in a crystal. It is the amount of energy that must be supplied to break up an ionic solid into its individual gaseous ions.   (Section 6.8)

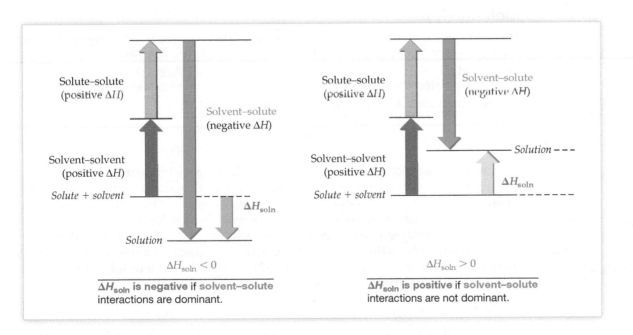

Figure 11.4
Components of ΔH_{soln}. The value of ΔH_{soln} is the sum of three terms: solvent–solvent, solute–solute, and solvent–solute.

Pentane

1-Butanol

WORKED EXAMPLE 11.1

CORRELATING SOLUBILITY AND CHEMICAL STRUCTURE

Pentane (C_5H_{12}) and 1-butanol (C_4H_9OH) are organic liquids with similar molecular masses but substantially different solubility behavior. Which of the two would you expect to be more soluble in water? Explain.

STRATEGY

Look at the two structures and decide on the kinds of intermolecular forces present between molecules in each case. The substance with intermolecular forces more like those in water will probably be more soluble in water.

SOLUTION

Pentane is a nonpolar molecule and is unlikely to have strong intermolecular interactions with polar water molecules. 1-Butanol, however, has an −OH part just as water does and can form hydrogen bonds with water. As a result, 1-butanol is more soluble in water.

▶ **PROBLEM 11.1** Arrange the following compounds in order of their expected increasing solubility in water: Br_2, KBr, toluene (C_7H_8, a constituent of gasoline).

▶ **PROBLEM 11.2** Which would you expect to have the larger (more negative) hydration energy?
(a) Na^+ or Cs^+ **(b)** K^+ or Ba^{2+}

11.3 UNITS OF CONCENTRATION

In daily life, it's often sufficient to describe a solution as either *dilute* or *concentrated*. In scientific work, though, it's usually necessary to know the exact concentration of a solution—that is, to know the exact amount of solute dissolved in a given amount of solvent. There are many ways of expressing concentration, each of which has its own advantages and disadvantages. We'll look briefly at four of the most common methods: *molarity, mole fraction, mass percent,* and *molality*.

Molarity (M)

The most common way of expressing concentration in a chemistry laboratory is to use **molarity (M)**. As discussed in Section 3.6, a solution's molarity is given by the number of moles of solute per liter of solution (mol/L, abbreviated M). If, for example, you dissolve 0.500 mol (20.0 g) of NaOH in enough water to give 1.000 L of solution, then the solution has a concentration of 0.500 M.

$$\text{Molarity (M)} = \frac{\text{Moles of solute}}{\text{Liters of solution}}$$

> **Remember...**
> A solution of a given **molarity** is prepared by dissolving a solute in a small amount of solvent and then diluting with solvent to the desired volume. The solution is not made by dissolving the solute in the desired volume of solvent. (Section 3.6)

The advantages of using molarity are twofold: (1) Stoichiometry calculations are simplified because numbers of moles are used rather than mass, and (2) amounts of solution (and therefore of solute) are conveniently measured by volume rather than by mass. As a result, **titrations** are particularly easy (Section 3.9).

The disadvantages of using molarity are also twofold: (1) The exact solute concentration depends on the temperature because the volume of a solution expands or contracts as the temperature changes, and (2) the exact amount of solvent in a given volume can't be determined unless the density of the solution is known.

> **Remember...**
> **Titration** is a procedure for determining the concentration of a solution by allowing a carefully measured amount of the solution to react with a standard solution of another substance whose concentration is known. (Section 3.9)

Mole Fraction (X)

As discussed in Section 9.5, the mole fraction (X) of any component in a solution is given by the number of moles of the component divided by the total number of moles making up the solution (including solvent):

$$\text{Mole fraction (X)} = \frac{\text{Moles of component}}{\text{Total moles making up the solution}}$$

For example, a solution prepared by dissolving 1.00 mol (32.0 g) of methyl alcohol (CH_3OH) in 5.00 mol (90.0 g) of water has a methyl alcohol concentration $X = 1.00 \text{ mol}/(1.00 \text{ mol} + 5.00 \text{ mol}) = 0.167$. Note that mole fractions are dimensionless because the units cancel.

Mole fractions are independent of temperature and are particularly useful for calculations involving gas mixtures. Except in special situations, mole fractions are not often used for liquid solutions because other units are generally more convenient.

Mass Percent (Mass %)

As the name suggests, the **mass percent** of any component in a solution is the mass of that component divided by the total mass of the solution times 100%:

$$\text{Mass percent} = \frac{\text{Mass of component}}{\text{Total mass of solution}} \times 100\%$$

For example, a solution prepared by dissolving 10.0 g of glucose in 100.0 g of water has a glucose concentration of 9.09 mass %:

$$\text{Mass \% glucose} = \frac{10.0 \text{ g}}{10.0 \text{ g} + 100.0 \text{ g}} \times 100\% = 9.09 \text{ mass \%}$$

Closely related to mass percent, and particularly useful for very dilute solutions, are the concentration units **parts per million (ppm)** and **parts per billion (ppb)**:

$$\text{Parts per million (ppm)} = \frac{\text{Mass of component}}{\text{Total mass of solution}} \times 10^6$$

$$\text{Parts per billion (ppb)} = \frac{\text{Mass of component}}{\text{Total mass of solution}} \times 10^9$$

A concentration of 1 ppm for a substance means that each kilogram of solution contains 1 mg of solute. For dilute aqueous solutions near room temperature, where 1 kg has a volume of 1 L, 1 ppm also means that each liter of solution contains 1 mg of solute. In the same way, a concentration of 1 ppb means that each liter of an aqueous solution contains 0.001 mg of solute.

Values in ppm and ppb are frequently used for expressing the concentrations of trace amounts of impurities in air or water. Thus, you might express the maximum allowable concentration of lead in drinking water as 15 ppb, or about 1 g per 67,000 L.

The advantage of using mass percent (or ppm) for expressing concentration is that the values are independent of temperature because masses don't change when substances are heated or cooled. The disadvantage of using mass percent is that it is generally less convenient when working with liquid solutions to measure amounts by mass rather than by volume. Furthermore, the density of a solution must be known before a concentration in mass percent can be converted into molarity. Worked Example 11.3 shows how to make the conversion.

▲ Dissolving a quarter teaspoon of table sugar in this modest backyard swimming pool would give a concentration of about 1 ppb.

WORKED EXAMPLE 11.2

USING A MASS PERCENT CONCENTRATION

Assume that you have a 5.75 mass % solution of LiCl in water. What mass of solution in grams contains 1.60 g of LiCl?

STRATEGY

Describing a concentration as 5.75 mass % means that 100.0 g of aqueous solution contains 5.75 g of LiCl (and 94.25 g of H_2O), a relationship that can be used as a conversion factor.

SOLUTION

$$\text{Mass of soln} = 1.60 \text{ g LiCl} \times \frac{100 \text{ g soln}}{5.75 \text{ g LiCl}} = 27.8 \text{ g soln}$$

WORKED EXAMPLE 11.3

USING DENSITY TO CONVERT MASS PERCENT CONCENTRATION TO MOLARITY

The density of a 25.0 mass % solution of sulfuric acid (H_2SO_4) in water is 1.1783 g/mL at 25.0 °C. What is the molarity of the solution?

STRATEGY

Describing a solution as 25.0 mass % sulfuric acid in water means that 100.0 g of solution contains 25.0 g of H_2SO_4 and 75.0 g of water. Since we want to calculate the concentration in molarity, we first need to find the number of moles of sulfuric acid dissolved in a specific mass of solution. We next use density as a conversion factor to find the volume of that solution and then calculate molarity by dividing the number of moles by the volume.

SOLUTION

First, convert the 25.0 g of H_2SO_4 into moles:

$$\frac{\text{Moles } H_2SO_4}{100.0 \text{ g solution}} = \frac{25.0 \text{ g } H_2SO_4}{100.0 \text{ g solution}} \times \frac{1 \text{ mol } H_2SO_4}{98.1 \text{ g } H_2SO_4} = \frac{0.255 \text{ mol } H_2SO_4}{100.0 \text{ g solution}}$$

Next, find the volume of 100.0 g of solution, using density as the conversion factor:

$$\text{Volume} = 100.0 \text{ g soln} \times \frac{1 \text{ mL}}{1.1783 \text{ g soln}} = 84.87 \text{ mL} = 0.084\ 87 \text{ L}$$

Then, calculate the molarity of the solution:

$$\text{Molarity} = \frac{\text{moles } H_2SO_4}{\text{liters of solution}} = \frac{0.255 \text{ mol } H_2SO_4}{0.084\ 87 \text{ L}} = 3.00 \text{ M}$$

The molarity of the 25.0 mass % sulfuric acid solution is 3.00 M.

▸ **PROBLEM 11.3**   What is the mass percent concentration of a saline solution prepared by dissolving 1.00 mol of NaCl in 1.00 L of water?

▸ **PROBLEM 11.4**   The legal limit for human exposure to carbon monoxide in the workplace is 35 ppm. Assuming that the density of air is 1.3 g/L, how many grams of carbon monoxide are in 1.0 L of air at the maximum allowable concentration?

▸ **PROBLEM 11.5**   Assuming that seawater is an aqueous solution of NaCl, what is its molarity? The density of seawater is 1.025 g/mL at 20 °C, and the NaCl concentration is 3.50 mass %.

Molality (*m*)

The **molality (*m*)** of a solution is defined as the number of moles of solute per kilogram of solvent (mol/kg):

$$\text{Molality } (m) = \frac{\text{Moles of solute}}{\text{Mass of solvent (kg)}}$$

To prepare a 1.000 *m* solution of KBr in water, for example, you might dissolve 1.000 mol of KBr (119.0 g) in 1.000 kg (1000 mL) of water. You can't say for sure what the final volume of the solution will be, although it will probably be a bit larger than 1000 mL. Although the names sound similar, note the differences between molarity and molality. Molarity is the number of moles of solute per *volume* (liter) of *solution*, whereas molality is the number of moles of solute per *mass* (kilogram) of *solvent*.

The main advantage of using molality is that it is temperature-independent because masses don't change when substances are heated or cooled. Thus, it is well suited for calculating certain properties of solutions that we'll discuss later in this chapter. The disadvantages of using molality are that amounts of solution must be measured by mass rather than by volume and that the density of the solution must be known to convert molality into molarity (see Worked Example 11.5).

A summary of the four methods of expressing concentration, together with a comparison of their relative advantages and disadvantages, is given in Table 11.3.

TABLE 11.3 A Comparison of Various Concentration Units

Name	Units	Advantages	Disadvantages
Molarity (M)	$\dfrac{\text{mol solute}}{\text{L solution}}$	Useful in stoichiometry; measure by volume	Temperature-dependent; must know density to find solvent mass
Mole fraction (X)	none	Temperature-independent; useful in special applications	Measure by mass; must know density to convert to molarity
Mass %	%	Temperature-independent; useful for small amounts	Measure by mass; must know density to convert to molarity
Molality (m)	$\dfrac{\text{mol solute}}{\text{kg solvent}}$	Temperature-independent; useful in special applications	Measure by mass; must know density to convert to molarity

WORKED EXAMPLE 11.4

CALCULATING THE MOLALITY OF A SOLUTION

What is the molality of a solution made by dissolving 1.45 g of table sugar (sucrose, $C_{12}H_{22}O_{11}$) in 30.0 mL of water? The molar mass of sucrose is 342.3 g/mol.

STRATEGY

Molality is the number of moles of solute per kilogram of solvent. Thus, we need to find how many moles are in 1.45 g of sucrose and how many kilograms are in 30.0 mL of water.

SOLUTION

The number of moles of sucrose is

$$1.45 \text{ g sucrose} \times \frac{1 \text{ mol sucrose}}{342.3 \text{ g sucrose}} = 4.24 \times 10^{-3} \text{ mol sucrose}$$

Since the density of water is 1.00 g/mL, 30.0 mL of water has a mass of 30.0 g, or 0.0300 kg. Thus, the molality of the solution is

$$\text{Molality} = \frac{4.24 \times 10^{-3} \text{ mol}}{0.0300 \text{ kg}} = 0.141 \, m$$

WORKED EXAMPLE 11.5

USING DENSITY TO CONVERT FROM MOLALITY TO MOLARITY

Ethylene glycol, $C_2H_4(OH)_2$, is a colorless liquid used as automobile antifreeze. If the density at 20 °C of a 4.028 m solution of ethylene glycol in water is 1.0241 g/mL, what is the molarity of the solution? The molar mass of ethylene glycol is 62.07 g/mol.

STRATEGY

A 4.028 m solution of ethylene glycol in water contains 4.028 mol of ethylene glycol per kilogram of water. To find the solution's molarity, we need to find the number of moles of solute per volume (liter) of solution. The volume, in turn, can be found from the mass of the solution by using density as a conversion factor.

Ethylene glycol

SOLUTION

The mass of the solution is the sum of the masses of solute and solvent. Assuming that 1.000 kg of solvent is used to dissolve 4.028 mol of ethylene glycol, the mass of the ethylene glycol is

$$\text{Mass of ethylene glycol} = 4.028 \text{ mol} \times 62.07 \frac{g}{\text{mol}} = 250.0 \text{ g}$$

Dissolving this 250.0 g of ethylene glycol in 1.000 kg (or 1000 g) of water gives the total mass of the solution:

$$\text{Mass of solution} = 250.0 \text{ g} + 1000 \text{ g} = 1250 \text{ g}$$

continued on next page

The volume of the solution is obtained from its mass by using density as a conversion factor:

$$\text{Volume of solution} = 1250 \text{ g} \times \frac{1 \text{ mL}}{1.0241 \text{ g}} = 1221 \text{ mL} = 1.221 \text{ L}$$

The molarity of the solution is the number of moles of solute divided by the volume of solution:

$$\text{Molarity of solution} = \frac{4.028 \text{ mol}}{1.221 \text{ L}} = 3.299 \text{ M}$$

WORKED EXAMPLE 11.6

USING DENSITY TO CONVERT MOLARITY TO OTHER MEASURES OF CONCENTRATION

A 0.750 M solution of H_2SO_4 in water has a density of 1.046 g/mL at 20 °C. What is the concentration of this solution in **(a)** mole fraction, **(b)** mass percent, and **(c)** molality? The molar mass of H_2SO_4 is 98.1 g/mol.

STRATEGY AND SOLUTION

(a) Let's pick an arbitrary amount of the solution that will make the calculations easy, say 1.00 L. Since the concentration of the solution is 0.750 mol/L and the density is 1.046 g/mL (or 1.046 kg/L), 1.00 L of the solution contains 0.750 mol (73.6 g) of H_2SO_4 and has a mass of 1.046 kg:

$$\text{Moles of } H_2SO_4 \text{ in 1.00 L soln} = 0.750 \frac{\text{mol}}{\text{L}} \times 1.00 \text{ L} = 0.750 \text{ mol}$$

$$\text{Mass of } H_2SO_4 \text{ in 1.00 L soln} = 0.750 \text{ mol} \times 98.1 \frac{\text{g}}{\text{mol}} = 73.6 \text{ g}$$

$$\text{Mass of 1.00 L soln} = 1.00 \text{ L} \times 1.046 \frac{\text{kg}}{\text{L}} = 1.046 \text{ kg}$$

Subtracting the mass of H_2SO_4 from the total mass of the solution gives 0.972 kg, or 54.0 mol, of water in 1.00 L of solution:

$$\text{Mass of } H_2O \text{ in 1.00 L soln} = (1.046 \text{ kg}) - (0.0736 \text{ kg}) = 0.972 \text{ kg } H_2O$$

$$\text{Moles of } H_2O \text{ in 1.00 L of soln} = 972 \text{ g} \times \frac{1 \text{ mol}}{18.0 \text{ g}} = 54.0 \text{ mol } H_2O$$

Thus, the mole fraction of H_2SO_4 is

$$X_{H_2SO_4} = \frac{0.750 \text{ mol } H_2SO_4}{0.750 \text{ mol } H_2SO_4 + 54.0 \text{ mol } H_2O} = 0.0137$$

(b) The mass percent concentration can be determined from the calculations in part **(a)**:

$$\text{Mass \% of } H_2SO_4 = \frac{0.0736 \text{ kg } H_2SO_4}{1.046 \text{ kg total}} \times 100\% = 7.04\%$$

(c) The molality of the solution can also be determined from the calculations in part **(a)**. Since 0.972 kg of water has 0.750 mol of H_2SO_4 dissolved in it, 1.00 kg of water would have 0.772 mol of H_2SO_4 dissolved in it:

$$1.00 \text{ kg } H_2O \times \frac{0.750 \text{ mol } H_2SO_4}{0.972 \text{ kg } H_2O} = 0.772 \text{ mol } H_2SO_4$$

Thus, the molality of the sulfuric acid solution is 0.772 *m*.

▶ **PROBLEM 11.6** What is the molality of a solution prepared by dissolving 0.385 g of cholesterol, $C_{27}H_{46}O$, in 40.0 g of chloroform, $CHCl_3$? What is the mole fraction of cholesterol in the solution?

▶ **PROBLEM 11.7** What mass in grams of a 0.500 *m* solution of sodium acetate, CH_3CO_2Na, in water would you use to obtain 0.150 mol of sodium acetate?

▶ **PROBLEM 11.8** The density at 20 °C of a 0.258 m solution of glucose in water is 1.0173 g/mL, and the molar mass of glucose is 180.2 g/mol. What is the molarity of the solution?

▶ **PROBLEM 11.9** The density at 20 °C of a 0.500 M solution of acetic acid in water is 1.0042 g/mL. What is the molality of the solution? The molar mass of acetic acid, CH_3CO_2H, is 60.05 g/mol.

▶ **PROBLEM 11.10** Assuming that seawater is a 3.50 mass % aqueous solution of NaCl, what is the molality of seawater?

11.4 SOME FACTORS AFFECTING SOLUBILITY

If you take solid NaCl and add it to water, dissolution occurs rapidly at first but then slows down as more and more NaCl is added. Eventually the dissolution stops because a dynamic equilibrium is reached where the number of Na^+ and Cl^- ions leaving a crystal to go into solution is equal to the number of ions returning from the solution to the crystal. At this point, the maximum possible amount of NaCl has dissolved and the solution is said to be **saturated** in that solute.

$$\text{Solute} + \text{Solvent} \underset{\text{crystallize}}{\overset{\text{dissolve}}{\rightleftharpoons}} \text{Solution}$$

Note that this definition requires a saturated solution to be at *equilibrium* with undissolved solid at a given temperature. Some substances, however, can form what are called **supersaturated** solutions, which contain a greater-than-equilibrium amount of solute. For example, when a saturated solution of sodium acetate is prepared at high temperature and then cooled slowly, a supersaturated solution results, as shown in Figure 11.5. Such a solution is unstable, however, and precipitation occurs when a tiny seed crystal of sodium acetate is added to initiate crystallization.

| A supersaturated solution of sodium acetate in water. | When a tiny seed crystal is added, larger crystals begin to grow and precipitate from the solution until equilibrium is reached. |

Figure 11.5
Precipitation from a supersaturated solution.

Effect of Temperature on Solubility

The solubility of a substance—that is, the amount of the substance per unit volume of solvent needed to form a saturated solution at a given temperature—is a physical property characteristic of that substance. Different substances can have greatly different solubilities, as shown in **Figure 11.6**. Sodium chloride, for instance, has a solubility of 35.9 g/100 mL of water at 20 °C, and sodium nitrate has a solubility of 87.3 g/100 mL of water at 20 °C. Sometimes, particularly when two liquids are involved, the solvent and solute are **miscible**, meaning that they are mutually soluble in all proportions. A solution of ethyl alcohol and water is an example.

Figure 11.6
Solubilities of some common solids in water as a function of temperature.

Most substances become more soluble as temperature rises, although the exact relationship is often complex and nonlinear.

Solubilities are temperature-dependent, so the temperature at which a specific measurement is made must be reported. As Figure 11.6 shows, there is no obvious correlation between structure and solubility or between solubility and temperature. The solubilities of most molecular and ionic solids increase with increasing temperature, although the solubilities of some (NaCl) are almost unchanged and the solubilities of others [$Ce_2(SO_4)_3$] decrease.

The effect of temperature on the solubility of gases is more predictable than its effect on the solubility of solids: Gases become less soluble in water as the temperature increases (**Figure 11.7**). One consequence of this decreased solubility is that carbonated drinks bubble continuously as they warm up to room temperature after being refrigerated. Soon, they lose so much dissolved CO_2 that they go flat. A much more important consequence is the damage to aquatic life that can result from the decrease in concentration of dissolved oxygen in lakes and rivers when hot water is discharged from industrial plants, an effect known as thermal pollution.

Effect of Pressure on Solubility

Pressure has practically no effect on the solubility of liquids and solids but has a profound effect on the solubility of gases. According to **Henry's law**, the solubility of a gas in a liquid at a given temperature is directly proportional to the partial pressure of the gas over the solution:

Henry's law   Solubility $= k \cdot P$

The constant k in this expression is characteristic of a specific gas, and P is the partial pressure of the gas over the solution. Doubling the partial pressure doubles the solubility, tripling the partial pressure triples the solubility, and so forth. Henry's-law constants are usually given in units of mol/(L·atm), and measurements are

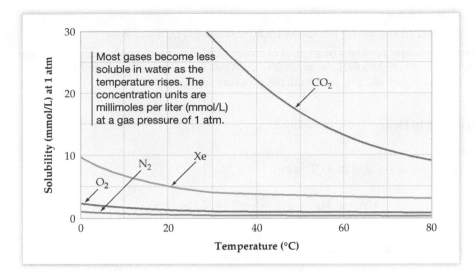

Figure 11.7
Solubilities of some gases in water as a function of temperature.

The graph shows solubility (mmol/L) at 1 atm versus temperature (°C). A text box reads: "Most gases become less soluble in water as the temperature rises. The concentration units are millimoles per liter (mmol/L) at a gas pressure of 1 atm." Curves are labeled CO_2, N_2, Xe, and O_2.

reported at 25 °C. Note that when the gas partial pressure P is 1 atm, the Henry's-law constant k is numerically equal to the solubility of the gas in moles per liter.

Perhaps the most common example of Henry's-law behavior occurs when you open a can of soda or other carbonated drink. Bubbles of gas immediately come fizzing out of solution because the pressure of CO_2 in the can drops and CO_2 suddenly becomes less soluble. A more serious example of Henry's-law behavior occurs when a deep-sea diver surfaces too quickly and develops a painful and life-threatening condition called decompression sickness (DCS) or the *bends*. The bends occur because large amounts of nitrogen dissolve in the blood at high underwater pressures. When the diver ascends and pressure decreases too rapidly, bubbles of nitrogen form in the blood, blocking capillaries and inhibiting blood flow. The condition can be prevented by using an oxygen/helium mixture for breathing rather than air (oxygen/nitrogen), because helium has a much lower solubility in blood than nitrogen.

On a molecular level, the increase in gas solubility with increasing pressure occurs because of a change in the position of the equilibrium between dissolved and undissolved gas. At a given pressure, an equilibrium is established in which equal numbers of gas particles enter and leave the solution. When the pressure is increased, however, more particles are forced into solution than leave it, so gas solubility increases until a new equilibrium is established (Figure 11.8).

▲ Divers who ascend too quickly can develop the bends, a condition caused by the formation of nitrogen bubbles in the blood. Treatment involves placing the diver into this decompression chamber and slowly changing the pressure.

Equilibrium	Pressure increase	Equilibrium restored
At a given pressure, an **equilibrium** exists in which equal numbers of gas particles enter and leave the solution.	When **pressure is increased** by pushing on the piston, more gas particles are temporarily forced into solution than are able to leave.	Solubility therefore increases until a **new equilibrium** is reached.

Figure 11.8
A molecular view of Henry's law.

WORKED EXAMPLE 11.7

USING HENRY'S LAW TO CALCULATE GAS SOLUBILITY

The Henry's-law constant of methyl bromide (CH_3Br), a gas used as a soil fumigating agent, is $k = 0.159$ mol/(L·atm) at 25 °C. What is the solubility in mol/L of methyl bromide in water at 25 °C and a partial pressure of 125 mm Hg?

STRATEGY

According to Henry's law, solubility $= k \cdot P$.

SOLUTION

$$k = 0.159 \text{ mol/(L·atm)}$$

$$P = 125 \text{ mm Hg} \times \frac{1 \text{ atm}}{760 \text{ mm Hg}} = 0.164 \text{ atm}$$

$$\text{Solubility} = k \cdot P = 0.159 \frac{\text{mol}}{\text{L·atm}} \times 0.164 \text{ atm} = 0.0261 \text{ M}$$

The solubility of methyl bromide in water at a partial pressure of 125 mm Hg is 0.0261 M.

▶ **PROBLEM 11.11** The solubility of CO_2 in water is 3.2×10^{-2} M at 25 °C and 1 atm pressure. What is the Henry's-law constant for CO_2 in mol/(L·atm)?

▶ **PROBLEM 11.12** The partial pressure of CO_2 in air is approximately 4.0×10^{-4} atm. Use the Henry's-law constant you calculated in Problem 11.11 to find the concentration of CO_2 in:

(a) A can of soda under a CO_2 pressure of 2.5 atm at 25 °C

(b) A can of soda open to the atmosphere at 25 °C

11.5 PHYSICAL BEHAVIOR OF SOLUTIONS: COLLIGATIVE PROPERTIES

The behavior of solutions is qualitatively similar to that of pure solvents but is quantitatively different. Pure water boils at 100.0 °C and freezes at 0.0 °C, for instance, but a 1.00 *m* (molal) solution of NaCl in water boils at 101.0 °C and freezes at −3.7 °C.

The higher boiling point and lower freezing point observed for a solution compared to a pure solvent are examples of **colligative properties**, which depend only on the amount of dissolved solute but not on the solute's chemical identity. The word *colligative* means "bound together in a collection" and is used because a collection of solute particles is responsible for the observed effects. Other colligative properties are a lower vapor pressure for a solution compared with the pure solvent and *osmosis*, the migration of solvent and other small molecules through a semipermeable membrane.

In comparing the properties of a pure solvent with those of a solution . . .

Colligative properties
- The vapor pressure of the solution is lower.
- The boiling point of the solution is higher.
- The freezing (or melting) point of the solution is lower.
- The solution gives rise to osmosis, the migration of solvent molecules through a semipermeable membrane.

We'll look at each of the four colligative properties in more detail in Sections 11.6–11.8.

11.6 VAPOR-PRESSURE LOWERING OF SOLUTIONS: RAOULT'S LAW

Recall from Section 10.5 that a liquid in a closed container is in equilibrium with its vapor and that the amount of pressure exerted by the vapor is called the **vapor pressure**. When you compare the vapor pressure of a pure solvent with that of a solution at the same temperature, however, you find that the two values are different. If the solute is nonvolatile and has no appreciable vapor pressure of its own, as occurs when a solid is dissolved, then the vapor pressure of the solution is always lower than that of the pure solvent. If the solute *is* volatile and has a significant vapor pressure of its own, as occurs in a mixture of two liquids, then the vapor pressure of the mixture is intermediate between the vapor pressures of the two pure liquids.

Solutions with a Nonvolatile Solute

It's easy to demonstrate with **manometers** that a solution of a nonvolatile solute has a lower vapor pressure than the pure solvent (**Figure 11.9**). Alternatively, you can show the same effect by comparing the evaporation rate of a pure solvent with the evaporation rate of a solution. A solution always evaporates more slowly than a pure solvent does because its vapor pressure is lower and its molecules therefore escape less readily.

Remember...
At equilibrium, the rate of evaporation from the liquid to the vapor is equal to the rate of condensation from the vapor back to the liquid. The resulting **vapor pressure** is the partial pressure of the gas in the equilibrium. (Section 10.5)

Remember...
A **manometer** is a mercury-filled U-tube used for reading pressure. One end of the tube is connected to the sample container and the other end is open to the atmosphere. (Section 9.1)

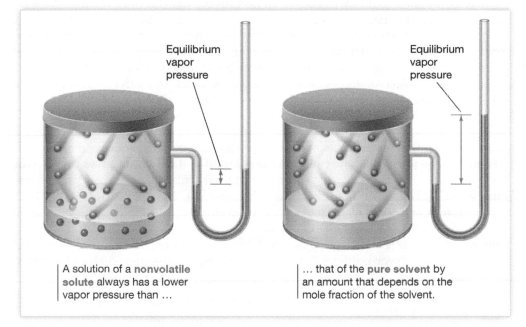

Equilibrium vapor pressure

Equilibrium vapor pressure

A solution of a **nonvolatile solute** always has a lower vapor pressure than ...

... that of the **pure solvent** by an amount that depends on the mole fraction of the solvent.

Figure 11.9
The equilibrium vapor pressure of solutions.

According to **Raoult's law**, the vapor pressure of a solution containing a nonvolatile solute is equal to the vapor pressure of the pure solvent times the mole fraction of the solvent. That is,

Raoult's law $P_{soln} = P_{solv} \times X_{solv}$

where P_{soln} is the vapor pressure of the solution, P_{solv} is the vapor pressure of pure solvent at the same temperature, and X_{solv} is the mole fraction of the solvent in the solution.

Take a solution of 1.00 mol of glucose in 15.0 mol of water at 25 °C, for instance. The vapor pressure of pure water at 25 °C is 23.76 mm Hg, and the mole fraction of water in the solution is 15.0 mol/(1.00 mol + 15.0 mol) = 0.938. Thus, Raoult's law predicts a vapor pressure for the solution of 23.76 mm Hg × 0.938 = 22.3 mm Hg, which corresponds to a vapor-pressure lowering, ΔP_{soln}, of 1.5 mm Hg:

$$P_{soln} = P_{solv} \times X_{solv} = 23.76 \text{ mm Hg} \times \frac{15.0 \text{ mol}}{1.00 \text{ mol} + 15.0 \text{ mol}} = 22.3 \text{ mm Hg}$$

$$\Delta P_{soln} = P_{solv} - P_{soln} = 23.76 \text{ mm Hg} - 22.3 \text{ mm Hg} = 1.5 \text{ mm Hg}$$

Alternatively, the extent of vapor pressure lowering (ΔP) can be calculated directly by multiplying the mole fraction of the *solute* times the vapor pressure of the pure solvent. That is,

$$\Delta P_{\text{soln}} = P_{\text{solv}} \times X_{\text{solute}} = 23.76 \text{ mm Hg} \times \frac{1.00 \text{ mol}}{1.00 \text{ mol} + 15.0 \text{ mol}}$$

$$= 1.49 \text{ mm Hg}$$

If an ionic substance such as NaCl is the solute rather than a molecular substance, we have to calculate mole fractions based on the total concentration of solute *particles* (ions) rather than NaCl formula units. A solution of 1.00 mol of NaCl in 15.0 mol of water at 25 °C, for example, contains 2.00 mol of dissolved particles, assuming complete dissociation, resulting in a mole fraction for water of 0.882 and a solution vapor pressure of 21.0 mm Hg.

$$X_{\text{water}} = \frac{15.0 \text{ mol } H_2O}{1.00 \text{ mol } Na^+ + 1.00 \text{ mol } Cl^- + 15.0 \text{ mol } H_2O} = 0.882$$

$$P_{\text{soln}} = P_{\text{solv}} \times X_{\text{solv}} = 23.76 \text{ mm Hg} \times 0.882 = 21.0 \text{ mm Hg}$$

Because the mole fraction of water is smaller in the NaCl solution than in the glucose solution, the vapor pressure of the NaCl solution is lower: 21.0 mm Hg for NaCl versus 22.3 mm Hg for glucose at 25 °C.

Just as the ideal gas law discussed in Section 9.3 applies only to "ideal" gases, Raoult's law applies only to ideal solutions. Raoult's law approximates the behavior of most real solutions, but significant deviations from ideality occur as the solute concentration increases. The law works best when solute concentrations are low and when solute and solvent particles have similar intermolecular forces.

If the intermolecular forces between solute particles and solvent molecules are weaker than the forces between solvent molecules alone, then the solvent molecules are less tightly held in the solution and the vapor pressure is higher than Raoult's law predicts. Conversely, if the intermolecular forces between solute and solvent molecules are stronger than the forces between solvent molecules alone, then the solvent molecules are more tightly held in the solution and the vapor pressure is lower than predicted. Solutions of ionic substances, in particular, often have a vapor pressure significantly lower than predicted, because the ion–dipole forces between dissolved ions and polar water molecules are so strong.

A further complication in predicting the extent of vapor-pressure lowering is that ionic substances rarely dissociate completely, so a solution of an ionic compound usually contains fewer particles than the formula of the compound would suggest. The actual extent of dissociation can be expressed as a **van't Hoff factor (i)**:

van't Hoff factor $i = \dfrac{\text{Moles of particles in solution}}{\text{Moles of solute dissolved}}$

Rearranging this equation thus shows that the number of moles of particles dissolved in a solution is equal to number of moles dissolved times the van't Hoff factor.

$$\text{Moles of particles in solution} = i \times \text{Moles of solute dissolved}$$

To take a solution of NaCl as an example, the experimentally determined van't Hoff factor for 0.05 m NaCl is 1.9, meaning that each mole of NaCl gives only 1.9 mol of particles rather than the 2.0 mol expected for complete dissociation. Of the 1.9 mol of particles, 0.1 mol is undissociated NaCl, 0.9 mol is Cl^-, and 0.9 mol is Na^+. Thus, NaCl is only $(0.9/1.0) \times 100\% = 90\%$ dissociated in a 0.05 m solution, and the extent of vapor pressure lowering is less than expected.

What accounts for the lowering of the vapor pressure when a nonvolatile solute is dissolved in a solvent? As we've noted on many prior occasions, a physical process such as the vaporization of a liquid to a gas is accompanied by a free-energy change, $\Delta G_{\text{vap}} = \Delta H_{\text{vap}} - T\Delta S_{\text{vap}}$. The more negative the value of ΔG_{vap}, the more favored the vaporization process. Thus, if we want to compare the ease of vaporization of a pure solvent with that of the solvent in a solution, we have to compare the signs and relative magnitudes of the ΔH_{vap} and ΔS_{vap} terms in the two cases.

The vaporization of a liquid to a gas is disfavored by enthalpy (positive ΔH_{vap}) because energy is required to overcome intermolecular attractions in the liquid. At the same time, however, vaporization is favored by entropy (positive ΔS_{vap}) because randomness increases when molecules go from a liquid state to a gaseous state.

The *enthalpies* of vaporization for a pure solvent and a solvent in a solution are similar because similar intermolecular forces must be overcome in both cases for solvent molecules to escape from the liquid. The *entropies* of vaporization for a pure solvent and a solvent in a solution are *not* similar, however. Because a solvent in a solution has more molecular randomness and higher entropy than a pure solvent does, the entropy change on going from liquid to vapor is smaller for the solvent in a solution than for the pure solvent. Subtracting a smaller $T\Delta S_{vap}$ from ΔH_{vap} thus results in a larger (less negative) ΔG_{vap} for the solution. As a result, vaporization is less favored for the solution and the vapor pressure of the solution at equilibrium is lower (Figure 11.10).

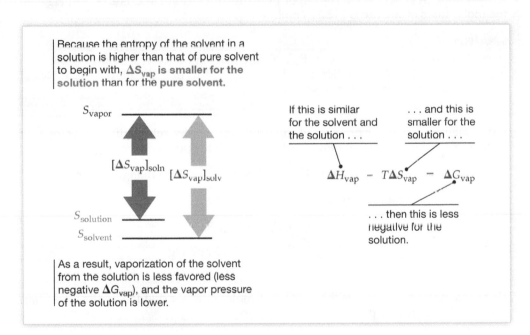

Figure 11.10
Vapor-pressure lowering. The lower vapor pressure of a solution relative to that of a pure solvent is due to the difference in their entropies of vaporization, ΔS_{vap}.

WORKED EXAMPLE 11.8

CALCULATING THE VAPOR PRESSURE OF A SOLUTION

What is the vapor pressure in mm Hg of a solution made by dissolving 18.3 g of NaCl in 500.0 g of H_2O at 70 °C, assuming a van't Hoff factor of 1.9? The vapor pressure of pure water at 70 °C is 233.7 mm Hg.

STRATEGY

According to Raoult's law, the vapor pressure of the solution equals the vapor pressure of pure solvent times the mole fraction of the solvent in the solution. Thus, we have to find the numbers of moles of solvent and solute and then calculate the mole fraction of solvent.

SOLUTION

First, use molar mass to calculate the number of moles of NaCl and H_2O.

$$\text{Moles of NaCl} = 18.3 \text{ g NaCl} \times \frac{1 \text{ mol NaCl}}{58.44 \text{ g NaCl}} = 0.313 \text{ mol NaCl}$$

$$\text{Moles of } H_2O = 500.0 \text{ g } H_2O \times \frac{1 \text{ mol } H_2O}{18.02 \text{ g } H_2O} = 27.75 \text{ mol } H_2O$$

continued on next page

Next, calculate the mole fraction of water in the solution. A van't Hoff factor of 1.9 means that the NaCl dissociates incompletely and gives only 1.9 particles per formula unit. Thus, the solution contains 1.9×0.313 mol $= 0.59$ mol of dissolved particles and the mole fraction of water is

$$\text{Mole fraction of } H_2O = \frac{27.75 \text{ mol}}{0.59 \text{ mol} + 27.75 \text{ mol}} = 0.9792$$

From Raoult's law, the vapor pressure of the solution is

$$P_{soln} = P_{solv} \times X_{solv} = 233.7 \text{ mm Hg} \times 0.9792 = 228.8 \text{ mm Hg}$$

WORKED EXAMPLE 11.9

CALCULATING VAPOR-PRESSURE LOWERING

How many grams of sucrose must be added to 320 g of water to lower the vapor pressure by 1.5 mm Hg at 25 °C? The vapor pressure of water at 25 °C is 23.8 mm Hg, and the molar mass of sucrose is 342.3 g/mol.

STRATEGY

According to Raoult's law, $P_{soln} = P_{solv} \times X_{solv}$, which can be rearranged to the form $X_{solv} = P_{soln}/P_{solv}$. This equation can then be solved to find the number of moles of sucrose and hence the number of grams.

SOLUTION

First, calculate the vapor pressure of the solution, P_{soln}, by subtracting the amount of vapor-pressure lowering from the vapor pressure of the pure solvent, P_{solv}:

$$P_{soln} = 23.8 \text{ mm Hg} - 1.5 \text{ mm Hg} = 22.3 \text{ mm Hg}$$

Now calculate the mole fraction of water, X_{solv}.

Since $$P_{soln} = P_{solv} \times X_{solv}$$

then $$X_{solv} = \frac{P_{soln}}{P_{solv}} = \frac{22.3 \text{ mm Hg}}{23.8 \text{ mm Hg}} = 0.937$$

This mole fraction of water is the number of moles of water divided by the total number of moles of sucrose plus water:

$$X_{solv} = \frac{\text{Moles of water}}{\text{Total moles}}$$

Since the number of moles of water is

$$\text{Moles of water} = 320 \text{ g} \times \frac{1 \text{ mol}}{18.0 \text{ g}} = 17.8 \text{ mol}$$

then the total number of moles of sucrose plus water is

$$\text{Total moles} = \frac{\text{moles of water}}{X_{solv}} = \frac{17.8 \text{ mol}}{0.937} = 19.0 \text{ mol}$$

Subtracting the number of moles of water from the total number of moles gives the number of moles of sucrose needed:

$$\text{Moles of sucrose} = 19.0 \text{ mol} - 17.8 \text{ mol} = 1.2 \text{ mol}$$

Converting moles into grams then gives the mass of sucrose needed:

$$\text{Grams of sucrose} = 1.2 \text{ mol} \times 342.3 \frac{g}{mol} = 4.1 \times 10^2 \text{ g}$$

▶ **PROBLEM 11.13**   What is the vapor pressure in mm Hg of a solution prepared by dissolving 5.00 g of benzoic acid ($C_7H_6O_2$) in 100.00 g of ethyl alcohol (C_2H_6O) at 35 °C? The vapor pressure of pure ethyl alcohol at 35 °C is 100.5 mm Hg.

▶ **PROBLEM 11.14**   How many grams of NaBr must be added to 250 g of water to lower the vapor pressure by 1.30 mm Hg at 40 °C assuming complete dissociation? The vapor pressure of water at 40 °C is 55.3 mm Hg.

CONCEPTUAL PROBLEM 11.15   The following diagram shows a close-up view of part of the vapor-pressure curve for a pure solvent and a solution of a nonvolatile solute. Which curve represents the pure solvent, and which the solution?

T (°C)

Solutions with a Volatile Solute

As you might expect from **Dalton's law of partial pressures** (Section 9.5), the overall vapor pressure P_{total} of a mixture of two volatile liquids, A and B, is the sum of the vapor-pressure contributions of the individual components, P_A and P_B:

$$P_{total} = P_A + P_B$$

The individual vapor pressures P_A and P_B are calculated by Raoult's law. That is, the vapor pressure of A is equal to the mole fraction of A (X_A) times the vapor pressure of pure A ($P°_A$), and the vapor pressure of B is equal to the mole fraction of B (X_B) times the vapor pressure of pure B ($P°_B$). Thus, the total vapor pressure of the solution is

$$P_{total} = P_A + P_B = (P°_A \cdot X_A) + (P°_B \cdot X_B)$$

Take a mixture of the two similar organic liquids benzene (C_6H_6, bp = 80.1 °C) and toluene (C_7H_8, bp = 110.6 °C), as an example. Pure benzene has a vapor pressure $P° = 96.0$ mm Hg at 25 °C, and pure toluene has $P° = 30.3$ mm Hg at the same temperature. In a 1:1 molar mixture of the two, where the mole fraction of each is $X = 0.500$, the vapor pressure of the solution is 63.1 mm Hg:

Remember...

Dalton's law of partial pressures states that the total pressure exerted by a mixture of gases in a container at constant volume and temperature is equal to the sum of the pressures of each individual gas in the container.   (Section 9.5)

Benzene   Toluene

$$P_{total} = (P°_{benzene})(X_{benzene}) + (P°_{toluene})(X_{toluene})$$
$$= (96.0 \text{ mm Hg} \times 0.500) + (30.3 \text{ mm Hg} \times 0.500)$$
$$= 48.0 \text{ mm Hg} + 15.1 \text{ mm Hg} = 63.1 \text{ mm Hg}$$

Note that the vapor pressure of the mixture is intermediate between the vapor pressures of the two pure liquids (Figure 11.11).

Figure 11.11

Raoult's law for a mixture of volatile liquids. The vapor pressure of a solution of the two volatile liquids benzene and toluene at 25 °C is the sum of the two individual contributions, each calculated by Raoult's law.

As with nonvolatile solutes, Raoult's law for a mixture of volatile liquids applies only to ideal solutions. Most real solutions show behaviors that deviate slightly from the ideal in either a positive or negative way, depending on the kinds and strengths of intermolecular forces present in the solution.

WORKED CONCEPTUAL EXAMPLE 11.10

INTERPRETING VAPOR PRESSURE CURVES

The following diagram shows a close-up view of part of the vapor-pressure curves for two pure liquids and a mixture of the two. Which curves represent pure liquids, and which represents the mixture?

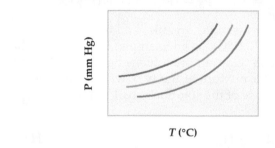

STRATEGY AND SOLUTION

The vapor pressure of a mixture of two volatile liquids is always intermediate between the vapor pressures of the two pure liquids. Thus, the top (red) and bottom (blue) curves represent pure liquids, and the middle curve (green) represents the mixture.

▶ **PROBLEM 11.16**

(a) What is the vapor pressure in mm Hg of a solution prepared by dissolving 25.0 g of ethyl alcohol (C_2H_5OH) in 100.0 g of water at 25 °C? The vapor pressure of pure water is 23.8 mm Hg, and the vapor pressure of ethyl alcohol is 61.2 mm Hg at 25 °C.

(b) What is the vapor pressure of the solution if 25.0 g of water is dissolved in 100.0 g of ethyl alcohol at 25 °C?

CONCEPTUAL PROBLEM 11.17 The following phase diagram shows part of the vapor-pressure curves for a pure liquid (green curve) and a solution of the first liquid with a second volatile liquid (red curve).

(a) Is the boiling point of the second liquid higher or lower than that of the first liquid?
(b) Draw on the diagram the approximate position of the vapor-pressure curve for the second liquid.

11.7 BOILING-POINT ELEVATION AND FREEZING-POINT DEPRESSION OF SOLUTIONS

We saw in Section 10.5 that the vapor pressure of a liquid rises with increasing temperature and that the liquid boils when its vapor pressure equals atmospheric pressure. Because a solution of a nonvolatile solute has a lower vapor pressure than a pure solvent has at a given temperature, the solution must be heated to a higher temperature to cause it to boil. Furthermore, the lower vapor pressure of the solution means that the liquid/vapor phase transition line on a **phase diagram** (Section 10.11) is always lower for the solution than for the pure solvent. As a result, the triple-point temperature T_t is lower for the solution, the solid/liquid phase transition line is shifted to a lower temperature for the solution, and the solution must be cooled to a lower temperature to freeze. **Figure 11.12** shows the situation.

Remember...

The **phase diagram** of a substance is a plot of pressure versus temperature, showing which phases are stable at any given combination of P and T. (Section 10.11)

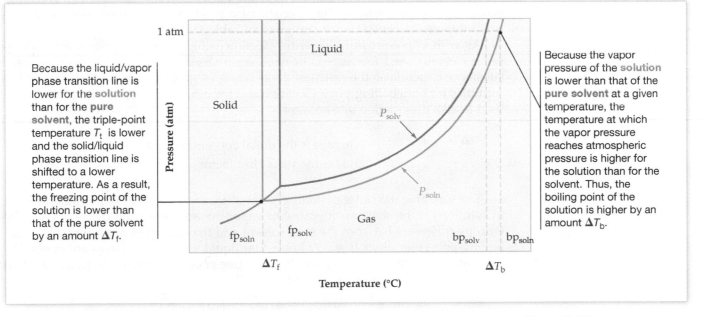

Because the liquid/vapor phase transition line is lower for the **solution** than for the **pure solvent**, the triple-point temperature T_t is lower and the solid/liquid phase transition line is shifted to a lower temperature. As a result, the freezing point of the solution is lower than that of the pure solvent by an amount ΔT_f.

Because the vapor pressure of the **solution** is lower than that of the **pure solvent** at a given temperature, the temperature at which the vapor pressure reaches atmospheric pressure is higher for the solution than for the solvent. Thus, the boiling point of the solution is higher by an amount ΔT_b.

Figure 11.12
Phase diagrams for a pure solvent (red) and a solution of a nonvolatile solute (green).

The boiling-point elevation of a solution relative to that of a pure solvent depends on the concentration of dissolved particles, just as vapor-pressure lowering does. Thus, a 1.00 m solution of glucose in water boils at approximately 100.51 °C at 1 atm pressure (0.51 °C above normal), but a 1.00 m solution of NaCl in water boils at approximately 101.02 °C (1.02 °C above normal) because there are twice as many particles (ions) dissolved in the NaCl solution as there are in the glucose solution.

The change in boiling point ΔT_b for a solution is

$$\Delta T_b = K_b \cdot m$$

where m is the *molal* (not molar) concentration of solute particles and K_b is the **molal boiling-point-elevation constant** characteristic of a given liquid. The concentration must be expressed in molality—the number of moles of solute particles per kilogram of solvent—rather than molarity so that the solute concentration is independent of temperature. Molal boiling-point-elevation constants are given in Table 11.4 for some common substances.

TABLE 11.4 Molal Boiling-Point-Elevation Constants (K_b) and Molal Freezing-Point-Depression Constants (K_f) for Some Common Substances

Substance	$K_b [(°C \cdot kg)/mol]$	$K_f [(°C \cdot kg)/mol]$
Benzene (C_6H_6)	2.64	5.07
Camphor ($C_{10}H_{16}O$)	5.95	37.8
Chloroform ($CHCl_3$)	3.63	4.70
Diethyl ether ($C_4H_{10}O$)	2.02	1.79
Ethyl alcohol (C_2H_6O)	1.22	1.99
Water (H_2O)	0.51	1.86

The freezing-point depression for a solution relative to that of a pure solvent depends on the concentration of solute particles, just as boiling-point elevation does. For example, a 1.00 m solution of glucose in water freezes at $-1.86\,°C$, and a 1.00 m solution of NaCl in water freezes at approximately $-3.72\,°C$. The change in freezing point ΔT_f for a solution is

$$\Delta T_f = K_f \cdot m$$

where m is the molal concentration of solute particles and K_f is the **molal freezing-point-depression constant** characteristic of a given solvent. Some molal freezing-point-depression constants are also given in Table 11.4.

As with vapor-pressure lowering (Section 11.6), the actual amount of boiling-point elevation and freezing-point depression observed for a solution of an ionic substance depends on the extent of dissociation, as given by a van't Hoff factor. The formulas for both boiling-point elevation and freezing-point depression can be modified to take dissociation into account:

$$\Delta T_b = K_b \cdot m \cdot i \quad \text{where } m \text{ is the molal concentration of formula units}$$
$$\Delta T_f = K_f \cdot m \cdot i \quad \text{and } i \text{ is the van't Hoff factor}$$

The fundamental cause of boiling-point elevation and freezing-point depression in solutions is the same as the cause of vapor-pressure lowering (Section 11.6): the entropy difference between the pure solvent and the solvent in a solution. Let's take boiling-point elevations first. We know that liquid and vapor phases are in equilibrium at the boiling point (T_b) and that the free-energy difference between the two phases (ΔG_{vap}) is therefore zero (Section 8.13).

$$\text{Since} \quad \Delta G_{vap} = \Delta H_{vap} - T_b \Delta S_{vap} = 0$$

$$\text{then} \quad \Delta H_{vap} = T_b \Delta S_{vap} \quad \text{and} \quad T_b = \frac{\Delta H_{vap}}{\Delta S_{vap}}$$

In comparing the enthalpies of vaporization (ΔH_{vap}) for a pure solvent and for a solvent in a solution, the values are similar because similar intermolecular forces holding the solvent molecules must be overcome in both cases. In comparing the entropies of vaporization, however, the values are not similar. Because the solvent in a solution has more molecular randomness than a pure solvent has, the entropy change between solution and vapor is smaller than the entropy change between pure solvent and vapor. But if ΔS_{vap} is smaller for the solution, then T_b must be correspondingly larger. In other words, the boiling point of the solution (T_b) is higher than that of the pure solvent (**Figure 11.13**).

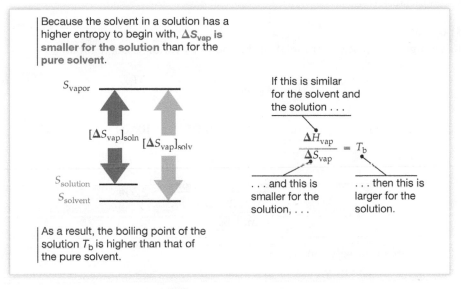

Figure 11.13
Boiling-point elevation. The higher boiling point of a solution relative to that of a pure solvent is due to a difference in their entropies of vaporization, ΔS_{vap}.

A similar explanation accounts for freezing-point depression. Because liquid and solid phases are in equilibrium at the freezing point, the free-energy difference between the phases (ΔG_{fusion}) is zero:

Since $\quad \Delta G_{fusion} = \Delta H_{fusion} - T_f \Delta S_{fusion} = 0$

then $\quad \Delta H_{fusion} = T_f \Delta S_{fusion} \quad$ and $\quad T_f - \dfrac{\Delta H_{fusion}}{\Delta S_{fusion}}$

In comparing the solvent in a solution with a pure solvent, the enthalpies of fusion (ΔH_{fusion}) are similar because similar intermolecular forces between solvent molecules are involved. The entropies of fusion (ΔS_{fusion}), however, are not similar. Because the solvent in a solution has more molecular randomness than a pure solvent has, the entropy change between the solvent in the solution and the solid is larger than the entropy change between pure solvent and the solid. With ΔS_{fusion} larger for the solution, T_f must be correspondingly smaller, meaning that the freezing point of the solution (T_f) is lower than that of the pure solvent (**Figure 11.14**).

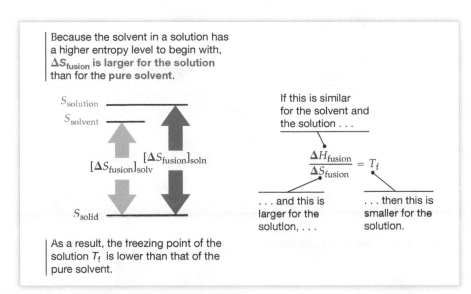

Figure 11.14
Freezing-point lowering. The lower freezing point of a solution relative to that of a pure solvent is due to a difference in their entropies of fusion, ΔS_{fusion}.

WORKED EXAMPLE 11.11

USING BOILING-POINT ELEVATION TO CALCULATE THE MOLALITY OF A SOLUTION

What is the molality of an aqueous glucose solution if the boiling point of the solution at 1 atm pressure is 101.27 °C? The molal boiling-point-elevation constant for water is given in Table 11.4.

STRATEGY

Rearrange the equation for molal boiling-point elevation to solve for m:

$$\Delta T_b = K_b \cdot m \qquad \text{so} \qquad m = \frac{\Delta T_b}{K_b}$$

where $K_b = 0.51 \ (\text{°C} \cdot \text{kg})/\text{mol}$ and $\Delta T_b = 101.27 \ \text{°C} - 100.00 \ \text{°C} = 1.27 \ \text{°C}$.

SOLUTION

$$m = \frac{1.27 \ \text{°C}}{0.51 \ \dfrac{\text{°C} \cdot \text{kg}}{\text{mol}}} = 2.5 \ \frac{\text{mol}}{\text{kg}} = 2.5 \ m$$

The molality of the solution is 2.5 m.

▶ **PROBLEM 11.18** What is the normal boiling point in °C of a solution prepared by dissolving 1.50 g of aspirin (acetylsalicylic acid, $C_9H_8O_4$) in 75.00 g of chloroform ($CHCl_3$)? The normal boiling point of chloroform is 61.7 °C, and K_b for chloroform is given in Table 11.4.

▶ **PROBLEM 11.19** What is the freezing point in °C of a solution prepared by dissolving 7.40 g of $MgCl_2$ in 110 g of water? The value of K_f for water is given in Table 11.4, and the van't Hoff factor for $MgCl_2$ is $i = 2.7$.

▶ **PROBLEM 11.20** Assuming complete dissociation, what is the molality of an aqueous solution of KBr whose freezing point is −2.95 °C? The molal freezing-point-depression constant of water is given in Table 11.4.

▶ **PROBLEM 11.21** When 9.12 g of HCl was dissolved in 190 g of water, the freezing point of the solution was −4.65 °C. What is the value of the van't Hoff factor for HCl?

CONCEPTUAL PROBLEM 11.22 The following phase diagram shows a close-up view of the liquid/vapor phase transition boundaries for pure chloroform and a solution of a nonvolatile solute in chloroform.

(a) What is the approximate boiling point of pure chloroform?
(b) What is the approximate molal concentration of the nonvolatile solute? See Table 11.4 to find K_b for chloroform.

11.8 OSMOSIS AND OSMOTIC PRESSURE

Certain materials, including those that make up the membranes around living cells, are *semipermeable*, meaning that they allow water or other smaller molecules to pass through, but they block the passage of larger solute molecules or solvated ions. When a solution and a pure solvent, or two solutions of different concentration, are separated by the right kind of semipermeable membrane, solvent molecules pass through the membrane in a process called **osmosis**. Although the passage of solvent through the membrane takes place in both directions, passage from the pure solvent side to the solution side is more favored and occurs faster. As a result, the amount of liquid on the pure solvent side of the membrane decreases, the amount of liquid on the solution side increases, and the concentration of the solution decreases.

Osmosis can be demonstrated with the experimental setup shown in Figure 11.15, in which a solution inside the bulb is separated from pure solvent in the beaker by a semipermeable membrane. Solvent passes through the membrane from the beaker to the bulb, causing the liquid level in the attached tube to rise. The increased weight of liquid in the tube creates an increased pressure that pushes solvent back through the membrane until the rates of forward and reverse passage become equal and the liquid level stops rising.

A **solution** inside the bulb is separated from pure **solvent** in the beaker by a semipermeable membrane.

Net passage of **solvent** from the beaker through the membrane occurs, and the liquid in the tube rises until an equilibrium is reached.

More concentrated solution

Solvent

Less concentrated solution

Osmotic pressure

At equilibrium, the **osmotic pressure** exerted by the column of liquid in the tube is sufficient to prevent further net passage of solvent.

Time

Semipermeable membrane

Solvent molecules on the **solution** side have a lower concentration and therefore pass through the **membrane** less frequently.

Membrane

Solvent molecules on the **pure solvent** side have a higher concentration and therefore pass through the membrane more frequently.

Figure 11.15
The phenomenon of osmosis.

The amount of pressure necessary to achieve this equilibrium passage of solvent molecules through the membrane is called the solution's **osmotic pressure**, **Π** (Greek capital pi). Osmotic pressures can be extremely high, even for relatively dilute solutions. The osmotic pressure of a 0.15 M NaCl solution at 25 °C, for example, is 7.3 atm, a value that will support a difference in water level of approximately 250 ft! The amount of osmotic pressure at equilibrium depends on the concentration of solute particles in the solution according to the equation

$$\Pi = MRT$$

where M is the molar concentration of solute particles, R is the gas constant [0.082 06 (L·atm)/(K·mol)], and T is the temperature in kelvin. For example, a 1.00 M solution of glucose in water at 300 K has an osmotic pressure of 24.6 atm:

$$\Pi = MRT = \left(1.00 \frac{mol}{L}\right)\left(0.082\ 06 \frac{L \cdot atm}{K \cdot mol}\right)(300\ K) = 24.6\ atm$$

Note that the solute concentration is given in *molarity* when calculating osmotic pressure rather than in molality as for other colligative properties. Because osmotic-pressure measurements are made at the specific temperature given in the equation $\Pi = MRT$, it's not necessary to express concentration in a temperature-independent unit like molality.

(a)   **(b)**

▲ **(a)** Normal red blood cells in plasma **(b)** rupture when immersed in pure water because osmotic pressure drives water into the cells and increases the internal pressure.

Osmosis, like all colligative properties, results from a favorable increase in entropy of the pure solvent as it passes through the membrane and mixes with the solution. We can also explain osmosis on a molecular level by noting that molecules on the solvent side of the membrane, because of their greater concentration, approach the membrane a bit more frequently than molecules on the solution side, thereby passing through more often (Figure 11.15).

WORKED EXAMPLE 11.12

CALCULATING THE OSMOTIC PRESSURE OF A SOLUTION

The total concentration of dissolved particles inside red blood cells and in the surrounding plasma is approximately 0.30 M, and the membrane surrounding the cells is semipermeable. What would the maximum osmotic pressure in atmospheres inside the cells be if the cells were removed from blood plasma and placed in pure water at 298 K?

STRATEGY

If red blood cells were removed from plasma and placed in pure water, water would pass through the cell membrane, causing a pressure increase inside the cells. The maximum amount of this pressure would be

$$\Pi = MRT$$

where M = 0.30 mol/L, R = 0.082 06 (L · atm)/(K · mol), T = 298 K.

SOLUTION

$$\Pi = \left(0.30 \frac{mol}{L}\right)\left(0.082\ 06 \frac{L \cdot atm}{K \cdot mol}\right)(298\ K) = 7.3\ atm$$

In fact, red blood cells rupture if the pressure differential across their membrane is greater than 5 atm, so the cells would burst if placed in pure water.

WORKED EXAMPLE 11.13

USING OSMOTIC PRESSURE TO CALCULATE THE MOLARITY OF A SOLUTION

A solution of an unknown substance in water at 293 K gives rise to an osmotic pressure of 5.66 atm. What is the molarity of the solution?

STRATEGY

We are given values for Π and T, and we need to solve for M in the equation $\Pi = MRT$. Rearranging this equation, we get

$$M = \frac{\Pi}{RT}$$

where $\Pi = 5.66$ atm, $R = 0.082\ 06$ (L·atm)/(K·mol), and $T = 293$ K.

SOLUTION

$$M = \frac{5.66\ \text{atm}}{\left(0.082\ 06\ \dfrac{\text{L}\cdot\text{atm}}{\text{K}\cdot\text{mol}}\right)(293\ \text{K})} = 0.235\ \text{M}$$

▶ **PROBLEM 11.23**   What osmotic pressure in atmospheres would you expect for a solution of 0.125 M $CaCl_2$ that is separated from pure water by a semipermeable membrane at 310 K? Assume 100% dissociation for $CaCl_2$.

▶ **PROBLEM 11.24**   A solution of an unknown substance in water at 300 K gives rise to an osmotic pressure of 3.85 atm. What is the molarity of the solution?

11.9 SOME USES OF COLLIGATIVE PROPERTIES

Colligative properties may seem somewhat obscure, but in fact they have many practical uses, both in the chemical laboratory and in everyday life. Motorists in winter, for instance, take advantage of freezing-point lowering when they drive on streets where the snow has been melted by a sprinkling of salt. The antifreeze added to automobile radiators and the deicer solution sprayed on airplane wings also work by lowering the freezing point of water. That same automobile antifreeze keeps radiator water from boiling over in summer by raising its boiling point.

One of the more interesting uses of colligative properties is the desalination of seawater by *reverse osmosis*. When pure water and seawater are separated by a suitable membrane, the passage of water molecules from the pure side to the solution side is faster than passage in the reverse direction. As osmotic pressure builds up, though, the rates of forward and reverse water passage eventually become equal at an osmotic pressure of about 30 atm at 25 °C. If, however, a pressure even *greater* than 30 atm is applied to the solution side, then the reverse passage of water becomes favored. As a result, pure water can be obtained from seawater (**Figure 11.16**).

▲ Freshwater is obtained from seawater by desalination using reverse osmosis.

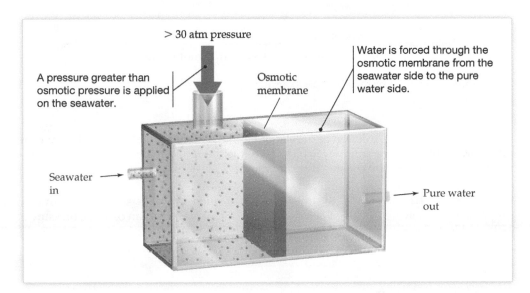

Figure 11.16
Desalination of seawater by reverse osmosis at high pressure.

In the laboratory, colligative properties are sometimes used for determining the molecular mass of an unknown substance. Any of the four colligative properties we've discussed can be used, but the most accurate values are obtained from osmotic-pressure measurements because the magnitude of the osmosis effect is so great. For example, a solution of 0.0200 M glucose in water at 300 K will give an osmotic-pressure reading of 374.2 mm Hg, a value that can easily be read to four significant figures. The same solution, however, will lower the freezing point by only 0.04 °C, a value that can be read to only one significant figure. Worked Example 11.14 shows how osmotic pressure can be used to find molecular mass.

WORKED EXAMPLE 11.14

USING OSMOTIC PRESSURE TO CALCULATE THE MOLECULAR MASS OF A SOLUTE

A solution prepared by dissolving 20.0 mg of insulin in water and diluting to a volume of 5.00 mL gives an osmotic pressure of 12.5 mm Hg at 300 K. What is the molecular mass of insulin?

STRATEGY

To determine molecular mass, we need to know the number of moles of insulin represented by the 20.0 mg sample. We can do this by first rearranging the equation for osmotic pressure to find the molar concentration of the insulin solution and then multiplying by the volume of the solution to obtain the number of moles of insulin.

SOLUTION

$$\text{Since} \quad \Pi = MRT, \quad \text{then} \quad M = \frac{\Pi}{RT}$$

$$M = \frac{12.5 \text{ mm Hg} \times \dfrac{1 \text{ atm}}{760 \text{ mm Hg}}}{0.082\,06 \dfrac{\text{L} \cdot \text{atm}}{\text{K} \cdot \text{mol}} \times 300 \text{ K}} = 6.68 \times 10^{-4} \text{ M}$$

Since the volume of the solution is 5.00 mL, the number of moles of insulin is

$$\text{Moles insulin} = 6.68 \times 10^{-4} \frac{\text{mol}}{\text{L}} \times \frac{1 \text{ L}}{1000 \text{ mL}} \times 5.00 \text{ mL} = 3.34 \times 10^{-6} \text{ mol}$$

Knowing both the mass and the number of moles of insulin, we can calculate the molar mass and thus the molecular mass:

$$\text{Molar mass} = \frac{\text{mass insulin}}{\text{moles of insulin}} = \frac{0.0200 \text{ g insulin}}{3.34 \times 10^{-6} \text{ mol insulin}} = 5990 \text{ g/mol}$$

The molecular mass of insulin is 5990 amu.

▶ **PROBLEM 11.25** A solution of 0.250 g of naphthalene (mothballs) in 35.00 g of camphor lowers the freezing point by 2.10 °C. What is the molar mass of naphthalene? The freezing-point-depression constant for camphor is 37.7 (°C · kg)/mol.

▶ **PROBLEM 11.26** What is the molar mass of sucrose (table sugar) if a solution prepared by dissolving 0.822 g of sucrose in 300.0 mL of water has an osmotic pressure of 149 mm Hg at 298 K?

11.10 FRACTIONAL DISTILLATION OF LIQUID MIXTURES

Undoubtedly the most important of all commercial applications of colligative properties is in the refining of petroleum to make gasoline. Although petroleum refineries appear as a vast maze of pipes, tanks, and towers, the pipes are just for transferring the petroleum or its products and the tanks are just for storage. It's in the towers that the separation of crude petroleum into usable fractions takes place. As we saw in Section 8.11, petroleum is a complex mixture of hydrocarbon molecules that are refined by distillation into different fractions: straight-run gasoline (bp 30–200 °C), kerosene (bp 175–300 °C), and gas oil (bp 275–400 °C).

Called **fractional distillation**, the separation of a mixture of different liquids into fractions with different boiling points occurs when the mixture is boiled and the vapors are condensed. Because the vapor is enriched in the component with the higher vapor pressure according to Raoult's law (Section 11.6), the condensed vapors are also enriched in that component and a partial purification can be effected. If the boil/condense cycle is repeated a large number of times, complete purification of the more volatile liquid component can be achieved.

As an example, let's look at the separation by fractional distillation of a 1:1 molar mixture of benzene and toluene ($X_{benzene}$ and $X_{toluene}$ are both 0.500). If we begin by heating the mixture, boiling occurs when the sum of the vapor pressures equals atmospheric pressure—that is, when $X \cdot P°_{benzene} + X \cdot P°_{toluene} = 760$ mm Hg. Reading from the vapor-pressure curves in **Figure 11.17** (or calculating values with the **Clausius–Clapeyron equation** as discussed in Section 10.5), we find that boiling occurs at 365.3 K (92.2 °C), where $P°_{benzene} = 1084$ mm Hg and $P°_{toluene} = 436$ mm Hg:

$$P_{mixt} = X \cdot P°_{benzene} + X \cdot P°_{toluene}$$
$$= (0.500)(1084 \text{ mm Hg}) + (0.500)(436 \text{ mm Hg})$$
$$= 542 \text{ mm Hg} + 218 \text{ mm Hg}$$
$$= 760 \text{ mm Hg}$$

▲ Distillation of petroleum into fractions according to boiling point is carried out in the large towers of this refinery.

Remember...

The **Clausius–Clapeyron equation** describes the relationship between vapor pressure and heat of vaporization, according to the expression $\ln P_{vap} = (-\Delta H_{vap}/R)(1/T) + C$. (Section 10.5)

Figure 11.17
Vapor-pressure curves for pure benzene (blue), pure toluene (red), and a 1:1 mixture of the two (green).

Although the starting *liquid* mixture of benzene and toluene has a 1:1 molar composition, the composition of the *vapor* is not 1:1. Of the 760 mm Hg total vapor pressure for the boiling mixture, 542/760 = 71.3% is due to benzene and 218/760 = 28.7% is due to toluene. If we now condense the vapor, the liquid we get has this same 71.3:28.7 composition. On boiling this new liquid mixture, the composition of the vapor now becomes 86.4% benzene and 13.6% toluene. A third condense/boil cycle brings the composition of the vapor to 94.4% benzene/5.6% toluene, and so on through further cycles until the desired level of purity is reached.

Fractional distillation can be represented on a liquid/vapor phase diagram by plotting temperature versus composition, as shown in **Figure 11.18**. The lower region of the diagram represents the liquid phase, and the upper region represents the vapor phase. Between the two is a thin equilibrium region where liquid and vapor coexist.

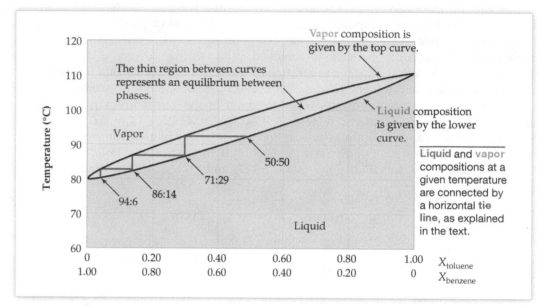

Figure 11.18

A phase diagram of temperature versus composition (mole fraction) for a mixture of benzene and toluene.

To understand how the diagram works, let's imagine starting in the middle of Figure 11.18 with the 50:50 benzene/toluene mixture and heating it to its boiling point (92.2 °C on the diagram). The lower curve represents the liquid composition (50:50), but the upper curve represents the vapor composition (approximately 71:29 at 92.2 °C). The two points are connected by a short horizontal line called a *tie line* to indicate that the temperature is the same at both points. Condensing the 71:29 vapor mixture by lowering the temperature gives a 71:29 liquid mixture that, when heated to *its* boiling point (86.6 °C), has an 86:14 vapor composition, as represented by another tie line. In essence, fractional distillation is simply a stairstep walk across successive tie lines in whatever number of steps is necessary to reach the desired purity.

In practice, the successive boil/condense cycles occur naturally in the distillation column, and there is no need to isolate liquid mixtures at intermediate stages of purification. Fractional distillation is therefore relatively simple to carry out and is used on a daily basis in refineries, chemical plants, and laboratories throughout the world (**Figure 11.19**).

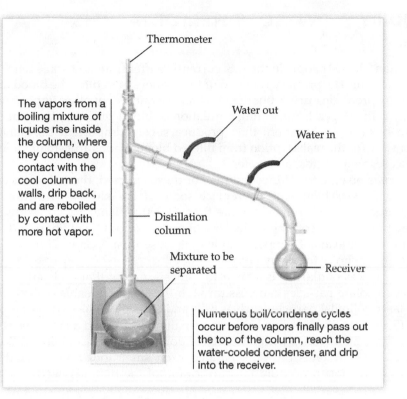

Figure 11.19
A simple fractional distillation column used in a chemistry laboratory.

Thermometer

The vapors from a boiling mixture of liquids rise inside the column, where they condense on contact with the cool column walls, drip back, and are reboiled by contact with more hot vapor.

Water out

Water in

Distillation column

Mixture to be separated

Receiver

Numerous boil/condense cycles occur before vapors finally pass out the top of the column, reach the water-cooled condenser, and drip into the receiver.

CONCEPTUAL PROBLEM 11.27   The following graph is a phase diagram of temperature versus composition for mixtures of the two liquids chloroform and dichloromethane.

(a) Label the regions on the diagram corresponding to liquid and vapor.
(b) Assume that you begin with a mixture of 60% chloroform and 40% dichloromethane. At what approximate temperature will the mixture begin to boil? Mark as point **A** on the diagram the liquid composition at the boiling point, and mark as point **B** the vapor composition at the boiling point.
(c) Assume that the vapor at point **B** condenses and is reboiled. Mark as point **C** on the diagram the liquid composition of the condensed vapor and as point **D** on the diagram the vapor composition of the reboiled material.
(d) What will the approximate composition of the liquid be after carrying out two cycles of boiling and condensing?

INQUIRY HOW DOES HEMODIALYSIS CLEANSE THE BLOOD?

▲ Hemodialysis on this artificial kidney machine cleanses the blood of individuals whose kidneys no longer function.

More than 330,000 people in the U.S. currently suffer from end-stage renal disease, or kidney failure. The primary function of the kidneys is to filter the blood and remove wastes by producing urine, but they also have a number of other important functions on which life depends, including regulation of blood pressure, body pH, and electrolyte balance. In addition, they produce several important hormones and are responsible for the reabsorption from filtered blood of ions and small molecules such as glucose, amino acids, and water.

There is no cure for kidney failure. For those afflicted, the only choices are regular hemodialysis treatments to replace some of the kidney's functions or organ transplantation. Unfortunately, more than 71,000 patients are currently awaiting a kidney transplant according to the United Network for Organ Sharing (UNOS), and the number of available organs is nowhere close to sufficient. Thus, dialysis is the only realistic choice for many people.

The process of dialysis is similar to osmosis, except that both solvent molecules and small solute particles can pass through the semipermeable dialysis membrane. Only large colloidal particles such as cells and large molecules such as proteins can't pass. (The exact dividing line between a small molecule and a large one is imprecise, and dialysis membranes with a variety of pore sizes can be obtained.) Because they don't dialyze, proteins can be separated from small ions and molecules, making dialysis a valuable procedure for purification of the proteins needed in laboratory studies.

The most important medical use of dialysis is in artificial kidney machines, where *hemodialysis* is used to cleanse the blood of patients, removing waste products like urea and controlling the potassium/sodium ion balance. Blood is diverted from the body and pumped through a dialysis tube suspended in a solution formulated to contain many of the same components as blood plasma. These substances—$NaCl$, $NaHCO_3$, KCl, and glucose—have the same concentrations in the dialysis solution as they do in blood, so that they have no net passage through the membrane.

Small waste products pass through the dialysis membrane from the blood to the solution side, where they are washed away, but cells, proteins, and other important blood components are prevented by their size from passing through the membrane. A typical hemodialysis treatment lasts for approximately 3–4 hours, and treatments are usually repeated 3–4 times per week.

And by the way: Please consider signing the necessary authorization card indicating your willingness to become an organ donor. In most states, all that's needed is to sign the back of your driver's license.

▸ **PROBLEM 11.28** What is the difference between a dialysis membrane and the typical semipermeable membrane used for osmosis?

SUMMARY

Solutions are homogeneous mixtures that contain particles the size of a typical ion or small molecule. Any one state of matter can mix with any other state, leading to seven possible kinds of solutions. For solutions in which a gas or solid is dissolved in a liquid, the dissolved substance is called the **solute** and the liquid is called the **solvent**.

The dissolution of a solute in a solvent has associated with it a free-energy change, $\Delta G = \Delta H - T\Delta S$. The enthalpy change is the **enthalpy of solution (ΔH_{soln})**, and the entropy change is the **entropy of solution (ΔS_{soln})**. Enthalpies of solution can be either positive or negative, depending on the relative strengths of solvent–solvent, solute–solute, and solvent–solute intermolecular forces. Entropies of solution are usually positive because molecular randomness increases when a pure solute dissolves in a pure solvent.

The concentration of a solution can be expressed in many ways, including **molarity** (moles of solute per liter of solution), **mole fraction** (moles of solute per mole of solution), **mass percent** (mass of solute per mass of solution times 100%), and **molality** (moles of solute per kilogram of solvent). When equilibrium is reached and no further solute dissolves in a given amount of solvent, a solution is said to be **saturated**. Solubilities are usually temperature-dependent, although often not in a simple way. Gas solubilities usually decrease with increasing temperature, but the solubilities of solids can either increase or decrease. The solubilities of gases also depend on pressure. According to **Henry's law** the solubility of a gas in a liquid at a given temperature is proportional to the partial pressure of the gas over the solution.

In comparison with a pure solvent, a solution has a lower vapor pressure at a given temperature, a lower freezing point, and a higher boiling point. In addition, a solution that is separated from solvent by a semipermeable membrane gives rise to the phenomenon of **osmosis**. All four of these properties of solutions depend only on the concentration of dissolved solute particles rather than on the chemical identity of those particles and are therefore called **colligative properties**. The fundamental cause of all colligative properties is the same: the higher entropy of the solvent in a solution relative to that of the pure solvent.

Colligative properties have many practical uses, including the melting of snow by salt, the desalination of seawater by reverse osmosis, the separation and purification of volatile liquids by fractional distillation, and the determination of molecular mass by osmotic pressure measurement.

KEY WORDS

colligative property *406*
colloid *393*
enthalpy of solution
     (ΔH_{soln}) *394*
entropy of solution
     (ΔS_{soln}) *394*
fractional distillation *421*

Henry's law *404*
mass percent (mass %) *399*
miscible *404*
molal boiling-point-elevation
     constant (K_b) *414*
molal freezing-point-depres-
     sion constant (K_f) *414*

molality (m) *400*
osmosis *417*
osmotic pressure (Π) *417*
parts per billion (ppb) *399*
parts per million (ppm) *399*
Raoult's law *407*
saturated *403*

solute *393*
solution *393*
solvent *393*
supersaturated *403*
van't Hoff factor (i) *408*

CONCEPTUAL PROBLEMS

Problems 11.1–11.28 appear within the chapter.

11.29 The following phase diagram shows part of the liquid/vapor phase-transition boundaries for pure ether and a solution of a nonvolatile solute in ether.

(a) What is the approximate normal boiling point of pure ether?

(b) What is the approximate molal concentration of the solute? [K_b for ether is 2.02 (°C · kg)/mol.]

11.30 Rank the situations represented by the following drawings according to increasing entropy.

(a) **(b)** **(c)**

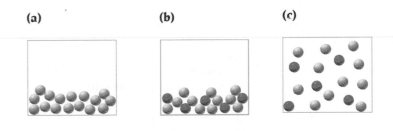

11.31 The following diagram shows a close-up view of part of the vapor-pressure curves for a solvent (red curve) and a solution of the solvent with a second liquid (green curve). Is the second liquid more volatile or less volatile than the solvent?

11.32 Assume that two liquids are separated by a semipermeable membrane. Make a drawing that shows the situation after equilibrium is reached.

Before equilibrium

11.33 Assume that you are distilling a 1:1 molar mixture of chloroform ($CHCl_3$; bp = 61.7 °C) and tetrachloromethane (CCl_4; bp = 76.5 °C). After the mixture has been heated to its boiling point and vapor has reached the top of the column, predict the approximate temperatures at the three points indicated.

Thermometer

1

2 — Distillation column

3

Heater

11.34 Two beakers, one with pure water (blue) and the other with a solution of NaCl in water (green), are placed in a closed container as represented by drawing **(a)**. Which of the drawings **(b)**–**(d)** represents what the beakers will look like after a substantial amount of time has passed?

(a)   (b)

(c)   (d)

11.35 A phase diagram of temperature versus composition for a mixture of the two volatile liquids hexane (bp = 69 °C) and decane (bp = 126 °C) is shown. Assume that you begin with a mixture containing 0.60 mol of decane and 0.40 mol of hexane.

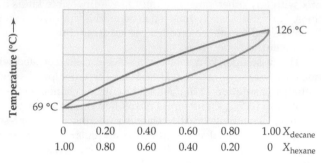

(a) What region on the diagram corresponds to vapor, and what region corresponds to liquid?

(b) At what approximate temperature will the mixture begin to boil? Mark as point **A** on the diagram the liquid composition at the boiling point, and mark as point **B** the vapor composition at the boiling point.

(c) Assume that the vapor at point **B** condenses and is reboiled. Mark as point **C** on the diagram the liquid composition of the condensed vapor and as point **D** on the diagram the vapor composition of the reboiled material.

11.36 The following phase diagram shows a very small part of the solid–liquid phase-transition boundaries for two solutions of equal concentration. Substance **A** has $i = 1$, and substance **B** has $i = 3$.

(a) Which line, red or blue, represents a solution of **A**, and which represents a solution of **B**?

(b) What is the approximate melting point of the pure liquid solvent?

(c) What is the approximate molal concentration of each solution, assuming the solvent has $K_f = 3.0$ °C/m?

11.37 The following phase diagram shows part of the liquid–vapor phase-transition boundaries for two solutions of equal concentration, one containing a nonvolatile solute and the other containing a volatile solute whose vapor pressure at a given temperature is approximately half that of the pure solvent.

(a) Which curve, red or green, represents the solution of the nonvolatile solute and which represents the solution of the volatile solute?

(b) Draw on the diagram the approximate position of the vapor-pressure curve for the pure solvent.

(c) Based on your drawing, what is the approximate molal concentration of the nonvolatile solute, assuming the solvent has $K_b = 2.0\ ^\circ C/m$?

(d) Based on your drawing, what is the approximate normal boiling point of the pure solvent?

SECTION PROBLEMS

Solutions and Energy Changes (Sections 11.1 and 11.2)

11.38 If a single 5 g block of NaCl is placed in water, it dissolves slowly, but if 5 g of powdered NaCl is placed in water, it dissolves rapidly. Explain.

11.39 Br_2 is much more soluble in tetrachloromethane, CCl_4, than in water. Explain.

11.40 Why do ionic substances with higher lattice energies tend to be less soluble in water than substances with lower lattice energies?

11.41 Which would you expect to have the larger hydration energy, SO_4^{2-} or ClO_4^-? Explain.

11.42 Ethyl alcohol, CH_3CH_2OH, is miscible with water at 20 °C, but pentyl alcohol, $CH_3CH_2CH_2CH_2CH_2OH$, is soluble in water only to the extent of 2.7 g/100 mL. Explain.

11.43 Pentyl alcohol (Problem 11.42) is miscible with octane, C_8H_{18}, but methyl alcohol, CH_3OH, is insoluble in octane. Explain.

11.44 The dissolution of $CaCl_2(s)$ in water is exothermic, with $\Delta H_{soln} = -81.3\ kJ/mol$. If you were to prepare a 1.00 m solution of $CaCl_2$ beginning with water at 25.0 °C, what would the final temperature of the solution be in °C? Assume that the specific heats of both pure H_2O and the solution are the same, 4.18 J/(K·g).

11.45 The dissolution of $NH_4ClO_4(s)$ in water is endothermic, with $\Delta H_{soln} = +33.5\ kJ/mol$. If you prepare a 1.00 m solution of NH_4ClO_4 beginning with water at 25.0 °C, what is the final temperature of the solution in °C? Assume that the specific heats of both pure H_2O and the solution are the same, 4.18 J/(K·g).

Units of Concentration (Section 11.3)

11.46 Propranolol ($C_{16}H_{21}NO_2$), a so-called beta-blocker that is used for treatment of high blood pressure, is effective at a blood plasma concentration of 50 ng/L. Express this concentration of propranolol in the following units:

(a) parts per billion (assume a plasma density of 1.025 g/mL)

(b) molarity

11.47 Residues of the herbicide atrazine ($C_8H_{14}ClN_5$) in water can be detected at concentrations as low as 0.050 μg/L. Express this concentration of atrazine in the following units:

(a) parts per billion (assume a solution density of 1.00 g/mL)

(b) molarity

11.48 How would you prepare each of the following solutions?

(a) A 0.150 M solution of glucose in water

(b) A 1.135 m solution of KBr in water

(c) A solution of methyl alcohol (methanol) and water in which $X_{methanol} = 0.15$ and $X_{water} = 0.85$

11.49 How would you prepare each of the following solutions?

(a) 100 mL of a 155 ppm solution of urea, CH_4N_2O, in water

(b) 100 mL of an aqueous solution whose K^+ concentration is 0.075 M

11.50 How would you prepare 165 mL of a 0.0268 M solution of benzoic acid ($C_7H_6O_2$) in chloroform ($CHCl_3$)?

11.51 How would you prepare 165 mL of a 0.0268 m solution of benzoic acid ($C_7H_6O_2$) in chloroform ($CHCl_3$)?

Benzoic acid

11.52 Which of the following solutions is more concentrated?

(a) 0.500 M KCl or 0.500 mass % KCl in water

(b) 1.75 M glucose or 1.75 m glucose in water

11.53 Which of the following solutions has the higher molarity?

(a) 10 ppm KI in water or 10,000 ppb KBr in water

(b) 0.25 mass % KCl in water or 0.25 mass % citric acid ($C_6H_8O_7$) in water

11.54 What is the mass percent concentration of the following solutions?

(a) Dissolve 0.655 mol of citric acid, $C_6H_8O_7$, in 1.00 kg of water.

(b) Dissolve 0.135 mg of KBr in 5.00 mL of water.

(c) Dissolve 5.50 g of aspirin, $C_9H_8O_4$, in 145 g of dichloromethane, CH_2Cl_2.

11.55 What is the molality of each solution prepared in Problem 11.54?

11.56 The so-called ozone layer in the Earth's stratosphere has an average total pressure of 10 mm Hg (1.3×10^{-2} atm). The partial pressure of ozone in the layer is about 1.2×10^{-6} mm Hg (1.6×10^{-9} atm). What is the concentration of ozone in parts per million, assuming that the average molar mass of air is 29 g/mol?

11.57 Persons are medically considered to have lead poisoning if they have a concentration of greater than 10 micrograms of lead per deciliter of blood. What is this concentration in parts per billion?

11.58 What is the concentration of each of the following solutions?

(a) The molality of a solution prepared by dissolving 25.0 g of H_2SO_4 in 1.30 L of water

(b) The mole fraction of each component of a solution prepared by dissolving 2.25 g of nicotine, $C_{10}H_{14}N_2$, in 80.0 g of CH_2Cl_2

11.59 Household bleach is a 5.0 mass % aqueous solution of sodium hypochlorite, NaOCl. What is the molality of the bleach? What is the mole fraction of NaOCl in the bleach?

11.60 The density of a 16.0 mass % solution of sulfuric acid in water is 1.1094 g/mL at 25.0 °C. What is the molarity of the solution?

11.61 Ethylene glycol, $C_2H_6O_2$, is the principal constituent of automobile antifreeze. If the density of a 40.0 mass % solution of ethylene glycol in water is 1.0514 g/mL at 20 °C, what is the molarity?

Ethylene glycol

11.62 What is the molality of the 40.0 mass % ethylene glycol solution used for automobile antifreeze (Problem 11.61)?

11.63 What is the molality of the 16.0 mass % solution of sulfuric acid in Problem 11.60?

11.64 Nalorphine ($C_{19}H_{21}NO_3$), a relative of morphine, is used to combat withdrawal symptoms in narcotics users. How many grams of a $1.3 \times 10^{-3}\, m$ aqueous solution of nalorphine are needed to obtain a dose of 1.5 mg?

Nalorphine

11.65 How many grams of water should you add to 32.5 g of sucrose, $C_{12}H_{22}O_{11}$, to get a 0.850 m solution?

11.66 A 0.944 M solution of glucose, $C_6H_{12}O_6$, in water has a density of 1.0624 g/mL at 20 °C. What is the concentration of this solution in the following units?
  (a) Mole fraction **(b)** Mass percent **(c)** Molality

11.67 Lactose, $C_{12}H_{22}O_{11}$, is a naturally occurring sugar found in mammalian milk. A 0.335 M solution of lactose in water has a density of 1.0432 g/mL at 20 °C. What is the concentration of this solution in the following units?
  (a) Mole fraction **(b)** Mass percent **(c)** Molality

Solubility and Henry's Law (Section 11.4)

11.68 Look at the solubility graph in Figure 11.6 on page 404, and estimate which member of each of the following pairs has the higher molar solubility at the given temperature:
  (a) $CuSO_4$ or NH_4Cl at 60 °C
  (b) CH_3CO_2Na or glucose at 20 °C

11.69 Look at the solubility graph in Figure 11.6, and estimate which member of each of the following pairs has the higher molar solubility at the given temperature:

  (a) NaCl or NH_4Cl at 40 °C
  (b) K_2SO_4 or $CuSO_4$ at 20 °C

11.70 Vinyl chloride ($H_2C{=}CHCl$), the starting material from which PVC polymer is made, has a Henry's-law constant of 0.091 mol/(L·atm) at 25 °C. What is the solubility of vinyl chloride in water in mol/L at 25 °C and a partial pressure of 0.75 atm?

11.71 Hydrogen sulfide, H_2S, is a toxic gas responsible for the odor of rotten eggs. The solubility of $H_2S(g)$ in water at STP is 0.195 M. What is the Henry's-law constant of H_2S at 0 °C? What is the solubility of H_2S in water at 0 °C and a partial pressure of 25.5 mm Hg?

11.72 Fish generally need an O_2 concentration in water of at least 4 mg/L for survival. What partial pressure of oxygen above the water in atmospheres at 0 °C is needed to obtain this concentration? The solubility of O_2 in water at 0 °C and 1 atm partial pressure is 2.21×10^{-3} mol/L.

11.73 At an altitude of 10,000 ft, the partial pressure of oxygen in the lungs is about 68 mm Hg. What is the concentration in mg/L of dissolved O_2 in blood (or water) at this partial pressure and a normal body temperature of 37 °C? The solubility of O_2 in water at 37 °C and 1 atm partial pressure is 1.93×10^{-3} mol/L.

11.74 Sulfur hexafluoride, which is used as a nonflammable insulator in high-voltage transformers, has a Henry's-law constant of 2.4×10^{-4} mol/(L·atm) at 25 °C. What is the solubility in mol/L of sulfur hexafluoride in water at 25 °C and a partial pressure of 2.00 atm?

11.75 The nonstick polymer Teflon is made from tetrafluoroethylene, C_2F_4. If C_2F_4 is a gas that dissolves in water at 298 K to the extent of 1.01×10^{-3} M with a partial pressure of 0.63 atm, what is its Henry's-law constant at 298 K?

Colligative Properties (Section 11.5–11.8)

11.76 When 1 mol of NaCl is added to 1 L of water, the boiling point increases. When 1 mol of methyl alcohol is added to 1 L of water, the boiling point decreases. Explain.

11.77 When 100 mL of 9 M H_2SO_4 at 0 °C is added to 100 mL of liquid water at 0 °C, the temperature rises to 12 °C. When 100 mL of 9 M H_2SO_4 at 0 °C is added to 100 g of solid ice at 0 °C, the temperature falls to −12 °C. Explain the difference in behavior.

11.78 Draw a phase diagram showing how the phase boundaries differ for a pure solvent compared with a solution.

11.79 A solution concentration must be expressed in molality when considering boiling-point elevation or freezing-point depression but can be expressed in molarity when considering osmotic pressure. Why?

11.80 What is the vapor pressure in mm Hg of the following solutions, each of which contains a nonvolatile solute? The vapor pressure of water at 45.0 °C is 71.93 mm Hg.
  (a) A solution of 10.0 g of urea, CH_4N_2O, in 150.0 g of water at 45.0 °C
  (b) A solution of 10.0 g of LiCl in 150.0 g of water at 45.0 °C, assuming complete dissociation

11.81 What is the vapor pressure in mm Hg of a solution of 16.0 g of glucose ($C_6H_{12}O_6$) in 80.0 g of methanol (CH_3OH) at 27 °C? The vapor pressure of pure methanol at 27 °C is 140 mm Hg.

11.82 What is the boiling point in °C of each of the solutions in Problem 11.80? For water, $K_b = 0.51$ (°C·kg)/mol.

11.83 What is the freezing point in °C of each of the solutions in Problem 11.80? For water, $K_f = 1.86\ (°C \cdot kg)/mol$.

11.84 A 1.0 m solution of K_2SO_4 in water has a freezing point of $-4.3\ °C$. What is the value of the van't Hoff factor i for K_2SO_4?

11.85 The van't Hoff factor for KCl is $i = 1.85$. What is the boiling point of a 0.75 m solution of KCl in water? For water, $K_b = 0.51\ (°C \cdot kg)/mol$.

11.86 Heptane (C_7H_{16}) and octane (C_8H_{18}) are constituents of gasoline. At 80.0 °C, the vapor pressure of heptane is 428 mm Hg and the vapor pressure of octane is 175 mm Hg. What is $X_{heptane}$ in a mixture of heptane and octane that has a vapor pressure of 305 mm Hg at 80.0 °C?

11.87 Cyclopentane (C_5H_{10}) and cyclohexane (C_6H_{12}) are volatile, nonpolar hydrocarbons. At 30.0 °C, the vapor pressure of cyclopentane is 385 mm Hg and the vapor pressure of cyclohexane is 122 mm Hg. What is $X_{pentane}$ in a mixture of C_5H_{10} and C_6H_{12} that has a vapor pressure of 212 mm Hg at 30.0 °C?

11.88 Acetone, C_3H_6O, and ethyl acetate, $C_4H_8O_2$, are organic liquids often used as solvents. At 30 °C, the vapor pressure of acetone is 285 mm Hg and the vapor pressure of ethyl acetate is 118 mm Hg. What is the vapor pressure in mm Hg at 30 °C of a solution prepared by dissolving 25.0 g of acetone in 25.0 g of ethyl acetate?

Acetone   Ethyl acetate

11.89 The industrial solvents chloroform, $CHCl_3$, and dichloromethane, CH_2Cl_2, are prepared commercially by reaction of methane with chlorine, followed by fractional distillation of the product mixture. At 25 °C, the vapor pressure of $CHCl_3$ is 205 mm Hg and the vapor pressure of CH_2Cl_2 is 415 mm Hg. What is the vapor pressure in mm Hg at 25 °C of a mixture of 15.0 g of $CHCl_3$ and 37.5 g of CH_2Cl_2?

11.90 What is the mole fraction of each component in the liquid mixture in Problem 11.88, and what is the mole fraction of each component in the vapor at 30 °C?

11.91 What is the mole fraction of each component in the liquid mixture in Problem 11.89, and what is the mole fraction of each component in the vapor at 25 °C?

11.92 A solution prepared by dissolving 5.00 g of aspirin, $C_9H_8O_4$, in 215 g of chloroform has a normal boiling point that is elevated by $\Delta T = 0.47\ °C$ over that of pure chloroform. What is the value of the molal boiling-point-elevation constant for chloroform?

11.93 A solution prepared by dissolving 3.00 g of ascorbic acid (vitamin C, $C_6H_8O_6$) in 50.0 g of acetic acid has a freezing point that is depressed by $\Delta T = 1.33\ °C$ below that of pure acetic acid. What is the value of the molal freezing-point-depression constant for acetic acid?

11.94 A solution of citric acid, $C_6H_8O_7$, in 50.0 g of acetic acid has a boiling point elevation of $\Delta T = 1.76\ °C$. What is the molality of the solution if the molal boiling-point-elevation constant for acetic acid is $K_b = 3.07\ (°C \cdot kg)/mol$?

11.95 What is the normal boiling point in °C of ethyl alcohol if a solution prepared by dissolving 26.0 g of glucose ($C_6H_{12}O_6$) in 285 g of ethyl alcohol has a boiling point of 79.1 °C? See Table 11.4 on page 414 to find K_b for ethyl alcohol.

11.96 What osmotic pressure in atmospheres would you expect for each of the following solutions?
(a) 5.00 g of NaCl in 350.0 mL of aqueous solution at 50 °C
(b) 6.33 g of sodium acetate, CH_3CO_2Na, in 55.0 mL of aqueous solution at 10 °C

11.97 What osmotic pressure in mm Hg would you expect for an aqueous solution of 11.5 mg of insulin (mol. mass = 5990 amu) in 6.60 mL of solution at 298 K? What would the height of the water column be in meters? The density of mercury is 13.534 g/mL at 298 K.

11.98 A solution of an unknown molecular substance in water at 300 K gives rise to an osmotic pressure of 4.85 atm. What is the molarity of the solution?

11.99 Human blood gives rise to an osmotic pressure of approximately 7.7 atm at body temperature, 37.0 °C. What must the molarity of an intravenous glucose solution be to give rise to the same osmotic pressure as blood?

Uses of Colligative Properties (Section 11.9)

11.100 When salt is spread on snow-covered roads at $-2\ °C$, the snow melts. When salt is spread on snow-covered roads at $-30\ °C$, nothing happens. Explain.

11.101 If cost per gram were not a concern, which of the following substances would be the most efficient per unit mass for melting snow from sidewalks and roads: glucose ($C_6H_{12}O_6$), LiCl, NaCl, or $CaCl_2$? Explain.

11.102 Cellobiose is a sugar obtained by degradation of cellulose. If 200.0 mL of an aqueous solution containing 1.500 g of cellobiose at 25.0 °C gives rise to an osmotic pressure of 407.2 mm Hg, what is the molecular mass of cellobiose?

11.103 Met-enkephalin is one of the so-called endorphins, a class of naturally occurring morphinelike chemicals in the brain. What is the molecular mass of met-enkephalin if 20.0 mL of an aqueous solution containing 15.0 mg of met-enkephalin at 298 K supports a column of water 32.9 cm high? The density of mercury at 298 K is 13.534 g/mL.

11.104 The freezing point of a solution prepared by dissolving 1.00 mol of hydrogen fluoride, HF, in 500 g of water is $-3.8\ °C$, but the freezing point of a solution prepared by dissolving 1.00 mol of hydrogen chloride, HCl, in 500 g of water is $-7.4\ °C$. Explain.

11.105 The boiling point of a solution prepared by dissolving 71 g of Na_2SO_4 in 1.00 kg of water is 100.8 °C. Explain.

11.106 Elemental analysis of β-carotene, a dietary source of vitamin A, shows that it contains 10.51% H and 89.49% C. Dissolving 0.0250 g of β-carotene in 1.50 g of camphor gives a freezing-point depression of 1.17 °C. What are the molecular mass and formula of β-carotene? [K_f for camphor is 37.7 $(°C \cdot kg)/mol$.]

11.107 Lysine, one of the amino acid building blocks found in proteins, contains 49.29% C, 9.65% H, 19.16% N, and 21.89% O by elemental analysis. A solution prepared by dissolving 30.0 mg of lysine in 1.200 g of the organic solvent biphenyl gives a freezing-point depression of 1.37 °C. What are the molecular mass and formula of lysine? [K_f for biphenyl is 8.00 $(°C \cdot kg)/mol$.]

CHAPTER PROBLEMS

11.108 How many grams of ethylene glycol (automobile antifreeze, $C_2H_6O_2$) dissolved in 3.55 kg of water is needed to lower the freezing point of water in an automobile radiator to $-22.0\ °C$?

11.109 When 1 mL of toluene is added to 100 mL of benzene (bp 80.1 °C), the boiling point of the benzene solution rises, but when 1 mL of benzene is added to 100 mL of toluene (bp 110.6 °C), the boiling point of the toluene solution falls. Explain.

11.110 When solid $CaCl_2$ is added to liquid water, the temperature rises. When solid $CaCl_2$ is added to ice at 0 °C, the temperature falls. Explain.

11.111 Silver chloride has a solubility of 0.007 mg/mL in water at 5 °C. What is the osmotic pressure in atmospheres of a saturated solution of AgCl?

11.112 When a 2.850 g mixture of the sugars sucrose ($C_{12}H_{22}O_{11}$) and fructose ($C_6H_{12}O_6$) was dissolved in water to a volume of 1.50 L, the resultant solution gave an osmotic pressure of 0.1843 atm at 298.0 K. What is X_{sucrose} of the mixture?

11.113 Glycerol ($C_3H_8O_3$) and diethylformamide ($C_5H_{11}NO$) are nonvolatile, miscible liquids. If the volume of a solution made by dissolving 10.208 g of a glycerol–diethylformamide mixture in water is 1.75 L and the solution has an osmotic pressure of 1.466 atm at 298.0 K, what is X_{glycerol} of the mixture?

11.114 How many grams of naphthalene, $C_{10}H_8$ (commonly used as household mothballs), should be added to 150.0 g of benzene to depress its freezing point by 0.35 °C? See Table 11.4 on page 414 to find K_f for benzene.

11.115 Bromine is sometimes used as a solution in tetrachloromethane, CCl_4. What is the vapor pressure in mm Hg of a solution of 1.50 g of Br_2 in 145.0 g of CCl_4 at 300 K? The vapor pressure of pure bromine at 300 K is 30.5 kPa, and the vapor pressure of CCl_4 is 16.5 kPa.

11.116 Assuming that seawater is a 3.5 mass % solution of NaCl and that its density is 1.00 g/mL, calculate both its boiling point and its freezing point in °C.

11.117 There's actually much more in seawater than just dissolved NaCl. Major ions present include 19,000 ppm Cl^-, 10,500 ppm Na^+, 2650 ppm SO_4^{2-}, 1350 ppm Mg^{2+}, 400 ppm Ca^{2+}, 380 ppm K^+, 140 ppm HCO_3^-, and 65 ppm Br^-.

(a) What is the total molality of all ions present in seawater?

(b) Assuming molality and molarity to be equal, what amount of osmotic pressure in atmospheres would seawater give rise to at 300 K?

11.118 Rubbing alcohol is a 90 mass % solution of isopropyl alcohol, C_3H_8O, in water.

(a) How many grams of rubbing alcohol contains 10.5 g of isopropyl alcohol?

(b) How many moles of isopropyl alcohol are in 50.0 g of rubbing alcohol?

11.119 Although not particularly convenient, it's possible to use osmotic pressure to measure temperature. What is the Kelvin temperature if a solution prepared by dissolving 17.5 mg of glucose ($C_6H_{12}O_6$) in 50.0 mL of aqueous solution gives rise to an osmotic pressure of 37.8 mm Hg?

11.120 The van't Hoff factor for $CaCl_2$ is 2.71. What is its mass % in an aqueous solution that has $T_f = -1.14\ °C$?

11.121 What is the van't Hoff factor for K_2SO_4 in an aqueous solution that is 5.00% K_2SO_4 by mass and freezes at $-1.21\ °C$?

11.122 If the van't Hoff factor for LiCl in a 0.62 m solution is 1.96, what is the vapor pressure depression in mm Hg of the solution at 298 K? (The vapor pressure of water at 298 K is 23.76 mm Hg.)

11.123 What is the value of the van't Hoff factor for KCl if a 1.00 m aqueous solution shows a vapor pressure depression of 0.734 mm Hg at 298 °C? (The vapor pressure of water at 298 K is 23.76 mm Hg.)

11.124 The steroid hormone *estradiol* contains only C, H, and O; combustion analysis of a 3.47 mg sample yields 10.10 mg CO_2 and 2.76 mg H_2O. On dissolving 7.55 mg of estradiol in 0.500 g of camphor, the melting point of camphor is depressed by 2.10 °C. What is the molecular mass of estradiol, and what is a probable formula? [For camphor, $K_f = 37.7\ (°C \cdot kg)/mol$.]

Estradiol

11.125 Many acids are partially dissociated into ions in aqueous solution. Trichloroacetic acid (CCl_3CO_2H), for instance, is partially dissociated in water according to the equation

$$CCl_3CO_2H(aq) \rightleftharpoons H^+(aq) + CCl_3CO_2^-(aq)$$

What is the percentage of molecules dissociated if the freezing point of a 1.00 m solution of trichloroacetic acid in water is $-2.53\ °C$?

11.126 Addition of 50.00 mL of 2.238 m H_2SO_4 (solution density = 1.1243 g/mL) to 50.00 mL of 2.238 M $BaCl_2$ gives a white precipitate.

(a) What is the mass of the precipitate in grams?

(b) If you filter the mixture and add more H_2SO_4 solution to the filtrate, would you obtain more precipitate? Explain.

11.127 A solid mixture of KCl, KNO_3, and $Ba(NO_3)_2$ is 20.92 mass % chlorine, and a 1.000 g sample of the mixture in 500.0 mL of aqueous solution at 25 °C has an osmotic pressure of 744.7 mm Hg. What are the mass percents of KCl, KNO_3, and $Ba(NO_3)_2$ in the mixture?

11.128 A solution of LiCl in a mixture of water and methanol (CH_3OH) has a vapor pressure of 39.4 mm Hg at 17 °C and 68.2 mm Hg at 27 °C. The vapor pressure of pure water is 14.5 mm Hg at 17 °C and 26.8 mm Hg at 27 °C, and the vapor pressure of pure methanol is 82.5 mm Hg at 17 °C and 140.3 mm Hg at 27 °C. What is the composition of the solution in mass percent?

11.129 An aqueous solution of KI has a freezing point of −1.95 °C and an osmotic pressure of 25.0 atm at 25.0 °C. Assuming that the KI completely dissociates in water, what is the density of the solution?

11.130 An aqueous solution of a certain organic compound has a density of 1.063 g/mL, an osmotic pressure of 12.16 atm at 25.0 °C, and a freezing point of −1.03 °C. The compound is known not to dissociate in water. What is the molar mass of the compound?

11.131 At 60 °C, compound X has a vapor pressure of 96 mm Hg, benzene (C_6H_6) has a vapor pressure of 395 mm Hg, and a 50:50 mixture by mass of benzene and X has a vapor pressure of 299 mm Hg. What is the molar mass of X?

11.132 An aqueous solution containing 100.0 g of NaCl and 100.0 g of $CaCl_2$ has a volume of 1.00 L and a density of 1.15 g/mL. The vapor pressure of pure water at 25 °C is 23.8 mm Hg, and you can assume complete dissociation for both solutes.

(a) What is the boiling point of the solution?

(b) What is the vapor pressure of the solution at 25 °C?

11.133 Iodic acid, HIO_3, is a weak acid that undergoes only partial dissociation in water. If a 1.00 M solution of HIO_3 has a density of 1.07 g/mL and a freezing point of −2.78 °C, what percent of the HIO_3 is dissociated?

11.134 A 1.24 M solution of KI has a density of 1.15 g/cm^3.

(a) What is the molality of the solution?

(b) What is the freezing point of the solution, assuming complete dissociation of KI?

(c) The actual freezing point of the solution is −4.46 °C. What percent of the KI is dissociated?

11.135 Desert countries like Saudi Arabia have built reverse osmosis plants to produce freshwater from seawater. Assume that seawater has the composition 0.470 M NaCl and 0.068 M $MgCl_2$ and that both compounds are completely dissociated.

(a) What is the osmotic pressure of seawater at 25 °C?

(b) If the reverse osmosis equipment can exert a maximum pressure of 100.0 atm at 25.0 °C, what is the maximum volume of freshwater that can be obtained from 1.00 L of seawater?

11.136 A solution prepared by dissolving 100.0 g of a mixture of sugar ($C_{12}H_{22}O_{11}$) and table salt (NaCl) in 500.0 g of water has a freezing point of −2.25 °C. What is the mass of each individual solute? Assume that NaCl is completely dissociated.

MULTICONCEPT PROBLEMS

11.137 Treatment of 1.385 g of an unknown metal M with an excess of aqueous HCl evolved a gas that was found to have a volume of 382.6 mL at 20.0 °C and 755 mm Hg pressure. Heating the reaction mixture to evaporate the water and remaining HCl then gave a white crystalline compound, MCl_x. After dissolving the compound in 25.0 g of water, the melting point of the resulting solution was −3.53 °C.

(a) How many moles of H_2 gas are evolved?

(b) What mass of MCl_x is formed?

(c) What is the molality of particles (ions) in the solution of MCl_x?

(d) How many moles of ions are in solution?

(e) What are the formula and molecular mass of MCl_x?

(f) What is the identity of the metal M?

11.138 A compound that contains only C and H was burned in excess O_2 to give CO_2 and H_2O. When 0.270 g of the compound was burned, the amount of CO_2 formed reacted completely with 20.0 mL of 2.00 M NaOH solution according to the equation

$$2\,OH^-(aq) + CO_2(g) \longrightarrow CO_3^{2-}(aq) + H_2O(l)$$

When 0.270 g of the compound was dissolved in 50.0 g of camphor, the resulting solution had a freezing point of 177.9 °C. (Pure camphor freezes at 179.8 °C and has $K_f = 37.7\ °C/m$.)

(a) What is the empirical formula of the compound?

(b) What is the molecular mass of the compound?

(c) What is the molecular formula of the compound?

11.139 Combustion analysis of a 36.72 mg sample of the male hormone testosterone gave 106.43 mg CO_2 and 32.100 mg H_2O as the only combustion products. When 5.00 mg of testosterone was dissolved in 15.0 mL of a suitable solvent at 25 °C, an osmotic pressure of 21.5 mm Hg was measured. What is the molecular formula of testosterone?

11.140 When 8.900 g of a mixture of an alkali metal chloride (XCl) and an alkaline earth chloride (YCl_2) was dissolved in 150.0 g of water, the freezing point of the resultant solution was −4.42 °C. Addition of an excess of aqueous $AgNO_3$ to the solution yielded a white precipitate with a mass of 27.575 g. How much of each metal chloride was present in the original mixture, and what are the identities of the two metals X and Y?

11.141 Combustion analysis of a 3.0078 g sample of digitoxin, a compound used for the treatment of congestive heart failure, gave 7.0950 g of CO_2 and 2.2668 g of H_2O. When 0.6617 g of digitoxin was dissolved in water to a total volume of 0.800 L, the osmotic pressure of the solution at 298 K was 0.026 44 atm. What is the molecular formula of digitoxin, which contains only C, H, and O?

CHAPTER 12

Chemical Kinetics

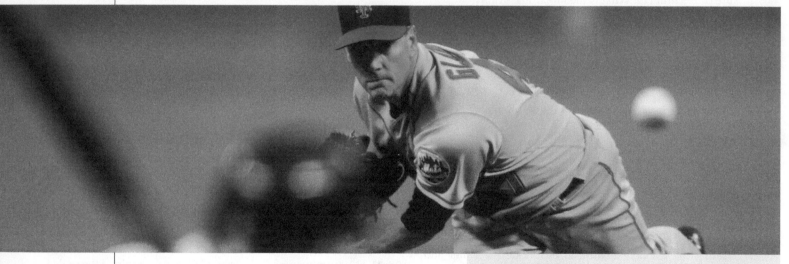

The speed of this pitch is defined as the change in the baseball's location per unit time (meters per second, m/s). Similarly, the speed, or rate, of a chemical reaction is defined as a change in concentration per unit time (molar per second, M/s).

CONTENTS

Chemists ask three fundamental questions when they study chemical reactions: What happens? To what extent does it happen? How fast and by what mechanism does it happen? The answer to the first question is given by the balanced chemical equation, which identifies the reactants, the products, and the stoichiometry of the reaction. The answer to the second question is addressed in Chapter 13, which deals with chemical equilibrium. In this chapter, we'll look at the answer to the third question—the speeds, or rates, and the mechanisms of chemical reactions. The area of chemistry concerned with reaction rates and the sequence of steps by which reactions occur is called **chemical kinetics**.

Chemical kinetics is a subject of crucial environmental, biological, and economic importance. In the upper atmosphere, for example, maintenance or depletion of the ozone layer, which protects us from the sun's harmful ultraviolet radiation, depends on the relative rates of reactions that produce and destroy O_3 molecules. In our bodies, large protein molecules called *enzymes* increase the rates of numerous reactions essential to life processes. In the chemical industry, the profitability of many processes requires fast reaction rates. For example, the economical synthesis of ammonia, used as a fertilizer, depends on the rate at which gaseous N_2 and H_2 can be converted to NH_3.

In this chapter, we'll describe reaction rates and examine how they are affected by variables such as concentrations and temperature. We'll also see how chemists use rate data to propose a *mechanism*, or pathway, by which a reaction takes place. By understanding reaction mechanisms, we can control known reactions and predict new ones.

12.1 REACTION RATES

The rates of chemical reactions differ greatly. Some reactions, such as the combination of sodium and bromine, occur instantly. Other reactions, such as the rusting of iron, are imperceptibly slow.

The reaction between sodium   or   The rusting of iron?
and bromine

◀ Which of these reactions is faster?

To describe a reaction rate quantitatively, we must specify how fast the concentration of a reactant or a product changes per unit time.

$$\text{Rate} = \frac{\text{Concentration change}}{\text{Time change}}$$

Look, for example, at the thermal decomposition of gaseous dinitrogen pentoxide, N_2O_5, to give the brown gas nitrogen dioxide, a common air pollutant, and molecular oxygen:

$$2\,N_2O_5(g) \longrightarrow 4\,NO_2(g) + O_2(g)$$

Colorless   Brown   Colorless

Changes in concentration as a function of time can be determined by measuring the increase in pressure as 2 gas molecules are converted to 5 gas molecules. Alternatively, concentration changes can be monitored by measuring the intensity of the brown color due to NO_2. Reactant and product concentrations as a function of time at 55 °C are listed in Table 12.1.

TABLE 12.1	Concentrations as a Function of Time at 55 °C for the Reaction $2 N_2O_5(g) \longrightarrow 4 NO_2(g) + O_2(g)$		
	Concentration (M)		
Time (s)	N_2O_5	NO_2	O_2
0	0.0200	0	0
100	0.0169	0.0063	0.0016
200	0.0142	0.0115	0.0029
300	0.0120	0.0160	0.0040
400	0.0101	0.0197	0.0049
500	0.0086	0.0229	0.0057
600	0.0072	0.0256	0.0064
700	0.0061	0.0278	0.0070

Note that the concentrations of NO_2 and O_2 increase as the concentration of N_2O_5 decreases.

The **reaction rate** is defined either as the *increase* in the concentration of a *product* per unit time or as the *decrease* in the concentration of a *reactant* per unit time. Let's look first at product formation. In the decomposition of N_2O_5, the rate of formation of O_2 is given by the equation

$$\text{Rate of formation of } O_2 = \frac{\Delta[O_2]}{\Delta t} = \frac{\text{Conc. of } O_2 \text{ at time } t_2 - \text{Conc. of } O_2 \text{ at time } t_1}{t_2 - t_1}$$

where the square brackets surrounding O_2 denote its molar concentration; $\Delta[O_2]$ is the change in the molar concentration of O_2; Δt is the change in the time; and $\Delta[O_2]/\Delta t$ is the average rate of change in the molar concentration of O_2 during the interval from time t_1 to t_2. During the time period 300 to 400 s, for example, the average rate of formation of O_2 is 9×10^{-6} M/s:

$$\text{Rate of formation of } O_2 = \frac{\Delta[O_2]}{\Delta t} = \frac{0.0049 \text{ M} - 0.0040 \text{ M}}{400 \text{ s} - 300 \text{ s}} = 9 \times 10^{-6} \text{ M/s}$$

The most common units of reaction rate are molar per second, M/s, or, equivalently, moles per liter second, mol/(L·s). We define reaction rate in terms of concentration (moles per liter) rather than amount (moles) because we want the rate to be independent of the scale of the reaction. When twice as much 0.0200 M N_2O_5 decomposes in a vessel of twice the volume, twice the number of moles of O_2 form per second, but the number of moles of O_2 *per liter* that form per second is unchanged.

Plotting the data of Table 12.1 to give the three curves in **Figure 12.1** affords additional insight into the concept of a reaction rate. Looking at the time period 300–400 s on the O_2 curve, $\Delta[O_2]$ and Δt are represented, respectively, by the vertical and horizontal sides of a right triangle. The slope of the third side, the hypotenuse of the triangle, is $\Delta[O_2]/\Delta t$, the average rate of O_2 formation during that time period. The steeper the slope of the hypotenuse, the faster the rate. Look, for example, at the triangle defined by $\Delta[NO_2]$ and Δt. The average rate of formation of NO_2 during the time period 300–400 s is 3.7×10^{-5} M/s, which is four times the rate of formation of O_2, in accord with the 4:1 ratio of the coefficients of NO_2 and O_2 in the chemical equation for the decomposition of N_2O_5.

$$\text{Rate of formation of } NO_2 = \frac{\Delta[NO_2]}{\Delta t} = \frac{0.0197 \text{ M} - 0.0160 \text{ M}}{400 \text{ s} - 300 \text{ s}} = 3.7 \times 10^{-5} \text{ M/s}$$

The concentrations of O_2 and NO_2 increase as the concentration of N_2O_5 decreases.

$\Delta[NO_2] = 0.0022$ M
$\Delta t = 100$ s

$\Delta[NO_2] = 0.0037$ M
$\Delta t = 100$ s

The slope of the hypotenuse of each triangle gives the average rate of change of the product or reactant concentration during the indicated time interval.

$\Delta[N_2O_5] = -0.0019$ M
$\Delta t = 100$ s

$\Delta[O_2] = 0.0009$ M
$\Delta t = 100$ s

The rate of formation of O_2 is one-fourth the rate of formation of NO_2 and one-half the rate of decomposition of N_2O_5.

As O_2 and NO_2 form, N_2O_5 disappears. Consequently, $\Delta[N_2O_5]/\Delta t$ is negative, in accord with the negative slope of the hypotenuse of the triangle defined by $\Delta[N_2O_5]$ and Δt in Figure 12.1. Because *reaction rate is defined as a positive quantity*, we must always introduce a minus sign when calculating the rate of disappearance of a reactant. During the time period 300–400 s, for example, the average rate of decomposition of N_2O_5 is 1.9×10^{-5} M/s:

$$\text{Rate of decomposition of } N_2O_5 = \frac{-\Delta[N_2O_5]}{\Delta t} = \frac{-(0.0101\text{ M} - 0.0120\text{ M})}{400\text{ s} - 300\text{ s}} = 1.9 \times 10^{-5}\text{ M/s}$$

When quoting a reaction rate, it's important to specify the reactant or product on which the rate is based because the rates of product formation and reactant consumption may differ, depending on the coefficients in the balanced chemical equation. For the decomposition of N_2O_5, 4 mol of NO_2 form and 2 mol of N_2O_5 disappear for each mole of O_2 that forms. Therefore, the rate of formation of O_2 is 1/4 the rate of formation of NO_2 and 1/2 the rate of decomposition of N_2O_5:

$$\left(\begin{array}{c}\text{Rate of formation}\\\text{of }O_2\end{array}\right) = \frac{1}{4}\left(\begin{array}{c}\text{Rate of formation}\\\text{of }NO_2\end{array}\right) = \frac{1}{2}\left(\begin{array}{c}\text{Rate of decomposition}\\\text{of }N_2O_5\end{array}\right)$$

or

$$\frac{\Delta[O_2]}{\Delta t} = \frac{1}{4}\left(\frac{\Delta[NO_2]}{\Delta t}\right) = -\frac{1}{2}\left(\frac{\Delta[N_2O_5]}{\Delta t}\right)$$

To avoid the ambiguity of more than one rate, chemists have defined a *general* rate of reaction equal to the rate of consumption of a reactant or formation of a product divided by its coefficient in the balanced chemical equation. Thus, for the reaction

$$2\,N_2O_5(g) \longrightarrow 4\,NO_2(g) + O_2(g)$$

the general rate of reaction has a single value given by the equation

$$\text{General rate of reaction} = -\frac{1}{2}\left(\frac{\Delta[N_2O_5]}{\Delta t}\right) = \frac{1}{4}\left(\frac{\Delta[NO_2]}{\Delta t}\right) = \frac{\Delta[O_2]}{\Delta t}$$

In this book, however, we will usually quote reaction rates in terms of the rate of consumption or formation of a specific substance, and will be careful to specify the substance on which the rate is based.

It's also important to specify the time when quoting a rate because the rate changes as the reaction proceeds. For example, the average rate of formation of NO_2 is 3.7×10^{-5} M/s during the time period 300–400 s, but it is only 2.2×10^{-5} M/s during the period 600–700 s (Figure 12.1). Ordinarily, reaction rates depend on the concentrations of at least some of the reactants and therefore decrease as the reaction mixture runs out of reactants, as indicated by the decreasing slopes of the curves in Figure 12.1 as time passes.

Often, chemists want to know the rate of a reaction at a specific time t rather than the rate averaged over a time interval Δt. For example, what is the rate of formation of NO_2 at time $t = 350$ s? If we make our measurements at shorter and shorter time intervals, the triangle defined by $\Delta[NO_2]$ and Δt will shrink to a point, and the slope of the hypotenuse of the triangle will approach the slope of the tangent to the curve, as shown in **Figure 12.2**. The slope of the tangent to a concentration-versus-time curve at a time t is called the **instantaneous rate** at that particular time. The instantaneous rate at the beginning of a reaction ($t = 0$) is called the **initial rate**.

Figure 12.2

Concentration of NO_2 versus time when N_2O_5 decomposes at 55 °C. As measurements are made at shorter and shorter time intervals, the triangle defined by $\Delta[NO_2]$ and Δt becomes smaller and smaller, and the slope of the hypotenuse of the triangle approaches the slope of the tangent to the curve.

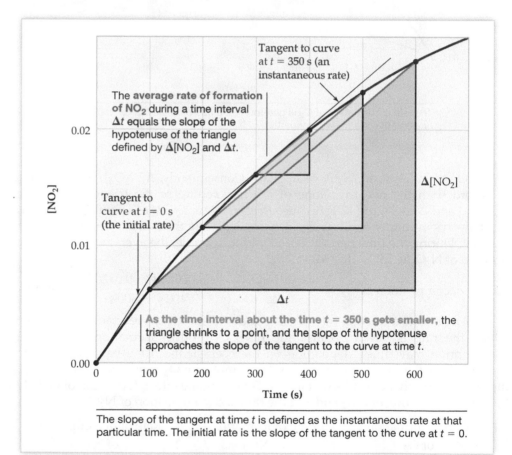

The slope of the tangent at time t is defined as the instantaneous rate at that particular time. The initial rate is the slope of the tangent to the curve at $t = 0$.

WORKED EXAMPLE 12.1

FINDING RELATIVE RATES OF PRODUCT FORMATION AND REACTANT CONSUMPTION

Ethanol (C_2H_5OH), the active ingredient in alcoholic beverages and an octane booster in gasoline, is produced by the fermentation of glucose. The balanced equation is

$$C_6H_{12}O_6(aq) \longrightarrow 2\,C_2H_5OH(aq) + 2\,CO_2(g)$$

(a) How is the rate of formation of ethanol related to the rate of consumption of glucose?
(b) Write this relationship in terms of $\Delta[C_2H_5OH]/\Delta t$ and $\Delta[C_6H_{12}O_6]/\Delta t$.

STRATEGY

To find the relative rates, look at the coefficients in the balanced chemical equation.

SOLUTION

(a) According to the balanced equation, 2 mol of ethanol are produced for each mole of glucose that reacts. Therefore, the rate of formation of ethanol is twice the rate of consumption of glucose.

(b) Since the rate of formation of ethanol is $\Delta[C_2H_5OH]/\Delta t$ and the rate of consumption of glucose is $-\Delta[C_6H_{12}O_6]/\Delta t$ (note the minus sign), we can write

$$\frac{\Delta[C_2H_5OH]}{\Delta t} = -2\frac{\Delta[C_6H_{12}O_6]}{\Delta t}$$

▶ **PROBLEM 12.1** The oxidation of iodide ion by arsenic acid, H_3AsO_4, is described by the balanced equation

$$3\,I^-(aq) + H_3AsO_4(aq) + 2\,H^+(aq) \longrightarrow I_3^-(aq) + H_3AsO_3(aq) + H_2O(l)$$

(a) If $-\Delta[I^-]/\Delta t = 4.8 \times 10^{-4}$ M/s, what is the value of $\Delta[I_3^-]/\Delta t$ during the same time interval?

(b) What is the average rate of consumption of H^+ during that time interval?

▶ **PROBLEM 12.2** Use the data in Table 12.1 to calculate the average rate of decomposition of N_2O_5 and the average rate of formation of O_2 during the time interval 200–300 s.

12.2 RATE LAWS AND REACTION ORDER

We noted in Section 12.1 that the rate of decomposition of N_2O_5 depends on its concentration, slowing down as the N_2O_5 concentration decreases. To explore further how reaction rates depend on concentrations, let's consider the general reaction

$$a\,A + b\,B \longrightarrow \text{Products}$$

where A and B are the reactants and a and b are stoichiometric coefficients in the balanced chemical equation. The dependence of the reaction rate on the concentration of each reactant is given by an equation called the **rate law**:

Rate Law $\quad \text{Rate} = -\dfrac{\Delta[A]}{\Delta t} = k[A]^m[B]^n$

In this equation, k is a proportionality constant called the **rate constant**. We've arbitrarily expressed the rate as the rate of disappearance of A ($-\Delta[A]/\Delta t$), but we could equally well have written it as the rate of disappearance of any reactant (say, $-\Delta[B]/\Delta t$) or as the rate of appearance of any product. The exponents m and n in the rate law indicate how sensitive the rate is to changes in [A] and [B], and they are generally unrelated to the coefficients a and b in the balanced equation. For the simple reactions discussed in this book, the exponents are usually small positive integers. For more complex reactions, however, the exponents can be negative, zero, or even fractions.

Figure 12.3 shows how the rate changes when the concentration of A is doubled for various values of the exponent m. An exponent of 1 means that the rate depends linearly on the concentration of the corresponding reactant: if $m = 1$ and [A] is doubled, the rate doubles. If $m = 2$ and [A] is doubled, $[A]^2$ quadruples and the rate increases by a factor of 4. If m is zero, the rate is independent of the concentration of A because any number raised to the zeroth power equals one ($[A]^0 = 1$). If m is negative, the rate *decreases* as [A] increases. For example, if $m = -1$ and [A] is doubled, $[A]^{-1}$ is halved and the rate decreases by a factor of 2. In general, the rate is proportional to $[A]^m$.

Figure 12.3

Change in reaction rate when the concentration of reactant A is doubled for different values of the exponent m in the rate law, rate $= k[A]^m[B]^n$.

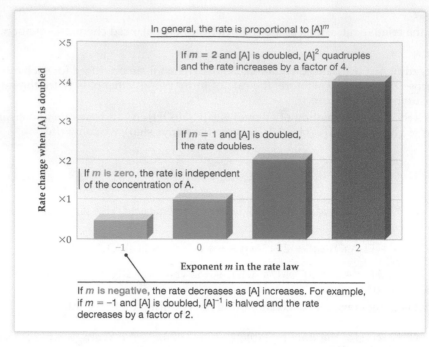

The values of the exponents m and n determine the **reaction order** with respect to A and B, respectively. The sum of the exponents $(m + n)$ defines the *overall* reaction order. Thus, if the rate law is

$$\text{Rate} = k[A]^2[B] \qquad m = 2; n = 1; \text{and } m + n = 3$$

we say that the reaction is second order in A, first order in B, and third order overall.

The values of the exponents in a rate law must be determined by experiment; they cannot be deduced from the stoichiometry of the reaction. As Table 12.2 shows, there is no general relationship between the stoichiometric coefficients in the balanced chemical equation and the exponents in the rate law. In the first reaction in Table 12.2, for example, the coefficients of $(CH_3)_3CBr$ and H_2O in the balanced equation are both 1, but the exponents in the rate law are 1 for $(CH_3)_3CBr$ and 0 for H_2O:

$$\text{Rate} = k[(CH_3)_3CBr]^1[H_2O]^0 = k[(CH_3)_3CBr]$$

In Section 12.11, we'll see that the exponents in a rate law depend on the reaction mechanism.

TABLE 12.2   Balanced Chemical Equations and Experimentally Determined Rate Laws for Some Reactions

Reaction*	Rate Law
$(CH_3)_3CBr(soln) + H_2O(soln) \longrightarrow (CH_3)_3COH(soln) + H^+(soln) + Br^-(soln)$	Rate $= k[(CH_3)_3CBr]$
$HCO_2H(aq) + Br_2(aq) \longrightarrow 2 H^+(aq) + 2 Br^-(aq) + CO_2(g)$	Rate $= k[Br_2]$
$BrO_3^-(aq) + 5 Br^-(aq) + 6 H^+(aq) \longrightarrow 3 Br_2(aq) + 3 H_2O(l)$	Rate $= k[BrO_3^-][Br^-][H^+]^2$
$H_2(g) + I_2(g) \longrightarrow 2 HI(g)$	Rate $= k[H_2][I_2]$

In general, the exponents in the rate law are not the same as the stoichiometric coefficients in the balanced chemical equation for the reaction.

*In the first reaction, "(*soln*)" denotes a nonaqueous solution.

WORKED EXAMPLE 12.2

FINDING REACTION ORDER FROM A RATE LAW

The second reaction in Table 12.2, shown in progress in **Figure 12.4**, is

$$HCO_2H(aq) + Br_2(aq) \longrightarrow 2 H^+(aq) + 2 Br^-(aq) + CO_2(g)$$

Colorless   Red   Colorless

What is the order of the reaction with respect to each of the reactants? What is the over-all reaction order?

Figure 12.4

The reaction of formic acid (HCO_2H) and bromine (Br_2). As time passes (left to right), the red color of bromine disappears because Br_2 is reduced to the colorless Br^- ion. The concentration of Br_2 as a function of time, and thus the reaction rate, can be determined by measuring the intensity of the color.

STRATEGY

To find the reaction order with respect to each reactant, look at the exponents in the rate law, not the coefficients in the balanced chemical equation. Then sum the exponents to obtain the overall reaction order.

SOLUTION

The rate law for the second reaction in Table 12.2 is

$$Rate = k[Br_2]$$

Because HCO_2H (formic acid) does not appear in the rate law, the rate is independent of the HCO_2H concentration, and so the reaction is zeroth order in HCO_2H. Because the exponent on $[Br_2]$ is 1 (it is understood to be 1 when no exponent is given), the reaction is first order in Br_2. The reaction is first order overall because the sum of the exponents is 1.

▶ **PROBLEM 12.3** Consider the last two reactions in Table 12.2. What is the order of each reaction in the various reactants? What is the overall reaction order for each?

12.3 EXPERIMENTAL DETERMINATION OF A RATE LAW

One method of determining the values of the exponents in a rate law—the *method of initial rates*—is to carry out a series of experiments in which the initial rate of a reaction is measured as a function of different sets of initial concentrations. Take, for example, the air oxidation of nitric oxide, one of the reactions that contributes to the formation of acid rain:

$$2\,NO(g) + O_2(g) \longrightarrow 2\,NO_2(g)$$

Some initial rate data are collected in Table 12.3.

TABLE 12.3 Initial Concentration and Rate Data for the Reaction $2\,NO(g) + O_2(g) \longrightarrow 2\,NO_2(g)$

Experiment	Initial [NO]	Initial [O_2]	Initial Rate of Formation of NO_2 (M/s)
1	0.015	0.015	0.048
2	0.030	0.015	0.192
3	0.015	0.030	0.096
4	0.030	0.030	0.384

Note that pairs of experiments are designed to investigate the effect on the initial rate of a change in the initial concentration of a single reactant. In the first two experiments, for example, the concentration of NO is doubled from 0.015 M to 0.030 M while the concentration of O_2 is held constant. The initial rate increases by a factor of 4, from 0.048 M/s to 0.192 M/s, indicating that the rate depends on the concentration of NO squared, $[NO]^2$. When [NO] is held constant and $[O_2]$ is doubled (experiments 1 and 3), the initial rate doubles from 0.048 M/s to 0.096 M/s, indicating that the rate depends on the concentration of O_2 to the first power, $[O_2]^1$. Therefore, the rate law for the formation of NO_2 is

$$\text{Rate} = \frac{\Delta[NO_2]}{\Delta t} = k[NO]^2[O_2]$$

In accord with this rate law, which is second order in NO, first order in O_2, and third order overall, the initial rate increases by a factor of 8 when the concentrations of both NO and O_2 are doubled (experiments 1 and 4).

The preceding method uses initial rates rather than rates at a later stage of the reaction because chemical reactions are reversible and we want to avoid complications from the reverse reaction: reactants ← products. As the product concentrations build up, the rate of the reverse reaction increases and the measured rate is affected by the concentrations of both reactants and products. At the beginning of the reaction, however, the product concentrations are zero, and therefore the products can't affect the measured rate. When we measure an initial rate, we are measuring the rate of only the forward reaction, so only reactants (and catalysts; see Section 12.14) can appear in the rate law.

One aspect of determining a rate law, as we've just seen, is to establish the reaction order. Another is to evaluate the numerical value of the rate constant k. Each reaction has its own characteristic value of the rate constant, which depends on temperature but does not depend on concentrations. To evaluate k for the formation of NO_2, for instance, we can use the data from any one of the experiments in Table 12.3. Solving the rate law for k and substituting the initial rate and concentrations from the first experiment, we obtain

$$k = \frac{\text{Rate}}{[NO]^2[O_2]} = \frac{0.048\,\frac{M}{s}}{(0.015\,M)^2(0.015\,M)} = 1.4 \times 10^4/(M^2 \cdot s)$$

Try repeating the calculation for experiments 2–4, and show that you get the same value of k. Note that the units of k in this example are $1/(M^2 \cdot s)$, read as "one over molar squared second." In general, the units of k depend on the number of concentration terms in the rate law and on the values of their exponents. Units for some common cases are given as follows:

Rate Law	Overall Reaction Order	Units for k
Rate = k	Zeroth order	M/s or M s^{-1}
Rate = k[A]	First order	1/s or s^{-1}
Rate = k[A][B]	Second order	$1/(M \cdot s)$ or M^{-1} s^{-1}
Rate = k[A][B]^2	Third order	$1/(M^2 \cdot s)$ or M^{-2} s^{-1}

Be careful not to confuse the rate of a reaction and its rate constant. The *rate* depends on concentrations, whereas the rate *constant* does not (it is a constant). The rate is usually expressed in units of M/s, whereas the units of the rate constant depend on the overall reaction order.

Worked Example 12.3 gives another instance of how a rate law can be determined from initial rates.

WORKED EXAMPLE 12.3

DETERMINING A RATE LAW FROM INITIAL RATES

Initial rate data for the decomposition of gaseous N_2O_5 at 55 °C are as follows:

Experiment	Initial [N_2O_5]	Initial Rate of Decomposition of N_2O_5 (M/s)
1	0.020	3.4×10^{-5}
2	0.050	8.5×10^{-5}

(a) What is the rate law?

(b) What is the value of the rate constant?

(c) What is the initial rate of decomposition of N_2O_5 at 55 °C when its initial concentration is 0.030 M?

STRATEGY

(a) The rate law for the decomposition of N_2O_5 can be written as

$$\text{Rate} = -\frac{\Delta[N_2O_5]}{\Delta t} = k[N_2O_5]^m$$

where m is both the order of the reaction in N_2O_5 and the overall reaction order. To find the value of the exponent m, compare the change in the initial concentration of N_2O_5 for experiments 1 and 2 with the change in the initial rate.

(b) To find the value of the rate constant k, solve the rate law for k and then substitute in the data from either experiment.

(c) To calculate the initial rate, substitute the rate constant found in part **(b)** and the given initial concentration (0.030 M) into the rate law.

SOLUTION

(a) Comparing experiments 1 and 2 shows that an increase in the initial concentration of N_2O_5 by a factor of 2.5 increases the initial rate by a factor of 2.5:

$$\frac{[N_2O_5]_2}{[N_2O_5]_1} = \frac{0.050 \text{ M}}{0.020 \text{ M}} = 2.5 \qquad \frac{(\text{Rate})_2}{(\text{Rate})_1} = \frac{8.5 \times 10^{-5} \text{ M/s}}{3.4 \times 10^{-5} \text{ M/s}} = 2.5$$

The rate is proportional to the concentration of N_2O_5, and therefore the rate law is first order in N_2O_5:

$$\text{Rate} = -\frac{\Delta[N_2O_5]}{\Delta t} = k[N_2O_5]$$

If the rate had increased by a factor of $(2.5)^2 = 6.25$, the reaction would have been second order in N_2O_5. If the rate had increased by a factor of $(2.5)^3 = 15.6$, the reaction would have been third order in N_2O_5, and so forth.

A more formal way to approach this problem is to write the rate law for each experiment:

$$(\text{Rate})_1 = k[N_2O_5]_1 = k(0.020 \text{ M})^m \qquad (\text{Rate})_2 = k[N_2O_5]_2 = k(0.050 \text{ M})^m$$

If we then divide the second equation by the first, we obtain

$$\frac{(\text{Rate})_2}{(\text{Rate})_1} = \frac{k(0.050 \text{ M})^m}{k(0.020 \text{ M})^m} = (2.5)^m$$

Comparing this ratio to the ratio of the experimental rates,

$$\frac{(\text{Rate})_2}{(\text{Rate})_1} = \frac{8.5 \times 10^{-5} \text{ M/s}}{3.4 \times 10^{-5} \text{ M/s}} = 2.5$$

continued on next page

shows that the exponent m must have a value of 1. Therefore, the rate law is

$$\text{Rate} = -\frac{\Delta[N_2O_5]}{\Delta t} = k[N_2O_5]$$

(b) Solving the rate law for k and substituting in the data from the first experiment gives

$$k = \frac{\text{Rate}}{[N_2O_5]} = \frac{3.4 \times 10^{-5} \frac{M}{s}}{0.020 \text{ M}} = 1.7 \times 10^{-3} \text{ s}^{-1}$$

(c) Substituting the initial concentration (0.030 M) and the rate constant from part **(b)** $(1.7 \times 10^{-3} \text{ s}^{-1})$ into the rate law gives

$$\text{Rate} = -\frac{\Delta[N_2O_5]}{\Delta t} = k[N_2O_5] = \left(\frac{1.7 \times 10^{-3}}{s}\right)(0.030 \text{ M}) = 5.1 \times 10^{-5} \text{ M/s}$$

BALLPARK CHECK

(b) It's a good idea to check the units of the rate constant. The units of k, $1/s$ or s^{-1}, are the expected units for a first-order reaction.

(c) Because the reaction is first order in N_2O_5 and the initial concentration of N_2O_5 is 3/2 times that in experiment 1, the decomposition rate will increase by a factor of 3/2 from 3.4×10^{-5} M/s to about 5×10^{-5} M/s, which agrees with the detailed solution.

WORKED CONCEPTUAL EXAMPLE 12.4

USING THE METHOD OF INITIAL RATES

The relative rates of the reaction $A + 2B \rightarrow$ products in vessels (1)–(4) are $1:2:2:4$. Red spheres represent A molecules, and blue spheres represent B molecules.

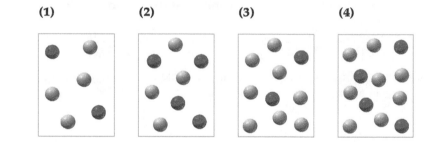

(1)   **(2)**   **(3)**   **(4)**

(a) What is the order of the reaction in A and B? What is the overall reaction order?

(b) Write the rate law.

STRATEGY

(a) To find the reaction order, apply the method of initial rates. Count the number of A and B molecules in vessels (1)–(4), and compare the relative rates with the relative number of molecules of each type. Assume that all four vessels have the same volume, so the concentrations are proportional to the number of molecules.

(b) The rate law can be written as rate $= k[A]^m [B]^n$, where the exponents m and n are the orders of the reaction in A and B, respectively.

SOLUTION

(a) Compare pairs of vessels in which the concentration of one reactant varies while the concentration of the other reactant remains constant. The concentration of A molecules in vessel (2) is twice that in vessel (1) while the concentration of B remains constant. Because the reaction rate in vessel (2) is twice that in vessel (1), the rate is proportional to [A], and therefore the reaction is first order in A. When the concentration of B is doubled while the concentration of A remains constant [compare vessels (1) and (3)], the rate doubles, so the reaction is first order in B.

When the concentrations of both A and B are doubled, the rate increases by a factor of 4 [compare vessels (1) and (4)], in accord with a reaction that is first order in A and first order in B. The overall reaction order is the sum of the orders in A and B, or $1 + 1 = 2$.

(b) Since the reaction is first order in A and first order in B, the rate law is rate $= k[A][B]$. Note that the exponents in the rate law differ from the coefficients in the balanced chemical equation, $A + 2B \longrightarrow$ products.

▶ **PROBLEM 12.4**   The oxidation of iodide ion by hydrogen peroxide in an acidic solution is described by the balanced equation

$$H_2O_2(aq) + 3I^-(aq) + 2H^+(aq) \longrightarrow I_3^-(aq) + 2H_2O(l)$$

The rate of formation of the red triiodide ion, $\Delta[I_3^-]/\Delta t$, can be determined by measuring the rate of appearance of the color (**Figure 12.5**). Initial rate data at 25 °C are as follows:

Experiment	Initial [H$_2$O$_2$]	Initial [I$^-$]	Initial Rate of Formation of [I$_3^-$] (M/s)
1	0.100	0.100	1.15×10^{-4}
2	0.100	0.200	2.30×10^{-4}
3	0.200	0.100	2.30×10^{-4}
4	0.200	0.200	4.60×10^{-4}

(a) What is the rate law for the formation of I_3^-?

(b) What is the value of the rate constant?

(c) What is the initial rate of formation of I_3^- when the initial concentrations are $[H_2O_2] = 0.300$ M and $[I^-] = 0.400$ M?

Figure 12.5
A sequence of photographs showing the progress of the reaction of hydrogen peroxide (H$_2$O$_2$) and iodide ion (I$^-$). As time passes (left to right), the red color due to the triiodide ion (I$_3^-$) increases in intensity.

▶ **PROBLEM 12.5**   What are the units of the rate constant for each of the reactions in Table 12.2?

CONCEPTUAL PROBLEM 12.6   The relative rates of the reaction $A + B \longrightarrow$ products in vessels (1)–(4) are 1:1:4:4. Red spheres represent A molecules, and blue spheres represent B molecules.

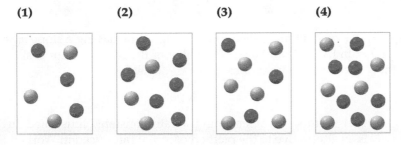

(a) What is the order of the reaction in A and B? What is the overall reaction order?

(b) Write the rate law.

12.4 INTEGRATED RATE LAW FOR A FIRST-ORDER REACTION

Thus far we've focused on the rate law, an equation that tells how a reaction rate depends on reactant concentrations. We're also interested, however, in how reactant and product concentrations vary with time. For example, it's important to know the rate at which the atmospheric ozone layer is being destroyed by air pollutants, but we also want to know what the ozone concentration will be 20 years from now and how long it will take for the concentration to change by a given amount, say, 10%.

Because the kinetics of the pollution-induced decomposition of ozone is a very complicated process, let's consider instead a simple, general first-order reaction:

$$A \longrightarrow Products$$

A **first-order reaction** is one whose rate depends on the concentration of a single reactant raised to the first power.

$$Rate = -\frac{\Delta[A]}{\Delta t} = k[A]$$

An example is the decomposition of hydrogen peroxide in basic solution, which we'll discuss in Worked Example 12.5 at the end of this section:

$$2\,H_2O_2(aq) \longrightarrow 2\,H_2O(l) + O_2(g)$$

Using calculus, it's possible to convert the rate law to another form, called the **integrated rate law**:

$$\ln \frac{[A]_t}{[A]_0} = -kt$$

In this equation, ln denotes the natural logarithm, $[A]_0$ is the concentration of A at some initial time, arbitrarily considered to be $t = 0$, and $[A]_t$ is the concentration of A at any time t thereafter. (See Appendix A.2 for a review of logarithms.) The ratio $[A]_t/[A]_0$ is the fraction of A that remains at time t. Thus, the integrated rate law is a *concentration–time equation* that lets us calculate the concentration of A or the fraction of A that remains at any time t. It can also be used to calculate the time required for the initial concentration of A to drop to any particular value or to any particular fraction of its initial concentration (**Figure 12.6a**). Worked Example 12.5 shows how to use the integrated rate law.

Since $\ln ([A]_t/[A]_0) = \ln [A]_t - \ln [A]_0$, we can rewrite the integrated rate law as

$$\ln [A]_t = -kt + \ln [A]_0$$

This equation is of the form $y = mx + b$, the equation for a straight line, so $\ln [A]_t$ is a linear function of time:

$$\underset{y}{\ln [A]_t} = \underset{m\ x}{(-k)t} + \underset{b}{\ln [A]_0}$$

A graph $\ln [A]$ versus time is therefore a straight line having a slope $m = -k$ and an intercept $b = \ln [A]_0$ (**Figure 12.6b**). The value of the rate constant is simply equal to minus the slope of the straight line:

$$k = -(Slope)$$

This graphical method of determining a rate constant, illustrated in Worked Example 12.6, is an alternative to the method of initial rates used in Worked Example 12.3. An $\ln [A]$-versus-time plot, however, will give a straight line only if the reaction is first order in A. Indeed, a good way of testing whether a reaction is first order is to examine the appearance of such a plot.

Figure 12.6
Plots for a first-order reaction.

WORKED EXAMPLE 12.5

USING THE INTEGRATED RATE LAW FOR A FIRST-ORDER REACTION

The decomposition of hydrogen peroxide in dilute sodium hydroxide solution is described by the equation

$$2 H_2O_2(aq) \longrightarrow 2 H_2O(l) + O_2(g)$$

The reaction is first order in H_2O_2, the rate constant for the consumption of H_2O_2 at 20 °C is $1.8 \times 10^{-5}\,s^{-1}$, and the initial concentration of H_2O_2 is 0.30 M.

(a) What is the concentration of H_2O_2 after 4.00 h?

(b) How long will it take for the H_2O_2 concentration to drop to 0.12 M?

(c) How long will it take for 90% of the H_2O_2 to decompose?

STRATEGY

Since this reaction has a first-order rate law, $-\Delta[H_2O_2]/\Delta t = k[H_2O_2]$, we can use the corresponding concentration–time equation for a first-order reaction:

$$\ln \frac{[H_2O_2]_t}{[H_2O_2]_0} = -kt$$

In each part, we substitute the known quantities into this equation and solve for the unknown.

SOLUTION

(a) Because k has units of s^{-1}, we must first convert the time from hours to seconds:

$$t = (4.00\,h)\left(\frac{60\,min}{h}\right)\left(\frac{60\,s}{min}\right) = 1.44 \times 10^4\,s$$

Then, substitute the values of $[H_2O_2]_0$, k, and t into the concentration–time equation:

$$\ln \frac{[H_2O_2]_t}{0.30\,M} = -(1.8 \times 10^{-5}\,s^{-1})(1.44 \times 10^4\,s) = -0.259$$

Taking the natural antilogarithm (antiln) of both sides gives

$$\frac{[H_2O_2]_t}{0.30\,M} = e^{-0.259} = 0.772$$

where the number $e = 2.718\,28...$ is the base of natural logarithms (see Appendix A.2). Therefore,

$$[H_2O_2]_t = (0.772)(0.30\,M) = 0.23\,M$$

continued on next page

(b) First, solve the concentration–time equation for the time:

$$t = -\frac{1}{k} \ln \frac{[H_2O_2]_t}{[H_2O_2]_0}$$

Then evaluate the time by substituting the concentrations and the value of k:

$$t = -\left(\frac{1}{1.8 \times 10^{-5}\,\text{s}^{-1}}\right)\left(\ln \frac{0.12\,\text{M}}{0.30\,\text{M}}\right) = -\left(\frac{1}{1.8 \times 10^{-5}\,\text{s}^{-1}}\right)(-0.916) = 5.1 \times 10^4\,\text{s}$$

Thus, the H_2O_2 concentration reaches 0.12 M at a time of 5.1×10^4 s (14 h).

(c) When 90% of the H_2O_2 has decomposed, 10% remains. Therefore,

$$\frac{[H_2O_2]_t}{[H_2O_2]_0} = \frac{(0.10)(0.30\,\text{M})}{0.30\,\text{M}} = 0.10$$

The time required for 90% decomposition is

$$t = -\left(\frac{1}{1.8 \times 10^{-5}\,\text{s}^{-1}}\right)(\ln 0.10) = -\left(\frac{1}{1.8 \times 10^{-5}\,\text{s}^{-1}}\right)(-2.30) = 1.3 \times 10^5\,\text{s} \text{ (36 h)}$$

BALLPARK CHECK

The concentration of H_2O_2 (0.23 M) after 4.00 h is less than the initial concentration (0.30 M). A longer period of time (14 h) is required for the concentration to drop to 0.12 M, and still more time (36 h) is needed for the concentration to fall to 0.030 M (10% of the original concentration). These results look reasonable. A plot of $[H_2O_2]$ versus time would exhibit an exponential decay of the H_2O_2 concentration, as expected for a first-order reaction.

WORKED EXAMPLE 12.6

PLOTTING DATA FOR A FIRST-ORDER REACTION

Experimental concentration-versus-time data for the decomposition of gaseous N_2O_5 at 55 °C are listed in Table 12.1 and are plotted in Figure 12.1. Use those data to confirm that the decomposition of N_2O_5 is a first-order reaction. What is the value of the rate constant for the consumption of N_2O_5?

STRATEGY

To confirm that the reaction is first order, check to see whether a plot of $\ln [N_2O_5]$ versus time gives a straight line. The rate constant for a first-order reaction equals minus the slope of the straight line.

SOLUTION

Values of $\ln [N_2O_5]$ are listed in the following table and are plotted versus time in the graph:

Time (s)	$[N_2O_5]$	$\ln [N_2O_5]$
0	0.0200	−3.912
100	0.0169	−4.080
200	0.0142	−4.255
300	0.0120	−4.423
400	0.0101	−4.595
500	0.0086	−4.756
600	0.0072	−4.934
700	0.0061	−5.099

Because the data points lie on a straight line, the reaction is first order in N_2O_5. The slope of the line can be determined from the coordinates of any two widely separated points on the line, and the rate constant k can be calculated from the slope:

$$\text{Slope} = \frac{\Delta y}{\Delta x} = \frac{(-5.02) - (-4.17)}{650\,\text{s} - 150\,\text{s}} = \frac{-0.85}{500\,\text{s}} = -1.7 \times 10^{-3}\,\text{s}^{-1}$$

$$k = -(\text{Slope}) = 1.7 \times 10^{-3}\,\text{s}^{-1}$$

Note that the slope is negative, k is positive, and the value of k agrees with the value obtained earlier in Worked Example 12.3 by the method of initial rates.

▶ **PROBLEM 12.7**   In acidic aqueous solution, the purple complex ion $Co(NH_3)_5Br^{2+}$ undergoes a slow reaction in which the bromide ion is replaced by a water molecule, yielding the pinkish-orange complex ion $Co(NH_3)_5(H_2O)^{3+}$:

$$Co(NH_3)_5Br^{2+}(aq) + H_2O(l) \longrightarrow Co(NH_3)_5(H_2O)^{3+}(aq) + Br^-(aq)$$

Purple   Pinkish-orange

The reaction is first order in $Co(NH_3)_5Br^{2+}$, the rate constant at 25 °C is $6.3 \times 10^{-6}\,s^{-1}$, and the initial concentration of $Co(NH_3)_5Br^{2+}$ is 0.100 M.

   (a) What is the molarity of $Co(NH_3)_5Br^{2+}$ after a reaction time of 10.0 h?

   (b) How many hours are required for 75% of the $Co(NH_3)_5Br^{2+}$ to react?

▶ **PROBLEM 12.8**   At high temperatures, cyclopropane is converted to propene, the material from which polypropylene plastics are made:

▲ Aqueous solutions of $Co(NH_3)_5Br^{2+}$ (left) and $Co(NH_3)_5(H_2O)^{3+}$ (right).

CH₂ structure (Cyclopropane) $\longrightarrow$ $CH_3-CH=CH_2$ (Propene)

Cyclopropane   Propene

Cyclopropane   Propene

   Given the following concentration data, test whether the reaction is first order and calculate the value of the rate constant.

Time (min)	0	5.0	10.0	15.0	20.0
[Cyclopropane]	0.098	0.080	0.066	0.054	0.044

12.5 HALF-LIFE OF A FIRST-ORDER REACTION

The **half-life** of a reaction, symbolized by $t_{1/2}$, is the time required for the reactant concentration to drop to one-half of its initial value. Consider the first-order reaction

$$A \longrightarrow Products$$

To relate the reaction's half-life to the rate constant, let's begin with the integrated rate law:

$$\ln \frac{[A]_t}{[A]_0} = -kt$$

When $t = t_{1/2}$, the fraction of A that remains, $[A]_t/[A]_0$, is 1/2. Therefore,

$$\ln \frac{1}{2} = -kt_{1/2}$$

$$so \quad t_{1/2} = \frac{-\ln \frac{1}{2}}{k} = \frac{\ln 2}{k}$$

$$or \quad t_{1/2} = \frac{0.693}{k}$$

Thus, the half-life of a first-order reaction is readily calculated from the rate constant, and vice versa.

The half-life of a first-order reaction is a constant because it depends only on the rate constant and not on the reactant concentration. This point is worth noting because reactions that are not first order have half-lives that *do* depend on concentration; that is, the amount of time in one half-life changes as the reactant concentration changes for a non-first-order reaction.

Because the half-life of a first-order reaction is a constant, each successive half-life is an equal period of time in which the reactant concentration decreases by a factor of 2 (**Figure 12.7**).

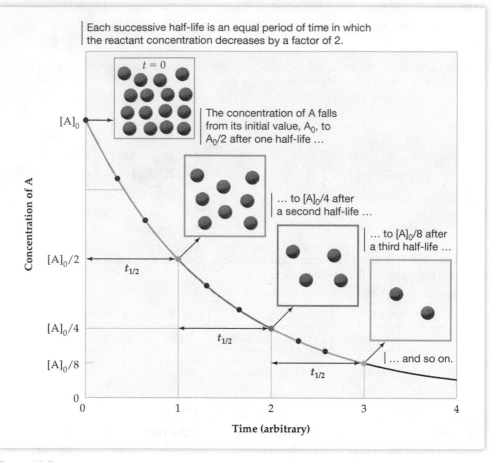

Figure 12.7
Concentration of a reactant A as a function of time for a first-order reaction.
Each half-life represents an equal amount of time.

WORKED EXAMPLE 12.7

DETERMINING THE HALF-LIFE FOR A FIRST-ORDER REACTION

(a) Estimate the half-life for the decomposition of gaseous N_2O_5 at 55 °C from the concentration-versus-time plot in Figure 12.1.

(b) Calculate the half-life from the rate constant ($1.7 \times 10^{-3}\,s^{-1}$).

(c) If the initial concentration of N_2O_5 is 0.020 M, what is the concentration of N_2O_5 after five half-lives?

(d) How long will it take for the N_2O_5 concentration to fall to 12.5% of its initial value?

STRATEGY

Because the decomposition of N_2O_5 is a first-order reaction (Worked Example 12.6), we can determine its half-life either from the time required for $[N_2O_5]$ to drop to 1/2 of its initial value or from the equation $t_{1/2} = 0.693/k$. To find $[N_2O_5]$ after n half-lives, multiply its initial concentration by $(1/2)^n$ because $[N_2O_5]$ drops by a factor of 2 during each successive half-life.

SOLUTION

(a) Figure 12.1 shows that the concentration of N_2O_5 falls from 0.020 M to 0.010 M during a time period of approximately 400 s. At 800 s, $[N_2O_5]$ has decreased by another factor of 2, to 0.0050 M. Therefore, $t_{1/2} \approx 400$ s.

(b) Based on the value of the rate constant,

$$t_{1/2} = \frac{\ln 2}{k} = \frac{0.693}{1.7 \times 10^{-3}\,\text{s}^{-1}} = 4.1 \times 10^2\,\text{s}\ (6.8\ \text{min})$$

(c) At $5t_{1/2}$, $[N_2O_5]$ will be $(1/2)^5 = 1/32$ of its initial value. Therefore,

$$[N_2O_5] = \frac{0.020\ \text{M}}{32} = 0.000\,62\ \text{M}$$

(d) Since 12.5% of the initial concentration corresponds to 1/8 or $(1/2)^3$ of the initial concentration, the time required is three half-lives:

$$t = 3t_{1/2} = 3(4.1 \times 10^2\,\text{s}) = 1.2 \times 10^3\,\text{s}\ (20\ \text{min})$$

▶ **PROBLEM 12.9** Consider the first-order decomposition of H_2O_2 in Worked Example 12.5.

(a) What is the half-life (in hours) of the reaction at 20 °C?

(b) What is the molarity of H_2O_2 after four half-lives if the initial concentration of H_2O_2 is 0.30 M?

(c) How many hours will it take for the concentration to drop to 25% of its initial value?

CONCEPTUAL PROBLEM 12.10 Consider the first-order reaction $A \rightarrow B$ in which A molecules (red spheres) are converted to B molecules (blue spheres).

(a) Given the following pictures at $t = 0$ min and $t = 10$ min, what is the half-life of the reaction?

(b) Draw a picture that shows the number of A and B molecules present at $t = 15$ min.

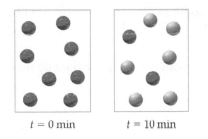

$t = 0$ min $t = 10$ min

12.6 RADIOACTIVE DECAY RATES

In Sections 2.8 and 2.9 we saw that many nuclei are radioactive. The rate at which a radioactive nucleus decays is characterized by its half-life, $t_{1/2}$. For example, carbon-14 decays to nitrogen-14 by emission of a β^- particle with a half-life of 5715 years:

$$^{14}_{6}\text{C} \longrightarrow\ ^{14}_{7}\text{N} + \ ^{0}_{-1}\text{e} \qquad t_{1/2} = 5715\ \text{y}$$

Radioactive decay is a first-order process, whose rate is proportional to the number of radioactive nuclei N in a sample times a first-order rate constant k, called the **decay constant**:

$$\text{Decay rate} = -\frac{\Delta N}{\Delta t} = kN$$

This rate law is strictly analogous to the rate law for a first-order chemical reaction, as can be seen by replacing the chemical reactant concentration $[A]$ in Section 12.4 with the number of radioactive nuclei N. Consequently, the integrated rate law for radioactive

▲ The rate of radioactive decay of carbon-14 has been used to determine that the Dead Sea Scrolls are approximately 1900 years old.

decay and the relationship between the half-life and the decay constant are also analogous to the equations given in Sections 12.4 and 12.5 for a first-order chemical reaction.

The integrated rate law for radioactive decay is

$$\ln\left(\frac{N_t}{N_0}\right) = -kt$$

where N_0 is the number of radioactive nuclei originally present in a sample and N_t is the number remaining at time t.

The relationship between the half-life and the decay constant is

$$t_{1/2} = \frac{\ln 2}{k} \quad \text{and} \quad k = \frac{\ln 2}{t_{1/2}}$$

Thus, if we know the value of either the decay constant k or the half-life $t_{1/2}$, we can calculate the value of the other. Furthermore, if we know the value of $t_{1/2}$, we can calculate the ratio of remaining and initial amounts of a radioactive sample N_t/N_0 at any time t by substituting the expression for k into the integrated rate law:

$$\text{Since} \quad \ln\left(\frac{N_t}{N_0}\right) = -kt \quad \text{and} \quad k = \frac{\ln 2}{t_{1/2}}$$

$$\text{then} \quad \ln\left(\frac{N_t}{N_0}\right) = (-\ln 2)\left(\frac{t}{t_{1/2}}\right)$$

Worked Example 12.8 shows how to calculate a half-life from a decay constant, and Worked Example 12.10 shows how to determine the percentage of a radioactive sample remaining at time t. Applications of radioactive decay rates will be further explored in Section 22.5.

Remember...

A **radioisotope** is an isotope that undergoes spontaneous radioactive decay (Section 2.8).

WORKED EXAMPLE 12.8

CALCULATING A HALF-LIFE FROM A DECAY CONSTANT

The decay constant for sodium-24, a **radioisotope** used medically in blood studies, is $4.63 \times 10^{-2}\,\text{h}^{-1}$. What is the half-life of ^{24}Na?

STRATEGY

Half-life can be calculated from the decay constant by using the equation

$$t_{1/2} = \frac{\ln 2}{k}$$

SOLUTION

Substituting the values $k = 4.63 \times 10^{-2}\,\text{h}^{-1}$ and $\ln 2 = 0.693$ into the equation gives

$$t_{1/2} = \frac{0.693}{4.63 \times 10^{-2}\,\text{h}^{-1}} = 15.0\,\text{h}$$

WORKED EXAMPLE 12.9

CALCULATING A DECAY CONSTANT FROM A HALF-LIFE

The half-life of radon-222, a radioactive gas of concern as a health hazard in some homes, is 3.82 days. What is the decay constant of ^{222}Rn?

STRATEGY

A decay constant can be calculated from the half-life by using the equation

$$k = \frac{\ln 2}{t_{1/2}}$$

SOLUTION

Substituting the values $t_{1/2} = 3.82$ days and $\ln 2 = 0.693$ into the equation gives

$$k = \frac{0.693}{3.82\,\text{days}} = 0.181\,\text{day}^{-1}$$

WORKED EXAMPLE 12.10

USING HALF-LIFE TO CALCULATE AN AMOUNT REMAINING

Phosphorus-32, a radioisotope used in leukemia therapy, has a half-life of 14.26 days. What percent of a sample remains after 35.0 days?

STRATEGY

The ratio of remaining (N_t) and initial (N_0) amounts of a radioactive sample at time t is given by the equation

$$\ln\left(\frac{N_t}{N_0}\right) = (-\ln 2)\left(\frac{t}{t_{1/2}}\right)$$

Taking N_0 as 100%, N_t can then be obtained.

SOLUTION

Substituting values for t and for $t_{1/2}$ into the equation gives

$$\ln\left(\frac{N_t}{N_0}\right) = (-0.693)\left(\frac{35.0\text{ days}}{14.26\text{ days}}\right) = -1.70$$

Taking the natural antilogarithm of -1.70 then gives the ratio N_t/N_0:

$$\frac{N_t}{N_0} = \text{antiln}\,(-1.70) = e^{-1.70} = 0.183$$

Since the initial amount of ^{32}P was 100%, we can set $N_0 = 100\%$ and solve for N_t:

$$\frac{N_t}{100\%} = 0.183 \quad \text{so} \quad N_t = (0.183)(100\%) = 18.3\%$$

After 35.0 days, 18.3% of a ^{32}P sample remains and $100\% - 18.3\% = 81.7\%$ has decayed.

WORKED EXAMPLE 12.11

USING DECAY RATES TO CALCULATE A HALF-LIFE

A sample of ^{41}Ar, a radioisotope used to measure the flow of gases from smokestacks, decays initially at a rate of 34,500 disintegrations/min, but the decay rate falls to 21,500 disintegrations/min after 75.0 min. What is the half-life of ^{41}Ar?

STRATEGY

The half-life of a radioactive decay process is obtained by finding $t_{1/2}$ in the equation

$$\ln\left(\frac{N_t}{N_0}\right) = (-\ln 2)\left(\frac{t}{t_{1/2}}\right)$$

In the present instance, though, we are given decay rates at two different times rather than values of N_t and N_0. Nevertheless, for a first-order process like radioactive decay, in which rate = kN, the ratio of the decay rate at any time t to the decay rate at time $t = 0$ is the same as the ratio of N_t to N_0:

$$\frac{\text{Decay rate at time } t}{\text{Decay rate at time } t = 0} = \frac{kN_t}{kN_0} = \frac{N_t}{N_0}$$

SOLUTION

Substituting the proper values into the equation gives

$$\ln\left(\frac{21{,}500}{34{,}500}\right) = (-0.693)\left(\frac{75.0\text{ min}}{t_{1/2}}\right) \quad \text{or} \quad -0.473 = \frac{-52.0\text{ min}}{t_{1/2}}$$

$$\text{so} \quad t_{1/2} = \frac{-52.0\text{ min}}{0.473} = 110\text{ min}$$

The half-life of ^{41}Ar is 110 min.

▲ The flow of gases from a smokestack can be measured by releasing ^{41}Ar and monitoring its passage.

▶ **PROBLEM 12.11** The decay constant for mercury-197, a radioisotope used medically in kidney scans, is $1.08 \times 10^{-2}\,h^{-1}$. What is the half-life of mercury-197?

▶ **PROBLEM 12.12** The half-life of carbon-14 is 5715 years. What is its decay constant?

▶ **PROBLEM 12.13** What percentage of $^{14}_{6}C$ ($t_{1/2}$ = 5715 years) remains in a sample estimated to be 16,230 years old?

▶ **PROBLEM 12.14** What is the half-life of iron-59, a radioisotope used medically in the diagnosis of anemia, if a sample with an initial decay rate of 16,800 disintegrations/min decays at a rate of 10,860 disintegrations/min after 28.0 days?

12.7 SECOND-ORDER REACTIONS

A **second-order reaction** is one whose rate depends either on the concentration of a single reactant raised to the second power or on the concentrations of two different reactants, each raised to the first power. For the simpler type, A → Products, the rate law is

$$\text{Rate} = -\frac{\Delta[A]}{\Delta t} = k[A]^2$$

An example is the thermal decomposition of nitrogen dioxide to yield NO and O_2:

$$2\,NO_2(g) \longrightarrow 2\,NO(g) + O_2(g)$$

Using calculus, it's possible to convert the rate law to the integrated rate law:

$$\frac{1}{[A]_t} = kt + \frac{1}{[A]_0}$$

This integrated rate law allows us to calculate the concentration of A at any time t if the initial concentration $[A]_0$ is known.

Since the integrated rate law has the form $y = mx + b$, a graph of $1/[A]$ versus time is a straight line if the reaction is second order:

$$\underset{y}{\frac{1}{[A]_t}} = \underset{mx}{kt} + \underset{b}{\frac{1}{[A]_0}}$$

The slope of the straight line is the rate constant k, and the intercept is $1/[A]_0$. Thus, by plotting $1/[A]$ versus time, we can test whether the reaction is second order and can determine the value of the rate constant (see Worked Example 12.12). We can also obtain an expression for the half-life of a second-order reaction by substituting $[A]_t = [A]_0/2$ and $t = t_{1/2}$ into the integrated rate law:

$$\frac{1}{\left(\frac{[A]_0}{2}\right)} = kt_{1/2} + \frac{1}{[A]_0}$$

so $\quad t_{1/2} = \frac{1}{k}\left(\frac{2}{[A]_0} - \frac{1}{[A]_0}\right)$

or $\quad t_{1/2} = \frac{1}{k[A]_0}$

In contrast with a first-order reaction, the time required for the concentration of A to drop to one-half of its initial value in a second-order reaction depends on both the rate constant and the initial concentration. Thus, the value of $t_{1/2}$ increases as the reaction proceeds because the value of $[A]_0$ at the beginning of each successive half-life is smaller by a factor of 2. Consequently, each half-life for a second-order reaction is twice as long as the preceding one (**Figure 12.8**).

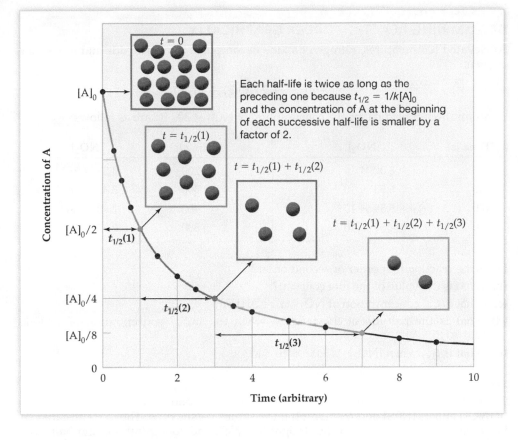

Figure 12.8
Concentration of a reactant A as a function of time for a second-order reaction.

Table 12.4 summarizes some important differences between first-order and second-order reactions of the type A → Products.

TABLE 12.4	Characteristics of First- and Second-Order Reactions of the Type A → Products	

	First-Order	**Second-Order**
Rate law	$-\dfrac{\Delta[A]}{\Delta t} = k[A]$	$-\dfrac{\Delta[A]}{\Delta t} = k[A]^2$
Concentration–time equation	$\ln[A]_t = -kt + \ln[A]_0$	$\dfrac{1}{[A]_t} = kt + \dfrac{1}{[A]_0}$
Linear graph	$\ln[A]$ versus t	$\dfrac{1}{[A]}$ versus t
	(graph: $\ln[A]$ vs Time, with $\ln[A]_0$ intercept, Slope $= -k$)	(graph: $\dfrac{1}{[A]}$ vs Time, with $\dfrac{1}{[A]_0}$ intercept, Slope $= k$)
Graphical determination of k	$k = -(\text{Slope})$	$k = \text{Slope}$
Half-life	$t_{1/2} = \dfrac{0.693}{k}$ (constant)	$t_{1/2} = \dfrac{1}{k[A]_0}$ (not constant)

WORKED EXAMPLE 12.12

DETERMINING REACTION ORDER GRAPHICALLY

At elevated temperatures, nitrogen dioxide decomposes to nitric oxide and molecular oxygen:

$$2\,NO_2(g) \longrightarrow 2\,NO(g) + O_2(g)$$

Concentration–time data for the consumption of NO_2 at 300 °C are as follows:

Time (s)	[NO$_2$]	Time (s)	[NO$_2$]
0	8.00×10^{-3}	200	4.29×10^{-3}
50	6.58×10^{-3}	300	3.48×10^{-3}
100	5.59×10^{-3}	400	2.93×10^{-3}
150	4.85×10^{-3}	500	2.53×10^{-3}

(a) Is the reaction first order or second order?

(b) What is the value of the rate constant?

(c) What is the concentration of NO_2 at $t = 20.0$ min?

(d) What is the half-life of the reaction when the initial concentration of NO_2 is 6.00×10^{-3} M?

(e) What is $t_{1/2}$ when $[NO_2]_0$ is 3.00×10^{-3} M?

STRATEGY

To determine whether the reaction is first order or second order, calculate values of $\ln [NO_2]$ and $1/[NO_2]$ and then graph these values versus time. The rate constant can be obtained from the slope of the straight-line plot, and concentrations and half-lives can be calculated from the appropriate equation in Table 12.4.

SOLUTION

Time (s)	[NO$_2$]	ln [NO$_2$]	1/[NO$_2$]
0	8.00×10^{-3}	-4.828	125
50	6.58×10^{-3}	-5.024	152
100	5.59×10^{-3}	-5.187	179
150	4.85×10^{-3}	-5.329	206
200	4.29×10^{-3}	-5.451	233
300	3.48×10^{-3}	-5.661	287
400	2.93×10^{-3}	-5.833	341
500	2.53×10^{-3}	-5.980	395

(a) The plot of $\ln [NO_2]$ versus time is curved, but the plot of $1/[NO_2]$ versus time is a straight line. The reaction is therefore second order in NO_2.

(b) The rate constant equals the slope of the straight line in the plot of $1/[NO_2]$ versus time, which we can estimate from the coordinates of two widely separated points on the line:

$$k = \text{Slope} = \frac{\Delta y}{\Delta x} = \frac{340 \text{ M}^{-1} - 150 \text{ M}^{-1}}{400 \text{ s} - 50 \text{ s}} = \frac{190 \text{ M}^{-1}}{350 \text{ s}} = 0.54/(\text{M} \cdot \text{s})$$

(c) The concentration of NO_2 at $t = 20.0$ min $(1.20 \times 10^3 \text{ s})$ can be calculated using the integrated rate law:

$$\frac{1}{[NO_2]_t} = kt + \frac{1}{[NO_2]_0}$$

Substituting the values of k, t, and $[NO_2]_0$ gives

$$\frac{1}{[NO_2]_t} = \left(\frac{0.54}{\text{M} \cdot \text{s}}\right)(1.20 \times 10^3 \text{ s}) + \frac{1}{8.00 \times 10^{-3} \text{ M}}$$

$$= \frac{648}{\text{M}} + \frac{125}{\text{M}} = \frac{773}{\text{M}}$$

$$[NO_2]_t = 1.3 \times 10^{-3} \text{ M}$$

(d) The half-life of this second-order reaction when the initial concentration of NO_2 is 6.00×10^{-3} M can be calculated from the rate constant and the initial concentration:

$$t_{1/2} = \frac{1}{k[NO_2]_0} = \frac{1}{\left(\dfrac{0.54}{\text{M} \cdot \text{s}}\right)(6.00 \times 10^{-3} \text{ M})} = 3.1 \times 10^2 \text{ s}$$

(e) When $[NO_2]_0$ is 3.00×10^{-3} M, $t_{1/2} = 6.2 \times 10^2$ s (twice as long as when $[NO_2]_0$ is 6.00×10^{-3} M because $[NO_2]_0$ is now smaller by a factor of 2).

▶ **PROBLEM 12.15** Hydrogen iodide gas decomposes at 410 °C:

$$2 \text{ HI}(g) \longrightarrow H_2(g) + I_2(g)$$

The following data describe this decomposition:

Time (min)	0	20	40	60	80
[HI]	0.500	0.382	0.310	0.260	0.224

(a) Is the reaction first order or second order?
(b) What is the value of the rate constant for consumption of HI?
(c) At what time (in minutes) does the HI concentration reach 0.100 M?
(d) In how many minutes does the HI concentration drop from 0.400 M to 0.200 M?

12.8   ZEROTH-ORDER REACTIONS

A **zeroth-order reaction** of the type A → Products is one that has the rate law

$$\text{Rate} = -\frac{\Delta[A]}{\Delta t} = k[A]^0 = k(1) = k$$

Throughout the course of the reaction, the rate remains constant ($= k$), independent of the concentration of the reactant. The integrated rate law is

$$[A] = -kt + [A]_0$$

This is another equation of the form $y = mx + b$, so a graph of [A] versus time is a straight line with a slope $-k$ (**Figure 12.9**). Note that both the rate constant k and the rate of a zeroth-order reaction have a constant value equal to minus the slope of the [A] versus time plot.

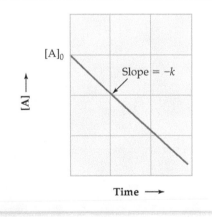

Figure 12.9
Concentration of a reactant A as a function of time for a zeroth-order reaction.

Zeroth-order reactions are relatively uncommon, but they can occur under special circumstances. Take, for example, the decomposition of gaseous ammonia on a hot platinum surface:

$$2\,NH_3(g) \xrightarrow[\text{Pt catalyst}]{1130\ K} N_2(g) + 3\,H_2(g)$$

The platinum surface is completely covered by a layer of NH_3 molecules (**Figure 12.10**), but the number of NH_3 molecules that can fit on the surface is limited by size constraints and is very small compared with the total number of NH_3 molecules. Most of the NH_3 is in the gas phase above the surface. Because only the NH_3 molecules on the surface can react, the reaction rate is constant and independent of the total concentration of NH_3:

$$\text{Rate} = -\frac{\Delta[NH_3]}{\Delta t} = k[NH_3]^0 = k$$

Figure 12.10

Decomposition of ammonia on a hot platinum surface. Only the NH_3 molecules attached to the surface can react.

Most of the NH_3 molecules are in the gas phase above the surface and are unable to react.

As NH_3 molecules on the surface decompose, they are replaced by molecules from the gas phase, so the number of NH_3 molecules on the surface remains constant.

NH₃ H₂ N₂

Because only the NH_3 molecules on the surface react under these conditions, the reaction rate is independent of the total concentration of NH_3.

12.9   REACTION MECHANISMS

Thus far, our discussion of chemical kinetics has centered on reaction rates. We've seen that the rate of a reaction usually depends on both reactant concentrations and the value of the rate constant. An equally important issue in chemical kinetics is the **reaction mechanism**, the sequence of molecular events, or reaction steps, that describes the pathway from reactants to products. Chemists want to know the sequence in which the various reaction steps take place so that they can better control known reactions and predict new ones.

◁▨▷ **Reaction Mechanism**   The sequence of reaction steps that describes the pathway from reactants to products.

A single step in a reaction mechanism is called an **elementary reaction**, or **elementary step**. To clarify the crucial distinction between an elementary reaction and an overall reaction, let's consider the gas-phase reaction of nitrogen dioxide and carbon monoxide to give nitric oxide and carbon dioxide:

$$NO_2(g) + CO(g) \longrightarrow NO(g) + CO_2(g) \qquad \text{Overall reaction}$$

Experimental evidence suggests that this reaction takes place by a two-step mechanism:

Step 1. $NO_2(g) + NO_2(g) \longrightarrow NO(g) + NO_3(g)$ Elementary reaction

Step 2. $NO_3(g) + CO(g) \longrightarrow NO_2(g) + CO_2(g)$ Elementary reaction

In the first elementary step, two NO_2 molecules collide with enough energy to break one N—O bond and form another, resulting in the transfer of an oxygen atom from one NO_2 molecule to the other. In the second step, the NO_3 molecule formed in the first step collides with a CO molecule, and the transfer of an oxygen atom from NO_3 to CO yields an NO_2 molecule and a CO_2 molecule (**Figure 12.11**).

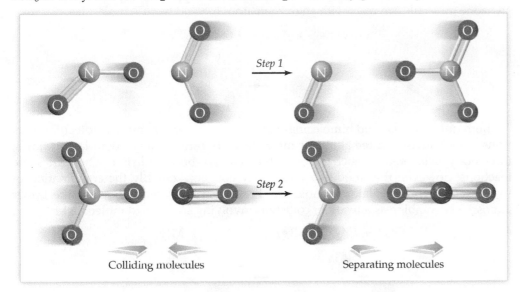

Colliding molecules   Separating molecules

Figure 12.11
Elementary steps in the reaction of NO_2 with CO.

The chemical equation for an elementary reaction is a description of an individual molecular event that involves breaking and/or making chemical bonds. By contrast, the balanced equation for an overall reaction describes only the stoichiometry of the overall process but provides no information about how the reaction occurs. The equation for the overall reaction of NO_2 with CO, for example, doesn't tell us that the reaction occurs by the direct transfer of an oxygen atom from an NO_2 molecule to a CO molecule.

Elementary reaction—describes an individual molecular event.

Overall reaction—describes the reaction stoichiometry.

The elementary steps in a proposed reaction mechanism must sum to give the overall reaction. When we sum the elementary steps in the reaction of NO_2 with CO and then cancel the molecules that appear on both sides of the resulting equation, for instance, we obtain the overall reaction:

Step 1. $NO_2(g) + NO_2(g) \longrightarrow NO(g) + NO_3(g)$ Elementary reaction
Step 2. $NO_3(g) + CO(g) \longrightarrow NO_2(g) + CO_2(g)$ Elementary reaction

$NO_2(g) + \cancel{NO_2(g)} + \cancel{NO_3(g)} + CO(g) \longrightarrow NO(g) + \cancel{NO_3(g)} + \cancel{NO_2(g)} + CO_2(g)$

$NO_2(g) + CO(g) \longrightarrow NO(g) + CO_2(g)$ Overall reaction

A species that is formed in one step of a reaction mechanism and consumed in a subsequent step, such as NO_3 in our example, is called a **reaction intermediate**. Reaction intermediates don't appear in the net equation for the overall reaction, and it's only by looking at the elementary steps that their presence is noticed.

Elementary reactions are classified on the basis of their **molecularity**, the number of molecules (or atoms) on the reactant side of the chemical equation. A **unimolecular reaction**, for instance, is an elementary reaction that involves a single reactant molecule—for example, the unimolecular decomposition of ozone in the upper atmosphere:

$$O_3{}^*(g) \longrightarrow O_2(g) + O(g)$$

▲ The beautiful northern lights, or aurora borealis, are often observed in the northern hemisphere at high latitudes. The light is partly produced by excited O atoms in the upper atmosphere.

The asterisk on O_3 indicates that the ozone molecule is in an energetically excited state because it has absorbed ultraviolet light from the sun. The absorbed energy causes one of the two O—O bonds to break, with the loss of an oxygen atom.

A **bimolecular reaction** is an elementary reaction that results from an energetic collision between two reactant atoms or molecules. In the upper atmosphere, for example, an ozone molecule can react with an oxygen atom to yield two O_2 molecules:

$$O_3(g) \;+\; O(g) \longrightarrow 2\,O_2(g)$$

Both unimolecular and bimolecular reactions are common, but **termolecular reactions**, which involve three atoms or molecules, are rare. As any pool player knows, three-body collisions are much less probable than two-body collisions. There are some reactions, however, that require a three-body collision, notably the combination of two atoms to form a diatomic molecule. For example, oxygen atoms in the upper atmosphere combine as a result of collisions involving some third molecule M:

$$O(g) + O(g) \;+\; M(g) \longrightarrow O_2(g) \;+\; M(g)$$

In the atmosphere, M is most likely N_2, but in principle it could be any atom or molecule. The role of M is to carry away the energy that is released when the O—O bond is formed. If M were not involved in the collision, the two oxygen atoms would simply bounce off each other, and no reaction would occur.

WORKED EXAMPLE 12.13

IDENTIFYING INTERMEDIATES AND MOLECULARITY IN A REACTION MECHANISM

The following two-step mechanism has been proposed for the gas-phase decomposition of nitrous oxide (N_2O):

Step 1. $\qquad\qquad\qquad N_2O(g) \longrightarrow N_2(g) \;+\; O(g)$

Step 2. $\qquad N_2O(g) \;+\; O(g) \longrightarrow N_2(g) \;+\; O_2(g)$

(a) Write the chemical equation for the overall reaction.
(b) Identify any reaction intermediates.
(c) What is the molecularity of each of the elementary reactions?
(d) What is the molecularity of the overall reaction?

STRATEGY

To find the overall reaction, sum the elementary steps. To identify intermediates and molecularity, look at the individual steps.

SOLUTION

(a) The overall reaction is the sum of the two elementary steps:

Step 1. $\qquad N_2O(g) \longrightarrow N_2(g) + O(g)$	Elementary reaction
Step 2. $N_2O(g) + O(g) \longrightarrow N_2(g) + O_2(g)$	Elementary reaction

$$\overline{2\,N_2O(g) + \cancel{O(g)} \longrightarrow 2\,N_2(g) + \cancel{O(g)} + O_2(g)}$$

$2\,N_2O(g) \longrightarrow 2\,N_2(g) + O_2(g) \qquad$ Overall reaction

(b) The oxygen atom is a reaction intermediate because it is formed in the first elementary step and consumed in the second step.

(c) The first elementary reaction is unimolecular because it involves a single reactant molecule. The second step is bimolecular because it involves two reactant atoms or molecules.

(d) It's inappropriate to use the word *molecularity* in connection with the overall reaction because the overall reaction does not describe an individual molecular event. Only an elementary reaction can have a molecularity.

▶ **PROBLEM 12.16** A suggested mechanism for the reaction of nitrogen dioxide and molecular fluorine is

Step 1. $NO_2(g) + F_2(g) \longrightarrow NO_2F(g) + F(g)$

Step 2. $NO_2(g) + F(g) \longrightarrow NO_2F(g)$

(a) Write the chemical equation for the overall reaction, and identify any reaction intermediates.

(b) What is the molecularity of each elementary reaction?

12.10 RATE LAWS FOR ELEMENTARY REACTIONS

Recall from Section 12.2 that the rate law for an overall chemical reaction must be determined experimentally. It can't be deduced from the stoichiometric coefficients in the balanced equation for the overall reaction. By contrast, the rate law for an elementary reaction follows directly from its molecularity because an elementary reaction is an individual molecular event. The concentration of each reactant in an elementary reaction appears in the rate law, with an exponent equal to its coefficient in the chemical equation for the elementary reaction.

Consider, for example, the unimolecular decomposition of ozone:

$$O_3(g) \longrightarrow O_2(g) + O(g)$$

The number of moles of O_3 per liter that decompose per unit time is directly proportional to the molar concentration of O_3:

$$\text{Rate} = -\frac{\Delta[O_3]}{\Delta t} = k[O_3]$$

The rate of a unimolecular reaction is always first order in the concentration of the reactant molecule.

For a bimolecular elementary reaction of the type $A + B \rightarrow$ Products, the reaction rate depends on the frequency of collisions between A and B molecules. The frequency of AB collisions involving any *particular* A molecule is proportional to the molar concentration of B, and the total frequency of AB collisions involving *all* A molecules is proportional to the molar concentration of A times the molar concentration of B (**Figure 12.12**). Therefore, the reaction obeys the second-order rate law

$$\text{Rate} = -\frac{\Delta[A]}{\Delta t} = -\frac{\Delta[B]}{\Delta t} = k[A][B]$$

(a) The frequency of AB collisions involving any one **A molecule** is proportional to the concentration of **B molecules**.

(b) Doubling the concentration of **A molecules** (from 1 to 2 per unit volume) doubles the total frequency of AB collisions.

(c) Doubling the concentration of **B molecules** doubles the frequency of AB collisions involving any one **A molecule**.

(d) Doubling the concentration of **A molecules** and doubling the concentration of **B molecules** quadruples the total frequency of AB collisions.

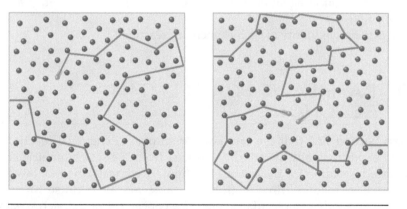

Thus, the total frequency of AB collisions is proportional to the concentration of **A molecules** times the concentration of **B molecules**.

Figure 12.12
The effect of concentration on the frequency of collisions between A molecules (blue) and B molecules (red).

An example is the conversion of bromomethane to methanol in a basic solution:

$$CH_3Br(aq) + OH^-(aq) \longrightarrow Br^-(aq) + CH_3OH(aq)$$

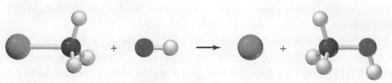

Bromomethane   Hydroxide ion   Bromide ion   Methanol

This reaction occurs in a single bimolecular step in which a new C—O bond forms at the same time as the C—Br bond breaks. The experimental rate law is

$$\text{Rate} = -\frac{\Delta[CH_3Br]}{\Delta t} = k[CH_3Br][OH^-]$$

By a similar line of reasoning, a bimolecular reaction of the type

$$A + A \longrightarrow \text{Products}$$

has the second-order rate law:

$$\text{Rate} = -\frac{\Delta[A]}{\Delta t} = k[A][A] = k[A]^2$$

Rate laws for elementary reactions are summarized in Table 12.5. Note that the overall reaction order for an elementary reaction always equals its molecularity.

TABLE 12.5   Rate Laws for Elementary Reactions

Elementary Reaction	Molecularity	Rate Law
A → Products	Unimolecular	Rate = $k[A]$
A + A → Products	Bimolecular	Rate = $k[A]^2$
A + B → Products	Bimolecular	Rate = $k[A][B]$
A + A + B → Products	Termolecular	Rate = $k[A]^2[B]$
A + B + C → Products	Termolecular	Rate = $k[A][B][C]$

▶ **PROBLEM 12.17**   Write the rate law for each of the following elementary reactions:
(a) $O_3(g) + O(g) \longrightarrow 2\,O_2(g)$
(b) $Br(g) + Br(g) + Ar(g) \longrightarrow Br_2(g) + Ar(g)$
(c) $Co(CN)_5(H_2O)^{2-}(aq) \longrightarrow Co(CN)_5^{2-}(aq) + H_2O(l)$

12.11 RATE LAWS FOR OVERALL REACTIONS

We saw in the previous section that the rate law for a single-step, elementary reaction follows directly from its molecularity. By contrast, the rate law for a multistep, overall reaction depends on the reaction mechanism—that is, on the sequence of elementary steps and their relative rates.

When an overall reaction occurs in two or more elementary steps, one of the steps is often much slower than the others. This slowest step in a reaction mechanism is called the **rate-determining step** because it acts as a bottleneck, limiting the rate at which reactants can be converted to products. In this respect, a chemical reaction is somewhat like the cafeteria line in a dining hall. The rate at which the line moves is determined not by the faster steps, perhaps picking up a salad or a beverage, but by the slowest step, perhaps waiting for a well-done hamburger. The overall reaction can occur no faster than the speed of the rate-determining step.

▲ Which is more likely to slow down this line: picking up a beverage or waiting for a well-done hamburger?

Multistep Reactions with an Initial Slow Step

The rate-determining step might occur anywhere in the multistep sequence. In the reaction of nitrogen dioxide with carbon monoxide, for instance, the first step in the mechanism is slower and rate-determining, whereas the second step occurs more rapidly:

$$NO_2(g) + NO_2(g) \xrightarrow{\;k_1\;} NO(g) + NO_3(g) \quad \text{Slower, rate-determining}$$
$$\underline{NO_3(g) + CO(g) \xrightarrow{\;k_2\;} NO_2(g) + CO_2(g) \quad \text{Faster}}$$
$$NO_2(g) + CO(g) \longrightarrow NO(g) + CO_2(g) \quad \text{Overall reaction}$$

The constants k_1 and k_2, written above the arrows in the preceding equations, are the rate constants for the elementary reactions. The rate of the overall reaction is determined by the rate of the first, slower step. In the second step, the unstable inter-mediate (NO_3) reacts as soon as it is formed.

Because the rate law for an overall reaction depends on the reaction mechanism, it provides important clues to the mechanism. A plausible mechanism must meet two criteria: (1) The elementary steps must sum up to give the overall reaction, and (2) the mechanism must be consistent with the experimental rate law for the overall reaction.

For the reaction of NO_2 with CO, for example, the experimental rate law is

$$\text{Rate} = -\frac{\Delta[NO_2]}{\Delta t} = k[NO_2]^2$$

The rate law predicted by the proposed mechanism is that for the rate-determining step (first step) and follows directly from the molecularity of that step:

$$\text{Rate} = -\frac{\Delta[NO_2]}{\Delta t} = k_1[NO_2]^2$$

Because the experimental and predicted rate laws have the same form (second-order dependence on $[NO_2]$), the proposed mechanism is consistent with the experimental rate law. The observed rate constant k equals k_1, the rate constant for the first elementary step.

Multistep Reactions with an Initial Fast Step

In contrast to reactions in which the first step is slow and rate-determining, the following three-step mechanism has been proposed for the reaction of nitric oxide with hydrogen:

$$2\,NO(g) \underset{k_{-1}}{\overset{k_1}{\rightleftharpoons}} N_2O_2(g) \qquad\qquad \text{Fast, reversible}$$

$$N_2O_2(g) + H_2(g) \xrightarrow{k_2} N_2O(g) + H_2O(g) \quad \text{Slow, rate-determining}$$

$$N_2O(g) + H_2(g) \xrightarrow{k_3} N_2(g) + H_2O(g) \qquad \text{Fast}$$

$$2\,NO(g) + 2\,H_2(g) \longrightarrow N_2(g) + 2\,H_2O(g) \quad \text{Overall reaction}$$

The first step, which is fast and reversible, produces a small concentration of the unstable intermediate, N_2O_2. This intermediate decomposes rapidly to NO in the reverse of the first step and reacts only slowly with H_2 in the second step, yielding a second intermediate, N_2O. The second step is the rate-determining step. In the third step, the N_2O reacts rapidly with H_2 to give N_2 and H_2O. On summing the three elementary steps, both intermediates cancel and we obtain the balanced equation for the overall reaction. The predicted rate law for the proposed mechanism is the rate law for the rate-determining step:

$$\text{Rate} = -\frac{\Delta[N_2O_2]}{\Delta t} = k_2[N_2O_2][H_2]$$

where k_2 is the rate constant for that step. Note that fast steps subsequent to the rate-determining step (the third step in our example) do not affect the rate of the reaction.

The experimental rate law for the formation of N_2 is

$$\text{Rate} = \frac{\Delta[N_2]}{\Delta t} = k[NO]^2[H_2]$$

where k is the observed rate constant for the overall reaction. To decide whether the proposed mechanism is plausible, we need to compare the experimental and predicted rate laws. The concentrations of reaction intermediates, such as N_2O_2, do not appear in the experimental rate law because their concentrations are usually very small and undetermined. Only reactants and products (and catalysts, if present) appear in the rate law for an overall reaction. Therefore, we must eliminate $[N_2O_2]$ from the predicted rate law. Because the mechanism indicates that the rate of formation of N_2 equals the rate of disappearance of N_2O_2, $\Delta[N_2]/\Delta t = -\Delta[N_2O_2]/\Delta t$, we can rewrite the predicted rate law as

$$\text{Rate} = \frac{\Delta[N_2]}{\Delta t} = k_2[N_2O_2][H_2]$$

To eliminate N_2O_2 from the right side of this equation, we assume that the fast, reversible, first step in the mechanism reaches a dynamic equilibrium. (We'll have more to say about chemical equilibrium in Chapter 13.) The rates of the forward and reverse reactions in the first step are given by

$$\text{Rate}_{forward} = k_1[NO]^2 \qquad \text{Rate}_{reverse} = k_{-1}[N_2O_2]$$

Just as the rates of vaporization and condensation are equal for a liquid–vapor equilibrium (Section 10.5), so the rates of the forward and reverse reactions are equal for a chemical equilibrium. Therefore,

$$k_1[NO]^2 = k_{-1}[N_2O_2] \qquad \text{and} \qquad [N_2O_2] = \frac{k_1}{k_{-1}}[NO]^2$$

Substituting this expression for $[N_2O_2]$ into the equation for the predicted rate eliminates the intermediate and gives the final predicted rate law in terms of only reactants and products:

$$\text{Rate} = \frac{\Delta[N_2]}{\Delta t} = k_2[N_2O_2][H_2] = k_2\frac{k_1}{k_{-1}}[NO]^2[H_2]$$

The predicted and experimental rate laws now have the same form: Both are second order in NO and first order in H_2. Therefore, the proposed mechanism is consistent with experiment and is a plausible mechanism for the reaction. Comparison of the two rate laws indicates that the observed rate constant k equals k_2k_1/k_{-1}.

Procedure Used in Studies of Reaction Mechanisms

Let's summarize the procedure that chemists use in establishing a reaction mechanism. First, the rate law is determined by experiment. Then, a series of elementary steps is proposed, and the rate law predicted by the proposed mechanism is worked out. If the observed and predicted rate laws do not agree, the mechanism must be discarded and another one must be devised. If the observed and predicted rate laws *do* agree, the proposed mechanism is a plausible (though not necessarily correct) pathway for the reaction. **Figure 12.13** summarizes the procedure.

Remember...

In a **liquid–vapor equilibrium** the number of molecules escaping from the liquid per unit time (vaporization) equals the number returning to the liquid per unit time (condensation). (Section 10.5)

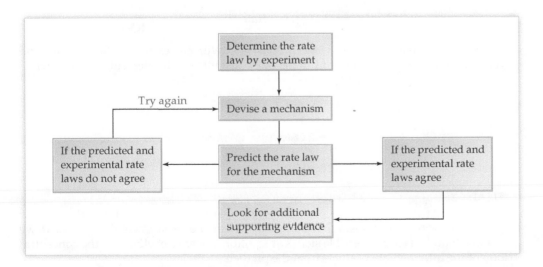

Figure 12.13
Flowchart illustrating the logic used in studies of reaction mechanisms.

The case for a particular mechanism is strengthened considerably if a reaction intermediate can be isolated or if an unstable intermediate can be detected. It's easy to disprove a mechanism, but it's seldom possible to finally prove a mechanism because there may be an alternative reaction pathway—not yet imagined—that also fits the experimental facts. The best we can do to establish a mechanism is to accumulate a convincing body of experimental evidence that supports it. Proving a reaction mechanism is more like proving a case in a court of law than like proving a theorem in mathematics.

WORKED EXAMPLE 12.14

SUGGESTING A MECHANISM GIVEN THE RATE LAW: REACTIONS WITH AN INITIAL SLOW STEP

The following reaction has a second-order rate law:

$$H_2(g) + 2\,ICl(g) \longrightarrow I_2(g) + 2\,HCl(g) \qquad Rate = k[H_2][ICl]$$

Devise a possible reaction mechanism.

STRATEGY

The reaction doesn't occur in a single elementary step because, if it did, the rate law would be third order: Rate $= k[H_2][ICl]^2$. The observed rate law will be obtained if the rate-determining step involves the bimolecular reaction of H_2 and ICl.

SOLUTION

A plausible sequence of elementary steps is

$$H_2(g) + ICl(g) \xrightarrow{k_1} HI(g) + HCl(g) \qquad \text{Slow, rate-determining}$$

$$HI(g) + ICl(g) \xrightarrow{k_2} I_2(g) + HCl(g) \qquad \text{Faster}$$

$$H_2(g) + 2\,ICl(g) \longrightarrow I_2(g) + 2\,HCl(g) \qquad \text{Overall reaction}$$

The rate law predicted by this mechanism, rate $= k_1[H_2][ICl]$, agrees with the observed rate law.

WORKED EXAMPLE 12.15

SUPPORTING A MECHANISM GIVEN THE RATE LAW: REACTIONS WITH AN INITIAL FAST STEP

The experimental rate law for the decomposition of ozone is second order in ozone and inverse first order in molecular oxygen:

$$2\,O_3(g) \longrightarrow 3\,O_2(g) \qquad Rate = -\frac{\Delta[O_3]}{\Delta t} = k\frac{[O_3]^2}{[O_2]}$$

Show that the following mechanism is consistent with the experimental rate law, and relate the observed rate constant k to the rate constants for the elementary reactions:

$$O_3(g) \underset{k_{-1}}{\overset{k_1}{\rightleftharpoons}} O_2(g) + O(g) \qquad \text{Fast, reversible}$$

$$O(g) + O_3(g) \xrightarrow{k_2} 2\,O_2(g) \qquad \text{Slow, rate-determining}$$

$$2\,O_3(g) \longrightarrow 3\,O_2(g) \qquad \text{Overall reaction}$$

STRATEGY

To show that the mechanism is consistent with experiment, we must derive the rate law predicted by the mechanism and compare it with the experimental rate law. If we assume that the faster, reversible step is at equilibrium, we can eliminate the concentration of the intermediate O atoms from the predicted rate law.

SOLUTION

The rate law for the rate-determining step is rate = $k_2[O][O_3]$, but the stoichiometry of the reaction indicates that the overall rate of consumption of ozone is twice the rate of the rate-determining step:

$$\text{Rate} = -\frac{\Delta[O_3]}{\Delta t} = 2k_2[O][O_3]$$

(When one O atom and one O_3 molecule react in the rate-determining step, two O_3 molecules are consumed in the overall reaction.)

The rates of the forward and reverse reactions in the faster, reversible step are given by

$$\text{Rate}_{\text{forward}} = k_1[O_3] \qquad \text{Rate}_{\text{reverse}} = k_{-1}[O_2][O]$$

Assuming that the first step is at equilibrium, we can equate the rates of the forward and reverse reactions and then solve for the concentration of the intermediate O atoms:

$$k_1[O_3] = k_{-1}[O_2][O] \qquad \text{so, } [O] = \frac{k_1[O_3]}{k_{-1}[O_2]}$$

Substituting this expression for [O] into the predicted rate law for overall consumption of ozone gives the predicted rate law in terms of only reactants and products:

$$\text{Rate} = -\frac{\Delta[O_3]}{\Delta t} = 2k_2[O][O_3] = 2k_2\frac{k_1}{k_{-1}}\frac{[O_3]^2}{[O_2]}$$

Because the predicted and experimental rate laws have the same reaction orders in O_3 and O_2, the proposed mechanism is consistent with the experimental rate law and is a plausible mechanism for the reaction. Comparison of the predicted and experimental rate laws indicates that the observed rate constant k equals $2k_2k_1/k_{-1}$.

▶ **PROBLEM 12.18**   The following reaction has a first-order rate law:

$$Co(CN)_5(H_2O)^{2-}(aq) + I^-(aq) \longrightarrow Co(CN)_5I^{3-}(aq) + H_2O(l)$$

$$\text{Rate} = k[Co(CN)_5(H_2O)^{2-}]$$

Suggest a possible reaction mechanism, and show that your mechanism agrees with the observed rate law.

▶ **PROBLEM 12.19**   The following mechanism has been proposed for the oxidation of nitric oxide to nitrogen dioxide:

$$NO(g) + O_2(g) \underset{k_{-1}}{\overset{k_1}{\rightleftharpoons}} NO_3(g) \qquad \text{Faster, reversible}$$

$$NO_3(g) + NO(g) \xrightarrow{k_2} 2\,NO_2(g) \qquad \text{Slower, rate-determining}$$

The experimental rate law for the overall reaction is

$$\text{Rate} = -\frac{\Delta[NO]}{\Delta t} = k[NO]^2[O_2]$$

(a) Write a balanced equation for the overall reaction.
(b) Show that the proposed mechanism is consistent with the experimental rate law.
(c) Relate the rate constant k to the rate constants for the elementary reactions.

12.12 REACTION RATES AND TEMPERATURE: THE ARRHENIUS EQUATION

Everyday experience tells us that the rates of chemical reactions increase with increasing temperature. Familiar fuels such as gas, oil, and coal are relatively inert at room temperature but burn rapidly at elevated temperatures. Many foods last almost indefinitely when stored in a freezer but spoil quickly at room temperature. Metallic magnesium is inert in cold water but reacts with hot water (**Figure 12.14**).

Figure 12.14
Magnesium is inert in cold water (left) but reacts with hot water (right).

Magnesium is inert
in cold water.

Magnesium reacts
in hot water.

$$Mg(s) + 2\,H_2O(l) \longrightarrow Mg^{2+}(aq) + 2\,OH^-(aq) + H_2(g)$$

The formation of bubbles of gas and the pink color of phenolphthalein, which indicates an alkaline solution, provide evidence of the reaction.

As a rule of thumb, reaction rates tend to double when the temperature is increased by 10 °C.

To understand why reaction rates depend on temperature, we need a picture, or model, of how reactions take place. According to the **collision theory** model, a bimolecular reaction occurs when two properly oriented reactant molecules come together in a sufficiently energetic collision. To be specific, let's consider one of the simplest possible reactions, the reaction of an atom A with a diatomic molecule BC to give a diatomic molecule AB and an atom C:

$$A + BC \longrightarrow AB + C$$

An example from atmospheric chemistry is the reaction of an oxygen atom with an HCl molecule to give an OH molecule and a chlorine atom:

$$O(g) + HCl(g) \longrightarrow OH(g) + Cl(g)$$

If the reaction occurs in a single step, the electron distribution about the three nuclei must change in the course of the collision such that a new bond, A—B, develops at the same time the old bond, B—C, breaks. Between the reactant and product stages, the nuclei pass through a configuration in which all three atoms are weakly linked together. We can picture the progress of the reaction as

$$A + B{-}C \longrightarrow A{\text{---}}B{\text{---}}C \longrightarrow A{-}B + C$$

A   B   C   A   B   C   A   B   C

If A and BC have filled shells of electrons (no unpaired electrons or vacant, low-energy orbitals), they will repel each other. To achieve the configuration A---B---C, then, the atoms require energy to overcome this repulsion. The energy comes from the kinetic energy of the colliding particles and is converted to potential energy in A---B---C. In fact, A---B---C has more potential energy than either the reactants or the products. Thus, there is a potential energy barrier that must be surmounted before reactants can be converted to products, as depicted graphically on the potential energy profile in **Figure 12.15**.

The height of the barrier is called the **activation energy (E_a)**, and the configuration of atoms at the maximum in the potential energy profile is called the **transition state**, or the *activated complex*. Since energy is conserved in the collision, all the energy needed to climb the potential energy hill must come from the kinetic energy of the colliding molecules. If the collision energy is less than E_a, the reactant molecules can't surmount

Figure 12.15
Potential energy profile for the reaction
$A + BC \rightarrow AB + C$.

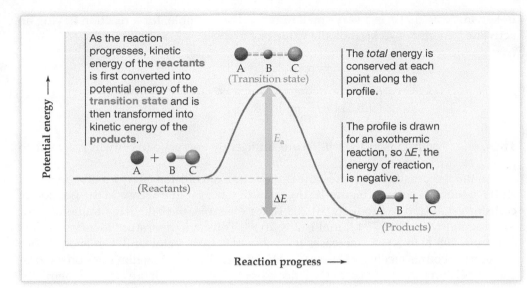

the barrier and they simply bounce apart. If the collision energy is at least as great as E_a, however, the reactants can climb over the barrier and be converted to products.

Experimental evidence for the notion of an activation energy barrier comes from a comparison of collision rates and reaction rates. Collision rates in gases can be calculated from **kinetic–molecular theory** (Section 9.6). For a gas at room temperature (298 K) and 1 atm pressure, each molecule undergoes approximately 10^9 collisions per second, or 1 collision every 10^{-9} s. Thus, if every collision resulted in reaction, every gas-phase reaction would be complete in about 10^{-9} s. By contrast, observed reactions often have half-lives of minutes or hours, so only a tiny fraction of the collisions lead to reaction.

Very few collisions are productive because very few occur with a collision energy as large as the activation energy. The fraction of collisions with an energy equal to or greater than the activation energy E_a is represented in **Figure 12.16** at two different temperatures by the areas under the curves to the right of E_a. When E_a is large compared to RT, this fraction f is approximated by the equation

$$f = e^{-E_a/RT}$$

where R is the gas constant [8.314 J/(K·mol)] and T is the absolute temperature

Remember...
According to the **kinetic–molecular theory**, the average kinetic energy and thus the average speed of gas molecules depends on the Kelvin temperature. Collision rates increase with increasing concentration, diameter, and average speed of the colliding molecules.   (Section 9.6)

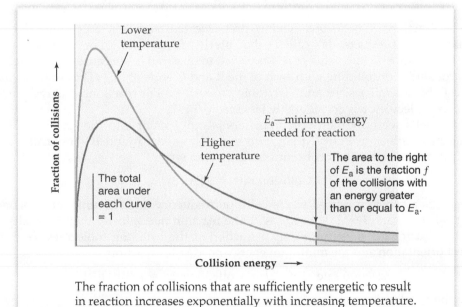

The fraction of collisions that are sufficiently energetic to result in reaction increases exponentially with increasing temperature.

Figure 12.16
Plots of the fraction of collisions with a particular energy at two different temperatures.

in kelvin. Note that f is a very small number. For example, for a reaction having an activation energy of 75 kJ/mol, the value of f at 298 K is 7×10^{-14}:

$$f = \exp\left[\frac{-75{,}000\ \dfrac{J}{mol}}{\left(8.314\ \dfrac{J}{K \cdot mol}\right)(298\ K)}\right] = e^{-30.3} = 7 \times 10^{-14}$$

Thus, only 7 collisions in 100 trillion are sufficiently energetic to convert reactants to products.

As the temperature increases, the distribution of collision energies broadens and shifts to higher energies (Figure 12.16), resulting in a rapid increase in the fraction of collisions that lead to products. At 308 K, for example, the calculated value of f for the reaction with $E_a = 75$ kJ/mol is 2×10^{-13}. Thus, a temperature increase of just 3%, from 298 K to 308 K, increases the value of f by a factor of 3. Collision theory therefore accounts nicely for the exponential dependence of reaction rates on reciprocal temperature. As T increases ($1/T$ decreases), $f = e^{-E_a/RT}$ increases exponentially. Collision theory also explains why reaction rates are so much lower than collision rates. Collision rates also increase with increasing temperature, but only by a small amount—less than 2% on going from 298 K to 308 K.

The fraction of collisions that lead to products is further reduced by an orientation requirement. Even if the reactants collide with sufficient energy, they won't react unless the orientation of the reaction partners is correct for formation of the transition state. For example, a collision of A with the C end of the molecule BC can't result in formation of AB:

The reactant molecules would simply collide and then separate without reaction:

The fraction of collisions having proper orientation for the conversion of reactants to products is called the **steric factor** (*p*). For the reaction, $A + BC \rightarrow AB + C$, the value of p is expected to be about 0.5 because A has a nearly 1:1 probability of colliding with each of the B and C ends of BC. (This assumes that B and C have similar sizes and electronic properties.) For reactions of larger, more complex molecules, p is considerably less than 0.5.

Now let's see how the two parameters p and f enter into the rate law. Since bimolecular collisions between any two molecules—say, A and B—occur at a rate that is proportional to their concentrations, we can write

$$\text{Collision rate} = Z[A][B]$$

where Z is a constant related to the collision frequency and has units of a second-order rate constant, $1/(M \cdot s)$ or $M^{-1} s^{-1}$. The reaction rate is lower than the collision rate by a factor $p \times f$ because only a fraction of the colliding molecules have the correct orientation and the minimum energy needed for reaction:

$$\text{Reaction rate} = p \times f \times \text{Collision rate} = pfZ[A][B]$$

Since the rate law is

$$\text{Reaction rate} = k[A][B]$$

the rate constant predicted by collision theory is $k = pfZ$, or $k = pZe^{-E_a/RT}$:

This expression is usually written in a form called the **Arrhenius equation**, named after Svante Arrhenius, the Swedish chemist who proposed it in 1889 on the basis of experimental studies of reaction rates:

$$\text{Arrhenius equation} \quad k = Ae^{-E_a/RT}$$

The parameter $A(= pZ)$ is called the **frequency factor**, or pre-exponential factor. In accord with the minus sign in the exponent, the rate constant decreases as E_a increases and increases as T increases.

CONCEPTUAL PROBLEM 12.20   The potential energy profile for the one-step reaction $AB + CD \rightarrow AC + BD$ follows. The energies are in kJ/mol relative to an arbitrary zero of energy.

(a) What is the value of the activation energy for this reaction?
(b) Is the reaction exothermic or endothermic?
(c) Suggest a plausible structure for the transition state.

12.13   USING THE ARRHENIUS EQUATION

As we saw in Section 12.12, the activation energy E_a is one of the most important factors affecting the rate of a chemical reaction. Its value can be determined using the Arrhenius equation if values of the rate constant are known at different temperatures.

Taking the natural logarithm of both sides of the Arrhenius equation, we obtain the logarithmic form

$$\ln k = \ln A - \frac{E_a}{RT}$$

This equation can be rearranged into the form $y = mx + b$, so a graph of $\ln k$ versus $1/T$, called an Arrhenius plot, gives a straight line with slope $m = -E_a/R$ and intercept $b = \ln A$:

$$\underset{\underset{y}{\uparrow}}{\ln k} = \underset{\underset{m}{\uparrow}\;\underset{x}{\uparrow}}{-\left(\frac{-E_a}{R}\right)\left(\frac{1}{T}\right)} + \underset{\underset{b}{\uparrow}}{\ln A}$$

The experimental value of the activation energy can be determined from the slope of the straight line, as shown in Worked Example 12.16.

$$E_a = -R(\text{Slope})$$

Still another form of the Arrhenius equation can be derived that allows us to estimate the activation energy from rate constants at just two temperatures. At temperature T_1,

$$\ln k_1 = \left(\frac{-E_a}{R}\right)\left(\frac{1}{T_1}\right) + \ln A$$

and at temperature T_2,

$$\ln k_2 = \left(\frac{-E_a}{R}\right)\left(\frac{1}{T_2}\right) + \ln A$$

Subtracting the first equation from the second, and remembering that $(\ln k_2 - \ln k_1) = \ln (k_2/k_1)$, we obtain

$$\ln \left(\frac{k_2}{k_1}\right) = \left(\frac{-E_a}{R}\right)\left(\frac{1}{T_2} - \frac{1}{T_1}\right)$$

This equation can be used to calculate E_a from rate constants k_1 and k_2 at temperatures T_1 and T_2. By the same token, if we know E_a and the rate constant k_1 at one temperature T_1, we can calculate the rate constant k_2 at another temperature T_2. Worked Example 12.16 shows how this is done.

WORKED EXAMPLE 12.16

USING THE ARRHENIUS EQUATION

Rate constants for the gas-phase decomposition of hydrogen iodide, $2\,HI(g) \rightarrow H_2(g) + I_2(g)$, are listed in the following table:

Temperature (°C)	$k\ (\text{M}^{-1}\text{s}^{-1})$	Temperature (°C)	$k\ (\text{M}^{-1}\text{s}^{-1})$
283	3.52×10^{-7}	427	1.16×10^{-3}
356	3.02×10^{-5}	508	3.95×10^{-2}
393	2.19×10^{-4}		

(a) Find the activation energy (in kJ/mol) using all five data points.

(b) Calculate E_a from the rate constants at 283 °C and 508 °C.

(c) Given the rate constant at 283 °C and the value of E_a obtained in part (b), what is the rate constant at 293 °C?

STRATEGY

(a) The activation energy E_a can be determined from the slope of a linear plot of $\ln k$ versus $1/T$.

(b) To calculate E_a from values of the rate constant at two temperatures, use the equation

$$\ln \left(\frac{k_2}{k_1}\right) = \left(\frac{-E_a}{R}\right)\left(\frac{1}{T_2} - \frac{1}{T_1}\right)$$

(c) Use the same equation and the known values of E_a and k_1 at T_1 to calculate k_2 at T_2.

SOLUTION

(a) Because the temperature in the Arrhenius equation is expressed in kelvin, we must first convert the Celsius temperatures to absolute temperatures. Then calculate values of $1/T$ and $\ln k$, and plot $\ln k$ versus $1/T$. The results are shown in the following table and graph:

t (°C)	T (K)	k (M^{-1}s^{-1})	$1/T$ (1/K)	$\ln k$
283	556	3.52×10^{-7}	0.001 80	-14.860
356	629	3.02×10^{-5}	0.001 59	-10.408
393	666	2.19×10^{-4}	0.001 50	-8.426
427	700	1.16×10^{-3}	0.001 43	-6.759
508	781	3.95×10^{-2}	0.001 28	-3.231

The slope of the straight-line plot can be determined from the coordinates of any two widely separated points on the line:

$$\text{Slope} = \frac{\Delta y}{\Delta x} = \frac{(-14.0) - (-3.9)}{(0.001\ 75\ \text{K}^{-1}) - (0.001\ 30\ \text{K}^{-1})} = \frac{-10.1}{0.000\ 45\ \text{K}^{-1}} = -2.24 \times 10^4\ \text{K}$$

Finally, calculate the activation energy from the slope:

$$E_a = -R(\text{Slope}) = -\left(8.314\ \frac{\text{J}}{\text{K} \cdot \text{mol}}\right)(-2.24 \times 10^4\ \text{K})$$

$$= 1.9 \times 10^5\ \text{J/mol} = 190\ \text{kJ/mol}$$

Note that the slope of the Arrhenius plot is negative and the activation energy is positive. The greater the activation energy for a particular reaction, the steeper the slope of the $\ln k$ versus $1/T$ plot and the greater the increase in the rate constant for a given increase in temperature.

(b) Substituting the values of $k_1 = 3.52 \times 10^{-7}\ \text{M}^{-1}\text{s}^{-1}$ at $T_1 = 556$ K (283 °C) and $k_2 = 3.95 \times 10^{-2}\ \text{M}^{-1}\text{s}^{-1}$ at $T_2 = 781$ K (508 °C) into the equation

$$\ln\left(\frac{k_2}{k_1}\right) = \left(\frac{-E_a}{R}\right)\left(\frac{1}{T_2} - \frac{1}{T_1}\right)$$

gives

$$\ln\left(\frac{3.95 \times 10^{-2}\ \text{M}^{-1}\ \text{s}^{-1}}{3.52 \times 10^{-7}\ \text{M}^{-1}\ \text{s}^{-1}}\right) = \left(\frac{-E_a}{8.314\ \dfrac{\text{J}}{\text{K} \cdot \text{mol}}}\right)\left(\frac{1}{781\ \text{K}} - \frac{1}{556\ \text{K}}\right)$$

continued on next page

Simplifying this equation gives

$$11.628 = \left(\frac{-E_a}{8.314 \dfrac{J}{K \cdot mol}}\right)\left(\frac{-5.18 \times 10^{-4}}{K}\right)$$

$$E_a = 1.87 \times 10^5 \, J/mol = 187 \, kJ/mol$$

(c) Use the same equation as in part **(b)**, but now the known values are

$$k_1 = 3.52 \times 10^{-7} \, M^{-1}s^{-1} \text{ at } T_1 = 556 \, K \, (283 \, °C)$$

$$E_a = 1.87 \times 10^5 \, J/mol$$

and k_2 at $T_2 = 566 \, K \, (293 \, °C)$ is the unknown.

$$\ln\left(\frac{k_2}{3.52 \times 10^{-7} \, M^{-1}s^{-1}}\right) = \left(\frac{-1.87 \times 10^5 \dfrac{J}{mol}}{8.314 \dfrac{J}{K \cdot mol}}\right)\left(\frac{1}{566 \, K} - \frac{1}{556 \, K}\right) = 0.715$$

Taking the antiln of both sides gives

$$\frac{k_2}{3.52 \times 10^{-7} \, M^{-1}s^{-1}} = e^{0.715} = 2.04$$

$$k_2 = 7.18 \times 10^{-7} \, M^{-1}s^{-1}$$

In this temperature range, a rise in temperature of 10 K doubles the rate constant.

▶ **PROBLEM 12.21**   Rate constants for the decomposition of gaseous dinitrogen pentoxide are $3.7 \times 10^{-5} \, s^{-1}$ at 25 °C and $1.7 \times 10^{-3} \, s^{-1}$ at 55 °C.

$$2 \, N_2O_5(g) \longrightarrow 4 \, NO_2(g) + O_2(g)$$

(a) What is the activation energy for this reaction in kJ/mol?
(b) What is the rate constant at 35 °C?

12.14   CATALYSIS

Reaction rates are affected not only by reactant concentrations and temperature but also by the presence of *catalysts*. A **catalyst** is a substance that increases the rate of a transformation without itself being consumed in the process. An example is manganese dioxide, a black powder that speeds up the thermal decomposition of potassium chlorate:

$$2 \, KClO_3(s) \xrightarrow[\text{Heat}]{\text{MnO}_2 \text{ catalyst}} 2 \, KCl(s) + 3 \, O_2(g)$$

In the absence of a catalyst, $KClO_3$ decomposes very slowly, even when heated, but when a small amount of MnO_2 is mixed with the $KClO_3$ before heating, rapid evolution of oxygen ensues. The MnO_2 can be recovered unchanged after the reaction is complete.

Catalysts are enormously important, both in the chemical industry and in living organisms. Nearly all industrial processes for the manufacture of essential chemicals use catalysts to favor formation of specific products and to lower reaction temperatures, thus reducing energy costs. In environmental chemistry, catalysts such as nitric oxide play a role in the formation of air pollutants, while other catalysts, such as platinum in automobile catalytic converters, are potent weapons in the battle to control air pollution.

In living organisms, almost all the hundreds of thousands of chemical reactions that take place constantly are catalyzed by large molecules called *enzymes* (see the

▲ MnO_2 catalyzes the thermal decomposition of $KClO_3$ to KCl and O_2 gas.

Inquiry at the end of this chapter). Nitrogenase, for example, an enzyme present in bacteria on the root nodules of leguminous plants such as peas and beans, catalyzes the conversion of atmospheric nitrogen to ammonia. The ammonia then serves as a fertilizer for plant growth. In the human body, the enzyme carbonic anhydrase catalyzes the reaction of carbon dioxide with water:

$$CO_2(aq) + H_2O(l) \rightleftharpoons H^+(aq) + HCO_3^-(aq)$$

The forward reaction occurs when the blood takes up CO_2 in the tissues, and the reverse reaction occurs when the blood releases CO_2 in the lungs. Remarkably, carbonic anhydrase increases the rate of these reactions by a factor of about 10^6!

How does a catalyst work? A catalyst accelerates the rate of a reaction by making available a different, lower-energy mechanism for the conversion of reactants to products. Take the decomposition of hydrogen peroxide in a basic, aqueous solution, for instance:

$$2 H_2O_2(aq) \longrightarrow 2 H_2O(l) + O_2(g)$$

Although unstable with respect to water and oxygen, hydrogen peroxide decomposes only very slowly at room temperature because the reaction has a high activation energy (76 kJ/mol). In the presence of iodide ion, however, the reaction is appreciably faster (Figure 12.17) because it can proceed by a different, lower-energy pathway:

Step 1.	$H_2O_2(aq) + I^-(aq) \longrightarrow H_2O(l) + IO^-(aq)$	Slower, rate-determining
Step 2.	$H_2O_2(aq) + IO^-(aq) \longrightarrow H_2O(l) + O_2(g) + I^-(aq)$	Faster
	$2 H_2O_2(aq) \longrightarrow 2 H_2O(l) + O_2(g)$	Overall reaction

The rate of decomposition of aqueous hydrogen peroxide can be monitored qualitatively by collecting the evolved oxygen gas in a balloon.

NaI(*aq*)

$O_2(g)$

NaI(*aq*)

$H_2O_2(aq)$

$H_2O_2(aq)$

In the absence of a catalyst, little O_2 is produced.

After addition of aqueous sodium iodide, the balloon rapidly inflates with O_2.

Figure 12.17
Decomposition of aqueous hydrogen peroxide.

The H_2O_2 first oxidizes the catalyst (I^-) to hypoiodite ion (IO^-) and then reduces the intermediate IO^- back to I^-. The catalyst does not appear in the overall reaction because it is consumed in step 1 and regenerated in step 2. The catalyst is, however, intimately involved in the reaction and appears in the observed rate law:

$$\text{Rate} = -\frac{\Delta[H_2O_2]}{\Delta t} = k[H_2O_2][I^-]$$

The rate law is consistent with the reaction of H_2O_2 and I^- as the rate-determining step. In general, a catalyst is consumed in one step of a reaction and is regenerated in a subsequent step, whereas an intermediate is formed in one step and is consumed in a subsequent step.

The catalyzed pathway for a reaction might have a faster rate than the uncatalyzed pathway either because of a larger frequency factor (A) or a smaller activation energy (E_a) in the Arrhenius equation. Usually, though, catalysts function by making available a reaction pathway with a lower activation energy (**Figure 12.18**). In the decomposition of hydrogen peroxide, for example, catalysis by I^- lowers E_a for the overall reaction by 19 kJ/mol.

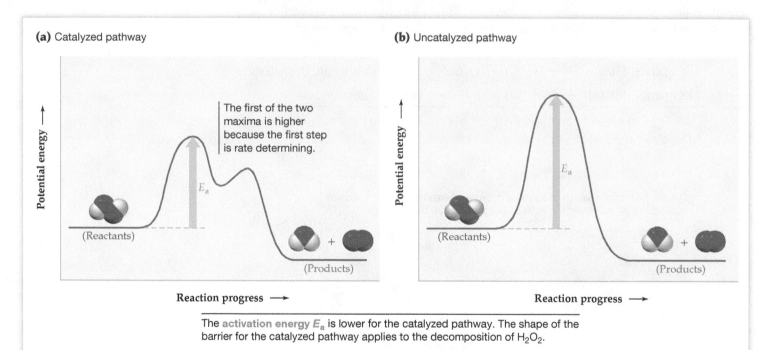

(a) Catalyzed pathway

The first of the two maxima is higher because the first step is rate determining.

(b) Uncatalyzed pathway

The activation energy E_a is lower for the catalyzed pathway. The shape of the barrier for the catalyzed pathway applies to the decomposition of H_2O_2.

Figure 12.18
Typical potential energy profiles for a reaction whose activation energy is lowered by the presence of a catalyst.

Because the reaction occurs in two steps, the energy profile for the catalyzed pathway shown in Figure 12.18 exhibits two maxima (two transition states) with a minimum between them that represents the energy of the intermediate species present after the first step. The first maximum is higher than the second because the first step is rate-determining, and the activation energy for the overall reaction is E_a for the first step. Maxima for both steps, though, are lower than E_a for the uncatalyzed pathway. Note that a catalyst does not affect the energies of the reactants and products, which are the same for both catalyzed and uncatalyzed pathways.

WORKED CONCEPTUAL EXAMPLE 12.17

USING THE METHOD OF INITIAL RATES FOR A CATALYZED REACTION

The relative rates of the reaction $A + B \rightarrow AB$ in vessels (1)–(4) are 1:2:1:2. Red spheres represent A molecules, blue spheres represent B molecules, and yellow spheres represent molecules of a third substance C.

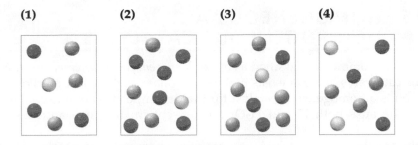

(a) What is the order of the reaction in A, B, and C?

(b) Write the rate law.

(c) Write a mechanism that agrees with the rate law.

(d) Why doesn't C appear in the equation for the overall reaction?

STRATEGY AND SOLUTION

(a) Count the number of molecules of each type in vessels (1)–(4), and compare the relative rates with the relative numbers of molecules. The concentration of A molecules in vessel (2) is twice that in vessel (1), while the concentrations of B and C remain constant. Because the reaction rate in vessel (2) is twice that in vessel (1), the rate is proportional to [A], and so the reaction is first order in A. When [B] is doubled [compare vessels (1) and (3)], the rate is unchanged, so the reaction is zeroth order in B. When [C] is doubled [compare vessels (1) and (4)], the rate doubles, so the reaction is first order in C.

(b) The rate law can be written as rate $= k[A]^m[B]^n[C]^p$, where the exponents m, n, and p specify the reaction orders in A, B, and C, respectively. Since the reaction is first order in A and C, and zeroth order in B, the rate law is rate $= k[A][C]$.

(c) The rate law tells us that A and C collide in the rate-determining step because the rate law for the overall reaction is the rate law for the rate-determining step. Subsequent steps in the mechanism are faster than the rate-determining step, and the various steps must sum up to give the overall reaction. Therefore, a plausible mechanism is

$$
\begin{array}{ll}
A + C \longrightarrow AC & \text{Slower, rate-determining} \\
\underline{AC + B \longrightarrow AB + C} & \text{Faster} \\
A + B \longrightarrow AB & \text{Overall reaction}
\end{array}
$$

(d) C doesn't appear in the overall reaction because it is consumed in the first step and regenerated in the second step. C is therefore a catalyst. AC is an intermediate because it is formed in the first step and consumed in the second step.

CONCEPTUAL PROBLEM 12.22   The relative rates of the reaction $2\,A + C_2 \longrightarrow 2\,AC$ in vessels (1)–(4) are $1:1:2:3$. Red spheres represent A molecules, blue spheres represent B molecules, and connected yellow spheres represent C_2 molecules.

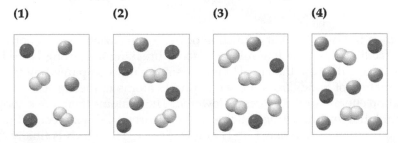

(a) What is the order of the reaction in A, B, and C_2?

(b) Write the rate law.

(c) Write a mechanism that agrees with the rate law.

(d) Identify all catalysts and intermediates in your mechanism.

12.15 HOMOGENEOUS AND HETEROGENEOUS CATALYSTS

Catalysts are commonly classified as either *homogeneous* or *heterogeneous*. A **homogeneous catalyst** is one that exists in the same phase as the reactants. For example, iodide ion is a homogeneous catalyst for the decomposition of aqueous hydrogen peroxide because both I^- and H_2O_2 are present in the same aqueous solution phase.

In the atmosphere, nitric oxide is a gas-phase homogeneous catalyst for the conversion of molecular oxygen to ozone, a process described by the following series of reactions:

$$1/2\ O_2(g) + NO(g) \longrightarrow NO_2(g)$$

$$NO_2(g) \xrightarrow{\text{Sunlight}} NO(g) + O(g)$$

$$\underline{O(g) + O_2(g) \longrightarrow O_3(g)}$$

$$3/2\ O_2(g) \longrightarrow O_3(g) \qquad \text{Overall reaction}$$

Nitric oxide first reacts with atmospheric O_2 to give nitrogen dioxide, a poisonous brown gas. Subsequently, NO_2 absorbs sunlight and dissociates to give an oxygen atom, which then reacts with O_2 to form ozone. As usual, the catalyst (NO) and the intermediates (NO_2 and O) do not appear in the chemical equation for the overall reaction.

A **heterogeneous catalyst** is one that exists in a different phase from that of the reactants. Ordinarily, the heterogeneous catalyst is a solid, and the reactants are either gases or liquids. In the Fischer–Tropsch process for manufacturing synthetic gasoline, for example, tiny particles of a metal such as iron or cobalt coated on alumina (Al_2O_3) catalyze the conversion of gaseous carbon monoxide and hydrogen to hydrocarbons such as octane (C_8H_{18}):

$$8\ CO(g) + 17\ H_2(g) \xrightarrow[\text{catalyst}]{Co/Al_2O_3} C_8H_{18}(l) + 8\ H_2O(l)$$

The mechanism of heterogeneous catalysis is often complex and not well understood. Important steps, however, frequently involve (1) attachment of reactants to the surface of the catalyst, a process called *adsorption*, (2) conversion of reactants to products on the surface, and (3) desorption of products from the surface. The adsorption step is thought to involve chemical bonding of the reactants to the highly reactive metal atoms on the surface with accompanying breaking, or at least weakening, of bonds in the reactants.

To illustrate, take the catalytic hydrogenation of compounds with C=C double bonds, a reaction used in the food industry to convert unsaturated vegetable oils to solid fats. The reaction is catalyzed by tiny particles of metals such as Ni, Pd, or Pt:

$$H_2C{=}CH_2(g) + H_2(g) \xrightarrow[\text{catalyst}]{\text{Metal}} H_3C{-}CH_3(g)$$
$$\text{Ethylene} \qquad\qquad\qquad\qquad \text{Ethane}$$

As shown in **Figure 12.19**, the function of the metal surface is to adsorb the reactants and facilitate the rate-determining step by breaking the strong H—H bond in the H_2 molecule. Because the H—H bond breaking is accompanied by the simultaneous formation of bonds from the separating H atoms to the surface metal atoms, the activation energy for the process is lowered. The H atoms then move about on the surface until they encounter the C atoms of the adsorbed C_2H_4 molecule. Subsequent stepwise formation of two new C—H bonds gives C_2H_6, which is finally desorbed from the surface.

Most of the catalysts used in industrial chemical processes are heterogeneous, in part because such catalysts can be easily separated from the reaction products. Table 12.6 lists some commercial processes that employ heterogeneous catalysts.

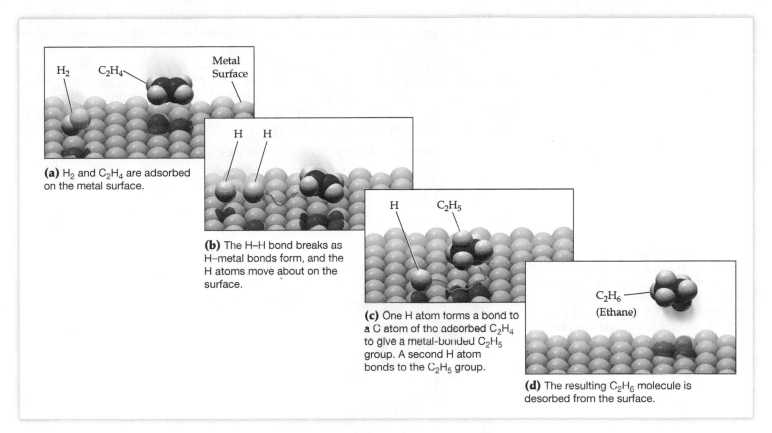

(a) H_2 and C_2H_4 are adsorbed on the metal surface.

(b) The H–H bond breaks as H–metal bonds form, and the H atoms move about on the surface.

(c) One H atom forms a bond to a C atom of the adsorbed C_2H_4 to give a metal-bonded C_2H_5 group. A second H atom bonds to the C_2H_5 group.

(d) The resulting C_2H_6 molecule is desorbed from the surface.

Figure 12.19
Proposed mechanism for the catalytic hydrogenation of ethylene (C_2H_4) on a metal surface.

TABLE 12.6   Some Heterogeneous Catalysts Used in Commercially Important Reactions

Reaction	Catalyst	Commercial Process	Product: Commercial Uses
$2\,SO_2 + O_2 \longrightarrow 2\,SO_3$	Pt or V_2O_5	Intermediate step in the contact process for synthesis of sulfuric acid	H_2SO_4: Manufacture of fertilizers, chemicals; oil refining
$4\,NH_3 + 5\,O_2 \longrightarrow 4\,NO + 6\,H_2O$	Pt and Rh	First step in the Ostwald process for synthesis of nitric acid	HNO_3: Manufacture of explosives, fertilizers, plastics, dyes, lacquers
$N_2 + 3\,H_2 \longrightarrow 2\,NH_3$	Fe, K_2O, and Al_2O_3	Haber process for synthesis of ammonia	NH_3: Manufacture of fertilizers, nitric acid
$H_2O + CH_4 \longrightarrow CO + 3\,H_2$	Ni	Steam–hydrocarbon re-forming process for synthesis of hydrogen	H_2: Manufacture of ammonia, methanol
$CO + H_2O \longrightarrow CO_2 + H_2$	ZnO and CuO	Water-gas shift reaction to improve yield in the synthesis of H_2	H_2: Manufacture of ammonia, methanol
$CO + 2\,H_2 \longrightarrow CH_3OH$	Cu, ZnO, and Al_2O_3	Industrial synthesis of methanol	CH_3OH: Manufacture of plastics, adhesives, gasoline additives; industrial solvent
$\begin{matrix} & & H & H \\ & & | & | \\ C{=}C + H_2 \longrightarrow & C{-}C \\ & & | & | \end{matrix}$	Ni, Pd, or Pt	Catalytic hydrogenation of compounds with C=C bonds as in conversion of unsaturated vegetable oils to solid fats	Food products: margarine, shortening

Another important application of heterogeneous catalysts is in automobile catalytic converters. Despite much work on engine design and fuel composition, automotive exhaust emissions contain air pollutants such as unburned hydrocarbons (C_xH_y), carbon monoxide, and nitric oxide. Carbon monoxide results from the incomplete combustion of hydrocarbon fuels, and nitric oxide is produced when atmospheric nitrogen and oxygen combine at the high temperatures present in an automobile engine. Catalytic converters help convert the offending pollutants to carbon dioxide, water, nitrogen, and oxygen (**Figure 12.20**):

$$C_xH_y(g) + (x + y/4)\,O_2(g) \longrightarrow x\,CO_2(g) + (y/2)\,H_2O(g)$$

$$2\,CO(g) + O_2(g) \longrightarrow 2\,CO_2(g)$$

$$2\,NO(g) \longrightarrow N_2(g) + O_2(g)$$

Figure 12.20
An automobile catalytic converter. The gases exhausted from an automobile engine pass through a catalytic converter where air pollutants such as unburned hydrocarbons (C_xH_y), CO, and NO are converted to CO_2, H_2O, N_2, and O_2. The catalytic converter contains beads that are impregnated with the heterogeneous catalyst.

Exhaust pipe

C_xH_y, CO, NO, O_2

Catalytic converter

To tail pipe

CO_2, H_2O, N_2, O_2

Typical catalysts for these reactions are the so-called noble metals Pt, Pd, and Rh and the transition metal oxides V_2O_5, Cr_2O_3, and CuO. The surface of the catalyst is rendered ineffective, or poisoned, by the adsorption of lead, which is why automobiles with catalytic converters (all those built since 1975) use unleaded gasoline.

INQUIRY HOW DO ENZYMES WORK?

Enzymes are large protein molecules that act as catalysts for biological reactions. They differ from simple inorganic catalysts in two important respects. First, enzymes have much larger and more complex structures than inorganic catalysts, with molecular masses ranging from about 10^4 to greater than 10^6 amu. Second, enzymes are far more specific in their action than inorganic catalysts, often catalyzing only a single reaction of a single compound, called the enzyme's *substrate*. For example, the enzyme *amylase* found in human digestive systems is able to catalyze the breakdown of starch to yield glucose but has no effect on cellulose, even though starch and cellulose are structurally similar. Thus, humans can digest potatoes (starch) but not grass (cellulose).

$$\text{Starch} + H_2O \xrightarrow{\text{Amylase}} \text{Many glucose molecules}$$

$$\text{Cellulose} + H_2O \xrightarrow{\text{Amylase}} \text{No reaction}$$

The catalytic activity of an enzyme is measured by its *turnover number*, which is defined as the number of substrate molecules acted on by one molecule of enzyme per second. Most enzymes have turnover numbers in the range 1–20,000, but some have much higher values. Carbonic anhydrase, which catalyzes the reaction of CO_2 with water to yield HCO_3^- ion, acts on *600,000* substrate molecules per second.

How do enzymes work? According to the *lock-and-key model*, an enzyme is pictured as a large, irregularly shaped molecule with a cleft, or crevice, in its middle. Inside the crevice is an *active site*, a small region with the shape and chemical composition necessary to bind the substrate and catalyze the appropriate reaction. In other words, the active site acts like a lock into which only a specific key (substrate) can fit (Figure 12.21). An enzyme's active site is lined by various acidic, basic, and neutral amino acid side chains, all properly positioned for maximum interaction with the substrate.

Substrate within the enzyme's active site

hexose kinase

Figure 12.21
An enzyme's active site. An enzyme is a large, three-dimensional molecule containing a crevice with an active site. Only a substrate whose shape and structure are complementary to those of the active site can fit into the enzyme. This computer-generated structure depicts the active site of the enzyme hexose kinase.

Enzyme-catalyzed reactions begin when the substrate migrates into the active site to form an *enzyme–substrate complex*. Often, no covalent bonds are formed; the enzyme and substrate are held together only by hydrogen bonds and by weak intermolecular attractions. With enzyme and substrate thus held together in a precisely defined arrangement, the appropriately positioned atoms in the active site facilitate a chemical reaction of the substrate molecule, and the enzyme plus the product then separate.

The reaction can be described by the following simplified mechanism:

$$E + S \underset{k_{-1}}{\overset{k_1}{\rightleftharpoons}} ES$$

$$ES \xrightarrow{k_2} E + P$$

where E, S, and P represent the enzyme, substrate, and product, respectively, and ES represents the enzyme–substrate complex. The rate of product formation is given by

$$\frac{\Delta[P]}{\Delta t} = k_2[ES]$$

At low concentrations of the substrate, the concentration of the enzyme–substrate complex is proportional to the concentration of the substrate, and the rate of product formation is therefore first order in S. At high concentrations of the substrate, however, the enzyme becomes saturated with the substrate—that is, all the enzyme is in the form of the enzyme–substrate complex. At that point, the reaction rate reaches a maximum value and becomes independent of the concentration of the substrate (zeroth order in S) because only substrate bound to the enzyme can react. The dependence of the rate on substrate concentration is shown in **Figure 12.22**.

Figure 12.22
Rate of product formation as a function of substrate concentration for an enzyme-catalyzed reaction.

▶ **PROBLEM 12.23** Given the preceding mechanism for an enzyme-catalyzed reaction, sketch a potential energy profile for the reaction and label the appropriate parts of your graph with E, S, P, ES, and the activation energy E_a.

SUMMARY

Chemical kinetics is the area of chemistry concerned with reaction rates. A **reaction rate** is defined as the increase in the concentration of a product or the decrease in the concentration of a reactant, per unit time. It can be expressed as the average rate during a given time interval, the **instantaneous rate** at a particular time, or the **initial rate** at the beginning of the reaction.

Reaction rates depend on reactant concentrations, temperature, and the presence of catalysts. The concentration dependence is given by the **rate law**, rate $= k[A]^m[B]^n$, where k is the **rate constant**, m and n specify the **reaction order** with respect to reactants A and B, and $m + n$ is the overall reaction order. The values of m and n must be determined by experiment; they can't be deduced from the stoichiometry of the overall reaction.

The **integrated rate law** is a concentration–time equation that lets us calculate concentrations at any time t or the time required for an initial concentration to reach any particular value. For a **first-order reaction**, the integrated rate law is $\ln [A]_t = -kt + \ln [A]_0$. A graph of $\ln [A]$ versus time is a straight line with a slope equal to $-k$. For a **second-order reaction**, the integrated rate law is $1/[A]_t = kt + 1/[A]_0$. A graph of $1/[A]$ versus time is linear with a slope equal to k. For a **zeroth-order reaction,** the integrated rate law is $[A]_t = -kt + [A]_0$, and a graph of $[A]$ versus time is linear with a slope equal to $-k$. The **half-life** ($t_{1/2}$) of a reaction is the time required for the reactant concentration to drop to one-half its initial value.

Radioactive decay is a first-order process, whose rate is proportional to the number of radioactive nuclei N in a sample times the **decay constant**, k. The number N_t of radioactive nuclei remaining at time t can be calculated from the integrated rate law $\ln (N_t/N_0) = -kt$, where N_0 is the number of radioactive nuclei originally present.

A **reaction mechanism** is the sequence of **elementary reactions**, or **elementary steps**, that defines the pathway from reactants to products. Elementary reactions are classified as **unimolecular, bimolecular,** or **termolecular**, depending on whether one, two, or three reactant molecules (or atoms) are involved. The rate law for an elementary reaction follows directly from its **molecularity**: rate $= k[A]$ for a unimolecular reaction, and rate $= k [A]^2$ or rate $= k [A][B]$ for a bimolecular reaction. The observed rate law for a multistep, overall reaction depends on the sequence of elementary steps and their relative rates. The slowest step is called the **rate-determining step**. A chemical species that is formed in one elementary step and consumed in a subsequent step is called a **reaction intermediate**. An acceptable mechanism must meet two criteria: (1) The elementary steps must sum to give the overall reaction, and (2) the mechanism must be consistent with the observed rate law.

The temperature dependence of rate constants is described by the **Arrhenius equation**, $k = Ae^{-E_a/RT}$, where A is the **frequency factor** and E_a is the **activation energy**. The value of E_a can be determined from the slope of a linear plot of $\ln k$ versus $1/T$, and it can be interpreted as the height of the potential energy barrier between the reactants and products. The configuration of atoms at the top of the barrier is called the **transition state**. According to **collision theory**, the rate constant is given by $k = pZe^{-E_a/RT}$, where p is a **steric factor** (the fraction of collisions in which the molecules have the proper orientation for reaction), Z is a constant related to the collision frequency, and $e^{-E_a/RT}$ is the fraction of collisions with energy equal to or greater than E_a.

A **catalyst** is a substance that increases the rate of a reaction without being consumed in the reaction. It functions by making available an alternative reaction pathway that has a lower activation energy. A **homogeneous catalyst** is present in the same phase as the reactants, whereas a **heterogeneous catalyst** is present in a different phase. **Enzymes** are large protein molecules that act as catalysts for biological reactions.

KEY WORDS

activation energy (E_a)   *466*
Arrhenius equation   *469*
bimolecular reaction   *458*
catalyst   *472*
chemical kinetics   *433*
collision theory   *466*
decay constant   *449*
elementary reaction   *456*

elementary step   *456*
enzyme   *479*
first-order reaction   *444*
frequency factor   *469*
half-life   *447*
heterogeneous catalyst   *476*
homogeneous catalyst   *476*
initial rate   *436*

instantaneous rate   *436*
integrated rate law   *444*
molecularity   *457*
rate constant   *437*
rate-determining step   *461*
rate law   *437*
reaction intermediate   *457*
reaction mechanism   *456*

reaction order   *438*
reaction rate   *434*
second-order reaction   *452*
steric factor (p)   *468*
termolecular reaction   *458*
transition state   *466*
unimolecular reaction   *457*
zeroth-order reaction   *455*

CONCEPTUAL PROBLEMS

Problems 12.1–12.23 appear within the chapter.

12.24 The following reaction is first order in A (red spheres) and first order in B (blue spheres):

$$A + B \longrightarrow Products \qquad Rate = k[A][B]$$

(a) What are the relative rates of this reaction in vessels (1)–(4)? Each vessel has the same volume.

(b) What are the relative values of the rate constant k for cases (1)–(4)?

(1)   **(2)**   **(3)**   **(4)**

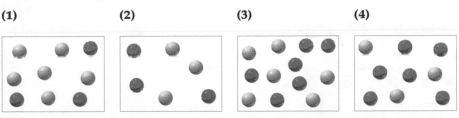

12.25 Consider the first-order decomposition of A molecules (red spheres) in three vessels of equal volume.

(1) (2) (3)

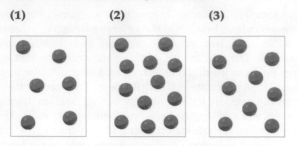

(a) What are the relative rates of decomposition in vessels (1)–(3)?

(b) What are the relative half-lives of the reactions in vessels (1)–(3)?

(c) How will the rates and half-lives be affected if the volume of each vessel is decreased by a factor of 2?

12.26 Consider the first-order reaction A → B in which A molecules (red spheres) are converted to B molecules (blue spheres).

(a) Given the following pictures at $t = 0$ min and $t = 1$ min, draw pictures that show the number of A and B molecules present at $t = 2$ min and $t = 3$ min.

(b) What is the half-life of the reaction?

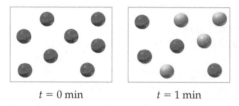

$t = 0$ min $t = 1$ min

12.27 The following pictures represent the progress of the reaction A → B in which A molecules (red spheres) are converted to B molecules (blue spheres).

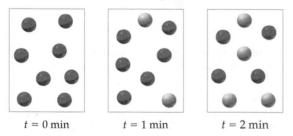

$t = 0$ min $t = 1$ min $t = 2$ min

(a) What is the order of the reaction?

(b) Draw a picture that shows the number of A and B molecules present at $t = 3$ min.

(c) Suppose that each sphere represents 6.0×10^{21} molecules and that the volume of the container is 1.0 L. What is the rate constant for the reaction in the usual units?

12.28 The following pictures represent the progress of a reaction in which two A molecules combine to give a more complex molecule A_2, $2 A \rightarrow A_2$.

$t = 0$ min $t = 1$ min $t = 3$ min $t = ?$ min

(a) Is the reaction first order or second order in A?

(b) What is the rate law?

(c) Draw an appropriate picture in the last box, and specify the time.

12.29 What is the molecularity of each of the following elementary reactions?

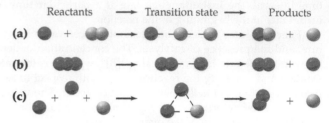

Reactants ⟶ Transition state ⟶ Products

(a)
(b)
(c)

12.30 The relative rates of the reaction A + B → AB in vessels (1)–(3) are 4:4:1. Red spheres represent A molecules, and blue spheres represent B molecules.

(1) (2) (3)

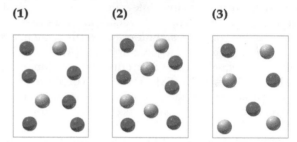

(a) What is the order of the reaction in A and B?

(b) Write the rate law.

(c) Write a mechanism that agrees with the rate law.

(d) Identify all intermediates in your mechanism.

12.31 The relative rates of the reaction AB + B → A + B_2 in vessels (1)–(4) are 2:1:1:4. Red spheres represent A, blue spheres represent B, and green spheres represent C.

(1) (2)

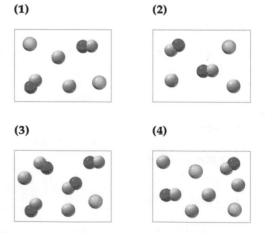

(3) (4)

(a) Write the rate law.

(b) Write a mechanism that agrees with the rate law.

(c) Identify all intermediates and catalysts in your mechanism.

12.32 Consider a reaction that occurs by the following mechanism:

$$A + BC \longrightarrow AC + B$$
$$AC + D \longrightarrow A + CD$$

The potential energy profile for this reaction is as follows:

Potential energy →

Reaction progress →

(a) What is the equation for the overall reaction?

(b) Write structural formulas for all species present at reaction stages 1–5. Identify each species as a reactant, product, catalyst, intermediate, or transition state.

(c) Which of the two steps in the mechanism is the rate-determining step? Write the rate law for the overall reaction.

(d) Is the reaction endothermic or exothermic? Add labels to the diagram that show the values of the energy of reaction ΔE and the activation energy E_a for the overall reaction.

12.33 Draw a plausible transition state for the bimolecular reaction of nitric oxide with ozone. Use dashed lines to indicate the atoms that are weakly linked together in the transition state.

$$NO(g) + O_3(g) \longrightarrow NO_2(g) + O_2(g)$$

SECTION PROBLEMS

Reaction Rates (Section 12.1)

12.34 Use the information in Table 12.1 and Figure 12.1 to estimate the instantaneous rate of appearance of NO_2 at $t = 350$ s by calculating the average rate of appearance of NO_2 over the following time intervals centered on $t = 350$ s:

(a) 0 to 700 s   (b) 100 to 600 s

(c) 200 to 500 s   (d) 300 to 400 s.

Which is the best estimate and why?

12.35 Concentration–time data for the decomposition of nitrogen dioxide are given in Worked Example 12.12. Estimate the instantaneous rate of disappearance of NO_2 at $t = 250$ s by calculating the average rate of disappearance of NO_2 over the following time intervals centered on $t = 250$ s:

(a) 0 to 500 s   (b) 100 to 400 s   (c) 200 to 300 s

Which is the best estimate and why?

12.36 From the plot of concentration–time data in Figure 12.1, estimate:

(a) the instantaneous rate of decomposition of N_2O_5 at $t = 200$ s

(b) the initial rate of decomposition of N_2O_5

12.37 From a plot of the concentration–time data in Worked Example 12.12, estimate:

(a) the instantaneous rate of decomposition of NO_2 at $t = 100$ s

(b) the initial rate of decomposition of NO_2

12.38 Ammonia is manufactured in large amounts by the reaction

$$N_2(g) + 3\,H_2(g) \longrightarrow 2\,NH_3(g)$$

(a) How is the rate of consumption of H_2 related to the rate of consumption of N_2?

(b) How is the rate of formation of NH_3 related to the rate of consumption of N_2?

12.39 In the first step of the Ostwald process for the synthesis of nitric acid, ammonia is converted to nitric oxide by the high-temperature reaction

$$4\,NH_3(g) + 5\,O_2(g) \longrightarrow 4\,NO(g) + 6\,H_2O(g)$$

(a) How is the rate of consumption of O_2 related to the rate of consumption of NH_3?

(b) How are the rates of formation of NO and H_2O related to the rate of consumption of NH_3?

12.40 Chlorite is reduced by bromide in acidic solution according to the following balanced equation:

$$ClO_2^-\,(aq) + 4\,Br^-(aq) + 4\,H^+(aq) \longrightarrow Cl^-(aq) + 2\,Br_2(aq) + 2\,H_2O(l)$$

(a) If $\Delta[Br_2]/\Delta t = 4.8 \times 10^{-6}$ M/s, what is the value of $\Delta[ClO_2^-]/\Delta t$ during the same time interval?

(b) What is the average rate of consumption of Br^- during the same time interval?

12.41 The oxidation of 2-butanone ($CH_3COC_2H_5$) by the cerium(IV) ion in aqueous solution to form acetic acid (CH_3CO_2H) occurs according to the following balanced equation:

$$CH_3COC_2H_5(aq) + 6\,Ce^{4+}(aq) + 3\,H_2O(l) \longrightarrow$$
$$2\,CH_3CO_2H(aq) + 6\,Ce^{3+}(aq) + 6\,H^+(aq)$$

(a) If acetic acid appears at an average rate of 5.0×10^{-8} M/s what is $\Delta[H^+]/\Delta t$ during the same time interval?

(b) What is the average rate of consumption of Ce^{4+} during the same time interval?

Rate Laws (Sections 12.2–12.3)

12.42 The gas-phase reaction of hydrogen and iodine monochloride is first order in H_2 and first order in ICl. What is the rate law, and what are the units of the rate constant?

$$H_2(g) + 2\,ICl(g) \longrightarrow 2\,HCl(g) + I_2(g)$$

12.43 The reaction $2\,NO(g) + 2\,H_2(g) \longrightarrow N_2(g) + 2\,H_2O(g)$ is first order in H_2 and second order in NO. Write the rate law, and specify the units of the rate constant.

12.44 Bromomethane is converted to methanol in an alkaline solution. The reaction is first order in each reactant.

$$CH_3Br(aq) + OH^-(aq) \longrightarrow CH_3OH(aq) + Br^-(aq)$$

(a) Write the rate law.

(b) How does the reaction rate change if the OH^- concentration is decreased by a factor of 5?

(c) What is the change in rate if the concentrations of both reactants are doubled?

12.45 The oxidation of Br^- by BrO_3^- in acidic solution is described by the equation

$$5\,Br^-(aq) + BrO_3^-(aq) + 6\,H^+(aq) \longrightarrow 3\,Br_2(aq) + 3\,H_2O(l)$$

The reaction is first order in Br^-, first order in BrO_3^-, and second order in H^+.

(a) Write the rate law.

(b) What is the overall reaction order?

(c) How does the reaction rate change if the H^+ concentration is tripled?

(d) What is the change in rate if the concentrations of both Br^- and BrO_3^- are halved?

12.46 Oxidation of bis(bipyridine)copper(I) ion by molecular oxygen is described by the equation:

$$Cu(C_{10}H_8N_2)_2{}^+(aq) + O_2(aq) \longrightarrow products$$

The reaction is first order in oxygen and second order in $Cu(C_{10}H_8N_2)_2{}^+$.

(a) Write the rate law.

(b) What is the overall reaction order?

(c) How does the reaction rate change if the concentration of $Cu(C_{10}H_8N_2)_2{}^+$ is decreased by a factor of 4?

12.47 In aqueous solution the oxidation of nitric oxide occurs according to the equation:

$$4\,NO(aq) + O_2(aq) + 2\,H_2O(l) \longrightarrow 4\,HNO_2(aq)$$

The reaction is second order in nitric oxide and first order in oxygen.

(a) Write the rate law.

(b) What is the overall reaction order?

(c) How does the reaction rate change when the concentration of oxygen is doubled?

(d) How does the reaction rate change when the concentration of nitric oxide is doubled and the concentration of oxygen is halved?

12.48 Initial rate data at 25 °C are listed in the table for the reaction

$$NH_4{}^+(aq) + NO_2{}^-(aq) \longrightarrow N_2(g) + 2\,H_2O(l)$$

Experiment	Initial [$NH_4{}^+$]	Initial [$NO_2{}^-$]	Initial Rate of Consumption of $NH_4{}^+$ (M/s)
1	0.24	0.10	7.2×10^{-6}
2	0.12	0.10	3.6×10^{-6}
3	0.12	0.15	5.4×10^{-6}

(a) What is the rate law?

(b) What is the value of the rate constant?

(c) What is the initial rate when the initial concentrations are [$NH_4{}^+$] = 0.39 M and [$NO_2{}^-$] = 0.052 M?

12.49 The initial rates listed in the following table were determined for the reaction

$$2\,NO(g) + Cl_2(g) \longrightarrow 2\,NOCl(g)$$

Experiment	Initial [NO]	Initial [Cl_2]	Initial Rate of Consumption of Cl_2 (M/s)
1	0.13	0.20	1.0×10^{-2}
2	0.26	0.20	4.0×10^{-2}
3	0.13	0.10	5.0×10^{-3}

(a) What is the rate law?

(b) What is the value of the rate constant?

(c) What is the initial rate when the initial concentrations of both reactants are 0.12 M?

Integrated Rate Law; Half-Life (Sections 12.4–12.5; 12.7–12.8)

12.50 At 500 °C, cyclopropane (C_3H_6) rearranges to propene (CH_3—CH=CH_2). The reaction is first order, and the rate constant is $6.7 \times 10^{-4}\,s^{-1}$. If the initial concentration of C_3H_6 is 0.0500 M:

(a) What is the molarity of C_3H_6 after 30 min?

(b) How many minutes does it take for the C_3H_6 concentration to drop to 0.0100 M?

(c) How many minutes does it take for 25% of the C_3H_6 to react?

12.51 The rearrangement of methyl isonitrile (CH_3NC) to acetonitrile (CH_3CN) is a first-order reaction and has a rate constant of $5.11 \times 10^{-5}\,s^{-1}$ at 472 K.

$$CH_3-N\equiv C \longrightarrow CH_3-C\equiv N$$

| Methyl isonitrile | Acetonitrile |

If the initial concentration of CH_3NC is 0.0340 M:

(a) What is the molarity of CH_3NC after 2.00 h?

(b) How many minutes does it take for the CH_3NC concentration to drop to 0.0300 M?

(c) How many minutes does it take for 20% of the CH_3NC to react?

12.52 What is the half-life (in minutes) of the reaction in Problem 12.50? How many minutes will it take for the concentration of cyclopropane to drop to 6.25% of its initial value?

12.53 What is the half-life (in hours) of the reaction in Problem 12.51? How many hours will it take for the concentration of methyl isonitrile to drop to 12.5% of its initial value?

12.54 Butadiene (C_4H_6) reacts with itself to form a dimer with the formula C_8H_{12}. The reaction is second order in C_4H_6. Assume the rate constant at a particular temperature is $4.0 \times 10^{-2}\,M^{-1}\,s^{-1}$ and the initial concentration of C_4H_6 is 0.0200 M.

(a) What is its molarity after a reaction time of 1.00 h?

(b) What is the time (in hours) when the C_4H_6 concentration reaches a value of 0.0020 M?

12.55 Hydrogen iodide decomposes slowly to H_2 and I_2 at 600 K. The reaction is second order in HI and the rate constant is $9.7 \times 10^{-6}\,M^{-1}\,s^{-1}$. Assume the initial concentration of HI is 0.100 M.

(a) What is its molarity after a reaction time of 6.00 days?

(b) What is the time (in days) when the HI concentration reaches a value of 0.085 M?

12.56 What is the half-life (in minutes) of the reaction in Problem 12.54 when the initial C_4H_6 concentration is 0.0200 M? How many minutes does it take for the concentration of C_4H_6 to drop from 0.0100 M to 0.0050 M?

12.57 What is the half-life (in days) of the reaction in Problem 12.55 when the initial HI concentration is 0.100 M? How many days does it take for the concentration of HI to drop from 0.200 M to 0.100 M?

12.58 At elevated temperatures, nitrous oxide decomposes according to the equation

$$2\,N_2O(g) \longrightarrow 2\,N_2(g) + O_2(g)$$

Given the following data, plot the appropriate graphs to determine whether the reaction is zeroth, first, or second order. What is the value of the rate constant for the consumption of N_2O?

Time (min)	0	60	90	300	600
[N$_2$O]	0.250	0.228	0.216	0.128	0.0630

12.59 Nitrosyl bromide decomposes at 10 °C:

$$2\,NOBr(g) \longrightarrow 2\,NO(g) + Br_2(g)$$

Use the following kinetic data to determine the order of the reaction and the value of the rate constant for consumption of NOBr.

Time (s)	0	10	40	120	320
[NOBr]	0.0390	0.0315	0.0175	0.007 84	0.003 76

12.60 At 25 °C, the half-life of a certain first-order reaction is 248 s. What is the value of the rate constant at this temperature?

12.61 *trans*-Cycloheptene (C_7H_{12}), a strained cyclic hydrocarbon, converts to *cis*-cycloheptene at low temperatures. This molecular rearrangement is a second-order process with a rate constant of 0.030 $M^{-1}\,s^{-1}$ at 60 °C. If the initial concentration of *trans*-cycloheptene is 0.035 M:

(a) What is the concentration of *trans*-cycloheptene after a reaction time of 1600 s?

(b) At what time will the concentration drop to one-twentieth of its initial value?

(c) What is the half-life of *trans*-cycloheptene at an initial concentration of 0.075 M?

12.62 A reaction of the type $A \rightarrow B + C$ has a rate constant $k = 3.6 \times 10^{-5}\,M/s$.

(a) What is the order of the reaction?

(b) What is the molarity of A after a reaction time of 30.0 min if the initial concentration of A is 0.096 M?

(c) What is the half-life (in minutes) of the reaction in part (b)?

12.63 Consider the following concentration–time data for the decomposition reaction $AB \rightarrow A + B$.

Time (min)	0	20	40	120	220
[AB]	0.206	0.186	0.181	0.117	0.036

(a) Determine the order of the reaction and the value of the rate constant.

(b) What is the molarity of AB after a reaction time of 192 min?

(c) What is the time (in minutes) when the AB concentration reaches a value of 0.0250 M?

Radioactive Decay Rates (Section 12.6)

12.64 The half-life of indium-111, a radioisotope used in studying the distribution of white blood cells, is $t_{1/2} = 2.805$ days. What is the decay constant of ^{111}In?

12.65 The decay constant of plutonium-239, a waste product from nuclear reactors, is 2.88×10^{-5} year^{-1}. What is the half-life of ^{239}Pu?

12.66 The decay constant of ^{35}S is 7.95×10^{-3} day^{-1}. What percentage of an ^{35}S sample remains after 185 days?

12.67 Plutonium-239 has a decay constant of 2.88×10^{-5} year^{-1}. What percentage of a ^{239}Pu sample remains after 1000 years? After 25,000 years? After 100,000 years?

12.68 Polonium-209, an α emitter, has a half-life of 102 years. How many α particles are emitted in 1.0 s from a 1.0 ng sample of ^{209}Po?

12.69 Chlorine-36 is a β emitter, with a half-life of 3.0×10^5 years. How many β particles are emitted in 1.0 min from a 5.0 mg sample of ^{36}Cl?

12.70 A 1.0 mg sample of ^{79}Se decays initially at a rate of 1.5×10^5 disintegrations/s. What is the half-life of ^{79}Se in years?

12.71 What is the half-life (in years) of ^{44}Ti if a 1.0 ng sample decays initially at a rate of 4.8×10^3 disintegrations/s?

12.72 A sample of ^{37}Ar undergoes 8540 disintegrations/min initially but undergoes 6990 disintegrations/min after 10.0 days. What is the half-life of ^{37}Ar in days?

12.73 A sample of ^{28}Mg decays initially at a rate of 53,500 disintegrations/min, but the decay rate falls to 10,980 disintegrations/min after 48.0 hours. What is the half-life of ^{28}Mg in hours?

Reaction Mechanisms (Sections 12.9–12.11)

12.74 What is the relationship between the coefficients in a balanced chemical equation for an overall reaction and the exponents in the rate law?

12.75 What distinguishes the rate-determining step from the other steps in a reaction mechanism? How does the rate-determining step affect the observed rate law?

12.76 Consider the following mechanism for the reaction of hydrogen and iodine monochloride:

Step 1. $H_2(g) + ICl(g) \longrightarrow HI(g) + HCl(g)$

Step 2. $HI(g) + ICl(g) \longrightarrow I_2(g) + HCl(g)$

(a) Write the equation for the overall reaction.

(b) Identify any reaction intermediates.

(c) What is the molecularity of each elementary step?

12.77 The following mechanism has been proposed for the reaction of nitric oxide and chlorine:

> Step 1. $NO(g) + Cl_2(g) \longrightarrow NOCl_2(g)$
>
> Step 2. $NOCl_2(g) + NO(g) \longrightarrow 2\ NOCl(g)$

(a) What is the overall reaction?

(b) Identify any reaction intermediates.

(c) What is the molecularity of each elementary step?

12.78 Give the molecularity and the rate law for each of the following elementary reactions:

(a) $O_3(g) + Cl(g) \longrightarrow O_2(g) + ClO(g)$

(b) $NO_2(g) \longrightarrow NO(g) + O(g)$

(c) $ClO(g) + O(g) \longrightarrow Cl(g) + O_2(g)$

(d) $Cl(g) + Cl(g) + N_2(g) \longrightarrow Cl_2(g) + N_2(g)$

12.79 Identify the molecularity and write the rate law for each of the following elementary reactions:

(a) $I_2(g) \longrightarrow 2\ I(g)$

(b) $2\ NO(g) + Br_2(g) \longrightarrow 2\ NOBr(g)$

(c) $N_2O_5(g) \longrightarrow NO_2(g) + NO_3(g)$

12.80 The thermal decomposition of nitryl chloride, NO_2Cl, is believed to occur by the following mechanism:

$$NO_2Cl(g) \xrightarrow{k_1} NO_2(g) + Cl(g)$$

$$Cl(g) + NO_2Cl(g) \xrightarrow{k_2} NO_2(g) + Cl_2(g)$$

(a) What is the overall reaction?

(b) What is the molecularity of each of the elementary steps?

(c) What rate law is predicted by this mechanism if the first step is rate-determining?

12.81 The substitution reactions of molybdenum hexacarbonyl, $Mo(CO)_6$, with a variety of other molecules L are believed to occur by the following mechanism:

$$Mo(CO)_6 \xrightarrow{k_1} Mo(CO)_5 + CO$$

$$Mo(CO)_5 + L \xrightarrow{k_2} Mo(CO)_5L$$

(a) What is the overall reaction?

(b) What is the molecularity of each of the elementary steps?

(c) Write the rate law, assuming that the first step is rate-determining.

12.82 The reaction $2\ NO_2(g) + F_2(g) \rightarrow 2\ NO_2F(g)$ has a second-order rate law, rate $= k[NO_2][F_2]$. Suggest a mechanism that is consistent with this rate law.

12.83 The decomposition of ozone in the upper atmosphere is facilitated by NO. The overall reaction and the rate law are

$$O_3(g) + O(g) \longrightarrow 2\ O_2(g) \qquad \text{Rate} = k[O_3][NO]$$

Write a mechanism that is consistent with the rate law.

12.84 A proposed mechanism for the oxidation of nitric oxide to nitrogen dioxide was described in Problem 12.19. Another possible mechanism for this reaction is

$$2\ NO(g) \underset{k_{-1}}{\overset{k_1}{\rightleftharpoons}} N_2O_2(g) \qquad \text{Faster, reversible}$$

$$N_2O_2(g) + O_2(g) \xrightarrow{k_2} 2\ NO_2(g) \quad \text{Slower, rate-determining}$$

(a) Write a balanced equation for the overall reaction.

(b) Show that this mechanism is consistent with the experimental rate law, rate $= -\Delta[NO]/\Delta t = k[NO]^2[O_2]$.

(c) Relate the rate constant k to the rate constants for the elementary reactions.

12.85 The following mechanism has been proposed for the decomposition of dinitrogen pentoxide, which has the experimental rate law, rate $= -\Delta[N_2O_5]/\Delta t = k[N_2O_5]$:

$$N_2O_5(g) \underset{k_{-1}}{\overset{k_1}{\rightleftharpoons}} NO_2(g) + NO_3(g) \qquad \text{Fast, reversible}$$

$$NO_2(g) + NO_3(g) \xrightarrow{k_2} NO(g) + NO_2(g) + O_2(g) \quad \text{Slow, rate-determining}$$

$$NO(g) + NO_3(g) \xrightarrow{k_3} 2\ NO_2(g) \qquad \text{Fast}$$

Note that the first step must be multiplied by 2 to obtain the overall reaction.

(a) Write a balanced equation for the overall reaction.

(b) Identify all reaction intermediates.

(c) Show that the proposed mechanism is consistent with the experimental rate law.

(d) Relate the rate constant k to the rate constants for the elementary reactions.

The Arrhenius Equation (Sections 12.12–12.13)

12.86 Why don't all collisions between reactant molecules lead to a chemical reaction?

12.87 Two reactions have the same activation energy, but their rates at the same temperature differ by a factor of 10. Explain.

12.88 Rate constants for the reaction $2\ N_2O_5(g) \rightarrow 4\ NO_2(g) + O_2(g)$ exhibit the following temperature dependence:

Temperature (°C)	k (s^{-1})	Temperature (°C)	k (s^{-1})
25	3.7×10^{-5}	55	1.7×10^{-3}
45	5.1×10^{-4}	65	5.2×10^{-3}

Plot an appropriate graph of the data, and determine the activation energy for this reaction in kJ/mol.

12.89 The following rate constants describe the thermal decomposition of nitrogen dioxide:

$$2\ NO_2(g) \longrightarrow 2\ NO(g) + O_2(g)$$

Temperature (°C)	k (M^{-1}s^{-1})	Temperature (°C)	k (M^{-1}s^{-1})
330	0.77	378	4.1
354	1.8	383	4.7

Plot an appropriate graph of the data, and calculate the value of E_a for this reaction in kJ/mol.

12.90 Rate constants for the reaction $NO_2(g) + CO(g) \rightarrow NO(g) + CO_2(g)$ are 1.3 M^{-1}s^{-1} at 700 K and 23.0 M^{-1}s^{-1} at 800 K.

(a) What is the value of the activation energy in kJ/mol?

(b) What is the rate constant at 750 K?

12.91 A certain first-order reaction has a rate constant of $1.0 \times 10^{-3} \, s^{-1}$ at 25 °C.

    (a) If the reaction rate doubles when the temperature is increased to 35 °C, what is the activation energy for this reaction in kJ/mol?

    (b) What is the E_a (in kJ/mol) if the same temperature change causes the rate to triple?

12.92 Reaction of the anti-cancer drug cisplatin, $Pt(NH_3)_2Cl_2$, with water is described by the equation

$$Pt(NH_3)_2Cl_2(aq) + H_2O(l) \longrightarrow$$
$$Pt(NH_3)_2(H_2O)Cl^+(aq) + Cl^-(aq)$$

The rate of this reaction increases by a factor of 15 on raising the temperature from 25 °C to 50 °C. What is the value of the activation energy in kJ/mol?

12.93 The widely used solvent ethyl acetate undergoes the following reaction in basic solution:

$$CH_3CO_2C_2H_5(aq) + OH^-(aq) \longrightarrow CH_3CO_2^-(aq) + C_2H_5OH(aq)$$

The rate of this reaction increases by a factor of 6.37 on raising the temperature from 15 °C to 45 °C. Calculate the value of the activation energy in kJ/mol.

Ethyl acetate

12.94 The values of $E_a = 183$ kJ/mol and $\Delta E = 9$ kJ/mol have been measured for the reaction

$$2 \, HI(g) \longrightarrow H_2(g) + I_2(g)$$

Sketch a potential energy profile for this reaction that shows the potential energy of reactants, products, and the transition state. Include labels that define E_a and ΔE.

12.95 The values of $E_a = 248$ kJ/mol and $\Delta E = 41$ kJ/mol have been measured for the reaction

$$H_2(g) + CO_2(g) \longrightarrow H_2O(g) + CO(g)$$

    (a) Sketch a potential energy profile for this reaction that shows the potential energy of reactants, products, and the transition state. Include labels that define E_a and ΔE.

    (b) Considering the geometry of the reactants and products, suggest a plausible structure for the transition state.

Catalysis (Sections 12.14–12.15)

12.96 Comment on the following statement: "A catalyst increases the rate of a reaction, but it is not consumed because it does not participate in the reaction."

12.97 Why doesn't a catalyst appear in the overall chemical equation for a reaction?

12.98 In the upper atmosphere, chlorofluorocarbons such as $CFCl_3$ absorb sunlight and subsequently fragment, yielding Cl atoms. The Cl atoms then destroy ozone by the following mechanism:

$$Cl(g) + O_3(g) \longrightarrow ClO(g) + O_2(g)$$
$$ClO(g) + O(g) \longrightarrow Cl(g) + O_2(g)$$

    (a) Write the chemical equation for the overall reaction.

    (b) What is the role of the Cl atoms in this reaction?

    (c) Is ClO a catalyst or a reaction intermediate?

    (d) What distinguishes a catalyst from an intermediate?

12.99 Sulfur dioxide is oxidized to sulfur trioxide in the following sequence of reactions:

$$2 \, SO_2(g) + 2 \, NO_2(g) \longrightarrow 2 \, SO_3(g) + 2 \, NO(g)$$
$$2 \, NO(g) + O_2(g) \longrightarrow 2 \, NO_2(g)$$

    (a) Write the chemical equation for the overall reaction.

    (b) Identify any molecule that acts as a catalyst or intermediate in this reaction.

12.100 Consider the following mechanism for the decomposition of nitramide (NH_2NO_2) in aqueous solution:

$$NH_2NO_2(aq) + OH^-(aq) \longrightarrow NHNO_2^-(aq) + H_2O(l)$$
$$NHNO_2^-(aq) \longrightarrow N_2O(g) + OH^-(aq)$$

    (a) Write the chemical equation for the overall reaction.

    (b) Identify the catalyst and the reaction intermediate.

    (c) How will the rate of the overall reaction be affected if HCl is added to the solution?

12.101 In Problem 12.83, you wrote a mechanism for the nitric oxide-facilitated decomposition of ozone. Does your mechanism involve a catalyst or a reaction intermediate? Explain.

CHAPTER PROBLEMS

12.102 You wish to determine the reaction order and rate constant for the following thermal decomposition reaction:

$$2\ AB_2 \longrightarrow A_2 + 2\ B_2$$

(a) What data would you collect?

(b) How would you use these data to determine whether the reaction is zeroth order, first order, or second order?

(c) Describe how you would determine the value of the rate constant.

12.103 You wish to determine the activation energy for the following first-order reaction:

$$A \longrightarrow B + C$$

(a) What data would you collect?

(b) How would you use these data to determine the activation energy?

12.104 The rate of the reaction $A + B_2 \rightarrow AB + B$ is directly proportional to the concentration of B_2, independent of the concentration of A, and directly proportional to the concentration of a substance C.

(a) What is the rate law?

(b) Write a mechanism that agrees with the experimental facts.

(c) What is the role of C in this reaction? Why doesn't C appear in the chemical equation for the overall reaction?

12.105 Consider three reactions with different values of E_a and ΔE:

Reaction 1. $E_a = 20\ kJ/mol$; $\Delta E = -60\ kJ/mol$

Reaction 2. $E_a = 10\ kJ/mol$; $\Delta E = -20\ kJ/mol$

Reaction 3. $E_a = 40\ kJ/mol$; $\Delta E = +15\ kJ/mol$

(a) Sketch a potential energy profile for each reaction that shows the potential energy of reactants, products, and the transition state. Include labels that define E_a and ΔE.

(b) Assuming that all three reactions are carried out at the same temperature and that all three have the same frequency factor A, which reaction is the fastest and which is the slowest?

(c) Which reaction is the most endothermic, and which is the most exothermic?

12.106 Consider the potential energy profile in Figure 12.18 for the iodide ion-catalyzed decomposition of H_2O_2. What point on the profile represents the potential energy of the transition state for the first step in the reaction? What point represents the potential energy of the transition state for the second step? What point represents the potential energy of the intermediate products $H_2O(l) + IO^-(aq)$?

12.107 The decomposition of N_2O_5 is a first-order reaction. At 25 °C, it takes 5.2 h for the concentration to drop from 0.120 M to 0.060 M. How many hours does it take for the concentration to drop from 0.030 M to 0.015 M? From 0.480 M to 0.015 M?

12.108 Consider the reaction $H_2(g) + I_2(g) \rightarrow 2\ HI(g)$. The reaction of a fixed amount of H_2 and I_2 is studied in a cylinder fitted with a movable piston. Indicate the effect of each of the following changes on the rate of the reaction:

(a) An increase in temperature at constant volume

(b) An increase in volume at constant temperature

(c) The addition of a catalyst

(d) The addition of argon (an inert gas) at constant volume

12.109 When the temperature of a gas is raised by 10 °C, the collision frequency increases by only about 2%, but the reaction rate increases by 100% (a factor of 2) or more. Explain.

12.110 The initial rates listed in the following table were measured in methanol solution for the reaction

$$C_2H_4Br_2 + 3\ I^- \longrightarrow C_2H_4 + 2\ Br^- + I_3^-$$

Experiment	Initial $[C_2H_4Br_2]$	Initial $[I^-]$	Initial Rate of Formation of I_3^- (M/s)
1	0.127	0.102	6.45×10^{-5}
2	0.343	0.102	1.74×10^{-4}
3	0.203	0.125	1.26×10^{-4}

(a) What is the rate law?

(b) What is the value of the rate constant?

(c) What is the initial rate when the concentrations of both reactants are 0.150 M?

12.111 Trimethylamine and chlorine dioxide react in water in an electron transfer reaction to form the trimethylamine cation and chlorite ion:

$$(CH_3)_3N(aq) + ClO_2(aq) + H_2O(l) \longrightarrow$$
$$(CH_3)_3NH^+(aq) + ClO_2^-(aq) + OH^-(aq)$$

Initial rate data obtained at 23 °C are listed in the following table:

Experiment	$[(CH_3)_3N]$	$[ClO_2]$	Initial Rate of Formation of ClO_2^- (M/s)
1	3.25×10^{-3}	4.60×10^{-3}	0.90
2	6.50×10^{-3}	2.30×10^{-3}	0.90
3	1.30×10^{-2}	2.30×10^{-3}	1.79
4	2.60×10^{-2}	9.20×10^{-3}	14.4

(a) What is the rate law, including the value of the rate constant?

(b) What would be the initial rate in an experiment with initial concentrations $[(CH_3)_3N] = 4.2 \times 10^{-2}$ M and $[ClO_2] = 3.4 \times 10^{-2}$ M?

12.112 The light-stimulated conversion of 11-*cis*-retinal to 11-*trans*-retinal is central to the vision process in humans. This reaction also occurs (more slowly) in the absence of light. At 80.0 °C in heptane solution, the reaction is first order with a rate constant of 1.02×10^{-5}/s.

(a) What is the molarity of 11-*cis*-retinal after 6.00 h if its initial concentration is 3.50×10^{-3} M?

(b) How many minutes does it take for 25% of the 11-*cis*-retinal to react?

(c) How many hours does it take for the concentration of 11-*trans*-retinal to reach 3.15×10^{-3} M?

12.113 Concentration–time data for the conversion of A and B to D are listed in the following table:

Experiment	Time (s)	[A]	[B]	[C]	[D]
1	0	5.00	2.00	1.00	0.00
	60	4.80	1.90	1.00	0.10
2	0	10.00	2.00	1.00	0.00
	60	9.60	1.80	1.00	0.20
3	0	5.00	4.00	1.00	0.00
	60	4.80	3.90	1.00	0.10
4	0	5.00	2.00	2.00	0.00
	60	4.60	1.80	2.00	0.20

(a) Write a balanced equation for the reaction.

(b) What is the reaction order with respect to A, B, and C? What is the overall reaction order?

(c) What is the rate law?

(d) Is a catalyst involved in this reaction? Explain.

(e) Suggest a mechanism that is consistent with the data.

(f) Calculate the rate constant for the formation of D.

12.114 What fraction of the molecules in a gas at 300 K collide with an energy equal to or greater than E_a when E_a equals 50 kJ/mol? What is the value of this fraction when E_a is 100 kJ/mol?

12.115 If the rate of a reaction increases by a factor of 2.5 when the temperature is raised from 20 °C to 30 °C, what is the value of the activation energy in kJ/mol? By what factor does the rate of this reaction increase when the temperature is raised from 120 °C to 130 °C.

12.116 Beginning with the integrated rate law, derive a general equation for the half-life of a zeroth-order reaction of the type A → Products. How does the length of each half-life compare with the length of the previous one? Make the same comparison for first-order and second-order reactions.

12.117 Consider the following concentration–time data for the reaction of iodide ion and hypochlorite ion (OCl^-). The products are chloride ion and hypoiodite ion (OI^-).

Experiment	Time (s)	[I^-]	[OCl^-]	[OH^-]
1	0	2.40×10^{-4}	1.60×10^{-4}	1.00
	10	2.17×10^{-4}	1.37×10^{-4}	1.00
2	0	1.20×10^{-4}	1.60×10^{-4}	1.00
	10	1.08×10^{-4}	1.48×10^{-4}	1.00
3	0	2.40×10^{-4}	4.00×10^{-5}	1.00
	10	2.34×10^{-4}	3.40×10^{-5}	1.00
4	0	1.20×10^{-4}	1.60×10^{-4}	2.00
	10	1.14×10^{-4}	1.54×10^{-4}	2.00

(a) Write a balanced equation for the reaction.

(b) Determine the rate law, and calculate the value of the rate constant.

(c) Does the reaction occur by a single-step mechanism? Explain.

(d) Propose a mechanism that is consistent with the rate law, and express the rate constant in terms of the rate constants for the elementary steps in your mechanism. (Hint: Transfer of an H^+ ion between H_2O and OCl^- is a rapid reversible reaction.)

12.118 Consider the reversible, first-order interconversion of two molecules A and B:

$$A \underset{k_r}{\overset{k_f}{\rightleftharpoons}} B$$

where $k_f = 3.0 \times 10^{-3}\,s^{-1}$ is the rate constant for the forward reaction and $k_r = 1.0 \times 10^{-3}\,s^{-1}$ is the rate constant for the reverse reaction. We'll see in Chapter 13 that a reaction does not go to completion but instead reaches a state of equilibrium with comparable concentrations of reactants and products if the rate constants k_f and k_r have comparable values.

(a) What are the rate laws for the forward and reverse reactions?

(b) Draw a qualitative graph that shows how the rates of the forward and reverse reactions vary with time.

(c) What are the relative concentrations of B and A when the rates of the forward and reverse reactions become equal?

12.119 Radioactive decay exhibits a first-order rate law, rate $= -\Delta N/\Delta t = kN$, where N denotes the number of radioactive nuclei present at time t. The half-life of strontium-90, a dangerous nuclear fission product, is 29 years.

(a) What fraction of the strontium-90 remains after three half-lives?

(b) What is the value of the decay constant for strontium-90?

(c) How many years are required for 99% of the strontium-90 to disappear?

12.120 The age of any remains from a once-living organism can be determined by *radiocarbon dating*, a procedure that works by determining the concentration of radioactive ^{14}C in the remains. All living organisms contain an equilibrium concentration of radioactive ^{14}C that gives rise to an average of 15.3 nuclear decay events per minute per gram of carbon. At death, however, no additional ^{14}C is taken in, so the concentration slowly drops as radioactive decay occurs. What is the age of a bone fragment from an archaeological dig if the bone shows an average of 2.3 radioactive events per minute per gram of carbon? For ^{14}C, $t_{1/2} = 5715$ years.

12.121 Potassium ion, K^+, is present in most foods and is an essential nutrient in the human body. Potassium-40, however, which has a natural abundance of 0.0117%, is radioactive with $t_{1/2} = 1.25 \times 10^9$ years. What is the decay constant of ^{40}K? How many $^{40}K^+$ ions are present in 1.00 g of KCl? How many disintegrations/s does 1.00 g of KCl undergo?

12.122 Assume that you are studying the first-order conversion of a reactant X to products in a reaction vessel with a constant volume of 1.000 L. At 1:00 p.m., you start the reaction at 25 °C with 1.000 mol of X. At 2:00 p.m., you find that 0.600 mol of X remains, and you immediately increase the temperature of the reaction mixture to 35 °C. At 3:00 p.m., you discover that 0.200 mol of X is still present. You want to finish the reaction by 4:00 p.m. but need to continue it until only 0.010 mol of X remains, so you decide to increase the temperature once again. What is the minimum temperature required to convert all but 0.010 mol of X to products by 4:00 p.m.?

12.123 The half-life for the first-order decomposition of N_2O_4 is 1.3×10^{-5} s.

$$N_2O_4(g) \longrightarrow 2\,NO_2(g)$$

If N_2O_4 is introduced into an evacuated flask at a pressure of 17.0 mm Hg, how many seconds are required for the pressure of NO_2 to reach 1.3 mm Hg?

12.124 Some reactions are so rapid that they are said to be diffusion-controlled; that is, the reactants react as quickly as they can collide. An example is the neutralization of H_3O^+ by OH^-, which has a second-order rate constant of $1.3 \times 10^{11}\ M^{-1}\,s^{-1}$ at 25 °C.

(a) If equal volumes of 2.0 M HCl and 2.0 M NaOH are mixed instantaneously, how much time is required for 99.999% of the acid to be neutralized?

(b) Under normal laboratory conditions, would you expect the rate of the acid–base neutralization to be limited by the rate of the reaction or by the speed of mixing?

12.125 The reaction $2\,NO(g) + O_2(g) \rightarrow 2\,NO_2(g)$ has the third-order rate law: rate $= k[NO]^2[O_2]$, where $k = 25\ M^{-2}\,s^{-1}$. Under the condition that $[NO] = 2\,[O_2]$, the integrated rate law is

$$\frac{1}{[O_2]^2} = 8\,kt + \frac{1}{([O_2]_0)^2}$$

What are the concentrations of NO, O_2, and NO_2 after 100.0 s if the initial concentrations are $[NO] = 0.0200$ M and $[O_2] = 0.0100$ M?

12.126 Consider the following data for the gas-phase decomposition of NO_2:

$$2\,NO_2(g) \longrightarrow 2\,NO(g) + O_2(g)$$

Temperature (K)	Initial [NO$_2$]	Initial Rate of Decomposition of NO$_2$ (M/s)
600	0.0010	5.4×10^{-7}
600	0.0020	2.2×10^{-6}
700	0.0020	5.2×10^{-5}

If 0.0050 mol of NO_2 is introduced into a 1.0 L flask and allowed to decompose at 650 K, how many seconds does it take for the NO_2 concentration to drop to 0.0010 M?

12.127 Use the following initial rate data to determine the activation energy (in kJ/mol) for the reaction $A + B \rightarrow C$:

Experiment	Temperature (K)	Initial [A]	Initial [B]	Initial Rate of Formation of C (M/s)
1	700	0.20	0.10	1.8×10^{-5}
2	700	0.40	0.10	3.6×10^{-5}
3	700	0.10	0.20	3.6×10^{-5}
4	600	0.50	0.50	4.3×10^{-5}

12.128 The reaction $A \rightarrow C$ is first order in the reactant A and is known to go to completion. The product C is colored and absorbs light strongly at 550 nm, while the reactant and intermediates are colorless. A solution of A was prepared, and the absorbance of C at 550 nm was measured as a func-

tion of time. (Note that the absorbance of C is directly proportional to its concentration.) Use the following data to determine the half-life of the reaction:

Time (s)	Absorbance
0	0.000
10	0.444
20	0.724
100	1.188
200	1.200
500	1.200

12.129 The following experimental data were obtained in a study of the reaction $2\,HI(g) \rightarrow H_2(g) + I_2(g)$. Predict the concentration of HI that would give a rate of 1.0×10^{-5} M/s at 650 K.

Experiment	Temperature (K)	Initial [HI]	Initial Rate (M/s)
1	700	0.10	1.8×10^{-5}
2	700	0.30	1.6×10^{-4}
3	800	0.20	3.9×10^{-3}
4	650	?	1.0×10^{-5}

12.130 A proposed nuclear theory suggests that the relative abundances of the uranium isotopes ^{235}U and ^{238}U were approximately equal at the time they were formed. Today, the observed ratio of these isotopes $^{235}U/^{238}U$ is 7.25×10^{-3}. Given that the half-lives for radioactive decay are 7.04×10^8 y for ^{235}U and 4.47×10^9 y for ^{238}U, calculate the age of the elements.

12.131 *Mycobacterium avium*, a human pathogen responsible for respiratory infections, is sometimes found in hot tubs. *M. avium* can be inactivated by many disinfectants including chlorine, chlorine dioxide, and ozone. For inactivation by chlorine dioxide, the following rate constants were obtained. What is the activation energy (in kJ) for the inactivation of *M. avium* by chlorine dioxide?

Temperature (°C)	k [L/(mg·min)]
5	0.267
30	3.45

12.132 The half-life of a typical peptide bond (the C—N bond in a protein backbone) in neutral aqueous solution is about 500 years. When a protease enzyme acts on a peptide bond, the bond's half-life is about 0.010 s. Assuming that these half-lives correspond to first-order reactions, by what factor does the enzyme increase the rate of the peptide bond breaking reaction?

12.133 Poly(ethylene terephthalate) is a synthetic plastic used for fibers, bottles, and packaging. This material can be broken down for recycling by treatment with water at elevated temperatures (230–270 °C) and pressures according to the following equation:

Repeating unit

$$2n \; H_2O \; + \qquad\qquad \longrightarrow$$

$$n \qquad\qquad + \; n \;\; HO-CH_2-CH_2-OH$$

The reaction was carried out at different temperatures, and the following rate constants were obtained.

Temperature (°C)	$k \; (M^{-3/2} \, s^{-1})$
235	2.95×10^{-5}
250	5.77×10^{-5}
265	1.44×10^{-4}

Plot an appropriate graph of the data, and calculate the activation energy for this reaction in kJ/mol.

12.134 Polytetrafluoroethylene (Teflon) decomposes when heated above 500 °C. Rate constants for the decomposition are $2.60 \times 10^{-4} \, s^{-1}$ at 530 °C and $9.45 \times 10^{-3} \, s^{-1}$ at 620 °C.

(a) What is the activation energy in kJ/mol?

(b) What is the half-life of this substance at 580 °C?

MULTICONCEPT PROBLEMS

12.135 Values of $E_a = 6.3$ kJ/mol and $A = 6.0 \times 10^8/(M \cdot s)$ have been measured for the bimolecular reaction:

$$NO(g) + F_2(g) \longrightarrow NOF(g) + F(g)$$

(a) Calculate the rate constant at 25 °C.

(b) The product of the reaction is nitrosyl fluoride. Its formula is usually written as NOF, but its structure is actually ONF. Is the ONF molecule linear or bent?

(c) Draw a plausible transition state for the reaction. Use dashed lines to indicate the atoms that are weakly linked together in the transition state.

(d) Why does the reaction have such a low activation energy?

12.136 A 1.50 L sample of gaseous HI having a density of $0.0101 \; g/cm^3$ is heated at 410 °C. As time passes, the HI decomposes to gaseous H_2 and I_2. The rate law is $-\Delta[HI]/\Delta t = k[HI]^2$, where $k = 0.031/(M \cdot min)$ at 410 °C.

(a) What is the initial rate of production of I_2 in molecules/min?

(b) What is the partial pressure of H_2 after a reaction time of 8.00 h?

12.137 The rate constant for the decomposition of gaseous NO_2 to NO and O_2 is $4.7/(M \cdot s)$ at 383 °C. Consider the decomposition of a sample of pure NO_2 having an initial pressure of 746 mm Hg in a 5.00 L reaction vessel at 383 °C.

(a) What is the order of the reaction?

(b) What is the initial rate of formation of O_2 in $g/(L \cdot s)$?

(c) What is the mass of O_2 in the vessel after a reaction time of 1.00 min?

12.138 The rate constant for the first-order decomposition of gaseous N_2O_5 to NO_2 and O_2 is $1.7 \times 10^{-3} \, s^{-1}$ at 55 °C.

(a) If 2.70 g of gaseous N_2O_5 is introduced into an evacuated 2.00 L container maintained at a constant temperature of 55 °C, what is the total pressure in the container after a reaction time of 13.0 minutes?

(b) Use the data in Appendix B to calculate the initial rate at which the reaction mixture absorbs heat (in J/s). You may assume that the heat of the reaction is independent of temperature.

(c) What is the total amount of heat absorbed (in kilojoules) after a reaction time of 10.0 min?

12.139 For the thermal decomposition of nitrous oxide, $2 \, N_2O(g) \rightarrow 2 \, N_2(g) + O_2(g)$, values of the parameters in the Arrhenius equation are $A = 4.2 \times 10^9 \, s^{-1}$ and $E_a = 222$ kJ/mol. If a stream of N_2O is passed through a tube 25 mm in diameter and 20 cm long at a flow rate of 0.75 L/min, at what temperature should the tube be maintained to have a partial pressure of 1.0 mm of O_2 in the exit gas? Assume that the total pressure of the gas in the tube is 1.50 atm.

12.140 A 0.500 L reaction vessel equipped with a movable piston is filled completely with a 3.00% aqueous solution of hydrogen peroxide. The H_2O_2 decomposes to water and O_2 gas in a first-order reaction that has a half-life of 10.7 h. As the reaction proceeds, the gas formed pushes the piston against a constant external atmospheric pressure of 738 mm Hg. Calculate the PV work done (in joules) after a reaction time of 4.02 h. (You may assume that the density of the solution is 1.00 g/mL and that the temperature of the system is maintained at 20 °C.)

12.141 At 791 K and relatively low pressures, the gas-phase decomposition of acetaldehyde (CH_3CHO) is second order in acetaldehyde.

$$CH_3CHO(g) \longrightarrow CH_4(g) + CO(g)$$

The total pressure of a particular reaction mixture was found to vary as follows:

Time (s)	0	75	148	308	605
Total pressure (atm)	0.500	0.583	0.641	0.724	0.808

(a) Use the pressure data to determine the value of the rate constant in units of $atm^{-1} \, s^{-1}$.

(b) What is the rate constant in the usual units of $M^{-1} \, s^{-1}$?

(c) If the volume of the reaction mixture is 1.00 L, what is the total amount of heat liberated (in joules) after a reaction time of 605 s?

CHAPTER

13

Chemical Equilibrium

In a championship match, the muscles of tennis players need extra oxygen. The transfer of O_2 from the lungs to the blood and then to the muscle tissues depends on chemical equilibria involving hemoglobin, an oxygen-carrying protein.

CONTENTS

492

At the beginning of Chapter 12, we raised three key questions about chemical reactions: What happens? How fast and by what mechanism does it happen? To what extent does it happen? The answer to the first question is given by the stoichiometry of the balanced chemical equation, and the answer to the second question is given by the kinetics of the reaction. In this chapter, we'll look at the answer to the third question: How far does a reaction proceed toward completion before it reaches a state of **chemical equilibrium**—a state in which the concentrations of reactants and products no longer change?

> 🔊 **Chemical Equilibrium** The state reached when the concentrations of reactants and products remain constant over time

We've already touched on the concept of equilibrium in connection with our study of the evaporation of liquids (Section 10.5). When a liquid evaporates in a closed container, it soon gives rise to a constant vapor pressure because of a dynamic equilibrium in which the number of molecules leaving the liquid equals the number returning from the vapor. Chemical reactions behave similarly. They can occur in both forward and reverse directions, and when the rates of the forward and reverse reactions become equal, the concentrations of reactants and products remain constant. At that point, the chemical system is at equilibrium.

Chemical equilibria are important in numerous biological and environmental processes. For example, equilibria involving O_2 molecules and the protein hemoglobin play a crucial role in the transport and delivery of oxygen from our lungs to cells throughout our body. Similar equilibria involving CO molecules and hemoglobin account for the toxicity of carbon monoxide.

A mixture of reactants and products in the equilibrium state is called an **equilibrium mixture**. In this chapter, we'll address a number of important questions about the composition of equilibrium mixtures: What is the relationship between the concentrations of reactants and products in an equilibrium mixture? How can we determine equilibrium concentrations from initial concentrations? What factors can we exploit to alter the composition of an equilibrium mixture? This last question is particularly important when choosing conditions for the synthesis of industrial chemicals such as hydrogen, ammonia, and methanol (CH_3OH).

▲ In a closed container, liquid bromine and its vapor are in a dynamic equilibrium.

13.1 THE EQUILIBRIUM STATE

In previous chapters, we've generally assumed that chemical reactions result in complete conversion of reactants to products. Many reactions, however, do not go to completion. Take, for example, the decomposition of the colorless gas dinitrogen tetroxide (N_2O_4) to the dark brown gas nitrogen dioxide (NO_2).

$$N_2O_4(g) \rightleftharpoons 2\,NO_2(g)$$

Colorless   Brown

Figure 13.1 shows the results of two experiments at 25 °C that illustrate the interconversion of N_2O_4 and NO_2. In the first experiment (Figure 13.1a), we begin with N_2O_4 at an initial concentration of 0.0400 M. The formation of NO_2 is indicated by the appearance of a brown color, and its concentration can be monitored by measuring the intensity of the color with a spectrophotometer. According to the balanced equation, 2.0 mol of NO_2 forms for each mole of N_2O_4 that disappears, so the concentration of N_2O_4 at any time equals the initial concentration of N_2O_4 minus half the concentration of NO_2. As time passes, the concentration of N_2O_4 decreases and the

▲ Mexico City on a smoggy day and on a clear day. The brown color of the smog is due primarily to NO_2 that results from automobile exhausts.

(a) Only N_2O_4 is present initially.

(b) Only NO_2 is present initially.

[NO$_2$] increases as [N$_2$O$_4$] decreases.

[N$_2$O$_4$] increases as [NO$_2$] decreases.

Chemical Equilibrium

In both experiments, a state of chemical equilibrium is reached when the concentrations level off at constant values: $[N_2O_4]$ = 0.0337 M; $[NO_2]$ = 0.0125 M.

Figure 13.1
Change in the concentrations of N_2O_4 and NO_2 with time in two experiments at 25 °C.

concentration of NO_2 increases until both concentrations level off at constant, equilibrium values: $[N_2O_4]$ = 0.0337 M; $[NO_2]$ = 0.0125 M.

In the second experiment, shown in Figure 13.1b, we begin with NO_2 as the sole reactant at a concentration of 0.0800 M. The conversion of NO_2 to N_2O_4 proceeds until the concentrations level off at the same values as obtained in the first experiment. Taken together, the two experiments demonstrate that the interconversion of N_2O_4 and NO_2 is reversible and that the same equilibrium state is reached starting from either substance.

$$N_2O_4(g) \rightleftharpoons 2\,NO_2(g) \qquad \text{Reaction occurs in both directions}$$

To indicate that the reaction can proceed in both forward and reverse directions, we write the balanced equation with two arrows, one pointing from reactants to products and the other pointing from products to reactants. (The terms "reactants" and "products" could be confusing in this context because the products of the forward reaction are the reactants in the reverse reaction. To avoid confusion, we'll restrict the term *reactants* to the substances on the left side of the chemical equation and the term *products* to the substances on the right side of the equation.)

Strictly speaking, *all* chemical reactions are reversible. What we sometimes call irreversible reactions are simply those that proceed *nearly* to completion, so that the equilibrium mixture contains almost all products and almost no reactants. For such reactions, the reverse reaction is often too slow to be detected.

Why do the reactions of N_2O_4 and NO_2 appear to stop after the concentrations reach their equilibrium values? We'll explore that question in more detail in Section 13.11, but note for now that the concentrations reach constant values, not because the reactions stop, but because the rates of the forward and reverse reactions become equal. Take, for example, the experiment in which N_2O_4 is converted to an equilibrium mixture of NO_2 and N_2O_4. Because reaction rates depend on concentrations (Section 12.2), the rate of the forward reaction ($N_2O_4 \rightarrow 2\,NO_2$) decreases as the concentration of N_2O_4 decreases, while the rate of the reverse reaction

Remember...

The **reaction rate** is given by the rate law and ordinarily depends on the concentrations of at least some of the reacting species, usually increasing with increasing concentration and decreasing with decreasing concentration.   (Section 12.2)

($N_2O_4 \leftarrow 2\,NO_2$) increases as the concentration of NO_2 increases. Eventually, the decreasing rate of the forward reaction and the increasing rate of the reverse reaction become equal. At that point, there are no further changes in concentrations because N_2O_4 and NO_2 both disappear as fast as they're formed. Thus, chemical equilibrium is a dynamic state in which forward and reverse reactions continue at equal rates so that there is no net conversion of reactants to products (Figure 13.2).

Figure 13.2
Rates of the forward and reverse reactions for the decomposition of N_2O_4 to NO_2.

▲ If the rate at which people move from the first floor to the second equals the rate at which people move from the second floor to the first, the number of people on each floor remains constant and the two populations are in dynamic equilibrium.

13.2 THE EQUILIBRIUM CONSTANT K_c

Table 13.1 lists concentration data for the experiments in Figure 13.1 along with data for three additional experiments. In experiments 1 and 2, the equilibrium mixtures have identical compositions because the initial concentration of N_2O_4 in experiment 1 is half the initial concentration of NO_2 in experiment 2; that is, the total number of N and O atoms is the same in both experiments. In experiments 3–5, different initial concentrations of N_2O_4 and/or NO_2 give different equilibrium concentrations. In all the experiments, however, the equilibrium concentrations are related. The last column of Table 13.1 shows that, at equilibrium, the expression $[NO_2]^2/[N_2O_4]$ has a constant value of approximately 4.64×10^{-3} M.

TABLE 13.1 Concentration Data at 25 °C for the Reaction $N_2O_4(g) \rightleftharpoons 2\,NO_2(g)$

Experiment	Initial Concentrations (M)		Equilibrium Concentrations (M)		Equilibrium Constant Expression
	$[N_2O_4]$	$[NO_2]$	$[N_2O_4]$	$[NO_2]$	$[NO_2]^2/[N_2O_4]$
1	0.0400	0.0000	0.0337	0.0125	4.64×10^{-3}
2	0.0000	0.0800	0.0337	0.0125	4.64×10^{-3}
3	0.0600	0.0000	0.0522	0.0156	4.66×10^{-3}
4	0.0000	0.0600	0.0246	0.0107	4.65×10^{-3}
5	0.0200	0.0600	0.0429	0.0141	4.63×10^{-3}

The expression $[NO_2]^2/[N_2O_4]$ appears to be related to the balanced equation for the reaction $N_2O_4(g) \rightleftharpoons 2\,NO_2(g)$ in that the concentration of the product is in the numerator, raised to the power of its coefficient in the balanced equation, and the concentration of the reactant is in the denominator. Is there an analogous expression with a constant value for every chemical reaction? If so, how is the form of that expression related to the balanced equation for the reaction?

To answer those questions, let's consider a general reversible reaction:

$$a\,A + b\,B \rightleftharpoons c\,C + d\,D$$

where A and B are the reactants, C and D are the products, and a, b, c, and d are their respective stoichiometric coefficients in the balanced chemical equation. In 1864 on the basis of experimental studies of many reversible reactions, the Norwegian chemists Cato Maximilian Guldberg and Peter Waage proposed that the concentrations in an equilibrium mixture are related by the following **equilibrium equation**, where K_c is the *equilibrium constant* and the expression on the right side is called the *equilibrium constant expression*.

$$\text{Equilibrium equation:} \quad K_c = \frac{[C]^c[D]^d}{[A]^a[B]^b} \quad \begin{matrix}\longleftarrow \text{Products} \\ \longleftarrow \text{Reactants}\end{matrix}$$

Equilibrium constant   Equilibrium constant expression

As usual, square brackets indicate the molar concentration of the substance within the brackets, hence the subscript c for "concentration" in K_c. The substances in the equilibrium constant expression may be gases or molecules and ions in a solution, but may not be pure solids or pure liquids for reasons that we'll explain in Section 13.4. The equilibrium equation is also known as the *law of mass action* because in the early days of chemistry, concentration was called "active mass."

The **equilibrium constant K_c** is the number obtained by multiplying the equilibrium concentrations of all the products and dividing by the product of the equilibrium concentrations of all the reactants, with the concentration of each substance raised to the power of its coefficient in the balanced chemical equation. No matter what the individual equilibrium concentrations may be in a particular experiment, *the equilibrium constant for a reaction at a particular temperature always has the same value.* Thus, the equilibrium equation for the decomposition reaction $N_2O_4(g) \rightleftharpoons 2\,NO_2$ is

$$K_c = \frac{[NO_2]^2}{[N_2O_4]} = 4.64 \times 10^{-3} \quad \text{at 25 °C}$$

where the equilibrium constant expression is $[NO_2]^2/[N_2O_4]$ and the equilibrium constant K_c has a value of 4.64×10^{-3} at 25 °C (Table 13.1).

Values of K_c are generally reported without units because the concentrations in the equilibrium constant expression are considered to be concentration ratios in which the molarity of each substance is divided by its molarity (1 M) in the **thermodynamic standard state** (Section 8.5). Because the units cancel, the concentration ratios and the values of K_c are dimensionless. For experiment 1 in Table 13.1, for example,

$$K_c = \frac{[NO_2]^2}{[N_2O_4]} = \frac{\left(\dfrac{0.0125\ \cancel{M}}{1\ \cancel{M}}\right)^2}{\left(\dfrac{0.0337\ \cancel{M}}{1\ \cancel{M}}\right)} = 4.64 \times 10^{-3} \quad \text{at 25 °C}$$

Equilibrium constants are temperature-dependent, so the temperature must be given when citing a value of K_c. For example, K_c for the decomposition of N_2O_4 increases from 4.64×10^{-3} at 25 °C to 1.53 at 127 °C.

Remember...

The **thermodynamic standard state** is the set of conditions under which thermodynamic measurements are reported: 1 M concentration for each solute in solution, 1 atm pressure for each gas, and a specified temperature, usually 25 °C. (Section 8.5)

The form of the equilibrium constant expression and the numerical value of the equilibrium constant depend on the form of the balanced chemical equation. Look again at the chemical equation and the equilibrium equation for a general reaction:

$$a\,A + b\,B \rightleftharpoons c\,C + d\,D \qquad K_c = \frac{[C]^c[D]^d}{[A]^a[B]^b}$$

If we write the chemical equation in the reverse direction, the new equilibrium constant expression is the reciprocal of the original expression and the new equilibrium constant K_c' is the reciprocal of the original equilibrium constant K_c. (The prime distinguishes K_c' from K_c.)

$$c\,C + d\,D \rightleftharpoons a\,A + b\,B \qquad K_c' = \frac{[A]^a[B]^b}{[C]^c[D]^d} = \frac{1}{K_c}$$

Because the equilibrium constants K_c and K_c' have different numerical values, it's important to specify the form of the balanced chemical equation when quoting the value of an equilibrium constant.

WORKED EXAMPLE 13.1

WRITING EQUILIBRIUM EQUATIONS FOR GAS-PHASE REACTIONS

Write the equilibrium equation for each of the following reactions:

(a) $N_2(g) + 3\,H_2(g) \rightleftharpoons 2\,NH_3(g)$

(b) $2\,NH_3(g) \rightleftharpoons N_2(g) + 3\,H_2(g)$

STRATEGY

Put the concentrations of the reaction products in the numerator of the equilibrium constant expression and the concentrations of the reactants in the denominator. Then raise the concentration of each substance to the power of its coefficient in the balanced chemical equation.

SOLUTION

(a) $K_c = \dfrac{[NH_3]^2}{[N_2][H_2]^3}$ — Coefficient of NH_3; Coefficient of H_2

(b) $K_c' = \dfrac{[N_2][H_2]^3}{[NH_3]^2}$ — Coefficient of H_2; Coefficient of NH_3 $\qquad K_c' = \dfrac{1}{K_c}$

Because the balanced equation in part **(b)** is the reverse of that in part **(a)**, the equilibrium constant expression in part **(b)** is the reciprocal of the expression in part **(a)** and the equilibrium constant K_c' is the reciprocal of K_c.

WORKED EXAMPLE 13.2

CALCULATING THE EQUILIBRIUM CONSTANT K_c

The following concentrations were measured for an equilibrium mixture at 500 K: $[N_2] = 3.0 \times 10^{-2}$ M; $[H_2] = 3.7 \times 10^{-2}$ M; $[NH_3] = 1.6 \times 10^{-2}$ M. Calculate the equilibrium constant at 500 K for each of the reactions in Worked Example 13.1.

STRATEGY

To calculate the value of the equilibrium constant, substitute the equilibrium concentrations into the equilibrium equation.

continued on next page

SOLUTION

(a) $K_c = \dfrac{[NH_3]^2}{[N_2][H_2]^3} = \dfrac{(1.6 \times 10^{-2})^2}{(3.0 \times 10^{-2})(3.7 \times 10^{-2})^3} = 1.7 \times 10^2$

(b) $K_c' = \dfrac{[N_2][H_2]^3}{[NH_3]^2} = \dfrac{(3.0 \times 10^{-2})(3.7 \times 10^{-2})^3}{(1.6 \times 10^{-2})^2} = 5.9 \times 10^{-3}$

Note that K_c' is the reciprocal of K_c. That is,

$$5.9 \times 10^{-3} = \dfrac{1}{1.7 \times 10^2}$$

▲ MTBE is a component of some gasolines but is being phased out because it has been found to be an unsafe contaminant of groundwater.

WORKED EXAMPLE 13.3

WRITING EQUILIBRIUM EQUATIONS FOR SOLUTION REACTIONS

Methyl *tert*-butyl ether (MTBE), a substance once used as a gasoline additive but now being phased out because of safety concerns, can be synthesized by heating methanol and *tert*-butyl alcohol with a catalytic amount of sulfuric acid:

$$\underset{\text{Methanol}}{CH_3OH(soln)} + \underset{\textit{tert}\text{-Butyl alcohol}}{C_4H_9OH(soln)} \underset{\text{catalyst}}{\overset{H^+}{\rightleftharpoons}} \underset{\text{Methyl }\textit{tert}\text{-butyl ether}}{C_4H_9OCH_3(soln)} + H_2O(soln)$$

In this equation, *soln* denotes a largely organic solution that also contains water. Write the equilibrium constant expression for the reaction.

STRATEGY

The rules for writing the equilibrium constant expression apply to reactions in liquid solutions as well as to gas-phase reactions (reactions in gaseous solutions). Put the concentrations of the products in the numerator and the concentrations of the reactants in the denominator. No exponents are needed because all the coefficients in the balanced chemical equation equal 1.

SOLUTION

$$K_c = \dfrac{[C_4H_9OCH_3]\,[H_2O]}{[CH_3OH]\,[C_4H_9OH]} \overset{\longleftarrow\text{ Products}}{\underset{\longleftarrow\text{ Reactants}}{}}$$

▶ **PROBLEM 13.1** The oxidation of sulfur dioxide to give sulfur trioxide is an important step in the industrial process for the synthesis of sulfuric acid. Write the equilibrium equation for each of the following reactions:

    (a) $2\,SO_2(g) + O_2(g) \rightleftharpoons 2\,SO_3(g)$ (b) $2\,SO_3(g) \rightleftharpoons 2\,SO_2(g) + O_2(g)$

▶ **PROBLEM 13.2** The following equilibrium concentrations were measured at 800 K: $[SO_2] = 3.0 \times 10^{-3}$ M; $[O_2] = 3.5 \times 10^{-3}$ M; $[SO_3] = 5.0 \times 10^{-2}$ M. Calculate the equilibrium constant at 800 K for each of the reactions in Problem 13.1.

▶ **PROBLEM 13.3** Lactic acid, which builds up in muscle tissue upon strenuous exercise, is partially dissociated in aqueous solution:

Lactic acid   Lactate ion

(a) Write the equilibrium constant expression for K_c.

(b) What is the value of K_c if the extent of dissociation in 0.100 M lactic acid is 3.65% at 25 °C?

Lactic acid

WORKED CONCEPTUAL EXAMPLE 13.4

JUDGING WHETHER A MIXTURE IS AT EQUILIBRIUM

The following pictures represent mixtures of A molecules (red spheres) and B molecules (blue spheres), which interconvert according to the equation A $\rightleftharpoons$ B. If mixture (1) is at equilibrium, which of the other mixtures are also at equilibrium? Explain.

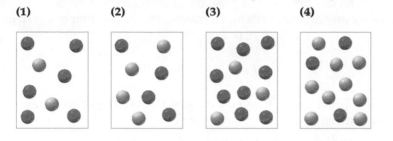

(1)   **(2)**   **(3)**   **(4)**

STRATEGY

The equilibrium constant for the reaction is given by K_c = [B]/[A], where the concentrations are equilibrium concentrations in units of mol/L. Since the equilibrium constant expression has the same number of concentration terms in the numerator and denominator, the volume cancels and K_c = (moles of B)/(moles of A). Because the number of moles is directly proportional to the number of molecules, K_c = (molecules of B)/(molecules of A) in the equilibrium mixture, mixture (1). To determine whether the other mixtures are at equilibrium, count the number of molecules and compare the B/A ratio in mixtures (2)–(4) with the B/A ratio in the equilibrium mixture.

SOLUTION

For mixture (1), K_c = [B]/[A] = 2/6 = 1/3.
For mixture (2), [B]/[A] = 4/4 = 1 ≠ K_c.
For mixture (3), [B]/[A] = 3/9 = 1/3 = K_c.
For mixture (4), [B]/[A] = 9/3 = 3 ≠ K_c.

Mixture (3) is at equilibrium, but mixtures (2) and (4) are not at equilibrium because their equilibrium constant expression [B]/[A] does not equal K_c.

CONCEPTUAL PROBLEM 13.4   The following pictures represent mixtures that contain A atoms (red), B atoms (blue), and AB and B_2 molecules, which interconvert according to the equation A + B_2 $\rightleftharpoons$ AB + B. If mixture (1) is at equilibrium, which of the other mixtures are also at equilibrium? Explain.

(1)   **(2)**   **(3)**   **(4)**

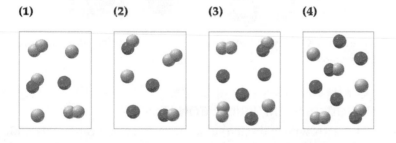

13.3 THE EQUILIBRIUM CONSTANT K_p

Because gas pressures are easily measured, equilibrium equations for gas-phase reactions are often written using **partial pressures** (Section 9.5) rather than molar concentrations. For example, the equilibrium equation for the decomposition of N_2O_4 can be written as

$$K_p = \frac{(P_{NO_2})^2}{P_{N_2O_4}} \quad \text{for the reaction } N_2O_4(g) \rightleftharpoons 2\,NO_2(g)$$

where $P_{N_2O_4}$ and P_{NO_2} are the partial pressures (in atmospheres) of reactants and products at equilibrium, and the subscript p on K reminds us that the **equilibrium constant** K_p is defined using partial pressures. As for K_c, values of K_p are dimensionless because

Remember...
The **partial pressure** of a gas in a mixture is the pressure the gas would exert if it were the only one present. Its partial pressure is independent of the partial pressures of the other gases in the mixture. (Section 9.5)

the partial pressures in the equilibrium equation are actually ratios of partial pressures in atmospheres to the standard-state partial pressure of 1 atm. Thus, the units cancel. Note that the equilibrium equations for K_p and K_c have the same form except that the expression for K_p contains partial pressures instead of molar concentrations.

The constants K_p and K_c for the general gas-phase reaction $a\,A + b\,B \rightleftharpoons c\,C + d\,D$ are related because the pressure of each component in a mixture of ideal gases is directly proportional to its molar concentration. For component A, for example,

$$P_A V = n_A RT$$

so

$$P_A = \frac{n_A}{V} RT = [A]RT$$

Similarly, $P_B = [B]RT$, $P_C = [C]RT$, and $P_D = [D]RT$. The equilibrium equation for K_p is therefore given by

$$K_p = \frac{(P_C)^c (P_D)^d}{(P_A)^a (P_B)^b} = \frac{([C]RT)^c([D]RT)^d}{([A]RT)^a([B]RT)^b} = \frac{[C]^c[D]^d}{[A]^a[B]^b} \times (RT)^{(c+d)-(a+b)}$$

Because the first term on the right side equals K_c, the values of K_p and K_c are related by the equation

$$K_p = K_c(RT)^{\Delta n} \qquad \text{for the reaction } a\,A + b\,B \rightleftharpoons c\,C + d\,D$$

Here, R is the gas constant, $0.082\ 06\ (L \cdot atm)/(K \cdot mol)$, T is the absolute temperature, and $\Delta n = (c + d) - (a + b)$ is the number of moles of gaseous products minus the number of moles of gaseous reactants.

For the decomposition of 1 mol of N_2O_4 to 2 mol of NO_2, $\Delta n = 2 - 1 = 1$, and $K_p = K_c(RT)$:

$$N_2O_4(g) \rightleftharpoons 2\,NO_2(g) \qquad K_p = K_c(RT)$$

For the reaction of 1 mol of hydrogen with 1 mol of iodine to give 2 mol of hydrogen iodide, $\Delta n = 2 - (1 + 1) = 0$, and $K_p = K_c(RT)^0 = K_c$:

$$H_2(g) + I_2(g) \rightleftharpoons 2\,HI(g) \qquad K_p = K_c$$

In general, K_p equals K_c only if the same number of moles of gases appear on both sides of the balanced chemical equation so that $\Delta n = 0$.

WORKED EXAMPLE 13.5

DETERMINING THE EQUILIBRIUM CONSTANT K_p

Methane (CH_4) reacts with hydrogen sulfide to yield H_2 and carbon disulfide, a solvent used in manufacturing rayon and cellophane:

$$CH_4(g) + 2\,H_2S(g) \rightleftharpoons CS_2(g) + 4\,H_2(g)$$

What is the value of K_p at 1000 K if the partial pressures in an equilibrium mixture at 1000 K are 0.20 atm of CH_4, 0.25 atm of H_2S, 0.52 atm of CS_2, and 0.10 atm of H_2?

STRATEGY

Write the equilibrium equation by setting K_p equal to the equilibrium constant expression using partial pressures. Put the partial pressures of products in the numerator and the partial pressures of reactants in the denominator, with the pressure of each substance raised to the power of its coefficient in the balanced chemical equation. Then substitute the partial pressures into the equilibrium equation and solve for K_p.

SOLUTION

Coefficient of H_2

$$K_p = \frac{(P_{CS_2})(P_{H_2})^4}{(P_{CH_4})(P_{H_2S})^2}$$

Coefficient of H_2S

$$K_p = \frac{(P_{CS_2})(P_{H_2})^4}{(P_{CH_4})(P_{H_2S})^2} = \frac{(0.52)(0.10)^4}{(0.20)(0.25)^2} = 4.2 \times 10^{-3}$$

Note that the partial pressures must be in units of atmospheres (not mm Hg) because the standard-state partial pressure for gases is 1 atm.

WORKED EXAMPLE 13.6

RELATING THE EQUILIBRIUM CONSTANTS K_p AND K_c

Hydrogen is produced industrially by the steam hydrocarbon re-forming process. The reaction that takes place in the first step of this process is

$$H_2O(g) + CH_4(g) \rightleftharpoons CO(g) + 3\,H_2(g)$$

(a) If $K_c = 3.8 \times 10^{-3}$ at 1000 K, what is the value of K_p at the same temperature?

(b) If $K_p = 6.1 \times 10^4$ at 1125 °C, what is the value of K_c at 1125 °C?

STRATEGY

To calculate K_p from K_c, or vice versa, use the equation $K_p = K_c(RT)^{\Delta n}$, where R must be in units of $(L \cdot atm)/(K \cdot mol)$, T is the temperature in kelvin, and Δn is the number of moles of gaseous products minus the number of moles of gaseous reactants.

SOLUTION

(a) For this reaction, $\Delta n = (1 + 3) - (1 + 1) = 2$. Therefore,

$$K_p = K_c(RT)^{\Delta n} = K_c(RT)^2 = (3.8 \times 10^{-3})[(0.082\,06)(1000)]^2 = 26$$

(b) Solving the equation $K_p = K_c(RT)^2$ for K_c gives

$$K_c = \frac{K_p}{(RT)^2} = \frac{6.1 \times 10^4}{[(0.082\,06)(1398)]^2} = 4.6$$

Note that the temperature in these equations is the absolute temperature; 1125 °C corresponds to $1125 + 273 = 1398$ K.

▶ **PROBLEM 13.5**   In the industrial synthesis of hydrogen, mixtures of CO and H_2 are enriched in H_2 by allowing the CO to react with steam. The chemical equation for this so-called water-gas shift reaction is

$$CO(g) + H_2O(g) \rightleftharpoons CO_2(g) + H_2(g)$$

What is the value of K_p at 700 K if the partial pressures in an equilibrium mixture at 700 K are 1.31 atm of CO, 10.0 atm of H_2O, 6.12 atm of CO_2, and 20.3 atm of H_2?

▶ **PROBLEM 13.6**   Nitric oxide reacts with oxygen to give nitrogen dioxide, an important reaction in the Ostwald process for the industrial synthesis of nitric acid:

$$2\,NO(g) + O_2(g) \rightleftharpoons 2\,NO_2(g)$$

If $K_c = 6.9 \times 10^5$ at 227 °C, what is the value of K_p at this temperature? If $K_p = 1.3 \times 10^{-2}$ at 1000 K, what is the value of K_c at 1000 K?

13.4 HETEROGENEOUS EQUILIBRIA

Thus far we've been discussing **homogeneous equilibria**, in which all reactants and products are in a single phase, usually either gaseous or solution. **Heterogeneous equilibria**, by contrast, are those in which reactants and products are present in more than one phase. Take, for example, the thermal decomposition of solid calcium carbonate, a reaction used in manufacturing cement:

$$\underset{\text{Limestone}}{CaCO_3(s)} \rightleftharpoons \underset{\text{Lime}}{CaO(s)} + CO_2(g)$$

When the reaction is carried out in a closed container, three phases are present at equilibrium: solid calcium carbonate, solid calcium oxide, and gaseous carbon dioxide. If we were to write the usual equilibrium equation for the reaction, including all the reactants and products, we would have

$$K_c = \frac{[CaO][CO_2]}{[CaCO_3]}$$

Once again, though, the concentrations in the equilibrium equation are ratios of actual concentrations to concentrations in the standard state. Because the standard state of a pure solid is the pure solid itself, the concentration ratio for a pure solid (and also for a pure liquid) is equal to 1. Thus, $[CaO] = 1$ and $[CaCO_3] = 1$, and so these concentrations can be omitted from the equilibrium equation:

$$K_c = \frac{[CaO][CO_2]}{[CaCO_3]} = \frac{(1)[CO_2]}{(1)} = [CO_2]$$

The analogous equilibrium equation in terms of pressure is $K_p = P_{CO_2}$ where P_{CO_2} is the equilibrium pressure of CO_2 in atmospheres:

$$K_c = [CO_2] \qquad K_p = P_{CO_2}$$

As a general rule, the concentrations of pure solids and pure liquids are not included when writing an equilibrium equation. We include only the concentrations of gases and the concentrations of solutes in solutions because only those concentrations can be varied.

To establish equilibrium between solid $CaCO_3$, solid CaO, and gaseous CO_2, all three components must be present. It follows from the equations $K_c = [CO_2]$ and $K_p = P_{CO_2}$, however, that the concentration and pressure of CO_2 at equilibrium are constant, independent of how much solid CaO and $CaCO_3$ is present (**Figure 13.3**). If the temperature is changed, however, the concentration and pressure of CO_2 will also change because the values of K_c and K_p depend on temperature.

▲ The manufacture of cement begins with the thermal decomposition of limestone, $CaCO_3$, in large kilns.

(a) Small amount of $CaCO_3$; large amount of CaO

CO_2

P_{CO_2}

$CaCO_3$ CaO

(b) Large amount of $CaCO_3$; small amount of CaO

CO_2

P_{CO_2}

$CaCO_3$ CaO

At the same temperature, the equilibrium pressure of CO_2 is the same in **(a)** and **(b)**, independent of how much solid $CaCO_3$ and CaO is present.

Figure 13.3
Thermal decomposition of calcium carbonate:
$CaCO_3(s) \rightleftharpoons CaO(s) + CO_2(g)$.

WORKED EXAMPLE 13.7

WRITING EQUILIBRIUM EQUATIONS FOR HETEROGENEOUS EQUILIBRIA

Write the equilibrium equation for each of the following reactions:

(a) $CO_2(g) + C(s) \rightleftharpoons 2\,CO(g)$

(b) $Hg(l) + Hg^{2+}(aq) \rightleftharpoons Hg_2^{2+}(aq)$

STRATEGY

Write the usual equilibrium constant expressions but omit the pure solid carbon in part **(a)** and the pure liquid mercury in part **(b)** because the ratio of their concentrations to their concentrations in the standard state is equal to 1.

SOLUTION

(a) $K_c = \dfrac{[CO]^2}{[CO_2]}$

Alternatively, because CO and CO_2 are gases, the equilibrium equation can be written using partial pressures:

$$K_p = \frac{(P_{CO})^2}{P_{CO_2}}$$

The relationship between K_p and K_c is $K_p = K_c(RT)^{\Delta n} = K_c(RT)$, because $\Delta n = 2 - 1 = 1$.

(b) $K_c = \dfrac{[Hg_2^{2+}]}{[Hg^{2+}]}$

In this case, it's not appropriate to write an expression for K_p because none of the reactants and products is a gas.

▶ **PROBLEM 13.7** For each of the following reactions, write the equilibrium constant expression for K_c. Where appropriate, also write the equilibrium constant expression for K_p and relate K_p to K_c.

(a) $2\,Fe(s) + 3\,H_2O(g) \rightleftharpoons Fe_2O_3(s) + 3\,H_2(g)$

(b) $2\,H_2O(l) \rightleftharpoons 2\,H_2(g) + O_2(g)$

(c) $SiCl_4(g) + 2\,H_2(g) \rightleftharpoons Si(s) + 4\,HCl(g)$

(d) $Hg_2^{2+}(aq) + 2\,Cl^-(aq) \rightleftharpoons Hg_2Cl_2(s)$

13.5 USING THE EQUILIBRIUM CONSTANT

Knowing the value of the equilibrium constant for a chemical reaction lets us judge the extent of the reaction, predict the direction of the reaction, and calculate equilibrium concentrations from initial concentrations. Let's look at each possibility.

Judging the Extent of Reaction

The numerical value of the equilibrium constant for a reaction indicates the extent to which reactants are converted to products; that is, it measures how far the reaction proceeds before the equilibrium state is reached. Consider, for example, the reaction of H_2 with O_2, which has a very large equilibrium constant ($K_c = 2.4 \times 10^{47}$ at 500 K):

$$2\,H_2(g) + O_2(g) \rightleftharpoons 2\,H_2O(g)$$

$$K_c = \frac{[H_2O]^2}{[H_2]^2[O_2]} = 2.4 \times 10^{47} \qquad \text{at 500 K}$$

Because products appear in the numerator of the equilibrium constant expression and reactants are in the denominator, a very large value of K_c means that the equilibrium ratio of products to reactants is very large. In other words, the reaction proceeds nearly to completion. For example, if stoichiometric amounts of H_2 and O_2 are allowed to react and [H₂O] = 0.10 M at equilibrium, then the concentrations of H₂ and O₂ that remain at equilibrium are negligibly small: $[H_2] = 4.4 \times 10^{-17}$ M and $[O_2] = 2.2 \times 10^{-17}$ M. (Try substituting these concentrations into the equilibrium equation to show that they satisfy the equation.)

By contrast, if a reaction has a very small value of K_c, the equilibrium ratio of products to reactants is very small and the reaction proceeds hardly at all before equilibrium is reached. For example, the reverse of the reaction of H₂ with O₂ gives the same equilibrium mixture as obtained from the forward reaction ($[H_2] = 4.4 \times 10^{-17}$ M, $[O_2] = 2.2 \times 10^{-17}$ M, [H₂O] = 0.10 M). The reverse reaction does not occur to any appreciable extent, however, because its equilibrium constant is so small: $K_c' = 1/K_c = 1/(2.4 \times 10^{47}) = 4.2 \times 10^{-48}$.

$$2\,H_2O(g) \rightleftharpoons 2\,H_2(g) + O_2(g)$$

$$K_c = \frac{[H_2]^2[O_2]}{[H_2O]^2} = 4.2 \times 10^{-48} \qquad \text{at 500 K}$$

If a reaction has an intermediate value of K_c—say, a value in the range of 10^3 to 10^{-3}—then appreciable concentrations of both reactants and products are present in the equilibrium mixture. The reaction of hydrogen with iodine, for example, has $K_c = 57.0$ at 700 K:

$$H_2(g) + I_2(g) \rightleftharpoons 2\,HI(g)$$

$$K_c = \frac{[HI]^2}{[H_2][I_2]} = 57.0 \qquad \text{at 700 K}$$

If the equilibrium concentrations of H₂ and I₂ are both 0.010 M, then the concentration of HI at equilibrium is 0.075 M:

$$[HI]^2 = K_c[H_2][I_2]$$

$$[HI] = \sqrt{K_c[H_2][I_2]} = \sqrt{(57.0)(0.010)(0.010)} = 0.075 \text{ M}$$

Thus, the concentrations of both reactants and products—0.010 M and 0.075 M—are appreciable.

(Note that pressing the $\sqrt{x}$ key on a calculator gives a positive number. Remember, though, that the square root of a positive number can be positive or negative. Of the two roots for the concentration of HI, ±0.075 M, we choose the positive one because the concentration of a chemical substance is always a positive quantity.)

The gas-phase decomposition of N₂O₄ to NO₂ is another reaction with a value of K_c that is neither large nor small: $K_c = 4.64 \times 10^{-3}$ at 25 °C. Accordingly, equilibrium mixtures contain appreciable concentrations of both N₂O₄ and NO₂, as shown previously in Table 13.1.

We can make the following generalizations concerning the composition of equilibrium mixtures:

- If $K_c > 10^3$, products predominate over reactants. If K_c is very large, the reaction proceeds nearly to completion.

- If $K_c < 10^{-3}$, reactants predominate over products. If K_c is very small, the reaction proceeds hardly at all.

- If K_c is in the range 10^{-3} to 10^3, appreciable concentrations of both reactants and products are present.

These points are illustrated in **Figure 13.4.**

The larger the value of the equilibrium constant K_c, the farther the reaction proceeds to the right before reaching the equilibrium state:

K_c

Very small — Very large

10^{-3} 1 10^3

Reaction proceeds hardly at all.

Appreciable concentrations of both reactants and products are present at equilibrium.

Reaction proceeds nearly to completion.

Figure 13.4
Judging the extent of a reaction.

▶ **PROBLEM 13.8** The value of K_c for the dissociation reaction $H_2(g) \rightleftharpoons 2\,H(g)$ is 1.2×10^{-42} at 500 K. Does the equilibrium mixture contain mainly H_2 molecules or H atoms? Explain in light of the electron configuration of hydrogen.

Hydrogen

Predicting the Direction of Reaction

Let's look again at the gaseous reaction of hydrogen with iodine:

$$H_2(g) + I_2(g) \rightleftharpoons 2\,HI(g) \qquad K_c = 57.0 \text{ at } 700 \text{ K}$$

Suppose that we have a mixture of $H_2(g)$, $I_2(g)$, and $HI(g)$ at 700 K with concentrations $[H_2]_t = 0.10$ M, $[I_2]_t = 0.20$ M, and $[HI]_t = 0.40$ M. (The subscript t on the concentration symbols means that the concentrations were measured at some arbitrary time t, not necessarily at equilibrium.) If we substitute these concentrations into the equilibrium constant expression, we obtain a value called the **reaction quotient** Q_c.

Reaction quotient $\quad Q_c = \dfrac{[HI]_t^{\,2}}{[H_2]_t[I_2]_t} = \dfrac{(0.40)^2}{(0.10)(0.20)} = 8.0$

The reaction quotient Q_c is defined in the same way as the equilibrium constant K_c except that the concentrations in Q_c are not necessarily equilibrium values.

For the case at hand, the numerical value of Q_c (8.0) does not equal K_c (57.0), so the mixture of $H_2(g)$, $I_2(g)$, and $HI(g)$ is not at equilibrium. As time passes, though, reaction will occur, changing the concentrations and thus changing the value of Q_c in the direction of K_c. After a sufficiently long time, an equilibrium state will be reached and $Q_c = K_c$.

The reaction quotient Q_c is useful because it lets us predict the direction of reaction by comparing the values of Q_c and K_c. If Q_c is less than K_c, movement toward equilibrium increases Q_c by converting reactants to products (that is, net reaction proceeds from left to right). If Q_c is greater than K_c, movement toward equilibrium decreases Q_c by converting products to reactants (that is, net reaction proceeds from right to left). If Q_c equals K_c, the reaction mixture is already at equilibrium, and no net reaction occurs.

Thus, we can make the following generalizations concerning the direction of the reaction:

• If $Q_c < K_c$, net reaction goes from left to right (reactants to products).
• If $Q_c > K_c$, net reaction goes from right to left (products to reactants).
• If $Q_c = K_c$, no net reaction occurs.

These points are illustrated in **Figure 13.5**.

Figure 13.5
Predicting the direction of reaction.

The direction of net reaction depends on the relative values of Q_c and K_c.

Reactants → Products

Reactants and products are at equilibrium.

Reactants ← Products

Movement toward equilibrium changes the value of Q_c until it equals K_c, but the **value of K_c** remains constant.

WORKED EXAMPLE 13.8

PREDICTING THE DIRECTION OF REACTION

A mixture of 1.57 mol of N_2, 1.92 mol of H_2, and 8.13 mol of NH_3 is introduced into a 20.0 L reaction vessel at 500 K. At this temperature, the equilibrium constant K_c for the reaction $N_2(g) + 3\,H_2(g) \rightleftharpoons 2\,NH_3(g)$ is 1.7×10^2. Is the reaction mixture at equilibrium? If not, what is the direction of the net reaction?

STRATEGY

To determine whether the reaction mixture is at equilibrium, we need to calculate the value of the reaction quotient Q_c and then compare it with the equilibrium constant K_c. If the mixture is not at equilibrium, the relative values of Q_c and K_c tell us the direction of the net reaction. Because we are given amounts in moles, we must first convert moles to molar concentrations before substituting into the expression for Q_c.

SOLUTION

The initial concentration of N_2 is $(1.57\ \text{mol})/(20.0\ \text{L}) = 0.0785$ M. Similarly, $[H_2] = 0.0960$ M and $[NH_3] = 0.406$ M. Substituting these concentrations into the equilibrium constant expression gives

$$Q_c = \frac{[NH_3]_t^{\,2}}{[N_2]_t[H_2]_t^{\,3}} = \frac{(0.406)^2}{(0.0785)(0.0960)^3} = 2.37 \times 10^3$$

Because Q_c does not equal K_c (1.7×10^2), the reaction mixture is not at equilibrium. Because Q_c is greater than K_c, net reaction will proceed from right to left, decreasing the concentration of NH_3 and increasing the concentrations of N_2 and H_2 until $Q_c = K_c = 1.7 \times 10^2$.

BALLPARK CHECK

Approximate initial concentrations can be calculated by dividing rounded values of the number of moles of each substance by the volume; $[N_2] \approx (1.6\ \text{mol})/(20\ \text{L}) \approx 0.08$ M, $[H_2] \approx (2\ \text{mol})/(20\ \text{L}) \approx 0.1$ M, and $[NH_3] \approx (8\ \text{mol})/(20\ \text{L}) \approx 0.4$ M. Substituting these concentrations into the expression for Q_c gives a ballpark estimate of Q_c:

$$Q_c = \frac{[NH_3]_t^{\,2}}{[N_2]_t[H_2]_t^{\,3}} \approx \frac{(0.4)^2}{(0.08)(0.1)^3} \approx 2 \times 10^3$$

You can calculate this value without a calculator because it equals $(16 \times 10^{-2})/(8 \times 10^{-5})$. The ballpark estimate of Q_c, like the more exact value (2.37×10^3), exceeds K_c, so the reaction mixture is not at equilibrium.

▶ **PROBLEM 13.9** The equilibrium constant K_c for the reaction $2\,NO(g) + O_2(g) \rightleftharpoons 2\,NO_2(g)$ is 6.9×10^5 at 500 K. A 5.0 L reaction vessel at 500 K was filled with 0.060 mol of NO, 1.0 mol of O_2, and 0.80 mol of NO_2.

(a) Is the reaction mixture at equilibrium? If not, in which direction does the net reaction proceed?

(b) What is the direction of the net reaction if the initial amounts are 5.0×10^{-3} mol of NO, 0.20 mol of O_2, and 4.0 mol of NO_2?

CONCEPTUAL PROBLEM 13.10 The reaction $A_2 + B_2 \rightleftharpoons 2\,AB$ has an equilibrium constant $K_c = 4$. The following pictures represent reaction mixtures that contain A_2 molecules (red), B_2 molecules (blue), and AB molecules:

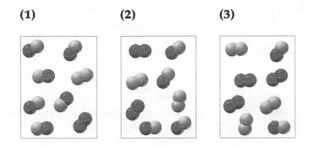

(1)   (2)   (3)

(a) Which reaction mixture is at equilibrium?

(b) For those reaction mixtures that are not at equilibrium, will the net reaction go in the forward or reverse direction to reach equilibrium?

Calculating Equilibrium Concentrations

If the equilibrium constant and all the equilibrium concentrations but one are known, the unknown concentration can be calculated directly from the equilibrium equation. To illustrate, let's consider the following problem: What is the concentration of NO in an equilibrium mixture of gaseous NO, O_2, and NO_2 at 500 K that contains 1.0×10^{-3} M O_2 and 5.0×10^{-2} M NO_2? At this temperature, the equilibrium constant K_c for the reaction $2\,NO(g) + O_2(g) \rightleftharpoons 2\,NO_2(g)$ is 6.9×10^5.

In this problem, K_c and all the equilibrium concentrations except one are known and we're asked to calculate the unknown equilibrium concentration. First, we write the equilibrium equation for the reaction and solve for the unknown concentration:

$$K_c = \frac{[NO_2]^2}{[NO]^2[O_2]} \qquad [NO] = \sqrt{\frac{[NO_2]^2}{[O_2]K_c}}$$

Then we substitute the known values of K_c, $[O_2]$, and $[NO_2]$ into the expression for [NO]. Taking the positive square root because the concentration of NO is a positive quantity, we obtain:

$$[NO] = \sqrt{\frac{(5.0 \times 10^{-2})^2}{(1.0 \times 10^{-3})(6.9 \times 10^5)}} = \sqrt{3.6 \times 10^{-6}} = 1.9 \times 10^{-3}\ M$$

To be sure that we haven't made any errors, it's a good idea to check the result by substituting it into the equilibrium equation:

$$K_c = 6.9 \times 10^5 = \frac{[NO_2]^2}{[NO]^2[O_2]} = \frac{(5.0 \times 10^{-2})^2}{(1.9 \times 10^{-3})^2(1.0 \times 10^{-3})} = 6.9 \times 10^5$$

Another type of problem is one in which we know the initial concentrations but do not know any of the equilibrium concentrations. To solve this kind of problem, follow the series of steps summarized in **Figure 13.6** and illustrated in Worked Examples 13.9 and 13.10. The same approach can be used to calculate equilibrium partial pressures from initial partial pressures and K_p, as shown in Worked Example 13.11.

Figure 13.6
Steps to follow in calculating equilibrium concentrations from initial concentrations.

Step 1. Write the balanced equation for the reaction.

Step 2. Under the balanced equation, make a table that lists for each substance involved in the reaction:
    (a) The initial concentration
    (b) The change in concentration on going to equilibrium
    (c) The equilibrium concentration
In constructing the table, define x as the concentration (mol/L) of one of the substances that reacts on going to equilibrium and then use the stoichiometry of the reaction to determine the concentrations of the other substances in terms of x.

Step 3. Substitute the equilibrium concentrations into the equilibrium equation for the reaction and solve for x. If you must solve a quadratic equation, choose the mathematical solution that makes chemical sense.

Step 4. Calculate the equilibrium concentrations from the calculated value of x.

Step 5. Check your results by substituting them into the equilibrium equation.

WORKED EXAMPLE 13.9

CALCULATING EQUILIBRIUM CONCENTRATIONS FROM INITIAL CONCENTRATIONS

The equilibrium constant K_c for the reaction of H_2 with I_2 is 57.0 at 700 K:

$$H_2(g) + I_2(g) \rightleftharpoons 2\,HI(g) \qquad K_c = 57.0 \text{ at } 700 \text{ K}$$

If 1.00 mol of H_2 is allowed to react with 1.00 mol of I_2 in a 10.0 L reaction vessel at 700 K, what are the concentrations of H_2, I_2, and HI at equilibrium? What is the composition of the equilibrium mixture in moles?

STRATEGY

We need to calculate equilibrium concentrations from initial concentrations, so we use the method outlined in Figure 13.6.

SOLUTION

Step 1. The balanced equation is given: $H_2(g) + I_2(g) \rightleftharpoons 2\,HI(g)$.

Step 2. The initial concentrations are $[H_2] = [I_2] = (1.00 \text{ mol})/(10.0 \text{ L}) = 0.100$ M. For convenience, define an unknown, x, as the concentration (mol/L) of H_2 that reacts. According to the balanced equation for the reaction, x mol/L of H_2 reacts with x mol/L of I_2 to give $2x$ mol/L of HI. This reduces the initial concentrations of H_2 and I_2 from 0.100 mol/L to $(0.100 - x)$ mol/L at equilibrium. Let's summarize these results in a table under the balanced equation:

Initial state   Equilibrium state

	$H_2(g)$	+	$I_2(g)$	$\rightleftharpoons$	$2\,HI(g)$
Initial concentration (M)	0.100		0.100		0
Change (M)	$-x$		$-x$		$+2x$
Equilibrium concentration (M)	$(0.100 - x)$		$(0.100 - x)$		$2x$

Step 3. Substitute the equilibrium concentrations into the equilibrium equation for the reaction:

$$K_c = 57.0 = \frac{[HI]^2}{[H_2][I_2]} = \frac{(2x)^2}{(0.100 - x)(0.100 - x)} = \left(\frac{2x}{0.100 - x}\right)^2$$

Because the right side of this equation is a perfect square, we can take the square root of both sides:

$$\sqrt{57.0} = \pm 7.55 = \frac{2x}{0.100 - x}$$

Solving for x, we obtain two solutions. The equation with the positive square root of 57.0 gives

$$+7.55(0.100 - x) = 2x$$
$$0.755 = 2x + 7.55x$$
$$x = \frac{0.755}{9.55} = 0.0791 \text{ M}$$

The equation with the negative square root of 57.0 gives

$$-7.55(0.100 - x) = 2x$$
$$-0.755 = 2x - 7.55x$$
$$x = \frac{-0.755}{-5.55} = 0.136 \text{ M}$$

Because the initial concentrations of H_2 and I_2 are 0.100 M, x can't exceed 0.100 M. Therefore, discard $x = 0.136$ M as chemically unreasonable and choose the first solution, $x = 0.0791$ M.

Step 4. Calculate the equilibrium concentrations from the calculated value of x:

$$[H_2] = [I_2] = 0.100 - x = 0.100 - 0.0791 = 0.021 \text{ M}$$
$$[HI] = 2x = (2)(0.0791) = 0.158 \text{ M}$$

Step 5. Check the results by substituting them into the equilibrium equation:

$$K_c = 57.0 = \frac{[HI]^2}{[H_2][I_2]} = \frac{(0.158)^2}{(0.021)(0.021)} = 57$$

The number of moles of each substance in the equilibrium mixture is obtained by multiplying each concentration by the volume of the reaction vessel:

$$\text{Moles of } H_2 = \text{Moles of } I_2 = (0.021 \text{ mol/L})(10.0 \text{ L}) = 0.21 \text{ mol}$$
$$\text{Moles of HI} = (0.158 \text{ mol/L})(10.0 \text{ L}) = 1.58 \text{ mol}$$

WORKED EXAMPLE 13.10

CALCULATING EQUILIBRIUM CONCENTRATIONS FROM INITIAL CONCENTRATIONS

Calculate the equilibrium concentrations of H_2, I_2, and HI at 700 K if the initial concentrations are $[H_2] = 0.100$ M and $[I_2] = 0.200$ M. The equilibrium constant K_c for the reaction $H_2(g) + I_2(g) \rightleftharpoons 2 HI(g)$ is 57.0 at 700 K.

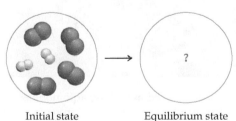

Initial state   Equilibrium state

STRATEGY

This problem is similar to Worked Example 13.9 except that the initial concentrations of H_2 and I_2 are unequal. Again, we follow the steps in Figure 13.6.

SOLUTION

Step 1. The balanced equation is $H_2(g) + I_2(g) \rightleftharpoons 2 HI(g)$.

Step 2. Again, define x as the concentration of H_2 that reacts. Set up a table of concentrations under the balanced equation:

	$H_2(g)$	+	$I_2(g)$	$\rightleftharpoons$	$2 HI(g)$
Initial concentration (M)	0.100		0.200		0
Change (M)	$-x$		$-x$		$+2x$
Equilibrium concentration (M)	$(0.100 - x)$		$(0.200 - x)$		$2x$

continued on next page

Step 3. Substitute the equilibrium concentrations into the equilibrium equation:

$$K_c = 57.0 = \frac{[HI]^2}{[H_2][I_2]} = \frac{(2x)^2}{(0.100 - x)(0.200 - x)}$$

Because the right side of this equation is not a perfect square, we must put the equation into the standard quadratic form, $ax^2 + bx + c = 0$, and then solve for x using the quadratic formula (Appendix A.4):

$$x = \frac{-b \pm \sqrt{b^2 - 4ac}}{2a}$$

Rearranging the equilibrium equation gives

$$(57.0)(0.0200 - 0.300x + x^2) = 4x^2$$

or

$$53.0x^2 - 17.1x + 1.14 = 0$$

Substituting the values of a, b, and c into the quadratic formula gives two solutions:

$$x = \frac{17.1 \pm \sqrt{(-17.1)^2 - 4(53.0)(1.14)}}{2(53.0)} = \frac{17.1 \pm 7.1}{106} = 0.228 \quad \text{and} \quad 0.0943$$

Discard the solution that uses the positive square root ($x = 0.228$) because the H_2 concentration can't change by more than its initial value (0.100 M). Therefore, choose the solution that uses the negative square root ($x = 0.0943$).

Step 4. Calculate the equilibrium concentrations from the calculated value of x:

$$[H_2] = 0.100 - x = 0.100 - 0.0943 = 0.006 \text{ M}$$
$$[I_2] = 0.200 - x = 0.200 - 0.0943 = 0.106 \text{ M}$$
$$[HI] = 2x = (2)(0.0943) = 0.189 \text{ M}$$

Step 5. Check the results by substituting them into the equilibrium equation:

$$K_c = 57.0 = \frac{[HI]^2}{[H_2][I_2]} = \frac{(0.189)^2}{(0.006)(0.106)} = 56.2$$

The calculated value of K_c (56.2), which should be rounded to one significant figure (6×10^1), agrees with the value given in the problem (57.0).

CALCULATING EQUILIBRIUM PARTIAL PRESSURES FROM INITIAL PARTIAL PRESSURES

One reaction that occurs in producing steel from iron ore is the reduction of iron(II) oxide by carbon monoxide to give iron metal and carbon dioxide. The equilibrium constant K_p for the reaction at 1000 K is 0.259.

$$FeO(s) + CO(g) \rightleftharpoons Fe(s) + CO_2(g) \qquad K_p = 0.259 \text{ at } 1000 \text{ K}$$

What are the equilibrium partial pressures of CO and CO_2 at 1000 K if the initial partial pressures are $P_{CO} = 1.000$ atm and $P_{CO_2} = 0.500$ atm?

STRATEGY

We can calculate equilibrium partial pressures from initial partial pressures and K_p in the same way that we calculate equilibrium concentrations from initial concentrations and K_c. Follow the steps in Figure 13.6, but substitute partial pressures for concentrations.

SOLUTION

Step 1. The balanced equation is $FeO(s) + CO(g) \rightleftharpoons Fe(s) + CO_2(g)$.

Step 2. Define x as the partial pressure of CO that reacts. Set up a table of partial pressures of the gases under the balanced equation:

	FeO(s) +	CO(g) $\rightleftharpoons$	Fe(s) +	CO$_2$(g)
Initial pressure (atm)		1.000		0.500
Change (atm)		$-x$		$+x$
Equilibrium pressure (atm)		$(0.1000 - x)$		$(0.500 + x)$

▲ The steel used in making automobiles is produced by the reaction of iron ore with carbon monoxide.

Step 3. Substitute the equilibrium partial pressures into the equilibrium equation for K_p:

$$K_p = 0.259 = \frac{P_{CO_2}}{P_{CO}} = \frac{0.500 + x}{1.000 - x}$$

As usual for a heterogeneous equilibrium, we omit the pure solids from the equilibrium equation. Rearranging the equilibrium equation and solving for x gives

$$0.259 - 0.259x = 0.500 + x$$

$$x = \frac{-0.241}{1.259} = -0.191$$

Step 4. Calculate the equilibrium partial pressures from the calculated value of x:

$$P_{CO} = 1.000 - x = 1.000 - (-0.191) = 1.191 \text{ atm}$$
$$P_{CO_2} = 0.500 + x = 0.500 + (-0.191) = 0.309 \text{ atm}$$

Step 5. Check the results by substituting them into the equilibrium equation:

$$K_p = 0.259 = \frac{P_{CO_2}}{P_{CO}} = \frac{0.309}{1.191} = 0.259$$

A negative value for x means that the reaction goes from products to reactants to reach equilibrium. This makes sense because the initial reaction quotient, $Q_p = 0.500/1.000 = 0.500$, is greater than the equilibrium constant, $K_p = 0.259$. When $Q_p > K_p$, the net reaction always goes from products to reactants (right to left).

▶ **PROBLEM 13.11**   In Problem 13.8, we found that an equilibrium mixture of H_2 molecules and H atoms at 500 K contains mainly H_2 molecules because the equilibrium constant for the dissociation reaction $H_2(g) \rightleftharpoons 2\,H(g)$ is very small ($K_c = 1.2 \times 10^{-42}$).
    (a) What is the molar concentration of H atoms at equilibrium if the equilibrium concentration of H_2 is 0.10 M?
    (b) How many H atoms and H_2 molecules are present in 1.0 L of 0.10 M H_2 at 500 K?

▶ **PROBLEM 13.12**   The H_2/CO ratio in mixtures of carbon monoxide and hydrogen (called *synthesis gas*) is increased by the water-gas shift reaction $CO(g) + H_2O(g) \rightleftharpoons CO_2(g) + H_2(g)$, which has an equilibrium constant $K_c = 4.24$ at 800 K. Calculate the equilibrium concentrations of CO_2, H_2, CO, and H_2O at 800 K if only CO and H_2O are present initially at concentrations of 0.150 M.

▶ **PROBLEM 13.13**   Calculate the equilibrium concentrations of N_2O_4 and NO_2 at 25 °C in a vessel that contains an initial N_2O_4 concentration of 0.0500 M. The equilibrium constant K_c for the reaction $N_2O_4(g) \rightleftharpoons 2\,NO_2(g)$ is 4.64×10^{-3} at 25 °C.

▶ **PROBLEM 13.14**   Calculate the equilibrium concentrations at 25 °C for the reaction in Problem 13.13 if the initial concentrations are $[N_2O_4] = 0.0200$ M and $[NO_2] = 0.0300$ M.

▶ **PROBLEM 13.15**   The equilibrium constant K_p for the reaction $C(s) + H_2O(g) \rightleftharpoons CO(g) + H_2(g)$ is 2.44 at 1000 K. What are the equilibrium partial pressures of H_2O, CO, and H_2 if the initial partial pressures are $P_{H_2O} = 1.20$ atm, $P_{CO} = 1.00$ atm, and $P_{H_2} = 1.40$ atm?

13.6 FACTORS THAT ALTER THE COMPOSITION OF AN EQUILIBRIUM MIXTURE: LE CHÂTELIER'S PRINCIPLE

One of the main goals of chemical synthesis is to maximize the conversion of reactants to products while minimizing the expenditure of energy. This objective is achieved easily if the reaction goes nearly to completion at mild temperature and pressure. If the reaction gives an equilibrium mixture that is rich in reactants and poor in products, however, then the experimental conditions must be adjusted.

For example, in the Haber process for the synthesis of ammonia from N_2 and H_2 (Figure 13.7), the choice of experimental conditions is of real economic importance. Annual worldwide production of ammonia is about 120 million metric tons, primarily for use as fertilizer.

Figure 13.7

Representation of the Haber process for the industrial production of ammonia. A mixture of gaseous N_2 and H_2 at 130–300 atm pressure is passed over a catalyst at 400–500 °C, and ammonia is produced by the reaction $N_2(g) + 3 H_2(g) \rightleftharpoons 2 NH_3(g)$. The NH_3 in the gaseous mixture of reactants and products is liquefied, and the unreacted N_2 and H_2 are recycled.

Pump to circulate gases

N_2, H_2 inlet →

Pump to compress gases

Expanding gases cool

Heat exchanger

Heat exchanger

Recycled unreacted N_2 and H_2

Catalyst (400–500 °C)

Heating coil

Refrigeration unit

Preheated feed gases (130–300 atm)

NH_3 outlet to storage tank

Several factors can be exploited to alter the composition of an equilibrium mixture:

- The concentration of reactants or products can be changed.
- The pressure and volume can be changed.
- The temperature can be changed.

A possible fourth factor, addition of a catalyst, increases only the rate at which equilibrium is reached. As we'll see in Section 13.10, a catalyst does not affect the equilibrium concentrations.

The qualitative effect of the listed changes on the composition of an equilibrium mixture can be predicted using a principle first described by the French chemist Henri-Louis Le Châtelier (pronounced Li Sha–tell–**yea**):

Le Châtelier's Principle   If a stress is applied to a reaction mixture at equilibrium, net reaction occurs in the direction that relieves the stress.

The word "stress" in this context means a change in concentration, pressure, volume, or temperature that disturbs the original equilibrium. Reaction then occurs to change the composition of the mixture until a new state of equilibrium is reached. The direction that the reaction takes (reactants to products or vice versa) is the one that reduces the stress. In the next three sections, we'll look at the different kinds of stress that can change the composition of an equilibrium mixture.

13.7 ALTERING AN EQUILIBRIUM MIXTURE: CHANGES IN CONCENTRATION

Let's consider the equilibrium that occurs in the Haber process for the synthesis of ammonia:

$$N_2(g) + 3\,H_2(g) \rightleftharpoons 2\,NH_3(g) \qquad K_c = 0.291 \text{ at } 700 \text{ K}$$

Suppose that we have an equilibrium mixture of 0.50 M N_2, 3.00 M H_2, and 1.98 M NH_3 at 700 K and that we disturb the equilibrium by increasing the N_2 concentration to 1.50 M. Le Châtelier's principle tells us that reaction will occur to relieve the stress of the increased concentration of N_2 by converting some of the N_2 to NH_3. As the N_2 concentration decreases, the H_2 concentration must also decrease and the NH_3 concentration must increase in accord with the stoichiometry of the balanced equation. These changes are illustrated in **Figure 13.8**.

Net conversion of N_2 and H_2 to NH_3 occurs until a new equilibrium is established. That is, the N_2 and H_2 concentrations decrease, while the NH_3 concentration increases.

Figure 13.8
Changes in concentrations when N_2 is added to an equilibrium mixture of N_2, H_2, and NH_3.

In general, when an equilibrium is disturbed by the addition or removal of any reactant or product, Le Châtelier's principle predicts that

- The concentration stress of an *added* reactant or product is relieved by net reaction in the direction that *consumes* the added substance.
- The concentration stress of a *removed* reactant or product is relieved by net reaction in the direction that *replenishes* the removed substance.

If these rules are applied to the equilibrium $N_2(g) + 3 H_2(g) \rightleftharpoons 2 NH_3(g)$, then the yield of ammonia is increased by an increase in the N_2 or H_2 concentration or by a decrease in the NH_3 concentration (**Figure 13.9**). In the industrial production of ammonia, the concentration of gaseous NH_3 is decreased by liquefying the ammonia (bp $-33\ °C$) as it's formed, and so more ammonia is produced.

Figure 13.9

Effect of concentration changes on the equilibrium $N_2(g) + 3 H_2(g) \rightleftharpoons 2 NH_3(g)$. An increase in the N_2 or H_2 concentration or a decrease in the NH_3 concentration shifts the equilibrium from left to right. A decrease in the N_2 or H_2 concentration or an increase in the NH_3 concentration shifts the equilibrium from right to left.

Le Châtelier's principle is a handy rule for predicting changes in the composition of an equilibrium mixture, but it doesn't explain *why* those changes occur. To see why Le Châtelier's principle works, let's look again at the reaction quotient Q_c. For the initial equilibrium mixture of 0.50 M N_2, 3.00 M H_2, and 1.98 M NH_3 at 700 K, Q_c equals the equilibrium constant K_c (0.291) because the system is at equilibrium:

$$Q_c = \frac{[NH_3]_t^2}{[N_2]_t[H_2]_t^3} = \frac{(1.98)^2}{(0.50)(3.00)^3} = 0.29 = K_c$$

When we disturb the equilibrium by increasing the N_2 concentration to 1.50 M, the denominator of the equilibrium constant expression increases and Q_c decreases to a value less than K_c:

$$Q_c = \frac{[NH_3]_t^2}{[N_2]_t[H_2]_t^3} = \frac{(1.98)^2}{(1.50)(3.00)^3} = 0.0968 < K_c$$

For the system to move to a new state of equilibrium, Q_c must increase; that is, the numerator of the equilibrium constant expression must increase and the denominator must decrease. This implies the net conversion of N_2 and H_2 to NH_3, just as predicted by Le Châtelier's principle. When the new equilibrium is established (Figure 13.8), the concentrations are 1.31 M N_2, 2.43 M H_2, and 2.36 M NH_3, and Q_c again equals K_c:

$$Q_c = \frac{[NH_3]_t^2}{[N_2]_t[H_2]_t^3} = \frac{(2.36)^2}{(1.31)(2.43)^3} = 0.296 = K_c$$

As another example of how a change in concentration affects an equilibrium, let's consider the reaction in aqueous solution of iron(III) ions and thiocyanate (SCN⁻) ions to give an equilibrium mixture that contains the Fe–N bonded red complex ion $FeNCS^{2+}$:

$$\underset{\text{Pale yellow}}{Fe^{3+}(aq)} + \underset{\text{Colorless}}{SCN^-(aq)} \rightleftharpoons \underset{\text{Red}}{FeNCS^{2+}(aq)}$$

Shifts in the position of this equilibrium can be detected by observing how the color of the solution changes when we add various reagents (**Figure 13.10**). If we add aqueous $FeCl_3$, the red color gets darker, as predicted by Le Châtelier's principle. The

(a) Original solution: Fe^{3+} (pale yellow), SCN^- (colorless), and $FeNCS^{2+}$ (red).

(b) After adding $FeCl_3$ to **(a)**: $[FeNCS^{2+}]$ increases.

(c) After adding KSCN to **(a)**: $[FeNCS^{2+}]$ increases.

(d) After adding $H_2C_2O_4$ to **(a)**: $[FeNCS^{2+}]$ decreases as $[Fe(C_2O_4)_3^{3-}]$ increases.

(e) After adding $HgCl_2$ to **(a)**: $[FeNCS^{2+}]$ decreases as $[Hg(SCN)_4^{2-}]$ increases.

Figure 13.10
Color changes produced by adding various reagents to an equilibrium mixture of Fe^{3+} (pale yellow), SCN^- (colorless), and $FeNCS^{2+}$ (red).

concentration stress of added Fe^{3+} is relieved by net reaction from left to right, which consumes some of the Fe^{3+} and increases the concentration of $FeNCS^{2+}$. (Note that the Cl^- ions are not involved in the reaction.) Similarly, if we add aqueous KSCN, the stress of added SCN^- shifts the equilibrium from left to right and again the red color gets darker.

The equilibrium can be shifted in the opposite direction by adding reagents that remove Fe^{3+} or SCN^- ions. For example, oxalic acid ($H_2C_2O_4$), a poisonous substance present in the leaves of plants such as rhubarb, reacts with Fe^{3+} to form the stable, yellow complex ion $Fe(C_2O_4)_3^{3-}$, thus decreasing the concentration of free $Fe^{3+}(aq)$. In accord with Le Châtelier's principle, the concentration stress of removed Fe^{3+} is relieved by the dissociation of $FeNCS^{2+}$ to replenish the Fe^{3+} ions. Because the concentration of $FeNCS^{2+}$ decreases, the red color disappears.

$$3 H_2C_2O_4(aq) + Fe^{3+}(aq) \longrightarrow Fe(C_2O_4)_3^{3-}(aq) + 6 H^+(aq)$$

$$FeNCS^{2+}(aq) \longrightarrow Fe^{3+}(aq) + SCN^-(aq)$$

Addition of aqueous $HgCl_2$ also eliminates the red color because $HgCl_2$ reacts with SCN^- ions to form the stable, colorless Hg–S bonded complex ion $Hg(SCN)_4^{2-}$. Removal of free $SCN^-(aq)$ results in dissociation of the red $FeNCS^{2+}$ ions so as to replenish the SCN^- ions.

$$HgCl_2(aq) + 4 SCN^-(aq) \longrightarrow Hg(SCN)_4^{2-}(aq) + 2 Cl^-(aq)$$

$$FeNCS^{2+}(aq) \longrightarrow Fe^{3+}(aq) + SCN^-(aq)$$

▲ The extremely sour leaves of rhubarb contain toxins such as oxalic acid, but the stalks and roots are nutritious.

WORKED EXAMPLE 13.12

APPLYING LE CHÂTELIER'S PRINCIPLE TO CONCENTRATION CHANGES

The reaction of iron(III) oxide with carbon monoxide occurs in a blast furnace when iron ore is reduced to iron metal:

$$Fe_2O_3(s) + 3 CO(g) \rightleftharpoons 2 Fe(l) + 3 CO_2(g)$$

Use Le Châtelier's principle to predict the direction of the net reaction when an equilibrium mixture is disturbed by:

(a) Adding Fe_2O_3

(b) Removing CO_2

(c) Removing CO; also account for the change using the reaction quotient Q_c.

continued on next page

STRATEGY

To predict the direction of net reaction, recall that a concentration stress is relieved by reaction in the direction that consumes an added substance or replenishes a removed substance. This rule does not apply to pure solids or pure liquids because their concentrations have a constant value equal to 1.

SOLUTION

(a) Because Fe_2O_3 is a pure solid, its concentration is equal to 1 and doesn't change when more Fe_2O_3 is added. Therefore, there is no concentration stress and the original equilibrium is undisturbed.

(b) Le Châtelier's principle predicts that the concentration stress of removed CO_2 will be relieved by net reaction from reactants to products to replenish the CO_2.

(c) Le Châtelier's principle predicts that the concentration stress of removed CO will be relieved by net reaction from products to reactants to replenish the CO. The reaction quotient is

$$Q_c = \frac{[CO_2]_t^3}{[CO]_t^3}$$

When the equilibrium is disturbed by reducing [CO], Q_c increases, so that $Q_c > K_c$. For the system to move to a new state of equilibrium, Q_c must decrease—that is, $[CO_2]$ must decrease and [CO] must increase. Therefore, the net reaction goes from products to reactants, as predicted by Le Châtelier's principle.

▶ **PROBLEM 13.16** Consider the equilibrium for the water-gas shift reaction:

$$CO(g) + H_2O(g) \rightleftharpoons CO_2(g) + H_2(g)$$

Use Le Châtelier's principle to predict how the concentration of H_2 will change when the equilibrium is disturbed by:

(a) Adding CO

(b) Adding CO_2

(c) Removing H_2O

(d) Removing CO_2; also account for the change using the reaction quotient Q_c.

13.8 ALTERING AN EQUILIBRIUM MIXTURE: CHANGES IN PRESSURE AND VOLUME

To illustrate how an equilibrium mixture is affected by a change in pressure as a result of a change in the volume, let's return to the Haber synthesis of ammonia. The balanced equation for the reaction has 4 mol of gas on the reactant side of the equation and 2 mol on the product side:

$$N_2(g) + 3\,H_2(g) \rightleftharpoons 2\,NH_3(g) \qquad K_c = 0.291 \text{ at } 700 \text{ K}$$

What happens to the composition of the equilibrium mixture if we increase the pressure by decreasing the volume? (Recall from Sections 9.2 and 9.3 that the pressure of an ideal gas is inversely proportional to the volume at constant temperature and constant number of moles of gas; $P = nRT/V$.) According to Le Châtelier's principle, net reaction will occur in the direction that relieves the stress of the increased pressure, which means that the number of moles of gas must decrease. Therefore, we predict that the net reaction will proceed from left to right because the forward reaction converts 4 mol of gaseous reactants to 2 mol of gaseous products.

In general, Le Châtelier's principle predicts that

- An *increase* in pressure by reducing the volume will bring about net reaction in the direction that *decreases* the number of moles of gas.

- A *decrease* in pressure by expanding the volume will bring about net reaction in the direction that *increases* the number of moles of gas.

To see why Le Châtelier's principle works for pressure (volume) changes, let's look again at the reaction quotient for the equilibrium mixture of 0.50 M N_2, 3.00 M H_2, and 1.98 M NH_3 at 700 K:

$$Q_c = \frac{[NH_3]_t^2}{[N_2]_t[H_2]_t^3} = \frac{(1.98)^2}{(0.50)(3.00)^3} = 0.29 = K_c$$

If we disturb the equilibrium by reducing the volume by a factor of 2, we not only double the total pressure, we also double the partial pressure and thus the molar concentration of each reactant and product (because molarity $= n/V = P/RT$). Because the balanced equation has more moles of gaseous reactants than gaseous products, the increase in the denominator of the equilibrium constant expression is greater than the increase in the numerator and the new value of Q_c is less than the equilibrium constant K_c:

$$Q_c = \frac{[NH_3]_t^2}{[N_2]_t[H_2]_t^3} = \frac{(3.96)^2}{(1.00)(6.00)^3} = 0.0726 < K_c$$

For the system to move to a new state of equilibrium, Q_c must increase, which means that the net reaction must go from reactants to products, as predicted by Le Châtelier's principle (**Figure 13.11**). In practice, the yield of ammonia in the Haber process is increased by running the reaction at high pressure, typically 130–300 atm.

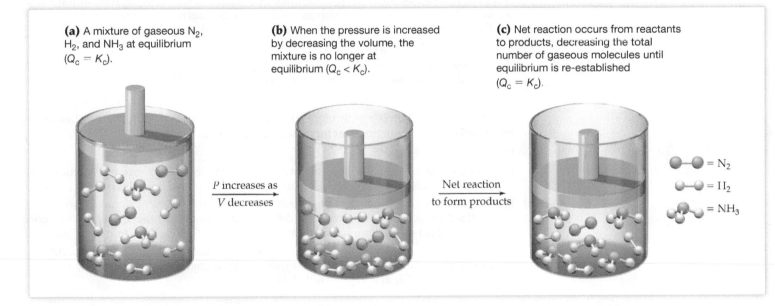

(a) A mixture of gaseous N_2, H_2, and NH_3 at equilibrium $(Q_c = K_c)$.

(b) When the pressure is increased by decreasing the volume, the mixture is no longer at equilibrium $(Q_c < K_c)$.

(c) Net reaction occurs from reactants to products, decreasing the total number of gaseous molecules until equilibrium is re-established $(Q_c = K_c)$.

P increases as
V decreases

Net reaction
to form products

●—● $= N_2$
●—● $= H_2$
●●● $= NH_3$

Figure 13.11
Qualitative effect of pressure and volume on the equilibrium
$N_2(g) + 3\, H_2(g) \rightleftharpoons 2\, NH_3(g)$.

The composition of an equilibrium mixture is unaffected by a change in pressure if the reaction involves no change in the number of moles of gas. For example, the reaction of hydrogen with gaseous iodine has 2 mol of gas on both sides of the balanced equation:

$$H_2(g) + I_2(g) \rightleftharpoons 2\, HI(g)$$

If we double the pressure by halving the volume, the numerator and denominator of the reaction quotient change by the same factor and Q_c remains unchanged:

$$Q_c = \frac{[HI]_t^2}{[H_2]_t[I_2]_t}$$

In applying Le Châtelier's principle to a heterogeneous equilibrium, the effect of pressure changes on solids and liquids can be ignored because the volume (and concentration) of a solid or a liquid is nearly independent of pressure. Consider, for example, the high-temperature reaction of carbon with steam, the first step in converting coal to gaseous fuels:

$$C(s) + H_2O(g) \rightleftharpoons CO(g) + H_2(g)$$

Ignoring the carbon because it's a solid, we predict that a decrease in volume (increase in pressure) will shift the equilibrium from products to reactants because the reverse reaction decreases the amount of gas from 2 mol to 1 mol.

Throughout this section, we've been careful to limit the application of Le Châtelier's principle to pressure changes that result from a change in *volume*. What happens, though, if we keep the volume constant but increase the total pressure by adding a gas that is not involved in the reaction—say, an inert gas such as argon? In that case, the equilibrium remains undisturbed because adding an inert gas at constant volume does not change the partial pressures or the molar concentrations of the substances involved in the reaction. Only if the added gas is a reactant or product does the reaction quotient change.

WORKED EXAMPLE 13.13

APPLYING LE CHÂTELIER'S PRINCIPLE TO PRESSURE AND VOLUME CHANGES

Does the number of moles of reaction products increase, decrease, or remain the same when each of the following equilibria is subjected to a decrease in pressure by increasing the volume?

(a) $PCl_5(g) \rightleftharpoons PCl_3(g) + Cl_2(g)$

(b) $CaO(s) + CO_2(g) \rightleftharpoons CaCO_3(s)$

(c) $3 Fe(s) + 4 H_2O(g) \rightleftharpoons Fe_3O_4(s) + 4 H_2(g)$

STRATEGY

According to Le Châtelier's principle, the stress of a decrease in pressure is relieved by net reaction in the direction that increases the number of moles of gas.

SOLUTION

(a) Because the forward reaction converts 1 mol of gas to 2 mol of gas, net reaction will go from reactants to products, thus increasing the number of moles of PCl_3 and Cl_2.

(b) Because there is 1 mol of gas on the reactant side of the balanced equation and none on the product side, the stress of a decrease in pressure is relieved by net reaction from products to reactants. The number of moles of $CaCO_3$ therefore decreases.

(c) Because there are 4 mol of gas on both sides of the balanced equation, the composition of the equilibrium mixture is unaffected by a change in pressure. The number of moles of Fe_3O_4 and H_2 remains the same.

▶ **PROBLEM 13.17** Does the number of moles of products increase, decrease, or remain the same when each of the following equilibria is subjected to an increase in pressure by decreasing the volume?

(a) $CO(g) + H_2O(g) \rightleftharpoons CO_2(g) + H_2(g)$

(b) $2 CO(g) \rightleftharpoons C(s) + CO_2(g)$

(c) $N_2O_4(g) \rightleftharpoons 2 NO_2(g)$

CONCEPTUAL PROBLEM 13.18 The following picture represents the equilibrium mixture for the gas-phase reaction $A_2 \rightleftharpoons 2 A$:

Draw a picture that shows how the concentrations change when the pressure is increased by reducing the volume.

13.9 ALTERING AN EQUILIBRIUM MIXTURE: CHANGES IN TEMPERATURE

When an equilibrium is disturbed by a change in concentration, pressure, or volume, the composition of the equilibrium mixture changes because the reaction quotient Q_c no longer equals the equilibrium constant K_c. As long as the temperature remains constant, however, concentration, pressure, or volume changes don't change the value of the equilibrium constant.

By contrast, a change in temperature nearly always changes the value of the equilibrium constant. For the Haber synthesis of ammonia, which is an exothermic reaction, the equilibrium constant K_c decreases by a factor of 10^{11} over the temperature range 300–1000 K (**Figure 13.12**).

$$N_2(g) + 3\,H_2(g) \rightleftharpoons 2\,NH_3(g) + 92.2\ kJ \qquad \Delta H° = -92.2\ kJ$$

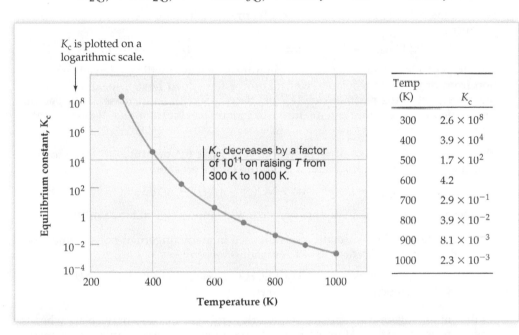

K_c is plotted on a logarithmic scale.

K_c decreases by a factor of 10^{11} on raising T from 300 K to 1000 K.

Temp (K)	K_c
300	2.6×10^8
400	3.9×10^4
500	1.7×10^2
600	4.2
700	2.9×10^{-1}
800	3.9×10^{-2}
900	8.1×10^{-3}
1000	2.3×10^{-3}

Figure 13.12

Temperature dependence of the equilibrium constant for the reaction $N_2(g) + 3\,H_2(g) \rightleftharpoons 2\,NH_3(g)$.

At low temperatures, the equilibrium mixture is rich in NH_3 because K_c is large. At high temperatures, the equilibrium shifts in the direction of N_2 and H_2.

In general, the temperature dependence of an equilibrium constant depends on the sign of $\Delta H°$ for the reaction.

- The equilibrium constant for an exothermic reaction (negative $\Delta H°$) decreases as the temperature increases.
- The equilibrium constant for an endothermic reaction (positive $\Delta H°$) increases as the temperature increases.

You can predict the way in which K_c depends on temperature by using Le Châtelier's principle. Take the endothermic decomposition of N_2O_4, for example:

$$\underset{\text{Colorless}}{N_2O_4(g)} + 55.3\ kJ \rightleftharpoons \underset{\text{Brown}}{2\,NO_2(g)} \qquad \Delta H° = +55.3\ kJ$$

Le Châtelier's principle says that if heat is added to an equilibrium mixture, thus increasing its temperature, net reaction occurs in the direction that relieves the stress of the added heat. For an endothermic reaction, such as the decomposition of N_2O_4, heat is absorbed by reaction in the forward direction. The equilibrium therefore shifts to the product side at the higher temperature, which means that K_c increases with increasing temperature.

Because N_2O_4 is colorless and NO_2 has a brown color, the effect of temperature on the N_2O_4–NO_2 equilibrium is readily apparent from the color of the mixture (**Figure 13.13**). For an exothermic reaction, such as the Haber synthesis of NH_3, heat is absorbed by net reaction in the reverse direction, so K_c decreases with increasing temperature.

$$N_2O_4(g) \rightleftharpoons 2\,NO_2(g);\ \Delta H > 0$$

K_c increases as T increases

The darker **brown** color of the sample at the highest temperature indicates that the equilibrium $N_2O_4(g) \rightleftharpoons 2\,NO_2(g)$ shifts from reactants to products with increasing temperature, as expected for an endothermic reaction.

Figure 13.13

Sample tubes containing an equilibrium mixture of N_2O_4 and NO_2 immersed in ice water (left), at room temperature (center), and immersed in hot water (right).

▲ Fingernail polish can be removed by dissolving it in ethyl acetate.

WORKED EXAMPLE 13.14

APPLYING LE CHÂTELIER'S PRINCIPLE TO TEMPERATURE CHANGES

In the first step of the Ostwald process for the synthesis of nitric acid, ammonia is oxidized to nitric oxide by the reaction

$$4 NH_3(g) + 5 O_2(g) \rightleftharpoons 4 NO(g) + 6 H_2O(g) \qquad \Delta H° = -901.2 \text{ kJ}$$

How does the equilibrium amount of NO vary with an increase in temperature?

STRATEGY

Le Châtelier's principle predicts that the stress of added heat when the temperature is increased will be relieved by net reaction in the direction that absorbs the heat. It's helpful to include the heat in the balanced equation—on the reactant side if the reaction is endothermic, or on the product side if the reaction is exothermic.

SOLUTION

Because the oxidation of ammonia is exothermic, we include the heat (901.2 kJ) on the product side:

$$4 NH_3(g) + 5 O_2(g) \rightleftharpoons 4 NO(g) + 6 H_2O(g) + 901.2 \text{ kJ}$$

The stress of added heat when the temperature is increased will be relieved by net reaction from products to reactants, which absorbs the added heat. The equilibrium will therefore shift to the reactant side (K_c will decrease) with an increase in temperature. Consequently, the equilibrium mixture will contain less NO at higher temperatures.

▶ **PROBLEM 13.19** When air is heated at very high temperatures in an automobile engine, the air pollutant nitric oxide is produced by the reaction

$$N_2(g) + O_2(g) \rightleftharpoons 2 NO(g) \qquad \Delta H° = +182.6 \text{ kJ}$$

How does the equilibrium amount of NO vary with an increase in temperature?

▶ **PROBLEM 13.20** Ethyl acetate, a solvent used in many fingernail-polish removers, is made by the reaction of acetic acid with ethanol:

$$CH_3CO_2H(soln) + CH_3CH_2OH(soln) \rightleftharpoons CH_3CO_2CH_2CH_3(soln) + H_2O(soln) \qquad \Delta H° = -2.9 \text{ kJ}$$

Acetic acid   Ethanol   Ethyl acetate

Does the amount of ethyl acetate in an equilibrium mixture increase or decrease when the temperature is increased? How does K_c change when the temperature is decreased? Justify your answers using Le Châtelier's principle.

WORKED CONCEPTUAL EXAMPLE 13.15

APPLYING LE CHÂTELIER'S PRINCIPLE TO TEMPERATURE CHANGES

The following pictures represent the composition of the equilibrium mixture at 600 K and 650 K for the combination of two A molecules, $2 A(g) \rightleftharpoons A_2(g)$:

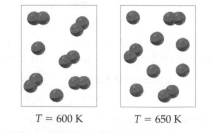

$T = 600 \text{ K}$ $T = 650 \text{ K}$

Is the reaction endothermic or exothermic? Explain using Le Châtelier's principle.

STRATEGY

We can determine the direction of net reaction on raising the temperature by counting the number of A and A_2 molecules at each temperature. According to Le Châtelier's principle, if the net reaction converts reactants to products on raising the temperature, heat is on the reactant side of the chemical equation and the reaction is endothermic. Conversely, if the net reaction converts products to reactants on raising the temperature, heat is on the product side and the reaction is exothermic.

SOLUTION

Two A and five A_2 molecules are present at 600 K, and six A and three A_2 molecules are present at 650 K. On raising the temperature, the net reaction converts products to reactants, and so heat is on the product side of the chemical equation:

$$2 A(g) \rightleftharpoons A_2(g) + \text{heat}$$

The reaction is therefore exothermic, as expected for a reaction in which a chemical bond is formed. Note that Le Châtelier's principle predicts that net reaction will occur in the direction that uses up the added heat.

CONCEPTUAL PROBLEM 13.21 The following pictures represent the composition of the equilibrium mixture for the reaction $A(g) + B(s) \rightleftharpoons AB(g)$ at 400 K and 500 K:

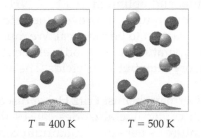

$T = 400$ K $T = 500$ K

Is the reaction endothermic or exothermic? Explain using Le Châtelier's principle.

13.10 THE EFFECT OF A CATALYST ON EQUILIBRIUM

Recall from Section 12.14 that a catalyst increases the rate of a chemical reaction by making available a new, lower-energy pathway for the conversion of reactants to products. Because the forward and reverse reactions pass through the same transition state, a catalyst lowers the activation energy for the forward and reverse reactions by exactly the same amount. As a result, the rates of the forward and reverse reactions increase by the same factor (Figure 13.14).

Remember...

A catalyst is a substance that increases the rate of a transformation without being consumed in the process. (Section 12.14)

The activation energy for the **catalyzed pathway** (red curve) is lower than that for the **uncatalyzed pathway** (blue curve) by an amount ΔE_a.

Because the forward and reverse reactions pass through the same transition state, the catalyst lowers the activation energy barrier for the forward and reverse reactions by the same amount. The catalyst therefore accelerates the forward and reverse reactions by the same factor, and the composition of the equilibrium mixture is unchanged.

Figure 13.14

Potential energy profiles for a reaction whose activation energy is lowered by the presence of a catalyst.

If a reaction mixture is at equilibrium in the absence of a catalyst (that is, the forward and reverse rates are equal), it will still be at equilibrium after a catalyst is added because the forward and reverse rates, though faster, remain equal. If a reaction mixture is not at equilibrium, a catalyst accelerates the rate at which equilibrium is reached, but it does not affect the composition of the equilibrium mixture. Because a catalyst has no effect on the equilibrium concentrations, it does not appear in the balanced chemical equation or in the equilibrium constant expression.

Even though a catalyst doesn't change the position of an equilibrium, it can nevertheless significantly influence the choice of optimum conditions for a reaction. Look again at the Haber synthesis of ammonia. Because the reaction $N_2(g) + 3 H_2(g) \rightleftharpoons 2 NH_3(g)$ is exothermic, its equilibrium constant decreases with increasing temperature, and optimum yields of NH_3 are obtained at low temperatures. At those low temperatures, however, the rate at which equilibrium is reached is too slow for the reaction to be practical. We thus have what appears to be a no-win situation: Low temperatures give good yields but slow rates, whereas high temperatures give satisfactory rates but poor yields. The answer to the dilemma is to find a catalyst.

In the early 1900s, the German chemist Fritz Haber discovered that a catalyst consisting of iron mixed with certain metal oxides causes the reaction to occur at a satisfactory rate at temperatures where the equilibrium concentration of NH_3 is reasonably favorable. The yield of NH_3 can be improved further by running the reaction at high pressures. Typical reaction conditions for the industrial synthesis of ammonia are 400–500 °C and 130–300 atm.

▶ **PROBLEM 13.22** A platinum catalyst is used in automobile catalytic converters to hasten the oxidation of carbon monoxide:

$$2 CO(g) + O_2(g) \xrightarrow{\text{Pt}} 2 CO_2(g) \qquad \Delta H° = -566 \text{ kJ}$$

Suppose that you have a reaction vessel containing an equilibrium mixture of $CO(g)$, $O_2(g)$, and $CO_2(g)$. Under the following conditions, will the amount of CO increase, decrease, or remain the same?

(a) A platinum catalyst is added.

(b) The temperature is increased.

(c) The pressure is increased by decreasing the volume.

(d) The pressure is increased by adding argon gas.

(e) The pressure is increased by adding O_2 gas.

13.11 THE LINK BETWEEN CHEMICAL EQUILIBRIUM AND CHEMICAL KINETICS

We emphasized in Section 13.1 that the equilibrium state is a dynamic one in which reactant and product concentrations remain constant, not because the reaction stops but because the rates of the forward and reverse reactions are equal. To explore this idea further, let's consider the general, reversible reaction

$$A + B \rightleftharpoons C + D$$

Remember...

Because an **elementary reaction** describes an individual molecular event, its rate law follows directly from its stoichiometry. (Sections 12.9 and 12.10)

Let's assume that the forward and reverse reactions occur in a single bimolecular step; that is, they are **elementary reactions** (Section 12.9). We can then write the following rate laws:

$$\text{Rate forward} = k_f[A][B]$$
$$\text{Rate reverse} = k_r[C][D]$$

If we begin with a mixture that contains all reactants and no products, the initial rate of the reverse reaction is zero because [C] = [D] = 0. As A and B are converted to C and D by the forward reaction, the rate of the forward reaction decreases because [A] and [B] are getting smaller. At the same time, the rate of the reverse reaction increases because [C] and [D] are getting larger. Eventually, the decreasing rate of the forward reaction and the increasing rate of the reverse reaction become equal, and thereafter the concentrations remain constant; that is, the system is at chemical equilibrium (Figure 13.2, page 495).

Because the forward and reverse rates are equal at equilibrium, we can write

$$k_f[A][B] = k_r[C][D] \qquad \text{at equilibrium}$$

which can be rearranged to give

$$\frac{k_f}{k_r} = \frac{[C][D]}{[A][B]}$$

The right side of this equation is the equilibrium constant expression for the forward reaction, which equals the equilibrium constant K_c since the reaction mixture is at equilibrium.

$$K_c = \frac{[C][D]}{[A][B]}$$

Therefore, the equilibrium constant is simply the ratio of the rate constants for the forward and reverse reactions:

$$K_c = \frac{k_f}{k_r}$$

In deriving this equation for K_c, we have assumed a single-step mechanism. For a multistep mechanism, each step has a characteristic rate constant ratio, k_f/k_r. When equilibrium is reached, each step in the mechanism must be at equilibrium, and K_c for the overall reaction is equal to the product of the rate constant ratios for the individual steps.

The equation relating K_c to k_f and k_r provides a fundamental link between chemical equilibrium and chemical kinetics: The relative values of the rate constants for the forward and reverse reactions determine the composition of the equilibrium mixture. When k_f is much larger than k_r, K_c is very large and the reaction goes almost to completion. Such a reaction is sometimes said to be irreversible because the reverse reaction is often too slow to be detected. When k_f and k_r have comparable values, K_c has a value near 1, and comparable concentrations of both reactants and products are present at equilibrium. This is the usual situation for a reversible reaction.

Addition of a catalyst to a reaction mixture increases both rate constants k_f and k_r because the reaction takes place by a different, lower-energy mechanism. Because k_f and k_r increase by the same factor, though, the ratio k_f/k_r is unaffected, and the value of the equilibrium constant $K_c = k_f/k_r$ remains unchanged. Thus, addition of a catalyst does not alter the composition of an equilibrium mixture.

The equation $K_c = k_f/k_r$ also helps explain why equilibrium constants depend on temperature. Recall from Section 12.12 that the rate constant increases as the temperature increases, in accord with the **Arrhenius equation** $k = Ae^{-E_a/RT}$. In general, the forward and reverse reactions have different values of the activation energy, so k_f and k_r increase by different amounts as the temperature increases. The ratio $k_f/k_r = K_c$ is therefore temperature-dependent. For an exothermic reaction, E_a for the reverse reaction is greater than E_a for the forward reaction. Consequently, as the temperature increases, k_r increases by more than k_f increases, and so $K_c = k_f/k_r$ for an exothermic reaction decreases as the temperature increases. Conversely, K_c for an endothermic reaction increases as the temperature increases. These results are in accord with Le Châtelier's principle (Section 13.9).

Remember...

Because the fraction of collisions with sufficient energy for reaction is given by $e^{-E_a/RT}$, the **Arrhenius equation** indicates that the rate constant decreases as E_a increases and increases as T increases.   (Section 12.12)

WORKED EXAMPLE 13.16

EXPLORING THE LINK BETWEEN EQUILIBRIUM AND KINETICS

The equilibrium constant K_c for the reaction of hydrogen with iodine is 57.0 at 700 K, and the reaction is endothermic ($\Delta E = 9$ kJ).

$$H_2(g) + I_2(g) \underset{k_r}{\overset{k_f}{\rightleftharpoons}} 2\,HI(g) \qquad K_c = 57.0 \text{ at } 700 \text{ K}$$

(a) Is the rate constant k_f for the formation of HI larger or smaller than the rate constant k_r for the decomposition of HI?

(b) The value of k_r at 700 K is $1.16 \times 10^{-3}\,M^{-1}\,s^{-1}$. What is the value of k_f at the same temperature?

(c) How are the values of k_f, k_r, and K_c affected by the addition of a catalyst?

(d) How are the values of k_f, k_r, and K_c affected by an increase in temperature?

STRATEGY

To answer these questions, make use of the relationship $K_c = k_f/k_r$. Also, remember that a catalyst increases k_f and k_r by the same factor, and recall that the temperature dependence of a rate constant increases with increasing value of the **activation energy** (Section 12.13).

SOLUTION

(a) Because $K_c = k_f/k_r = 57.0$, the rate constant for the formation of HI (forward reaction) is larger than the rate constant for the decomposition of HI (reverse reaction) by a factor of 57.0.

(b) Because $K_c = k_f/k_r$,

$$k_f = (K_c)(k_r) = (57.0)(1.16 \times 10^{-3}\,M^{-1}\,s^{-1}) = 6.61 \times 10^{-2}\,M^{-1}\,s^{-1}$$

(c) A catalyst lowers the activation energy barrier for the forward and reverse reactions by the same amount, thus increasing the rate constants k_f and k_r by the same factor. Because the equilibrium constant K_c equals the ratio of k_f to k_r, the value of K_c is unaffected by the addition of a catalyst.

(d) Because the reaction is endothermic, E_a for the forward reaction is greater than E_a for the reverse reaction. Consequently, as the temperature increases, k_f increases by more than k_r increases, and therefore $K_c = k_f/k_r$ increases, consistent with Le Châtelier's principle.

Remember...

The greater the **activation energy**, the steeper the slope of an Arrhenius plot (a graph of ln k versus $1/T$) and the greater the increase in k for a given increase in T. (Section 12.13)

▸ **PROBLEM 13.23** Nitric oxide emitted from the engines of supersonic aircraft can contribute to the destruction of stratospheric ozone:

$$NO(g) + O_3(g) \underset{k_r}{\overset{k_f}{\rightleftharpoons}} NO_2(g) + O_2(g)$$

This reaction is highly exothermic ($\Delta E = -201$ kJ), and its equilibrium constant K_c is 3.4×10^{34} at 300 K.

(a) Which rate constant is larger, k_f or k_r?

(b) The value of k_f at 300 K is $8.5 \times 10^6\,M^{-1}\,s^{-1}$. What is the value of k_r at the same temperature?

(c) A typical temperature in the stratosphere is 230 K. Do the values of k_f, k_r, and K_c increase or decrease when the temperature is lowered from 300 K to 230 K?

▲ Nitric oxide emissions from supersonic aircraft can contribute to destruction of the ozone layer.

INQUIRY HOW DOES EQUILIBRIUM AFFECT OXYGEN TRANSPORT IN THE BLOODSTREAM?

Humans, like all animals, need oxygen. The oxygen comes from breathing: About 500 mL of air is drawn into the lungs of an average person with each breath. When the freshly inspired air travels through the bronchial passages and enters the approximately 150 million alveolar sacs of the lungs, it picks up moisture and mixes with air remaining from the previous breath. As it mixes, the concentrations of both water vapor and carbon dioxide increase. These gas concentrations are measured by their partial pressures, with the partial pressure of oxygen in the lungs usually around 100 mm Hg (Table 13.2). Oxygen then diffuses through the delicate walls of the lung alveoli and into arterial blood, which transports it to all body tissues.

Only about 3% of the oxygen in blood is dissolved; the rest is chemically bound to *hemoglobin* molecules (Hb), large proteins that contain *heme* groups embedded in them. Each hemoglobin molecule contains four heme groups, and each heme group contains an iron atom that can bind to one O_2 molecule. Thus, a single hemoglobin molecule can bind four molecules of oxygen.

TABLE 13.2	Partial Pressure of Oxygen in Human Lungs and Blood at Sea Level
Source	P_{O_2} **(mm Hg)**
Dry air	159
Alveolar air	100
Arterial blood	95
Venous blood	40

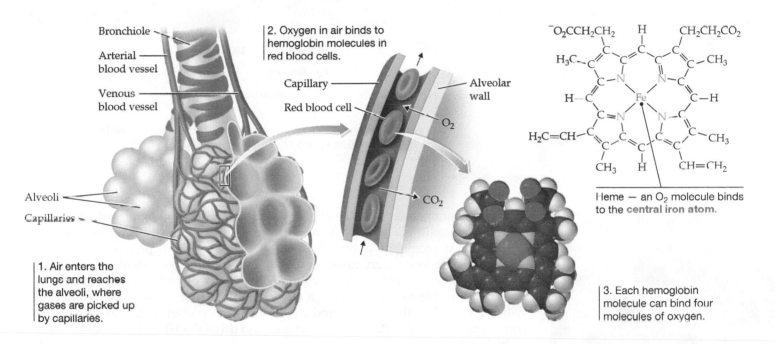

Bronchiole
Arterial blood vessel
Venous blood vessel
Alveoli
Capillaries

1. Air enters the lungs and reaches the alveoli, where gases are picked up by capillaries.

2. Oxygen in air binds to hemoglobin molecules in red blood cells.

Capillary
Red blood cell
Alveolar wall
O_2
CO_2

Heme — an O_2 molecule binds to the **central iron atom**.

3. Each hemoglobin molecule can bind four molecules of oxygen.

The entire system of oxygen transport and delivery in the body depends on the pickup and release of O_2 by hemoglobin according to the following series of equilibria:

$$Hb + O_2 \rightleftharpoons Hb(O_2)$$
$$Hb(O_2) + O_2 \rightleftharpoons Hb(O_2)_2$$
$$Hb(O_2)_2 + O_2 \rightleftharpoons Hb(O_2)_3$$
$$Hb(O_2)_3 + O_2 \rightleftharpoons Hb(O_2)_4$$

The positions of the different equilibria depend on the partial pressures of O_2 (P_{O_2}) in the various tissues. In hard-working, oxygen-starved muscles, where P_{O_2} is low, oxygen is released from hemoglobin as the equilibria shift toward the left, according to Le Châtelier's principle. In the lungs, where P_{O_2} is high, oxygen is absorbed by hemoglobin as the equilibria shift toward the right.

The amount of oxygen carried by hemoglobin at any given value of P_{O_2} is usually expressed as a percent saturation and can be found from the curve shown in **Figure 13.15**. The saturation is 97.5% in the lungs, where $P_{O_2} = 100$ mm Hg, meaning that each hemoglobin molecule is carrying close to its maximum possible amount of 4 O_2 molecules. When $P_{O_2} = 26$ mm Hg, however, the saturation drops to 50%.

The saturation is 97.5% in the lungs, where $P_{O_2} = 100$ mm Hg, meaning that each hemoglobin molecule is carrying close to its maximum possible amount of 4 O_2 molecules.

When $P_{O_2} = 26$ mm Hg, however, the saturation drops to 50%.

Figure 13.15
An oxygen-carrying curve for hemoglobin. The percent saturation of the oxygen-binding sites on hemoglobin depends on the partial pressure of oxygen (P_{O_2}).

▲ The bodies of mountain dwellers produce increased amounts of hemoglobin to cope with the low O_2 pressures at high altitudes.

What about people who live at high altitudes? In Leadville, Colorado, for example, where the altitude is 10,156 ft, the partial pressure of O_2 in the lungs is only about 68 mm Hg. Hemoglobin is only 90% saturated with O_2 at this pressure, so less oxygen is available for delivery to the tissues. People who climb suddenly from sea level to high altitude thus experience a feeling of oxygen deprivation, or *hypoxia*, as their bodies are unable to supply enough oxygen to their tissues. The body soon copes with the situation, though, by producing more hemoglobin molecules, which both provide more capacity for O_2 transport and also drive the Hb + O_2 equilibria to the right. The time required to adapt to the lower O_2 pressures is typically days to weeks, so athletes and hikers must train at high altitudes for some time.

▶ **PROBLEM 13.24** The affinity of hemoglobin (Hb) for CO is greater than its affinity for O_2. Use Le Châtelier's principle to predict how CO affects the equilibrium Hb + $O_2 \rightleftharpoons$ Hb(O_2). Suggest a reason for the toxicity of CO.

▶ **PROBLEM 13.25** How many O_2 molecules are drawn into the lungs of an average person with each breath? Assume that the ambient air pressure is 1.00 atm and the temperature is 25 °C.

SUMMARY

Chemical equilibrium is a dynamic state in which the concentrations of reactants and products remain constant because the rates of the forward and reverse reactions are equal. For the general reaction $a A + b B \rightleftharpoons c C + d D$, concentrations in the **equilibrium mixture** are related by the **equilibrium equation**:

$$K_c = \frac{[C]^c[D]^d}{[A]^a[B]^b}$$

The quotient on the right side of the equation is called the *equilibrium constant expression*. The **equilibrium constant K_c** is the number obtained when equilibrium concentrations (in mol/L) are substituted into the equilibrium constant expression. The value of K_c varies with temperature and depends on the form of the balanced chemical equation.

The **equilibrium constant K_p** can be used for gas-phase reactions. It is defined in the same way as K_c except that the equilibrium constant expression contains partial pressures (in atmospheres) instead of molar concentrations. The constants K_p and K_c are related by the equation $K_p = K_c(RT)^{\Delta n}$, where $\Delta n = (c + d) - (a + b)$.

Homogeneous equilibria are those in which all reactants and products are in a single phase; **heterogeneous equilibria** are those in which reactants and products are present in more than one phase. The equilibrium equation for a heterogeneous equilibrium does not include concentrations of pure solids or pure liquids.

The value of the equilibrium constant for a reaction makes it possible to judge the extent of reaction, predict the direction of reaction, and calculate equilibrium concentrations (or partial pressures) from initial concentrations (or partial pressures). The farther the reaction proceeds toward completion, the larger the value of K_c. The direction of a reaction not at equilibrium depends on the relative values of K_c and the **reaction quotient Q_c**, which is defined in the same way as K_c except that the concentrations in the equilibrium constant expression are not necessarily equilibrium concentrations. If $Q_c < K_c$, the net reaction goes from reactants to products to attain equilibrium; if $Q_c > K_c$, the net reaction goes from products to reactants; if $Q_c = K_c$, the system is at equilibrium.

The composition of an equilibrium mixture can be altered by changes in concentration, pressure (volume), or temperature. The qualitative effect of these changes is predicted by **Le Châtelier's principle**, which says that if a stress is applied to a reaction mixture at equilibrium, net reaction occurs in the direction that relieves the stress. Temperature changes affect equilibrium concentrations because K_c is temperature-dependent. As the temperature increases, K_c for an exothermic reaction decreases and K_c for an endothermic reaction increases.

A catalyst increases the rate at which chemical equilibrium is reached, but it does not affect the equilibrium constant or the equilibrium concentrations. The equilibrium constant for a single-step reaction equals the ratio of the rate constants for the forward and reverse reactions: $K_c = k_f/k_r$.

KEY WORDS

CONCEPTUAL PROBLEMS

Problems 13.1–13.25 appear within the chapter.

13.26 Consider the interconversion of A molecules (red spheres) and B molecules (blue spheres) according to the reaction A $\rightleftharpoons$ B. Each of the series of pictures at the right represents a separate experiment in which time increases from left to right:

(a) Which of the experiments has resulted in an equilibrium state?

(b) What is the value of the equilibrium constant K_c for the reaction A $\rightleftharpoons$ B?

(c) Explain why you can calculate K_c without knowing the volume of the reaction vessel.

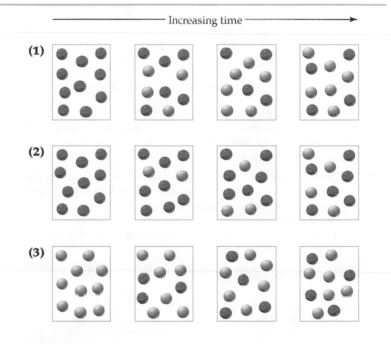

Increasing time →

(1)

(2)

(3)

13.27 The following pictures represent the equilibrium state for three different reactions of the type $A_2 + X_2 \rightleftharpoons 2\,AX$ (X = B, C, or D):

$A_2 + B_2 \rightleftharpoons 2\,AB$ $A_2 + C_2 \rightleftharpoons 2\,AC$ $A_2 + D_2 \rightleftharpoons 2\,AD$

    (a) Which reaction has the largest equilibrium constant?

    (b) Which reaction has the smallest equilibrium constant?

13.28 The reaction $A_2 + B \rightleftharpoons A + AB$ has an equilibrium constant $K_c = 2$. The following pictures represent reaction mixtures that contain A atoms (red), B atoms (blue), and A_2 and AB molecules:

(1)   **(2)**   **(3)**

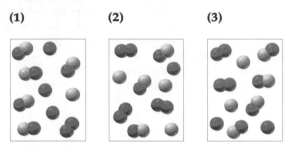

    (a) Which reaction mixture is at equilibrium?

    (b) For those mixtures that are not at equilibrium, will the reaction go in the forward or reverse direction to reach equilibrium?

13.29 The following pictures represent the initial state and the equilibrium state for the reaction of A_2 molecules (red) with B atoms (blue) to give AB molecules:

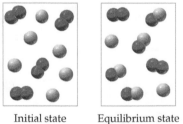

Initial state   Equilibrium state

    (a) Write a balanced chemical equation for the reaction.

    (b) If the volume of the equilibrium mixture is decreased, will the number of AB molecules increase, decrease, or remain the same? Explain.

13.30 Consider the reaction $A + B \rightleftharpoons AB$. The vessel on the right contains an equilibrium mixture of A molecules (red spheres), B molecules (blue spheres), and AB molecules. If the stopcock is opened and the contents of the two vessels are allowed to mix, will the reaction go in the forward or reverse direction? Explain.

13.31 The following pictures represent the composition of the equilibrium mixture for the reaction $A + B \rightleftharpoons AB$ at 300 K and at 400 K:

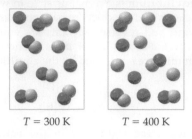

$T = 300\text{ K}$ $T = 400\text{ K}$

    Is the reaction exothermic or endothermic? Explain using Le Châtelier's principle.

13.32 The following pictures represent equilibrium mixtures at 325 K and 350 K for a reaction involving A atoms (red), B atoms (blue), and AB molecules:

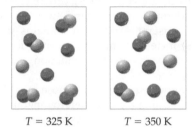

$T = 325\text{ K}$ $T = 350\text{ K}$

    (a) Write a balanced equation for the reaction that occurs on raising the temperature.

    (b) Is the reaction exothermic or endothermic? Explain using Le Châtelier's principle.

    (c) If the volume of the container is increased, will the number of A atoms increase, decrease, or remain the same? Explain.

13.33 The following picture represents an equilibrium mixture of solid $BaCO_3$, solid BaO, and gaseous CO_2 obtained as a result of the endothermic decomposition of $BaCO_3$:

    (a) Draw a picture that represents the equilibrium mixture after addition of four more CO_2 molecules.

    (b) Draw a picture that represents the equilibrium mixture at a higher temperature.

13.34 The following picture represents the composition of the equilibrium mixture for the endothermic reaction $A_2 \rightleftharpoons 2\,A$ at 500 K:

    Draw a picture that represents the equilibrium mixture after each of the following changes:

(a) Adding a catalyst

(b) Increasing the volume

(c) Decreasing the temperature

13.35 The following picture represents the equilibrium state for the reaction $2\,AB \rightleftharpoons A_2 + B_2$:

Which rate constant is larger, k_f or k_r? Explain.

13.36 The following pictures represent the initial and equilibrium states for the exothermic decomposition of gaseous A molecules (red) to give gaseous B molecules (blue):

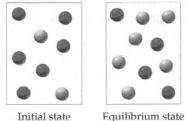

Initial state   Equilibrium state

(a) Write a balanced chemical equation for the reaction.

(b) Will the number of A molecules in the equilibrium mixture increase, decrease, or remain the same after each of the following changes? Explain.

(1) Increasing the temperature

(2) Decreasing the volume

(3) Increasing the pressure by adding an inert gas

(4) Adding a catalyst

13.37 The following pictures represent the initial and equilibrium states for the exothermic reaction of solid A (red) with gaseous B_2 (blue) to give gaseous AB:

Initial state   Equilibrium state

(a) Write a balanced chemical equation for the reaction.

(b) Will the number of AB molecules in the equilibrium mixture increase, decrease, or remain the same after each of the following changes? Explain.

(1) Increasing the partial pressure of B_2

(2) Adding more solid A

(3) Increasing the volume

(4) Increasing the temperature

SECTION PROBLEMS

Equilibrium Constant Expressions and Equilibrium Constants (Sections 13.1–13.4)

13.38 For the reaction $A_2 + 2\,B \rightleftharpoons 2\,AB$, the rate of the forward reaction is 18 M/s and the rate of the reverse reaction is 12 M/s. The reaction is not at equilibrium. Will the reaction proceed in the forward or reverse direction to attain equilibrium?

13.39 For the reaction $2\,A_3 + B_2 \rightleftharpoons 2\,A_3B$, the rate of the forward reaction is 0.35 M/s and the rate of the reverse reaction is 0.65 M/s. The reaction is not at equilibrium. Will the reaction proceed in the forward or reverse direction to attain equilibrium?

13.40 For each of the following equilibria, write the equilibrium constant expression for K_c:

(a) $CH_4(g) + H_2O(g) \rightleftharpoons CO(g) + 3\,H_2(g)$

(b) $3\,F_2(g) + Cl_2(g) \rightleftharpoons 2\,ClF_3(g)$

(c) $H_2(g) + F_2(g) \rightleftharpoons 2\,HF(g)$

13.41 For each of the following equilibria, write the equilibrium constant expression for K_c:

(a) $2\,C_2H_4(g) + O_2(g) \rightleftharpoons 2\,CH_3CHO(g)$

(b) $2\,NO(g) \rightleftharpoons N_2(g) + O_2(g)$

(c) $4\,NH_3(g) + 5\,O_2(g) \rightleftharpoons 4\,NO(g) + 6\,H_2O(g)$

13.42 For each of the equilibria in Problem 13.40, write the equilibrium constant expression for K_p and give the equation that relates K_p and K_c.

13.43 For each of the equilibria in Problem 13.41, write the equilibrium constant expression for K_p and give the equation that relates K_p and K_c.

13.44 Diethyl ether, used as an anesthetic, is synthesized by heating ethanol with concentrated sulfuric acid. Write the equilibrium constant expression for K_c.

$$2\,C_2H_5OH(soln) \rightleftharpoons C_2H_5OC_2H_5(soln) + H_2O(soln)$$

Ethanol   Diethyl ether

13.45 Ethylene glycol, used as antifreeze in automobile radiators, is manufactured by the hydration of ethylene oxide. Write the equilibrium constant expression for K_c.

$$H_2C{-}CH_2(soln) + H_2O(soln) \rightleftharpoons HOCH_2CH_2OH(soln)$$

Ethylene oxide   Ethylene glycol

13.46 If $K_c = 7.5 \times 10^{-9}$ at 1000 K for the reaction $N_2(g) + O_2(g) \rightleftharpoons 2 NO(g)$, what is K_c at 1000 K for the reaction $2 NO(g) \rightleftharpoons N_2(g) + O_2(g)$?

13.47 At 400 K, $K_p = 50.2$ for the reaction $N_2O_4(g) \rightleftharpoons 2 NO_2(g)$ What is K_p at 400 K for the reaction $2 NO_2(g) \rightleftharpoons N_2O_4(g)$?

13.48 An equilibrium mixture of PCl_5, PCl_3, and Cl_2 at a certain temperature contains 8.3×10^{-3} M PCl_5, 1.5×10^{-2} M PCl_3, and 3.2×10^{-2} M Cl_2. Calculate the equilibrium constant K_c for the reaction $PCl_5(g) \rightleftharpoons PCl_3(g) + Cl_2(g)$.

13.49 The partial pressures in an equilibrium mixture of NO, Cl_2, and NOCl at 500 K are as follows: $P_{NO} = 0.240$ atm; $P_{Cl_2} = 0.608$ atm; $P_{NOCl} = 1.35$ atm. What is K_p at 500 K for the reaction $2 NO(g) + Cl_2(g) \rightleftharpoons 2 NOCl(g)$?

13.50 A sample of HI (9.30×10^{-3} mol) was placed in an empty 2.00 L container at 1000 K. After equilibrium was reached, the concentration of I_2 was 6.29×10^{-4} M. Calculate the value of K_c at 1000 K for the reaction $H_2(g) + I_2(g) \rightleftharpoons 2 HI(g)$.

13.51 Vinegar contains acetic acid, a weak acid that is partially dissociated in aqueous solution:

$$CH_3CO_2H(aq) \rightleftharpoons H^+(aq) + CH_3CO_2^-(aq)$$

Acetic acid

(a) Write the equilibrium constant expression for K_c.

(b) What is the value of K_c if the extent of dissociation in 1.0 M CH_3CO_2H is 0.42%?

13.52 The industrial solvent ethyl acetate is produced by the reaction of acetic acid with ethanol:

$$CH_3CO_2H(soln) + CH_3CH_2OH(soln) \rightleftharpoons$$

Acetic acid   Ethanol

$$CH_3CO_2CH_2CH_3(soln) + H_2O(soln)$$

Ethyl acetate

(a) Write the equilibrium constant expression for K_c.

(b) A solution prepared by mixing 1.00 mol of acetic acid and 1.00 mol of ethanol contains 0.65 mol of ethyl acetate at equilibrium. Calculate the value of K_c. Explain why you can calculate K_c without knowing the volume of the solution.

13.53 A characteristic reaction of ethyl acetate is hydrolysis, the reverse of the reaction in Problem 13.52. Write the equilibrium equation for the hydrolysis of ethyl acetate, and use the data in Problem 13.52 to calculate K_c for the hydrolysis reaction.

13.54 At 298 K, K_c is 2.2×10^5 for the reaction $F(g) + O_2(g) \rightleftharpoons O_2F(g)$. What is the value of K_p at this temperature?

13.55 At 298 K, K_p is 1.6×10^{-6} for the reaction $2 NOCl(g) \rightleftharpoons 2 NO(g) + Cl_2(g)$. What is the value of K_c at this temperature?

13.56 The vapor pressure of water at 25 °C is 0.0313 atm. Calculate the values of K_p and K_c at 25 °C for the equilibrium $H_2O(l) \rightleftharpoons H_2O(g)$.

13.57 Naphthalene, a white solid used to make mothballs, has a vapor pressure of 0.10 mm Hg at 27 °C. Calculate the values of K_p and K_c at 27 °C for the equilibrium $C_{10}H_8(s) \rightleftharpoons C_{10}H_8(g)$.

Naphthalene

13.58 For each of the following equilibria, write the equilibrium constant expression for K_c. Where appropriate, also write the equilibrium constant expression for K_p.

(a) $Fe_2O_3(s) + 3 CO(g) \rightleftharpoons 2 Fe(l) + 3 CO_2(g)$

(b) $4 Fe(s) + 3 O_2(g) \rightleftharpoons 2 Fe_2O_3(s)$

(c) $BaSO_4(s) \rightleftharpoons BaO(s) + SO_3(g)$

(d) $BaSO_4(s) \rightleftharpoons Ba^{2+}(aq) + SO_4^{2-}(aq)$

13.59 For each of the following equilibria, write the equilibrium constant expression for K_c. Where appropriate, also write the equilibrium constant expression for K_p.

(a) $WO_3(s) + 3 H_2(g) \rightleftharpoons W(s) + 3 H_2O(g)$

(b) $Ag^+(aq) + Cl^-(aq) \rightleftharpoons AgCl(s)$

(c) $2 FeCl_3(s) + 3 H_2O(g) \rightleftharpoons Fe_2O_3(s) + 6 HCl(g)$

(d) $MgCO_3(s) \rightleftharpoons MgO(s) + CO_2(g)$

Using the Equilibrium Constant (Section 13.5)

13.60 When the following reactions come to equilibrium, does the equilibrium mixture contain mostly reactants or mostly products?

(a) $H_2(g) + S(s) \rightleftharpoons H_2S(g)$; $K_c = 7.8 \times 10^5$

(b) $N_2(g) + 2 H_2(g) \rightleftharpoons N_2H_4(g)$; $K_c = 7.4 \times 10^{-26}$

13.61 Which of the following reactions yield appreciable equilibrium concentrations of both reactants and products?

(a) $2 Cu(s) + O_2(g) \rightleftharpoons 2 CuO(s)$; $K_c = 4 \times 10^{45}$

(b) $H_3PO_4(aq) \rightleftharpoons H^+(aq) + H_2PO_4^-(aq)$; $K_c = 7.5 \times 10^{-3}$

(c) $2 HBr(g) \rightleftharpoons H_2(g) + Br_2(g)$; $K_c = 2 \times 10^{-19}$

13.62 When wine spoils, ethanol is oxidized to acetic acid as O_2 from the air reacts with the wine:

$$CH_3CH_2OH(aq) + O_2(aq) \rightleftharpoons CH_3CO_2H(aq) + H_2O(l)$$

Ethanol   Acetic acid

The value of K_c for this reaction at 25 °C is 1.2×10^{82}. Will much ethanol remain when the reaction has reached equilibrium? Explain.

13.63 The value of K_c for the reaction $3 O_2(g) \rightleftharpoons 2 O_3(g)$ is 1.7×10^{-56} at 25 °C. Do you expect pure air at 25 °C to contain much O_3 (ozone) when O_2 and O_3 are in equilibrium? If the equilibrium concentration of O_2 in air at 25 °C is 8×10^{-3} M, what is the equilibrium concentration of O_3?

13.64 At 1400 K, $K_c = 2.5 \times 10^{-3}$ for the reaction $CH_4(g) + 2\,H_2S(g) \rightleftharpoons CS_2(g) + 4\,H_2(g)$. A 10.0 L reaction vessel at 1400 K contains 2.0 mol of CH_4, 3.0 mol of CS_2, 3.0 mol of H_2, and 4.0 mol of H_2S. Is the reaction mixture at equilibrium? If not, in which direction does the reaction proceed to reach equilibrium?

13.65 The first step in the industrial synthesis of hydrogen is the reaction of steam and methane to give synthesis gas, a mixture of carbon monoxide and hydrogen:

$$H_2O(g) + CH_4(g) \rightleftharpoons CO(g) + 3\,H_2(g) \qquad K_c = 4.7 \text{ at } 1400 \text{ K}$$

A mixture of reactants and products at 1400 K contains 0.035 M H_2O, 0.050 M CH_4, 0.15 M CO, and 0.20 M H_2. In which direction does the reaction proceed to reach equilibrium?

13.66 Phosphine (PH_3) decomposes at elevated temperatures, yielding gaseous P_2 and H_2:

$$2\,PH_3(g) \rightleftharpoons P_2(g) + 3\,H_2(g) \qquad K_p = 398 \text{ at } 873 \text{ K}$$

If the initial partial pressures are $P_{PH_3} = 0.0260$ atm, $P_{P_2} = 0.871$ atm, $P_{H_2} = 0.517$ atm, calculate Q_p and determine the direction of reaction to attain equilibrium.

13.67 When a mixture of PH_3, P_2, and H_2 comes to equilibrium at 873 K according to the reaction in Problem 13.66, $P_{P_2} = 0.412$ atm and $P_{H_2} = 0.822$ atm. What is P_{PH_3}?

13.68 Gaseous indium dihydride is formed from the elements at elevated temperature:

$$In(g) + H_2(g) \rightleftharpoons InH_2(g) \qquad K_p = 1.48 \text{ at } 973 \text{ K}$$

Partial pressures measured in a reaction vessel are: $P_{In} = 0.0600$ atm, $P_{H_2} = 0.0350$ atm, $P_{InH_2} = 0.0760$ atm.

(a) Calculate Q_p, and determine the direction of reaction to attain equilibrium.

(b) Determine the equilibrium partial pressures of all the gases.

13.69 The following reaction, which has $K_c = 0.145$ at 298 K, takes place in carbon tetrachloride solution:

$$2\,BrCl(soln) \rightleftharpoons Br_2(soln) + Cl_2(soln)$$

A measurement of the concentrations shows [BrCl] = 0.050 M, [Br_2] = 0.035 M, and [Cl_2] = 0.030 M.

(a) Calculate Q_c, and determine the direction of reaction to attain equilibrium.

(a) Determine the equilibrium concentrations of BrCl, Br_2, and Cl_2.

13.70 An equilibrium mixture of N_2, H_2, and NH_3 at 700 K contains 0.036 M N_2 and 0.15 M H_2. At this temperature, K_c for the reaction $N_2(g) + 3\,H_2(g) \rightleftharpoons 2\,NH_3(g)$ is 0.29. What is the concentration of NH_3?

13.71 An equilibrium mixture of O_2, SO_2, and SO_3 contains equal concentrations of SO_2 and SO_3. Calculate the concentration of O_2 if $K_c = 2.7 \times 10^2$ for the reaction $2\,SO_2(g) + O_2(g) \rightleftharpoons 2\,SO_3(g)$.

13.72 The air pollutant NO is produced in automobile engines from the high temperature reaction $N_2(g) + O_2(g) \rightleftharpoons 2\,NO(g)$; $K_c = 1.7 \times 10^{-3}$ at 2300 K. If the initial concentrations of N_2 and O_2 at 2300 K are both 1.40 M, what are the concentrations of NO, N_2, and O_2 when the reaction mixture reaches equilibrium?

13.73 Recalculate the equilibrium concentrations in Problem 13.72 if the initial concentrations are 2.24 M N_2 and 0.56 M O_2. (This N_2/O_2 concentration ratio is the ratio found in air.)

13.74 The interconversion of L-α-lysine and L-β-lysine, for which $K_c = 7.20$ at 333 K, is catalyzed by the enzyme lysine 2,3-aminomutase.

L-α-Lysine

L-β-Lysine

L-α-Lysine occurs in proteins while L-β-lysine is a precursor to certain antibiotics. At 333 K, a solution of L-α-lysine at a concentration of 3.00×10^{-3} M is placed in contact with lysine 2,3-aminomutase. What are the equilibrium concentrations of L-α-lysine and L-β-lysine?

13.75 Chlorine monoxide and dichlorine dioxide are involved in the catalytic destruction of stratospheric ozone. They are related by the equation

$$2\,ClO(g) \rightleftharpoons Cl_2O_2(g)$$

for which K_c is 4.96×10^{11} at 253 K. For an equilibrium mixture in which [Cl_2O_2] is 6.00×10^{-6} M, what is [ClO]?

13.76 The value of K_c for the reaction of acetic acid with ethanol is 3.4 at 25 °C:

$$CH_3CO_2H(soln) + CH_3CH_2OH(soln) \rightleftharpoons$$

Acetic acid   Ethanol

$$CH_3CO_2CH_2CH_3(soln) + H_2O(soln) \qquad K_c = 3.4$$

Ethyl acetate

(a) How many moles of ethyl acetate are present in an equilibrium mixture that contains 4.0 mol of acetic acid, 6.0 mol of ethanol, and 12.0 mol of water at 25 °C?

(b) Calculate the number of moles of all reactants and products in an equilibrium mixture prepared by mixing 1.00 mol of acetic acid and 10.00 mol of ethanol.

13.77 In a basic aqueous solution, chloromethane undergoes a substitution reaction in which Cl^- is replaced by OH^-:

$$CH_3Cl(aq) + OH^-(aq) \rightleftharpoons CH_3OH(aq) + Cl^-(aq)$$

Chloromethane   Methanol

The equilibrium constant K_c is 1×10^{16}. Calculate the equilibrium concentrations of CH_3Cl, CH_3OH, OH^-, and Cl^- in a solution prepared by mixing equal volumes of 0.1 M CH_3Cl and 0.2 M NaOH. (Hint: In defining x, assume that the reaction goes 100% to completion, and then take account of a small amount of the reverse reaction.)

13.78 At 700 K, $K_p = 0.140$ for the reaction $ClF_3(g) \rightleftharpoons ClF(g) + F_2(g)$. Calculate the equilibrium partial pressures of ClF_3, ClF, and F_2 if only ClF_3 is present initially, at a partial pressure of 1.47 atm.

13.79 The reaction of iron(III) oxide with carbon monoxide is important in making steel. At 1000 K, $K_p = 19.9$ for the reaction $Fe_2O_3(s) + 3\,CO(g) \rightleftharpoons 2\,Fe(s) + 3\,CO_2(g)$. What are the equilibrium partial pressures of CO and CO_2 if CO is the only gas present initially, at a partial pressure of 0.978 atm?

Le Châtelier's Principle (Sections 13.6–13.10)

13.80 Consider the following equilibrium: $Ag^+(aq) + Cl^-(aq) \rightleftharpoons AgCl(s)$. Use Le Châtelier's principle to predict how the amount of solid silver chloride will change when the equilibrium is disturbed by:
(a) Adding NaCl   (b) Adding $AgNO_3$
(c) Adding NH_3, which reacts with Ag^+ to form the complex ion $Ag(NH_3)_2^+$
(d) Removing Cl^-; also account for the change using the reaction quotient Q_c.

13.81 Will the concentration of NO_2 increase, decrease, or remain the same when the equilibrium $NO_2Cl(g) + NO(g) \rightleftharpoons NOCl(g) + NO_2(g)$ is disturbed by the following changes?
(a) Adding NOCl   (b) Adding NO   (c) Removing NO
(d) Adding NO_2Cl; also account for the change using the reaction quotient Q_c.

13.82 When each of the following equilibria is disturbed by increasing the pressure as a result of decreasing the volume, does the number of moles of reaction products increase, decrease, or remain the same?
(a) $2\,CO_2(g) \rightleftharpoons 2\,CO(g) + O_2(g)$
(b) $N_2(g) + O_2(g) \rightleftharpoons 2\,NO(g)$
(c) $Si(s) + 2\,Cl_2(g) \rightleftharpoons SiCl_4(g)$

13.83 For each of the following equilibria, use Le Châtelier's principle to predict the direction of reaction when the volume is increased.
(a) $C(s) + H_2O(g) \rightleftharpoons CO(g) + H_2(g)$
(b) $2\,H_2(g) + O_2(g) \rightleftharpoons 2\,H_2O(g)$
(c) $2\,Fe(s) + 3\,H_2O(g) \rightleftharpoons Fe_2O_3(s) + 3\,H_2(g)$

13.84 For the water-gas shift reaction $CO(g) + H_2O(g) \rightleftharpoons CO_2(g) + H_2(g)$, $\Delta H° = -41.2$ kJ, does the amount of H_2 in an equilibrium mixture increase or decrease when the temperature is increased? How does K_c change when the temperature is decreased? Justify your answers using Le Châtelier's principle.

13.85 The value of $\Delta H°$ for the reaction $3\,O_2(g) \rightleftharpoons 2\,O_3(g)$ is $+285$ kJ. Does the equilibrium constant for this reaction increase or decrease when the temperature increases? Justify your answer using Le Châtelier's principle.

13.86 Consider the exothermic reaction $CoCl_4^{2-}(aq) + 6\,H_2O(l) \rightleftharpoons Co(H_2O)_6^{2+}(aq) + 4\,Cl^-(aq)$, which interconverts the blue $CoCl_4^{2-}$ ion and the pink $Co(H_2O)_6^{2+}$ ion. Will the equilibrium concentration of $CoCl_4^{2-}$ increase or decrease when the following changes occur?
(a) HCl is added
(b) $Co(NO_3)_2$ is added

(c) The solution is diluted with water
(d) The temperature is increased

13.87 Consider the endothermic reaction $Fe^{3+}(aq) + Cl^-(aq) \rightleftharpoons FeCl^{2+}(aq)$. Use Le Châtelier's principle to predict how the equilibrium concentration of the complex ion $FeCl^{2+}$ will change when:
(a) $Fe(NO_3)_3$ is added
(b) Cl^- is precipitated as AgCl by addition of $AgNO_3$
(c) The temperature is increased
(d) A catalyst is added

13.88 Methanol (CH_3OH) is manufactured by the reaction of carbon monoxide with hydrogen in the presence of a $Cu/ZnO/Al_2O_3$ catalyst:

$$CO(g) + 2\,H_2(g) \underset{\text{catalyst}}{\overset{Cu/ZnO/Al_2O_3}{\rightleftharpoons}} CH_3OH(g) \qquad \Delta H° = -91 \text{ kJ}$$

Does the amount of methanol increase, decrease, or remain the same when an equilibrium mixture of reactants and products is subjected to the following changes?
(a) The temperature is increased
(b) The volume is decreased
(c) Helium is added
(d) CO is added
(e) The catalyst is removed

13.89 In the gas phase at 400 °C, isopropyl alcohol (rubbing alcohol) decomposes to acetone, an important industrial solvent:

$$\underset{\text{Isopropyl alcohol}}{(CH_3)_2CHOH(g)} \rightleftharpoons \underset{\text{Acetone}}{(CH_3)_2CO(g)} + H_2(g) \qquad \Delta H° = +57.3 \text{ kJ}$$

Does the amount of acetone increase, decrease, or remain the same when an equilibrium mixture of reactants and products is subjected to the following changes?
(a) The temperature is increased
(b) The volume is increased   (c) Argon is added
(d) H_2 is added   (e) A catalyst is added

13.90 The following reaction is important in gold mining:

$$4\,Au(s) + 8\,CN^-(aq) + O_2(g) + 2\,H_2O(l) \rightleftharpoons$$
$$4\,Au(CN)_2^-(aq) + 4\,OH^-$$

For a reaction mixture at equilibrium, in which direction would the reaction go to re-establish equilibrium after each of the following changes?
(a) Adding gold
(b) Increasing the hydroxide concentration

(c) Increasing the partial pressure of oxygen

(d) Adding $Fe^{3+}(aq)$, which reacts with cyanide to form $Fe(CN)_6^{3-}(aq)$

13.91 The following reaction, catalyzed by iridium, is endothermic at 700 K:

$$CaO(s) + CH_4(g) + 2 H_2O(g) \rightleftharpoons CaCO_3(s) + 4 H_2(g)$$

For a reaction mixture at equilibrium at 700 K, how would the following changes affect the total quantity of $CaCO_3$ in the reaction mixture once equilibrium is re-established?

(a) Increasing the temperature

(b) Adding calcium oxide

(c) Removing methane (CH_4)

(d) Increasing the total volume

(e) Adding iridium

Chemical Equilibrium and Chemical Kinetics (Section 13.11)

13.92 Consider a general, single-step reaction of the type $A + B \rightleftharpoons C$. Show that the equilibrium constant is equal to the ratio of the rate constants for the forward and reverse reactions, $K_c = k_f/k_r$.

13.93 Which of the following relative values of k_f and k_r results in an equilibrium mixture that contains large amounts of reactants and small amounts of products?

(a) $k_f > k_r$ (b) $k_f = k_r$ (c) $k_f < k_r$

13.94 Consider the gas-phase hydration of hexafluoroacetone, $(CF_3)_2CO$:

$$(CF_3)_2CO(g) + H_2O(g) \underset{k_r}{\overset{k_f}{\rightleftharpoons}} (CF_3)_2C(OH)_2(g)$$

At 76 °C, the forward and reverse rate constants are $k_f = 0.13\ M^{-1}\ s^{-1}$ and $k_r = 6.2 \times 10^{-4}\ s^{-1}$. What is the value of the equilibrium constant K_c?

13.95 Consider the reaction of chloromethane with OH^- in aqueous solution:

$$CH_3Cl(aq) + OH^-(aq) \underset{k_r}{\overset{k_f}{\rightleftharpoons}} CH_3OH(aq) + Cl^-(aq)$$

At 25 °C, the rate constant for the forward reaction is $6 \times 10^{-6}\ M^{-1}\ s^{-1}$, and the equilibrium constant K_c is 1×10^{16}. Calculate the rate constant for the reverse reaction at 25 °C.

13.96 In automobile catalytic converters, the air pollutant nitric oxide is converted to nitrogen and oxygen. Listed in the table are forward and reverse rate constants for the reaction $2 NO(g) \rightleftharpoons N_2(g) + O_2(g)$.

Temperature (K)	$k_f\ (M^{-1}s^{-1})$	$k_r\ (M^{-1}s^{-1})$
1400	0.29	1.1×10^{-6}
1500	1.3	1.4×10^{-5}

Is the reaction endothermic or exothermic? Explain in terms of kinetics.

13.97 Forward and reverse rate constants for the reaction $CO_2(g) + N_2(g) \rightleftharpoons CO(g) + N_2O(g)$ exhibit the following temperature dependence:

Temperature (K)	$k_f\ (M^{-1}s^{-1})$	$k_r\ (M^{-1}s^{-1})$
1200	9.1×10^{-11}	1.5×10^5
1300	2.7×10^{-9}	2.6×10^5

Is the reaction endothermic or exothermic? Explain in terms of kinetics.

CHAPTER PROBLEMS

13.98 The equilibrium concentrations in a gas mixture at a particular temperature are 0.13 M H_2, 0.70 M I_2, and 2.1 M HI. What equilibrium concentrations are obtained at the same temperature when 0.20 mol of HI is injected into an empty 500.0 mL container?

13.99 A 5.00 L reaction vessel is filled with 1.00 mol of H_2, 1.00 mol of I_2, and 2.50 mol of HI. Calculate the equilibrium concentrations of H_2, I_2, and HI at 500 K. The equilibrium constant K_c at 500 K for the reaction $H_2(g) + I_2(g) \rightleftharpoons 2 HI(g)$ is 129.

13.100 At 1000 K, the value of K_c for the reaction $C(s) + H_2O(g) \rightleftharpoons CO(g) + H_2(g)$ is 3.0×10^{-2}. Calculate the equilibrium concentrations of H_2O, CO_2, and H_2 in a reaction mixture obtained by heating 6.00 mol of steam and an excess of solid carbon in a 5.00 L container. What is the molar composition of the equilibrium mixture?

13.101 The equilibrium constant K_p for the reaction $PCl_5(g) \rightleftharpoons PCl_3(g) + Cl_2(g)$ is 3.81×10^2 at 600 K and 2.69×10^3 at 700 K.

(a) Is the reaction endothermic or exothermic?

(b) How are the equilibrium amounts of reactants and products affected by (i) an increase in volume, (ii) addition of an inert gas, and (iii) addition of a catalyst?

13.102 Consider the following gas-phase reaction: $2 A(g) + B(g) \rightleftharpoons C(g) + D(g)$. An equilibrium mixture of reactants and products is subjected to the following changes:

(a) A decrease in volume   (b) An increase in temperature

(c) Addition of reactants   (d) Addition of a catalyst

(e) Addition of an inert gas

Which of these changes affect the composition of the equilibrium mixture but leave the value of the equilibrium constant K_c unchanged? Which of the changes affect the value of K_c? Which affect neither the composition of the equilibrium mixture nor K_c?

13.103 Baking soda (sodium bicarbonate) decomposes when it is heated:

$$2 NaHCO_3(s) \rightleftharpoons Na_2CO_3(s) + CO_2(g) + H_2O(g)$$
$$\Delta H° = +136\ kJ$$

Consider an equilibrium mixture of reactants and products in a closed container. How does the number of moles of CO_2 change when the mixture is disturbed by the following:

(a) Adding solid $NaHCO_3$ (b) Adding water vapor

(c) Decreasing the volume of the container

(d) Increasing the temperature

13.104 The reaction $2 \text{AsH}_3(g) \rightleftharpoons \text{As}_2(g) + 3\text{H}_2(g)$ has $K_p = 7.2 \times 10^7$ at 1073 K. At the same temperature, what is K_p for each of the following reactions?
(a) $\text{As}_2(g) + 3\text{H}_2(g) \rightleftharpoons 2\text{AsH}_3(g)$
(b) $4\text{AsH}_3(g) \rightleftharpoons 2\text{As}_2(g) + 6\text{H}_2(g)$
(c) $9\text{H}_2(g) + 3\text{As}_2(g) \rightleftharpoons 6\text{AsH}_3(g)$

13.105 The reaction $2\text{PH}_3(g) + \text{As}_2(g) \rightleftharpoons 2\text{AsH}_3(g) + \text{P}_2(g)$ has $K_p = 2.9 \times 10^{-5}$ at 873 K. At the same temperature, what is K_p for each of the following reactions?
(a) $2\text{AsH}_3(g) + \text{P}_2(g) \rightleftharpoons 2\text{PH}_3(g) + \text{As}_2(g)$
(b) $6\text{PH}_3(g) + 3\text{As}_2(g) \rightleftharpoons 3\text{P}_2(g) + 6\text{AsH}_3(g)$
(c) $2\text{P}_2(g) + 4\text{AsH}_3(g) \rightleftharpoons 2\text{As}_2(g) + 4\text{PH}_3(g)$

13.106 When 1.000 mol of PCl_5 is introduced into a 5.000 L container at 500 K, 78.50% of the PCl_5 dissociates to give an equilibrium mixture of PCl_5, PCl_3, and Cl_2:

$$\text{PCl}_5(g) \rightleftharpoons \text{PCl}_3(g) + \text{Cl}_2(g)$$

(a) Calculate the values of K_c and K_p.
(b) If the initial concentrations in a particular mixture of reactants and products are $[\text{PCl}_5] = 0.500$ M, $[\text{PCl}_3] = 0.150$ M, and $[\text{Cl}_2] = 0.600$ M, in which direction does the reaction proceed to reach equilibrium? What are the concentrations when the mixture reaches equilibrium?

13.107 Heavy water, symbolized D_2O (D = ^{2}H) finds use as a neutron moderator in nuclear reactors. In a mixture with ordinary water, exchange of isotopes occurs according to the following equation:

$$\text{H}_2\text{O} + \text{D}_2\text{O} \rightleftharpoons 2\text{HDO} \qquad K_c = 3.86 \text{ at } 298 \text{ K}$$

When 1.00 mol of H_2O is combined with 1.00 mol of D_2O, what are the equilibrium amounts of H_2O, D_2O, and HDO (in moles) at 298 K? Assume the density of the mixture is constant at 1.05 g/cm^3.

13.108 Refining petroleum involves cracking large hydrocarbon molecules into smaller, more volatile pieces. A simple example of hydrocarbon cracking is the gas-phase thermal decomposition of butane to give ethane and ethylene:

Butane, C_4H_{10} Ethane, C_2H_6 Ethylene, C_2H_4

(a) Write the equilibrium constant expressions for K_p and K_c.
(b) The value of K_p at 500 °C is 12. What is the value of K_c?
(c) A sample of butane having a pressure of 50 atm is heated at 500 °C in a closed container at constant volume. When equilibrium is reached, what percentage of the butane has been converted to ethane and ethylene? What is the total pressure at equilibrium?
(d) How would the percent conversion in part (c) be affected by a decrease in volume?

13.109 Consider the reaction $\text{C}(s) + \text{CO}_2(g) \rightleftharpoons 2\text{CO}(g)$. When 1.50 mol of CO_2 and an excess of solid carbon are heated in a 20.0 L container at 1100 K, the equilibrium concentration of CO is 7.00×10^{-2} M.
(a) What is the equilibrium concentration of CO_2?
(b) What is the value of the equilibrium constant K_c at 1100 K?

13.110 The equilibrium constant K_p for the gas-phase thermal decomposition of *tert*-butyl chloride is 3.45 at 500 K:

$$(\text{CH}_3)_3\text{CCl}(g) \rightleftharpoons (\text{CH}_3)_2\text{C}=\text{CH}_2(g) + \text{HCl}(g)$$

tert-Butyl chloride   Isobutylene

(a) Calculate the value of K_c at 500 K.
(b) Calculate the molar concentrations of reactants and products in an equilibrium mixture obtained by heating 1.00 mol of *tert*-butyl chloride in a 5.00 L vessel at 500 K.
(c) A mixture of isobutylene (0.400 atm partial pressure at 500 K) and HCl (0.600 atm partial pressure at 500 K) is allowed to reach equilibrium at 500 K. What are the equilibrium partial pressures of *tert*-butyl chloride, isobutylene, and HCl?

13.111 As shown in Figure 13.14, a catalyst lowers the activation energy for the forward and reverse reactions by the same amount, ΔE_a.
(a) Apply the Arrhenius equation, $k = Ae^{-E_a/RT}$, to the forward and reverse reactions, and show that a catalyst increases the rates of both reactions by the same factor.
(b) Use the relation between the equilibrium constant and the forward and reverse rate constants, $K_c = k_f/k_r$, to show that a catalyst does not affect the value of the equilibrium constant.

13.112 Given the Arrhenius equation, $k = Ae^{-E_a/RT}$, and the relation between the equilibrium constant and the forward and reverse rate constants, $K_c = k_f/k_r$, explain why K_c for an exothermic reaction decreases with increasing temperature.

13.113 At 1000 K, $K_p = 2.1 \times 10^6$ and $\Delta H° = -107.7$ kJ for the reaction $\text{H}_2(g) + \text{Br}_2(g) \rightleftharpoons 2\text{HBr}(g)$.
(a) A 0.974 mol quantity of Br_2 is added to a 1.00 L reaction vessel that contains 1.22 mol of H_2 gas at 1000 K. What are the partial pressures of H_2, Br_2, and HBr at equilibrium?
(b) For the equilibrium in part (a), each of the following changes will increase the equilibrium partial pressure of HBr. Choose the change that will cause the greatest increase in the pressure of HBr, and explain your choice.
   (i) Adding 0.10 mol of H_2
   (ii) Adding 0.10 mol of Br_2
   (iii) Decreasing the temperature to 700 K.

13.114 Consider the gas-phase decomposition of NOBr:

$$2\,NOBr(g) \rightleftharpoons 2\,NO(g) + Br_2(g)$$

(a) When 0.0200 mol of NOBr is added to an empty 1.00 L flask and the decomposition reaction is allowed to reach equilibrium at 300 K, the total pressure in the flask is 0.588 atm. What is the equilibrium constant K_c for this reaction at 300 K?

(b) What is the value of K_p for this reaction at 300 K?

13.115 At 100 °C, $K_c = 4.72$ for the reaction $2\,NO_2(g) \rightleftharpoons N_2O_4(g)$. An empty 10.0 L flask is filled with 4.60 g of NO_2 at 100 °C. What is the total pressure in the flask at equilibrium?

13.116 Halogen lamps are ordinary tungsten filament lamps in which the lamp bulb contains a small amount of a halogen (often bromine). At the high temperatures of the lamp, the halogens dissociate and exist as single atoms.

(a) In an ordinary tungsten lamp, the hot tungsten filament is constantly evaporating and the tungsten condenses on the relatively cool walls of the bulb. In a Br-containing halogen lamp, the tungsten reacts with the Br atoms to give gaseous WBr_4:

$$W(s) + 4\,Br(g) \rightleftharpoons WBr_4(g)$$

At the walls of the lamp, where the temperature is about 900 K, this reaction has an equilibrium constant K_p of about 100. If the equilibrium pressure of $Br(g)$ is 0.010 atm, what is the equilibrium pressure of $WBr_4(g)$ near the walls of the bulb?

(b) Near the tungsten filament, where the temperature is about 2800 K, the reaction in part (a) has a K_p value of about 5.0. Is the reaction exothermic or endothermic?

(c) When the $WBr_4(g)$ diffuses back toward the filament, it decomposes, depositing tungsten back onto the filament. Show quantitatively that the pressure of WBr_4 from part (a) will cause the reaction in part (a) to go in reverse direction at 2800 K. [The pressure of $Br(g)$ is still 0.010 atm.] Thus, tungsten is continually recycled from the walls of the bulb back to the filament, allowing the bulb to last longer and burn brighter.

13.117 The decomposition of solid ammonium carbamate, $(NH_4)(NH_2CO_2)$, to gaseous ammonia and carbon dioxide is an endothermic reaction.

$$(NH_4)(NH_2CO_2)(s) \rightleftharpoons 2\,NH_3(g) + CO_2(g)$$

(a) When solid $(NH_4)(NH_2CO_2)$ is introduced into an evacuated flask at 25 °C, the total pressure of gas at equilibrium is 0.116 atm. What is the value of K_p at 25 °C?

(b) Given that the decomposition reaction is at equilibrium, how would the following changes affect the total quantity of NH_3 in the flask once equilibrium is reestablished?

   (i) Adding CO_2 (ii) Adding $(NH_4)(NH_2CO_2)$

   (iii) Removing CO_2 (iv) Increasing the total volume

   (v) Adding neon   (vi) Increasing the temperature

13.118 At 25 °C, $K_c = 216$ for the reaction $2\,NO_2(g) \rightleftharpoons N_2O_4(g)$. A 1.00 L flask containing a mixture of NO_2 and N_2O_4 at 25 °C has a total pressure of 1.50 atm. What is the partial pressure of each gas?

13.119 At 500 °C, F_2 gas is stable and does not dissociate, but at 840 °C, some dissociation occurs: $F_2(g) \rightleftharpoons 2\,F(g)$. A flask filled with 0.600 atm of F_2 at 500 °C was heated to 840 °C, and the pressure at equilibrium was measured to be 0.984 atm. What is the equilibrium constant K_p for the dissociation of F_2 gas at 840 °C?

13.120 The reaction $NO(g) + NO_2(g) \rightleftharpoons N_2O_3(g)$ takes place in the atmosphere with $K_c = 13$ at 298 K. A gas mixture is prepared with 2.0 mol NO and 3.0 mol NO_2 and an initial total pressure of 1.65 atm.

(a) What are the equilibrium partial pressures of NO, NO_2, and N_2O_3 at 298 K?

(b) What is the volume of the container?

13.121 Phosgene ($COCl_2$) is a toxic gas that damages the lungs. At 360 °C, $K_c = 8.4 \times 10^{-4}$ for the decomposition of phosgene:

$$COCl_2(g) \rightleftharpoons CO(g) + Cl_2(g)$$

If an empty 50.0 L container is charged with 1.00 mol of phosgene at 360 °C, what is the total pressure in the container after the system comes to equilibrium?

13.122 The equilibrium constant K_c for the reaction $N_2(g) + 3\,H_2(g) \rightleftharpoons 2\,NH_3(g)$ is 4.20 at 600 K. When a quantity of gaseous NH_3 was placed in a 1.00 L reaction vessel at 600 K and the reaction was allowed to reach equilibrium, the vessel was found to contain 0.200 mol of N_2. How many moles of NH_3 were placed in the vessel?

13.123 At 45 °C, $K_c = 0.619$ for the reaction $N_2O_4(g) \rightleftharpoons 2\,NO_2(g)$. If 46.0 g of N_2O_4 is introduced into an empty 2.00 L container, what are the partial pressures of NO_2 and N_2O_4 after equilibrium has been achieved at 45 °C?

13.124 When 9.25 g of ClF_3 was introduced into an empty 2.00 L container at 700.0 K, 19.8% of the ClF_3 decomposed to give an equilibrium mixture of ClF_3, ClF, and F_2.

$$ClF_3(g) \rightleftharpoons ClF(g) + F_2(g)$$

(a) What is the value of the equilibrium constant K_c at 700.0 K?

(b) What is the value of the equilibrium constant K_p at 700.0 K?

(c) In a separate experiment, 39.4 g of ClF_3 was introduced into an empty 2.00 L container at 700.0 K. What are the concentrations of ClF_3, ClF, and F_2 when the mixture reaches equilibrium?

13.125 The following reaction in aqueous solution is catalyzed by the enzyme aspartase and has $K_c = 6.95 \times 10^{-3}$ at 37 °C:

If the initial concentration of L-aspartate is 8.32×10^{-3} M, what are the equilibrium concentrations of L-aspartate, fumarate, and ammonium ion at 37 °C?

13.126 The reaction of fumarate (Problem 13.125) with water to form L-malate is catalyzed by the enzyme fumarase; $K_c = 3.3$ at 37 °C.

Fumarate   L-Malate

When a reaction mixture with [fumarate] = 1.56×10^{-3} M and [L-malate] = 2.27×10^{-3} M comes to equilibrium in the presence of fumarase at 37 °C, what are the equilibrium concentrations of fumarate and L-malate? (Water can be omitted from the equilibrium equation because its concentration in dilute solutions is essentially the same as that in pure water.)

MULTICONCEPT PROBLEMS

13.127 The F—F bond in F_2 is relatively weak because the lone pairs of electrons on one F atom repel the lone pairs on the other F atom; $K_p = 7.83$ at 1500 K for the reaction $F_2(g) \rightleftharpoons 2\,F(g)$.
   (a) If the equilibrium partial pressure of F_2 molecules at 1500 K is 0.200 atm, what is the equilibrium partial pressure of F atoms in atm?
   (b) What fraction of the F_2 molecules dissociate at 1500 K?
   (c) Why is the F—F bond in F_2 weaker than the Cl—Cl bond in Cl_2?

13.128 When 0.500 mol of N_2O_4 is placed in a 4.00 L reaction vessel and heated at 400 K, 79.3% of the N_2O_4 decomposes to NO_2.
   (a) Calculate K_c and K_p at 400 K for the reaction $N_2O_4(g) \rightleftharpoons 2\,NO_2(g)$.
   (b) Draw an electron-dot structure for NO_2, and rationalize the structure of N_2O_4.

13.129 The equilibrium constant K_c for the gas-phase thermal decomposition of cyclopropane to propene is 1.0×10^5 at 500 K:

$$\underset{\text{CH}_2}{\overset{/\backslash}{\text{H}_2\text{C}-\text{CH}_2}} \rightleftharpoons \text{CH}_3-\text{CH}=\text{CH}_2 \quad K_c = 1.0 \times 10^5$$

Cyclopropane   Propene

   (a) What is the value of K_p at 500 K?
   (b) What is the equilibrium partial pressure of cyclopropane at 500 K when the partial pressure of propene is 5.0 atm?
   (c) Can you alter the ratio of the two concentrations at equilibrium by adding cyclopropane or by decreasing the volume of the container? Explain.
   (d) Which has the larger rate constant, the forward reaction or the reverse reaction?
   (e) Why is cyclopropane so reactive? (Hint: Consider the hybrid orbitals used by the C atoms.)

13.130 Acetic acid tends to form dimers, $(CH_3CO_2H)_2$, because of hydrogen bonding:

$$2\,CH_3-C\overset{O}{\underset{O-H}{\diagup}} \rightleftharpoons CH_3-C\overset{O\cdots H-O}{\underset{O-H\cdots O}{\diagup}}C-CH_3$$

Monomer   Dimer

The equilibrium constant K_c for this reaction is 1.51×10^2 in benzene solution, but only 3.7×10^{-2} in water solution.
   (a) Calculate the ratio of dimers to monomers for 0.100 M acetic acid in benzene.
   (b) Calculate the ratio of dimers to monomers for 0.100 M acetic acid in water.
   (c) Why is K_c for the water solution so much smaller than K_c for the benzene solution?

13.131 A 125.4 g quantity of water and an equal molar amount of carbon monoxide were placed in an empty 10.0 L vessel, and the mixture was heated to 700 K. At equilibrium, the partial pressure of CO was 9.80 atm. The reaction is

$$CO(g) + H_2O(g) \rightleftharpoons CO_2(g) + H_2(g)$$

   (a) What is the value of K_p at 700 K?
   (b) An additional 31.4 g of water was added to the reaction vessel, and a new state of equilibrium was achieved. What are the equilibrium partial pressures of each gas in the mixture? What is the concentration of H_2 in molecules/cm³?

13.132 A 79.2 g chunk of dry ice (solid CO_2) and 30.0 g of graphite (carbon) were placed in an empty 5.00 L container, and the mixture was heated to achieve equilibrium. The reaction is

$$CO_2(g) + C(s) \rightleftharpoons 2\,CO(g)$$

   (a) What is the value of K_p at 1000 K if the gas density at 1000 K is 16.3 g/L?
   (b) What is the value of K_p at 1100 K if the gas density at 1100 K is 16.9 g/L?
   (c) Is the reaction exothermic or endothermic? Explain.

13.133 The amount of carbon dioxide in a gaseous mixture of CO_2 and CO can be determined by passing the gas into an aqueous solution that contains an excess of $Ba(OH)_2$. The CO_2 reacts, yielding a precipitate of $BaCO_3$, but the CO does not react. This method was used to analyze the equilibrium composition of the gas obtained when 1.77 g of CO_2 reacted with 2.0 g of graphite in a 1.000 L container at 1100 K. The analysis yielded 3.41 g of $BaCO_3$. Use these data to calculate K_p at 1100 K for the reaction

$$CO_2(g) + C(s) \rightleftharpoons 2\ CO(g)$$

13.134 A 14.58 g quantity of N_2O_4 was placed in a 1.000 L reaction vessel at 400 K. The N_2O_4 decomposed to an equilibrium mixture of N_2O_4 and NO_2 that had a total pressure of 9.15 atm.

(a) What is the value of K_c for the reaction $N_2O_4(g) \rightleftharpoons 2\ NO_2(g)$ at 400 K?

(b) How much heat (in kilojoules) was absorbed when the N_2O_4 decomposed to give the equilibrium mixture? (Standard heats of formation may be found in Appendix B.)

13.135 Consider the sublimation of mothballs at 27 °C in a room having dimensions 8.0 ft × 10.0 ft × 8.0 ft. Assume that the mothballs are pure solid naphthalene (density 1.16 g/cm^3) and that they are spheres with a diameter of 12.0 mm. The equilibrium constant K_c for the sublimation of naphthalene is 5.40×10^{-6} at 27 °C.

$$C_{10}H_8(s) \rightleftharpoons C_{10}H_8(g)$$

(a) When excess mothballs are present, how many gaseous naphthalene molecules are in the room at equilibrium?

(b) How many mothballs are required to saturate the room with gaseous naphthalene?

13.136 Ozone is unstable with respect to decomposition to ordinary oxygen:

$$2\ O_3(g) \rightleftharpoons 3\ O_2(g) \qquad K_p = 1.3 \times 10^{57}$$

How many O_3 molecules are present at equilibrium in 10 million cubic meters of air at 25 °C and 720 mm Hg pressure?

13.137 The equilibrium constant for the dimerization of acetic acid in benzene solution is 1.51×10^2 at 25 °C (see Problem 13.130).

$$2\ CH_3CO_2H \rightleftharpoons (CH_3CO_2H)_2 \qquad K_c = 1.51 \times 10^2 \text{ at } 25 \text{ °C}$$

(a) What are the equilibrium concentrations of monomer and dimer at 25 °C in a solution prepared by dissolving 0.0300 mol of pure acetic acid in enough benzene to make 250.0 mL of solution?

(b) What is the osmotic pressure of the solution at 25 °C?

13.138 For the decomposition reaction $PCl_5(g) \rightleftharpoons PCl_3(g) + Cl_2(g)$, $K_p = 381$ at 600 K and $K_c = 46.9$ at 700 K.

(a) Is the reaction endothermic or exothermic? Explain. Does your answer agree with what you would predict based on bond energies?

(b) If 1.25 g of PCl_5 is introduced into an evacuated 0.500 L flask at 700 K and the decomposition reaction is allowed to reach equilibrium, what percent of the PCl_5 will decompose and what will be the total pressure in the flask?

(c) Write electron-dot structures for PCl_5 and PCl_3, and indicate whether these molecules have a dipole moment. Explain.

13.139 Propanol (PrOH) and methyl methacrylate (MMA) associate in solution by an intermolecular force, forming an adduct represented as PrOH·MMA. The equilibrium constant for the association reaction is $K_c = 0.701$ at 298 K.

$$\rightleftharpoons \text{PrOH} \cdot \text{MMA}$$

(a) What is the predominant intermolecular force accounting for the interaction between PrOH and MMA?

(b) Draw a plausible structure for the PrOH·MMA adduct. Use $\cdots$ to signify an intermolecular interaction.

(c) If the initial concentrations are [PrOH] = 0.100 M and [MMA] = 0.0500 M, what are the equilibrium concentrations of PrOH, MMA, and PrOH·MMA?

CHAPTER

14

Aqueous Equilibria: Acids and Bases

The sour taste of citrus fruits is due to acids such as citric acid and ascorbic acid (vitamin C).

CONTENTS

A cids and bases are among the most familiar of all chemical compounds. Acetic acid in vinegar, citric acid in lemons and other citrus fruits, magnesium hydroxide in commercial antacids, and ammonia in household cleaning products are among the acids and bases that we encounter in everyday life. Hydrochloric acid of approximately 0.15 M concentration is the acid in gastric juice; it is essential to digestion and is secreted by the lining of our stomachs in quantities of 1.2–1.5 L per day.

The characteristic properties of acids and bases have been known for centuries. Acids react with metals such as iron and zinc to yield H_2 gas, and they change the color of the plant dye *litmus* from blue to red. By contrast, bases feel slippery, and they change the color of litmus from red to blue. When acids and bases are mixed in the right proportion, the characteristic acidic and basic properties disappear and new substances known as *salts* are obtained.

What is it that makes an acid an acid and a base a base? We first raised those questions in Section 4.5, and we'll now take a closer look at some of the concepts that chemists have developed to describe the chemical behavior of acids and bases. We'll also apply the principles of chemical equilibrium discussed in Chapter 13 to determine the concentrations of the substances present in aqueous solutions of acids and bases. An enormous amount of chemistry can be understood in terms of acid–base reactions, perhaps the most important reaction type in all of chemistry.

14.1 ACID–BASE CONCEPTS: THE BRØNSTED–LOWRY THEORY

Thus far, we've been using the Arrhenius theory of acids and bases (Section 4.5). According to Arrhenius, acids are substances that dissociate in water to produce hydrogen ions (H^+) and bases are substances that dissociate in water to yield hydroxide ions (OH^-). Thus, HCl and H_2SO_4 are acids, and NaOH and $Ba(OH)_2$ are bases.

- A generalized Arrhenius acid $HA(aq) \rightleftharpoons H^+(aq) + A^-(aq)$

- A generalized Arrhenius base $MOH(aq) \rightleftharpoons M^+(aq) + OH^-(aq)$

In this book, we'll refer to these reactions as dissociation reactions rather than ionization reactions and reserve the term ionization for processes that involve loss of an electron.

The Arrhenius theory accounts for the properties of many common acids and bases, but it has important limitations. For one thing, the Arrhenius theory is restricted to aqueous solutions; for another, it doesn't account for the basicity of substances like ammonia (NH_3) that don't contain OH groups. In 1923, a more general theory of acids and bases was proposed independently by the Danish chemist Johannes Brønsted and the English chemist Thomas Lowry. According to the **Brønsted–Lowry theory**, an acid is any substance (molecule or ion) that can transfer a proton (H^+ ion) to another substance and a base is any substance that can accept a proton. In short, acids are proton donors, bases are proton acceptors, and acid–base reactions are proton-transfer reactions:

- Brønsted–Lowry acid   A substance that can transfer H^+

- Brønsted–Lowry base   A substance that can accept H^+

$$HA \quad + \quad B \quad \rightleftharpoons \quad BH^+ \quad + \quad A^-$$

HA	+	B		BH+	+	A⁻
H⁺ donor		H⁺ acceptor		H⁺ donor		H⁺ acceptor
Acid		Base		Acid		Base

Conjugate acid–base pairs

It follows from this equation that the products of a Brønsted–Lowry acid–base reaction, BH^+ and A^-, are themselves acids and bases. The species BH^+ produced when the base B accepts a proton from HA can itself donate a proton back to A^-, meaning that it is a Brønsted–Lowry acid. Similarly, the species A^- produced when HA loses a proton can itself accept a proton back from BH^+, meaning that it is a Brønsted–Lowry base. Chemical species whose formulas differ only by one proton are said to be **conjugate acid–base pairs**. Thus, A^- is the **conjugate base** of the acid HA, and HA is the **conjugate acid** of the base A^-. Similarly, B is the conjugate base of the acid BH^+, and BH^+ is the conjugate acid of the base B.

To see what's going on in an acid–base reaction, keep your eye on the proton. For example, when a Brønsted–Lowry acid HA dissolves in water, it reacts reversibly with water in an *acid-dissociation equilibrium*. The acid transfers a proton to the solvent, which acts as a base (a proton acceptor). The products are the **hydronium ion, H_3O^+** (the conjugate acid of H_2O), and A^- (the conjugate base of HA):

In the reverse reaction, H_3O^+ acts as the proton donor (acid) and A^- acts as the proton acceptor (base). Typical examples of Brønsted–Lowry acids include not only electrically neutral molecules, such as HCl, HNO_3, and HF, but also cations and anions of salts that contain transferable protons, such as NH_4^+, HSO_4^-, and HCO_3^-.

When a Brønsted–Lowry base such as NH_3 dissolves in water, it accepts a proton from the solvent, which acts as an acid. The products are the hydroxide ion, OH^- (the conjugate base of water), and the ammonium ion, NH_4^+ (the conjugate acid of NH_3). In the reverse reaction, NH_4^+ acts as the proton donor and OH^- acts as the proton acceptor:

For a molecule or ion to accept a proton, it must have at least one unshared pair of electrons that it can use for bonding to the proton. As shown by the following electron-dot structures, all Brønsted–Lowry bases have one or more lone pairs of electrons:

$$:\overset{\displaystyle .}{\underset{\displaystyle H}{O}}\!-\!H \qquad :\overset{\displaystyle ..}{\underset{\displaystyle ..}{F}}:^{-} \qquad H\!-\!\overset{\displaystyle .}{\underset{\displaystyle H}{N}}\!-\!H \qquad \left[:\overset{\displaystyle ..}{\underset{\displaystyle ..}{O}}\!-\!H\right]^{-}$$

Some Brønsted–Lowry bases

WORKED EXAMPLE 14.1

EXPLAINING ACIDITY WITH THE ARRHENIUS AND BRØNSTED–LOWRY THEORIES

Account for the acidic properties of nitrous acid (HNO_2) using the Arrhenius theory and the Brønsted–Lowry theory, and identify the conjugate base of HNO_2.

Nitrous acid

STRATEGY

To account for the acidity of a substance, consider how it can produce H^+ ions in water (Arrhenius theory) and how it can act as a proton donor (Brønsted–Lowry theory).

SOLUTION

HNO_2 is an Arrhenius acid because it dissociates in water to produce H^+ ions:

$$HNO_2(aq) \rightleftharpoons H^+(aq) + NO_2^-(aq)$$

Nitrous acid is a Brønsted–Lowry acid because it acts as a proton donor when it dissociates, transferring a proton to water to give the hydronium ion, H_3O^+:

$$\underset{\text{Acid}}{HNO_2(aq)} + \underset{\text{Base}}{H_2O(l)} \rightleftharpoons \underset{\text{Acid}}{H_3O^+(aq)} + \underset{\text{Base}}{NO_2^-(aq)}$$

Conjugate acid–base pairs

The conjugate base of HNO_2 is NO_2^-, the species that remains after HNO_2 has lost a proton.

▶ **PROBLEM 14.1** Write a balanced equation for the dissociation of each of the following Brønsted–Lowry acids in water:

(a) H_2SO_4 **(b)** HSO_4^- **(c)** H_3O^+ **(d)** NH_4^+

What is the conjugate base of each acid?

▶ **PROBLEM 14.2** What is the conjugate acid of each of the following Brønsted–Lowry bases?

(a) HCO_3^- **(b)** CO_3^{2-} **(c)** OH^- **(d)** $H_2PO_4^-$

WORKED EXAMPLE 14.2

IDENTIFYING BRØNSTED–LOWRY ACIDS, BASES, AND CONJUGATE ACID–BASE PAIRS

For the following reaction in aqueous solution, identify the Brønsted–Lowry acids, bases, and conjugate acid–base pairs:

= H = S = F

STRATEGY

The simplest approach is to identify the conjugate acid–base pairs, the species whose formulas differ by just one proton.

continued on next page

SOLUTION

The second reactant is HF, and the first product is its conjugate base F^-. The second product is H_2S, and the first reactant is its conjugate base HS^-. Therefore, the Brønsted–Lowry acids, bases, and conjugate acid–base pairs are as follows:

$$HS^-(aq) + HF(aq) \rightleftharpoons F^-(aq) + H_2S(aq)$$

Base   Acid   Base   Acid

Conjugate acid–base pairs

CONCEPTUAL PROBLEM 14.3   For the following reaction in aqueous solution, identify the Brønsted–Lowry acids, bases, and conjugate acid–base pairs:

⬤ = H   ⬤ = N   ⬤ = Cl

14.2   ACID STRENGTH AND BASE STRENGTH

A helpful way of viewing an acid-dissociation equilibrium is to realize that the two bases, H_2O and A^-, are competing for protons:

$$HA(aq) + H_2O(l) \rightleftharpoons H_3O^+(aq) + A^-(aq)$$

Acid   Base   Acid   Base

If H_2O is a stronger base (a stronger proton acceptor) than A^-, the H_2O molecules will get the protons and the solution will contain mainly H_3O^+ and A^-. If A^- is a stronger base than H_2O, the A^- ions will get the protons and the solution will contain mainly HA and H_2O. When beginning with equal concentrations of reactants and products, *the proton is always transferred to the stronger base*. This means that the direction of reaction to reach equilibrium is proton transfer from the stronger acid to the stronger base to give the weaker acid and the weaker base:

Stronger acid + Stronger base ⟶ Weaker acid + Weaker base

Different acids differ in their ability to donate protons. A **strong acid** is one that is almost completely dissociated in water and is therefore a strong electrolyte (Section 4.2). Thus, the acid-dissociation equilibrium of a strong acid lies nearly 100% to the right, and the solution contains almost entirely H_3O^+ and A^- ions with only a negligible amount of undissociated HA molecules. Typical strong acids are perchloric acid ($HClO_4$), hydrochloric acid (HCl), hydrobromic acid (HBr), hydroiodic acid (HI), nitric acid (HNO_3), and sulfuric acid (H_2SO_4). It follows from this definition that strong acids have very weak conjugate bases. The ions ClO_4^-, Cl^-, Br^-, I^-, NO_3^-, and HSO_4^- have only a negligible tendency to combine with a proton in aqueous solution, and they are therefore much weaker bases than H_2O.

A **weak acid** is one that is only partially dissociated in water and is thus a weak electrolyte. Only a small fraction of the weak acid molecules transfer a proton to water, and the solution therefore contains mainly undissociated HA molecules along with small amounts of H_3O^+ and the conjugate base A^-. Typical weak acids are nitrous acid (HNO_2), hydrofluoric acid (HF), and acetic acid (CH_3CO_2H). In the case of very weak acids, such as NH_3, OH^-, and H_2, the acid has practically no tendency to transfer a proton to water and the acid-dissociation equilibrium lies essentially 100% to the left. It follows from this definition that very weak acids have strong

Remember...

Substances that dissolve in water to produce solutions that conduct electricity are called electrolytes. Molecular substances that dissociate into ions to a large extent are strong electrolytes, while those that dissociate to only a small extent are weak electrolytes.   (Section 4.2)

conjugate bases. For example, the NH_2^-, O^{2-}, and H^- ions are essentially 100% protonated in aqueous solution and are much stronger bases than H_2O.

The equilibrium concentrations of HA, H_3O^+, and A^- for strong acids, weak acids, and very weak acids are represented in **Figure 14.1**. The inverse relationship between the strength of an acid and the strength of its conjugate base is illustrated in Table 14.1.

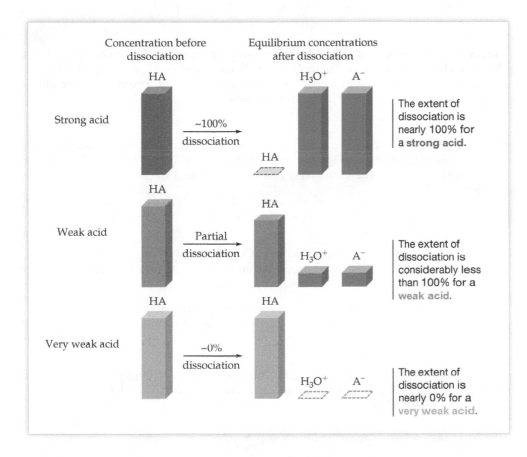

Figure 14.1
Dissociation of HA involves H^+ transfer to H_2O, yielding H_3O^+ and A^-.

TABLE 14.1 Relative Strengths of Conjugate Acid–Base Pairs

	Acid, HA		Base, A⁻		
Stronger acid	$HClO_4$ HCl H_2SO_4 HNO_3	**Strong acids:** 100% dissociated in aqueous solution.	ClO_4^- Cl^- HSO_4^- NO_3^-	**Very weak bases:** Negligible tendency to be protonated in aqueous solution.	Weaker base
	H_3O^+		H_2O		
	HSO_4^- H_3PO_4 HNO_2 HF CH_3CO_2H H_2CO_3 H_2S NH_4^+ HCN HCO_3^-	**Weak acids:** Exist in solution as a mixture of HA, A⁻, and H_3O^+.	SO_4^{2-} $H_2PO_4^-$ NO_2^- F^- $CH_3CO_2^-$ HCO_3^- HS^- NH_3 CN^- CO_3^{2-}	**Weak bases:** Moderate tendency to be protonated in aqueous solution.	
	H_2O		OH^-		
Weaker acid	NH_3 OH^- H_2	**Very weak acids:** Negligible tendency to dissociate.	NH_2^- O^{2-} H^-	**Strong bases:** 100% protonated in aqueous solution.	Stronger base

WORKED EXAMPLE 14.3

PREDICTING THE DIRECTION OF ACID–BASE REACTIONS

If you mix equal concentrations of reactants and products, which of the following reactions proceed to the right and which proceed to the left?

(a) $H_2SO_4(aq) + NH_3(aq) \rightleftharpoons NH_4^+(aq) + HSO_4^-(aq)$

(b) $HCO_3^-(aq) + SO_4^{2-}(aq) \rightleftharpoons HSO_4^-(aq) + CO_3^{2-}(aq)$

STRATEGY

To predict the direction of reaction, use the balanced equation to identify the acids and bases, and then use Table 14.1 to identify the stronger acid and the stronger base. When equal concentrations of reactants and products are present, proton transfer always occurs from the stronger acid to the stronger base.

SOLUTION

(a) In this reaction, H_2SO_4 and NH_4^+ are the acids, and NH_3 and HSO_4^- are the bases. According to Table 14.1, H_2SO_4 is a stronger acid than NH_4^+ and NH_3 is a stronger base than HSO_4^-. Therefore, NH_3 gets the proton and the reaction proceeds from left to right.

$$H_2SO_4(aq) + NH_3(aq) \longrightarrow NH_4^+(aq) + HSO_4^-(aq)$$

Stronger acid　　Stronger base　　Weaker acid　　Weaker base

(b) HCO_3^- and HSO_4^- are the acids, and SO_4^{2-} and CO_3^{2-} are the bases. Table 14.1 indicates that HSO_4^- is the stronger acid and CO_3^{2-} is the stronger base. Therefore, CO_3^{2-} gets the proton and the reaction proceeds from right to left.

$$HCO_3^-(aq) + SO_4^{2-}(aq) \longleftarrow HSO_4^-(aq) + CO_3^{2-}(aq)$$

Weaker acid　　Weaker base　　Stronger acid　　Stronger base

▶ **PROBLEM 14.4** If you mix equal concentrations of reactants and products, which of the following reactions proceed to the right and which proceed to the left?

(a) $HF(aq) + NO_3^-(aq) \rightleftharpoons HNO_3(aq) + F^-(aq)$

(b) $NH_4^+(aq) + CO_3^{2-}(aq) \rightleftharpoons HCO_3^-(aq) + NH_3(aq)$

CONCEPTUAL PROBLEM 14.5 The following pictures represent aqueous solutions of two acids HA (A = X or Y); water molecules have been omitted for clarity.

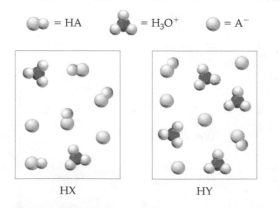

　　　　　= HA　　　　= H$_3$O$^+$　　　　= A$^-$

HX　　　　　　　　HY

(a) Which is the stronger acid, HX or HY?

(b) Which is the stronger base, X$^-$ or Y$^-$?

(c) If you mix equal concentrations of reactants and products, will the following reaction proceed to the right or to the left?

$$HX + Y^- \rightleftharpoons HY + X^-$$

14.3 HYDRATED PROTONS AND HYDRONIUM IONS

As we've seen, the proton is fundamental to both the Arrhenius and the Brønsted–Lowry definitions of an acid. Dissociation of an Arrhenius acid HA gives an aqueous hydrogen ion, or hydrated proton, written as $H^+(aq)$:

$$HA(aq) \rightleftharpoons H^+(aq) + A^-(aq)$$

As a bare proton, the positively charged H^+ ion is too reactive to exist in aqueous solution and so it bonds to the oxygen atom of a solvent water molecule to give the trigonal pyramidal hydronium ion, H_3O^+. The H_3O^+ ion, which can be regarded as the simplest hydrate of the proton, $[H(H_2O)]^+$, can associate through hydrogen bonding with additional water molecules to give higher hydrates with the general formula $[H(H_2O)_n]^+$ (n = 2, 3, or 4), such as $H_5O_2^+$, $H_7O_3^+$, and $H_9O_4^+$. It's likely that acidic aqueous solutions contain a distribution of $[H(H_2O)_n]^+$ ions having different values of n. In this book, though, we'll use the symbols $H^+(aq)$ and $H_3O^+(aq)$ to mean the same thing—namely, a proton hydrated by an unspecified number of water molecules. Ordinarily, we use H_3O^+ in acid–base reactions to emphasize the proton-transfer character of those reactions.

H_3O^+ — the hydronium ion, or hydrated H^+

▶ **PROBLEM 14.6** Some of the following ions have been detected by mass spectrometry:

$$H_9O_4^+, H_{13}O_5^+, H_{19}O_9^+, H_{25}O_{11}^+, H_{43}O_{21}^+$$

(a) Which should be considered as hydrates of the proton?
(b) For the ions that are hydrates, tell how many water molecules are present in addition to the proton.

14.4 DISSOCIATION OF WATER

One of the most important properties of water is its ability to act both as an acid and as a base. In the presence of an acid, water acts as a base, whereas in the presence of a base, water acts as an acid. It's not surprising, therefore, that in pure water one molecule can donate a proton to another in a reaction in which water acts as both an acid and a base in the same reaction:

Called the *dissociation of water*, this reaction is characterized by the equilibrium equation $K_w = [H_3O^+][OH^-]$, where the equilibrium constant K_w is called the *ion-product constant for water*.

◀⊨ **Dissociation of Water** $2 H_2O(l) \rightleftharpoons H_3O^+(aq) + OH^-(aq)$

◀⊨ **Ion-Product Constant for water** $K_w = [H_3O^+][OH^-]$

As discussed in Section 13.4, the **concentration** of water is omitted from the equilibrium constant expression because water is a pure liquid.

There are two important aspects of the dynamic equilibrium in the dissociation of water. First, the forward and reverse reactions are rapid: H_2O molecules, H_3O^+ ions, and OH^- ions continually interconvert as protons transfer quickly from one species to another. Second, the position of the equilibrium lies far to the left. At any given instant, only a tiny fraction of the water molecules are dissociated into H_3O^+ and OH^- ions. The vast majority of the H_2O molecules are undissociated.

Remember...

The **concentration** of a pure liquid or a pure solid is omitted from the equilibrium constant expression because the ratio of its actual concentration to its concentration in the thermodynamic standard state is equal to 1.   (Section 13.4)

We can calculate the extent of the dissociation of the water molecules starting from experimental measurements that show the H_3O^+ concentration in pure water to be 1.0×10^{-7} M at 25 °C:

$$[H_3O^+] = 1.0 \times 10^{-7} \text{ M} \qquad \text{at 25 °C}$$

Since the dissociation reaction of water produces equal concentrations of H_3O^+ and OH^- ions, the OH^- concentration in pure water is also 1.0×10^{-7} M at 25 °C:

$$[H_3O^+] = [OH^-] = 1.0 \times 10^{-7} \text{ M} \qquad \text{at 25 °C}$$

Furthermore, we know that the molar concentration of pure water, calculated from its density and molar mass, is 55.4 M at 25 °C:

$$[H_2O] = \left(\frac{997 \text{ g}}{\text{L}}\right)\left(\frac{1 \text{ mol}}{18.0 \text{ g}}\right) = 55.4 \text{ mol/L} \qquad \text{at 25 °C}$$

From these facts, we conclude that the ratio of dissociated to undissociated water molecules is about 2 in 10^9, a very small number indeed:

$$\frac{[H_2O]_{\text{dissociated}}}{[H_2O]_{\text{undissociated}}} = \frac{1.0 \times 10^{-7} \text{ M}}{55.4 \text{ M}} = 1.8 \times 10^{-9} \qquad \text{about 2 in } 10^9$$

In addition, we can calculate that the numerical value of K_w at 25 °C is 1.0×10^{-14}:

$$K_w = [H_3O^+][OH^-] = (1.0 \times 10^{-7})(1.0 \times 10^{-7})$$
$$= 1.0 \times 10^{-14} \qquad \text{at 25 °C}$$

In very dilute solutions, the water is almost a pure liquid and the product of the H_3O^+ and OH^- concentrations is unaffected by the presence of solutes. This is not true in more concentrated solutions, but we'll neglect that complication and assume that the product of the H_3O^+ and OH^- concentrations is always 1.0×10^{-14} at 25 °C in any aqueous solution.

We can distinguish acidic, neutral, and basic aqueous solutions by the relative values of the H_3O^+ and OH^- concentrations:

$$\textbf{Acidic:} \quad [H_3O^+] > [OH^-]$$
$$\textbf{Neutral:} \quad [H_3O^+] = [OH^-]$$
$$\textbf{Basic:} \quad [H_3O^+] < [OH^-]$$

At 25 °C, $[H_3O^+] > 1.0 \times 10^{-7}$ M in an acidic solution, $[H_3O^+] = [OH^-] = 1.0 \times 10^{-7}$ M in a neutral solution, and $[H_3O^+] < 1.0 \times 10^{-7}$ M in a basic solution (**Figure 14.2**). If one of the concentrations, $[H_3O^+]$ or $[OH^-]$, is known, the other is readily calculated:

$$\text{Since} \quad [H_3O^+][OH^-] = K_w = 1.0 \times 10^{-14}$$

$$\text{then} \quad [H_3O^+] = \frac{1.0 \times 10^{-14}}{[OH^-]} \quad \text{and} \quad [OH^-] = \frac{1.0 \times 10^{-14}}{[H_3O^+]}$$

Figure 14.2
Values of the H_3O^+ and OH^- concentrations at 25 °C in acidic, neutral, and basic solutions.

In the previous discussion, we were careful to emphasize that the value of $K_w = 1.0 \times 10^{-14}$ applies only at 25 °C. This is because K_w, like all equilibrium constants, is affected by temperature and the H_3O^+ and OH^- concentrations in neutral aqueous solutions at temperatures other than 25 °C deviate from 1.0×10^{-7} M (see Problem 14.9). Unless otherwise indicated, we'll always assume a temperature of 25 °C.

WORKED EXAMPLE 14.4

CALCULATING [OH⁻] FROM K_w AND [H₃O⁺]

The concentration of H_3O^+ ions in a sample of lemon juice is 2.5×10^{-3} M. Calculate the concentration of OH^- ions, and classify the solution as acidic, neutral, or basic.

STRATEGY

When $[H_3O^+]$ is known, the OH^- concentration can be found from the expression $[OH^-] = K_w/[H_3O^+]$.

SOLUTION

$$[OH^-] = \frac{K_w}{[H_3O^-]} = \frac{1.0 \times 10^{-14}}{2.5 \times 10^{-3}} = 4.0 \times 10^{-12} \text{ M}$$

Because $[H_3O^+] > [OH^-]$, the solution is acidic.

BALLPARK CHECK

Because the product of the H_3O^+ and OH^- concentrations must equal 10^{-14}, and because the H_3O^+ concentration is in the range 10^{-3} M to 10^{-2} M, the OH^- concentration must be in the range 10^{-11} M to 10^{-12} M. The ballpark check and the solution agree.

▶ **PROBLEM 14.7** The concentration of H_3O^+ ions in the runoff from a coal mine is 1.4×10^{-4} M. Calculate the concentration of OH^- ions, and classify the solution as acidic, neutral, or basic.

▶ **PROBLEM 14.8** The concentration of OH^- in a sample of seawater is 2.0×10^{-6} M. Calculate the concentration of H_3O^+ ions, and classify the solution as acidic, neutral, or basic.

▶ **PROBLEM 14.9** At 50 °C the value of K_w is 5.5×10^{-14}. What are the concentrations of H_3O^+ and OH^- in a neutral solution at 50 °C?

14.5 THE pH SCALE

Rather than write hydronium ion concentrations in molarity, it's more convenient to express them on a logarithmic scale known as the *pH scale*. The term **pH** is derived from the French *puissance d'hydrogène* ("power of hydrogen") and refers to the power of 10 (the exponent) used to express the molar H_3O^+ concentration. The pH of a solution is defined as the negative base-10 logarithm (log) of the molar hydronium ion concentration:

$$pH = -\log [H_3O^+] \quad \text{or} \quad [H_3O^+] = \text{antilog} (-pH) = 10^{-pH}$$

Thus, an acidic solution having $[H_3O^+] = 10^{-2}$ M has a pH of 2, a basic solution having $[OH^-] = 10^{-2}$ M and $[H_3O^+] = 10^{-12}$ M has a pH of 12, and a neutral solution having $[H_3O^+] = 10^{-7}$ M has a pH of 7. Note that we can take the log of $[H_3O^+]$ because $[H_3O^+]$ is a dimensionless ratio of the actual concentration to the concentration (1 M) in the standard state. Although much less frequently used than pH, a pOH can be defined in the same way as pH and used to express the molar OH^- concentration. Just as $pH = -\log [H_3O^+]$, so $pOH = -\log [OH^-]$. It follows from the equation $[H_3O^+][OH^-] = 1.0 \times 10^{-14}$ that $pH + pOH = 14.00$.

If you use a calculator to find the pH from the H_3O^+ concentration, your answer will have more decimal places than the proper number of significant figures. For example, the pH of the lemon juice in Worked Example 14.4 ($[H_3O^+] = 2.5 \times 10^{-3}$ M) is found on a calculator to be

$$pH = -\log (2.5 \times 10^{-3}) = 2.602\,06$$

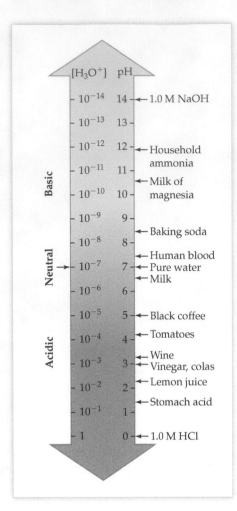

Figure 14.3
The pH scale and pH values for some common substances.

This result should be rounded to pH 2.60 (two significant figures) because $[H_3O^+]$ has only two significant figures. Note that the only significant figures in a logarithm are the digits to the right of the decimal point; the number to the left of the decimal point is an exact number related to the integral power of 10 in the exponential expression for $[H_3O^+]$:

$$pH = -\log(2.5 \times 10^{-3}) = -\log 10^{-3} - \log 2.5 = 3 - 0.40 = 2.60$$

| 2 significant figures (2 SF's) | Exact number | Exact number | 2 SF's | Exact number | 2 SF's |

Because the pH scale is logarithmic, the pH changes by 1 unit when $[H_3O^+]$ changes by a factor of 10, by 2 units when $[H_3O^+]$ changes by a factor of 100, and by 6 units when $[H_3O^+]$ changes by a factor of 1,000,000. To appreciate the extent to which the pH scale is a compression of the $[H_3O^+]$ scale, compare the amounts of 12 M HCl required to change the pH of the water in a backyard swimming pool: Only about 100 mL of 12 M HCl is needed to change the pH from 7 to 6, but a 10,000 L truckload of 12 M HCl is needed to change the pH from 7 to 1.

The pH scale and pH values for some common substances are shown in **Figure 14.3**. Because the pH is the *negative* log of $[H_3O^+]$, the pH decreases as $[H_3O^+]$ increases. Thus, when $[H_3O^+]$ increases from 10^{-7} M to 10^{-6} M, the pH decreases from 7 to 6. As a result, acidic solutions have pH less than 7, and basic solutions have pH greater than 7.

Acidic solution:	$pH < 7$
Neutral solution:	$pH = 7$
Basic solution:	$pH > 7$

WORKED EXAMPLE 14.5

CALCULATING THE pH FROM THE H_3O^+ CONCENTRATION

Calculate the pH of an aqueous ammonia solution that has an OH^- concentration of 1.9×10^{-3} M.

STRATEGY

First, calculate the H_3O^+ concentration from the OH^- concentration, and then take the negative logarithm of $[H_3O^+]$ to convert to pH.

SOLUTION

$$[H_3O^+] = \frac{K_w}{[OH^-]} = \frac{1.0 \times 10^{-14}}{1.9 \times 10^{-3}} = 5.3 \times 10^{-12} \text{ M}$$

$$pH = -\log[H_3O^+] = -\log(5.3 \times 10^{-12}) = 11.28$$

The pH is quoted to two significant figures (.28) because $[H_3O^+]$ is known to two significant figures (5.3).

BALLPARK CHECK

Because $[OH^-]$ is between 10^{-3} M and 10^{-2} M, $[H_3O^+]$ is between 10^{-11} M and 10^{-12} M. Therefore, the pH is between 11 and 12, in agreement with the solution.

WORKED EXAMPLE 14.6

CALCULATING THE H_3O^+ CONCENTRATION FROM THE pH

Acid rain is a matter of serious concern because most species of fish die in waters having a pH lower than 4.5–5.0. Calculate the H_3O^+ concentration in a lake that has a pH of 4.5.

STRATEGY

Calculate the H_3O^+ concentration by taking the antilogarithm of the negative of the pH.

SOLUTION

$$[H_3O^+] = \text{antilog}\,(-pH) = 10^{-pH} = 10^{-4.5} = 3 \times 10^{-5}\,M$$

$[H_3O^+]$ is reported to only one significant figure because the pH has only one digit beyond the decimal point. (If you need help in finding the antilog of a number, see Appendix A.2.)

BALLPARK CHECK

Because a pH of 4.5 is between 4 and 5, $[H_3O^+]$ is between 10^{-4} M and 10^{-5} M, in agreement with the solution.

▶ **PROBLEM 14.10** Calculate the pH of each of the following solutions:

(a) A sample of seawater that has an OH^- concentration of 1.58×10^{-6} M

(b) A sample of acid rain that has an H_3O^+ concentration of 6.0×10^{-5} M

▶ **PROBLEM 14.11** Calculate the concentrations of H_3O^+ and OH^- in each of the following solutions:

(a) Human blood (pH 7.40)   **(b)** A cola beverage (pH 2.8)

14.6 MEASURING pH

The approximate pH of a solution can be determined by using an **acid–base indicator**, a substance that changes color in a specific pH range (**Figure 14.4**). Indicators (abbreviated HIn) exhibit pH-dependent color changes because they are weak acids and have different colors in their acid (HIn) and conjugate base (In⁻) forms:

$$\underset{\text{Color A}}{HIn(aq)} + H_2O(l) \rightleftharpoons H_3O^+(aq) + \underset{\text{Color B}}{In^-(aq)}$$

Bromthymol blue, for example, changes color in the pH range 6.0–7.6, from yellow in its acid form to blue in its base form.

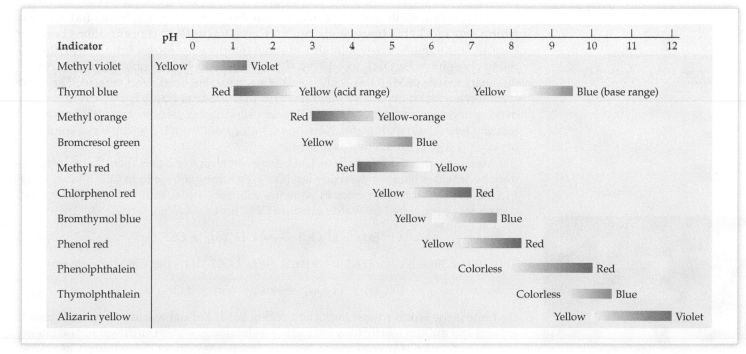

Figure 14.4

Some common acid–base indicators and their color changes. The color of an indicator changes over a range of about 2 pH units.

Figure 14.5
A pH meter with its electrical probe dipping into milk of magnesia. An accurate value of the pH (10.52) is shown on the meter.

Especially convenient for making approximate pH measurements is a commercially available mixture of indicators known as *universal indicator* that exhibits various colors depending on the pH (see Figure 14.8 on page 566). More accurate pH values can be determined with an electronic instrument called a *pH meter* (Figure 14.5), a device that measures the pH-dependent electrical potential of the test solution. We'll learn more about pH meters in Section 17.7.

14.7 THE pH IN SOLUTIONS OF STRONG ACIDS AND STRONG BASES

The commonly encountered strong acids listed in Table 14.1 include three *monoprotic acids* ($HClO_4$, HCl, and HNO_3), which contain a single dissociable proton, and one *diprotic acid* (H_2SO_4), which has two dissociable protons. Because strong monoprotic acids are nearly 100% dissociated in aqueous solution, the H_3O^+ and A^- concentrations are equal to the initial concentration of the acid and the concentration of undissociated HA molecules is essentially zero.

$$HA(aq) + H_2O(l) \xrightarrow{100\%} H_3O^+(aq) + A^-(aq)$$

The pH of a solution of a strong monoprotic acid is easily calculated from the H_3O^+ concentration, as shown in Worked Example 14.7. Calculation of the pH of an H_2SO_4 solution is more complicated because essentially 100% of the H_2SO_4 molecules dissociate to give H_3O^+ and HSO_4^- ions but much less than 100% of the resulting HSO_4^- ions dissociate to give H_3O^+ and SO_4^{2-} ions. We'll have more to say about diprotic acids in Section 14.11.

The most familiar examples of strong bases are alkali metal hydroxides, MOH, such as NaOH (*caustic soda*) and KOH (*caustic potash*). These compounds are water-soluble ionic solids that exist in aqueous solution as alkali metal cations (M^+) and OH^- anions:

$$MOH(s) \xrightarrow{H_2O} MOH(aq) \xrightarrow{100\%} M^+(aq) + OH^-(aq)$$

Thus, 0.10 M NaOH contains 0.10 M Na^+ and 0.10 M OH^-, and the pH is readily calculated from the OH^- concentration, as shown in Worked Example 14.8a.

The alkaline earth metal hydroxides $M(OH)_2$ (M = Mg, Ca, Sr, or Ba) are also strong bases (~100% dissociated), but they give lower OH^- concentrations because they are less soluble. Their solubility at room temperature varies from 38 g/L for the relatively soluble $Ba(OH)_2$ to ~10^{-2} g/L for the relatively insoluble $Mg(OH)_2$. Aqueous suspensions of $Mg(OH)_2$, called *milk of magnesia*, are used as an antacid. The most common and least expensive alkaline earth hydroxide is $Ca(OH)_2$, which is used in making mortars and cements. $Ca(OH)_2$ is called *slaked lime* because it is made by treating *lime* (CaO) with water. Aqueous solutions of $Ca(OH)_2$, which has a solubility of only ~1.3 g/L, are known as *limewater*.

Alkaline earth oxides, such as CaO, are even stronger bases than the corresponding hydroxides because the oxide ion (O^{2-}) is a stronger base than OH^- (Table 14.1). In fact, the O^{2-} ion can't exist in aqueous solutions because it is immediately and completely protonated by water, yielding OH^- ions:

$$O^{2-}(aq) + H_2O(l) \xrightarrow{100\%} OH^-(aq) + OH^-(aq)$$

Thus, when lime is dissolved in water, it gives 2 OH^- ions per CaO formula unit:

$$CaO(s) + H_2O(l) \longrightarrow Ca^{2+}(aq) + 2 OH^-(aq)$$

Lime is the world's most important strong base. Annual worldwide production is around 283 million metric tons for use in steelmaking, water purification, and chemical manufacture. Lime is made by the decomposition of limestone, $CaCO_3$, at temperatures of 800–1000 °C:

▲ Lime is spread on lawns and gardens to raise the pH of acidic soils.

$$CaCO_3(s) \xrightarrow{Heat} CaO(s) + CO_2(g)$$

WORKED EXAMPLE 14.7

CALCULATING THE pH OF A STRONG ACID SOLUTION

Calculate the pH of a 0.025 M HNO_3 solution.

STRATEGY

Because nitric acid is a strong acid, it is almost completely dissociated in aqueous solution. Therefore, the $[H_3O^+]$ equals the initial concentration of the HNO_3, and the pH equals the negative log of the $[H_3O^+]$.

SOLUTION

$$HNO_3(aq) + H_2O(l) \xrightarrow{100\%} H_3O^+(aq) + NO_3^-(aq)$$

$$pH = -\log [H_3O^+] = -\log (2.5 \times 10^{-2}) = 1.60$$

BALLPARK CHECK

Because the $[H_3O^+]$ is between 10^{-1} M and 10^{-2} M, the pH is between 1 and 2, in agreement with the solution.

WORKED EXAMPLE 14.8

CALCULATING THE pH OF A STRONG BASE SOLUTION

Calculate the pH of each of the following solutions:

(a) A 0.10 M solution of NaOH

(b) A 0.0050 M solution of slaked lime $[Ca(OH)_2]$

(c) A solution prepared by dissolving 0.28 g of lime (CaO) in enough water to make 1.00 L of limewater $[Ca(OH)_2(aq)]$

STRATEGY

Because NaOH and $Ca(OH)_2$ are strong bases, they are essentially 100% dissociated and their $[OH^-]$ is directly related to their initial concentrations. To calculate the $[OH^-]$ in a solution prepared by dissolving CaO, we must first do a mass-to-mole conversion and then use the balanced equation for the reaction of CaO with water to find the number of moles of OH^- in the solution. In each case, $[H_3O^+] = K_w/[OH^-]$ and $pH = -\log [H_3O^+]$.

SOLUTION

(a) Because NaOH is a strong base, $[OH^-] = 0.10$ M, $[H_3O^+] = 1.0 \times 10^{-13}$ M, and pH = 13.00.

$$[H_3O^+] = \frac{K_w}{[OH^-]} = \frac{1.0 \times 10^{-14}}{0.10} = 1.0 \times 10^{-13} \text{ M}$$

$$pH = -\log (1.0 \times 10^{-13}) = 13.00$$

(b) Because slaked lime is a strong base, it provides $2\,OH^-$ ions per $Ca(OH)_2$ formula unit. Therefore, $[OH^-] = 2(0.0050 \text{ M}) = 0.010$ M, $[H_3O^+] = 1.0 \times 10^{-12}$ M, and pH = 12.00:

$$[H_3O^+] = \frac{K_w}{[OH^-]} = \frac{1.0 \times 10^{-14}}{0.010} = 1.0 \times 10^{-12} \text{ M}$$

$$pH = -\log (1.0 \times 10^{-12}) = 12.00$$

(c) First calculate the number of moles of CaO dissolved from the given mass of CaO and its molar mass (56.1 g/mol):

$$\text{Moles of CaO} = 0.28 \text{ g CaO} \times \frac{1 \text{ mol CaO}}{56.1 \text{ g CaO}} = 0.0050 \text{ mol CaO}$$

Protonation of the O^{2-} ion produces 2 mol of OH^- per mole of CaO dissolved:

$$CaO(s) + H_2O(l) \longrightarrow Ca^{2+}(aq) + 2\,OH^-(aq)$$

$$\text{Moles of } OH^- \text{ produced} = 2(0.0050 \text{ mol}) = 0.010 \text{ mol}$$

Since the solution volume is 1.00 L,

$$[OH^-] = \frac{0.010 \text{ mol}}{1.00 \text{ L}} = 0.010 \text{ M}$$

The $[OH^-]$ happens to be identical to that in part (b). Therefore, pH = 12.00.

▶ **PROBLEM 14.12** Calculate the pH of the following solutions:
(a) 0.050 M $HClO_4$ (b) 6.0 M HCl   (c) 4.0 M KOH   (d) 0.010 M $Ba(OH)_2$

▶ **PROBLEM 14.13** Calculate the pH of a solution prepared by dissolving 0.25 g of BaO in enough water to make 0.500 L of solution.

14.8 EQUILIBRIA IN SOLUTIONS OF WEAK ACIDS

It's important to realize that a weak acid is not the same thing as a dilute solution of a strong acid. Whereas a strong acid is 100% dissociated in aqueous solution, a weak acid is only partially dissociated. It might therefore happen that the H_3O^+ concentration from complete dissociation of a dilute strong acid is the same as that from partial dissociation of a more concentrated weak acid.

Like the equilibrium reactions discussed in Chapter 13, the dissociation of a weak acid in water is characterized by an equilibrium equation. The equilibrium constant for the dissociation reaction, denoted K_a, is called the **acid-dissociation constant**:

$$HA(aq) + H_2O(l) \rightleftharpoons H_3O^+(aq) + A^-(aq)$$

$$K_a = \frac{[H_3O^+][A^-]}{[HA]}$$

Note that water has been omitted from the equilibrium equation because its concentration in dilute solutions is essentially the same as that in pure water (55.4 M) and pure liquids are always omitted from equilibrium equations (Section 13.4).

Values of K_a and pK_a for some typical weak acids are listed in Table 14.2. Just as the pH is defined as $-\log [H^+]$, so the pK_a of an acid is defined as $-\log K_a$. Note that the pK_a decreases as K_a increases. As indicated by the equilibrium equation, the larger the value of K_a, the stronger the acid. Thus, methanol ($K_a = 2.9 \times 10^{-16}$; $pK_a = 15.54$) is the weakest of the acids listed in Table 14.2, and nitrous acid ($K_a = 4.5 \times 10^{-4}$; $pK_a = 3.35$) is the strongest of the weak acids. Strong acids, such as HCl, have K_a values that are much greater than 1 and pK_a values that are negative. A more complete list of K_a values for weak acids is given in Appendix C.

TABLE 14.2   Acid-Dissociation Constants at 25 °C

	Acid	Molecular Formula	Structural Formula*	K_a	$pK_a^\dagger$
Stronger acid	Hydrochloric	HCl	H—Cl	2×10^6	-6.3
	Nitrous	HNO_2	H—O—N=O	4.5×10^{-4}	3.35
	Hydrofluoric	HF	H—F	3.5×10^{-4}	3.46
	Formic	HCO_2H	H—C(=O)—O—H	1.8×10^{-4}	3.74
	Ascorbic (vitamin C)	$C_6H_8O_6$		8.0×10^{-5}	4.10
	Acetic	CH_3CO_2H	CH_3—C(=O)—O—H	1.8×10^{-5}	4.74
	Hypochlorous	HOCl	H—O—Cl	3.5×10^{-8}	7.46
Weaker acid	Hydrocyanic	HCN	H—C≡N	4.9×10^{-10}	9.31
	Methanol	CH_3OH	CH_3—O—H	2.9×10^{-16}	15.54

* The proton that is transferred to water when the acid dissociates is shown in red. $^\dagger pK_a = -\log K_a$.

Numerical values of acid-dissociation constants are determined from pH measurements, as shown in Worked Example 14.9.

WORKED EXAMPLE 14.9

CALCULATING K_a AND pK_a FOR A WEAK ACID FROM THE pH OF THE SOLUTION

The pH of 0.250 M HF is 2.036. What are the values of K_a and pK_a for hydrofluoric acid?

STRATEGY

First, write the balanced equation for the dissociation equilibrium. Then, define x as the concentration of HF that dissociates and make the usual table under the balanced equation (Figure 13.6 (p. 508), Steps 1 and 2). Because x equals the H_3O^+ concentration, its value can be calculated from the pH. Finally, substitute the equilibrium concentrations into the equilibrium equation to obtain the value of K_a and take the negative log of K_a to obtain the pK_a.

SOLUTION

	$HF(aq)$ + $H_2O(l)$ $\rightleftharpoons$ $H_3O^+(aq)$ + $F^-(aq)$		
Initial concentration (M)	0.250	~0*	0
Change (M)	$-x$	$+x$	$+x$
Equilibrium concentration (M)	$(0.250 - x)$	x	x

*A very small concentration of H_3O^+ is present initially because of the dissociation of water.

We can calculate the value of x from the pH:

$$x = [H_3O^+] = \text{antilog}\,(-pH) = 10^{-pH} = 10^{-2.036} = 9.20 \times 10^{-3}\,M$$

The other equilibrium concentrations are

$$[F^-] = x = 9.20 \times 10^{-3}\,M$$

$$[HF] = 0.250 - x = 0.250 - 0.009\,20 = 0.241\,M$$

Substituting these concentrations into the equilibrium equation gives the value of K_a:

$$K_a = \frac{[H_3O^+][F^-]}{[HF]} = \frac{(x)(x)}{(0.250 - x)} = \frac{(9.20 \times 10^{-3})(9.20 \times 10^{-3})}{0.241} = 3.51 \times 10^{-4}$$

$$pK_a = -\log K_a = -\log\,(3.51 \times 10^{-4}) = 3.455$$

BALLPARK CHECK

Because the pH is about 2, $[H_3O^+]$ and $[F^-]$ are about $10^{-2}\,M$, and $[HF]$ is about 0.25 M $(0.250\,M - 10^{-2}\,M)$. The value of K_a is therefore about $(10^{-2})(10^{-2})/0.25$, or 4×10^{-4}, and the pK_a is between 3 and 4. The ballpark check and the solution agree.

▲ Of the hydrohalic acids HF, HCl, HBr, and HI, hydrofluoric acid is the only weak acid. Which of these acids has a positive value of pK_a?

▶ **PROBLEM 14.14** The pH of 0.10 M HOCl is 4.23. Calculate K_a and pK_a for hypochlorous acid, and check your answers against the values given in Table 14.2.

CONCEPTUAL PROBLEM 14.15 The following pictures represent aqueous solutions of three acids HA (A = X, Y, or Z); water molecules have been omitted for clarity:

- = HA
- = H_3O^+
- = A^-

HX   HY   HZ

(a) Arrange the three acids in order of increasing value of K_a.

(b) Which acid, if any, is a strong acid?

(c) Which solution has the highest pH, and which has the lowest pH?

14.9 CALCULATING EQUILIBRIUM CONCENTRATIONS IN SOLUTIONS OF WEAK ACIDS

Once the K_a value for a weak acid has been measured, it can be used to calculate equilibrium concentrations and the pH in a solution of the acid. We'll illustrate the approach to such a problem by calculating the concentrations of all species present (H_3O^+, CN^-, HCN, and OH^-) and the pH in a 0.10 M HCN solution. The approach we'll take is quite general and will be useful on numerous later occasions.

The key to solving acid–base equilibrium problems is to think about the chemistry—that is, to consider the possible proton-transfer reactions that can take place between Brønsted–Lowry acids and bases.

Step 1. Let's begin by listing the species present initially before any dissociation and by identifying them as acids or bases. Since water can behave either as an acid or a base, our list of species present initially is

$$\underset{\text{Acid}}{\text{HCN}} \qquad \underset{\text{Acid or base}}{\text{H}_2\text{O}}$$

Step 2. Because we have two acids (HCN and H_2O) and just one base (H_2O), two proton-transfer reactions are possible:

$$\text{HCN}(aq) + \text{H}_2\text{O}(l) \rightleftharpoons \text{H}_3\text{O}^+(aq) + \text{CN}^-(aq) \quad K_a = 4.9 \times 10^{-10}$$
$$\text{H}_2\text{O}(l) + \text{H}_2\text{O}(l) \rightleftharpoons \text{H}_3\text{O}^+(aq) + \text{OH}^-(aq) \quad K_w = 1.0 \times 10^{-14}$$

The value of K_a for HCN comes from Table 14.2.

Step 3. The proton-transfer reaction that proceeds farther to the right—the one that has the larger equilibrium constant—is called the **principal reaction**. Any other proton-transfer reactions are called **subsidiary reactions**. Since K_a for HCN is more than 10,000 times greater than K_w, the principal reaction in this case is dissociation of HCN and dissociation of water is a subsidiary reaction.

Although the principal reaction and the subsidiary reaction both produce H_3O^+ ions, there is only one H_3O^+ concentration in the solution, which must simultaneously satisfy the equilibrium equations for both reactions. To make life simple, we'll assume that essentially all the H_3O^+ comes from the principal reaction:

$$[\text{H}_3\text{O}^+] \text{ (total)} = [\text{H}_3\text{O}^+] \text{ (from principal reaction)} + [\text{H}_3\text{O}^+] \text{ (from subsidiary reaction)}$$

$$\approx [\text{H}_3\text{O}^+] \text{ (from principal reaction)}$$

In other words, we'll assume that the equilibrium concentration of H_3O^+ is established entirely by the dissociation of the stronger acid, HCN, while dissociation of the weaker acid, H_2O, makes a negligible contribution.

$$[\text{H}_3\text{O}^+] \text{ (total)} \approx [\text{H}_3\text{O}^+] \text{ (from HCN)}$$

Step 4. Next, we express the concentrations of the species involved in the principal reaction in terms of the concentration of HCN that dissociates—say, x mol/L. According to the balanced equation for the dissociation of HCN, if x mol/L of HCN dissociates, then x mol/L of H_3O^+ and x mol/L of CN^- are formed and the initial concentration of HCN before dissociation (0.10 mol/L in our example) is reduced to $(0.10 - x)$ mol/L at equilibrium. Let's summarize these considerations in the usual table under the principal reaction:

Principal reaction:	$\text{HCN}(aq)$ + $\text{H}_2\text{O}(l)$ $\rightleftharpoons$ $\text{H}_3\text{O}^+(aq)$ + $\text{CN}^-(aq)$		
Initial concentration (M)	0.10	~0	0
Change (M)	$-x$	$+x$	$+x$
Equilibrium concentration (M)	$0.10 - x$	x	x

Step 5. Substituting the equilibrium concentrations into the equilibrium equation for the principal reaction gives

$$K_a = 4.9 \times 10^{-10} = \frac{[H_3O^+][CN^-]}{[HCN]} = \frac{(x)(x)}{(0.10 - x)}$$

Because K_a is very small, the principal reaction will not proceed very far to the right and x will be negligibly small compared to 0.10. Therefore, we can make the approximation that $(0.10 - x) \approx 0.10$, which greatly simplifies the solution:

$$4.9 \times 10^{-10} = \frac{(x)(x)}{(0.10 - x)} = \frac{x^2}{0.10}$$

$$x^2 = 4.9 \times 10^{-11}$$

$$x = 7.0 \times 10^{-6}$$

Step 6. Next, we use the calculated value of x to obtain the equilibrium concentration of all species involved in the principal reaction:

$$[H_3O^+] = [CN^-] = x = 7.0 \times 10^{-6}\,M$$

$$[HCN] = 0.10 - x = 0.10 - (7.0 \times 10^{-6}) = 0.10\,M$$

Note that our simplifying approximation, $0.10 - x \approx 0.10$, is valid because x is only 7.0×10^{-6} and the initial [HCN] is known to only the second decimal place (0.10). In general, x can be neglected if the value of the initial concentration doesn't change when x is subtracted from it. In this example, x could not be neglected if it were greater than or equal to 0.01. *It's important to check the validity of the simplifying approximation in every problem* because x is not always negligible compared to the initial concentration of the acid. Worked Example 14.10 illustrates such a case.

Step 7. The species involved in the principal reaction are present in "big" concentrations. The species involved in the subsidiary reaction(s) are present in smaller concentrations that can be calculated from equilibrium equations for the subsidiary reaction(s) and the big concentrations already determined. In the present problem, only the OH^- concentration remains to be calculated. It is determined from the subsidiary equilibrium equation, $[H_3O^+][OH^-] = K_w$, and the H_3O^+ concentration $(7.0 \times 10^{-6}\,M)$ already calculated from the principal reaction:

$$[OH^-] = \frac{K_w}{[H_3O^+]} = \frac{1.0 \times 10^{-14}}{7.0 \times 10^{-6}} = 1.4 \times 10^{-9}\,M$$

Note that $[OH^-]$ is 5000 times smaller than $[H_3O^+]$.

At this point, we can check the initial assumption that essentially all the H_3O^+ comes from the principal reaction. Because the dissociation of water gives one H_3O^+ ion for each OH^- ion and because water is the only source of OH^-, $[H_3O^+]$ from the dissociation of water is equal to $[OH^-]$, which we just calculated to be $1.4 \times 10^{-9}\,M$. This value is negligible compared with $[H_3O^+]$ from the dissociation of HCN $(7.0 \times 10^{-6}\,M)$.

$$[H_3O^+]\,(\text{total}) = [H_3O^+]\,(\text{from HCN}) + [H_3O^+]\,(\text{from } H_2O)$$

$$= (7.0 \times 10^{-6}\,M) + (1.4 \times 10^{-9}\,M) = 7.0 \times 10^{-6}\,M$$

Step 8. Finally, we can calculate the pH:

$$pH = -\log(\text{total }[H_3O^+]) = -\log(7.0 \times 10^{-6}) = 5.15$$

Figure 14.6 summarizes the steps followed in solving this problem. This same systematic approach is applied to all acid–base equilibrium problems in this chapter and in Chapter 15.

Figure 14.6

Steps to follow in solving problems involving weak acids.

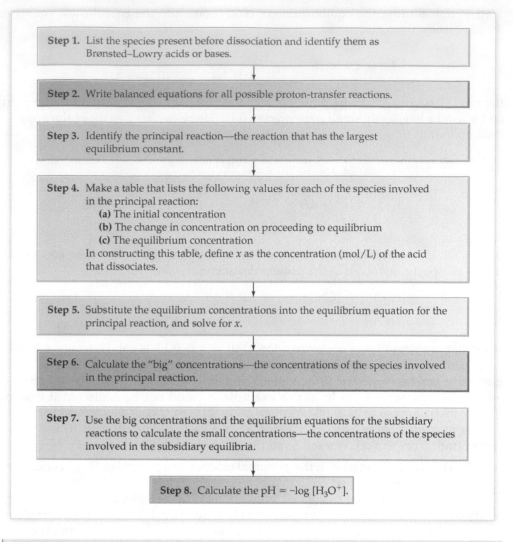

Step 1. List the species present before dissociation and identify them as Brønsted–Lowry acids or bases.

Step 2. Write balanced equations for all possible proton-transfer reactions.

Step 3. Identify the principal reaction—the reaction that has the largest equilibrium constant.

Step 4. Make a table that lists the following values for each of the species involved in the principal reaction:
  (a) The initial concentration
  (b) The change in concentration on proceeding to equilibrium
  (c) The equilibrium concentration
In constructing this table, define x as the concentration (mol/L) of the acid that dissociates.

Step 5. Substitute the equilibrium concentrations into the equilibrium equation for the principal reaction, and solve for x.

Step 6. Calculate the "big" concentrations—the concentrations of the species involved in the principal reaction.

Step 7. Use the big concentrations and the equilibrium equations for the subsidiary reactions to calculate the small concentrations—the concentrations of the species involved in the subsidiary equilibria.

Step 8. Calculate the pH = $-\log [H_3O^+]$.

WORKED EXAMPLE 14.10

CALCULATING THE pH AND THE EQUILIBRIUM CONCENTRATIONS IN A SOLUTION OF A WEAK ACID

Calculate the pH and the concentrations of all species present (H_3O^+, F^-, HF, and OH^-) in 0.050 M HF.

STRATEGY

Follow the eight-step sequence outlined in Figure 14.6.

SOLUTION

Step 1. The species present initially are

$$\underset{\text{Acid}}{HF} \qquad \underset{\text{Acid or base}}{H_2O}$$

Step 2. The possible proton-transfer reactions are

$$HF(aq) + H_2O(l) \rightleftharpoons H_3O^+(aq) + F^-(aq) \qquad K_a = 3.5 \times 10^{-4}$$
$$H_2O(l) + H_2O(l) \rightleftharpoons H_3O^+(aq) + OH^-(aq) \qquad K_w = 1.0 \times 10^{-14}$$

Step 3. Since $K_a \gg K_w$, the principal reaction is the dissociation of HF.

Step 4.

Principal reaction:	$HF(aq) + H_2O(l) \rightleftharpoons H_3O^+(aq) + F^-(aq)$		
Initial concentration (M)	0.050	~0	0
Change (M)	$-x$	$+x$	$+x$
Equilibrium concentration (M)	$0.050 - x$	x	x

Step 5. Substituting the equilibrium concentrations into the equilibrium equation for the principal reaction gives

$$K_a = 3.5 \times 10^{-4} = \frac{[H_3O^+][F^-]}{[HF]} = \frac{(x)(x)}{(0.050 - x)}$$

Making the usual approximation that x is negligible compared with the initial concentration of the acid, we assume that $(0.050 - x) \approx 0.050$ and then solve for an approximate value of x:

$$x^2 \approx (3.5 \times 10^{-4})(0.050)$$

$$x \approx 4.2 \times 10^{-3}$$

Since the initial concentration of HF (0.050 M) is known to the third decimal place, x is negligible compared with the initial [HF] only if x is less than 0.001 M. Our approximate value of x (0.0042 M) is not negligible compared with 0.050 M because 0.050 M − 0.0042 M = 0.046 M. Therefore, our approximation, $0.050 - x \approx 0.050$, is invalid, and we must solve the quadratic equation without making approximations:

$$3.5 \times 10^{-4} = \frac{x^2}{(0.050 - x)}$$

$$x^2 + (3.5 \times 10^{-4})x - (1.75 \times 10^{-5}) = 0$$

We use the standard quadratic formula (Appendix A.4):

$$x = \frac{-b \pm \sqrt{b^2 - 4ac}}{2a}$$

$$= \frac{-(3.5 \times 10^{-4}) \pm \sqrt{(3.5 \times 10^{-4})^2 - 4(1)(-1.75 \times 10^{-5})}}{2(1)}$$

$$= \frac{-(3.5 \times 10^{-4}) \pm (8.37 \times 10^{-3})}{2}$$

$$= +4.0 \times 10^{-3} \quad \text{or} \quad -4.4 \times 10^{-3}$$

Of the two solutions for x, only the positive value has physical meaning, since x is the H_3O^+ concentration. Therefore,

$$x = 4.0 \times 10^{-3}$$

Note that whether we must solve the quadratic equation depends on both the size of x and the number of significant figures in the initial concentration.

Step 6. The big concentrations are

$$[H_3O^+] = [F^-] = x = 4.0 \times 10^{-3} \, M$$
$$[HF] = (0.050 - x) = (0.050 - 0.0040) = 0.046 \, M$$

Step 7. The small concentration, $[OH^-]$, is obtained from the subsidiary equilibrium, the dissociation of water:

$$[OH^-] = \frac{K_w}{[H_3O^+]} = \frac{1.0 \times 10^{-14}}{4.0 \times 10^{-3}} = 2.5 \times 10^{-12} \, M$$

Step 8. $pH = -\log [H_3O^+] = -\log (4.0 \times 10^{-3}) = 2.40$

BALLPARK CHECK

Arithmetic errors in solving quadratic equations are common, so it's a good idea to check that the value of x obtained from the quadratic equation is reasonable. If the approximate value of x (4.2×10^{-3}) is fairly small compared to the initial concentration of the acid (0.050 M), as is the case in this problem, then the value of x obtained from the quadratic equation (4.0×10^{-3}) should be fairly close to the approximate value of x. The approximate and more exact values of x agree.

Acetic acid

▶ **PROBLEM 14.16** Acetic acid, CH_3CO_2H, is the solute that gives vinegar its characteristic odor and sour taste. Calculate the pH and the concentrations of all species present (H_3O^+, $CH_3CO_2^-$, CH_3CO_2H, and OH^-) in:

(a) 1.00 M CH_3CO_2H (b) 0.0100 M CH_3CO_2H

▶ **PROBLEM 14.17** A vitamin C tablet containing 250 mg of ascorbic acid ($C_6H_8O_6$; $K_a = 8.0 \times 10^{-5}$) is dissolved in a 250 mL glass of water. What is the pH of the solution?

14.10 PERCENT DISSOCIATION IN SOLUTIONS OF WEAK ACIDS

In addition to K_a, another useful measure of the strength of a weak acid is the **percent dissociation**, defined as the concentration of the acid that dissociates divided by the initial concentration of the acid times 100%:

$$\text{Percent dissociation} = \frac{[HA]_{\text{dissociated}}}{[HA]_{\text{initial}}} \times 100\%$$

Take, for example, the 1.00 M acetic acid solution in Problem 14.16a. If you solved that problem correctly, you found that 1.00 M CH_3CO_2H has $[H_3O^+] = 4.2 \times 10^{-3}$ M. Because $[H_3O^+]$ equals the concentration of CH_3CO_2H that dissociates, the percent dissociation in 1.00 M CH_3CO_2H is 0.42%:

$$\text{Percent dissociation} = \frac{[CH_3CO_2H]_{\text{dissociated}}}{[CH_3CO_2H]_{\text{initial}}} \times 100\%$$

$$= \frac{4.2 \times 10^{-3}\text{ M}}{1.00\text{ M}} \times 100\% = 0.42\%$$

In general, the percent dissociation depends on the acid and increases with increasing value of K_a. For a given weak acid, the percent dissociation increases with decreasing concentration, as shown in **Figure 14.7**. The 0.0100 M CH_3CO_2H solution in Problem 14.16b, for example, has $[H_3O^+] = 4.2 \times 10^{-4}$ M, and the percent dissociation is 4.2%:

$$\text{Percent dissociation} = \frac{[CH_3CO_2H]_{\text{dissociated}}}{[CH_3CO_2H]_{\text{initial}}} \times 100\%$$

$$= \frac{4.2 \times 10^{-4}\text{ M}}{0.0100\text{ M}} \times 100\% = 4.2\%$$

Figure 14.7
The percent dissociation of acetic acid increases as the concentration of the acid decreases.

▶ **PROBLEM 14.18** Calculate the percent dissociation of HF ($K_a = 3.5 \times 10^{-4}$) in:
(a) 0.050 M HF   (b) 0.50 M HF

14.11 POLYPROTIC ACIDS

Acids that contain more than one dissociable proton are called **polyprotic acids**. Polyprotic acids dissociate in a stepwise manner, and each dissociation step is characterized by its own acid-dissociation constant, K_{a1}, K_{a2}, and so forth. For example, carbonic acid (H_2CO_3), the diprotic acid that forms when gaseous carbon dioxide dissolves in water, is important in maintaining a constant pH in human blood. It undergoes the following dissociation reactions:

$$H_2CO_3(aq) + H_2O(l) \rightleftharpoons H_3O^+(aq) + HCO_3^-(aq) \quad K_{a1} = \frac{[H_3O^+][HCO_3^-]}{[H_2CO_3]} = 4.3 \times 10^{-7}$$

$$HCO_3^-(aq) + H_2O(l) \rightleftharpoons H_3O^+(aq) + CO_3^{2-}(aq) \quad K_{a2} = \frac{[H_3O^+][CO_3^{2-}]}{[HCO_3^-]} = 5.6 \times 10^{-11}$$

As shown in Table 14.3, the values of stepwise dissociation constants of polyprotic acids decrease, typically by a factor of 10^4 to 10^6, in the order $K_{a1} > K_{a2} > K_{a3}$. Because of electrostatic forces, it's more difficult to remove a positively charged proton from a negative ion such as HCO_3^- than from an uncharged molecule such as H_2CO_3, so $K_{a2} < K_{a1}$. In the case of triprotic acids (such as H_3PO_4), it's more difficult to remove H^+ from an anion with a double negative charge (such as HPO_4^{2-}) than from an anion with a single negative charge (such as $H_2PO_4^-$), so $K_{a3} < K_{a2}$.

TABLE 14.3 Stepwise Dissociation Constants for Polyprotic Acids at 25 °C

Name	Formula	K_{a1}	K_{a2}	K_{a3}
Carbonic acid	H_2CO_3	4.3×10^{-7}	5.6×10^{-11}	
Hydrogen sulfide*	H_2S	1.0×10^{-7}	$\sim 10^{-19}$	
Oxalic acid	$H_2C_2O_4$	5.9×10^{-2}	6.4×10^{-5}	
Phosphoric acid	H_3PO_4	7.5×10^{-3}	6.2×10^{-8}	4.8×10^{-13}
Sulfuric acid	H_2SO_4	Very large	1.2×10^{-2}	
Sulfurous acid	H_2SO_3	1.5×10^{-2}	6.3×10^{-8}	

*Because of its very small size, K_{a2} for H_2S is difficult to measure and its value is uncertain.

Polyprotic acid solutions contain a mixture of acids—H_2A, HA^-, and H_2O in the case of a diprotic acid. Because H_2A is by far the strongest acid, the principal reaction is the dissociation of H_2A and essentially all the H_3O^+ in the solution comes from the first dissociation step. Worked Example 14.11 shows how calculations are done.

Sulfuric acid (H_2SO_4), a strong acid, differs from most other polyprotic acids because it has a very large value of K_{a1}. Essentially all the H_2SO_4 molecules dissociate to give H_3O^+ and HSO_4^- ions, but only a fraction of the resulting HSO_4^- ions dissociate to give additional H_3O^+ ions and SO_4^{2-} ions. Worked Example 14.12 shows how to calculate the equilibrium concentrations and the pH.

▲ Carbonated beverages contain polyprotic acids such as carbonic acid and phosphoric acid.

WORKED EXAMPLE 14.11

CALCULATING THE pH AND THE EQUILIBRIUM CONCENTRATIONS IN A SOLUTION OF A DIPROTIC ACID

Calculate the pH and the concentrations of all species present (H_2CO_3, HCO_3^-, CO_3^{2-}, H_3O^+, and OH^-) in a 0.020 M carbonic acid solution.

STRATEGY

Use the eight-step procedure summarized in Figure 14.6. The values of K_{a1} and K_{a2} may be found in Table 14.3.

continued on next page

Carbonic acid

SOLUTION

Steps 1–3. The species present initially are H_2CO_3 (acid) and H_2O (acid or base). Because $K_{a1} \gg K_w$, the principal reaction is the dissociation of H_2CO_3.

Step 4.

Principal reaction	$H_2CO_3(aq) + H_2O(l) \rightleftharpoons H_3O^+(aq) + HCO_3^-(aq)$		
Initial concentration (M)	0.020	~0	0
Change (M)	$-x$	$+x$	$+x$
Equilibrium concentration (M)	$0.020 - x$	x	x

Step 5. Substituting the equilibrium concentrations into the equilibrium equation for the principal reaction gives

$$K_{a1} = 4.3 \times 10^{-7} = \frac{[H_3O^+][HCO_3^-]}{[H_2CO_3]} = \frac{(x)(x)}{(0.020 - x)}$$

Assuming that $(0.020 - x) \approx 0.020$,

$$x^2 = (4.3 \times 10^{-7})(0.020)$$

$$x = 9.3 \times 10^{-5} \qquad \text{Approximation } (0.020 - x) \approx 0.020 \text{ is justified.}$$

Step 6. The big concentrations are

$$[H_3O^+] = [HCO_3^-] = x = 9.3 \times 10^{-5} \text{ M}$$

$$[H_2CO_3] = 0.020 - x = 0.020 - 0.000\,093 = 0.020 \text{ M}$$

Step 7. The small concentrations are obtained from the subsidiary equilibria—(1) dissociation of HCO_3^- and (2) dissociation of water—and from the big concentrations already determined:

$$(1) \quad HCO_3^-(aq) + H_2O(l) \rightleftharpoons H_3O^+(aq) + CO_3^{2-}(aq)$$

$$K_{a2} = 5.6 \times 10^{-11} = \frac{[H_3O^+][CO_3^{2-}]}{[HCO_3^-]} = \frac{(9.3 \times 10^{-5})[CO_3^{2-}]}{9.3 \times 10^{-5}}$$

$$[CO_3^{2-}] = K_{a2} = 5.6 \times 10^{-11} \text{ M}$$

(In general, for a solution of a weak diprotic acid that has a very small value of K_{a2}, $[A^{2-}] = K_{a2}$.)

$$(2) \quad [OH^-] = \frac{K_w}{[H_3O^+]} = \frac{1.0 \times 10^{-14}}{9.3 \times 10^{-5}} = 1.1 \times 10^{-10} \text{ M}$$

The second dissociation of H_2CO_3 produces a negligible amount of H_3O^+ compared with the H_3O^+ obtained from the first dissociation. Of the 9.3×10^{-5} mol/L of HCO_3^- produced by the first dissociation, only 5.6×10^{-11} mol/L dissociates to form H_3O^+ and CO_3^{2-}.

Step 8. $pH = -\log [H_3O^+] = -\log (9.3 \times 10^{-5}) = 4.03$

BALLPARK CHECK

When the value of x can be neglected compared with the initial concentration of the acid (Step 5), the $[H_3O^+]$ equals the square root of the product of K_{a1} and the initial concentration of the acid. In this problem, $[H_3O^+]$ is the square root of approximately $(4 \times 10^{-7})(2 \times 10^{-2})$, or about 10^{-4} M. Therefore, the pH ≈ 4, in agreement with the solution.

WORKED EXAMPLE 14.12

CALCULATING THE pH AND THE EQUILIBRIUM CONCENTRATIONS IN A SULFURIC ACID SOLUTION

Calculate the pH and the concentrations of all species present (HSO_4^-, SO_4^{2-}, H_3O^+, and OH^-) in 0.10 M H_2SO_4.

STRATEGY

Use the eight-step procedure summarized in Figure 14.6.

Sulfuric acid

SOLUTION

Steps 1–3. Because H_2SO_4 is essentially 100% dissociated to give H_3O^+ and HSO_4^- (K_{a1} is very large), the species present initially are H_3O^+ (acid), HSO_4^- (acid), and H_2O (acid or base). Although H_3O^+ is the strongest acid present, proton transfer from H_3O^+ to H_2O to give H_2O and H_3O^+ is not considered to be the principal reaction because it does not change any of the concentrations. The next strongest acid present is HSO_4^- ($K_{a2} > K_w$), so we consider the principal reaction to be dissociation of HSO_4^-.

Step 4.

Principal reaction	$HSO_4^-(aq) + H_2O(l) \rightleftharpoons H_3O^+(aq) + SO_4^{2-}(aq)$		
Initial concentration (M)	0.10	0.10	0
Change (M)	$-x$	$+x$	$+x$
Equilibrium concentration (M)	$0.10 - x$	$0.10 + x$	x

▲ The brightness of the planet Venus is due in part to thick, highly reflective clouds in its upper atmosphere. These clouds consist of sulfur dioxide and droplets of sulfuric acid.

Note that the second dissociation step takes place in the presence of 0.10 M H_3O^+ from the first dissociation step.

Step 5. Substituting the equilibrium concentrations into the equilibrium equation for the principal reaction gives

$$K_{a2} = 1.2 \times 10^{-2} = \frac{[H_3O^+][SO_4^{2-}]}{[HSO_4^-]} = \frac{(0.10 + x)(x)}{(0.10 - x)}$$

Neglecting x compared with 0.10 and solving this equation would give $x = K_{a2} = 0.012$, which is not negligible compared with 0.10. Therefore, we use the quadratic equation to obtain the value of x:

$$0.0012 - 0.012x = 0.10x + x^2$$
$$x^2 + 0.112x - 0.0012 = 0$$
$$x = \frac{-b \pm \sqrt{b^2 - 4ac}}{2a} = \frac{-0.112 \pm \sqrt{(0.112)^2 - 4(1)(-0.0012)}}{2(1)}$$
$$= \frac{-0.112 \pm 0.132}{2}$$
$$= +0.010 \quad \text{or} \quad -0.122$$

Because x is the SO_4^{2-} concentration, it must be positive. Therefore,

$$x = 0.010$$

Step 6. The big concentrations are

$$[SO_4^{2-}] = x = 0.010 \text{ M}$$
$$[HSO_4^-] = 0.10 - x = 0.10 - 0.010 = 0.09 \text{ M}$$
$$[H_3O^+] = 0.10 + x = 0.10 + 0.010 = 0.11 \text{ M}$$

Step 7. The small concentration, $[OH^-]$, is obtained from the subsidiary equilibrium, dissociation of water:

$$[OH^-] = \frac{K_w}{[H_3O^+]} = \frac{1.0 \times 10^{-14}}{0.11} = 9.1 \times 10^{-14} \text{ M}$$

Step 8. $pH = -\log [H_3O^+] = -\log 0.11 = 0.96$

BALLPARK CHECK

The easiest check in this case is to substitute the big concentrations obtained in Step 6 into the equilibrium equation for the second dissociation step and show that the equilibrium constant expression equals K_{a2}:

$$\frac{[H_3O^+][SO_4^{2-}]}{[HSO_4^-]} = \frac{(0.11)(0.010)}{0.09} = 0.012 = K_{a2}$$

Since $[H_3O^+]$ is approximately 10^{-1} M, the pH should be about 1, in agreement with the detailed solution.

▶ **PROBLEM 14.19** Calculate the pH and the concentrations of all species present in 0.10 M H_2SO_3. Values of K_a are in Table 14.3.

▶ **PROBLEM 14.20** Like sulfuric acid, selenic acid (H_2SeO_4) is a diprotic acid that has a very large value of K_{a1}. Calculate the pH and the concentrations of all species present in 0.50 M H_2SeO_4 ($K_{a2} = 1.2 \times 10^{-2}$).

14.12 EQUILIBRIA IN SOLUTIONS OF WEAK BASES

Weak bases, such as ammonia, accept a proton from water to give the conjugate acid of the base and OH^- ions:

$$NH_3(aq) + H_2O(l) \rightleftharpoons NH_4^+(aq) + OH^-(aq)$$

The equilibrium reaction of any base B with water is characterized by an equilibrium equation similar in form to that for the dissociation of a weak acid. The equilibrium constant is called the **base-dissociation constant, K_b**:

$$B(aq) + H_2O(l) \rightleftharpoons BH^+(aq) + OH^-(aq)$$

$$K_b = \frac{[BH^+][OH^-]}{[B]}$$

As usual, $[H_2O]$ is omitted from the equilibrium constant expression. Table 14.4 lists some typical weak bases and gives their K_b values at 25 °C. (The term *base-protonation constant* might be a more descriptive name for K_b, but the term *base-dissociation constant* is still widely used.)

TABLE 14.4 K_b Values for Some Weak Bases and K_a Values for Their Conjugate Acids at 25 °C

Base	Formula, B	K_b	Conjugate Acid, BH^+	K_a
Ammonia	NH_3	1.8×10^{-5}	NH_4^+	5.6×10^{-10}
Aniline	$C_6H_5NH_2$	4.3×10^{-10}	$C_6H_5NH_3^+$	2.3×10^{-5}
Dimethylamine	$(CH_3)_2NH$	5.4×10^{-4}	$(CH_3)_2NH_2^+$	1.9×10^{-11}
Hydrazine	N_2H_4	8.9×10^{-7}	$N_2H_5^+$	1.1×10^{-8}
Hydroxylamine	NH_2OH	9.1×10^{-9}	NH_3OH^+	1.1×10^{-6}
Methylamine	CH_3NH_2	3.7×10^{-4}	$CH_3NH_3^+$	2.7×10^{-11}

Many weak bases are organic compounds called *amines*, derivatives of ammonia in which one or more hydrogen atoms are replaced by an organic, carbon-based group, such as a methyl group (CH_3). Methylamine (CH_3NH_2), for example, is an organic amine responsible for the odor of rotting fish.

▲ Many over-the-counter drugs contain salts formed from amines and hydrochloric acid.

Amines are organic compounds in which one, two, or three substituents, such as a methyl group, are attached to a basic nitrogen atom.

Methyl group

$CH_3-\overset{..}{N}-H$ $CH_3-\overset{..}{N}-CH_3$ $CH_3-\overset{..}{N}-CH_3$
$\quad\quad |$ $|$ $|$
$\quad\quad H$ H CH_3

Methylamine   Dimethylamine   Trimethylamine

The basicity of an amine is due to the lone pair of electrons on the nitrogen atom, which can be used for bonding to a proton.

Equilibria in solutions of weak bases are treated by the same procedure used for solving problems involving weak acids. Worked Example 14.13 illustrates the procedure.

WORKED EXAMPLE 14.13

CALCULATING THE pH AND THE EQUILIBRIUM CONCENTRATIONS IN A SOLUTION OF A WEAK BASE

Codeine ($C_{18}H_{21}NO_3$), a drug used in painkillers and cough medicines, is a naturally occurring amine that has $K_b = 1.6 \times 10^{-6}$. Calculate the pH and the concentrations of all species present in a 0.0012 M solution of codeine.

STRATEGY

Use the procedure outlined in Figure 14.6.

SOLUTION

Step 1. Let's use Cod as an abbreviation for codeine and $CodH^+$ for its conjugate acid. The species present initially are Cod (base) and H_2O (acid or base).

Step 2. There are two possible proton-transfer reactions:

$$Cod(aq) + H_2O(l) \rightleftharpoons CodH^+(aq) + OH^-(aq) \qquad K_b = 1.6 \times 10^{-6}$$
$$H_2O(l) + H_2O(l) \rightleftharpoons H_3O^+(aq) + OH^-(aq) \qquad K_w = 1.0 \times 10^{-14}$$

Codeine

Step 3. Since Cod is a much stronger base than H_2O ($K_b \gg K_w$), the principal reaction involves the protonation of codeine.

Step 4.

Principal reaction	$Cod(aq) + H_2O(l) \rightleftharpoons CodH^+(aq) + OH^-(aq)$		
Initial concentration (M)	0.0012	0	~0
Change (M)	$-x$	$+x$	$+x$
Equilibrium concentration (M)	$0.0012 - x$	x	x

Step 5. The value of x is obtained from the equilibrium equation:

$$K_b = 1.6 \times 10^{-6} = \frac{[CodH^+][OH^-]}{[Cod]} = \frac{(x)(x)}{(0.0012 - x)}$$

Assuming that $(0.0012 - x) \approx 0.0012$,

$$x^2 - (1.6 \times 10^{-6})(0.0012)$$

$$x = 4.4 \times 10^{-5} \qquad \text{Approximation } (0.0012 - x) \approx 0.0012 \text{ is justified.}$$

Step 6. The big concentrations are

$$[CodH^+] = [OH^-] = x = 4.4 \times 10^{-5} \text{ M}$$
$$[Cod] = 0.0012 - x = 0.0012 - 0.000\,044 = 0.0012 \text{ M}$$

Step 7. The small concentration is obtained from the subsidiary equilibrium, the dissociation of water:

$$[H_3O^+] = \frac{K_w}{[OH^-]} = \frac{1.0 \times 10^{-14}}{4.4 \times 10^{-5}} = 2.3 \times 10^{-10} \text{ M}$$

Step 8. $pH = -\log [H_3O^+] = -\log (2.3 \times 10^{-10}) = 9.64$

The pH is greater than 7, as expected for a solution of a weak base.

BALLPARK CHECK

Because x is negligible compared with the initial concentration of codeine (Step 5), the $[OH^-]$ equals the square root of the product of K_b and the initial concentration of codeine. Therefore, $[OH^-]$ equals the square root of approximately $(16 \times 10^{-7}) \times (1 \times 10^{-3})$, or about 4×10^{-5}. Since the $[OH^-]$ is between 10^{-5} M and 10^{-4} M, the $[H_3O^+]$ is between 10^{-9} M and 10^{-10} M, and so the pH is between 9 and 10. The ballpark check and the solution agree.

Strychnine

▶ **PROBLEM 14.21** Calculate the pH and the concentrations of all species present in 0.40 M NH_3 ($K_b = 1.8 \times 10^{-5}$).

▶ **PROBLEM 14.22** Strychnine ($C_{21}H_{22}N_2O_2$), a deadly poison used for killing rodents, is a weak base having $K_b = 1.8 \times 10^{-6}$. Calculate the pH of a saturated solution of strychnine (16 mg/100 mL).

14.13 RELATION BETWEEN K_a AND K_b

We've seen in previous sections that the strength of an acid can be expressed by its value of K_a and the strength of a base can be expressed by its value of K_b. For a conjugate acid–base pair, the two equilibrium constants are related in a simple way that makes it possible to calculate either one from the other. Let's consider the conjugate acid–base pair NH_4^+ and NH_3, for example, where K_a refers to proton transfer from the acid NH_4^+ to water and K_b refers to proton transfer from water to the base NH_3. The sum of the two reactions is simply the dissociation of water:

$$\cancel{NH_4^+}(aq) + H_2O(l) \rightleftharpoons H_3O^+(aq) + \cancel{NH_3}(aq) \qquad K_a = \frac{[H_3O^+][NH_3]}{[NH_4^+]} = 5.6 \times 10^{-10}$$

$$\cancel{NH_3}(aq) + H_2O(l) \rightleftharpoons \cancel{NH_4^+}(aq) + OH^-(aq) \qquad K_b = \frac{[NH_4^+][OH^-]}{[NH_3]} = 1.8 \times 10^{-5}$$

Net: $\quad 2 H_2O(l) \rightleftharpoons H_3O^+(aq) + OH^-(aq) \qquad K_w = [H_3O^+][OH^-] = 1.0 \times 10^{-14}$

The equilibrium constant for the net reaction equals the product of the equilibrium constants for the reactions added:

$$K_a \times K_b = \frac{[H_3O^+]\cancel{[NH_3]}}{\cancel{[NH_4^+]}} \times \frac{\cancel{[NH_4^+]}[OH^-]}{\cancel{[NH_3]}} = [H_3O^+][OH^-] = K_w$$

$$= (5.6 \times 10^{-10})(1.8 \times 10^{-5}) = 1.0 \times 10^{-14}$$

What we've shown in this particular case is true in general. *Whenever chemical equations for two (or more) reactions are added to get the equation for a net reaction, the equilibrium constant for the net reaction equals the product of the equilibrium constants for the individual reactions:*

$$K_{net} = K_1 \times K_2 \times \cdots$$

For any conjugate acid–base pair, the product of the acid-dissociation constant for the acid and the base-dissociation constant for the base always equals the ion-product constant for water:

$$K_a \times K_b = K_w$$

As the strength of an acid increases (larger K_a), the strength of its conjugate base decreases (smaller K_b) because the product $K_a \times K_b$ remains constant at 1.0×10^{-14}. This inverse relationship between the strength of an acid and the strength of its conjugate base was illustrated qualitatively in Table 14.1. Taking the negative base-10 logarithm of both sides of the equation $K_a \times K_b = K_w$ gives another useful relationship:

$$pK_a + pK_b = pK_w = 14.00$$

where $pK_a = -\log K_a$, $pK_b = -\log K_b$, and $pK_w = -\log K_w$.

Compilations of equilibrium constants, such as Appendix C, generally list either K_a or K_b, but not both, because K_a is easily calculated from K_b and vice versa:

$$K_a = \frac{K_w}{K_b} \qquad \text{and} \qquad K_b = \frac{K_w}{K_a}$$

Similarly, pK_a can be calculated from pK_b and vice versa:

$$pK_a = 14.00 - pK_b \quad \text{and} \quad pK_b = 14.00 - pK_a$$

WORKED EXAMPLE 14.14

RELATING K_a, K_b, pK_a, AND pK_b

(a) K_b for trimethylamine is 6.5×10^{-5}. Calculate K_a for the trimethylammonium ion, $(CH_3)_3NH^+$.

(b) K_a for HCN is 4.9×10^{-10}. Calculate K_b for CN^-.

(c) Pyridine (C_5H_5N), an organic solvent, has $pK_b = 8.74$. What is the value of pK_a for the pyridinium ion, $C_5H_5NH^+$?

Pyridine

STRATEGY

To calculate K_a from K_b (or vice versa), use the equation $K_a = K_w/K_b$ or $K_b = K_w/K_a$. To calculate pK_a from pK_b, use the equation $pK_a = 14.00 - pK_b$.

SOLUTION

(a) K_a for $(CH_3)_3NH^+$ is the equilibrium constant for the acid-dissociation reaction

$$(CH_3)_3NH^+(aq) + H_2O(l) \rightleftharpoons H_3O^+(aq) + (CH_3)_3N(aq)$$

Because $K_a = K_w/K_b$, we can find K_a for $(CH_3)_3NH^+$ from K_b for its conjugate base $(CH_3)_3N$:

$$K_a = \frac{K_w}{K_b} = \frac{1.0 \times 10^{-14}}{6.5 \times 10^{-5}} = 1.5 \times 10^{-10}$$

(b) K_b for CN^- is the equilibrium constant for the base-protonation reaction

$$CN^-(aq) + H_2O(l) \rightleftharpoons HCN(aq) + OH^-(aq)$$

Because $K_b = K_w/K_a$, we can find K_b for CN^- from K_a for its conjugate acid HCN:

$$K_b = \frac{K_w}{K_a} = \frac{1.0 \times 10^{-14}}{4.9 \times 10^{-10}} = 2.0 \times 10^{-5}$$

(c) We can find pK_a for $C_5H_5NH^+$ from pK_b for C_5H_5N:

$$pK_a = 14.00 - pK_b = 14.00 - 8.74 = 5.26$$

▸ **PROBLEM 14.23**

(a) Piperidine ($C_5H_{11}N$) is an amine found in black pepper. Find K_b for piperidine in Appendix C, and then calculate K_a for the $C_5H_{11}NH^+$ cation.

(b) Find K_a for HOCl in Appendix C, and then calculate K_b for OCl^-.

(c) The value of pK_a for formic acid (HCO_2H) is 3.74. What is the value of pK_b for the formate ion (HCO_2^-)?

Piperidine

14.14 ACID–BASE PROPERTIES OF SALTS

When an acid neutralizes a base (Section 4.1), an ionic compound called a *salt* is formed. Salt solutions can be neutral, acidic, or basic, depending on the acid–base properties of the constituent cations and anions (**Figure 14.8**). As a general rule, salts formed by the reaction of a strong acid with a strong base give neutral solutions, salts formed by the reaction of a strong acid with a weak base give acidic solutions, and salts formed by the reaction of a weak acid with a strong base give basic solutions. It's as if the influence of the stronger partner dominates:

Strong acid + Strong base ⟶ Neutral solution

Strong acid + Weak base ⟶ **Acidic** solution

Weak acid + Strong base ⟶ **Basic** solution

Figure 14.8

Aqueous salt solutions (0.10 M) of NaCl, NH₄Cl, AlCl₃, NaCN, and (NH₄)₂CO₃. A few drops of universal indicator have been added to each solution. Universal indicator is red at pH 3, yellow at pH 5, green at pH 7, and blue at pH ≥ 10.

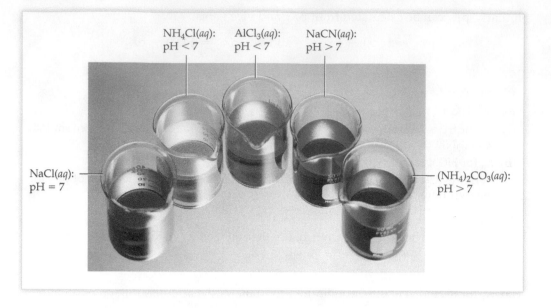

Salts That Yield Neutral Solutions

Salts such as NaCl that are derived from a strong base (NaOH) and a strong acid (HCl) yield neutral solutions because neither the cation nor the anion reacts appreciably with water to produce H_3O^+ or OH^- ions. As the conjugate base of a strong acid, Cl^- has no tendency to make the solution basic by picking up a proton from water. As the cation of a strong base, the hydrated Na^+ ion has only a negligible tendency to make the solution acidic by transferring a proton to a solvent water molecule.

The following ions do not react appreciably with water to produce either H_3O^+ or OH^- ions:

• Cations from strong bases:

  Alkali metal cations of group 1A (Li^+, Na^+, K^+)

  Alkaline earth cations of group 2A (Mg^{2+}, Ca^{2+}, Sr^{2+}, Ba^{2+}), except for Be^{2+}

• Anions from strong monoprotic acids:

  Cl^-, Br^-, I^-, NO_3^-, and ClO_4^-

Salts that contain only these ions give neutral solutions in pure water (pH = 7).

Salts That Yield Acidic Solutions

Salts such as NH_4Cl that are derived from a weak base (NH_3) and a strong acid (HCl) produce acidic solutions. In such a case, the anion is neither an acid nor a base, but the cation is a weak acid:

$$NH_4^+(aq) + H_2O(l) \rightleftharpoons H_3O^+(aq) + NH_3(aq)$$

Related ammonium salts derived from amines, such as [CH₃NH₃]Cl, [(CH₃)₂NH₂]Cl, and [(CH₃)₃NH]Cl, also give acidic solutions because they too have cations with at least one dissociable proton. The pH of a solution that contains an acidic cation can be calculated by the standard procedure outlined in Figure 14.6. For a 0.10 M NH_4Cl solution, the pH is 5.12. Although the reaction of a cation or anion of a salt with water to produce H_3O^+ or OH^- ions is sometimes called a *salt hydrolysis reaction*, there is no fundamental difference between a salt hydrolysis reaction and any other Brønsted–Lowry acid–base reaction.

Another type of acidic cation is the hydrated cation of a small, highly charged metal ion, such as Al^{3+}. In aqueous solution, the Al^{3+} ion bonds to six water molecules to give the hydrated cation $Al(H_2O)_6^{3+}$. As shown in **Figure 14.9**, the negative (oxygen) end of each dipolar water molecule bonds to the positive metal cation and the six water molecules are located at the vertices of a regular octahedron.

Figure 14.9
Octahedral structure of the $Al(H_2O)_6^{3+}$ cation.

A regular octahedron has eight equilateral triangular faces and six vertices.

The six Al–O bonds point toward the six vertices of the octahedron.

A model of the $Al(H_2O)_6^{3+}$ cation, showing the octahedral arrangement of bonds to the six H_2O molecules.

All metal ions exist in aqueous solution as hydrated cations, but the acidity of these cations varies greatly depending on the charge and size of the unhydrated metal ion. Because of the high (3+) charge on the Al^{3+} ion, electrons in the O—H bonds of the bound water molecules are attracted toward the Al^{3+} ion. The attraction is strong because the Al^{3+} ion is small and the electrons in the O—H bonds are relatively close to the center of positive charge. As a result, electron density shifts from the O—H bonds toward the Al^{3+} ion, thus weakening the O—H bonds and increasing their polarity, which in turn eases the transfer of a proton to a solvent water molecule:

Electrons are attracted toward Al^{3+}, thus weakening the O–H bonds.

This O–H bond breaks, and H^+ is transferred to H_2O.

$$Al(H_2O)_6^{3+}(aq) \quad + \quad H_2O(l) \quad \rightleftharpoons \quad Al(H_2O)_5(OH)^{2+}(aq) \quad + \quad H_3O^+(aq)$$

The acid-dissociation constant for $Al(H_2O)_6^{3+}$, $K_a = 1.4 \times 10^{-5}$, is much larger than $K_w = 1.0 \times 10^{-14}$, which means that the water molecules in the hydrated cation are much stronger proton donors than are free solvent water molecules. In fact, the acid strength of $Al(H_2O)_6^{3+}$ is comparable to that of acetic acid, which has $K_a = 1.8 \times 10^{-5}$. In general, the acidity of hydrated main-group cations increases from left to right in the periodic table as the metal ion charge increases and the metal ion size decreases ($Li^+ < Be^{2+}$, $Na^+ < Mg^{2+} < Al^{3+}$). Transition metal cations, such as Zn^{2+}, Cr^{3+}, and Fe^{3+}, also give acidic solutions; their K_a values are listed in Table C.2 of Appendix C.

WORKED EXAMPLE 14.15

CALCULATING THE pH OF AN ACIDIC SALT SOLUTION

Calculate the pH of a 0.10 M solution of $AlCl_3$; K_a for $Al(H_2O)_6^{3+}$ is 1.4×10^{-5}.

STRATEGY

Because this problem is similar to others done earlier, we'll abbreviate the procedure in Figure 14.6.

SOLUTION

Steps 1–4. The species present initially are $Al(H_2O)_6^{3+}$ (acid), Cl^- (inert), and H_2O (acid or base). Because $Al(H_2O)_6^{3+}$ is a much stronger acid than water ($K_a \gg K_w$), the principal reaction is dissociation of $Al(H_2O)_6^{3+}$:

Principal reaction	$Al(H_2O)_6^{3+}(aq) + H_2O(l) \rightleftharpoons H_3O^+(aq) + Al(H_2O)_5(OH)^{2+}(aq)$		
Equilibrium concentration (M)	$0.10 - x$	x	x

Step 5. The value of x is obtained from the equilibrium equation:

$$K_a = 1.4 \times 10^{-5} = \frac{[H_3O^+][Al(H_2O)_5(OH)^{2+}]}{[Al(H_2O)_6^{3+}]} = \frac{(x)(x)}{(0.10 - x)} \approx \frac{x^2}{0.10}$$

$$x = [H_3O^+] = 1.2 \times 10^{-3} \, M$$

Step 8. $pH = -\log(1.2 \times 10^{-3}) = 2.92$

Thus, $Al(H_2O)_6^{3+}$ is a much stronger acid than NH_4^+, which agrees with the colors of the indicator in Figure 14.8.

▶ **PROBLEM 14.24** Predict whether the following salt solutions are neutral or acidic, and calculate the pH of each:
(a) 0.25 M NH_4Br **(b)** 0.40 M $ZnCl_2$; K_a for $Zn(H_2O)_6^{2+}$ is 2.5×10^{-10}.

Salts That Yield Basic Solutions

Salts such as NaCN that are derived from a strong base (NaOH) and a weak acid (HCN) yield basic solutions. In this case, the cation is neither an acid nor a base but the anion is a weak base:

$$CN^-(aq) + H_2O(l) \rightleftharpoons HCN(aq) + OH^-(aq)$$

Other anions that exhibit basic properties are listed in Table 14.1 and include NO_2^-, F^-, $CH_3CO_2^-$, and CO_3^{2-}. The pH of a basic salt solution can be calculated by the standard procedure, as shown in Worked Example 14.16.

WORKED EXAMPLE 14.16

CALCULATING THE pH OF A BASIC SALT SOLUTION

Calculate the pH of a 0.10 M solution of NaCN; K_a for HCN is 4.9×10^{-10}.

STRATEGY

Use the procedure summarized in Figure 14.6.

SOLUTION

Step 1. The species present initially are Na^+ (inert), CN^- (base), and H_2O (acid or base).

Step 2. There are two possible proton-transfer reactions:

$$CN^-(aq) + H_2O(l) \rightleftharpoons HCN(aq) + OH^-(aq) \qquad K_b$$

$$H_2O(l) + H_2O(l) \rightleftharpoons H_3O^+(aq) + OH^-(aq) \qquad K_w$$

Step 3. As shown in Worked Example 14.14b, $K_b = K_w/(K_a$ for HCN$) = 2.0 \times 10^{-5}$. Because $K_b \gg K_w$, CN^- is a stronger base than H_2O and the principal reaction is proton transfer from H_2O to CN^-.

Step 4.

Principal reaction	$CN^-(aq) + H_2O(l) \rightleftharpoons HCN(aq) + OH^-(aq)$		
Equilibrium concentration (M)	$0.10 - x$	x	x

Step 5. The value of x is obtained from the equilibrium equation:

$$K_b = 2.0 \times 10^{-5} = \frac{[HCN][OH^-]}{[CN^-]} = \frac{(x)(x)}{(0.10 - x)} \approx \frac{x^2}{0.10}$$

$$x = [OH^-] = 1.4 \times 10^{-3}\ M$$

Step 7. $[H_3O^+] = \dfrac{K_w}{[OH^-]} = \dfrac{1.0 \times 10^{-14}}{1.4 \times 10^{-3}} = 7.1 \times 10^{-12}$

Step 8. pH $= -\log(7.1 \times 10^{-12}) = 11.15$

The solution is basic, which agrees with the color of the indicator in Figure 14.8.

▶ **PROBLEM 14.25** Calculate the pH of 0.20 M NaNO$_2$; K_a for HNO$_2$ is 4.6×10^{-4}.

Salts That Contain Acidic Cations and Basic Anions

Finally, let's look at a salt such as $(NH_4)_2CO_3$ in which both the cation and the anion can undergo proton-transfer reactions. Because NH_4^+ is a weak acid and CO_3^{2-} is a weak base, the pH of an $(NH_4)_2CO_3$ solution depends on the relative acid strength of the cation and base strength of the anion:

$$NH_4^+(aq) + H_2O(l) \rightleftharpoons H_3O^+(aq) + NH_3(aq) \qquad \text{Acid strength } (K_a)$$

$$CO_3^{2-}(aq) + H_2O(l) \rightleftharpoons HCO_3^-(aq) + OH^-(aq) \qquad \text{Base strength } (K_b)$$

We can distinguish three possible cases:

- $K_a > K_b$: If K_a for the cation is greater than K_b for the anion, the solution will contain an excess of H_3O^+ ions (pH < 7).
- $K_a < K_b$: If K_a for the cation is less than K_b for the anion, the solution will contain an excess of OH^- ions (pH > 7).
- $K_a \approx K_b$: If K_a for the cation and K_b for the anion are comparable, the solution will contain approximately equal concentrations of H_3O^+ and OH^- ions (pH ≈ 7).

To determine whether an $(NH_4)_2CO_3$ solution is acidic, basic, or neutral, let's work out the values of K_a for NH_4^+ and K_b for CO_3^{2-}:

$$K_a \text{ for } NH_4^+ = \frac{K_w}{K_b \text{ for } NH_3} = \frac{1.0 \times 10^{-14}}{1.8 \times 10^{-5}} = 5.6 \times 10^{-10}$$

$$K_b \text{ for } CO_3^{2-} = \frac{K_w}{K_a \text{ for } HCO_3^-} = \frac{K_w}{K_{a2} \text{ for } H_2CO_3} = \frac{1.0 \times 10^{-14}}{5.6 \times 10^{-11}} = 1.8 \times 10^{-4}$$

Because $K_a < K_b$, the solution is basic (pH > 7), in accord with the color of the indicator in Figure 14.8.

A summary of the acid–base properties of salts is given in Table 14.5.

TABLE 14.5   Acid–Base Properties of Salts

Type of Salt	Examples	Ions That React with Water	pH of Solution
Cation from strong base; anion from strong acid	NaCl, KNO₃, BaI₂	None	~7
Cation from weak base; anion from strong acid	NH₄Cl, NH₄NO₃, [(CH₃)₃NH]Cl	Cation	<7
Small, highly charged, cation; anion from strong acid	AlCl₃, Cr(NO₃)₃, Fe(ClO₄)₃	Hydrated cation	<7
Cation from strong base; anion from weak acid	NaCN, KF, Na₂CO₃	Anion	>7
Cation from weak base; anion from weak acid	NH₄CN, NH₄F, (NH₄)₂CO₃	Cation and anion	<7 if $K_a > K_b$ >7 if $K_a < K_b$ ~7 if $K_a \approx K_b$

▸ **PROBLEM 14.26**   Calculate K_a for the cation and K_b for the anion in an aqueous NH₄CN solution. Is the solution acidic, basic, or neutral?

▸ **PROBLEM 14.27**   Classify each of the following salt solutions as acidic, basic, or neutral:
   (a) KBr   **(b)** NaNO₂   **(c)** NH₄Br   **(d)** ZnCl₂   **(e)** NH₄F

14.15   FACTORS THAT AFFECT ACID STRENGTH

Remember...

The **strength of a bond** is measured by the bond dissociation energy, which for an H—A bond equals $\Delta H°$ for the reaction $HA(g) \rightarrow H(g) + A(g)$.   (Section 8.10)

Remember...

Electrostatic potential maps use color to portray the calculated electron distribution in a molecule. Electron-rich regions are red, and electron-poor regions are blue. Intermediate regions may be yellow, orange, or green.   (Section 7.4)

Why is one acid stronger than another? Although a complete analysis of the factors that determine the strength of an acid is complex, the extent of dissociation of an acid HA is often determined by the strength and polarity of the H—A bond. The **strength of the H–A bond**, as we saw in Section 8.10, is the enthalpy required to dissociate HA into an H atom and an A atom. The polarity of the H—A bond increases with an increase in the electronegativity of A and is related to the ease of electron transfer from an H atom to an A atom to give an H⁺ cation and an A⁻ anion. In general, the weaker and more polar the H—A bond, the stronger the acid.

Let's look first at the hydrohalic acids HF, HCl, HBr, and HI. **Electrostatic potential maps** (Section 7.4) show that all these molecules are polar, with the halogen atom being electron rich (red) and the H atom being electron poor (blue).

HF   HCl   HBr   HI

The variation in polarity in this series, however, is much less important than the variation in bond strength, which decreases markedly from 570 kJ/mol for HF to 298 kJ/mol for HI.

In general, for binary acids of elements in the same group of the periodic table, the H—A bond strength is the most important determinant of acidity. The H—A bond strength generally decreases with increasing size of element A down a group, so acidity increases. For HA (A = F, Cl, Br, or I), for example, the size of A increases from F to I, so bond strength decreases and acidity increases from HF to HI. Hydrofluoric acid is a weak acid ($K_a = 3.5 \times 10^{-4}$), whereas HCl, HBr, and HI are strong acids.

As a further example of this effect, H_2S ($K_{a1} = 1.0 \times 10^{-7}$) is a stronger acid than H_2O.

For binary acids of elements in the same row of the periodic table, changes in the H—A bond strength are smaller and the polarity of the H—A bond is the most important determinant of acid strength. The strengths of binary acids of the second-row elements, for example, increase as the electronegativity of A increases:

As the electrostatic potential maps show, the C—H bond is relatively nonpolar and methane has no tendency to dissociate in water into H_3O^+ and CH_3^- ions. The N—H bond is more polar, but dissociation of NH_3 into H_3O^+ and NH_2^- ions is still negligibly small. Water and hydrofluoric acid, however, are increasingly stronger acids. Periodic trends in the strength binary acids are summarized in **Figure 14.10**.

Oxoacids, such as H_2CO_3, HNO_3, H_2SO_4, and $HClO$, have the general formula H_nYO_m, where Y is a nonmetallic atom, such as C, N, S, or Cl, and n and m are integers. The atom Y is always bonded to one or more hydroxyl (OH) groups and can be bonded, in addition, to one or more oxygen atoms:

Because the dissociation of an oxoacid requires breaking an O—H bond, any factor that weakens the O—H bond or increases its polarity increases the strength of the acid. Two such factors are the electronegativity of Y and the oxidation number of Y in the general reaction

$$-Y-O-H + H_2O \rightleftharpoons H_3O^+ + -Y-O^-$$

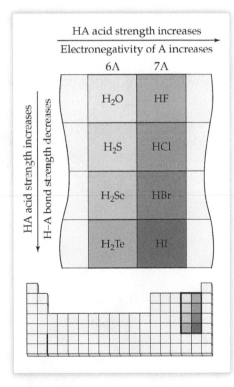

Figure 14.10
Periodic trends in the strength of binary acids. The acid strength of a binary acid HA increases from left to right in the periodic table, with increasing electronegativity of A, and from top to bottom, with decreasing H—A bond strength.

- *For oxoacids that contain the same number of OH groups and the same number of O atoms, acid strength increases as the electronegativity of Y increases.* For example, the acid strength of the hypohalous acids HOY (Y = Cl, Br, or I) increases as the electronegativity of the halogen increases:

Acid strength →

$$H-O-I \quad < \quad H-O-Br \quad < \quad H-O-Cl$$

Dissociation constant, K_a	2.3×10^{-11}	2.0×10^{-9}	3.5×10^{-8}
Electronegativity of Y	2.5	2.8	3.0

Electronegativity of Y →

As the halogen becomes more electronegative, an increasing amount of electron density shifts from the O—H bond toward the halogen, thus weakening the O—H bond and increasing its polarity. As a result, the proton is more easily transferred to a solvent water molecule, and so the acid strength increases.

- *For oxoacids that contain the same atom Y but different numbers of oxygen atoms, acid strength increases as the oxidation number of Y increases.* The oxidation number of Y increases, in turn, as the number of oxygen atoms increases. This effect is illustrated by the oxoacids of chlorine:

Acid strength; number of O atoms →

$$H-O-Cl \;<\; H-O-Cl-O \;<\; H-O-\overset{\displaystyle O}{\underset{}{Cl}}-O \;<\; H-O-\overset{\displaystyle O}{\underset{\displaystyle O}{Cl}}-O$$

Name of acid	Hypochlorous	Chlorous	Chloric	Perchloric
Dissociation constant, K_a	3.5×10^{-8}	1.2×10^{-2}	~1	Very large
Oxidation number of Cl	+1	+3	+5	+7

Oxidation number of Cl

As the number of O atoms in $HClO_m$ increases, an increasing amount of electron density shifts from the Cl atom toward the more electronegative O atoms. The amount of positive charge on the Cl atom therefore increases as its oxidation number increases. The increased positive charge on the Cl atom in turn attracts an increasing amount of electron density from the O—H bond, thus weakening the O—H bond and increasing its polarity. As a result, the proton is more easily transferred to a solvent water molecule. [Recall that this same charge effect was discussed in Section 14.14 for $Al(H_2O)_6^{3+}$.]

Another factor that affects the acid strength of oxoacids is the relative stability of the corresponding oxoanions. The ClO_m^- anion becomes more stable as the number of O atoms increases in the series $ClO^- < ClO_2^- < ClO_3^- < ClO_4^-$ because a larger number of electronegative O atoms can better accommodate the anion's negative charge. As the stability of the anion increases, the corresponding acid has a greater tendency to dissociate. The increase in acid strength with increasing number of O atoms is further illustrated by the oxoacids of sulfur: H_2SO_4 is a stronger acid than H_2SO_3.

▶ **PROBLEM 14.28** Identify the stronger acid in each of the following pairs:
(a) H_2S or H_2Se (b) HI or H_2Te
(c) HNO_2 or HNO_3 (d) H_2SO_3 or H_2SeO_3

14.16 LEWIS ACIDS AND BASES

In 1923, the same year in which Brønsted and Lowry defined acids and bases in terms of their proton donor/acceptor properties, the American chemist G. N. Lewis proposed an even more general concept of acids and bases. Lewis noticed that when a base accepts a proton, it does so by sharing a lone pair of electrons with the proton to form a new covalent bond. Using ammonia as an example, the reaction can be written in the following format, in which the curved arrow represents the donation of the nitrogen lone pair to form a bond with H^+:

In this reaction, the proton behaves as an electron-pair acceptor and the ammonia molecule behaves as an electron-pair donor. Consequently, the Lewis definition of acids and bases states that a *Lewis acid* is an electron-pair acceptor and a *Lewis base* is an electron-pair donor.

◁▭ **Lewis acid**   An electron-pair acceptor
◁▭ **Lewis base**   An electron-pair donor

Because all proton acceptors have an unshared pair of electrons and all electron-pair donors can accept a proton, the Lewis and the Brønsted–Lowry definitions of a base are simply different ways of looking at the same property. All Lewis bases are Brønsted–Lowry bases, and all Brønsted–Lowry bases are Lewis bases. The Lewis definition of an acid, however, is considerably more general than the Brønsted–Lowry definition. Lewis acids include not only H^+ but also other cations and neutral molecules having vacant valence orbitals that can accept a share in a pair of electrons donated by a Lewis base.

Common examples of cationic Lewis acids are metal ions, such as Al^{3+} and Cu^{2+}. Hydration of the Al^{3+} ion, for example, is a Lewis acid–base reaction in which each of six H_2O molecules donates a pair of electrons to Al^{3+} to form the hydrated cation $Al(H_2O)_6^{3+}$:

Lewis acid   Lewis base

Similarly, the reaction of Cu^{2+} ion with ammonia is a Lewis acid–base reaction in which each of four NH_3 molecules donates a pair of electrons to Cu^{2+} to form the deep blue $Cu(NH_3)_4^{2+}$ ion (**Figure 14.11**).

$$Cu^{2+} + 4 : NH_3 \longrightarrow Cu(NH_3)_4^{2+}$$

Lewis acid   Lewis base

Examples of neutral Lewis acids are halides of group 3A elements, such as BF_3. Boron trifluoride, a colorless gas, is an excellent Lewis acid because the boron atom

Figure 14.11

The addition of aqueous ammonia to a solution of the $Cu^{2+}(aq)$ ion is a Lewis acid–base reaction.

(a) Light blue $Cu^{2+}(aq)$

(b) Addition of $NH_3(aq)$ to **(a)** gives a light blue precipitate of $Cu(OH)_2$.

(c) Addition of excess $NH_3(aq)$ to **(a)** or **(b)** yields the deep blue $Cu(NH_3)_4{}^{2+}$ ion.

in the trigonal planar BF_3 molecule is surrounded by only six valence electrons (**Figure 14.12**). The boron atom uses three sp^2 hybrid orbitals to bond to the three F atoms and has a vacant $2p$ valence orbital that can accept a share in a pair of electrons from a Lewis base, such as NH_3. The Lewis acid and base sites are evident in electrostatic potential maps, which show the electron-poor B atom (blue) and the electron-rich N atom (red). In the product, called an *acid–base adduct*, the boron atom has acquired a stable octet of electrons.

Figure 14.12

The reaction of the Lewis acid BF_3 with the Lewis base NH_3.

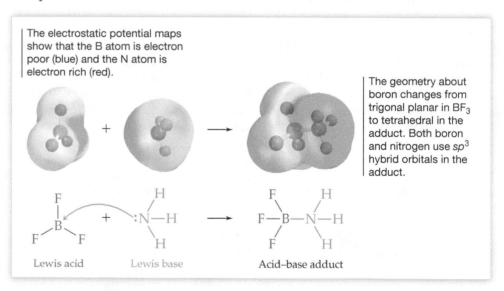

The electrostatic potential maps show that the B atom is electron poor (blue) and the N atom is electron rich (red).

The geometry about boron changes from trigonal planar in BF_3 to tetrahedral in the adduct. Both boron and nitrogen use sp^3 hybrid orbitals in the adduct.

Lewis acid   Lewis base   Acid–base adduct

Additional examples of neutral Lewis acids are oxides of nonmetals, such as CO_2, SO_2, and SO_3. The reaction of SO_3 with water, for example, can be viewed as a Lewis acid–base reaction in which SO_3 accepts a share in a lone pair of electrons from a water molecule:

Lewis acid   Lewis base

Sulfuric acid

Because the sulfur–oxygen bonds are polar, with a partial positive charge ($\delta+$) on the less electronegative S atom, the S atom attracts an electron pair from H_2O. Formation of a bond from the water O atom to the S atom in the first step is helped along by the shift of a shared pair of electrons to oxygen. In the second step, a proton shifts from one oxygen atom to another, yielding sulfuric acid (H_2SO_4).

WORKED EXAMPLE 14.17

IDENTIFYING LEWIS ACIDS AND BASES

For each of the following reactions, identify the Lewis acid and the Lewis base.

(a) $CO_2 + OH^- \longrightarrow HCO_3^-$

(b) $B(OH)_3 + OH^- \longrightarrow B(OH)_4^-$

(c) $6\,CN^- + Fe^{3+} \longrightarrow Fe(CN)_6^{3-}$

STRATEGY

To identify the Lewis acid and the Lewis base, determine which molecule or ion can accept an electron pair (the Lewis acid) and which can donate an electron pair (the Lewis base).

SOLUTION

(a) The carbon atom of $O{=}C{=}O$ bears a partial positive charge ($\delta+$) because carbon is less electronegative than oxygen. Therefore, the carbon atom attracts an electron pair from OH^-. Formation of a covalent bond from OH^- to CO_2 is helped along by a shift of a shared electron pair to oxygen:

The Lewis acid (electron-pair acceptor) is CO_2; the Lewis base (electron-pair donor) is OH^-.

(b) The Lewis acid is boric acid, $B(OH)_3$, a weak acid and mild antiseptic used in eyewash. The boron atom in $B(OH)_3$ has a vacant valence orbital and completes its octet by accepting a share in a pair of electrons from the Lewis base, OH^-.

(c) The Lewis acid is Fe^{3+}, and the Lewis base is CN^-. Each of the six $:C{\equiv}N:^-$ ions bond to the Fe^{3+} ion by donating a lone pair of electrons on the C atom.

▶ **PROBLEM 14.29** For each of the following reactions, identify the Lewis acid and the Lewis base.

(a) $AlCl_3 + Cl^- \longrightarrow AlCl_4^-$ **(b)** $2\,NH_3 + Ag^+ \longrightarrow Ag(NH_3)_2^+$

(c) $SO_2 + OH^- \longrightarrow HSO_3^-$ **(d)** $6\,H_2O + Cr^{3+} \longrightarrow Cr(H_2O)_6^{3+}$

CONCEPTUAL PROBLEM 14.30 For the following Lewis acid–base reaction, draw electron-dot structures for the reactants and products, and use the curved arrow notation to represent the donation of a lone pair of electrons from the Lewis base to the Lewis acid.

$$BeCl_2 + 2\,Cl^- \rightarrow BeCl_4^{2-}$$

▲ Plants that burn sulfur-containing coal and oil release large quantities of sulfur oxides into the atmosphere, ultimately leading to acid rain.

▲ A marble statue is being slowly dissolved by reaction of calcium carbonate with acid rain.

INQUIRY WHAT IS ACID RAIN AND WHAT ARE ITS EFFECTS?

The problem of acid rain is one of the more important environmental issues of recent times. Both the causes and the effects of acid rain are well understood. The problem is what to do about it.

As the water that has evaporated from oceans and lakes condenses into rain-drops, it dissolves small quantities of gases from the atmosphere. Under normal conditions, rain is slightly acidic, with a pH close to 5.6, because of dissolved CO_2. In recent decades, however, the acidity of rainwater in many industrialized areas of the world has increased by a factor of over 100, to a pH between 3 and 3.5.

The primary cause of acid rain is industrial and automotive pollution. Each year in industrialized countries, large power plants and smelters that burn sulfur-containing fossil fuels pour millions of tons of sulfur dioxide (SO_2) gas into the atmosphere, where some is oxidized by air to produce sulfur trioxide (SO_3). Sulfur oxides then dissolve in rain to form dilute sulfurous acid and sulfuric acid:

$$SO_2(g) + H_2O(l) \longrightarrow H_2SO_3(aq) \qquad \text{Sulfurous acid}$$
$$SO_3(g) + H_2O(l) \longrightarrow H_2SO_4(aq) \qquad \text{Sulfuric acid}$$

Nitrogen oxides, produced by the high-temperature reaction of N_2 with O_2 in coal-burning plants and in automobile engines, further contribute to the problem. Nitrogen dioxide (NO_2) reacts with water to form dilute nitric acid (HNO_3) and nitric oxide (NO):

$$3\,NO_2(g) + H_2O(l) \longrightarrow 2\,HNO_3(aq) + NO(g)$$

The NO is subsequently oxidized to NO_2 by atmospheric oxygen, and reaction of the resulting NO_2 and water produces still more HNO_3.

Oxides of both sulfur and nitrogen have always been present in the atmosphere, produced by such natural sources as volcanoes and lightning bolts, but their amounts have increased dramatically over the last century because of industrialization.

Many processes in nature require such a fine pH balance that they are dramatically upset by the shift that has occurred in the pH of rain. Thousands of lakes in the Adirondack region of upper New York state and in southeastern Canada have become so acidic that all fish life has disappeared. Massive tree die-offs have occurred throughout central and eastern Europe as acid rain has lowered the pH of the soil and leached nutrients from leaves. Countless marble statues have been slowly dissolved away as their calcium carbonate has been attacked by acid rain.

$$CaCO_3(s) + 2\,H^+(aq) \longrightarrow Ca^{2+}(aq) + H_2O(l) + CO_2(g)$$

Acid rain also contributes to the death of fish by leaching Al^{3+} from rocks into lakes. Though the lakes are acidic, the gills of fish are basic because fish excrete nitrogenous waste as NH_3 from their gills. The Al^{3+} then precipitates as $Al(OH)_3$ and clogs the gills:

$$NH_3(aq) + H_2O(l) \rightleftharpoons NH_4^+(aq) + OH^-(aq)$$
$$Al^{3+}(aq) + 3\,OH^-(aq) \rightleftharpoons Al(OH)_3(s)$$

Fortunately, acidic emissions from automobiles and power plants have been greatly reduced in recent years. Nitrogen oxide emissions have been lowered by equipping automobiles with catalytic converters (Section 12.15), which catalyze the decomposition of nitrogen oxides to N_2 and O_2. Sulfur dioxide emissions from power plants have been reduced by scrubbing combustion products before they are emitted from plant smoke stacks. In this process an aqueous suspension of lime (CaO) is added to the combustion chamber and the stack. The lime reacts with SO_2 to give calcium sulfite ($CaSO_3$):

$$CaO(s) + SO_2(g) \longrightarrow CaSO_3(s)$$

Unfortunately, scrubbers are expensive, and the $CaSO_3$, which has no commercial uses, must be disposed of in landfills. Much more work on methods to control acidic emissions remains to be done because the problem will grow more serious as sources of low-sulfur coal are exhausted and power plants are forced to rely on more abundant sources of high-sulfur coal.

Current research and development efforts center on *coal gasification*, a promising approach to producing electric power with nearly zero harmful emissions. In a coal gasifier, coal is treated with steam and oxygen at high temperature and pressure, producing a gaseous mixture of hydrogen and carbon monoxide along with methane and carbon dioxide. Combustion of this mixture, a synthetic fuel, is used to drive gas and steam turbines, which in turn generate electricity. Because sulfur and other impurities can be removed from the gas stream prior to combustion, air pollution is minimized. Moreover, compared to conventional coal-fired power plants, coal gasification plants would contribute less to global warming because carbon dioxide could be more easily captured for underground storage. Electric power companies, though, have been slow to adopt this technology because of higher costs for construction of coal gasification plants.

Unfortunately, it takes many years for lakes and streams to recover from the damage done by acid rain, even after sulfur and nitrogen oxide emissions have been reduced and the pH of rainwater has returned to normal levels. One approach to accelerating the process and mitigating the effects of continued oxide emissions employs lime and limestone to neutralize the acidity:

$$CaO(s) + 2\,H^+(aq) \longrightarrow Ca^{2+}(aq) + H_2O(l)$$

$$CaCO_3(s) + 2\,H^+(aq) \longrightarrow Ca^{2+}(aq) + H_2O(l) + CO_2(g)$$

This approach, called liming, has been widely used in Norway and Sweden but only infrequently in the United States. It is an expensive, short-term remediation procedure, but it does allow fish to survive in lakes and streams while longer-term solutions to the acid-rain problem are being pursued.

▶ **PROBLEM 14.31** The reaction of lime (CaO) with SO_2 in the scrubber of a power plant is a Lewis acid–base reaction. Explain.

▶ **PROBLEM 14.32** What is the pH of 1.00 L of rainwater that has dissolved 5.47 mg of NO_2? Assume that all of the NO_2 has reacted with water to give nitric acid.

SUMMARY

According to the Arrhenius theory, acids (HA) are substances that dissociate in water to produce $H^+(aq)$ and bases (MOH) are substances that dissociate to yield $OH^-(aq)$. The more general **Brønsted–Lowry theory** defines an acid as a proton donor, a base as a proton acceptor, and an acid–base reaction as a proton-transfer reaction. Examples of Brønsted–Lowry acids are HCl, NH_4^+, and HSO_4^-; examples of Brønsted–Lowry bases are OH^-, F^-, and NH_3.

A **strong acid** HA is nearly 100% dissociated, whereas a **weak acid** HA is only partially dissociated, existing as an equilibrium mixture of HA, H_3O^+, and A^-:

$$HA(aq) + H_2O(l) \rightleftharpoons H_3O^+(aq) + A^-(aq)$$

The strength of an acid (HA) and the strength of its **conjugate base** (A^-) are inversely related. The H_3O^+ ion, a hydrated proton, is called the **hydronium ion**.

Water, which can act both as an acid and as a base, undergoes the dissociation reaction $H_2O + H_2O \rightleftharpoons H_3O^+ + OH^-$. In pure water at 25 °C, $[H_3O^+] = [OH^-] = 1.0 \times 10^{-7}$ M. The **ion-product constant for water**, K_w, is given by $K_w = [H_3O^+][OH^-] = 1.0 \times 10^{-14}$. The acidity of an aqueous solution is expressed on the **pH** scale, where $pH = -\log [H_3O^+]$. At 25 °C, acidic solutions have pH < 7, basic solutions have pH > 7, and neutral solutions have pH = 7. The pH of a solution can be determined using an **acid–base indicator** or a pH meter. The extent of dissociation of a weak acid HA is measured by its **acid-dissociation constant**, K_a:

$$K_a = \frac{[H_3O^+][A^-]}{[HA]}$$

Polyprotic acids contain more than one dissociable proton and dissociate in a stepwise manner. Because the stepwise dissociation constants decrease in the order $K_{a1} \gg K_{a2} \gg K_{a3}$, nearly all the H_3O^+ in a polyprotic acid solution comes from the first dissociation step.

The extent of dissociation of a weak base B is measured by its **base-dissociation constant**, K_b:

$$B(aq) + H_2O(l) \rightleftharpoons BH^+(aq) + OH^-(aq) \qquad K_b = \frac{[BH^+][OH^-]}{[B]}$$

Examples of weak bases are NH_3 and derivatives of NH_3 called *amines*. For any conjugate acid–base pair, (K_a for the acid) $\times$ (K_b for the base) $= K_w$.

Aqueous solutions of salts can be neutral, acidic, or basic, depending on the acid–base properties of the constituent ions. Group 1A and 2A cations (except Be^{2+}) and anions that are conjugate bases of strong acids, such as Cl^-, do not react appreciably with water to produce H_3O^+ or OH^- ions. Cations that are conjugate acids of weak bases, such as NH_4^+, and hydrated cations of small, highly charged metal ions, such as Al^{3+}, yield acidic solutions. Anions that are conjugate bases of weak acids, such as CN^-, yield basic solutions.

The acid strength of a binary acid HA increases down a group of the periodic table with decreasing strength of the H—A bond and increases from left to right across a row with increasing polarity of the H—A bond. The acid strength of an oxoacid, H_nYO_m (Y = C, N, S, Cl), increases with increasing electronegativity and increasing oxidation number of the central atom Y.

A **Lewis acid** is an electron-pair acceptor, and a **Lewis base** is an electron-pair donor. Lewis acids include not only H^+ but also other cations and neutral molecules that can accept a share in a pair of electrons from a Lewis base. Examples of Lewis acids are Al^{3+}, Cu^{2+}, BF_3, SO_3, and CO_2.

KEY WORDS

acid–base indicator *549*
acid-dissociation
   constant (K_a) *552*
Arrhenius acid *539*
Arrhenius base *539*
base-dissociation
   constant (K_b) *562*

Brønsted–Lowry acid *539*
Brønsted–Lowry base *539*
Brønsted–Lowry
   theory *539*
conjugate acid *540*
conjugate acid–base
   pair *540*

conjugate base *540*
dissociation of water *545*
hydronium ion, H_3O^+ *540*
ion-product constant for
   water (K_w) *545*
Lewis acid *573*
Lewis base *573*

percent dissociation *558*
pH *547*
polyprotic acid *559*
principal reaction *554*
strong acid *542*
subsidiary reaction *554*
weak acid *542*

CONCEPTUAL PROBLEMS

Problems 14.1–14.32 appear within the chapter.

14.33 For each of the following reactions, identify the Brønsted–Lowry acids and bases:

14.34 The following pictures represent aqueous solutions of three acids HA (A = X, Y, or Z); water molecules have been omitted for clarity:

(a) What is the conjugate base of each acid?

(b) Arrange the three acids in order of increasing acid strength.

(c) Which acid, if any, is a strong acid?

(d) Which acid has the smallest value of K_a?

(e) What is the percent dissociation in the solution of HZ?

14.35 Which of the following pictures represents a solution of a weak diprotic acid H_2A? (Water molecules are omitted for clarity.) Which pictures represent an impossible situation? Explain.

 $= H_2A$ $= H_3O^+$ $= HA^-$ $= A^{2-}$

(a)   **(b)**

(c)   **(d)**

14.36 Which of the following pictures best represents an aqueous solution of sulfuric acid? Explain. (Water molecules have been omitted for clarity.)

$= H_2SO_4$ $= H_3O^+$ $= HSO_4^-$ $= SO_4^{2-}$

(a)   **(b)**   **(c)**

14.37 The following pictures represent aqueous solutions of three acids HA (A = X, Y, or Z); water molecules have been omitted for clarity:

$= HA$ $= H_3O^+$ $= A^-$

HX   HY   HZ

(a) Which conjugate base ($A^- = X^-$, Y^-, or Z^-) has the largest value of K_b?

(b) Which A^- ion is the weakest base?

14.38 The following pictures represent solutions of three salts NaA ($A^- = X^-$, Y^-, or Z^-); water molecules and Na^+ ions have been omitted for clarity:

$= A^-$ $= HA$ $= OH^-$

NaX   NaY

NaZ

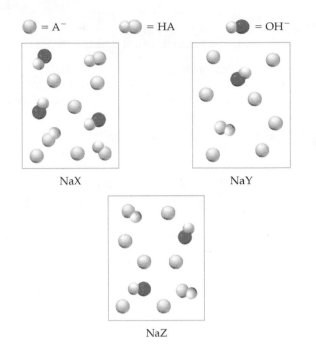

(a) Arrange the three A^- anions in order of increasing base strength.

(b) Which A^- anion has the strongest conjugate acid?

(c) Which A^- anion has the smallest value of pK_b?

(d) Why, within each box, is the number of HA molecules and OH^- anions the same?

14.39 The following picture represents the hydrated metal cation $M(H_2O)_6{}^{n+}$, where $n = 1, 2$, or 3.

(a) Write a balanced equation for the reaction of $M(H_2O)_6{}^{n+}$ with water, and write the equilibrium equation for the reaction.

(b) Does the equilibrium constant increase, decrease, or remain the same as the value of n increases? Explain.

(c) Which $M(H_2O)_6{}^{n+}$ ion ($n = 1, 2$, or 3) is the strongest acid, and which has the strongest conjugate base?

14.40 Locate sulfur, selenium, chlorine, and bromine in the periodic table:

(a) Which binary acid (H_2S, H_2Se, HCl, or HBr) is the strongest? Which is the weakest? Explain.

(b) Which oxoacid (H_2SO_3, H_2SeO_3, $HClO_3$, or $HBrO_3$) is the strongest? Which is the weakest? Explain.

14.41 Look at the electron-dot structures of the following molecules and ions:

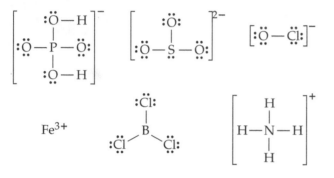

(a) Which of these molecules and ions can behave as a Brønsted–Lowry acid? Which can behave as a Brønsted–Lowry base?

(b) Which can behave as a Lewis acid? Which can behave as a Lewis base?

14.42 Boric acid (H_3BO_3) is a weak monoprotic acid that yields H_3O^+ ions in water. H_3BO_3 might behave either as a Brønsted–Lowry acid or as a Lewis acid, though it is, in fact, a Lewis acid.

(a) Write a balanced equation for the reaction with water in which H_3BO_3 behaves as a Brønsted–Lowry acid.

(b) Write a balanced equation for the reaction with water in which H_3BO_3 behaves as a Lewis acid. Hint: One of the reaction products contains a tetrahedral boron atom.

14.43 The reaction of PCl_4^+ with Cl^- is a Lewis acid–base reaction. Draw electron-dot structures for the reactants and products, and use the curved arrow notation (Section 14.16) to represent the donation of a lone pair of electrons from the Lewis base to the Lewis acid.

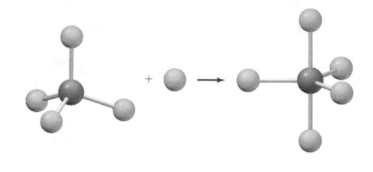

SECTION PROBLEMS

Acid–Base Concepts (Sections 14.1–14.2)

14.44 Give three examples of molecules or ions that are Brønsted–Lowry bases but not Arrhenius bases.

14.45 Give an example of an anion that can behave both as a Brønsted–Lowry acid and as a Brønsted–Lowry base.

14.46 Give the formula for the conjugate base of each of the following Brønsted–Lowry acids:
(a) HSO_4^- (b) H_2SO_3 (c) $H_2PO_4^-$
(d) NH_4^+ (e) H_2O (f) NH_3

14.47 Give the formula for the conjugate acid of each of the following Brønsted–Lowry bases:
(a) SO_3^{2-} (b) H_2O (c) CH_3NH_2
(d) OH^- (e) HCO_3^- (f) H^-

14.48 For each of the following reactions, identify the Brønsted–Lowry acids and bases and the conjugate acid–base pairs:
(a) $CH_3CO_2H(aq) + NH_3(aq) \rightleftharpoons$
$$NH_4^+(aq) + CH_3CO_2^-(aq)$$
(b) $CO_3^{2-}(aq) + H_3O^+(aq) \rightleftharpoons H_2O(l) + HCO_3^-(aq)$

(c) $HSO_3^-(aq) + H_2O(l) \rightleftharpoons H_3O^+(aq) + SO_3^{2-}(aq)$
(d) $HSO_3^-(aq) + H_2O(l) \rightleftharpoons H_2SO_3(aq) + OH^-(aq)$

14.49 For each of the following reactions, identify the Brønsted–Lowry acids and bases and the conjugate acid–base pairs:
(a) $CN^-(aq) + H_2O(l) \rightleftharpoons OH^-(aq) + HCN(aq)$
(b) $H_2PO_4^-(aq) + H_2O(l) \rightleftharpoons H_3O^+(aq) + HPO_4^{2-}(aq)$
(c) $HPO_4^{2-}(aq) + H_2O(l) \rightleftharpoons OH^-(aq) + H_2PO_4^-(aq)$
(d) $NH_4^+(aq) + NO_2^-(aq) \rightleftharpoons HNO_2(aq) + NH_3(aq)$

14.50 Which of the following species behave as strong acids or as strong bases in aqueous solution? See Table 14.1 to check your answers.
(a) HNO_2 (b) HNO_3 (c) NH_4^+ (d) Cl^-
(e) H^- (f) O^{2-} (g) H_2SO_4

14.51 Which acid in each of the following pairs has the stronger conjugate base? See Table 14.1 for help with parts (c) and (d).
(a) H_2CO_3 or H_2SO_4 (b) HCl or HF
(c) HF or NH_4^+ (d) HCN or HSO_4^-

14.52 Of the conjugate acid–base pairs HF/F⁻, HCl/Cl⁻, and HCN/CN⁻, complete the following equation with the pair that gives an equilibrium constant $K_c > 1$.

$$\underline{\hspace{2cm}} + H_2PO_4^- \longrightarrow \underline{\hspace{2cm}} + H_3PO_4.$$

14.53 Of the conjugate acid–base pairs HSO_4^-/SO_4^{2-}, NH_4^+/NH_3, and HNO_3/NO_3^-, complete the following equation with the pair that gives an equilibrium constant $K_c > 1$.

$$\underline{\hspace{2cm}} + H_2S \longrightarrow \underline{\hspace{2cm}} + HS^-$$

Dissociation of Water; pH (Sections 14.4–14.6)

14.54 For each of the following solutions, calculate $[OH^-]$ from $[H_3O^+]$, or $[H_3O^+]$ from $[OH^-]$. Classify each solution as acidic, basic, or neutral.
(a) $[H_3O^+] = 3.4 \times 10^{-9}$ M   (b) $[OH^-] = 0.010$ M
(c) $[OH^-] = 1.0 \times 10^{-10}$ M   (d) $[H_3O^+] = 1.0 \times 10^{-7}$ M
(e) $[H_3O^+] = 8.6 \times 10^{-5}$ M

14.55 For each of the following solutions, calculate $[OH^-]$ from $[H_3O^+]$, or $[H_3O^+]$ from $[OH^-]$. Classify each solution as acidic, basic, or neutral.
(a) $[H_3O^+] = 2.5 \times 10^{-4}$ M   (b) $[H_3O^+] = 2.0$ M
(c) $[OH^-] = 5.6 \times 10^{-9}$ M   (d) $[OH^-] = 1.5 \times 10^{-3}$ M
(e) $[OH^-] = 1.0 \times 10^{-7}$ M

14.56 Water superheated under pressure to 200 °C and 750 atm has $K_w = 1.5 \times 10^{-11}$. What is $[H_3O^+]$ and $[OH^-]$ at 200 °C? Is the water acidic, basic, or neutral?

14.57 Water at 500 °C and 250 atm is a supercritical fluid. Under these conditions, K_w is approximately 1.7×10^{-19}. Estimate $[H_3O^+]$ and $[OH^-]$ at 500 °C. Is the water acidic, basic, or neutral?

14.58 Calculate the pH to the correct number of significant figures for solutions with the following concentrations of H_3O^+ or OH^-:
(a) $[H_3O^+] = 2.0 \times 10^{-5}$ M   (b) $[OH^-] = 4 \times 10^{-3}$ M
(c) $[H_3O^+] = 3.56 \times 10^{-9}$ M   (d) $[H_3O^+] = 10^{-3}$ M
(e) $[OH^-] = 12$ M

14.59 What is the pH to the correct number of significant figures for solutions with the following concentrations of H_3O^+ or OH^-?
(a) $[OH^-] = 7.6 \times 10^{-3}$ M   (b) $[H_3O^+] = 10^{-8}$ M
(c) $[H_3O^+] = 5.0$ M   (d) $[OH^-] = 1.0 \times 10^{-7}$ M
(e) $[H_3O^+] = 2.18 \times 10^{-10}$ M

14.60 Calculate the H_3O^+ concentration to the correct number of significant figures for solutions with the following pH values:
(a) 4.1   (b) 10.82   (c) 0.00
(d) 14.25   (e) −1.0   (f) 5.238

14.61 What is the H_3O^+ concentration to the correct number of significant figures for solutions with the following pH values?
(a) 9.0   (b) 7.00   (c) −0.3
(d) 15.18   (e) 2.63   (f) 10.756

14.62 Which of the indicators thymol blue, alizarin yellow, chlorphenol red, or methyl orange would be most appropriate to detect a pH change from:
(a) 7 to 5?   (b) 8 to 10?   (c) 3 to 5?

14.63 Which of the indicators methyl violet, bromcresol green, phenol red, or thymolphthalein, would be most appropriate to detect a pH change from:
(a) 4 to 6?   (b) 8 to 10?   (c) 2 to 0?

Strong Acids and Strong Bases (Section 14.7)

14.64 A solution of NaOH has a pH of 10.50. How many grams of CaO should be dissolved in sufficient water to make 1.00 L of a solution having the same pH?

14.65 A solution of KOH has a pH of 10.00. How many grams of SrO should be dissolved in sufficient water to make 2.00 L of a solution having the same pH?

14.66 Calculate the pH of solutions prepared by:
(a) Dissolving 4.8 g of lithium hydroxide in water to give 250 mL of solution
(b) Dissolving 0.93 g of hydrogen chloride in water to give 0.40 L of solution
(c) Diluting 50.0 mL of 0.10 M HCl to a volume of 1.00 L
(d) Mixing 100.0 mL of 2.0×10^{-3} M HCl and 400.0 mL of 1.0×10^{-3} M $HClO_4$ (Assume that volumes are additive.)

14.67 Calculate the pH of solutions prepared by:
(a) Dissolving 0.20 g of sodium oxide in water to give 100.0 mL of solution
(b) Dissolving 1.26 g of pure nitric acid in water to give 0.500 L of solution
(c) Diluting 40.0 mL of 0.075 M $Ba(OH)_2$ to a volume of 300.0 mL
(d) Mixing equal volumes of 0.20 M HCl and 0.50 M HNO_3 (Assume that volumes are additive.)

Weak Acids (Sections 14.8–14.10)

14.68 Look up the values of K_a in Appendix C for C_6H_5OH, HNO_3, CH_3CO_2H, and $HOCl$, and arrange these acids in order of:
(a) Increasing acid strength
(b) Decreasing percent dissociation
Also estimate $[H_3O^+]$ in a 1.0 M solution of each acid.

14.69 Look up the values of K_a in Appendix C for HCO_2H, HCN, $HClO_4$, and HOBr, and arrange these acids in order of:
(a) Increasing acid strength
(b) Decreasing percent dissociation
Also estimate $[H_3O^+]$ in a 1.0 M solution of each acid.

14.70 The pH of 0.040 M hypobromous acid (HOBr) is 5.05. Set up the equilibrium equation for the dissociation of HOBr, and calculate the value of the acid-dissociation constant.

14.71 Lactic acid ($C_3H_6O_3$), which occurs in sour milk and foods such as sauerkraut, is a weak monoprotic acid. The pH of a 0.10 M solution of lactic acid is 2.43. What are the values of K_a and pK_a for lactic acid?

Lactic acid

14.72 Acrylic acid ($HC_3H_3O_2$) is used in the manufacture of paints and plastics. The pK_a of acrylic acid is 4.25.

(a) Calculate the pH and the concentrations of all species (H_3O^+, $C_3H_3O_2^-$, $HC_3H_3O_2$, and OH^-) in 0.150 M acrylic acid.

(b) Calculate the percent dissociation in 0.0500 M acrylic acid.

14.73 Hippuric acid ($HC_9H_8NO_3$), found in horse urine, has $pK_a = 3.62$.

(a) Calculate the pH and the concentrations of all species (H_3O^+, $C_9H_8NO_3^-$, $HC_9H_8NO_3$, and OH^-) in 0.100 M hippuric acid.

(b) Calculate the percent dissociation in 0.0750 M hippuric acid.

14.74 Calculate the pH and the percent dissociation in 1.5 M HNO_2 ($K_a = 4.5 \times 10^{-4}$).

14.75 A typical aspirin tablet contains 324 mg of aspirin (acetylsalicylic acid, $C_9H_8O_4$), a monoprotic acid having $K_a = 3.0 \times 10^{-4}$. If you dissolve two aspirin tablets in a 300 mL glass of water, what is the pH of the solution and the percent dissociation?

Polyprotic Acids (Section 14.11)

14.76 Write balanced net ionic equations and the corresponding equilibrium equations for the stepwise dissociation of the diprotic acid H_2SeO_4.

14.77 Write balanced net ionic equations and the corresponding equilibrium equations for the stepwise dissociation of the triprotic acid H_3PO_4.

14.78 Calculate the pH and the concentrations of all species present (H_2CO_3, HCO_3^-, CO_3^{2-}, H_3O^+, and OH^-) in 0.010 M H_2CO_3 ($K_{a1} = 4.3 \times 10^{-7}$; $K_{a2} = 5.6 \times 10^{-11}$).

14.79 Calculate the pH and the concentrations of H_2SO_3, HSO_3^-, SO_3^{2-}, H_3O^+, and OH^- in 0.025 M H_2SO_3 ($K_{a1} = 1.5 \times 10^{-2}$; $K_{a2} = 6.3 \times 10^{-8}$).

14.80 Oxalic acid ($H_2C_2O_4$) is a diprotic acid that occurs in plants such as rhubarb and spinach. Calculate the pH and the concentration of $C_2O_4^{2-}$ ions in 0.20 M $H_2C_2O_4$ ($K_{a1} = 5.9 \times 10^{-2}$; $K_{a2} = 6.4 \times 10^{-5}$).

Oxalic acid

14.81 Calculate the concentrations of H_3O^+ and SO_4^{2-} in a solution prepared by mixing equal volumes of 0.2 M HCl and 0.6 M H_2SO_4 (K_{a2} for H_2SO_4 is 1.2×10^{-2}).

Weak Bases; Relation between K_a and K_b (Sections 14.12–14.13)

14.82 Write a balanced net ionic equation and the corresponding equilibrium equation for the reaction of the following weak bases with water:

(a) Dimethylamine, $(CH_3)_2NH$ (b) Aniline, $C_6H_5NH_2$

(c) Cyanide ion, CN^-

Dimethylamine   Aniline

14.83 Write a balanced net ionic equation and the corresponding equilibrium equation for the reaction of the following weak bases with water:

(a) Pyridine, C_5H_5N

(b) Ethylamine, $C_2H_5NH_2$

(c) Acetate ion, $CH_3CO_2^-$

Pyridine   Ethylamine

14.84 Morphine ($C_{17}H_{19}NO_3$), a narcotic used in painkillers, is a weak organic base. If the pH of a 7.0×10^{-4} M solution of morphine is 9.50, what are the values of K_b and pK_b?

14.85 A 1.00×10^{-3} M solution of quinine, a drug used in treating malaria, has a pH of 9.75. What are the values of K_b and pK_b?

14.86 Oxycodone ($C_{18}H_{21}NO_4$), a narcotic analgesic, is a weak base with $pK_b = 5.47$. Calculate the pH and the concentrations of all species present ($C_{18}H_{21}NO_4$, $HC_{18}H_{21}NO_4^+$, H_3O^+, and OH^-) in a 0.002 50 M oxycodone solution.

14.87 Morpholine (C_4H_9NO) is a weak organic base with $pK_b = 5.68$. Calculate the pH and the concentrations of all species present (C_4H_9NO, $HC_4H_9NO^+$, H_3O^+, and OH^-) in a 0.0100 M morpholine solution.

14.88 Using values of K_b in Appendix C, calculate values of K_a for each of the following ions:

(a) Propylammonium ion, $C_3H_7NH_3^+$

(b) Hydroxylammonium ion, NH_3OH^+

(c) Anilinium ion, $C_6H_5NH_3^+$

(d) Pyridinium ion, $C_5H_5NH^+$

14.89 Using values of K_a in Appendix C, calculate values of K_b for each of the following ions:

(a) Fluoride ion, F^-

(b) Hypobromite ion, OBr^-

(c) Hydrogen sulfide ion, HS^-

(d) Sulfide ion, S^{2-}

Acid–Base Properties of Salts (Section 14.14)

14.90 Write a balanced net ionic equation for the reaction of each of the following ions with water. In each case, identify the Brønsted–Lowry acids and bases and the conjugate acid–base pairs.

(a) $CH_3NH_3^+$ (b) $Cr(H_2O)_6^{3+}$

(c) $CH_3CO_2^-$ (d) PO_4^{3-}

14.91 Write a balanced net ionic equation for the principal reaction in solutions of each of the following salts. In each case, identify the Brønsted–Lowry acids and bases and the conjugate acid–base pairs.
(a) Na_2CO_3 **(b)** NH_4NO_3 **(c)** NaCl **(d)** $ZnCl_2$

14.92 Classify each of the following ions according to whether they react with water to give a neutral, acidic, or basic solution:
(a) F^- **(b)** Br^- **(c)** NH_4^+
(d) $K(H_2O)_6^+$ **(e)** SO_3^{2-} **(f)** $Cr(H_2O)_6^{3+}$

14.93 Classify each of the following salt solutions as neutral, acidic, or basic. See Appendix C for values of equilibrium constants.
(a) $Fe(NO_3)_3$ **(b)** $Ba(NO_3)_2$ **(c)** NaOCl
(d) NH_4I **(e)** NH_4NO_2 **(f)** $(CH_3NH_3)Cl$

14.94 Calculate the concentrations of all species present and the pH in 0.10 M solutions of the following substances. See Appendix C for values of equilibrium constants.
(a) Ethylammonium nitrate, $(C_2H_5NH_3)NO_3$
(b) Sodium acetate, $Na(CH_3CO_2)$
(c) Sodium nitrate, $NaNO_3$

14.95 Calculate the pH and the percent dissociation of the hydrated cation in 0.020 M solutions of the following substances. See Appendix C for values of equilibrium constants.
(a) $Fe(NO_3)_2$ **(b)** $Fe(NO_3)_3$

Factors That Affect Acid Strength (Section 14.15)

14.96 Arrange each group of compounds in order of increasing acid strength. Explain your reasoning.
(a) HCl, H_2S, PH_3 **(b)** NH_3, PH_3, AsH_3
(c) HBrO, $HBrO_3$, $HBrO_4$

14.97 Arrange each group of compounds in order of decreasing acid strength. Explain your reasoning.
(a) H_2O, H_2S, H_2Se **(b)** $HClO_3$, $HBrO_3$, HIO_3
(c) PH_3, H_2S, HCl

14.98 Identify the strongest acid in each of the following sets. Explain your reasoning.
(a) H_2O, HF, or HCl **(b)** $HClO_2$, $HClO_3$, or $HBrO_3$
(c) HBr, H_2S, or H_2Se

14.99 Identify the weakest acid in each of the following sets. Explain your reasoning.

(a) H_2SO_3, $HClO_3$, $HClO_4$ **(b)** NH_3, H_2O, H_2S
(c) $B(OH)_3$, $Al(OH)_3$, $Ga(OH)_3$

14.100 Identify the stronger acid in each of the following pairs. Explain your reasoning.
(a) H_2Se or H_2Te **(b)** H_3PO_4 or H_3AsO_4
(c) $H_2PO_4^-$ or HPO_4^{2-} **(d)** CH_4 or NH_4^+

14.101 Identify the stronger base in each of the following pairs. Explain your reasoning.
(a) ClO_2^- or ClO_3^- **(b)** HSO_4^- or $HSeO_4^-$
(c) HS^- or OH^- **(d)** HS^- or Br^-

Lewis Acids and Bases (Section 14.16)

14.102 For each of the following reactions, identify the Lewis acid and the Lewis base:
(a) $SiF_4 + 2F^- \longrightarrow SiF_6^{2-}$
(b) $4NH_3 + Zn^{2+} \longrightarrow Zn(NH_3)_4^{2+}$
(c) $2Cl^- + HgCl_2 \longrightarrow HgCl_4^{2-}$
(d) $CO_2 + H_2O \longrightarrow H_2CO_3$

14.103 For each of the following reactions, identify the Lewis acid and the Lewis base:
(a) $2Cl^- + BeCl_2 \longrightarrow BeCl_4^{2-}$
(b) $Mg^{2+} + 6H_2O \longrightarrow Mg(H_2O)_6^{2+}$
(c) $SO_3 + OH^- \longrightarrow HSO_4^-$ **(d)** $F^- + BF_3 \longrightarrow BF_4^-$

14.104 For each of the Lewis acid–base reactions in Problem 14.102, draw electron-dot structures for the reactants and products, and use the curved arrow notation (Section 14.16) to represent the donation of a lone pair of electrons from the Lewis base to the Lewis acid.

14.105 For each of the Lewis acid–base reactions in Problem 14.103, draw electron-dot structures for the reactants and products, and use the curved arrow notation (Section 14.16) to represent the donation of a lone pair of electrons from the Lewis base to the Lewis acid.

14.106 Classify each of the following as a Lewis acid or a Lewis base:
(a) CN^- **(b)** H^+ **(c)** H_2O
(d) Fe^{3+} **(e)** OH^- **(f)** CO_2
(g) $P(CH_3)_3$ **(h)** $B(CH_3)_3$

14.107 Which would you expect to be the stronger Lewis acid in each of the following pairs? Explain.
(a) BF_3 or BH_3 **(b)** SO_2 or SO_3
(c) Sn^{2+} or Sn^{4+} **(d)** CH_3^+ or CH_4

CHAPTER PROBLEMS

14.108 Aqueous solutions of hydrogen sulfide contain H_2S, HS^-, S^{2-}, H_3O^+, OH^-, and H_2O in varying concentrations. Which of these species can act only as an acid? Which can act only as a base? Which can act both as an acid and as a base?

14.109 The hydronium ion H_3O^+ is the strongest acid that can exist in aqueous solution because stronger acids dissociate by transferring a proton to water. What is the strongest base that can exist in aqueous solution?

14.110 Baking powder contains baking soda ($NaHCO_3$) and an acidic substance such as sodium alum, $NaAl(SO_4)_2 \cdot 12 H_2O$. These components react in an aqueous medium to produce

CO_2 gas, which "raises" the dough. Write a balanced net ionic equation for the reaction.

14.111 Arrange the following substances in order of increasing $[H_3O^+]$ for a 0.10 M solution of each:
(a) $Zn(NO_3)_2$ **(b)** Na_2O **(c)** NaOCl
(d) $NaClO_4$ **(e)** $HClO_4$

14.112 At 0 °C, the density of liquid water is 0.9998 g/mL and the value of K_w is 1.14×10^{-15}. What fraction of the molecules in liquid water are dissociated at 0 °C? What is the percent dissociation at 0 °C? What is the pH of a neutral solution at 0 °C?

14.113 Use the conjugate acid–base pair HCN and CN⁻ to derive the relationship between K_a and K_b.

14.114 The pH of 0.050 M gallic acid, an acid found in tea leaves, is 2.86. Calculate K_a and pK_a for gallic acid.

14.115 The pH of 0.040 M pyruvic acid, a compound involved in metabolic pathways, is 1.96. Calculate K_a and pK_a for pyruvic acid.

14.116 Nicotine ($C_{10}H_{14}N_2$) can accept two protons because it has two basic N atoms ($K_{b1} = 1.0 \times 10^{-6}$; $K_{b2} = 1.3 \times 10^{-11}$). Calculate the values of K_a for the conjugate acids $C_{10}H_{14}N_2H^+$ and $C_{10}H_{14}N_2H_2^{2+}$.

Nicotine

14.117 Sodium benzoate ($C_6H_5CO_2Na$) is used as a food preservative. Calculate the pH and the concentrations of all species present (Na^+, $C_6H_5CO_2^-$, $C_6H_5CO_2H$, H_3O^+, and OH^-) in 0.050 M sodium benzoate; K_a for benzoic acid ($C_6H_5CO_2H$) is 6.5×10^{-5}.

14.118 The hydrated cation $M(H_2O)_6^{3+}$ has $K_a = 10^{-4}$, and the acid HA has $K_a = 10^{-5}$. Identify the principal reaction in an aqueous solution of each of the following salts, and classify each solution as acidic, basic, or neutral:

(a) NaA   (b) M(NO₃)₃   (c) NaNO₃   (d) MA₃

14.119 Calculate the pH and the concentrations of all species present (H_3O^+, F^-, HF, Cl^-, and OH^-) in a solution that contains 0.10 M HF ($K_a = 3.5 \times 10^{-4}$) and 0.10 M HCl.

14.120 Calculate the pH and the concentrations of all species present (H_3O^+, OH^-, HIO_3, and IO_3^-) in 0.0500 M HIO_3. K_a for HIO_3 is 1.7×10^{-1}.

14.121 Quinolinic acid, $H_2C_7H_3NO_4$ ($pK_{a1} = 2.43$; $pK_{a2} = 4.78$), has been implicated in the progression of Alzheimer's disease. Calculate the pH and the concentrations of all species present ($H_2C_7H_3NO_4$, $HC_7H_3NO_4^-$, $C_7H_3NO_4^{2-}$, H_3O^+, and OH^-) in a 0.050 M solution of quinolinic acid.

14.122 Calculate the pH and the concentrations of all species present ($H_2C_8H_4O_4$, $HC_8H_4O_4^-$, $C_8H_4O_4^{2-}$, H_3O^+, and OH^-) in a 0.0250 M solution of phthalic acid, $H_2C_8H_4O_4$ ($pK_{a1} = 2.89$; $pK_{a2} = 5.51$).

14.123 Sulfur dioxide is quite soluble in water:

$$SO_2(g) + H_2O(l) \rightleftharpoons H_2SO_3(aq) \qquad K = 1.33$$

The H_2SO_3 produced is a weak diprotic acid ($K_{a1} = 1.5 \times 10^{-2}$; $K_{a2} = 6.3 \times 10^{-8}$). Calculate the pH and the concentrations of H_2SO_3, HSO_3^-, and SO_3^{2-} in a solution prepared by continuously bubbling SO_2 at a pressure of 1.00 atm into pure water.

14.124 Classify each of the following salt solutions as neutral, acidic, or basic. See Appendix C for values of equilibrium constants.

(a) NH_4F

(b) $(NH_4)_2SO_3$

14.125 Calculate the pH and the percent dissociation of the hydrated cation in the following solutions. See Appendix C for the value of the equilibrium constant.

(a) 0.010 M $Cr(NO_3)_3$

(b) 0.0050 M $Cr(NO_3)_3$

(c) 0.0010 M $Cr(NO_3)_3$

14.126 Beginning with the equilibrium equation for the dissociation of a weak acid HA, show that the percent dissociation varies directly as the square root of K_a and inversely as the square root of the initial concentration of HA when the concentration of HA that dissociates is negligible compared with its initial concentration.

14.127 Calculate the pH and the concentrations of all species present in 0.25 M solutions of each of the salts in Problem 14.124. (Hint: The principal reaction is proton transfer from the cation to the anion.)

14.128 For a solution of two weak acids with comparable values of K_a, there is no single principal reaction. The two acid-dissociation equilibrium equations must therefore be solved simultaneously. Calculate the pH in a solution that is 0.10 M in acetic acid (CH_3CO_2H, $K_a = 1.8 \times 10^{-5}$) and 0.10 M in benzoic acid ($C_6H_5CO_2H$, $K_a = 6.5 \times 10^{-5}$). (Hint: Let $x = [CH_3CO_2H]$ that dissociates and $y = [C_6H_5CO_2H]$ that dissociates; then $[H_3O^+] = x + y$.)

14.129 What is the pH and the principal source of H_3O^+ ions in 1.0×10^{-10} M HCl? (Hint: The pH of an acid solution can't exceed 7.) What is the pH of 1.0×10^{-7} M HCl?

14.130 When NO_2 is bubbled into water, it is completely converted to HNO_3 and HNO_2:

$$2\,NO_2(g) + H_2O(l) \longrightarrow HNO_3(aq) + HNO_2(aq)$$

Calculate the pH and the concentrations of all species present (H_3O^+, OH^-, HNO_2, NO_2^-, and NO_3^-) in a solution prepared by dissolving 0.0500 mol of NO_2 in 1.00 L of water. K_a for HNO_2 is 4.5×10^{-4}.

14.131 Acid and base behavior can be observed in solvents other than water. One commonly used solvent is dimethyl sulfoxide (DMSO), which can be treated as a monoprotic acid "HSol." Just as water can behave either as an acid or a base, so HSol can behave either as a Brønsted–Lowry acid or base.

(a) The equilibrium constant for self-dissociation of HSol (call it K_{HSol}) is 1×10^{-35}. Write the chemical equation for the self-dissociation reaction and the corresponding equilibrium equation. (Hint: The equilibrium equation is analogous to the equilibrium equation for K_w in the case of water.)

(b) The weak acid HCN has an acid dissociation constant $K_a = 1.3 \times 10^{-13}$ in the solvent HSol. If 0.010 mol of NaCN is dissolved in 1.00 L of HSol, what is the equilibrium concentration of H_2Sol^+?

MULTICONCEPT PROBLEMS

14.132 A 7.0 mass % solution of H_3PO_4 in water has a density of 1.0353 g/mL. Calculate the pH and the molar concentrations of all species present (H_3PO_4, $H_2PO_4^-$, HPO_4^{2-}, PO_4^{3-}, H_3O^+, and OH^-) in the solution. Values of equilibrium constants are listed in Appendix C.

14.133 In the case of very weak acids, $[H_3O^+]$ from the dissociation of water is significant compared with $[H_3O^+]$ from the dissociation of the weak acid. The sugar substitute saccharin ($C_7H_5NO_3S$), for example, is a very weak acid having $K_a = 2.1 \times 10^{-12}$ and a solubility in water of 348 mg/100 mL. Calculate $[H_3O^+]$ in a saturated solution of saccharin. (Hint: Equilibrium equations for the dissociation of saccharin and water must be solved simultaneously.)

14.134 In aqueous solution, sodium acetate behaves as a strong electrolyte, yielding Na^+ cations and $CH_3CO_2^-$ anions. A particular solution of sodium acetate has a pH of 9.07 and a density of 1.0085 g/mL. What is the molality of this solution, and what is its freezing point?

14.135 During a certain time period, 4.0 million tons of SO_2 was released into the atmosphere and was subsequently oxidized to SO_3. As explained in the Inquiry, the acid rain produced when the SO_3 dissolves in water can damage marble statues:

$$CaCO_3(s) + H_2SO_4(aq) \longrightarrow CaSO_4(aq) + CO_2(g) + H_2O(l)$$

(a) How many 500 pound marble statues could be damaged by the acid rain? (Assume that the statues are pure $CaCO_3$ and that a statue is damaged when 3.0% of its mass is dissolved.)

(b) How many liters of CO_2 gas at 20 °C and 735 mm Hg is produced as a byproduct?

(c) The cation in aqueous H_2SO_4 is trigonal pyramidal rather than trigonal planar. Explain.

14.136 Neutralization reactions involving either a strong acid or a strong base go essentially to completion, and therefore we must take such neutralizations into account before calculating concentrations in mixtures of acids and bases. Consider a mixture of 3.28 g of Na_3PO_4 and 300.0 mL of 0.180 M HCl. Write balanced net ionic equations for the neutralization reactions, and calculate the pH of the solution.

14.137 We've said that alkali metal cations do not react appreciably with water to produce H_3O^+ ions, but in fact, all cations are acidic to some extent. The most acidic alkali metal cation is the smallest one, Li^+, which has $K_a = 2.5 \times 10^{-14}$ for the reaction

$$Li(H_2O)_4^+(aq) + H_2O(l) \rightleftharpoons H_3O^+(aq) + Li(H_2O)_3(OH)(aq)$$

This reaction and the dissociation of water must be considered simultaneously in calculating the pH of Li^+ solutions, which nevertheless have pH $\approx$ 7. Check this by calculating the pH of 0.10 M LiCl.

14.138 A 1.000 L sample of HF gas at 20.0 °C and 0.601 atm pressure was dissolved in enough water to make 50.0 mL of hydrofluoric acid.

(a) What is the pH of the solution?

(b) To what volume must you dilute the solution to triple the percent dissociation. Why can't you solve this problem by using the result obtained in Problem 14.126?

14.139 A 200.0 mL sample of 0.350 M acetic acid (CH_3CO_2H) was allowed to react with 2.000 L of gaseous ammonia at 25 °C and a pressure of 650.8 mm Hg. Assuming no change in the volume of the solution, calculate the pH and the equilibrium concentrations of all species present (CH_3CO_2H, $CH_3CO_2^-$, NH_3, NH_4^+, H_3O^+, and OH^-). Values of equilibrium constants are listed in Appendix C.

14.140 You may have been told not to mix bleach and ammonia. The reason is that bleach (sodium hypochlorite) reacts with ammonia to produce toxic chloramines, such as NH_2Cl. For example, in basic solution:

$$OCl^-(aq) + NH_3(aq) \longrightarrow OH^-(aq) + NH_2Cl(aq)$$

(a) The following initial rate data for this reaction were obtained in basic solution at 25 °C:

pH	Initial $[OCl^-]$	Initial $[NH_3]$	Initial Rate (M/s)
12	0.001	0.01	0.017
12	0.002	0.01	0.033
12	0.002	0.03	0.100
13	0.002	0.03	0.010

What is the rate law for the reaction? What is the numerical value of the rate constant k, including the correct units?

(b) The following mechanism has been proposed for this reaction in basic solution:

$$H_2O + OCl^- \rightleftharpoons HOCl + OH^- \quad \text{Fast, equilibrium constant } K_1$$
$$HOCl + NH_3 \longrightarrow H_2O + NH_2Cl \quad \text{Slow, rate constant } k_2$$

Assuming that the first step is in equilibrium and the second step is rate-determining, calculate the value of the rate constant k_2 for the second step. K_a for HOCl is 3.5×10^{-8}.

CHAPTER 15

Applications of Aqueous Equilibria

The limestone (CaCO₃) framework of a coral reef is in equilibrium with Ca²⁺ and CO₃²⁻ ions in the ocean.

The limestone (CaCO$_3$) framework of a coral reef is in equilibrium with Ca^{2+} and CO$_3^{2-}$ ions in the ocean.

CONTENTS

A queous equilibria play a crucial role in many biological and environmental processes. The pH of human blood, for example, is carefully controlled at a value of 7.4 by equilibria involving primarily the conjugate acid–base pair H_2CO_3 and HCO_3^-. The pH of many lakes and streams must remain near 5.5 for plant and aquatic life to flourish.

We began a study of aqueous equilibria in Chapter 14, where we examined the dissociation of weak acids and weak bases. In this chapter, we'll continue the study by focusing on some applications of aqueous equilibria. First we'll see how to calculate the pH of mixtures of acids and bases. Then we'll look at the dissolution and precipitation of slightly soluble ionic compounds and the factors that affect solubility. Aqueous equilibria involving the dissolution and precipitation of ionic compounds are important in a great many natural processes, from tooth decay to the formation of coral reefs and limestone caves.

15.1 NEUTRALIZATION REACTIONS

We've seen on numerous occasions that the neutralization reaction of an acid with a base produces water and a salt. But to what extent does a neutralization reaction go to completion? We must answer that question before we can make pH calculations on mixtures of acids and bases. We'll look at four types of neutralization reactions: (1) strong acid–strong base, (2) weak acid–strong base, (3) strong acid–weak base, and (4) weak acid–weak base.

Strong Acid–Strong Base

As an example of a strong acid–strong base reaction, let's consider the reaction of hydrochloric acid with aqueous sodium hydroxide to give water and an aqueous solution of sodium chloride:

$$HCl(aq) + NaOH(aq) \longrightarrow H_2O(l) + NaCl(aq)$$

Because $HCl(aq)$, $NaOH(aq)$, and $NaCl(aq)$ are all completely dissociated, the net ionic equation for the neutralization reaction is

$$H_3O^+(aq) + OH^-(aq) \rightleftharpoons 2\,H_2O(l)$$

If we mix equal numbers of moles of $HCl(aq)$ and $NaOH(aq)$, the concentrations of H_3O^+ and OH^- remaining in the NaCl solution after neutralization will be the same as those in pure water, $[H_3O^+] = [OH^-] = 1.0 \times 10^{-7}$ M. In other words, the reaction of HCl with NaOH proceeds far to the right.

We come to the same conclusion by looking at the equilibrium constant for the reaction. Because the neutralization reaction of any strong acid with a strong base is the reverse of the dissociation of water, its equilibrium constant, K_n ("n" for neutralization), is just the reciprocal of the ion-product constant for water, $K_n = 1/K_w$:

$$H_3O^+(aq) + OH^-(aq) \rightleftharpoons 2\,H_2O(l)$$

$$K_n = \frac{1}{[H_3O^+][OH^-]} = \frac{1}{K_w} = \frac{1}{1.0 \times 10^{-14}} = 1.0 \times 10^{14}$$

The value of K_n (1.0×10^{14}) for a strong acid–strong base reaction is a very large number, which means that the neutralization reaction proceeds essentially 100% to completion. After neutralization of equal molar amounts of acid and base, **the solution contains a salt** derived from a strong base and a strong acid. Because neither the cation nor the anion of the salt has acidic or basic properties, the pH is 7 (Section 14.14).

Remember...

Salt solutions can be neutral, acidic, or basic, depending on the acid–base properties of the constituent cations and anions. (Section 14.14)

Weak Acid–Strong Base

Because a weak acid HA is largely undissociated, the net ionic equation for the neutralization reaction of a weak acid with a strong base involves proton transfer from HA to the strong base, OH^-:

$$HA(aq) + OH^-(aq) \rightleftharpoons H_2O(l) + A^-(aq)$$

Acetic acid (CH_3CO_2H), for example, reacts with aqueous NaOH to give water and aqueous sodium acetate (CH_3CO_2Na):

$$CH_3CO_2H(aq) + OH^-(aq) \rightleftharpoons H_2O(l) + CH_3CO_2^-(aq)$$

Na^+ ions do not appear in the net ionic equation because both NaOH and CH_3CO_2Na are completely dissociated.

To obtain the equilibrium constant K_n for the neutralization of acetic acid, we multiply known equilibrium constants for reactions that add to give the net ionic equation for the neutralization reaction. Because CH_3CO_2H is on the left side of the equation and $CH_3CO_2^-$ is on the right side, one of the reactions needed is the dissociation of CH_3CO_2H. Because H_2O is on the right side of the equation and OH^- is on the left side, the other reaction needed is the reverse of the dissociation of H_2O. Note that H_3O^+ and one H_2O molecule cancel when the two equations are added:

$$CH_3CO_2H(aq) + \cancel{H_2O(l)} \rightleftharpoons \cancel{H_3O^+(aq)} + CH_3CO_2^-(aq) \qquad K_a = 1.8 \times 10^{-5}$$

$$\cancel{H_3O^+(aq)} + OH^-(aq) \rightleftharpoons \cancel{2}\, H_2O(l) \qquad 1/K_w = 1.0 \times 10^{14}$$

$$\text{Net:} \quad CH_3CO_2H(aq) + OH^-(aq) \rightleftharpoons H_2O(l) + CH_3CO_2^-(aq) \qquad K_n = (K_a)(1/K_w) = (1.8 \times 10^{-5})(1.0 \times 10^{14})$$
$$= 1.8 \times 10^9$$

Weak acid–strong base neutralization
$$CH_3CO_2H(aq) + OH^-(aq) \rightleftharpoons$$
$$H_2O(l) + CH_3CO_2^-(aq)$$

▲ When NaOH(aq) is added to $CH_3CO_2H(aq)$ containing the acid–base indicator phenolphthalein, the color of the indicator changes from colorless to pink in the pH range 8.2–9.8 because of neutralization of the acetic acid.

As we saw in Section 14.13, the equilibrium constant for the net reaction equals the product of the equilibrium constants for the reactions added, Therefore, we multiply K_a for CH_3CO_2H by the reciprocal of K_w to get K_n for the neutralization reaction. (We use $1/K_w$ because the H_2O dissociation reaction is written in the reverse direction.) The resulting large value of K_n (1.8×10^9) means that the neutralization reaction proceeds nearly 100% to completion.

As a general rule, the neutralization of any weak acid with a strong base will go 100% to completion because OH^- has a great affinity for protons. After neutralization of equal molar amounts of CH_3CO_2H and NaOH, the solution contains Na^+, which has no acidic or basic properties, and $CH_3CO_2^-$, which is a weak base. Therefore, the pH is greater than 7 (Section 14.14).

Strong Acid–Weak Base

A strong acid HA is completely dissociated into H_3O^+ and A^- ions, and its neutralization reaction with a weak base therefore involves proton transfer from H_3O^+ to the weak base B:

$$H_3O^+(aq) + B(aq) \rightleftharpoons H_2O(l) + BH^+(aq)$$

For example, the net ionic equation for the neutralization of hydrochloric acid with aqueous ammonia is

$$H_3O^+(aq) + NH_3(aq) \rightleftharpoons H_2O(l) + NH_4^+(aq)$$

As in the weak acid–strong base case, we can obtain the equilibrium constant for the neutralization reaction by multiplying known equilibrium constants for reactions that add to give the net ionic equation:

$$NH_3(aq) + \cancel{H_2O(l)} \rightleftharpoons NH_4^+(aq) + \cancel{OH^-(aq)} \qquad K_b = 1.8 \times 10^{-5}$$

$$H_3O^+(aq) + \cancel{OH^-(aq)} \rightleftharpoons \cancel{2}\, H_2O(l) \qquad 1/K_w = 1.0 \times 10^{14}$$

$$\text{Net:} \quad H_3O^+(aq) + NH_3(aq) \rightleftharpoons H_2O(l) + NH_4^+(aq) \qquad K_n = (K_b)(1/K_w)$$
$$= (1.8 \times 10^{-5})(1.0 \times 10^{14})$$
$$= 1.8 \times 10^9$$

Again, the neutralization reaction proceeds nearly 100% to the right because its equilibrium constant K_n is a very large number (1.8×10^9). (It's purely coincidental that the neutralization reactions of CH_3CO_2H with NaOH and of HCl with NH_3 have the same value of K_n. The two K_n values are the same because K_a for CH_3CO_2H happens to have the same value as K_b for NH_3.)

The neutralization of any weak base with a strong acid generally goes 100% to completion because H_3O^+ is a powerful proton donor. After the neutralization of equal molar amounts of NH_3 and HCl, the solution contains NH_4^+, which is a weak acid, and Cl^-, which has no acidic or basic properties. Therefore, the pH is less than 7 (Section 14.14).

Weak Acid–Weak Base

Both a weak acid HA and a weak base B are largely undissociated, and the neutralization reaction between them therefore involves proton transfer from the weak acid to the weak base. For example, the net ionic equation for the neutralization of acetic acid with aqueous ammonia is

$$CH_3CO_2H(aq) + NH_3(aq) \rightleftharpoons NH_4^+(aq) + CH_3CO_2^-(aq)$$

The equilibrium constant K_n can be obtained by multiplying equilibrium constants for (1) the acid dissociation of acetic acid, (2) the base protonation of ammonia, and (3) the reverse of the dissociation of water:

$$CH_3CO_2H(aq) + H_2O(l) \rightleftharpoons H_3O^+(aq) + CH_3CO_2^-(aq) \qquad K_a = 1.8 \times 10^{-5}$$

$$NH_3(aq) + H_2O(l) \rightleftharpoons NH_4^+(aq) + OH^-(aq) \qquad K_b = 1.8 \times 10^{-5}$$

$$H_3O^+(aq) + OH^-(aq) \rightleftharpoons 2\,H_2O(l) \qquad 1/K_w = 1.0 \times 10^{14}$$

Net: $CH_3CO_2H(aq) + NH_3(aq) \rightleftharpoons NH_4^+(aq) + CH_3CO_2^-(aq) \qquad K_n = (K_a)(K_b)(1/K_w)$

$$K_n = (K_a)(K_b)\left(\frac{1}{K_w}\right) = (1.8 \times 10^{-5})(1.8 \times 10^{-5})(1.0 \times 10^{14}) = 3.2 \times 10^4$$

The value of K_n in this case is smaller than it is for the preceding three cases, so the neutralization does not proceed as far toward completion.

In general, weak acid–weak base neutralizations have less tendency to proceed to completion than neutralizations involving strong acids or strong bases. The neutralization of HCN with aqueous ammonia, for example, has a value of K_n less than one, which means that the reaction proceeds less than halfway to completion:

$$HCN(aq) + NH_3(aq) \rightleftharpoons NH_4^+(aq) + CN^-(aq) \qquad K_n = 0.88$$

Strong acid–weak base neutralization
$$H_3O^+(aq) + NH_3(aq) \rightleftharpoons H_2O(l) + NH_4^+(aq)$$

▲ When hydrochloric acid is added to aqueous ammonia containing the acid–base indicator methyl red, the color of the indicator changes from yellow to red in the pH range 6.0–4.2 because of the neutralization of the NH_3.

WORKED EXAMPLE 15.1

WRITING EQUATIONS FOR NEUTRALIZATION REACTIONS, AND ESTIMATING THE pH OF THE RESULTING SOLUTION

Write a balanced net ionic equation for the neutralization of equal molar amounts of nitric acid and methylamine (CH_3NH_2). Indicate whether the pH after neutralization is greater than, equal to, or less than 7.

STRATEGY

The formulas that should appear in the net ionic equation depend on whether the acid and base are strong (completely dissociated) or weak (largely undissociated). The pH after neutralization depends on the acid–base properties of the cation and anion in the resulting salt solution (Section 14.14).

SOLUTION

Because HNO_3 is a strong acid and CH_3NH_2 is a weak base, the neutralization proceeds to completion and the net ionic equation is

$$H_3O^+(aq) + CH_3NH_2(aq) \rightleftharpoons H_2O(l) + CH_3NH_3^+(aq)$$

After neutralization, the solution contains $CH_3NH_3^+$, a weak acid, and NO_3^-, which has no acidic or basic properties. Therefore, the pH is less than 7.

▶ **PROBLEM 15.1** Write balanced net ionic equations for the neutralization of equal molar amounts of the following acids and bases. Indicate whether the pH after neutralization is greater than, equal to, or less than 7. Values of K_a and K_b are listed in Appendix C.

(a) HNO_2 and KOH   (b) HBr and NH_3 (c) KOH and $HClO_4$

▶ **PROBLEM 15.2** Write balanced net ionic equations for the neutralization of the following acids and bases, calculate the value of K_n for each neutralization reaction, and arrange the reactions in order of increasing tendency to proceed to completion. Values of K_a and K_b are listed in Appendix C.

(a) HF and NaOH   (b) HCl and KOH   (c) HF and NH_3

15.2 THE COMMON-ION EFFECT

A solution of a weak acid and its conjugate base is an important acid–base mixture because such mixtures regulate the pH in biological systems. To illustrate pH calculations for weak acid–conjugate base mixtures, let's calculate the pH of a solution prepared by dissolving 0.10 mol of acetic acid and 0.10 mol of sodium acetate in water and then diluting the solution to a volume of 1.00 L. This problem, like those discussed in Chapter 14, can be solved by thinking about the chemistry involved. First, identify the acid–base properties of the various species in solution, and then consider the possible proton-transfer reactions these species can undergo. We'll follow the procedure outlined in Figure 14.6 on page 556.

Step 1. Because acetic acid is largely undissociated in aqueous solution and the salt sodium acetate is essentially 100% dissociated, the species present initially are

$$CH_3CO_2H \quad Na^+ \quad CH_3CO_2^- \quad H_2O$$
$$\text{Acid} \qquad \text{Inert} \qquad \text{Base} \qquad \text{Acid or base}$$

Steps 2–3. Because we have two acids and two bases, there are four possible proton-transfer reactions. We know, however, that acetic acid is a stronger acid than water and that the principal reaction therefore involves proton transfer from CH_3CO_2H to either $CH_3CO_2^-$ or H_2O:

$$CH_3CO_2H(aq) + CH_3CO_2^-(aq) \rightleftharpoons CH_3CO_2^-(aq) + CH_3CO_2H(aq) \qquad K = 1$$

$$CH_3CO_2H(aq) + H_2O(l) \rightleftharpoons H_3O^+(aq) + CH_3CO_2^-(aq) \qquad K_a = 1.8 \times 10^{-5}$$

Although the first of these reactions has the larger equilibrium constant, we can't consider it to be the principal reaction because the reactants and products are identical. Proton transfer from acetic acid to its conjugate base is constantly occurring, but that reaction doesn't change any concentrations and therefore can't be used to calculate equilibrium concentrations. Consequently, the principal reaction is the dissociation of acetic acid.

Step 4. Now we can set up a table of concentrations for the species involved in the principal reaction. As in Section 14.9, we define x as the concentration of acid that dissociates—here, acetic acid—but we need to remember that the acetate ions come from two sources: 0.10 mol/L of acetate comes from the sodium acetate present initially, and x mol/L comes from the dissociation of acetic acid.

Principal reaction	$CH_3CO_2H(aq) + H_2O(l) \rightleftharpoons H_3O^+(aq) + CH_3CO_2^-(aq)$		
Initial concentration (M)	0.10	~0	0.10
Change (M)	$-x$	$+x$	$+x$
Equilibrium concentration (M)	$0.10 - x$	x	$0.10 + x$

Step 5. Substituting the equilibrium concentrations into the equilibrium equation for the principal reaction, we obtain

$$K_a = 1.8 \times 10^{-5} = \frac{[H_3O^+][CH_3CO_2^-]}{[CH_3CO_2H]} = \frac{(x)(0.10 + x)}{0.10 - x}$$

Because K_a is small, x is small compared to 0.10 and we can make the approximation that $(0.10 + x) \approx (0.10 - x) \approx 0.10$, which simplifies the solution of the equation:

$$1.8 \times 10^{-5} = \frac{(x)(0.10 + x)}{0.10 - x} \approx \frac{(x)(0.10)}{0.10}$$

$$x = [H_3O^+] = 1.8 \times 10^{-5} \, M$$

Step 6. $pH = -\log(1.8 \times 10^{-5}) = 4.74$

It's interesting to compare the $[H_3O^+]$ in a 0.10 M acetic acid–0.10 M sodium acetate solution with the $[H_3O^+]$ in a 0.10 M solution of pure acetic acid. The principal reaction is the same in both cases, but in 0.10 M acetic acid all the acetate ions come from the dissociation of acetic acid:

Principal reaction	$CH_3CO_2H(aq) + H_2O(l) \rightleftharpoons H_3O^+(aq) + CH_3CO_2^-(aq)$		
Equilibrium concentration (M)	$0.10 - x$	x	x

The calculated $[H_3O^+]$ of 0.10 M acetic acid is $1.3 \times 10^{-3} \, M$, and the pH is 2.89 versus a pH of 4.74 for the acetic acid–sodium acetate solution. The difference in pH is illustrated in **Figure 15.1**.

$CH_3CO_2H(aq)$–$CH_3CO_2Na(aq)$
$[H_3O^+] = 1.8 \times 10^{-5} \, M$
$pH = 4.74$

$CH_3CO_2H(aq)$
$[H_3O^+] = 1.3 \times 10^{-3} \, M$
$pH = 2.89$

The difference in pH is revealed by the color of the indicator methyl orange, which changes from yellow to red in the pH range 4.4–3.2.

Figure 15.1
A demonstration of the common-ion effect. The 0.10 M acetic acid–0.10 M sodium acetate solution on the left has a lower H_3O^+ concentration and a higher pH than the 0.10 M acetic acid solution on the right.

The decrease in $[H_3O^+]$ on adding acetate ions to an acetic acid solution is an example of the **common-ion effect**, the shift in an equilibrium on adding a substance that provides more of an ion already involved in the equilibrium. Thus, added acetate ions shift the acetic acid-dissociation equilibrium to the left, as shown in **Figure 15.2**.

$$CH_3CO_2H(aq) + H_2O(l) \rightleftharpoons H_3O^+(aq) + CH_3CO_2^-(aq)$$

The common-ion effect is just another example of Le Châtelier's principle (Section 13.6), in which the stress on the equilibrium of raising one of the product concentrations is relieved by shifting the equilibrium to the reactant side. Another case is discussed in Worked Example 15.2.

Remember...
Le Châtelier's principle says that if a concentration, pressure, or temperature stress is applied to a reaction mixture at equilibrium, net reaction occurs in the direction that relieves the stress. Net reaction continues until a new state of equilibrium is achieved. (Section 13.6)

Figure 15.2
The common-ion effect. Note that $[H_3O^+]$ is plotted on a logarithmic scale.

The concentration of H_3O^+ in a 0.10 M acetic acid solution decreases as the concentration of added sodium acetate increases because added acetate ions shift the acid-dissociation equilibrium to the left.

0.10 M CH_3CO_2H
+ 0.10 M $CH_3CO_2^-$

Concentration of added $CH_3CO_2^-$ (mol/L)

WORKED EXAMPLE 15.2

CALCULATING THE EFFECT OF A COMMON ION ON CONCENTRATIONS, pH, AND PERCENT DISSOCIATION

In 0.15 M NH_3 ($K_b = 1.8 \times 10^{-5}$), the pH is 11.21 and the percent dissociation is 1.1%. Calculate the concentrations of all species present, the pH, and the percent dissociation of ammonia in a solution that is 0.15 M in NH_3 and 0.45 M in NH_4Cl.

STRATEGY

The solution contains a weak base (NH_3) and its conjugate acid (NH_4^+), the common ion. Because this problem is similar to the acetic acid–sodium acetate problem, we'll abbreviate the procedure shown in Figure 14.6.

SOLUTION

Steps 1–3. The principal reaction is proton transfer to NH_3 from H_2O:

$$NH_3(aq) + H_2O(l) \rightleftharpoons NH_4^+(aq) + OH^-(aq)$$

Step 4. Since NH_4^+ ions come both from the NH_4Cl present initially (0.45 M) and from the reaction of NH_3 with H_2O, the concentrations of the species involved in the principal reaction are as follows:

Principal reaction	$NH_3(aq)$ + $H_2O(l)$ $\rightleftharpoons$	$NH_4^+(aq)$ +	$OH^-(aq)$
Initial concentration (M)	0.15	0.45	~0
Change (M)	$-x$	$+x$	$+x$
Equilibrium concentration (M)	$0.15 - x$	$0.45 + x$	x

Steps 5–6. The equilibrium equation for the principal reaction is

$$K_b = 1.8 \times 10^{-5} = \frac{[NH_4^+][OH^-]}{[NH_3]} = \frac{(0.45 + x)(x)}{0.15 - x} \approx \frac{(0.45)(x)}{0.15}$$

We assume x is negligible compared to 0.45 and 0.15 because (1) the equilibrium constant K_b is small and (2) the equilibrium is shifted to the left by the common-ion effect. Therefore,

$$x = [OH^-] = \frac{(1.8 \times 10^{-5})(0.15)}{0.45} = 6.0 \times 10^{-6} M$$

$$[NH_3] = 0.15 - x = 0.15 - (6.0 \times 10^{-6}) = 0.15 M$$

$$[NH_4^+] = 0.45 + x = 0.45 + (6.0 \times 10^{-6}) = 0.45 M$$

Thus, the assumption concerning the negligible size of x is justified.

Steps 7–8. The H_3O^+ concentration and the pH are

$$[H_3O^+] = \frac{K_w}{[OH^-]} = \frac{1.0 \times 10^{-14}}{6.0 \times 10^{-6}} = 1.7 \times 10^{-9} \text{ M}$$

$$pH = -\log (1.7 \times 10^{-9}) = 8.77$$

The percent dissociation of ammonia is

$$\text{Percent dissociation} = \frac{[NH_3]_{\text{dissociated}}}{[NH_3]_{\text{initial}}} \times 100\% = \frac{6.0 \times 10^{-6}}{0.15} \times 100\% = 0.0040\%$$

BALLPARK CHECK

In the NH_3–NH_4Cl solution, NH_4^+ is the common ion, and raising its concentration shifts the equilibrium for the principal reaction to the left.

$$NH_3(aq) + H_2O(l) \rightleftharpoons NH_4^+(aq) + OH^-(aq)$$

Thus, the percent dissociation in the 0.15 M NH_3–0.45 M NH_4Cl solution will be less than the 1.1% in 0.15 M NH_3. Also, the $[OH^-]$ will be less than that in 0.15 M NH_3, and so the pH will be less than 11.21.

▶ **PROBLEM 15.3** Calculate the concentrations of all species present, the pH, and the percent dissociation of HCN ($K_a = 4.9 \times 10^{-10}$) in a solution that is 0.025 M in HCN and 0.010 M in NaCN.

▶ **PROBLEM 15.4** Calculate the pH in a solution prepared by dissolving 0.10 mol of solid NH_4Cl in 0.500 L of 0.40 M NH_3. Assume that there is no volume change.

WORKED CONCEPTUAL EXAMPLE 15.3

DETERMINING THE EFFECT OF A COMMON ION ON pH AND PERCENT DISSOCIATION

The following pictures represent solutions of a weak acid HA that may also contain the sodium salt NaA. Which solution has the highest pH? Which has the largest percent dissociation of HA? (Na^+ ions and solvent water molecules have been omitted for clarity.)

STRATEGY

The pH and the percent dissociation of HA are determined by the extent of the reaction $HA(aq) + H_2O(l) \rightleftharpoons H_3O^+(aq) + A^-(aq)$. The dissociation equilibrium shifts to the left on adding more of the common ion A^-, thus decreasing the H_3O^+ concentration (increasing the pH) and decreasing the percent dissociation. To answer the questions posed, simply count the number of A^- ions.

SOLUTION

All three solutions contain the same number of HA molecules, but different numbers of A^- ions—none for solution 1, three for solution 2, and six for solution 3. The dissociation equilibrium lies farthest to the left for solution 3, and therefore solution 3 has the lowest H_3O^+ concentration and the highest pH. For solution 1, no common ion is present to suppress the dissociation of HA, and therefore solution 1 has the largest percent dissociation.

CONCEPTUAL PROBLEM 15.5 The following pictures represent solutions of a weak base B that may also contain the chloride salt BH^+Cl^-. Which solution has the lowest pH: Which has the largest percent dissociation of B? (Cl^- ions and solvent water molecules have been omitted for clarity.)

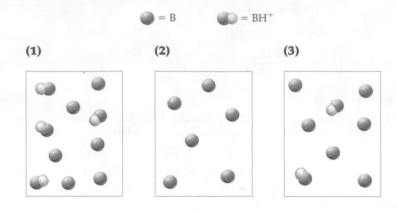

15.3 BUFFER SOLUTIONS

Solutions like those discussed in Section 15.2, which contain a weak acid and its conjugate base, are called **buffer solutions** because they resist drastic changes in pH. If a small amount of OH^- is added to a buffer solution, the pH increases, but not by much because the acid component of the buffer solution neutralizes the added OH^-. If a small amount of H_3O^+ is added to a buffer solution, the pH decreases, but again not by much because the base component of the buffer solution neutralizes the added H_3O^+.

$$
\text{Buffer solution} \quad
\begin{array}{c}
\text{Weak acid} \\
+ \\
\text{Conjugate base}
\end{array}
\quad
\begin{array}{c}
\text{For} \\
\text{example:}
\end{array}
\quad
\left\{
\begin{array}{l}
CH_3CO_2H + CH_3CO_2^- \\
HF + F^- \\
NH_4^+ + NH_3 \\
H_2PO_4^- + HPO_4^{2-}
\end{array}
\right.
$$

Buffer solutions are very important in biological systems. Blood, for example, is a buffer solution that can soak up the acids and bases produced in biological reactions. The pH of human blood is carefully controlled at a value very close to 7.4 by conjugate acid–base pairs, primarily H_2CO_3 and its conjugate base HCO_3^-. The oxygen-carrying ability of blood depends on control of the pH to within 0.1 pH unit.

To see how a buffer solution works, let's return to the 0.10 M acetic acid−0.10 M sodium acetate solution discussed in Section 15.2. The principal reaction and the equilibrium concentrations for the solution are

Principal reaction	$CH_3CO_2H(aq) + H_2O(l) \rightleftharpoons H_3O^+(aq) + CH_3CO_2^-(aq)$		
Equilibrium concentration (M)	$0.10 - x$	x	$0.10 + x$

If we solve the equilibrium equation for $[H_3O^+]$, we obtain

$$K_a = \frac{[H_3O^+][CH_3CO_2^-]}{[CH_3CO_2H]}$$

$$[H_3O^+] = K_a \frac{[CH_3CO_2H]}{[CH_3CO_2^-]}$$

Thus, the H_3O^+ concentration in a buffer solution has a value close to the value of K_a for the weak acid but differs by a factor equal to the concentration ratio [weak acid]/ [conjugate base]. In the 0.10 M acetic acid−0.10 M sodium acetate solution, where the concentration ratio is 1.0, $[H_3O^+]$ equals K_a:

$$[H_3O^+] = K_a \frac{(0.10 - x)}{(0.10 + x)} = K_a\left(\frac{0.10}{0.10}\right) = K_a = 1.8 \times 10^{-5}\,M$$

$$pH = pK_a = -\log (1.8 \times 10^{-5}) = 4.74$$

Note that in calculating this result we have set the *equilibrium* concentrations, $(0.10 - x)$ and $(0.10 + x)$, equal to the *initial* concentrations, 0.10, because x is negligible compared with the initial concentrations. For commonly used buffer solutions, K_a is small and the initial concentrations are relatively large. As a result, x is generally negligible compared with the initial concentrations, and we can use initial concentrations in the calculations.

Addition of OH⁻ to a Buffer

Now let's consider what happens when we add H_3O^+ or OH^- to a buffer solution. First, suppose that we add 0.01 mol of solid NaOH to 1.00 L of the 0.10 M acetic acid–0.10 M sodium acetate solution. Because neutralization reactions involving strong acids or strong bases go essentially 100% to completion (Section 15.1), we must take account of neutralization before calculating $[H_3O^+]$. Initially, we have (1.00 L)(0.10 mol/L) = 0.10 mol of acetic acid and an equal amount of acetate ion. When we add 0.01 mol of NaOH, the neutralization reaction will alter the numbers of moles:

Neutralization reaction	$CH_3CO_2H(aq)$ +	$OH^-(aq)$ $\xrightarrow{100\%}$	$H_2O(l)$ +	$CH_3CO_2^-(aq)$
Before reaction (mol)	0.10	0.01		0.10
Change (mol)	−0.01	−0.01		+0.01
After reaction (mol)	0.09	~0		0.11

If we assume that the solution volume remains constant at 1.00 L, the concentrations of the buffer components after neutralization are

$$[CH_3CO_2H] = \frac{0.09\text{ mol}}{1.00\text{ L}} = 0.09\text{ M}$$

$$[CH_3CO_2^-] = \frac{0.11\text{ mol}}{1.00\text{ L}} = 0.11\text{ M}$$

Substituting these concentrations into the expression for $[H_3O^+]$, we can then calculate the pH:

$$[H_3O^+] = K_a \frac{[CH_3CO_2H]}{[CH_3CO_2^-]}$$

$$= (1.8 \times 10^{-5})\left(\frac{0.09}{0.11}\right) = 1.5 \times 10^{-5}\,M$$

$$pH = 4.82$$

Adding 0.01 mol of NaOH changes $[H_3O^+]$ by only a small amount because the concentration ratio [weak acid]/[conjugate base] changes by only a small amount, from 1.0 to 9/11 (**Figure 15.3a**). The corresponding change in pH, from 4.74 to 4.82, is only 0.08 pH unit.

Addition of H₃O⁺ to a Buffer

Now suppose that we add 0.01 mol of HCl to 1.00 L of the 0.10 M acetic acid–0.10 M sodium acetate buffer solution. The added strong acid will convert 0.01 mol of acetate ions to 0.01 mol of acetic acid because of the neutralization reaction

$$H_3O^+(aq) + CH_3CO_2^-(aq) \xrightarrow{100\%} H_2O(l) + CH_3CO_2H(aq)$$

Figure 15.3
The addition of (a) OH⁻ and (b) H₃O⁺ to a buffer solution.

(a)   Original buffer solution   (b)

Weak acid

When OH⁻ is added to a buffer solution, some of the weak acid is neutralized and thus converted to the conjugate base.

Weak acid

When H₃O⁺ is added to a buffer solution, some of the conjugate base is neutralized and thus converted to the weak acid.

Weak acid

Conju-gate base

Conju-gate base

Conju-gate base

Buffer solution after addition of OH⁻

Buffer solution after addition of H₃O⁺

As long as the concentration ratio [weak acid]/[conjugate base] stays close to its original value, [H₃O⁺] and the pH won't change very much in either of these cases.

The concentrations after neutralization will be $[CH_3CO_2H] = 0.11$ M and $[CH_3CO_2^-] = 0.09$ M, and the pH of the solution will be 4.66:

$$[H_3O^+] = K_a \frac{[CH_3CO_2H]}{[CH_3CO_2^-]}$$

$$= (1.8 \times 10^{-5})\left(\frac{0.11}{0.09}\right) = 2.2 \times 10^{-5} \text{ M}$$

$$pH = 4.66$$

Again, the change in pH, from 4.74 to 4.66, is small because the concentration ratio [weak acid]/[conjugate base] remains close to its original value (**Figure 15.3b**).

Buffer Capacity

To appreciate the ability of a buffer solution to maintain a nearly constant pH, let's contrast the behavior of the 0.10 M acetic acid–0.10 M sodium acetate buffer with that of a 1.8×10^{-5} M HCl solution. This very dilute solution of a strong acid has the same pH (4.74) as the buffer solution, but it doesn't have the capacity to soak up added acid or base. For example, if we add 0.01 mol of solid NaOH to 1.00 L of 1.8×10^{-5} M HCl, a negligible amount of the OH⁻ (1.8×10^{-5} mol) is neutralized and the concentration of OH⁻ after neutralization is 0.01 mol/1.00 L = 0.01 M. As a result, the pH rises from 4.74 to 12.0:

$$[H_3O^+] = \frac{K_w}{[OH^-]} = \frac{(1.0 \times 10^{-14})}{(0.01)} = 1 \times 10^{-12} \text{ M}$$

$$pH = 12.0$$

The abilities of the HCl solution and the buffer solution to absorb added base are contrasted in **Figure 15.4**.

We sometimes talk about the buffering ability of a solution using the term **buffer capacity** as a measure of the amount of acid or base that the solution can absorb without a significant change in pH. Buffer capacity is also a measure of how little the pH changes with the addition of a given amount of acid or base. Buffer capacity depends on how many moles of weak acid and conjugate base are present. For equal volumes of solution, the more concentrated the solution, the greater the buffer capacity. For solutions having the same concentration, the greater the volume, the greater the buffer capacity.

(a) 1.00 L of 1.8 × 10⁻⁵ M HCl (pH = 4.74)

(b) The solution from **(a)** turns yellow (pH > 5.4) after addition of only a few drops of 0.10 M NaOH.

(c) 1.00 L of a 0.10 M acetic acid–0.10 M sodium acetate buffer solution (pH = 4.74)

(d) The solution from **(c)** is still red (pH < 5.4) after addition of 100 mL of 0.10 M NaOH.

Figure 15.4
The abilities of a strong acid solution and a buffer solution to absorb added base. The color of each solution is due to the presence of a few drops of methyl red, an acid–base indicator that is red at pH less than about 5.4 and yellow at pH greater than about 5.4.

CONCEPTUAL PROBLEM 15.6   The following pictures represent solutions that contain a weak acid HA and/or its sodium salt NaA. (Na⁺ ions and solvent water molecules have been omitted for clarity.)

⬤⬤ = HA   ⬤ = A⁻

(1)   **(2)**   **(3)**   **(4)**

(a) Which of the solutions are buffer solutions?
(b) Which solution has the greatest buffer capacity?

▶ **PROBLEM 15.7**   Calculate the pH of 0.100 L of a buffer solution that is 0.25 M in HF and 0.50 M in NaF. What is the change in pH on addition of the following?
   (a) 0.002 mol of HNO₃   **(b)** 0.004 mol of KOH

▶ **PROBLEM 15.8**   Calculate the change in pH when 0.002 mol of HNO₃ is added to 0.100 L of a buffer solution that is 0.050 M in HF and 0.100 M in NaF. Does this solution have more or less buffer capacity than the one in Problem 15.7?

15.4 THE HENDERSON–HASSELBALCH EQUATION

We saw in Section 15.3 that the H_3O^+ concentration in a buffer solution depends on the dissociation constant of the weak acid and on the concentration ratio [weak acid]/[conjugate base]:

$$[H_3O^+] = K_a \frac{[\text{Acid}]}{[\text{Base}]}$$

This equation can be rewritten in logarithmic form by taking the negative base-10 logarithm of both sides:

$$pH = -\log[H_3O^+] = -\log\left(K_a \frac{[\text{Acid}]}{[\text{Base}]}\right) = -\log K_a - \log\frac{[\text{Acid}]}{[\text{Base}]}$$

Because $pK_a = -\log K_a$ and

$$-\log\frac{[\text{Acid}]}{[\text{Base}]} = \log\frac{[\text{Base}]}{[\text{Acid}]}$$

we obtain an expression called the **Henderson–Hasselbalch equation**:

Henderson-Hasselbalch Equation $\quad pH = pK_a + \log\dfrac{[\text{Base}]}{[\text{Acid}]}$

The Henderson–Hasselbalch equation says that the pH of a buffer solution has a value close to the pK_a of the weak acid, differing only by the amount log [base]/[acid]. When [base]/[acid] = 1, then log [base]/[acid] = 0 and the pH equals the pK_a.

The real importance of the Henderson–Hasselbalch equation, particularly in biochemistry, is that it tells us how the pH affects the percent dissociation of a weak acid. Suppose, for example, that you have a solution containing the amino acid glycine, one of the molecules from which proteins are made, and that the pH of the solution is 2.00 pH units greater than the pK_a of glycine:

Glycine

$$\underset{\text{Glycine}}{\overset{+}{H_3}NCH_2\overset{\displaystyle \overset{O}{\|}}{C}O^-(aq)} + H_2O(l) \rightleftharpoons H_2NCH_2\overset{\displaystyle \overset{O}{\|}}{C}O^-(aq) + H_3O^+(aq) \qquad \begin{array}{l} K_a = 2.5 \times 10^{-10} \\ pK_a = 9.60 \end{array}$$

$$pH = pK_a + 2.00 = 11.60$$

Since pH = pK_a + 2.00, then log [base]/[acid] = 2.00 and [base]/[acid] = 1.0×10^2 = 100/1. According to the Henderson–Hasselbalch equation, therefore, 100 of every 101 glycine molecules are dissociated, which corresponds to 99% dissociation:

$$\log\frac{[\text{Base}]}{[\text{Acid}]} = pH - pK_a = 2.00$$

$$\frac{[\text{Base}]}{[\text{Acid}]} = 1.0 \times 10^2 = \frac{100}{1} \qquad 99\% \text{ dissociation}$$

The Henderson–Hasselbalch equation thus gives the following relationships:

At pH = pK_a + 2.00: $\quad \dfrac{[\text{Base}]}{[\text{Acid}]} = 1.0 \times 10^2 = \dfrac{100}{1} \qquad$ 99% dissociation

At pH = pK_a + 1.00: $\quad \dfrac{[\text{Base}]}{[\text{Acid}]} = 1.0 \times 10^1 = \dfrac{10}{1} \qquad$ 91% dissociation

At pH = pK_a + 0.00: $\quad \dfrac{[\text{Base}]}{[\text{Acid}]} = 1.0 \times 10^0 = \dfrac{1}{1} \qquad$ 50% dissociation

At pH = pK_a − 1.00: $\quad \dfrac{[\text{Base}]}{[\text{Acid}]} = 1.0 \times 10^{-1} = \dfrac{1}{10} \qquad$ 9% dissociation

At pH = pK_a − 2.00: $\quad \dfrac{[\text{Base}]}{[\text{Acid}]} = 1.0 \times 10^{-2} = \dfrac{1}{100} \qquad$ 1% dissociation

The Henderson–Hasselbalch equation also tells us how to prepare a buffer solution with a given pH. The general idea is to select a weak acid whose pK_a is close to the desired pH and then adjust the [base]/[acid] ratio to the value specified by the Henderson–Hasselbalch equation. For example, to prepare a buffer having a pH near 7, we might use the $H_2PO_4^- - HPO_4^{2-}$ conjugate acid–base pair because the pK_a for $H_2PO_4^-$ is $-\log(6.2 \times 10^{-8}) = 7.21$. Similarly, a mixture of NH_4Cl and NH_3 would be a good choice for a buffer having a pH near 9 because the pK_a for NH_4^+ is $-\log(5.6 \times 10^{-10}) = 9.25$. As a rule of thumb, the pK_a of the weak acid component of a buffer should be within ± 1 pH unit of the desired pH.

Because buffer solutions are widely used in the laboratory and in medicine, prepackaged buffers having a variety of precisely known pH values are commercially available (Figure 15.5). The manufacturer prepares these buffers by choosing a buffer system having an appropriate pK_a value and then adjusting the amounts of the ingredients so that the [base]/[acid] ratio has the proper value.

The pH of a buffer solution does not depend on the volume of the solution because a change in solution volume changes the concentrations of the acid and base by the same amount. Thus, the [base]/[acid] ratio and the pH remain unchanged. As a result, the volume of water used to prepare a buffer solution is not critical and you can dilute a buffer without changing its pH. The pH depends only on pK_a and on the relative molar amounts of the weak acid and the conjugate base.

Figure 15.5
Prepackaged buffer solutions of known pH and solid ingredients for preparing buffer solutions of known pH.

WORKED EXAMPLE 15.4

USING THE HENDERSON–HASSELBALCH EQUATION

(a) Use the Henderson–Hasselbalch equation to calculate the pH of a buffer solution that is 0.45 M in NH_4Cl and 0.15 M in NH_3.

(b) How would you prepare an NH_4Cl-NH_3 buffer that has a pH of 9.00?

STRATEGY

(a) We've already solved this problem by another method in Worked Example 15.2. Now that we've discussed equilibria in buffer solutions, though, we can use the Henderson–Hasselbalch equation as a shortcut. Since NH_4^+ is the weak acid in an $NH_4^+-NH_3$ buffer solution, we need to find the pK_a for NH_4^+ from the tabulated K_b value for NH_3 (Appendix C). Then, substitute $[NH_3]$, $[NH_4^+]$, and the pK_a value into the Henderson–Hasselbalch equation to find the pH.

(b) Use the Henderson–Hasselbalch equation to calculate the $[NH_3]/[NH_4^+]$ ratio from the desired pH and the pK_a value for NH_4^+.

SOLUTION

(a) Since K_b for NH_3 is 1.8×10^{-5}, K_a for NH_4^+ is 5.6×10^{-10} and $pK_a = 9.25$.

$$K_a = \frac{K_w}{K_b} = \frac{1.0 \times 10^{-14}}{1.8 \times 10^{-5}} = 5.6 \times 10^{-10}$$

$$pK_a = -\log K_a = -\log(5.6 \times 10^{-10}) = 9.25$$

Since [base] = $[NH_3]$ = 0.15 M and [acid] = $[NH_4^+]$ = 0.45 M,

$$pH = pK_a + \log\frac{[Base]}{[Acid]} = 9.25 + \log\left(\frac{0.15}{0.45}\right) = 9.25 - 0.48 = 8.77$$

The pH of the buffer solution is 8.77.

(b) Rearrange the Henderson–Hasselbalch equation to obtain an expression for the relative amounts of NH_3 and NH_4^+ in a solution having pH = 9.00:

$$\log\frac{[Base]}{[Acid]} = pH - pK_a = 9.00 - 9.25 = -0.25$$

Therefore,

$$\frac{[NH_3]}{[NH_4^+]} = \text{antilog}(-0.25) = 10^{-0.25} = 0.56$$

The solution must contain 0.56 mol of NH_3 for every 1.00 mol of NH_4Cl, but the volume of the solution isn't critical. One way of preparing the buffer would be to combine 1.00 mol of NH_4Cl (53.5 g) with 0.56 mol of NH_3 (say, 560 mL of 1.00 M NH_3).

continued on next page

BALLPARK CHECK

A common error in using the Henderson–Hasselbalch equation is to invert the [base]/[acid] ratio. It is therefore wise to check that your answer makes chemical sense. If the concentrations of the acid and its conjugate base are equal, the pH will equal the pK_a. If the acid predominates, the pH will be less than the pK_a, and if the conjugate base predominates, the pH will be greater than the pK_a. In part **(a)**, [acid] = $[NH_4^+]$ is greater than [base] = $[NH_3]$ and so the calculated pH (8.77) should be less than the pK_a (9.25). In part **(b)**, the desired pH is less than the pK_a so the buffer should contain more moles of acid than base, in agreement with the solution.

WORKED EXAMPLE 15.5

USING THE HENDERSON–HASSELBALCH EQUATION TO DETERMINE THE EFFECTIVENESS OF A BUFFER SOLUTION

What $[NH_3]/[NH_4^+]$ ratio is required for a buffer solution that has pH = 7.00? Why is a mixture of NH_3 and NH_4Cl a poor choice for a buffer having pH = 7.00?

STRATEGY

We can calculate the required $[NH_3]/[NH_4^+]$ ratio from the Henderson–Hasselbalch equation.

SOLUTION

$$\log \frac{[NH_3]}{[NH_4^+]} = pH - pK_a = 7.00 - 9.25 = -2.25$$

$$\frac{[NH_3]}{[NH_4^+]} = \text{antilog}\,(-2.25) = 10^{-2.25} = 5.6 \times 10^{-3}$$

For a typical value of $[NH_4^+]$—say, 1.0 M—the NH_3 concentration would have to be very small (0.0056 M). Such a solution is a poor buffer because it has little capacity to absorb added acid. Also, because the $[NH_3]/[NH_4^+]$ ratio is far from 1.0, addition of a small amount of H_3O^+ or OH^- will result in a large change in the pH.

BALLPARK CHECK

Because the desired pH is much less than the pK_a value, the buffer must contain much more weak acid than conjugate base, in agreement with the solution.

▶ **PROBLEM 15.9** Use the Henderson–Hasselbalch equation to calculate the pH of a buffer solution prepared by mixing equal volumes of 0.20 M $NaHCO_3$ and 0.10 M Na_2CO_3. (K_a values are given in Appendix C.)

▶ **PROBLEM 15.10** How would you prepare a $NaHCO_3$–Na_2CO_3 buffer solution that has pH = 10.40?

▶ **PROBLEM 15.11** Suppose you are performing an experiment that requires a constant pH of 7.50. Suggest an appropriate buffer system based on the K_a values in Appendix C.

▶ **PROBLEM 15.12** The pK_a of the amino acid serine is 9.15. At what pH is serine:
(a) 66% dissociated?   **(b)** 5% dissociated?

Serine

$$\underset{\text{CH}_2\text{OH}}{\overset{\displaystyle \overset{\text{O}}{\overset{\|}{\text{H}_3\overset{+}{\text{N}}\text{CHCO}^-}}}{}}$$

Serine
$pK_a = 9.15$

15.5 pH TITRATION CURVES

In a typical acid–base titration (Section 3.9), a solution containing a known concentration of base (or acid) is added slowly from a buret to a second solution containing an unknown concentration of acid (or base). The progress of the titration is monitored, either by using a pH meter (Figure 15.6a) or by observing the color of a suitable acid–base indicator. With a pH meter, you can record data to produce a **pH titration curve**, a plot of the pH of the solution as a function of the volume of added titrant (Figure 15.6b).

Remember ...

Titration is a procedure for determining the concentration of a solution by allowing a carefully measured volume to react with a standard solution of another substance, whose concentration is known. (Section 3.9)

(a) A pH titration in which 0.100 M NaOH is added slowly from a buret to an HCl solution of unknown concentration. The pH of the solution is measured with a pH meter and is recorded as a function of the volume of NaOH added.

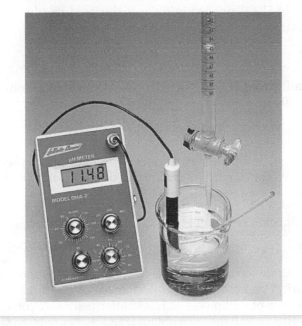

(b) The pH titration curve for titration of 40.0 mL of 0.100 M HCl with 0.100 M NaOH.

The pH increases gradually in the regions before and after the equivalence point, but increases rapidly in the region near the equivalence point.

← Equivalence point

The equivalence point comes after addition of 40.0 mL of 0.100 M NaOH. The pH at the equivalence point is 7.00.

Figure 15.6
A strong acid–strong base titration.

Why study titration curves? The shape of a pH titration curve makes it possible to identify the **equivalence point** in a titration, the point at which stoichiometrically equivalent quantities of acid and base have been mixed together. Knowing the shape of the titration curve is also useful in selecting a suitable indicator to signal the equivalence point. We'll explore both of these points later.

We can calculate pH titration curves using the principles of aqueous solution equilibria. To understand why titration curves have certain characteristic shapes, let's calculate these curves for four common types of titration: (1) strong acid–strong base, (2) weak acid–strong base, (3) weak base–strong acid, and (4) polyprotic acid–strong base. For convenience, we'll express amounts of solute in millimoles (mmol) and solution volumes in milliliters (mL). Molar concentration can thus be expressed in mmol/mL, a unit that is equivalent to mol/L:

$$\text{Molarity} = \frac{\text{mmol of solute}}{\text{mL of solution}} = \frac{10^{-3} \text{ mol of soulte}}{10^{-3} \text{ L of solution}} = \frac{\text{mol of solute}}{\text{L of solution}}$$

15.6 STRONG ACID–STRONG BASE TITRATIONS

As an example of a strong acid–strong base titration, let's consider the titration of 40.0 mL of 0.100 M HCl with 0.100 M NaOH. We'll calculate the pH at selected points in the course of the titration to illustrate the procedures we use to calculate the entire curve.

1. **Before addition of any NaOH.** Since HCl is a strong acid, the initial concentration of H_3O^+ is 0.100 M and the pH is 1.00. (We've rounded the value of the pH to two significant figures.)

2. **Before the equivalence point.** Let's calculate the pH after addition of 10.0 mL of 0.100 M NaOH. The added OH^- ions will decrease $[H_3O^+]$ because of the neutralization reaction

$$H_3O^+(aq) + OH^-(aq) \xrightarrow{100\%} 2\,H_2O(l)$$

The number of millimoles of H_3O^+ present initially is the product of the initial volume of HCl and its molarity:

$$\text{mmol } H_3O^+ \text{ initial} = (40.0 \text{ mL})(0.100 \text{ mmol/mL}) = 4.00 \text{ mmol}$$

Similarly, the number of millimoles of OH^- added is the product of the volume of NaOH added and its molarity:

$$\text{mmol } OH^- \text{ added} = (10.0 \text{ mL})(0.100 \text{ mmol/mL}) = 1.00 \text{ mmol}$$

For each mmol of OH^- added, an equal amount of H_3O^+ will disappear because of the neutralization reaction. The number of millimoles of H_3O^+ remaining after neutralization is therefore

$$\text{mmol } H_3O^+ \text{ after neutralization} = \text{mmol } H_3O^+_{\text{initial}} - \text{mmol } OH^-_{\text{added}}$$
$$= 4.00 \text{ mmol} - 1.00 \text{ mmol} = 3.00 \text{ mmol}$$

We've carried out this calculation using *amounts* of acid and base (mmol) rather than concentrations (molarity) because the volume changes as the titration proceeds. If we divide the number of millimoles of H_3O^+ after neutralization by the total volume (now 40.0 + 10.0 = 50.0 mL), we obtain $[H_3O^+]$ after neutralization:

$$[H_3O^+] \text{ after neutralization} = \frac{3.00 \text{ mmol}}{50.0 \text{ mL}} = 6.00 \times 10^{-2} \text{ M}$$
$$pH = -\log(6.00 \times 10^{-2}) = 1.22$$

This same procedure can be used to calculate the pH at other points prior to the equivalence point, giving the results summarized in the top part of Table 15.1.

3. **At the equivalence point.** After addition of 40.0 mL of 0.100 M NaOH, we have added (40.0 mL)(0.100 mmol/mL) = 4.00 mmol of NaOH, which is just enough OH^- to neutralize all the 4.00 mmol of HCl present initially. This is the equivalence point of the titration, and the pH is 7.00 because the solution contains only water and NaCl, a salt derived from a strong base and a strong acid.

4. **Beyond the equivalence point.** After addition of 60.0 mL of 0.100 M NaOH, we have added (60.0 mL)(0.100 mmol/mL) = 6.00 mmol of NaOH, which is more than enough to neutralize the 4.00 mmol of HCl present initially. Consequently, an excess of OH^- (6.00 − 4.00 = 2.00 mmol) is present. Since the total volume is now 40.0 + 60.0 = 100.0 mL, the concentration of OH^- is

$$[OH^-] \text{ after neutralization} = \frac{2.00 \text{ mmol}}{100.0 \text{ mL}} = 2.00 \times 10^{-2} \text{ M}$$

The H_3O^+ concentration and the pH are

$$[H_3O^+] = \frac{K_w}{[OH^-]} = \frac{1.0 \times 10^{-14}}{2.00 \times 10^{-2}} = 5.0 \times 10^{-13}\,M$$

$$pH = -\log(5.0 \times 10^{-13}) = 12.30$$

Sample results for pH calculations at other places beyond the equivalence point are also included in the bottom part of Table 15.1.

TABLE 15.1 Sample Results for pH Calculations at Various Points in the Titration of 40.0 mL of 0.100 M HCl with 0.100 M NaOH

mL NaOH Added	mmol OH⁻ Added	mmol H_3O^+ After Neutralization	Total Volume (mL)		[H_3O^+] After Neutralization	pH
Before the equivalence point:						
0.0	0.0	4.00	40.0		1.00×10^{-1}	1.00
10.0	1.00	3.00	50.0		6.00×10^{-2}	1.22
20.0	2.00	2.00	60.0		3.33×10^{-2}	1.48
30.0	3.00	1.00	70.0		1.43×10^{-2}	1.84
39.0	3.90	0.10	79.0		1.27×10^{-3}	2.90
39.9	3.99	0.01	79.9		1.3×10^{-4}	3.9
At the equivalence point:						
40.0	4.00	0.00	80.0		1.0×10^{-7}	7.00

Beyond the equivalence point:

mL NaOH Added	mmol OH⁻ Added	mmol OH⁻ After Neutralization	Total Volume (mL)	[OH⁻] After Neutralization	[H_3O^+] After Neutralization	pH
40.1	4.01	0.01	80.1	1.2×10^{-4}	8.3×10^{-11}	10.1
41.0	4.10	0.10	81.0	1.2×10^{-3}	8.3×10^{-12}	11.08
50.0	5.00	1.00	90.0	1.11×10^{-2}	9.0×10^{-13}	12.05
60.0	6.00	2.00	100.0	2.00×10^{-2}	5.0×10^{-13}	12.30
70.0	7.00	3.00	110.0	2.73×10^{-2}	3.7×10^{-13}	12.43
80.0	8.00	4.00	120.0	3.33×10^{-2}	3.0×10^{-13}	12.52

Plotting the pH data in Table 15.1 as a function of milliliters of NaOH added gives the pH titration curve shown previously in Figure 15.6b (page 601). This curve exhibits a gradual increase in pH in the regions before and after the equivalence point but a very sharp increase in pH in the region near the equivalence point. Thus, when the volume of added NaOH increases from 39.9 to 40.1 mL (0.2 mL is only about 4 drops), the pH increases from 3.9 to 10.1 (Table 15.1). This very sharp increase in pH in the region of the equivalence point is characteristic of the titration curve for any strong acid–strong base reaction, a feature that allows us to identify the equivalence point when the concentration of the acid is unknown.

The pH curve for the titration of a strong base with a strong acid is similar except that the initial pH is high and then decreases as acid is added (Figure 15.7).

▶ **PROBLEM 15.13** A 40.0 mL volume of 0.100 M HCl is titrated with 0.100 M NaOH. Calculate the pH of the solution after addition of **(a)** 35.0 mL and **(b)** 45.0 mL of base. Are your results consistent with the pH data in Table 15.1?

▶ **PROBLEM 15.14** A 40.0 mL volume of 0.100 M NaOH is titrated with 0.0500 M HCl. Calculate the pH after addition of the following volumes of acid:
(a) 60.0 mL   **(b)** 80.2 mL   **(c)** 100.0 mL

Figure 15.7
A strong base–strong acid titration curve. The curve shown is for the titration of 40.0 mL of 0.100 M NaOH with 0.100 M HCl.

15.7 WEAK ACID–STRONG BASE TITRATIONS

As an example of a weak acid–strong base titration, let's consider the titration of 40.0 mL of 0.100 M acetic acid with 0.100 M NaOH. Calculating the pH at selected points along the titration curve is straightforward because we've already met all the equilibrium problems that arise.

Remember...

The step-by-step procedure for solving equilibrium problems involving **weak acids** is outlined in Figure 14.6. (Section 14.9)

1. **Before addition of any NaOH.** The equilibrium problem at this point is the familiar one of calculating the pH of a solution of a **weak acid**. The calculated pH of 0.100 M acetic acid is 2.89.

2. **Before the equivalence point.** Since acetic acid is largely undissociated and NaOH is completely dissociated, the neutralization reaction is

$$CH_3CO_2H(aq) + OH^-(aq) \xrightarrow{100\%} H_2O(l) + CH_3CO_2^-(aq)$$

After addition of 20.0 mL of 0.100 M NaOH, we have added $(20.0 \text{ mL}) \times (0.100 \text{ mmol/mL}) = 2.00$ mmol of NaOH, which is enough OH^- to neutralize exactly half the 4.00 mmol of CH_3CO_2H present initially. Neutralization gives a buffer solution that contains 2.00 mmol of $CH_3CO_2^-$ and $4.00 - 2.00 = 2.00$ mmol of CH_3CO_2H. Consequently, the [base]/[acid] ratio is 1.00, and $pH = pK_a$:

$$pH = pK_a + \log \frac{[\text{Base}]}{[\text{Acid}]} = pK_a = 4.74$$

3. **At the equivalence point.** The equivalence point is reached after adding 40.0 mL of 0.100 M NaOH (4.00 mmol), which is just enough OH^- to neutralize all the 4.00 mmol of CH_3CO_2H present initially. After neutralization, the solution contains 0.0500 M $CH_3CO_2^-$:

$$[Na^+] = [CH_3CO_2^-] = \frac{4.00 \text{ mmol}}{40.0 \text{ mL} + 40.0 \text{ mL}} = 0.0500 \text{ M}$$

Remember...

Acetate ion ($CH_3CO_2^-$) gives a **basic salt solution** because it can accept a proton from water, yielding OH^-: $CH_3CO_2^-(aq) + H_2O(l) \rightleftharpoons CH_3CO_2H(aq) + OH^-(aq)$. (Section 14.14)

Because Na^+ is neither an acid nor a base and $CH_3CO_2^-$ is a weak base, we have a **basic salt solution** (Section 14.14), whose pH can be calculated as 8.72 by the method outlined in Worked Example 14.16. For a weak monoprotic acid–strong base titration, the pH at the equivalence point is always greater than 7 because the anion of the weak acid is a base.

4. **After the equivalence point.** After addition of 60.0 mL of 0.100 M NaOH, we have added $(60.0 \text{ mL})(0.100 \text{ mmol/mL}) = 6.00$ mmol of NaOH, which is more than enough OH^- to neutralize the 4.00 mmol of CH_3CO_2H present initially. The total volume is $40.0 + 60.0 = 100.0$ mL, and the concentrations after neutralization are

$$[CH_3CO_2^-] = \frac{4.00 \text{ mmol}}{100.0 \text{ mL}} = 0.0400 \text{ M}$$

$$[OH^-] = \frac{6.00 \text{ mmol} - 4.00 \text{ mmol}}{100.0 \text{ mL}} = 0.0200 \text{ M}$$

The principal reaction is the same as that at the equivalence point:

$$CH_3CO_2^-(aq) + H_2O(l) \rightleftharpoons CH_3CO_2H(aq) + OH^-(aq)$$

In this case, however, $[OH^-]$ from the principal reaction is negligible compared with $[OH^-]$ from the excess NaOH. The hydronium ion concentration and the pH can be calculated from that $[OH^-]$:

$$[H_3O^+] = \frac{K_w}{[OH^-]} = \frac{1.0 \times 10^{-14}}{0.0200} = 5.0 \times 10^{-13} \text{ M}$$

$$pH = 12.30$$

In general, [OH⁻] from the reaction of the anion of a weak acid with water is negligible beyond the equivalence point, and the pH is determined by the concentration of OH⁻ from the excess NaOH.

The results of pH calculations for the titration of 0.100 M CH_3CO_2H with 0.100 M NaOH are plotted in **Figure 15.8**. Comparison of the titration curves for the weak acid–strong base titration and the strong acid–strong base case shows several significant differences:

- The initial rise in pH is greater for the titration of the weak acid than for the strong acid, but the curve then becomes more level in the region midway to the equivalence point. Both effects are due to the buffering action of the weak acid–conjugate base mixture. The curve has its minimum slope exactly halfway to the equivalence point, where the buffering action is maximized and the pH = pK_a for the weak acid.

- The increase in pH in the region near the equivalence point is smaller in the weak acid case than in the strong acid case. The weaker the acid, the smaller the increase in the pH, as illustrated in **Figure 15.9** (page 606).

- The pH at the equivalence point is greater than 7 in the weak acid titration because the anion of a weak acid is a base.

Beyond the equivalence point, the curves for the weak acid–strong base and strong acid–strong base titrations are identical because the pH in both cases is determined by the concentration of OH⁻ from the excess NaOH.

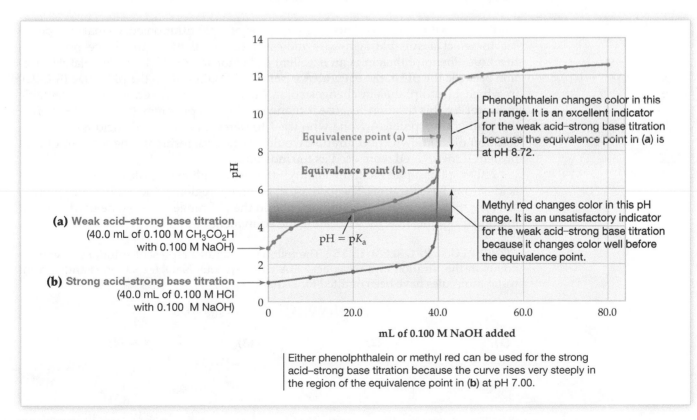

Figure 15.8
(a) A weak acid–strong base titration curve (blue) compared with (b) a strong acid–strong base curve (red). The pH ranges in which the acid–base indicators phenolphthalein and methyl red change color are indicated.

Figure 15.9
Various weak acid–strong base pH titration curves.

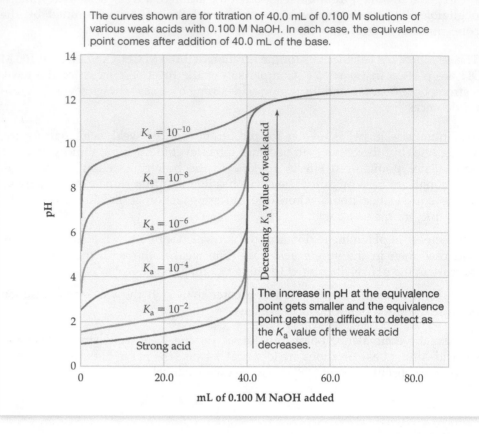

The curves shown are for titration of 40.0 mL of 0.100 M solutions of various weak acids with 0.100 M NaOH. In each case, the equivalence point comes after addition of 40.0 mL of the base.

$K_a = 10^{-10}$

$K_a = 10^{-8}$

$K_a = 10^{-6}$

$K_a = 10^{-4}$

$K_a = 10^{-2}$

Strong acid

Decreasing K_a value of weak acid

The increase in pH at the equivalence point gets smaller and the equivalence point gets more difficult to detect as the K_a value of the weak acid decreases.

pH

mL of 0.100 M NaOH added

Figure 15.8 shows how knowing the shape of a pH titration curve makes it possible to select a suitable acid–base indicator to signal the equivalence point of a titration. Phenolphthalein is an excellent indicator for the $CH_3CO_2H-NaOH$ titration because the pH at the equivalence point (8.72) falls within the pH range (8.2–9.8) in which phenolphthalein changes color. Methyl red, however, is an unacceptable indicator for this titration because it changes color in a pH range (4.2–6.0) well before the equivalence point. Anyone who tried to determine the acetic acid content in a solution of unknown concentration would badly underestimate the amount of acid present if methyl red were used as the indicator.

Either phenolphthalein or methyl red is a suitable indicator for a strong acid–strong base titration. The increase in pH in the region of the equivalence point is so steep that any indicator changing color in the pH range 4–10 can be used without making a significant error in locating the equivalence point.

CONCEPTUAL PROBLEM 15.15 The following pictures represent solutions at various points in the titration of a weak acid HA with aqueous NaOH. (Na^+ ions and solvent water molecules have been omitted for clarity.)

= HA   = A⁻   = OH⁻

(1)   **(2)**   **(3)**   **(4)**

Which picture corresponds to each of the following points in the titration?

(a) Before the addition of any NaOH   (b) Before the equivalence point

(c) At the equivalence point   (d) After the equivalence point

▶ **PROBLEM 15.16** Consider the titration of 100.0 mL of 0.016 M HOCl ($K_a = 3.5 \times 10^{-8}$) with 0.0400 M NaOH. How many milliliters of 0.0400 M NaOH are required to reach the equivalence point? Calculate the pH:

(a) After the addition of 10.0 mL of 0.0400 M NaOH

(b) Halfway to the equivalence point

(c) At the equivalence point

▶ **PROBLEM 15.17** The following acid–base indicators change color in the indicated pH ranges: bromthymol blue (6.0–7.6), thymolphthalein (9.4–10.6), and alizarin yellow (10.1–12.0). Which indicator is best for the titration in Problem 15.16? Which indicator is unacceptable? Explain.

15.8 WEAK BASE–STRONG ACID TITRATIONS

Figure 15.10 shows the pH titration curve for a typical weak base–strong acid titration, the titration of 40.0 mL of 0.100 M NH_3 with 0.100 M HCl. The pH calculations are simply outlined to save space; you should verify the results yourself.

Figure 15.10
A weak base–strong acid titration curve.

1. **Before addition of any HCl.** The equilibrium problem at the start of the titration is the familiar one of calculating the pH of a solution of a weak base (Section 14.12). The principal reaction at this point is the reaction of ammonia with water:

$$NH_3(aq) + H_2O(l) \rightleftharpoons NH_4^+(aq) + OH^-(aq) \qquad K_b = 1.8 \times 10^{-5}$$

The initial pH is 11.12.

2. **Before the equivalence point.** As HCl is added to the NH_3 solution, NH_3 is converted to NH_4^+ because of the neutralization reaction

$$NH_3(aq) + H_3O^+(aq) \xrightarrow{100\%} NH_4^+(aq) + H_2O(l)$$

Remember...

Equilibria in **solutions of weak bases** are treated by the same procedure used for solving problems involving weak acids. (Section 14.12)

The neutralization reaction goes to completion, but the amount of H_3O^+ added before the equivalence point is insufficient to convert all the NH_3 to NH_4^+. We therefore have an NH_4^+–NH_3 buffer solution, which accounts for the leveling of the titration curve in the buffer region between the start of the titration and the equivalence point. The pH at any specific point can be calculated from the Henderson–Hasselbalch equation. After addition of 20.0 mL of 0.100 M HCl (halfway to the equivalence point), $[NH_3] = [NH_4^+]$ and the pH equals pK_a for NH_4^+ (9.25).

3. **At the equivalence point.** The equivalence point is reached after adding 40.0 mL of 0.100 M HCl (4.00 mmol). At this point, the 4.00 mmol of NH_3 present initially has been converted to 4.00 mmol of NH_4^+; $[NH_4^+] = (4.00 \text{ mmol})/(80.0 \text{ mL}) = 0.0500$ M. Since NH_4^+ is a weak acid and Cl^- is neither an acid nor a base, we have an acidic salt solution (Section 14.14). The principal reaction is

$$NH_4^+(aq) + H_2O(l) \rightleftharpoons H_3O^+(aq) + NH_3(aq) \qquad K_a = K_w/K_b = 5.6 \times 10^{-10}$$

The pH at the equivalence point is 5.28.

4. **Beyond the equivalence point.** In this region, all the NH_3 has been converted to NH_4^+, and excess H_3O^+ is present from the excess HCl. Because the acid dissociation of NH_4^+ produces a negligible $[H_3O^+]$ compared with $[H_3O^+]$ from the excess HCl, the pH can be calculated directly from the concentration of the excess HCl. For example, after addition of 60.0 mL of 0.100 M HCl:

$$[H_3O^+] = \frac{6.00 \text{ mmol} - 4.00 \text{ mmol}}{100.0 \text{ mL}} = 0.0200 \text{ M}$$

$$pH = 1.70$$

15.9 POLYPROTIC ACID–STRONG BASE TITRATIONS

As a final example of an acid–base titration, let's consider the gradual addition of NaOH to the protonated form of the amino acid alanine (H_2A^+), a substance that behaves as a diprotic acid. Amino acids are both acidic and basic and can be protonated by strong acids such as HCl, yielding salts such as $H_2A^+Cl^-$. The protonated form of the amino acid has two dissociable protons and can react with two molar amounts of OH^- to give first the neutral form and then the anionic form:

Alanine cation (H_2A^+)

The proton of the $-CO_2H$ group is more acidic than the proton of the $-NH_3^+$ group and is neutralized first. The neutral form of alanine (HA) that results has a plus charge on the $-NH_3^+$ group and a minus charge on the $-CO_2^-$ group but is electrically neutral overall. In a second step, the proton of the $-NH_3^+$ group is neutralized, yielding the anionic form of alanine (A^-). The dissociation equilibria and their K_a values are

$$H_2A^+(aq) + H_2O(l) \rightleftharpoons H_3O^+(aq) + HA(aq) \qquad K_{a1} = 4.6 \times 10^{-3}; pK_{a1} = 2.34$$

$$HA(aq) + H_2O(l) \rightleftharpoons H_3O^+(aq) + A^-(aq) \qquad K_{a2} = 2.0 \times 10^{-10}; pK_{a2} = 9.69$$

Figure 15.11 shows the pH titration curve for the addition of solid NaOH to 1.00 L of a 1.00 M solution of H_2A^+ (1.00 mol). Because K_{a1} and K_{a2} are separated by several powers of 10, the titration curve exhibits two well-defined equivalence points and two buffer regions.

Figure 15.11
A diprotic acid–strong base titration curve. The change in the pH of 1.00 L of a 1.00 M solution of the protonated form of alanine (H_2A^+) on the addition of solid NaOH.

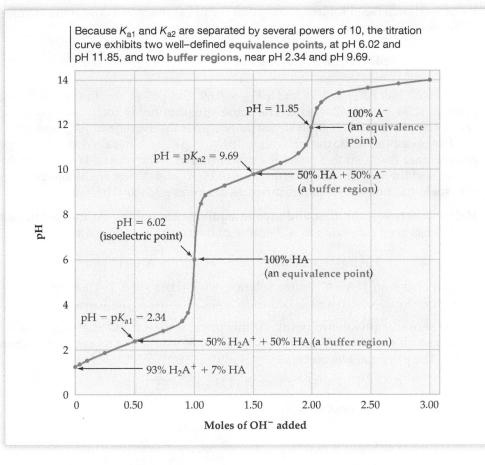

Because K_{a1} and K_{a2} are separated by several powers of 10, the titration curve exhibits two well–defined **equivalence points**, at pH 6.02 and pH 11.85, and two **buffer regions**, near pH 2.34 and pH 9.69.

pH = 11.85
100% A^- (an equivalence point)
pH = pK_{a2} = 9.69
50% HA + 50% A^- (a buffer region)
pH = 6.02 (isoelectric point)
100% HA (an equivalence point)
pH = pK_{a1} = 2.34
50% H_2A^+ + 50% HA (a buffer region)
93% H_2A^+ + 7% HA

Moles of OH⁻ added

Calculations for Diprotic Acid–Strong Base Titrations

As a review of many of the acid–base problems we've encountered in this chapter and in Chapter 14, let's calculate the pH at several points on the curve for titration of the protonated form of alanine, H_2A^+, with NaOH. We've met all these equilibrium problems previously, except for the situation at the first equivalence point. To simplify the calculations, we'll assume that the added base is solid NaOH so that we can neglect volume changes in the course of the titration.

1. **Before addition of any NaOH.** The equilibrium problem at the start of the titration is the familiar one of calculating the pH of a diprotic acid (Section 14.11). The principal reaction is the dissociation of H_2A^+, and $[H_3O^+]$ can be calculated from the equilibrium equation

$$K_{a1} = 4.6 \times 10^{-3} = \frac{[H_3O^+][HA]}{[H_2A^+]} = \frac{(x)(x)}{1.00 - x}$$

Solving the quadratic equation gives $[H_3O^+]$ = 0.066 M and pH = 1.18.

2. **Halfway to the first equivalence point.** As NaOH is added, H_2A^+ is converted to HA because of the neutralization reaction

$$H_2A^+(aq) + OH^-(aq) \xrightarrow{100\%} H_2O(l) + HA(aq)$$

Halfway to the first equivalence point, we have an H_2A^+–HA buffer solution with $[H_2A^+]$ = [HA]. The Henderson–Hasselbalch equation gives pH = pK_{a1} = 2.34.

3. **At the first equivalence point.** At this point, we have added just enough NaOH to convert all the H_2A^+ to HA. The principal reaction at the first equivalence point is proton transfer between HA molecules:

$$2 HA(aq) \rightleftharpoons H_2A^+(aq) + A^-(aq) \qquad K = K_{a2}/K_{a1} = 4.3 \times 10^{-8}$$

Remember ...
Because K_{a1} for H_2A^+ is much greater than K_{a2}, **the principal reaction is the dissociation of H_2A^+** and essentially all the H_3O^+ in the solution comes from the first dissociation step. (Section 14.11)

It can be shown (see Problem 15.140) that the pH at this point equals the average of the two pK_a values:

$$\text{pH (at first equivalence point)} = \frac{pK_{a1} + pK_{a2}}{2}$$

Since H_2A^+ has $pK_{a1} = 2.34$ and $pK_{a2} = 9.69$, the pH at the first equivalence point is $(2.34 + 9.69)/2 = 6.02$. The same situation holds for most polyprotic acids: The pH at the first equivalence point equals the average of pK_{a1} and pK_{a2}.

For an amino acid, the pH value, $(pK_{a1} + pK_{a2})/2$, is called the *isoelectric point* (Figure 15.11). At that point, the concentration of the neutral HA is at a maximum, and the very small concentrations of H_2A^+ and A^- are equal. Biochemists use isoelectric points to separate mixtures of amino acids and proteins.

4. **Halfway between the first and second equivalence points.** At this point, half the HA has been converted to A^- because of the neutralization reaction

$$HA(aq) + OH^-(aq) \xrightarrow{100\%} H_2O(l) + A^-(aq)$$

We thus have an $HA-A^-$ buffer solution with $[HA] = [A^-]$. Therefore, pH = $pK_{a2} = 9.69$.

5. **At the second equivalence point.** At this point, we have added enough NaOH to convert all the HA to A^-, and we have a 1.00 M solution of a **basic salt** (Section 14.14). The principal reaction is

$$A^-(aq) + H_2O(l) \rightleftharpoons HA(aq) + OH^-(aq)$$

and its equilibrium constant is

$$K_b = \frac{K_w}{K_a \text{ for HA}} = \frac{K_w}{K_{a2}} = \frac{1.0 \times 10^{-14}}{2.0 \times 10^{-10}} = 5.0 \times 10^{-5}$$

We can obtain $[OH^-]$ from the equilibrium equation for the principal reaction and then calculate $[H_3O^+]$ and the pH in the usual way:

$$K_b = 5.0 \times 10^{-5} = \frac{[HA][OH^-]}{[A^-]} = \frac{(x)(x)}{1.00 - x} \qquad x = [OH^-] = 7.1 \times 10^{-3} \, M$$

$$[H_3O^+] = \frac{K_w}{[OH^-]} = \frac{1.0 \times 10^{-14}}{7.1 \times 10^{-3}} = 1.4 \times 10^{-12} \, M$$

$$\text{pH} = 11.85$$

Since the initial solution of H_2A^+ contained 1.00 mol of H_2A^+, the amount of NaOH required to reach the second equivalence point is 2.00 mol. Beyond the second equivalence point, the pH is determined by $[OH^-]$ from the excess NaOH.

WORKED EXAMPLE 15.6

CALCULATING THE pH FOR A DIPROTIC ACID–STRONG BASE TITRATION

Assume that you are titrating 30.0 mL of a 0.0600 M solution of the protonated form of the amino acid methionine (H_2A^+) with 0.0900 M NaOH. Calculate the pH after addition of 20.0 mL of base.

$$\overset{\displaystyle O}{\underset{\displaystyle \underset{CH_2CH_2SCH_3}{|}}{\overset{\displaystyle \|}{H_3NCHCOH}}}$$

Methionine cation (H_2A^+)
$K_{a1} = 5.2 \times 10^{-3}$
$K_{a2} = 6.2 \times 10^{-10}$

Methionine cation

STRATEGY

First calculate the number of millimoles of H_2A^+ present initially and of NaOH added. Then you can tell which species remain after neutralization and therefore what type of equilibrium problem you must solve.

SOLUTION

The number of millimoles of H_2A^+ present initially and of NaOH added are

$$\text{mmol } H_2A^+ \text{ initial} = (30.0 \text{ mL})(0.0600 \text{ mmol/mL}) = 1.80 \text{ mmol}$$
$$\text{mmol NaOH added} = (20.0 \text{ mL})(0.0900 \text{ mmol/mL}) = 1.80 \text{ mmol}$$

The added base is just enough to reach the first equivalence point, converting all the H_2A^+ to HA because of the neutralization reaction

$$H_2A^+(aq) + OH^-(aq) \xrightarrow{100\%} H_2O(l) + HA(aq)$$

Therefore, the pH equals the average of pK_{a1} and pK_{a2}:

$$pH = \frac{pK_{a1} + pK_{a2}}{2} = \frac{[-\log (5.2 \times 10^{-3})] + [-\log (6.2 \times 10^{-10})]}{2}$$

$$= \frac{2.28 + 9.21}{2} = 5.74$$

▶ **PROBLEM 15.18** Assume that 40.0 mL of 0.0800 M H_2SO_3 ($K_{a1} = 1.5 \times 10^{-2}$, $K_{a2} = 6.3 \times 10^{-8}$) is titrated with 0.160 M NaOH. Calculate the pH after addition of the following volumes of 0.160 M NaOH:
(a) 20.0 mL   (b) 30.0 mL   (c) 35.0 mL

▶ **PROBLEM 15.19** Assume that 40.0 mL of a 0.0250 M solution of the protonated form of the amino acid valine (H_2A^+) is titrated with 0.100 M NaOH. Calculate the pH after addition of the following volumes of 0.100 M NaOH:
(a) 10.0 mL   (b) 15.0 mL   (c) 20.0 mL

$$\overset{\overset{\displaystyle O}{\overset{\displaystyle \|}{}}}{\underset{\underset{\displaystyle CHCH_3}{\underset{\displaystyle |}{}}}{\overset{+}{H_3}NCHCOH}}$$
$$\underset{\displaystyle CH_3}{|}$$

Valine cation (H_2A^+)
$K_{a1} = 4.8 \times 10^{-3}$
$K_{a2} = 2.4 \times 10^{-10}$

Valine cation

15.10 SOLUBILITY EQUILIBRIA

Many biological and environmental processes involve the dissolution or precipitation of a sparingly soluble ionic compound. Tooth decay, for example, begins when tooth enamel, composed of the mineral hydroxyapatite, $Ca_5(PO_4)_3OH$, dissolves on reaction with organic acids produced by the bacterial decomposition of foods rich in sugar. Kidney stones form when moderately insoluble calcium salts, such as calcium oxalate, CaC_2O_4, precipitate slowly over a long period of time. To understand the quantitative aspects of such solubility and precipitation phenomena, we must examine the principles of solubility equilibria.

Let's consider the solubility equilibrium in a saturated solution of calcium fluoride in contact with an excess of solid calcium fluoride. Like most sparingly soluble ionic solutes, calcium fluoride is a strong electrolyte in water and exists in the aqueous phase as dissociated hydrated ions, $Ca^{2+}(aq)$ and $F^-(aq)$. At equilibrium, the ion concentrations remain constant because the rate at which solid CaF_2 dissolves to

▲ Most kidney stones consist of insoluble calcium salts, such as calcium oxalate.

give $Ca^{2+}(aq)$ and $F^-(aq)$ exactly equals the rate at which the ions crystallize to form solid CaF_2:

$$CaF_2(s) \rightleftharpoons Ca^{2+}(aq) + 2\,F^-(aq)$$

The equilibrium equation for the dissolution reaction is

$$K_{sp} = [Ca^{2+}][F^-]^2$$

where the equilibrium constant K_{sp} is called the *solubility product constant*, or simply the **solubility product**. As usual for a heterogeneous equilibrium, the concentration of the solid, CaF_2, is omitted from the equilibrium equation (Section 13.4).

For the general solubility equilibrium

$$M_mX_x(s) \rightleftharpoons m\,M^{n+}(aq) + x\,X^{y-}(aq)$$

the equilibrium constant expression for K_{sp} is

$$K_{sp} = [M^{n+}]^m[X^{y-}]^x$$

Thus, K_{sp} always equals the product of the equilibrium concentrations of all the ions on the right side of the chemical equation, with the concentration of each ion raised to the power of its coefficient in the balanced equation.

WORKED EXAMPLE 15.7

WRITING EQUILIBRIUM CONSTANT EXPRESSIONS FOR K_{sp}

Write the equilibrium constant expression for the solubility product of silver chromate, Ag_2CrO_4.

STRATEGY AND SOLUTION

First write the balanced equation for the solubility equilibrium:

$$Ag_2CrO_4(s) \rightleftharpoons 2\,Ag^+(aq) + CrO_4{}^{2-}(aq)$$

The exponents in the equilibrium constant expression for K_{sp} are the coefficients in the balanced equation. Therefore,

$$K_{sp} = [Ag^+]^2[CrO_4{}^{2-}]$$

▶ **PROBLEM 15.20** Write the equilibrium constant expression for K_{sp} of:
(a) AgCl **(b)** PbI_2 **(c)** $Ca_3(PO_4)_2$ **(d)** $Cr(OH)_3$

15.11 MEASURING K_{sp} AND CALCULATING SOLUBILITY FROM K_{sp}

◀ A saturated solution of calcium fluoride in contact with solid CaF_2 contains constant equilibrium concentrations of $Ca^{2+}(aq)$ and $F^-(aq)$ because at equilibrium the ions crystallize at the same rate as the solid dissolves.

The numerical value of a solubility product K_{sp} is measured by experiment. For example, we could determine K_{sp} for CaF_2 by adding an excess of solid CaF_2 to water, stirring the mixture to give a saturated solution of CaF_2, and then measuring the concentrations of Ca^{2+} and F^- in the saturated solution. To make sure that the concentrations had reached constant equilibrium values, we would want to stir the mixture for an additional period of time and then repeat the measurements. Suppose that we found $[Ca^{2+}] = 2.0 \times 10^{-4}$ M and $[F^-] = 4.1 \times 10^{-4}$ M. (The value of $[F^-]$ is twice the value of $[Ca^{2+}]$ because each mole of CaF_2 that dissolves yields 1 mol of Ca^{2+} ions and 2 mol of F^- ions.) We could then calculate K_{sp} for CaF_2:

$$K_{sp} = [Ca^{2+}][F^-]^2 = (2.0 \times 10^{-4})(4.1 \times 10^{-4})^2 = 3.4 \times 10^{-11}$$

Another way to measure K_{sp} for CaF_2 is to approach the equilibrium from the opposite direction—that is, by mixing sources of Ca^{2+} and F^- ions to give a precipitate of solid CaF_2 and a saturated solution of CaF_2. Suppose, for example, that we mix solutions of $CaCl_2$ and NaF, allow time for equilibrium to be reached, and then measure $[Ca^{2+}] = 3.5 \times 10^{-5}$ M and $[F^-] = 1.0 \times 10^{-3}$ M. Within experimental error, these ion concentrations yield the same value of K_{sp}:

$$K_{sp} = [Ca^{2+}][F^-]^2 = (3.5 \times 10^{-5})(1.0 \times 10^{-3})^2 = 3.5 \times 10^{-11}$$

The value of K_{sp} is unaffected by the presence of other ions in solution, such as Na^+ from NaF and Cl^- from $CaCl_2$, as long as the solution is very dilute. As ion concentrations increase, K_{sp} values are somewhat modified because of electrostatic interactions between ions, but we'll ignore that complication here.

If the saturated solution is prepared by a method other than the dissolution of CaF_2 in pure water, there are no separate restrictions on $[Ca^{2+}]$ and $[F^-]$; the only restriction on the ion concentrations is that the value of the equilibrium constant expression $[Ca^{2+}][F^-]^2$ must equal the K_{sp}. That condition is satisfied by an infinite number of combinations of $[Ca^{2+}]$ and $[F^-]$, and therefore we can prepare many different solutions that are saturated with respect to CaF_2. For example, if $[F^-]$ is 1.0×10^{-2} M, then $[Ca^{2+}]$ must be 3.5×10^{-7} M:

$$[Ca^{2+}] = \frac{K_{sp}}{[F^-]^2} = \frac{3.5 \times 10^{-11}}{(1.0 \times 10^{-2})^2} = 3.5 \times 10^{-7}$$

Selected values of K_{sp} for various ionic compounds at 25 °C are listed in Table 15.2, and additional values can be found in Appendix C. Like all equilibrium constants, values of K_{sp} depend on temperature (Section 13.9).

TABLE 15.2 K_{sp} Values for Some Ionic Compounds at 25 °C

Name	Formula	K_{sp}
Aluminum hydroxide	$Al(OH)_3$	1.9×10^{-33}
Barium carbonate	$BaCO_3$	2.6×10^{-9}
Calcium carbonate	$CaCO_3$	5.0×10^{-9}
Calcium fluoride	CaF_2	3.5×10^{-11}
Lead(II) chloride	$PbCl_2$	1.2×10^{-5}
Lead(II) chromate	$PbCrO_4$	2.8×10^{-13}
Silver chloride	$AgCl$	1.8×10^{-10}
Silver sulfate	Ag_2SO_4	1.2×10^{-5}

Once the K_{sp} value for a compound has been measured, you can use it to calculate the solubility of the compound—the amount of compound that dissolves per unit volume of saturated solution. Because of two complications, however, calculated solubilities are often approximate. First, K_{sp} values can be difficult to measure, and values listed in different sources might differ by as much as a factor of 10 or more. Second, calculated solubilities can be less than observed solubilities because of side reactions. For example, dissolution of $PbCl_2$ gives both Pb^{2+} and $PbCl^+$ because of some ion association between Pb^{2+} and Cl^- ions:

$$(1)\ PbCl_2(s) \rightleftharpoons Pb^{2+}(aq) + 2\ Cl^-(aq)$$
$$(2)\ Pb^{2+}(aq) + Cl^-(aq) \rightleftharpoons PbCl^+(aq)$$

In this book, we will calculate approximate solubilities assuming that ionic solutes are completely dissociated (reaction 1). In the case of $PbCl_2$, ignoring the second equilibrium gives a calculated solubility that is too low by a factor of about 2.

▲ Addition of aqueous K_2CrO_4 to aqueous $AgNO_3$ gives a red precipitate of Ag_2CrO_4 and a saturated solution of Ag_2CrO_4.

WORKED EXAMPLE 15.8

CALCULATING K_{sp} FROM ION CONCENTRATIONS

A particular saturated solution of silver chromate, Ag_2CrO_4, has $[Ag^+] = 5.0 \times 10^{-5}$ M and $[CrO_4^{2-}] = 4.4 \times 10^{-4}$ M. What is the value of K_{sp} for Ag_2CrO_4?

STRATEGY

Substituting the equilibrium concentrations into the expression for K_{sp} of Ag_2CrO_4 (Worked Example 15.7) gives the value of K_{sp}.

SOLUTION

$$K_{sp} = [Ag^+]^2[CrO_4^{2-}] = (5.0 \times 10^{-5})^2(4.4 \times 10^{-4}) = 1.1 \times 10^{-12}$$

BALLPARK CHECK

K_{sp} is approximately $(5)^2(4) = 100$ times $(10^{-5})^2(10^{-4})$. So K_{sp} is about 10^{-12}, in agreement with the solution.

WORKED EXAMPLE 15.9

CALCULATING K_{sp} FROM SOLUBILITY

A saturated solution of Ag_2CrO_4 prepared by dissolving solid Ag_2CrO_4 in water has $[CrO_4^{2-}] = 6.5 \times 10^{-5}$ M. Calculate K_{sp} for Ag_2CrO_4.

STRATEGY

Because both the Ag^+ and CrO_4^{2-} ions come from the dissolution of solid Ag_2CrO_4, $[Ag^+]$ must be twice $[CrO_4^{2-}]$.

$$Ag_2CrO_4(s) \rightleftharpoons 2\,Ag^+(aq) + CrO_4^{2-}(aq)$$

Substituting $[Ag^+]$ and $[CrO_4^{2-}]$ into the equilibrium equation gives the value of K_{sp}.

SOLUTION

$$[Ag^+] = (2)[CrO_4^{2-}] = (2)(6.5 \times 10^{-5}) = 1.3 \times 10^{-4}\,M$$
$$K_{sp} = [Ag^+]^2[CrO_4^{2-}] = (1.3 \times 10^{-4})^2(6.5 \times 10^{-5}) = 1.1 \times 10^{-12}$$

WORKED EXAMPLE 15.10

CALCULATING SOLUBILITY FROM K_{SP}

Calculate the solubility of MgF_2 in water at 25 °C in units of:

(a) Moles per liter   **(b)** Grams per liter

STRATEGY

(a) Write the balanced equation for the solubility equilibrium assuming the complete dissociation of MgF_2, and look up K_{sp} for MgF_2 in Appendix C. If we define x as the number of moles per liter of MgF_2 that dissolves, then the saturated solution contains x mol/L of Mg^{2+} and $2x$ mol/L of F^-. Substituting these equilibrium concentrations into the expression for K_{sp} and solving for x gives the molar solubility.

(b) To convert the solubility from units of moles per liter to units of grams per liter, multiply the molar solubility of MgF_2 by its molar mass (62.3 g/mol).

SOLUTION

(a) It's helpful to summarize the equilibrium concentrations under the balanced equation:

Solubility Equilibrium	$MgF_2(s) \rightleftharpoons Mg^{2+}(aq) + 2\,F^-(aq)$	
Equilibrium concentration (M)	x	$2x$

Substituting the equilibrium concentrations into the expression for K_{sp} gives

$K_{sp} = 7.4 \times 10^{-11} = [Mg^{2+}][F^-]^2 = (x)(2x)^2$

$4x^3 = 7.4 \times 10^{-11}$

$x^3 = 1.8 \times 10^{-11}$

$x = [Mg^{2+}] = $ Molar solubility $= 2.6 \times 10^{-4}$ mol/L

Thus, the molar solubility of MgF_2 in water at 25 °C is 2.6×10^{-4} M. (Taking account of the side reaction that produces MgF^+ would increase the calculated solubility by about 6%.)

Note that the number 2 appears twice in the expression $(x)(2x)^2$. The exponent 2 is required because of the equilibrium equation, $K_{sp} = [Mg^{2+}][F^-]^2$. The coefficient 2 in $2x$ is required because each mole of MgF_2 that dissolves gives 2 mol of $F^-(aq)$.

(b) Solubility (in g/L) $= \dfrac{2.6 \times 10^{-4} \text{ mol}}{L} \times \dfrac{62.3 \text{ g}}{mol} = 1.6 \times 10^{-2}$ g/L

BALLPARK CHECK

(a) The molar solubility of MgF_2 is the cube root of $K_{sp}/4$, which equals the cube root of approximately 20×10^{-12}. Because $(2)^3 = 8$, $(3)^3 = 27$, and $(10^{-4})^3 = 10^{-12}$, the molar solubility is between 2×10^{-4} M and 3×10^{-4} M. The ballpark check and the solution agree.

▶ **PROBLEM 15.21** A saturated solution of $Ca_3(PO_4)_2$ has $[Ca^{2+}] = 2.01 \times 10^{-8}$ M and $[PO_4^{3-}] = 1.6 \times 10^{-5}$ M. Calculate K_{sp} for $Ca_3(PO_4)_2$.

▶ **PROBLEM 15.22** Prior to having an X-ray exam of the upper gastrointestinal tract, a patient drinks an aqueous suspension of solid $BaSO_4$. (Scattering of X rays by barium greatly enhances the quality of the photograph.) Although Ba^{2+} is toxic, ingestion of $BaSO_4$ is safe because it is quite insoluble. If a saturated solution prepared by dissolving solid $BaSO_4$ in water has $[Ba^{2+}] = 1.05 \times 10^{-5}$ M, what is the value of K_{sp} for $BaSO_4$?

▶ **PROBLEM 15.23** Which has the greater molar solubility: AgCl with $K_{sp} = 1.8 \times 10^{-10}$ or Ag_2CrO_4 with $K_{sp} = 1.1 \times 10^{-12}$? Which has the greater solubility in grams per liter?

CONCEPTUAL PROBLEM 15.24 The following pictures represent saturated solutions of three silver salts: AgX, AgY, and AgZ. (Other ions and solvent water molecules have been omitted for clarity.)

▲ This X-ray photograph of the small intestine was taken soon after the patient drank a barium sulfate "cocktail."

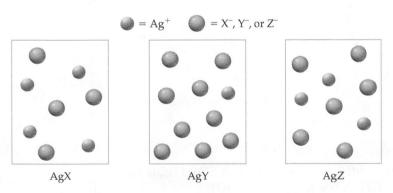

= Ag^+ = $X^-, Y^-,$ or Z^-

AgX   AgY   AgZ

(a) Which salt has the largest value of K_{sp}?

(b) Which salt has the smallest value of K_{sp}?

15.12 FACTORS THAT AFFECT SOLUBILITY

Solubility and the Common-Ion Effect

We've already discussed the common-ion effect in connection with the dissociation of weak acids and bases (Section 15.2). To see how a common ion affects the position of a solubility equilibrium, let's look again at the solubility of MgF_2:

$$MgF_2(s) \rightleftharpoons Mg^{2+}(aq) + 2\,F^-(aq)$$

In Worked Example 15.10, we found that the molar solubility of MgF_2 in pure water at 25 °C is 2.6×10^{-4} M. Thus,

$$[Mg^{2+}] = 2.6 \times 10^{-4}\,\text{M} \qquad [F^-] = 5.2 \times 10^{-4}\,\text{M}$$

When MgF_2 dissolves in a solution that contains a common ion from another source—say, F^- from NaF—the position of the solubility equilibrium is shifted to the left by the common-ion effect. If $[F^-]$ is larger than 5.2×10^{-4} M, then $[Mg^{2+}]$ must be correspondingly smaller than 2.6×10^{-4} M to maintain the equilibrium expression $[Mg^{2+}][F^-]^2$ at a constant value of $K_{sp} = 7.4 \times 10^{-11}$. A smaller value of $[Mg^{2+}]$ means that MgF_2 is less soluble in a sodium fluoride solution than it is in pure water. Similarly, the presence of Mg^{2+} from another source—say, $MgCl_2$—shifts the solubility equilibrium to the left and decreases the solubility of MgF_2.

In general, the solubility of a slightly soluble ionic compound is decreased by the presence of a common ion in the solution, as illustrated in Figure 15.12. The quantitative aspects of the common-ion effect are explored in Worked Example 15.11.

Figure 15.12
The common-ion effect. The calculated solubility of MgF_2 is plotted on a logarithmic scale.

WORKED EXAMPLE 15.11

CALCULATING SOLUBILITY IN A SOLUTION THAT CONTAINS A COMMON ION

Calculate the molar solubility of MgF_2 in 0.10 M NaF at 25 °C.

STRATEGY

Once again, we define x as the molar solubility of MgF_2. The dissolution of x mol/L of MgF_2 provides x mol/L of Mg^{2+} and $2x$ mol/L of F^-, but the total concentration of F^-

is $(0.10 + 2x)$ mol/L because the solution already contains 0.10 mol/L of F^- from the completely dissociated NaF. Substituting the equilibrium concentrations into the expression for K_{sp} and solving for x gives the molar solubility.

SOLUTION

Again, we summarize the equilibrium concentrations under the balanced equation:

Solubility Equilibrium	$MgF_2(s) \rightleftharpoons Mg^{2+}(aq) + 2\,F^-(aq)$	
Equilibrium concentration (M)	x	$0.10 + 2x$

Substituting the equilibrium concentrations into the expression for K_{sp} gives

$$K_{sp} = 7.4 \times 10^{-11} = [Mg^{2+}][F^-]^2 = (x)(0.10 + 2x)^2$$

Because K_{sp} is small, $2x$ will be small compared to 0.10 and we can make the approximation that $(0.10 + 2x) \approx 0.10$. Therefore,

$$7.4 \times 10^{-11} = (x)(0.10 + 2x)^2 \approx (x)(0.10)^2$$

$$x = [Mg^{2+}] = \text{Molar solubility} = \frac{7.4 \times 10^{-11}}{(0.10)^2} = 7.4 \times 10^{-9}\,M$$

Note that the calculated solubility of MgF_2 in 0.10 M NaF is less than that in pure water by a factor of about 35,000! (See Figure 15.12.) (Taking account of the equilibrium $Mg^{2+} + F^- \rightleftharpoons MgF^+$ would increase the calculated solubility by a factor of about 10. In this case, quite a bit of the Mg^{2+} is converted to MgF^+ because of the relatively high F^- concentration in 0.10 M NaF.)

BALLPARK CHECK

We can check our results by substituting the calculated equilibrium concentrations into the expression for K_{sp}:

$$K_{sp} = 7.4 \times 10^{-11} = [Mg^{2+}][F^-]^2 = (7.4 \times 10^{-9})(0.10)^2 = 7.4 \times 10^{-11}$$

▶ **PROBLEM 15.25** Calculate the molar solubility of MgF_2 in 0.10 M $MgCl_2$ at 25 °C.

Solubility and the pH of the Solution

An ionic compound that contains a basic anion becomes more soluble as the acidity of the solution increases. The solubility of $CaCO_3$, for example, increases with decreasing pH (Figure 15.13) because the CO_3^{2-} ions combine with protons to give HCO_3^- ions. As CO_3^{2-} ions are removed from the solution, the solubility equilibrium shifts to

Figure 15.13
Plot of the solubility of $CaCO_3$ at 25 °C versus the pH of the solution. The solubility is plotted on a logarithmic scale.

▲ These downward-growing, icicle-shaped structures, called stalactites, and the upward growing columns, called stalagmites, are formed in limestone caves by the slow precipitation of calcium carbonate from dripping water.

Remember ...

A **coordinate covalent bond** forms when one atom donates two electrons (a lone pair) to another atom that has a vacant orbital.   (Section 7.5)

The electron-pair donor is a **Lewis base**. (Section 14.16)

the right, as predicted by Le Châtelier's principle. The net reaction is the dissolution of $CaCO_3$ in acidic solution to give Ca^{2+} ions and HCO_3^- ions:

$$CaCO_3(s) \rightleftharpoons Ca^{2+}(aq) + CO_3^{2-}(aq)$$

$$H_3O^+(aq) + CO_3^{2-}(aq) \rightleftharpoons HCO_3^-(aq) + H_2O(l)$$

Net: $$CaCO_3(s) + H_3O^+(aq) \rightleftharpoons Ca^{2+}(aq) + HCO_3^-(aq) + H_2O(l)$$

Other salts that contain basic anions, such as CN^-, PO_4^{3-}, S^{2-}, or F^-, behave similarly. By contrast, pH has no effect on the solubility of salts that contain anions of strong acids (Cl^-, Br^-, I^-, NO_3^-, and ClO_4^-) because these anions are not protonated by H_3O^+.

The effect of pH on the solubility of $CaCO_3$ has important environmental consequences. For instance, the formation of limestone caves, such as Mammoth Cave in Kentucky, is due to the slow dissolution of limestone ($CaCO_3$) in the slightly acidic natural water of underground streams, and the formation of stalactites and stalagmites in these caves is due to the slow precipitation of $CaCO_3$ from dripping water. Marble, another form of $CaCO_3$, also dissolves in acid, which accounts for the deterioration of marble monuments on exposure to acid rain (Inquiry, pages 576–577).

The effect of pH on solubility is also important in understanding how fluoride ion reduces tooth decay. When tooth enamel, mainly hydroxyapatite, $Ca_5(PO_4)_3OH$, comes in contact with F^- ions in drinking water or fluoride-containing toothpaste, OH^- ions in $Ca_5(PO_4)_3OH$ are replaced by F^- ions, giving the mineral fluorapatite, $Ca_5(PO_4)_3F$. Because F^- is a much weaker base than OH^-, $Ca_5(PO_4)_3F$ is much more resistant than $Ca_5(PO_4)_3OH$ to dissolving in acids. (See the Inquiry at the end of this chapter.)

▶ **PROBLEM 15.26** Which of the following compounds are more soluble in acidic solution than in pure water?

(a) AgCN   (b) PbI_2 (c) $Al(OH)_3$ (d) ZnS

Solubility and the Formation of Complex Ions

The solubility of an ionic compound increases dramatically if the solution contains a **Lewis base** that can form a **coordinate covalent bond** to the metal cation (Section 7.5). Silver chloride, for example, is quite insoluble in water and in acid, but it dissolves in an excess of aqueous ammonia, forming the *complex ion* $Ag(NH_3)_2^+$ (**Figure 15.14**). A **complex ion** is an ion that contains a metal cation bonded to one or more small molecules or ions, such as NH_3, CN^-, or OH^-. In accord with Le Châtelier's principle, ammonia shifts the solubility equilibrium to the right by tying up the Ag^+ ion in the form of the complex ion:

$$AgCl(s) \rightleftharpoons Ag^+(aq) + Cl^-(aq)$$

$$Ag^+(aq) + 2\,NH_3(aq) \rightleftharpoons Ag(NH_3)_2^+(aq)$$

The formation of a complex ion is a stepwise process, and each step has its own characteristic equilibrium constant. For the formation of $Ag(NH_3)_2^+$, the reactions are

$$Ag^+(aq) + NH_3(aq) \rightleftharpoons Ag(NH_3)^+(aq) \qquad K_1 = 2.1 \times 10^3$$

$$Ag(NH_3)^+(aq) + NH_3(aq) \rightleftharpoons Ag(NH_3)_2^+(aq) \qquad K_2 = 8.1 \times 10^3$$

Net: $$Ag^+(aq) + 2\,NH_3(aq) \rightleftharpoons Ag(NH_3)_2^+(aq) \qquad K_f = 1.7 \times 10^7$$

$$K_1 = \frac{[Ag(NH_3)^+]}{[Ag^+][NH_3]} = 2.1 \times 10^3 \qquad K_2 = \frac{[Ag(NH_3)_2^+]}{[Ag(NH_3)^+][NH_3]} = 8.1 \times 10^3$$

$$K_f = K_1 K_2 = \frac{[Ag(NH_3)_2^+]}{[Ag^+][NH_3]^2} = 1.7 \times 10^7 \qquad \text{at } 25\,°C$$

Silver chloride is quite insoluble in water . . .

. . . but dissolves on addition of an excess of aqueous ammonia.

Figure 15.14
The reaction of silver chloride with aqueous ammonia.

The stability of a complex ion is measured by its **formation constant K_f** (or *stability constant*), the equilibrium constant for the formation of the complex ion from the hydrated metal cation. The large value of K_f for $Ag(NH_3)_2^+$ means that this complex ion is quite stable, and nearly all the Ag^+ ion in an aqueous ammonia solution is therefore present in the form of $Ag(NH_3)_2^+$ (see Worked Example 15.12).

The net reaction for dissolution of AgCl in aqueous ammonia is the sum of the equations for the dissolution of AgCl in water and the reaction of $Ag^+(aq)$ with $NH_3(aq)$ to give $Ag(NH_3)_2^+$:

$$AgCl(s) \rightleftharpoons Ag^+(aq) + Cl^-(aq)$$

$$\underline{Ag^+(aq) + 2\,NH_3(aq) \rightleftharpoons Ag(NH_3)_2^+(aq)}$$

$$\text{Net:}\quad AgCl(s) + 2\,NH_3(aq) \rightleftharpoons Ag(NH_3)_2^+(aq) + Cl^-(aq)$$

The equilibrium constant K for the net reaction is the product of the equilibrium constants for the reactions added:

$$K = \frac{[Ag(NH_3)_2^+][Cl^-]}{[NH_3]^2} = (K_{sp})(K_f) = (1.8 \times 10^{-10})(1.7 \times 10^7) = 3.1 \times 10^{-3}$$

Because K is much larger than K_{sp}, the solubility equilibrium for AgCl lies much farther to the right in the presence of ammonia than it does in the absence of ammonia. The increase in the solubility of AgCl on the addition of ammonia is shown graphically in **Figure 15.15**. In general, the solubility of an ionic compound increases when the metal cation is tied up in the form of a complex ion. The quantitative effect of complex formation on the solubility of AgCl is explored in Worked Example 15.13.

Figure 15.15

Plot of the solubility of AgCl in aqueous ammonia at 25 °C versus the concentration of ammonia. The solubility is plotted on a logarithmic scale.

The solubility of AgCl in $NH_3(aq)$ increases with increasing $[NH_3]$ owing to formation of the complex ion $Ag(NH_3)_2^+$.

Pure water

WORKED EXAMPLE 15.12

CALCULATING THE CONCENTRATIONS OF COMPLEX IONS

What are the concentrations of Ag^+, $Ag(NH_3)^+$, and $Ag(NH_3)_2^+$ in a solution prepared by adding 0.10 mol of $AgNO_3$ to 1.0 L of 3.0 M NH_3? $K_f = 1.7 \times 10^7$, $K_1 = 2.1 \times 10^3$, and $K_2 = 8.1 \times 10^3$.

STRATEGY

Because K_1, K_2, and K_f for $Ag(NH_3)_2^+$ are all large numbers, nearly all the Ag^+ from $AgNO_3$ will be converted to $Ag(NH_3)_2^+$:

$$Ag^+(aq) + 2\,NH_3(aq) \rightleftharpoons Ag(NH_3)_2^+(aq) \qquad K_f = 1.7 \times 10^7$$

To calculate the concentrations, it's convenient to imagine that 100% of the Ag^+ is converted to $Ag(NH_3)_2^+$, followed by a tiny amount of back-reaction [dissociation of $Ag(NH_3)_2^+$] to give a small equilibrium concentration of Ag^+.

SOLUTION

The conversion of 0.10 mol/L of Ag^+ to $Ag(NH_3)_2^+$ consumes 0.20 mol/L of NH_3. Assuming 100% conversion to $Ag(NH_3)_2^+$, the following concentrations are obtained:

$$[Ag^+] = 0\ M$$

$$[Ag(NH_3)_2^+] = 0.10\ M$$

$$[NH_3] = 3.0 - 0.20 = 2.8\ M$$

The dissociation of x mol/L of $Ag(NH_3)_2^+$ in the back-reaction produces x mol/L of Ag^+ and $2x$ mol/L of NH_3. Therefore, the equilibrium concentrations (in mol/L) are

$$[Ag(NH_3)_2^+] = 0.10 - x$$

$$[Ag^+] = x$$

$$[NH_3] = 2.8 + 2x$$

Let's summarize our reasoning in a table under the balanced equation:

	$Ag^+(aq)$ +	$2\,NH_3(aq)$ $\rightleftharpoons$	$Ag(NH_3)_2^+(aq)$
Initial concentration (M)	0.10	3.0	0
After 100% reaction (M)	0	2.8	0.10
Equilibrium concentration (M)	x	$2.8 + 2x$	$0.10 - x$

Substituting the equilibrium concentrations into the expression for K_f and making the approximation that x is negligible compared to 0.10 (and to 2.8) gives

$$K_f = 1.7 \times 10^7 = \frac{[Ag(NH_3)_2^+]}{[Ag^+][NH_3]^2} = \frac{0.10 - x}{(x)(2.8 + 2x)^2} \approx \frac{0.10}{(x)(2.8)^2}$$

$$[Ag^+] = x = \frac{0.10}{(1.7 \times 10^7)(2.8)^2} = 7.5 \times 10^{-10} \text{ M}$$

$$[Ag(NH_3)_2^+] = 0.10 - x = 0.10 - (7.5 \times 10^{-10}) = 0.10 \text{ M}$$

The concentration of $Ag(NH_3)^+$ can be calculated from either of the stepwise equilibria. Let's use the equilibrium equation for the formation of $Ag(NH_3)^+$ from Ag^+:

$$K_1 = \frac{[Ag(NH_3)^+]}{[Ag^+][NH_3]} = 2.1 \times 10^3$$

$$[Ag(NH_3)^+] = K_1[Ag^+][NH_3] = (2.1 \times 10^3)(7.5 \times 10^{-10})(2.8) = 4.4 \times 10^{-6} \text{ M}$$

Thus, nearly all the Ag^+ is in the form of $Ag(NH_3)_2^+$.

BALLPARK CHECK

The approximate equilibrium concentrations are $[Ag^+] = 7 \times 10^{-10}$ M, $[Ag(NH_3)^+] = 4 \times 10^{-6}$ M, $[Ag(NH_3)_2^+] = 0.1$ M, and $[NH_3] = 3$ M. We can check these results by substituting them into the equilibrium constant expressions for K_f and K_1:

$$K_f = 1.7 \times 10^7 = \frac{[Ag(NH_3)_2^+]}{[Ag^+][NH_3]^2} \approx \frac{0.1}{(7 \times 10^{-10})(3)^2} = 2 \times 10^7$$

$$K_1 = 2.1 \times 10^3 = \frac{[Ag(NH_3)^+]}{[Ag^+][NH_3]} \approx \frac{4 \times 10^{-6}}{(7 \times 10^{-10})(3)} = 2 \times 10^3$$

The ballpark estimates of K_f and K_1 agree with the experimental values.

WORKED EXAMPLE 15.13

EXPLORING THE EFFECT OF COMPLEX FORMATION ON SOLUBILITY

Calculate the molar solubility of AgCl at 25 °C in:

(a) Pure water   (b) 3.0 M NH_3

STRATEGY

Write the balanced equation for the dissolution reaction, and define x as the number of moles per liter of AgCl that dissolves. Then express the equilibrium concentrations in terms of x, and substitute them into the appropriate equilibrium equation. Solving for x gives the molar solubility.

SOLUTION

(a) In pure water, the solubility equilibrium is

$$AgCl(s) \rightleftharpoons Ag^+(aq) + Cl^-(aq)$$

Substituting the equilibrium concentrations (x mol/L) into the expression for K_{sp} gives

$$K_{sp} = 1.8 \times 10^{-10} = [Ag^+][Cl^-] = (x)(x)$$

$$x = \text{Molar solubility} = \sqrt{1.8 \times 10^{-10}} = 1.3 \times 10^{-5} \text{ M}$$

(b) The balanced equation for the dissolution of AgCl in aqueous NH_3 is

$$AgCl(s) + 2\,NH_3(aq) \rightleftharpoons Ag(NH_3)_2^+(aq) + Cl^-(aq) \qquad K = 3.1 \times 10^{-3}$$

If we define x as the number of moles per liter of AgCl that dissolves, then the saturated solution contains x mol/L of $Ag(NH_3)_2^+$, x mol/L of Cl^-, and $(3.0 - 2x)$ mol/L of NH_3. (We're assuming that essentially all the Ag^+ is in the form

continued on next page

of $Ag(NH_3)_2^+$, as proved in Worked Example 15.12.) Substituting the equilibrium concentrations into the equilibrium equation gives

$$K = 3.1 \times 10^{-3} = \frac{[Ag(NH_3)_2^+][Cl^-]}{[NH_3]^2} = \frac{(x)(x)}{(3.0 - 2x)^2}$$

Taking the square root of both sides, we obtain

$$5.6 \times 10^{-2} = \frac{x}{3.0 - 2x}$$

$$x = (5.6 \times 10^{-2})(3.0 - 2x) = 0.17 - 0.11x$$

$$x = \frac{0.17}{1.11} = 0.15 \text{ M}$$

The molar solubility of AgCl in 3.0 M NH_3 is 0.15 M. Thus, AgCl is much more soluble in aqueous NH_3 than in pure water, as shown in Figure 15.15.

BALLPARK CHECK

Check the calculated equilibrium concentrations by substituting them into the appropriate equilibrium equation. For part **(b)**, for example, $[Ag(NH_3)_2^+] = [Cl^-] = x = 0.15$ M and $[NH_3] = 3.0 - 2x = 2.7$ M. Since $[NH_3]$ is 10% less than 3 M, $K = [Ag(NH_3)_2^+][Cl^-]/[NH_3]^2$ is about 20% greater than $(0.15/3)^2 = (0.05)^2 = 2.5 \times 10^{-3}$. The ballpark estimate and the experimental value of $K = 3.1 \times 10^{-3}$ agree.

▶ **PROBLEM 15.27** In an excess of $NH_3(aq)$, Cu^{2+} ion forms a deep blue complex ion, $Cu(NH_3)_4^{2+}$, which has a formation constant $K_f = 5.6 \times 10^{11}$. Calculate the concentration of Cu^{2+} in a solution prepared by adding 5.0×10^{-3} mol of $CuSO_4$ to 0.500 L of 0.40 M NH_3.

▶ **PROBLEM 15.28** Silver bromide dissolves in aqueous sodium thiosulfate, $Na_2S_2O_3$, yielding the complex ion $Ag(S_2O_3)_2^{3-}$:

$$AgBr(s) + 2 S_2O_3^{2-}(aq) \rightleftharpoons Ag(S_2O_3)_2^{3-}(aq) + Br^-(aq) \qquad K = ?$$

Calculate the equilibrium constant K for the dissolution reaction, and calculate the molar solubility of AgBr in 0.10 M $Na_2S_2O_3$. $K_{sp} = 5.4 \times 10^{-13}$ for AgBr and $K_f = 4.7 \times 10^{13}$ for $Ag(S_2O_3)_2^{3-}$.

Solubility and Amphoterism

Certain metal hydroxides, such as aluminum hydroxide (**Figure 15.16**), are soluble both in strongly acidic and in strongly basic solutions:

In acid: $\quad Al(OH)_3(s) + 3 H_3O^+(aq) \rightleftharpoons Al^{3+}(aq) + 6 H_2O(l)$

In base: $\quad Al(OH)_3(s) + OH^-(aq) \rightleftharpoons Al(OH)_4^-(aq)$

Such hydroxides are said to be **amphoteric** (am-fo-**tare**-ic), a term that comes from the Greek word *amphoteros*, meaning "in both ways."

Figure 15.16
The amphoteric behavior of Al(OH)₃.

Aluminum hydroxide, a gelatinous white precipitate, forms on addition of aqueous NaOH to $Al^{3+}(aq)$.

The precipitate dissolves on addition of excess aqueous NaOH, yielding the colorless $Al(OH)_4^-$ ion. The precipitate also dissolves in aqueous HCl, yielding the colorless Al^{3+} ion.

The dissolution of $Al(OH)_3$ in excess base is just a special case of the effect of complex-ion formation on solubility: $Al(OH)_3$ dissolves because excess OH^- ions convert it to the soluble complex ion $Al(OH)_4^-$ (aluminate ion). The effect of pH on the solubility of $Al(OH)_3$ is shown in **Figure 15.17**.

Al(OH)$_3$ dissolves in strongly acidic solutions.

Al(OH)$_3$ dissolves in strongly basic solutions.

Al(OH)$_3$ is essentially insoluble between pH 4 and 10.

Figure 15.17
A plot of solubility versus pH shows that Al(OH)₃ is an amphoteric hydroxide.

Other examples of amphoteric hydroxides include $Zn(OH)_2$, $Cr(OH)_3$, $Sn(OH)_2$, and $Pb(OH)_2$, which react with excess OH^- ions to form the soluble complex ions $Zn(OH)_4^{2-}$ (zincate ion), $Cr(OH)_4^-$ (chromite ion), $Sn(OH)_3^-$ (stannite ion), and $Pb(OH)_3^-$ (plumbite ion), respectively. By contrast, basic hydroxides, such as $Mn(OH)_2$, $Fe(OH)_2$, and $Fe(OH)_3$, dissolve in strong acid but not in strong base.

15.13 PRECIPITATION OF IONIC COMPOUNDS

A common problem in chemistry is to decide whether a precipitate of an ionic compound will form when solutions that contain the constituent ions are mixed. For example, will CaF_2 precipitate on mixing solutions of $CaCl_2$ and NaF? In other words, will the dissolution reaction proceed in the reverse direction, from right to left?

$$CaF_2(s) \rightleftharpoons Ca^{2+}(aq) + 2\,F^-(aq)$$

We touched on this question briefly in Section 4.4 when we looked at solubility guidelines, but we can now get a more quantitative view. The answer depends on the value of the **ion product (IP)**, a number defined by the expression

$$IP = [Ca^{2+}]_t[F^-]_t^2$$

The IP is defined in the same way as K_{sp}, except that the concentrations in the expression for IP are initial concentrations—that is, arbitrary concentrations at time t, not necessarily equilibrium concentrations. Thus, the IP is actually a **reaction quotient** Q_c (Section 13.5), but the term *ion product* is more descriptive because, as usual, solid CaF_2 is omitted from the equilibrium constant expression.

If the value of IP is greater than K_{sp}, the solution is supersaturated with respect to CaF_2—a nonequilibrium situation. In that case, CaF_2 will precipitate, thus reducing the ion concentrations until IP equals K_{sp}. At that point, solubility equilibrium is reached and the solution is saturated.

Remember ...
The **reaction quotient** Q_c is defined in the same way as the equilibrium constant K_c except that the concentrations in the equilibrium constant expression are not necessarily equilibrium values. (Section 13.5)

In general, we only need to calculate the value of IP and then compare it with K_{sp} to decide whether an ionic compound will precipitate. Three cases arise:

1. If $IP > K_{sp}$, the solution is supersaturated and precipitation will occur.
2. If $IP = K_{sp}$, the solution is saturated and equilibrium exists already.
3. If $IP < K_{sp}$, the solution is unsaturated and precipitation will not occur.

▲ When 0.150 L of 0.10 M $Pb(NO_3)_2$ and 0.100 L of 0.20 M NaCl are mixed, a white precipitate of $PbCl_2$ forms because the ion product is greater than K_{sp}.

WORKED EXAMPLE 15.14

DECIDING WHETHER A PRECIPITATE WILL FORM WHEN SOLUTIONS ARE MIXED

Will a precipitate form when 0.150 L of 0.10 M $Pb(NO_3)_2$ and 0.100 L of 0.20 M NaCl are mixed?

STRATEGY

Since ionic compounds are strong electrolytes, $Pb(NO_3)_2$ and NaCl exist in solution as separate cations and anions. Use the solubility guidelines discussed in Section 4.4 to decide which ions might form a precipitate, and calculate their concentrations after mixing. Then calculate the IP for the possible precipitate and compare it with the value of K_{sp}.

SOLUTION

After the two solutions are mixed, the combined solution contains Pb^{2+}, NO_3^-, Na^+, and Cl^- ions and has a volume of $0.150 \text{ L} + 0.100 \text{ L} = 0.250 \text{ L}$. Because sodium salts and nitrate salts are soluble in water, the only compound that might precipitate is $PbCl_2$, which has $K_{sp} = 1.2 \times 10^{-5}$ (Appendix C). To calculate the value of IP for $PbCl_2$, first calculate the number of moles of Pb^{2+} and Cl^- in the combined solution:

$$\text{Moles } Pb^{2+} = (0.150 \text{ L})(0.10 \text{ mol/L}) = 1.5 \times 10^{-2} \text{ mol}$$

$$\text{Moles } Cl^- = (0.100 \text{ L})(0.20 \text{ mol/L}) = 2.0 \times 10^{-2} \text{ mol}$$

Then convert moles to molar concentrations:

$$[Pb^{2+}] = \frac{1.5 \times 10^{-2} \text{ mol}}{0.250 \text{ L}} = 6.0 \times 10^{-2} \text{ M}$$

$$[Cl^-] = \frac{2.0 \times 10^{-2} \text{ mol}}{0.250 \text{ L}} = 8.0 \times 10^{-2} \text{ M}$$

The ion product is

$$IP = [Pb^{2+}]_t[Cl^-]_t^2 = (6.0 \times 10^{-2})(8.0 \times 10^{-2})^2 = 3.8 \times 10^{-4}$$

Since $K_{sp} = 1.2 \times 10^{-5}$, IP is greater than K_{sp} and $PbCl_2$ will therefore precipitate.

▸ **PROBLEM 15.29** Will a precipitate form on mixing equal volumes of the following solutions?
  (a) 3.0×10^{-3} M $BaCl_2$ and 2.0×10^{-3} M Na_2CO_3
  (b) 1.0×10^{-5} M $Ba(NO_3)_2$ and 4.0×10^{-5} M Na_2CO_3

▸ **PROBLEM 15.30** Will a precipitate form on mixing 25 mL of 1.0×10^{-3} M $MnSO_4$, 25 mL of 1.0×10^{-3} M $FeSO_4$, and 200 mL of a buffer solution that is 0.20 M in NH_4Cl and 0.20 M in NH_3? Values of K_{sp} can be found in Appendix C.

15.14 SEPARATION OF IONS BY SELECTIVE PRECIPITATION

A convenient method for separating a mixture of ions is to add a solution that will precipitate some of the ions but not others. The anions SO_4^{2-} and Cl^-, for example, can be separated by addition of a solution of $Ba(NO_3)_2$. Insoluble $BaSO_4$ precipitates, but Cl^- remains in solution because $BaCl_2$ is soluble. Similarly, the cations Ag^+ and Zn^{2+} can be separated by addition of dilute HCl. Silver chloride, AgCl, precipitates, but Zn^{2+} stays in solution because $ZnCl_2$ is soluble.

In Section 15.15, we'll see that mixtures of metal cations, M^{2+}, can be separated into two groups by the selective precipitation of metal sulfides, MS. For example, Pb^{2+}, Cu^{2+}, and Hg^{2+}, which form very insoluble sulfides, can be separated from Mn^{2+}, Fe^{2+}, Co^{2+}, Ni^{2+}, and Zn^{2+}, which form more soluble sulfides. The separation is carried out in an acidic solution and makes use of the following solubility equilibrium:

$$MS(s) + 2\,H_3O^+(aq) \rightleftharpoons M^{2+}(aq) + H_2S(aq) + 2\,H_2O(l)$$

The equilibrium constant for this reaction, called the *solubility product in acid*, is given the symbol K_{spa}:

$$K_{spa} = \frac{[M^{2+}][H_2S]}{[H_3O^+]^2}$$

The separation depends on adjusting the H_3O^+ concentration so that the reaction quotient Q_c exceeds K_{spa} for the very insoluble sulfides but not for the more soluble ones (Table 15.3).

We use K_{spa} for metal sulfides rather than K_{sp} for two reasons. First, the ion separations are carried out in acidic solution, so use of K_{spa} is more convenient. Second, because the value of K_{a2} for H_2S ($\sim 10^{-19}$) is very small, S^{2-}, like O^{2-}, is highly basic and is not an important species in aqueous solutions. The principal sulfide-containing species in aqueous solutions are H_2S in acidic solutions and HS^- in basic solutions.

In a typical experiment, the M^{2+} concentrations are about 0.01 M, and the H_3O^+ concentration is adjusted to about 0.3 M by adding HCl. The solution is then saturated with H_2S gas, which gives an H_2S concentration of about 0.10 M. Substituting these concentrations into the equilibrium constant expression, we find that the reaction quotient Q_c is 1×10^{-2}:

$$Q_c = \frac{[M^{2+}]_t[H_2S]_t}{[H_3O^+]_t^2} = \frac{(0.01)(0.10)}{(0.3)^2} = 1 \times 10^{-2}$$

This value of Q_c exceeds K_{spa} for PbS, CuS, and HgS (Table 15.3) but does not exceed K_{spa} for MnS, FeS, CoS, NiS, or ZnS. As a result, PbS, CuS, and HgS precipitate under these acidic conditions, but Mn^{2+}, Fe^{2+}, Co^{2+}, Ni^{2+}, and Zn^{2+} remain in solution.

▶ **PROBLEM 15.31** Determine whether Cd^{2+} can be separated from Zn^{2+} by bubbling H_2S through a 0.3 M HCl solution that contains 0.005 M Cd^{2+} and 0.005 M Zn^{2+}. (K_{spa} for CdS is 8×10^{-7}.)

TABLE 15.3 Solubility Products in Acid (K_{spa}) at 25 °C for Metal Sulfides

Metal Sulfide, MS	K_{spa}
MnS	3×10^7
FeS	6×10^2
CoS	3
NiS	8×10^{-1}
ZnS	3×10^{-2}
PbS	3×10^{-7}
CuS	6×10^{-16}
HgS	2×10^{-32}

▲ Adding H_2S to an acidic solution of Hg^{2+} and Ni^{2+} precipitates Hg^{2+} as black HgS but leaves green Ni^{2+} in solution.

15.15 QUALITATIVE ANALYSIS

Qualitative analysis is a procedure for identifying the ions present in an unknown solution. The ions are identified by specific chemical tests, but because one ion can interfere with the test for another, the ions must first be separated. In the traditional scheme of analysis for metal cations, some 20 cations are separated initially into five groups by selective precipitation (**Figure 15.18**).

• **Group I: Ag^+, Hg_2^{2+}, and Pb^{2+}.** When aqueous HCl is added to the unknown solution, the cations of group I precipitate as insoluble chlorides: AgCl, Hg_2Cl_2, and $PbCl_2$. The cations of groups II–V, which form soluble chlorides, remain in solution. A small amount of the Pb^{2+} also remains in solution because $PbCl_2$ is slightly soluble.

• **Group II: Pb^{2+}, Cu^{2+}, Hg^{2+}, Cd^{2+}, Bi^{3+}, and Sn^{4+}.** After the insoluble chlorides have been removed, the solution is treated with H_2S to precipitate the cations of group II as insoluble sulfides: PbS, CuS, HgS, CdS, Bi_2S_3, and SnS_2. Because the solution is strongly acidic at this point ($[H_3O^+] \approx 0.3$ M), only the most insoluble sulfides precipitate. The acid-insoluble sulfides are then removed from the solution.

Figure 15.18
Flowchart for the separation of metal cations in qualitative analysis.

▲ When aqueous potassium chromate is added to a solution that contains Pb^{2+}, a yellow precipitate of $PbCrO_4$ forms.

- **Group III: Mn^{2+}, Fe^{2+}, Co^{2+}, Ni^{2+}, Zn^{2+}, Al^{3+}, and Cr^{3+}.** At this point, aqueous NH_3 is added, neutralizing the acidic solution and giving an NH_4^+–NH_3 buffer that is slightly basic (pH $\approx$ 8). The decrease in $[H_3O^+]$ shifts the metal sulfide solubility equilibrium to the left, thus precipitating the 2+ cations of group III as insoluble sulfides: MnS, FeS, CoS, NiS, and ZnS. The 3+ cations precipitate from the basic solution, not as sulfides, but as insoluble hydroxides: $Al(OH)_3$ and $Cr(OH)_3$.

- **Group IV: Ca^{2+} and Ba^{2+}.** After the base-insoluble sulfides and the insoluble hydroxides have been removed, the solution is treated with $(NH_4)_2CO_3$ to precipitate the cations of group IV as insoluble carbonates: $CaCO_3$ and $BaCO_3$. Magnesium carbonate does not precipitate at this point because $[CO_3^{2-}]$ in the NH_4^+–NH_3 buffer is maintained at a low value.

- **Group V: Na^+, K^+, and Mg^{2+}.** The only ions remaining in solution at this point are those whose chlorides, sulfides, and carbonates are soluble under the conditions of the previous reactions. Magnesium ion is separated and identified by the addition of a solution of $(NH_4)_2HPO_4$; if Mg^{2+} is present, a white precipitate of $Mg(NH_4)PO_4$ forms. The alkali metal ions are usually identified by the characteristic colors that they impart to a Bunsen flame (**Figure 15.19**).

Once the cations have been separated into groups, further separations and specific tests are carried out to determine the presence or absence of the ions in each group. In group I, for example, lead can be separated from silver and mercury by treating the precipitate with hot water. The more soluble $PbCl_2$ dissolves, but the less soluble AgCl and Hg_2Cl_2 do not. To test for Pb^{2+}, the solid chlorides are removed, and the solution is treated with a solution of K_2CrO_4. If Pb^{2+} is present, a yellow precipitate of $PbCrO_4$ forms.

Figure 15.19
Flame tests for sodium and potassium.

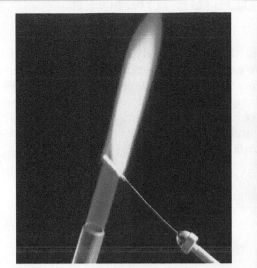

Sodium imparts a persistent yellow color to the flame.

Potassium turns the flame a fleeting violet color.

Detailed procedures for separating and identifying all the ions can be found in general chemistry laboratory manuals. Although modern methods of metal-ion analysis employ sophisticated analytical instruments, qualitative analysis is still included in many general chemistry laboratory courses because it is an excellent vehicle for developing laboratory skills and for learning about acid–base, solubility, and complex-ion equilibria.

INQUIRY HOW DOES FLUORIDE ION HELP TO PREVENT DENTAL CAVITIES?

Tooth enamel, the hardest substance in the human body, comes under constant chemical attack, both from the foods we eat and from bacterial infections. Made of the mineral hydroxyapatite, enamel forms the hard outer layer of the tooth where it protects the tooth from abrasion. Although it stands up well to the mechanical process of chewing, tooth enamel is nevertheless susceptible to erosion by acids. This erosion eventually leads to tooth decay and to the subsequent cavities that affect an estimated 75% of schoolchildren and virtually all adults.

▲ Better take care of your teeth. A result of poor dental hygene.

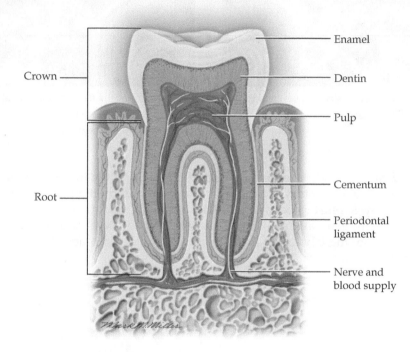

▲ Structure of a tooth.

Like calcium phosphate, $Ca_3(PO_4)_2$, hydroxyapatite, $Ca_5(PO_4)_3(OH)$ is a very insoluble compound, with $K_{sp} = 2.3 \times 10^{-59}$. Despite its small K_{sp}, hydroxyapatite can be demineralized, or dissolved, by reaction with acid:

$$Ca_5(PO_4)_3(OH)(s) + 4\,H^+(aq) \xrightleftharpoons[\text{Remineralization}]{\text{Demineralization}} 5\,Ca^{2+}(aq) + 3\,HPO_4{}^{2-}(aq) + H_2O(l)$$

Saliva, which contains relatively high concentrations Ca^{2+}, $PO_4{}^{3-}$, and $HPO_4{}^{2-}$, gives some protection to enamel, and some remineralization, or precipitation, of enamel from the ions in saliva can also take place. Thus, small erosions heal naturally before becoming cavities.

Unfortunately, this dynamic, balanced system in the mouth is overwhelmed by the presence of large amounts of acid. Both acidic beverages like sodas and bacterial metabolism of the sugars and starches left on teeth after eating are common sources of acid. When the initial decay can't be fully reversed by remineralization, small erosions, called dental caries (or, more commonly, "cavities"), reach and penetrate the softer dentin layer beneath the enamel causing considerable pain when they reach nerves in the underlying pulp.

The simplest and most common way to protect teeth from cavities is to brush them regularly, which physically removes the food that can feed bacteria. In addition, teeth can be protected by chemical treatment with a dilute solution of fluoride ion, which makes the enamel more resistant to attack by acid. Fluoride functions both by increasing the rate at which enamel remineralizes and by causing the partial conversion of hydroxyapatite to fluorapatite through exchange of F^- for OH^- in healthy enamel.

$$Ca_5(PO_4)_3(OH)(s) + F^-(aq) \rightleftharpoons Ca_5(PO_4)_3(F)(s) + OH^-(aq)$$

The K_{sp} of fluorapatite is about 10 times smaller than that of hydroxyapatite:

$$Ca_5(PO_4)_3(OH)(s) \rightleftharpoons 5\,Ca^{2+}(aq) + 3\,PO_4^{3-}(aq) + OH^-(aq) \qquad K_{sp} = 2.3 \times 10^{-59}$$
$$Ca_5(PO_4)_3(F)(s) \rightleftharpoons 5\,Ca^{2+}(aq) + 3\,PO_4^{3-}(aq) + F^-(aq) \qquad K_{sp} = 3.2 \times 10^{-60}$$

Thus, fluorapatite is less soluble than hydroxyapatite, and substitution of F^- for OH^- in tooth enamel is favored when the F^- concentration exceeds the OH^- concentration. In addition, the fluorapatite is less susceptible to dissolution by acid because F^- is a weaker base than OH^-.

Many communities now fluoridate their water supplies; just 1 mg/L (1.0 ppm) of fluoride ion in drinking water is sufficient to cause a 20–40% reduction in cavities among children. In regions where the water is not fluoridated, similar results can be obtained by brushing with toothpastes that contain a fluoride compound such as NaF, SnF_2, or Na_2PO_3F. Periodic treatments in a dentist's office with fluoride-containing gels or rinses also help to strengthen tooth enamel.

▶ **PROBLEM 15.32** Express the concentration of 1.0 ppm fluoride in units of molarity (assume that the solution density is 1.0 g/mL).

▶ **PROBLEM 15.33** Estimate the equilibrium constant for the conversion of hydroxyapatite to fluorapatite.

SUMMARY

Neutralization reactions involving a strong acid and/or a strong base have very large equilibrium constants (K_n) and proceed nearly 100% to completion. Weak acid–weak base neutralizations do not go to completion.

The **common-ion effect** is the shift in the position of an equilibrium that occurs when a substance is added that provides more of an ion already involved in the equilibrium. An example is the decrease in percent dissociation of a weak acid on the addition of its conjugate base.

A solution of a weak acid and its conjugate base is called a **buffer solution** because it resists drastic changes in pH. **Buffer capacity**, the ability of a buffer solution to absorb small amounts of added H_3O^+ or OH^- without a significant change in pH, increases with increasing amounts of weak acid and conjugate base. The pH of a buffer solution has a value close to the pK_a ($-\log K_a$) of the weak acid and can be calculated from the **Henderson–Hasselbalch equation**:

$$pH = pK_a + \log \frac{[\text{Conjugate base}]}{[\text{Weak acid}]}$$

A **pH titration curve** is a plot of the pH of a solution as a function of the volume of base (or acid) added in the course of an acid–base titration. For a strong acid–strong base titration, the titration curve exhibits a sharp change in pH in the region of the **equivalence point**, the point at which stoichiometrically equivalent amounts of acid and base have been mixed together. For weak acid–strong base and weak base–strong acid titrations, the titration curves display a relatively flat buffer region midway to the equivalence point, a smaller change in pH in the region of the equivalence point, and a pH at the equivalence point that is not equal to 7.00. The titration curve for a diprotic acid–strong base titration exhibits two equivalence points and two buffer regions.

The **solubility product (K_{sp})** for an ionic compound is the equilibrium constant for dissolution of the compound in water. The solubility of the compound and K_{sp} are related by the equilibrium equation for the dissolution reaction. The solubility of an ionic compound is (1) suppressed by the presence of a common ion in the solution, (2) increased by decreasing the pH if the compound contains a basic anion, such as OH^-, S^{2-}, or CO_3^{2-}, and (3) increased by the presence of a Lewis base, such as NH_3, CN^-, or OH^-, that can bond to the metal cation to form a **complex ion**. The stability of a complex ion is measured by its **formation constant (K_f)**.

When solutions of soluble ionic compounds are mixed, an insoluble compound will precipitate if the **ion product (IP)** for the insoluble compound exceeds its K_{sp}. The IP is defined in the same way as K_{sp}, except that the concentrations in the expression for IP are not necessarily equilibrium concentrations. Certain metal cations can be separated by the selective precipitation of metal sulfides. Selective precipitation is important in **qualitative analysis**, a procedure for identifying the ions present in an unknown solution.

KEY WORDS

amphoteric *622*
buffer capacity *596*
buffer solution *594*
common-ion effect *591*

complex ion *618*
equivalence point *601*
formation constant
  (K_f) *619*

Henderson–Hasselbalch
  equation *598*
ion product (IP) *623*
pH titration curve *601*

qualitative analysis *625*
solubility product
  (K_{sp}) *612*

CONCEPTUAL PROBLEMS

Problems 15.1–15.33 appear within the chapter.

15.34 The following pictures represent solutions that contain one or more of the compounds H_2A, NaHA, and Na_2A, where

H_2A is a weak diprotic acid. (Na^+ ions and solvent water molecules have been omitted for clarity.)

(a) Which of the solutions are buffer solutions?

(b) Which solution has the greatest buffer capacity?

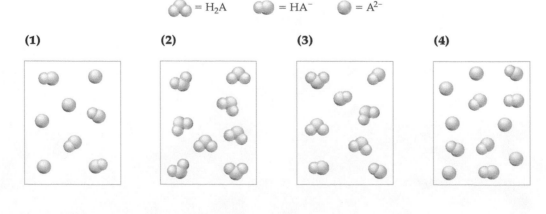

= H_2A = HA^- = A^{2-}

(1)   (2)   (3)   (4)

15.35 The following pictures represent solutions that contain a weak acid HA ($pK_a = 6.0$) and its sodium salt NaA. (Na^+ ions and solvent water molecules have been omitted for clarity.)

= HA   = A^-

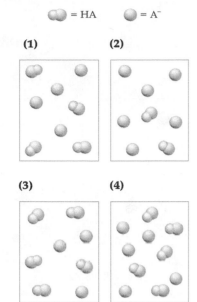

(1)   **(2)**

(3)   **(4)**

(a) Which solution has the highest pH? Which has the lowest pH?

(b) Draw a picture that represents the equilibrium state of solution (1) after the addition of two H_3O^+ ions.

(c) Draw a picture that represents the equilibrium state of solution (1) after the addition of two OH^- ions.

15.36 The strong acid HA is mixed with an equal molar amount of aqueous NaOH. Which of the following pictures represents the equilibrium state of the solution? (Na^+ ions and solvent water molecules have been omitted for clarity.)

= HA   = H_3O^+

= A^- = OH^- = H_2O

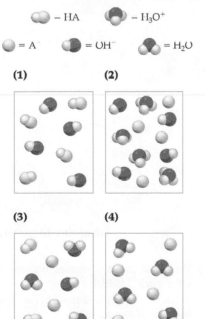

(1)   **(2)**

(3)   **(4)**

15.37 The following pictures represent solutions at various stages in the titration of a weak diprotic acid H_2A with aqueous NaOH. (Na^+ ions and water molecules have been omitted for clarity.)

= OH^- = HA^-

= A^{2-} = H_2A

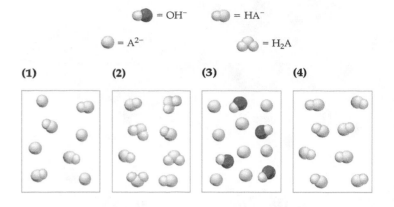

(1)   **(2)**   **(3)**   **(4)**

(a) To which of the following stages do solutions 1–4 correspond?
  (i) Halfway to the first equivalence point
  (ii) At the first equivalence point
  (iii) Halfway between the first and second equivalence points
  (iv) Beyond the second equivalence point

(b) Which solution has the highest pH? Which has the lowest pH?

15.38 The following pictures represent solutions at various stages in the titration of sulfuric acid H_2A ($A^{2-} = SO_4{}^{2-}$) with aqueous NaOH. (Na^+ ions and water molecules have been omitted for clarity.)

= H_2A = HA^-

= A^{2-} = OH^- = H_3O^+

(1)   **(2)**   **(3)**   **(4)**

(a) To which of the following stages do solutions 1–4 correspond?
  (i) Halfway to the first equivalence point
  (ii) Halfway between the first and second equivalence points
  (iii) At the second equivalence point
  (iv) Beyond the second equivalence point

(b) Draw a picture that represents the solution prior to addition of any NaOH.

15.39 The following pictures represent solutions at various stages in the titration of a weak base B with aqueous HCl. (Cl⁻ ions and solvent water molecules have been omitted for clarity.)

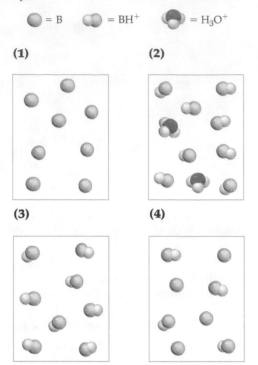

(a) To which of the following stages do solutions 1–4 correspond?
   (i) The initial solution before addition of any HCl
   (ii) Halfway to the equivalence point
   (iii) At the equivalence point
   (iv) Beyond the equivalence point
(b) Is the pH at the equivalence point more or less than 7?

15.40 The following pictures represent solutions of AgCl, which also may contain ions other than Ag^+ and Cl^- that are not shown. If solution 1 is a saturated solution of AgCl, classify solutions 2–4 as unsaturated, saturated, or supersaturated.

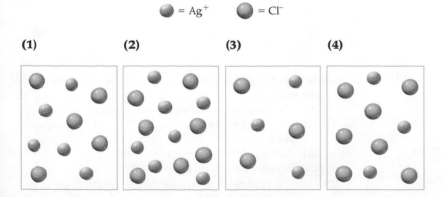

15.41 The following pictures represent solutions of Ag_2CrO_4, which also may contain ions other than Ag^+ and CrO_4^{2-} that are not shown. Solution 1 is in equilibrium with solid Ag_2CrO_4. Will a precipitate of solid Ag_2CrO_4 form in solutions 2–4? Explain.

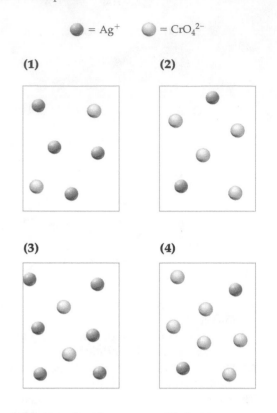

15.42 The following plot shows two pH titration curves, each representing the titration of 50.0 mL of 0.100 M acid with 0.100 M NaOH:

(a) Which of the two curves represents the titration of a strong acid? Which represents a weak acid?
(b) What is the approximate pH at the equivalence point for each of the acids?
(c) What is the approximate pK_a of the weak acid?

15.43 The following pH titration curve applies to the titration of 40.0 mL of a 0.100 M solution of a diprotic acid with 0.100 M NaOH:

mL of 0.100 M NaOH added

(a) How many equivalence points are present, and how many milliliters of base are required to reach each equivalence point?

(b) What is the approximate pH at each equivalence point?

(c) What are the approximate pK_a values for this acid?

SECTION PROBLEMS

Neutralization Reactions (Section 15.1)

15.44 Is the pH greater than, equal to, or less than 7 after the neutralization of each of the following pairs of acids and bases?
  (a) HI and NaOH
  (b) HOCl and $Ba(OH)_2$
  (c) HNO_3 and aniline ($C_6H_5NH_2$)
  (d) Benzoic acid ($C_6H_5CO_2H$) and KOH

15.45 Is the pH greater than, equal to, or less than 7 after the neutralization of each of the following pairs of acids and bases?
  (a) CsOH and HNO_2 **(b)** NH_3 and HBr
  (c) KOH and $HClO_4$ **(d)** NH_3 and HOBr

15.46 Which of the following mixtures has the higher pH?
  (a) Equal volumes of 0.10 M HF and 0.10 M NaOH
  (b) Equal volumes of 0.10 M HCl and 0.10 M NaOH

15.47 Which of the following mixtures has the lower pH?
  (a) Equal volumes of 0.10 M $HClO_4$ and 0.10 M NaOH
  (b) Equal volumes of 0.10 M $HClO_4$ and 0.10 M NH_3

15.48 Phenol (C_6H_5OH, $K_a = 1.3 \times 10^{-10}$) is a weak acid used in mouthwashes, and pyridine (C_5H_5N, $K_b = 1.8 \times 10^{-9}$) is a weak base used as a solvent. Calculate the value of K_n for the neutralization of phenol by pyridine. Does the neutralization reaction proceed very far toward completion?

Phenol   Pyridine

15.49 Aniline ($C_6H_5NH_2$, $K_b = 4.3 \times 10^{-10}$) is a weak base used in the manufacture of dyes. Calculate the value of K_n for the neutralization of aniline by vitamin C (ascorbic acid, $C_6H_8O_6$, $K_a = 8.0 \times 10^{-5}$). Does much aniline remain at equilibrium?

Aniline   Ascorbic acid

15.50 The equilibrium constant K_n for the neutralization of lactic acid ($HC_3H_5O_3$) and urea (CH_4N_2O) is 2.1×10^{-4}. What is K_b for urea? See Appendix C for the K_a of lactic acid.

15.51 The equilibrium constant K_n for the neutralization of boric acid (H_3BO_3) and caffeine ($C_8H_{10}N_4O_2$) is 24. What is K_b for caffeine? See Appendix C for the K_a of boric acid.

The Common-Ion Effect (Section 15.2)

15.52 Does the pH increase, decrease, or remain the same on the addition of each of the following?
  (a) LiF to an HF solution
  (b) KI to an HI solution
  (c) NH_4Cl to an NH_3 solution

15.53 Does the pH increase, decrease, or remain the same on the addition of each of the following?

   (a) NH_4NO_3 to an NH_3 solution

   (b) Na_2CO_3 to an $NaHCO_3$ solution

   (c) $NaClO_4$ to an $NaOH$ solution

15.54 Calculate the pH of a solution that is 0.25 M in HF and 0.10 M in NaF.

15.55 Calculate the pH of a solution prepared by mixing equal volumes of 0.20 M methylamine (CH_3NH_2, $K_b = 3.7 \times 10^{-4}$) and 0.60 M CH_3NH_3Cl.

Methylamine   Methylammonium cation

15.56 The pH of a solution of HN_3 ($K_a = 1.9 \times 10^{-5}$) and NaN_3 is 4.86. What is the molarity of NaN_3 if the molarity of HN_3 is 0.016 M?

15.57 The pH of a solution of NH_3 and NH_4Br is 8.90. What is the molarity of NH_4Br if the molarity of NH_3 is 0.016 M?

15.58 Calculate the percent dissociation of 0.10 M hydrazoic acid (HN_3, $K_a = 1.9 \times 10^{-5}$). Recalculate the percent dissociation of 0.10 M HN_3 in the presence of 0.10 M HCl, and explain the change.

15.59 Calculate the pH of 100 mL of 0.30 M NH_3 before and after the addition of 4.0 g of NH_4NO_3, and account for the change. Assume that the volume remains constant.

Buffer Solutions (Sections 15.3–15.4)

15.60 Which of the following gives a buffer solution when equal volumes of the two solutions are mixed?

   (a) 0.10 M HF and 0.10 M NaF

   (b) 0.10 M HF and 0.10 M NaOH

   (c) 0.20 M HF and 0.10 M NaOH

   (d) 0.10 M HCl and 0.20 M NaF

15.61 Which of the following gives a buffer solution when equal volumes of the two solutions are mixed?

   (a) 0.10 M NH_3 and 0.10 M HCl

   (b) 0.20 M NH_3 and 0.10 M HCl

   (c) 0.10 M NH_4Cl and 0.10 M NH_3

   (d) 0.20 M NH_4Cl and 0.10 M NaOH

15.62 Which of the following solutions has the greater buffer capacity: (a) 100 mL of 0.30 M HNO_2–0.30 M $NaNO_2$ or (b) 100 mL of 0.10 M HNO_2–0.10 M $NaNO_2$? Explain.

15.63 Which of the following solutions has the greater buffer capacity: (a) 50 mL of 0.20 M NH_4Br–0.30 M NH_3 or (b) 50 mL of 0.40 M NH_4Br–0.60 M NH_3? Explain.

15.64 Calculate the pH of a buffer solution that is 0.20 M in HCN and 0.12 M in NaCN. Will the pH change if the solution is diluted by a factor of 2? Explain.

15.65 Calculate the pH of a buffer solution prepared by dissolving 4.2 g of $NaHCO_3$ and 5.3 g of Na_2CO_3 in 0.20 L of water. Will the pH change if the solution volume is increased by a factor of 10? Explain.

15.66 Calculate the pH of 0.250 L of a 0.36 M formic acid–0.30 M sodium formate buffer before and after the addition of (a) 0.0050 mol of NaOH and (b) 0.0050 mol of HCl. Assume that the volume remains constant.

15.67 Calculate the pH of 0.375 L of a 0.18 M acetic acid–0.29 M sodium acetate buffer before and after the addition of (a) 0.0060 mol of KOH and (b) 0.0060 mol of HBr. Assume that the volume remains constant.

15.68 Use the Henderson–Hasselbalch equation to calculate the pH of a buffer solution that is 0.25 M in formic acid (HCO_2H) and 0.50 M in sodium formate (HCO_2Na).

15.69 Use the Henderson–Hasselbalch equation to calculate the ratio of H_2CO_3 to HCO_3^- in blood having a pH of 7.40.

15.70 In what volume ratio should you mix 1.0 M solutions of NH_4Cl and NH_3 to produce a buffer solution having pH = 9.80?

15.71 Give a recipe for preparing a CH_3CO_2H–CH_3CO_2Na buffer solution that has pH = 4.44.

15.72 You need a buffer solution that has pH = 7.00. Which of the following buffer systems should you choose? Explain.

   (a) H_3PO_4 and $H_2PO_4^-$ (b) $H_2PO_4^-$ and HPO_4^{2-}

   (c) HPO_4^{2-} and PO_4^{3-}

15.73 Which of the following conjugate acid–base pairs should you choose to prepare a buffer solution that has pH = 4.50? Explain.

   (a) HSO_4^- and SO_4^{2-} (b) $HOCl$ and OCl^-

   (c) $C_6H_5CO_2H$ and $C_6H_5CO_2^-$

15.74 What is the K_a of the amino acid leucine if it is 34.5% dissociated at pH = 9.46?

15.75 What is the K_a of the amino acid serine if it is 86.3% dissociated at pH = 9.95?

pH Titration Curves (Sections 15.5–15.9)

15.76 Consider the titration of 60.0 mL of 0.150 M HNO_3 with 0.450 M NaOH.

   (a) How many millimoles of HNO_3 are present at the start of the titration?

   (b) How many milliliters of NaOH are required to reach the equivalence point?

   (c) What is the pH at the equivalence point?

   (d) Sketch the general shape of the pH titration curve.

15.77 Make a rough plot of pH versus milliliters of acid added for the titration of 50.0 mL of 1.0 M NaOH with 1.0 M HCl. Indicate the pH at the following points, and tell how many milliliters of acid are required to reach the equivalence point.

   (a) At the start of the titration

   (b) At the equivalence point

   (c) After the addition of a large excess of acid

15.78 Consider the titration of 25.0 mL of 0.125 M HCl with 0.100 M KOH. Calculate the pH after the addition of each of the following volumes of base:

   (a) 3.0 mL   (b) 20 mL   (c) 65 mL

15.79 Consider the titration of 50.0 mL of 0.116 M NaOH with 0.0750 M HCl. Calculate the pH after the addition of each of the following volumes of acid:

   (a) 5.0 mL   (b) 50 mL   (c) 0.10 L

15.80 Consider the titration of 40.0 mL of 0.250 M HF with 0.200 M NaOH. How many milliliters of base are required to reach the equivalence point? Calculate the pH at each of the following points:

(a) After the addition of 10.0 mL of base

(b) Halfway to the equivalence point

(c) At the equivalence point

(d) After the addition of 80.0 mL of base

15.81 A 100.0 mL sample of 0.100 M methylamine (CH_3NH_2, $K_b = 3.7 \times 10^{-4}$) is titrated with 0.250 M HNO_3. Calculate the pH after the addition of each of the following volumes of acid:

(a) 0.0 mL   (b) 20.0 mL

(c) 40.0 mL   (d) 60.0 mL

15.82 Consider the titration of 50.0 mL of a 0.100 M solution of the protonated form of the amino acid alanine (H_2A^+; $K_{a1} = 4.6 \times 10^{-3}$, $K_{a2} = 2.0 \times 10^{-10}$) with 0.100 M NaOH. Calculate the pH after the addition of each of the following volumes of base:

(a) 10.0 mL   (b) 25.0 mL   (c) 50.0 mL

(d) 75.0 mL   (e) 100.0 mL

15.83 Consider the titration of 25.0 mL of 0.0200 M H_2CO_3 with 0.0250 M KOH. Calculate the pH after the addition of each of the following volumes of base:

(a) 10.0 mL   (b) 20.0 mL   (c) 30.0 mL

(d) 40.0 mL   (e) 50.0 mL

15.84 The equivalence point was reached in titrations of three unknown acids at pH 9.16 (acid A), 8.88 (acid B), and 8.19 (acid C).

(a) Which is the strongest acid?

(b) Which is the weakest acid?

15.85 The equivalence point was reached in titrations of three unknown bases at pH 5.53 (base A), 4.11 (base B), and 6.00 (base C).

(a) Which is the strongest base?

(b) Which is the weakest base?

15.86 What is the pH at the equivalence point for the titration of 0.10 M solutions of the following acids and bases, and which of the indicators in Figure 14.4 would be suitable for each titration?

(a) HNO_2 and NaOH

(b) HI and NaOH

(c) CH_3NH_2 (methylamine) and HCl

15.87 What is the pH at the equivalence point for the titration of 0.20 M solutions of the following acids and bases? Which of the indicators in Figure 14.4 would be suitable for each titration?

(a) $C_5H_{11}N$ (piperidine) and HNO_3

(b) $NaHSO_3$ and NaOH

(c) $Ba(OH)_2$ and HBr

Solubility Equilibria (Sections 15.10–15.11)

15.88 For each of the following compounds, write a balanced net ionic equation for the dissolution of the compound in water, and write the equilibrium expression for K_{sp}:

(a) Ag_2CO_3 (b) $PbCrO_4$

(c) $Al(OH)_3$ (d) Hg_2Cl_2

15.89 For each of the following, write the equilibrium expression for K_{sp}:

(a) $Ca(OH)_2$ (b) Ag_3PO_4

(c) $BaCO_3$ (d) $Ca_5(PO_4)_3OH$

15.90 A particular saturated solution of PbI_2 has $[Pb^{2+}] = 5.0 \times 10^{-3}$ M and $[I^-] = 1.3 \times 10^{-3}$ M.

(a) What is the value of K_{sp} for PbI_2?

(b) What is $[I^-]$ in a saturated solution of PbI_2 that has $[Pb^{2+}] = 2.5 \times 10^{-4}$ M?

(c) What is $[Pb^{2+}]$ in a saturated solution that has $[I^-] = 2.5 \times 10^{-4}$ M?

15.91 A particular saturated solution of $Ca_3(PO_4)_2$ has $[Ca^{2+}] = [PO_4^{3-}] = 2.9 \times 10^{-7}$ M.

(a) What is the value of K_{sp} for $Ca_3(PO_4)_2$?

(b) What is $[Ca^{2+}]$ in a saturated solution of $Ca_3(PO_4)_2$ that has $[PO_4^{3-}] = 0.010$ M?

(c) What is $[PO_4^{3-}]$ in a saturated solution that has $[Ca^{2+}] = 0.010$ M?

15.92 If a saturated solution prepared by dissolving Ag_2CO_3 in water has $[Ag^+] = 2.56 \times 10^{-4}$ M, what is the value of K_{sp} for Ag_2CO_3?

15.93 If a saturated aqueous solution of the shock-sensitive compound lead(II) azide, $Pb(N_3)_2$, has $[Pb^{2+}] = 8.5 \times 10^{-4}$ M, what is the value of K_{sp} for $Pb(N_3)_2$?

15.94 Use the following solubility data to calculate a value of K_{sp} for each compound:

(a) SrF_2: 1.03×10^{-3} M   (b) CuI: 1.05×10^{-6} M

(c) MgC_2O_4: 0.094 g/L   (d) $Zn(CN)_2$: 4.95×10^{-4} g/L

15.95 Use the following solubility data to calculate a value of K_{sp} for each compound:

(a) $CdCO_3$; 1.0×10^{-6} M   (b) $Ca(OH)_2$; 1.06×10^{-2} M

(c) $PbBr_2$; 4.34 g/L   (d) $BaCrO_4$; 2.8×10^{-3} g/L

15.96 Use the values of K_{sp} in Appendix C to calculate the molar solubility of the following compounds:

(a) $BaCrO_4$ (b) $Mg(OH)_2$ (c) Ag_2SO_3

15.97 Use the values of K_{sp} in Appendix C to calculate the solubility of the following compounds (in g/L):

(a) Ag_2CO_3 (b) CuBr   (c) $Cu_3(PO_4)_2$

Factors That Affect Solubility (Section 15.12)

15.98 Use Le Châtelier's principle to explain the following changes in the solubility of Ag_2CO_3 in water:

(a) Decrease on addition of $AgNO_3$

(b) Increase on addition of HNO_3

(c) Decrease on addition of Na_2CO_3

(d) Increase on addition of NH_3

15.99 Use Le Châtelier's principle to predict whether the solubility of BaF_2 will increase, decrease, or remain the same on addition of each of the following substances:

(a) HCl   (b) KF

(c) $NaNO_3$ (d) $Ba(NO_3)_2$

15.100 Calculate the molar solubility of $PbCrO_4$ in:

(a) Pure water   (b) 1.0×10^{-3} M K_2CrO_4

15.101 Calculate the molar solubility of SrF_2 in:

(a) 0.010 M $Sr(NO_3)_2$ (b) 0.010 M NaF

15.102 Which of the following compounds are more soluble in acidic solution than in pure water? Write a balanced net ionic equation for each dissolution reaction.

(a) AgBr   (b) $CaCO_3$

(c) $Ni(OH)_2$ (d) $Ca_3(PO_4)_2$

15.103 Which of the following compounds are more soluble in acidic solution than in pure water? Write a balanced net ionic equation for each dissolution reaction.

(a) MnS   (b) $Fe(OH)_3$ (c) AgCl   (d) $BaCO_3$

15.104 Is the solubility of $Zn(OH)_2$ increased, decreased, or unchanged on addition of each of the following substances? Write a balanced net ionic equation for each dissolution reaction. (See Appendix C.6 for formulas of complex ions.)

(a) HCl   (b) KOH   (c) NaCN

15.105 Is the solubility of $Fe(OH)_3$ increased, decreased, or unchanged on addition of each of the following substances? Write a balanced net ionic equation for each dissolution reaction. (See Appendix C.6 for formulas of complex ions.)

(a) HBr(aq)   (b) NaOH(aq)   (c) KCN(aq)

15.106 Silver ion reacts with excess CN^- to form a colorless complex ion, $Ag(CN)_2^-$, which has a formation constant $K_f = 3.0 \times 10^{20}$. Calculate the concentration of Ag^+ in a solution prepared by mixing equal volumes of 2.0×10^{-3} M $AgNO_3$ and 0.20 M NaCN.

15.107 Dissolution of 5.0×10^{-3} mol of $Cr(OH)_3$ in 1.0 L of 1.0 M NaOH gives a solution of the complex ion $Cr(OH)_4^-$ ($K_f = 8 \times 10^{29}$). What fraction of the chromium in such a solution is present as uncomplexed Cr^{3+}?

15.108 Write a balanced net ionic equation for each of the following dissolution reactions, and use the appropriate K_{sp} and K_f values in Appendix C to calculate the equilibrium constant for each.

(a) AgI in aqueous NaCN to form $Ag(CN)_2^-$

(b) $Al(OH)_3$ in aqueous NaOH to form $Al(OH)_4^-$

(c) $Zn(OH)_2$ in aqueous NH_3 to form $Zn(NH_3)_4^{2+}$

15.109 Write a balanced net ionic equation for each of the following dissolution reactions, and use the appropriate K_{sp} and K_f values in Appendix C to calculate the equilibrium constant for each.

(a) $Zn(OH)_2$ in aqueous NaOH to form $Zn(OH)_4^{2-}$

(b) $Cu(OH)_2$ in aqueous NH_3 to form $Cu(NH_3)_4^{2+}$

(c) AgBr in aqueous NH_3 to form $Ag(NH_3)_2^+$

15.110 Calculate the molar solubility of AgI in:

(a) Pure water

(b) 0.10 M NaCN; K_f for $Ag(CN)_2^-$ is 3.0×10^{20}

15.111 Calculate the molar solubility of $Cr(OH)_3$ in 0.50 M NaOH; K_f for $Cr(OH)_4^-$ is 8×10^{29}.

Precipitation; Qualitative Analysis (Sections 15.13–15.15)

15.112 What compound, if any, will precipitate when 80 mL of 1.0×10^{-5} M $Ba(OH)_2$ is added to 20 mL of 1.0×10^{-5} M $Fe_2(SO_4)_3$?

15.113 "Hard" water contains alkaline earth cations such as Ca^{2+}, which reacts with CO_3^{2-} to form insoluble deposits of $CaCO_3$. Will a precipitate of $CaCO_3$ form if a 250 mL sample of hard water having $[Ca^{2+}] = 8.0 \times 10^{-4}$ M is treated with the following?

(a) 0.10 mL of 2.0×10^{-3} M Na_2CO_3

(b) 10 mg of solid Na_2CO_3

15.114 The pH of a sample of hard water (Problem 15.113) having $[Mg^{2+}] = 2.5 \times 10^{-4}$ M is adjusted to pH 10.80. Will $Mg(OH)_2$ precipitate?

15.115 In qualitative analysis, Al^{3+} and Mg^{2+} are separated in an NH_4^+–NH_3 buffer having pH ≈ 8. Assuming cation concentrations of 0.010 M, show why $Al(OH)_3$ precipitates but $Mg(OH)_2$ does not.

15.116 Can Fe^{2+} be separated from Sn^{2+} by bubbling H_2S through a 0.3 M HCl solution that contains 0.01 M Fe^{2+} and 0.01 M Sn^{2+}? A saturated solution of H_2S has $[H_2S] ≈ 0.10$ M. Values of K_{spa} are 6×10^2 for FeS and 1×10^{-5} for SnS.

15.117 Can Co^{2+} be separated from Zn^{2+} by bubbling H_2S through a 0.3 M HCl solution that contains 0.01 M Co^{2+} and 0.01 M Zn^{2+}? A saturated solution of H_2S has $[H_2S] ≈ 0.10$ M. Values of K_{spa} are 3 for CoS and 3×10^{-2} for ZnS.

15.118 Will FeS precipitate in a solution that is 0.10 M in $Fe(NO_3)_2$, 0.4 M in HCl, and 0.10 M in H_2S? Will FeS precipitate if the pH of the solution is adjusted to pH 8 with an NH_4^+–NH_3 buffer? $K_{spa} = 6 \times 10^2$ for FeS.

15.119 Will CoS precipitate in a solution that is 0.10 M in $Co(NO_3)_2$, 0.5 M in HCl, and 0.10 M in H_2S? Will CoS precipitate if the pH of the solution is adjusted to pH 8 with an NH_4^+–NH_3 buffer? $K_{spa} = 3$ for CoS.

15.120 Using the qualitative analysis flowchart in Figure 15.18, tell how you could separate the following pairs of ions:

(a) Ag^+ and Cu^{2+} (b) Na^+ and Ca^{2+}

(c) Mg^{2+} and Mn^{2+} (d) K^+ and Cr^{3+}

15.121 Give a method for separating the following pairs of ions by the addition of no more than two substances:

(a) Hg_2^{2+} and Co^{2+} (b) Na^+ and Mg^{2+}

(c) Fe^{2+} and Hg^{2+} (d) Ba^{2+} and Pb^{2+}

CHAPTER PROBLEMS

15.122 Assume that you have three white solids: NaCl, KCl, and $MgCl_2$. What tests could you do to tell which is which?

15.123 On the same graph, sketch pH titration curves for the titration of (1) a strong acid with a strong base and (2) a weak acid with a strong base. How do the two curves differ with respect to the following?

(a) The initial pH

(b) The pH in the region between the start of the titration and the equivalence point

(c) The pH at the equivalence point

(d) The pH beyond the equivalence point

(e) The volume of base required to reach the equivalence point

15.124 Consider the titration of 50.0 mL of 0.010 M HA (K_a = 1.0×10^{-4}) with 0.010 M NaOH.

(a) Sketch the pH titration curve, and label the equivalence point.

(b) How many milliliters of 0.010 M NaOH are required to reach the equivalence point?

(c) Is the pH at the equivalence point greater than, equal to, or less than 7?

(d) What is the pH exactly halfway to the equivalence point?

15.125 Consider saturated solutions of the slightly soluble salts AgBr and $BaCO_3$.

(a) Is the solubility of AgBr increased, decreased, or unaffected by the addition of each of the following substances?

(i) HBr   **(ii)** HNO_3

(iii) $AgNO_3$ **(iv)** NH_3

(b) Is the solubility of $BaCO_3$ increased, decreased, or unaffected by the addition of each of the following substances?

(i) HNO_3 **(ii)** $Ba(NO_3)_2$

(iii) Na_2CO_3 **(iv)** CH_3CO_2H

15.126 A saturated solution of $Mg(OH)_2$ in water has pH = 10.35. Calculate K_{sp} for $Mg(OH)_2$.

15.127 Consider a buffer solution that contains equal concentrations of $H_2PO_4^-$ and HPO_4^{2-}. Will the pH increase, decrease, or remain the same when each of the following substances is added?

(a) Na_2HPO_4 **(b)** HBr   **(c)** KOH

(d) KI   **(e)** H_3PO_4 **(f)** Na_3PO_4

15.128 Calculate the concentrations of NH_4^+ and NH_3 and the pH in a solution prepared by mixing 20.0 g of NaOH and 0.500 L of 1.5 M NH_4Cl. Assume that the volume remains constant.

15.129 In qualitative analysis, Ag^+, Hg_2^{2+}, and Pb^{2+} are separated from other cations by the addition of HCl. Calculate the concentration of Cl^- required to just begin the precipitation of **(a)** AgCl, **(b)** Hg_2Cl_2, and **(c)** $PbCl_2$ in a solution having metal-ion concentrations of 0.030 M. What fraction of the Pb^{2+} remains in solution when the Ag^+ just begins to precipitate?

15.130 Calculate the molar solubility of MnS in a 0.30 M NH_4Cl–0.50 M NH_3 buffer solution that is saturated with H_2S ($[H_2S] \approx 0.10$ M). What is the solubility of MnS (in g/L)? (K_{spa} for MnS is 3×10^7.)

15.131 The titration of 0.02500 L of a diprotic acid solution with 0.1000 M NaOH requires 34.72 mL of titrant to reach the second equivalence point. The pH is 3.95 at the first equivalence point and 9.27 at the second equivalence point. If the acid solution contained 0.2015 g of the acid, what is the molar mass, pK_{a1}, and pK_{a2} of the acid?

15.132 What is the pH of a solution prepared by mixing 60.0 mL of 1.00 M H_3PO_4 and 1.00 L of 0.100 M LiOH?

15.133 A student dilutes a solution of 0.100 mol of H_3PO_4 and 0.150 mol of NaOH with water to a volume of 1.00 L but then realizes that the distilled water used was in fact dilute hydrochloric acid.

(a) If the pH of the final solution is 6.73, what are the concentrations of H_3PO_4, $H_2PO_4^-$, and HPO_4^{2-}?

(b) How many moles of HCl were inadvertently added to the original solution?

15.134 Given a buret filled with 0.10 M acetic acid and a second buret filled with 0.15 M sodium acetate, how many milliliters of each solution should be mixed together to produce 20.0 mL of a solution with a pH of 4.85?

15.135 The acidity of lemon juice is derived primarily from citric acid (H_3Cit), a triprotic acid. What are the concentrations of H_3Cit, H_2Cit^-, $HCit^{2-}$, and Cit^{3-} in a sample of lemon juice that has a pH of 2.37 and a total concentration of the four citrate-containing species of 0.350 M?

Citric acid

15.136 A 100.0 mL sample of a solution that is 0.100 M in HCl and 0.100 M in HCN is titrated with 0.100 M NaOH. Calculate the pH after the addition of the following volumes of NaOH:

(a) 0.0 mL   **(b)** 75.0 mL

(c) 100.0 mL   **(d)** 125.0 mL

15.137 A 0.0100 mol sample of solid $Cd(OH)_2$ (K_{sp} = 5.3×10^{-15}) in 100.0 mL of water is titrated with 0.100 M HNO_3.

(a) What is the molar solubility of $Cd(OH)_2$ in pure water? What is the pH of the solution before the addition of any HNO_3?

(b) What is the pH of the solution after the addition of 90.0 mL of 0.100 M HNO_3?

(c) How many milliliters of 0.100 M HNO_3 must be added to completely neutralize the $Cd(OH)_2$?

15.138 Zinc hydroxide, $Zn(OH)_2$ (K_{sp} = 4.1×10^{-17}), is nearly insoluble in water but is more soluble in strong base because Zn^{2+} forms the soluble complex ion $Zn(OH)_4^{2-}$ (K_f = 3×10^{15}).

(a) What is the molar solubility of $Zn(OH)_2$ in pure water? (You may ignore OH^- from the self-dissociation of water.)

(b) What is the pH of the solution in part **(a)**?

(c) What is the molar solubility of $Zn(OH)_2$ in 0.10 M NaOH?

15.139 Citric acid (H_3Cit) can be used as a household cleaning agent to dissolve rust stains. The rust, represented as $Fe(OH)_3$, dissolves because the citrate ion forms a soluble complex with Fe^{3+}:

$$Fe(OH)_3(s) + H_3Cit(aq) \rightleftharpoons Fe(Cit)(aq) + 3 H_2O(l)$$

(a) Using the equilibrium constants in Appendix C and K_f = 6.3×10^{11} for Fe(Cit), calculate the equilibrium constant K for the reaction.

(b) Calculate the molar solubility of $Fe(OH)_3$ in a 0.500 M solution of H_3Cit.

MULTICONCEPT PROBLEMS

15.140 When a typical diprotic acid H_2A ($K_{a1} = 10^{-4}$; $K_{a2} = 10^{-10}$) is titrated with NaOH, the principal A-containing species at the first equivalence point is HA^-.

 (a) By considering all four proton-transfer reactions that can occur in an aqueous solution of HA^-, show that the principal reaction is $2 HA^- \rightleftharpoons H_2A + A^{2-}$.

 (b) Assuming that this is the principal reaction, show that the pH at the first equivalence point equals the average of pK_{a1} and pK_{a2}.

 (c) How many A^{2-} ions are present in 50.0 mL of 1.0 M NaHA?

15.141 Ethylenediamine ($NH_2CH_2CH_2NH_2$, abbreviated en) is an organic base that can accept two protons:

$$en(aq) + H_2O(l) \rightleftharpoons enH^+(aq) + OH^-(aq) \qquad K_{b1} = 5.2 \times 10^{-4}$$

$$enH^+(aq) + H_2O(l) \rightleftharpoons enH_2^{2+}(aq) + OH^-(aq) \quad K_{b2} = 3.7 \times 10^{-7}$$

 (a) Consider the titration of 30.0 mL of 0.100 M ethylenediamine with 0.100 M HCl. Calculate the pH after the addition of the following volumes of acid, and construct a qualitative plot of pH versus milliliters of HCl added:

 (i)   0.0 mL   (ii) 15.0 mL
 (iii) 30.0 mL   (iv) 45.0 mL
 (v) 60.0 mL   (vi) 75.0 mL

 (b) Draw the structure of ethylenediamine, and explain why it can accept two protons.

 (c) What hybrid orbitals do the N atoms use for bonding?

15.142 A 40.0 mL sample of a mixture of HCl and H_3PO_4 was titrated with 0.100 M NaOH. The first equivalence point was reached after 88.0 mL of base, and the second equivalence point was reached after 126.4 mL of base.

 (a) What is the concentration of H_3O^+ at the first equivalence point?

 (b) What are the initial concentrations of HCl and H_3PO_4 in the mixture?

 (c) What percent of the HCl is neutralized at the first equivalence point?

 (d) What is the pH of the mixture before the addition of any base?

 (e) Sketch the pH titration curve, and label the buffer regions and equivalence points.

 (f) What indicators would you select to signal the equivalence points?

15.143 A 1.000 L sample of HCl gas at 25 °C and 732.0 mm Hg was absorbed completely in an aqueous solution that contained 6.954 g of Na_2CO_3 and 250.0 g of water.

 (a) What is the pH of the solution?

 (b) What is the freezing point of the solution?

 (c) What is the vapor pressure of the solution? (The vapor pressure of pure water at 25 °C is 23.76 mm Hg.)

15.144 A saturated solution of an ionic salt MX exhibits an osmotic pressure of 74.4 mm Hg at 25 °C. Assuming that MX is completely dissociated in solution, what is the value of its K_{sp}?

15.145 Consider the reaction that occurs on mixing 50.0 mL of 0.560 M $NaHCO_3$ and 50.0 mL of 0.400 M NaOH at 25 °C.

 (a) Write a balanced net ionic equation for the reaction.

 (b) What is the pH of the resulting solution?

 (c) How much heat (in joules) is liberated by the reaction? (Standard heats of formation are given in Appendix B.)

 (d) What is the final temperature of the solution to the nearest 0.1 °C? You may assume that all the heat liberated is absorbed by the solution, the mass of the solution is 100.0 g, and its specific heat is $4.18 \, J/(g \cdot °C)$.

15.146 In qualitative analysis, Ca^{2+} and Ba^{2+} are separated from Na^+, K^+, and Mg^{2+} by adding aqueous $(NH_4)_2CO_3$ to a solution that also contains aqueous NH_3 (Figure 15.18). Assume that the concentrations after mixing are 0.080 M $(NH_4)_2CO_3$ and 0.16 M NH_3.

 (a) List all the Brønsted–Lowry acids and bases present initially, and identify the principal reaction.

 (b) Calculate the pH and the concentrations of all species present in the solution.

 (c) In order for the human eye to detect the appearance of a precipitate, a very large number of ions must come together to form solid particles. For this and other reasons, the ion product must often exceed K_{sp} by a factor of about 10^3 before a precipitate can be detected in a typical qualitative analysis experiment. Taking this fact into account, show quantitatively that the CO_3^{2-} concentration is large enough to give observable precipitation of $CaCO_3$ and $BaCO_3$, but not $MgCO_3$. Assume that the metal-ion concentrations are 0.010 M.

 (d) Show quantitatively which of the Mg^{2+}, Ca^{2+}, and Ba^{2+} ions, if any, should give an observable precipitate of the metal hydroxide.

 (e) Could the separation of Ca^{2+} and Ba^{2+} from Mg^{2+} be accomplished using 0.08 M Na_2CO_3 in place of 0.080 M $(NH_4)_2CO_3$? Show quantitatively why or why not.

(The left column is partially cut off at the page fold.)

What facto
reaction
pletion.
at all. Still others—
at 400–500 °C—res
of both reactants a

As we saw in S
value of its equilib
reaction goes far to
the reaction does n
determines the val
out measuring the
Put another way, w
extent of a particu
thermodynamics,
other forms of ener

16.1 SPON

We have defined a
any external influe
nonspontaneous a
influence. Conside
stopcock in the ap
spontaneously into
same. The reverse
occur spontaneous
have to push on the

As a second exa
presence of a platin

The forward reactic
of water into its ele
Chapter 17 that we
reverse process is
energy.

In general, whe
the temperature, p
example, the Haber

15.147 A railroad tank car derails and spills 36 tons of concentrated sulfuric acid. The acid is 98.0 mass % H_2SO_4 and has a density of 1.836 g/mL.

(a) What is the molarity of the acid?

(b) How many kilograms of sodium carbonate are needed to completely neutralize the acid?

(c) How many liters of carbon dioxide at 18 °C and 745 mm Hg are produced as a byproduct?

15.148 Some progressive hair dyes marketed to men, such as Grecian Formula 16, contain lead acetate, $Pb(CH_3CO_2)_2$. As the dye solution is rubbed on the hair, the Pb^{2+} ions react with the sulfur atoms in hair proteins to give lead(II) sulfide (PbS), which is black. A typical dye solution contains 0.3 mass % $Pb(CH_3CO_2)_2$, and about 2 mL of dye solution is used per application.

(a) Assuming that 30% of the $Pb(CH_3CO_2)_2$ is converted to PbS, how many milligrams of PbS are formed per application of the dye?

(b) Suppose the hair is washed with shampoo and water that has pH = 5.50. How many washings would be required to remove 50% of the black color? Assume that 3 gal of water is used per washing and that the water becomes saturated with PbS.

(c) Does the calculated number of washings look reasonable, given that frequent application of the dye is recommended? What process(es) in addition to dissolution might contribute to the loss of color?

Remember...

The **reaction quotient** Q is defined in the same way as the equilibrium constant K except that the concentrations or partial pressures in the equilibrium constant expression are not necessarily equilibrium values. (Section 13.5)

Remember...

The **activation energy** E_a, the energy difference between the transition state and the reactants, is the minimum collision energy needed for reaction. (Section 12.12)

A mixture of gaseous N_2, H_2, and NH_3, each at a partial pressure of 1 atm, reacts spontaneously at 300 K to convert some of the N_2 and H_2 to NH_3. We can predict the direction of spontaneous reaction from the relative values of the equilibrium constant K and the **reaction quotient** Q (Section 13.5). Since $K_p = 4.4 \times 10^5$ at 300 K and $Q_p = 1$ for partial pressures of 1 atm, the reaction will proceed in the forward direction because Q_p is less than K_p. Under these conditions, the reverse reaction is nonspontaneous. At 700 K, however, $K_p = 8.8 \times 10^{-5}$ and the reverse reaction is spontaneous because Q_p is greater than K_p.

A spontaneous reaction always moves a reaction mixture toward equilibrium. By contrast, a nonspontaneous reaction moves the composition of a mixture away from the equilibrium composition. Remember, though, that the word spontaneous doesn't necessarily mean "fast." A spontaneous reaction can be either fast or slow—for example, the gradual rusting of iron metal is a slow spontaneous reaction. Thermodynamics tells us where a reaction is headed, but it says nothing about how long it takes to get there. As discussed in Section 12.12, the rate at which equilibrium is achieved depends on kinetics, especially on the height of the **activation energy** barrier between the reactants and products (**Figure 16.2**).

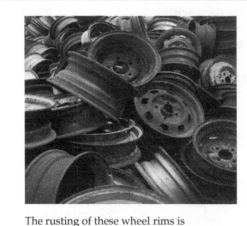

The rusting of these wheel rims is a slow but spontaneous reaction.

Figure 16.2
The rate of a spontaneous reaction depends on kinetics.

▶ **PROBLEM 16.1** Which of the following processes are spontaneous? Which are nonspontaneous?
(a) Diffusion of perfume molecules from one side of a room to the other
(b) Heat flow from a cold object to a hot object
(c) Decomposition of rust ($Fe_2O_3 \cdot H_2O$) to iron metal, oxygen, and water
(d) Decomposition of solid $CaCO_3$ to solid CaO and gaseous CO_2 at 25 °C and 1 atm pressure ($K_p = 1.4 \times 10^{-23}$)

16.2 ENTHALPY, ENTROPY, AND SPONTANEOUS PROCESSES: A BRIEF REVIEW

Let's look more closely at spontaneous processes and at the thermodynamic factors that cause them to occur. We saw in Chapter 8 that most spontaneous chemical reactions are accompanied by the conversion of potential energy to heat. For example, when methane burns in air, the potential energy stored in the chemical bonds of CH_4

and O_2 is partly converted to heat, which flows from the system (reactants plus products) to the surroundings:

$$CH_4(g) + 2\,O_2(g) \longrightarrow CO_2(g) + 2\,H_2O(l) \qquad \Delta H° = -890.3 \text{ kJ}$$

Because heat is lost by the system, the reaction is exothermic and the standard enthalpy of reaction is negative ($\Delta H° = -890.3$ kJ). The total energy is conserved, so all the energy lost by the system shows up as heat gained by the surroundings.

Because spontaneous reactions so often give off heat, the nineteenth-century French chemist Marcellin Berthelot proposed that spontaneous chemical or physical changes are *always* exothermic. But Berthelot's proposal can't be correct. Ice, for example, spontaneously absorbs heat from the surroundings and melts at temperatures above 0 °C. Similarly, liquid water absorbs heat and spontaneously boils at temperatures above 100 °C. As further examples, gaseous N_2O_4 absorbs heat when it decomposes to NO_2 at 400 K, and table salt absorbs heat when it dissolves in water at room temperature:

$$\begin{aligned} H_2O(s) &\longrightarrow H_2O(l) & \Delta H_{fusion} &= +6.01 \text{ kJ} \\ H_2O(l) &\longrightarrow H_2O(g) & \Delta H_{vap} &= +40.7 \text{ kJ} \\ N_2O_4(g) &\longrightarrow 2\,NO_2(g) & \Delta H° &= +55.3 \text{ kJ} \\ NaCl(s) &\longrightarrow Na^+(aq) + Cl^-(aq) & \Delta H° &= +3.88 \text{ kJ} \end{aligned}$$

All these processes are endothermic, yet all are spontaneous. In all cases, the system moves spontaneously to a state of *higher* enthalpy by absorbing heat from the surroundings.

Because some spontaneous reactions are exothermic and others are endothermic, enthalpy alone can't account for the direction of spontaneous change; a second factor must be involved. This second determinant of spontaneous change is nature's tendency to move to a condition of maximum randomness (Section 8.12).

Molecular randomness is called **entropy** and is denoted by the symbol S. Entropy is a **state function** (Section 8.2), and the entropy change ΔS for a process thus depends only on the initial and final states of the system:

$$\Delta S = S_{final} - S_{initial}$$

When the randomness of a system increases, ΔS has a positive value; when randomness decreases, ΔS is negative.

The randomness of a system comes about because the particles in the system (atoms, ions, and molecules) are in incessant motion, moving about in the accessible volume, colliding with each other and continually exchanging energy. Randomness—and thus entropy—is a probability concept, related to the number of ways that a particular state of a system can be achieved. A particular state of a macroscopic system, characterized by its temperature, pressure, volume, and number of particles, can be achieved in a vast number of ways in which the fluctuating positions and energies of the individual particles differ but the volume and total energy are constant.

We'll examine the relationship between entropy and probability in the next section, but first let's take a qualitative look at the four spontaneous endothermic processes mentioned previously (melting of ice, boiling of liquid water, decomposition of N_2O_4, and dissolving of NaCl in water). Each of these processes involves an increase in the randomness of the system. When ice melts, for example, randomness increases because the highly ordered crystalline arrangement of tightly held water molecules collapses and the molecules become free to move about in the liquid. When liquid water vaporizes, randomness further increases because the molecules can now move independently in the much larger volume of the gas. In general, processes that convert a solid to a liquid or a liquid to a gas involve an increase in randomness and thus an increase in entropy (**Figure 16.3**).

▲ The combustion of natural gas (mainly CH_4) in air is a spontaneous, exothermic reaction.

Remember...

A **state function** is a function or property whose value depends only on the present state (condition) of the system, not on the path used to arrive at that condition. Pressure, volume, temperature, enthalpy, and entropy are state functions. (Section 8.2)

Figure 16.3
How molecular randomness—and thus entropy—changes when solids, liquids, and gases interconvert.

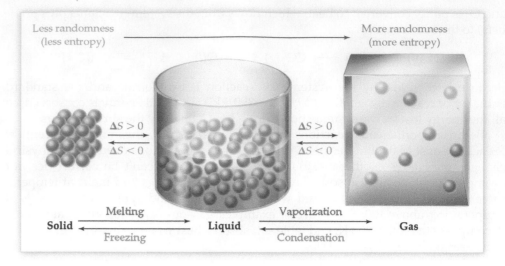

The decomposition of N_2O_4 (O_2N-NO_2) is accompanied by an increase in randomness because breaking the N—N bond allows the two gaseous NO_2 fragments to move independently. Whenever a molecule breaks into two or more pieces, the amount of molecular randomness increases. More specifically, randomness—and thus entropy—increases whenever a reaction results in an increase in the number of gaseous particles (**Figure 16.4**).

Figure 16.4
How molecular randomness—and thus entropy—changes when the number of gaseous particles changes.

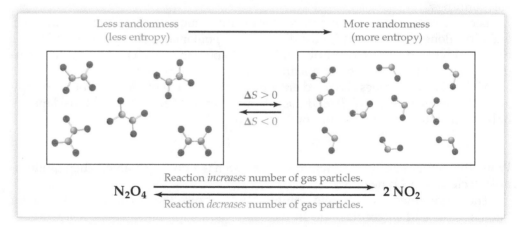

Remember...

Hydrated ions are surrounded and stabilized by an ordered shell of solvent water molecules. The stabilization results from ion–dipole attractions.   (Section 11.2)

The entropy change on dissolving sodium chloride in water occurs because the crystal structure of solid NaCl is disrupted and the Na^+ and Cl^- ions become **hydrated** (Section 11.2). Disruption of the crystal increases randomness because the Na^+ and Cl^- ions are tightly held in the solid but are free to move about in the liquid. The hydration process, however, *decreases* randomness because the polar, hydrating water molecules adopt an orderly arrangement about the Na^+ and Cl^- ions. It turns out that the overall dissolution process for NaCl results in a net increase in randomness, and ΔS is thus positive (**Figure 16.5**). This is usually the case for the dissolution of molecular solids, such as $HgCl_2$, and salts that contain +1 cations and −1 anions. For salts such as $CaSO_4$, which contain more highly charged ions, the hydrating water molecules are more strongly attached to the ions and the dissolution process often results in a net decrease in entropy. The following dissolution reactions illustrate the point:

$$HgCl_2(s) \longrightarrow HgCl_2(aq) \qquad \Delta S = +9 \text{ J/(K·mol)}$$
$$NaCl(s) \longrightarrow Na^+(aq) + Cl^-(aq) \qquad \Delta S = +43 \text{ J/(K·mol)}$$
$$CaSO_4(s) \longrightarrow Ca^{2+}(aq) + SO_4^{2-}(aq) \qquad \Delta S = -140 \text{ J/(K·mol)}$$

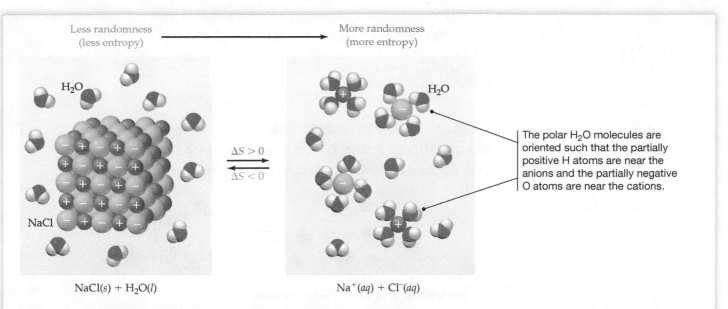

Less randomness → More randomness
(less entropy) (more entropy)

$\Delta S > 0$
$\Delta S < 0$

The polar H_2O molecules are oriented such that the partially positive H atoms are near the anions and the partially negative O atoms are near the cations.

$NaCl(s) + H_2O(l)$ $Na^+(aq) + Cl^-(aq)$

Disruption of the crystal increases the entropy, but the hydration process decreases the entropy. For the dissolution of NaCl, the net effect is an entropy increase.

Figure 16.5
Dissolution of sodium chloride. When NaCl dissolves in water, the crystal breaks up, and the Na^+ and Cl^- ions are surrounded by hydrating water molecules.

WORKED EXAMPLE 16.1

PREDICTING THE SIGN OF ΔS

Predict the sign of ΔS in the system for each of the following processes:

(a) $CO_2(s) \longrightarrow CO_2(g)$ (sublimation of dry ice)

(b) $CaSO_4(s) \longrightarrow CaO(s) + SO_3(g)$

(c) $N_2(g) + 3\,H_2(g) \longrightarrow 2\,NH_3(g)$

(d) $I_2(s) \longrightarrow I_2(aq)$ (dissolution of iodine in water)

STRATEGY

To predict the sign of ΔS, look to see whether the process involves a phase change, a change in the number of gaseous molecules, or the dissolution (or precipitation) of a solid. Entropy generally increases for phase transitions that convert a solid to a liquid or a liquid to a gas, for reactions that increase the number of gaseous molecules, and for the dissolution of molecular solids or salts with +1 cations and −1 anions.

SOLUTION

(a) The molecules in a gas are free to move about randomly, whereas the molecules in a solid are tightly held in a highly ordered arrangement. Therefore, randomness increases when a solid sublimes and ΔS is positive.

(b) One mole of gaseous molecules appears on the product side of the equation and none appears on the reactant side. Because the reaction increases the number of gaseous molecules, the entropy change is positive.

(c) The entropy change is negative because the reaction decreases the number of gaseous molecules from 4 mol to 2 mol. Fewer particles can move independently after reaction than before.

(d) Iodine molecules are electrically neutral and form a molecular solid. The dissolution process destroys the order of the crystal and enables the iodine molecules to move about randomly in the liquid. Therefore, ΔS is positive.

▶ **PROBLEM 16.2**   Predict the sign of ΔS in the system for each of the following processes:
(a) $H_2O(g) \longrightarrow H_2O(l)$ (formation of rain droplets)
(b) $I_2(g) \longrightarrow 2\,I(g)$
(c) $CaCO_3(s) \longrightarrow CaO(s) + CO_2(g)$
(d) $Ag^+(aq) + Br^-(aq) \longrightarrow AgBr(s)$

WORKED CONCEPTUAL EXAMPLE 16.2

PREDICTING THE SIGN OF ΔS FOR A GAS-PHASE REACTION

Consider the gas-phase reaction of A_2 molecules (red) with B atoms (blue):

(a) Write a balanced equation for the reaction.
(b) Predict the sign of ΔS for the reaction.

STRATEGY

To determine the stoichiometry of the reaction, count the number of reactant A_2 molecules and B atoms and the number of product AB molecules. To predict the sign of the entropy change, see if the reaction increases or decreases the number of gaseous particles.

SOLUTION

(a) In this reaction, 3 A_2 molecules and 6 B atoms are consumed and 6 AB molecules are formed ($3\,A_2 + 6\,B \rightarrow 6\,AB$). Dividing by 3 to reduce the coefficients to their smallest whole number values gives the balanced equation $A_2(g) + 2\,B(g) \rightarrow 2\,AB(g)$.

(b) Because the reaction decreases the number of gaseous particles from 3 mol to 2 mol, the entropy change is negative.

CONCEPTUAL PROBLEM 16.3   Consider the gas-phase reaction of AB_3 and A_2 molecules:

(a) Write a balanced equation for the reaction.
(b) What is the sign of the entropy change for the reaction?

16.3   ENTROPY AND PROBABILITY

Why do systems tend to move spontaneously to a state of maximum randomness? The answer is that a random arrangement of particles is more probable than an ordered arrangement because a random arrangement can be achieved in more ways. To begin with a simple example, suppose that you shake a box containing 20 identical coins and then count the number of heads (H) and tails (T). It's very unlikely that all 20 coins will come up heads; that is, a perfectly ordered arrangement of 20 heads (or 20 tails) is much less probable than a random mixture of heads and tails.

The probabilities of the ordered and random arrangements are proportional to the number of ways that the arrangements can be achieved. The perfectly ordered arrangement of 20 heads can be achieved in only one way because it consists of a

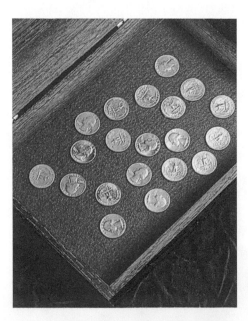

▲ Shaking a box that contains 20 quarters gives a random arrangement of heads and tails.

single configuration. In how many ways, though, can a random arrangement be achieved? If there were just two coins in the box, each of them could come up in one of two ways (H or T), and the two together could come up in $2 \times 2 = 2^2 = 4$ ways (HH, HT, TH, or TT). Three coins could come up in $2 \times 2 \times 2 = 2^3 = 8$ ways (HHH, THH, HTH, HHT, HTT, THT, TTH, or TTT), and so on. For the case of 20 coins, the number of possible arrangements is $2^{20} = 1,048,576$.

Because the ordered arrangement of 20 heads (or 20 tails) can be achieved in only one way and a random mixture of heads and tails can be achieved in $2^{20} - 2 \approx 2^{20}$ ways, a random arrangement is 2^{20} times more probable than a perfectly ordered arrangement. If you begin with an ordered arrangement of 20 heads and shake the box, the system will move to a state with a random mixture of heads and tails because that state is more probable. (Note that the state with a random arrangement of coins includes all possible arrangements except the two perfectly ordered arrangements.)

An analogous chemical example is a crystal containing diatomic molecules such as carbon monoxide in which the two distinct ends of the CO molecule correspond to the heads and tails of a coin. Let's suppose that the long dimensions of the molecules are oriented vertically (**Figure 16.6**) and that the temperature is 0 K, so that the molecules are locked into a fixed arrangement. The state in which the molecules pack together in a perfectly ordered "heads-up" arrangement (Figure 16.6a) can be achieved in only one way, whereas the state in which the molecules are arranged randomly with respect to the vertical direction can be achieved in many ways—2^{20} ways for a hypothetical crystal containing 20 CO molecules (Figure 16.6b). Therefore, a structure in which the molecules are arranged randomly is 2^{20} times more probable than the perfectly ordered heads-up structure.

The Austrian physicist Ludwig Boltzmann proposed that the entropy of a particular state is related to the number of ways that the state can be achieved, according to the formula

$$S = k \ln W$$

where S is the entropy of the state, $\ln W$ is the natural logarithm of the number of ways that the state can be achieved, and k, now known as *Boltzmann's constant*, is a universal constant equal to the gas constant R divided by Avogadro's number ($k = R/N_A = 1.38 \times 10^{-23}$ J/K). Because a logarithm is dimensionless, the Boltzmann equation implies that entropy has the same units as the constant k, joules per kelvin.

Now let's apply Boltzmann's formula to our hypothetical crystal containing 20 CO molecules. Because a perfectly ordered state can be achieved in only one way ($W = 1$ in the Boltzmann equation) and because $\ln 1 = 0$, the entropy of the perfectly ordered state is zero:

$$S = k \ln W = k \ln 1$$
$$= 0$$

The more probable state in which the molecules are arranged randomly can be achieved in 2^{20} ways and thus has a higher entropy:

$$S = k \ln W = k \ln 2^{20}$$
$$= (1.38 \times 10^{-23} \text{ J/K})(20)(\ln 2)$$
$$= 1.91 \times 10^{-22} \text{ J/K}$$

where we have made use of the relation $\ln x^a = a \ln x$ (Appendix A.2).

If our crystal contained 1 mol of CO molecules, the entropy of the perfectly ordered state (6.02×10^{23} C atoms up) would still be zero, but the entropy of the state with a random arrangement of CO molecules would be much higher because Avogadro's number of molecules can be arranged randomly in a huge number of ways ($W = 2^{N_A} = 2^{6.02 \times 10^{23}}$).

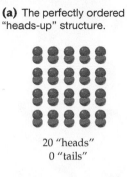

(a) The perfectly ordered "heads-up" structure.

20 "heads"
0 "tails"

(b) The molecules arranged randomly in one of the 2^{20} ways in which a disordered structure can be obtained.

9 "heads"
11 "tails"

Figure 16.6
A hypothetical crystal containing 20 CO molecules.

According to Boltzmann's formula, the entropy of the state with a random arrangement of CO molecules is

$$S = k \ln W = k \ln 2^{N_A} = k N_A \ln 2$$

Because $k = R/N_A$,

$$S = R \ln 2 = (8.314 \text{ J/K})(0.693)$$
$$= 5.76 \text{ J/K}$$

Based on experimental measurements, the entropy of 1 mol of solid carbon monoxide near 0 K is about 5 J/K, indicating that the CO molecules adopt a nearly random arrangement. Entropy associated with a random arrangement of molecules in space is sometimes called positional, or configurational, entropy.

The nearly random arrangement of CO molecules in crystalline carbon monoxide is unusual but can be understood in terms of molecular structure. Because CO molecules have a **dipole moment** of only 0.11 D, intermolecular **dipole–dipole forces** are unusually weak (Sections 10.1 and 10.2), and the molecules therefore have little preference for a slightly lower energy, completely ordered arrangement. By contrast, HCl, with a larger dipole moment of 1.11 D, forms an ordered crystalline solid, and so the entropy of 1 mol of solid HCl at 0 K is 0 J/K.

Boltzmann's formula also explains why a gas expands into a vacuum. If the two bulbs in Figure 16.1 have equal volumes, each molecule has one chance in two of being in bulb A (heads, in our coin example) and one chance in two of being in bulb B (tails) when the stopcock is opened. It's exceedingly unlikely that all the molecules in 1 mol of gas will be in bulb A because that state can be achieved in only one way. The state in which Avogadro's number of molecules are randomly distributed between bulbs A and B can be achieved in $2^{6.02 \times 10^{23}}$ ways, and the entropy of that state is therefore higher than the entropy of the ordered state by the now familiar amount, $R \ln 2 = 5.76 \text{ J/K}$. Thus, a gas expands spontaneously because the state of greater volume is more probable.

We can derive a general equation for the entropy change that occurs on the expansion of an ideal gas at constant temperature by considering the distribution of N molecules among B hypothetical boxes, or cells, each having an equal volume v.

Volume per box = v
Number of accessible boxes = B
Total volume, $V = Bv$

Since the **energy of an ideal gas** depends only on the temperature (Section 9.6), ΔE for the expansion of an ideal gas at constant temperature is zero. To calculate the entropy change $\Delta S = S_{\text{final}} - S_{\text{initial}}$ using the Boltzmann equation, we have only to find the number of ways N molecules can be distributed among the B boxes.

A single molecule can go into any one of the boxes and can thus be assigned to B boxes in B ways. Two molecules can occupy the boxes in $B \times B = B^2$ ways, three molecules can fill the boxes in $B \times B \times B = B^3$ ways, and so on. The number of ways that N molecules can occupy B boxes is $W = B^N$.

Now suppose that the initial volume comprises B_{initial} boxes and the final volume consists of B_{final} boxes:

$$V_{\text{initial}} = B_{\text{initial}}v \qquad \text{and} \qquad V_{\text{final}} = B_{\text{final}}v$$

Then the probabilities of the initial and final states—that is, the number of ways they can be achieved—are

$$W_{\text{initial}} = (B_{\text{initial}})^N \qquad \text{and} \qquad W_{\text{final}} = (B_{\text{final}})^N$$

According to the Boltzmann equation, the entropy change due to a change in volume is

$$\Delta S = S_{final} - S_{initial} = k \ln W_{final} - k \ln W_{initial} = k \ln \frac{W_{final}}{W_{initial}}$$

$$= k \ln \left(\frac{B_{final}}{B_{initial}} \right)^N = kN \ln \frac{B_{final}}{B_{initial}}$$

Because $V_{initial} = B_{initial}v$ and $V_{final} = B_{final}v$,

$$\Delta S = kN \ln \left(\frac{V_{final}/v}{V_{initial}/v} \right) = kN \ln \frac{V_{final}}{V_{initial}}$$

Finally, because $k = R/N_A$ and the number of particles equals the number of moles of gas times Avogadro's number ($N = nN_A$), then

$$kN = \left(\frac{R}{N_A} \right)(nN_A) = nR$$

and so the entropy change for expansion (or compression) of n moles of an ideal gas at constant temperature is

$$\Delta S = nR \ln \frac{V_{final}}{V_{initial}}$$

For a twofold expansion of 1 mol of an ideal gas at constant temperature, $\Delta S = R \ln 2$, the same result as we obtained previously.

Because the pressure and volume of an ideal gas are related inversely ($P = nRT/V$), we can also write

$$\Delta S = nR \ln \frac{P_{initial}}{P_{final}}$$

Thus, the entropy of a gas *increases* when its pressure *decreases* at constant temperature, and the entropy *decreases* when its pressure *increases*. Common sense tells us that the more we squeeze the gas, the less space the gas molecules have and so randomness decreases.

▶ **PROBLEM 16.4**   Which state has the higher entropy? Explain in terms of probability.
   (a) A perfectly ordered crystal of solid nitrous oxide (N≡N—O) or a disordered crystal in which the molecules are oriented randomly
   (b) Quartz glass (Section 10.10) or a quartz crystal
   (c) 1 mol of N_2 gas at STP or 1 mol of N_2 gas at 273 K in a volume of 11.2 L
   (d) 1 mol of N_2 gas at STP or 1 mol of N_2 gas at 273 K and 0.25 atm

16.4   ENTROPY AND TEMPERATURE

Thus far we've seen that entropy is associated with the orientation and distribution of molecules in space. Disordered crystals have higher entropy than ordered crystals, and expanded gases have higher entropy than compressed gases.

Entropy is also associated with molecular motion. As the temperature of a substance increases, random molecular motion increases and there is a corresponding increase in the average kinetic energy of the molecules. But not all the molecules have the same energy. As we saw in Section 9.6, there is a distribution of molecular speeds in a gas, a distribution that broadens and shifts to higher speeds with increasing temperature (Figure 9.12, page 328). In solids, liquids, and gases, the total energy of a substance can be distributed among the individual molecules in a number of ways that increases as the total energy increases. According to Boltzmann's formula, the more ways that the energy can be distributed, the greater the randomness of the state and the higher its entropy. Therefore, the entropy of a substance increases with increasing temperature (**Figure 16.7**).

Higher temperature:
•Greater molecular motion
•Broader distribution of individual molecular energies
•More randomness
•Higher entropy

Lower temperature:
•Less molecular motion
•Narrower distribution of individual molecular energies
•Less randomness
•Lower entropy

Figure 16.7
A substance at a higher temperature has greater entropy than the same substance at a lower temperature.

A typical plot of entropy versus temperature is shown in **Figure 16.8**. At absolute zero, every substance is a solid whose particles are tightly held in a crystalline structure. If there is no residual orientational disorder, like that in carbon monoxide (Figure 16.6b), the entropy of the substance at 0 K will be zero, a general result summarized in the **third law of thermodynamics**:

Third Law of Thermodynamics   The entropy of a perfectly ordered crystalline substance at 0 K is zero.

(The first law of thermodynamics was discussed in Section 8.1. We'll review the first law and discuss the second law in Section 16.6.)

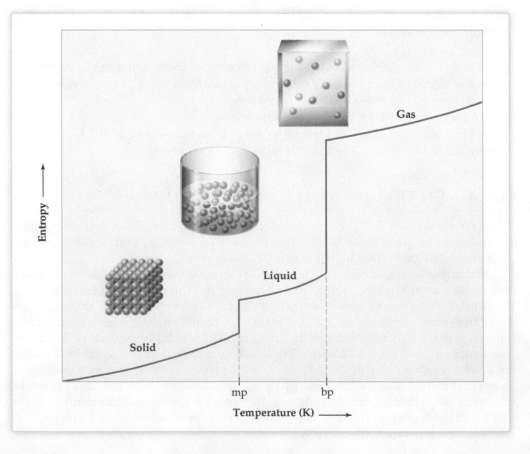

Figure 16.8
Entropy versus temperature. The entropy of a pure substance, equal to zero at 0 K, shows a steady increase with rising temperature, punctuated by discontinuous jumps in entropy at the temperatures of the phase transitions.

As the temperature of a solid is raised, the added energy increases the vibrational motion of the molecules about their equilibrium positions in the crystal. The number of ways in which the vibrational energy can be distributed increases with rising temperature, and the entropy of the solid thus increases steadily as the temperature increases.

At the melting point, there is a discontinuous jump in entropy because there are many more ways of arranging the molecules in the liquid than in the solid. Furthermore, the molecules in the liquid can undergo translational and rotational as well as vibrational motion, and so there are many more ways of distributing the total energy in the liquid. (Translational motion is motion of the center of mass.) An even greater jump in entropy is observed at the boiling point because molecules in the gas are free to occupy a much larger volume. Between the melting point and the boiling point, the entropy of a liquid increases steadily as molecular motion increases and the number of ways of distributing the total energy among the individual molecules increases. For the same reason, the entropy of a gas rises steadily as its temperature increases.

16.5 STANDARD MOLAR ENTROPIES AND STANDARD ENTROPIES OF REACTION

We won't describe how the entropy of a substance is determined, except to note that two approaches are available: (1) calculations based on Boltzmann's formula and (2) experimental measurements of heat capacities (Section 8.7) down to very low temperatures. Suffice it to say that **standard molar entropies**, denoted by $S°$, are known for many substances.

Remember...
The molar **heat capacity** is the amount of heat needed to raise the temperature of 1 mol of a substance by 1 °C. (Section 8.7)

◁▭ **Standard Molar Entropy, $S°$**   The entropy of 1 mol of the pure substance at 1 atm pressure and a specified temperature, usually 25 °C.

Values of $S°$ for some common substances at 25 °C are listed in Table 16.1, and additional values are given in Appendix B. Note that the units of $S°$ are *joules* (not kilojoules) per kelvin mole [J/(K · mol)]. Standard molar entropies are often called *absolute entropies* because they are measured with respect to an absolute reference point—the entropy of the perfectly ordered crystalline substance at 0 K [$S° = 0$ J/(K · mol) at $T = 0$ K].

Standard molar entropies make it possible to compare the entropies of different substances under the same conditions of temperature and pressure. It's apparent from Table 16.1, for example, that the entropies of gaseous substances tend to be

TABLE 16.1   Standard Molar Entropies for Some Common Substances at 25 °C

Substance	Formula	$S°$ [J/(K · mol)]	Substance	Formula	$S°$ [J/(K · mol)]
Gases			**Liquids**		
Acetylene	C_2H_2	200.8	Acetic acid	CH_3CO_2H	160
Ammonia	NH_3	192.3	Ethanol	CH_3CH_2OH	161
Carbon dioxide	CO_2	213.6	Methanol	CH_3OH	127
Carbon monoxide	CO	197.6	Water	H_2O	69.9
Ethylene	C_2H_4	219.5	**Solids**		
Hydrogen	H_2	130.6	Calcium carbonate	$CaCO_3$	91.7
Methane	CH_4	186.2	Calcium oxide	CaO	38.1
Nitrogen	N_2	191.5	Diamond	C	2.4
Nitrogen dioxide	NO_2	240.0	Graphite	C	5.7
Dinitrogen tetroxide	N_2O_4	304.3	Iron	Fe	27.3
Oxygen	O_2	205.0	Iron(III) oxide	Fe_2O_3	87.4

larger than those of liquids, which, in turn, tend to be larger than those of solids. Table 16.1 also shows that $S°$ values increase with increasing molecular complexity. Compare, for example, CH_3OH, which has $S° = 127$ J/(K·mol), and CH_3CH_2OH, which has $S° = 161$ J/(K·mol).

Once we have values for standard molar entropies, it's easy to calculate the entropy change for a chemical reaction. The **standard entropy of reaction ($\Delta S°$)** can be obtained simply by subtracting the standard molar entropies of all the reactants from the standard molar entropies of all the products:

$$\Delta S° = S°(\text{products}) - S°(\text{reactants})$$

Because $S°$ values are quoted on a per-mole basis, the $S°$ value for each substance must be multiplied by the stoichiometric coefficient of that substance in the balanced chemical equation. Thus, for the general reaction

$$a\,A + b\,B \longrightarrow c\,C + d\,D$$

the standard entropy of reaction is

$$\Delta S° = [c\,S°(C) + d\,S°(D)] - [a\,S°(A) + b\,S°(B)]$$

where the units of the coefficients are moles, the units of $S°$ are J/(K·mol), and the units of $\Delta S°$ are J/K.

As an example, let's calculate the standard entropy change for the reaction

$$N_2O_4(g) \longrightarrow 2\,NO_2(g)$$

Using the appropriate $S°$ values from Table 16.1, we find that $\Delta S° = 175.7$ J/K:

$$\Delta S° = 2\,S°(NO_2) - S°(N_2O_4)$$
$$= (2\text{ mol})\left(240.0\,\frac{J}{K \cdot mol}\right) - (1\text{ mol})\left(304.3\,\frac{J}{K \cdot mol}\right)$$
$$= 175.7\text{ J/K}$$

Although the standard molar entropy of N_2O_4 is larger than that of NO_2, as expected for a more complex molecule, $\Delta S°$ for the reaction is positive because 1 mol of N_2O_4 is converted to 2 mol of NO_2. As noted earlier, we expect an increase in entropy whenever a molecule breaks into two or more pieces.

WORKED EXAMPLE 16.3

CALCULATING THE STANDARD ENTROPY OF REACTION

Calculate the standard entropy of reaction at 25 °C for the Haber synthesis of ammonia:

$$N_2(g) + 3\,H_2(g) \longrightarrow 2\,NH_3(g)$$

STRATEGY

To calculate $\Delta S°$ for the reaction, subtract the standard molar entropies of all the reactants from the standard molar entropies of all the products. Look up the $S°$ values in Table 16.1 or Appendix B, and remember to multiply the $S°$ value for each substance by its coefficient in the balanced chemical equation.

SOLUTION

$$\Delta S° = 2\,S°(NH_3) - [S°(N_2) + 3\,S°(H_2)]$$
$$= (2\text{ mol})\left(192.3\,\frac{J}{K \cdot mol}\right) - \left[(1\text{ mol})\left(191.5\,\frac{J}{K \cdot mol}\right) + (3\text{ mol})\left(130.6\,\frac{J}{K \cdot mol}\right)\right]$$
$$= -198.7\text{ J/K}$$

BALLPARK CHECK

As predicted in Worked Example 16.1c, $\Delta S°$ should be negative because the reaction decreases the number of gaseous molecules from 4 mol to 2 mol.

▶ **PROBLEM 16.5**   Calculate the standard entropy of reaction at 25 °C for the decomposition of calcium carbonate:

$$CaCO_3(s) \longrightarrow CaO(s) + CO_2(g)$$

16.6   ENTROPY AND THE SECOND LAW OF THERMODYNAMICS

We've seen thus far that molecular systems tend to move spontaneously toward a state of minimum enthalpy and maximum entropy. In any particular reaction, though, the enthalpy of the system can either increase or decrease. Similarly, the entropy of the system can either increase or decrease. How, then, can we decide whether a reaction will occur spontaneously? In Section 8.13, we said that it is the value of the *free-energy change*, ΔG, that is the criterion for spontaneity, where $\Delta G = \Delta H - T\Delta S$. If $\Delta G < 0$, the reaction is spontaneous; if $\Delta G > 0$, the reaction is nonspontaneous; and if $\Delta G = 0$, the reaction is at equilibrium. In this section and the next, we'll see how that conclusion was reached. Let's begin by looking at the first and second laws of thermodynamics:

◀═▶ **First Law of Thermodynamics**	In any process, spontaneous or non-spontaneous, the total energy of a system and its surroundings is constant.
◀═▶ **Second Law of Thermodynamics**	In any *spontaneous* process, the total entropy of a system and its surroundings always increases.

The first law is simply a statement of the conservation of energy (Section 8.1). It says that energy (or enthalpy) can flow between a system and its surroundings but the total energy of the system plus the surroundings always remains constant. In an exothermic reaction, the system loses enthalpy to the surroundings; in an endothermic reaction, the system gains enthalpy from the surroundings. Because energy is conserved in *all* chemical processes, spontaneous and nonspontaneous, the first law helps us keep track of energy flow between the system and the surroundings but it doesn't tell us whether a particular reaction will be spontaneous or nonspontaneous.

The second law, however, provides a clear-cut criterion of spontaneity. It says that the direction of spontaneous change is always determined by the sign of the total entropy change:

$$\Delta S_{total} = \Delta S_{system} + \Delta S_{surroundings}$$

Specifically,

If $\Delta S_{total} > 0$, the reaction is spontaneous.

If $\Delta S_{total} < 0$, the reaction is nonspontaneous.

If $\Delta S_{total} = 0$, the reaction mixture is at equilibrium.

All reactions proceed spontaneously in the direction that increases the entropy of the system plus surroundings. A reaction that is nonspontaneous in the forward direction is spontaneous in the reverse direction because ΔS_{total} for the reverse reaction equals $-\Delta S_{total}$ for the forward reaction. If ΔS_{total} is zero, the reaction doesn't go spontaneously in either direction, and so the reaction mixture is at equilibrium.

To determine the value of ΔS_{total}, we need values for the entropy changes in the system and the surroundings. The entropy change in the system, ΔS_{sys}, is just the entropy of reaction, which can be calculated from standard molar entropies (Table 16.1), as described in Section 16.5. For a reaction that occurs at constant pressure, the entropy change in the surroundings is directly proportional to the enthalpy change for the reaction (ΔH) and inversely proportional to the kelvin temperature (T) of the surroundings, according to the equation

$$\Delta S_{surr} = \frac{-\Delta H}{T}$$

Although we won't derive this equation to calculate ΔS_{surr}, we can nevertheless justify its form. To see why ΔS_{surr} is proportional to $-\Delta H$, recall that for an exothermic reaction ($\Delta H < 0$), the system loses heat to the surroundings (**Figure 16.9a**). As a result, the random motion of the molecules in the surroundings increases and the entropy of the surroundings also increases ($\Delta S_{surr} > 0$). Conversely, for an endothermic reaction ($\Delta H > 0$), the system gains heat from the surroundings (**Figure 16.9b**) and the entropy of the surroundings therefore decreases ($\Delta S_{surr} < 0$). Because ΔS_{surr} is positive when ΔH is negative, and vice versa, ΔS_{surr} is proportional to $-\Delta H$:

$$\Delta S_{surr} \propto -\Delta H$$

(a) When an exothermic reaction occurs in the system ($\Delta H < 0$), the surroundings gains heat and its entropy increases ($\Delta S_{surr} > 0$).

(b) When an endothermic reaction occurs in the system ($\Delta H > 0$), the surroundings loses heat and its entropy decreases ($\Delta S_{surr} < 0$).

Figure 16.9
The relationship between the enthalpy change in the system (ΔH) and the entropy change in the surroundings (ΔS_{surr}).

The reason why ΔS_{surr} is inversely proportional to the absolute temperature T is more subtle. We can think of the surroundings as an infinitely large constant-temperature bath to which heat can be added without changing its temperature. If the surroundings has a low temperature, it has only a small amount of randomness, in which case the addition of a given quantity of heat results in a substantial increase in the amount of randomness (a relatively large value of ΔS_{surr}). If the surroundings has a high temperature, it already has a large amount of randomness, and the addition of the same quantity of heat produces only a marginal increase in the amount of randomness (a relatively small value of ΔS_{surr}). Thus, ΔS_{surr} varies inversely with temperature:

$$\Delta S_{surr} \propto \frac{1}{T}$$

Adding heat to the surroundings is somewhat analogous to tossing a rock into a lake. If the lake exhibits little motion (calm, smooth surface) before the rock is thrown, the rock's impact produces considerable motion, evident in a circular pattern of waves. If the lake already exhibits appreciable motion (rough, choppy surface), the additional motion produced when the rock hits the water is hardly noticeable.

▲ Adding heat to cold surroundings is analogous to tossing a rock into calm waters. Both processes produce a considerable increase in the amount of motion and thus a relatively large increase in entropy.

▲ Adding heat to hot surroundings is analogous to tossing a rock into rough waters. Both processes produce a relatively small increase in the amount of motion and thus a relatively small increase in entropy.

WORKED EXAMPLE 16.4

DETERMINING WHETHER A REACTION IS SPONTANEOUS

Consider the oxidation of iron metal:

$$4\,Fe(s) + 3\,O_2(g) \longrightarrow 2\,Fe_2O_3(s)$$

By determining the sign of ΔS_{total}, show whether the reaction is spontaneous at 25 °C.

STRATEGY

To determine the sign of $\Delta S_{total} = \Delta S_{sys} + \Delta S_{surr}$, we need to calculate the values of ΔS_{sys} and ΔS_{surr}. The entropy change in the system equals the standard entropy of reaction and can be calculated using the standard molar entropies in Table 16.1. To obtain $\Delta S_{surr} = -\Delta H°/T$, calculate $\Delta H°$ for the reaction from standard enthalpies of formation (Section 8.9).

SOLUTION

$\Delta S_{sys} = \Delta S° = 2\,S°(Fe_2O_3) - [4\,S°(Fe) + 3\,S°(O_2)]$

$$= (2\,mol)\left(87.4\,\frac{J}{K\cdot mol}\right) - \left[(4\,mol)\left(27.3\,\frac{J}{K\cdot mol}\right) + (3\,mol)\left(205.0\,\frac{J}{K\cdot mol}\right)\right]$$

$$= -549.5\,J/K$$

$\Delta H° = 2\,\Delta H°_f(Fe_2O_3) - [4\,\Delta H°_f(Fe) + 3\,\Delta H°_f(O_2)]$

Because $\Delta H°_f = 0$ for elements and $\Delta H°_f = -824.2$ kJ/mol for Fe_2O_3 (Appendix B), $\Delta H°$ for the reaction is

$$\Delta H° = 2\,\Delta H°_f(Fe_2O_3) = (2\,mol)(-824.2\,kJ/mol) = -1648.4\,kJ$$

Therefore, at 25 °C = 298.15 K,

$$\Delta S_{surr} = \frac{-\Delta H°}{T} = \frac{-(-1,648,400\,J)}{298.15\,K} = 5529\,J/K$$

$$\Delta S_{total} = \Delta S_{sys} + \Delta S_{surr} = -549.5\,J/K + 5529\,J/K = 4980\,J/K$$

Because the total entropy change is positive, the reaction is spontaneous under standard-state conditions at 25 °C.

BALLPARK CHECK

Since the reaction consumes 3 mol of gas, ΔS_{sys} is negative. Because the oxidation (burning) of iron metal is highly exothermic, $\Delta S_{surr} = -\Delta H°/T$ is positive and very large. The value of ΔS_{surr} is greater than the absolute value of ΔS_{sys}, and so ΔS_{total} is positive, in agreement with the solution.

▶ **PROBLEM 16.6** By determining the sign of ΔS_{total}, show whether the decomposition of calcium carbonate is spontaneous under standard-state conditions at 25 °C.

$$CaCO_3(s) \longrightarrow CaO(s) + CO_2(g)$$

16.7 FREE ENERGY

Chemists are generally more interested in the system (the reaction mixture) than the surroundings, and it's therefore convenient to restate the second law in terms of the thermodynamic properties of the system, without regard to the surroundings. For this purpose, we use the thermodynamic property called **free energy**, denoted by G in honor of J. Willard Gibbs (1839–1903), the American mathematical physicist who laid the foundations of chemical thermodynamics. The free energy G of a system is defined as

◁▧ **Free Energy** $G = H - TS$

As you might expect from its name, free energy has units of energy (J or kJ).

Because enthalpy, entropy, and temperature are state functions, free energy is also a state function, and the change in free energy (ΔG) for a process is independent of path. As we saw in Section 8.13, ΔG for a reaction at constant temperature equals the change in enthalpy minus the product of temperature times the change in entropy:

$$\Delta G = \Delta H - T\Delta S$$

To see what this equation for free-energy change has to do with spontaneity, let's return to the relationship

$$\Delta S_{total} = \Delta S_{sys} + \Delta S_{surr} = \Delta S + \Delta S_{surr}$$

where we have now dropped the subscript *sys*. (It's generally understood that symbols without a subscript refer to the system, not the surroundings.) Since $\Delta S_{surr} = -\Delta H/T$, where ΔH is the heat gained by the system at constant pressure, we can also write

$$\Delta S_{total} = \Delta S - \frac{\Delta H}{T}$$

Multiplying both sides by $-T$ gives

$$-T\Delta S_{total} = \Delta H - T\Delta S$$

The right side of this equation is just ΔG, the change in the free energy of the system at constant temperature and pressure. Therefore,

$$-T\Delta S_{total} = \Delta G$$

Note that ΔG and ΔS_{total} have opposite signs because the absolute temperature T is always positive.

According to the second law of thermodynamics, a reaction is spontaneous if ΔS_{total} is positive, nonspontaneous if ΔS_{total} is negative, and at equilibrium if ΔS_{total} is zero. Because $-T\Delta S_{total} = \Delta G$, and because ΔG and ΔS_{total} have opposite signs, we can restate the thermodynamic criterion for the spontaneity of a reaction carried out at constant temperature and pressure in the following way:

> If $\Delta G < 0$, the reaction is spontaneous.
>
> If $\Delta G > 0$, the reaction is nonspontaneous.
>
> If $\Delta G = 0$, the reaction mixture is at equilibrium.

In other words, *in any spontaneous process at constant temperature and pressure, the free energy of the system always decreases.*

As discussed in Section 8.13, the temperature T acts as a weighting factor that determines the relative importance of the enthalpy and entropy contributions to ΔG in the free-energy equation $\Delta G = \Delta H - T\Delta S$. If ΔH and ΔS are either both negative or both positive, the sign of ΔG (and therefore the spontaneity of the reaction) depends on the temperature (Table 16.2). If ΔH and ΔS are both negative, the

TABLE 16.2 Signs of Enthalpy, Entropy, and Free-Energy Changes and Reaction Spontaneity for a Reaction at Constant Temperature and Pressure

ΔH	ΔS	$\Delta G = \Delta H - T\Delta S$	Reaction Spontaneity	Example
$-$	$+$	$-$	Spontaneous at all temperatures	$2\,NO_2(g) \rightarrow N_2(g) + 2\,O_2(g)$
$-$	$-$	$-$ or $+$	Spontaneous at low temperatures where ΔH outweighs $T\Delta S$	$N_2(g) + 3\,H_2(g) \rightarrow 2\,NH_3(g)$
			Nonspontaneous at high temperatures where $T\Delta S$ outweighs ΔH	
$+$	$-$	$+$	Nonspontaneous at all temperatures	$3\,O_2(g) \rightarrow 2\,O_3(g)$
$+$	$+$	$-$ or $+$	Spontaneous at high temperatures where $T\Delta S$ outweighs ΔH	$2\,HgO(s) \rightarrow 2\,Hg(l) + O_2(g)$
			Nonspontaneous at low temperatures where ΔH outweighs $T\Delta S$	

reaction will be spontaneous only if the absolute value of ΔH is larger than the absolute value of $T\Delta S$. This is most likely at low temperatures, where the weighting factor T in $T\Delta S$ is small. If ΔH and ΔS are both positive, the reaction will be spontaneous only if $T\Delta S$ is larger than ΔH, which is most likely at high temperatures. We've already seen how these considerations apply to phase changes (Section 10.4).

Remember...

The **melting** of ice, for example, is spontaneous above 0 °C where $T\Delta S$ outweighs ΔH and ΔG is negative but is nonspontaneous below 0 °C where ΔH outweighs $T\Delta S$ and ΔG is positive. (Section 10.4)

WORKED EXAMPLE 16.5

DETERMINING THE TEMPERATURE AT WHICH A REACTION BECOMES SPONTANEOUS

Iron metal can be produced by reducing iron(III) oxide with hydrogen:

$$Fe_2O_3(s) + 3\,H_2(g) \longrightarrow 2\,Fe(s) + 3\,H_2O(g) \qquad \Delta H° = +98.8\,kJ; \Delta S° = +141.5\,J/K$$

(a) Is this reaction spontaneous under standard-state conditions at 25 °C?

(b) At what temperature will the reaction become spontaneous?

STRATEGY AND SOLUTION

(a) To determine whether the reaction is spontaneous at 25 °C, we need to determine the sign of $\Delta G = \Delta H - T\Delta S$. At 25 °C (298 K), ΔG for the reaction is

$$\Delta G = \Delta H - T\Delta S = (98.8\,kJ) - (298\,K)(0.1415\,kJ/K)$$
$$= (98.8\,kJ) - (42.2\,kJ)$$
$$= 56.6\,kJ$$

Because the positive ΔH term is larger than the positive $T\Delta S$ term, ΔG is positive and the reaction is nonspontaneous at 298 K.

(b) At sufficiently high temperatures, $T\Delta S$ becomes larger than ΔH, ΔG becomes negative, and the reaction becomes spontaneous. We can estimate the temperature at which ΔG changes from positive to negative by setting $\Delta G = \Delta H - T\Delta S = 0$. Solving for T, we find that the reaction becomes spontaneous at 698 K:

$$T = \frac{\Delta H}{\Delta S} = \frac{98.8\,kJ}{0.1415\,kJ/K} = 698\,K$$

This calculation assumes the values of ΔH and ΔS are unchanged on going from 298 K to 698 K. In general, the enthalpies and entropies of both reactants and products increase with increasing temperature, but the increases for the products tend to cancel the increases for the reactants. As a result, values of ΔH and ΔS for a reaction are relatively independent of temperature, at least over a small temperature range. In this example, the temperature range is quite large (400 K), and so the calculated value of T is only an estimate.

BALLPARK CHECK

(a) Let's use rounded values of ΔH (100 kJ), T (300 K), and ΔS (0.14 kJ/K) to estimate the relative values of ΔH and $T\Delta S$. Because $T\Delta S = 300\,K \times 0.14\,kJ/K = 42\,kJ$ is smaller than ΔH (100 kJ), $\Delta G = \Delta H - T\Delta S$ is positive and the reaction is nonspontaneous at 300 K. The ballpark check agrees with the solution.

(b) The temperature at which the reaction becomes spontaneous is approximately $(100\,kJ)/(0.14\,kJ/K) \approx 700\,K$, in agreement with the solution.

▶ **PROBLEM 16.7** Consider the decomposition of gaseous N_2O_4:

$$N_2O_4(g) \longrightarrow 2\,NO_2(g) \qquad \Delta H° = +55.3\,kJ; \Delta S° = +175.7\,J/K$$

(a) Is this reaction spontaneous under standard-state conditions at 25 °C?

(b) Estimate the temperature at which the reaction becomes spontaneous.

▶ **PROBLEM 16.8** The following data apply to the vaporization of mercury: $\Delta H_{vap} = 59.11\,kJ/mol$; $\Delta S_{vap} = 93.9\,J/(K \cdot mol)$.

(a) Does mercury boil at 325 °C and 1 atm pressure?

(b) What is the normal boiling point of mercury?

CONCEPTUAL PROBLEM 16.9 What are the signs (+, −, or 0) of ΔH, ΔS, and ΔG for the following spontaneous reaction of A atoms (red) and B atoms (blue)?

16.8 STANDARD FREE-ENERGY CHANGES FOR REACTIONS

The free energy of a substance, like its enthalpy and entropy, depends on its temperature, pressure, physical state (solid, liquid, or gas), and concentration (in the case of solutions). As a result, free-energy changes for chemical reactions must be compared under a well-defined set of standard-state conditions, as discussed in Section 8.5.

Standard-State Conditions { Solids, liquids, and gases in pure form at 1 atm pressure
Solutes at 1 M concentration
A specified temperature, usually 25 °C

The **standard free-energy change** ($\Delta G°$) for a reaction is the change in free energy that occurs when reactants in their standard states are converted to products in their standard states. As with $\Delta H°$ (Section 8.9), the value of $\Delta G°$ is an extensive property that refers to the number of moles indicated in the balanced chemical equation. For example, $\Delta G°$ at 25 °C for the reaction

$$2\,Na(s) + 2\,H_2O(l) \longrightarrow H_2(g) + 2\,Na^+(aq) + 2\,OH^-(aq)$$

is the change in free energy that occurs when 2 mol of solid sodium reacts completely with 2 mol of liquid water to give 1 mol of hydrogen gas at 1 atm pressure, along with an aqueous solution that contains 2 mol of Na^+ ions and 2 mol of OH^- ions at concentrations of 1 M, with all reactants and products at a temperature of 25 °C. For this reaction, $\Delta G° = -364$ kJ.

Because the free-energy change for any process at constant temperature and pressure is $\Delta G = \Delta H - T\Delta S$, we can calculate the standard free-energy change $\Delta G°$ for a reaction from the standard enthalpy change $\Delta H°$ and the standard entropy change $\Delta S°$. Consider again the Haber synthesis of ammonia:

$$N_2(g) + 3\,H_2(g) \longrightarrow 2\,NH_3(g) \qquad \Delta H° = -92.2\ \text{kJ}; \Delta S° = -198.7\ \text{J/K}$$

The standard free-energy change at 25 °C (298 K) is

$$\Delta G° = \Delta H° - T\Delta S° = (-92.2 \times 10^3\,\text{J}) - (298\,\text{K})(-198.7\,\text{J/K})$$
$$= (-92.2 \times 10^3\,\text{J}) - (-59.2 \times 10^3\,\text{J})$$
$$= -33.0 \times 10^3\,\text{J} \quad \text{or} \quad -33.0\ \text{kJ}$$

Because the negative $\Delta H°$ term is larger than the negative $T\Delta S°$ term at 25 °C, $\Delta G°$ is negative and the reaction is spontaneous under standard-state conditions.

It's important to note that a standard free-energy change applies to a hypothetical process rather than an actual process. In the hypothetical process, separate reactants in their standard states are completely converted to separate products in their standard states. In an actual process, however, reactants and products are mixed together and the reaction may not go to completion.

Take the Haber synthesis, for example. The hypothetical process is

| 1 mol N₂(g) (1 atm, 25 °C) | + | 3 mol H₂(g) (1 atm, 25 °C) | $\Delta G° = -33.0$ kJ | 2 mol NH₃(g) (1 atm, 25 °C) |

State 1   State 2

where $\Delta G^\circ = -33.0$ kJ is the change in the free energy of the system on going from state 1 to state 2. In an actual synthesis of ammonia, however, the reactants N_2 and H_2 are not separate but are mixed together. Moreover, the reaction doesn't go to completion; it reaches an equilibrium state in which both reactants and products are present together.

How, then, should we think about the meaning of ΔG° in the context of an actual reaction? One way would be to suppose that we have a mixture of N_2, H_2, and NH_3, with each substance present at a partial pressure of 1 atm. Suppose further that the mixture behaves as an ideal gas so that the free energy of each component in the mixture is the same as the free energy of the pure substance. Finally, suppose that the number of moles of each component—say x, y, and z—is very large so that the partial pressures don't change appreciably when 1 mol of N_2 and 3 mol of H_2 are converted to 2 mol of NH_3. In other words, we are imagining the following real process:

x mol $N_2(g)$ (1 atm, 25 °C) y mol $H_2(g)$ (1 atm, 25 °C) z mol $NH_3(g)$ (1 atm, 25 °C)	$\xrightarrow{\Delta G^\circ = -33.0 \text{ kJ}}$	$(x-1)$ mol $N_2(g)$ (1 atm, 25 °C) $(y-3)$ mol $H_2(g)$ (1 atm, 25 °C) $(z+2)$ mol $NH_3(g)$ (1 atm, 25 °C)
State 1		State 2

The free-energy change for this process is the standard free-energy change ΔG° because each reactant and product is present at 1 atm pressure. If ΔG° is negative, the reaction will proceed spontaneously to give more products. If ΔG° is positive, the reaction will proceed in the reverse direction to give more reactants. As always, the value of ΔG° indicates only whether the reaction is spontaneous and provides no information about its rate.

WORKED EXAMPLE 16.6

CALCULATING ΔG° FOR A REACTION FROM ΔH° AND ΔS°

Iron metal is produced commercially by reducing iron(III) oxide in iron ore with carbon monoxide:

$$Fe_2O_3(s) + 3\, CO(g) \longrightarrow 2\, Fe(s) + 3\, CO_2(g)$$

(a) Calculate the standard free-energy change for this reaction at 25 °C.

(b) Is the reaction spontaneous under standard-state conditions at 25 °C?

(c) Does the reverse reaction become spontaneous at higher temperatures? Explain.

STRATEGY

(a) We can calculate the standard free-energy change from the relation $\Delta G^\circ = \Delta H^\circ - T\Delta S^\circ$, but first we must find ΔH° and ΔS° from standard enthalpies of formation (ΔH°_f) and standard molar entropies (S°).

(b) The reaction is spontaneous under standard-state conditions if ΔG° is negative.

(c) The spontaneity of the reaction at higher temperatures depends on the signs and magnitudes of ΔH° and ΔS°.

SOLUTION

(a) The following values of ΔH°_f and S° are found in Appendix B:

	$Fe_2O_3(s)$	$CO(g)$	$Fe(s)$	$CO_2(g)$
ΔH°_f (kJ/mol)	−824.2	−110.5	0	−393.5
S° [J/(K·mol)]	87.4	197.6	27.3	213.6

So we have

$$\Delta H^\circ = [2\,\Delta H^\circ_f(Fe) + 3\,\Delta H^\circ_f(CO_2)] - [\Delta H^\circ_f(Fe_2O_3) + 3\,\Delta H^\circ_f(CO)]$$

$$= [(2\,\text{mol})(0\,\text{kJ/mol}) + (3\,\text{mol})(-393.5\,\text{kJ/mol})]$$

$$- [(1\,\text{mol})(-824.2\,\text{kJ/mol}) + (3\,\text{mol})(-110.5\,\text{kJ/mol})]$$

$$\Delta H^\circ = -24.8\,\text{kJ}$$

continued on next page

and

$$\Delta S° = [2 \, S°(\text{Fe}) + 3 \, S°(\text{CO}_2)] - [S°(\text{Fe}_2\text{O}_3) + 3 \, S°(\text{CO})]$$

$$= \left[(2 \, \text{mol})\left(27.3 \, \frac{\text{J}}{\text{K} \cdot \text{mol}}\right) + (3 \, \text{mol})\left(213.6 \, \frac{\text{J}}{\text{K} \cdot \text{mol}}\right) \right]$$

$$- \left[(1 \, \text{mol})\left(87.4 \, \frac{\text{J}}{\text{K} \cdot \text{mol}}\right) + (3 \, \text{mol})\left(197.6 \, \frac{\text{J}}{\text{K} \cdot \text{mol}}\right) \right]$$

$$\Delta S° = +15.2 \, \text{J/K} \quad \text{or} \quad 0.0152 \, \text{kJ/K}$$

Therefore,

$$\Delta G° = \Delta H° - T\Delta S°$$

$$= (-24.8 \, \text{kJ}) - (298 \, \text{K})(0.0152 \, \text{kJ/K})$$

$$\Delta G° = -29.3 \, \text{kJ}$$

(b) Because $\Delta G°$ is negative, the reaction is spontaneous at 25 °C. This means that a mixture of $\text{Fe}_2\text{O}_3(s)$, $\text{CO}(g)$, $\text{Fe}(s)$, and $\text{CO}_2(g)$, with each gas at a partial pressure of 1 atm, will react at 25 °C to produce more iron metal.

(c) Because $\Delta H°$ is negative and $\Delta S°$ is positive, $\Delta G°$ will be negative at all temperatures. The forward reaction is therefore spontaneous at all temperatures, and the reverse reaction does not become spontaneous at higher temperatures.

▶ **PROBLEM 16.10** Consider the thermal decomposition of calcium carbonate:

$$\text{CaCO}_3(s) \longrightarrow \text{CaO}(s) + \text{CO}_2(g)$$

(a) Use the data in Appendix B to calculate the standard free-energy change for this reaction at 25 °C.

(b) Will a mixture of solid CaCO_3, solid CaO, and gaseous CO_2 at 1 atm pressure react spontaneously at 25 °C to produce more CaO and CO_2?

(c) Assuming that $\Delta H°$ and $\Delta S°$ are independent of temperature, estimate the temperature at which the reaction becomes spontaneous.

CONCEPTUAL PROBLEM 16.11 Consider the following endothermic decomposition of AB_2 molecules:

(a) What is the sign (+, −, or 0) of $\Delta S°$ for the reaction?

(b) Is the reaction more likely to be spontaneous at high temperatures or at low temperatures? Explain.

16.9 STANDARD FREE ENERGIES OF FORMATION

The **standard free energy of formation ($\Delta G°_f$)** of a substance is the free-energy change for the formation of 1 mol of the substance in its standard state from the most stable form of its constituent elements in their standard states. For example, we found in Section 16.8 that the standard free-energy change $\Delta G°$ for the synthesis of 2 mol of NH_3 from its constituent elements is −33.0 kJ:

$$\text{N}_2(g) + 3 \, \text{H}_2(g) \longrightarrow 2 \, \text{NH}_3(g) \qquad \Delta G° = -33.0 \, \text{kJ}$$

Therefore, $\Delta G°_f$ for ammonia is −33.0 kJ/2 mol, or −16.5 kJ/mol.

Values of $\Delta G°_f$ at 25 °C for some common substances are listed in Table 16.3, and additional values are given in Appendix B. Note that $\Delta G°_f$ for an element in its most

TABLE 16.3 Standard Free Energies of Formation for Some Common Substances at 25 °C

Substance	Formula	$\Delta G°_f$ (kJ/mol)	Substance	Formula	$\Delta G°_f$ (kJ/mol)
Gases			**Liquids**		
Acetylene	C_2H_2	209.9	Acetic acid	CH_3CO_2H	−390
Ammonia	NH_3	−16.5	Ethanol	CH_3CH_2OH	−174.9
Carbon dioxide	CO_2	−394.4	Methanol	CH_3OH	−166.6
Carbon monoxide	CO	−137.2	Water	H_2O	−237.2
Ethylene	C_2H_4	68.1	**Solids**		
Hydrogen	H_2	0	Calcium carbonate	$CaCO_3$	−1129.1
Methane	CH_4	−50.8	Calcium oxide	CaO	−603.3
Nitrogen	N_2	0	Diamond	C	2.9
Nitrogen dioxide	NO_2	51.3	Graphite	C	0
Dinitrogen tetroxide	N_2O_4	99.8	Iron(III) oxide	Fe_2O_3	−742.2

stable form at 25 °C is defined to be zero. Thus, solid graphite has $\Delta G°_f = 0$ kJ/mol, but diamond, a less stable form of solid carbon at 25 °C, has $\Delta G°_f = 2.9$ kJ/mol.

As with standard enthalpies of formation, $\Delta H°_f$, a zero value of $\Delta G°_f$ for elements in their most stable form establishes a thermochemical "sea level," or reference point, with respect to which the standard free energies of other substances are measured. We can't measure the absolute value of a substance's free energy (as we can the entropy), but that's not a problem because we are interested only in free-energy *differences* between reactants and products.

The standard free energy of formation of a substance measures its thermodynamic stability with respect to its constituent elements. Substances that have a negative value of $\Delta G°_f$, such as carbon dioxide and water, are stable and do not decompose to their constituent elements under standard-state conditions. Substances that have a positive value of $\Delta G°_f$, such as ethylene and nitrogen dioxide, are thermodynamically unstable with respect to their constituent elements and can, in principle, decompose. In fact, however, such substances can exist for long periods of time if the rate of their decomposition is slow.

There's no point in trying to synthesize a substance from its elements under standard-state conditions if the substance has a positive value of $\Delta G°_f$. Such a substance would have to be prepared at other temperatures and/or pressures, or it would have to be made from alternative starting materials using a reaction that has a negative free-energy change. Thus, a knowledge of thermodynamics can save considerable time in chemical synthesis.

In Section 16.8, we calculated standard free-energy changes for reactions from the equation $\Delta G° = \Delta H° - T\Delta S°$, using tabulated values of $\Delta H°_f$ and $S°$ to find $\Delta H°$ and $\Delta S°$. Alternatively, we can calculate $\Delta G°$ more directly by subtracting the standard free energies of formation of all the reactants from the standard free energies of formation of all the products:

$$\Delta G° = \Delta G°_f(\text{products}) - \Delta G°_f(\text{reactants})$$

For the general reaction

$$a\,A + b\,B \longrightarrow c\,C + d\,D$$

the standard free-energy change is

$$\Delta G° = [c\,\Delta G°_f(C) + d\,\Delta G°_f(D)] - [a\,\Delta G°_f(A) + b\,\Delta G°_f(B)]$$

To illustrate, let's calculate the standard free-energy change for the reaction in Worked Example 16.6—the reduction of iron(III) oxide with carbon monoxide:

$$Fe_2O_3(s) + 3\,CO(g) \longrightarrow 2\,Fe(s) + 3\,CO_2(g)$$

Using the ΔG°_{f} values in Table 16.3, we obtain

$$\Delta G^{\circ} = [2\,\Delta G^{\circ}_{f}(Fe) + 3\,\Delta G^{\circ}_{f}(CO_2)] - [\Delta G^{\circ}_{f}(Fe_2O_3) + 3\,\Delta G^{\circ}_{f}(CO)]$$

$$= [(2\text{ mol})(0\text{ kJ/mol}) + (3\text{ mol})(-394.4\text{ kJ/mol})]$$

$$-[(1\text{ mol})(-742.2\text{ kJ/mol}) + (3\text{ mol})(-137.2\text{ kJ/mol})]$$

$$\Delta G^{\circ} = -29.4\text{ kJ}$$

This result agrees well with the value of -29.3 kJ calculated from $\Delta G^{\circ} = \Delta H^{\circ} - T\Delta S^{\circ}$ in Worked Example 16.6.

WORKED EXAMPLE 16.7

CALCULATING ΔG° FOR A REACTION FROM ΔG°_{f} VALUES

(a) Calculate the standard free-energy change for the oxidation of ammonia to give nitric oxide (NO) and water. Is it worth trying to find a catalyst for this reaction under standard-state conditions at 25 °C?

$$4\,NH_3(g) + 5\,O_2(g) \longrightarrow 4\,NO(g) + 6\,H_2O(l)$$

(b) Is it worth trying to find a catalyst for the synthesis of NO from gaseous N_2 and O_2 under standard-state conditions at 25 °C?

STRATEGY

We can calculate ΔG° most easily from tabulated standard free energies of formation (Appendix B). It's worth trying to find a catalyst for a reaction only if the reaction has a negative free-energy change.

SOLUTION

(a) $\Delta G^{\circ} = [4\,\Delta G^{\circ}_{f}(NO) + 6\,\Delta G^{\circ}_{f}(H_2O)] - [4\,\Delta G^{\circ}_{f}(NH_3) + 5\,\Delta G^{\circ}_{f}(O_2)]$

$$= [(4\text{ mol})(87.6\text{ kJ/mol}) + (6\text{ mol})(-237.2\text{ kJ/mol})]$$

$$-[(4\text{ mol})(-16.5\text{ kJ/mol}) + (5\text{ mol})(0\text{ kJ/mol})]$$

$$\Delta G^{\circ} = -1006.8\text{ kJ}$$

It is worth looking for a catalyst because the negative value of ΔG° indicates that the reaction is spontaneous under standard-state conditions. (This reaction is the first step in the Ostwald process for the production of nitric acid. In industry, the reaction is carried out using a platinum–rhodium catalyst.)

(b) It's not worth looking for a catalyst for the reaction $N_2(g) + O_2(g) \rightarrow 2\,NO(g)$ because the standard free energy of formation of NO is positive ($\Delta G^{\circ}_{f} = 87.6$ kJ/mol). This means that NO is unstable with respect to decomposition to N_2 and O_2 under standard-state conditions at 25 °C. A catalyst could only increase the rate of decomposition. It can't affect the composition of the equilibrium mixture (Section 13.10), and so it can't affect the direction of the reaction.

▸ **PROBLEM 16.12**

(a) Using values of ΔG°_{f} in Appendix B, calculate the standard free-energy change for the reaction of calcium carbide (CaC_2) with water. Might this reaction be used for synthesis of acetylene (HC≡CH, or C_2H_2)?

$$CaC_2(s) + 2\,H_2O(l) \longrightarrow C_2H_2(g) + Ca(OH)_2(s)$$

(b) Is it possible to synthesize acetylene from solid graphite and gaseous H_2 at 25 °C and 1 atm pressure?

16.10 FREE-ENERGY CHANGES AND COMPOSITION OF THE REACTION MIXTURE

The sign of the standard free-energy change ΔG° tells us the direction of spontaneous reaction when both reactants and products are present at standard-state conditions. In actual reactions, however, the composition of the reaction mixture seldom corresponds to standard-state pressures and concentrations. Moreover, the partial pressures and concentrations change as a reaction proceeds. How, then, do we calculate the free-energy change ΔG for a reaction when the reactants and products are present at nonstandard-state pressures and concentrations?

The answer is given by the relation

$$\Delta G = \Delta G° + RT \ln Q$$

where ΔG is the free-energy change under nonstandard-state conditions, $\Delta G°$ is the free-energy change under standard-state conditions, R is the gas constant, T is the absolute temperature in kelvin, and Q is the reaction quotient (Q_p for reactions involving gases because the standard state for gases is 1 atm pressure, or Q_c for reactions involving solutes in solution because the standard state for solutes is 1 M concentration). Recall from Section 13.5 that the reaction quotient Q_c is an expression having the same form as the equilibrium constant expression K_c except that the concentrations do not necessarily have equilibrium values. Similarly, Q_p has the same form as K_p except that the partial pressures have arbitrary values. For example, for the Haber synthesis of ammonia:

$$N_2(g) + 3\,H_2(g) \rightleftharpoons 2\,NH_3(g) \qquad Q_p = \frac{(P_{NH_3})^2}{(P_{N_2})(P_{H_2})^3}$$

For reactions that involve both gases and solutes in solution, the reaction quotient Q contains partial pressures of gases in atmospheres and molar concentrations of solutes.

We won't derive the equation for ΔG under nonstandard-state conditions. It's hardly surprising, however, that ΔG and Q should turn out to be related because both predict the direction of a reaction. Worked Example 16.8 shows how to use this equation.

WORKED EXAMPLE 16.8

CALCULATING ΔG FOR A REACTION UNDER NONSTANDARD-STATE CONDITIONS

Calculate the free-energy change for ammonia synthesis at 25 °C (298 K) given the following sets of partial pressures:

(a) 1.0 atm N_2, 3.0 atm H_2, 0.020 atm NH_3

(b) 0.010 atm N_2, 0.030 atm H_2, 2.0 atm NH_3

$$N_2(g) + 3\,H_2(g) \rightleftharpoons 2\,NH_3(g) \qquad \Delta G° = -33.0 \text{ kJ}$$

STRATEGY

We can calculate ΔG from the relation $\Delta G = \Delta G° + RT \ln Q$, where Q is Q_p for the reaction $N_2(g) + 3\,H_2(g) \rightleftharpoons 2\,NH_3(g)$.

SOLUTION

(a) The value of Q_p is

$$Q_p = \frac{(P_{NH_3})^2}{(P_{N_2})(P_{H_2})^3} = \frac{(0.020)^2}{(1.0)(3.0)^3} = 1.5 \times 10^{-5}$$

Substituting this value of Q_p into the equation for ΔG gives

$$\Delta G = \Delta G° + RT \ln Q_p$$
$$= (-33.0 \times 10^3 \text{ J/mol}) + [8.314 \text{ J/(K·mol)}](298 \text{ K})(\ln 1.5 \times 10^{-5})$$
$$= (-33.0 \times 10^3 \text{ J/mol}) + (-27.5 \times 10^3 \text{ J/mol})$$

$$\Delta G = -60.5 \text{ kJ/mol}$$

To maintain consistent units in this calculation, we have expressed ΔG and $\Delta G°$ in units of J/mol because R has units of J/(K·mol). The phrase *per mole* in this context means per molar amounts of reactants and products indicated by the coefficients in

continued on next page

the balanced equation. Thus, the free-energy change is -60.5 kJ when 1 mol of N_2 and 3 mol of H_2 are converted to 2 mol of NH_3 under the specified conditions.

ΔG is more negative than $\Delta G°$ because Q_p is less than 1 and $\ln Q_p$ is therefore a negative number. Thus, the reaction has a greater thermodynamic tendency to occur under the cited conditions than it does under standard-state conditions. When each reactant and product is present at a partial pressure of 1 atm, $Q_p = 1$, $\ln Q_p = 0$, and $\Delta G = \Delta G°$.

(b) The value of Q_p is

$$Q_p = \frac{(P_{NH_3})^2}{(P_{N_2})(P_{H_2})^3} = \frac{(2.0)^2}{(0.010)(0.030)^3} = 1.5 \times 10^7$$

The corresponding value of ΔG is

$$\Delta G = \Delta G° + RT \ln Q_p$$

$$= (-33.0 \times 10^3 \text{ J/mol}) + [8.314 \text{ J/(K} \cdot \text{mol)}](298 \text{ K})(\ln 1.5 \times 10^7)$$

$$= (-33.0 \times 10^3 \text{ J/mol}) + (40.9 \times 10^3 \text{ J/mol})$$

$$\Delta G = 7.9 \text{ kJ/mol}$$

Because Q_p is large enough to give a positive value for ΔG, the reaction is non-spontaneous in the forward direction but spontaneous in the reverse direction. Thus, as we saw already in Section 13.5, the direction in which a reaction proceeds spontaneously depends on the composition of the reaction mixture.

BALLPARK CHECK

(a) Based on Le Châtelier's principle (Section 13.6), we expect that the reaction will have a greater tendency to occur under the cited conditions than under standard-state conditions because one of the reactant partial pressures is greater than 1 atm and the product partial pressure is less than 1 atm. We therefore predict that Q_p will be less than 1 and ΔG will be more negative than $\Delta G°$, in agreement with the solution.

(b) In this case, the reaction mixture is rich in the product and poor in the reactants. Therefore, Q_p is expected to be greater than 1 and ΔG should be more positive than $\Delta G°$, in agreement with the solution.

▶ **PROBLEM 16.13** Calculate ΔG for the formation of ethylene (C_2H_4) from carbon and hydrogen at 25 °C when the partial pressures are 100 atm H_2 and 0.10 atm C_2H_4.

$$2 \text{ C}(s) + 2 \text{ H}_2(g) \longrightarrow \text{C}_2\text{H}_4(g) \qquad \Delta G° = 68.1 \text{ kJ}$$

Is the reaction spontaneous in the forward or the reverse direction?

CONCEPTUAL PROBLEM 16.14 Consider the following gas-phase reaction of A_2 (red) and B_2 (blue) molecules:

$$A_2 + B_2 \rightleftharpoons 2 \text{ AB} \qquad \Delta G° = 15 \text{ kJ}$$

(a) Which of the following reaction mixtures has the largest ΔG of reaction? Which has the smallest?

(1)   **(2)**   **(3)**

(b) If the partial pressure of each reactant and product in reaction mixture 1 is equal to 1 atm, what is the value of ΔG for the reaction in mixture 1?

16.11 FREE ENERGY AND CHEMICAL EQUILIBRIUM

Now that we've seen how ΔG for a reaction depends on composition, we can understand how the total free energy of a reaction mixture changes as the reaction progresses toward equilibrium. Look again at the expression for calculating ΔG:

$$\Delta G = \Delta G^\circ + RT \ln Q$$

If the reaction mixture contains mainly reactants and almost no products, Q will be much less than 1 and $RT \ln Q$ will be a very large negative number (minus infinity when $Q = 0$). Consequently, no matter what the value of ΔG° (positive or negative), the negative $RT \ln Q$ term will dominate the ΔG° term and ΔG will be negative. This means that the forward reaction is always spontaneous when the concentration of products is very small. Conversely, if the reaction mixture contains mainly products and almost no reactants, Q will be much greater than 1 and $RT \ln Q$ will be a very large positive number (plus infinity when no reactants are present). Consequently, the positive $RT \ln Q$ term will dominate the ΔG° term and ΔG will be positive. Thus, the reverse reaction is always spontaneous when the concentration of reactants is very small. These conditions are summarized as follows:

- When the reaction mixture is mostly reactants,

    $Q \ll 1$ $RT \ln Q \ll 0$ $\Delta G < 0$

    the total free energy decreases as the reaction proceeds spontaneously in the forward direction.

- When the reaction mixture is mostly products,

    $Q \gg 1$ $RT \ln Q \gg 0$ $\Delta G > 0$

    the total free energy decreases as the reaction proceeds spontaneously in the reverse direction.

Figure 16.10 shows how the total free energy of a reaction mixture changes as the reaction progresses. Because the free energy decreases as pure reactants form products and also decreases as pure products form reactants, the free-energy curve must go through a minimum somewhere between pure reactants and pure products.

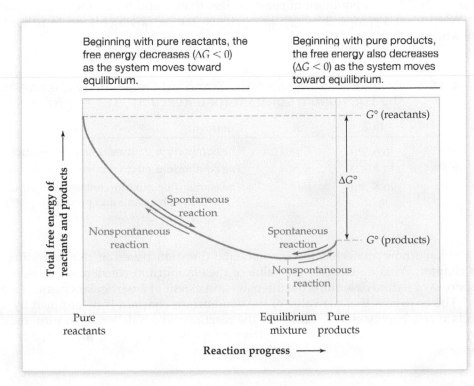

Beginning with pure reactants, the free energy decreases ($\Delta G < 0$) as the system moves toward equilibrium.

Beginning with pure products, the free energy also decreases ($\Delta G < 0$) as the system moves toward equilibrium.

G° (reactants)

ΔG°

G° (products)

Spontaneous reaction

Nonspontaneous reaction

Spontaneous reaction

Nonspontaneous reaction

Total free energy of reactants and products

Pure reactants

Equilibrium mixture

Pure products

Reaction progress ⟶

Figure 16.10
The total free energy of a reaction mixture as a function of the progress of the reaction. The graph is drawn assuming that the pure reactants and pure products are in their standard states and that ΔG° for the reaction is negative, so the equilibrium composition is rich in products.

At that minimum free-energy composition, the system is at equilibrium because the conversion of either reactants to products or products to reactants would involve an increase in free energy. The equilibrium composition persists indefinitely unless the system is disturbed by an external influence.

The sign of ΔG for the reaction is the same as the sign of the slope of the free-energy curve (Figure 16.10). To the left of the equilibrium composition, ΔG and the slope of the curve are negative and the free energy decreases as reactants are converted to products. To the right of the equilibrium composition, ΔG and the slope of the curve are positive. Exactly at the equilibrium composition, ΔG and the slope of the curve are zero and no net reaction occurs.

We can now derive a relationship between free energy and the equilibrium constant. At equilibrium, ΔG for a reaction is zero and the reaction quotient Q equals the equilibrium constant K. Substituting $\Delta G = 0$ and $Q = K$ into the equation

$$\Delta G = \Delta G° + RT \ln Q$$

gives $\qquad 0 = \Delta G° + RT \ln K$

or $\qquad \Delta G° = -RT \ln K$

In this equation, K is K_p for reactions involving gases and K_c for reactions involving solutes in solution. For reactions involving both gases and solutes in solution, the equilibrium constant expression contains partial pressures of gases and molar concentrations of solutes.

The equation $\Delta G° = -RT \ln K$ is one of the most important relationships in chemical thermodynamics because it allows us to calculate the equilibrium constant for a reaction from the standard free-energy change, or vice versa. This relationship is especially useful when K is difficult to measure. Consider a reaction so slow that it takes more than an experimenter's lifetime to reach equilibrium or a reaction that goes essentially to completion, so that the equilibrium concentrations of the reactants are extremely small and hard to measure. We can't measure K directly in such cases, but we can calculate its value from $\Delta G°$.

The relationship between $\Delta G°$ and the equilibrium constant K is summarized in Table 16.4. A reaction with a negative value of $\Delta G°$ has an equilibrium constant greater than 1, which corresponds to a minimum in the free-energy curve of Figure 16.10 at a composition rich in products. Conversely, a reaction that has a positive value of $\Delta G°$ has an equilibrium constant less than 1 and a minimum in the free-energy curve at a composition rich in reactants. Try redrawing Figure 16.10 for the case where $\Delta G° > 0$.

TABLE 16.4 Relationship between the Standard Free-Energy Change and the Equilibrium Constant for a Reaction: $\Delta G° = -RT \ln K$

$\Delta G°$	$\ln K$	K	Comment
$\Delta G° < 0$	$\ln K > 0$	$K > 1$	The equilibrium mixture is mainly products.
$\Delta G° > 0$	$\ln K < 0$	$K < 1$	The equilibrium mixture is mainly reactants.
$\Delta G° = 0$	$\ln K = 0$	$K = 1$	The equilibrium mixture contains comparable amounts of reactants and products.

We have now answered the fundamental question posed at the beginning of this chapter: What determines the value of the equilibrium constant—that is, what properties of nature determine the direction and extent of a particular chemical reaction? The answer is that the value of the equilibrium constant is determined by the standard free-energy change ($\Delta G°$) for the reaction, which depends, in turn, on the standard heats of formation and the standard molar entropies of the reactants and products.

WORKED EXAMPLE 16.9

CALCULATING AN EQUILIBRIUM CONSTANT FROM $\Delta G°$ FOR THE REACTION

Methanol (CH_3OH), an important alcohol used in the manufacture of adhesives, fibers, and plastics, is synthesized industrially by the reaction

$$CO(g) + 2\,H_2(g) \rightleftharpoons CH_3OH(g)$$

Use the thermodynamic data in Appendix B to calculate the equilibrium constant for this reaction at 25 °C.

Carbon monoxide   Hydrogen   Methanol

STRATEGY

First calculate $\Delta G°$ for the reaction from the tabulated values of $\Delta G°_f$ for reactants and products. Then use the equation $\Delta G° = -RT \ln K$ to find the value of the equilibrium constant.

SOLUTION

$$\Delta G° = \Delta G°_f(CH_3OH) - [\Delta G°_f(CO) + 2\,\Delta G°_f(H_2)]$$
$$= (1\,\text{mol})(-162.3\,\text{kJ/mol}) - [(1\,\text{mol})(-137.2\,\text{kJ/mol}) + (2\,\text{mol})(0\,\text{kJ/mol})]$$
$$\Delta G° = -25.1\,\text{kJ}$$

Solving the equation $\Delta G° = -RT \ln K$

for $\ln K$ gives $\ln K = \dfrac{-\Delta G°}{RT} = \dfrac{-(-25.1 \times 10^3\,\text{J/mol})}{[8.314\,\text{J/(K}\cdot\text{mol)}](298\,\text{K})} = 10.1$

Therefore, $K = K_p = \text{antiln}\,10.1 = e^{10.1} = 2 \times 10^4$

    The equilibrium constant obtained by this procedure is K_p because the reactants and products are gases and their standard states are defined in terms of pressure. If we want the value of K_c, we must calculate it from the relation $K_p = K_c(RT)^{\Delta n}$ (Section 13.3), where R must be expressed in the proper units [$R = 0.082\,06\,(\text{L}\cdot\text{atm})/(\text{K}\cdot\text{mol})$].

BALLPARK CHECK

$\Delta G°$ is negative, so the equilibrium mixture should be mainly products ($K > 1$), in agreement with the solution.

WORKED EXAMPLE 16.10

CALCULATING A VAPOR PRESSURE FROM $\Delta G°$

The value of $\Delta G°_f$ at 25 °C for gaseous mercury is 31.85 kJ/mol. What is the vapor pressure of mercury at 25 °C?

STRATEGY

The vapor pressure (in atm) equals K_p for the reaction

$$Hg(l) \rightleftharpoons Hg(g) \qquad K_p = P_{Hg}$$

$Hg(l)$ is omitted from the equilibrium constant expression because it is a pure liquid. Because the standard state for elemental mercury is the pure liquid, $\Delta G°_f = 0$ for $Hg(l)$ and $\Delta G°$ for the vaporization reaction simply equals $\Delta G°_f$ for $Hg(g)$ (31.85 kJ/mol). We can calculate K_p from the equation $\Delta G° = -RT \ln K_p$, as in Worked Example 16.9.

continued on next page

▲ Mercury has an appreciable vapor pressure at room temperature, and its handling requires adequate ventilation.

SOLUTION

$$\ln K_p = \frac{-\Delta G°}{RT} = \frac{-(31.85 \times 10^3 \text{ J/mol})}{[8.314 \text{ J/(K} \cdot \text{mol)}](298 \text{ K})} = -12.86$$

$$K_p = \text{antiln} (-12.86) = e^{-12.86} = 2.6 \times 10^{-6}$$

Since K_p is defined in units of atmospheres, the vapor pressure of mercury at 25 °C is 2.6×10^{-6} atm (0.0020 mm Hg). Because the vapor pressure is appreciable and mercury is toxic in the lungs, mercury should not be handled without adequate ventilation.

BALLPARK CHECK

$\Delta G°$ is positive, so the vaporization reaction should not proceed very far before reaching equilibrium. Thus, K_p should be less than 1, in agreement with the solution.

WORKED EXAMPLE 16.11

CALCULATING $\Delta G°$ FROM K_{sp}

At 25 °C, K_{sp} for $PbCrO_4$ is 2.8×10^{-13}. Calculate the standard free-energy change at 25 °C for the reaction $PbCrO_4(s) \rightleftharpoons Pb^{2+}(aq) + CrO_4^{2-}(aq)$.

STRATEGY AND SOLUTION

We can calculate $\Delta G°$ directly from the equilibrium constant K_{sp}:

$$\Delta G° = -RT \ln K_{sp} = -[8.314 \text{ J/(K} \cdot \text{mol)}](298 \text{ K})(\ln 2.8 \times 10^{-13})$$

$$= 71.6 \times 10^3 \text{ J/mol} = 71.6 \text{ kJ/mol}$$

BALLPARK CHECK

The K_{sp} value is much less than 1, so $\Delta G°$ should be a large positive number, in agreement with the solution.

▶ **PROBLEM 16.15** Given the data in Appendix B, calculate K_p at 25 °C for the reaction $CaCO_3(s) \rightleftharpoons CaO(s) + CO_2(g)$.

▶ **PROBLEM 16.16** Use the data in Appendix B to calculate the vapor pressure of water at 25 °C.

▶ **PROBLEM 16.17** At 25 °C, K_w for the dissociation of water is 1.0×10^{-14}. Calculate $\Delta G°$ for the reaction $2 H_2O(l) \rightleftharpoons H_3O^+(aq) + OH^-(aq)$.

INQUIRY DOES ENTROPY PREVENT THE EVOLUTION OF BIOLOGICAL COMPLEXITY?

The idea of entropy has intrigued thinkers for more than a century. Poets, philosophers, physicists, and biologists have all struggled to understand the consequences of entropy.

Poets and philosophers have spoken of entropy as "time's arrow," a metaphor that arises out of the second law of thermodynamics. According to the second law, all spontaneously occurring processes are accompanied by an increase in the entropy of the universe. At some far distant time, when all matter and energy is randomly distributed and there is no available energy left, the universe as we know it must end.

Physicists speak of entropy as giving a directionality to time. There is a symmetry to basic physical laws that makes them equally valid when the signs of the quantities are reversed. Thus, the attraction between a positively charged proton and a negatively charged electron, for example, is exactly the same as the attraction between a negatively charged proton (a so-called *antiproton*) and a positively charged electron (a *positron*). Time, however, cannot be reversed because of entropy. Any process that takes place spontaneously over time must increase the entropy of the universe. The reverse process, which would have to go backward over time, can't occur because it would decrease the entropy of the universe. Thus, there is a one-way nature to time that is not shared by other quantities.

Biologists, too, have been intrigued by entropy and its consequences. Their problem is that if the randomness of the universe is always increasing, how is it possible for enormously complex and increasingly sophisticated life forms to evolve? After all, the more complex the organism, the less the amount of randomness and the *lower* the entropy. The answer to the biologists' question again arises from the second law of thermodynamics: All spontaneous processes increase the randomness of the universe—that is, the total randomness of both system and surroundings. It's perfectly possible, however, for the randomness of any *system* to decrease spontaneously as long as the randomness of the *surroundings* increases by an even greater amount.

The energy used to power living organisms comes from sunlight, caused ultimately by nuclear reactions in the sun. Photosynthetic cells in plants use the Sun's energy to make glucose, which is then used by animals as their primary source of energy. The energy an animal obtains from glucose is then used to build and organize complex molecules, resulting in a decrease in entropy for the animal. At the same time, however, the entropy of the surroundings increases as the animal releases small, simple waste products such as CO_2 and H_2O. Furthermore, heat is released by the animal, further increasing the entropy of the surroundings. Thus, an organism pays for its decrease in entropy by increasing the entropy of the rest of the universe.

▲ At some distant time, when all is disorder, the universe as we know it must end.

▶ **PROBLEM 16.18** Consider the growth of a human adult from a single cell. Does this process violate the second law of thermodynamics? Explain.

▶ **PROBLEM 16.19** If you watched a movie run backward, would you expect to see violations of the second law? Explain.

SUMMARY

Thermodynamics deals with the interconversion of heat and other forms of energy and allows us to predict the direction and extent of chemical reactions and other spontaneous processes. A **spontaneous process** proceeds on its own without any external influence. All spontaneous reactions move toward equilibrium.

Entropy, denoted by S, is a state function that measures molecular randomness. The entropy of a system (reactants plus products) increases (ΔS is positive) for the following processes: phase transitions that convert a solid to a liquid or a liquid to a gas, reactions that increase the number of gaseous molecules, dissolution of molecular solids and certain salts in water, raising the temperature of a substance, and the expansion of a gas at constant temperature. For a change in the volume of n mol of an ideal gas at constant temperature, $\Delta S = nR \ln(V_{final}/V_{initial})$.

A state of a system with a random distribution of molecules and molecular energies (a state of high entropy) can be achieved in more ways (W) than an ordered state and is therefore more probable. The entropy of a state can be calculated from Boltzmann's formula, $S = k \ln W$. According to the **third law of thermodynamics**, the entropy of a pure, perfectly ordered crystalline substance at 0 K is zero.

The **standard molar entropy ($S°$)** of a substance is the absolute entropy of 1 mol of the pure substance at 1 atm pressure and a specified temperature, usually 25 °C. The **standard entropy of reaction ($\Delta S°$)** can be calculated from the relation $\Delta S° = S°(\text{products}) - S°(\text{reactants})$.

The **first law of thermodynamics** states that in any process, the total energy of a system and its surroundings remains constant. The **second law of thermodynamics** says that in any *spontaneous* process, the total entropy of a system and its surroundings ($\Delta S_{total} = \Delta S_{sys} + \Delta S_{surr}$) always increases. A chemical reaction is spontaneous if $\Delta S_{total} > 0$, nonspontaneous if $\Delta S_{total} < 0$, and at equilibrium if $\Delta S_{total} = 0$. Reactions that are nonspontaneous in the forward direction are spontaneous in the reverse direction. For a reaction at constant pressure, $\Delta S_{surr} = -\Delta H/T$, and ΔS_{sys} is ΔS for the reaction.

Free energy, $G = H - TS$, is a state function that indicates whether a reaction is spontaneous or nonspontaneous. A reaction at constant temperature and pressure is spontaneous if $\Delta G < 0$, nonspontaneous if $\Delta G > 0$, and at equilibrium if $\Delta G = 0$. In the equation $\Delta G = \Delta H - T\Delta S$, temperature is a weighting factor that determines the relative importance of the enthalpy and entropy contributions to ΔG.

The **standard free-energy change ($\Delta G°$)** for a reaction is the change in free energy that occurs when reactants in their standard states are completely converted to products in their standard states. The **standard free energy of formation ($\Delta G°_f$)** of a substance is the free-energy change for formation of 1 mol of the substance in its standard state from the most stable form of the constituent elements in their standard states. Substances with a negative value of $\Delta G°_f$ are thermodynamically stable with respect to the constituent elements. We can calculate $\Delta G°$ for a reaction in either of two ways: (1) $\Delta G° = \Delta G°_f(\text{products}) - \Delta G°_f(\text{reactants})$ or (2) $\Delta G° = \Delta H° - T\Delta S°$.

The free-energy change, ΔG, for a reaction under nonstandard-state conditions is given by $\Delta G = \Delta G° + RT \ln Q$, where Q is the reaction quotient. At equilibrium, $\Delta G = 0$ and $Q = K$. As a result, $\Delta G° = -RT \ln K$, which allows us to calculate the equilibrium constant from $\Delta G°$ and vice versa.

KEY WORDS

CONCEPTUAL PROBLEMS

Problems 16.1–16.19 appear within the chapter.

16.20 Ideal gases A (red spheres) and B (blue spheres) occupy two separate bulbs. The contents of both bulbs constitute the initial state of an isolated system. Consider the process that occurs when the stopcock is opened.

(a) Sketch the final (equilibrium) state of the system.

(b) What are the signs (+, −, or 0) of ΔH, ΔS, and ΔG for this process? Explain.

(c) How does this process illustrate the second law of thermodynamics?

(d) Is the reverse process spontaneous or nonspontaneous? Explain.

16.21 What are the signs (+, −, or 0) of ΔH, ΔS, and ΔG for the spontaneous sublimation of a crystalline solid? Explain.

16.22 What are the signs (+, −, or 0) of ΔH, ΔS, and ΔG for the spontaneous condensation of a vapor to a liquid? Explain.

16.23 An ideal gas is compressed at constant temperature. What are the signs (+, −, or 0) of ΔH, ΔS, and ΔG for the process? Explain.

16.24 Consider the following spontaneous reaction of A_2 molecules (red) and B_2 molecules (blue):

(a) Write a balanced equation for the reaction.

(b) What are the signs (+, −, or 0) of ΔH, ΔS, and ΔG for the reaction? Explain.

16.25 Consider the dissociation reaction $A_2(g) \rightleftharpoons 2\,A(g)$. The following pictures represent two possible initial states and the equilibrium state of the system:

Initial state 1   Initial state 2

Equilibrium state

(a) Is the reaction quotient Q_p for initial state 1 greater than, less than, or equal to the equilibrium constant K_p? Is Q_p for initial state 2 greater than, less than, or equal to K_p?

(b) What are the signs (+, −, or 0) of ΔH, ΔS, and ΔG when the system goes from initial state 1 to the equilibrium state? Explain. Is this a spontaneous process?

(c) What are the signs (+, −, or 0) of ΔH, ΔS, and ΔG when the system goes from initial state 2 to the equilibrium state? Explain. Is this a spontaneous process?

(d) Relate each of the pictures to the graph in Figure 16.10.

16.26 Consider again the dissociation reaction $A_2(g) \rightleftharpoons 2\,A(g)$ (Problem 16.25).

(a) What are the signs (+, −, or 0) of the standard enthalpy change, $\Delta H°$, and the standard entropy change, $\Delta S°$, for the forward reaction?

(b) Distinguish between the meaning of $\Delta S°$ for the dissociation reaction and ΔS for the process in which the system goes from initial state 1 to the equilibrium state (pictured in Problem 16.25).

(c) Can you say anything about the sign of $\Delta G°$ for the dissociation reaction? How does $\Delta G°$ depend on temperature? Will $\Delta G°$ increase, decrease, or remain the same if the temperature increases?

(d) Will the equilibrium constant K_p increase, decrease, or remain the same if the temperature increases? How will the picture for the equilibrium state (Problem 16.25) change if the temperature increases?

(e) What is the value of ΔG for the dissociation reaction when the system is at equilibrium?

16.27 Consider the following graph of the total free energy of reactants and products versus reaction progress for a general reaction, Reactants $\longrightarrow$ Products:

(a) Account for the shape of the curve, and identify the point at which $\Delta G = 0$. What is the significance of that point?

(b) Why is the minimum in the plot on the left side of the graph?

16.28 The following pictures represent equilibrium mixtures for the interconversion of A molecules (red) and X, Y, or Z molecules (blue):

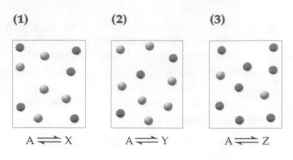

(1)   (2)   (3)

A ⇌ X   A ⇌ Y   A ⇌ Z

What is the sign of $\Delta G°$ for each of the three reactions?

16.29 The following pictures represent the composition of the equilibrium mixture at 25 °C and 45 °C for the reaction A ⇌ B, where A molecules are represented by red spheres and B molecules by blue spheres:

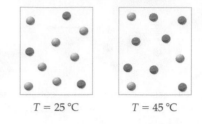

$T = 25\,°C$ $T = 45\,°C$

What are the signs of $\Delta H°$ and $\Delta S°$ for the forward reaction A ⟶ B? Explain. (Assume that $\Delta H°$ and $\Delta S°$ are independent of temperature.)

SECTION PROBLEMS

Spontaneous Processes (Section 16.1)

16.30 Which of the following processes are spontaneous, and which are nonspontaneous?

(a) Freezing of water at 2 °C

(b) Corrosion of iron metal

(c) Expansion of a gas to fill the available volume

(d) Separation of an unsaturated aqueous solution of potassium chloride into solid KCl and liquid water

16.31 Tell whether the following processes are spontaneous or nonspontaneous:

(a) Dissolving sugar in hot coffee

(b) Decomposition of NaCl to solid sodium and gaseous chlorine at 25 °C and 1 atm pressure

(c) Uniform mixing of bromine vapor and nitrogen gas

(d) Boiling of gasoline at 25 °C and 1 atm pressure

16.32 Assuming that gaseous reactants and products are present at 1 atm partial pressure, which of the following reactions are spontaneous in the forward direction?

(a) $N_2(g) + 2\,H_2(g) \longrightarrow N_2H_4(l)$; $K_p = 7 \times 10^{-27}$

(b) $2\,Mg(s) + O_2(g) \longrightarrow 2\,MgO(s)$; $K_p = 2 \times 10^{198}$

(c) $MgCO_3(s) \longrightarrow MgO(s) + CO_2(g)$; $K_p = 9 \times 10^{-10}$

(d) $2\,CO(g) + O_2(g) \longrightarrow 2\,CO_2(g)$; $K_p = 1 \times 10^{90}$

16.33 Assuming that dissolved reactants and products are present at 1 M concentrations, which of the following reactions are nonspontaneous in the forward direction?

(a) $HCN(aq) + H_2O(l) \longrightarrow H_3O^+(aq) + CN^-(aq)$;
$K = 4.9 \times 10^{-10}$

(b) $H_3O^+(aq) + OH^-(aq) \longrightarrow 2\,H_2O(l)$; $K = 1.0 \times 10^{14}$

(c) $Ba^{2+}(aq) + CO_3^{2-}(aq) \longrightarrow BaCO_3(s)$; $K = 3.8 \times 10^8$

(d) $AgCl(s) \longrightarrow Ag^+(aq) + Cl^-(aq)$; $K = 1.8 \times 10^{-10}$

Entropy (Sections 16.2–16.4)

16.34 Define entropy, and give an example of a process in which the entropy of a system increases.

16.35 Comment on the following statement: Exothermic reactions are spontaneous, but endothermic reactions are nonspontaneous.

16.36 Predict the sign of the entropy change in the system for each of the following processes:

(a) A solid sublimes   (b) A liquid freezes

(c) AgI precipitates from a solution containing Ag^+ and I^- ions

(d) Gaseous CO_2 bubbles out of a carbonated beverage

16.37 Predict the sign of ΔS in the system for each of the following reactions:

(a) $PCl_5(s) \longrightarrow PCl_3(l) + Cl_2(g)$

(b) $CH_4(g) + 2\,O_2(g) \longrightarrow CO_2(g) + 2\,H_2O(l)$

(c) $2\,H_3O^+(aq) + CO_3^{2-}(aq) \longrightarrow CO_2(g) + 3\,H_2O(l)$

(d) $Mg(s) + Cl_2(g) \longrightarrow MgCl_2(s)$

16.38 Predict the sign of ΔS for each process in Problem 16.30.

16.39 Predict the sign of ΔS for each process in Problem 16.31.

16.40 Consider a disordered crystal of monodeuteriomethane in which each tetrahedral CH_3D molecule is oriented randomly in one of four possible ways. Use Boltzmann's formula to calculate the entropy of the disordered state of the crystal if the crystal contains:

(a) 12 molecules   (b) 120 molecules

(c) 1 mol of molecules

What is the entropy of the crystal if the C—D bond of each of the CH_3D molecules points in the same direction?

16.41 Consider the distribution of ideal gas molecules among three bulbs (A, B, and C) of equal volume. For each of the following states, determine the number of ways (W) that the state can be achieved, and use Boltzmann's formula to calculate the entropy of the state:

(a) 2 molecules in bulb A

(b) 2 molecules randomly distributed among bulbs A, B, and C

(c) 3 molecules in bulb A

(d) 3 molecules randomly distributed among bulbs A, B, and C

(e) 1 mol of molecules in bulb A

(f) 1 mol of molecules randomly distributed among bulbs A, B, and C

What is ΔS on going from state **(e)** to state **(f)**? Compare your result with ΔS calculated from the equation $\Delta S = nR \ln(V_{final}/V_{initial})$.

16.42 What is the entropy of 100 molecules in a system of 1000 boxes?

16.43 What is the entropy of 100 molecules in a system of 10,000 boxes?

16.44 By what factor does the entropy increase for a collection of 1000 molecules moved from 1×10^6 boxes to 1×10^7 boxes? For a move from 1×10^{16} to 1×10^{17} boxes? (Express your answers to three significant figures.)

16.45 If the entropy of a collection of molecules in 50,000 boxes is 3.73×10^{-20} J/K, how many molecules are there?

16.46 Which state in each of the following pairs has the higher entropy per mole of substance?

(a) H_2 at 25 °C in a volume of 10 L or H_2 at 25 °C in a volume of 50 L

(b) O_2 at 25 °C and 1 atm or O_2 at 25 °C and 10 atm

(c) H_2 at 25 °C and 1 atm or H_2 at 100 °C and 1 atm

(d) CO_2 at STP or CO_2 at 100 °C and 0.1 atm

16.47 Which state in each of the following pairs has the higher entropy per mole of substance?

(a) Ice at −40 °C or ice at 0 °C

(b) N_2 at STP or N_2 at 0 °C and 10 atm

(c) N_2 at STP or N_2 at 0 °C in a volume of 50 L

(d) Water vapor at 150 °C and 1 atm or water vapor at 100 °C and 2 atm

16.48 What is the entropy change when the volume of 1.6 g of O_2 increases from 2.5 L to 3.5 L at a constant temperature of 75 °C? Assume that O_2 behaves as an ideal gas.

16.49 What is the value of ΔS when 2.4 g of CH_4 is compressed from 30.0 L to 20.0 L at a constant temperature of 100 °C? Assume that CH_4 behaves as an ideal gas.

Standard Molar Entropies and Standard Entropies of Reaction (Section 16.5)

16.50 Which substance in each of the following pairs would you expect to have the higher standard molar entropy? Explain.

(a) $C_2H_2(g)$ or $C_2H_6(g)$ **(b)** $CO_2(g)$ or $CO(g)$

(c) $I_2(s)$ or $I_2(g)$ **(d)** $CH_3OH(g)$ or $CH_3OH(l)$

16.51 Which substance in each of the following pairs would you expect to have the higher standard molar entropy? Explain.

(a) $NO(g)$ or $NO_2(g)$ **(b)** $CH_3CO_2H(l)$ or $HCO_2H(l)$

(c) $Br_2(l)$ or $Br_2(s)$ **(d)** $S(s)$ or $SO_3(g)$

16.52 Use the standard molar entropies in Appendix B to calculate the standard entropy of reaction for the oxidation of carbon monoxide to carbon dioxide:

$$2\,CO(g) + O_2(g) \longrightarrow 2\,CO_2(g)$$

16.53 Use the standard molar entropies in Appendix B to calculate the standard entropy of reaction for the oxidation of graphite to carbon dioxide:

$$C(s) + O_2(g) \longrightarrow 2\,CO_2(g)$$

16.54 Use the standard molar entropies in Appendix B to calculate $\Delta S°$ at 25 °C for each of the following reactions. Account for the sign of the entropy change in each case.

(a) $2\,H_2O_2(l) \longrightarrow 2\,H_2O(l) + O_2(g)$

(b) $2\,Na(s) + Cl_2(g) \longrightarrow 2\,NaCl(s)$

(c) $2\,O_3(g) \longrightarrow 3\,O_2(g)$

(d) $4\,Al(s) + 3\,O_2(g) \longrightarrow 2\,Al_2O_3(s)$

16.55 Use the $S°$ values in Appendix B to calculate $\Delta S°$ at 25 °C for each of the following reactions. Suggest a reason for the sign of $\Delta S°$ in each case.

(a) $2\,S(s) + 3\,O_2(g) \longrightarrow 2\,SO_3(g)$

(b) $SO_3(g) + H_2O(l) \longrightarrow H_2SO_4(aq)$

(c) $AgCl(s) \longrightarrow Ag^+(aq) + Cl^-(aq)$

(d) $NH_4NO_3(s) \longrightarrow N_2O(g) + 2\,H_2O(g)$

Entropy and the Second Law of Thermodynamics (Section 16.6)

16.56 State the second law of thermodynamics.

16.57 An isolated system is one that exchanges neither matter nor energy with the surroundings. What is the entropy criterion for spontaneous change in an isolated system? Give an example of a spontaneous process in an isolated system.

16.58 Give an equation that relates the entropy change in the surroundings to the enthalpy change in the system. What is the sign of ΔS_{surr} for the following?

(a) An exothermic reaction

(b) An endothermic reaction

16.59 When heat is added to the surroundings, the entropy of the surroundings increases. How does ΔS_{surr} depend on the temperature of the surroundings? Explain.

16.60 Reduction of mercury(II) oxide with zinc gives metallic mercury:

$$HgO(s) + Zn(s) \longrightarrow ZnO(s) + Hg(l)$$

(a) If $\Delta H° = -259.7$ kJ/mol and $\Delta S° = +7.8$ J/K, what is ΔS_{total} for this reaction? Is the reaction spontaneous under standard-state conditions at 25 °C?

(b) Estimate at what temperature, if any, the reaction will become nonspontaneous.

16.61 Elemental sulfur is formed by the reaction of zinc sulfide with oxygen:

$$2\,ZnS(s) + O_2(g) \longrightarrow 2\,ZnO(s) + 2\,S(s)$$

(a) If $\Delta H° = -289.0$ kJ/mol and $\Delta S° = -169.4$ J/K, what is ΔS_{total} for this reaction? Is the reaction spontaneous under standard-state conditions at 25 °C?

(b) At what temperature, if any, will the reaction become nonspontaneous?

16.62 In lightning storms, oxygen is converted to ozone:

$$3\,O_2(g) \longrightarrow 2\,O_3(g)$$

By determining the sign of ΔS_{total}, show whether the reaction is spontaneous at 25 °C.

16.63 Sulfur dioxide emitted from coal-fired power plants is oxidized to sulfur trioxide in the atmosphere:

$$2\,SO_2(g) + O_2(g) \longrightarrow 2\,SO_3(g)$$

By determining the sign of ΔS_{total}, show whether the reaction is spontaneous at 25 °C.

16.64 Elemental mercury can be produced from its oxide:

$$2\,HgO(s) \longrightarrow 2\,Hg(l) + O_2(g)$$

(a) Use data in Appendix B to calculate ΔS_{sys}, ΔS_{surr}, and ΔS_{total} for this reaction. Is the reaction spontaneous under standard-state conditions at 25 °C?

(b) Estimate the temperature at which the reaction will become spontaneous.

16.65 Phosphorus pentachloride forms from phosphorus trichloride and chlorine:

$$PCl_3(g) + Cl_2(g) \longrightarrow PCl_5(g)$$

(a) Use data in Appendix B to calculate ΔS_{sys}, ΔS_{surr}, and ΔS_{total} for this reaction. Is the reaction spontaneous under standard-state conditions at 25 °C?

(b) Estimate the temperature at which the reaction will become nonspontaneous.

16.66 For the vaporization of benzene, $\Delta H_{vap} = 30.7$ kJ/mol and $\Delta S_{vap} = 87.0$ J/(K·mol). Calculate ΔS_{surr} and ΔS_{total} at:

(a) 70 °C   (b) 80 °C   (c) 90 °C

Does benzene boil at 70 °C and 1 atm pressure? Calculate the normal boiling point of benzene.

16.67 For the melting of sodium chloride, $\Delta H_{fusion} = 28.16$ kJ/mol and $\Delta S_{fusion} = 26.22$ J/(K·mol). Calculate ΔS_{surr} and ΔS_{total} at:

(a) 1050 K   (b) 1074 K   (c) 1100 K

Does NaCl melt at 1100 K? Calculate the melting point of NaCl.

Free Energy (Section 16.7)

16.68 Describe how the signs of ΔH and ΔS determine whether a reaction is spontaneous or nonspontaneous at constant temperature and pressure.

16.69 What determines the direction of a spontaneous reaction when ΔH and ΔS are both positive or both negative? Explain.

16.70 The melting point of benzene is 5.5 °C. Predict the signs of ΔH, ΔS, and ΔG for melting of benzene at:

(a) 0 °C   (b) 15 °C

16.71 Consider a twofold expansion of 1 mol of an ideal gas at 25 °C in the isolated system shown in Figure 16.1 on page 641.

(a) What are the values of ΔH, ΔS, and ΔG for the process?

(b) How does this process illustrate the second law of thermodynamics?

16.72 Given the data in Problem 16.66, calculate ΔG for the vaporization of benzene at:

(a) 70 °C   (b) 80 °C   (c) 90 °C

Predict whether benzene will boil at each of these temperatures and 1 atm pressure.

16.73 Given the data in Problem 16.67, calculate ΔG for the melting of sodium chloride at:

(a) 1050 K   (b) 1074 K   (c) 1100 K

Predict whether NaCl will melt at each of these temperatures and 1 atm pressure.

16.74 Calculate the melting point of benzoic acid ($C_6H_5CO_2H$), given the following data: $\Delta H_{fusion} = 18.02$ kJ/mol and $\Delta S_{fusion} = 45.56$ J/(K·mol).

Benzoic acid

16.75 Calculate the enthalpy of fusion of naphthalene ($C_{10}H_8$), given that its melting point is 128 °C and its entropy of fusion is 47.7 J/(K·mol).

Naphthalene

Standard Free-Energy Changes and Standard Free Energies of Formation (Sections 16.8–16.9)

16.76 Define (a) the standard free-energy change, $\Delta G°$, for a reaction and (b) the standard free energy of formation, $\Delta G°_f$, of a substance.

16.77 What is meant by the standard state of a substance?

16.78 Use the data in Appendix B to calculate $\Delta H°$ and $\Delta S°$ for each of the following reactions. From the values of $\Delta H°$ and $\Delta S°$, calculate $\Delta G°$ at 25 °C and predict whether each reaction is spontaneous under standard-state conditions.

(a) $N_2(g) + 2\,O_2(g) \longrightarrow 2\,NO_2(g)$

(b) $2\,KClO_3(s) \longrightarrow 2\,KCl(s) + 3\,O_2(g)$

(c) $CH_3CH_2OH(l) + O_2(g) \longrightarrow CH_3CO_2H(l) + H_2O(l)$

16.79 Use the data in Appendix B to calculate $\Delta H°$ and $\Delta S°$ for each of the following reactions. From the values of $\Delta H°$ and $\Delta S°$, calculate $\Delta G°$ at 25 °C and predict whether each reaction is spontaneous under standard-state conditions.

(a) $2\,SO_2(g) + O_2(g) \longrightarrow 2\,SO_3(g)$

(b) $N_2(g) + 2\,H_2(g) \longrightarrow N_2H_4(l)$

(c) $CH_3OH(l) + O_2(g) \longrightarrow HCO_2H(l) + H_2O(l)$

16.80 Use the standard free energies of formation in Appendix B to calculate $\Delta G°$ at 25 °C for each reaction in Problem 16.78.

16.81 Use the standard free energies of formation in Appendix B to calculate $\Delta G°$ at 25 °C for each reaction in Problem 16.79.

16.82 Use the data in Appendix B to tell which of the following compounds are thermodynamically stable with respect to their constituent elements at 25 °C:

(a) $BaCO_3(s)$ (b) $HBr(g)$

(c) $N_2O(g)$ (d) $C_2H_4(g)$

16.83 Use the data in Appendix B to decide whether synthesis of the following compounds from their constituent elements is thermodynamically feasible at 25 °C:

(a) $C_6H_6(l)$ (b) $NO(g)$

(c) $PH_3(g)$ (d) $FeO(s)$

16.84 Use the values of $\Delta G°_f$ in Appendix B to calculate the standard free-energy change for the synthesis of dichloroethane from ethylene and chlorine.

$$C_2H_4(g) + Cl_2(g) \longrightarrow CH_2ClCH_2Cl(l)$$

Is it possible to synthesize dichloroethane from gaseous C_2H_4 and Cl_2, each at 25 °C and 1 atm pressure?

16.85 Use the values of $\Delta G°_f$ in Appendix B to calculate the standard free-energy change for the conversion of ammonia to hydrazine:

$$2 NH_3(g) \longrightarrow H_2(g) + N_2H_4(l)$$

Is it worth trying to find a catalyst for this reaction under standard-state conditions at 25 °C?

16.86 Use the data in Appendix B to calculate ΔG for the decomposition of nitrosyl chloride at 25 °C when the partial pressures are 2.00 atm of NOCl, 1.00×10^{-3} atm of NO, and 1.00×10^{-3} atm of Cl_2.

$$2 NO(g) + Cl_2(g) \longrightarrow 2 NOCl(g)$$

Is the reaction spontaneous in the forward or the reverse direction under these conditions?

16.87 What is ΔG for the formation of solid uranium hexafluoride from uranium and fluorine at 25 °C when the partial pressure of F_2 is 0.045 atm? The standard free energy of formation of $UF_6(s)$ is -2068 kJ/mol.

$$U(s) + 3 F_2(g) \longrightarrow UF_6(s)$$

Is the reaction spontaneous in the forward or the reverse direction under these conditions?

16.88 Ethanol is manufactured in industry by the hydration of ethylene:

$$CH_2{=}CH_2(g) + H_2O(l) \longrightarrow CH_3CH_2OH(l)$$

Ethylene   Ethanol

Using the data in Appendix B, calculate $\Delta G°$ and show that this reaction is spontaneous at 25 °C. Why does this reaction become nonspontaneous at higher temperatures? Estimate the temperature at which the reaction becomes nonspontaneous.

16.89 Sulfur dioxide in the effluent gases from coal-burning electric power plants is one of the principal causes of acid rain. One method for reducing SO_2 emissions involves partial conversion of SO_2 to H_2S, followed by catalytic conversion of the H_2S and the remaining SO_2 to elemental sulfur:

$$2 H_2S(g) + SO_2(g) \longrightarrow 3 S(s) + 2 H_2O(g)$$

Using the data in Appendix B, calculate $\Delta G°$ and show that this reaction is spontaneous at 25 °C. Why does this reaction become nonspontaneous at high temperatures? Estimate the temperature at which the reaction becomes nonspontaneous.

16.90 Consider the conversion of acetylene to benzene:

$$3 C_2H_2(g) \longrightarrow C_6H_6(l)$$

Acetylene   Benzene

Is a catalyst for this reaction possible? Is it possible to synthesize benzene from graphite and gaseous H_2 at 25 °C and 1 atm pressure?

16.91 Consider the conversion of 1,2-dichloroethane to vinyl chloride, the starting material for manufacturing poly(vinyl chloride) (PVC) plastics:

$$CH_2ClCH_2Cl(l) \longrightarrow CH_2{=}CHCl(g) + HCl(g)$$

1,2-Dichloroethane   Vinyl chloride

Is this reaction spontaneous under standard state conditions? Would it help to carry out the reaction in the presence of base to remove HCl? Explain. Is it possible to synthesize vinyl chloride from graphite, gaseous H_2, and gaseous Cl_2 at 25 °C and 1 atm pressure?

Free Energy, Composition, and Chemical Equilibrium (Sections 16.10–16.11)

16.92 What is the relationship between the free-energy change under nonstandard-state conditions, ΔG, the free-energy change under standard-state conditions, $\Delta G°$, and the reaction quotient, Q?

16.93 Compare the values of ΔG and $\Delta G°$ when:

(a) $Q < 1$ (b) $Q = 1$ (c) $Q > 1$

Does the thermodynamic tendency for the reaction to occur increase or decrease as Q increases?

16.94 Sulfuric acid is produced in larger amounts by weight than any other chemical. It is used in manufacturing fertilizers, oil refining, and hundreds of other processes. An intermediate step in the industrial process for the synthesis of H_2SO_4 is the catalytic oxidation of sulfur dioxide:

$$2 SO_2(g) + O_2(g) \longrightarrow 2 SO_3(g) \qquad \Delta G° = -141.8 \text{ kJ}$$

Calculate ΔG at 25 °C, given the following sets of partial pressures:

(a) 100 atm SO_2, 100 atm O_2, 1.0 atm SO_3

(b) 2.0 atm SO_2, 1.0 atm O_2, 10 atm SO_3

(c) Each reactant and product at a partial pressure of 1.0 atm

16.95 Urea (NH_2CONH_2), an important nitrogen fertilizer, is produced industrially by the reaction

$$2\,NH_3(g) + CO_2(g) \longrightarrow NH_2CONH_2(aq) + H_2O(l)$$

Urea

Given that $\Delta G^\circ = -13.6$ kJ, calculate ΔG at 25 °C for the following sets of conditions:

(a) 10 atm NH_3, 10 atm CO_2, 1.0 M NH_2CONH_2

(b) 0.10 atm NH_3, 0.10 atm CO_2, 1.0 M NH_2CONH_2

Is the reaction spontaneous for the conditions in part **(a)** and/or part **(b)**?

16.96 What is the relationship between the standard free-energy change, ΔG°, for a reaction and the equilibrium constant, K? What is the sign of ΔG° when:

(a) $K > 1$ **(b)** $K = 1$ **(c)** $K < 1$

16.97 Do you expect a large or small value of the equilibrium constant for a reaction with the following values of ΔG°?

(a) ΔG° is positive.

(b) ΔG° is negative.

16.98 Calculate the equilibrium constant K_p at 25 °C for the reaction in Problem 16.94.

16.99 Calculate the equilibrium constant at 25 °C for the reaction in Problem 16.95.

16.100 Given values of ΔG°_f at 25 °C for liquid ethanol (−174.9 kJ/mol) and gaseous ethanol (−167.9 kJ/mol), calculate the vapor pressure of ethanol at 25 °C.

16.101 At 25 °C, K_a for acid dissociation of aspirin ($C_9H_8O_4$) is 3.0×10^{-4}. Calculate ΔG° for the reaction $C_9H_8O_4(aq) + H_2O(l) \rightleftharpoons H_3O^+(aq) + C_9H_7O_4^-(aq)$

16.102 If ΔG°_f for gaseous bromine is 3.14 kJ/mol at 25 °C, what is the vapor pressure of bromine at 25 °C?

16.103 Calculate the equilibrium partial pressure of iodine vapor above solid iodine at 25 °C if ΔG°_f for gaseous iodine is 19.4 kJ/mol at 25 °C.

16.104 Ethylene oxide, C_2H_4O, is used to make antifreeze (ethylene glycol, $HOCH_2CH_2OH$). It is produced industrially by the catalyzed air oxidation of ethylene:

$$2\,CH_2{=}CH_2(g) + O_2(g) \longrightarrow 2\,CH_2{-}CH_2(g)$$

Ethylene oxide

Use the data in Appendix B to calculate ΔG° and K_p for this reaction at 25 °C.

16.105 The first step in the commercial production of titanium metal is the reaction of rutile (TiO_2) with chlorine and graphite:

$$TiO_2(s) + 2\,Cl_2(g) + 2\,C(s) \longrightarrow TiCl_4(l) + 2\,CO(g)$$

Use the data in Appendix B to calculate ΔG° and the equilibrium constant for this reaction at 25 °C.

CHAPTER PROBLEMS

16.106 What is the entropy change when 1.32 g of propane (C_3H_8) at 0.100 atm pressure is compressed by a factor of five at a constant temperature of 20 °C? Assume that propane behaves as an ideal gas.

16.107 Indicate whether the following processes are spontaneous or nonspontaneous:

(a) Heat transfer from a block of ice to a room maintained at 25 °C

(b) Evaporation of water from an open beaker

(c) Conversion of iron(III) oxide to iron metal and oxygen

(d) Uphill motion of an automobile

16.108 Do you agree with the following statements? If not, explain.

(a) Spontaneous reactions are always fast.

(b) In any spontaneous process, the entropy of the system always increases.

(c) An endothermic reaction is always nonspontaneous.

(d) A reaction that is nonspontaneous in the forward direction is always spontaneous in the reverse direction.

16.109 When rolling a pair of dice, there are two ways to get a point total of 3 (1 + 2; 2 + 1) but only one way to get a point total of 2 (1 + 1). How many ways are there of getting point totals of 4–12? What is the most probable point total?

16.110 Make a rough, qualitative plot of the standard molar entropy versus temperature for methane from 0 K to 298 K. Incorporate the following data into your plot: mp = −182 °C; bp = −164 °C; $S^\circ = 186.2$ J/(K·mol) at 25 °C.

16.111 The standard free-energy change at 25 °C for the dissociation of water is 79.9 kJ:

$$2\,H_2O(l) \rightleftharpoons H_3O^+(aq) + OH^-(aq) \qquad \Delta G^\circ = 79.9 \text{ kJ}$$

For each of the following sets of concentrations, calculate ΔG at 25 °C and indicate whether the reaction is spontaneous in the forward or reverse direction:

(a) $[H_3O^+] = [OH^-] = 1.0$ M

(b) $[H_3O^+] = [OH^-] = 1.0 \times 10^{-7}$ M

(c) $[H_3O^+] = 1.0 \times 10^{-7}$ M, $[OH^-] = 1.0 \times 10^{-10}$ M

Are your results consistent with Le Châtelier's principle? Use the thermodynamic data to calculate the equilibrium constant for the reaction.

16.112 Calculate the normal boiling point of ethanol (CH_3CH_2OH), given that its enthalpy of vaporization is 38.6 kJ/mol and its entropy of vaporization is 110 J/(K·mol).

16.113 Chloroform ($CHCl_3$) has a normal boiling point of 61 °C and an enthalpy of vaporization of 29.24 kJ/mol. What are its values of ΔG_{vap} and ΔS_{vap} at 61 °C?

16.114 The entropy change for a certain nonspontaneous reaction at 50 °C is 104 J/K.

   (a) Is the reaction endothermic or exothermic?

   (b) What is the minimum value of ΔH (in kJ) for the reaction?

16.115 Ammonium nitrate is dangerous because it decomposes (sometimes explosively) when heated:

$$NH_4NO_3(s) \longrightarrow N_2O(g) + 2\,H_2O(g)$$

   (a) Using the data in Appendix B, show that this reaction is spontaneous at 25 °C.

   (b) How does $\Delta G°$ for the reaction change when the temperature is raised?

   (c) Calculate the equilibrium constant K_p at 25 °C.

   (d) Calculate ΔG for the reaction when the partial pressure of each gas is 30 atm.

16.116 Use the data in Appendix B to calculate $\Delta H°$, $\Delta S°$, and $\Delta G°$ at 25 °C for each of the following reactions:

   (a) $2\,Mg(s) + O_2(g) \longrightarrow 2\,MgO(s)$

   (b) $MgCO_3(s) \longrightarrow MgO(s) + CO_2(g)$

   (c) $Fe_2O_3(s) + 2\,Al(s) \longrightarrow Al_2O_3(s) + 2\,Fe(s)$

   (d) $2\,NaHCO_3(s) \longrightarrow Na_2CO_3(s) + CO_2(g) + H_2O(g)$

   Are these reactions spontaneous or nonspontaneous at 25 °C and 1 atm pressure? How does $\Delta G°$ change when the temperature is raised?

16.117 *Trouton's rule* says that the ratio of the molar heat of vaporization of a liquid to its normal boiling point (in kelvin) is approximately the same for all liquids: $\Delta H_{vap}/T_{bp} \approx 88\ J/(K \cdot mol)$.

   (a) Check the reliability of Trouton's rule for the liquids listed in the following table.

   (b) Explain why liquids tend to have the same value of $\Delta H_{vap}/T_{bp}$.

   (c) Which of the liquids in the table deviate(s) from Trouton's rule? Explain.

Liquid	bp (°C)	ΔH_{vap} (kJ/mol)
Ammonia	−33.3	23.4
Benzene	80.1	30.8
Carbon tetrachloride	76.8	29.8
Chloroform	61.1	29.2
Mercury	356.6	59.11

16.118 Ammonium hydrogen sulfide, a stink bomb ingredient, decomposes to ammonia and hydrogen sulfide.

$$NH_4HS(s) \longrightarrow NH_3(g) + H_2S(g)$$

Calculate the standard free energy of formation of $NH_4HS(s)$ at 25 °C if the total pressure resulting from NH_4HS placed in an evacuated container is 0.658 atm at 25 °C.

16.119 Nickel tetracarbonyl, a volatile liquid used to purify nickel, forms when carbon monoxide contacts nickel. For $Ni(CO)_4(l)$, $\Delta H°_f = -633.0\ kJ/mol$ and $S° = 313.4\ J/(K \cdot mol)$.

$$Ni(s) + 4\,CO(g) \longrightarrow Ni(CO)_4(l)$$

   (a) Calculate $\Delta H°$, $\Delta S°$, and $\Delta G°$ for the reaction under standard-state conditions at 25 °C.

   (b) Estimate the temperature at which the reaction becomes nonspontaneous.

   (c) Calculate $\Delta G°_f$ for $Ni(CO)_4(l)$.

16.120 Just as we can define a standard enthalpy of formation ($\Delta H°_f$) and a standard free energy of formation ($\Delta G°_f$), we can define an analogous standard entropy of formation ($\Delta S°_f$) as being the entropy change for the formation of a substance in its standard state from its constituent elements in their standard states. Use the standard molar entropies given in Appendix B to calculate $\Delta S°_f$ for the following substances:

   (a) Benzene, $C_6H_6(l)$ **(b)** $CaSO_4(s)$

   (c) Ethanol, $CH_3CH_2OH(l)$

   Check your answers by calculating $\Delta S°_f$ from the values given in Appendix B for $\Delta H°_f$ and $\Delta G°_f$.

16.121 Use the data in Appendix B to calculate the equilibrium pressure of CO_2 in a closed 1 L vessel that contains each of the following samples:

   (a) 15 g of $MgCO_3$ and 1.0 g of MgO at 25 °C

   (b) 15 g of $MgCO_3$ and 1.0 g of MgO at 280 °C

   (c) 30 g of $MgCO_3$ and 1.0 g of MgO at 280 °C

   Assume that $\Delta H°$ and $\Delta S°$ are independent of temperature.

16.122 The equilibrium constant K_b for dissociation of aqueous ammonia is 1.710×10^{-5} at 20 °C and 1.892×10^{-5} at 50 °C. What are the values of $\Delta H°$ and $\Delta S°$ for the reaction?

$$NH_3(aq) + H_2O(l) \rightleftharpoons NH_4^+(aq) + OH^-(aq)$$

16.123 Consider the Haber synthesis of gaseous NH_3 ($\Delta H°_f = -46.1\ kJ/mol$; $\Delta G°_f = -16.5\ kJ/mol$):

$$N_2(g) + 3\,H_2(g) \longrightarrow 2\,NH_3(g)$$

   (a) Use only these data to calculate $\Delta H°$ and $\Delta S°$ for the reaction at 25 °C.

   (b) Account for the sign of $\Delta S°$.

   (c) Is the reaction spontaneous under standard-state conditions at 25 °C? Explain.

   (d) What are the equilibrium constants K_p and K_c for the reaction at 350 K? Assume that $\Delta H°$ and $\Delta S°$ are independent of temperature.

16.124 Consider the dissolution of AgBr in water at 25 °C:

$$AgBr(s) \rightleftharpoons Ag^+(aq) + Br^-(aq)$$

   (a) Use the standard heats of formation and standard molar entropies in Appendix B to calculate $\Delta G°$ for the reaction at 25 °C.

   (b) Calculate K_{sp} for AgBr at 25 °C.

   (c) Calculate ΔG for the dissolution of AgBr at 25 °C when $[Ag^+] = [Br^-] = 1.00 \times 10^{-5}$ M. Is your result consistent with the relative values of Q and K_{sp}?

16.125 The temperature dependence of the equilibrium constant is given by the equation

$$\ln K = \frac{-\Delta H°}{R}\left(\frac{1}{T}\right) + \frac{\Delta S°}{R}$$

where $\Delta H°$ and $\Delta S°$ are assumed to be independent of temperature.

(a) Derive this equation from equations given in this chapter.

(b) Explain how this equation can be used to determine experimental values of $\Delta H°$ and $\Delta S°$ from values of K at several different temperatures.

(c) Use this equation to predict the sign of $\Delta H°$ for a reaction whose equilibrium constant increases with increasing temperature. Is the reaction endothermic or exothermic? Is your prediction in accord with Le Châtelier's principle?

16.126 The normal boiling point of bromine is 58.8 °C, and the standard entropies of the liquid and vapor are $S°[Br_2(l)] = 152.2 \text{ J/(K·mol)}$; $S°[Br_2(g)] = 245.4 \text{ J/(K·mol)}$. At what temperature does bromine have a vapor pressure of 227 mm Hg?

16.127 The molar solubility of lead iodide is 1.45×10^{-3} M at 20 °C and 6.85×10^{-3} M at 80 °C. What are the values of $\Delta H°$ and $\Delta S°$ for dissolution of PbI_2?

$$PbI_2(s) \longrightarrow Pb^{2+}(aq) + 2\,I^-(aq)$$

Assume that $\Delta H°$ and $\Delta S°$ are independent of temperature.

16.128 Use the data in Appendix B to calculate the equilibrium constant K for the following reaction at 80 °C:

$$2\,Br^-(aq) + Cl_2(g) \longrightarrow Br_2(l) + 2\,Cl^-(aq)$$

Assume that $\Delta H°$ and $\Delta S°$ are independent of temperature.

16.129 Use the data from Appendix B to determine the normal boiling point of carbon disulfide (CS_2).

16.130 A humidity sensor consists of a cardboard square that is colored blue in dry weather and red in humid weather. The color change is due to the reaction:

$$CoCl_2(s) + 6\,H_2O(g) \rightleftharpoons [Co(H_2O)_6]Cl_2(s)$$
$$\text{Blue} \qquad\qquad\qquad\qquad \text{Red}$$

For this reaction at 25 °C, $\Delta H° = -352 \text{ kJ/mol}$ and $\Delta S° = -899 \text{ J/(K·mol)}$. Assuming that $\Delta H°$ and $\Delta S°$ are independent of temperature, what is the vapor pressure of water (in mm Hg) at equilibrium for the above reaction at 35 °C on a hot summer day?

16.131 The following reaction, sometimes used in the laboratory to generate small quantities of oxygen gas, has $\Delta G° = -224.4 \text{ kJ/mol}$ at 25 °C:

$$2\,KClO_3(s) \longrightarrow 2\,KCl(s) + 3\,O_2(g)$$

Use the following additional data at 25 °C to calculate the standard molar entropy $S°$ of O_2 at 25 °C: $\Delta H°_f(KClO_3) = -397.7 \text{ kJ/mol}$, $\Delta H°_f(KCl) = -436.5 \text{ kJ/mol}$, $S°(KClO_3) = 143.1 \text{ J/(K·mol)}$, and $S°(KCl) = 82.6 \text{ J/(K·mol)}$.

16.132 Consider the equilibrium $N_2O_4(g) \rightleftharpoons 2\,NO_2(g)$.

(a) Use the thermodynamic data in Appendix B to determine the temperature at which an equilibrium mixture with a total pressure of 1.00 atm will contain twice as much NO_2 as N_2O_4. Assume that $\Delta H°$ and $\Delta S°$ are independent of temperature.

(b) At what temperature will an equilibrium mixture with a total pressure of 1.00 atm contain equal amounts of NO_2 and N_2O_4?

MULTICONCEPT PROBLEMS

16.133 Sorbitol ($C_6H_{14}O_6$), a substance used as a sweetener in foods, is prepared by the reaction of glucose with hydrogen in the presence of a catalyst:

$$C_6H_{12}O_6(aq) + H_2(g) \longrightarrow C_6H_{14}O_6(aq)$$

Which of the following quantities are affected by the catalyst?

(a) Rate of the forward reaction

(b) Rate of the reverse reaction

(c) Spontaneity of the reaction

(d) $\Delta H°$

(e) $\Delta S°$

(f) $\Delta G°$

(g) The equilibrium constant

(h) Time required to reach equilibrium

16.134 A mixture of 14.0 g of N_2 and 3.024 g of H_2 in a 5.00 L container is heated to 400 °C. Use the data in Appendix B to calculate the molar concentrations of N_2, H_2, and NH_3 at

equilibrium. Assume that $\Delta H°$ and $\Delta S°$ are independent of temperature, and remember that the standard state of a gas is defined in terms of pressure.

$$N_2(g) + 3\,H_2(g) \rightleftharpoons 2\,NH_3(g)$$

16.135 One step in the commercial synthesis of sulfuric acid is the catalytic oxidation of sulfur dioxide:

$$2\,SO_2(g) + O_2(g) \rightleftharpoons 2\,SO_3(g)$$

(a) A mixture of 192 g of SO_2, 48.0 g of O_2, and a V_2O_5 catalyst is heated to 800 K in a 15.0 L vessel. Use the data in Appendix B to calculate the partial pressures of SO_3, SO_2, and O_2 at equilibrium. Assume that $\Delta H°$ and $\Delta S°$ are independent of temperature.

(b) Does the percent yield of SO_3 increase or decrease on raising the temperature from 800 K to 1000 K? Explain.

(c) Does the total pressure increase or decrease on raising the temperature from 800 K to 1000 K? Calculate the total pressure (in atm) at 1000 K.

16.136 The lead storage battery uses the reaction

$$Pb(s) + PbO_2(s) + 2\,H^+(aq) + 2\,HSO_4^-(aq) \longrightarrow$$
$$2\,PbSO_4(s) + 2\,H_2O(l)$$

(a) Use the data in Appendix B to calculate $\Delta G°$ for this reaction.

(b) Calculate ΔG for this reaction on a cold winter's day (10 °F) in a battery that has run down to the point where the sulfuric acid concentration is only 0.100 M.

16.137 What is the molar solubility of $CaCO_3$ at 50 °C in a solution prepared by dissolving 1.000 L of CO_2 gas (at 20 °C and 731 mm Hg) and 3.335 g of solid $Ca(OH)_2$ in enough water to make 500.0 mL of solution at 50 °C? Is the solubility of $CaCO_3$ at 50 °C larger or smaller than at 25 °C? Explain. You may assume that $\Delta H°$ and $\Delta S°$ are independent of temperature.

16.138 A 1.00 L volume of gaseous ammonia at 25.0 °C and 744 mm Hg was dissolved in enough water to make 500.0 mL of aqueous ammonia at 2.0 °C. What is K_b for NH_3 at 2.0 °C, and what is the pH of the solution? Assume that $\Delta H°$ and $\Delta S°$ are independent of temperature.

16.139 Consider the unbalanced equation:

$$I_2(s) \longrightarrow I^-(aq) + IO_3^-(aq).$$

(a) Balance the equation for this reaction in basic solution.

(b) Use the data in Appendix B and $\Delta G°_f$ for $IO_3^-(aq) = -128.0$ kJ/mol to calculate $\Delta G°$ for the reaction at 25 °C.

(c) Is the reaction spontaneous or nonspontaneous under standard-state conditions?

(d) What pH is required for the reaction to be at equilibrium at 25 °C when $[I^-] = 0.10$ M and $[IO_3^-] = 0.50$ M?

16.140 A mixture of NO_2 and N_2O_4, each at an initial partial pressure of 1.00 atm and a temperature of 100 °C, is allowed to react. Use the data in Appendix B to calculate the partial pressure of each gas at equilibrium. Assume that $\Delta H°$ and $\Delta S°$ are independent of temperature.

$$N_2O_4(g) \rightleftharpoons 2\,NO_2(g)$$

Electrochemistry

A major focus in the field of electrochemistry is the development of new and more efficient batteries. This Tesla Motors roadster, a zero-emission electric vehicle, is powered by 6831 lithium-ion batteries. It has a top speed of 125 mph, a 0-to-60 mph acceleration time of 3.9 s, and a 245 mile range.

CONTENTS

Batteries are everywhere. They provide the electric current to start our automobiles and to power a host of products such as digital watches and cameras, electronic calculators and laptop computers, heart pacemakers, radios, and cell phones. In hybrid and all-electric vehicles, batteries power an electric motor that supplements or replaces a gasoline engine. A battery is an *electrochemical cell*, a device for interconverting chemical and electrical energy. A battery takes the energy released by a spontaneous chemical reaction and uses it to produce electricity.

Electrochemistry, the area of chemistry concerned with the interconversion of chemical and electrical energy, is enormously important in modern science and technology not only because of batteries but also because it makes possible the manufacture of essential industrial chemicals and materials. Sodium hydroxide, for example, which is used in the manufacture of paper, textiles, soaps, and detergents, is produced by passing an electric current through an aqueous solution of sodium chloride. Chlorine, essential to the manufacture of plastics such as poly(vinyl chloride) (PVC), is obtained in the same process. Aluminum metal is also produced in an electrochemical process, as is pure copper for use in electrical wiring.

In this chapter, we'll look at the principles involved in the design and operation of electrochemical cells. In addition, we'll explore some important connections between electrochemistry and thermodynamics.

17.1 GALVANIC CELLS

Electrochemical cells are of two types: **galvanic cells** (also called *voltaic cells* and commonly known as batteries) and **electrolytic cells**. The names "galvanic" and "voltaic" honor the Italian scientists Luigi Galvani (1737–1798) and Alessandro Volta (1745–1827), who conducted pioneering work in the field of electrochemistry. In a galvanic cell, a spontaneous chemical reaction generates an electric current. In an electrolytic cell, an electric current drives a nonspontaneous reaction. The two types are therefore the reverse of each other. We'll take up galvanic cells in this section and will examine electrolytic cells later. First, though, let's review some of the basics of oxidation–reduction, or redox, reactions, first described in Section 4.6.

If you immerse a strip of zinc metal in an aqueous solution of copper sulfate, you find that a dark colored solid deposits on the surface of the zinc and that the blue color characteristic of the Cu^{2+} ion slowly disappears from the solution (Figure 17.1). Chemical analysis shows that the dark colored deposit consists of tiny particles of copper metal and that the solution now contains zinc ions. Therefore, the reaction is

$$Zn(s) + Cu^{2+}(aq) \longrightarrow Zn^{2+}(aq) + Cu(s)$$

This is a redox reaction in which Zn is oxidized to Zn^{2+} and Cu^{2+} is reduced to Cu. Recall that an *oxidation* is a loss of electrons (an increase in oxidation number) and a *reduction* is a gain of electrons (a decrease in oxidation number).

As discussed in Section 4.9, we can represent the oxidation and reduction aspects of the reaction by separating the overall process into *half-reactions*, one representing the oxidation reaction and the other representing the reduction:

Oxidation half-reaction: $\quad Zn(s) \longrightarrow Zn^{2+}(aq) + 2\,e^-$

Reduction half-reaction: $\quad Cu^{2+}(aq) + 2\,e^- \longrightarrow Cu(s)$

We say that Cu^{2+} is the *oxidizing agent* because, in gaining electrons from Zn, it causes the oxidation of Zn to Zn^{2+}. Similarly, we say that Zn is the *reducing agent* because, in losing electrons to Cu^{2+}, it causes the reduction of Cu^{2+} to Cu.

If the reaction is carried out as shown in Figure 17.1, electrons are transferred directly from Zn to Cu^{2+} and the enthalpy of reaction is lost to the surroundings as heat. If, however, the reaction is carried out using the electrochemical cell depicted in

Figure 17.1
The redox reaction of zinc metal with aqueous Cu^{2+} ions.

A strip of zinc metal is immersed in an aqueous copper sulfate solution.

The redox reaction takes place at the metal–solution interface and directly transfers two electrons from Zn atoms to Cu^{2+} ions to produce Zn^{2+} ions and copper metal.

As time passes, a dark colored deposit of copper metal appears on the zinc, and the blue color due to $Cu^{2+}(aq)$ fades from the solution.

The surface of the zinc becomes covered with copper atoms, and Zn^{2+} ions replace Cu^{2+} ions in the solution.

Figure 17.2, then some of the chemical energy released by the reaction is converted to electrical energy, which can be used to light a lightbulb or run an electric motor.

The apparatus shown in Figure 17.2 is a type of galvanic cell called a *Daniell cell*, after John Frederick Daniell, the English chemist who first constructed it in 1836. It consists of two separate *half-cells*, a beaker containing a strip of zinc that dips into an aqueous solution of zinc sulfate and a second beaker containing a strip of copper that dips into aqueous copper sulfate. The strips of zinc and copper are called **electrodes** and are connected by an electrically conducting wire. In addition, the two solutions are connected by a **salt bridge**, a U-shaped tube that contains a gel permeated with a solution of an inert electrolyte, such as Na_2SO_4. The ions of the inert electrolyte do not react with the other ions in the solutions, and they are not oxidized or reduced at the electrodes.

The reaction that occurs in the Daniell cell is the same one that occurs when Zn reacts directly with Cu^{2+}, but now, because the Zn metal and Cu^{2+} ions are in separate compartments, the electrons are transferred from Zn to Cu^{2+} through the wire. Consequently, the oxidation and reduction half-reactions occur at separate electrodes and an electric current flows through the wire. Electrons are not transferred through the solution because the metal wire is a much better conductor of electrons than is water. In fact, free electrons react rapidly with water and are therefore unstable in aqueous solutions.

(a) A galvanic cell

The negative particles (electrons in the wire and anions in solution) travel around the circuit in the same counterclockwise direction.

The resulting electric current can be used to light a lightbulb.

$$Cu^{2+}(aq) + 2\,e^- \longrightarrow Cu(s) \qquad Zn(s) \longrightarrow Zn^{2+}(aq) + 2\,e^-$$

(b) An operating Daniell cell

The salt bridge in part **(a)** is replaced by a porous glass disk that allows ions to flow between the anode and cathode compartments but prevents bulk mixing, which would bring Cu^{2+} ions into direct contact with zinc and short-circuit the cell.

Figure 17.2
A Daniell cell, an example of a galvanic cell. **(a)** A Daniell cell uses the oxidation of zinc metal to Zn^{2+} ions and the reduction of Cu^{2+} ions to copper metal. **(b)** In this operating Daniell cell, the lightbulb in part **(a)** is replaced with a digital voltmeter (more about that in Section 17.3).

The electrode at which oxidation takes place is called the **anode** (the zinc strip in this example), and the electrode at which reduction takes place is called the **cathode** (the copper strip). The anode and cathode half-reactions must add to give the overall cell reaction:

Anode (oxidation) half-reaction:	$Zn(s) \longrightarrow Zn^{2+}(aq) + 2\,e^-$
Cathode (reduction) half-reaction:	$Cu^{2+}(aq) + 2\,e^- \longrightarrow Cu(s)$
Overall cell reaction:	$Zn(s) + Cu^{2+}(aq) \longrightarrow Zn^{2+}(aq) + Cu(s)$

The salt bridge is necessary to complete the electrical circuit. Without it, the solution in the anode compartment would become positively charged as Zn^{2+} ions appeared in it, and the solution in the cathode compartment would become negatively charged as Cu^{2+} ions were removed from it. Because of the charge imbalance, the electrode reactions would quickly come to a halt and electron flow through the wire would cease.

With the salt bridge in place, electrical neutrality is maintained in both compartments by a flow of ions. Anions (in this case SO_4^{2-}) flow through the salt bridge from the cathode compartment to the anode compartment, and cations migrate through the salt bridge from the anode compartment to the cathode compartment. For the cell shown in Figure 17.2, Na^+ ions move out of the salt bridge into the cathode compartment and Zn^{2+} ions move into the salt bridge from the anode compartment. The anode and cathode get their names from the direction of ion flow between the two compartments: *Anions* move toward the *anode*, and *cations* move toward the *cathode*.

The electrodes of commercial galvanic cells are generally labeled with plus (+) and minus (−) signs, although the magnitude of the actual charge on the electrodes is infinitesimally small and the sign of the charge associated with each electrode depends on the point of view. From the perspective of the wire, the anode looks negative because a stream of negatively charged electrons comes from it. From the perspective of the solution, however, the anode looks positive because a stream of positively charged Zn^{2+} ions move from it. Because galvanic cells are used to supply electric current to an external circuit, it makes sense to adopt the perspective of the wire. Consequently, we regard the anode as the negative ($-$) electrode and the cathode as the positive ($+$) electrode. Thus, electrons move through the external circuit from the negative electrode, where they are produced by the anode half-reaction, to the positive electrode, where they are consumed by the cathode half-reaction.

Anode:
- Is where oxidation occurs
- Is where electrons are produced
- Is what anions migrate toward
- Has a negative sign

Cathode:
- Is where reduction occurs
- Is where electrons are consumed
- Is what cations migrate toward
- Has a positive sign

Why do anions move toward the anode? Shouldn't the negative ions be repelled by the negative charge of the anode? The answer is that the anode's negative charge is shielded by the surrounding Zn^{2+} cations, which enter the solution from the surface of the electrode when zinc is oxidized. From the perspective of the anions, the solution around the anode looks positive, and so the anions move toward the anode to neutralize the positive charge of the Zn^{2+} cations (**Figure 17.3**).

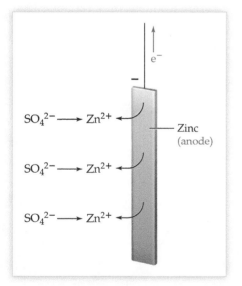

Figure 17.3
Why do negative ions move toward the negative electrode?

WORKED EXAMPLE 17.1

DESIGNING A GALVANIC CELL

Design a galvanic cell that uses the redox reaction

$$Fe(s) + 2\ Fe^{3+}(aq) \longrightarrow 3\ Fe^{2+}(aq)$$

Identify the anode and cathode half-reactions, and sketch the experimental setup. Label the anode and cathode, indicate the direction of electron and ion flow, and identify the sign of each electrode.

STRATEGY

First, separate the overall cell reaction into anode (oxidation) and cathode (reduction) half-reactions. Then, set up two half-cells that use these half-reactions and connect the half-cells with a conducting wire and a salt bridge.

SOLUTION

In the overall cell reaction, iron metal is oxidized to iron(II) ions and iron(III) ions are reduced to iron(II) ions. Therefore, the cell half-reactions are

Anode (oxidation):	$Fe(s) \longrightarrow Fe^{2+}(aq) + 2\ e^{-}$
Cathode (reduction):	$2 \times [Fe^{3+}(aq) + e^{-} \longrightarrow Fe^{2+}(aq)]$
Overall cell reaction:	$Fe(s) + 2\ Fe^{3+}(aq) \longrightarrow 3\ Fe^{2+}(aq)$

The cathode half-reaction is multiplied by a factor of 2 so that the two half-reactions will add to give the overall cell reaction. Whenever half-reactions are added, the electrons must cancel. No electrons can appear in the overall reaction because all the electrons lost by the reducing agent are gained by the oxidizing agent.

A possible experimental setup is shown below. The anode compartment consists of an iron metal electrode dipping into an aqueous solution of $Fe(NO_3)_2$. Note, though, that any inert electrolyte can be used to carry the current in the anode compartment; Fe^{2+} does not need to be present initially because it's not a reactant in the anode half-reaction.

Since Fe^{3+} is a reactant in the cathode half-reaction, $Fe(NO_3)_3$ would be a good electrolyte for the cathode compartment. The cathode can be any electrical conductor that doesn't react with the ions in the solution. A platinum wire is a common inert electrode, but iron metal can't be used because it would react directly with Fe^{3+}, thus short-circuiting the cell. The salt bridge contains $NaNO_3$, but any inert electrolyte would do. Electrons flow through the wire from the iron anode ($-$) to the platinum cathode ($+$). Anions move from the cathode compartment toward the anode while cations migrate from the anode compartment toward the cathode.

$$Fe(s) \longrightarrow Fe^{2+}(aq) + 2\,e^- \qquad Fe^{3+}(aq) + e^- \longrightarrow Fe^{2+}(aq)$$

▶ **PROBLEM 17.1** Describe a galvanic cell that uses the reaction

$$2\,Ag^+(aq) + Ni(s) \longrightarrow 2\,Ag(s) + Ni^{2+}(aq)$$

Identify the anode and cathode half-reactions, and sketch the experimental setup. Label the anode and cathode, indicate the direction of electron and ion flow, and identify the sign of each electrode.

17.2 SHORTHAND NOTATION FOR GALVANIC CELLS

Rather than describing a galvanic cell in words, it's convenient to use a shorthand notation for representing the cell. For the Daniell cell in Figure 17.2, which uses the reaction

$$Zn(s) + Cu^{2+}(aq) \longrightarrow Zn^{2+}(aq) + Cu(s)$$

we can write the following expression:

$$Zn(s)|Zn^{2+}(aq)||Cu^{2+}(aq)|Cu(s)$$

In this notation, a single vertical line (|) represents a phase boundary, such as that between a solid electrode and an aqueous solution, and the double vertical line (||) denotes a salt bridge. The shorthand for the anode half-cell is always written on the left of the salt-bridge symbol, followed on the right by the shorthand for the cathode half-cell. The electrodes are written on the extreme left (anode) and on the extreme right (cathode), and the reactants in each half-cell are always written first, followed by the products. With these arbitrary conventions, electrons move through the external circuit from left to right (from anode to cathode). Reading the shorthand thus suggests the overall cell reaction: Zn is oxidized to Zn^{2+}, and Cu^{2+} is reduced to Cu.

For the galvanic cell in Worked Example 17.1, based on the reaction

$$Fe(s) + 2\ Fe^{3+}(aq) \longrightarrow 3\ Fe^{2+}(aq)$$

the shorthand notation is

$$Fe(s)|Fe^{2+}(aq)||Fe^{3+}(aq), Fe^{2+}(aq)|Pt(s)$$

The shorthand for the cathode half-cell includes both reactant (Fe^{3+}) and product (Fe^{2+}) as well as the electrode (Pt). The two ions $Fe^{3+}(aq)$ and $Fe^{2+}(aq)$ are separated by a comma rather than a vertical line because they are in the same phase.

The notation for a cell involving a gas has an additional vertical line because an additional phase is present. Thus, the notation

$$Cu(s)|Cu^{2+}(aq)||Cl_2(g)|Cl^-(aq)|C(s)$$

specifies a cell in which copper is oxidized to Cu^{2+} at a copper anode and Cl_2 gas is reduced to Cl^- at a graphite (carbon) cathode. The cell reaction is

$$Cu(s) + Cl_2(g) \longrightarrow Cu^{2+}(aq) + 2\ Cl^-(aq)$$

A more detailed notation would include ion concentrations and gas pressures, as in the following:

$$Cu(s)|Cu^{2+}(1.0\ M)||Cl_2(1\ atm)|Cl^-(1.0\ M)|C(s)$$

WORKED EXAMPLE 17.2

INTERPRETING THE SHORTHAND NOTATION FOR A GALVANIC CELL

Given the following shorthand notation

$$Pt(s)|Sn^{2+}(aq), Sn^{4+}(aq)||Ag^+(aq)|Ag(s)$$

write a balanced equation for the cell reaction, and give a brief description of the cell.

STRATEGY

We can obtain the cell half-reactions simply by reading the shorthand notation. To find the balanced equation for the cell reaction, add the two half-reactions after multiplying each by an appropriate factor so that the electrons will cancel. The shorthand notation specifies the anode on the extreme left, the cathode on the extreme right, and the reactants in the half-cell compartments.

SOLUTION

Because the anode always appears at the left in the shorthand notation, the anode (oxidation) half-reaction is

$$Sn^{2+}(aq) \longrightarrow Sn^{4+}(aq) + 2\ e^-$$

The platinum electrode is inert and serves only to conduct electrons. The cathode (reduction) half-reaction is

$$2 \times [Ag^+(aq) + e^- \longrightarrow Ag(s)]$$

We multiply the cathode half-reaction by a factor of 2 so that the electrons will cancel when we sum the two half-reactions to give the cell reaction:

$$Sn^{2+}(aq) + 2\,Ag^+(aq) \longrightarrow Sn^{4+}(aq) + 2\,Ag(s)$$

The cell consists of a platinum wire anode dipping into an Sn^{2+} solution—say, $Sn(NO_3)_2(aq)$—and a silver cathode dipping into an Ag^+ solution—say, $AgNO_3(aq)$. As usual, the anode and cathode half-cells must be connected by a wire and a salt bridge containing inert ions.

Although the anode half-cell always appears on the left in the shorthand notation, its location in a cell drawing is arbitrary. This means that you can't infer which electrode is the anode and which is the cathode from the location of the electrodes in a cell drawing. You must identify the electrodes based on whether each electrode half-reaction is an oxidation or a reduction.

▶ **PROBLEM 17.2**   Write a balanced equation for the overall cell reaction, and give a brief description of a galvanic cell represented by the following shorthand notation:

$$Pb(s)|Pb^{2+}(aq)||Br_2(l)|Br^-(aq)|Pt(s)$$

▶ **PROBLEM 17.3**   Write the shorthand notation for a galvanic cell that uses the reaction

$$Fe(s) + Sn^{2+}(aq) \longrightarrow Fe^{2+}(aq) + Sn(s)$$

CONCEPTUAL PROBLEM 17.4   Consider the following galvanic cell:

(a) Complete the drawing by adding any components essential for a functioning cell.
(b) Label the anode and cathode, and indicate the direction of ion flow.
(c) Write a balanced equation for the cell reaction.
(d) Write the shorthand notation for the cell.

17.3   CELL POTENTIALS AND FREE-ENERGY CHANGES FOR CELL REACTIONS

Let's return to the Daniell cell shown in Figure 17.2 to find an electrical measure of the tendency for a cell reaction to occur. Electrons move through the external circuit from the zinc anode to the copper cathode because they have lower energy when on copper than on zinc. The force that pushes the negatively charged electrons away from the anode (− electrode) and pulls them toward the cathode (+ electrode) is an electrical potential called the **electromotive force (emf)**, also known as the **cell potential (E)** or the **cell voltage**. The SI unit of electrical potential is the volt (V), and the potential of a galvanic cell is defined as a positive quantity.

The relationship between the volt and the SI units of energy (joule, J) and electric charge (coulomb, C) is given by the equation

$$1\,J = 1\,C \times 1\,V$$

where 1 C is the amount of charge transferred when a current of 1 **ampere (A)** flows for 1 second (s) (Section 1.5). When 1 C of charge moves between two electrodes that differ in electrical potential by 1 V, 1 J of energy is released by the cell and can be used to do electrical work.

The relationship between the watt (W), the ampere, and the volt is given by

$$1\,W = \frac{1\,J}{s} = \frac{1\,C \times 1\,V}{s} = 1\,A \times 1\,V$$

Remember ...

The **ampere** (1 A = 1 C/s) is the SI unit of electric current   (Section 1.5).

where 1 W is 1 J/s and 1 A is 1 C/s. Thus, the current passing through a 100 W household lightbulb at a household voltage of 110 V is about 1 A, which means that the electric charge of the electrons passing through the bulb in 1 s is 1 C.

A cell potential is measured with an electronic instrument called a *voltmeter* (Figure 17.2b), which is designed to give a positive reading when the + and − terminals of the voltmeter are connected to the + (cathode) and − (anode) electrodes of the cell, respectively. Thus, the voltmeter–cell connections required to get a positive reading on the voltmeter indicate which electrode is the anode and which is the cathode.

We've now seen two quantitative measures of the tendency for a chemical reaction to occur: the cell potential E, an electrochemical quantity, and the **free-energy change ΔG**, a thermochemical quantity (Section 16.7). The values of ΔG and E are directly proportional and are related by the equation

Remember...

If the **free-energy change ΔG** for a reaction is negative, the reaction is spontaneous. The greater the negative value of ΔG, the greater the tendency for the reaction to occur.   (Section 16.7)

$$\Delta G = -nFE$$

where n is the number of moles of electrons transferred in the reaction and F is the **faraday** (or *Faraday constant*), the electric charge on 1 mol of electrons (96,485 C/mol e$^-$). In our calculations, we'll round the value of F to three significant figures:

$$F = 96,500\,C/mol\,e^-$$

The faraday is named in honor of Michael Faraday (1791–1867), the nineteenth-century English scientist who laid the foundations for our current understanding of electricity.

Two features of the equation $\Delta G = -nFE$ are worth noting: the units and the minus sign. When we multiply the charge transferred (nF) in coulombs by the cell potential (E) in volts, we obtain an energy (ΔG) in joules, in accord with the relationship $1\,J = 1\,C \times 1\,V$. The minus sign is required because E and ΔG have opposite signs: The spontaneous reaction in a galvanic cell has a positive cell potential but a negative free-energy change (Section 16.7).

Later in this chapter, we'll see that cell potentials, like free-energy changes, depend on the composition of the reaction mixture. The **standard cell potential $E°$** is the cell potential when both reactants and products are in their standard states— solutes at 1 M concentrations, gases at a partial pressure of 1 atm, solids and liquids in pure form, with all at a specified temperature, usually 25 °C. For example, $E°$ for the reaction

$$Zn(s) + Cu^{2+}(aq) \longrightarrow Zn^{2+}(aq) + Cu(s) \qquad E° = 1.10\,V$$

is the cell potential measured at 25 °C for a cell that has pure Zn and Cu metal electrodes and 1 M concentrations of Zn^{2+} and Cu^{2+}.

The standard free-energy change and the standard cell potential are related by the equation

$$\Delta G° = -nFE°$$

Because $\Delta G°$ and $E°$ are directly proportional, a voltmeter can be regarded as a "free-energy meter." When a voltmeter measures $E°$, it also indirectly measures $\Delta G°$.

WORKED EXAMPLE 17.3

CALCULATING A STANDARD FREE-ENERGY CHANGE FROM A STANDARD CELL POTENTIAL

The standard cell potential at 25 °C is 1.10 V for the reaction

$$Zn(s) + Cu^{2+}(aq) \longrightarrow Zn^{2+}(aq) + Cu(s)$$

Calculate the standard free-energy change for this reaction at 25 °C.

STRATEGY

To calculate $\Delta G°$, we use the equation $\Delta G° = -nFE°$, where n can be inferred from the balanced chemical equation, F is 96,500 C/mol e⁻, and $E°$ is given.

SOLUTION

Two moles of electrons are transferred from Zn to Cu^{2+} in this reaction, so n = 2 mol e⁻ and the standard free-energy change is

$$\Delta G° = -nFE° = -(2 \text{ mol e}^-)\left(\frac{96,500 \text{ C}}{\text{mol e}^-} \right)(1.10 \text{ V})\left(\frac{1 \text{ J}}{1 \text{ C} \cdot \text{V}} \right)$$

$$= -212{,}000 \text{ J} = -212 \text{ kJ}$$

BALLPARK CHECK

F is about 10^5 C/mol e⁻ and $E°$ is about 1 V, so $\Delta G° = -nFE°$ is approximately $-(2 \text{ mol e}^-)(10^5 \text{ C/mol e}^-)(1 \text{ V}) = -2 \times 10^5$ J, or -200 kJ. The ballpark check and the solution agree. Note that $\Delta G°$ is negative, as expected for a spontaneous reaction.

▶ **PROBLEM 17.5** The standard cell potential at 25 °C is 0.92 V for the reaction

$$Al(s) + Cr^{3+}(aq) \longrightarrow Al^{3+}(aq) + Cr(s)$$

What is the standard free-energy change for this reaction at 25 °C?

17.4 STANDARD REDUCTION POTENTIALS

The standard potential of any galvanic cell is the sum of the standard half-cell potentials for oxidation at the anode and reduction at the cathode:

$$E°_{cell} = E°_{ox} + E°_{red}$$

Consider, for example, a cell in which H_2 gas is oxidized to H^+ ions at the anode and Cu^{2+} ions are reduced to copper metal at the cathode (**Figure 17.4**):

Anode (oxidation):	$H_2(g) \longrightarrow 2 H^+(aq) + 2 e^-$
Cathode (reduction):	$Cu^{2+}(aq) + 2 e^- \longrightarrow Cu(s)$
Overall cell reaction:	$H_2(g) + Cu^{2+}(aq) \longrightarrow 2 H^+(aq) + Cu(s)$

[In this chapter we represent the hydrated proton as $H^+(aq)$ rather than $H_3O^+(aq)$ because we're interested here in electron transfer, not proton transfer as in Chapter 14.] The standard potential for this cell, 0.34 V at 25 °C, measures the sum of the reaction tendencies of the oxidation and reduction half-reactions:

$$E°_{cell} = E°_{ox} + E°_{red} = E°_{H_2 \to H^+} + E°_{Cu^{2+} \to Cu} = 0.34 \text{ V}$$

If we could determine $E°$ values for individual half-reactions, we could combine those values to obtain $E°$ values for a host of cell reactions. Unfortunately, it's not possible to measure the potential of a single electrode; we can measure only a potential *difference* by placing a voltmeter between *two* electrodes. Nevertheless, we can develop a set of standard half-cell potentials by choosing an arbitrary standard half-cell as a reference point, assigning it an arbitrary potential, and then expressing

Figure 17.4

A galvanic cell consisting of a Cu^{2+}(1 M)/Cu half-cell and a standard hydrogen electrode (S.H.E.). The measured standard cell potential at 25 °C is 0.34 V.

Voltmeter

0.34 V

Electrons flow from the S.H.E. (anode) to the copper cathode.

Copper (cathode)

Na$^+$ NO$_3$$^-$
Salt bridge

H$_2$(g) (1 atm)

Standard hydrogen electrode (anode)

NO$_3$$^-$
Cu^{2+} (1 M)
NO$_3$$^-$

H$^+$ (1 M)
NO$_3$$^-$
H$^+$ NO$_3$$^-$

The S.H.E. is a piece of platinum foil that is in contact with bubbles of H$_2$(g) at 1 atm pressure and with H$^+$(aq) at 1 M concentration.

$Cu^{2+}(aq) + 2e^- \longrightarrow Cu(s)$ $H_2(g) \longrightarrow 2H^+(aq) + 2e^-$

Remember...

The **standard enthalpy of formation**, $\Delta H°_f$, of a substance is expressed relative to an arbitrary reference of $\Delta H°_f = 0$ kJ/mol for its constituent elements in their standard states.   (Section 8.9)

the potential of all other half-cells relative to the reference half-cell. Recall that this same approach was used in Section 8.9 for determining standard enthalpies of formation, $\Delta H°_f$.

To define an electrochemical "sea level," chemists have chosen a reference half-cell called the **standard hydrogen electrode (S.H.E.)**, shown in Figure 17.4. It consists of a platinum electrode in contact with H_2 gas and aqueous H^+ ions at standard-state conditions [1 atm H_2(g), 1 M H^+(aq), 25 °C]. The corresponding half-reaction, written in either direction, is assigned an arbitrary potential of exactly 0 V:

$$2H^+(aq, 1\text{ M}) + 2e^- \longrightarrow H_2(g, 1\text{ atm}) \qquad E° = 0\text{ V}$$
$$H_2(g, 1\text{ atm}) \longrightarrow 2H^+(aq, 1\text{ M}) + 2e^- \qquad E° = 0\text{ V}$$

With this choice of standard reference electrode, the entire potential of the cell

$$Pt(s)|H_2(1\text{ atm})|H^+(1\text{ M})||Cu^{2+}(1\text{ M})|Cu(s)$$

can be attributed to the Cu^{2+}/Cu half-cell:

$$E°_{cell} = E°_{H_2 \rightarrow H^+} + E°_{Cu^{2+} \rightarrow Cu} = 0.34\text{ V}$$
$$\qquad\quad \uparrow \qquad\quad \uparrow \qquad\qquad \uparrow$$
$$\qquad 0.34\text{ V} \quad 0\text{ V} \qquad\quad 0.34\text{ V}$$

Because the Cu^{2+}/Cu half-reaction is a reduction, the corresponding half-cell potential, $E° = 0.34$ V, is called a **standard reduction potential**:

$$Cu^{2+}(aq) + 2e^- \longrightarrow Cu(s) \qquad \text{Standard reduction potential: } E° = 0.34\text{ V}$$

In a cell in which this half-reaction occurs in the opposite direction, the corresponding half-cell potential has the same magnitude but opposite sign:

$$Cu(s) \longrightarrow Cu^{2+}(aq) + 2e^- \qquad E° = -0.34\text{ V}$$

Whenever the direction of a half-reaction is reversed, the sign of $E°$ must also be reversed. Thus, the standard potential for an oxidation half-reaction is the negative of the standard reduction potential.

We can determine standard potentials for other half-cells simply by constructing galvanic cells in which each half-cell of interest is paired up with the S.H.E. For example, to find the potential of a half-cell consisting of a zinc electrode dipping into a 1 M Zn^{2+} solution, we would build the cell shown in **Figure 17.5**. The voltmeter–electrode connections required to get a positive reading on the voltmeter (0.76 V) tell us that the zinc electrode is the anode and the S.H.E. is the cathode. Therefore, the half-cell reactions involve oxidation of Zn and reduction of H^+. Alternatively, we could identify the direction of the half-reactions by noting that the H^+ concentration decreases as the cell reaction progresses.

Anode (oxidation):	$Zn(s) \longrightarrow Zn^{2+}(aq) + 2\,e^-$	$E° = ?$
Cathode (reduction):	$2\,H^+(aq) + 2\,e^- \longrightarrow H_2(g)$	$E° = 0\,V$
Overall cell reaction:	$Zn(s) + 2\,H^+(aq) \longrightarrow Zn^{2+}(aq) + H_2(g)$	$E° = 0.76\,V$

Since the anode and cathode half-cell potentials must sum to give the overall cell potential, the $E°$ value for oxidation of Zn to Zn^{2+} Must be 0.76 V and the standard *reduction* potential for the Zn^{2+}/Zn half-cell is therefore -0.76 V.

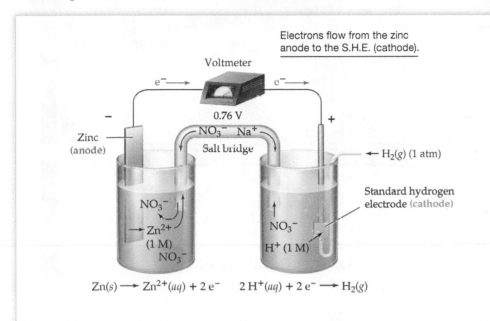

Figure 17.5

A galvanic cell consisting of a Zn/Zn^{2+} (1 M) half-cell and a standard hydrogen electrode. The measured standard cell potential at 25 °C is 0.76 V.

We could also have calculated the standard reduction potential for the Zn^{2+}/Zn half-cell from the observed standard potential of the Daniell cell (1.10 V) and the standard reduction potential for the Cu^{2+}/Cu half-cell (0.34 V):

Anode (oxidation):	$Zn(s) \longrightarrow Zn^{2+}(aq) + 2\,e^-$	$E° - ?$
Cathode (reduction):	$Cu^{2+}(aq) + 2\,e^- \longrightarrow Cu(s)$	$E° = 0.34\,V$
Overall cell reaction:	$Zn(s) + Cu^{2+}(aq) \longrightarrow Zn^{2+}(aq) + Cu(s)$	$E° = 1.10\,V$

Since 1.10 V = 0.76 V + 0.34 V, we would again conclude that the $E°$ value for oxidation of Zn to Zn^{2+} is 0.76 V and the standard reduction potential for the Zn^{2+}/Zn half-cell is therefore -0.76 V.

From experiments of the sort just described, hundreds of half-cell potentials have been determined. A short list is presented in Table 17.1, and a more complete tabulation is given in Appendix D. The following conventions are observed when constructing a table of half-cell potentials:

• **The half-reactions are written as reductions** rather than as oxidations. This means that oxidizing agents and electrons are on the left side of each half-reaction and reducing agents are on the right side.

• **The listed half-cell potentials are standard reduction potentials,** also known as **standard electrode potentials**.

• **The half-reactions are listed in order of decreasing standard reduction potential,** meaning a decreasing tendency to occur in the forward direction and an increasing tendency to occur in the reverse direction. Consequently, the strongest oxidizing agents are located in the upper left of the table (F_2, H_2O_2, MnO_4^-, and so forth), and the strongest reducing agents are found in the lower right of the table (Li, Na, Mg, and so forth).

TABLE 17.1 Standard Reduction Potentials at 25 °C

	Reduction Half-Reaction		$E°$ (V)	
Stronger oxidizing agent	$F_2(g) + 2\,e^-$	$\longrightarrow 2\,F^-(aq)$	2.87	Weaker reducing agent
	$H_2O_2(aq) + 2\,H^+(aq) + 2\,e^-$	$\longrightarrow 2\,H_2O(l)$	1.78	
	$MnO_4^-(aq) + 8\,H^+(aq) + 5\,e^-$	$\longrightarrow Mn^{2+}(aq) + 4\,H_2O(l)$	1.51	
	$Cl_2(g) + 2\,e^-$	$\longrightarrow 2\,Cl^-(aq)$	1.36	
	$Cr_2O_7^{2-}(aq) + 14\,H^+(aq) + 6\,e^-$	$\longrightarrow 2\,Cr^{3+}(aq) + 7\,H_2O(l)$	1.36	
	$O_2(g) + 4\,H^+(aq) + 4\,e^-$	$\longrightarrow 2\,H_2O(l)$	1.23	
	$Br_2(aq) + 2\,e^-$	$\longrightarrow 2\,Br^-(aq)$	1.09	
	$Ag^+(aq) + e^-$	$\longrightarrow Ag(s)$	0.80	
	$Fe^{3+}(aq) + e^-$	$\longrightarrow Fe^{2+}(aq)$	0.77	
	$O_2(g) + 2\,H^+(aq) + 2\,e^-$	$\longrightarrow H_2O_2(aq)$	0.70	
	$I_2(s) + 2\,e^-$	$\longrightarrow 2\,I^-(aq)$	0.54	
	$O_2(g) + 2\,H_2O(l) + 4\,e^-$	$\longrightarrow 4\,OH^-(aq)$	0.40	
	$Cu^{2+}(aq) + 2\,e^-$	$\longrightarrow Cu(s)$	0.34	
	$Sn^{4+}(aq) + 2\,e^-$	$\longrightarrow Sn^{2+}(aq)$	0.15	
	$2\,H^+(aq) + 2\,e^-$	$\longrightarrow H_2(g)$	0	
	$Pb^{2+}(aq) + 2\,e^-$	$\longrightarrow Pb(s)$	-0.13	
	$Ni^{2+}(aq) + 2\,e^-$	$\longrightarrow Ni(s)$	-0.26	
	$Cd^{2+}(aq) + 2\,e^-$	$\longrightarrow Cd(s)$	-0.40	
	$Fe^{2+}(aq) + 2\,e^-$	$\longrightarrow Fe(s)$	-0.45	
	$Zn^{2+}(aq) + 2\,e^-$	$\longrightarrow Zn(s)$	-0.76	
	$2\,H_2O(l) + 2\,e^-$	$\longrightarrow H_2(g) + 2\,OH^-(aq)$	-0.83	
	$Al^{3+}(aq) + 3\,e^-$	$\longrightarrow Al(s)$	-1.66	
Weaker oxidizing agent	$Mg^{2+}(aq) + 2\,e^-$	$\longrightarrow Mg(s)$	-2.37	Stronger reducing agent
	$Na^+(aq) + e^-$	$\longrightarrow Na(s)$	-2.71	
	$Li^+(aq) + e^-$	$\longrightarrow Li(s)$	-3.04	

By choosing $E° = 0$ V for the standard hydrogen electrode, we obtain standard reduction potentials that range from about +3 V to −3 V.

Note how the ordering of the half-reactions in Table 17.1 corresponds to their ordering in the activity series in Table 4.5 (page 130). The more active metals at the top of the activity series have the more positive oxidation potentials and therefore the more negative standard reduction potentials.

▶ **PROBLEM 17.6** The standard potential for the following galvanic cell is 0.92 V:

$$Al(s)\,|\,Al^{3+}(aq)\,||\,Cr^{3+}(aq)\,|\,Cr(s)$$

Look up the standard reduction potential for the Al^{3+}/Al half-cell in Table 17.1, and calculate the standard reduction potential for the Cr^{3+}/Cr half-cell.

17.5 USING STANDARD REDUCTION POTENTIALS

A table of standard reduction potentials summarizes an enormous amount of chemical information in a very small space. It enables us to arrange oxidizing or reducing agents in order of increasing strength, and it permits us to predict the spontaneity or nonspontaneity of thousands of redox reactions. Suppose, for example, that the table contains just 100 half-reactions. We can pair each reduction half-reaction with any one of the remaining 99 oxidation half-reactions to give a total of $100 \times 99 = 9900$ cell reactions. By calculating the $E°$ values for these cell reactions, we would find that half of them are spontaneous and the other half are nonspontaneous. (Can you see why?)

To illustrate how to use the tabulated $E°$ values, let's calculate $E°$ for the oxidation of $Zn(s)$ by $Ag^+(aq)$:

$$2\,Ag^+(aq) + Zn(s) \longrightarrow 2\,Ag(s) + Zn^{2+}(aq)$$

First, we find the relevant half-reactions in Table 17.1 and write them in the appropriate direction for reduction of Ag^+ and oxidation of Zn. Next, we add the half-reactions to get the overall reaction. Before adding, though, we must multiply the Ag^+/Ag half-reaction by a factor of 2 so that the electrons will cancel:

Reduction:	$2 \times [Ag^+(aq) + e^- \longrightarrow Ag(s)]$	$E° = 0.80\ V$
Oxidation:	$Zn(s) \longrightarrow Zn^{2+}(aq) + 2\,e^-$	$E° = -(-0.76\ V)$
Overall reaction:	$2\,Ag^+(aq) + Zn(s) \longrightarrow 2\,Ag(s) + Zn^{2+}(aq)$	$E° = 1.56\ V$

Then, we tabulate the $E°$ values for the half-reactions, remembering that $E°$ for oxidation of zinc is the negative of the standard reduction potential ($-0.76\ V$). We do not multiply the $E°$ value for reduction of Ag^+ ($0.80\ V$) by a factor of 2, however, because an electrical potential does not depend on how much reaction occurs.

The reason why $E°$ values are independent of the amount of reaction can be understood by looking at the equation $\Delta G° = -nFE°$. Free energy is an **extensive property** (Section 1.4) because it depends on the amount of substance. If we double the amount of Ag^+ reduced, the free-energy change, $\Delta G°$, doubles. The number of electrons transferred, n, also doubles, however, so the ratio $E° = -\Delta G°/nF$ is constant. Electrical potential is therefore an **intensive property**, which does not depend on the amount of substance.

The $E°$ value for the overall reaction of $Zn(s)$ with $Ag^+(aq)$ is the sum of the $E°$ values for the two half-reactions: $0.80\ V + 0.76\ V = 1.56\ V$. Because $E°$ is positive (and $\Delta G°$ is negative), oxidation of zinc by Ag^+ is a spontaneous reaction under standard-state conditions. Just as Ag^+ can oxidize Zn, it's evident from Table 17.1 that Ag^+ can oxidize any reducing agent that lies below it in the table (Fe^{2+}, H_2O_2, Cu, and so forth). Summing $E°$ for the Ag^+/Ag reduction ($0.80\ V$) and $-E°$ for any half-reaction that lies below the Ag^+/Ag half-reaction always gives a positive $E°$ for the overall reaction.

In general, an oxidizing agent can oxidize any reducing agent that lies below it in the table but can't oxidize a reducing agent that appears above it in the table. Thus, Ag^+ can't oxidize Br^-, H_2O, Cr^{3+}, and so forth because $E°$ for the overall reaction is negative. Simply by glancing at the locations of the oxidizing and reducing agents in the table, we can predict whether a reaction is spontaneous or nonspontaneous.

Remember...

Extensive properties, like mass and volume, have values that depend on the sample size. **Intensive properties**, like temperature and melting point, have values that do not depend on the sample size. (Section 1.4)

WORKED EXAMPLE 17.4

ARRANGING OXIDIZING AND REDUCING AGENTS IN ORDER OF INCREASING STRENGTH

(a) Arrange the following oxidizing agents in order of increasing strength under standard-state conditions: $Br_2(aq)$, $Fe^{3+}(aq)$, $Cr_2O_7{}^{2-}(aq)$.
(b) Arrange the following reducing agents in order of increasing strength under standard-state conditions: $Al(s)$, $Na(s)$, $Zn(s)$.

STRATEGY

Pick out the half-reactions in Table 17.1 that involve the given oxidizing or reducing agents, and list them, along with their $E°$ values, in the order in which they occur in the table. The strength of an oxidizing agent increases as the $E°$ value increases, and the strength of a reducing agent increases as the $E°$ value decreases.

continued on next page

SOLUTION

(a) List the half-reactions that involve Br_2, Fe^{3+}, and $Cr_2O_7^{2-}$ in the order in which they occur in Table 17.1:

$$Cr_2O_7^{2-}(aq) + 14\,H^+(aq) + 6\,e^- \longrightarrow 2\,Cr^{3+}(aq) + 7\,H_2O(l) \qquad E° = 1.36\,V$$
$$Br_2(aq) + 2\,e^- \longrightarrow 2\,Br^-(aq) \qquad E° = 1.09\,V$$
$$Fe^{3+}(aq) + e^- \longrightarrow Fe^{2+}(aq) \qquad E° = 0.77\,V$$

We can see that $Cr_2O_7^{2-}$ has the greatest tendency to be reduced (largest $E°$) and Fe^{3+} has the least tendency to be reduced (smallest $E°$). The species that has the greatest tendency to be reduced is the strongest oxidizing agent, so oxidizing strength increases in the order $Fe^{3+} < Br_2 < Cr_2O_7^{2-}$. As a shortcut, simply note that the strength of the oxidizing agents, listed on the left side of Table 17.1, increases on moving up in the table.

(b) List the half-reactions that involve $Al(s)$, $Na(s)$, and $Zn(s)$ in the order in which they occur in Table 17.1:

$$Zn^{2+}(aq) + 2\,e^- \longrightarrow Zn(s) \qquad E° = -0.76\,V$$
$$Al^{3+}(aq) + 3\,e^- \longrightarrow Al(s) \qquad E° = -1.66\,V$$
$$Na^+(aq) + e^- \longrightarrow Na(s) \qquad E° = -2.71\,V$$

The last half-reaction has the least tendency to occur in the forward direction (most negative $E°$) and the greatest tendency to occur in the reverse direction. Therefore, Na is the strongest reducing agent, and reducing strength increases in the order $Zn < Al < Na$. As a shortcut, note that the strength of the reducing agents, listed on the right side of Table 17.1, increases on moving down in the table.

WORKED EXAMPLE 17.5

PREDICTING WHETHER A REDOX REACTION IS SPONTANEOUS

Predict from Table 17.1 whether $Pb^{2+}(aq)$ can oxidize $Al(s)$ or $Cu(s)$ under standard-state conditions. Calculate $E°$ for each reaction at 25 °C.

STRATEGY

To predict whether a redox reaction is spontaneous, remember that an oxidizing agent can oxidize any reducing agent that lies below it in the table but can't oxidize one that lies above it. To calculate $E°$ for a redox reaction, sum the $E°$ values for the reduction and oxidation half-reactions.

SOLUTION

$Pb^{2+}(aq)$ is above $Al(s)$ in the table but below $Cu(s)$. Therefore, $Pb^{2+}(aq)$ can oxidize $Al(s)$ but can't oxidize $Cu(s)$. To confirm these predictions, calculate $E°$ values for the overall reactions.

For the oxidation of Al by Pb^{2+}, $E°$ is positive (1.53 V) and the reaction is therefore spontaneous:

$$3 \times [Pb^{2+}(aq) + 2\,e^- \longrightarrow Pb(s)] \qquad\qquad E° = -0.13\,V$$
$$\underline{2 \times [Al(s) \longrightarrow Al^{3+}(aq) + 3\,e^-] \qquad\qquad E° = 1.66\,V}$$
$$3\,Pb^{2+}(aq) + 2\,Al(s) \longrightarrow 3\,Pb(s) + 2\,Al^{3+}(aq) \qquad E° = 1.53\,V$$

Note that we have multiplied the Pb^{2+}/Pb half-reaction by a factor of 3 and the Al/Al^{3+} half-reaction by a factor of 2 so that the electrons will cancel, but we do not multiply the $E°$ values by these factors because electrical potential is an intensive property.

For the oxidation of Cu by Pb^{2+}, $E°$ is negative (-0.47 V) and the reaction is therefore nonspontaneous:

$$Pb^{2+}(aq) + 2\,e^- \longrightarrow Pb(s) \qquad\qquad E° = -0.13\,V$$
$$\underline{Cu(s) \longrightarrow Cu^{2+}(aq) + 2\,e^- \qquad\qquad E° = -0.34\,V}$$
$$Pb^{2+}(aq) + Cu(s) \longrightarrow Pb(s) + Cu^{2+}(aq) \qquad E° = -0.47\,V$$

▶ **PROBLEM 17.7**   Which is the stronger oxidizing agent, $Cl_2(g)$ or $Ag^+(aq)$? Which is the stronger reducing agent, $Fe(s)$ or $Mg(s)$?

▶ **PROBLEM 17.8**   Predict from Table 17.1 whether each of the following reactions can occur under standard-state conditions:

(a) $2\,Fe^{3+}(aq) + 2\,I^-(aq) \longrightarrow 2\,Fe^{2+}(aq) + I_2(s)$

(b) $3\,Ni(s) + 2\,Al^{3+}(aq) \longrightarrow 3\,Ni^{2+}(aq) + 2\,Al(s)$

Confirm your predictions by calculating the value of E° for each reaction. Which reaction(s) can occur in the reverse direction under standard-state conditions?

CONCEPTUAL PROBLEM 17.9   Consider the following table of standard reduction potentials:

Reduction Half-Reaction	E° (V)
$A^{3+} + 2\,e^- \longrightarrow A^+$	1.47
$B^{2+} + 2\,e^- \longrightarrow B$	0.60
$C^{2+} + 2\,e^- \longrightarrow C$	−0.21
$D^+ + e^- \longrightarrow D$	−1.38

(a) Which substance is the strongest reducing agent? Which is the strongest oxidizing agent?

(b) Which substances can be oxidized by B^{2+}? Which can be reduced by C?

(c) Write a balanced equation for the overall cell reaction that delivers the highest voltage, and calculate E° for the reaction.

17.6   CELL POTENTIALS AND COMPOSITION OF THE REACTION MIXTURE: THE NERNST EQUATION

Cell potentials, like free-energy changes, depend on temperature and on the composition of the reaction mixture—that is, on the concentrations of solutes and the partial pressures of gases. This dependence can be derived from the equation

$$\Delta G = \Delta G^\circ + RT \ln Q$$

Recall from Section 16.10 that ΔG is the free-energy change for a reaction under nonstandard-state conditions, ΔG° is the free-energy change under standard-state conditions, and Q is the reaction quotient. Since $\Delta G = -nFE$ and $\Delta G^\circ = -nFE^\circ$, we can rewrite the equation for ΔG in the form

$$-nFE = -nFE^\circ + RT \ln Q$$

Dividing by $-nF$, we obtain the **Nernst equation**, named after Walther Nernst (1864–1941), the German chemist who first derived it:

Remember...

The **reaction quotient Q** is an expression having the same form as the equilibrium constant expression K except that the concentrations and partial pressures do not necessarily have equilibrium values. (Section 16.10)

◀⇒ **Nernst equation** $E = E^\circ - \dfrac{RT}{nF} \ln Q$ or $E = E^\circ - \dfrac{2.303RT}{nF} \log Q$

Because of an intimate connection between the cell voltage and pH (Section 17.7), we will write the Nernst equation in terms of base-10 logarithms, $\log Q$ rather than $\ln Q$. At 25 °C, $2.303RT/F$ has a value of 0.0592 V, and therefore

$$E = E^\circ - \frac{0.0592\ V}{n}\log Q \quad \text{in volts, at 25 °C}$$

In actual galvanic cells, the concentrations and partial pressures of reactants and products seldom have standard-state values, and the values change as the cell reaction proceeds. The Nernst equation is useful because it enables us to calculate cell potentials under nonstandard-state conditions, as shown in Worked Example 17.6.

WORKED EXAMPLE 17.6

USING THE NERNST EQUATION TO CALCULATE THE CELL POTENTIAL UNDER NONSTANDARD-STATE CONDITIONS

Consider a galvanic cell that uses the reaction

$$Zn(s) + 2\,H^+(aq) \longrightarrow Zn^{2+}(aq) + H_2(g)$$

Calculate the cell potential at 25 °C when $[H^+] = 1.0$ M, $[Zn^{2+}] = 0.0010$ M, and $P_{H_2} = 0.10$ atm.

STRATEGY

We can calculate the standard cell potential $E°$ from the standard reduction potentials in Table 17.1 and then use the Nernst equation to find the cell potential E under the cited conditions.

SOLUTION

The standard cell potential is

$$E° = E°_{Zn \to Zn^{2+}} + E°_{H^+ \to H_2} = -(-0.76\ \text{V}) + 0\ \text{V} = 0.76\ \text{V}$$

The cell potential at 25 °C under nonstandard-state conditions is given by the Nernst equation:

$$E = E° - \frac{0.0592\ \text{V}}{n} \log\ Q$$

$$= E° - \left(\frac{0.0592\ \text{V}}{n} \right) \left(\log \frac{[Zn^{2+}](P_{H_2})}{[H^+]^2} \right)$$

where the reaction quotient contains both molar concentrations of solutes and the partial pressure of a gas (in atm). As usual, zinc has been omitted from the reaction quotient because it is a pure solid. For this reaction, 2 mol of electrons are transferred, so $n = 2$. Substituting into the Nernst equation the appropriate values of $E°$, n, $[H^+]$, $[Zn^{2+}]$, and P_{H_2} gives

$$E = (0.76\ \text{V}) - \left(\frac{0.0592\ \text{V}}{2} \right) \left(\log \frac{(0.0010)(0.10)}{(1.0)^2} \right) = (0.76\ \text{V}) - \left(\frac{0.0592\ \text{V}}{2} \right)(-4.0)$$

$$= 0.76\ \text{V} + 0.12\ \text{V}$$

$$= 0.88\ \text{V} \quad \text{at } 25\,°C$$

BALLPARK CHECK

We expect that the reaction will have a greater tendency to occur under the cited conditions than under standard-state conditions because the product concentrations are lower than standard-state values. We therefore predict that the cell potential E will be greater than the standard cell potential $E°$, in agreement with the solution.

▶ **PROBLEM 17.10** Consider a galvanic cell that uses the reaction

$$Cu(s) + 2\,Fe^{3+}(aq) \longrightarrow Cu^{2+}(aq) + 2\,Fe^{2+}(aq)$$

What is the potential of a cell at 25 °C that has the following ion concentrations?

$$[Fe^{3+}] = 1.0 \times 10^{-4}\ \text{M} \quad [Cu^{2+}] = 0.25\ \text{M} \quad [Fe^{2+}] = 0.20\ \text{M}$$

WORKED CONCEPTUAL EXAMPLE 17.7

EXPLORING HOW CHANGES IN CONCENTRATIONS AFFECT CELL VOLTAGE

Consider the following galvanic cell:

(a) What is the change in the cell voltage on increasing the ion concentrations in the anode compartment by a factor of 10?

(b) What is the change in the cell voltage on increasing the ion concentrations in the cathode compartment by a factor of 10?

STRATEGY

The direction of electron flow in the picture tells us that lead is the anode and silver is the cathode. Therefore, the cell reaction is $Pb(s) + 2 Ag^+(aq) \rightarrow Pb^{2+}(aq) + 2 Ag(s)$. The cell potential at 25 °C is given by the Nernst equation, where $n = 2$ and $Q = [Pb^{2+}]/[Ag^+]^2$:

$$E = E° - \frac{0.0592 \text{ V}}{n} \log Q$$

$$= E° - \left(\frac{0.0592 \text{ V}}{2}\right)\left(\log \frac{[Pb^{2+}]}{[Ag^+]^2}\right)$$

The change in E on changing the ion concentrations will be determined by the change in the log term in the Nernst equation.

SOLUTION

(a) Pb^{2+} is in the anode compartment, and Ag^+ is in the cathode compartment. Suppose that the original concentrations of Pb^{2+} and Ag^+ are 1 M, so that $E = E°$. Increasing $[Pb^{2+}]$ to 10 M gives

$$E = E° - \left(\frac{0.0592 \text{ V}}{2}\right)\left(\log \frac{(10)}{(1)^2}\right)$$

Because $\log 10 = 1.0$, $E = E° - 0.03$ V. Thus, increasing the Pb^{2+} concentration by a factor of 10 decreases the cell voltage by 0.03 V.

(b) Increasing $[Ag^+]$ to 10 M gives

$$E = E° - \left(\frac{0.0592 \text{ V}}{2}\right)\left(\log \frac{(1)}{(10)^2}\right)$$

Because $\log (10)^{-2} = -2.0$, $E = E° + 0.06$ V. Thus, increasing the Ag^+ concentration by a factor of 10 increases the cell voltage by 0.06 V.

BALLPARK CHECK

We expect that the reaction will have a lesser tendency to occur when the product ion concentration, $[Pb^{2+}]$, is increased and a greater tendency to occur when the reactant ion concentration, $[Ag^+]$, is increased. Therefore, the cell voltage E will decrease when $[Pb^{2+}]$ is increased and will increase when $[Ag^+]$ is increased. The ballpark check and the solution agree.

CONCEPTUAL PROBLEM 17.11   Consider the following galvanic cell:

(a) What is the change in the cell voltage on decreasing the ion concentrations in the anode compartment by a factor of 100?

(b) What is the change in the cell voltage on decreasing the ion concentrations in the cathode compartment by a factor of 100?

17.7   ELECTROCHEMICAL DETERMINATION OF pH

The electrochemical determination of pH using a pH meter is a particularly important application of the Nernst equation. Consider, for example, a cell with a hydrogen electrode as the anode and a second reference electrode as the cathode:

$$Pt\,|\,H_2(1 \text{ atm})\,|\,H^+(? \text{ M})\,||\,\text{Reference cathode}$$

The hydrogen electrode consists of a platinum wire that is in contact with H_2 at 1 atm and dips into a solution of unknown pH. The potential of this cell is

$$E_{cell} = E_{H_2 \rightarrow H^+} + E_{ref}$$

We can calculate the potential for the hydrogen electrode half-reaction

$$H_2(g) \longrightarrow 2\,H^+(aq) + 2\,e^-$$

by applying the Nernst equation to this half-reaction:

$$E_{H_2 \rightarrow H^+} = (E°_{H_2 \rightarrow H^+}) - \left(\frac{0.0592 \text{ V}}{n}\right)\left(\log \frac{[H^+]^2}{P_{H_2}}\right)$$

Since $E° = 0$ V for the standard hydrogen electrode, $n = 2$, and $P_{H_2} = 1$ atm, we can rewrite this equation as

$$E_{H_2 \rightarrow H^+} = -\left(\frac{0.0592 \text{ V}}{2}\right)(\log [H^+]^2)$$

Further, because $\log [H^+]^2 = 2 \log [H^+]$ and $-\log [H^+] = $ pH, the half-cell potential for the hydrogen electrode is directly proportional to the pH:

$$E_{H_2 \rightarrow H^+} = -\left(\frac{0.0592 \text{ V}}{2}\right)(2)(\log [H^+]) = (0.0592 \text{ V})(-\log [H^+])$$

$$= (0.0592 \text{ V})(pH)$$

The overall cell potential is

$$E_{cell} = (0.0592 \text{ V})(pH) + E_{ref}$$

and the pH is therefore a linear function of the cell potential:

$$pH = \frac{E_{cell} - E_{ref}}{0.0592 \text{ V}}$$

Thus, a higher cell potential indicates a higher pH, meaning that we can measure the pH of a solution simply by measuring E_{cell}.

In actual pH measurements, a *glass electrode* replaces the cumbersome hydrogen electrode and a *calomel electrode* is used as the reference. A glass electrode consists of a silver wire coated with silver chloride that dips into a reference solution of dilute hydrochloric acid (**Figure 17.6**). The hydrochloric acid is separated from the test solution of unknown pH by a thin glass membrane. For rugged applications, the exterior of the electrode is made of an epoxy resin, which protects the glass tip. A calomel electrode consists of mercury(I) chloride (Hg_2Cl_2, commonly called calomel) in contact with liquid mercury and aqueous KCl. The cell half-reactions are

$$2 \times [Ag(s) + Cl^-(aq) \longrightarrow AgCl(s) + e^-] \qquad E° = -0.22 \text{ V}$$
$$Hg_2Cl_2(s) + 2\,e^- \longrightarrow 2\,Hg(l) + 2\,Cl^-(aq) \qquad E° = 0.28 \text{ V}$$

The overall cell potential, E_{cell}, depends not only on the potentials of these two half-reactions but also on the boundary potential that develops across the thin glass membrane separating the reference HCl solution from the test solution. Because the boundary potential depends linearly on the difference in the pH of the solutions on the two sides of the membrane, the pH of the test solution can be determined by measuring E_{cell}. The cell potential is measured with a pH meter, a voltage-measuring device that electronically converts E_{cell} to pH and displays the result in pH units.

When a glass electrode is immersed in the test solution, its electrical potential depends linearly on the difference in the pH of the solutions on the two sides of the membrane.

Ag wire coated with AgCl

Reference solution of dilute HCl

Thin glass membrane separating reference solution from test solution of unknown pH

Figure 17.6
A glass electrode consists of a silver wire coated with silver chloride that dips into a reference solution of dilute hydrochloric acid.

WORKED EXAMPLE 17.8

USING THE NERNST EQUATION IN THE ELECTROCHEMICAL DETERMINATION OF pH

The following cell has a potential of 0.55 V at 25 °C:

$$Pt(s)|H_2(1 \text{ atm})|H^+(?\ M)||Cl^-(1\ M)|Hg_2Cl_2(s)|Hg(l)$$

What is the pH of the solution in the anode compartment?

STRATEGY

First, read the shorthand notation to obtain the cell reaction. Then, calculate the half-cell potential for the hydrogen electrode from the observed cell potential and the half-cell potential for the calomel reference electrode. Finally, apply the Nernst equation to find the pH.

SOLUTION

The cell reaction is

$$H_2(g) + Hg_2Cl_2(s) \longrightarrow 2\,H^+(aq) + 2\,Hg(l) + 2\,Cl^-(aq)$$

and the cell potential is

$$E_{cell} = E_{H_2 \rightarrow H^+} + E_{Hg_2Cl_2 \rightarrow Hg} = 0.55 \text{ V}$$

Because the reference electrode is the standard calomel electrode, which has $E = E° = 0.28$ V (Appendix D), the half-cell potential for the hydrogen electrode is 0.27 V:

$$E_{H_2 \rightarrow H^+} = E_{cell} - E_{Hg_2Cl_2 \rightarrow Hg} = 0.55 \text{ V} - 0.28 \text{ V} = 0.27 \text{ V}$$

We can then apply the Nernst equation to the half-reaction $H_2(g) \rightarrow 2\,H^+(aq) + 2\,e^-$:

$$E_{H_2 \rightarrow H^+} = (E°_{H_2 \rightarrow H^+}) - \left(\frac{0.0592 \text{ V}}{n}\right)\left(\log \frac{[H^+]^2}{P_{H_2}}\right)$$

Substituting in the values of E, $E°$, n, and P_{H_2} gives

$$0.27 \text{ V} = (0 \text{ V}) - \left(\frac{0.0592 \text{ V}}{2}\right)\left(\log \frac{[H^+]^2}{1}\right) = (0.0592 \text{ V})(\text{pH})$$

Therefore, the pH is

$$\text{pH} = \frac{0.27 \text{ V}}{0.0592 \text{ V}} = 4.6$$

▶ **PROBLEM 17.12**   What is the pH of the solution in the anode compartment of the following cell if the measured cell potential at 25 °C is 0.28 V?

$$Pt(s)|H_2(1 \text{ atm})|H^+(? \text{ M})||Pb^{2+}(1 \text{ M})|Pb(s)$$

17.8   STANDARD CELL POTENTIALS AND EQUILIBRIUM CONSTANTS

Remember...

The equation $\Delta G° = -RT \ln K$ follows directly from the equation $\Delta G = \Delta G° + RT \ln Q$ because, at equilibrium, $\Delta G = 0$ and $Q = K$.   (Section 16.11)

We saw in Section 17.3 that the standard free-energy change for a reaction is related to the standard cell potential by the equation

$$\Delta G° = -nFE°$$

In addition, we showed in Section 16.11 that the standard free-energy change is also related to the equilibrium constant for the reaction:

$$\Delta G° = -RT \ln K$$

Combining these two equations, we obtain

$$-nFE° = -RT \ln K$$

or

$$E° = \frac{RT}{nF} \ln K = \frac{2.303RT}{nF} \log K$$

Since $2.303 \, RT/F$ has a value of 0.0592 V at 25 °C, we can rewrite this equation in the following simplified form, which relates the standard cell potential and the equilibrium constant for a redox reaction:

$$E° = \frac{0.0592 \text{ V}}{n} \log K \qquad \text{in volts, at 25 °C}$$

Very small concentrations are difficult to measure, so the determination of an equilibrium constant from concentration measurements is not feasible when K is either very large or very small. Standard cell potentials, however, are relatively easy to measure. Consequently, the most common use of this equation is in calculating equilibrium constants from standard cell potentials.

As an example, let's calculate the value of K for the reaction in the Daniell cell:

$$Zn(s) + Cu^{2+}(aq) \longrightarrow Zn^{2+}(aq) + Cu(s) \qquad E° = 1.10 \text{ V}$$

Solving for log K in the equation that relates $E°$ and log K and substituting in the appropriate values of $E°$ and n, we obtain

$$E° = \frac{0.0592 \text{ V}}{n} \log K$$

$$\log K = \frac{nE°}{0.0592 \text{ V}} = \frac{(2)(1.10 \text{ V})}{0.0592 \text{ V}} = 37.2$$

$$K = \text{antilog } 37.2 = 10^{37.2} = 2 \times 10^{37} \qquad \text{at 25 °C}$$

Because $K = [Zn^{2+}]/[Cu^{2+}]$ is a very large number, the reaction goes essentially to completion. When $[Zn^{2+}] = 1$ M, for example, $[Cu^{2+}]$ is less than 10^{-37} M.

The preceding calculation shows that even a relatively small value of $E°$ (+1.10 V) corresponds to a huge value of K (2×10^{37}). A positive value of $E°$ corresponds to a positive value of log K and therefore $K > 1$, and a negative value of $E°$ corresponds to a negative value of log K and therefore $K < 1$. Because the standard reduction potentials in Table 17.1 span a range of about 6 V, $E°$ for a redox reaction can range from +6 V for reaction of the strongest oxidizing agent with the strongest reducing agent to -6 V for reaction of the weakest oxidizing agent with the weakest reducing agent.

However, $E°$ values outside the range $+3$ V to -3 V are uncommon. For the case of $n = 2$, the correspondence between the values of $E°$ and K is indicated in **Figure 17.7**. Equilibrium constants for redox reactions tend to be either very large or very small compared to equilibrium constants for acid–base reactions, which are in the range of 10^{14} to 10^{-14}. Thus, redox reactions typically go either essentially to completion or almost not at all.

Figure 17.7
The relationship between the equilibrium constant K for a redox reaction with $n = 2$ and the standard cell potential $E°$. Note that K is plotted on a logarithmic scale.

In previous chapters, we discussed two different ways to determine the value of an equilibrium constant K: from concentration data (Section 13.2) and from thermochemical data (Section 16.11). In this section, we've added a third way: from electrochemical data. The following are the key relationships needed for each approach:

1. K from concentration data for solutes: $K = \dfrac{[C]^c[D]^d}{[A]^a[B]^b}$

2. K from thermochemical data: $\Delta G° = -RT \ln K; \qquad \ln K = \dfrac{-\Delta G°}{RT}$

3. K from electrochemical data: $E° = \dfrac{RT}{nF} \ln K; \qquad \ln K = \dfrac{nFE°}{RT}$

WORKED EXAMPLE 17.9

USING STANDARD REDUCTION POTENTIALS TO CALCULATE AN EQUILIBRIUM CONSTANT

Use the standard reduction potentials in Table 17.1 to calculate the equilibrium constant at 25 °C for the reaction

$$6\,Br^-(aq) + Cr_2O_7^{2-}(aq) + 14\,H^+(aq) \longrightarrow 3\,Br_2(aq) + 2\,Cr^{3+}(aq) + 7\,H_2O(l)$$

STRATEGY

Calculate $E°$ for the reaction from standard reduction potentials, as in Worked Example 17.5. Then use the equation $\log K = nE°/0.0592$ V to determine the equilibrium constant.

SOLUTION

Find the relevant half-reactions in Table 17.1, and write them in the proper direction for oxidation of Br^- and reduction of $Cr_2O_7^{2-}$. Before adding the half-reactions to get the

continued on next page

overall reaction, multiply the Br^-/Br_2 half-reaction by a factor of 3 so that the electrons will cancel:

$$
\begin{array}{ll}
3 \times [2\,Br^-(aq) \longrightarrow Br_2(aq) + 2\,e^-] & E^\circ = -1.09\ V \\
Cr_2O_7^{2-}(aq) + 14\,H^+(aq) + 6\,e^- \longrightarrow 2\,Cr^{3+}(aq) + 7\,H_2O(l) & E^\circ = \ \ \ 1.36\ V \\
\hline
6\,Br^-(aq) + Cr_2O_7^{2-}(aq) + 14\,H^+(aq) \longrightarrow 3\,Br_2(aq) + 2\,Cr^{3+}(aq) + 7\,H_2O(l) & E^\circ = \ \ \ 0.27\ V
\end{array}
$$

Note that E° for the Br^-/Br_2 oxidation is the negative of the tabulated standard reduction potential (1.09 V), and remember that we don't multiply this E° value by a factor of 3 because electrical potential is an intensive property. The E° value for the overall reaction is the sum of the E° values for the half-reactions: $-1.09\ V + 1.36\ V = 0.27\ V$. To calculate the equilibrium constant, use the relation between $\log K$ and nE°, with $n = 6$:

$$
\log\ K = \frac{nE^\circ}{0.0592\ V} = \frac{(6)(0.27\ V)}{0.0592\ V} = 27 \qquad K = 1 \times 10^{27} \qquad \text{at } 25\ ^\circ C
$$

BALLPARK CHECK

E° is positive, so K should be greater than 1, in agreement with the solution.

▶ **PROBLEM 17.13**   Use the data in Table 17.1 to calculate the equilibrium constant at 25 °C for the reaction

$$4\,Fe^{2+}(aq) + O_2(g) + 4\,H^+(aq) \longrightarrow 4\,Fe^{3+}(aq) + 2\,H_2O(l)$$

▶ **PROBLEM 17.14**   What is the value of E° for a redox reaction involving the transfer of 2 mol of electrons if its equilibrium constant is 1.8×10^{-5}?

17.9   BATTERIES

By far the most important practical application of galvanic cells is their use as *batteries*. In multicell batteries, such as those in automobiles, the individual galvanic cells are linked in series, with the anode of each cell connected to the cathode of the adjacent cell. The voltage provided by the battery is the sum of the individual cell voltages.

The features required in a battery depend on the application. In general, though, a commercially successful battery should be compact, lightweight, physically rugged, and inexpensive, and it must provide a stable source of power for relatively long periods of time. Battery design is an active area of research that requires considerable ingenuity as well as a solid understanding of electrochemistry. Let's look at several of the most common types of commercial batteries.

Lead Storage Battery

The *lead storage battery* is perhaps the most familiar of all galvanic cells because it has been used as a reliable source of power for starting automobiles for nearly a century. A typical 12 V battery consists of six cells connected in series, each cell providing a potential of about 2 V. The cell design is illustrated in **Figure 17.8**. The anode, a series of lead grids packed with spongy lead, and the cathode, a second series of grids packed with lead dioxide, dip into the electrolyte, an aqueous solution of sulfuric acid (38% by weight). When the cell is discharging (providing current) the electrode half-reactions and the overall cell reaction are:

Anode:	$Pb(s) + HSO_4^-(aq) \longrightarrow PbSO_4(s) + H^+(aq) + 2\,e^-$	$E^\circ = 0.296\ V$
Cathode:	$PbO_2(s) + 3\,H^+(aq) + HSO_4^-(aq) + 2\,e^- \longrightarrow PbSO_4(s) + 2\,H_2O(l)$	$E^\circ = 1.628\ V$
Overall:	$Pb(s) + PbO_2(s) + 2\,H^+(aq) + 2\,HSO_4^-(aq) \longrightarrow 2\,PbSO_4(s) + 2\,H_2O(l)$	$E^\circ = 1.924\ V$

Note that these equations contain HSO_4^- ions rather than SO_4^{2-} because SO_4^{2-} is protonated in strongly acidic solutions.

Each electrode consists of several grids with a large surface area so that the battery can deliver the high currents required to start an automobile engine.

$H_2SO_4(aq)$ (electrolyte)

Lead grid packed with spongy lead (anode)

Lead grid packed with PbO_2 (cathode)

Figure 17.8
A lead storage battery and a cutaway view of one cell.

Lead is oxidized to lead sulfate at the anode, and lead dioxide is reduced to lead sulfate at the cathode. The cell doesn't need to have separate anode and cathode compartments because the oxidizing and reducing agents are both solids (PbO_2 and Pb) that are kept from coming in contact by the presence of insulating spacers between the grids.

Because the reaction product, solid $PbSO_4$, adheres to the surface of the electrodes, a run-down lead storage battery can be recharged by using an external source of direct current to drive the cell reaction in the reverse, nonspontaneous direction. In an automobile, the battery is continuously recharged by a device called an *alternator*, which is driven by the engine.

A lead storage battery typically provides good service for several years, but eventually the spongy $PbSO_4$ deposits on the electrodes turn into a hard, crystalline form that can't be converted back to Pb and PbO_2. Then it's no longer possible to recharge the battery and it must be replaced. Because lead is extremely toxic, replaced batteries should be recycled, as is mandated by most states.

Dry-Cell Batteries

The *dry cell*, or *Leclanché cell*, was patented in 1866 by the Frenchman George Leclanché. Used for many years as a power source for flashlights and portable radios, it consists of a zinc metal can, which serves as the anode, and an inert graphite rod surrounded by a paste of solid manganese dioxide and carbon black, which functions as the cathode (**Figure 17.9**). Surrounding the MnO_2-containing paste

Insulator

Graphite rod (cathode)

MnO_2 and carbon black paste

NH_4Cl and $ZnCl_2$ paste (electrolyte)

Zinc metal can (anode)

Figure 17.9
Leclanché dry cell and a cutaway view.

is the electrolyte, a moist paste of ammonium chloride and zinc chloride in starch. A dry cell is not completely dry but gets its name because the electrolyte is a viscous, aqueous paste rather than a liquid solution. The electrode reactions, which are rather complicated, can be represented in simplified form by the following equations:

Anode: $Zn(s) \longrightarrow Zn^{2+}(aq) + 2\,e^-$

Cathode: $2\,MnO_2(s) + 2\,NH_4^+(aq) + 2\,e^- \longrightarrow Mn_2O_3(s) + 2\,NH_3(aq) + H_2O(l)$

The Leclanché cell is largely of historical interest and has been displaced by the *alkaline dry cell*, a modified version in which the acidic NH_4Cl electrolyte of the Leclanché cell is replaced by a basic electrolyte, either NaOH or KOH. As in the Leclanché cell, the electrode reactions involve oxidation of zinc and reduction of manganese dioxide, but the oxidation product is zinc oxide, as is appropriate to the basic conditions:

Anode: $Zn(s) + 2\,OH^-(aq) \longrightarrow ZnO(s) + H_2O(l) + 2\,e^-$

Cathode: $2\,MnO_2(s) + H_2O(l) + 2\,e^- \longrightarrow Mn_2O_3(s) + 2\,OH^-(aq)$

Corrosion of the zinc anode is a significant side reaction under acidic conditions because zinc reacts with $H^+(aq)$ to give $Zn^{2+}(aq)$ and $H_2(g)$. Under basic conditions, however, the cell has a longer life because zinc corrodes more slowly. The alkaline cell also produces higher power and a more stable current and voltage because of more efficient ion transport in the alkaline electrolyte. The voltage of an alkaline cell is about 1.5 V.

Nickel–Cadmium Batteries

Nickel–cadmium, or *"ni–cad," batteries* are popular for use in calculators and portable power tools because, unlike most other dry-cell batteries, they are rechargeable. The anode of a ni–cad battery is cadmium metal, and the cathode is the nickel(III) compound NiO(OH) supported on nickel metal. The electrode reactions are

Anode: $Cd(s) + 2\,OH^-(aq) \longrightarrow Cd(OH)_2(s) + 2\,e^-$

Cathode: $NiO(OH)(s) + H_2O(l) + e^- \longrightarrow Ni(OH)_2(s) + OH^-(aq)$

Ni–cad batteries can be recharged hundreds of times because the solid products of the electrode reactions adhere to the surface of the electrodes.

Nickel–Metal Hydride Batteries

Because cadmium is an expensive, toxic, heavy metal, ni–cad batteries have been replaced in many applications by lighter, more environmentally friendly *nickel–metal hydride*, or *NiMH, batteries* (**Figure 17.10**). An NiMH battery delivers about the same voltage (1.2 V) as a ni–cad battery but has about twice the energy density, the amount of energy stored per unit mass. Though both batteries have the same cathode, they have different anodes. In an NiMH battery, the anode is a special metal alloy, such as $LaNi_5$, that is capable of absorbing and releasing large amounts of hydrogen at ordinary temperatures and pressures. When the cell is discharging, the electrode and overall cell reactions can be written as

Anode: $MH_{ab}(s) + OH^-(aq) \longrightarrow M(s) + H_2O(l) + e^-$

Cathode: $NiO(OH)(s) + H_2O(l) + e^- \longrightarrow Ni(OH)_2(s) + OH^-(aq)$

Overall: $MH_{ab}(s) + NiO(OH)(s) \longrightarrow M(s) + Ni(OH)_2(s)$

Figure 17.10
Rechargeable nickel–metal hydride batteries.

where M represents the hydrogen-absorbing metal alloy and H_{ab} denotes the absorbed hydrogen. Thus, the metal hydride is oxidized at the anode, NiO(OH) is reduced at the cathode, and the overall cell reaction transfers hydrogen from the anode to the cathode with no change in the KOH electrolyte.

NiMH batteries are used in a host of consumer electronic products and also in hybrid gas-electric automobiles, which are powered by both a gasoline engine and an electric motor. Battery packs consisting of many NiMH batteries supply energy to the electric motor and also store energy that is captured on braking. When the brakes are applied, the electric motor acts as a generator and recharges the batteries. Some of the car's kinetic energy, which would otherwise be dissipated as heat, is converted to electrical energy, thus reducing use of the gasoline engine and increasing gas mileage.

Lithium and Lithium-Ion Batteries

Lithium and lithium-ion batteries are even more popular for portable electronic products than nickel-based batteries because of their light weight and high voltage (about 3.0 V). Lithium has a higher $E°$ value for oxidation and a lower atomic mass than any other metal; only 6.94 g of lithium is needed to provide 1 mol of electrons.

Lithium batteries use a lithium metal anode and an electrolyte consisting of a lithium salt, such as $LiClO_4$, in an organic solvent. Most lithium batteries have a manganese dioxide cathode, which can absorb a variable number of Li^+ ions into its solid-state structure. The electrode reactions involve oxidation of lithium at the anode and reduction of MnO_2 at the cathode:

Anode: $x\,Li(s) \longrightarrow x\,Li^+(soln) + x\,e^-$

Cathode: $MnO_2(s) + x\,Li^+(soln) + x\,e^- \longrightarrow Li_xMnO_2(s)$

Li^+ ions migrate through the electrolyte from the anode to the cathode, while electrons move from the anode to the cathode through the external circuit. Lithium batteries are used in watches, calculators, and other small consumer devices.

The distinction between a lithium battery and a lithium-ion battery lies in the nature of the anode. Whereas a lithium battery uses a lithium metal anode, a lithium-ion battery uses a graphite anode that has lithium atoms inserted between its layers of carbon atoms. This so-called lithiated graphite, written as Li_xC_6, contains no lithium metal as such, which is why a lithium-ion battery isn't called a lithium battery. The usual cathode in a lithium-ion battery is CoO_2, another metal oxide that can incorporate Li^+ ions into its structure. The electrolyte is either a solution of a lithium salt in an organic solvent or a solid-state polymer electrolyte that can transport Li^+ ions.

Because an uncharged lithium-ion battery has a graphite anode and a $LiCoO_2$ cathode, the electrode reactions on discharging the battery can be written as

Anode: $Li_xC_6(s) \longrightarrow x\,Li^+(soln) + 6\,C(s) + x\,e^-$

Cathode: $Li_{1-x}CoO_2(s) + x\,Li^+(soln) + x\,e^- \longrightarrow LiCoO_2(s)$

When the battery is charged initially or recharged subsequently, the electrode reactions occur in the reverse direction.

Lithium-ion batteries are used in cell phones, laptop computers, digital cameras, power tools, and in Tesla Motors electric cars. Recent concerns about the possible overheating and explosion of lithium ion batteries are being addressed by the development of alternative electrode materials, such as lithium titanate (Li_2TiO_3) and lithium iron phosphate ($LiFePO_4$), which have greater thermal stability than Li_xC_6 and $LiCoO_2$.

▶ **PROBLEM 17.15** Write a balanced equation for the overall cell reaction when each of the following batteries is producing current:
(a) Leclanché dry cell (b) Alkaline dry cell (c) Nickel–cadmium battery
(d) Lithium battery (e) Lithium-ion battery

17.10 FUEL CELLS

A **fuel cell** is a galvanic cell in which one of the reactants is a fuel such as hydrogen or methanol. Traditional hydrocarbon fuels, such as methane or propane, can't be used directly but must first be converted to hydrogen by the steam–hydrocarbon reforming process described in Section 18.3. A fuel cell differs from an ordinary battery in that the reactants are not contained within the cell but instead are continuously supplied from an external reservoir.

Perhaps the best-known example is the hydrogen–oxygen fuel cell that is used as a source of electric power in space vehicles (**Figure 17.11**). This cell contains porous carbon electrodes impregnated with metallic catalysts and an electrolyte consisting of hot, aqueous KOH. The fuel, gaseous H_2, and the oxidizing agent, gaseous O_2, don't react directly but instead flow into separate cell compartments where H_2 is oxidized at the anode and O_2 is reduced at the cathode. The overall cell reaction is simply the conversion of hydrogen and oxygen to water:

$$\text{Anode:} \qquad 2\,H_2(g) + 4\,OH^-(aq) \longrightarrow 4\,H_2O(l) + 4\,e^-$$
$$\text{Cathode:} \qquad O_2(g) + 2\,H_2O(l) + 4\,e^- \longrightarrow 4\,OH^-(aq)$$
$$\text{Overall:} \qquad 2\,H_2(g) + O_2(g) \longrightarrow 2\,H_2O(l)$$

Figure 17.11
A hydrogen–oxygen fuel cell.

$H_2(g)$ is oxidized to $H_2O(l)$ at the anode.

Anode −

Cathode +

$O_2(g)$ is reduced to $OH^-(aq)$ at the cathode.

H_2 inlet

O_2 inlet

Porous carbon electrodes containing metallic catalysts

H_2O outlet

Hot aqueous KOH

Excess O_2 outlet

The net reaction is the conversion of H_2 and O_2 to water.

In fuel cells designed to power environmentally clean electric vehicles, the aqueous KOH electrolyte is replaced by a special, polymer membrane that conducts protons but not electrons. The electrode and overall cell reactions in these so-called *proton-exchange membrane (PEM) fuel cells* are

$$\text{Anode:} \qquad 2\,H_2(g) \longrightarrow 4\,H^+(aq) + 4\,e^-$$
$$\text{Cathode:} \qquad O_2(g) + 4\,H^+(aq) + 4\,e^- \longrightarrow 2\,H_2O(l)$$
$$\text{Overall:} \qquad 2\,H_2(g) + O_2(g) \longrightarrow 2\,H_2O(l)$$

Protons pass through the membrane from the anode to the cathode, while electrons move through the external circuit from the anode to the cathode, driving an electric motor that powers the vehicle. Because the only reaction product is water, the vehicle itself doesn't produce environmental pollutants or CO_2, although CO_2 is produced in the steam–hydrocarbon reforming process used to obtain hydrogen.

Fuel-cell powered demonstration vehicles have been in existence for several years: Buses have been tested in several North American and European cities, the first fuel-cell powered truck has been delivered to the U.S. Army, and General

Motors has recently unveiled a fuel-cell concept car that accelerates from 0 to 60 mph in 10 s and has a range of 300 mi. Despite these advances and vigorous current research efforts, mass marketing of commercial fuel-cell vehicles that are competitive with internal combustion vehicles is at least a decade away. Among the developments needed for commercialization are improvements in the performance and a decrease in the cost of proton-exchange membranes, development of less expensive catalysts for the electrode reactions, discovery of new and safer methods for onboard storage of hydrogen, and development of a hydrogen-fuel infrastructure.

Consumer applications of fuel cells might also become available in small electronic products, such as cell phones and laptop computers. The cell proposed for use in these products is the *direct methanol fuel cell* (DMFC). It is similar to the PEM fuel cell but uses aqueous methanol (CH_3OH) as the fuel, rather than gaseous hydrogen:

Anode: $2\,CH_3OH(aq) + 2\,H_2O(l) \longrightarrow 2\,CO_2(g) + 12\,H^+(aq) + 12\,e^-$

Cathode: $3\,O_2(g) + 12\,H^+(aq) + 12\,e^- \longrightarrow 6\,H_2O(l)$

Overall: $2\,CH_3OH(aq) + 3\,O_2(g) \longrightarrow 2\,CO_2(g) + 4\,H_2O(l)$

The DMFC is lighter and has a higher energy density than conventional batteries. Moreover, methanol is more available, safer, and easier to store than hydrogen.

Fuel cells are also likely to find use as power generators for hospitals, hotels, and apartment buildings. Indeed, for some time now, the Tokyo Electric Power Company in Japan has been operating an 11 megawatt fuel-cell power plant capable of supplying electricity to about 4000 households.

▸ **PROBLEM 17.16** In what ways are fuel cells and batteries similar, and in what ways are they different?

▸ **PROBLEM 17.17** What is the standard potential for the cell reaction in
(a) the hydrogen–oxygen fuel cell used in space vehicles?
(b) the PEM fuel cell used in electric automobiles?

17.11 CORROSION

Corrosion is the oxidative deterioration of a metal, such as the conversion of iron to rust, a hydrated iron(III) oxide of approximate composition $Fe_2O_3 \cdot H_2O$. The rusting of iron has enormous economic consequences. It has been estimated that as much as one-fourth of the steel produced in the United States goes to replace steel structures and products that have been destroyed by corrosion.

To prevent corrosion, we first have to understand how it occurs. One important fact is that the rusting of iron requires both oxygen and water; it doesn't occur in oxygen-free water or in dry air. Another clue is the observation that rusting involves pitting of the metal surface, but the rust is deposited at a location physically separated from the pits. This suggests that rust does not form by direct reaction of iron and oxygen but rather by an electrochemical process in which iron is oxidized in one region of the surface and oxygen is reduced in another region.

A possible mechanism for rusting, consistent with the known facts, is illustrated in **Figure 17.12**. The surface of the iron and a droplet of surface water constitute a tiny galvanic cell in which different regions of the surface act as anode and cathode while the aqueous phase serves as the electrolyte. Iron is oxidized more readily in some regions (anode regions) than in others (cathode regions) because the composition of the metal is somewhat inhomogeneous and the surface is irregular. Factors such as impurities, phase boundaries, and mechanical stress may influence the ease of oxidation in a particular region of the surface.

At an anode region, iron is oxidized to Fe^{2+} ions,

$$Fe(s) \longrightarrow Fe^{2+}(aq) + 2\,e^- \qquad E° = 0.45\ V$$

while at a cathode region, oxygen is reduced to water:

$$O_2(g) + 4\,H^+(aq) + 4\,e^- \longrightarrow 2\,H_2O(l) \qquad E° = 1.23\ V$$

▲ The steel support column of this bridge has corroded because the iron has been oxidized by moist air, yielding $Fe_2O_3 \cdot H_2O$ (rust).

The metal and a surface water droplet constitute a tiny galvanic cell in which iron is oxidized to Fe^{2+} in a region of the surface (**anode region**) remote from atmospheric O_2, and O_2 is reduced near the edge of the droplet at another region of the surface (**cathode region**).

Water droplet

Rust

Air

O_2

O_2 Fe^{3+}

Dissolved O_2 oxidizes Fe^{2+} further to Fe^{3+} before it is deposited as rust ($Fe_2O_3 \cdot H_2O$).

Fe^{2+}

O_2

Iron metal

Anode region

$Fe \longrightarrow Fe^{2+} + 2\,e^-$

Cathode region

$O_2 + 4\,H^+ + 4\,e^- \longrightarrow 2\,H_2O$

Electrons flow from anode to cathode through the metal, while ions flow through the water droplet.

e^-

Figure 17.12
Why does iron corrode?

The actual potential for the reduction half-reaction is less than the standard potential (1.23 V) because the water droplet is not 1 M in H^+ ions. (In fact, the water is only slightly acidic because the main source of H^+ ions is the reaction of water with dissolved atmospheric carbon dioxide.) Even at pH 7, however, the potential for the reduction half-reaction is 0.81 V, which means that the cell potential is highly positive, indicative of a spontaneous reaction.

The electrons required for reduction of O_2 at the cathode region are supplied by a current that flows through the metal from the more easily oxidized anode region (Figure 17.12). The electrical circuit is completed by migration of ions in the water droplet. When Fe^{2+} ions migrate away from the pitted anode region, they come in contact with O_2 dissolved in the surface portion of the water droplet and are further oxidized to Fe^{3+} ions:

$$4\,Fe^{2+}(aq) + O_2(g) + 4\,H^+(aq) \longrightarrow 4\,Fe^{3+}(aq) + 2\,H_2O(l)$$

Iron(III) forms a very insoluble hydrated oxide even in moderately acidic solutions, and so the iron(III) is deposited as the familiar red-brown material that we call rust:

$$2\,Fe^{3+}(aq) + 4\,H_2O(l) \longrightarrow Fe_2O_3 \cdot H_2O(s) + 6\,H^+(aq)$$
$$\text{Rust}$$

An electrochemical mechanism for corrosion also explains nicely why automobiles rust more rapidly in places where road salt is used to melt snow and ice. Dissolved salts in the water droplet greatly increase the conductivity of the electrolyte, thus accelerating the pace of corrosion.

A glance at a table of standard reduction potentials indicates that the O_2/H_2O half-reaction lies above the M^{n+}/M half-reaction for nearly all metals, so O_2 can oxidize all metals except a few, such as gold and platinum. Aluminum, for example, has $E^\circ = -1.66$ V for the Al^{3+}/Al half-reaction and is oxidized more readily than iron. In other words, the corrosion of aluminum products such as aircraft and automobile parts, window frames, cooking utensils, and soda cans should be a serious problem. Fortunately, it isn't, because oxidation of aluminum gives a very hard, almost impenetrable film of Al_2O_3 that adheres to the surface of the metal and protects it from further contact and reaction with oxygen. Other metals such as magnesium, chromium, titanium, and zinc form similar protective oxide coatings. In the case of iron, however, rust is too porous to shield the underlying metal from further oxidation.

▲ This titanium bicycle doesn't corrode because of a hard, impenetrable layer of TiO_2 that adheres to the surface and protects the metal from further oxidation.

Prevention of Corrosion

Corrosion of iron can be prevented, or at least minimized, by shielding the metal surface from oxygen and moisture. A coat of paint is effective for a while, but rust begins to form as soon as the paint is scratched or chipped. Metals such as chromium, tin, or zinc afford a more durable surface coating for iron. The steel used in making automobiles, for example, is coated by dipping it into a bath of molten zinc, a process known as **galvanizing**. As the potentials indicate, zinc is oxidized more easily than iron, and therefore, when the metal corrodes, zinc is oxidized instead of iron. Any incipient oxidation of iron would be reversed immediately because Zn can reduce Fe^{2+} to Fe. As long as the zinc and iron are in contact, the zinc protects the iron from oxidation even if the zinc layer becomes scratched (**Figure 17.13**).

$$Fe^{2+}(aq) + 2\,e^- \longrightarrow Fe(s) \qquad E° = -0.45\text{ V}$$
$$Zn^{2+}(aq) + 2\,e^- \longrightarrow Zn(s) \qquad E° = -0.76\text{ V}$$

The zinc (**anode**), iron (**cathode**), and water droplet (**electrolyte**) constitute a tiny galvanic cell.

Air

Water droplet

O_2

Scratch in zinc layer

Zn^{2+}

Zinc metal

Zinc (anode) $Zn \longrightarrow Zn^{2+} + 2\,e^-$

e^-

Iron (cathode)

Iron metal

$O_2 + 4\,H^+ + 4\,e^- \longrightarrow 2\,H_2O$

Oxygen is reduced at the cathode, and zinc is oxidized at the anode, thus protecting the iron from oxidation.

Figure 17.13
Galvanized iron. A layer of zinc protects iron from oxidation, even when the zinc layer becomes scratched.

The technique of protecting a metal from corrosion by connecting it to a second metal that is more easily oxidized is called **cathodic protection**. It's unnecessary to cover the entire surface of the metal with a second metal, as in galvanizing iron. All that's required is electrical contact with the second metal. An underground steel pipeline, for example, can be protected by connecting it through an insulated wire to a stake of magnesium, which acts as a *sacrificial anode* and corrodes instead of the iron. In effect, the arrangement is a galvanic cell in which the easily oxidized magnesium acts as the anode, the pipeline behaves as the cathode, and moist soil is the electrolyte. The cell half-reactions are

Anode: $Mg(s) \longrightarrow Mg^{2+}(aq) + 2\,e^-$ $\qquad E° = 2.37\text{ V}$
Cathode: $O_2(g) + 4\,H^+(aq) + 4\,e^- \longrightarrow 2\,H_2O(l)$ $\qquad E° = 1.23\text{ V}$

For large steel structures such as pipelines, storage tanks, bridges, and ships, cathodic protection is the best defense against premature rusting.

▶ **PROBLEM 17.18** Magnesium is often attached to the steel hulls of ships to protect the steel from rusting. Write balanced equations for the corrosion reactions that occur **(a)** in the presence of Mg and **(b)** in the absence of Mg.

17.12 ELECTROLYSIS AND ELECTROLYTIC CELLS

Thus far, we've been concerned only with galvanic cells—electrochemical cells in which a spontaneous redox reaction produces an electric current. A second important kind of electrochemical cell is the electrolytic cell, in which an electric current is used to drive a nonspontaneous reaction. Thus, the processes occurring in galvanic and electrolytic cells are the reverse of each other: A galvanic cell converts chemical energy to electrical energy when a reaction with a positive value of E (and a negative value of ΔG) proceeds toward equilibrium; an electrolytic cell converts electrical energy to chemical energy when an electric current drives a reaction with a negative value of E (and a positive value of ΔG) in a direction away from equilibrium.

The process of using an electric current to bring about chemical change is called **electrolysis**. The opposite signs of E and $\Delta G = -nFE$ for the two kinds of cells are summarized in Table 17.2, along with the situation for a reaction that has reached equilibrium—a dead battery!

TABLE 17.2   Relationship between Cell Potentials E and Free-Energy Changes ΔG

Reaction Type	E	ΔG	Cell Type
Spontaneous	+	−	Galvanic
Nonspontaneous	−	+	Electrolytic
Equilibrium	0	0	Dead battery

Electrolysis of Molten Sodium Chloride

An electrolytic cell has two electrodes that dip into an electrolyte and are connected to a battery or some other source of direct electric current. A cell for electrolysis of molten sodium chloride, for example, is illustrated in **Figure 17.14**. The battery serves as an electron pump, pushing electrons into one electrode and pulling them out of the other. The negative electrode attracts Na^+ cations, which combine with the electrons supplied by the battery and are thereby reduced to liquid sodium metal. Similarly, the positive electrode attracts Cl^- anions, which replenish the electrons removed by the battery and are thereby oxidized to chlorine gas. The electrode reactions and overall cell reaction are

Anode (oxidation): $2\,Cl^-(l) \longrightarrow Cl_2(g) + 2\,e^-$

Cathode (reduction): $2\,Na^+(l) + 2\,e^- \longrightarrow 2\,Na(l)$

Overall cell reaction: $2\,Na^+(l) + 2\,Cl^-(l) \longrightarrow 2\,Na(l) + Cl_2(g)$

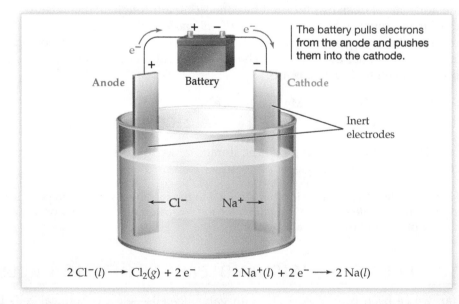

Figure 17.14
Electrolysis of molten sodium chloride. Chloride ions are oxidized to Cl_2 gas at the anode, and Na^+ ions are reduced to sodium metal at the cathode.

As in a galvanic cell, the anode is the electrode where oxidation takes place and the cathode is the electrode where reduction takes place. The signs of the electrodes, however, are opposite for galvanic and electrolytic cells. In a galvanic cell, the anode is considered to be negative because it supplies electrons to the external circuit, but in an electrolytic cell, the anode is considered to be positive because electrons are pulled out of it by the battery. The sign of each electrode in the electrolytic cell is the same as the sign of the battery electrode to which it is attached.

Electrolysis of Aqueous Sodium Chloride

When an aqueous salt solution is electrolyzed, the electrode reactions may differ from those for electrolysis of the molten salt because water may be involved. In the electrolysis of aqueous sodium chloride, for example, the cathode half-reaction might be either the reduction of Na^+ to sodium metal, as in the case of molten sodium chloride, or the reduction of water to hydrogen gas:

$$Na^+(aq) + e^- \longrightarrow Na(s) \qquad E° = -2.71 \text{ V}$$
$$2 H_2O(l) + 2 e^- \longrightarrow H_2(g) + 2 OH^-(aq) \qquad E° = -0.83 \text{ V}$$

Because the standard potential is much less negative for the reduction of water than for the reduction of Na^+, water is reduced preferentially and bubbles of hydrogen gas are produced at the cathode.

The anode half-reaction might be either oxidation of Cl^- to Cl_2 gas, as in the case of molten sodium chloride, or oxidation of water to oxygen gas:

$$2 Cl^-(aq) \longrightarrow Cl_2(g) + 2 e^- \qquad E° = -1.36 \text{ V}$$
$$2 H_2O(l) \longrightarrow O_2(g) + 4 H^+(aq) + 4 e^- \qquad E° = -1.23 \text{ V}$$

Based on the $E°$ values, we might expect a slight preference for oxidation of water in a solution having 1 M ion concentrations. For a neutral solution ($[H^+] = 10^{-7}$ M), the preference for water oxidation will be even greater because its oxidation potential at pH 7 is -0.81 V. The observed product at the anode, however, is Cl_2, not O_2, because of a phenomenon called *overvoltage*.

Experiments indicate that the applied voltage required for an electrolysis is always greater than the voltage calculated from standard oxidation and reduction potentials. The additional voltage required is the **overvoltage**. The overvoltage is needed because the rate of electron transfer at the electrode–solution interface for one or both of the cell half-reactions is often slow, thus limiting the amount of current that passes through an electrolytic cell. For electrode half-reactions involving solution or deposition of metals, the overvoltage is quite small, but for half-reactions involving formation of O_2 (or H_2) gas, the overvoltage can be as large as 1 V. Present theory is unable to predict the magnitude of the overvoltage, but it's known that the overvoltage for the formation of O_2 is much larger than that for the formation of Cl_2. Because of overvoltage, it's sometimes difficult to predict which half-reaction will occur when $E°$ values for the competing half-reactions are similar. In such cases, only experiment can tell what actually happens.

The observed electrode reactions and overall cell reaction for electrolysis of aqueous sodium chloride are

Anode (oxidation):	$2 Cl^-(aq) \longrightarrow Cl_2(g) + 2 e^-$	$E° = -1.36 \text{ V}$
Cathode (reduction):	$2 H_2O(l) + 2 e^- \longrightarrow H_2(g) + 2 OH^-(aq)$	$E° = -0.83 \text{ V}$
Overall cell reaction:	$2 Cl^-(aq) + 2 H_2O(l) \longrightarrow Cl_2(g) + H_2(g) + 2 OH^-(aq)$	$E° = -2.19 \text{ V}$

Sodium ion acts as a spectator ion and is not involved in the electrode reactions. Thus, the sodium chloride solution is converted to a sodium hydroxide solution as the electrolysis proceeds. The minimum potential required to force this non-spontaneous reaction to occur under standard-state conditions is 2.19 V plus the overvoltage.

Electrolysis of Water

The electrolysis of any aqueous solution requires the presence of an electrolyte to carry the current in solution. If the ions of the electrolyte are less easily oxidized and reduced than water, however, then water will react at both electrodes. Consider, for example, the electrolysis of an aqueous solution of the inert electrolyte Na_2SO_4.

Water is oxidized at the anode in preference to SO_4^{2-} ions and is reduced at the cathode in preference to Na^+ ions. The electrode and overall cell reactions are

Anode (oxidation):
$$2\,H_2O(l) \longrightarrow O_2(g) + 4\,H^+(aq) + 4\,e^-$$

Cathode (reduction):
$$4\,H_2O(l) + 4\,e^- \longrightarrow 2\,H_2(g) + 4\,OH^-(aq)$$

Overall cell reaction:
$$6\,H_2O(l) \longrightarrow 2\,H_2(g) + O_2(g) + 4\,H^+(aq) + 4\,OH^-(aq)$$

If the anode and cathode solutions are mixed, the H^+ and OH^- ions react to form water:

$$4\,H^+(aq) + 4\,OH^-(aq) \longrightarrow 4\,H_2O(l)$$

The net electrolysis reaction is therefore the decomposition of water, a process sometimes used in the laboratory to produce small amounts of pure H_2 and O_2:

$$2\,H_2O(l) \longrightarrow 2\,H_2(g) + O_2(g)$$

CONCEPTUAL PROBLEM 17.19   Metallic potassium was first prepared by Humphrey Davy in 1807 by electrolysis of molten potassium hydroxide:

(a) Label the anode and cathode, and show the direction of ion flow.
(b) Write balanced equations for the anode, cathode, and overall cell reactions.

▶ **PROBLEM 17.20**   Predict the half-cell reactions that occur when aqueous solutions of the following salts are electrolyzed in a cell with inert electrodes. What is the overall cell reaction in each case?
   (a) LiCl   (b) $CuSO_4$ (c) K_2SO_4

17.13   COMMERCIAL APPLICATIONS OF ELECTROLYSIS

Electrolysis is used in the manufacture of many important chemicals and in numerous processes for purification and electroplating of metals. Let's look at some examples.

Manufacture of Sodium

Sodium metal is produced commercially in a *Downs cell* by electrolysis of a molten mixture of sodium chloride and calcium chloride (**Figure 17.15**). The presence of $CaCl_2$ allows the cell to be operated at a lower temperature because the melting point of the $NaCl$–$CaCl_2$ mixture (about 580 °C) is depressed well below that of pure NaCl (801 °C). The liquid sodium produced at the cylindrical steel cathode is less dense than the molten salt and thus floats to the top part of the cell, where it is drawn off into a suitable container. Chlorine gas forms at the graphite anode, which is separated from the cathode by an iron screen to keep the highly reactive sodium and chlorine away from each other. Because the Downs process requires high currents (typically 25,000–40,000 A), plants for producing sodium are located near sources of inexpensive hydroelectric power, such as Niagara Falls, New York.

Figure 17.15
Cross-sectional view of a Downs cell for commercial production of sodium metal by electrolysis of molten sodium chloride. The cell design keeps the sodium and chlorine apart from each other and out of contact with air.

Manufacture of Chlorine and Sodium Hydroxide

Production of chlorine and sodium hydroxide by electrolysis of aqueous sodium chloride is the basis of the *chlor-alkali industry*, a business that generates annual sales of approximately $4 billion in the United States alone. Annual U.S. production is about 8 million metric tons for chlorine and 6 million metric tons for sodium hydroxide. Chlorine is used in water and sewage treatment, as a bleaching agent in manufacturing paper, and in the manufacture of plastics such as poly(vinyl chloride) (PVC). Sodium hydroxide is employed in making paper, textiles, soaps, and detergents.

Figure 17.16 shows the essential features of a membrane cell for commercial production of chlorine and sodium hydroxide. A saturated aqueous solution of sodium chloride (*brine*) flows into the anode compartment, where Cl^- is oxidized to Cl_2 gas,

Sodium ions move from the anode compartment to the cathode compartment through a cation-permeable membrane and then flow out of the cell as an aqueous solution of NaOH.

Figure 17.16
A membrane cell for electrolytic production of Cl_2 and NaOH. Chloride ion is oxidized to Cl_2 gas at the anode, and water is converted to H_2 gas and OH^- ions at the cathode.

and water enters the cathode compartment, where it is converted to H_2 gas and OH^- ions. Between the anode and cathode compartments is a special polymer membrane that is permeable to cations but not to anions or water. The membrane keeps the Cl_2 and OH^- ions apart but allows a current of Na^+ ions to flow into the cathode compartment, thus carrying the current in the solution and maintaining electrical neutrality in both compartments. The Na^+ and OH^- ions flow out of the cathode compartment as an aqueous solution of NaOH.

Manufacture of Aluminum

Although aluminum is the third most abundant element in the Earth's crust at 8.23% by mass, it remained a rare and expensive metal until 1886, when a 22-year-old American, Charles Martin Hall, and a 23-year-old Frenchman, Paul Heroult, independently devised a practical process for the electrolytic production of aluminum. Still used today, the **Hall–Heroult process** involves electrolysis of a molten mixture of aluminum oxide (Al_2O_3) and cryolite (Na_3AlF_6) at about 1000 °C in a cell with graphite electrodes (**Figure 17.17**). Electrolysis of pure Al_2O_3 is impractical because it melts at a very high temperature (2045 °C), and electrolysis of aqueous Al^{3+} solutions is not feasible because water is reduced in preference to Al^{3+} ions. Thus, the use of cryolite as a solvent for Al_2O_3 is the key to the success of the Hall–Heroult process.

Figure 17.17
An electrolytic cell for production of aluminum by the Hall–Heroult process.

Because molten aluminum is more dense than the Al_2O_3–Na_3AlF_6 mixture, it collects at the bottom of the cell and is drawn off periodically.

The electrode reactions are still not fully understood, but they probably involve complex anions of the type $AlF_xO_y^{+3-x-2y}$, formed by the reaction of Al_2O_3 and Na_3AlF_6. The complex anions are reduced at the cathode to molten aluminum metal and are oxidized at the anode to O_2 gas, which reacts with the graphite anodes to give CO_2 gas. As a result, the anodes are chewed up rapidly and must be replaced frequently. The cell operates at a low voltage (5−6 V) but with very high currents (up to 250,000 A) because 1 mol of electrons produces only 9.0 g of aluminum. Electrolytic production of aluminum is the largest single consumer of electricity in the United States, making recycling of aluminum products highly desirable. As with the manufacture of sodium, aluminum production generally takes place near hydroelectric plants, such as those along the Columbia River in Washington.

Electrorefining and Electroplating

The purification of a metal by means of electrolysis is called **electrorefining**. For example, impure copper obtained from ores is converted to pure copper in an electrolytic cell that has impure copper as the anode and pure copper as the cathode (**Figure 17.18**). The electrolyte is an aqueous solution of copper sulfate.

At the impure Cu anode, copper is oxidized along with more easily oxidized metallic impurities such as zinc and iron. Less easily oxidized impurities such as silver, gold, and platinum fall to the bottom of the cell as *anode mud*, which is reprocessed to recover the precious metals. At the pure Cu cathode, Cu^{2+} ions are

Copper is transferred through the $CuSO_4$ solution from the impure Cu anode to the pure Cu cathode.

Alternating slabs of impure copper and pure copper serve as the electrodes in electrolytic cells for the refining of copper.

Noble metal impurities (Ag, Au, Pt) are not oxidized and collect as anode mud.

More easily oxidized impurities (Zn, Fe) remain in solution as cations.

Figure 17.18
Electrorefining of copper metal.

reduced to pure copper metal, but the less easily reduced metal ions (Zn^{2+}, Fe^{2+}, and so forth) remain in the solution.

Anode (oxidation):	$M(s) \longrightarrow M^{2+}(aq) + 2\,e^-$ (M = Cu, Zn, Fe)
Cathode (reduction):	$Cu^{2+}(aq) + 2\,e^- \longrightarrow Cu(s)$

Thus, the net cell reaction simply transfers copper metal from the impure anode to the pure cathode. The copper obtained by this process is 99.95% pure.

Closely related to electrorefining is **electroplating**, the coating of one metal on the surface of another using electrolysis. For example, steel motorcycle parts are often plated with chromium to protect them from corrosion, and silver-plating is commonly used to make items of fine table service. The object to be plated is carefully cleaned and then set up as the cathode of an electrolytic cell that contains a solution of ions of the metal to be deposited.

▶ **PROBLEM 17.21**   Sketch an electrolytic cell suitable for electroplating a silver spoon. Describe the electrodes and the electrolyte, label the anode and cathode, and indicate the direction of electron and ion flow. Write balanced equations for the anode and cathode half-reactions. What is the overall cell reaction?

▲ Silver-plated objects such as this teapot are made by electroplating pure silver metal onto steel.

17.14   QUANTITATIVE ASPECTS OF ELECTROLYSIS

In the 1830s, Michael Faraday showed that the amount of substance produced at an electrode by electrolysis depends on the quantity of charge passed through the cell. For example, passing 1 mol of electrons through a Downs cell yields 1 mol (23.0 g) of sodium at the cathode:

$$Na^+(l) + e^- \longrightarrow Na(l)$$

1 mol   1 mol   1 mol (23.0 g)

Similarly, passing 1 mol of electrons in the Hall–Heroult process produces 1/3 mol (9.0 g) of aluminum, because 3 mol of electrons are required to reduce 1 mol of Al^{3+} to aluminum metal:

$$Al^{3+}(l) + 3\,e^- \longrightarrow Al(l)$$

1/3 mol   1 mol   1/3 mol (9.0 g)

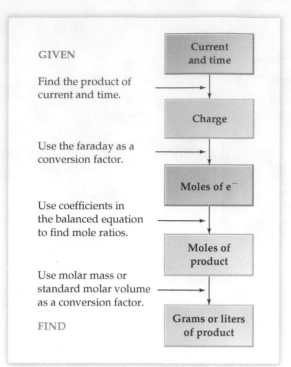

Figure 17.19
Sequence of conversions used to calculate the amount of product produced by passing a current through an electrolytic cell for a fixed period of time.

In general, the amount of product formed in an electrode reaction follows directly from the stoichiometry of the reaction and the molar mass of the product.

To find out how many moles of electrons pass through a cell in a particular experiment, we need to measure the electric current and the time that the current flows. The number of coulombs of charge passed through the cell equals the product of the current in amperes (coulombs per second) and the time in seconds:

$$\text{Charge (C)} = \text{Current (A)} \times \text{Time (s)}$$

Because the charge on 1 mol of electrons is 96,500 C (Section 17.3), the number of moles of electrons passed through the cell is

$$\text{Moles of e}^- = \text{Charge (C)} \times \frac{1 \text{ mol e}^-}{96,500 \text{ C}}$$

The sequence of conversions in **Figure 17.19** is used to calculate the mass or volume of product produced by passing a known current through a cell for a fixed period of time. The key is to think of the electrons as a reactant in a balanced chemical equation and then to proceed as with any other stoichiometry problem. Worked Example 17.10 illustrates the calculations. Alternatively, we can calculate the current (or time) required to produce a given amount of product by working through the sequence in Figure 17.19 in the reverse direction, as shown in Worked Example 17.11.

WORKED EXAMPLE 17.10

CALCULATING THE AMOUNT OF PRODUCT PRODUCED BY ELECTROLYSIS

A constant current of 30.0 A is passed through an aqueous solution of NaCl for 1.00 h. How many grams of NaOH and how many liters of Cl_2 gas at STP are produced?

STRATEGY

To convert the current and time to grams or liters of product, carry out the sequence of conversions in Figure 17.19.

SOLUTION

Because electrons can be thought of as a reactant in the electrolysis process, the first step is to calculate the charge and the number of moles of electrons passed through the cell:

$$\text{Charge} = \left(30.0\,\frac{C}{s}\right)(1.00\text{ h})\left(\frac{60\text{ min}}{h}\right)\left(\frac{60\text{ s}}{\text{min}}\right) = 1.08 \times 10^5\,C$$

$$\text{Moles of e}^- = (1.08 \times 10^5\,C)\left(\frac{1\text{ mol e}^-}{96,500\text{ C}}\right) = 1.12\text{ mol e}^-$$

The cathode reaction yields 2 mol of OH^- per 2 mol of electrons (Section 17.12), so 1.12 mol of NaOH will be obtained:

$$2\,H_2O(l) + 2\,e^- \longrightarrow H_2(g) + 2\,OH^-(aq)$$

$$\text{Moles of NaOH} = (1.12\text{ mol e}^-)\left(\frac{2\text{ mol NaOH}}{2\text{ mol e}^-}\right) = 1.12\text{ mol NaOH}$$

Converting the number of moles of NaOH to grams of NaOH gives

$$\text{Grams of NaOH} = (1.12\text{ mol NaOH})\left(\frac{40.0\text{ g NaOH}}{\text{mol NaOH}}\right) = 44.8\text{ g NaOH}$$

The anode reaction gives 1 mol of Cl_2 per 2 mol of electrons, so 0.560 mol of Cl_2 will be obtained:

$$2 \, Cl^-(aq) \longrightarrow Cl_2(g) + 2 \, e^-$$

$$\text{Moles of } Cl_2 = (1.12 \text{ mol } e^-)\left(\frac{1 \text{ mol } Cl_2}{2 \text{ mol } e^-}\right) = 0.560 \text{ mol } Cl_2$$

Since 1 mol of an ideal gas occupies 22.4 L at STP, the volume of Cl_2 obtained is

$$\text{Litres of } Cl_2 = (0.560 \text{ mol } Cl_2)\left(\frac{22.4 \text{ L } Cl_2}{\text{mol } Cl_2}\right) = 12.5 \text{ L } Cl_2$$

As a shortcut, the entire sequence of conversions can be carried out in one step. For example, the volume of Cl_2 produced at the anode is

$$\left(30.0 \, \frac{C}{s}\right)(1.00 \text{ h})\left(\frac{3600 \text{ s}}{h}\right)\left(\frac{1 \text{ mol } e^-}{96,500 \text{ C}}\right)\left(\frac{1 \text{ mol } Cl_2}{2 \text{ mol } e^-}\right)\left(\frac{22.4 \text{ L } Cl_2}{\text{mol } Cl_2}\right) = 12.5 \text{ L } Cl_2$$

BALLPARK CHECK

Since approximately 1 mol of electrons is passed through the cell and the electrode reactions yield 1 mol of NaOH and 0.5 mol of Cl_2 per mole of electrons, 1 mol of NaOH (~40 g) and 0.5 mol of Cl_2 (~11 L at STP) will be formed. The ballpark check and the solution agree.

WORKED EXAMPLE 17.11

CALCULATING THE CURRENT REQUIRED TO PRODUCE A GIVEN AMOUNT OF PRODUCT IN A GIVEN TIME

How many amperes must be passed through a Downs cell to produce sodium metal at a rate of 30.0 kg/h?

STRATEGY

Proceed through a sequence of conversions similar to that in Worked Example 17.10, but in reverse order.

SOLUTION

Because the molar mass of sodium is 23.0 g/mol, the number of moles of sodium produced per hour is

$$\text{Moles of Na} = (30.0 \text{ kg Na})\left(\frac{1000 \text{ g}}{1 \text{ kg}}\right)\left(\frac{1 \text{ mol Na}}{23.0 \text{ g Na}}\right) = 1.30 \times 10^3 \text{ mol Na}$$

To produce each mole of sodium, 1 mol of electrons must be passed through the cell:

$$Na^+(l) + e^- \longrightarrow Na(l)$$

Therefore, the charge passed per hour is

$$\text{Charge} = (1.30 \times 10^3 \text{ mol Na})\left(\frac{1 \text{ mol } e^-}{1 \text{ mol Na}}\right)\left(\frac{96,500 \text{ C}}{\text{mol } e^-}\right) = 1.25 \times 10^8 \text{ C}$$

Since there are 3600 s in 1 h, the current required is

$$\text{Current} = \frac{1.25 \times 10^8 \text{ C}}{3600 \text{ s}} = 3.47 \times 10^4 \text{ C/s} = 34,700 \text{ A}$$

▶ **PROBLEM 17.22**   How many kilograms of aluminum can be produced in 8.00 h by passing a constant current of 1.00×10^5 A through a molten mixture of aluminum oxide and cryolite?

▶ **PROBLEM 17.23**   A layer of silver is electroplated on a coffee server using a constant current of 0.100 A. How much time is required to deposit 3.00 g of silver?

INQUIRY WHY ARE SOME METAL OBJECTS BRIGHTLY COLORED?

▲ Anodized aluminum sports bottles.

If you're like many people, you may have used a brightly colored aluminum sports bottle. These bottles are lightweight, inexpensive, and impart no taste or odor to their contents. Or perhaps you know someone who has had a total joint replacement. If so, the titanium screws used to implant the artificial joint may have been colored because color coding of the components of orthopedic implants increases efficiency and accuracy during surgery. Given that aluminum and titanium are silvery metals, how do aluminum and titanium objects become brightly colored?

Aluminum, titanium, and several other metals can be colored by an electrochemical process called *anodizing*. Unlike electroplating, in which a metal ion in the electrolyte is *reduced* and the metal is coated onto the surface of the cathode, anodizing *oxidizes* a metal anode to yield a metal oxide coating. In the oxidation of aluminum, for instance, the electrode reactions are

Cathode (reduction):	$6\,H^+(aq) + 6\,e^- \longrightarrow 3\,H_2(g)$
Anode (oxidation):	$2\,Al(s) + 3\,H_2O(l) \longrightarrow Al_2O_3(s) + 6\,H^+(aq) + 6\,e^-$
Overall cell reaction:	$2\,Al(s) + 3\,H_2O(l) \longrightarrow Al_2O_3(s) + 3\,H_2(g)$

The thickness of the aluminum oxide coating that forms on the anode can be controlled by varying the current flow curing the electrolysis. Typically, the coating is about 0.01 mm thick, which corresponds to about 4×10^4 atomic layers of Al_2O_3 on top of the underlying aluminum metal. The porosity of the coating can also be controlled by varying the electrochemical conditions, and it's this porosity that makes coloring possible. When an organic dye is added to the electrolyte, dye molecules soak into the spongy surface coating as it forms and become trapped when the surface hardens. A broad range of dyes is available, so anodized aluminum objects like water bottles, bicycle parts, and key chains come in a wide variety of colors.

Titanium anodizing proceeds much like that of aluminum, but the resultant coat of TiO_2 is much thinner (10^{-4} mm) than the corresponding coat of Al_2O_3 (10^{-2} mm). Furthermore, the iridescent colors of anodized titanium result not from the absorption of organic dyes but from the interference of light as it is reflected by the anodized surface. When a beam of white light strikes the anodized surface, part of the light is reflected from the outer TiO_2, while part penetrates through the semitransparent TiO_2 and is reflected from the inner metal. If the two reflections of a particular wavelength are out of phase, they interfere destructively and that wavelength is canceled from the reflected light. As a result, the light that remains is colored. Similar effects are responsible for the diffraction of X-rays (Section 10.7).

▲ Anodized titanium medical implant components such as bone screws are color coded to assist the surgeon during surgery.

Anodized titanium is particularly useful for biomedical applications because bone cells adhere to the microscopically rough surface of the TiO_2 coating about 10 times better than they do to the smooth surface of bare titanium metal, thus hastening the integration of the implant into the body. Moreover, postoperative infections, which occur in up to 4% of total joint replacements, can be minimized by incorporating antibiotics into the rough surface of the TiO_2 coating. Locating antibiotics at the site of the implant is more effective than administering them either orally or intravenously.

▶ **PROBLEM 17.24** What is the overall cell reaction and cell potential for anodizing titanium if the anode half-reaction is

$$Ti(s) + 2\,H_2O(l) \longrightarrow TiO_2(s) + 4\,H^+(aq) + 4\,e^- \qquad E° = +1.066\ V$$

▶ **PROBLEM 17.25** How many minutes are required to produce a 0.0100 mm thick coating of Al_2O_3 (density 3.97 g/cm^3) on a square piece of aluminum metal 10.0 cm on an edge if the current passed through the piece is 0.600 A?

SUMMARY

Electrochemistry is the area of chemistry concerned with the interconversion of chemical and electrical energy. Chemical energy is converted to electrical energy in a **galvanic cell**, a device in which a spontaneous redox reaction is used to produce an electric current. Electrical energy is converted to chemical energy in an **electrolytic cell**, a cell in which an electric current drives a nonspontaneous reaction. It's convenient to separate cell reactions into half-reactions because oxidation and reduction occur at separate **electrodes**. The electrode at which oxidation occurs is called the **anode**, and the electrode at which reduction occurs is called the **cathode**.

The **cell potential** E (also called the **cell voltage** or **electromotive force**) is an electrical measure of the cell reaction's tendency to occur. Cell potentials depend on temperature, ion concentrations, and gas pressures. The **standard cell potential $E°$** is the cell potential when reactants and products are in their standard states. Cell potentials are related to free-energy changes by the equations $\Delta G = -nFE$ and $\Delta G° = -nFE°$, where n is the number of moles of electrons transferred in the cell reaction and $F = 96,500$ C/ mol e^- is the **faraday**, the charge on 1 mol of electrons.

The **standard reduction potential** for a half-reaction is defined relative to an arbitrary value of 0 V for the **standard hydrogen electrode (S.H.E.)**:

$$2\,H^+(aq, 1\,M) + 2\,e^- \longrightarrow H_2(g, 1\,atm) \qquad E° = 0\,V$$

Tables of standard reduction potentials—also called **standard electrode potentials**—are used to arrange oxidizing and reducing agents in order of increasing strength, to calculate $E°$ values for cell reactions, and to decide whether a particular redox reaction is spontaneous.

Cell potentials under nonstandard-state conditions can be calculated using the **Nernst equation**,

$$E = E° - \frac{0.0592\,V}{n} \log Q \qquad \text{in volts, at 25 °C}$$

where Q is the reaction quotient. The equilibrium constant K and the standard cell potential $E°$ are related by the equation

$$E° = \frac{0.0592\,V}{n} \log K \qquad \text{in volts, at 25 °C}$$

A **battery** consists of one or more galvanic cells. A **fuel cell** differs from a battery in that the reactants are continuously supplied to the cell.

Corrosion of iron (rusting) is an electrochemical process in which iron is oxidized in an anode region of the metal surface and oxygen is reduced in a cathode region. Corrosion can be prevented by covering iron with another metal, such as zinc in the process called **galvanizing**, or simply by putting the iron in electrical contact with a second metal that is more easily oxidized, a process called **cathodic protection**.

Electrolysis, the process of using an electric current to bring about chemical change, is employed to produce sodium, chlorine, sodium hydroxide, and aluminum (**Hall–Heroult process**) and is used in **electrorefining** and **electroplating**.

The product obtained at an electrode depends on the reduction potentials and **overvoltage**. The amount of product obtained is related to the number of moles of electrons passed through the cell, which depends on the current and the time that the current flows.

KEY WORDS

CONCEPTUAL PROBLEMS

Problems 17.1–17.25 appear within the chapter.

17.26 The following picture of a galvanic cell has lead and zinc electrodes:

(a) Label the electrodes, and identify the ions present in the solutions.

(b) Label the anode and cathode.

(c) Indicate the direction of electron flow in the wire and ion flow in the solutions.

(d) Tell what electrolyte could be used in the salt bridge, and indicate the direction of ion flow.

(e) Write balanced equations for the electrode and overall cell reactions.

17.27 Consider the following galvanic cell:

(a) Identify the anode and cathode.

(b) Write a balanced equation for the cell reaction.

(c) Write the shorthand notation for the cell.

17.28 Consider the following galvanic cells:

(1) $Cu(s)|Cu^{2+}(1\ M)||Fe^{3+}(1\ M), Fe^{2+}(1\ M)|Pt(s)$

(2) $Cu(s)|Cu^{2+}(1\ M)||Fe^{3+}(1\ M), Fe^{2+}(5\ M)|Pt(s)$

(3) $Cu(s)|Cu^{2+}(0.1\ M)||Fe^{3+}(0.1\ M), Fe^{2+}(0.1\ M)|Pt(s)$

(a) Write a balanced equation for each cell reaction.

(b) Sketch each cell. Label the anode and cathode, and indicate the direction of electron and ion flow.

(c) Which of the three cells has the largest cell potential? Which has the smallest cell potential? Explain.

17.29 Sketch a cell with inert electrodes suitable for electrolysis of aqueous $CuBr_2$.

(a) Label the anode and cathode.

(b) Indicate the direction of electron and ion flow.

(c) Write balanced equations for the anode, cathode, and overall cell reactions.

17.30 Consider the following electrochemical cell:

(a) Is the cell a galvanic or an electrolytic cell? Explain.

(b) Label the anode and cathode, and show the direction of ion flow.

(c) Write balanced equations for the anode, cathode, and overall cell reactions.

17.31 It has recently been reported that porous pellets of TiO_2 can be reduced to titanium metal at the cathode of an electrochemical cell containing molten $CaCl_2$ as the electrolyte.

When the TiO_2 is reduced, the O^{2-} ions dissolve in the $CaCl_2$ and are subsequently oxidized to O_2 gas at the anode. This approach may be the basis for a less expensive process than the one currently used for producing titanium.

(a) Label the anode and cathode, and indicate the signs of the electrodes.

(b) Indicate the direction of electron and ion flow.

(c) Write balanced equations for the anode, cathode, and overall cell reactions.

17.32 Consider a Daniell cell with 1.0 M ion concentrations:

Does the cell voltage increase, decrease, or remain the same when each of the following changes is made? Explain.

(a) 5.0 M $CuSO_4$ is added to the cathode compartment.

(b) 5.0 M H_2SO_4 is added to the cathode compartment.

(c) 5.0 M $Zn(NO_3)_2$ is added to the anode compartment.

(d) 1.0 M $Zn(NO_3)_2$ is added to the anode compartment.

17.33 Consider the following galvanic cell with 0.10 M concentrations:

Does the cell voltage increase, decrease, or remain the same when each of the following changes is made? Explain.

(a) 0.10 M NaCl is added to the cathode compartment.

(b) 0.10 M NaCl is added to the anode compartment.

(c) 1.0 M NH_3 is added to the cathode compartment.

(d) 1.0 M NH_3 is added to the anode compartment.

17.34 Consider a PEM fuel cell, consisting of a sandwich of two porous graphite electrodes and the proton-exchange membrane, with separate compartments for entrance of H_2 and O_2:

Fuel H_2 →

← O_2 from air

Porous graphite electrodes containing metallic catalysts

Proton-exchange membrane

(a) Label the anode and cathode, and indicate the signs of the electrodes.

SECTION PROBLEMS

Galvanic Cells (Sections 17.1–17.2)

17.36 Why is the cathode of a galvanic cell considered to be the positive electrode?

17.37 What is the function of a salt bridge in a galvanic cell?

17.38 Describe galvanic cells that use the following reactions. In each case, write the anode and cathode half-reactions and sketch the experimental setup. Label the anode and cathode, identify the sign of each electrode, and indicate the direction of electron and ion flow.

(a) $Cd(s) + Sn^{2+}(aq) \longrightarrow Cd^{2+}(aq) + Sn(s)$

(b) $2 Al(s) + 3 Cd^{2+}(aq) \longrightarrow 2 Al^{3+}(aq) + 3 Cd(s)$

(c) $Cr_2O_7{}^{2-}(aq) + 6 Fe^{2+}(aq) + 14 H^+(aq) \longrightarrow$
$$2 Cr^{3+}(aq) + 6 Fe^{3+}(aq) + 7 H_2O(l)$$

17.39 Describe galvanic cells that use the following reactions. In each case, write the anode and cathode half-reactions and sketch the experimental setup. Label the anode and cathode, identify the sign of each electrode, and indicate the direction of electron and ion flow.

(a) $3 Cu^{2+}(aq) + 2 Cr(s) \longrightarrow 3 Cu(s) + 2 Cr^{3+}(aq)$

(b) $Pb(s) + 2 H^+(aq) \longrightarrow Pb^{2+}(aq) + H_2(g)$

(c) $Cl_2(g) + Sn^{2+}(aq) \longrightarrow Sn^{4+}(aq) + 2 Cl^-(aq)$

17.40 Write the standard shorthand notation for each cell in Problem 17.38.

17.41 Write the standard shorthand notation for each cell in Problem 17.39.

17.42 Write a balanced equation for the overall cell reaction in the following galvanic cell, and tell why inert electrodes are required at the anode and cathode.

$$Pt(s)|Br^-(aq)|Br_2(l)||Cl_2(g)|Cl^-(aq)|Pt(s)$$

(b) Indicate the direction of electron and ion flow.

(c) Identify the substances that exit from each cell compartment.

(d) Write balanced equations for the anode, cathode, and overall cell reactions, and calculate the standard cell potential.

17.35 Consider the following table of standard reduction potentials:

Reduction Half-Reaction	$E°$ (V)
$A^+ + e^- \longrightarrow A$	0.80
$B^{2+} + 2 e^- \longrightarrow B$	0.38
$C_2 + 2 e^- \longrightarrow 2 C^-$	0.17
$D^{3+} + 3 e^- \longrightarrow D$	−1.36

(a) Which substance is the strongest oxidizing agent? Which is the strongest reducing agent?

(b) Which substances can be oxidized by B^{2+}? Which can be reduced by D?

(c) Write a balanced equation for the overall cell reaction that delivers a voltage of 1.53 V under standard-state conditions.

17.43 Write the standard shorthand notation for a galvanic cell that uses the following cell reaction. Include inert electrodes if necessary.

$$Fe(s) + I_2(s) \longrightarrow Fe^{2+}(aq) + 2 I^-(aq)$$

17.44 An H_2/H^+ half-cell (anode) and an Ag^+/Ag half-cell (cathode) are connected by a wire and a salt bridge.

(a) Sketch the cell, indicating the direction of electron and ion flow.

(b) Write balanced equations for the electrode and overall cell reactions.

(c) Give the shorthand notation for the cell.

17.45 A galvanic cell is constructed from a Zn/Zn^{2+} half-cell (anode) and a Cl_2/Cl^- half-cell (cathode).

(a) Sketch the cell, indicating the direction of electron and ion flow.

(b) Write balanced equations for the electrode and overall cell reactions.

(c) Give the shorthand notation for the cell.

17.46 Write balanced equations for the electrode and overall cell reactions in the following galvanic cells. Sketch each cell, labeling the anode and cathode and showing the direction of electron and ion flow.

(a) $Co(s)|Co^{2+}(aq)||Cu^{2+}(aq)|Cu(s)$

(b) $Fe(s)|Fe^{2+}(aq)||O_2(g)|H^+(aq), H_2O(l)|Pt(s)$

17.47 Write balanced equations for the electrode and overall cell reactions in the following galvanic cells. Sketch each cell, labeling the anode and cathode and showing the direction of electron and ion flow.

(a) $Mn(s)|Mn^{2+}(aq)||Pb^{2+}(aq)|Pb(s)$

(b) $Pt(s)|H_2(g)|H^+(aq)||Cl^-(aq)|AgCl(s)|Ag(s)$

Cell Potentials and Free-Energy Changes; Standard Reduction Potentials (Sections 17.3–17.5)

17.48 What conditions must be met for a cell potential E to qualify as a standard cell potential $E°$?

17.49 How are standard reduction potentials defined?

17.50 The silver oxide–zinc battery used in watches delivers a voltage of 1.60 V. Calculate the free-energy change (in kilojoules) for the cell reaction

$$Zn(s) + Ag_2O(s) \longrightarrow ZnO(s) + 2\,Ag(s)$$

17.51 The standard cell potential for a lead storage battery is 1.924 V. Calculate $\Delta G°$ (in kilojoules) for the cell reaction

$$Pb(s) + PbO_2(s) + 2\,H^+(aq) + 2\,HSO_4^-(aq) \longrightarrow$$
$$2\,PbSO_4(s) + 2\,H_2O(l)$$

17.52 What is the value of x for the following reaction if $E° = 1.43$ V and $\Delta G° = -414$ kJ?

$$A + B^{x+} \longrightarrow A^{x+} + B$$

17.53 What are the values of x and y for the following reaction if $E° = 0.91$ V and $\Delta G° = -527$ kJ?

$$2\,A^{x+} + 3\,B \longrightarrow 2\,A + 3\,B^{y+}$$

17.54 Use the standard free energies of formation in Appendix B to calculate the standard cell potential for the reaction in the hydrogen–oxygen fuel cell:

$$2\,H_2(g) + O_2(g) \longrightarrow 2\,H_2O(l)$$

17.55 Consider a fuel cell that uses the reaction

$$CH_4(g) + 2\,O_2(g) \longrightarrow CO_2(g) + 2\,H_2O(l)$$

Given the standard free energies of formation in Appendix B, what is the value of $E°$ for the cell reaction?

17.56 The standard potential for the following galvanic cell is 0.40 V:

$$Zn(s)|Zn^{2+}(aq)||Eu^{3+}(aq), Eu^{2+}(aq)|Pt(s)$$

(Europium, Eu, is one of the lanthanide elements.) Use the data in Table 17.1 to calculate the standard reduction potential for the Eu^{3+}/Eu^{2+} half-cell.

17.57 The following reaction has an $E°$ value of 0.27 V:

$$Cu^{2+}(aq) + 2\,Ag(s) + 2\,Br^-(aq) \longrightarrow Cu(s) + 2\,AgBr(s)$$

Use the data in Table 17.1 to calculate the standard reduction potential for the half-reaction

$$AgBr(s) + e^- \longrightarrow Ag(s) + Br^-(aq)$$

17.58 Arrange the following oxidizing agents in order of increasing strength under standard-state conditions: $Br_2(aq)$, $MnO_4^-(aq)$, $Sn^{4+}(aq)$.

17.59 List the following reducing agents in order of increasing strength under standard-state conditions: $Al(s)$, $Pb(s)$, $Fe(s)$.

17.60 Consider the following substances: $I_2\,(s)$, $Fe^{2+}(aq)$, $Cr_2O_7^{2-}(aq)$. Which is the strongest oxidizing agent? Which is the weakest oxidizing agent?

17.61 Consider the following substances: $Fe^{2+}(aq)$, $Sn^{2+}(aq)$, $I^-(aq)$. Identify the strongest reducing agent and the weakest reducing agent.

17.62 Given the following half-reactions, combine the two that give the cell reaction with the most positive $E°$. Write a balanced equation for the cell reaction, and calculate $E°$ and $\Delta G°$.

$$
\begin{array}{ll}
Co^{2+}(aq) + 2\,e^- \longrightarrow Co(s) & E° = -0.28 \text{ V} \\
I_2(s) + 2\,e^- \longrightarrow 2\,I^-(aq) & E° = 0.54 \text{ V} \\
Cu^{2+}(aq) + 2\,e^- \longrightarrow Cu(s) & E° = 0.34 \text{ V}
\end{array}
$$

17.63 Combine the two half-reactions in Problem 17.62 that give the spontaneous cell reaction with the smallest $E°$. Write a balanced equation for the cell reaction, and calculate $E°$ and $\Delta G°$.

17.64 Calculate the standard cell potential and the standard free-energy change (in kilojoules) for each reaction in Problem 17.38. (See Appendix D for standard reduction potentials.)

17.65 Calculate $E°$ and $\Delta G°$ (in kilojoules) for the cell reactions in Problem 17.39. (See Appendix D for standard reduction potentials.)

17.66 Calculate $E°$ for each of the following reactions, and tell which are spontaneous under standard-state conditions:

(a) $2\,Fe^{2+}(aq) + Pb^{2+}(aq) \longrightarrow 2\,Fe^{3+}(aq) + Pb(s)$

(b) $Mg(s) + Ni^{2+}(aq) \longrightarrow Mg^{2+}(aq) + Ni(s)$

17.67 Calculate $E°$ for each of the following reactions, and tell which are spontaneous under standard-state conditions:

(a) $5\,Ag^+(aq) + Mn^{2+}(aq) + 4\,H_2O(l) \longrightarrow$
$$5\,Ag(s) + MnO_4^-(aq) + 8\,H^+(aq)$$

(b) $2\,H_2O_2(aq) \longrightarrow O_2(g) + 2\,H_2O(l)$

17.68 Use the data in Appendix D to predict whether the following reactions can occur under standard-state conditions:

(a) Oxidation of $Sn^{2+}(aq)$ by $Br_2(aq)$

(b) Reduction of $Ni^{2+}(aq)$ by $Sn^{2+}(aq)$

(c) Oxidation of $Ag(s)$ by $Pb^{2+}(aq)$

(d) Reduction of $I_2(s)$ by $H_2SO_3(aq)$

17.69 Use the data in Appendix D to predict whether the following reactions can occur under standard-state conditions:

(a) Reduction of $Pb^{2+}(aq)$ by $Ni(s)$

(b) Oxidation of $Au^+(aq)$ by $Mn^{2+}(aq)$

(c) Reduction of $I_2(s)$ by $Mn(s)$

(d) Oxidation of $Fe^{2+}(aq)$ by $Br_2(aq)$

17.70 What reaction can occur, if any, when the following experiments are carried out under standard-state conditions?

(a) Oxygen gas is bubbled through an acidic solution of $Cr(NO_3)_3$.

(b) A strip of lead is dipped into an aqueous solution of $AgNO_3$.

(c) Chlorine gas is bubbled through aqueous $H_2C_2O_4$.

(d) A nickel wire is dipped into an aqueous solution of $HClO$.

17.71 What reaction can occur, if any, when the following experiments are carried out under standard-state conditions?

(a) A strip of zinc is dipped into an aqueous solution of $Pb(NO_3)_2$.

(b) An acidic solution of $FeSO_4$ is exposed to oxygen.

(c) A silver wire is immersed in an aqueous solution of $NiCl_2$.

(d) Hydrogen gas is bubbled through aqueous $Cd(NO_3)_2$.

The Nernst Equation (Sections 17.6–17.7)

17.72 Consider a galvanic cell that uses the reaction

$$2 Ag^+(aq) + Sn(s) \longrightarrow 2 Ag(s) + Sn^{2+}(aq)$$

Calculate the potential at 25 °C for a cell that has the following ion concentrations: $[Ag^+] = 0.010$ M, $[Sn^{2+}] = 0.020$ M.

17.73 Consider a galvanic cell based on the reaction

$$2 Fe^{2+}(aq) + Cl_2(g) \longrightarrow 2 Fe^{3+}(aq) + 2 Cl^-(aq)$$

Calculate the cell potential at 25 °C when $[Fe^{2+}] = 1.0$ M, $[Fe^{3+}] = 1.0 \times 10^{-3}$ M, $[Cl^-] = 3.0 \times 10^{-3}$ M, and $P_{Cl_2} = 0.50$ atm.

17.74 What is the cell potential at 25 °C for the following galvanic cell?

$$Pb(s)|Pb^{2+}(1.0 \text{ M})||Cu^{2+}(1.0 \times 10^{-4} \text{ M})|Cu(s)$$

If the Pb^{2+} concentration is maintained at 1.0 M, what is the Cu^{2+} concentration when the cell potential drops to zero?

17.75 A galvanic cell has an iron electrode in contact with 0.10 M $FeSO_4$ and a copper electrode in contact with a $CuSO_4$ solution. If the measured cell potential at 25 °C is 0.67 V, what is the concentration of Cu^{2+} in the $CuSO_4$ solution?

17.76 What is the $Zn^{2+}:Cu^{2+}$ concentration ratio in the following cell at 25 °C if the measured cell potential is 1.07 V?

$$Zn(s)|Zn^{2+}(aq)||Cu^{2+}(aq)|Cu(s)$$

17.77 What is the $Fe^{2+}:Sn^{2+}$ concentration ratio in the following cell at 25 °C if the measured cell potential is 0.35 V?

$$Fe(s)|Fe^{2+}(aq)||Sn^{2+}(aq)|Sn(s)$$

17.78 The Nernst equation applies to both cell reactions and half-reactions. For the conditions specified, calculate the potential for the following half-reactions at 25 °C:

(a) $I_2(s) + 2 e^- \longrightarrow 2 I^-(aq)$; $[I^-] = 0.020$ M

(b) $Fe^{3+}(aq) + e^- \longrightarrow Fe^{2+}(aq)$; $[Fe^{3+}] = [Fe^{2+}] = 0.10$ M

(c) $Sn^{2+}(aq) \longrightarrow Sn^{4+}(aq) + 2 e^-$; $[Sn^{2+}] = 1.0 \times 10^{-3}$ M, $[Sn^{4+}] = 0.40$ M

(d) $2 Cr^{3+}(aq) + 7 H_2O(l) \longrightarrow Cr_2O_7^{2-}(aq) + 14 H^+(aq) + 6 e^-$; $[Cr^{3+}] = [Cr_2O_7^{2-}] = 1.0$ M, $[H^+] = 0.010$ M

17.79 What is the reduction potential at 25 °C for the hydrogen electrode in each of the following solutions? The half-reaction is

$$2 H^+(aq) + 2 e^- \longrightarrow H_2(g, 1 \text{ atm})$$

(a) 1.0 M HCl **(b)** A solution having pH 4.00
(c) Pure water **(d)** 1.0 M NaOH

17.80 The following cell has a potential of 0.27 V at 25 °C:

$$Pt(s)|H_2(1 \text{ atm})|H^+(? \text{ M})||Ni^{2+}(1 \text{ M})|Ni(s)$$

What is the pH of the solution in the anode compartment?

17.81 What is the pH of the solution in the cathode compartment of the following cell if the measured cell potential at 25 °C is 0.58 V?

$$Zn(s)|Zn^{2+}(1 \text{ M})||H^+(? \text{ M})|H_2(1 \text{ atm})|Pt(s)$$

Standard Cell Potentials and Equilibrium Constants (Section 17.8)

17.82 Beginning with the equations that relate $E°$, $\Delta G°$, and K, show that $\Delta G°$ is negative and $K > 1$ for a reaction that has a positive value of $E°$.

17.83 If a reaction has an equilibrium constant $K < 1$, is $E°$ positive or negative? What is the value of K when $E° = 0$ V?

17.84 Use the data in Table 17.1 to calculate the equilibrium constant at 25 °C for the reaction

$$Ni(s) + 2 Ag^+(aq) \longrightarrow Ni^{2+}(aq) + 2 Ag(s)$$

17.85 From standard reduction potentials, calculate the equilibrium constant at 25 °C for the reaction

$$2 MnO_4^-(aq) + 10 Cl^-(aq) + 16 H^+(aq) \longrightarrow 2 Mn^{2+}(aq) + 5 Cl_2(g) + 8 H_2O(l)$$

17.86 Calculate the equilibrium constant at 25 °C for each reaction in Problem 17.38.

17.87 Calculate the equilibrium constant at 25 °C for each reaction in Problem 17.39.

17.88 Calculate the equilibrium constant at 25 °C for the reaction

$$Hg_2^{2+}(aq) \longrightarrow Hg(l) + Hg^{2+}(aq)$$

See Appendix D for standard reduction potentials.

17.89 Use standard reduction potentials to calculate the equilibrium constant at 25 °C for decomposition of hydrogen peroxide:

$$2 H_2O_2(l) \longrightarrow 2 H_2O(l) + O_2(g)$$

Batteries; Fuel Cells; Corrosion (Sections 17.9–17.11)

17.90 For a lead storage battery:

(a) Sketch one cell that shows the anode, cathode, electrolyte, direction of electron and ion flow, and sign of the electrodes.

(b) Write the anode, cathode, and overall cell reactions.

(c) Calculate the equilibrium constant for the cell reaction ($E° = 1.924$V).

(d) What is the cell voltage when the cell reaction reaches equilibrium?

17.91 A mercury battery uses the following electrode half-reactions:

$$HgO(s) + H_2O(l) + 2 e^- \longrightarrow Hg(l) + 2 OH^-(aq) \quad E° = 0.098 \text{ V}$$
$$ZnO(s) + H_2O(l) + 2 e^- \longrightarrow Zn(s) + 2 OH^-(aq) \quad E° = -1.260 \text{ V}$$

(a) Write a balanced equation for the overall cell reaction.

(b) Calculate $\Delta G°$ (in kilojoules) and K at 25 °C for the cell reaction.

(c) What is the effect on the cell voltage of a tenfold change in the concentration of KOH in the electrolyte? Explain.

17.92 Calculate the values of $E°$, $\Delta G°$ (in kilojoules), and K at 25 °C for the cell reaction in a hydrogen–oxygen fuel cell: $2 H_2(g) + O_2(g) \longrightarrow 2 H_2O(l)$. What is the cell voltage at 25 °C if the partial pressure of each gas is 25 atm?

17.93 Use the thermodynamic data in Appendix B to calculate the standard cell potential and the equilibrium constant at 25 °C for the cell reaction in a direct methanol fuel cell:

$$2 CH_3OH(l) + 3 O_2(g) \longrightarrow 2 CO_2(g) + 4 H_2O(l)$$

17.94 What is rust? What causes it to form? What can be done to prevent its formation?

17.95 The standard oxidation potential for the reaction $Cr(s) \longrightarrow Cr^{3+}(aq) + 3\,e^-$ is 0.74 V. Despite the large, positive oxidation potential, chromium is sometimes used as a protective coating on steel. Why doesn't the chromium corrode?

17.96 What is meant by cathodic protection? Which of the following metals can offer cathodic protection to iron?

Zn, Ni, Al, Sn

17.97 What is a sacrificial anode? Give an example.

Electrolysis (Sections 17.12–17.14)

17.98 Magnesium metal is produced by the electrolysis of molten magnesium chloride using inert electrodes.
   (a) Sketch the cell, label the anode and cathode, indicate the sign of the electrodes, and show the direction of electron and ion flow.
   (b) Write balanced equations for the anode, cathode, and overall cell reactions.

17.99 **(a)** Sketch a cell with inert electrodes suitable for the electrolysis of an aqueous solution of sulfuric acid. Label the anode and cathode, and indicate the direction of electron and ion flow. Identify the positive and negative electrodes.
   (b) Write balanced equations for the anode, cathode, and overall cell reactions.

17.100 List the anode and cathode half-reactions that might occur when an aqueous solution of $MgCl_2$ is electrolyzed in a cell having inert electrodes. Predict which half-reactions will occur, and justify your answers.

17.101 What products should be formed when the following reactants are electrolyzed in a cell having inert electrodes? Account for any differences.
   (a) Molten KCl   **(b)** Aqueous KCl

17.102 Predict the anode, cathode, and overall cell reactions when an aqueous solution of each of the following salts is electrolyzed in a cell having inert electrodes:
   (a) NaBr   **(b)** $CuCl_2$ **(c)** LiOH

17.103 Predict the anode, cathode, and overall cell reactions when an aqueous solution of each of the following salts is electrolyzed in a cell having inert electrodes:
   (a) Ag_2SO_4 **(b)** $Ca(OH)_2$ **(c)** KI

17.104 How many grams of silver will be obtained when an aqueous silver nitrate solution is electrolyzed for 20.0 min with a constant current of 2.40 A?

17.105 A constant current of 100.0 A is passed through an electrolytic cell having an impure copper anode, a pure copper cathode, and an aqueous $CuSO_4$ electrolyte. How many kilograms of copper are refined by transfer from the anode to the cathode in a 24.0 h period?

17.106 How many hours are required to produce 1.00×10^3 kg of sodium by the electrolysis of molten NaCl with a constant current of 3.00×10^4 A? How many liters of Cl_2 at STP will be obtained as a byproduct?

17.107 What constant current (in amperes) is required to produce aluminum by the Hall–Heroult process at a rate of 40.0 kg/h?

17.108 Electrolysis of a metal nitrate solution $M(NO_3)_2(aq)$ for 325 min with a constant current of 20.0 A gives 111 g of the metal. Identify the metal ion M^{2+}.

17.109 What is the metal ion in a metal nitrate solution $M(NO_3)_3(aq)$ if 90.52 g of metal was recovered from a 4.00 h electrolysis at a constant current of 35.0 A?

CHAPTER PROBLEMS

17.110 Consider a galvanic cell that uses the following half-reactions:

$$MnO_4^-(aq) + 8\,H^+(aq) + 5\,e^- \longrightarrow Mn^{2+}(aq) + 4\,H_2O(l)$$
$$Sn^{4+}(aq) + 2\,e^- \longrightarrow Sn^{2+}(aq)$$

   (a) Write a balanced equation for the overall cell reaction.
   (b) What is the oxidizing agent, and what is the reducing agent?
   (c) Calculate the standard cell potential.

17.111 Given the following half-reactions and $E°$ values,

$$Mn^{3+}(aq) + e^- \longrightarrow Mn^{2+}(aq) \qquad E° = 1.54\ V$$
$$MnO_2(s) + 4\,H^+(aq) + e^- \longrightarrow Mn^{3+}(aq) + 2\,H_2O(l) \quad E° = 0.95\ V$$

   write a balanced equation for the formation of Mn^{2+} and MnO_2 from Mn^{3+}, and calculate the value of $E°$ for this reaction. Is the reaction spontaneous under standard-state conditions?

17.112 Consider the following half-reactions and $E°$ values:

$$Ag^+(aq) + e^- \longrightarrow Ag(s) \qquad E° = 0.80\ V$$
$$Cu^{2+}(aq) + 2\,e^- \longrightarrow Cu(s) \qquad E° = 0.34\ V$$
$$Pb^{2+}(aq) + 2\,e^- \longrightarrow Pb(s) \qquad E° = -0.13\ V$$

   (a) Which of these metals or ions is the strongest oxidizing agent? Which is the strongest reducing agent?
   (b) The half-reactions can be used to construct three different galvanic cells. Tell which cell delivers the highest voltage, identify the anode and cathode, and tell the direction of electron and ion flow.
   (c) Write the cell reaction for part **(b)**, and calculate the values of $E°$, $\Delta G°$ (in kilojoules), and K for this reaction at 25 °C.
   (d) Calculate the voltage for the cell in part **(b)** if both ion concentrations are 0.010 M.

17.113 Standard reduction potentials for the Pb^{2+}/Pb and Cd^{2+}/Cd half-reactions are -0.13 V and -0.40 V, respectively. At what relative concentrations of Pb^{2+} and Cd^{2+} will these half-reactions have the same reduction potential?

17.114 Consider a galvanic cell that uses the following half-reactions:

$$2\,H^+(aq) + 2\,e^- \longrightarrow H_2(g)$$
$$Al^{3+}(aq) + 3\,e^- \longrightarrow Al(s)$$

(a) What materials are used for the electrodes? Identify the anode and cathode, and indicate the direction of electron and ion flow.

(b) Write a balanced equation for the cell reaction, and calculate the standard cell potential.

(c) Calculate the cell potential at 25 °C if the ion concentrations are 0.10 M and the partial pressure of H_2 is 10.0 atm.

(d) Calculate $\Delta G°$ (in kilojoules) and K for the cell reaction at 25 °C.

(e) Calculate the mass change (in grams) of the aluminum electrode after the cell has supplied a constant current of 10.0 A for 25.0 min.

17.115 When the nickel–zinc battery, used in digital cameras, is recharged, the following cell reaction occurs:

$$2\,Ni(OH)_2(s) + Zn(OH)_2(s) \longrightarrow 2\,Ni(OH)_3(s) + Zn(s)$$

(a) How many grams of zinc are formed when 3.35×10^{-2} g of $Ni(OH)_2$ are consumed?

(b) How many minutes are required to fully recharge a dead battery that contains 6.17×10^{-2} g of Zn with a constant current of 0.100 A?

17.116 Chlorine can be prepared in the laboratory by the reaction of hydrochloric acid and potassium permanganate.

(a) Use data in Appendix D to write a balanced equation for the reaction. The reduction product is Mn^{2+}.

(b) Calculate $E°$ and $\Delta G°$ for the reaction.

(c) How many liters of Cl_2 at 1.0 atm and 25 °C will result from the reaction of 179 g $KMnO_4$ with an excess of HCl?

17.117 The following cell reactions occur spontaneously:

$$B \mid A^+ \quad \textgreater B^+ \mid A$$
$$C + A^+ \longrightarrow C^+ + A$$
$$B + C^+ \longrightarrow B^+ + C$$

(a) Arrange the following reduction half-reactions in order of decreasing tendency to occur: $A^+ + e^- \rightarrow A$, $B^+ + e^- \rightarrow B$, and $C^+ + e^- \rightarrow C$.

(b) Which of these substances (A, A^+, B, B^+, C, C^+) is the strongest oxidizing agent? Which is the strongest reducing agent?

(c) Which of the three cell reactions delivers the highest voltage?

17.118 Consider the following substances: $Fe(s)$, $PbO_2(s)$, $H^+(aq)$, $Al(s)$, $Ag(s)$, $Cr_2O_7^{2-}(aq)$.

(a) Look at the $E°$ values in Appendix D, and classify each substance as an oxidizing agent or a reducing agent.

(b) Which is the strongest oxidizing agent? Which is the weakest oxidizing agent?

(c) Which is the strongest reducing agent? Which is the weakest reducing agent?

(d) Which substances can be oxidized by $Cu^{2+}(aq)$? Which can be reduced by $H_2O_2(aq)$?

17.119 The sodium–sulfur battery has molybdenum electrodes with anode and cathode compartments separated by β-alumina, a ceramic through which sodium ions can pass. Because the battery operates at temperatures above 300 °C, all the reactants and products are present in a molten solution. The cell voltage is about 2.0 V.

(a) What is the cell reaction if the shorthand notation is $Mo(s)|Na(soln)|Na^+(soln)||S(soln)|S^{2-}(soln)|Mo(s)$?

(b) How many kilograms of sodium are consumed when a 25 kW sodium–sulfur battery produces current for 32 minutes?

17.120 When suspected drunk drivers are tested with a Breathalyzer, the alcohol (ethanol) in the exhaled breath is oxidized to acetic acid with an acidic solution of potassium dichromate:

$$3\,CH_3CH_2OH(aq) + 2\,Cr_2O_7^{2-}(aq) + 16\,H^+(aq) \longrightarrow$$

Ethanol $\qquad\qquad 3\,CH_3CO_2H(aq) + 4\,Cr^{3+}(aq) + 11\,H_2O(l)$

Acetic acid

The color of the solution changes because some of the orange $Cr_2O_7^{2-}$ is converted to the green Cr^{3+}. The Breathalyzer measures the color change and produces a meter reading calibrated in blood alcohol content.

(a) What is $E°$ for the reaction if the standard half-cell potential for the reduction of acetic acid to ethanol is 0.058 V?

(b) What is the value of E for the reaction when the concentrations of ethanol, acetic acid, $Cr_2O_7^{2-}$, and Cr^{3+} are 1.0 M and the pH is 4.00?

17.121 Consider the addition of the following half-reactions:

(1) $Fe^{3+}(aq) + 3\,e^- \longrightarrow Fe(s)$	$E°_1 = -0.04$ V
(2) $Fe(s) \longrightarrow Fe^{2+}(aq) + 2\,e^-$	$E°_2 = 0.45$ V
(3) $Fe^{3+}(aq) + e^- \longrightarrow Fe^{2+}(aq)$	$E°_3 = ?$

Because half-reactions (1) and (2) contain a different number of electrons, the net reaction (3) is another half-reaction, and $E°_3$ can't be obtained simply by adding $E°_1$ and $E°_2$. The free-energy changes, however, are additive because G is a state function:

$$\Delta G°_3 = \Delta G°_1 + \Delta G°_2$$

(a) Starting with the relationship between $\Delta G°$ and $E°$, derive a general equation that relates the $E°$ values for half-reactions (1), (2), and (3).

(b) Calculate the value of $E°_3$ for the Fe^{3+}/Fe^{2+} half-reaction.

(c) Explain why the $E°$ values would be additive ($E°_3 = E°_1 + E°_2$) if reaction (3) were an overall cell reaction rather than a half-reaction.

17.122 The following galvanic cell has a potential of 0.578 V at 25 °C:

$$Ag(s)|AgCl(s)|Cl^-(1.0\ M)||Ag^+(1.0\ M)|Ag(s)$$

Use this information to calculate K_{sp} for AgCl at 25 °C.

17.123 A galvanic cell has a silver electrode in contact with 0.050 M $AgNO_3$ and a copper electrode in contact with 1.0 M $Cu(NO_3)_2$.

(a) Write a balanced equation for the cell reaction, and calculate the cell potential at 25 °C.

(b) Excess $NaBr(aq)$ is added to the $AgNO_3$ solution to precipitate AgBr. What is the cell potential at 25 °C after the precipitation of AgBr if the concentration of excess Br^- is 1.0 M? Write a balanced equation for the cell reaction under these conditions. (K_{sp} for AgBr at 25 °C is 5.4×10^{-13}.)

(c) Use the result in part (b) to calculate the standard reduction potential $E°$ for the half-reaction

$$AgBr(s) + e^- \longrightarrow Ag(s) + Br^-(aq).$$

17.124 At one time on Earth, iron was present mostly as iron(II). Later, once plants had produced a significant quantity of oxygen in the atmosphere, the iron became oxidized to iron(III). Show that $Fe^{2+}(aq)$ can be spontaneously oxidized to $Fe^{3+}(aq)$ by $O_2(g)$ at 25 °C assuming the following reasonable environmental conditions: $[Fe^{2+}] = [Fe^{3+}] = 1 \times 10^{-7}$ M; pH = 7.0; $P_{O_2} = 160$ mm Hg.

17.125 Given the following standard reduction potentials at 25 °C, (a) balance the equation for the reaction of H_2MoO_4 with elemental arsenic in acidic solution to give Mo^{3+} and H_3AsO_4, and (b) calculate $E°$ for this reaction.

Half-Reaction	$E°$ (V)
$H_3AsO_4(aq) + 2 H^+(aq) + 2 e^- \longrightarrow H_3AsO_3(aq) + H_2O(l)$	+0.560
$H_3AsO_3(aq) + 3 H^+(aq) + 3 e^- \longrightarrow As(s) + 3 H_2O(l)$	+0.240
$H_2MoO_4(aq) + 2 H^+(aq) + 2 e^- \longrightarrow MoO_2(s) + 2 H_2O(l)$	+0.646
$MoO_2(s) + 4 H^+(aq) + e^- \longrightarrow Mo^{3+}(aq) + 2 H_2O(l)$	+0.008

17.126 The following galvanic cell has a potential of 1.214 V at 25 °C:

$$Hg(l)|Hg_2Br_2(s)|Br^-(0.10 \text{ M})||MnO_4^-(0.10 \text{ M}),$$
$$Mn^{2+}(0.10 \text{ M}), H^+(0.10 \text{ M})|Pt(s)$$

Calculate the value of K_{sp} for Hg_2Br_2 at 25 °C.

17.127 For the following half-reaction, $E° = 1.103$ V:

$$Cu^{2+}(aq) + 2 CN^-(aq) + e^- \longrightarrow Cu(CN)_2^-(aq)$$

Calculate the formation constant K_f for $Cu(CN)_2^-$.

17.128 Accidentally chewing on a stray fragment of aluminum foil can cause a sharp tooth pain if the aluminum comes in contact with an amalgam filling. The filling, an alloy of silver, tin, and mercury, acts as the cathode of a tiny galvanic cell, the aluminum behaves as the anode, and saliva serves as the electrolyte. When the aluminum and the filling come in contact, an electric current passes from the aluminum to the filling, which is sensed by a nerve in the tooth. Aluminum is oxidized at the anode, and O_2 gas is reduced to water at the cathode.

(a) Write balanced equations for the anode, cathode, and overall cell reactions.

(b) Write the Nernst equation in a form that applies at body temperature (37 °C).

(c) Calculate the cell voltage at 37 °C. You may assume that $[Al^{3+}] = 1.0 \times 10^{-9}$ M, $P_{O_2} = 0.20$ atm, and that saliva has a pH of 7.0. Also assume that the $E°$ values in Appendix D apply at 37 °C.

17.129 Copper reduces dilute nitric acid to nitric oxide (NO) but reduces concentrated nitric acid to nitrogen dioxide (NO_2):

(1) $3 Cu(s) + 2 NO_3^-(aq) + 8 H^+(aq) \longrightarrow$
$\qquad 3 Cu^{2+}(aq) + 2 NO(g) + 4 H_2O(l) \qquad E° = 0.62$ V

(2) $Cu(s) + 2 NO_3^-(aq) + 4 H^+(aq) \longrightarrow$
$\qquad Cu^{2+}(aq) + 2 NO_2(g) + 2 H_2O(l) \qquad E° = 0.45$ V.

Assuming that $[Cu^{2+}] = 0.10$ M and that the partial pressures of NO and NO_2 are 1.0×10^{-3} atm, calculate the potential (E) for reactions (1) and (2) at 25 °C and show which reaction has the greater thermodynamic tendency to occur when the concentration of HNO_3 is

(a) 1.0 M   (b) 10.0 M

(c) At what HNO_3 concentration do reactions (1) and (2) have the same value of E?

MULTICONCEPT PROBLEMS

17.130 Adiponitrile, a key intermediate in the manufacture of nylon, is made industrially by an electrolytic process that reduces acrylonitrile:

Anode (oxidation): $2 H_2O \longrightarrow O_2 + 4 H^+ + 4 e^-$

Cathode (reduction):
$\quad 2 CH_2{=}CHCN + 2 H^+ + 2 e^- \longrightarrow NC(CH_2)_4CN$
$\qquad$ Acrylonitrile $\qquad\qquad\qquad\qquad$ Adiponitrile

(a) Write a balanced equation for the overall cell reaction.

(b) How many kilograms of adiponitrile are produced in 10.0 h in a cell that has a constant current of 3.00×10^3 A?

(c) How many liters of O_2 at 740 mm Hg and 25 °C are produced as a byproduct?

17.131 The reaction of MnO_4^- with oxalic acid ($H_2C_2O_4$) in acidic solution, yielding Mn^{2+} and CO_2 gas, is widely used to determine the concentration of permanganate solutions:

(a) Write a balanced net ionic equation for the reaction.

(b) Use the data in Appendix D to calculate $E°$ for the reaction.

(c) Show that the reaction goes to completion by calculating the values of $\Delta G°$ and K at 25 °C.

(d) A 1.200 g sample of sodium oxalate ($Na_2C_2O_4$) is dissolved in dilute H_2SO_4 and then titrated with a $KMnO_4$ solution. If 32.50 mL of the $KMnO_4$ solution is required to reach the equivalence point, what is the molarity of the $KMnO_4$ solution?

17.132 Calculate the standard reduction potential for $Ba^{2+}(aq) + 2 e^- \rightarrow Ba(s)$ given that $\Delta G° = 16.7$ kJ for the reaction $Ba^{2+}(aq) + 2 Cl^-(aq) \rightarrow BaCl_2(s)$. Use any data needed from Appendixes B and D.

17.133 A concentration cell has the same half-reactions at the anode and cathode, but a voltage results from different concentrations in the two electrode compartments.

(a) What is x in the concentration cell $Cu(s)|Cu^{2+}(x \text{ M})||Cu^{2+}(0.10 \text{ M})|Cu(s)$ if the measured cell potential is 0.0965 V?

(b) A similar cell has 0.10 M Cu^{2+} in both compartments. When a stoichiometric amount of ethylenediamine

$(NH_2CH_2CH_2NH_2)$ is added to one compartment, the measured cell potential is 0.179 V. Calculate the formation constant K_f for the complex ion $Cu(NH_2CH_2CH_2NH_2)_2^{2+}$. Assume there is no volume change.

17.134 Consider the redox titration (Section 4.10) of 120.0 mL of 0.100 M $FeSO_4$ with 0.120 M $K_2Cr_2O_7$ at 25 °C, assuming that the pH of the solution is maintained at 2.00 with a suitable buffer. The solution is in contact with a platinum electrode and constitutes one half-cell of an electrochemical cell. The other half-cell is a standard hydrogen electrode. The two half-cells are connected with a wire and a salt bridge, and the progress of the titration is monitored by measuring the cell potential with a voltmeter.

(a) Write a balanced net ionic equation for the titration reaction, assuming that the products are Fe^{3+} and Cr^{3+}.

(b) What is the cell potential at the equivalence point?

17.135 Consider the reaction that occurs in the hydrogen–oxygen fuel cell:

$$2 H_2(g) + O_2(g) \longrightarrow 2 H_2O(l)$$

(a) Use the thermodynamic data in Appendix B to calculate the values of $\Delta G°$ and $E°$ at 95 °C, assuming that $\Delta H°$ and $\Delta S°$ are independent of temperature.

(b) Calculate the cell voltage at 95 °C when the partial pressures of H_2 and O_2 are 25 atm.

17.136 Consider a galvanic cell that utilizes the following half-reactions:

Anode: $Zn(s) + H_2O(l) \longrightarrow ZnO(s) + 2 H^+(aq) + 2 e^-$

Cathode: $Ag^+(aq) + e^- \longrightarrow Ag(s)$

(a) Write a balanced equation for the cell reaction, and use the thermodynamic data in Appendix B to calculate the values of $\Delta H°$, $\Delta S°$, and $\Delta G°$ for the reaction.

(b) What are the values of $E°$ and the equilibrium constant K for the cell reaction at 25 °C?

(c) What happens to the cell voltage if aqueous ammonia is added to the cathode compartment? Calculate the cell voltage assuming that the solution in the cathode compartment was prepared by mixing 50.0 mL of 0.100 M $AgNO_3$ and 50.0 mL of 4.00 M NH_3.

(d) Will AgCl precipitate if 10.0 mL of 0.200 M NaCl is added to the solution in part (c)? Will AgBr precipitate if 10.0 mL of 0.200 M KBr is added to the resulting solution?

17.137 The nickel–iron battery has an iron anode, an NiO(OH) cathode, and a KOH electrolyte. This battery uses the following half-reactions and has an $E°$ value of 1.37 V at 25 °C:

$$Fe(s) + 2 OH^-(aq) \longrightarrow Fe(OH)_2(s) + 2 e^-$$
$$NiO(OH)(s) + H_2O(l) + e^- \longrightarrow Ni(OH)_2(s) + OH^-(aq)$$

(a) Write a balanced equation for the cell reaction.

(b) Calculate $\Delta G°$ (in kilojoules) and the equilibrium constant K for the cell reaction at 25 °C.

(c) What is the cell voltage at 25 °C when the concentration of KOH in the electrolyte is 5.0 M?

(d) How many grams of $Fe(OH)_2$ are formed at the anode when the battery produces a constant current of 0.250 A for 40.0 min? How many water molecules are consumed in the process?

17.138 Experimental solid-oxide fuel cells that use butane (C_4H_{10}) as the fuel have been reported recently. These cells contain composite metal/metal oxide electrodes and a solid metal oxide electrolyte. The cell half-reactions are

Anode: $C_4H_{10}(g) + 13 O^{2-}(s) \longrightarrow 4 CO_2(g) + 5 H_2O(l) + 26 e^-$
Cathode: $O_2(g) + 4 e^- \longrightarrow 2 O^{2-}(s)$

(a) Write a balanced equation for the cell reaction.

(b) Use the thermodynamic data in Appendix B to calculate the values of $E°$ and the equilibrium constant K for the cell reaction at 25 °C. Will $E°$ and K increase, decrease, or remain the same on raising the temperature?

(c) How many grams of butane are required to produce a constant current of 10.5 A for 8.00 h? How many liters of gaseous butane at 20 °C and 815 mm Hg pressure are required?

17.139 The half-reactions that occur in ordinary alkaline batteries can be written as

Cathode: $MnO_2(s) + H_2O(l) + e^- \longrightarrow MnO(OH)(s) + OH^-(aq)$
Anode: $Zn(s) + 2 OH^-(aq) \longrightarrow Zn(OH)_2(s) + 2 e^-$

In 1999, researchers in Israel reported a new type of alkaline battery, called a "super-iron" battery. This battery uses the same anode reaction as an ordinary alkaline battery but involves the reduction of FeO_4^{2-} ion (from K_2FeO_4) to solid $Fe(OH)_3$ at the cathode.

(a) Use the following standard reduction potential and any data from Appendixes C and D to calculate the standard cell potential expected for an ordinary alkaline battery:

$$MnO(OH)(s) + H_2O(l) + e^- \longrightarrow Mn(OH)_2(s) + OH^-(aq)$$
$$E° = -0.380 \text{ V}$$

(b) Write a balanced equation for the cathode half-reaction in a super-iron battery. The half-reaction occurs in a basic environment.

(c) A super-iron battery should last longer than an ordinary alkaline battery of the same size and weight because its cathode can provide more charge per unit mass. Quantitatively compare the number of coulombs of charge released by the reduction of 10.0 g of K_2FeO_4 to $Fe(OH)_3$ with the number of coulombs of charge released by the reduction of 10.0 g of MnO_2 to MnO(OH).

17.140 Gold metal is extracted from its ore by treating the crushed rock with an aerated cyanide solution. The unbalanced equation for the reaction is

$$Au(s) + CN^-(aq) + O_2(g) \longrightarrow Au(CN)_2^-(aq)$$

(a) Balance the equation for this reaction in basic solution.

(b) Use any of the following data at 25 °C to calculate $\Delta G°$ for this reaction at 25 °C: K_f for $Au(CN)_2^- = 6.2 \times 10^{38}$, K_a for HCN = 4.9×10^{-10}, and standard reduction potentials are

$O_2(g) + 4 H^+(aq) + 4 e^- \longrightarrow 2 H_2O(l)$ $E° = 1.229$ V
$Au^{3+}(aq) + 3 e^- \longrightarrow Au(s)$ $E° = 1.498$ V
$Au^{3+}(aq) + 2 e^- \longrightarrow Au^+(aq)$ $E° = 1.401$ V

17.141 Consider the redox titration of 100.0 mL of a solution of 0.010 M Fe^{2+} in 1.50 M H_2SO_4 with a 0.010 M solution of $KMnO_4$, yielding Fe^{3+} and Mn^{2+}. The titration is carried out in an electrochemical cell equipped with a platinum electrode and a calomel reference electrode consisting of an Hg_2Cl_2/Hg electrode in contact with a saturated KCl solution having $[Cl^-] = 2.9$ M. Using any data in Appendixes C and D, calculate the cell potential after addition of (a) 5.0 mL, (b) 10.0 mL, (c) 19.0 mL, and (d) 21.0 mL of the $KMnO_4$ solution.

CHAPTER 20

Transition Elements and Coordination Chemistry

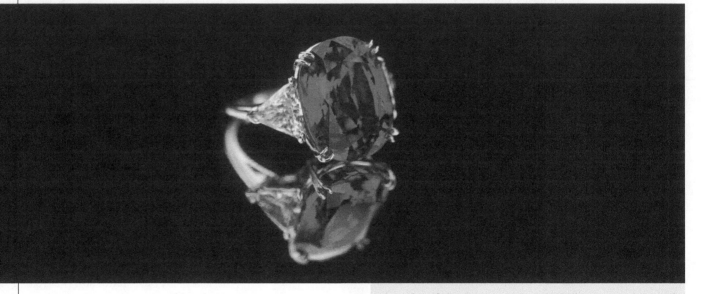

The color of the Carmen Lucia Ruby is due to transitions of *d* electrons in Cr^{3+} ions.

CONTENTS

he *transition elements* occupy the central part of the periodic table, bridging the gap between the active *s*-block metals of groups 1A and 2A on the left and the *p*-block metals, semimetals, and nonmetals of groups 3A–8A on the right (**Figure 20.1**). Because the *d* subshells are being filled in this region of the periodic table, the transition elements are also called the *d-block elements*.

Each *d* subshell consists of five orbitals and can accommodate 10 electrons, so each transition series consists of 10 elements. The first series extends from scandium through zinc and includes many familiar metals, such as chromium, iron, and copper. The second series runs from yttrium through cadmium, and the third series runs from lutecium through mercury. In addition, there is a fourth transition series made up of lawrencium through the recently discovered element 112, copernicium (Cn).

Figure 20.1
The transition elements are located in the central region of the periodic table.

Tucked into the periodic table between barium (atomic number 56) and lutecium (atomic number 71) are the *lanthanides*. In this series of 14 metallic elements, the seven 4*f* orbitals are progressively filled, as shown in Figure 5.16 (page 174). Following radium (atomic number 88) is a second series of 14 elements, the *actinides*, in which the 5*f* subshell is progressively filled. The lanthanides and actinides together comprise the *f-block elements*, or *inner transition elements*.

The transition metals iron and copper have been known since antiquity and have played an important role in the development of civilization. Iron, the main constituent of steel, is still important as a structural material. Worldwide production of steel was 1.22 billion metric tons in 2009. In newer technologies, other transition elements are useful. For example, the strong, lightweight metal titanium is a major component in modern jet aircraft and is used in manufacturing artificial joints and dental implants. Transition metals are also used as heterogeneous catalysts in automobile catalytic converters and in the industrial synthesis of essential chemicals such as sulfuric acid, nitric acid, and ammonia.

The role of the transition elements in living systems is equally important. Iron is present in biomolecules such as hemoglobin, which transports oxygen from our lungs to other parts of the body. Cobalt is an essential component of vitamin B_{12}. Nickel, copper, and zinc are vital constituents of many enzymes, the large protein molecules that catalyze biochemical reactions.

In this chapter, we'll look at the properties and chemical behavior of transition metal compounds, paying special attention to *coordination compounds*, in which a central metal ion or atom—usually a transition metal—is attached to a group of surrounding molecules or ions by coordinate covalent bonds (Section 7.5).

20.1 ELECTRON CONFIGURATIONS

Look at the electron configurations of potassium and calcium, the *s*-block elements immediately preceding the first transition series. These atoms have 4*s* valence electrons, but no *d* electrons:

$$\textbf{K } (Z = 19): [Ar] \, 3d^0 \, 4s^1 \qquad \textbf{Ca } (Z = 20): [Ar] \, 3d^0 \, 4s^2$$

The filling of the 3*d* subshell begins at atomic number 21 (scandium) and continues until the subshell is completely filled at atomic number 30 (zinc):

$$\textbf{Sc } (Z = 21): [Ar] \, 3d^1 \, 4s^2 \longrightarrow \textbf{Zn } (Z = 30): [Ar] \, 3d^{10} \, 4s^2$$

(It's convenient to list the valence electrons in order of principal quantum number rather than in order of orbital filling because the 4*s* electrons are lost first in forming ions.)

For main-group elements, the valence electrons are generally considered to be those in the outermost shell because they are the ones that are involved in chemical bonding. For transition elements, however, both the $(n - 1)d$ and the ns electrons are involved in bonding and are considered valence electrons.

The filling of the 3*d* subshell generally proceeds according to **Hund's rule** with one electron adding to each of the five 3*d* orbitals before a second electron adds to any one of them (Section 5.11). There are just two exceptions to the expected regular filling pattern, chromium and copper:

Remember...

According to **Hund's rule**, if two or more orbitals with the same energy are available, one electron goes into each until all are half-filled and the electrons in the half-filled orbitals all have the same spin. (Section 5.11)

	Cr (Z = 24)		Cu (Z = 29)	
Expected configuration	↑ ↑ ↑ ↑ — $3d^4$	↑↓ $4s^2$	↑↓ ↑↓ ↑↓ ↑↓ ↑ $3d^9$	↑↓ $4s^2$
Observed configuration	↑ ↑ ↑ ↑ ↑ $3d^5$	↑ $4s^1$	↑↓ ↑↓ ↑↓ ↑↓ ↑↓ $3d^{10}$	↑ $4s^1$

Electron configurations depend on both orbital energies and electron–electron repulsions. Consequently, it's not always possible to predict configurations when two valence subshells have similar energies. It's often found, however, that exceptions from the expected orbital filling pattern result in either half-filled or completely filled subshells. In the case of chromium, for example, the 3*d* and 4*s* subshells have similar energies. It's evidently advantageous to shift one electron from the 4*s* to the 3*d* subshell, which decreases electron–electron repulsions and gives two half-filled subshells. Because each valence electron is in a separate orbital, the electron–electron repulsion that would otherwise occur between the two 4*s* electrons in the expected configuration is eliminated. A similar shift of one electron from 4*s* to 3*d* in copper gives a completely filled 3*d* subshell and a half-filled 4*s* subshell.

When a neutral atom loses one or more electrons, the remaining electrons are less shielded and the effective nuclear charge (Z_{eff}) increases. Consequently, the remaining electrons are more strongly attracted to the nucleus and their orbital energies decrease. It turns out that the valence *d* orbitals experience a steeper drop in energy with increasing Z_{eff} than does the valence *s* orbital, making the *d* orbitals in cations lower in energy than the *s* orbital. As a result, the valence *s* orbital is vacant and all the valence electrons occupy the *d* orbitals in transition metal cations. Iron, for example, which forms 2+ and 3+ cations, has the following valence electron configurations:

Fe: ↑↓ ↑ ↑ ↑ ↑ $3d^6$ ↑↓ $4s^2$ Fe^{2+}: ↑↓ ↑ ↑ ↑ ↑ $3d^6$ Fe^{3+}: ↑ ↑ ↑ ↑ ↑ $3d^5$

In neutral molecules and complex anions, the metal atom usually has a positive oxidation state. It therefore has a partial positive charge and a higher Z_{eff} than that of the neutral atom. As a result, the valence d orbitals are again lower in energy than the valence s orbital, and so all the metal's valence electrons occupy the d orbitals. The metal atom in both VCl_4 and MnO_4^{2-}, for example, has the valence configuration $3d^1$. Electron configurations and other properties for atoms and common ions of first-series transition elements are summarized in Table 20.1.

TABLE 20.1 Selected Properties of First-Series Transition Elements

Group:	3B	4B	5B	6B	7B	8B			1B	2B
Element:	Sc	Ti	V	Cr	Mn	Fe	Co	Ni	Cu	Zn
Valence electron configuration										
M atom	$3d^1 4s^2$	$3d^2 4s^2$	$3d^3 4s^2$	$3d^5 4s^1$	$3d^5 4s^2$	$3d^6 4s^2$	$3d^7 4s^2$	$3d^8 4s^2$	$3d^{10} 4s^1$	$3d^{10} 4s^2$
M^{2+} ion		$3d^2$	$3d^3$	$3d^4$	$3d^5$	$3d^6$	$3d^7$	$3d^8$	$3d^9$	$3d^{10}$
M^{3+} ion	$3d^0$	$3d^1$	$3d^2$	$3d^3$	$3d^4$	$3d^5$	$3d^6$			
Elec. conductivity*	3	4	8	11	1	17	24	24	96	27
Melting point (°C)	1541	1668	1910	1907	1246	1538	1495	1455	1085	420
Boiling point (°C)	2836	3287	3407	2671	2061	2861	2927	2913	2562	907
Density (g/cm³)	2.99	4.51	6.0	7.15	7.3	7.87	8.86	8.90	8.96	7.13
Atomic radius (pm)	162	147	134	128	127	126	125	124	128	134
E_i (kJ/mol)†										
First	633	659	651	653	717	762	760	737	745	906
Second	1235	1310	1410	1591	1509	1562	1648	1753	1958	1733
Third	2389	2653	2828	2987	3248	2957	3232	3395	3555	3833

*Electrical conductivity relative to an arbitrary value of 100 for silver
†Ionization energy

Historically, transition elements are placed in groups of the periodic table designated 1B–8B because their valence electron configurations are similar to those of analogous elements in the main groups 1A–8A. Thus, copper in group 1B ([Ar] $3d^{10} 4s^1$) and zinc in group 2B ([Ar] $3d^{10} 4s^2$) have valence electron configurations similar to those of potassium in group 1A ([Ar] $4s^1$) and calcium in group 2A ([Ar] $4s^2$). Similarly, scandium in group 3B ([Ar] $3d^1 4s^2$) through iron in group 8B ([Ar] $3d^6 4s^2$) have the same number of valence electrons as the p-block elements aluminum in group 3A ([Ne] $3s^2 3p^1$) through argon in group 8A ([Ne] $3s^2 3p^6$). Cobalt ([Ar] $3d^7 4s^2$) and nickel ([Ar] $3d^8 4s^2$) are also assigned to group 8B although there are no main-group elements with 9 or 10 valence electrons.

WORKED EXAMPLE 20.1

WRITING ELECTRON CONFIGURATIONS OF TRANSITION METALS

Write the electron configuration of the metal in each of the following atoms or ions:

(a) Ni **(b)** Cr^{3+} **(c)** FeO_4^{2-} (ferrate ion)

STRATEGY

In neutral atoms of the first transition series, the $4s$ orbital is usually filled with 2 electrons and the remaining electrons occupy the $3d$ orbitals. In transition metal ions, all the valence electrons occupy the d orbitals. For polyatomic ions, first determine the oxidation number of the transition metal, and then assign the valence electrons to the d orbitals as you would if the metal were a simple ion.

continued on next page

SOLUTION

(a) Nickel ($Z = 28$) has a total of 28 electrons, including the argon core of 18. Two of the 10 valence electrons occupy the $4s$ orbital, and the remaining eight are assigned to the $3d$ orbitals. The electron configuration is therefore [Ar] $3d^8 4s^2$.

(b) A neutral Cr atom ($Z = 24$) has a total of 24 electrons; a Cr^{3+} ion has $24 - 3 = 21$ electrons. Because all the valence electrons occupy the $3d$ orbitals, the electron configuration of Cr^{3+} is [Ar] $3d^3$.

(c) The oxidation number of each of the four oxygens in FeO_4^{2-} is -2 and the overall charge on the oxoanion is -2, so the oxidation number of the iron must be $+6$. An iron(VI) atom has a total of 20 electrons, 6 less than a neutral iron atom ($Z = 26$). Because the valence electrons occupy the $3d$ orbitals, the electron configuration of Fe(VI) is [Ar] $3d^2$.

▶ **PROBLEM 20.1**   Write the electron configuration of the metal in each of the following:

(a) V   (b) Co^{2+} (c) MnO_2 (d) $CuCl_4^{2-}$

CONCEPTUAL PROBLEM 20.2   On the periodic table below, locate the transition metal atom or ion with the following electron configurations. Identify each atom or ion.

(a) An atom: [Ar] $3d^5 4s^2$ (b) A 2+ ion: [Ar] $3d^8$
(c) An atom: [Kr] $4d^{10} 5s^1$ (d) A 3+ ion: [Kr] $4d^3$

20.2   PROPERTIES OF TRANSITION ELEMENTS

Let's look at some trends in the properties of the transition elements shown in Table 20.1 and try to understand them in terms of electron configurations.

Metallic Properties

All the transition elements are metals. Like the metals of groups 1A and 2A, the transition metals are malleable, ductile, lustrous, and good conductors of heat and electricity. Silver has the highest electrical conductivity of any element at room temperature, with copper a close second. The transition metals are harder, have higher melting and boiling points, and are more dense than the group 1A and 2A metals, largely because the sharing of d, as well as s, electrons results in stronger bonding.

From left to right across the first transition series, melting points increase from 1541 °C for Sc to a maximum of 1910 °C for V in group 5B, then decrease to 420 °C for Zn (Table 20.1, **Figure 20.2**). The second- and third-series elements exhibit a similar maximum in melting point, but at group 6B rather than 5B: 2623 °C for Mo and 3422 °C for W, the metal with the highest melting point. The melting points increase as the number of unpaired d electrons available for bonding increases and then decrease as the d electrons pair up and become less available for bonding. Zinc ($3d^{10} 4s^2$), in which all the d and s electrons are paired, has a relatively low melting point (420 °C) and mercury ($4f^{14} 5d^{10} 6s^2$) is a liquid at room temperature (mp -39 °C). We'll look at bonding in metals in more detail in Section 21.4.

▲ Native copper.

Figure 20.2
Relative melting points of the transition elements.

Atomic Radii and Densities

Atomic radii are given in **Figure 20.3**. From left to right across a transition series, the atomic radii decrease, at first markedly and then more gradually after group 6B. Toward the end of each series, the radii increase again. The decrease in radii with increasing atomic number occurs because the added *d* electrons only partially **shield** the added nuclear charge (Section 5.14). As a result, the effective nuclear charge Z_{eff} increases. With increasing Z_{eff}, the electrons are more strongly attracted to the

Remember...
The valence electrons are only weakly **shielded** by electrons in the same subshell, which are at the same distance from the nucleus.   (Section 5.14)

Figure 20.3
Atomic radii (in pm) of the transition elements.

nucleus and atomic size decreases. The upturn in radii toward the end of each series is probably due to more effective shielding and increasing electron–electron repulsion as double occupation of the *d* orbitals is completed. In contrast to the large variation in radii for main-group elements, all transition metal atoms have quite similar radii, which accounts for their ability to blend together in forming alloys such as brass (mostly copper and zinc).

The atomic radii of the second- and third-series transition elements from group 4B on are nearly identical, though we would expect an increase in size on adding an entire principal quantum shell of electrons. The small sizes of the third-series atoms are associated with what is called the **lanthanide contraction**, the general decrease in atomic radii of the *f*-block lanthanide elements between the second and third transition series (**Figure 20.4**).

Figure 20.4
Atomic radii (in pm) of the lanthanide elements.

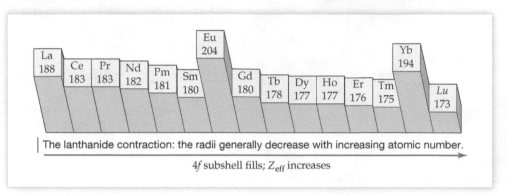

The lanthanide contraction: the radii generally decrease with increasing atomic number.

$4f$ subshell fills; Z_{eff} increases

The lanthanide contraction is due to the increase in effective nuclear charge with increasing atomic number as the $4f$ subshell is filled. By the end of the lanthanides, the size *decrease* due to a larger Z_{eff} almost exactly compensates for the expected size *increase* due to an added quantum shell of electrons. Consequently, atoms of the third transition series have radii very similar to those of the second transition series.

The densities of the transition metals are inversely related to their atomic radii (**Figure 20.5**). The densities initially increase from left to right across each transition series and then decrease toward the end of each series. Because the second- and third-series elements have nearly the same atomic volume, the much heavier third-series elements have unusually high densities: 22.6 g/cm³ for osmium and iridium, the most dense elements.

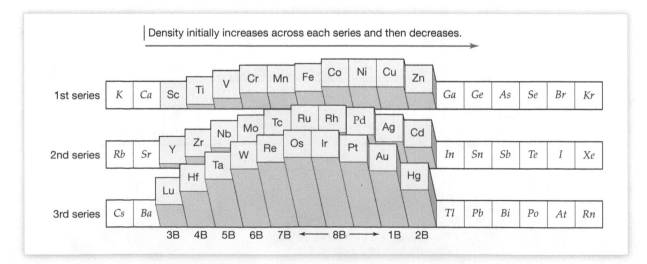

Density initially increases across each series and then decreases.

Figure 20.5
Relative densities of the transition metals.

Ionization Energies and Oxidation Potentials

Ionization energies generally increase from left to right across a transition series, though there are some irregularities, as indicated in Table 20.1, for the atoms of the first transition series. The general trend correlates with an increase in effective nuclear charge and a decrease in atomic radius.

Table 20.2 lists standard potentials $E°$ for oxidation of first-series transition metals. Note that these potentials are the negative of the corresponding standard reduction potentials that were given in Table 17.1 on page 692. Except for copper, all the $E°$ values are positive, which means that the solid metal is oxidized to its aqueous cation more readily than H_2 gas is oxidized to $H^+(aq)$.

$$M(s) \longrightarrow M^{2+}(aq) + 2\,e^- \qquad E° > 0\ V \qquad \text{Product is } M^{3+} \text{ for } M = Sc$$
$$H_2(g) \longrightarrow 2\,H^+(aq) + 2\,e^- \qquad E° = 0\ V$$

In other words, the first-series metals, except for copper, are stronger reducing agents than H_2 gas and can therefore be oxidized by the H^+ ion in acids like HCl that lack an oxidizing anion:

$$M(s) + 2\,H^+(aq) \longrightarrow M^{2+}(aq) + H_2(g) \qquad E° > 0\ V \text{ (except for } M = Cu)$$

Oxidation of copper requires a stronger oxidizing agent, such as HNO_3.

TABLE 20.2 Standard Potentials for Oxidation of First-Series Transition Metals

Oxidation Half-Reaction	$E°$ (V)	Oxidation Half-Reaction	$E°$ (V)
$Sc(s) \rightarrow Sc^{3+}(aq) + 3\,e^-$	2.08	$Fe(s) \rightarrow Fe^{2+}(aq) + 2\,e^-$	0.45
$Ti(s) \rightarrow Ti^{2+}(aq) + 2\,e^-$	1.63	$Co(s) \rightarrow Co^{2+}(aq) + 2\,e^-$	0.28
$V(s) \rightarrow V^{2+}(aq) + 2\,e^-$	1.18	$Ni(s) \rightarrow Ni^{2+}(aq) + 2\,e^-$	0.26
$Cr(s) \rightarrow Cr^{2+}(aq) + 2\,e^-$	0.91	$Cu(s) \rightarrow Cu^{2+}(aq) + 2\,e^-$	−0.34
$Mn(s) \rightarrow Mn^{2+}(aq) + 2\,e^-$	1.18	$Zn(s) \rightarrow Zn^{2+}(aq) + 2\,e^-$	0.76

The standard potential for the oxidation of a metal is a composite property that depends on $\Delta G°$ for the sublimation of the metal, the ionization energies of the metal atom, and $\Delta G°$ for the hydration of the metal ion:

$$M(s) \xrightarrow{\Delta G°_{subl}} M(g) \xrightarrow{E_i\,(-2\,e^-)} M^{2+}(g) \xrightarrow{\Delta G°_{hydr}} M^{2+}(aq)$$

Nevertheless, the general trend in the $E°$ values shown in Table 20.2 correlates with the general trend in the ionization energies in Table 20.1. The ease of oxidation of the metal decreases as the ionization energies increase across the transition series from Sc to Zn. (Only Mn and Zn deviate from the trend of decreasing $E°$ values.) Thus, the so-called *early transition metals*, those on the left side of the *d* block (Sc through Mn), are oxidized most easily and are the strongest reducing agents.

20.3 OXIDATION STATES OF TRANSITION ELEMENTS

The transition elements differ from most main-group metals in that they exhibit a variety of oxidation states. Sodium, magnesium, and aluminum, for example, have a single oxidation state equal to their periodic group number (Na^+, Mg^{2+}, and Al^{3+}), but the transition elements frequently have oxidation states less than their group number. For example, manganese in group 7B shows oxidation states of $+2$ in $Mn^{2+}(aq)$, $+3$ in $Mn(OH)_3(s)$, $+4$ in $MnO_2(s)$, $+6$ in $MnO_4^{2-}(aq)$ (manganate ion), and

▶ Manganese has different oxidation states and different colors in these ions and solid compounds.

Manganese species:	$Mn^{2+}(aq)$	$Mn(OH)_3(s)$	$MnO_2(s)$	$MnO_4^{2-}(aq)$	$MnO_4^-(aq)$
Oxidation state of manganese:	+2	+3	+4	+6	+7

+7 in $MnO_4^-(aq)$ (permanganate ion). **Figure 20.6** summarizes the common oxidation states for elements of the first transition series, with the most frequently encountered ones indicated in red.

Figure 20.6
Common oxidation states for first-series transition elements. The states encountered most frequently are shown in red. Most transition elements have more than one common oxidation state.

The highest oxidation state for the group 3B–7B metals is their periodic group number ...

... but the group 8B transition metals have a maximum oxidation state less than their group number.

All the first-series transition elements except scandium form a 2+ cation, corresponding to loss of the two $4s$ valence electrons. Because the $3d$ and $4s$ orbitals have similar energies, loss of a $3d$ electron is also possible, yielding 3+ cations such as $V^{3+}(aq)$, $Cr^{3+}(aq)$, and $Fe^{3+}(aq)$. Additional energy is required to remove the third electron, but this is more than compensated for by the larger (more negative) $\Delta G°$ of hydration of the more highly charged 3+ cation. Still higher oxidation states result from loss or sharing of additional d electrons. In their highest oxidation states, the transition elements are combined with the most electronegative elements (F and O): for example, $VF_5(l)$ and $V_2O_5(s)$ for vanadium in group 5B; CrO_4^{2-} (chromate ion) and $Cr_2O_7^{2-}$ (dichromate ion) for chromium in group 6B; MnO_4^- for manganese in group 7B.

Note in Figure 20.6 that the highest oxidation state for the group 3B–7B metals is the group number, corresponding to loss or sharing of all the valence s and d electrons. For the group 8B transition metals, though, loss or sharing of all the valence electrons is energetically prohibitive because of the increasing value of Z_{eff}. Consequently, only lower oxidation states are accessible for these transition metals—for example, +6 in FeO_4^{2-} and +3 in Co^{3+}. Even these species have a great tendency to be reduced to still lower oxidation states. For example, the aqueous Co^{3+} ion is unstable because it oxidizes water to O_2 gas and is thereby reduced to Co^{2+}:

$$4\,Co^{3+}(aq) + 2\,H_2O(l) \longrightarrow 4\,Co^{2+}(aq) + O_2(g) + 4\,H^+(aq) \qquad E° = +0.58\ \text{V}$$

In general, ions that have the transition metal in a high oxidation state tend to be good oxidizing agents—for example, $Cr_2O_7^{2-}$, MnO_4^-, and FeO_4^{2-}. Conversely, early transition metal ions with the metal in a low oxidation state are good reducing agents—for example, V^{2+} and Cr^{2+}. Divalent ions of the later transition metals on the right side of the d block, such as Co^{2+}, Ni^{2+}, Cu^{2+}, and Zn^{2+}, are poor reducing agents because of the larger value of Z_{eff}. In fact, zinc has only one stable oxidation state ($+2$).

CONCEPTUAL PROBLEM 20.3   How does the effective nuclear charge, Z_{eff}, vary from left to right across the first transition series?

Sc	Ti	V	Cr	Mn	Fe	Co	Ni	Cu	Zn

Based on the variation in Z_{eff},

(a) Which M^{2+} ion (M = Ti–Zn) should be the strongest reducing agent? Which should be the weakest?

(b) Which oxoanion (VO_4^{3-}, CrO_4^{2-}, MnO_4^{2-}, or FeO_4^{2-}) should be the strongest oxidizing agent? Which should be the weakest?

20.4 CHEMISTRY OF SELECTED TRANSITION ELEMENTS

Experimental work in transition metal chemistry is particularly enjoyable because most transition metal compounds have brilliant colors. In this section, we'll look at the chemistry of some representative elements commonly encountered in the laboratory.

Chromium

Chromium, which gets its name from the Greek word for color (*chroma*), is obtained from the ore chromite, a mixed metal oxide with the formula $FeO \cdot Cr_2O_3$, or $FeCr_2O_4$. Reduction of chromite with carbon gives the alloy ferrochrome, which is used to make stainless steel, a hard, corrosion-resistant steel that contains up to 30% chromium.

$$FeCr_2O_4(s) + 4\,C(s) \longrightarrow \underbrace{Fe(s) + 2\,Cr(s)}_{\text{Ferrochrome}} + 4\,CO(g)$$

Pure chromium is obtained by reducing chromium(III) oxide with aluminum:

$$Cr_2O_3(s) + 2\,Al(s) \longrightarrow 2\,Cr(s) + Al_2O_3(s)$$

In addition to its use in making steels, chromium is widely used to electroplate metallic objects with an attractive, protective coating (Section 17.13). Chromium is hard and lustrous, takes a high polish, and resists corrosion because an invisible, microscopic film of chromium(III) oxide shields the surface from further oxidation.

The aqueous solution chemistry of chromium can be systematized according to its oxidation states and the species that exist under acidic and basic conditions (Table 20.3). The common oxidation states are $+2$, $+3$, and $+6$, with the $+3$ state the most stable.

▲ This sculpture, *Herakles in Ithaka* by Jason Seley, was made from chromium-plated automobile bumpers.

TABLE 20.3   Chromium Species in Common Oxidation States

	Oxidation State		
	+2	**+3**	**+6**
Acidic solution:	$Cr^{2+}(aq)$ Chromium(II) ion (Chromous ion) Blue	$\xrightarrow{+0.41\ V}$ $Cr^{3+}(aq)$ Chromium(III) ion (Chromic ion) Violet	$\xrightarrow{+1.36\ V}$ $Cr_2O_7^{2-}(aq)$ Dichromate ion Orange
Basic solution:	$Cr(OH)_2(s)$ Light Blue	$Cr(OH)_3(s)$ Pale Green	$\xleftarrow{-0.13\ V}$ $CrO_4^{2-}(aq)$ Chromate ion Yellow
		$Cr(OH)_4^{-}(aq)$ Chromite ion Deep green	

Chromium metal reacts with aqueous acids in the absence of oxygen to give $Cr^{2+}(aq)$, the beautiful blue chromium(II) (chromous) ion, in which Cr^{2+} is bound to six water molecules, $Cr(H_2O)_6{}^{2+}$ (**Figure 20.7a**):

$$Cr(s) + 2\,H^+(aq) \longrightarrow Cr^{2+}(aq) + H_2(g) \qquad E° = +0.91\ V$$

In air, the reaction of chromium metal with acids yields chromium(III) because chromium(II) is rapidly oxidized by atmospheric oxygen:

$$4\,Cr^{2+}(aq) + O_2(g) + 4\,H^+(aq) \longrightarrow 4\,Cr^{3+}(aq) + 2\,H_2O(l) \qquad E° = +1.64\ V$$

Although the $Cr(H_2O)_6{}^{3+}$ ion is violet, chromium(III) solutions are often green because anions replace some of the bound water molecules to give green complex ions such as $Cr(H_2O)_5Cl^{2+}$ and $Cr(H_2O)_4Cl_2{}^+$ (**Figure 20.7b**).

Figure 20.7
Reaction of chromium metal with aqueous acids.

(a) Reaction of chromium metal with 6 M H_2SO_4 in the *absence* of air gives bubbles of H_2 gas and a solution containing the blue chromium(II) ion.

(b) Reaction of chromium metal with 6 M HCl in the *presence* of air yields a green solution containing chromium(III) species.

In basic solution, chromium(III) precipitates as chromium(III) hydroxide, a pale green solid that dissolves both in acid and in excess base (**Figure 20.8**):

In acid: $Cr(OH)_3(s) + 3\,H_3O^+(aq) \rightleftharpoons Cr^{3+}(aq) + 6\,H_2O(l)$

In excess base: $Cr(OH)_3(s) + OH^-(aq) \rightleftharpoons Cr(OH)_4{}^-(aq)$

Recall from Section 15.12 that this behavior is typical of amphoteric metal hydroxides.

Slow addition of aqueous NaOH to a solution of the violet $Cr(H_2O)_6^{3+}$ ion ...

... gives a pale green precipitate of chromium(III) hydroxide, $Cr(OH)_3$.

The $Cr(OH)_3$ dissolves on addition of H_2SO_4 ...

... re-forming the $Cr(H_2O)_6^{3+}$ ion.

$Cr(OH)_3$ also dissolves on addition of excess NaOH ...

... yielding the deep green chromite ion, $Cr(OH)_4^-$.

Figure 20.8
Amphoteric behavior of chromium(III) hydroxide.

In contrast to the amphoteric $Cr(OH)_3$, chromium(II) hydroxide is a typical basic hydroxide. It dissolves in acid but not in excess base. Conversely, the chromium(VI) compound, $CrO_2(OH)_2$, is a strong acid (chromic acid, H_2CrO_4). Recall from Section 14.15 that **acid strength** increases with increasing polarity of the O—H bonds, which increases, in turn, with increasing oxidation number of the chromium atom.

+2	+3	+6
$Cr(OH)_2$	$Cr(OH)_3$	$CrO_2(OH)_2$
Basic	Amphoteric	Acidic

————— Increasing strength as a proton donor —————⟶

Remember...
Acid strength increases with increasing oxidation number of the atom to which an OH group is attached. Electron density shifts from the OH group to the attached atom, thus weakening the O—H bond, increasing its polarity, and facilitating proton transfer to a solvent water molecule. (Section 14.15)

In the +6 oxidation state, the most important solution species are the yellow chromate ion (CrO_4^{2-}) and the orange dichromate ion ($Cr_2O_7^{2-}$). These ions are interconverted by the rapid equilibrium reaction

$$2\,CrO_4^{2-}(aq) + 2\,H^+(aq) \rightleftharpoons Cr_2O_7^{2-}(aq) + H_2O(l) \qquad K \approx 10^{14}$$

Because the equilibrium constant is about 10^{14}, CrO_4^{2-} ions predominate in basic solutions and $Cr_2O_7^{2-}$ ions predominate in acidic solutions (**Figure 20.9**). The CrO_4^{2-} ion is tetrahedral, and the $Cr_2O_7^{2-}$ ion has a structure in which two CrO_4^{2-} ions share a common oxygen atom.

The $Cr_2O_7^{2-}$ ion is a powerful oxidizing agent in acidic solution and is widely used as an oxidant in analytical chemistry.

$$Cr_2O_7^{2-}(aq) + 14\,H^+(aq) + 6\,e^- \longrightarrow 2\,Cr^{3+}(aq) + 7\,H_2O(l) \qquad E° = +1.36\ V$$

In basic solution, where CrO_4^{2-} is the predominant species, chromium(VI) is a much weaker oxidizing agent:

$$CrO_4^{2-}(aq) + 4\,H_2O(l) + 3\,e^- \longrightarrow Cr(OH)_3(s) + 5\,OH^-(aq) \qquad E° = -0.13\ V$$

Chromium(VI) compounds must be handled with care because they are highly toxic and are known to cause cancer.

Chromate ion, CrO_4^{2-}

Dichromate ion, $Cr_2O_7^{2-}$

Figure 20.9
Conversion of the yellow $CrO_4^{2-}(aq)$ ion to the orange $Cr_2O_7^{2-}(aq)$ ion.

$$2\,CrO_4^{2-}(aq) + 2\,H^+(aq) \longrightarrow Cr_2O_7^{2-}(aq) + H_2O(l)$$

| An aqueous solution of sodium chromate (Na_2CrO_4). | On addition of dilute sulfuric acid to a sodium chromate solution, the yellow CrO_4^{2-} ion is converted to the orange $Cr_2O_7^{2-}$ ion. |

Iron

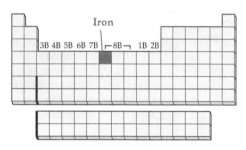

Iron, the fourth most abundant element in the Earth's crust at 5.6% by mass, is immensely important both in human civilization and in living systems. Because iron is relatively soft and easily corroded, it is combined with carbon and other metals, such as vanadium, chromium, and manganese, to make steel alloys that are harder and less reactive than pure iron. Iron is obtained from its most important ores, hematite (Fe_2O_3) and magnetite (Fe_3O_4), by reduction with coke in a blast furnace (see Section 21.3). In living systems, iron is an essential constituent of numerous biomolecules. The body of a healthy human adult contains about 4 g of iron, 65% of which is present in the oxygen-carrying protein hemoglobin (Chapter 13 Inquiry).

The most common oxidation states of iron are +2 (ferrous) and +3 (ferric). When iron metal reacts in the absence of air with an acid such as HCl, which lacks an oxidizing anion, the product is the light green iron(II) ion, $Fe(H_2O)_6^{2+}$:

$$Fe(s) + 2\,H^+(aq) \longrightarrow Fe^{2+}(aq) + H_2(g) \qquad E° = +0.45\ V$$

The oxidation stops at the iron(II) stage because the standard potential for oxidation of the iron(II) ion is negative:

$$Fe^{2+}(aq) \longrightarrow Fe^{3+}(aq) + e^- \qquad E° = -0.77\ V$$

In air, the iron(II) ion is slowly oxidized by atmospheric oxygen to the iron(III) ion, $Fe(H_2O)_6^{3+}$:

$$4\,Fe^{2+}(aq) + O_2(g) + 4\,H^+(aq) \longrightarrow 4\,Fe^{3+}(aq) + 2\,H_2O(l) \qquad E° = +0.46\ V$$

When iron is treated with an acid that has an oxidizing anion—for example, dilute nitric acid—the metal is oxidized directly to iron(III):

$$Fe(s) + NO_3^-(aq) + 4\,H^+(aq) \longrightarrow Fe^{3+}(aq) + NO(g) + 2\,H_2O(l) \qquad E° = +1.00\ V$$

The addition of a base to iron(III) solutions precipitates the gelatinous, red-brown hydrous oxide, $Fe_2O_3 \cdot x\,H_2O$, usually written as $Fe(OH)_3$ (**Figure 20.10**):

$$Fe^{3+}(aq) + 3\,OH^-(aq) \longrightarrow Fe(OH)_3(s)$$

Because $Fe(OH)_3$ is very insoluble ($K_{sp} = 2.6 \times 10^{-39}$), it forms as soon as the pH rises above pH 2. The red-brown rust stains that you've seen in sinks and bathtubs

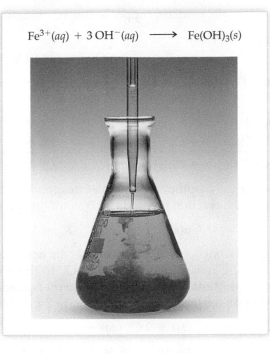

$$Fe^{3+}(aq) + 3\,OH^-(aq) \longrightarrow Fe(OH)_3(s)$$

Figure 20.10
When dilute NaOH is added to a solution of iron(III) sulfate, $Fe_2(SO_4)_3$, a gelatinous, red-brown precipitate of $Fe(OH)_3$ forms.

are due to air oxidation of $Fe^{2+}(aq)$ in hard water followed by deposition of hydrous iron(III) oxide. Unlike $Cr(OH)_3$, $Fe(OH)_3$ is not appreciably amphoteric. It dissolves in acid, but not in excess base.

Copper

Copper, a reddish metal, is a relatively rare element, accounting for only 0.0068% of the Earth's crust by mass. Like the other group 1B elements silver and gold, copper is found in nature in the elemental state. Copper's most important ores are sulfides, such as chalcopyrite, $CuFeS_2$. In a multistep process, copper sulfides are concentrated, separated from iron, and converted to molten copper(I) sulfide, which is then reduced to elemental copper by blowing air through the hot liquid:

$$Cu_2S(l) + O_2(g) \longrightarrow 2\,Cu(l) + SO_2(g)$$

The product, containing about 99% copper, is purified by electrolysis (Section 17.13).

Because of its high electrical conductivity and negative oxidation potential, copper is widely used to make electrical wiring and corrosion-resistant water pipes. Copper is also used in coins and is combined with other metals to make alloys such as brass (mostly copper and zinc) and bronze (mostly copper and tin). Though less reactive than other first-series transition metals, copper is oxidized on prolonged exposure to O_2, CO_2, and water in moist air, forming basic copper(II) carbonate, $Cu_2(OH)_2CO_3$. Subsequent reaction with dilute H_2SO_4 in acid rain then forms $Cu_2(OH)_2SO_4$, the green patina seen on bronze monuments.

$$2\,Cu(s) + O_2(g) + CO_2(g) + H_2O(g) \longrightarrow Cu_2(OH)_2CO_3(s)$$

$$Cu_2(OH)_2CO_3(s) + H_2SO_4(aq) \longrightarrow Cu_2(OH)_2SO_4(s) + CO_2(g) + H_2O(l)$$

In its compounds, copper exists in two common oxidation states, +1 (cuprous) and +2 (cupric). Because $E°$ for the Cu^+/Cu^{2+} half-reaction is less negative than that for the Cu/Cu^+ half-reaction, any oxidizing agent strong enough to oxidize copper to the copper(I) ion is also able to oxidize the copper(I) ion to the copper(II) ion.

$$Cu(s) \longrightarrow Cu^+(aq) + e^- \qquad E° = -0.52 \text{ V}$$

$$Cu^+(aq) \longrightarrow Cu^{2+}(aq) + e^- \qquad E° = -0.15 \text{ V}$$

▲ Why do statues made of copper or bronze turn green with age?

Dilute nitric acid, for example, oxidizes copper to the +2 oxidation state:

$$3\ Cu\ (s) + 2\ NO_3^-(aq) + 8\ H^+(aq) \longrightarrow$$
$$3\ Cu^{2+}(aq) + 2\ NO(g) + 4\ H_2O(l) \qquad E° = +0.62\ V$$

It follows from the $E°$ values that $Cu^+(aq)$ can disproportionate, oxidizing and reducing itself:

$$
\begin{array}{ll}
Cu^+(aq) + e^- \longrightarrow Cu(s) & E° = +0.52\ V \\
Cu^+(aq) \longrightarrow Cu^{2+}(aq) + e^- & E° = -0.15\ V \\
\hline
2\ Cu^+(aq) \longrightarrow Cu(s) + Cu^{2+}(aq) & E° = +0.37\ V
\end{array}
$$

The positive $E°$ value for the disproportionation corresponds to a large equilibrium constant, indicating that the reaction proceeds far toward completion:

$$2\ Cu^+(aq) \rightleftharpoons Cu(s) + Cu^{2+}(aq) \qquad K_c = 1.8 \times 10^6$$

Thus, the copper(I) ion is not an important species in aqueous solution, though copper(I) does exist in solid compounds such as CuCl. In the presence of Cl^- ions, the disproportionation equilibrium is reversed because precipitation of the insoluble, white copper(I) chloride drives the following reaction to the right:

$$Cu(s) + Cu^{2+}(aq) + 2\ Cl^-(aq) \longrightarrow 2\ CuCl(s)$$

The more common +2 oxidation state is found in the blue aqueous ion, $Cu(H_2O)_6^{2+}$, and in numerous solid compounds and complex ions. The addition of base (aqueous ammonia) to a solution of a copper(II) salt gives a blue precipitate of copper(II) hydroxide, which dissolves in excess aqueous ammonia, yielding the dark blue complex ion $Cu(NH_3)_4^{2+}$ (**Figure 20.11**):

$$Cu^{2+}(aq) + 2\ OH^-(aq) \longrightarrow Cu(OH)_2(s)$$
$$Cu(OH)_2(s) + 4\ NH_3(aq) \longrightarrow Cu(NH_3)_4^{2+}(aq) + 2\ OH^-(aq)$$

When an aqueous solution of $CuSO_4$ is treated with aqueous ammonia, a blue precipitate of $Cu(OH)_2$ forms.

$Cu^{2+}(aq)$

On the addition of excess ammonia, $Cu(OH)_2$ dissolves, yielding the deep blue $Cu(NH_3)_4^{2+}$ ion.

Figure 20.11
Reactions of $Cu^{2+}(aq)$ with aqueous ammonia.

▶ **PROBLEM 20.4** What product is formed when dilute H_2SO_4, a nonoxidizing acid, is added to each of the following ions or compounds?

(a) CrO_4^{2-} (b) $Cr(OH)_3$ (c) $Cr(OH)_2$
(d) $Fe(OH)_2$ (e) $Cu(OH)_2$

▶ **PROBLEM 20.5** What product is formed when excess aqueous NaOH is added to a solution of each of the following ions?

(a) Cr^{2+} (b) Cr^{3+} (c) $Cr_2O_7^{2-}$
(d) Fe^{2+} (e) Fe^{3+}

20.5 COORDINATION COMPOUNDS

A **coordination compound** is a compound in which a central metal ion or atom is attached to a group of surrounding molecules or ions by coordinate covalent bonds. A good example is the anticancer drug cisplatin, $Pt(NH_3)_2Cl_2$, in which two NH_3 molecules and two Cl^- ions use lone pairs of electrons to bond to the platinum(II) ion:

$$\begin{array}{c} \overset{..}{:}\overset{..}{Cl}\overset{..}{:} \\ :\overset{..}{Cl}:Pt:NH_3 \qquad \text{Cisplatin} \\ \overset{..}{NH_3} \end{array}$$

The molecules or ions that surround the central metal ion in a coordination compound are called **ligands**, and the atoms that are attached directly to the metal are called **ligand donor atoms**. In cisplatin, for example, the ligands are NH_3 and Cl^-, and the ligand donor atoms are N and Cl. The formation of a coordination compound is a Lewis acid–base interaction in which the ligands act as Lewis bases, or electron-pair donors, and the central metal ion behaves as a Lewis acid, an electron-pair acceptor.

Not all coordination compounds are neutral molecules like $Pt(NH_3)_2Cl_2$. Many are salts, such as $[Ni(NH_3)_6]Cl_2$ and $K_3[Fe(CN)_6]$, which contain a complex cation or anion along with enough ions of opposite charge to give a compound that is electrically neutral overall. To emphasize that the complex ion is a discrete structural unit, it is always enclosed in brackets in the formula of a salt. Thus, $[Ni(NH_3)_6]Cl_2$ contains $[Ni(NH_3)_6]^{2+}$ cations and Cl^- anions. The term **metal complex**, or simply complex, refers both to neutral molecules, such as $Pt(NH_3)_2Cl_2$, and to complex ions, such as $[Ni(NH_3)_6]^{2+}$ and $[Fe(CN)_6]^{3-}$.

The number of ligand donor atoms that surround a central metal ion in a complex is called the **coordination number** of the metal. Thus, platinum(II) has a coordination number of 4 in $Pt(NH_3)_2Cl_2$, and iron(III) has a coordination number of 6 in $[Fe(CN)_6]^{3-}$. The most common coordination numbers are 4 and 6, but others are well-known (Table 20.4). The coordination number of a metal ion in a particular complex depends on the metal ion's size, charge, and electron configuration, and on the size and shape of the ligands.

TABLE 20.4	**Examples of Complexes with Various Coordination Numbers**
Coordination Number	**Complex**
2	$[Ag(NH_3)_2]^+$, $[CuCl_2]^-$
3	$[HgI_3]^-$
4	$[Zn(NH_3)_4]^{2+}$, $[Ni(CN)_4]^{2-}$
5	$[Ni(CN)_5]^{3-}$, $Fe(CO)_5$
6	$[Cr(H_2O)_6]^{3+}$, $[Fe(CN)_6]^{3-}$
7	$[ZrF_7]^{3-}$
8	$[Mo(CN)_8]^{4-}$

Metal complexes have characteristic shapes that depend on the metal ion's coordination number. Two-coordinate complexes, such as $[Ag(NH_3)_2]^+$, are linear. Four-coordinate complexes are either tetrahedral or square planar; for example, $[Zn(NH_3)_4]^{2+}$ is tetrahedral, and $[Ni(CN)_4]^{2-}$ is square planar. Nearly all six-coordinate complexes are octahedral. The more common coordination geometries are illustrated in Figure 20.12. Coordination geometries were first deduced by the Swiss chemist Alfred Werner, who was awarded the 1913 Nobel Prize in Chemistry for his pioneering studies.

In the octahedral arrangement, four ligands are at the corners of a square, with one more above and one below the plane of the square.

Linear
(two-coordinate)

Tetrahedral
(four-coordinate)

Square planar
(four-coordinate)

Octahedral
(six-coordinate)

Figure 20.12
The arrangement of ligand donor atoms (L) in ML_n complexes with coordination numbers 2, 4, and 6.

The charge on a metal complex equals the charge on the metal ion (its oxidation state) plus the sum of the charges on the ligands. Thus, if we know the charge on each ligand and the charge on the complex, we can easily find the oxidation state of the metal.

WORKED EXAMPLE 20.2

DETERMINING THE FORMULA OF A METAL COMPLEX

A cobalt(III) ion forms a complex with four ammonia molecules and two chloride ions. What is the formula of the complex, including its charge?

STRATEGY

The charge on the complex is the sum of the charges on the Co^{3+} ion, the four electrically neutral NH_3 ligands, and the two Cl^- ligands:

$$\begin{array}{ccc} Co^{3+} & 4\,NH_3 & 2\,Cl^- \\ +3 \quad + & (4)(0) \quad + & (2)(-1) \quad = +1 \end{array}$$

SOLUTION

The formula of the complex is $[Co(NH_3)_4Cl_2]^+$.

WORKED EXAMPLE 20.3

DETERMINING THE OXIDATION STATE OF THE METAL IN A COORDINATION COMPOUND

What is the oxidation state of platinum in the coordination compound $K[Pt(NH_3)Cl_5]$?

STRATEGY

Because the compound is electrically neutral overall and contains one K^+ cation per complex anion, the anion must be $[Pt(NH_3)Cl_5]^-$. Since ammonia is neutral and chloride has a charge of -1, the sum of the oxidation numbers is $+1 + n + 0 + (5)(-1) = 0$, where n is the oxidation number of Pt:

$$\begin{array}{cccc} K^+ & Pt^{n+} & NH_3 & 5\,Cl^- \\ +1 \quad + & n \quad + & 0 \quad + & (5)(-1) = 0; \quad \text{so}, n = +4 \end{array}$$

SOLUTION

The oxidation state of platinum is $+4$.

$[Pt(NH_3)Cl_5]^-$

▶ **PROBLEM 20.6**   What is the formula of the chromium(III) complex that contains two ammonia and four thiocyanate (SCN^-) ligands?

▶ **PROBLEM 20.7**   What is the oxidation state of iron in $Na_4[Fe(CN)_6]$?

20.6   LIGANDS

The structures of some typical ligands are shown in **Figure 20.13**. They can be classified as *monodentate* or *polydentate*, depending on the number of ligand donor atoms that bond to the metal. Ligands such as H_2O, NH_3, or Cl^- that bond using an electron pair of a single donor atom are called **monodentate ligands** (literally, "one-toothed" ligands). Those that bond through electron pairs on more than one donor atom are termed **polydentate ligands** ("many-toothed" ligands). For example, ethylenediamine ($NH_2CH_2CH_2NH_2$, abbreviated en) is a **bidentate ligand** because it bonds to a metal using the electron pair on each of its two nitrogen atoms. The **hexadentate ligand** ethylenediaminetetraacetate ion ($EDTA^{4-}$) bonds to a metal ion through electron pairs on six donor atoms (two N atoms and four O atoms).

Figure 20.13
Structures of some common ligands. Ligand donor atoms are in color. The thiocyanate ion can bond to a metal through either the S atom or the N atom.

Polydentate ligands are known as **chelating agents** (pronounced **key**-late-ing, from the Greek word *chele*, meaning "claw") because their multipoint attachment to a metal ion resembles the grasping of an object by the claws of a crab. For example, ethylenediamine holds a cobalt(III) ion with two claws, its two nitrogen donor atoms (**Figure 20.14**). The resulting five-membered ring consisting of the Co(III) ion, two N atoms, and two C atoms of the ligand is called a **chelate ring**. A complex such as $[Co(en)_3]^{3+}$ or $[Co(EDTA)]^-$ that contains one or more chelate rings is known as a metal **chelate**.

Because $EDTA^{4-}$ bonds to a metal ion through six donor atoms, it forms especially stable complexes and is often used to hold metal ions in solution. For example, in the treatment of lead poisoning, $EDTA^{4-}$ bonds to Pb^{2+}, which is then excreted by the kidneys as the soluble chelate $[Pb(EDTA)]^{2-}$. $EDTA^{4-}$ is commonly added to food products such as commercial salad dressings to complex any metal cations that might be present in trace amounts. The free metal ions might otherwise catalyze the oxidation of oils, thus causing the dressing to become rancid.

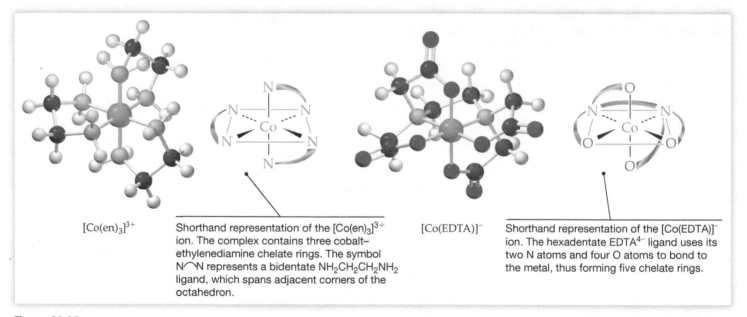

$[Co(en)_3]^{3+}$ — Shorthand representation of the $[Co(en)_3]^{3+}$ ion. The complex contains three cobalt–ethylenediamine chelate rings. The symbol N⌢N represents a bidentate $NH_2CH_2CH_2NH_2$ ligand, which spans adjacent corners of the octahedron.

$[Co(EDTA)]^-$ — Shorthand representation of the $[Co(EDTA)]^-$ ion. The hexadentate $EDTA^{4-}$ ligand uses its two N atoms and four O atoms to bond to the metal, thus forming five chelate rings.

Figure 20.14
The structures of $[Co(en)_3]^{3+}$ and $[Co(EDTA)]^-$.

Naturally occurring chelating ligands are essential constituents of many important biomolecules. For example, the heme group in hemoglobin contains a planar, tetradentate ligand that uses the lone pair of electrons on each of its four N atoms to bond to an iron(II) ion (Chapter 13 Inquiry). The ligand in heme is a *porphyrin*, a derivative of the porphine molecule (**Figure 20.15a**) in which the porphine's peripheral H atoms are replaced by various substituent groups ($-CH_3$, $-CH=CH_2$, and $-CH_2CH_2CO_2^-$ in heme). Bonding of the porphyrin to the Fe(II) ion involves the prior loss of the two NH protons, which makes room for the Fe(II) to occupy the cavity between the four N atoms.

In hemoglobin, the heme is linked to a protein (globin) through an additional Fe—N bond, as shown in **Figure 20.15b**. In addition, the Fe(II) can bond to an O_2 molecule to give the six-coordinate, octahedral complex present in oxyhemoglobin. The three-dimensional shape of the protein part of the molecule makes possible the reversible binding of O_2.

▶ **PROBLEM 20.8**   Using the abbreviation N⌢O for the glycinate (gly⁻) ligand shown in Figure 20.13,

(a) Draw a possible structure for $Cr(gly)_3$.

(b) Identify the Lewis acid, Lewis base, ligand donor atoms, and chelate rings.

(c) What is the coordination number, coordination geometry, and oxidation state of chromium?

(a) Loss of the two NH protons gives a planar, tetradentate 2− ligand that can bond to a metal cation.

(b) The Fe(II) ion has a six-coordinate, octahedral environment, and the O_2 acts as a monodentate ligand.

Heme

Protein (globin)

Figure 20.15
Chelating ligands in biomolecules. **(a)** The structure of the porphine molecule. The porphyrins are derivatives of porphine in which some of the peripheral H atoms are replaced by various substituent groups. **(b)** Schematic of the planar heme group, the attached protein chain, and the bound O_2 molecule in oxyhemoglobin.

20.7 NAMING COORDINATION COMPOUNDS

In the early days of coordination chemistry, coordination compounds were named after their discoverer or according to their color. Now, we use systematic names that specify the number of ligands of each particular type, the metal, and its oxidation state. Before listing the rules used to name coordination compounds, let's consider a few examples that will illustrate how to apply the rules:

$K_3[Fe(CN)_6]$ Potassium hexacyanoferrate(III)

Cation

6 CN^- ligands — Metal in +3 oxidation state

Anion

$Pt(NH_3)_2Cl_2$ Diamminedichloroplatinum(II)

2 NH_3 ligands — 2 Cl^- ligands — Metal in +2 oxidation state

$[Cr(H_2O)_4Cl_2]Cl$ Tetraaquadichlorochromium(III) chloride

4 H_2O ligands — 2 Cl^- ligands — Metal in +3 oxidation state — Anion

Cation

The following list summarizes the nomenclature rules recommended by the International Union of Pure and Applied Chemistry:

1. If the compound is a salt, name the cation first and then the anion, just as in naming simple salts. For example, $K_3[Fe(CN)_6]$ is potassium hexacyanoferrate(III).

2. In naming a complex ion or a neutral complex, name the ligands first and then the metal. The names of anionic ligands end in -o. As shown in Table 20.5, they are usually obtained by changing the anion endings -ide to -o and -ate to -ato. Neutral ligands are specified by their usual names, except for H_2O, NH_3, and CO, which are called aqua, ammine (note spelling), and carbonyl, respectively. The name of a complex is one word, with no space between the various ligand names and no space between the names of the last ligand and the metal.

TABLE 20.5 Names of Some Common Ligands

Anionic Ligand	Ligand Name	Neutral Ligand	Ligand Name
Bromide, Br^-	Bromo	Ammonia, NH_3	Ammine
Carbonate, CO_3^{2-}	Carbonato	Water, H_2O	Aqua
Chloride, Cl^-	Chloro	Carbon monoxide, CO	Carbonyl
Cyanide, CN^-	Cyano	Ethylenediamine, en	Ethylenediamine
Fluoride, F^-	Fluoro		
Glycinate, gly^-	Glycinato		
Hydroxide, OH^-	Hydroxo		
Oxalate, $C_2O_4^{2-}$	Oxalato		
Thiocyanate, SCN^-	Thiocyanato*		
	Isothiocyanato†		

* Ligand donor atom is S
† Ligand donor atom is N

3. If the complex contains more than one ligand of a particular type, indicate the number with the appropriate Greek prefix: di-, tri-, tetra-, penta-, hexa-, and so forth. The ligands are listed in alphabetical order, and the prefixes are ignored in determining the order. Thus, tetraaqua precedes dichloro in the name for $[Cr(H_2O)_4Cl_2]Cl$: tetraaquadichlorochromium(III) chloride.

4. If the name of a ligand itself contains a Greek prefix—for example, ethylenediamine—put the ligand name in parentheses and use one of the following alternative prefixes to specify the number of ligands: bis- (2), tris- (3), tetrakis- (4), and so forth. Thus, the name of $[Co(en)_3]Cl_3$ is tris(ethylenediamine)cobalt(III) chloride.

5. Use a Roman numeral in parentheses immediately following the name of the metal to indicate the metal's oxidation state. As shown by the preceding examples, there is no space between the name of the metal and the parenthesis.

6. In naming the metal, use the ending -ate if the metal is in an anionic complex. Thus, $[Fe(CN)_6]^{3-}$ is the hexacyanoferrate(III) anion. There are no simple rules for going from the name of the metal to the name of the metallate anion, partly because some of the anions have Latin names. Some common examples are given in Table 20.6.

▲ A sample of tris(ethylenediamine) cobalt(III) chloride, $[Co(en)_3]Cl_3$.

TABLE 20.6 Names of Some Common Metallate Anions

Metal	Anion Name	Metal	Anion Name
Aluminum	Aluminate	Iron	Ferrate
Chromium	Chromate	Manganese	Manganate
Cobalt	Cobaltate	Nickel	Nickelate
Copper	Cuprate	Platinum	Platinate
Gold	Aurate	Zinc	Zincate

The rules for naming coordination compounds make it possible to go from a formula to the systematic name or from a systematic name to the appropriate formula. Worked Examples 20.4 and 20.5 provide some practice.

WORKED EXAMPLE 20.4

DETERMINING THE NAME OF A COORDINATION COMPOUND FROM ITS FORMULA

Name each of the following:

(a) $[Co(NH_3)_6]Cl_3$, prepared in 1798 by B. M. Tassaert and generally considered to be the first coordination compound

(b) $[Rh(NH_3)_5I]I_2$, a yellow compound obtained by heating $[Rh(NH_3)_5(H_2O)]I_3$ at 100 °C

(c) $Fe(CO)_5$, a highly toxic, volatile liquid

(d) $[Fe(C_2O_4)_3]^{3-}$, the ion formed when Fe_2O_3 rust stains are dissolved in oxalic acid $(H_2C_2O_4)$

STRATEGY

First determine the oxidation state of the metal, as in Worked Example 20.3. Then apply the six rules above to name the compound or ion.

SOLUTION

(a) Because the chloride ion has a charge of -1 and ammonia is neutral, the oxidation state of cobalt is $+3$. Use the prefix *hexa-* to indicate that the cation contains six NH_3 ligands, and use a Roman numeral III in parentheses to indicate the oxidation state of cobalt. The name of $[Co(NH_3)_6]Cl_3$ is hexaamminecobalt(III) chloride.

(b) Because the iodide ion has a charge of -1, the complex cation is $[Rh(NH_3)_5I]^{2+}$ and the rhodium has an oxidation state of $+3$. List the *ammine* ligands before the *iodo* ligand, and use the prefix *penta-* to indicate the presence of five NH_3 ligands. The name of $[Rh(NH_3)_5I]I_2$ is pentaammineiodorhodium(III) iodide.

(c) Because the carbonyl ligand is neutral, the oxidation state of iron is zero. The systematic name of $Fe(CO)_5$ is pentacarbonyliron(0), but the common name iron pentacarbonyl is often used.

(d) Because each oxalate ligand $(C_2O_4^{2-})$ has a charge of -2 and because $[Fe(C_2O_4)_3]^{3-}$ has an overall charge of -3, iron must have an oxidation state of $+3$. Use the name ferrate(III) for the metal because the complex is an anion. The name of $[Fe(C_2O_4)_3]^{3-}$ is the trioxalatoferrate(III) ion.

▲ The compound $K_3[Fe(C_2O_4)_3] \cdot 3\,H_2O$ contains the trioxalatoferrate(III) anion.

WORKED EXAMPLE 20.5

DETERMINING THE FORMULA OF A COORDINATION COMPOUND FROM ITS NAME

Write the formula for each of the following:

(a) Potassium tetracyanonickelate(II)

(b) Aquachlorobis(ethylenediamine)cobalt(III) chloride

(c) Sodium hexafluoroaluminate

(d) Diamminesilver(I) ion

STRATEGY

To find the formula and charge of the complex cation or anion, note the number of ligands of each type, their charge, and the oxidation state of the metal in the name of the compound or ion. If the name refers to an electrically neutral compound, balance the charge of the complex cation or anion with the appropriate number of ions of opposite charge.

SOLUTION

(a) The bonding of four CN^- ligands to Ni^{2+} gives an $[Ni(CN)_4]^{2-}$ anion, which must be balanced by two K^+ cations. The compound's formula is therefore $K_2[Ni(CN)_4]$. This compound is obtained when excess KCN is added to a solution of a nickel(II) salt.

continued on next page

(b) Because the complex cation contains one H_2O, one Cl^-, and two neutral en ligands, and because the metal is Co^{3+}, the cation is $[Co(en)_2(H_2O)Cl]^{2+}$. The 2+ charge of the cation must be balanced by two Cl^- anions, so the formula of the compound is $[Co(en)_2(H_2O)Cl]Cl_2$. The cation is the first product formed when $[Co(en)_2Cl_2]^+$ reacts with water.

(c) Sodium hexafluoroaluminate, also called cryolite, is used in the electrolytic production of aluminum metal (Section 17.13) and is a coordination compound of a main-group element. The oxidation state of aluminum is omitted from the name because aluminum has only one oxidation state (+3). Because F^- has a charge of -1, the anion is $[AlF_6]^{3-}$. The charge of the anion must be balanced by three Na^+ cations; therefore, the formula for the compound is $Na_3[AlF_6]$.

(d) Diamminesilver(I) ion, formed when silver chloride dissolves in an excess of aqueous ammonia, has the formula $[Ag(NH_3)_2]^+$.

▶ **PROBLEM 20.9**   Name each of the following:

(a) $[Cu(NH_3)_4]SO_4$, a deep blue compound obtained when $CuSO_4$ is treated with an excess of ammonia

(b) $Na[Cr(OH)_4]$, the compound formed when $Cr(OH)_3$ is dissolved in an excess of aqueous NaOH

(c) $Co(gly)_3$, a complex that contains the anion of the amino acid glycine

(d) $[Fe(H_2O)_5(NCS)]^{2+}$, the red complex ion formed in a qualitative analysis test for iron

▶ **PROBLEM 20.10**   Write the formula for each of the following:

(a) Tetraamminezinc(II) nitrate, the compound formed when zinc nitrate is treated with an excess of ammonia

(b) Tetracarbonylnickel(0), the first metal carbonyl (prepared in 1888) and an important compound in the industrial refining of nickel metal

(c) Potassium amminetrichloroplatinate(II), a compound that contains a square planar anion

(d) The dicyanoaurate(I) ion, an ion important in the extraction of gold from its ores

20.8   ISOMERS

One of the more interesting aspects of coordination chemistry is the existence of **isomers**, compounds that have the same formula but a different arrangement of their constituent atoms. Because their atoms are arranged differently, isomers are different compounds with different chemical reactivity and different physical properties such as color, solubility, and melting point. Figure 20.16 shows a scheme for classifying some of the kinds of isomers in coordination chemistry. As we'll see in Chapter 23, isomers are also important in organic chemistry.

Figure 20.16

Classification scheme for the kinds of isomers in coordination chemistry. See the text for examples.

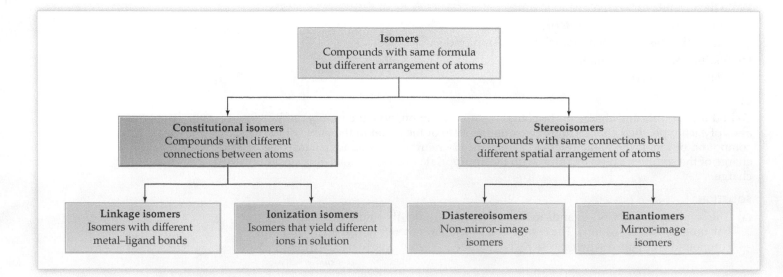

Constitutional Isomers

Isomers that have different connections among their constituent atoms are called **constitutional isomers**. Of the various types of constitutional isomers, we'll discuss just two: *linkage isomers* and *ionization isomers*.

Linkage isomers arise when a ligand can bond to a metal through either of two different donor atoms. For example, the nitrite (NO_2^-) ion forms two different pentaamminecobalt(III) complexes: a yellow *nitro* complex that contains a Co—N bond, $[Co(NH_3)_5(NO_2)]^{2+}$, and a red *nitrito* complex that contains a Co—O bond, $[Co(NH_3)_5(ONO)]^{2+}$ **(Figure 20.17)**. The ligand in the nitrito complex is written as ONO to emphasize that it's linked to the cobalt through an oxygen atom. The thiocyanate (SCN^-) ion is another ligand that gives linkage isomers because it can bond to a metal through either the sulfur atom to give a thiocyanato complex or the nitrogen atom to give an isothiocyanato complex.

(a) N-bonded NO_2^- ligand   **(b)** O-bonded NO_2^- ligand

Ionization isomers differ in the anion that is bonded to the metal ion. An example is the pair $[Co(NH_3)_5Br]SO_4$, a violet compound that has a Co—Br bond and a free sulfate anion, and $[Co(NH_3)_5SO_4]Br$, a red compound that has a Co—sulfate bond and a free bromide ion. Ionization isomers get their name because they yield different ions in solution.

Figure 20.17
Linkage isomers. Samples and structures of **(a)** the nitro complex $[Co(NH_3)_5(NO_2)]^{2+}$ and **(b)** the nitrito complex $[Co(NH_3)_5(ONO)]^{2+}$.

Stereoisomers

Isomers that have the same connections among atoms but a different arrangement of the atoms in space are called **stereoisomers**. In coordination chemistry, there are two kinds of stereoisomers: *diastereoisomers* and *enantiomers*. We'll discuss diastereoisomers in this section and enantiomers in Section 20.9.

Diastereoisomers, also called *geometric isomers*, are non-mirror-image stereoisomers. For example, in the square planar complex $Pt(NH_3)_2Cl_2$, the two Pt—Cl bonds can be oriented either adjacent at a 90° angle or opposite at a 180° angle, as shown in **Figure 20.18**. The isomer in which identical ligands occupy adjacent corners of the square is called the **cis isomer**, and the one in which identical ligands are across from each other is called the **trans isomer**. (The Latin word *cis* means "next to"; *trans* means "across".)

Figure 20.18
Diastereoisomers of the square planar complex $Pt(NH_3)_2Cl_2$. The two compounds have the same connections among atoms but different arrangements of the atoms in space.

cis isomer   trans isomer

Cis and trans isomers are different compounds with different properties. Thus, cis-Pt(NH$_3$)$_2$Cl$_2$ is a polar molecule and is more soluble in water than $trans$–Pt(NH$_3$)$_2$Cl$_2$. The trans isomer is nonpolar because the two Pt—Cl and the two Pt—NH$_3$ bond dipoles point in opposite directions and therefore cancel. It's also interesting that cis-Pt(NH$_3$)$_2$Cl$_2$ (cisplatin) is a widely prescribed anticancer drug, whereas the trans isomer is inactive as an antitumor agent.

In general, square planar complexes of the type MA$_2$B$_2$ and MA$_2$BC—where M is a metal ion and A, B, and C are ligands—can exist as cis–trans isomers. No cis–trans isomers are possible, however, for four-coordinate tetrahedral complexes because all four corners of a tetrahedron are adjacent to one another.

Octahedral complexes of the type MA$_4$B$_2$ can also exist as diastereoisomers because the two B ligands can be on either adjacent or opposite corners of the octahedron. Examples are the violet compound cis-[Co(NH$_3$)$_4$Cl$_2$]Cl and the green compound $trans$-[Co(NH$_3$)$_4$Cl$_2$]Cl. As **Figure 20.19** shows, there are several ways of drawing the cis and trans isomers because each complex can be rotated in space, changing the perspective but not the identity of the isomer.

(a) cis isomer
(b) cis isomer

Same as
=

Although they may appear different, cis isomers (**a**) and (**b**) are identical, as can be seen by rotating the entire complex by 90° about a Cl–Co–NH$_3$ axis.

(c) trans isomer
(d) trans isomer

Same as
=

Trans isomers (**c**) and (**d**) are also identical.

Figure 20.19
Diastereoisomers of the [Co(NH$_3$)$_4$Cl$_2$]$^+$ ion.

How can we be sure that there are only two diastereoisomers of the [Co(NH$_3$)$_4$Cl$_2$]$^+$ ion? The first Cl$^-$ ligand can be located at any one of the six corners of the octahedron. Once one Cl$^-$ is present, however, the five corners remaining are no longer equivalent. The second Cl$^-$ can be located either on one of the four corners adjacent to the first Cl$^-$, which gives the cis isomer, or on the unique corner opposite the first Cl$^-$, which gives the trans isomer. Thus, only two diastereoisomers are possible for complexes of the type MA$_4$B$_2$ (and MA$_4$BC).

WORKED EXAMPLE 20.6

ENUMERATING DIASTEREOISOMERS FOR SQUARE PLANAR AND OCTAHEDRAL COMPLEXES

Platinum(II) forms square planar complexes, and platinum(IV) gives octahedral complexes. How many diastereoisomers are possible for each of the following complexes? Draw their structures.

(a) $[Pt(NH_3)_3Cl]^+$ (b) $[Pt(NH_3)Cl_5]^-$

(c) $Pt(NH_3)_2Cl(NO_2)$ (d) $[Pt(NH_3)_4ClBr]^{2+}$

STRATEGY

Recall that cis and trans isomers are possible for square planar complexes of the type MA_2B_2 and MA_2BC and for octahedral complexes of the type MA_4B_2 and MA_4BC. Cis and trans isomers are not possible when only one ligand differs from the others, as in complexes of the type MA_3B and MA_5B.

SOLUTION

(a) No isomers are possible for $[Pt(NH_3)_3Cl]^+$, a square planar complex of the type MA_3B.

(b) No isomers are possible for $[Pt(NH_3)Cl_5]^-$, an octahedral complex of the type MA_5B.

(c) Cis and trans isomers are possible for $Pt(NH_3)_2Cl(NO_2)$, a square planar complex of the type MA_2BC. The Cl^- and NO_2^- ligands can be on either adjacent or opposite corners of the square.

(d) Cis and trans isomers are possible for $[Pt(NH_3)_4ClBr]^{2+}$, an octahedral complex of the type MA_4BC. The Cl^- and Br^- ligands can be on either adjacent or opposite corners of the octahedron.

WORKED EXAMPLE 20.7

DRAWING THE STRUCTURES OF DIASTEREOISOMERS

Draw the structures of all possible diastereoisomers of triamminetrichlorocobalt(III), $Co(NH_3)_3Cl_3$.

STRATEGY AND SOLUTION

Two diastereoisomers are possible for an octahedral complex of the type MA_3B_3. Isomer **(a)** shown below has the three Cl^- ligands in adjacent positions on one triangular face of the octahedron; isomer **(b)** has all three Cl^- ligands in a plane that contains the Co(III) ion. In isomer **(a)**, all three Cl—Co—Cl bond angles are 90°, whereas in isomer **(b)** two Cl—Co—Cl angles are 90° and the third is 180°.

(a)   **(b)**

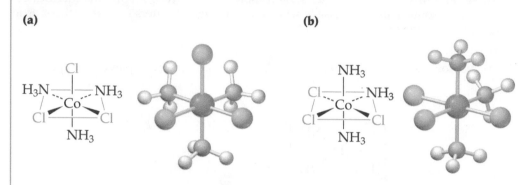

   To convince yourself that only two diastereoisomers of $Co(NH_3)_3Cl_3$ exist, look back at Figure 20.19 and consider the products obtained from *cis*- and *trans*-$[Co(NH_3)_4Cl_2]^+$ when one of the four NH_3 ligands is replaced by a Cl^-. There are two kinds of NH_3 ligands in *cis*-$[Co(NH_3)_4Cl_2]^+$: two NH_3 ligands that are trans to each other and two NH_3 ligands that are trans to a Cl^-. Replacing an NH_3 trans to another NH_3 with Cl^- gives $Co(NH_3)_3Cl_3$ isomer **(a)**, whereas replacing an NH_3 trans to a Cl^- with another Cl^- gives isomer **(b)**. All four NH_3 ligands in *trans*-$[Co(NH_3)_4Cl_2]^+$ are equivalent, and replacing any one of them with a Cl^- gives isomer **(b)**. [If you rotate the resulting $Co(NH_3)_3Cl_3$ complex, you can see that it is identical to the previous drawing of isomer **(b)**.] Thus, there are only two diastereoisomers for a complex of the type MA_3B_3.

▶ **PROBLEM 20.11**   How many diastereoisomers are possible for the following complexes? Draw the structure of each diastereoisomer.

(a) $Pt(NH_3)_2(SCN)_2$ **(b)** $[CoCl_2Br_2]^{2-}$ (tetrahedral)

(c) $Co(NH_3)_3(NO_2)_3$ **(d)** $Pt(en)Cl_2$

(e) $[Cr(en)_2Br_2]^+$ **(f)** $[Rh(en)_3]^{3+}$

WORKED CONCEPTUAL EXAMPLE 20.8

IDENTIFYING CIS AND TRANS ISOMERS

Consider the following isomers of the $[Co(NH_3)_4(H_2O)Cl]^{2+}$ ion:

= Co   = NH_3 = H_2O = Cl

(1)   **(2)**   **(3)**   **(4)**

(a) Label the isomers as cis or trans.

(b) Which isomers are identical, and which are different?

STRATEGY

Look at the location of the H_2O and Cl^- ligands. Isomers that have H_2O and Cl^- on adjacent corners of the octahedron are cis, whereas those that have H_2O and Cl^- on opposite corners are trans. Because only two isomers are possible for complexes of the type MA_4BC, all the cis isomers are identical and all the trans isomers are identical.

SOLUTION

(a) Isomers (1) and (4) have H_2O and Cl^- on opposite corners of the octahedron and are therefore trans isomers. Isomers (2) and (3) have H_2O and Cl^- on adjacent corners of the octahedron and are therefore cis isomers.

(b) Isomers (1) and (4) are identical, as can be seen by rotating (1) counterclockwise by 90° about the vertical (z) axis:

Isomers (2) and (3) differ from (1) and (4) and are identical, as can be seen by rotating (2) clockwise by 90° about the x axis and then counterclockwise by 90° about the y axis:

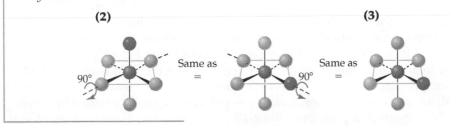

CONCEPTUAL PROBLEM 20.12 Which of the following $[Co(en)(NH_3)_3Cl]^{2+}$ isomers are identical, and which are different?

= Co   = $NH_2CH_2CH_2NH_2$ = NH_3 = Cl

(1)   **(2)**   **(3)**   **(4)**

20.9 ENANTIOMERS AND MOLECULAR HANDEDNESS

Diastereoisomers are relatively easy to distinguish because the various bonds in the cis and trans isomers point in different directions. *Enantiomers*, however, are stereoisomers that differ in a more subtle way: **Enantiomers** are molecules or ions that are nonidentical mirror images of each other; they differ because of their handedness.

Handedness affects almost everything we do. Anyone who has played much softball knows that the last available glove always fits the wrong hand. Any left-handed person sitting next to a right-handed person in a lecture knows that taking notes sometimes means bumping elbows. The reason for these difficulties is that our hands aren't identical—they're mirror images. When you hold your left hand up to a mirror, the image you see looks like your right hand. (Try it.)

Not all objects are handed. There's no such thing as a right-handed tennis ball or a left-handed coffee mug. When a tennis ball or a coffee mug is held up to a mirror, the image reflected is identical to the ball or mug itself. Objects that do have a handedness to them are said to be **chiral** (pronounced **ky**-ral, from the Greek *cheir*, meaning "hand"), and objects that lack handedness are said to be nonchiral, or **achiral**.

Why is it that some objects are chiral but others aren't? In general, an object is not chiral if, like the coffee mug, it has a **symmetry plane** cutting through its middle so that one half of the object is a mirror image of the other half. If you were to cut the mug in half, one half of the mug would be the mirror image of the other half. A hand, however, has no symmetry plane and is therefore chiral. If you were to cut a hand in two, one "half" of the hand would not be a mirror image of the other half (**Figure 20.20**).

Just as certain objects like a hand are chiral, certain molecules and ions are also chiral. Consider, for example, the tris(ethylenediamine)cobalt(III) ion, $[Co(en)_3]^{3+}$, an ion with the shape of a three-bladed propeller (**Figure 20.21**). The $[Co(en)_3]^{3+}$ cation has no symmetry plane because its two halves aren't mirror images. Thus, $[Co(en)_3]^{3+}$ is chiral and can exist in two nonidentical mirror-image forms. When viewed as drawn in Figure 20.21, one enantiomer is "right-handed" because the three ethylenediamine ligands appear to spiral in a clockwise direction and the other enantiomer is "left-handed" because the ethylenediamine ligands spiral in a counterclockwise direction. By contrast, the analogous ammonia complex $[Co(NH_3)_6]^{3+}$ is achiral because, like a coffee mug, it has a symmetry plane. (Actually, $[Co(NH_3)_6]^{3+}$ has several symmetry planes, though only one is shown in Figure 20.21.) Thus, $[Co(NH_3)_6]^{3+}$ exists in a single form and does not have enantiomers.

Enantiomers have identical properties except for their reactions with other chiral substances and their effect on *plane-polarized light*. In ordinary light, the electric vibrations occur in all planes parallel to the direction in which the light wave is traveling, but in plane-polarized light, the electric vibrations of the light wave are restricted to a single plane, as shown in **Figure 20.22**. Plane-polarized light is obtained by passing ordinary light through a polarizing filter, like that found in certain kinds of sunglasses. If the plane-polarized light is then passed through a solution of one enantiomer, the plane of polarization is rotated, either to the right (clockwise) or to the left (counterclockwise). If the light is passed through a solution of the other enantiomer, its plane of polarization is rotated through an equal angle, but in the opposite direction. Enantiomers are sometimes called *optical isomers* because of their effect on plane-polarized light.

Enantiomers are labeled (+) or (−), depending on the direction of rotation of the plane of polarization. For example, the isomer of $[Co(en)_3]^{3+}$ that rotates the plane of polarization to the right is labeled (+)-$[Co(en)_3]^{3+}$, and the isomer that rotates the plane of polarization to the left is designated (−)-$[Co(en)_3]^{3+}$. A 1:1 mixture of the (+) and (−) isomers, called a **racemic mixture**, produces no net optical rotation because the rotations produced by the individual enantiomers exactly cancel.

Symmetry plane

An achiral object like the coffee mug has a symmetry plane passing through it, making the two halves mirror images.

A chiral object like the hand has no symmetry plane because the two halves of the hand are not mirror images.

Figure 20.20
The meaning of a symmetry plane.

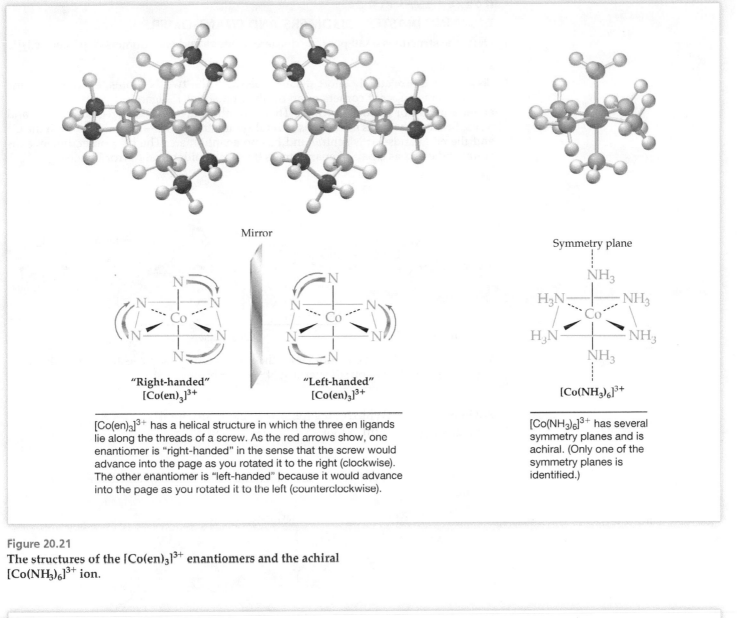

Mirror

"Right-handed"
$[Co(en)_3]^{3+}$

"Left-handed"
$[Co(en)_3]^{3+}$

$[Co(en)_3]^{3+}$ has a helical structure in which the three en ligands lie along the threads of a screw. As the red arrows show, one enantiomer is "right-handed" in the sense that the screw would advance into the page as you rotated it to the right (clockwise). The other enantiomer is "left-handed" because it would advance into the page as you rotated it to the left (counterclockwise).

Symmetry plane

$[Co(NH_3)_6]^{3+}$

$[Co(NH_3)_6]^{3+}$ has several symmetry planes and is achiral. (Only one of the symmetry planes is identified.)

Figure 20.21
The structures of the $[Co(en)_3]^{3+}$ enantiomers and the achiral $[Co(NH_3)_6]^{3+}$ ion.

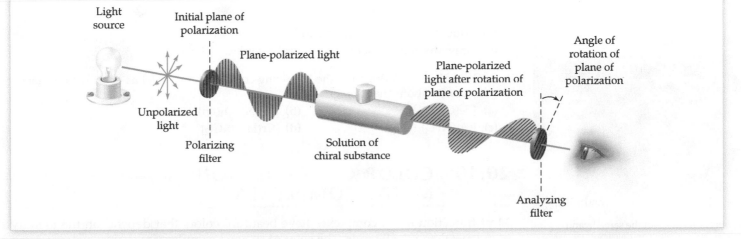

Light source

Initial plane of polarization

Plane-polarized light

Angle of rotation of plane of polarization

Unpolarized light

Polarizing filter

Solution of chiral substance

Plane-polarized light after rotation of plane of polarization

Analyzing filter

Figure 20.22
The essential features of a polarimeter. The polarimeter measures the angle through which the plane of plane-polarized light is rotated when the light is passed through a solution of a chiral substance.

WORKED EXAMPLE 20.9

DRAWING DIASTEREOISOMERS AND ENANTIOMERS

Draw the structures of all possible diastereoisomers and enantiomers of $[Co(en)_2Cl_2]^+$.

STRATEGY

Because of the relatively short distance between the two N atoms, ethylenediamine always spans adjacent corners of an octahedron. The Cl^- ligands, however, can be on either adjacent or opposite corners. Therefore, there are two diastereoisomers, cis and trans. Because the trans isomer has several symmetry planes—one cuts through the Co and the en ligands—it is achiral and has no enantiomers. The cis isomer, however, is chiral and exists as a pair of enantiomers that are nonidentical mirror images.

SOLUTION

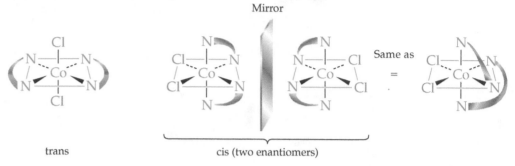

trans   cis (two enantiomers)

You can see that the cis enantiomer on the right is not the same as the one on the left if you rotate it by 180° about the vertical N—Co—N axis.

▶ **PROBLEM 20.13** Which of the following objects are chiral?
(a) A chair   (b) A foot   (c) A pencil
(d) A corkscrew (e) A banana   (f) A football

CONCEPTUAL PROBLEM 20.14 Consider the following ethylenediamine complexes of rhodium:

(a) Which complexes are chiral, and which are achiral?
(b) Draw the enantiomer of each chiral complex.

▶ **PROBLEM 20.15** Which of the following complexes can exist as enantiomers? Draw the structure of both enantiomers.
(a) $[Fe(C_2O_4)_3]^{3-}$ (b) $[Co(NH_3)_4(en)]^{3+}$
(c) $[Co(NH_3)_2(en)_2]^{3+}$ (d) $[Cr(H_2O)_4Cl_2]^+$

20.10 COLOR OF TRANSITION METAL COMPLEXES

Figure 20.23
Aqueous solutions of the nitrate salts of cobalt(II), nickel(II), copper(II), and zinc(II).

Most transition metal complexes have beautiful colors that depend on the identity of the metal and the ligands. The color of an aqua complex, for example, depends on the metal: $[Co(H_2O)_6]^{2+}$ is pink, $[Ni(H_2O)_6]^{2+}$ is green, $[Cu(H_2O)_6]^{2+}$ is blue, but $[Zn(H_2O)_6]^{2+}$ is colorless (**Figure 20.23**). If we keep the metal constant but vary the ligand, the color also changes. For example, $[Ni(H_2O)_6]^{2+}$ is green, $[Ni(NH_3)_6]^{2+}$ is blue, and $[Ni(en)_3]^{2+}$ is violet (**Figure 20.24**).

$[Ni(H_2O)_6]^{2+}$ $[Ni(NH_3)_6]^{2+}$ $[Ni(en)_3]^{2+}$

The same metal, but different ligands

Figure 20.24
Aqueous solutions that contain $[Ni(H_2O)_6]^{2+}$, $[Ni(NH_3)_6]^{2+}$, and $[Ni(en)_3]^{2+}$.

How can we account for the color of transition metal complexes? Let's begin by recalling that white light consists of a continuous spectrum of wavelengths corresponding to different colors (Section 5.1). When white light strikes a colored substance, some wavelengths are transmitted while others are absorbed. Just as atoms can absorb light by undergoing electronic transitions between atomic energy levels, thereby giving rise to atomic spectra, so a metal complex can absorb light by undergoing an electronic transition from its lowest (ground) energy state to a higher (excited) energy state.

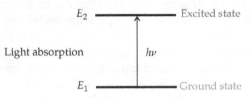

E_2 ———————— Excited state

Light absorption $h\nu$

E_1 ———————— Ground state

The wavelength λ of the light absorbed by a metal complex depends on the energy separation $\Delta E = E_2 - E_1$ between the two states, as given by the equation $\Delta E = h\nu = hc/\lambda$ (Section 5.3), where h is Planck's constant, ν is the frequency of the light, and c is the speed of light:

$$\Delta E = E_2 - E_1 = h\nu = \frac{hc}{\lambda} \qquad \text{or} \qquad \lambda = \frac{hc}{\Delta E}$$

The measure of the amount of light absorbed by a substance is called the *absorbance*, and a plot of absorbance versus wavelength is called an **absorption spectrum**. For example, the absorption spectrum of the red-violet $[Ti(H_2O)_6]^{3+}$ ion has a broad absorption band at about 500 nm, a wavelength in the blue-green part of the visible spectrum (**Figure 20.25**). In general, the color that we see is complementary to the color absorbed (**Figure 20.26**).

Violet

Because the absorbance is smaller in the red and violet regions of the spectrum, these colors are largely transmitted and we perceive the color of $[Ti(H_2O)_6]^{3+}$ to be red-violet.

Red

Absorbance

400   500   600   700

Wavelength (nm)

Figure 20.25
A solution that contains the $[Ti(H_2O)_6]^{3+}$ ion and its visible absorption spectrum.

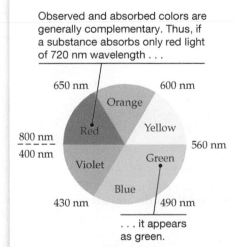

Observed and absorbed colors are generally complementary. Thus, if a substance absorbs only red light of 720 nm wavelength . . .

650 nm   600 nm
                  Orange
800 nm   Red   Yellow
400 nm   560 nm
            Violet   Green
                  Blue
430 nm   490 nm

. . . it appears as green.

Figure 20.26
An artist's color wheel. The observed color of a substance is complementary to the color of the light absorbed and appears on the opposite side of the wheel.

▶ **PROBLEM 20.16**   Consider a complex ion that has just one absorption band at 625 nm.

(a) What is the most likely color of this ion?

(b) What is the energy difference ΔE (in joules) between the ground and excited states for this ion?

20.11 BONDING IN COMPLEXES: VALENCE BOND THEORY

Remember...

The **valence bond theory** describes a covalent bond as a pair of electrons of opposite spin that are shared between two atoms as a result of orbital overlap. (Section 7.10)

According to the **valence bond theory** (Section 7.10), the bonding in metal complexes arises when a filled ligand orbital containing a pair of electrons overlaps a vacant hybrid orbital on the metal ion to give a coordinate covalent bond:

Vacant metal
hybrid atomic orbital

Occupied ligand
atomic orbital

Coordinate covalent
bond

Remember...

Hybrid orbitals are formed by a mathematical combination of atomic orbital wave functions. Combination of one *s* and one *p* orbital gives a set of two equivalent *sp* hybrids that are oriented at 180° to each other. The combination of one *s* and three *p* orbitals gives a set of four equivalent sp^3 hybrids that are oriented at 109.5° to each other and point toward the corners of a regular tetrahedron.   (Sections 7.11–7.12)

The **hybrid orbitals** that a metal ion uses to accept a share in the ligand electrons are those that point in the directions of the ligands. In linear complexes the metal uses *sp* hybrids, while in tetrahedral complexes the metal uses sp^3 hybrids. Remember that geometry and hybridization go together. Once you know the geometry of a complex, you automatically know which hybrid orbitals the metal ion uses.

In octahedral complexes, the metal ion uses valence *d* orbitals in addition to *s* and *p* orbitals to form six bonds to the ligands. Hybridization occurs by a combination of two *d* orbitals, one *s* orbital, and three *p* orbitals, resulting in either six d^2sp^3 hybrids or six sp^3d^2 hybrids. As we'll see later, the difference between d^2sp^3 and sp^3d^2 hybrids lies in the principal quantum number of the *d* orbitals. Both sets of hybrids, however, point toward the six corners of a regular octahedron, as shown in **Figure 20.27**. All six orbitals within each set are equivalent, and the angle between any two adjacent orbitals is 90°.

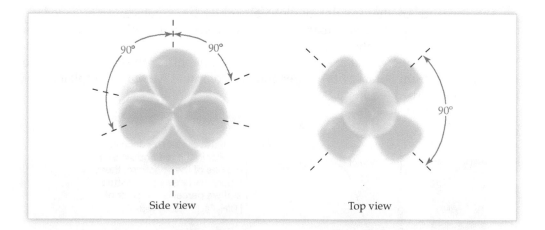

Side view

Top view

Figure 20.27
The octahedral geometry of the six d^2sp^3 and sp^3d^2 hybrid orbitals.

In square planar complexes, the metal ion uses a set of four equivalent dsp^2 hybrid orbitals formed by the hybridization of one *d* orbital, one *s* orbital, and two *p* orbitals. These hybrids point toward the four corners of a square, as shown in **Figure 20.28**.

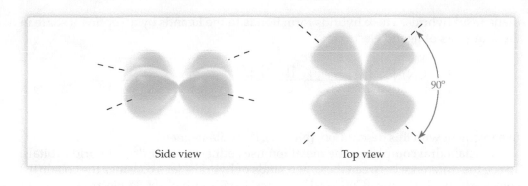

Figure 20.28
The square planar geometry of the four
dsp^2 **hybrid orbitals.**

Side view   Top view

The relationship between the geometry of a complex and the hybrid orbitals used by the metal ion is summarized in Table 20.7.

TABLE 20.7   Hybrid Orbitals for Common Coordination Geometries

Coordination Number	Geometry	Hybrid Orbitals	Example
2	Linear	sp	$[Ag(NH_3)_2]^+$
4	Tetrahedral	sp^3	$[CoCl_4]^{2-}$
4	Square planar	dsp^2	$[Ni(CN)_4]^{2-}$
6	Octahedral	d^2sp^3 or sp^3d^2	$[Cr(H_2O)_6]^{3+}$, $[Co(H_2O)_6]^{2+}$

To illustrate the relationship between geometry and hybridization, let's consider the tetrahedral complex $[CoCl_4]^{2-}$. A free Co^{2+} ion has the electron configuration [Ar] $3d^7$ and the following orbital diagram:

$$Co^{2+}:\ [Ar]\ \underset{3d}{\uparrow\downarrow\ \uparrow\downarrow\ \uparrow\ \uparrow\ \uparrow}\quad \underset{4s}{\rule{0.4cm}{0.4pt}}\quad \underset{4p}{\rule{0.4cm}{0.4pt}\ \rule{0.4cm}{0.4pt}\ \rule{0.4cm}{0.4pt}}$$

Because the geometry of $[CoCl_4]^{2-}$ is tetrahedral, the hybrid orbitals that Co^{2+} uses to accept a share in the four pairs of ligand electrons must be sp^3 hybrids formed from the vacant $4s$ and $4p$ orbitals. The following orbital diagram represents the bonding in the complex, showing the hybridization of the metal orbitals and the four pairs of ligand electrons, now shared in the bonds between the metal and the ligands:

$$[CoCl_4]^{2-}:\ [Ar]\ \underset{3d}{\uparrow\downarrow\ \uparrow\downarrow\ \uparrow\ \uparrow\ \uparrow}\quad \boxed{\underset{4s}{\uparrow\downarrow}\quad \underset{4p}{\uparrow\downarrow\ \uparrow\downarrow\ \uparrow\downarrow}}$$

Four sp^3 bonds to the ligands

In accord with this description, $[CoCl_4]^{2-}$ has three unpaired electrons and is paramagnetic. Recall from Section 7.14 that **paramagnetic** substances contain unpaired electrons and are attracted by magnetic fields, whereas diamagnetic substances contain only paired electrons and are weakly repelled by magnetic fields. The number of unpaired electrons in a transition metal complex can be determined by quantitatively measuring the force exerted on the complex by a magnetic field.

As an example of a square planar complex, consider $[Ni(CN)_4]^{2-}$. A free Ni^{2+} ion has eight $3d$ electrons, two of which are unpaired in accord with Hund's rule (Section 5.11):

$$Ni^{2+}:\ [Ar]\ \underset{3d}{\uparrow\downarrow\ \uparrow\downarrow\ \uparrow\downarrow\ \uparrow\ \uparrow}\quad \underset{4s}{\rule{0.4cm}{0.4pt}}\quad \underset{4p}{\rule{0.4cm}{0.4pt}\ \rule{0.4cm}{0.4pt}\ \rule{0.4cm}{0.4pt}}$$

Because $[Ni(CN)_4]^{2-}$ is square planar, the metal ion must use dsp^2 hybrids. By pairing up the two unpaired d electrons in one d orbital, we obtain a vacant $3d$ orbital that can be hybridized with the $4s$ orbital and two of the $4p$ orbitals to give the square

Remember...

The O_2 molecule has two unpaired π^*_{2p} electrons and is **paramagnetic**, whereas N_2 and F_2 have no unpaired electrons and are diamagnetic.   (Section 7.14)

planar dsp^2 hybrids. These hybrids form bonds to the ligands by accepting a share in the four pairs of ligand electrons:

$$[\text{Ni(CN)}_4]^{2-}: \text{[Ar]} \underset{3d}{\uparrow\downarrow\ \ \uparrow\downarrow\ \ \uparrow\downarrow\ \ \uparrow\downarrow}\ \boxed{\underset{4s}{\uparrow\downarrow}\quad \underset{4p}{\uparrow\downarrow\ \ \uparrow\downarrow\ \ \uparrow\downarrow}}\ \_\_$$

Four dsp^2 bonds to the ligands

In agreement with this description, $[\text{Ni(CN)}_4]^{2-}$ is diamagnetic.

In octahedral complexes, the metal ion uses either sp^3d^2 or d^2sp^3 hybrid orbitals. To see the difference between these two kinds of hybrids, let's consider the cobalt(III) complexes $[\text{CoF}_6]^{3-}$ and $[\text{Co(CN)}_6]^{3-}$. A free Co^{3+} ion has six $3d$ electrons, four of which are unpaired:

$$Co^{3+}: \text{[Ar]} \underset{3d}{\uparrow\downarrow\ \ \uparrow\ \ \uparrow\ \ \uparrow\ \ \uparrow}\ \ \underset{4s}{\_\_}\ \ \underset{4p}{\_\_\ \_\_\ \_\_}\ \ \underset{4d}{\_\_\ \_\_\ \_\_\ \_\_\ \_\_}$$

Magnetic measurements indicate that $[\text{CoF}_6]^{3-}$ is paramagnetic and contains four unpaired electrons. Evidently, none of the $3d$ orbitals is available to accept a share in the ligand electrons because each is already at least partially occupied. Consequently, the octahedral hybrids that Co^{3+} uses are formed from the vacant $4s$, $4p$, and $4d$ orbitals. These orbitals, called sp^3d^2 hybrids, share in the six pairs of ligand electrons, as shown in the following orbital diagram:

$$[\text{CoF}_6]^{3-}: \text{[Ar]} \underset{3d}{\uparrow\downarrow\ \ \uparrow\ \ \uparrow\ \ \uparrow\ \ \uparrow}\ \boxed{\underset{4s}{\uparrow\downarrow}\quad \underset{4p}{\uparrow\downarrow\ \ \uparrow\downarrow\ \ \uparrow\downarrow}\quad \underset{4d}{\uparrow\downarrow\ \ \uparrow\downarrow}}\underset{4d}{\_\_\ \_\_\ \_\_}$$

Six sp^3d^2 bonds to the ligands

In contrast to $[\text{CoF}_6]^{3-}$, magnetic measurements indicate that $[\text{Co(CN)}_6]^{3-}$ is diamagnetic. All six $3d$ electrons are therefore paired and occupy just three of the five $3d$ orbitals. That leaves two vacant $3d$ orbitals, which combine with the vacant $4s$ and $4p$ orbitals to give a set of six octahedral hybrid orbitals called d^2sp^3 hybrids. The d^2sp^3 hybrids form bonds to the ligands by accepting a share in the six pairs of ligand electrons:

$$[\text{Co(CN)}_6]^{3-}: \text{[Ar]} \underset{3d}{\uparrow\downarrow\ \ \uparrow\downarrow\ \ \uparrow\downarrow}\ \boxed{\underset{}{\uparrow\downarrow\ \ \uparrow\downarrow}\quad \underset{4s}{\uparrow\downarrow}\quad \underset{4p}{\uparrow\downarrow\ \ \uparrow\downarrow\ \ \uparrow\downarrow}}\ \underset{4d}{\_\_\ \_\_\ \_\_\ \_\_\ \_\_}$$

Six d^2sp^3 bonds to the ligands

The difference between d^2sp^3 and sp^3d^2 hybrids lies in the principal quantum number of the d orbitals. In d^2sp^3 hybrids, the principal quantum number of the d orbitals is one less than the principal quantum number of the s and p orbitals. In sp^3d^2 hybrids, the s, p, and d orbitals have the same principal quantum number. To determine which set of hybrids is used in any given complex, we must know the magnetic properties of the complex.

Complexes of metals like Co^{3+} that exhibit more than one spin state are classified as *high-spin* or *low-spin*. A **high-spin complex**, such as $[\text{CoF}_6]^{3-}$, is one in which the d electrons are arranged according to Hund's rule to give the maximum number of unpaired electrons. A **low-spin complex**, such as $[\text{Co(CN)}_6]^{3-}$, is one in which the d electrons are paired up to give a maximum number of doubly occupied d orbitals and a minimum number of unpaired electrons.

$[\text{V(NH}_3)_6]^{3+}$

WORKED EXAMPLE 20.10

DESCRIBING THE BONDING IN COMPLEXES IN TERMS OF VALENCE BOND HYBRID ORBITALS

Give a valence bond description of the bonding in $[\text{V(NH}_3)_6]^{3+}$. Include orbital diagrams for the free metal ion and the metal ion in the complex. Tell which hybrid orbitals the metal ion uses and the number of unpaired electrons present.

STRATEGY AND SOLUTION

The free V^{3+} ion has the electron configuration [Ar] $3d^2$ and the orbital diagram

$$V^{3+}: \ [Ar] \ \underset{3d}{\uparrow \ \uparrow \ \_\_ \ \_\_ \ \_\_} \quad \underset{4s}{\_\_} \quad \underset{4p}{\_\_ \ \_\_ \ \_\_}$$

Because $[V(NH_3)_6]^{3+}$ is octahedral, the V^{3+} ion must use either d^2sp^3 or sp^3d^2 hybrid orbitals in accepting a share in six pairs of electrons from the six NH_3 ligands. The preferred hybrids are d^2sp^3 because several $3d$ orbitals are vacant and d^2sp^3 hybrids have lower energy than sp^3d^2 hybrids (because the $3d$ orbitals have lower energy than the $4d$ orbitals). Thus, $[V(NH_3)_6]^{3+}$ has the following orbital diagram:

$$[V(NH_3)_6]^{3+}: \ [Ar] \ \underset{3d}{\uparrow \ \uparrow \ \_\_} \ \boxed{\underset{}{\uparrow\downarrow \ \uparrow\downarrow} \quad \underset{4s}{\uparrow\downarrow} \quad \underset{4p}{\uparrow\downarrow \ \uparrow\downarrow \ \uparrow\downarrow}}$$

Six d^2sp^3 bonds to the ligands

The complex has two unpaired electrons and is therefore paramagnetic.

▶ **PROBLEM 20.17** Give a valence bond description of the bonding in each of the following complexes. Include orbital diagrams for the free metal ion and the metal ion in the complex. Tell which hybrid orbitals the metal ion uses and the number of unpaired electrons in each complex.

(a) $[Fe(CN)_6]^{3-}$ (low-spin)   **(b)** $[Co(H_2O)_6]^{2+}$ (high-spin)

(c) $[VCl_4]^-$ (tetrahedral)   **(d)** $[PtCl_4]^{2-}$ (square planar)

20.12 CRYSTAL FIELD THEORY

Valence bond theory helps us visualize the bonding in complexes, but it doesn't account for their color or explain why some complexes are high-spin whereas others are low-spin. To explain these properties, we turn to the **crystal field theory**, a model that views the bonding in complexes as arising from electrostatic interactions and considers the effect of the ligand charges on the energies of the metal ion d orbitals. This model was first applied to transition metal ions in ionic crystals—hence the name crystal field theory—but it also applies to metal complexes where the "crystal field" is the electric field due to the charges or dipoles of the ligands.

Octahedral Complexes

Let's first consider an octahedral complex such as $[TiF_6]^{3-}$ (**Figure 20.29**). According to the crystal field theory, the bonding is ionic and involves electrostatic attraction between the positively charged Ti^{3+} ion and the negatively charged F^- ligands. Of course, the F^- ligands repel one another, which is why they adopt the geometry (octahedral) that locates them as far apart from one another as possible. Because the metal–ligand attractions are greater than the ligand–ligand repulsions, the complex is more stable than the separated ions, thus accounting for the bonding.

Note the differences between crystal field theory and valence bond theory. In crystal field theory, there are no covalent bonds, no shared electrons, and no hybrid orbitals—just electrostatic interactions within an array of ions. In complexes that contain neutral dipolar ligands, such as H_2O or NH_3, the electrostatic interactions are of the ion–dipole type (Section 10.2). For example, in $[Ti(H_2O)_6]^{3+}$, the Ti^{3+} ion attracts the negative end of the water dipoles.

Figure 20.29

Crystal field model of the octahedral $[TiF_6]^{3-}$ complex. The metal ion and ligands are regarded as charged particles held together by electrostatic attraction. The ligands lie along the $\pm x$, $\pm y$, and $\pm z$ directions.

Remember...

Although the *d* orbitals have different shapes, all five *d* orbitals have the same energy in a free metal ion.   (Section 5.7)

To explain why complexes are colored, we need to look at the effect of the ligand charges on the energies of the *d* orbitals. Recall that four of the *d orbitals* are shaped like a cloverleaf, while the fifth (d_{z^2}) is shaped like a dumbbell inside a donut (Section 5.7). **Figure 20.30** shows the spatial orientation of the *d* orbitals with respect to an octahedral array of charged ligands located along the x, y, and z coordinate axes.

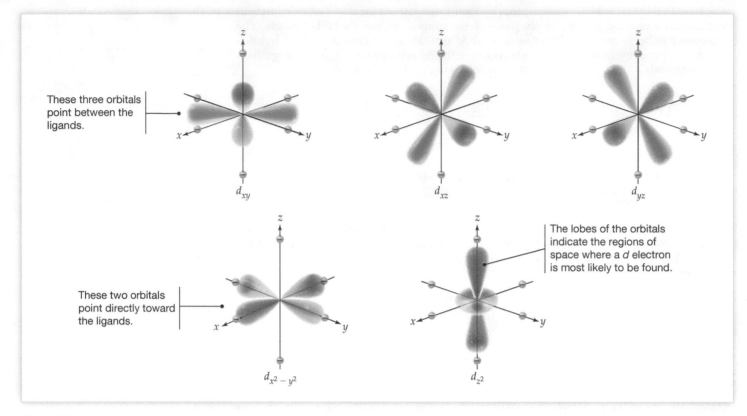

These three orbitals point between the ligands.

d_{xy} d_{xz} d_{yz}

These two orbitals point directly toward the ligands.

The lobes of the orbitals indicate the regions of space where a *d* electron is most likely to be found.

$d_{x^2-y^2}$ d_{z^2}

Figure 20.30
The shapes of the five *d* orbitals and their orientation with respect to an octahedral array of charged ligands.

Because the *d* electrons are negatively charged, they are repelled by the negatively charged ligands. Thus, their orbital energies are higher in the complex than in the free metal ion. But not all the *d* orbitals are raised in energy by the same amount. As shown in **Figure 20.31**, the d_{z^2} and $d_{x^2-y^2}$ orbitals, which point directly at the ligands, are raised in energy to a greater extent than the d_{xy}, d_{xz}, and d_{yz} orbitals, which point between the ligands. This energy splitting between the two sets of *d* orbitals is called the **crystal field splitting** and is represented by the Greek letter Δ.

In general, the crystal field splitting energy Δ corresponds to wavelengths of light in the visible region of the spectrum, and the colors of complexes can therefore be attributed to electronic transitions between the lower- and higher-energy sets of *d* orbitals. Consider, for example, $[Ti(H_2O)_6]^{3+}$, a complex that contains a single *d* electron (Ti^{3+} has the electron configuration [Ar] $3d^1$). In the ground-energy state, the *d* electron occupies one of the lower-energy orbitals—xy, xz, or yz (from now on we'll denote the *d* orbitals by their subscripts). When $[Ti(H_2O)_6]^{3+}$ absorbs blue-green light with a wavelength of about 500 nm, the absorbed energy promotes the *d* electron to one of the higher-energy orbitals, z^2 or $x^2 - y^2$:

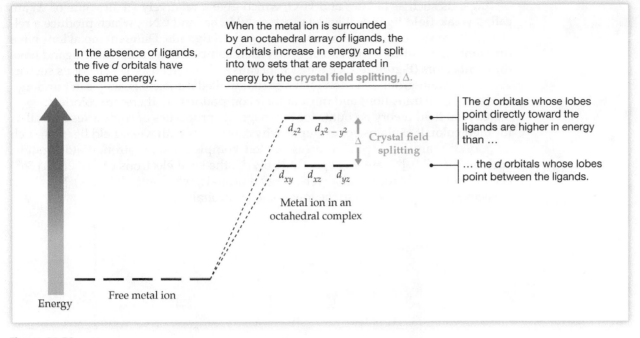

Figure 20.31
A *d*-orbital energy-level diagram for a free metal ion and a metal ion in an octahedral complex.

We can calculate the value of Δ from the wavelength of the absorbed light, about 500 nm for $[Ti(H_2O)_6]^{3+}$:

$$\Delta = h\nu = \frac{hc}{\lambda} = \frac{(6.626 \times 10^{-34}\, J\cdot s)(3.00 \times 10^8\, m/s)}{500 \times 10^{-9}\, m} = 4.0 \times 10^{-19}\, J$$

This is the energy needed to excite a single $[Ti(H_2O)_6]^{3+}$ ion. To express Δ on a per-mole basis, we multiply by Avogadro's number:

$$\Delta = \left(4.0 \times 10^{-19}\, \frac{J}{ion}\right)\left(6.02 \times 10^{23}\, \frac{ions}{mol}\right) = 2.4 \times 10^5\, J/mol = 240\, kJ/mol$$

The absorption spectra of different complexes indicate that the size of the crystal field splitting depends on the nature of the ligands. For example, Δ for Ni^{2+} ([Ar] $3d^8$) complexes increases as the ligand varies from H_2O to NH_3 to ethylenediamine (en). Accordingly, the electronic transitions shift to higher energy (shorter wavelength) as the ligand varies from H_2O to NH_3 to en, thus accounting for the observed variation in color (Figure 20.24; page 833):

In general, the crystal field splitting increases as the ligand varies in the following order, known as the **spectrochemical series**:

Weak-field ligands $I^- < Br^- < Cl^- < F^- < H_2O < NH_3 < en < CN^-$ Strong-field ligands

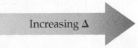

Increasing Δ

Ligands such as halides and H_2O, which give a relatively small value of Δ, are called **weak-field ligands**. Ligands such as NH_3, en, and CN^-, which produce a relatively large value of Δ, are known as **strong-field ligands**. Different metal ions have different values of Δ, which explains why their complexes with the same ligand have different colors (Figure 20.23; page 833). Because d^0 ions such as Ti^{4+}, d^{10} ions such as Zn^{2+}, and main-group ions don't have partially filled d subshells, they can't undergo d–d electronic transitions and most of their compounds are therefore colorless.

Crystal field theory accounts for the magnetic properties of complexes as well as for their color. It explains, for example, why complexes with weak-field ligands, such as $[CoF_6]^{3-}$, are high-spin, whereas related complexes with strong-field ligands, such as $[Co(CN)_6]^{3-}$, are low-spin. In $[CoF_6]^{3-}$, the six d electrons of Co^{3+} ($[Ar]\, 3d^6$) occupy both the higher- and lower-energy d orbitals, whereas in $[Co(CN)_6]^{3-}$, all six d electrons are spin-paired in the lower-energy orbitals:

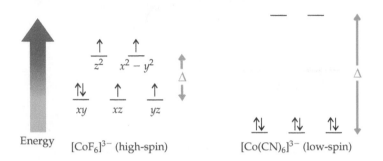

What determines which of the two spin states has the lower energy? In general, when an electron moves from a z^2 or $x^2 - y^2$ orbital to one of the lower-energy orbitals, the orbital energy decreases by Δ. But because of electron–electron repulsion, it costs energy to put the electron into an orbital that already contains another electron. The energy required is called the spin-pairing energy P. If Δ is greater than P, as it is for $[Co(CN)_6]^{3-}$, then the low-spin arrangement has lower energy. If Δ is less than P, as it is for $[CoF_6]^{3-}$, the high-spin arrangement has lower energy. Thus, the observed spin state depends on the relative values of Δ and P. In general, strong-field ligands give low-spin complexes, and weak-field ligands give high-spin complexes.

A choice between high-spin and low-spin electron configurations arises only for complexes of metal ions with four to seven d electrons, so-called d^4–d^7 complexes. For d^1–d^3 and d^8–d^{10} complexes, only one ground-state electron configuration is possible. In d^1–d^3 complexes, all the electrons occupy the lower-energy d orbitals, independent of the value of Δ. In d^8–d^{10} complexes, the lower-energy set of d orbitals is filled with three pairs of electrons, while the higher-energy set contains two, three, or four electrons, again independent of the value of Δ.

WORKED EXAMPLE 20.11

DRAWING CRYSTAL FIELD ENERGY-LEVEL DIAGRAMS FOR OCTAHEDRAL COMPLEXES

Draw a crystal field orbital energy-level diagram, and predict the number of unpaired electrons for each of the following complexes:

(a) $[Cr(en)_3]^{3+}$ **(b)** $[Mn(CN)_6]^{3-}$ **(c)** $[Co(H_2O)_6]^{2+}$

STRATEGY

All three complexes are octahedral, so the energy-level diagrams will show three lower-energy and two higher-energy d orbitals. For d^1–d^3 and d^8–d^{10} complexes, the electrons occupy the orbitals in accord with Hund's rule so as to give the maximum number of unpaired electrons. For d^4–d^7 complexes, the orbital occupancy and number of unpaired electrons depend on the position of the ligand in the spectrochemical series.

SOLUTION

(a) $Cr^{3+}([Ar] 3d^3)$ has three unpaired electrons. In the complex, they occupy the lower-energy set of d orbitals as shown below.

(b) $Mn^{3+}([Ar] 3d^4)$ can have a high-spin or a low-spin configuration. Because CN^- is a strong-field ligand, all four d electrons go into the lower-energy d orbitals. The complex is low-spin, with two unpaired electrons.

(c) $Co^{2+}([Ar] 3d^7)$ has a high-spin configuration with three unpaired electrons because H_2O is a weak-field ligand.

In the following orbital energy-level diagrams, the relative values of the crystal field splitting Δ agree with the positions of the ligands in the spectrochemical series ($H_2O <$ en $< CN^-$):

▶ **PROBLEM 20.18** Draw a crystal field d-orbital energy-level diagram, and predict the number of unpaired electrons for each of the following complexes:

(a) $[Fe(H_2O)_6]^{2+}$ (b) $[Fe(CN)_6]^{4-}$ (c) $[VF_6]^{3-}$ (d) $[Ni(en)_3]^{2+}$

Tetrahedral and Square Planar Complexes

Different geometric arrangements of the ligands give different energy splittings for the d orbitals. **Figure 20.32** shows d-orbital energy-level diagrams for tetrahedral and square planar complexes.

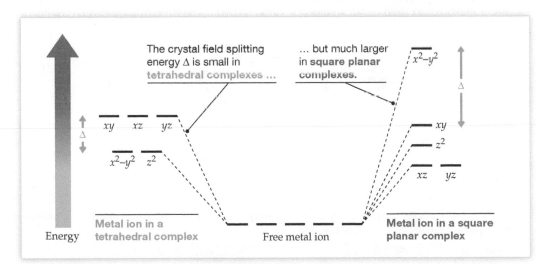

Figure 20.32
Energies of the d orbitals in tetrahedral and square planar complexes relative to their energy in the free metal ion.

The splitting pattern in tetrahedral complexes is just the opposite of that in octahedral complexes; that is, the xy, xz, and yz orbitals have higher energy than the $x^2 - y^2$ and z^2 orbitals. (As with octahedral complexes, the energy ordering follows from the relative orientation of the orbital lobes and the ligands, but we won't derive the result.) Because none of the orbitals points directly at the ligands in tetrahedral geometry and because there are only four ligands instead of six, the crystal field splitting in tetrahedral complexes is only about half of that in octahedral complexes. Consequently, Δ is almost always smaller than the spin-pairing energy P, and nearly all tetrahedral complexes are high-spin.

Square planar complexes look like octahedral ones (Figure 20.30) except that the two trans ligands along the z axis are missing. In square planar complexes, the $x^2 - y^2$ orbital is high in energy (Figure 20.32) because it points directly at all four ligands, which lie along the x and y axes. The splitting pattern is more complicated here than for the octahedral and tetrahedral cases, but the main point to remember is that a large energy gap exists between the $x^2 - y^2$ orbital and the four lower-energy orbitals. Square planar geometry is most common for metal ions with electron configuration d^8 because this configuration favors low-spin complexes in which all four lower-energy orbitals are filled and the higher-energy $x^2 - y^2$ orbital is vacant. Common examples are $[Ni(CN)_4]^{2-}$, $[PdCl_4]^{2-}$, and $Pt(NH_3)_2Cl_2$.

$[FeCl_4]^-$

$[PtCl_4]^{2-}$

WORKED EXAMPLE 20.12

DRAWING CRYSTAL FIELD ENERGY-LEVEL DIAGRAMS FOR TETRAHEDRAL AND SQUARE PLANAR COMPLEXES

Draw crystal field energy-level diagrams, and predict the number of unpaired electrons for the following complexes:

(a) $[FeCl_4]^-$ (tetrahedral)   **(b)** $[PtCl_4]^{2-}$ (square planar)

STRATEGY

Begin with the energy-level diagrams in Figure 20.32, and remember that nearly all tetrahedral complexes are high-spin (small Δ) while square planar complexes have a large energy gap (large Δ) between the $x^2 - y^2$ orbital and the four lower-energy orbitals.

SOLUTION

(a) The five d electrons of Fe^{3+}([Ar] $3d^5$) are distributed between the higher- and lower-energy orbitals as shown below. Because Δ is small in tetrahedral complexes, $[FeCl_4]^-$ is high-spin with five unpaired electrons.

(b) Pt^{2+}([Xe] $4f^{14} 5d^8$) has eight d electrons. Because Δ is large in square planar complexes, all the electrons occupy the four lower-energy d orbitals. There are no unpaired electrons, and the complex is diamagnetic.

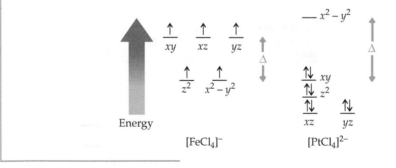

▶ **PROBLEM 20.19**   Draw a crystal field energy-level diagram, and predict the number of unpaired electrons for the following complexes:

(a) $[NiCl_4]^{2-}$ (tetrahedral)   **(b)** $[Ni(CN)_4]^{2-}$ (square planar)

INQUIRY HOW DO LIVING THINGS ACQUIRE NITROGEN?

As a constituent of DNA, RNA, and proteins, nitrogen is an essential element for every life form. Although elemental nitrogen (N_2) makes up some 78% of our atmosphere, it is not directly usable by plants and animals because its extremely strong $N\equiv N$ triple bond prevents easy conversion to nitrogen compounds that living organisms can use. Elemental nitrogen does engage in some chemical reactions, but overcoming the high activation energy barrier for breaking its triple bond requires an electric discharge, elevated temperature and pressure, or a metal catalyst. Converting elemental nitrogen into simple nitrogen compounds that plants and animals can use is referred to as "fixing nitrogen." Examples of compounds made by fixing nitrogen include ammonia, nitrites, nitrates, and organic compounds such as urea (H_2NCONH_2).

Nitrogen is fixed industrially by the Haber process (Section 13.6) in which elemental N_2 and H_2 are converted to ammonia at $400-500\,°C$ and $130-300$ atm pressure in the presence of an iron-containing catalyst. Produced on an immense scale—about 120 million metric tons per year worldwide—ammonia is used in cleaning products and chemical manufacture, but its most important use is as a fertilizer and as a starting material for synthesis of other nitrogen fertilizers such as urea. Global food production today is estimated to be double what it would be without the ammonia produced by the Haber process.

In addition to the Haber process, an equally important source of ammonia for agriculture is biological nitrogen fixation, a natural process in which certain bacteria—such as those of the genus *Rhizobium* found in the root nodules of leguminous plants like peas, beans, and clover—fix atmospheric N_2. Plants harboring these bacteria will grow in nitrogen-depleted soil and can be plowed under to serve as natural fertilizer for another crop. Whereas the Haber synthesis of ammonia requires high temperature and pressure, biological nitrogen fixation occurs under ambient conditions.

How do *Rhizobia* accomplish nitrogen fixation? The bacteria contain an enzyme complex called a *nitrogenase*, which catalyzes the reduction of N_2 to NH_3:

$$N_2 + 6\,H^+ + 6\,e^- \longrightarrow 2\,NH_3$$

Nitrogenases contain iron along with another transition metal such as molybdenum or vanadium. The well-studied molybdenum nitrogenase consists of two proteins: an iron protein containing a single Fe_4S_4 cluster with a tetrahedral iron environment and an iron-molybdenum protein containing Fe_7MoS_9 clusters with a tetrahedral environment for the iron and an octahedral environment for the molybdenum. The Mo atom is surrounded by three sulfur ligands and three other ligand donor atoms, and the Fe_7MoS_9 cluster is believed to be the active site where the N_2 is reduced (Figure 20.33). Precisely where the N_2 molecule binds in the active site is not known.

The iron–molybdenum protein has all the machinery needed to break the strong $N\equiv N$ bond of N_2 and produce NH_3, but it requires a steady stream of electrons—six electrons to break each $N\equiv N$ bond. With the help of the organic molecule adenosine triphosphate (ATP), electrons are pumped in a series of one-electron steps from the iron protein through a chain of iron–sulfur clusters to the active site of the iron–molybdenum protein. Compounds such as diimide ($HN=NH$) and hydrazine (H_2N-NH_2) have been suggested as intermediates, but the exact mechanism of the reaction is still unknown.

▶ **PROBLEM 20.20** Assume that hydrogenation of N_2 occurs in the following steps:

$$N_2(g) + H_2(g) \longrightarrow HN=NH(g) \qquad \Delta G°_1 = ?$$
$$HN=NH(g) + H_2(g) \longrightarrow H_2N-NH_2(g) \qquad \Delta G°_2 = ?$$
$$H_2N-NH_2(g) + H_2(g) \longrightarrow 2\,NH_3(g) \qquad \Delta G°_3 = ?$$

Use the data in Appendix B to calculate $\Delta G°$ for each step ($\Delta G°_f$ for $HN=NH(g)$ is $+213.8$ kJ/mol). Which step is the most favorable under standard-state conditions?

▶ **PROBLEM 20.21** Draw the two diastereoisomers of diimide, $HN=NH$.

▲ Ammonia is injected directly into a field from tanks containing liquid ammonia under pressure.

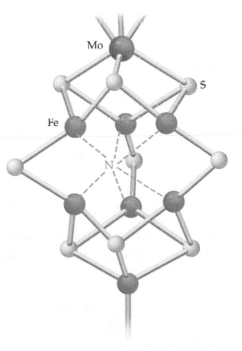

Figure 20.33
The Fe_7MoS_9 active site of nitrogenase as determined by x-ray crystallography (Section 10.7). The identity of the atom surrounded by six iron atoms (shown as N) is uncertain; it could be C, N, or O.

SUMMARY

Transition elements, or *d-block elements*, are the metallic elements in the central part of the periodic table. Most of the neutral atoms have a valence electron configuration $(n-1)d^{1-10}ns^2$, and the cations have a configuration $(n-1)d^{1-10}$. Transition metals exhibit a variety of oxidation states. Ions with the metal in a high oxidation state tend to be good oxidizing agents ($Cr_2O_7^{2-}$, MnO_4^-), while ions with an early transition metal in a low oxidation state are good reducing agents (V^{2+}, Cr^{2+}).

Coordination compounds (metal complexes) are compounds in which a central metal ion is attached to a group of surrounding **ligands** by coordinate covalent bonds. Ligands can be **monodentate** or **polydentate**, depending on the number of **ligand donor atoms** attached to the metal. Polydentate ligands are also called **chelating agents**. They form complexes known as metal **chelates** that contain rings of atoms known as **chelate rings**.

The number of ligand donor atoms bonded to a metal is called the **coordination number** of the metal. Common coordination numbers and geometries are 2 (linear), 4 (tetrahedral or square planar), and 6 (octahedral). Systematic names for complexes specify the number of ligands of each particular type, the metal, and its oxidation state.

Many complexes exist as **isomers**, compounds that have the same formula but a different arrangement of the constituent atoms. **Constitutional isomers**, such as **linkage isomers** and **ionization isomers**, have different connections between their constituent atoms. **Stereoisomers** have the same connections but a different spatial arrangement of the atoms. **Diastereoisomers** are non-mirror-image stereoisomers, such as the **cis** and **trans isomers** of square planar MA_2B_2 and octahedral MA_4B_2 complexes. **Enantiomers** are mirror-image stereoisomers, such as "right-handed" and "left-handed" $[Co(en)_3]^{3+}$. One enantiomer rotates the plane of plane-polarized light to the right, and the other rotates the plane through an equal angle but in the opposite direction. A 1:1 mixture of the two enantiomers is called a **racemic mixture**. Molecules that have handedness are said to be **chiral**. All other molecules are **achiral**.

Valence bond theory describes the bonding in complexes in terms of two-electron, coordinate covalent bonds resulting from the overlap of filled ligand orbitals with vacant metal hybrid orbitals that point in the direction of the ligands: sp (linear), sp^3 (tetrahedral), dsp^2 (square planar), and d^2sp^3 or sp^3d^2 (octahedral).

Crystal field theory assumes that the metal–ligand bonding is entirely ionic. Because of electrostatic repulsions between the d electrons and the ligands, the d orbitals are raised in energy and are differentiated by an energy separation called the **crystal field splitting**, Δ. In octahedral complexes, the d_{z^2} and $d_{x^2-y^2}$ orbitals have higher energy than the d_{xy}, d_{xz}, and d_{yz} orbitals. Tetrahedral and square planar complexes exhibit different splitting patterns. The colors of complexes are due to electronic transitions from one set of d orbitals to another, and the transition energies depend on the position of the ligand in the **spectrochemical series**. **Weak-field ligands** give small Δ values, and **strong-field ligands** give large Δ values. Crystal field theory accounts for the magnetic properties of complexes in terms of the relative values of Δ and the spin-pairing energy P. Small Δ values favor **high-spin complexes**, and large Δ values favor **low-spin complexes**.

KEY WORDS

absorption spectrum *833*	coordination compound *817*	high-spin complex *836*	monodentate ligand *819*
achiral *830*	coordination number *817*	ionization isomer *825*	polydentate ligand *819*
bidentate ligand *819*	crystal field splitting (Δ) *838*	isomer *824*	racemic mixture *830*
chelate *820*	crystal field theory *837*	lanthanide contraction *808*	spectrochemical series *839*
chelate ring *820*	diastereoisomer *825*	ligand *817*	stereoisomer *825*
chelating agent *820*	enantiomer *830*	ligand donor atom *817*	strong-field ligand *840*
chiral *830*	hexadentate ligand *819*	linkage isomer *825*	symmetry plane *830*
cis isomer *825*		low-spin complex *836*	trans isomer *825*
constitutional isomer *825*		metal complex *817*	weak-field ligand *840*

CONCEPTUAL PROBLEMS

Problems 20.1–20.21 appear within the chapter.

20.22 Locate on the periodic table the transition elements with the following electron configurations. Identify each element.

(a) [Ar] $3d^7\,4s^2$ **(b)** [Ar] $3d^5\,4s^1$

(c) [Kr] $4d^2\,5s^2$ **(d)** [Xe] $4f^3\,6s^2$

20.23 Look at the location in the periodic table of elements A, B, C, and D.

What is the electron configuration of the transition metal in each of the following ions?

(a) A^{2+} **(b)** B^+ **(c)** C^{3+} **(d)** DO_4^{2-}

20.24 What is the general trend in the following properties from left to right across the first transition series (Sc to Zn)? Explain each trend.
    (a) Atomic radius   **(b)** Density
    (c) Ionization energy   **(d)** Standard oxidation potential

Sc	Ti	V	Cr	Mn	Fe	Co	Ni	Cu	Zn

20.25 Classify the following ligands as monodentate, bidentate, or tridentate. Which can form chelate rings?

    (a) $NH_2CH_2CH_2NH_2$
    (b) $CH_3CH_2CH_2NH_2$

    (c) $NH_2CH_2CH_2NHCH_2CO_2^-$
    (d) $NH_2CH_2CH_2NH_3^+$

20.26 What is the systematic name for each of the following molecules or ions? Include *cis* or *trans* prefixes for diastereoisomers. Platinum is Pt(II) in square planar complexes and Pt(IV) in octahedral complexes.

    ● = Pt   = $NH_2CH_2CH_2NH_2$ = NH_3 = Cl   = H_2O
    (1)   **(2)**   **(3)**   **(4)**

20.27 Draw the structure of the following complexes. What are the oxidation state, coordination number, and coordination geometry of the metal in each?
    (a) $Na[Au(CN)_2]$ **(b)** $[Co(NH_3)_5Br]SO_4$
    (c) $Pt(en)Cl_2$ **(d)** $(NH_4)_2[PtCl_2(C_2O_4)_2]$

20.28 Consider the following isomers of $[Cr(NH_3)_2Cl_4]^-$

    ● = Cr   = NH_3 = Cl
    (1)   **(2)**   **(3)**   **(4)**

    (a) Label the isomers as cis or trans.
    (b) Which isomers are identical, and which are different?
    (c) Do any of these isomers exist as enantiomers? Explain.

20.29 Consider the following ethylenediamine complexes:

    ● = Cr   = $NH_2CH_2CH_2NH_2$ = Cl
    (1)   **(2)**   **(3)**   **(4)**

    (a) Which complexes are chiral, and which are achiral?
    (b) Draw the enantiomer of each chiral complex.
    (c) Which, if any, of the chiral complexes are enantiomers of one another?

20.30 Predict the crystal field energy-level diagram for a square pyramidal ML_5 complex that has two ligands along the $\pm x$ and $\pm y$ axes but only one ligand along the z axis. Your diagram should be intermediate between those for an octahedral ML_6 complex and a square planar ML_4 complex.

20.31 Imagine two complexes, one tetrahedral and one square planar, in which the central atom is bonded to four different ligands (shown here in four different colors). Is either complex chiral? Explain.

SECTION PROBLEMS

Electron Configurations and Properties of Transition Elements (Sections 20.1–20.2)

20.32 Use the periodic table to give the electron configuration for each of the following atoms and ions:
    (a) Cr   **(b)** Zr   **(c)** Co^{2+}
    (d) Fe^{3+} **(e)** Mo^{3+} **(f)** Cr(VI) in CrO_4^{2-}

20.33 Specify the electron configuration for each of the following atoms and ions:
    (a) Mn   **(b)** Cd   **(c)** Cr^{3+}
    (d) Ag^I **(e)** Rh^{3+} **(f)** Mn(VI) in MnO_4^{2-}

20.34 Predict the number of unpaired electrons for each of the following:
    (a) Cu^{2+} **(b)** Ti^{2+} **(c)** Zn^{2+} **(d)** Cr^{3+}

20.35 Predict the number of unpaired electrons for each of the following:

(a) Sc^{3+} (b) Co^{2+} (c) Mn^{3+} (d) Cr^{2+}

20.36 Titanium, used to make jet aircraft engines, is much harder than potassium or calcium. Explain.

20.37 Molybdenum (mp 2623 °C) has a higher melting point than yttrium (mp 1522 °C) or cadmium (321 °C). Explain.

20.38 Briefly account for each of the following observations:

(a) Atomic radii decrease in the order Sc > Ti > V.

(b) Densities increase in the order Ti < V < Cr.

20.39 Arrange the following atoms in order of decreasing atomic radius, and account for the trend:

(a) Cr   (b) Ti   (c) Mn   (d) V

20.40 What is the lanthanide contraction, and why does it occur?

20.41 The atomic radii of zirconium and hafnium are nearly identical. Explain.

20.42 Calculate the sum of the first two ionization energies for the first-series transition elements, and account for the general trend.

20.43 What is the general trend in standard potentials for the oxidation of first-series transition metals from Sc to Zn? What is the reason for the trend?

20.44 Write a balanced net ionic equation for the reaction of each of the following metals with hydrochloric acid in the absence of air. If no reaction occurs, indicate N.R.

(a) Cr   (b) Zn   (c) Cu   (d) Fe

20.45 Write a balanced net ionic equation for the reaction of each of the following metals with dilute sulfuric acid in the absence of air. If no reaction occurs, indicate N.R.

(a) Mn   (b) Ag   (c) Sc   (d) Ni

Oxidation States (Section 20.3)

20.46 Which of the following metals have more than one oxidation state?

(a) Zn   (b) Mn   (c) Sr   (d) Cu

20.47 Which of the following metals have only one oxidation state?

(a) V   (b) Al   (c) Co   (d) Sc

20.48 What is the highest oxidation state for each of the elements from Sc to Zn?

20.49 The highest oxidation state for the early transition metals Sc, Ti, V, Cr, and Mn is the periodic group number. The highest oxidation state for the later transition elements Fe, Co, and Ni is less than the periodic group number. Explain.

20.50 Which is the stronger oxidizing agent, Cr^{2+} or Cu^{2+}? Explain.

20.51 Which is the stronger reducing agent, Ti^{2+} or Ni^{2+}? Explain.

20.52 Do you expect a compound with vanadium in the +2 oxidation state to be an oxidizing or a reducing agent? Explain.

20.53 Will a compound that contains a Co^{3+} ion be an oxidizing agent or a reducing agent? Explain.

20.54 Arrange the following substances in order of increasing strength as an oxidizing agent, and account for the trend:

(a) Mn^{2+} (b) MnO_2 (c) MnO_4^-

20.55 Arrange the following ions in order of increasing strength as a reducing agent, and account for the trend:

(a) Cr^{2+} (b) Cr^{3+} (c) $Cr_2O_7^{2-}$

Chemistry of Selected Transition Elements (Section 20.4)

20.56 Write a balanced equation for the industrial production of:

(a) Chromium metal from chromium(III) oxide

(b) Copper metal from copper(I) sulfide

20.57 Write a balanced net ionic equation for the reaction of nitric acid with:

(a) Iron metal   (b) Copper metal   (c) Chromium metal

20.58 Choose the chromium hydroxide that is amphoteric, and write a balanced net ionic equation for its reaction with hydroxide ion. What is the oxidation state of the chromium and the color of the product?

(a) $CrO_2(OH)_2$ (b) $Cr(OH)_3$ (c) $Cr(OH)_2$

20.59 Explain how $Cr(OH)_3$ can act both as an acid and as a base.

20.60 Which of the following compounds is amphoteric?

(a) $Cr(OH)_2$ (b) $Fe(OH)_2$ (c) $Cr(OH)_3$ (d) $Fe(OH)_3$

20.61 Which of the following ions disproportionates in aqueous solution? Write a balanced net ionic equation for the reaction.

(a) Cr^{3+} (b) Fe^{3+} (c) Cu^+ (d) Cu^{2+}

20.62 How might you separate the following pairs of ions by the addition of a single reagent? Include formulas for the major products of the reactions.

(a) Fe^{3+} and Na^+ (b) Cr^{3+} and Fe^{3+} (c) Fe^{3+} and Cu^{2+}

20.63 Give a method for separating the following pairs of ions by the addition of a single reagent. Include formulas for the major products of the reactions.

(a) K^+ and Cu^{2+} (b) Cu^{2+} and Cr^{3+} (c) Fe^{3+} and Al^{3+}

20.64 Complete and balance the net ionic equation for each of the following reactions in acidic solution:

(a) $Cr_2O_7^{2-}(aq) + Fe^{2+}(aq) \longrightarrow$

(b) $Fe^{2+}(aq) + O_2(g) \longrightarrow$

(c) $Cu_2O(s) + H^+(aq) \longrightarrow$

(d) $Fe(s) + H^+(aq) \longrightarrow$

20.65 Complete and balance the net ionic equation for each of the following reactions in acidic solution:

(a) $Cr^{2+}(aq) + Cr_2O_7^{2-}(aq) \longrightarrow$

(b) $Cu(s) + conc\ HNO_3(aq) \longrightarrow$

(c) $Cu^{2+}(aq) + excess\ NH_3(aq) \longrightarrow$

(d) $Cr(OH)_4^-(aq) + excess\ H^+(aq) \longrightarrow$

20.66 Write a balanced net ionic equation for each of the following reactions:

(a) A CrO_4^{2-} solution turns from yellow to orange upon the addition of acid.

(b) $Fe^{3+}(aq)$ reacts with aqueous KSCN to give a deep red solution.

(c) Copper metal reacts with nitric acid to give NO gas and a blue solution.

(d) A deep green solution of $Cr(OH)_3$ in excess base turns yellow on the addition of hydrogen peroxide.

20.67 Write a balanced net ionic equation for each of the following reactions:

(a) A $CuSO_4$ solution becomes dark blue when excess ammonia is added.

(b) A solution of $Na_2Cr_2O_7$ turns from orange to yellow on the addition of base.

(c) When base is added to a solution of $Fe(NO_3)_3$, a red-brown precipitate forms.

(d) The dissolution of CuS in hot HNO_3 gives NO gas, a blue solution, and a yellow solid.

Coordination Compounds; Ligands (Sections 20.5–20.6)

20.68 Forming $[Ni(en)_3]^{2+}$ from Ni^{2+} and ethylenediamine is a Lewis acid–base reaction. Explain.

20.69 Identify the Lewis acid and the Lewis base in the reaction of oxalate ions $(C_2O_4{}^{2-})$ with Fe^{3+} to give $[Fe(C_2O_4)_3]^{3-}$.

20.70 Give an example of a coordination compound in which the metal exhibits a coordination number of:
(a) 2   (b) 4   (c) 6

20.71 What is the coordination number of the metal in each of the following complexes?
(a) $AgCl_2{}^-$
(b) $[Cr(H_2O)_5Cl]^{2+}$
(c) $[Co(NCS)_4]^{2-}$
(d) $[ZrF_8]^{4-}$
(e) $Co(NH_3)_3(NO_2)_3$
(f) $[Fe(EDTA)(H_2O)]^-$

20.72 What is the oxidation state of the metal in each of the complexes in Problem 20.71?

20.73 Identify the oxidation state of the metal in each of the following complexes:
(a) $[Ni(CN)_5]^{3-}$
(b) $Ni(CO)_4$
(c) $[Co(en)_2(H_2O)Br]^{2+}$
(d) $[Cu(H_2O)_2(C_2O_4)_2]^{2-}$

20.74 What is the formula of a complex that has each of the following geometries?
(a) Tetrahedral
(b) Linear
(c) Octahedral
(d) Square planar

20.75 What is the formula, including the charge, for each of the following complexes?
(a) An iridium(III) complex with three ammonia and three chloride ligands
(b) A chromium(III) complex with two water and two oxalate ligands
(c) A platinum(IV) complex with two ethylenediamine and two thiocyanate ligands

20.76 Draw the structure of the iron oxalate complex $[Fe(C_2O_4)_3]^{3-}$. Describe the coordination geometry, and identify any chelate rings. What are the coordination number and the oxidation number of the iron?

20.77 Draw the structure of the platinum ethylenediamine complex $[Pt(en)_2]^{2+}$. Describe the coordination geometry, and identify any chelate rings. What are the coordination number and the oxidation number of the platinum?

20.78 Identify the oxidation state of the metal in each of the following compounds:
(a) $Co(NH_3)_3(NO_2)_3$
(b) $[Ag(NH_3)_2]NO_3$
(c) $K_3[Cr(C_2O_4)_2Cl_2]$
(d) $Cs[CuCl_2]$

20.79 What is the oxidation state of the metal in each of the following compounds?
(a) $(NH_4)_3[RhCl_6]$
(b) $[Cr(NH_3)_4(SCN)_2]Br$
(c) $[Cu(en)_2]SO_4$
(d) $Na_2[Mn(EDTA)]$

Naming Coordination Compounds (Section 20.7)

20.80 What is the systematic name for each of the following ions?
(a) $[MnCl_4]^{2-}$
(b) $[Ni(NH_3)_6]^{2+}$
(c) $[Co(CO_3)_3]^{3-}$
(d) $[Pt(en)_2(SCN)_2]^{2+}$

20.81 Assign a systematic name to each of the following ions:
(a) $[AuCl_4]^-$
(b) $[Fe(CN)_6]^{4-}$
(c) $[Fe(H_2O)_5NCS]^{2+}$
(d) $[Cr(NH_3)_2(C_2O_4)_2]^-$

20.82 What is the systematic name for each of the following coordination compounds?
(a) $Cs[FeCl_4]$
(b) $[V(H_2O)_6](NO_3)_3$
(c) $[Co(NH_3)_4Br_2]Br$
(d) $Cu(gly)_2$

20.83 What is the systematic name for each of the following compounds?
(a) $[Cu(NH_3)_4]SO_4$
(b) $Cr(CO)_6$
(c) $K_3[Fe(C_2O_4)_3]$
(d) $[Co(en)_2(NH_3)CN]Cl_2$

20.84 Write the formula for each of the following compounds:
(a) Tetraammineplatinum(II) chloride
(b) Sodium hexacyanoferrate(III)
(c) Tris(ethylenediamine)platinum(IV) sulfate
(d) Triamminetrithiocyanatorhodium(III)

20.85 Write the formula for each of the following compounds:
(a) Diamminesilver(I) nitrate
(b) Potassium diaquadioxalatocobaltate(III)
(c) Hexacarbonylmolybdenum(0)
(d) Diamminebis(ethylenediamine)chromium(III) chloride

Isomers (Sections 20.8–20.9)

20.86 Draw all constitutional isomers of $[Ru(NH_3)_5(NO_2)]Cl$. Label the isomers as linkage isomers or ionization isomers.

20.87 There are six possible isomers for a square planar palladium(II) complex that contains two Cl^- and two SCN^- ligands. Sketch the structures of all six, and label them according to the isomer classification scheme in Figure 20.16.

20.88 Which of the following complexes can exist as diastereoisomers?
(a) $[Cr(NH_3)_2Cl_4]^-$
(b) $[Co(NH_3)_5Br]^{2+}$
(c) $[FeCl_2(NCS)_2]^{2-}$ (tetrahedral)
(d) $[PtCl_2Br_2]^{2-}$ (square planar)

20.89 Tell how many diastereoisomers are possible for each of the following complexes, and draw their structures:
(a) $Pt(NH_3)_2(CN)_2$
(b) $[Co(en)(SCN)_4]^-$
(c) $[Cr(H_2O)_4Cl_2]^+$
(d) $Ru(NH_3)_3I_3$

20.90 Which of the following complexes are chiral?
(a) $Pt(en)Cl_2$
(b) cis-$[Co(NH_3)_4Br_2]^+$
(c) cis-$[Cr(en)_2(H_2O)_2]^{3+}$
(d) $[Cr(C_2O_4)_3]^{3-}$

20.91 Which of the following complexes can exist as enantiomers? Draw their structures.
(a) $[Cr(en)_3]^{3+}$
(b) cis-$[Co(en)_2(NH_3)Cl]^{2+}$
(c) $trans$-$[Co(en)_2(NH_3)Cl]^{2+}$
(d) $[Pt(NH_3)_3Cl_3]^+$

20.92 Draw all possible diastereoisomers of $[Cr(C_2O_4)_2(H_2O)_2]^-$. Which can exist as a pair of enantiomers?

20.93 Draw the three possible diastereoisomers of the triethylenetetramine complex $[Co(trien)Cl_2]^+$. Abbreviate the flexible tetradentate trien ligand $H_2NCH_2CH_2NHCH_2CH_2NHCH_2$-$CH_2NH_2$ as N⌒N⌒N⌒N. Which of the isomers can exist as a pair of enantiomers?

20.94 How does plane-polarized light differ from ordinary light? Draw the structure of a chromium complex that rotates the plane of plane-polarized light.

20.95 What is a racemic mixture? Does it affect plane-polarized light? Explain.

Color of Complexes; Valence Bond and Crystal Field Theories (Sections 20.10–20.12)

20.96 What is an absorption spectrum? If the absorption spectrum of a complex has just one band at 455 nm, what is the color of the complex?

20.97 A red complex has just one absorption band in the visible region of the spectrum. Predict the approximate wavelength of this band.

20.98 Give a valence bond description of the bonding in each of the following complexes. Include orbital diagrams for the free metal ion and the metal ion in the complex. Indicate which hybrid orbitals the metal ion uses for bonding, and specify the number of unpaired electrons.

(a) $[Ti(H_2O)_6]^{3+}$ **(b)** $[NiBr_4]^{2-}$ (tetrahedral)

(c) $[Fe(CN)_6]^{3-}$ (low-spin)   **(d)** $[MnCl_6]^{3-}$ (high-spin)

20.99 For each of the following complexes, describe the bonding using valence bond theory. Include orbital diagrams for the free metal ion and the metal ion in the complex. Indicate which hybrid orbitals the metal ion uses for bonding, and specify the number of unpaired electrons.

(a) $[AuCl_4]^-$ (square planar)   **(b)** $[Ag(NH_3)_2]^+$

(c) $[Fe(H_2O)_6]^{2+}$ (high-spin)   **(d)** $[Fe(CN)_6]^{4-}$ (low-spin)

20.100 There are two possible $[M(OH)_4]^-$ complexes of first-series transition metals that have three unpaired electrons.

(a) What is the oxidation state and the identity of M in these complexes?

(b) Using orbital diagrams, give a valence bond description of the bonding in each complex.

(c) Based on common oxidation states of first-series transition metals (Figure 20.6), which $[M(OH)_4]^-$ complex is more likely to exist?

20.101 Two first-series transition metals have three unpaired electrons in complex ions of the type $[MCl_4]^{2-}$.

(a) What is the oxidation state and the identity of M in these ions?

(b) Draw valence bond orbital diagrams for the two possible ions.

(c) Based on common oxidation states of first-series transition metals (Figure 20.6), which ion is more likely to exist?

20.102 Draw a crystal field energy-level diagram for the $3d$ orbitals of titanium in $[Ti(H_2O)_6]^{3+}$. Indicate the crystal field splitting, and explain why $[Ti(H_2O)_6]^{3+}$ is colored.

20.103 Use a sketch to explain why the d_{xy} and $d_{x^2-y^2}$ orbitals have different energies in an octahedral complex. Which of the two orbitals has higher energy?

20.104 The $[Ti(NCS)_6]^{3-}$ ion exhibits a single absorption band at 544 nm. Calculate the crystal field splitting energy Δ in kJ/mol. Is NCS$^-$ a stronger or weaker field ligand than water? Predict the color of $[Ti(NCS)_6]^{3-}$.

20.105 The $[Cr(H_2O)_6]^{3+}$ ion is violet, and $[Cr(CN)_6]^{3-}$ is yellow. Explain this difference using crystal field theory. Use the colors to order H_2O and CN$^-$ in the spectrochemical series.

20.106 For each of the following complexes, draw a crystal field energy-level diagram, assign the electrons to orbitals, and predict the number of unpaired electrons:

(a) $[CrF_6]^{3-}$ **(b)** $[V(H_2O)_6]^{3+}$ **(c)** $[Fe(CN)_6]^{3-}$

20.107 Draw a crystal field energy-level diagram, assign the electrons to orbitals, and predict the number of unpaired electrons for each of the following:

(a) $[Cu(en)_3]^{2+}$ **(b)** $[FeF_6]^{3-}$ **(c)** $[Co(en)_3]^{3+}$ (low-spin)

20.108 The $Ni^{2+}(aq)$ cation is green, but $Zn^{2+}(aq)$ is colorless. Explain.

20.109 The $Cr^{3+}(aq)$ cation is violet, but $Y^{3+}(aq)$ is colorless. Explain.

20.110 Weak-field ligands tend to give high-spin complexes, but strong-field ligands tend to give low-spin complexes. Explain.

20.111 Explain why nearly all tetrahedral complexes are high-spin.

20.112 Draw a crystal field energy-level diagram for a square planar complex, and explain why square planar geometry is especially common for d^8 complexes.

20.113 For each of the following complexes, draw a crystal field energy-level diagram, assign the electrons to orbitals, and predict the number of unpaired electrons:

(a) $[Pt(NH_3)_4]^{2+}$ (square planar)

(b) $[MnCl_4]^{2-}$ (tetrahedral)

(c) $[Co(NCS)_4]^{2-}$ (tetrahedral)

(d) $[Cu(en)_2]^{2+}$ (square planar)

CHAPTER PROBLEMS

20.114 Which of the following complexes are paramagnetic?

(a) $[Mn(CN)_6]^{3-}$ **(b)** $[Zn(NH_3)_4]^{2+}$

(c) $[Fe(CN)_6]^{4-}$ **(d)** $[FeF_6]^{4-}$

20.115 Which of the following complexes are diamagnetic?

(a) $[Ni(H_2O)_6]^{2+}$ **(b)** $[Co(CN)_6]^{3-}$

(c) $[HgI_4]^{2-}$ **(d)** $[Cu(NH_3)_4]^{2+}$

20.116 For each of the following reactions in acidic solution, predict the products and write a balanced net ionic equation:

(a) $Co^{3+}(aq) + H_2O(l) \longrightarrow$

(b) $Cr^{2+}(aq) + O_2(g) \longrightarrow$

(c) $Cu(s) + Cr_2O_7^{2-}(aq) \longrightarrow$

(d) $CrO_4^{2-}(aq) + H^+(aq) \longrightarrow$

20.117 Write a balanced net ionic equation for each of the following reactions in acidic, basic, or neutral solution:

    (a) $MnO_4^-(aq) + C_2O_4^{2-}(aq) \xrightarrow{\text{Acidic}} Mn^{2+}(aq) + CO_2(g)$

    (b) $Cr_2O_7^{2-}(aq) + Ti^{3+}(aq) \xrightarrow{\text{Acidic}} Cr^{3+}(aq) + TiO^{2+}(aq)$

    (c) $MnO_4^-(aq) + SO_3^{2-}(aq) \xrightarrow{\text{Basic}} MnO_4^{2-}(aq) + SO_4^{2-}(aq)$

    (d) $Fe(OH)_2(s) + O_2(g) \xrightarrow{\text{Neutral}} Fe(OH)_3(s)$

20.118 What role does $EDTA^{4-}$ play as a trace additive to mayonnaise? Would the glycinate ion $(H_2NCH_2CO_2^-)$ be an effective substitute for $EDTA^{4-}$?

20.119 Tris(2-aminoethyl)amine, abbreviated tren, is the tetradentate ligand $N(CH_2CH_2NH_2)_3$. Using $N^\frown N$ to represent each of the three $NCH_2CH_2NH_2$ segments of the ligand, sketch all possible isomers of the octahedral complex $[Co(tren)BrCl]^+$.

20.120 Nickel(II) complexes with the formula NiX_2L_2, where X^- is Cl^- or N-bonded NCS^- and L is the monodentate triphenylphosphine ligand $P(C_6H_5)_3$, can be square planar or tetrahedral.

    (a) Draw crystal field energy-level diagrams for a square planar and a tetrahedral nickel(II) complex, and show the population of the orbitals.

    (b) If $NiCl_2L_2$ is paramagnetic and $Ni(NCS)_2L_2$ is diamagnetic, which of the two complexes is tetrahedral and which is square planar?

    (c) Draw possible structures for each of the NiX_2L_2 complexes, and tell which ones have a dipole moment.

20.121 Describe the bonding in $[Mn(CN)_6]^{3-}$, using both crystal field theory and valence bond theory. Include the appropriate crystal field d orbital energy-level diagram and the valence bond orbital diagram. Which model allows you to predict the number of unpaired electrons? How many do you expect?

20.122 The complex $[FeCl_6]^{3-}$ is more paramagnetic than $[Fe(CN)_6]^{3-}$. Explain.

20.123 Although Cl^- is a weak-field ligand and CN^- is a strong-field ligand, $[CrCl_6]^{3-}$ and $[Cr(CN)_6]^{3-}$ exhibit approximately the same amount of paramagnetism. Explain.

20.124 In octahedral complexes, the choice between high-spin and low-spin electron configurations arises only for d^4–d^7 complexes. Explain.

20.125 Draw a crystal field energy-level diagram, and predict the number of unpaired electrons for each of the following:

    (a) $[Mn(H_2O)_6]^{2+}$ **(b)** $Pt(NH_3)_2Cl_2$

    (c) $[FeO_4]^{2-}$ **(d)** $[Ru(NH_3)_6]^{2+}$ (low-spin)

20.126 Explain why $[CoCl_4]^{2-}$ (blue) and $[Co(H_2O)_6]^{2+}$ (pink) have different colors. Which complex has its absorption bands at longer wavelengths?

20.127 Draw the structure of all isomers of the octahedral complex $[NbX_2Cl_4]^-$ ($X^- = NCS^-$), and identify those that are linkage isomers.

20.128 The glycinate anion, $gly^- = NH_2CH_2CO_2^-$, bonds to metal ions through the N atom and one of the O atoms. Using $N^\frown O$ to represent gly^-, sketch the structures of the four stereoisomers of $Co(gly)_3$.

20.129 There are three coordination compounds with the empirical formula $Co(NH_3)_3(NO_2)_3$ in which all the nitrite ions are bonded through the N atom. Two isomers have the same molar mass but different non-zero dipole moments. The third compound is a salt with singly charged ions and a molar mass twice that of the other compounds.

    (a) Draw the structures of the isomeric compounds.

    (b) What is the chemical formula of the third compound?

20.130 Draw the structures of all possible diastereoisomers of an octahedral complex with the formula $MA_2B_2C_2$. Which of the diastereoisomers, if any, can exist as enantiomers?

20.131 Look at the colors of the isomeric complexes in Figure 20.17 on page 825, and predict which is the stronger field ligand, nitro ($-NO_2$) or nitrito ($-ONO$)? Explain.

20.132 The amount of paramagnetism for a first-series transition metal complex is related approximately to its spin-only magnetic moment. The spin-only value of the magnetic moment in units of Bohr magnetons (BM) is given by $\sqrt{n(n + 2)}$, where n is the number of unpaired electrons. Calculate the spin-only value of the magnetic moment for the 2+ ions of the first-series transition metals (except Sc) in octahedral complexes with **(a)** weak-field ligands and **(b)** strong-field ligands. For which electron configurations can the magnetic moment distinguish between high-spin and low-spin electron configurations?

20.133 Predict the crystal field energy-level diagram for a linear ML_2 complex that has two ligands along the $\pm z$ axis:

20.134 The reaction of the octahedral complex $Co(NH_3)_3(NO_2)_3$ with HCl yields a complex $[Co(NH_3)_3(H_2O)Cl_2]^+$ in which the two chloride ligands are trans to one another.

    (a) Draw the two possible stereoisomers of the starting material $[Co(NH_3)_3(NO_2)_3]$. (All three NO_2^- ligands are bonded to Co through the N atom.)

    (b) Assuming that the NH_3 groups remain in place, which of the two starting isomers could give rise to the observed product?

20.135 Consider the octahedral complex $[Co(en)(dien)Cl]^{2+}$, where dien $= H_2NCH_2CH_2NHCH_2CH_2NH_2$, which can be abbreviated $N^\frown N^\frown N$.

    (a) The dien (diethylenetriamine) ligand is a tridentate ligand. Explain what is meant by "tridentate" and why dien can act as a tridentate ligand.

    (b) Draw all possible stereoisomers of $[Co(en)(dien)Cl]^{2+}$ (dien is a flexible ligand). Which stereoisomers are chiral, and which are achiral?

20.136 For each of the following, (i) give the systematic name of the compound and specify the oxidation state of the transition metal, (ii) draw a crystal field energy-level diagram and assign the d electrons to orbitals, (iii) indicate whether the complex is high-spin or low-spin (for d^4–d^7 complexes), and (iv) specify the number of unpaired electrons.

(a) $(NH_4)[Cr(H_2O)_6](SO_4)_2$

(b) $Mo(CO)_6$ (CO is a strong-field ligand)

(c) $[Ni(NH_3)_4(H_2O)_2](NO_3)_2$

(d) $K_4[Os(CN)_6]$

(e) $[Pt(NH_3)_4](ClO_4)_2$

(f) $Na_2[Fe(CO)_4]$

20.137 The drug Nipride, $Na_2[Fe(CN)_5NO]$, is an inorganic complex used as a source of NO to lower blood pressure during surgery.

(a) The nitrosyl ligand in this complex is believed to be NO^+ rather than neutral NO. What is the oxidation state of iron, and what is the systematic name for $Na_2[Fe(CN)_5NO]$?

(b) Draw a crystal field energy-level diagram for $[Fe(CN)_5NO]^{2-}$, assign the electrons to orbitals, and predict the number of unpaired electrons.

20.138 Based on the colors of their Cr(III) complexes, arrange the following ligands in a spectrochemical series in order of increasing value of the crystal field splitting Δ: acac$^-$ (a bidentate ligand), $CH_3CO_2^-$ (acetate), Cl$^-$, H_2O, NH_3, and urea. The colors of the Cr(III) complexes are red for $Cr(acac)_3$, violet for $[Cr(H_2O)_6]^{3+}$, green for $[CrCl_2(H_2O)_4]^+$, green for $[Cr(urea)_6]^{3+}$, yellow for $[Cr(NH_3)_6]^{3+}$, and blue-violet for $Cr(CH_3CO_2)_3(H_2O)_3$.

MULTICONCEPT PROBLEMS

20.139 Spinach contains a lot of iron but is not a good source of dietary iron because nearly all the iron is tied up in the oxalate complex $[Fe(C_2O_4)_3]^{3-}$.

(a) The formation constant K_f for $[Fe(C_2O_4)_3]^{3-}$ is 3.3×10^{20}. Calculate the equilibrium concentration of free Fe^{3+} in a 0.100 M solution of $[Fe(C_2O_4)_3]^{3-}$. (Ignore any acid–base reactions.)

(b) Under the acidic conditions in the stomach, the Fe^{3+} concentration should be greater because of the reaction

$$[Fe(C_2O_4)_3]^{3-}(aq) + 6\,H_3O^+(aq) \rightleftharpoons$$
$$Fe^{3+}(aq) + 3\,H_2C_2O_4(aq) + 6\,H_2O(l)$$

Show, however, that this reaction is nonspontaneous under standard-state conditions. (For $H_2C_2O_4$, $K_{a1} = 5.9 \times 10^{-2}$ and $K_{a2} = 6.4 \times 10^{-5}$.)

(c) Draw a crystal field energy-level diagram for $[Fe(C_2O_4)_3]^{3-}$, and predict the number of unpaired electrons. ($C_2O_4^{2-}$ is a weak-field bidentate ligand.)

(d) Draw the structure of $[Fe(C_2O_4)_3]^{3-}$. Is the complex chiral or achiral?

20.140 Formation constants for the ammonia and ethylenediamine complexes of nickel(II) indicate that $Ni(en)_3^{2+}$ is much more stable than $Ni(NH_3)_6^{2+}$:

(1) $Ni(H_2O)_6^{2+}(aq) + 6\,NH_3(aq) \rightleftharpoons$
$\quad Ni(NH_3)_6^{2+}(aq) + 6\,H_2O(l) \qquad K_f = 2.0 \times 10^8$

(2) $Ni(H_2O)_6^{2+}(aq) + 3\,en(aq) \rightleftharpoons$
$\quad Ni(en)_3^{2+}(aq) + 6\,H_2O(l) \qquad K_f = 4 \times 10^{17}$

The enthalpy changes for the two reactions, ΔH°_1 and ΔH°_2, should be about the same because both complexes have six Ni—N bonds.

(a) Which of the two reactions should have the larger entropy change, ΔS°? Explain.

(b) Account for the greater stability of $Ni(en)_3^{2+}$ in terms of the relative values of ΔS° for the two reactions.

(c) Assuming that $\Delta H^\circ_2 - \Delta H^\circ_1$ is zero, calculate the value of $\Delta S^\circ_2 - \Delta S^\circ_1$.

20.141 The percent iron in iron ore can be determined by dissolving the ore in acid, then reducing the iron to Fe^{2+}, and finally titrating the Fe^{2+} with aqueous $KMnO_4$. The reaction products are Fe^{3+} and Mn^{2+}.

(a) Write a balanced net ionic equation for the titration reaction.

(b) Use the E° values in Appendix D to calculate ΔG° (in kilojoules) and the equilibrium constant for the reaction.

(c) Draw a crystal field energy-level diagram for the reactants and products, MnO_4^-, $[Fe(H_2O)_6]^{2+}$, $[Fe(H_2O)_6]^{3+}$, and $[Mn(H_2O)_6]^{2+}$, and predict the number of unpaired electrons for each.

(d) Does the paramagnetism of the solution increase or decrease as the reaction proceeds? Explain.

(e) What is the mass % Fe in the iron ore if titration of the Fe^{2+} from a 1.265 g sample of ore requires 34.83 mL of 0.051 32 M $KMnO_4$ to reach the equivalence point?

20.142 The complete reaction of 2.60 g of chromium metal with 50.00 mL of 1.200 M H_2SO_4 in the absence of air gave a blue solution and a colorless gas that was collected at 25 °C and a pressure of 735 mm Hg.

(a) Write a balanced net ionic equation for the reaction.

(b) How many liters of gas were produced?

(c) What is the pH of the solution?

(d) Describe the bonding in the blue-colored ion, using both the crystal field theory and the valence bond theory. Include the appropriate crystal field d-orbital energy-level diagram and the valence bond orbital diagram. Identify the hybrid orbitals used in the valence bond description.

(e) When an excess of KCN is added to the solution, the color changes and the paramagnetism of the solution decreases. Explain.

20.143 In acidic aqueous solution, the complex *trans*-$[Co(en)_2Cl_2]^+$ undergoes the following substitution reaction:

trans-$[Co(en)_2Cl_2]^+(aq) + H_2O(l) \longrightarrow$
$\quad$ *trans*-$[Co(en)_2(H_2O)Cl]^{2+}(aq) + Cl^-(aq)$

The reaction is first order in *trans*-$[Co(en)_2Cl_2]^+$, and the rate constant at 25 °C is $3.2 \times 10^{-5}\,s^{-1}$.

(a) What is the half-life of the reaction in hours?

(b) If the initial concentration of *trans*-[Co(en)$_2$Cl$_2$]$^+$ is 0.138 M, what is its molarity after a reaction time of 16.5 h?

(c) Devise a possible reaction mechanism with a unimolecular rate-determining step.

(d) Is the reaction product chiral or achiral? Explain.

(e) Draw a crystal field energy-level diagram for *trans*-[Co(en)$_2$Cl$_2$]$^+$ that takes account of the fact that Cl$^-$ is a weaker-field ligand than ethylenediamine.

20.144 Chromium forms three isomeric compounds A, B, and C with percent composition 19.52% Cr, 39.91% Cl, and 40.57% H$_2$O. When a sample of each compound was dissolved in water and aqueous AgNO$_3$ was added, a precipitate of AgCl formed immediately. A 0.225 g sample of compound A gave 0.363 g of AgCl, 0.263 g of B gave 0.283 g of AgCl, and 0.358 g of C gave 0.193 g of AgCl. One of the three compounds is violet, while the other two are green. In all three, chromium has coordination number 6.

(a) What are the empirical formulas of A, B, and C?

(b) What are the probable structural formulas of A, B, and C? Draw the structure of the cation in each compound. Which cation can exist as diastereoisomers?

(c) Which of the three compounds is likely to be the violet one? Explain.

(d) What are the approximate freezing points of 0.25 *m* solutions of A, B, and C, assuming complete dissociation?

20.145 Cobalt(III) trifluoroacetylacetonate, Co(tfac)$_3$, is a six–coordinate, octahedral metal chelate in which three planar, bidentate tfac ligands are attached to a central Co atom:

(a) Draw all possible diastereoisomers and enantiomers of Co(tfac)$_3$.

(b) Diastereoisomers A and B have dipole moments of 6.5 D and 3.8 D, respectively. Which of your diastereoisomers is A and which is B?

(c) The isomerization reaction A → B in chloroform solution has first-order rate constants of 0.0889 h^{-1} at 66.1 °C and 0.0870 min^{-1} at 99.2 °C. What is the activation energy for the reaction?

(d) Draw a crystal field energy-level diagram for Co(tfac)$_3$, and predict its magnetic properties. (In this complex, tfac is a strong-field ligand.)

20.146 Consider the following reaction, and assume that its equilibrium constant is 1.00×10^{14}:

$$2\,CrO_4^{2-}(aq) + 2\,H^+(aq) \rightleftharpoons Cr_2O_7^{2-}(aq) + H_2O(l)$$

(a) Write the equilibrium equation for the reaction, and explain why CrO$_4^{2-}$ ions predominate in basic solutions and Cr$_2$O$_7^{2-}$ ions predominate in acidic solutions.

(b) Calculate the CrO$_4^{2-}$ and Cr$_2$O$_7^{2-}$ concentrations in a solution that has a total chromium concentration of 0.100 M and a pH of 4.000.

(c) What are the CrO$_4^{2-}$ and Cr$_2$O$_7^{2-}$ concentrations if the pH is 2.000?

20.147 An alternative to cyanide leaching of gold ores is leaching with thiocyanate ion, which forms a square planar gold(III) complex, [Au(SCN)$_4$]$^-$.

(a) If the formation constant for [Au(SCN)$_4$]$^-$ is $K_f = 10^{37}$, what is the equilibrium concentration of Au^{3+} in a 0.050 M solution of [Au(SCN)$_4$]$^-$?

(b) Draw a crystal field energy-level diagram for [Au(SCN)$_4$]$^-$, and predict the number of unpaired electrons.

CHAPTER 21

Metals and Solid-State Materials

The exterior of the Water Cube, the Beijing 2008 Olympic National Swimming Center, is illuminated by approximately 496,000 light-emitting diodes (LEDs).

CONTENTS

The materials available for making tools and weapons, houses and skyscrapers, computers and lasers have had a profound effect on the development of human civilization. Indeed, archaeologists organize early human history in terms of materials—the Stone Age, in which only natural materials such as wood and stone were available; the Bronze Age, in which implements were made of copper alloyed with tin; and the Iron Age, in which ornaments, weapons, and tools were made of iron.

Copper and iron are still of enormous importance. Copper is used to make electrical wiring, and iron is the main constituent of steel. Today, metals unknown in ancient times, such as aluminum and titanium, play a leading role in modern technology. These metals are widely used, for instance, in the aircraft industry, because of their low densities and high resistance to corrosion.

Modern technology is made possible by a host of *solid-state materials* such as *semiconductors, superconductors, advanced ceramics, composites,* and *nanoparticles.* Semiconductors are used in the miniature solid-state electronic devices found in computers. Superconductors are used to make the powerful electromagnets found in the magnetic resonance imaging (MRI) instruments employed in medical diagnosis. Advanced ceramics and composites have numerous engineering, electronic, and biomedical applications and are likely to be among the more important materials in future technologies. Nanoparticles, used in sunscreens, cosmetics, and many other products, are being investigated as a possible weapon in the war on cancer.

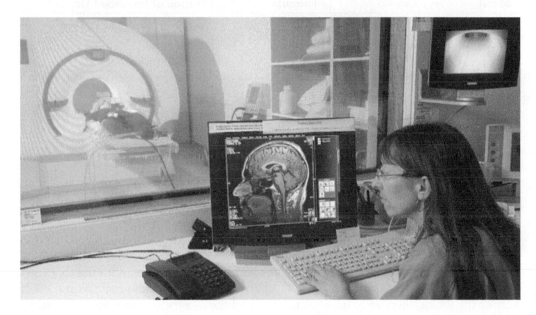

◀ The MRI instruments used in hospitals contain electromagnets made with superconductors.

In this chapter, we'll look at both metals and solid-state materials. We'll examine the natural sources of the metallic elements, the methods used to obtain metals from their ores, and the models used to describe the bonding in metals. We'll also look at the structure, bonding, properties, and applications of semiconductors, superconductors, ceramics, composites, and nanoparticles.

21.1 SOURCES OF THE METALLIC ELEMENTS

Most metals occur in nature as **minerals,** the crystalline, inorganic constituents of the rocks that make up the Earth's crust. Silicates and aluminosilicates (Section 19.8) are the most abundant minerals, but they are difficult to concentrate and reduce and are therefore generally unimportant as commercial sources of metals. More important are oxides and sulfides, such as hematite (Fe_2O_3), rutile (TiO_2), and cinnabar (HgS) (**Figure 21.1**), which yield iron, titanium, and mercury, respectively. Mineral deposits from which metals can be produced economically are called **ores** (Table 21.1).

Remember...

Silicates contain oxoanions in which one or more O atoms bridge Si atoms to give rings, chains, layers, and extended three-dimensional structures. Partial substitution of Si^{4+} with Al^{3+} gives **aluminosilicates**. (Section 19.8)

Figure 21.1
Samples of hematite (Fe$_2$O$_3$), rutile (TiO$_2$), and cinnabar (HgS).

TABLE 21.1   Principal Ores of Some Important Metals

Metal	Ore	Formula	Location of Important Deposits
Aluminum	Bauxite	$Al_2O_3 \cdot x\,H_2O$	Australia, Brazil, Jamaica
Chromium	Chromite	$FeCr_2O_4$	Russia, South Africa
Copper	Chalcopyrite	$CuFeS_2$	U.S., Chile, Canada
Iron	Hematite	Fe_2O_3	Australia, Ukraine, U.S.
Lead	Galena	PbS	U.S., Australia, Canada
Manganese	Pyrolusite	MnO_2	Russia, Gabon, South Africa
Mercury	Cinnabar	HgS	Spain, Algeria, Mexico
Tin	Cassiterite	SnO_2	Malaysia, Bolivia
Titanium	Rutile	TiO_2	Australia
	Ilmenite	$FeTiO_3$	Canada, U.S., Australia
Zinc	Sphalerite	ZnS	U.S., Canada, Australia

The chemical compositions of the most common ores correlate with the locations of the metals in the periodic table (**Figure 21.2**). The early transition metals on the left side of the *d* block generally occur as oxides, and the more electronegative, late transition metals on the right side of the *d* block occur as sulfides. This pattern makes sense because the less electronegative metals tend to form ionic compounds by losing electrons to highly electronegative nonmetals such as oxygen. By contrast, the more electronegative metals tend to form compounds with more covalent character by bonding to the less electronegative nonmetals such as sulfur.

We might also expect to find oxide ores for the *s*-block metals and sulfide ores for the more electronegative *p*-block metals. In fact, sulfide ores are common for the *p*-block metals, except for Al and Sn, but oxides of the *s*-block metals are strongly basic and far too reactive to exist in an environment that contains acidic oxides such as CO_2 and SiO_2. Consequently, *s*-block metals are found in nature as carbonates, as silicates, and, in the case of Na and K, as chlorides. Only gold (Au) and the platinum-group metals (Ru, Os, Rh, Ir, Pd, and Pt) are sufficiently unreactive to occur commonly in uncombined form as the free metals.

▶ **PROBLEM 21.1**   In view of the 3− charge on the PO_4^{3-} ion, explain why the group 3B transition metals are found in nature as phosphates.

The s-block metals occur as chlorides, silicates, and carbonates.

The d- and p-block metals are found as oxides and sulfides, except for the group 3B metals, which occur as phosphates, and the platinum-group metals and gold, which occur in uncombined form.

1A																	8A
	2A											3A	4A	5A	6A	7A	
Li	Be																
Na	Mg	3B	4B	5B	6B	7B		8B		1B	2B	Al					
K	Ca	Sc	Ti	V	Cr	Mn	Fe	Co	Ni	Cu	Zn	Ga					
Rb	Sr	Y	Zr	Nb	Mo	Tc	Ru	Rh	Pd	Ag	Cd	In	Sn				
Cs	Ba	Lu	Hf	Ta	W	Re	Os	Ir	Pt	Au	Hg	Tl	Pb	Bi			

There is no mineral source of technetium, a radioactive element that is made in nuclear reactors.

Chlorides   Silicates

Carbonates   Phosphates

Oxides   Free metals

Sulfides

Figure 21.2
Primary mineral sources of metals.

21.2 METALLURGY

An ore is a complex mixture of a metal-containing mineral and economically worthless material called **gangue** (pronounced "gang"), consisting of sand, clay, and other impurities. The extraction of a metal from its ore requires several steps: (1) concentration of the ore and, if necessary, chemical treatment prior to reduction; (2) reduction of the mineral to the free metal; and (3) refining or purification of the metal. These processes are a part of **metallurgy**, the science and technology of extracting metals from their ores. Another aspect of metallurgy is the making of **alloys**, solid metallic solutions composed of two or more elements. Steels and bronze are examples.

Concentration and Chemical Treatment of Ores

Ores are concentrated by separating the mineral from the gangue. The mineral and the gangue have different properties, which are exploited in various separation methods. Density differences, for example, are important in panning for gold, a procedure in which prospectors flush water over gold-bearing earth in a pan. The less dense gangue is washed away, and the more dense gold particles remain at the bottom of the pan. Differences in magnetic properties are used to concentrate the iron ore magnetite (Fe_3O_4). The Fe_3O_4 is strongly attracted by magnets, but the gangue is unaffected.

Metal sulfide ores are concentrated by **flotation**, a process that exploits differences in the ability of water and oil to wet the surfaces of the mineral and the gangue. A powdered ore such as chalcopyrite ($CuFeS_2$) is mixed with water, oil, and a detergent, and the mixture is vigorously agitated in a tank by blowing air through the liquid (**Figure 21.3**). The gangue, which contains ionic silicates, is moistened by the polar water molecules and sinks to the bottom of the tank. The mineral particles, which contain the less polar metal sulfide, are coated by the nonpolar oil molecules and become attached to the soapy air bubbles created by the detergent. The metal sulfide particles are thus carried to the surface in the soapy froth, which is skimmed off at the top of the tank.

Sometimes, ores are concentrated by chemical treatment. In the *Bayer process*, for instance, the Al_2O_3 in bauxite ($Al_2O_3 \cdot x\,H_2O$) is separated from Fe_2O_3 impurities by treating the ore with hot aqueous NaOH. The amphoteric Al_2O_3 dissolves as the aluminate ion, $Al(OH)_4^-$, but the basic Fe_2O_3 does not:

$$Al_2O_3(s) + 2\,OH^-(aq) + 3\,H_2O(l) \longrightarrow 2\,Al(OH)_4^-(aq)$$

The Bayer process was described in more detail in Section 18.9.

▲ In panning for gold, prospectors use density differences to separate gold from the gangue.

Figure 21.3
The flotation process for concentrating metal sulfide ores.

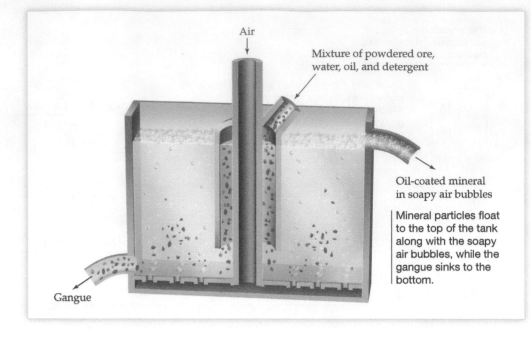

Chemical treatment is also used to convert minerals to compounds that are more easily reduced to the metal. For example, sulfide minerals, such as sphalerite (ZnS), are converted to oxides by **roasting**, a process that involves heating the mineral in air:

$$2\,ZnS(s) + 3\,O_2(g) \xrightarrow{\text{Heat}} 2\,ZnO(s) + 2\,SO_2(g)$$

Formerly, the sulfur dioxide byproduct was a source of acid rain because it is oxidized in the atmosphere to SO_3, which reacts with water vapor to yield sulfuric acid. In modern roasting facilities, however, the SO_2 is converted to sulfuric acid rather than being vented to the atmosphere.

Reduction

Once an ore has been concentrated, it is reduced to the free metal, either by chemical reduction or by electrolysis (Table 21.2). The method used depends on the activity of the metal, as measured by its standard reduction potential (Table 17.1). The most active metals have the most negative standard reduction potentials and are the most difficult to reduce; the least active metals have the most positive standard reduction potentials and are the easiest to reduce.

TABLE 21.2   Reduction Methods for Producing Some Common Metals

	Metal	Reduction Method
Least active	Au, Pt	None; found in nature as the free metal
	Cu, Ag, Hg	Roasting of the metal sulfide
	V, Cr, Mn, Fe, Ni, Zn, W, Pb	Reduction of the metal oxide with carbon, hydrogen, or a more active metal
	Al	Electrolysis of molten Al_2O_3 in cryolite
Most active	Li, Na, Mg	Electrolysis of the molten metal chloride

Gold and platinum are so inactive that they are usually found in nature in uncombined form, but copper and silver, which are slightly more active, are found in both combined and uncombined form. Copper, silver, and mercury commonly occur in sulfide ores that are easily reduced by roasting. Cinnabar (HgS), for example, yields elemental mercury when the ore is heated at 600 °C in a stream of air:

$$HgS(s) + O_2(g) \xrightarrow{600\,°C} Hg(g) + SO_2(g)$$

Although it may seem strange that heating a substance in oxygen reduces it to the metal, both oxidation and reduction of HgS occur in this reaction: Sulfide ions are oxidized and mercury(II) is reduced.

More active metals, such as chromium, zinc, and tungsten, are obtained by reducing their oxides with a chemical reducing agent such as carbon, hydrogen, or a more active metal (Na, Mg, or Al). Pure chromium, for example, is produced by reducing Cr_2O_3 with aluminum (Section 20.4). Zinc, used in the automobile industry for galvanizing steel (Section 17.11), is obtained by reducing ZnO with coke, a form of carbon produced by heating coal in the absence of air:

$$ZnO(s) + C(s) \xrightarrow{Heat} Zn(g) + CO(g)$$

Although carbon is the cheapest available reducing agent, it is unsatisfactory for reducing oxides of metals like tungsten that form very stable carbides. (Tungsten carbide, WC, is an extremely hard material used to make high-speed cutting tools.) The preferred method for producing tungsten reduces tungsten(VI) oxide with hydrogen:

$$WO_3(s) + 3\,H_2(g) \xrightarrow{850\,°C} W(s) + 3\,H_2O(g)$$

Because of its high strength, high melting point (3422 °C), low volatility, and high efficiency for converting electrical energy into light, tungsten is used to make filaments for electric lightbulbs (Figure 21.4).

There are no chemical reducing agents strong enough to reduce compounds of the most active metals, so these metals are produced by electrolytic reduction (Section 17.13). Lithium, sodium, and magnesium, for example, are obtained by the electrolysis of their molten chlorides. Aluminum is manufactured by the electrolysis of purified Al_2O_3 in molten cryolite (Na_3AlF_6).

Refining

For most applications, the metals obtained from processing and reducing ores need to be purified. The methods used include distillation, chemical purification, and electrorefining. Zinc (bp 907 °C), for example, is volatile enough to be separated from cadmium, lead, and other impurities by distillation. In this way, the purity of the zinc obtained from reduction of ZnO is increased from 99% to 99.99%. Nickel, used as a catalyst and as a battery material, is purified by the **Mond process**, a chemical method in which the volatile compound nickel tetracarbonyl, $Ni(CO)_4$ (bp 42 °C), is formed and subsequently decomposed. Carbon monoxide is passed over impure nickel at about 150 °C and 20 atm pressure, forming $Ni(CO)_4$ and leaving metal impurities behind. The $Ni(CO)_4$ is then decomposed at higher temperatures (about 230 °C) on pellets of pure nickel. The process works because the equilibrium shifts to the left with increasing temperature:

$$Ni(s) + 4\,CO(g) \underset{\text{Higher temp.}}{\overset{\text{Lower temp.}}{\rightleftharpoons}} Ni(CO)_4(g) \qquad \Delta H° = -160.8\ \text{kJ};\ \Delta S° = -410\ \text{J/K}$$

A similar strategy is employed to purify zirconium, which is used to make the cladding (metallic exterior) of the uranium oxide fuel rods in nuclear reactors. The crude metal is heated at about 200 °C with a small amount of iodine in an evacuated container to form the volatile ZrI_4. The ZrI_4 is then decomposed to pure zirconium by letting the vapor come in contact with an electrically heated tungsten or zirconium filament at about 1300 °C:

$$Zr(s) + 2\,I_2(g) \underset{1300\,°C}{\overset{200\,°C}{\rightleftharpoons}} ZrI_4(g)$$

Figure 21.4
The incandescent lightbulb. The bulb emits white light when an electric current passes through the tungsten wire filament, heating it to a high temperature. The glass bulb contains gases such as argon and nitrogen, which carry away heat from the filament. Although tungsten has the highest boiling point of any element (5555 °C), the tungsten slowly evaporates from the hot filament and condenses as the black spot of tungsten metal usually visible on the inside surface of a burned-out bulb.

▲ Zirconium is used as cladding for uranium dioxide fuel rods in nuclear reactors.

Copper from the reduction of ores must be purified for use in making electrical wiring because impurities increase its electrical resistance. The method used is electrorefining, an electrolytic process in which copper is oxidized to Cu^{2+} at an impure copper anode and Cu^{2+} from an aqueous copper sulfate solution is reduced to copper at a pure copper cathode. The process was described in Section 17.13.

▶ **PROBLEM 21.2** Write a balanced equation for the production of each of the following metals:

(a) Chromium by reducing Cr_2O_3 with aluminum
(b) Copper by roasting Cu_2S
(c) Lead by reducing PbO with coke
(d) Potassium by the electrolysis of molten KCl

21.3 IRON AND STEEL

The metallurgy of iron is of special technological importance because iron is the major constituent of steel, the most widely used of all metals. Worldwide steel production amounts to 1.4 billion metric tons per year. Iron is produced by carbon monoxide reduction of iron ore, usually hematite (Fe_2O_3), in a huge reactor called a *blast furnace* (**Figure 21.5**). A charge of iron ore, coke, and limestone ($CaCO_3$) is introduced at the top of the furnace, and a blast of hot air is sent in at the bottom, burning coke and yielding carbon monoxide at a temperature of about 2000 °C:

$$2\,C(s) + O_2(g) \longrightarrow 2\,CO(g) \qquad \Delta H^\circ = -221.0 \text{ kJ}$$

Figure 21.5
A diagram of a blast furnace for the reduction of iron ore. Modern blast furnaces are as large as 60 m in height and 14 m in diameter. They are designed for continuous operation and produce up to 9000 metric tons of iron per day. Note the approximate temperatures and the chemical reactions that occur in the various regions of the furnace.

Charge (ore, coke, limestone)

CO, CO_2

Solid charge descends

Hot gases rise

——— 200 °C ———
$3\,Fe_2O_3 + CO \longrightarrow 2\,Fe_3O_4 + CO_2$
$Fe_3O_4 + CO \longrightarrow 3\,FeO + CO_2$
$CaCO_3 \longrightarrow CaO + CO_2$
——— 700 °C ———
$C + CO_2 \longrightarrow 2\,CO$
$FeO + CO \longrightarrow Fe + CO_2$
——— 1200 °C ———
Impure iron melts. Molten slag forms.
——— 1500 °C ———
$2\,C + O_2 \longrightarrow 2\,CO$
——— 2000 °C ———
Hot air blast

Hot air blast

Slag

Molten iron

As the charge descends and the hot carbon monoxide rises, a complex series of high-temperature reactions occurs in the various regions of the furnace, as shown in Figure 21.5. The key overall reaction is the reduction of Fe_2O_3 to iron metal (mp 1538 °C), which is obtained as an impure liquid at the bottom of the furnace:

$$Fe_2O_3(s) + 3\,CO(g) \longrightarrow 2\,Fe(l) + 3\,CO_2(g)$$

The purpose of the limestone is to remove the gangue from the iron ore. At the high temperatures of the furnace, the limestone decomposes yielding lime (CaO), a basic oxide that reacts with SiO_2 and other acidic oxides present in the gangue. The product, called **slag**, is a molten material consisting mainly of calcium silicate:

$$CaCO_3(s) \longrightarrow CaO(s) + CO_2(g)$$
$$\underset{\text{Lime}}{CaO(s)} + \underset{\text{Sand}}{SiO_2(s)} \longrightarrow \underset{\text{Slag}}{CaSiO_3(l)}$$

The slag, which is less dense than the molten iron, floats on the surface of the iron, thus allowing the iron and the slag to be removed from the bottom of the furnace through separate taps.

The iron obtained from a blast furnace is a brittle material called *cast iron*, or *pig iron*. It contains about 4% elemental carbon and smaller amounts of other impurities such as elemental silicon, phosphorus, sulfur, and manganese, which are formed from their compounds in the reducing atmosphere of the furnace. The most important of several methods for purifying the iron and converting it to steel is the **basic oxygen process**. Molten iron from the blast furnace is exposed to a jet of pure oxygen gas for about 20 min in a furnace that is lined with basic oxides such as CaO. The impurities in the iron are oxidized, and the acidic oxides that form react with the basic CaO to yield a molten slag that can be poured off. Phosphorus, for example, is oxidized to P_4O_{10}, which then reacts with CaO to give molten calcium phosphate:

$$P_4(l) + 5\,O_2(g) \longrightarrow P_4O_{10}(l)$$
$$\underset{\text{Basic oxide}}{6\,CaO(s)} + \underset{\text{Acidic oxide}}{P_4O_{10}(l)} \longrightarrow \underset{\text{Slag}}{2\,Ca_3(PO_4)_2(l)}$$

Manganese also passes into the slag because its oxide is basic and reacts with added SiO_2, yielding molten manganese silicate:

$$2\,Mn(l) + O_2(g) \longrightarrow 2\,MnO(s)$$
$$\underset{\text{Basic oxide}}{MnO(s)} + \underset{\text{Acidic oxide}}{SiO_2(s)} \longrightarrow \underset{\text{Slag}}{MnSiO_3(l)}$$

The basic oxygen process produces steels that contain about 1% carbon but only very small amounts of phosphorus and sulfur. Usually, the composition of the liquid steel is monitored by chemical analysis, and the amounts of oxygen and impure iron used are adjusted to achieve the desired concentrations of carbon and other impurities. The hardness, strength, and malleability of the steel depend on its chemical composition, on the rate at which the liquid steel is cooled, and on subsequent heat treatment of the solid. The mechanical and chemical properties of a steel can also be altered by adding other metals. Stainless steel, for example, is a corrosion-resistant iron alloy that contains up to 30% chromium along with smaller amounts of nickel.

▶ **PROBLEM 21.3** The formation of $CaSiO_3$ slag in a blast furnace can be considered an acid–base reaction. Explain.

▲ Using the basic oxygen process to make steel.

21.4 BONDING IN METALS

Thus far, we've discussed the sources, production, and properties of some important metals. Some properties, such as hardness and melting point, vary considerably among metals, but other properties are characteristic of metals in general. For instance, all metals can be drawn into wires (ductility) or beaten into sheets (malleability) without breaking into pieces like glass or an ionic crystal. Furthermore, all metals have a high thermal and electrical conductivity. When you touch a metal, it feels cold because the metal efficiently conducts heat away from your hand, and when you connect a metal wire to the terminals of a battery, it conducts an electric current.

To understand those properties, we need to look at the bonding in metals. We'll consider two theoretical models that are commonly used: the *electron-sea model* and the *molecular orbital theory*.

▶ Because of its ductility, aluminum can be drawn into the wires used in electric power lines.

Electron-Sea Model of Metals

Remember...

A **body-centered cubic** unit cell has one atom at each of the eight corners of the cell and an additional atom at the center. Thus, each atom is surrounded by eight others. (Section 10.8)

If you try to draw an electron-dot structure for a metal, you'll quickly realize that there aren't enough valence electrons available to form an electron-pair bond between every pair of adjacent atoms. Sodium, for example, which has just one valence electron per atom ($3s^1$), crystallizes in a **body-centered cubic** structure in which each Na atom is surrounded by eight nearest neighbors (Section 10.8). Consequently, the valence electrons can't be localized in a bond between any particular pair of atoms. Instead, they are delocalized and belong to the crystal as a whole.

In the **electron-sea model**, a metal crystal is viewed as a three-dimensional array of metal cations immersed in a sea of delocalized electrons that are free to move throughout the crystal (Figure 21.6). The continuum of delocalized, mobile valence electrons acts as an electrostatic glue that holds the metal cations together.

Figure 21.6
A two-dimensional representation of the electron-sea model of a metal. An ordered array of cations is immersed in a continuous distribution of delocalized, mobile valence electrons.

The electron-sea model affords a simple qualitative explanation for the electrical and thermal conductivity of metals. Because the electrons are mobile, they are free to move away from a negative electrode and toward a positive electrode when a metal is subjected to an electrical potential. The mobile electrons can also conduct heat by carrying kinetic energy from one part of the crystal to another. Metals are malleable and ductile because the delocalized bonding extends in all directions; that is, it is not confined to oriented bond directions, as in covalent network solids like diamond or

SiO_2. When a metallic crystal is deformed, no localized bonds are broken. Instead, the electron sea simply adjusts to the new distribution of cations, and the energy of the deformed structure is similar to that of the original. Thus, the energy required to deform a metal like sodium is relatively small. The energy required to deform a transition metal like iron is greater because iron has more valence electrons ($4s^2\,3d^6$), and the electrostatic glue is therefore more dense.

Molecular Orbital Theory for Metals

A more detailed understanding of the bonding in metals is provided by the molecular orbital theory, a model that is a logical extension of the molecular orbital description of small molecules discussed in Sections 7.13–7.15. Recall that in the H_2 molecule the $1s$ orbitals of the two H atoms overlap to give a σ bonding MO and a higher-energy σ^* antibonding MO. The bonding in the gaseous Na_2 molecule is similar: The $3s$ orbitals of the two Na atoms combine to give a σ and a σ^* MO. Because each Na atom has just one $3s$ valence electron, the lower-energy bonding orbital is filled and the higher-energy antibonding orbital is empty:

Remember...

A molecular orbital (MO) is a wave function whose square gives the probability of finding an electron within a given region of space in a molecule. MOs are formed by mathematically combining atomic orbitals on different atoms. (Sections 7.13–7.15)

Now consider what happens if we bring together an increasingly larger number of Na atoms to build up a crystal of sodium metal. The key idea to remember from Section 7.13 is that the number of molecular orbitals formed is the same as the number of atomic orbitals combined. Thus, there will be three MOs for a triatomic Na_3 molecule, four MOs for Na_4, and so on. A cubic crystal of sodium metal, 1.5 mm on an edge, contains about 10^{20} Na atoms and therefore has about 10^{20} MOs, each of which is delocalized over all the atoms in the crystal.

As shown in **Figure 21.7**, the difference in energy between successive MOs in an Na_n molecule decreases as the number of Na atoms increases so that the MOs merge into an almost continuous band of energy levels for large values of n. Consequently, MO theory for metals is often called **band theory**. The bottom half of the band consists of bonding MOs and is filled, whereas the top half of the band consists of antibonding MOs and is empty.

Figure 21.7
Molecular orbital energy levels for Na_n molecules. A crystal of sodium metal can be regarded as a giant Na_n molecule, where n has a value of about 10^{20}. In this and subsequent figures, the red color denotes the filled portion of a band.

How does band theory account for the electrical conductivity of metals? Because each of the MOs in a metal has a definite energy (Figure 21.7), each electron in a metal has a specific kinetic energy and a specific velocity. These values depend on the particular MO energy level and increase from the bottom of a band to the top. For a one-dimensional metal wire, electrons traveling in opposite directions at the same speed have the same kinetic energy. Thus, the energy levels within a band occur in degenerate pairs; one set of energy levels applies to electrons moving to the right, and the other set applies to electrons moving to the left.

In the absence of an electrical potential, the two sets of levels are equally populated. That is, for each electron moving to the right, another electron moves to the left with exactly the same speed (Figure 21.8). As a result, there is no net electric current in either direction. In the presence of an electrical potential, however, those electrons moving to the right (toward the positive terminal of a battery) are accelerated, those moving to the left (toward the negative terminal) are slowed down, and those moving to the left with very slow speeds undergo a change of direction. Thus, the number of electrons moving to the right is now greater than the number moving to the left and there is a net electric current.

Remember...

Degenerate energy levels have the same energy. (Section 5.11)

Figure 21.8

Half-filled 3s band of MO energy levels for a one-dimensional sodium metal wire. The direction of electron motion for the two degenerate sets of energy levels is indicated by the horizontal arrows.

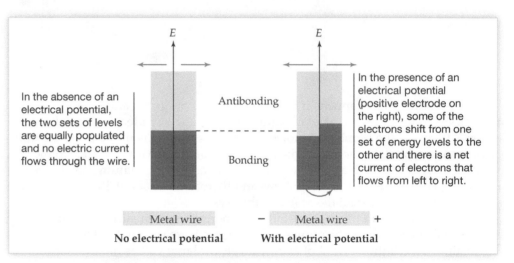

In the absence of an electrical potential, the two sets of levels are equally populated and no electric current flows through the wire.

Antibonding

Bonding

In the presence of an electrical potential (positive electrode on the right), some of the electrons shift from one set of energy levels to the other and there is a net current of electrons that flows from left to right.

Metal wire — Metal wire +

No electrical potential   **With electrical potential**

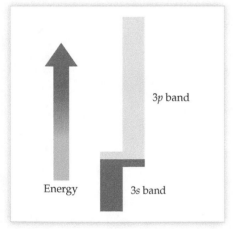

Figure 21.9

The composite 3s–3p band in magnesium metal. The 3s and 3p bands have similar energies and overlap to give a composite band consisting of four MOs per Mg atom. The composite band can accommodate eight electrons per Mg atom but is only partially filled, since each Mg atom has just two valence electrons. (In this and subsequent figures, the separate sets of energy levels for the right- and left-moving electrons aren't shown.)

3p band

Energy   3s band

Figure 21.8 shows that an electrical potential can shift electrons from one set of energy levels to the other only if the band is partially filled. If the band is completely filled, there are no available vacant energy levels to which electrons can be excited, and therefore the two sets of levels must remain equally populated, even in the presence of an electrical potential. This means that an electrical potential can't accelerate the electrons in a completely filled band, a result that applies to a three-dimensional crystal as well as to a one-dimensional wire. *Materials that have only completely filled bands are therefore electrical insulators*. By contrast, *materials that have partially filled bands are metallic conductors*.

Based on the preceding analysis, we would predict that magnesium should be an insulator because it has the electron configuration [Ar] $3s^2$ and should therefore have a completely filled 3s band. This prediction is wrong, however, because we have not yet considered the 3p valence orbitals. Just as the 3s orbitals combine to form a 3s band, so the 3p orbitals can combine to form a 3p band. If the 3s and 3p bands were widely separated in energy, the 3s band would be filled, the 3p band would be empty, and magnesium would be an insulator. In fact, though, the 3s and 3p bands overlap in energy, and the resulting composite band is only partially filled (Figure 21.9). Thus, magnesium and other alkaline earth elements are metallic conductors.

Transition metals have a *d* band that can overlap the *s* band to give a composite band consisting of six MOs per metal atom. Half of these MOs are bonding and half are antibonding. We might therefore expect maximum bonding for metals that have six valence electrons per metal atom because six electrons will just fill the bonding MOs and leave the antibonding MOs empty. In accord with this picture, maximum bonding near group 6B causes the melting points of the transition metals to also be at a maximum near group 6B (Section 20.2).

WORKED EXAMPLE 21.1

USING BAND THEORY TO ACCOUNT FOR MELTING POINTS

The melting points of chromium and zinc are 1907 °C and 420 °C, respectively. Use band theory to account for the difference.

STRATEGY

The electron configurations are [Ar] $3d^5 4s^1$ for Cr and [Ar] $3d^{10} 4s^2$ for Zn. Assume that the $3d$ and $4s$ bands overlap. The composite band, which can accommodate 12 valence electrons per metal atom, will be half-filled for Cr and completely filled for Zn. The melting points will depend on the occupancy of the bonding and antibonding MOs.

SOLUTION

Strong bonding and a consequent high melting point are expected for Cr because all the bonding MOs are occupied and all the antibonding MOs are empty. Weak bonding and a low melting point are expected for Zn because both the bonding and the antibonding MOs are occupied. (The fact that Zn is a metal suggests that the $4p$ orbitals also contribute to the composite band.)

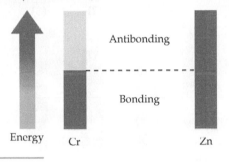

WORKED CONCEPTUAL EXAMPLE 21.2

USING BAND THEORY TO ACCOUNT FOR PHYSICAL PROPERTIES

The following pictures represent the electron population of the composite $s–d$ band for three metals—Ag, Mo, and Y:

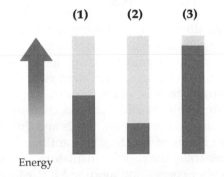

(a) Which picture corresponds to which metal? Explain.

(b) Which metal has the highest melting point, and which has the lowest? Explain.

(c) Molybdenum is very hard, whereas silver is relatively soft. Explain.

STRATEGY

As second-series transition metals, Ag, Mo, and Y have $5s$ and $4d$ valence electrons. All the valence electrons will occupy a composite $s–d$ band, which can accommodate 12 electrons per metal atom. To identify each metal, count the number of $5s$ and $4d$ valence electrons and compare that number with the population of the bands in pictures (1), (2), and (3) above. The melting point and hardness of a metal is expected to increase as the difference between the number of bonding and antibonding electrons increases.

continued on next page

SOLUTION

(a) Ag in group 1B has 11 valence electrons. Thus, its $s-d$ band is eleven-twelfths filled, which corresponds to picture (3). Mo in group 6B has six valence electrons. Its $s-d$ band is exactly half-filled, which corresponds to picture (1). Y in group 3B has three valence electrons. Its $s-d$ band is one-fourth filled, which corresponds to picture (2).

(b) Mo has the highest melting point because its bonding MOs are completely filled and its antibonding MOs are completely vacant. Ag has the lowest melting point because it has six bonding electrons and five antibonding electrons per Ag atom, an excess of only one bonding electron per Ag atom.

(c) Mo is very hard because it has an excess of six bonding electrons per Mo atom. Ag is very soft because it has an excess of only one bonding electron per Ag atom. Both hardness and melting point increase as metal–metal bonding increases.

▸ **PROBLEM 21.4** Mercury metal is a liquid at room temperature. Use band theory to suggest a reason for its low melting point (−39 °C).

CONCEPTUAL PROBLEM 21.5 The following pictures represent the electron population of the composite $s-d$ band for three metals—Hf, Pt, and Re:

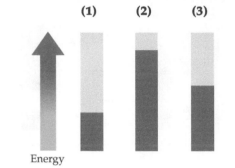

(1)   (2)   (3)

Energy

(a) Which picture corresponds to which metal? Explain.
(b) Which metal has the highest melting point, and which is the hardest? Explain.
(c) Which metal has the lowest melting point, and which is the softest? Explain.

21.5 SEMICONDUCTORS

A **semiconductor**, such as silicon or germanium, is a material that has an electrical conductivity intermediate between that of a metal and that of an insulator. To understand the electrical properties of semiconductors, let's look first at the bonding in insulators. Take diamond, for example, a covalent network solid in which each C atom is bonded tetrahedrally to four other C atoms (Figure 10.26). In a localized description of the bonding, C—C electron-pair bonds result from the overlap of sp^3 hybrid orbitals. In a delocalized description, the 2s and 2p valence orbitals of all the C atoms combine to give bands of bonding and antibonding MOs—a total of four MOs per C atom. As is generally the case for insulators, the bonding MOs, called the **valence band**, and the higher-energy antibonding MOs, called the **conduction band**, are separated in energy by a large **band gap**. The band gap in diamond is about 520 kJ/mol.

Each of the two bands in diamond can accommodate four electrons per C atom. Because carbon has just four valence electrons ($2s^2\,2p^2$), the valence band is completely filled and the conduction band is completely empty. Diamond is therefore an insulator because there are no vacant MOs in the valence band to which electrons can be excited by an electrical potential and because population of the vacant MOs of the conduction band is prevented by the large band gap. By contrast, metallic conductors have no energy gap between the highest occupied and lowest unoccupied MOs. This fundamental difference between the energy levels of metals and insulators is illustrated in **Figure 21.10**.

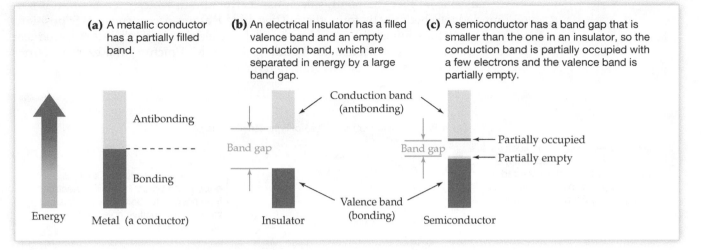

(a) A metallic conductor has a partially filled band.

(b) An electrical insulator has a filled valence band and an empty conduction band, which are separated in energy by a large band gap.

(c) A semiconductor has a band gap that is smaller than the one in an insulator, so the conduction band is partially occupied with a few electrons and the valence band is partially empty.

Figure 21.10

Bands of MO energy levels for (a) a metallic conductor, (b) an electrical insulator, and (c) a semiconductor. Electrical conductivity in metals and semiconductors results from the presence of partially filled bands.

The MOs of a semiconductor are similar to those of an insulator, but the band gap in a semiconductor is smaller (Figure 21.10). As a result, a few electrons have enough thermal energy to jump the gap and occupy the higher-energy conduction band. The conduction band is thus partially filled, and the valence band is partially empty because it now contains a few unoccupied MOs. When an electrical potential is applied to a semiconductor, it conducts a small amount of current because the potential can accelerate the electrons in the partially filled bands. Table 21.3 shows how the electrical properties of the group 4A elements vary with the size of the band gap.

TABLE 21.3   Band Gaps for the Group 4A Elements

Element*	Band Gap (kJ/mol)	Type of Material
C (diamond)	520	Insulator
Si	107	Semiconductor
Ge	65	Semiconductor
Sn (gray tin)	8	Semiconductor
Sn (white tin)	0	Metal
Pb	0	Metal

* Si, Ge, and gray Sn have the same structure as diamond.

The electrical conductivity of a semiconductor increases with increasing temperature because the number of electrons with sufficient thermal energy to occupy the conduction band increases as the temperature rises. At higher temperatures, there are more charge carriers (electrons) in the conduction band and more vacancies in the valence band. By contrast, the electrical conductivity of a metal decreases with increasing temperature. At higher temperatures, the metal cations undergo increased vibrational motion about their lattice sites and vibration of the cations disrupts the flow of electrons through the crystal. Thus, the temperature dependence of the electrical conductivity is the best criterion for distinguishing a metal from a semiconductor: As the temperature increases, the conductivity of a metal decreases, whereas the conductivity of a semiconductor increases.

The conductivity of a semiconductor can be greatly increased by adding small (ppm) amounts of certain impurities, a process called **doping**. Consider, for example, the addition of a group 5A element such as phosphorus to a group 4A semiconductor such as silicon. Like diamond, silicon has a structure in which each Si atom is surrounded tetrahedrally by four others. The added P atoms occupy normal Si positions in the structure, but each P atom has five valence electrons and therefore introduces an extra electron not needed for bonding. In the MO picture, the extra electrons occupy the conduction band, as shown in Figure 21.11a.

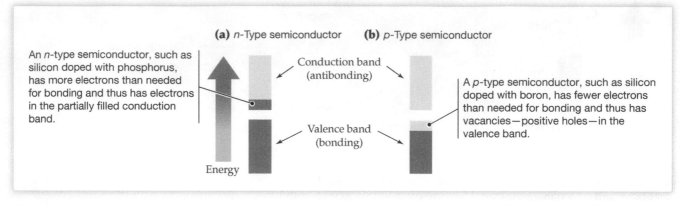

Figure 21.11
MO energy levels for doped semiconductors.

The number of electrons in the conduction band of the doped silicon is much greater than the number in pure silicon, and the conductivity of the doped semiconductor is therefore correspondingly higher. When just one of every one million Si atoms is replaced by P, the number of electrons in the conduction band increases from $\sim 10^{10}/cm^3$ to $\sim 10^{17}/cm^3$ and the conductivity increases by a factor of $\sim 10^7$. Because the charge carriers are electrons, which are *negatively* charged, the silicon doped with a group 5A element is called an **n-type semiconductor**.

Now let's consider a semiconductor in which silicon is doped with a group 3A element such as boron. Each B atom has just three valence electrons and therefore does not have enough electrons to form bonds to its four Si neighbors. In the MO picture, the bonding MOs of the valence band are only partially filled, as shown in Figure 21.11b.

The vacancies in the valence band can be thought of as positive holes in a filled band. When the electrons in the partially filled valence band move under the influence of an applied potential, the positive holes move in the opposite direction. Because the charge carriers can be regarded as the *positive* holes, silicon doped with a group 3A element is called a **p-type semiconductor**. In a localized picture, a positive hole is a missing electron in a B—Si electron-pair bond. When an electron from an adjacent Si—Si bond moves into the hole, the hole moves in the opposite direction.

WORKED EXAMPLE 21.3

IDENTIFYING THE TYPE OF A DOPED SEMICONDUCTOR

Consider a crystal of germanium that has been doped with a small amount of aluminum. Is the doped crystal an *n*-type or *p*-type semiconductor? Compare the conductivity of the doped crystal with that of pure germanium.

STRATEGY

Consider the location of germanium and aluminum in the periodic table and the number of valence electrons in the doped crystal relative to the number in pure germanium. Doped semiconductors with more electrons than the pure semiconductor are *n*-type, and those with fewer electrons are *p*-type.

SOLUTION

Germanium, like silicon, is a group 4A semiconductor, and aluminum, like boron, is a group 3A element. The doped germanium is therefore a *p*-type semiconductor because each Al atom has one less valence electron than needed for bonding to the four neighboring Ge atoms. (Like silicon, germanium has the diamond structure.) The valence band is thus partially filled, which accounts for the electrical conductivity. The conductivity is greater than that of pure germanium because the doped germanium has many more positive holes in the valence band. That is, it has more vacant MOs available to which electrons can be excited by an electrical potential.

▶ **PROBLEM 21.6**   Is germanium doped with arsenic an *n*-type or a *p*-type semiconductor? Why is its conductivity greater than that of pure germanium?

CONCEPTUAL PROBLEM 21.7   The following pictures show the electron population of the bands of MO energy levels for four materials—diamond, silicon, silicon doped with aluminum, and white tin:

Energy

(a) Which picture corresponds to which material?
(b) Arrange the four materials in order of increasing electrical conductivity. Explain.

21.6   SEMICONDUCTOR APPLICATIONS

Doped semiconductors are essential components in the modern solid-state electronic devices found in numerous commercial products. These devices include:

- *diodes* that convert alternating current to direct current
- *light-emitting diodes (LEDs)* that serve as light sources in traffic signals, vehicle brake lights, digital clocks, and hospital pulse oximeters that monitor the oxygen saturation of hemoglobin in blood
- *diode lasers* that produce the bright, red light of laser pointers and supermarket bar-code scanners
- *photovoltaic (solar) cells* that convert sunlight into electricity
- *transistors* that control and amplify electrical signals in the integrated circuits of computers, cell phones, and many other consumer electronic products.

All these devices are made from *n*- and *p*-type semiconductors.

Diodes

A diode is a device that permits electric current to flow in one direction but is highly resistant to current flow in the opposite direction. It consists of a *p*-type semiconductor in contact with an *n*-type semiconductor to give a *p*−*n* junction (**Figure 21.12**).

If the *n*-type semiconductor is connected to the negative terminal of a battery and the *p*-type semiconductor is connected to the positive terminal (Figure 21.12a), electrons in the conduction band of the *n*-type semiconductor are repelled by the negative terminal and are attracted to the positive terminal. Consequently, they move into the region of the *p*−*n* junction from the *n*-side to the *p*-side where they fall into vacancies (positive holes) in the valence band of the *p*-type semiconductor. At the same time, the positive holes move in the opposite direction, from the *p*-side to

Under a forward bias (negative battery terminal on the *n*-type side), a current flows through the *p*–*n* junction because the charge carriers, electrons and holes, combine in the region of the junction.

Wire to positive battery terminal

Wire to negative battery terminal

(a)　+

p-type　　　　*n*-type

Wire to negative battery terminal

Wire to positive battery terminal

(b)　–

Under a reverse bias (negative battery terminal on the *p*-type side), almost no current flows because the electrons and holes move away from one another.

p-type　　　　*n*-type

Figure 21.12
A semiconductor diode.

the *n*-side where they combine with electrons in the conduction band of the *n*-type semiconductor. The motion of the electrons and holes constitutes an electric current that persists as long as the device is connected to the battery because the battery continues to pump electrons into the *n*-side and holes into the *p*-side. When the device is connected to the battery in this way, the *p*−*n* junction is said to be under a *forward bias*.

If the connections to the battery are reversed (*reverse bias*, Figure 21.12b), the charge carriers move in the reverse directions: Negative electrons move toward the positive battery terminal, and positive holes move toward the negative terminal. Because the charge carriers move away from the *p*−*n* junction, almost no electric current can flow through the junction; current flows only when the junction is under a forward bias. A *p*−*n* junction that is part of a circuit and subjected to an alternating potential acts as a *rectifier*, allowing current to flow in only one direction, thereby converting alternating current to direct current.

Light-Emitting Diodes (LEDs)

Energy is released as light when electrons and holes combine in the *p*−*n* junction of a diode under a forward bias because of an electronic transition from the conduction band to the valence band. A schematic of a light-emitting diode, or LED, is shown in **Figure 21.13**, along with the corresponding band theory energy level diagram.

In the energy level diagram, the valence and conduction bands have different energies on the *n*- and *p*-type sides because migration of a few electrons from the *n*-side to the *p*-side in the absence of an external voltage gives the *n*-side a small positive charge and the *p*-side a small negative charge. This charge difference lowers the energy of the bands on the *n*-side, raises the energy of the bands on the *p*-side, and prevents current flow in the absence of an external voltage. In the presence of an external voltage, the energy required for electrons to climb the energy hill in the region of the *p*−*n* junction is provided by the forward bias from the battery. The energy of the light emitted by an LED is roughly equal to the band gap energy, E_g, and is related to the wavelength of the light by the equation, $E_g = h\nu = hc/\lambda$.

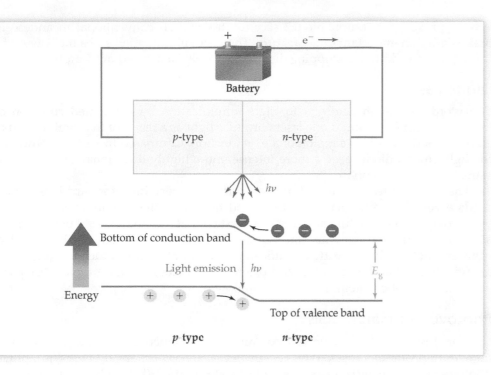

Figure 21.13
A schematic of a light-emitting diode (LED), along with the corresponding band theory energy level diagram.

The semiconductors commonly used for making LEDs are 1:1 compounds of group 3A and 5A elements, such as GaAs, GaP, AlAs, and InP. These so-called 3–5 semiconductors have the same diamond structure and the same number of valence electrons as the elemental semiconductors Si and Ge. In GaAs, for example, each Ga atom is surrounded tetrahedrally by four As atoms and each As atom is surrounded tetrahedrally by four Ga atoms. The average number of valence electrons per atom is four—three from Ga and five from As—so the valence band is nearly filled and the conduction band is nearly empty, as is the case for pure Si and Ge. n-Type GaAs can be made by doping with an element having one more valence electron than As (for example, Se), and p-type GaAs can be made by doping with an element having one less valence electron than Ga (for example, Zn).

In one method for manufacturing LEDs, thin films of n-type and p-type semiconductors are layered onto a transparent substrate by a process called *chemical vapor deposition*. For example, a GaAs layer can be deposited by bringing highly purified vapors of trimethylgallium, $Ga(CH_3)_3$, and arsine, AsH_3, into contact with the hot substrate at about 1000 °C.

$$Ga(CH_3)_3(g) + AsH_3(g) \xrightarrow{\text{1000 °C}} GaAs(s) + 3\,CH_4(g)$$

Because mixtures of different 3–5 semiconductors can form a continuous series of solid solutions, the band gap and thus the color of the light emitted by an LED can be tuned by varying the composition of the mixture. For example, GaAs and GaP form solid solutions having composition GaP_xAs_{1-x} ($0 \le x \le 1$). The band gaps of these solutions vary from ~135 kJ/mol, corresponding to infrared light, to ~222 kJ/mol, corresponding to green light, as the value of x increases from 0 to 1. The familiar red light emitted by many commercial LEDs is produced by $GaP_{0.40}As_{0.60}$, which has a band gap of 181 kJ/mol. Light in the blue and green regions of the spectrum can be obtained from solid solutions of gallium and indium nitrides, $Ga_xIn_{1-x}N$.

Red, green, and blue LEDs are combined to produce the numerous colors displayed on sports stadium JumboTrons and large, outdoor message boards. For example, the 120 × 90 foot display on the Nasdaq MarketSite Tower in New York's Times Square consists of almost 19 million LEDs that combine to produce more than one billion colors.

Compared with incandescent lightbulbs, LEDs are smaller, brighter, longer lived, and more energy efficient, and they have faster switching times. For example, LED

▲ LED vehicle brake lights.

vehicle brake lights illuminate 0.2 seconds faster than conventional incandescent brake lights, an important safety feature. The faster illumination gives the driver of a trailing car an additional stopping distance of 19 feet at a speed of 65 mph.

Diode Lasers

The word *laser* is an acronym for *l*ight *a*mplification by *s*timulated *e*mission of *r*adiation. Both LEDs and diode lasers produce light as a result of the combination of electrons and holes in the region of a $p-n$ junction. Compared to an LED, however, the light from a diode laser is more intense, more highly directional, and all of the same frequency and phase.

The essential features of a diode laser are (1) a very high forward bias, which sends a very large number of electrons and holes into the $p-n$ junction, and (2) a laser cavity with a structure and dimensions such that the emitted light bounces back and forth within the material, thus stimulating a cascade of combinations of electrons and holes, which greatly amplifies the amount of light produced. Diode lasers are widely used in laser pointers and printers, bar-code readers, compact disc players, and fiber optic systems for data transmission.

Photovoltaic (Solar) Cells

Like an LED, a photovoltaic cell contains a $p-n$ junction, but the two devices involve opposite processes. Whereas an LED converts electrical energy to light, a photovoltaic, or solar, cell converts light to electricity. When light with an energy greater than or equal to the band gap shines on a $p-n$ junction, electrons are excited from the valence band of the p-type semiconductor into the conduction band of the n-type semiconductor (Figure 21.14). If the $p-n$ junction is made part of an electrical circuit, electrons will flow through the junction from the p-side to the n-side because of the negative (downhill) slope of the conduction band in the region of the junction. Positive holes left behind in the valence band move in the opposite direction. The resulting current can be used to charge a battery or power an electrical device, such as a calculator or a lightbulb.

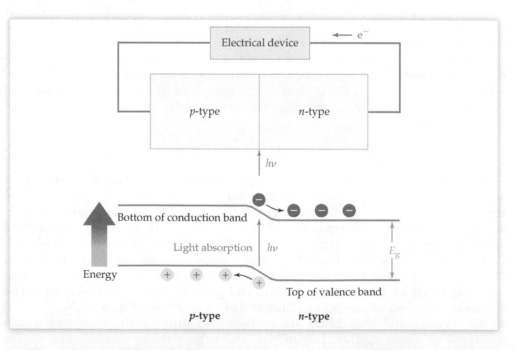

Figure 21.14
A schematic of a photovoltaic (solar) cell, along with the corresponding band theory energy level diagram.

Silicon, which has a band gap of 107 kJ/mol, is commonly used to make solar cells; it absorbs sunlight with a wavelength less than about 1100 nm (ultraviolet, visible, and some of the infrared). Because the efficiency of light-to-electricity conversion in presently available solar cells is only about 20%, current research focuses on increasing the efficiency of these cells and reducing their cost.

Transistors

The transistor, invented in 1947 at Bell Laboratories, is an essential component in radios, television sets, computers, cell phones, and a host of other electronic products. Transistors consist of $n-p-n$ or $p-n-p$ junctions that control and amplify electrical signals in modern integrated circuits. An amazing number of these extremely small devices can be packed into a small space, thus decreasing the size and increasing the speed of electrical equipment. For example, computer microprocessors now contain tens of billions of transistors on a silicon chip with a surface area of about 2 cm^2 and are able to execute more than 100 billion instructions per second.

▶ **PROBLEM 21.8** What is the wavelength of the light emitted by a GaP LED with a band gap of 222 kJ/mol?

▲ An Intel Core 2 Duo Processor.

21.7 SUPERCONDUCTORS

The discovery of high-temperature superconductors is one of the most exciting scientific developments in the last 25 years. It has stimulated an enormous amount of research in chemistry, physics, and materials science that could some day lead to a world of superfast computers, magnetically levitated trains, and power lines that carry electric current without loss of energy.

A **superconductor** is a material that loses all electrical resistance below a characteristic temperature called the **superconducting transition temperature**, T_c. This phenomenon was discovered in 1911 by the Dutch physicist Heike Kamerlingh Onnes, who found that mercury abruptly loses its electrical resistance when it is cooled with liquid helium to 4.2 K (**Figure 21.15**). Below its T_c, a superconductor becomes a perfect conductor and an electric current, once started, flows indefinitely without loss of energy.

Figure 21.15
The electrical resistance of mercury falls to zero at its superconducting transition temperature, T_c = 4.2 K.

Ever since the initial discovery in 1911, scientists have been searching for materials that superconduct at higher temperatures, and more than 6000 superconductors are now known. Until 1986, however, the record value of T_c was only 23.2 K, for the compound Nb$_3$Ge. The situation changed dramatically in 1986, when K. Alex Müller and J. Georg Bednorz of the IBM Zürich Research Laboratory reported a T_c of 35 K for the nonstoichiometric barium lanthanum copper oxide Ba$_x$La$_{2-x}$CuO$_4$, where x has a value of about 0.1. Soon thereafter, scientists found even higher values of T_c for other copper-containing oxides: 90 K for YBa$_2$Cu$_3$O$_7$, 125 K for Tl$_2$Ba$_2$Ca$_2$Cu$_3$O$_{10}$, 133 K for HgBa$_2$Ca$_2$Cu$_3$O$_{8+x}$, and 138 K for Hg$_{0.8}$Tl$_{0.2}$Ba$_2$Ca$_2$Cu$_3$O$_{8.33}$, the recordholder as of this writing. High values of T_c for these compounds were completely unexpected because most metal oxides—nonmetallic inorganic solids called *ceramics*—are electrical insulators. Within just one year of discovering the first ceramic superconductor, Müller and Bednorz were awarded the 1987 Nobel Prize in Physics.

The crystal structure of $YBa_2Cu_3O_7$, the so-called 1-2-3 compound (1 yttrium, 2 bariums, and 3 coppers), is illustrated in **Figure 21.16**, and one unit cell of the structure is shown in **Figure 21.17**. The crystal contains parallel planes of Y, Ba, and Cu atoms. Two-thirds of the Cu atoms are surrounded by a square pyramid of five O atoms, some of which are shared with neighboring CuO_5 groups to give two-dimensional layers of square pyramids. The remaining Cu atoms are surrounded by a square of four O atoms, two of which are shared with neighboring CuO_4 squares to give chains of CuO_4 groups. It's interesting to note that the Cu atoms have a fractional oxidation number of +2.33, based on the usual oxidation numbers of +3 for Y, +2 for Ba, and −2 for O. Both the infinitely extended layers of Cu and O atoms and the fractional oxidation number of Cu appear to play a role in the current flow, but a generally accepted theory of superconductivity in ceramic superconductors is not yet available. This is a field where experiment is far ahead of theory.

Figure 21.16

A computer graphics representation of the crystal structure of $YBa_2Cu_3O_7$.

Layers of Y atoms (yellow) and Ba atoms (blue) are sandwiched between layers of CuO_5 square pyramids (red) and chains of square planar CuO_4 groups (green).

Figure 21.17

One unit cell of the crystal structure of $YBa_2Cu_3O_7$. The unit cell contains one Y atom, two Ba atoms, three Cu atoms, and seven O atoms.

In counting the Cu and O atoms, recall that the unit cell contains 1/8 of each corner atom, 1/4 of each edge atom, and 1/2 of each face atom (Section 10.8).

The figure includes eight O atoms from neighboring unit cells to show the square pyramidal CuO_5 groups and square planar CuO_4 groups.

Yttrium
Barium
Copper
Oxygen

One of the most dramatic properties of a superconductor is its ability to levitate a magnet. When a superconductor is cooled below its T_c and a magnet is lowered toward it, the superconductor and the magnet repel each other, and the magnet hovers above the superconductor as though suspended in midair (Figure 21.18).

The force responsible for levitation arises in the following way: When the magnet moves toward the superconductor, it induces a supercurrent in the surface of the superconductor that continues to flow even after the magnet stops moving. The supercurrent, in turn, induces a magnetic field in the superconductor that exactly cancels the field from the magnet. Thus, the net magnetic field within the bulk of the superconductor is zero, a phenomenon called the *Meissner effect*. Outside the superconductor, however, the magnetic fields due to the magnet and the supercurrent repel each other, just as the north poles of two bar magnets do. The magnet therefore experiences an upward magnetic force as well as the usual downward gravitational force, and it remains suspended above the superconductor at the point where the two forces are equal. Potential applications of the Meissner effect include high-speed, magnetically levitated trains, such as the one now operating in Shanghai, China (Figure 21.19).

Other common applications of superconductors exist. For example, powerful superconducting magnets are essential components in the magnetic resonance imaging (MRI) instruments widely used in medical diagnosis. Superconductors are also used to make the magnets that bend the path of charged particles in high-energy particle accelerators. These applications, however, use conventional superconductors ($T_c \leq 20$ K) that are cooled to 4.2 K with liquid helium, an expensive substance that requires sophisticated cryogenic (cooling) equipment. Much of the excitement surrounding the high-temperature superconductors arises because their T_c values are above the boiling point of liquid nitrogen (bp 77 K), an abundant refrigerant that is cheaper than milk. Of course, the search goes on for materials with still higher values of T_c. For applications such as long-distance electric power transmission, the goal is a material that superconducts at room temperature.

Presently known high-temperature superconductors are brittle powders with high melting points, so they are not easily fabricated into the wires and coils needed for electrical equipment. Nevertheless, commercial applications of high-temperature superconductors are beginning to emerge. Superconducting thin films are used as microwave filters in cell-phone base stations, and superconducting wire 1 km in length is now commercially available.

In 1991, scientists at AT&T Bell Laboratories discovered a new class of high temperature superconductors based on fullerene, the allotrope of carbon that contains C_{60} molecules (Sections 10.10 and 19.7). These soccer ball-shaped C_{60} molecules react with potassium to give K_3C_{60}, a stable crystalline solid that contains a face-centered cubic array of C_{60}^{3-} ions, with K^+ ions in the cavities between them (Figure 21.20). At room temperature, K_3C_{60} is a metallic conductor, but it becomes a superconductor at 19.5 K. The related fullerides Rb_3C_{60} and Cs_3C_{60} have higher T_c values of 29.5 K and 40 K, respectively.

Still another class of high-temperature superconductors has been discovered very recently. In February of 2008 scientists at the Tokyo Institute of Technology reported that a fluorine-doped lanthanum oxide iron arsenide, $LaO_{1-x}F_xFeAs$ ($x = 0.11$), superconducts at 26 K. Subsequent replacement of lanthanum by other lanthanide elements has raised the value of T_c to a current maximum of 55 K for the fluorine-doped samarium compound.

▶ **PROBLEM 21.9** Show that one unit cell of $YBa_2Cu_3O_7$ (Figure 21.17) contains three Cu atoms and seven O atoms.

Figure 21.18
Levitation of a magnet above a pellet of $YBa_2Cu_3O_7$ cooled to 77 K with liquid nitrogen. $YBa_2Cu_3O_7$ becomes a superconductor at approximately 90 K.

Figure 21.19
A Maglev train is now in commercial operation in Shanghai, China, running at 430 km/h.

Remember...

Carbon exists in more than 40 known structural forms, or allotropes, most of which are amorphous. Three of the most common crystalline forms are graphite, diamond, and fullerene.   (Sections 10.10 and 19.7)

Figure 21.20
A portion of one unit cell of the face-centered cubic structure of K_3C_{60} viewed perpendicular to a cube face.

The C_{60}^{3-} ions are located at the cube corners and face centers, and the K^+ ions (red and blue spheres) are in two kinds of holes between the C_{60}^{3-} ions.

These K^+ ions lie in the plane of the cube face (the plane of the paper) and are surrounded octahedrally by six C_{60}^{3-} ions.

These K^+ ions lie in a plane one-fourth of a cell edge length below the plane of the paper and are surrounded tetrahedrally by four C_{60}^{3-} ions.

|← 1424 pm →|

21.8 CERAMICS

Ceramics are inorganic, nonmetallic, nonmolecular solids, including both crystalline materials such as quartz (SiO_2) and amorphous materials such as glasses. Known since ancient times, traditional silicate ceramics, such as pottery and porcelain, are made by heating aluminosilicate clays to high temperatures. Modern, so-called **advanced ceramics**—materials that have high-tech engineering, electronic, and biomedical applications—include *oxide ceramics*, such as alumina (Al_2O_3), and *nonoxide ceramics*, such as silicon carbide (SiC) and silicon nitride (Si_3N_4). Additional examples are listed in Table 21.4, which compares the properties of ceramics with those of aluminum and steel. Note that oxide ceramics are named by replacing the *-um* ending of the element name with an *-a*; thus, BeO is beryllia, ZrO_2 is zirconia, and so forth.

TABLE 21.4   Properties of Some Ceramic and Metallic Materials

Material	Melting Point (°C)	Density (g/cm³)	Elastic Modulus (GPa)*	Hardness (Mohs scale)†
Oxide ceramics				
Alumina, Al_2O_3	2054	3.99	380	9
Beryllia, BeO	2578	3.01	370	8
Zirconia, ZrO_2	2710	5.68	210	8
Nonoxide ceramics				
Boron carbide, B_4C	2350	2.50	280	9
Silicon carbide, SiC	2830	3.16	400	9
Silicon nitride, Si_3N_4	1900	3.17	310	9
Metals				
Aluminum	660	2.70	70	3
Plain carbon steel	1515	7.86	205	5

* The elastic modulus, measured in units of pressure (1 gigapascal = 1 GPa = 10^9 Pa) indicates the stiffness of a material when it is subjected to a load. The larger the value, the stiffer the material.

† Numbers on the Mohs hardness scale range from 1 for talc, a very soft material, to 10 for diamond, the hardest known natural substance.

In many respects, the properties of ceramics are superior to those of metals: Ceramics have higher melting points and are stiffer, harder, and more resistant to wear and corrosion. Moreover, they maintain much of their strength at high temperatures, where metals either melt or corrode because of oxidation. Silicon nitride and silicon carbide, for example, are stable to oxidation in air up to 1400–1500 °C, and oxide ceramics don't react with oxygen because they are already fully oxidized. Because ceramics are less dense than steel, they are attractive lightweight, high-temperature materials for replacing metal components in aircraft, space vehicles, and automotive engines.

Unfortunately, ceramics are brittle, as anyone who has dropped a coffee cup well knows. The brittleness, hardness, stiffness, and high melting points of ceramics are all due to strong chemical bonding. Take silicon carbide, for example, a covalent network solid that crystallizes in the diamond structure (**Figure 21.21**). Each Si atom is bonded tetrahedrally to four C atoms, and each C atom is bonded tetrahedrally to four Si atoms. The strong, highly directional covalent bonds ($D_{Si-C} = 435$ kJ/mol) prevent the planes of atoms from sliding over one another when the solid is subjected to the stress of a load or an impact. As a result, the solid can't deform to relieve the stress. It maintains its shape up to a point, but then the bonds give way suddenly, and the material fails catastrophically when the stress exceeds a certain threshold value. Oxide ceramics, in which the bonding is largely ionic, behave similarly. By contrast, metals are able to deform under stress because their planes of metal cations can slide easily in the electron sea (Section 21.4). As a result, metals dent but ceramics shatter.

▲ A silicon nitride rotor for use in gas-turbine engines.

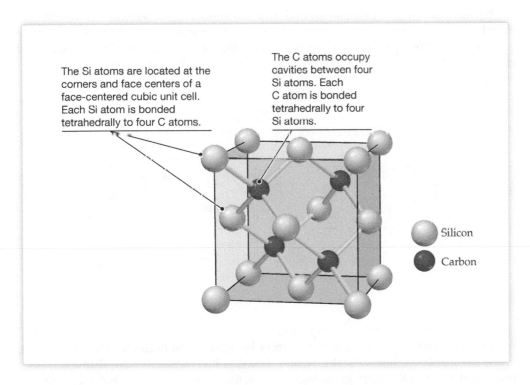

The Si atoms are located at the corners and face centers of a face-centered cubic unit cell. Each Si atom is bonded tetrahedrally to four C atoms.

The C atoms occupy cavities between four Si atoms. Each C atom is bonded tetrahedrally to four Si atoms.

Silicon

Carbon

Figure 21.21
One unit cell of the cubic form of silicon carbide, SiC. The crystal can't deform under stress because the bonds are strong and highly directional.

Ceramic processing, the series of steps that leads from raw material to the finished ceramic object, is important in determining the strength and the resistance to fracture of the product. Processing often begins with a fine powder, which is combined with an organic binder, shaped, compacted, and finally *sintered* at temperatures of 1300–2000 °C. **Sintering**, which occurs below the melting point, is a process in which the particles of the powder are welded together without completely melting. During sintering, the crystal grains grow larger and the density of the material increases as the void spaces between particles disappear. Unfortunately, impurities and remaining voids can lead to microscopic cracks that cause the material to fail under stress. It is therefore important to minimize impurities and voids by beginning with high-purity, fine powders that can be tightly compacted prior to sintering.

One approach to making such powders is the **sol–gel method**, in which a metal oxide powder is synthesized from a metal alkoxide, a compound derived from a metal and an alcohol. In the synthesis of titania (TiO_2) from titanium ethoxide, $Ti(OCH_2CH_3)_4$, for example, the $Ti(OCH_2CH_3)_4$ starting material is made by the reaction of titanium(IV) chloride with ethanol and ammonia in a benzene solution:

$$TiCl_4 + 4\ \underset{\text{Ethanol}}{HOCH_2CH_3} + 4\ NH_3(g) \xrightarrow{\text{Benzene}} \underset{\text{Titanium ethoxide}}{Ti(OCH_2CH_3)_4} + 4\ NH_4Cl(s)$$

Pure $Ti(OCH_2CH_3)_4$ is then dissolved in an appropriate organic solvent, and water is added to bring about a *hydrolysis* reaction:

$$Ti(OCH_2CH_3)_4 + 4\ H_2O \xrightarrow{\text{Solution}} Ti(OH)_4(s) + 4\ HOCH_2CH_3$$

In this reaction, Ti—OCH_2CH_3 bonds are broken, Ti—OH bonds are formed, and ethanol is regenerated. The $Ti(OH)_4$ forms in the solution as a colloidal dispersion called a *sol*, consisting of extremely fine particles having a diameter of only 0.001–$0.1\ \mu m$. Subsequent reactions eliminate water molecules and form oxygen bridges between Ti atoms:

$$(HO)_3Ti-O\boxed{-H\ +\ H-O}-Ti(OH)_3 \longrightarrow (HO)_3Ti-O-Ti(OH)_3\ +\ H_2O$$

Because all the OH groups can undergo this reaction, the particles of the sol link together through a three-dimensional network of oxygen bridges and the sol is converted to a more rigid, gelatinlike material called a *gel*. The remaining water and solvent are then removed by heating the gel, and TiO_2 is obtained as a fine powder consisting of high-purity particles with a diameter less than $1\ \mu m$ (**Figure 21.22**).

Figure 21.22
Electron micrographs of a titania powder (left) and the dense ceramic produced by sintering the powder (right). The powder, consisting of tightly packed particles of TiO_2 with a diameter less than $1\ \mu m$, was made by the sol–gel method.

Oxide ceramics have many important uses. Alumina, for example, is the material of choice for making spark-plug insulators because of its high electrical resistance, high strength, high thermal stability, and chemical inertness. Because alumina is nontoxic and essentially inert in biological systems, it is used in constructing dental crowns and the heads of artificial hips. Alumina is also used as a substrate material for electronic circuit boards. High purity silica (SiO_2) fibers are used to make the lightweight, heat-resistant ceramic tiles that protect the space shuttle on re-entry into the atmosphere. The shuttle is covered with more than 20,000 tiles that have a density less than that of styrofoam and are able to withstand temperatures up to 1600 °C.

In the military, ceramics are widely used because they are lightweight and are strong enough to shatter and deflect bullets and other projectiles. For example, body armor, once made of steel (density, $7.86\ g/cm^3$), is now made of light ceramic materials such as boron carbide (density, $2.50\ g/cm^3$). Use of lightweight ceramic armor panels in place of steel in combat vehicles and military aircraft has increased maneuverability and decreased fuel consumption.

WORKED EXAMPLE 21.4

SYNTHESIZING THE 1-2-3 SUPERCONDUCTOR BY HYDROLYSIS OF A MIXTURE OF METAL ETHOXIDES

The 1-2-3 ceramic superconductor $YBa_2Cu_3O_7$ has been synthesized by the sol–gel method from a stoichiometric mixture of yttrium ethoxide, barium ethoxide, and copper(II) ethoxide in an appropriate organic solvent. The oxide product, before being heated in oxygen, has the formula $YBa_2Cu_3O_{6.5}$. Write a balanced equation for the hydrolysis of the stoichiometric mixture of metal ethoxides.

STRATEGY

First, determine the chemical formulas of the metal ethoxides, and then write a balanced equation for the reaction of the mixture of metal ethoxides with water.

SOLUTION

The ethoxide ligand is the anion of ethanol, $HOCH_2CH_3$, and has a charge of -1. Because yttrium is a group 3B element and has an oxidation number of $+3$, the formula of yttrium ethoxide must be $Y(OCH_2CH_3)_3$. Similarly, because both barium (in group 2A) and copper(II) have an oxidation number of $+2$, the formulas of barium ethoxide and copper ethoxide must be $Ba(OCH_2CH_3)_2$ and $Cu(OCH_2CH_3)_2$, respectively.

Hydrolysis of $Y(OCH_2CH_3)_3$, which breaks the $Y-OCH_2CH_3$ bonds and forms $Y-OH$ bonds, requires one H_2O molecule for each ethoxide ligand:

$$Y(OCH_2CH_3)_3 + 3\,H_2O \longrightarrow Y(OH)_3 + 3\,HOCH_2CH_3$$

Similarly, hydrolysis of $Ba(OCH_2CH_3)_2$ and $Cu(OCH_2CH_3)_2$ yields $Ba(OH)_2$ and $Cu(OH)_2$, respectively:

$$Ba(OCH_2CH_3)_2 + 2\,H_2O \longrightarrow Ba(OH)_2 + 2\,HOCH_2CH_3$$
$$Cu(OCH_2CH_3)_2 + 2\,H_2O \longrightarrow Cu(OH)_2 + 2\,HOCH_2CH_3$$

Because the three metal ethoxides are present together in a 1:2:3 ratio in the synthesis of the superconductor, we can write the product of the hydrolysis as $Y(OH)_3 \cdot 2\,Ba(OH)_2 \cdot 3\,Cu(OH)_2$, or $YBa_2Cu_3(OH)_{13}$. Thus, the hydrolysis reaction requires 13 H_2O molecules for 13 OCH_2CH_3 ligands, and the balanced equation is

$$Y(OCH_2CH_3)_3 + 2\,Ba(OCH_2CH_3)_2 + 3\,Cu(OCH_2CH_3)_2 + 13\,H_2O \longrightarrow$$
$$YBa_2Cu_3(OH)_{13} + 13\,HOCH_2CH_3$$

Subsequent heating of $YBa_2Cu_3(OH)_{13}$ removes water, converting the mixed-metal hydroxide to the oxide $YBa_2Cu_3O_{6.5}$, which is then oxidized to $YBa_2Cu_3O_7$ by heating in O_2 gas.

▶ **PROBLEM 21.10** Silica glasses used in lenses, laser mirrors, and other optical components can be made by the sol–gel method. One step in the process is the hydrolysis of $Si(OCH_3)_4$. Write a balanced equation for the reaction.

▶ **PROBLEM 21.11** Crystals of the oxide ceramic barium titanate, $BaTiO_3$, have an unsymmetrical arrangement of ions, which gives the crystals an electric dipole moment. Such materials are called ferroelectrics and are used to make various electronic devices. Barium titanate can be made by the sol–gel method, which involves hydrolysis of a mixture of metal alkoxides. Write a balanced equation for the hydrolysis of a 1:1 mixture of barium isopropoxide and titanium isopropoxide, and explain how the resulting sol is converted to $BaTiO_3$. (The isopropoxide ligand is the anion of isopropyl alcohol, $HOCH(CH_3)_2$, also known as rubbing alcohol.)

21.9 COMPOSITES

In the previous section, we saw that ceramics are brittle and prone to fracture. They can be strengthened and toughened, though, by mixing the ceramic powder prior to sintering with fibers of a second ceramic material, such as carbon, boron, or silicon carbide. The resulting hybrid material, called a **ceramic composite**, combines the advantageous properties of both components. An example is the composite consisting of fine grains of alumina reinforced with *whiskers* of silicon carbide. Whiskers are tiny, fiber-shaped particles, about 0.5 μm in diameter and 50 μm long, that are very strong because they are single crystals. Silicon carbide-reinforced alumina possesses high strength and high shock resistance, even at high temperatures, and has therefore been used to make high-speed cutting tools for machining very hard steels.

How do fibers and whiskers increase the strength and fracture toughness of a composite material? First, fibers have great strength along the fiber axis because most of the chemical bonds are aligned in that direction. Second, there are several ways in which fibers can prevent microscopic cracks from propagating to the point that they lead to the fracture of the material. The fibers can deflect cracks, thus preventing them from moving cleanly in one direction, and they can bridge cracks, thus holding the two sides of a crack together.

Silicon carbide-reinforced alumina is a composite in which both the fibers and the surrounding matrix are ceramics. There are other composites, however, in which the two phases are different types of materials. Examples are **ceramic–metal composites**, or **cermets**, such as aluminum metal reinforced with boron fiber, and **ceramic–polymer composites**, such as boron/epoxy and carbon/epoxy. (Epoxy is a resin consisting of long-chain organic molecules.) These materials are popular for aerospace and military applications because of their high strength-to-weight ratios. Boron-reinforced aluminum, for example, is used as a lightweight structural material in the space shuttle, and boron/epoxy and carbon/epoxy skins are used on military aircraft. Increased use of composite materials in commercial aircraft could result in weight savings of 20–30% and corresponding savings in fuel, which accounts for as much as 40% of the cost of operating an airline. Carbon/epoxy composites are also used to make strong, lightweight sports equipment, such as golf clubs, tennis racquets, fishing rods, and bicycles.

▶ The skin of the B-2 advanced technology aircraft is a strong, lightweight composite material that contains carbon fibers.

Ceramic fibers used in composites are usually made by high-temperature methods. Carbon (graphite) fiber, for example, can be made by the thermal decomposition of fibers of polyacrylonitrile, a long-chain organic molecule also used to make the textile Orlon:

Polyacrylonitrile

Repeating unit

In the final step of the multistep process, the carbon in the fiber is converted to graphite by heating at 1400–2500 °C. Similarly, silicon carbide fiber can be made by heating fibers that contain long-chain molecules with alternating silicon and carbon atoms:

$$- SiH_2 - CH_2 \boxed{SiH_2 - CH_2} SiH_2 - CH_2 - \xrightarrow[-H_2]{Heat} SiC \text{ fiber}$$

Repeating unit

▶ **PROBLEM 21.12**   Classify each of these composites as ceramic–ceramic, ceramic–metal, or ceramic–polymer:

(a) Cobalt/tungsten carbide

(b) Silicon carbide/zirconia

(c) Boron nitride/epoxy

(d) Boron carbide/titanium

INQUIRY WHY IS IT SAID THAT THE NEXT BIG THING WILL BE REALLY SMALL?

Imagine a world of super-fast computers, cheap big-screen television sets, and drugs that target and kill cancer cells with a minimum of side effects. Those are but a few of the developments that might emerge from *nanotechnology*, one of the hottest research areas in science today.

Nanotechnology is the study and production of materials and structures that have at least one dimension between 1 nm and 100 nm, where one nanometer is one billionth of a meter (1 nm = 10^{-9} m). Nanoscale materials with just one dimension in the range 1–100 nm are called nanolayers; those with two are termed nanotubes or nanowires; and those with three are said to be nanoparticles. Nanotechnology is an explosively growing, multidisciplinary enterprise, spanning the fields of chemistry, physics, biology, medicine, materials science, environmental science, and engineering.

To appreciate the extremely small size of nanomaterials, it's helpful to note that 1 nm is the width of four H atoms laid side by side, one thousandth the length of a typical bacterium, and about 50,000 times smaller than the diameter of a human hair. Because of their small size, nanoparticles have unique properties. They tend to have lower melting points, different colors, and greater reactivity than bulk materials. For example, gold nanoparticles are red and chemically reactive, whereas the bulk metal is yellow and inert. The lower melting points and greater reactivity of nanoparticles result because a substantial percentage of the atoms in a nanoparticle are on the surface and are therefore bound less tightly than those within the bulk solid; for a 5 nm particle, about 30% of the atoms are on the surface.

Because nanoparticles have dimensions intermediate between those of individual atoms and bulk solids, they have intermediate electronic properties as well. Recall that atoms and small molecules have discrete, quantized energy levels (Sections 5.8, 7.13–7.14), whereas solid metals and semiconductors have broad bands of energy levels (Sections 21.4–21.5). This difference arises because electrons in atoms are confined to a very small volume whereas in solids they are delocalized throughout the entire crystal. For solid nanoparticles, the spacing between energy levels increases as the size of the particle decreases.

A particularly striking electronic effect is seen in so-called *quantum dots*, semiconductor nanoparticles that are about 1–10 nm in diameter and contain only hundreds to tens of thousands of atoms. When a quantum dot is irradiated with ultraviolet light, it emits visible light having a wavelength that depends on the size of the nanoparticle. For example, a 3 nm cadmium selenide particle emits green light at 520 nm, whereas a 5.5 nm particle of the same substance emits red light at 620 nm. An entire rainbow of colors can be emitted by differently sized nanoparticles of a single substance, with the wavelength of the emitted light decreasing from the red to the violet part of the spectrum as the size of the particle decreases.

Color, as we've seen in Sections 5.8 and 20.10, is due to electronic transitions. When a quantum dot is irradiated with ultraviolet light, an electron is excited from the valence band to an energy level within the conduction band. Subsequently, the electron undergoes a transition from the bottom of the conduction band to the top of the valence band. This transition produces a visible photon having an energy roughly equal to the band gap. The smaller the particle, the larger the band gap and the greater the shift in the color of the emitted light from the red to the violet.

Because of their distinctive optical properties, quantum dots may have numerous applications. For example, the surface of a quantum dot can be chemically modified by attaching an organic molecule that targets and bonds to a specific biomolecule, such as DNA or a protein. The modified quantum dots are thousands of times smaller than human cells and are able to penetrate cell membranes. When they bond to a biomolecule and are irradiated with ultraviolet light, they serve as fluorescent probes, or labels, for that particular biomolecule, with the color of the emitted light dependent on the size of the quantum dot. Thus, irradiation with a single light

▲ Wine-colored, 15 nm gold nanoparticles in solution (left) and a bar of bulk gold (right).

▲ The color of these semiconductor nanoparticles, called quantum dots, varies from red to violet as the size of the nanoparticles decreases.

source of a mixture of quantum dots having different sizes and different surface modifications allows simultaneous detection, tracking, and imaging in color of a number of different biomolecules within a cell. Already, quantum dots are available commercially for biomedical applications.

Several types of nanoparticles, including quantum dots, are being investigated as potential weapons in the fight against cancer. For example, nanoparticles can be modified by attaching antibodies that target and bond to receptors found on the outside of cancer cell membranes but have little affinity for the membranes of healthy cells. Because of their small size, the nanoparticles can enter the interior of cancer cells through the cell membranes. Prior attachment to the nanoparticles of magnetic resonance imaging (MRI) contrast agents, such as paramagnetic Gd^{3+} ions, greatly enhances the quality of MRI images and may allow cancer to be detected at its earliest and most curable stages.

▶ Upon excitation with light, nanoparticles that contain a ruthenium chelate generate a highly reactive form of oxygen that is lethal to rat cancer cells. Dead cells are shown in red, live cells in green.

Although human cancer applications are still in the future, low-tech applications of nanoparticles exist already. For example, metal oxide nanoparticles are widely used in sunscreens and cosmetics, stain-resistant fabrics, dirt-repellent paints, and coatings for self-cleaning windows. Carbon nanotubes are used as reinforcing rods and toughening elements in structural composite materials, and gold nanoparticles are effective as highly selective oxidation catalysts.

▶ **PROBLEM 21.13** You wish to track the motions of two proteins within a cell. To protein A you attach a quantum dot that emits yellow light, and to protein B, a quantum dot of the same substance that emits blue light. Which quantum dot is larger? Explain.

▶ **PROBLEM 21.14** Calculate the percentage of the atoms that are on the surface of a cubic nanoparticle if the diameter of the atoms is 250 pm and the edge length of the particle is

(a) 5.0 nm   (b) 10 nm

SUMMARY

Most metals occur in nature as **minerals**—the silicates, carbonates, oxides, sulfides, phosphates, and chlorides that make up the rocks of the Earth's crust. The type of mineral in which a metal is found depends on the metal's location in the periodic table. Minerals from which metals can be produced economically are called **ores**.

Metallurgy, the science and technology of extracting metals from their ores, involves three steps: (1) concentration and chemical treatment to separate the mineral from impurities called **gangue**; (2) reduction of the mineral to the free metal; and (3) refining or purification of the metal. The first step uses processes such as **flotation** and **roasting**. The reduction method (roasting, chemical reduction, or electrolysis) depends on the activity of the metal. The refining step involves distillation, chemical purification (for example, the **Mond process** for nickel), or electrorefining.

Iron is produced in a blast furnace by reducing iron oxide ores with CO. Added limestone ($CaCO_3$) decomposes to CaO, which reacts with SiO_2 and other acidic oxide impurities to yield a molten **slag** (mainly $CaSiO_3$) that is separated from the molten iron at the bottom of the furnace. The iron is converted to steel by the **basic oxygen process**, which removes impurities such as elemental Si, P, S, and most of the C.

Two bonding models are used for metals. The **electron-sea model** pictures a metal as an array of metal cations immersed in a sea of delocalized, mobile valence electrons that act as an electrostatic glue. In the molecular orbital theory for metals, also called **band theory**, the delocalized valence electrons occupy a vast number of MO energy levels that are so closely spaced that they merge into an almost continuous band. Both theories account for properties such as malleability, ductility, and high thermal and electrical conductivity, but band theory better explains how the number of valence electrons affects properties such as melting point and hardness.

Band theory also accounts for the electrical properties of metals, insulators, and semiconductors. Materials with partially filled bands are metallic conductors, and materials with only completely filled bands are electrical insulators. In insulators, the bonding MOs, called the **valence band**, and the antibonding MOs, called the **conduction band**, are separated in energy by a large **band gap**. In **semiconductors**, the band gap is smaller, and a few electrons have enough thermal energy to occupy the conduction band. The resulting partially filled valence and conduction bands give rise to a small conductivity. The conductivity can be increased by **doping**—adding a group 5A impurity to a group 4A element, which gives an **n-type semiconductor**, or adding a group 3A impurity to a group 4A element, which gives a **p-type semiconductor**. Doped semiconductors are essential components in modern solid-state electronic devices, such as diodes, light-emitting diodes (LEDs), diode lasers, photovoltaic (solar) cells, and transistors.

A **superconductor** is a material that loses all electrical resistance below a characteristic temperature called the **superconducting transition temperature**, T_c. An example is $YBa_2Cu_3O_7$ ($T_c = 90$ K). Below T_c, a superconductor can levitate a magnet, a consequence of the Meissner effect.

Ceramics are inorganic, nonmetallic, nonmolecular solids. Modern **advanced ceramics** include oxide ceramics such as Al_2O_3 and $YBa_2Cu_3O_7$ and nonoxide ceramics such as SiC and Si_3N_4. Ceramics are generally higher-melting, lighter, stiffer, harder, and more resistant to wear and corrosion than metals. One approach to ceramic processing is the **sol–gel method**, involving hydrolysis of a metal alkoxide. The strength and fracture toughness of ceramics can be increased by making **ceramic composites**, hybrid materials such as Al_2O_3/SiC in which fine grains of Al_2O_3 are reinforced by whiskers of SiC. Other types of composites include **ceramic–metal composites** and **ceramic–polymer composites**.

KEY WORDS

advanced ceramic   *874*
alloy   *855*
band gap   *864*
band theory   *861*
basic oxygen
   process   *859*
ceramic   *874*
ceramic composite   *877*

ceramic–metal composite
   (cermet)   *878*
ceramic–polymer
   composite   *878*
conduction band   *864*
doping   *865*
electron-sea model   *860*
flotation   *855*

gangue   *855*
metallurgy   *855*
mineral   *853*
Mond process   *857*
n-type semiconductor   *866*
ore   *853*
p-type semiconductor   *866*
roasting   *856*

semiconductor   *864*
sintering   *875*
slag   *859*
sol–gel method   *876*
superconducting transition
   temperature, T_c *871*
superconductor   *871*
valence band   *864*

CONCEPTUAL PROBLEMS

Problems 21.1–21.14 appear within the chapter.

21.15 Look at the location of elements A, B, C, and D in the following periodic table:

Without looking at Figure 21.2, predict whether these elements are likely to be found in nature as carbonates, oxides, sulfides, or in uncombined form. Explain.

21.16 The methods for extracting metals from their ores include (i) roasting a metal sulfide, (ii) chemical reduction of a metal oxide, and (iii) electrolysis. The preferred method depends on the $E°$ value for the reduction half-reaction $M^{n+}(aq) + n\,e^- \rightarrow M(s)$.

(a) Which method is appropriate for the metals with the most negative $E°$ values?

(b) Which method is appropriate for the metals with the most positive $E°$ values?

(c) Which method is appropriate for metals A, B, C, and D in the following periodic table?

21.17 The following pictures show the electron populations of the bands of MO energy levels for four different materials:

(a) Classify each material as an insulator, a semiconductor, or a metal.

(b) Arrange the four materials in order of increasing electrical conductivity. Explain.

(c) Tell whether the conductivity of each material increases or decreases when the temperature increases.

21.18 The following pictures show the electron populations of the composite $s–d$ bands for three different transition metals:

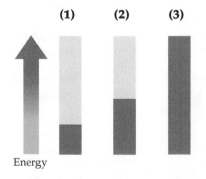

(a) Which metal has the highest melting point? Explain.

(b) Which metal has the lowest melting point? Explain.

(c) Arrange the metals in order of increasing hardness. Explain.

21.19 The following picture represents the electron population of the bands of MO energy levels for elemental silicon:

(a) Identify the valence band, conduction band, and band gap.

(b) In a drawing, show how the electron population changes when the silicon is doped with gallium.

(c) In a drawing, show how the electron population changes when the silicon is doped with arsenic.

(d) Compare the electrical conductivity of the doped silicon samples with that of pure silicon. Account for the differences.

21.20 Sketch the electron populations of the bands of MO energy levels for elemental carbon (diamond), silicon, germanium, gray tin, and white tin. (Band gap data are given in Table 21.3.) Your sketches should show how the populations of the different bands vary with a change in the group 4A element.

21.21 Pictures (1) and (2) are energy level diagrams for two different LEDs. One LED emits red light, and the other emits blue light. Which one emits red, and which blue? Explain.

SECTION PROBLEMS

Sources of the Metallic Elements (Section 21.1)

21.22 List three metals that are found in nature as oxide ores.

21.23 List three metals that are found in nature in uncombined form.

21.24 Locate the following metals in the periodic table, and predict whether they are likely to be found in nature as oxides, sulfides, or in uncombined form:

(a) Copper   (b) Zirconium

(c) Palladium   (d) Bismuth

21.25 Locate the following metals in the periodic table, and predict whether they are likely to be found in nature as oxides, sulfides, or in uncombined form:

(a) Vanadium   (b) Silver

(c) Rhodium   (d) Hafnium

21.26 Explain why early transition metals occur in nature as oxides but late transition metals occur as sulfides.

21.27 Explain why iron occurs in nature as an oxide but calcium occurs as a carbonate.

21.28 Name minerals that contain the following compounds:
(a) Fe_2O_3 (b) PbS (c) TiO_2 (d) $CuFeS_2$

21.29 Write chemical formulas for the following minerals:
(a) Cinnabar (b) Bauxite
(c) Sphalerite (d) Chromite

Metallurgy (Section 21.2)

21.30 Describe the flotation process for concentrating a metal sulfide ore, and explain why this process would not work well for concentrating a metal oxide ore.

21.31 Gallium is a minor constituent in bauxite, $Al_2O_3 \cdot x\, H_2O$, and like aluminum, forms an amphoteric oxide, Ga_2O_3. Explain how the Bayer process makes it possible to separate Ga_2O_3 from Fe_2O_3, which is also present in bauxite. Write a balanced net ionic equation for the reaction.

21.32 Zinc, cadmium, and mercury are found in nature as sulfide ores. Values of $E°$ for the reduction half-reaction $M^{2+}(aq) + 2\,e^- \rightarrow M(s)$ are -0.76 V for M = Zn, -0.40 V for M = Cd, and $+0.85$ V for M = Hg. Explain why roasting sphalerite (ZnS) gives ZnO but roasting cinnabar (HgS) gives elemental mercury. What product would you expect from roasting CdS?

21.33 Zinc metal is produced by reducing ZnO with coke, and magnesium metal is produced by the electrolysis of molten $MgCl_2$. Look at the standard reduction potentials in Appendix D, and explain why magnesium can't be prepared by the method used for zinc.

21.34 Complete and balance each of the following equations:
(a) $V_2O_5(s) + Ca(s) \longrightarrow$ (b) $PbS(s) + O_2(g) \longrightarrow$
(c) $MoO_3(s) + H_2(g) \longrightarrow$ (d) $MnO_2(s) + Al(s) \longrightarrow$
(e) $MgCl_2(l) \xrightarrow{\text{Electrolysis}}$

21.35 Complete and balance each of the following equations:
(a) $Fe_2O_3(s) + H_2(g) \longrightarrow$ (b) $Cr_2O_3(s) + Al(s) \longrightarrow$
(c) $Ag_2S(s) + O_2(g) \longrightarrow$ (d) $TiCl_4(g) + Mg(l) \longrightarrow$
(e) $LiCl(l) \xrightarrow{\text{Electrolysis}}$

21.36 Use the data in Appendix B to calculate $\Delta H°$ and $\Delta G°$ for the roasting of sphalerite, ZnS:
$$2\,ZnS(s) + 3\,O_2(g) \longrightarrow 2\,ZnO(s) + 2\,SO_2(g)$$
Explain why $\Delta H°$ and $\Delta G°$ have different values, and account for the sign of $(\Delta H° - \Delta G°)$.

21.37 Use the thermodynamic data in Appendix B to calculate $\Delta H°$ and $\Delta G°$ for the roasting of cinnabar, HgS:
$$HgS(s) + O_2(g) \longrightarrow Hg(l) + SO_2(g)$$
Explain why $\Delta H°$ and $\Delta G°$ have different values, and account for the sign of $(\Delta H° - \Delta G°)$.

21.38 Ferrochrome, an iron–chromium alloy used to make stainless steel, is produced by reducing chromite ($FeCr_2O_4$) with coke:
$$FeCr_2O_4(s) + 4\,C(s) \longrightarrow \underbrace{Fe(s) + 2\,Cr(s)}_{\text{Ferrochrome}} + 4\,CO(g)$$
(a) How many kilograms of chromium can be obtained by the reaction of 236 kg of chromite with an excess of coke?
(b) How many liters of carbon monoxide at 25 °C and 740 mm Hg are obtained as a byproduct?

21.39 In one step of the industrial process for producing copper from chalcopyrite ($CuFeS_2$), molten copper(I) sulfide is reduced with a blast of hot air:
$$Cu_2S(l) + O_2(g) \longrightarrow 2\,Cu(l) + SO_2(g)$$
(a) How many kilograms of Cu_2S must be reduced to account for the world's annual copper production of about 1.4×10^{10} kg?
(b) How many liters of SO_2 at STP are produced as a byproduct?
(c) If all the SO_2 escaped into the atmosphere and were converted to sulfuric acid in acid rain, how many kilograms of H_2SO_4 would there be in the rain?

21.40 Nickel, used to make stainless steel, can be purified by electrorefining. The electrolysis cell has an impure nickel anode, a pure nickel cathode, and an aqueous solution of nickel sulfate as the electrolyte. How many kilograms of nickel can be refined in 8.00 h if the current passed through the cell is held constant at 52.5 A?

21.41 Pure copper for use in electrical wiring is obtained by electrorefining. How many hours are required to transfer 7.50 kg of copper from an impure copper anode to a pure copper cathode if the current passed through the electrolysis cell is held constant at 40.0 A?

Iron and Steel (Section 21.3)

21.42 Write a balanced equation for the overall reaction that occurs in a blast furnace when iron ore is reduced to iron metal. Identify the oxidizing agent and the reducing agent.

21.43 What is the role of coke in the commercial process for producing iron? Write balanced equations for the relevant chemical reactions.

21.44 What is slag, and what is its role in the commercial process for producing iron?

21.45 Why is limestone added to the blast furnace in the commercial process for producing iron? Write balanced equations for the relevant chemical reactions.

21.46 Briefly describe the basic oxygen process. Write balanced equations for the relevant reactions.

21.47 Why does slag form in the basic oxygen process? Write balanced equations for the relevant reactions.

21.48 When iron ore is reduced in a blast furnace, some of the SiO_2 impurity is also reduced by reaction with carbon to give elemental silicon and carbon monoxide. The silicon is subsequently reoxidized in the basic oxygen process, and the resulting SiO_2 reacts with CaO, yielding slag, which is then separated from the molten steel. Write balanced equations for the three reactions involving SiO_2.

21.49 In a blast furnace, some of the $CaSO_4$ impurity in iron ore is reduced by carbon, yielding elemental sulfur and carbon monoxide. The sulfur is subsequently oxidized in the basic oxygen process, and the product reacts with CaO to give a molten slag. Write balanced equations for the reactions.

21.50 Could tungsten be produced in a blast furnace by the reduction of WO_3? Explain.

21.51 Could aluminum be produced in a blast furnace by the reduction of Al_2O_3? Explain.

Bonding In Metals (Section 21.4)

21.52 Potassium metal crystallizes in a body-centered cubic structure. Draw one unit cell, and try to draw an electron-dot structure for bonding of the central K atom to its nearest-neighbor K atoms. What is the problem?

21.53 Describe the electron-sea model of the bonding in cesium metal. Cesium has a body-centered cubic structure.

21.54 How does the electron-sea model account for the malleability and ductility of metals?

21.55 How does the electron-sea model account for the electrical and thermal conductivity of metals?

21.56 Cesium metal is very soft, and tungsten metal is very hard. Explain the difference using the electron-sea model.

21.57 Sodium melts at 98 °C, and magnesium melts at 650 °C. Account for the higher melting point of magnesium using the electron-sea model.

21.58 Why is the molecular orbital theory for metals called band theory?

21.59 Draw an MO energy-level diagram that shows the population of the 4s band for potassium metal.

21.60 How does band theory account for the electrical conductivity of metals?

21.61 Materials with partially filled bands are metallic conductors, and materials with only completely filled bands are electrical insulators. Explain why the population of the bands affects the conductivity.

21.62 Draw an MO energy-level diagram for beryllium metal, and show the population of the MOs for the following two cases:

(a) The 2s and 2p bands are well separated in energy.

(b) The 2s and 2p bands overlap in energy.

Which diagram agrees with the fact that beryllium has a high electrical conductivity? Explain.

21.63 Draw an MO energy-level diagram for calcium metal, and show the population of the MOs for the following two cases:

(a) The 4s and 3d bands are well separated in energy.

(b) The 4s and 3d bands overlap in energy.

Which diagram agrees with the fact that calcium has a high electrical conductivity? Explain.

21.64 The melting points for the second-series transition elements increase from 1522 °C for yttrium to 2623 °C for molybdenum and then decrease again to 321 °C for cadmium. Account for the trend using band theory.

21.65 Copper has a Mohs hardness value of 3, and iron has a Mohs hardness value of 5. Use band theory to explain why copper is softer than iron.

Semiconductors and Semiconductor Applications (Sections 21.5–21.6)

21.66 Define a semiconductor, and give three examples.

21.67 Tell what is meant by each of the following terms:

(a) Valence band   (b) Conduction band

(c) Band gap   (d) Doping

21.68 Draw the bands of MO energy levels and the electron population for:

(a) A semiconductor   (b) An electrical insulator

Explain why a semiconductor has the higher electrical conductivity.

21.69 Draw the bands of MO energy levels and the electron population for:

(a) A semiconductor   (b) A metallic conductor

Explain why a semiconductor has the lower electrical conductivity.

21.70 How does the electrical conductivity of a semiconductor change as the size of the band gap increases? Explain.

21.71 How does the electrical conductivity of a semiconductor change as the temperature increases? Explain.

21.72 Explain what an *n*-type semiconductor is, and give an example. Draw an MO energy-level diagram, and show the population of the valence band and the conduction band for an *n*-type semiconductor.

21.73 Explain what a *p*-type semiconductor is, and give an example. Draw an MO energy-level diagram, and show the population of the valence band and the conduction band for a *p*-type semiconductor.

21.74 Explain why germanium doped with phosphorus has a higher electrical conductivity than pure germanium.

21.75 Explain why silicon doped with gallium has a higher electrical conductivity than pure silicon.

21.76 Classify the following semiconductors as *n*-type or *p*-type:

(a) Si doped with In   (b) Ge doped with Sb

(c) Gray Sn doped with As

21.77 Classify the following semiconductors as *n*-type or *p*-type:

(a) Ge doped with As   (b) Ge doped with B

(c) Si doped with Sb

21.78 The so-called 2–6 semiconductors are 1:1 compounds of group 2A and 6A elements. Write a balanced equation for the synthesis of the 2–6 semiconductor CdSe by chemical vapor deposition from the molecular precursors $Cd(CH_3)_2(g)$ and $H_2Se(g)$.

21.79 Write a balanced equation for the synthesis of the 2–6 semiconductor ZnTe by chemical vapor deposition from dimethylzinc, $Zn(CH_3)_2$, and diethyltellurium, $Te(CH_2CH_3)_2$, assuming that the other product is gaseous propane $(CH_3CH_2CH_3)$.

21.80 Arrange the following materials in order of increasing electrical conductivity:

(a) Cu   (b) Al_2O_3 (c) Fe

(d) Pure Ge   (e) Ge doped with In

21.81 Arrange the following materials in order of increasing electrical conductivity:

(a) Pure gray Sn   (b) Gray Sn doped with Sb

(c) NaCl   (d) Ag   (e) Pure Si

21.82 Explain how a diode converts alternating current to direct current.

21.83 An LED produces light only when the *n*- and *p*-type semiconductors are connected to the proper terminals of a battery. Explain why no light is produced if you reverse the battery connections.

21.84 What are the main differences between an LED and a photovoltaic cell?

21.85 In what ways are LEDs and diode lasers similar, and in what ways are they different?

21.86 What is the wavelength and the color of the light emitted by a GaP_xAs_{1-x} LED with a band gap of 193 kJ/mol? (See Figure 20.26, page 833, for the relationship between wavelength and color.)

21.87 What band gap is needed for an LED to produce blue light with a wavelength of 470 nm?

Superconductors (Section 21.7)

21.88 What are the two most striking properties of a superconductor?

21.89 $YBa_2Cu_3O_7$ is a superconductor below its T_c of 90 K and a metallic conductor above 90 K. Make a rough plot of electrical resistance versus temperature for $YBa_2Cu_3O_7$.

21.90 What is the coordination environment of the K^+ ions in the fullerene-based superconductor K_3C_{60}.

21.91 Look at Figure 21.17, and identify the coordination numbers of the Cu, Y, and Ba atoms.

Ceramics and Composites (Sections 21.8–21.9)

21.92 What is a ceramic, and what properties distinguish a ceramic from a metal?

21.93 Contrast the bonding in ceramics with the bonding in metals.

21.94 Why are ceramics more wear-resistant than metals?

21.95 Why are oxide ceramics more corrosion-resistant than metals?

21.96 Silicon nitride (Si_3N_4), a high-temperature ceramic useful for making engine components, is a covalent network solid in which each Si atom is bonded to four N atoms and each N atom is bonded to three Si atoms. Explain why silicon nitride is more brittle than a metal like copper.

21.97 Magnesia (MgO), used as an insulator for electrical heating devices, has a face-centered cubic structure like that of NaCl. Draw one unit cell of the structure of MgO, and explain why MgO is more brittle than magnesium metal.

21.98 What is ceramic processing?

21.99 Describe what happens when a ceramic powder is sintered.

21.100 Zirconia (ZrO_2), an unusually tough oxide ceramic, has been used to make very sharp table knives. Write a balanced equation for the hydrolysis of zirconium isopropoxide in the sol–gel method for making zirconia powders. The isopropoxide ligand is the anion of isopropyl alcohol, $HOCH(CH_3)_2$.

21.101 Zinc oxide is a semiconducting ceramic used to make *varistors* (variable resistors). Write a balanced equation for the hydrolysis of zinc ethoxide in the sol–gel method for making ZnO powders.

21.102 Describe the reactions that occur when an $Si(OH)_4$ sol becomes a gel. What is the formula of the ceramic obtained when the gel is dried and sintered?

21.103 Describe the reactions that occur when a $Y(OH)_3$ sol becomes a gel. What is the chemical formula of the ceramic obtained when the gel is dried and sintered?

21.104 Some ceramics can be synthesized easily from molecular or ionic precursors. Titanium diboride (TiB_2) powder forms from the decomposition of titanium(III) borohydride dissolved in an organic solvent at 140 °C. Write a balanced equation for this reaction if the other products are diborane (B_2H_6) and molecular hydrogen. (The borohydride ion is BH_4^-.)

21.105 GeS_2 is a nonoxide ceramic accessible by the sol–gel method. Write a balanced equation for the preparation of GeS_2 from tetraethoxygermane, $Ge(OCH_2CH_3)_4$, and H_2S in an organic solvent.

21.106 Silicon nitride powder can be made by the reaction of silicon tetrachloride vapor with gaseous ammonia. The byproduct is gaseous hydrogen chloride. Write a balanced equation for the reaction.

21.107 Boron, which is used to make composites, is deposited on a tungsten wire when the wire is heated electrically in the presence of boron trichloride vapor and gaseous hydrogen. Write a balanced equation for the reaction.

21.108 Explain why graphite/epoxy composites are good materials for making tennis rackets and golf clubs.

21.109 Explain why silicon carbide-reinforced alumina is stronger and tougher than pure alumina.

CHAPTER PROBLEMS

21.110 Estimate the temperature at which the Mond reaction for the formation of $Ni(CO)_4$ becomes nonspontaneous. (See Section 21.2 for thermodynamic data.)

21.111 What is the standard free-energy change in kJ per mole of metal for decomposition of M_2O_3 (M = Fe or Al) to the metal and O_2 gas? Can these metals be obtained by decomposition of their oxides under standard-state conditions? (See Appendix B for thermodynamic data.)

21.112 To separate europium (Eu) from a mixture of lanthanides (symbolized by Ln) an aqueous solution of $Ln(NO_3)_3$ is treated with zinc amalgam, an alloy of zinc and mercury. Of all the Ln^{3+} ions, only Eu^{3+} is reduced by Zn (to Eu^{2+}). The Eu^{2+} ions can then be precipitated by addition of sulfate ions. Write balanced net ionic equations for the reduction and precipitation reactions.

21.113 Wide band gap semiconductors have a band gap between 2 and 7 electron volts (eV), where 1 eV = 96.485 kJ/mol. The wide-band gap semiconductor GaN, used to construct the laser in Blu-ray DVD players, has a band gap of 3.44 eV. The material in the laser, $Ga_xIn_{1-x}N$, has some indium substituted for gallium.
(a) What wavelength of light (in nm) would GaN emit, based on its band gap?

(b) If the light from the device is blue, does partial substitution of indium for gallium increase or decrease the band gap of $Ga_xIn_{1-x}N$ compared to GaN?

21.114 Imagine a planet with an atmosphere that contains O_2 and SO_2 but no CO_2. Give the chemical composition of the minerals you would expect to find for the alkaline earth metals on such a planet.

21.115 Superconductors with values of T_c above 77 K are of special interest. What's so special about 77 K?

21.116 What properties of metals are better explained by band theory than by the electron-sea model?

21.117 Tungsten is hard and has a very high melting point (3422 °C), and gold is soft and has a relatively low melting point (1064 °C). Are these facts in better agreement with the electron-sea model or the MO model (band theory)? Explain.

21.118 Explain why the enthalpy of vaporization of vanadium (460 kJ/mol) is much larger than that of zinc (114 kJ/mol).

21.119 Classify each of the following materials as a metallic conductor, an *n* type semiconductor, a *p*-type semiconductor, or an electrical insulator:
(a) MgO   (b) Si doped with Sb
(c) White tin   (d) Ge doped with Ga
(e) Stainless steel

21.120 Gallium arsenide, a material used to manufacture laser printers and compact disc players, has a band gap of 130 kJ/mol. Is GaAs a metallic conductor, a semiconductor, or an electrical insulator? With what group 4A element is GaAs isoelectronic? (Isoelectronic substances have the same number of electrons.)

21.121 A 3.4×10^3 kg batch of cast iron contains 0.45% by mass of phosphorus as an impurity. In the conversion of cast iron to steel by the basic oxygen process, the phosphorus is oxidized to P_4O_{10}, which then reacts with CaO and is removed as slag.

(a) Write balanced equations for the oxidation of P_4 and for the formation of slag.

(b) How many kilograms of CaO are required to react with all the P_4O_{10}?

21.122 The $YBa_2Cu_3O_7$ superconductor can be synthesized by the sol–gel method from a stoichiometric mixture of metal ethoxides followed by heating in oxygen. How many grams of $Y(OCH_2CH_3)_3$ and how many grams of $Ba(OCH_2CH_3)_2$ are required to react with 75.4 g of $Cu(OCH_2CH_3)_2$ and an excess of water? Assuming a 100% yield, how many grams of $YBa_2Cu_3O_7$ are obtained?

21.123 Does the conductivity increase, decrease, or remain the same when

(a) n-type InP is doped with Cd? Explain.

(b) p-type InP is doped with Se? Explain.

21.124 Mullite, $3\,Al_2O_3 \cdot 2\,SiO_2$, a high-temperature ceramic being considered for use in engines, can be made by the sol–gel method.

(a) Write a balanced equation for formation of the sol by hydrolysis of a stoichiometric mixture of aluminum ethoxide and tetraethoxysilane, $Si(OCH_2CH_3)_4$.

(b) Describe the reactions that convert the sol to a gel.

(c) What additional steps are required to convert the gel to the ceramic product?

21.125 The glass in photochromic sunglasses is called a nanocomposite because it contains tiny silver halide particles with a diameter of less than 10 nm. This glass darkens and becomes less transparent outdoors in sunlight but returns to its original transparency indoors, where there is less light. How might these reversible changes occur?

21.126 Small molecules with C=C double bonds, called monomers, can join with one another to form long chain molecules called polymers. Thus, acrylonitrile, $H_2C=CHCN$, polymerizes under appropriate conditions to give polyacrylonitrile, a common starting material for producing the carbon fibers used in composites.

Repeating unit

Polyacrylonitrile

(a) Write electron-dot structures for acrylonitrile and polyacrylonitrile, and show how rearranging the electrons can lead to formation of the polymer.

(b) Use the bond dissociation energies in Table 7.1 to calculate ΔH per $H_2C=CHCN$ unit for the conversion of acrylonitrile to polyacrylonitrile. Is the reaction endothermic or exothermic?

21.127 Zinc selenide (ZnSe) doped with Ga has some Ga atoms in place of Zn atoms and is an n-type semiconductor. Draw an MO energy-level diagram for doped ZnSe, show the population of the bands, and explain why Ga substitution gives an n-type semiconductor.

21.128 Consider a hypothetical material consisting of an infinite one-dimensional array of hydride ions (H^-).

(a) Show how a band of MOs could be formed from individual atomic orbitals, and explain why this material should be an electrical insulator.

(b) If some of the hydride ions in the above material were replaced with neutral hydrogen atoms, the resulting doped material should be a better electrical conductor. Draw an MO energy-level diagram for the doped material, show the population of the band, and explain why the doped material can conduct electricity.

(c) Would you describe the doped material as n-type or p-type? Explain.

21.129 The small size of cellular telephones results from the use of sophisticated gallium arsenide (GaAs) semiconductors instead of ordinary silicon-based semiconductors.

(a) Draw an MO energy-level diagram for GaAs, and show the population of the bands.

(b) Explain why the conductivity of GaAs increases as the temperature increases.

(c) Does the conductivity of GaAs increase or decrease when pure GaAs is doped with (i) Zn or (ii) S? Explain.

MULTICONCEPT PROBLEMS

21.130 An 8.894 g block of aluminum was pressed into a thin square of foil with 36.5 cm edge lengths.

(a) If the density of Al is 2.699 g/cm³, how thick is the foil in cm?

(b) How many unit cells thick is the foil? Aluminum crystallizes in a face-centered cubic structure and has an atomic radius of 143 pm.

21.131 Europium(II) oxide is a semiconductor with a band gap of 108 kJ/mol. Below 69 K, it is also ferromagnetic, meaning all the unpaired electrons on europium are aligned in the same direction.

(a) How many f electrons are present on each europium ion in EuO? (In lanthanide ions the 4f orbitals are lower in energy than the 6s orbitals.)

(b) All the f electrons are unpaired in EuO. Predict the spin-only magnetic moment of EuO, using the formula in Problem 20.132.

21.132 A 0.3249 g sample of stainless steel was analyzed for iron by dissolving the sample in sulfuric acid and titrating the Fe^{2+} in the resulting solution with 0.018 54 M $K_2Cr_2O_7$. If 38.89 mL of the $K_2Cr_2O_7$ solution was required to reach the equivalence point, what is the mass percentage of iron in the steel?

21.133 Red light with a wavelength of 660 nm from a 3.0 mW diode laser shines on a solar cell.

(a) How many photons per second are emitted by the laser? (1 W = 1 J/s)

(b) How much current (in amperes) flows in the circuit of the solar cell if all the photons are absorbed by the cell and each photon produces one electron?

21.134 The mineral wustite is a nonstoichiometric iron oxide with the empirical formula Fe_xO, where x is a number slightly less than 1. Wustite can be regarded as an FeO in which some of the Fe sites are vacant. It has a density of $5.75\ g/cm^3$, a cubic unit cell with an edge length of 431 pm, and a face-centered cubic arrangement of oxygen atoms.

(a) What is the value of x in the formula Fe_xO?

(b) Based on the formula in part (a), what is the average oxidation state of Fe?

(c) Each Fe atom in wustite is in either the +2 or the +3 oxidation state. What percent of the Fe atoms are in the +3 oxidation state?

(d) Using X rays with a wavelength of 70.93 pm, at what angle would third-order diffraction be observed from the planes of atoms that coincide with the faces of the unit cells? Third-order diffraction means that the value of n in the Bragg equation (Section 10.7) is equal to 3.

(e) Wustite is a semiconducting iron(II) oxide in which some of the Fe^{2+} has been replaced by Fe^{3+}. Should it be described as an n-type or a p-type semiconductor? Explain.

21.135 At high temperatures, coke reduces silica impurities in iron ore to elemental silicon:

$$SiO_2(s) + 2\,C(s) \longrightarrow Si(s) + 2\,CO(g)$$

(a) Use the data in Appendix B to calculate the values of $\Delta H°$, $\Delta S°$, and $\Delta G°$ for this reaction at 25 °C.

(b) Is the reaction endothermic or exothermic?

(c) Account for the sign of the entropy change.

(d) Is the reaction spontaneous at 25 °C and 1 atm pressure of CO?

(e) Assuming that $\Delta H°$ and $\Delta S°$ do not depend on temperature, estimate the temperature at which the reaction becomes spontaneous at 1 atm pressure of CO.

21.136 The Mond process for purifying nickel involves the reaction of impure nickel with carbon monoxide at about 150 °C to give nickel tetracarbonyl. The nickel tetracarbonyl then decomposes to pure nickel at about 230 °C:

$$Ni(s) + 4\,CO(g) \rightleftharpoons Ni(CO)_4(g)$$
$$\Delta H° = -160.8\ kJ;\ \Delta S° = -410\ J/K$$

The values of $\Delta H°$ and $\Delta S°$ apply at 25 °C, but they are relatively independent of temperature and can be used at 150 °C and 230 °C.

(a) Calculate $\Delta G°$ and the equilibrium constant K_p at 150 °C.

(b) Calculate $\Delta G°$ and the equilibrium constant K_p at 230 °C.

(c) Why does the reaction have a large negative value for $\Delta S°$? Show that the change in $\Delta G°$ with increasing temperature is consistent with a negative value of $\Delta S°$.

(d) Show that the change in K_p with increasing temperature is consistent with a negative value of $\Delta H°$.

21.137 Figure 21.5 indicates that carbon reacts with carbon dioxide to form carbon monoxide at high temperatures:

$$C(s) + CO_2(g) \longrightarrow 2\,CO(g)$$

(a) Use the thermodynamic data in Appendix B to calculate the total pressure and the molar concentrations of CO and CO_2 at 500 °C in a 50.00 L vessel that initially contains 100.0 g of CO_2 and an excess of solid carbon. Assume that the reaction mixture has reached equilibrium and that $\Delta H°$ and $\Delta S°$ are independent of temperature.

(b) Calculate the total pressure and the equilibrium concentrations at 1000 °C.

(c) Use $\Delta H°$ and $\Delta S°$ to explain why the concentrations increase or decrease on raising the temperature.

21.138 Zinc chromite ($ZnCr_2O_4$), once used to make magnetic tape for cassette recorders, can be prepared by the thermal decomposition of $(NH_4)_2Zn(CrO_4)_2$. The other reaction products are N_2 and water vapor.

(a) Write a balanced equation for the reaction.

(b) How many grams of $ZnCr_2O_4$ can be prepared from 10.36 g of $(NH_4)_2Zn(CrO_4)_2$?

(c) How many liters of gaseous byproducts are obtained at 292 °C and 745 mm pressure?

(d) $ZnCr_2O_4$ has the cubic spinel structure consisting of a cubic closest-packed (face-centered cubic) array of O^{2-} ions with Zn^{2+} ions in tetrahedral holes surrounded by four O^{2-} ions and Cr^{3+} ions in octahedral holes surrounded by six O^{2-} ions. The tetrahedral and octahedral holes are like those in K_3C_{60} (see Figure 21.20). What fraction of each of the two types of holes is occupied?

(e) Draw a crystal field d-orbital energy-level diagram for the Cr^{3+} ion in $ZnCr_2O_4$. Would you expect this compound to be colored? Explain. Does the Zn^{2+} ion contribute to the color? Explain.

21.139 The alkali metal fulleride superconductors M_3C_{60} have a cubic closest-packed (face-centered cubic) arrangement of nearly spherical C_{60}^{3-} anions with M^+ cations in the holes between the larger C_{60}^{3-} ions. The holes are of two types: octahedral holes, which are surrounded octahedrally by six C_{60}^{3-} ions, and tetrahedral holes, which are surrounded tetrahedrally by four C_{60}^{3-} ions.

(a) Sketch the three-dimensional structure of one unit cell.

(b) How many C_{60}^{3-} ions, octahedral holes, and tetrahedral holes are present per unit cell?

(c) Specify fractional coordinates for all the octahedral and tetrahedral holes. (Fractional coordinates are fractions of the unit cell edge lengths. For example, a hole at the center of the cell has fractional coordinates $\frac{1}{2}, \frac{1}{2}, \frac{1}{2}$.)

(d) The radius of a C_{60}^{3-} ion is about 500 pm. Assuming that the C_{60}^{3-} ions are in contact along the face diagonals of the unit cell, calculate the radii of the octahedral and tetrahedral holes.

(e) The ionic radii of Na^+, K^+, and Rb^+ are 102, 138, and 152 pm, respectively. Which of these ions will fit into the octahedral and tetrahedral holes? Which ions will fit only if the framework of C_{60}^{3-} ions expands?

21.140 A single-walled carbon nanotube can be regarded as a single sheet of graphite rolled into a cylinder (Figure 10.27b, page 379). Calculate the number of C atoms in a single-walled nanotube having a length of 1.0 mm and a diameter of 1.08 nm. The C—C bond length in graphite is 141.5 pm.

CHAPTER 22

Nuclear Chemistry

After 20 years and 9 billion dollars, work on the proposed national nuclear waste repository at Yucca Mountain, Nevada, was stopped in early 2010.

CONTENTS

We've seen repeatedly in previous chapters that only the bonds between atoms change when a chemical reaction takes place, while the identities of the atoms themselves remain unchanged. Yet we also saw in Sections 2.7–2.9 that atoms *can* change their identities when *nuclear* reactions occur. You may recall that five kinds of nuclear processes commonly take place, as summarized in Table 22.1.

TABLE 22.1   A Summary of Nuclear Decay Processes

Process	Symbol	Change in Atomic Number	Change in Mass Number	Change in Neutron Number
Alpha emission	^4_2He or α	−2	−4	−2
Beta emission	$^0_{-1}\text{e}$ or β^-	+1	0	−1
Gamma emission	$^0_0\gamma$ or γ	0	0	0
Positron emission	^0_1e or β^+	−1	0	+1
Electron capture	E. C.	−1	0	+1

You may also recall from Section 12.6 that radioactive decay is kinetically a **first-order process**, whose rate is proportional to the number of radioactive nuclei N in a sample times the first-order rate constant k. That is, decay rate $= k \times N$. Like all first-order processes, radioactive decay is characterized by a **half-life**, $t_{1/2}$, the time required for the number of radioactive nuclei in a sample to drop to half its initial value. The half-lives of different **radioisotopes** vary enormously. Some, such as uranium-238, decay at a barely perceptible rate over billions of years, while others, such as carbon-21, decay within microseconds.

Let's now look further into the nature of nuclear decay, focusing particularly on the energy changes that occur during nuclear transformations and on the uses and effects of radioactivity.

22.1   ENERGY CHANGES DURING NUCLEAR REACTIONS

We saw in Figure 2.8, repeated in **Figure 22.1** for convenience, that the band of nuclear stability obtained by plotting the number of protons versus the number of neutrons for observable nuclei is slightly curved. Lighter elements have an approximately 1:1 neutron/proton ratio, but heavier elements need a substantially higher ratio of neutrons to protons for stability.

Observations such as those in Figure 22.1 suggest that neutrons function as a kind of nuclear glue to overcome the proton–proton repulsions that would otherwise cause a nucleus to fly apart. The more protons there are in the nucleus, the more glue is needed.

In principle, it should be possible to measure the strength of the forces holding a nucleus together by measuring the amount of energy necessary to tear the nucleus apart into its component protons and neutrons. That is, the amount of energy that must be *added* to tear the nucleus apart is numerically equal to the amount of energy that is *released* when a stable nucleus forms from its constituent particles. The two processes are simply the reverse of one another. With a helium-4 nucleus, for instance, the energy change associated with combining two neutrons and two protons to form ^4_2He is a direct measure of helium-4 nuclear stability.

$$2\,^1_1\text{H} + 2\,^1_0\text{n} \longrightarrow \,^4_2\text{He} \qquad \Delta E = ?$$

Unfortunately, there is a problem with actually carrying out the measurement, because temperatures rivaling those in the interior of the Sun (10^7 K) are necessary for nuclei to form! That is, the **activation energy** (Section 12.12) required to force the elementary particles close enough for reaction is enormous. Nevertheless, the energy

Remember...

A **first-order process** is one whose rate depends on the concentration of only one substance raised to the first power. (Section 12.4)

The **half-life**, $t_{1/2}$ of a nuclear decay is the time required for the number of radioactive nuclei in the sample to drop to one-half its initial value and is related to the rate constant k by the equation $t_{1/2} = 0.693/k$. (Section 12.6)

A **radioisotope** is an isotope that undergoes spontaneous radioactive decay. (Section 2.8)

Remember...

Activation energy is the potential-energy barrier that must be surmounted before reactants can be converted to products. The height of the barrier controls the rate of the reaction.   (Section 12.12)

Figure 22.1
The band of nuclear stability. The band shows the various neutron/proton combinations occurring in nuclei that are either nonradioactive or are radioactive but decay slowly enough to exist for a measurable time.

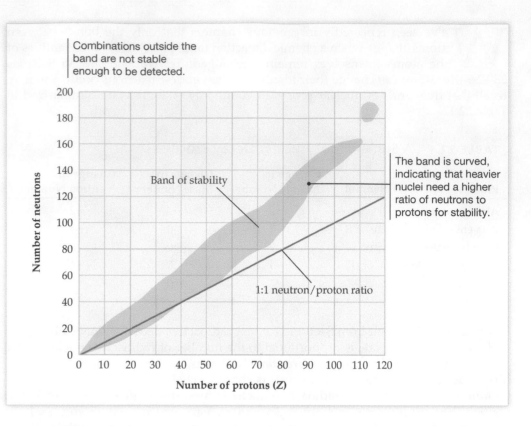

change for the process can be calculated using the now-famous equation $\Delta E = \Delta mc^2$, which was proposed by Albert Einstein in 1905 as part of his special theory of relativity and which relates the energy change ΔE of a nuclear process to a corresponding mass change Δm. (Recall that the symbol c represents the speed of light; its value is $c = 299\ 792\ 458$ m/s.)

Using the helium-4 nucleus for an example calculation, the mass of the two neutrons and two protons that combine to form the nucleus is 4.031 88 amu:

$$
\begin{array}{lll}
\text{Mass of 2 protons} & = (2)(1.008\ 66\ \text{amu}) & = 2.017\ 32\ \text{amu} \\
\underline{\text{Mass of 2 protons}} & \underline{= (2)(1.007\ 28\ \text{amu})} & \underline{= 2.014\ 56\ \text{amu}} \\
\text{Total mass of 2 n + 2 p} & & = 4.031\ 88\ \text{amu}
\end{array}
$$

The mass of the helium-4 *nucleus* can be found by subtracting the mass of two electrons from the experimentally measured mass of a helium-4 *atom* (4.002 60 amu).

$$
\begin{array}{lll}
\text{Mass of helium-4 atom} & & = \quad 4.002\ 60\ \text{amu} \\
\underline{-\text{Mass of 2 electrons} = -(2)(5.486 \times 10^{-4}\ \text{amu})} & & \underline{= -0.001\ 10\ \text{amu}} \\
\text{Mass of helium-4 nucleus} & & = \quad 4.001\ 50\ \text{amu}
\end{array}
$$

Subtracting the mass of the helium nucleus from the combined mass of its constituent particles shows a difference of 0.030 38 amu. That is, 0.030 38 amu (or 0.030 38 g/mol) is lost when two protons and two neutrons combine to form a helium-4 nucleus:

$$
\begin{array}{ll}
\text{Mass of 2 n + 2 p} & = \quad 4.031\ 88\ \text{amu} \\
\underline{-\text{Mass of } ^4\text{He nucleus}} & \underline{= -4.001\ 50\ \text{amu}} \\
\text{Mass difference in amu} & = \quad 0.030\ 38\ \text{amu}
\end{array}
$$

$$\text{Mass difference in grams} = (0.030\ 38\ \text{amu})\left(1.6605 \times 10^{-24}\ \frac{\text{g}}{\text{amu}}\right) = 5.045 \times 10^{-26}\ \text{g}$$

$$\text{Mass difference in g/mol} = \left(5.045 \times 10^{-26}\ \frac{\text{g}}{\text{atom}}\right)\left(6.022 \times 10^{23}\ \frac{\text{atom}}{\text{mol}}\right) = 3.038 \times 10^{-2}\ \frac{\text{g}}{\text{mol}}$$

The loss in mass that occurs when protons and neutrons combine to form a nucleus is called the **mass defect** of the nucleus. This lost mass is converted into energy that is released during the nuclear reaction and is thus a direct measure of the **binding energy** holding the nucleus together. The larger the binding energy, the more stable the nucleus. For a helium-4 nucleus, the binding energy is

$$\Delta E = \Delta mc^2 = (5.045 \times 10^{-26} \, g)\left(10^{-3} \, \frac{kg}{g}\right)\left(3.00 \times 10^8 \, \frac{m}{s}\right)^2$$

$$= 4.54 \times 10^{-12} \left(\frac{kg \cdot m^2}{s^2}\right) = 4.54 \times 10^{-12} \, J$$

The binding energy can be expressed on a kJ/mol basis by converting joules to kilojoules and multiplying by Avogadro's number:

$$\text{Binding energy} = \left(4.54 \times 10^{-12} \, \frac{J}{atom}\right)\left(\frac{1 \, kJ}{1000 \, J}\right)\left(6.022 \times 10^{23} \, \frac{atom}{mol}\right)$$

$$= 2.73 \times 10^9 \, \frac{kJ}{mol}$$

The binding energy of a helium-4 nucleus is 4.54×10^{-12} J, or 2.73×10^9 kJ/mol. In other words, 4.54×10^{-12} J is released when a helium-4 nucleus is formed from 2 protons and 2 neutrons, and 4.54×10^{-12} J must be supplied to disintegrate a helium-4 nucleus into isolated protons and neutrons. This amount of energy is more than *10 million times* the energy change associated with a typical chemical process!

To make comparisons among different nuclei easier, binding energies are usually expressed on a per-**nucleon** basis using *electron volts* (*eV*) as the energy unit, where $1 \, eV = 1.60 \times 10^{-19}$ J and 1 million electron volts (1 MeV) $= 1.60 \times 10^{-13}$ J. Thus, the helium-4 binding energy is 7.09 MeV/nucleon:

$$\text{Helium-4 binding energy} = \left(4.54 \times 10^{-12} \, \frac{J}{nucleus}\right)\left(\frac{1 \, MeV}{1.60 \times 10^{-13} \, J}\right)\left(\frac{1 \, nucleus}{4 \, nucleons}\right)$$

$$= 7.09 \, \text{MeV/nucleon}$$

A plot of binding energy per nucleon for the most stable isotope of each element is shown in **Figure 22.2**. Since a larger binding energy per nucleon corresponds to greater stability, the most stable nuclei are at the top of the curve and the least stable nuclei are at the bottom. Iron-56, with a binding energy of 8.79 MeV/nucleon, is the most stable isotope known. If all the mass in the universe were converted to its most stable form, the universe would become a chunk of iron!

Remember...

A **nucleon** is the general term for a nuclear particle, either proton or neutron. (Section 2.8)

Figure 22.2
The binding energy per nucleon for the most stable isotope of each naturally occurring element.

Remember...

The **law of mass conservation** says that mass is neither created nor destroyed in chemical reactions.   (Section 2.1)

The **law of energy conservation** says that energy can neither be created nor destroyed but only converted from one form to another. (Section 8.1)

The idea that mass and energy are interconvertible is potentially disturbing because it seems to overthrow two of the fundamental principles on which chemistry is based—the **law of mass conservation** and the **law of energy conservation**. In fact, what the mass–energy interconversion means is that neither mass nor energy is conserved independently; rather, it is the *combination* of mass and energy that is conserved. Every time we do a reaction, whether nuclear *or* chemical, mass and energy are interconverted, but the combination of the two is conserved. For the energy change involved in a typical chemical reaction, however, the effect is so small that the mass change can't be detected by even the best analytical balance. Worked Example 22.2 illustrates such a mass–energy calculation for a chemical reaction.

WORKED EXAMPLE 22.1

CALCULATING A MASS DEFECT AND A BINDING ENERGY

Helium-6 is a radioactive isotope with $t_{1/2} = 0.807$ s. Calculate the mass defect for the formation of a ^{6}He nucleus in both grams and g/mol, and calculate the binding energy in both MeV/nucleon and kJ/mol. Is a ^{6}He nucleus more stable or less stable than a ^{4}He nucleus? The mass of a ^{6}He atom is 6.018 89 amu.

STRATEGY

Find the mass defect by subtracting the mass of the ^{6}He nucleus from the mass of its constituent nucleons, and use the Einstein equation to find the ^{6}He binding energy. Then use Avogadro's number (6.022×10^{23} mol^{-1}) to find the per-mole value.

SOLUTION

First, calculate the total mass of the nucleons (4 n + 2 p):

$$
\begin{aligned}
\text{Mass of 4 neutrons} &= (4)(1.008\,66 \text{ amu}) = 4.034\,64 \text{ amu} \\
\text{Mass of 2 protons} &= (2)(1.007\,28 \text{ amu})\ = 2.014\,56 \text{ amu} \\
\hline
\text{Mass of 4 n + 2 p} &\qquad\qquad\qquad\quad = 6.049\,20 \text{ amu}
\end{aligned}
$$

Next, calculate the mass of a ^{6}He nucleus by subtracting the mass of two electrons from the mass of a ^{6}He atom:

$$
\begin{aligned}
\text{Mass of helium-6 atom} &= \ \ 6.018\,89 \text{ amu} \\
-\text{Mass of 2 electrons} = -(2)(5.486 \times 10^{-4} \text{ amu}) &= -0.001\,10 \text{ amu} \\
\hline
\text{Mass of helium-6 nucleus} &= \ \ 6.017\,79 \text{ amu}
\end{aligned}
$$

Then subtract the mass of the ^{6}He nucleus from the mass of the nucleons, and convert amu to grams to find the mass defect:

$$\text{Mass defect in amu } = \text{Mass of nucleons } - \text{ Mass of nucleus}$$
$$= (6.049\,20 \text{ amu}) - (6.017\,79 \text{ amu}) = 0.031\,41 \text{ amu}$$

$$\text{Mass difference in grams} = (0.031\,41 \text{ amu})\left(1.6605 \times 10^{-24} \frac{\text{g}}{\text{amu}}\right)$$
$$= 5.216 \times 10^{-26} \text{ g}$$

$$\text{Mass difference in g/mol} = \left(5.216 \times 10^{-26} \frac{\text{g}}{\text{atom}}\right)\left(6.022 \times 10^{23} \frac{\text{atom}}{\text{mol}}\right)$$
$$= 3.141 \times 10^{-2} \frac{\text{g}}{\text{mol}}$$

Now, use the Einstein equation to convert the mass defect into binding energy:

$$\Delta E = \Delta mc^2 = (5.216 \times 10^{-26} \text{ g})\left(\frac{1 \text{ kg}}{1000 \text{ g}}\right)\left(3.00 \times 10^8 \frac{\text{m}}{\text{s}}\right)^2 = 4.69 \times 10^{-12} \text{ J}$$

$$\text{Binding energy in MeV/nucleon} = \left(4.69 \times 10^{-12} \frac{\text{J}}{\text{nucleus}}\right)\left(\frac{1 \text{ MeV}}{1.60 \times 10^{-13} \text{ J}}\right)\left(\frac{1 \text{ nucleus}}{6 \text{ nucleons}}\right)$$
$$= 4.89 \text{ MeV/nucleon}$$

$$\text{Binding energy in kJ/mol} = \left(4.69 \times 10^{-12} \frac{\text{J}}{\text{atom}}\right)\left(\frac{1\,\text{kJ}}{1000\,\text{J}}\right)\left(6.022 \times 10^{23} \frac{\text{atom}}{\text{mol}}\right)$$

$$= 2.82 \times 10^9 \frac{\text{kJ}}{\text{mol}}$$

The binding energy of a radioactive ^{6}He nucleus is 4.89 MeV/nucleon, making ^{6}He less stable than ^{4}He, whose binding energy is 7.09 MeV/nucleon.

WORKED EXAMPLE 22.2

CALCULATING THE MASS DEFECT IN A CHEMICAL REACTION

What is the mass change in g/mol when hydrogen atoms (H) combine to form hydrogen molecules (H_2)?

$$2\,\text{H} \longrightarrow H_2 \qquad \Delta E = -436\;\text{kJ/mol}$$

STRATEGY

The problem asks us to calculate a mass defect Δm when the energy change ΔE is known. To do this, we have to rearrange the Einstein equation to solve for mass, remembering that $1\,\text{J} = 1\,\text{kg} \cdot \text{m}^2/\text{s}^2$.

SOLUTION

$$\Delta m = \frac{\Delta E}{c^2} = \frac{\left(-436\,\dfrac{\text{kJ}}{\text{mol}}\right)\left(\dfrac{1\,\text{kg}\cdot\text{m}^2/\text{s}^2}{\text{J}}\right)\left(\dfrac{1000\,\text{J}}{1\,\text{kJ}}\right)\left(\dfrac{1000\,\text{g}}{1\,\text{kg}}\right)}{\left(3.00 \times 10^8\,\dfrac{\text{m}}{\text{s}}\right)^2} = -4.84 \times 10^{-9}\,\frac{\text{g}}{\text{mol}}$$

The loss in mass accompanying formation of H_2 molecules from their constituent H atoms is 4.84×10^{-9} g/mol, much too small an amount to be detectable by any balance and far smaller than the mass defect of a stable nucleus, which we calculated to be approximately 10^{-2} g/mol.

▶ **PROBLEM 22.1** Calculate the mass defect for the formation of an oxygen-16 nucleus in both grams and g/mol, and calculate the binding energy in both MeV/nucleon and kJ/mol. The mass of an ^{16}O atom is 15.994 91 amu.

▶ **PROBLEM 22.2** What is the mass change in g/mol for the reaction of sodium metal with chlorine gas (Cl_2) to give sodium chloride?

$$2\,\text{Na}(s) + Cl_2(g) \longrightarrow 2\,\text{NaCl}(s) \quad \Delta E - -820\;\text{kJ}$$

22.2 NUCLEAR FISSION AND FUSION

A careful look at the plot of atomic number versus binding energy per nucleon in Figure 22.2 leads to some interesting and important conclusions. The fact that binding energy per nucleon begins at a relatively low value for $^2_1$H, reaches a maximum for $^{56}_{26}$Fe, and then gradually tails off implies that both lighter and heavier nuclei are less stable than midweight nuclei near iron-56. Very heavy nuclei can therefore gain stability and release energy if they fragment to yield midweight nuclei, while very light nuclei can gain stability and release energy if they fuse together. The two resultant processes—**fission** for the fragmenting of heavy nuclei and **fusion** for the joining together of light nuclei—have changed the world since their discovery in the late 1930s and early 1940s.

Nuclear Fission

Certain nuclei—uranium-233, uranium-235, and plutonium-239, for example—do more than undergo simple radioactive decay; they break into fragments when struck by neutrons. As illustrated in **Figure 22.3**, an incoming neutron causes the nucleus to split into two smaller pieces of roughly similar size.

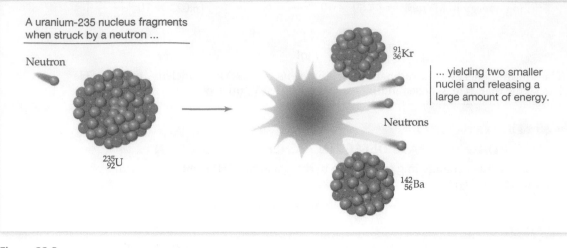

Figure 22.3
A representation of nuclear fission.

The fission of a given nucleus does not occur in exactly the same way each time, and nearly 800 different fission products have been identified from uranium-235. One of the more frequently occurring pathways generates barium-142 and krypton-91, along with two additional neutrons plus the one neutron that initiated the fission:

$$\ce{^1_0n + ^{235}_{92}U -> ^{142}_{56}Ba + ^{91}_{36}Kr + 3 ^1_0n}$$

The three neutrons released by fission of a ^{235}U nucleus can induce up to three more fissions yielding as many as nine neutrons, which can induce up to nine more fissions yielding 27 neutrons, and so on indefinitely. The result is a **chain reaction** that continues to occur even if the external supply of bombarding neutrons is cut off. If the sample size is small, many of the neutrons escape before initiating additional fission events, and the chain reaction soon stops. If there is a sufficient amount of ^{235}U, though—an amount called the **critical mass**—enough neutrons remain for the chain reaction to become self-sustaining. Under high-pressure conditions that confine the ^{235}U to a small volume, the chain reaction may even occur so rapidly that a nuclear explosion results. For ^{235}U, the critical mass is about 56 kg, although the amount can be reduced to 15 kg by placing a coating of ^{238}U around the ^{235}U to reflect back some of the escaping neutrons.

The amount of energy released during nuclear fission can be calculated as in Worked Example 22.3 by finding the accompanying mass change and then using the Einstein mass–energy relationship discussed in the previous section. (Note that when calculating the mass change for a nuclear reaction, it's simplest to use the masses of the *atoms* corresponding to the relevant nuclei, rather than the masses of the nuclei themselves, because the number of electrons is the same in both reactants and products and thus cancels from the calculation.)

▲ An enormous amount of energy is released in the explosion that accompanies an uncontrolled nuclear chain reaction.

WORKED EXAMPLE 22.3

CALCULATING THE ENERGY RELEASED IN A NUCLEAR REACTION

How much energy in both joules and kJ/mol is released by the fission of uranium-235 to form barium-142 and krypton-91? The atomic masses are ^{235}U (235.0439 amu), ^{142}Ba (141.9164 amu), ^{91}Kr (90.9234 amu), and ^1_0n (1.008 66 amu).

$$\ce{^1_0n + ^{235}_{92}U -> ^{142}_{56}Ba + ^{91}_{36}Kr + 3 ^1_0n}$$

STRATEGY

Calculate the mass change by subtracting the masses of the products from the mass of the ^{235}U reactant, and then use the Einstein equation to convert mass to energy.

SOLUTION

Mass of ^{235}U	$=$	235.0439 amu
$-$Mass of ^{142}Ba	$=$	-141.9164 amu
$-$Mass of ^{91}Kr	$=$	-90.9234 amu
$-$Mass of $2\,{}_{0}^{1}n = -(2)(1.008\,66\,\text{amu}) =$		-2.0173 amu
Mass change:	$=$	0.1868 amu

$$\text{Mass difference in grams} = (0.1868\ \text{amu})\left(1.6605 \times 10^{-24}\ \frac{g}{\text{amu}}\right) = 3.102 \times 10^{-25}\ g$$

$$\Delta E = \Delta mc^2 = (3.102 \times 10^{-25}\ g)\left(\frac{1\ \text{kg}}{1000\ g}\right)\left(3.00 \times 10^8\ \frac{m}{s}\right)^2$$

$$= 2.79 \times 10^{-11}\ J$$

$$\Delta E \text{ in kJ/mol} = \left(2.79 \times 10^{-11}\ \frac{J}{\text{atom}}\right)\left(\frac{1\ \text{kJ}}{1000\ J}\right)\left(6.022 \times 10^{23}\ \frac{\text{atom}}{\text{mol}}\right)$$

$$= 1.68 \times 10^{10}\ \frac{\text{kJ}}{\text{mol}}$$

Nuclear fission of a ^{235}U atom releases 2.79×10^{-11} J, or 1.68×10^{10} kJ/mol.

▸ **PROBLEM 22.3**   An alternative pathway for the nuclear fission of ^{235}U produces tellurium-137 and zirconium-97. How much energy in kJ/mol is released in this fission pathway?

$${}_{0}^{1}n + {}_{92}^{235}U \longrightarrow {}_{52}^{137}Te + {}_{40}^{97}Zr + 2\,{}_{0}^{1}n$$

The masses are ^{235}U (235.0439 amu), ^{137}Te (136.9254 amu), ^{97}Zr (96.9110 amu), and ${}_{0}^{1}n$ (1.008 66 amu).

Nuclear Reactors

The same fission process that leads to a nuclear explosion under uncontrolled conditions can be used to generate electric power when carried out in a controlled manner in a nuclear reactor (**Figure 22.4**). The principle behind a nuclear reactor is straightforward: uranium fuel is placed in a pressurized containment vessel surrounded by water, and *control rods* made of boron and cadmium are added. The water slows the neutrons released during fission so their escape is more difficult, and the control rods absorb and thus regulate the flow of neutrons when they are raised and lowered, maintaining the fission at a barely self-sustainable rate to prevent overheating. Energy from the controlled fission heats a circulating coolant, which in turn produces steam to drive a turbine and produce electricity.

Naturally occurring uranium is a mixture of two major isotopes. The nonfissionable ^{238}U isotope has a natural abundance of 99.3%, while the fissionable ^{235}U isotope is present only to the extent of 0.7%. In a typical nuclear reactor, the fuel is made of compressed pellets of UO_2 that have been isotopically enriched to a 3% concentration of ^{235}U and then encased in zirconium rods. The rods are placed in a pressure vessel filled with water, which acts as a moderator to slow the neutrons so they can be captured more readily.

No nuclear explosion can occur in a reactor because the amount and concentration of fissionable fuel is too low and because the fuel is not confined by pressure into a small volume. In a worst-case accident, however, uncontrolled fission could lead to enormous overheating that could melt the reactor and surrounding containment vessel, thereby releasing large amounts of radioactivity to the environment. Newer reactors get around this problem by adopting what are called *passive safety* designs that automatically slow runaway reactors without any electronic feedback or operator input.

Figure 22.4
A nuclear power plant.

Thirty-one countries around the world now obtain some of their electricity from nuclear energy (**Figure 22.5**). The United States produces more nuclear power than any other country—approximately 101,000 megawatts per year from 104 commercial generators. France produces the highest percentage of its electricity from nuclear plants—76% from 59 plants. Worldwide, 434 nuclear plants were in operation in 2008, with an additional 53 under construction and 134 more being planned. The total output was 371,000 megawatts, or approximately 15% of the world's electrical power.

The primary problem holding back future development is the yet unsolved matter of how to dispose of the radioactive wastes generated by the plants. It will take at least 600 years for waste strontium-90 to decay to safe levels, and at least 20,000 years for plutonium-239 to decay.

Nuclear Fusion

Just as heavy nuclei such as ^{235}U release energy when they undergo *fission*, very light nuclei such as the isotopes of hydrogen release enormous amounts of energy when they undergo *fusion*. In fact, it's just this fusion reaction of hydrogen nuclei to produce helium that powers our Sun and other stars. Among the processes thought to occur in the Sun are those in the following sequence leading to helium-4:

$$\ce{^1_1H + ^1_1H \longrightarrow ^2_1H + ^0_1e}$$

$$\ce{^1_1H + ^2_1H \longrightarrow ^3_2He}$$

$$\ce{^3_2He + ^3_2He \longrightarrow ^4_2He + 2\, ^1_1H}$$

$$\ce{^3_2He + ^1_1H \longrightarrow ^4_2He + ^0_1e}$$

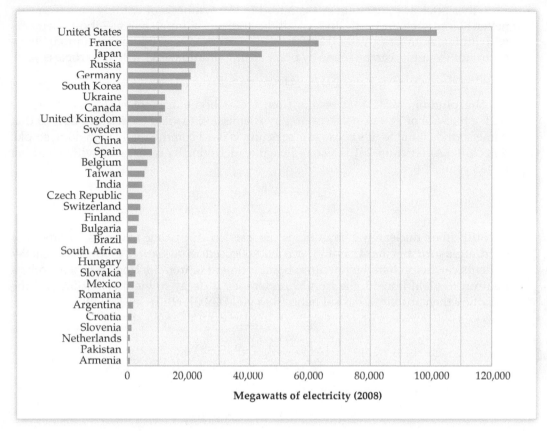

Figure 22.5
Megawatts of electricity generated by nuclear power in 2008.

The main appeal of nuclear fusion as a power source is that the hydrogen isotopes used as fuel are cheap and plentiful and that the fusion products are nonradioactive and nonpolluting. The technical problems that must be solved before achieving a practical and controllable fusion method are staggering, however. Not the least of the problems is that a temperature of approximately 40 *million* kelvin is needed to initiate the fusion process.

▶ **PROBLEM 22.4** Calculate the amount of energy released in kJ/mol for the fusion reaction of ^{1}H and ^{2}H atoms to yield a ^{3}He atom:

$$^1_1\text{H} + ^2_1\text{H} \longrightarrow ^3_2\text{He}$$

The atomic masses are ^{1}H (1.007 83 amu), ^{2}H (2.014 10 amu), and ^{3}He (3.016 03 amu).

22.3 NUCLEAR TRANSMUTATION

Fewer than 300 of the more than 3600 known isotopes occur naturally. The remainder have been made by **nuclear transmutation**, the change of one element into another. Such transmutation is often brought about by bombardment of an atom with a high-energy particle such as a proton, neutron, or α particle. In the ensuing collision between particle and atom, an unstable nucleus is momentarily created, a nuclear change occurs, and a different element is produced. The first nuclear transmutation was accomplished in 1917 by Ernest Rutherford, who bombarded ^{14}N nuclei with α particles and found that ^{17}O was produced:

$$^{14}_7\text{N} + ^4_2\text{He} \longrightarrow ^{17}_8\text{O} + ^1_1\text{H}$$

Other nuclear transmutations can lead to the synthesis of entirely new elements never before seen on Earth. In fact, all the transuranium elements—those elements with atomic numbers greater than 92—have been produced by transmutation. Plutonium, for example, can be made by bombarding uranium-238 with α particles:

$$^{238}_{92}U + {}^{4}_{2}He \longrightarrow {}^{241}_{94}Pu + {}^{1}_{0}n$$

The plutonium-241 that results from U-238 bombardment is itself radioactive with a half-life of 14.3 years, decaying by β emission to yield americium-241. (If that name sounds familiar, it's because americium is used commercially in making smoke detectors.) Americium-241 is also radioactive, decaying by α emission with a half-life of 433 years.

$$^{241}_{94}Pu \longrightarrow {}^{241}_{95}Am + {}^{0}_{-1}e$$
$$^{241}_{95}Am \longrightarrow {}^{237}_{93}Np + {}^{4}_{2}He$$

Still other nuclear transmutations are carried out using neutrons, protons, or even atoms for bombardment. The cobalt-60 used in radiation therapy for cancer patients can be prepared by neutron bombardment of iron-58. Iron-58 first absorbs a neutron to yield iron-59, the iron-59 undergoes β decay to yield cobalt-59, and the cobalt-59 then absorbs a second neutron to yield cobalt-60:

$$^{58}_{26}Fe + {}^{1}_{0}n \longrightarrow {}^{59}_{26}Fe$$
$$^{59}_{26}Fe \longrightarrow {}^{59}_{27}Co + {}^{0}_{-1}e$$
$$^{59}_{27}Co + {}^{1}_{0}n \longrightarrow {}^{60}_{27}Co$$

The overall change can be written as

$$^{58}_{26}Fe + 2\,{}^{1}_{0}n \longrightarrow {}^{60}_{27}Co + {}^{0}_{-1}e$$

▲ The Fermi National Accelerator Laboratory has a particle accelerator 4 mi in circumference that is able to accelerate protons to energies of 1 trillion eV.

WORKED EXAMPLE 22.4

BALANCING A NUCLEAR TRANSMUTATION EQUATION

The element berkelium was first prepared at the University of California at Berkeley in 1949 by α bombardment of $^{241}_{95}Am$. Two neutrons are also produced during the reaction. What isotope of berkelium results from this transmutation? Write a balanced nuclear equation.

STRATEGY AND SOLUTION

According to the periodic table, berkelium has $Z = 97$. Since the sum of the reactant mass numbers is $241 + 4 = 245$ and 2 neutrons are produced, the berkelium isotope must have a mass number of $245 - 2 = 243$.

$$^{241}_{95}Am + {}^{4}_{2}He \longrightarrow {}^{243}_{97}Bk + 2\,{}^{1}_{0}n$$

▶ **PROBLEM 22.5** Write a balanced nuclear equation for the reaction of argon-40 with a proton:

$$^{40}_{18}Ar + {}^{1}_{1}H \longrightarrow ? + {}^{1}_{0}n$$

▶ **PROBLEM 22.6** Write a balanced nuclear equation for the reaction of uranium-238 with a deuteron ($^{2}_{1}H$):

$$^{238}_{92}U + {}^{2}_{1}H \longrightarrow ? + 2\,{}^{1}_{0}n$$

22.4 DETECTING AND MEASURING RADIOACTIVITY

Radioactive emissions are invisible. We can't see, hear, smell, touch, or taste them, no matter how high the dose. We can, however, measure and detect radioactivity using a suitable instrument, such as a Geiger counter, and the effects of that radiation on living organisms can be readily observed.

A Geiger counter for detecting and measuring radiation. As radiation enters the argon-filled wand, it knocks loose electrons (blue), which conduct a tiny electric current that registers on the meter.

Battery

The current flow registers on the meter.

Amplifier and counter

Wire

Positively charged

Argon gas

Negatively charged

◀ A Geiger counter for detecting and measuring radiation.

Radiation intensity is expressed in different ways, depending on what is being measured. Some units measure the number of nuclear decay events, while others measure the amount of exposure to radiation or the biological consequences of radiation (Table 22.2).

TABLE 22.2   Units for Measuring Radiation

Unit	Quantity Measured	Description
Becquerel (Bq)	Decay events	1 Bq = 1 disintegration/s
Curie (Ci)	Decay events	1 Ci = 3.7×10^{10} disintegrations/s
Gray (Gy)	Energy absorbed per kilogram of tissue	1 Gy = 1 J/kg tissue
Rad	Energy absorbed per kilogram of tissue	1 rad = 0.01 Gy
Sievert (Sv)	Tissue damage	1 Sv = 1 J/kg
Rem	Tissue damage	1 rem = 0.01 Sv

- The *becquerel* (Bq) is the SI unit for measuring the number of nuclear disintegrations occurring per second in a sample: 1 Bq = 1 disintegration/s. The *curie* (Ci) and *millicurie* (mCi) also measure disintegrations per unit time, but they are far larger units than the becquerel and are more often used, particularly in medicine and biochemistry. One curie is the decay rate of 1 g of radium, equal to 3.7×10^{10} Bq:

$$1 \text{ Bq} = 1 \text{ disintegration/s}$$

$$1 \text{ Ci} = 3.7 \times 10^{10} \text{ Bq} = 3.7 \times 10^{10} \text{ disintegrations/s}$$

As an example, a 1.5 mCi sample of tritium is equal to 5.6×10^7 Bq, meaning that it undergoes 5.6×10^7 disintegrations/s.

- The *gray* (Gy) is the SI unit for measuring the amount of energy absorbed per kilogram of tissue exposed to a radiation source: 1 Gy = 1 J/kg. The *rad* (*radiation absorbed dose*) also measures tissue exposure and is more often used in medicine.

$$1 \text{ Gy} = 1 \text{ J/kg} \qquad 1 \text{ rad} = 0.01 \text{ Gy}$$

- The *sievert* (Sv) is the SI unit that measures the amount of tissue damage caused by radiation. It takes into account not just the energy absorbed per kilogram of tissue but also the different biological effects of different kinds of radiation. For example, 1 Gy of α radiation causes 20 times more tissue damage than 1 Gy of γ rays, but 1 Sv of α radiation and 1 Sv of γ rays cause the same amount of damage. The *rem* (*roentgen equivalent for man*) is an analogous non-SI unit that is more frequently used in medicine.

$$1 \text{ rem} = 0.01 \text{ Sv}$$

The effects of radiation on the human body vary with the energy and kind of radiation, as well as with the length of exposure and whether the radiation is from an external or internal source. When coming from an external source, X rays and γ radiation are more harmful than α and β particles because they penetrate clothing and skin. When coming from an internal source, however, α and β particles are particularly dangerous because all their energy is given up to surrounding tissue. Alpha emitters, although relatively harmless externally, are especially hazardous internally and are almost never used in medical applications.

Because of their relatively large mass, α particles move slowly—up to only one-tenth the speed of light—and can be stopped by a few sheets of paper or by the top layer of skin. Beta particles, because they are much lighter, move at up to nine-tenths the speed of light and have about 100 times the penetrating power of α particles. A block of wood or heavy protective clothing is necessary to stop β radiation, which would otherwise penetrate and burn the skin.

Gamma rays and X rays move at the speed of light and have about 1000 times the penetrating power of α particles. A lead block several inches thick is needed to stop γ and X radiation, which could otherwise penetrate and damage the body's internal organs. Some properties of different kinds of radiation are summarized in Table 22.3.

TABLE 22.3   Some Properties of Radiation

Type of Radiation	Energy Range	Penetrating Distance in Water*
α	3–9 MeV	0.02–0.04 mm
β	0–3 MeV	0–4 mm
X	100 eV–10 keV	0.01–1 cm
γ	10 keV–10 MeV	1–20 cm

* Distances at which one-half of the radiation has been stopped.

The biological effects of different radiation doses are given in Table 22.4. Although the effects sound fearful, the average radiation dose received annually by most people is only about 120 mrem. About 70% of this radiation comes from natural sources such as rocks and cosmic rays—energetic particles coming from interstellar space. The remaining 30% comes from medical procedures such as X rays. The amount due to emissions from nuclear power plants and to fallout from atmospheric testing of nuclear weapons in the 1950s is barely detectable.

TABLE 22.4   Biological Effects of Short-Term Radiation on Humans

Dose (rem)	Biological Effects
0–25	No detectable effects
25–100	Temporary decrease in white blood cell count
100–200	Nausea, vomiting, longer-term decrease in white blood cells
200–300	Vomiting, diarrhea, loss of appetite, listlessness
300–600	Vomiting, diarrhea, hemorrhaging, eventual death in some cases
Above 600	Eventual death in nearly all cases

22.5 APPLICATIONS OF NUCLEAR CHEMISTRY

Nuclear chemistry has many applications in daily life, in numerous scientific fields, and in medicine. Here are just a few:

Dating with Radioisotopes

Biblical scrolls are found in a cave near the Dead Sea. Are they authentic? A mummified body is discovered in a peat bog near Ramten, Denmark. How old is it? The burned bones of a man are dug up near Lubbock, Texas. How long have humans lived in the area? These and many other questions can be answered by archaeologists using a technique called *radiocarbon dating*. (The Dead Sea Scrolls are 1900 years old and authentic, the mummy is 2200 years old, and the human remains found in Texas are 9900 years old.)

Radiocarbon dating of archaeological artifacts depends on the slow and constant production of radioactive carbon-14 in the upper atmosphere by neutron bombardment of nitrogen atoms. (The neutrons come from the bombardment of other atoms by cosmic rays.)

$$^{14}_{7}\text{N} + ^{1}_{0}\text{n} \longrightarrow ^{14}_{6}\text{C} + ^{1}_{1}\text{H}$$

▲ Radiocarbon dating places the age of this bog mummy at 2200 years BP. The abbreviation BP means "Before Present," with 1950 taken as the reference point.

Carbon-14 atoms produced in the upper atmosphere combine with oxygen to yield $^{14}\text{CO}_2$, which slowly diffuses into the lower atmosphere, where it mixes with ordinary $^{12}\text{CO}_2$ and is taken up by plants during photosynthesis. When these plants are eaten, carbon-14 enters the food chain and is ultimately distributed throughout all living organisms.

As long as a plant or animal is living, a dynamic equilibrium exists in which an organism excretes or exhales the same ratio of ^{14}C to ^{12}C that it takes in. As a result, the ratio of ^{14}C to ^{12}C in the living organism remains constant and is the same as that in the atmosphere—about 1 part in 10^{12}. When the plant or animal dies, however, it no longer takes in more ^{14}C and the $^{14}\text{C}/^{12}\text{C}$ ratio in the organism slowly decreases as ^{14}C undergoes radioactive decay by β emission, with $t_{1/2} = 5715$ years.

$$^{14}_{6}\text{C} \longrightarrow ^{14}_{7}\text{N} + ^{0}_{-1}\text{e}$$

At 5715 years (one ^{14}C half-life) after the death of the organism, the $^{14}\text{C}/^{12}\text{C}$ ratio has decreased by a factor of 2; at 11,430 years after death, the $^{14}\text{C}/^{12}\text{C}$ ratio has decreased by a factor of 4; and so on. By measuring the present $^{14}\text{C}/^{12}\text{C}$ ratio in the traces of any once-living organism, archaeologists can determine how long ago the organism died. The results are usually given as the number of years BP, meaning "Before Present," with the year 1950 used as the reference point.

Human or animal hair from well-preserved remains, charcoal or wood fragments from once-living trees, and cotton or linen from once-living plants are all useful sources for radiocarbon dating. The technique becomes less accurate as samples get older and the amount of ^{14}C they contain diminishes, but artifacts with an age of 1000–20,000 years can be dated with reasonable accuracy. The outer limit of the technique is about 60,000 years.

Just as radiocarbon measurements allow dating of once-living organisms, similar measurements on other radioisotopes make possible the dating of rocks. Uranium-238, for example, has a half-life of 4.47×10^9 years and decays through a series of events to yield lead-206. The age of a uranium-containing rock can therefore be determined by measuring the $^{238}\text{U}/^{206}\text{Pb}$ ratio. Similarly, potassium-40 has a half-life of 1.25×10^9 years and decays through electron capture and positron emission to yield argon-40. (Both processes yield the same product.)

$$^{40}_{19}\text{K} + ^{0}_{-1}\text{e} \longrightarrow ^{40}_{18}\text{Ar}$$
$$^{40}_{19}\text{K} \longrightarrow ^{40}_{18}\text{Ar} + ^{0}_{1}\text{e}$$

The age of a rock can be found by crushing a sample, measuring the amount of ^{40}Ar gas that escapes, and comparing the amount of ^{40}Ar with the amount of ^{40}K remaining in the sample. It is through techniques such as these that the age of the Earth has been estimated at 4.54 billion years.

WORKED EXAMPLE 22.5

USING RADIOCARBON DATING

Radiocarbon measurements made in 1988 on the Shroud of Turin, a religious artifact thought by some to be the burial shroud of Christ, showed a ^{14}C decay rate of 14.2 disintegrations/min per gram of carbon. What age BP is implied by this result if currently living organisms decay at the rate of 15.3 disintegrations/min per gram of carbon? The half-life of ^{14}C is 5715 years.

STRATEGY

For a first-order process like radioactive decay, in which rate $= kN_t$, the ratio of the decay rate at any time t to the decay rate at time $t = 0$ is the same as the ratio of N_t to N_0:

$$\frac{\text{Decay rate at time } t}{\text{Decay rate at time } t = 0} = \frac{kN_t}{kN_0} = \frac{N_t}{N_0}$$

To date the shroud, we need to calculate the time t that corresponds to the observed decay rate. This can be done by solving for t in the integrated rate law, as explained in Section 12.6.

$$\ln\left(\frac{N_t}{N_0}\right) = (-\ln 2)\left(\frac{t}{t_{1/2}}\right)$$

SOLUTION

Substituting the proper values into the equation gives

$$\ln\left(\frac{14.2}{15.3}\right) = -0.693\left(\frac{t}{5715 \text{ years}}\right) \quad \text{or} \quad -0.0746 = -0.693\left(\frac{t}{5715 \text{ years}}\right)$$

$$\text{so} \quad t = \frac{(-0.0746)(5715 \text{ years})}{-0.693} = 615 \text{ years}$$

An age of 615 years in 1988 corresponds to an age of $615 - 38 = 577$ years in 1950, or 577 BP. These results imply that the Shroud of Turin comes from medieval times.

▶ **PROBLEM 22.7** Charcoal found in the Lascaux cave in France, site of many prehistoric cave paintings, was observed in 1950 to decay at a rate of 2.4 disintegrations/min per gram of carbon. What is the age of the charcoal BP if currently living organisms decay at the rate of 15.3 disintegrations/min per gram of carbon? The half-life of ^{14}C is 5715 years.

Medical Uses of Radioactivity

The origins of nuclear medicine date to 1901, when the French physician Henri Danlos first used radium in the treatment of a tuberculous skin lesion. Since that time, uses of radioactivity have become a crucial part of modern medical care, both diagnostic and therapeutic. Current nuclear techniques can be grouped into three classes: (1) in vivo procedures, (2) therapeutic procedures, and (3) imaging procedures.

In Vivo Procedures In vivo studies—those that take place *inside* the body—are carried out to assess the functioning of a particular organ or body system. A radiopharmaceutical agent is administered, and its path in the body—whether it is absorbed, excreted, diluted, or concentrated—is determined by analysis of blood or urine samples.

An example of the many in vivo procedures using radioactive agents is the determination of whole-blood volume by injecting a known quantity of red blood cells labeled with radioactive chromium-51. After a suitable interval to allow the labeled cells to be distributed evenly throughout the body, a blood sample is taken, the amount of dilution of the ^{51}Cr is measured, and the blood volume is calculated.

Therapeutic Procedures Therapeutic procedures—those in which radiation is used to kill diseased tissue—can involve either external or internal sources of radiation. External radiation therapy for the treatment of cancer is often carried out with γ rays from a cobalt-60 source. The highly radioactive source is shielded by a thick lead

▲ What is the age of this painting from the Lascaux cave in France?

▲ A person's blood volume can be found by injecting a small amount of radioactive chromium-51 and measuring the dilution factor.

container and has a small opening directed toward the site of the tumor. By focusing the radiation beam on the tumor and rotating the patient's body, the tumor receives the full exposure while the exposure of surrounding parts of the body is minimized. Nevertheless, sufficient exposure occurs so that most patients suffer some effects of radiation sickness.

Internal radiation therapy is a much more selective technique than external therapy. In the treatment of thyroid disease, for example, iodine-131, a powerful β emitter known to localize in the target tissue, is administered internally. Because β particles penetrate no farther than several millimeters, the localized ^{131}I produces a high radiation dose that destroys only the surrounding diseased tissue.

The half-lives of some medically useful radioisotopes are listed in Table 22.5. As you might expect if you think about it, the radioisotopes used internally in medical applications have fairly short half-lives so that they decay rapidly and don't cause long-term health hazards.

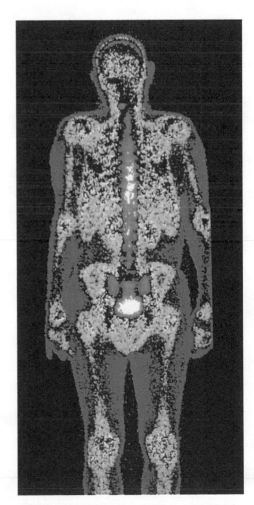

▲ Cancerous tumors can be treated by irradiation with γ rays from this cobalt-60 source.

TABLE 22.5   Half-Lives of Some Useful Radioisotopes

Radioisotope	Symbol	Radiation	Half-life	Use
Fluorine-18	$^{18}_{9}F$	β^+	110 minutes	PET scans
Phosphorus-32	$^{32}_{15}P$	β^-	14.28 days	Leukemia therapy
Cobalt-60	$^{60}_{27}Co$	β^-, γ	5.27 years	Cancer therapy
Technetium-99m*	$^{99m}_{43}Tc$	γ	6.01 hours	Brain scans
Iodine-123	$^{123}_{53}I$	γ	13.2 hours	Thyroid therapy

* The m in technetium-99m stands for *metastable*, meaning that it undergoes γ emission but does not change its mass number or atomic number.

◀ Technetium-99m, a short-lived radioisotope used for brain scans, is obtained from the decay of ^{99}Mo, which is itself prepared by neutron bombardment of ^{98}Mo and then stored in this "technetium cow" in the form of MoO_4^{2-}. Small amounts of ^{99m}Tc are removed by passing a saline solution through the cylinder.

Imaging Procedures Imaging procedures give diagnostic information about the health of body organs by analyzing the distribution pattern of radioisotopes introduced into the body. A radiopharmaceutical agent that is known to concentrate in a specific tissue or organ is injected into the body, and its distribution pattern is monitored by external radiation detectors. Depending on the disease and the organ, a diseased organ might concentrate more of the radiopharmaceutical than a normal organ and thus show up as a radioactive "hot" spot against a "cold" background. Alternatively, the diseased organ might concentrate less of the radiopharmaceutical than a normal organ and thus show up as a cold spot on a hot background.

The radioisotope most widely used today is technetium-99m, whose short half-life of 6.01 hours minimizes a patient's exposure to harmful effects. Bone scans using Tc-99m, such as that shown in **Figure 22.6**, are an important tool in the diagnosis of stress fractures, cancer, and other conditions.

Figure 22.6
A bone scan using radioactive technetium-99m.

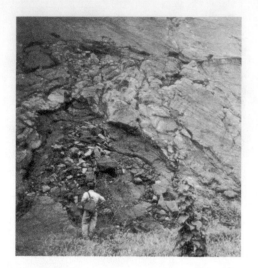

▲ Believe it or not, naturally occurring nuclear chain reactions took place 2 billion years ago at this site in west equatorial Africa near present-day Oklo, Gabon.

INQUIRY: DOES NATURE HAVE NUCLEAR REACTORS?

Nuclear reactors aren't easy to build. A critical mass of fissionable fuel has to be obtained, typically uranium-235, enriched from its 0.7% natural abundance to about 3%. Purified control rods have to be made, neutron moderators selected, and many safety precautions taken. The first man-made nuclear reactor was constructed in Chicago, Illinois, only 70 years ago, in 1942. Nevertheless, and as hard as it is to believe, the world's first true nuclear reactor is located in Gabon, Africa, and is approximately *2 billion* years old. Sixteen of these natural reactors are now known, collectively called the Oklo Fossil Reactors.

The reactors were discovered in early 1972 when chemical analysis of uranium ore samples from the Oklo mine in Gabon showed abnormally low amounts of ^{235}U. Although naturally occurring uranium typically contains 0.72% of the fissionable ^{235}U isotope, some of the samples from the Oklo mine contained as little as 0.44% of ^{235}U. Furthermore, the abundances of several other isotopes in the ore, including ^{142}Nd and ^{99}Ru, were also dramatically different from normal values. All these differences closely resemble those found in the spent fuel from modern nuclear reactors, leading investigators to conclude that spontaneous and self-sustaining nuclear chain reactions must have occurred at the mine site nearly 2 billion years ago.

The Oklo nuclear reactors are thought to have formed when unusually rich uranium deposits were flooded by groundwater, which acted as a moderator to slow the neutrons released by fission of ^{235}U and prevent their escape, thereby allowing a chain reaction to begin. As soon as the chain reaction started, though, the heat released rapidly boiled away the groundwater, which stopped the process and shut down the reactor until it cooled. Groundwater then returned, and the chain reaction restarted. Isotope measurements in nearby rocks indicate that the reactors cycled on and off every 2–3 hours for several hundred thousand years until the concentration of ^{235}U in the ore became too low to sustain a chain reaction. Up to 2 tons of ^{235}U underwent fission.

Could another natural reactor form today? When the Oklo reactors formed 2 billion years ago, the abundance of the fissionable ^{235}U isotope in uranium was about 3%, the same percentage as that used today in nuclear power plants. Today, however, the natural abundance of ^{235}U is only about 0.7% because of nuclear decay over the past few billion years, so present-day nuclear fuel has to be enriched before it can be used. Since a chain-reaction is no longer self-sustaining at the present 0.7% ^{235}U level, the conditions needed by natural reactors are no longer present on Earth.

SUMMARY

Nuclear chemistry is the study of the properties and reactions of atomic nuclei. Nuclear reactions differ from chemical reactions in that they involve a change in an atom's nucleus, often producing a different element. The rate of radioactive decay is characterized kinetically by a first-order decay constant and by a half-life, $t_{1/2}$, the time required for the number of radioactive nuclei in a sample to drop to half its initial value.

The stability of a given nucleus is related to its neutron/proton ratio. The strength of the forces involved can be measured by calculating an atom's **mass defect**—the difference in mass between a given nucleus and the total mass of its individual nucleons (protons and neutrons). Applying the Einstein equation $\Delta E = \Delta mc^2$ then allows calculation of the nuclear **binding energy**. The energy change accompanying a nuclear reaction is far greater than that accompanying any chemical reaction.

Certain heavy nuclei, such as uranium-235, undergo **nuclear fission** when struck by neutrons, breaking apart into fragment nuclei and releasing enormous amounts of energy. Light nuclei, such as the isotopes of hydrogen, undergo **nuclear fusion** when heated to sufficiently high temperatures, forming heavier nuclei and releasing energy.

Of the more than 3600 known isotopes, most have been made by **nuclear transmutation**, the change of one element into another. Such transmutation is often brought about by bombardment of an atom with a high-energy particle such as a proton, neutron, or α particle.

Radiation intensity is expressed in different ways, according to what property is being measured. The becquerel (Bq) and the curie (Ci) measure the number of radioactive disintegrations per second in a sample. The gray (Gy) and the rad measure the amount of radiation absorbed per kilogram of tissue. The sievert (Sv) and the rem measure the amount of tissue damage caused by radiation. Radiation effects become noticeable with a human exposure of 25 rem and become lethal at an exposure above 600 rem.

KEY WORDS

binding energy *891*	**critical mass** *894*	**fusion** *893*	**nuclear transmutation** *897*
chain reaction *894*	**fission** *893*	**mass defect** *891*	

SECTION PROBLEMS

Problems 22.1–22.7 appear within the chapter.

Energy Changes during Nuclear Reactions (Section 22.1)

22.8 Why does a given nucleus have less mass than the sum of its constituent protons and neutrons?

22.9 In an endothermic chemical reaction, do the products have more mass, less mass, or the same mass as the reactants? Explain.

22.10 What is the wavelength (in nm) of γ rays whose energy is 1.50 MeV?

22.11 What is the frequency (in Hz) of X rays whose energy is 6.82 keV?

22.12 Calculate the mass defect (in g/mol) for the following nuclei:
(a) ^{52}Fe (atomic mass = 51.948 11 amu)
(b) ^{92}Mo (atomic mass = 91.906 81 amu)

22.13 Calculate the mass defect (in g/mol) for the following nuclei:
(a) ^{32}S (atomic mass = 31.972 07 amu)
(b) ^{40}Ca (atomic mass = 39.962 59 amu)

22.14 Calculate the binding energy (in MeV/nucleon) for the following nuclei:
(a) ^{58}Ni (atomic mass = 57.935 35 amu)
(b) ^{84}Kr (atomic mass = 83.911 51 amu)

22.15 Calculate the binding energy (in MeV/nucleon) for the following nuclei:
(a) ^{63}Cu (atomic mass = 62.939 60 amu)
(b) ^{84}Sr (atomic mass = 83.913 43 amu)

22.16 What is the energy change ΔE (in kJ/mol) when an α particle is emitted from ^{174}Ir? The atomic mass of ^{174}Ir is 173.966 66 amu, the atomic mass of ^{170}Re is 169.958 04 amu, and the atomic mass of a ^{4}He atom is 4.002 60 amu.
$$^{174}_{77}\text{Ir} \longrightarrow {}^{170}_{75}\text{Re} + {}^{4}_{2}\text{He} \qquad \Delta E = ?$$

22.17 Magnesium-28 is a β emitter that decays to aluminum-28. How much energy is released in kJ/mol? The atomic mass of ^{28}Mg is 27.983 88 amu, and the atomic mass of ^{28}Al is 27.981 91 amu.

22.18 What is the mass change in grams accompanying the formation of NH_3 from H_2 and N_2?
$$N_2(g) + 3\,H_2(g) \longrightarrow 2\,NH_3(g) \qquad \Delta H° = -92.2 \text{ kJ}$$

22.19 What is the mass change in grams accompanying the formation of CO and H_2 in the water-gas reaction?
$$C(s) + H_2O(g) \longrightarrow CO(g) + H_2(g) \qquad \Delta H° = +131 \text{ kJ}$$

22.20 A positron has the same mass as an electron (9.109×10^{-31} kg) but an opposite charge. When the two particles encounter each other, annihilation occurs and only γ rays are produced. How much energy (in kJ/mol) is produced?

22.21 How much energy is released (in kJ) in the fusion reaction of ^{2}H to yield 1 mol of ^{3}He? The atomic mass of ^{2}H is 2.0141 amu, and the atomic mass of ^{3}He is 3.0160 amu.
$$2\,{}^{2}_{1}\text{H} \longrightarrow {}^{3}_{2}\text{He} + {}^{1}_{0}\text{n}$$

Nuclear Transmutation (Section 22.3)

22.22 Give the products of the following nuclear reactions:
(a) $^{109}_{47}\text{Ag} + {}^{4}_{2}\text{He} \longrightarrow ?$
(b) $^{10}_{5}\text{B} + {}^{4}_{2}\text{He} \longrightarrow ? + {}^{1}_{0}\text{n}$

22.23 Balance the following equations for the nuclear fission of ^{235}U:

(a) $^{235}_{92}U \longrightarrow ^{160}_{62}Sm + ^{72}_{30}Zn + ?\,^{1}_{0}n$

(b) $^{235}_{92}U \longrightarrow ^{87}_{35}Br + ? + 2\,^{1}_{0}n$

22.24 Element 109 ($^{266}_{109}Mt$) was prepared in 1982 by bombardment of ^{209}Bi atoms with ^{58}Fe atoms. Identify the other product that must have formed, and write a balanced nuclear equation assuming no other products were formed.

22.25 Molybdenum-99 is formed by neutron bombardment of a naturally occurring isotope. If one neutron is absorbed and no byproducts are formed, what is the starting isotope?

22.26 Californium-246 is formed by bombardment of uranium-238 atoms. If four neutrons are formed as byproducts, what particle is used for the bombardment?

22.27 Balance the following transmutation reactions:

(a) $^{246}_{96}Cm + ^{12}_{6}C \longrightarrow ? + 4\,^{1}_{0}n$

(b) $^{253}_{99}Es + ? \longrightarrow ^{256}_{101}Md + ^{1}_{0}n$

(c) $^{250}_{98}Cf + ^{11}_{5}B \longrightarrow ? + 4\,^{1}_{0}n$

CHAPTER PROBLEMS

22.28 The electronic systems on the New Horizons spacecraft, launched on January 19, 2006, and scheduled to reach Pluto on July 14, 2015, are powered by electricity generated by heat. The heat comes from the radioactive decay of ^{238}Pu in the 11 kg of $^{238}PuO_2$ fuel onboard. The generator provided 240 W when the spacecraft was launched. If the power output is directly proportional to the amount of ^{238}Pu in the generator, what will the power output be when the spacecraft reaches Pluto? The half life of ^{238}Pu is 87.7 y.

22.29 To treat a brain tumor with gamma knife radiosurgery, the patient's head is positioned within a hemispherical dome covered by 201 individual ^{60}Co sources directed inward toward the tumor target point. The tumor receives a very high dose of radiation because all the beams converge on it, while any irradiated healthy tissue receives only the radiation of a single beam. For a prescribed dose of 1800 rad, how long should the radiation treatment go if 2.2×10^{11} disintegrations of ^{60}Co are required to give a dose of 1.0 rad? Assume that all the sources are directed at the tumor with an activity of 30 Ci each.

22.30 Thorium-232 decays by a 10-step series of nuclear reactions, ultimately yielding lead-208, along with 6 α particles and 4 β particles. How much energy (in kJ/mol) is released during the overall process? The relevant masses are: ^{232}Th = 232.038 054 amu; ^{208}Pb = 207.976 627 amu; electron = $5.485\,799 \times 10^{-4}$ amu; ^{4}He = 4.002 603 amu.

22.31 Fraud in science is rare but does happen occasionally. In 1999, the creation of three superheavy elements (one new) was claimed when ^{208}Pb was bombarded with ^{86}Kr. The claim was subsequently found to be fraudulent and was withdrawn. Identify the isotopes X, Y, and Z that were claimed.

$$^{208}_{82}Pb + ^{86}_{36}Kr \xrightarrow{-n} X \xrightarrow{-\alpha} Y \xrightarrow{-\alpha} Z$$

22.32 Calculate the mass defect (in g/mol) and the binding energy (in MeV/nucleon) for the following nuclei. Which of the two is more stable?

(a) ^{50}Cr (atomic mass = 49.946 05 amu)

(b) ^{64}Zn (atomic mass = 63.929 15 amu)

22.33 What is the age BP of a bone fragment that shows an average of 2.9 disintegrations/min per gram of carbon in 2005? The carbon in living organisms undergoes an average of 15.3 disintegrations/min per gram, and the half-life of ^{14}C is 5715 years. (See Section 12.6.)

22.34 How much energy (in kJ/mol) is released in the fusion reaction of ^{2}H with ^{3}He?

$$^{2}_{1}H + ^{3}_{2}He \longrightarrow ^{4}_{2}He + ^{1}_{1}H$$

The relevant masses are ^{2}H (2.0141 amu), ^{3}He (3.0160 amu), ^{4}He (4.0026 amu), and ^{1}H (1.0078 amu).

22.35 What is the age of a rock whose $^{40}Ar/^{40}K$ ratio is 1.15? The half-life of ^{40}K is 1.28×10^{9} years.

22.36 The most abundant isotope of uranium, ^{238}U, does not undergo fission. In a *breeder reactor*, however, a ^{238}U atom captures a neutron and emits two β particles to make a fissionable isotope of plutonium, which can then be used as fuel in a nuclear reactor. Write a balanced nuclear equation.

22.37 It has been estimated that 3.9×10^{23} kJ/s is radiated into space by the Sun. What is the rate of the Sun's mass loss in kg/s?

22.38 In a cancer treatment called boron neutron-capture therapy, a drug containing boron-10 is injected into a patient where it selectively binds to cancer cells. Irradiating the affected area with neutrons then induces the following reaction:

$$^{10}B + ^{1}n \longrightarrow ^{4}He + ^{7}Li + \gamma$$

The α radiation kills the cancer cells, leaving the surrounding tissue unharmed. The reactants in this nuclear process have essentially no kinetic energy, but the products have a total kinetic energy of 2.31 MeV. What is the energy of the γ photon released? Relevant masses are: ^{4}He (4.002 603 amu), ^{7}Li (7.016 004 amu), ^{10}B (10.012 937 amu), e^{-} (0.000 548 6 amu), $^{1}_{0}n$ (1.008 665 amu).

22.39 Neptunium-237 decays by a series of steps to bismuth-209. How many α and β particles are produced by this decay process?

22.40 The radioactive isotope ^{100}Tc decays to form the stable isotope ^{100}Mo.

(a) There are two possible pathways for this decay. Write balanced equations for both.

(b) Only one of the pathways is observed. Calculate the energy released by both pathways, and explain why only one is observed. Relevant masses are: ^{100}Tc (99.907 657 amu), ^{100}Mo (99.907 48 amu), e^{-} (0.000 548 6 amu).

22.41 The radioisotope ^{226}Ac can decay by any of three different nuclear processes: α emission, β emission, or electron capture.

(a) Write a balanced nuclear equation for the decay of ^{226}Ac by each decay mode.

(b) For the decay of ^{226}Ac by all processes combined, the first-order rate constant is $k = 0.556\,d^{-1}$. How many days are required for 80.0% of a sample of ^{226}Ac to decay?

MULTICONCEPT PROBLEMS

22.42 A small sample of wood from an archeological site in Clovis, New Mexico, was burned in O_2, and the CO_2 produced was bubbled through a solution of $Ba(OH)_2$ to produce a precipitate of $BaCO_3$. When the $BaCO_3$ was collected by filtration, a 1.000 g sample was found to have a radioactivity of 4.0×10^{-3} Bq. The half-life of ^{14}C is 5715 y, and living organisms have a radioactivity due to ^{14}C of 15.3 disintegrations/min per gram of carbon. Assuming that the analysis was carried out in 1960, what is the age BP of the Clovis site?

22.43 Polonium-210, a naturally occurring radioisotope, is an α emitter, with $t_{1/2} = 138$ d. Assume that a sample of ^{210}Po with a mass of 0.700 mg was placed in a 250.0 mL flask, which was evacuated, sealed, and allowed to sit undisturbed. What would the pressure be inside the flask (in mm Hg) at 20 °C after 365 days if all the α particles emitted had become helium atoms?

22.44 A blood-volume determination was carried out on a patient by injection with 20.0 mL of blood that had been radioactively labeled with Cr-51 to an activity of 4.10 μCi/mL. After a brief period to allow for mixing in the body, blood was drawn from the patient for analysis. Unfortunately, a mixup in the laboratory prevented an immediate analysis, and it was not until 17.0 days later that a measurement on the blood was made. The radiation level was then determined to be 0.009 35 μCi/mL. If ^{51}Cr has $t_{1/2} = 27.7$ days, what is the volume of blood in the patient?

22.45 Imagine that you have a 0.007 50 M aqueous $MgCl_2$ solution, prepared so that it contains a small amount of radioactive ^{28}Mg. The half-life of ^{28}Mg is 20.91 h, and the initial activity of the $MgCl_2$ solution is 0.112 μCi/mL. Assume that 20.00 mL of this $MgCl_2$ solution is added to 15.00 mL of 0.012 50 M aqueous Na_2CO_3 solution and that the resultant precipitate is then removed by filtration to give a clear filtrate. After a long break to go for a run, you find that the activity of the filtrate measured 2.40 h after beginning the experiment is 0.029 μCi/mL. What are the molar concentrations of Mg^{2+} and CO_3^{2-} in the filtrate, and what is the solubility product constant of $MgCO_3$?

APPENDIX A

Mathematical Operations

A.1 SCIENTIFIC NOTATION

The numbers that you encounter in chemistry are often either very large or very small. For example, there are about 33,000,000,000,000,000,000,000 H_2O molecules in 1.0 mL of water, and the distance between the H and O atoms in an H_2O molecule is 0.000 000 000 095 7 m. These quantities are more conveniently written in scientific notation as 3.3×10^{22} molecules and 9.57×10^{-11} m, respectively. In scientific notation, numbers are written in the exponential format $A \times 10^n$, where A is a number between 1 and 10, and the exponent n is a positive or negative integer.

How do you convert a number from ordinary notation to scientific notation? If the number is greater than or equal to 10, shift the decimal point to the *left* by n places until you obtain a number between 1 and 10. Then, multiply the result by 10^n. For example, the number 8137.6 is written in scientific notation as 8.1376×10^3:

$$8137.6 = 8.1376 \times 10^3$$

Shift decimal point to the left by 3 places to get a number between 1 and 10

Number of places decimal point was shifted to the left

When you shift the decimal point to the left by three places, you are in effect dividing the number by $10 \times 10 \times 10 = 1000 = 10^3$. Therefore, you must multiply the result by 10^3 so that the value of the number is unchanged.

To convert a number less than 1 to scientific notation, shift the decimal point to the *right* by n places until you obtain a number between 1 and 10. Then, multiply the result by 10^{-n}. For example, the number 0.012 is written in scientific notation as 1.2×10^{-2}:

$$0.012 = 1.2 \times 10^{-2}$$

Shift decimal point to the right by 2 places to get a number between 1 and 10

Number of places decimal point was shifted to the right

When you shift the decimal point to the right by two places, you are in effect multiplying the number by $10 \times 10 = 100 = 10^2$. Therefore, you must multiply the result by 10^{-2} so that the value of the number is unchanged. ($10^2 \times 10^{-2} = 10^0 = 1$.)

The following table gives some additional examples. To convert from scientific notation to ordinary notation, simply reverse the preceding process. Thus, to write the number 5.84×10^4 in ordinary notation, drop the factor of 10^4 and move the decimal point by 4 places to the *right* ($5.84 \times 10^4 = 58,400$). To write the number 3.5×10^{-1} in ordinary notation, drop the factor of 10^{-1} and move the decimal point by 1 place to the *left* ($3.5 \times 10^{-1} = 0.35$). Note that you don't need scientific notation for numbers between 1 and 10 because $10^0 = 1$.

Number	Scientific Notation
58,400	5.84×10^4
0.35	3.5×10^{-1}
7.296	$7.296 \times 10^0 = 7.296$

Addition and Subtraction

To add or subtract two numbers expressed in scientific notation, both numbers must have the same exponent. Thus, to add 7.16×10^3 and 1.32×10^2, first write the latter number as 0.132×10^3 and then add:

$$\begin{array}{r} 7.16 \ \times 10^3 \\ +0.132 \times 10^3 \\ \hline 7.29 \ \times 10^3 \end{array}$$

The answer has three significant figures. (Significant figures are discussed in Section 1.12.) Alternatively, you can write the first number as 71.6×10^2 and then add:

$$\begin{array}{r} 71.6 \ \times 10^2 \\ +1.32 \times 10^2 \\ \hline 72.9 \ \times 10^2 = 7.29 \times 10^3 \end{array}$$

Multiplication and Division

To multiply two numbers expressed in scientific notation, multiply the factors in front of the powers of 10 and then add the exponents:

$$(A \times 10^n)(B \times 10^m) = AB \times 10^{n+m}$$

For example,

$$(2.5 \times 10^4)(4.7 \times 10^7) = (2.5)(4.7) \times 10^{4+7} = 12 \times 10^{11} = 1.2 \times 10^{12}$$

$$(3.46 \times 10^5)(2.2 \times 10^{-2}) = (3.46)(2.2) \times 10^{5+(-2)} = 7.6 \times 10^3$$

Both answers have two significant figures.

To divide two numbers expressed in scientific notation, divide the factors in front of the powers of 10 and then subtract the exponent in the denominator from the exponent in the numerator:

$$\frac{A \times 10^n}{B \times 10^m} = \frac{A}{B} \times 10^{n-m}$$

For example,

$$\frac{3 \times 10^6}{7.2 \times 10^2} = \frac{3}{7.2} \times 10^{6-2} = 0.4 \times 10^4 = 4 \times 10^3 \qquad \text{(1 significant figure)}$$

$$\frac{7.50 \times 10^{-5}}{2.5 \times 10^{-7}} = \frac{7.50}{2.5} \times 10^{-5-(-7)} = 3.0 \times 10^2 \qquad \text{(2 significant figures)}$$

Powers and Roots

To raise a number $A \times 10^n$ to a power m, raise the factor A to the power m and then multiply the exponent n by the power m:

$$(A \times 10^n)^m = A^m \times 10^{n \times m}$$

For example, 3.6×10^2 raised to the 3rd power is 4.7×10^7:

$$(3.6 \times 10^2)^3 = (3.6)^3 \times 10^{2 \times 3} = 47 \times 10^6 = 4.7 \times 10^7 \qquad \text{(2 significant figures)}$$

To take the mth root of a number $A \times 10^n$, raise the number to the power $1/m$. That is, raise factor A to the power $1/m$ and then divide the exponent n by the root m:

$$\sqrt[m]{A \times 10^n} = (A \times 10^n)^{1/m} = A^{1/m} \times 10^{n/m}$$

For example, the square root of 9.0×10^8 is 3.0×10^4:

$$\sqrt[2]{9.0 \times 10^8} = (9.0 \times 10^8)^{1/2} = (9.0)^{1/2} \times 10^{8/2} = 3.0 \times 10^4 \quad \text{(2 significant figures)}$$

Because the exponent in the answer (n/m) is an integer, we must sometimes rewrite the original number by shifting the decimal point so that the exponent n is an integral multiple of the root m. For example, to take the cube root of 6.4×10^{10}, we first rewrite this number as 64×10^9 so that the exponent (9) is an integral multiple of the root 3:

$$\sqrt[3]{6.4 \times 10^{10}} = \sqrt[3]{64 \times 10^9} = (64)^{1/3} \times 10^{9/3} = 4.0 \times 10^3$$

Scientific Notation and Electronic Calculators

With a scientific calculator you can carry out calculations in scientific notation. You should consult the instruction manual for your particular calculator to learn how to enter and manipulate numbers expressed in an exponential format. On most calculators, you enter the number $A \times 10^n$ by (i) entering the number A, (ii) pressing a key labeled EXP or EE, and (iii) entering the exponent n. If the exponent is negative, you press a key labeled $+/-$ before entering the value of n. (Note that you do not enter the number 10.) The calculator displays the number $A \times 10^n$ with the number A on the left followed by some space and then the exponent n. For example,

$$4.625 \times 10^2 \quad \text{is displayed as} \quad 4.625 \quad 02$$

To add, subtract, multiply, or divide exponential numbers, use the same sequence of keystrokes as you would in working with ordinary numbers. When you add or subtract on a calculator, the numbers need not have the same exponent; the calculator automatically takes account of the different exponents. Remember, though, that the calculator often gives more digits in the answer than the allowed number of significant figures. It's sometimes helpful to outline the calculation on paper, as in the preceding examples, in order to keep track of the number of significant figures.

Most calculators have x^2 and $\sqrt{x}$ keys for squaring a number and finding its square root. Just enter the number and press the appropriate key. You probably have a y^x (or a^x) key for raising a number to a power. To raise 4.625×10^2 to the 3rd power, for example, use the following keystrokes: (i) enter the number 4.625×10^2 in the usual way, (ii) press the y^x key, (iii) enter the power 3, and (iv) press the $=$ key. The result is displayed as 9.8931641 07, but it must be rounded to 4 significant figures. Therefore, $(4.625 \times 10^2)^3 = 9.893 \times 10^7$.

To take the mth root of a number, raise the number to the power $1/m$. For example, to take the 5th root of 4.52×10^{11}, use the following keystrokes: (i) enter the number 4.52×10^{11}, (ii) press the y^x key, (iii) enter the number 5 (for the 5th root), (iv) press the $1/x$ key (to convert the 5th root to the power 1/5), and (v) press the $=$ key. The result is

$$\sqrt[5]{4.52 \times 10^{11}} = (4.52 \times 10^{11})^{1/5} = 2.14 \times 10^2$$

The calculator is able to handle the nonintegral exponent 11/5, and there is therefore no need to enter the number as 45.2×10^{10} so that the exponent is an integral multiple of the root 5.

▶ **PROBLEM A.1** Perform the following calculations, expressing the result in scientific notation with the correct number of significant figures. (You don't need a calculator for these.)

(a) $(1.50 \times 10^4) + (5.04 \times 10^3)$ **(b)** $(2.5 \times 10^{-2}) - (5.0 \times 10^{-3})$

(c) $(4.0 \times 10^4)^2$ **(d)** $\sqrt[3]{8 \times 10^{12}}$ **(e)** $\sqrt{2.5 \times 10^5}$

ANSWERS:

(a) 2.00×10^4 **(b)** 2.0×10^{-2} **(c)** 1.6×10^9 **(d)** 2×10^4 **(e)** $\pm 5.0 \times 10^2$

▶ **PROBLEM A.2** Perform the following calculations, expressing the result in scientific notation with the correct number of significant figures. (Use a calculator for these.)

(a) $(9.72 \times 10^{-1}) + (3.4823 \times 10^2)$ **(b)** $(3.772 \times 10^3) - (2.891 \times 10^4)$

(c) $(7.62 \times 10^{-3})^4$ **(d)** $\sqrt[3]{8.2 \times 10^7}$ **(e)** $\sqrt[5]{3.47 \times 10^{-12}}$

ANSWERS:

(a) 3.4920×10^2 **(b)** -2.514×10^4 **(c)** 3.37×10^{-9}

(d) 4.3×10^2 **(e)** 5.11×10^{-3}

A.2 LOGARITHMS

Common Logarithms

Any positive number x can be written as 10 raised to some power z—that is, $x = 10^z$. The exponent z is called the *common*, or *base 10*, *logarithm* of the number x and is denoted $\log_{10} x$, or simply $\log x$:

$$x = 10^z \qquad \log x = z$$

For example, 100 can be written as 10^2, and log 100 is therefore equal to 2:

$$100 = 10^2 \qquad \log 100 = 2$$

Similarly,

$$10 = 10^1 \qquad \log 10 = 1$$
$$1 = 10^0 \qquad \log 1 = 0$$
$$0.1 = 10^{-1} \qquad \log 0.1 = -1$$

In general, the logarithm of a number x is the power z to which 10 must be raised to equal the number x.

As **Figure A.1** shows, the logarithm of a number greater than 1 is positive, the logarithm of 1 is zero, and the logarithm of a positive number less than 1 is negative. The logarithm of a *negative* number is undefined because 10 raised to any power is always positive ($x = 10^z > 0$).

You can use a calculator to find the logarithm of a number that is not an integral power of 10. For example, to find the logarithm of 61.2, simply enter 61.2, and press the LOG key. The logarithm should be between 1 and 2 because 61.2 is between 10^1 and 10^2. The calculator gives a value of 1.786751422, which must be rounded to 1.787 because 61.2 has three significant figures.

Significant Figures and Common Logarithms

The only significant figures in a logarithm are the digits to the right of the decimal point; the number to the left of the decimal point is an exact number related to the integral power of 10 in the exponential expression for the number whose logarithm is

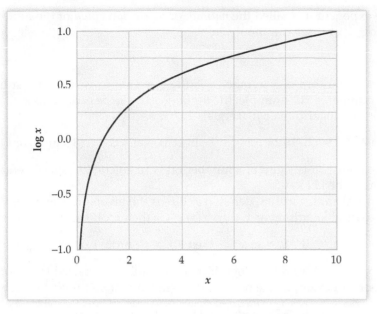

Figure A.1
Values of log x for values of x in the range 0.1 to 10.

to be found. Thus, the logarithm of 61.2, which has three significant figures, can be written as follows:

$$\log 61.2 = \log (6.12 \times 10^1) = \log 6.12 + \log 10^1 = 0.787 + 1 = 1.787$$

3 SF's	3 SF's	Exact number		3 SF's	Exact number	Exact number	3 SF's

The digit (1) to the left of the decimal point in the logarithm (1.787) is an exact number and is not a significant figure; it merely indicates the location of the decimal point in the number 61.2. There are only three significant figures in the logarithm (7, 8, 7) because 61.2 has only three significant figures. Similarly, log 61 = 1.79 (2 significant figures), and log (6 $\times$ 10¹) = 1.8 (1 significant figure).

Antilogarithms

The antilogarithm, denoted antilog, is the inverse of the common logarithm. If z is the logarithm of x, then x is the antilogarithm of z. But since x can be written as 10^z, the antilogarithm of z is 10^z:

$$\text{If } \quad z = \log x \quad \text{then} \quad x = \text{antilog } z = 10^z$$

In other words, the antilog of a number is 10 raised to a power equal to that number. For example, the antilog of 2 is $10^2 = 100$, and the antilog of 3.71 is $10^{3.71}$.

To find the value of antilog 3.71, use your calculator. If you have a 10^x key, enter 3.71 and press the 10^x key. If you have a y^x key, use the following keystrokes: (i) enter 10, (ii) press the y^x key, (iii) enter the exponent 3.71, and (iv) press the = key. If you have an INV (inverse) key, enter 3.71, press the INV key, and then press the LOG key. The calculator gives antilog 3.71 = 5.12861384×10^3, which must be rounded to 5.1×10^3 (2 significant figures) because the logarithm (3.71) has just two significant figures, the two digits to the right of the decimal point.

Natural Logarithms

The number $e = 2.718\ 28\ldots$, like $\pi = 3.141\ 59\ldots$, turns up in many scientific problems. It is therefore convenient to define a logarithm based on e, just as we defined a logarithm based on 10. Just as a number x can be written as 10^z, it can also be written as e^u. The exponent u is called the *natural*, or *base e*, *logarithm* of the number x and is denoted $\log_e x$, or more commonly, $\ln x$:

$$x = e^u \qquad \ln x = u$$

The natural logarithm of a number x is the power u to which e must be raised to equal the number x. For example, the number 10.0 can be written as $e^{2.303}$, and therefore the natural logarithm of 10.0 equals 2.303:

$$10.0 = e^{2.303} = (2.718\ 28\ldots)^{2.303} \qquad \ln 10.0 = 2.303 \qquad \text{(3 significant figures)}$$

To find the natural logarithm of a number on your calculator, simply enter the number, and press the LN key.

The natural antilogarithm, denoted antiln, is the inverse of the natural logarithm. If u is the natural logarithm of x, then $x (= e^u)$ is the natural antilogarithm of u:

$$\text{If} \quad u = \ln x \qquad \text{then} \qquad x = \text{antiln } u = e^u$$

In other words, the natural antilogarithm of a number is e raised to a power equal to that number. For example, the natural antilogarithm of 3.71 is $e^{3.71}$, which equals 41:

$$\text{antiln } 3.71 = e^{3.71} = 41 \qquad \text{(2 significant figures)}$$

Your calculator probably has an INV (inverse) key or an e^x key. To find the natural antilogarithm of a number—say, 3.71—enter 3.71, press the INV key, and then press the LN key. Alternatively, you can enter 3.71, and press the e^x key.

Some Mathematical Properties of Logarithms

Because logarithms are exponents, the algebraic properties of exponents can be used to derive the following useful relationships involving logarithms:

1. The logarithm (either common or natural) of a product xy equals the sum of the logarithm of x and the logarithm of y:

$$\log xy = \log x + \log y \qquad \ln xy = \ln x + \ln y$$

2. The logarithm of a quotient x/y equals the difference between the logarithm of x and the logarithm of y :

$$\log \frac{x}{y} = \log x - \log y \qquad \ln \frac{x}{y} = \ln x - \ln y$$

It follows from these relationships that

$$\log \frac{y}{x} = -\log \frac{x}{y} \qquad \ln \frac{y}{x} = -\ln \frac{x}{y}$$

Because $\log 1 = \ln 1 = 0$, it also follows that

$$\log \frac{1}{x} = -\log x \qquad \ln \frac{1}{x} = -\ln x$$

3. The logarithm of x raised to a power a equals a times the logarithm of x:

$$\log x^a = a \log x \qquad \ln x^a = a \ln x$$

Similarly,

$$\log x^{1/a} = \frac{1}{a} \log x \qquad \ln x^{1/a} = \frac{1}{a} \ln x$$

where

$$x^{1/a} = \sqrt[a]{x}.$$

What is the numerical relationship between the common logarithm and the natural logarithm? To derive it, we begin with the definitions of $\log x$ and $\ln x$:

$$\log x = z \qquad \text{where} \qquad x = 10^z$$
$$\log x = u \qquad \text{where} \qquad x = e^u$$

We then write $\ln x$ in terms of 10^z and make use of the property that $\ln x^a - a \ln x$:

$$\ln x = \ln 10^z = z \ln 10$$

Because $z = \log x$ and $\ln 10.0 = 2.303$, we find that the natural logarithm is 2.303 times the common logarithm:

$$\ln x = 2.303 \log x$$

Since the natural and common logarithms differ by a factor of only 2.303, the same rule can be used to find the number of significant figures in both: The only digits that are significant figures in both natural and common logarithms are those to the right of the decimal point.

▶ **PROBLEM A.3** Use a calculator to evaluate the following expressions, and round each result to the correct number of significant figures:

(a) $\log 705$ **(b)** $\ln (3.4 \times 10^{-6})$ **(c)** antilog (-2.56) **(d)** antiln 8.1

ANSWERS:

(a) 2.848   **(b)** −12.59   **(c)** 2.8×10^{-3} **(d)** 3×10^3

A.3 STRAIGHT-LINE GRAPHS AND LINEAR EQUATIONS

The results of a scientific experiment are often summarized in the form of a graph. Consider an experiment in which some property y is measured as a function of some variable x. (A real example would be measurement of the volume of a gas as a function of its temperature, but we'll use y and x to keep the discussion general.) Suppose that we obtain the following experimental data:

x	y
−1	−5
1	1
3	7
5	13

The graph in Figure A.2 shows values of x, called the independent variable, along the horizontal axis and values of y, the dependent variable, along the vertical axis. Each pair of experimental values of x and y is represented by a point on the graph. For this particular experiment, the four data points lie on a straight line.

The equation of a straight line can be written as

$$y = mx + b$$

where m is the slope of the line and b is the intercept, the value of y at the point where the line crosses the y axis—that is, the value of y when $x = 0$. The slope of the line is the change in y (Δy) for a given change in x (Δx):

$$m = \text{slope} = \frac{\Delta y}{\Delta x}$$

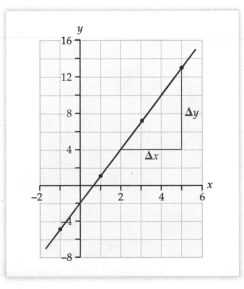

Figure A.2
A straight-line y versus x plot of the data in the table.

The right-triangle in Figure A.2 shows that y changes from 4 to 13 when x changes from 2 to 5. Therefore, the slope of the line is 3:

$$m = \text{slope} = \frac{\Delta y}{\Delta x} = \frac{13 - 4}{5 - 2} = \frac{9}{3} = 3$$

The graph shows a y intercept of -2 ($b = -2$), and the equation of the line is therefore

$$y = 3x - 2$$

An equation of the form $y = mx + b$ is called a *linear equation* because values of x and y that satisfy such an equation are the coordinates of points that lie on a straight line. We also say that y is a *linear function* of x, or that y is *directly proportional* to x. In our example, the rate of change of y is 3 times that of x.

A.4 QUADRATIC EQUATIONS

A quadratic equation is an equation that can be written in the form

$$ax^2 + bx + c = 0$$

where a, b, and c are constants. The equation contains only powers of x and is called quadratic because the highest power of x is 2. The solutions to a quadratic equation (values of x that satisfy the equation) are given by the *quadratic formula*:

$$x = \frac{-b \pm \sqrt{b^2 - 4ac}}{2a}$$

The $\pm$ indicates that there are two solutions, one given by the $+$ sign and the other given by the $-$ sign.

As an example, let's solve the equation

$$x^2 = \frac{2 - 6x}{3}$$

First, we put the equation into the form $ax^2 + bx + c = 0$ by multiplying it by 3 and moving $2 - 6x$ to the left side. The result is

$$3x^2 + 6x - 2 = 0$$

Then we apply the quadratic formula with $a = 3$, $b = 6$, and $c = -2$:

$$x = \frac{-6 \pm \sqrt{(6)^2 - 4(3)(-2)}}{2(3)}$$

$$= \frac{-6 \pm \sqrt{36 + 24}}{6} = \frac{-6 \pm \sqrt{60}}{6} = \frac{-6 \pm 7.746}{6}$$

The two solutions are

$$x = \frac{-6 + 7.746}{6} = \frac{1.746}{6} = 0.291 \quad \text{and} \quad x = \frac{-6 - 7.746}{6} = \frac{-13.746}{6} = -2.291$$

APPENDIX B

Thermodynamic Properties at 25 °C

TABLE B.1 Inorganic Substances

Substance and State	$\Delta H°_f$ (kJ/mol)	$\Delta G°_f$ (kJ/mol)	$S°$ [J/(K·mol)]	Substance and State	$\Delta H°_f$ (kJ/mol)	$\Delta G°_f$ (kJ/mol)	$S°$ [J/(K·mol)]
Aluminum				*Calcium*			
Al(s)	0	0	28.3	Ca(s)	0	0	41.4
Al(g)	330.0	289.4	164.5	Ca(g)	177.8	144.0	154.8
AlCl$_3$(s)	−704.2	−628.8	109.3	Ca^{2+}(aq)	−542.8	−553.6	−53.1
Al$_2$O$_3$(s)	1676	−1582	50.9	CaF$_2$(s)	−1228.0	−1175.6	68.5
				CaCl$_2$(s)	−795.4	−748.8	108.4
Barium				CaH$_2$(s)	−181.5	−142.5	41.4
Ba(s)	0	0	62.5	CaC$_2$(s)	−59.8	−64.8	70.0
Ba(g)	180.0	146.0	170.1	CaO(s)	−634.9	−603.3	38.1
Ba^{2+}(aq)	−537.6	−560.8	9.6	Ca(OH)$_2$(s)	−985.2	−897.5	83.4
BaCl$_2$(s)	−855.0	−806.7	123.7	CaCO$_3$(s)	−1207.6	−1129.1	91.7
BaO(s)	−548.0	−520.3	72.1	CaSO$_4$(s)	−1434.1	−1321.9	107
BaCO$_3$(s)	−1213.0	−1134.4	112.1	Ca$_3$(PO$_4$)$_2$(s)	−4120.8	−3884.7	236.0
BaSO$_4$(s)	−1473.2	−1362.2	132.2				
Beryllium							
Be(s)	0	0	9.5	*Carbon*			
BeO(s)	609.4	−580.1	13.8	C(s, graphite)	0	0	5.7
Be(OH)$_2$(s)	−902.5	−815.0	45.5	C(s, diamond)	1.9	2.9	2.4
				C(g)	716.7	671.3	158.0
Boron				CO(g)	−110.5	−137.2	197.6
B(s)	0	0	5.9	CO$_2$(g)	−393.5	−394.4	213.6
BF$_3$(g)	−1136.0	−1119.4	254.3	CO$_2$(aq)	−113.8	−386.0	117.6
BCl$_3$(g)	−403.8	−388.7	290.0	CO$_3{}^{2-}$(aq)	−677.1	−527.8	−56.9
B$_2$H$_6$(g)	36.4	87.6	232.0	HCO$_3{}^-$(aq)	−692.0	−586.8	91.2
B$_2$O$_3$(s)	−1273.5	−1194.3	54.0	H$_2$CO$_3$(aq)	−699.7	−623.2	187.4
H$_3$BO$_3$(s)	−1094.3	−968.9	90.0	HCN(l)	108.9	125.0	112.8
Bromine				HCN(g)	135.1	124.7	201.7
Br(g)	111.9	82.4	174.9	CS$_2$(l)	89.0	64.6	151.3
Br$^-$(aq)	−121.5	−104.0	82.4	CS$_2$(g)	116.7	67.1	237.7
Br$_2$(l)	0	0	152.2	COCl$_2$(g)	−219.1	−204.9	283.4
Br$_2$(g)	30.9	3.14	245.4				
HBr(g)	−36.3	−53.4	198.6				
Cadmium				*Cesium*			
Cd(s)	0	0	51.8	Cs(s)	0	0	85.2
Cd(g)	111.8	77.3	167.6	Cs(g)	76.5	49.6	175.6
Cd^{2+}(aq)	−75.9	−77.6	−73.2	Cs$^+$(aq)	−258.3	−292.0	133.1
CdCl$_2$(s)	−391.5	−343.9	115.3	CsF(s)	−553.5	−525.5	92.8
CdO(s)	−258.4	−228.7	54.8	CsCl(s)	−443.0	−414.5	101.2
CdS(s)	−161.9	−156.5	64.9	CsBr(s)	−405.8	−391.4	113.1
CdSO$_4$(s)	−933.3	−822.7	123.0	CsI(s)	−346.6	−340.6	123.1

(continued)

A-9

TABLE B.1   Inorganic Substances (*continued*)

Substance and State	$\Delta H°_f$ (kJ/mol)	$\Delta G°_f$ (kJ/mol)	$S°$ [J/(K · mol)]	Substance and State	$\Delta H°_f$ (kJ/mol)	$\Delta G°_f$ (kJ/mol)	$S°$ [J/(K · mol)]
Chlorine				*Iron*			
$Cl(g)$	121.3	105.3	165.1	$Fe(s)$	0	0	27.3
$Cl^-(aq)$	−167.2	−131.3	56.5	$Fe(g)$	416.3	370.3	180.5
$Cl_2(g)$	0	0	223.0	$FeCl_2(s)$	−341.8	−302.3	118.0
$HCl(g)$	−92.3	−95.3	186.8	$FeCl_3(s)$	−399.5	−334.0	142.3
$HCl(aq)$	−167.2	−131.2	56.5	$FeO(s)$	−272	−255	61
$ClO_2(g)$	102.5	120.5	256.7	$Fe_2O_3(s)$	−824.2	−742.2	87.4
$Cl_2O(g)$	80.3	97.9	266.1	$Fe_3O_4(s)$	−1118	−1015	146
Chromium				$FeS_2(s)$	−178.2	−166.9	52.9
$Cr(s)$	0	0	23.8	*Lead*			
$Cr(g)$	396.6	351.8	174.4	$Pb(s)$	0	0	64.8
$Cr_2O_3(s)$	−1140	−1058	81.2	$Pb(g)$	195.2	162.2	175.3
Cobalt				$PbCl_2(s)$	−359.4	−314.1	136.0
$Co(s)$	0	0	30.0	$PbBr_2(s)$	−278.7	−261.9	161.5
$Co(g)$	424.7	380.3	179.4	$PbO(s)$	−217.3	−187.9	68.7
$CoO(s)$	−237.9	−214.2	53.0	$PbO_2(s)$	−277	−217.4	68.6
Copper				$PbS(s)$	−100	−98.7	91.2
$Cu(s)$	0	0	33.1	$PbCO_3(s)$	−699.1	−625.5	131.0
$Cu(g)$	337.4	297.7	166.3	$PbSO_4(s)$	−919.9	−813.2	148.6
$Cu^{2+}(aq)$	64.8	65.5	−99.6	*Lithium*			
$CuCl(s)$	−137.2	−119.9	86.2	$Li(s)$	0	0	29.1
$CuCl_2(s)$	−220.1	−175.7	108.1	$Li(g)$	159.3	126.6	138.7
$CuO(s)$	−157.3	−129.7	42.6	$Li^+(aq)$	−278.5	−293.3	13
$Cu_2O(s)$	−168.6	−146.0	93.1	$LiF(s)$	−616.0	−587.7	35.7
$CuS(s)$	−53.1	−53.6	66.5	$LiCl(s)$	−408.6	−384.4	59.3
$Cu_2S(s)$	−79.5	−86.2	120.9	$LiBr(s)$	−351.2	−342.0	74.3
$CuSO_4(s)$	−771.4	−662.2	109.2	$LiI(s)$	−270.4	−270.3	86.8
Fluorine				$Li_2O(s)$	−597.9	−561.2	37.6
$F(g)$	79.4	62.3	158.7	$LiOH(s)$	−487.5	−441.5	42.8
$F^-(aq)$	−332.6	−278.8	−13.8	*Magnesium*			
$F_2(g)$	0	0	202.7	$Mg(s)$	0	0	32.7
$HF(g)$	−273.3	−275.4	173.7	$Mg(g)$	147.1	112.5	148.6
Hydrogen				$MgCl_2(s)$	−641.6	−591.8	89.6
$H(g)$	218.0	203.3	114.6	$MgO(s)$	−601.7	−569.4	26.9
$H^+(aq)$	0	0	0	$MgCO_3(s)$	−1096	−1012	65.7
$H_2(g)$	0	0	130.6	$MgSO_4(s)$	−1284.9	−1170.6	91.6
$OH^-(aq)$	−230.0	−157.3	−10.8	*Manganese*			
$H_2O(l)$	−285.8	−237.2	69.9	$Mn(s)$	0	0	32.0
$H_2O(g)$	−241.8	−228.6	188.7	$Mn(g)$	280.7	238.5	173.6
$H_2O_2(l)$	−187.8	−120.4	110	$MnO(s)$	−385.2	−362.9	59.7
$H_2O_2(g)$	−136.3	−105.6	232.6	$MnO_2(s)$	−520.0	−465.1	53.1
$H_2O_2(aq)$	−191.2	−134.1	144	*Mercury*			
Iodine				$Hg(l)$	0	0	76.0
$I(g)$	106.8	70.3	180.7	$Hg(g)$	61.32	31.85	174.8
$I^-(aq)$	−55.2	−51.6	111	$Hg^{2+}(aq)$	171.1	164.4	−32.2
$I_2(s)$	0	0	116.1	$Hg_2^{2+}(aq)$	172.4	153.5	84.5
$I_2(g)$	62.4	19.4	260.6	$HgCl_2(s)$	−224.3	−178.6	146.0
$HI(g)$	26.5	1.7	206.5	$Hg_2Cl_2(s)$	−265.4	−210.7	191.6

TABLE B.1 Inorganic Substances (*continued*)

Substance and State	$\Delta H°_f$ (kJ/mol)	$\Delta G°_f$ (kJ/mol)	$S°$ [J/(K·mol)]	Substance and State	$\Delta H°_f$ (kJ/mol)	$\Delta G°_f$ (kJ/mol)	$S°$ [J/(K·mol)]
$HgO(s)$	−90.8	−58.6	70.3	*Potassium*			
$HgS(s)$	−58.2	−50.6	82.4	$K(s)$	0	0	64.7
				$K(g)$	89.2	60.6	160.2
Nickel				$K^+(aq)$	−252.4	−283.3	102.5
$Ni(s)$	0	0	29.9	$KF(s)$	−567.3	−537.8	66.6
$Ni(g)$	429.7	384.5	182.1	$KCl(s)$	−436.5	−408.5	82.6
$NiCl_2(s)$	−305.3	−259.1	97.7	$KBr(s)$	−393.8	−380.7	95.9
$NiO(s)$	−240	−212	38.0	$KI(s)$	−327.9	−324.9	106.3
$NiS(s)$	−82.0	−79.5	53.0	$K_2O(s)$	−361.5		
				$K_2O_2(s)$	−494.1	−425.1	102.1
Nitrogen				$KO_2(s)$	−284.9	−239.4	116.7
$N(g)$	472.7	455.6	153.2	$KOH(s)$	−424.6	−379.4	81.2
$N_2(g)$	0	0	191.5	$KOH(aq)$	−482.4	−440.5	91.6
$NH_3(g)$	−46.1	−16.5	192.3	$KClO_3(s)$	−397.7	−296.3	143.1
$NH_3(aq)$	−80.3	−26.6	111	$KClO_4(s)$	−432.8	−303.1	151.0
$NH_4^+(aq)$	−132.5	−79.4	113	$KNO_3(s)$	−494.6	−394.9	133.1
$N_2H_4(l)$	50.6	149.2	121.2				
$N_2H_4(g)$	95.4	159.3	238.4	*Rubidium*			
$NO(g)$	91.3	87.6	210.7	$Rb(s)$	0	0	76.8
$NO_2(g)$	33.2	51.3	240.0	$Rb(g)$	80.9	53.1	170.0
$N_2O(g)$	82.0	104.2	219.7	$Rb^+(aq)$	−251.2	−284.0	121.5
$N_2O_4(g)$	11.1	99.8	304.3	$RbF(s)$	−557.7		
$N_2O_5(g)$	13.3	117.1	355.6	$RbCl(s)$	−435.4	−407.8	95.9
$NOCl(g)$	51.7	66.1	261.6	$RbBr(s)$	−394.6	−381.8	110.0
$NO_2Cl(g)$	12.6	54.4	272.1	$RbI(s)$	−333.8	328.9	118.4
$HNO_3(l)$	−174.1	−80.8	155.6				
$HNO_3(g)$	−133.9	−73.5	266.8	*Selenium*			
$HNO_2(aq)$	−119	−50.6	136	$Se(s, black)$	0	0	42.44
$HNO_3(aq)$	−207.4	−111.3	146.4	$H_2Se(g)$	29.7	15.9	219.0
$NO_3^-(aq)$	−207.4	−111.3	146.4				
$NH_4Cl(s)$	−314.4	−202.9	94.6	*Silicon*			
$NH_4NO_3(s)$	−365.6	−184.0	151.1	$Si(s)$	0	0	18.8
				$Si(g)$	450.0	405.5	167.9
Oxygen				$SiF_4(g)$	−1615.0	−1572.8	282.7
$O(g)$	249.2	231.7	160.9	$SiCl_4(l)$	−687.0	−619.8	239.7
$O_2(g)$	0	0	205.0	$SiO_2(s, quartz)$	−910.7	−856.3	41.5
$O_3(g)$	143	163	238.8				
				Silver			
Phosphorus				$Ag(s)$	0	0	42.6
$P(s, white)$	0	0	41.1	$Ag(g)$	284.9	246.0	173.0
$P(s, red)$	−18	−12	22.8	$Ag^+(aq)$	105.6	77.1	72.7
$P_4(g)$	58.9	24.5	279.9	$AgF(s)$	−204.6		
$PH_3(g)$	5.4	13.5	210.1	$AgCl(s)$	−127.1	−109.8	96.2
$PCl_3(l)$	−319.7	−272.3	217.1	$AgBr(s)$	−100.4	−96.9	107.1
$PCl_3(g)$	−287.0	−267.8	311.7	$AgI(s)$	−61.8	−66.2	115.5
$PCl_5(s)$	−443.5			$Ag_2O(s)$	−31.1	−11.2	121.3
$PCl_5(g)$	−374.9	−305.0	364.5	$Ag_2S(s)$	−32.6	−40.7	144.0
$P_4O_{10}(s)$	−2984	−2698	228.9	$AgNO_3(s)$	−124.4	−33.4	140.9
$PO_4^{3-}(aq)$	−1277.4	−1018.7	220.5				
$HPO_4^{2-}(aq)$	−1292.1	−1089.2	−33.5	*Sodium*			
$H_2PO_4^-(aq)$	−1296.3	−1130.2	90.4	$Na(s)$	0	0	51.2
$H_3PO_4(s)$	−1284.4	−1124.3	110.5	$Na(g)$	107.3	76.8	153.6

(*continued*)

TABLE B.1   Inorganic Substances (*continued*)

Substance and State	$\Delta H°_f$ (kJ/mol)	$\Delta G°_f$ (kJ/mol)	$S°$ [J/(K · mol)]	Substance and State	$\Delta H°_f$ (kJ/mol)	$\Delta G°_f$ (kJ/mol)	$S°$ [J/(K · mol)]
$Na^+(aq)$	−240.1	−261.9	59.0	*Tin*			
$NaF(s)$	−576.6	−546.3	51.1	Sn(s, white)	0	0	51.2
$NaCl(s)$	−411.2	−384.2	72.1	Sn(s, gray)	−2.1	0.1	44.1
$NaBr(s)$	−361.1	−349.0	86.8	$Sn(g)$	301.2	266.2	168.4
$NaI(s)$	−287.8	−286.1	98.5	$SnCl_4(l)$	−511.3	−440.1	258.6
$NaH(s)$	−56.3	−33.5	40.0	$SnCl_4(g)$	−471.5	−432.2	365.8
$Na_2O(s)$	−414.2	−375.5	75.1	$SnO(s)$	−280.7	−251.9	57.4
$Na_2O_2(s)$	−510.9	−447.7	95.0	$SnO_2(s)$	−577.6	−515.8	49.0
$NaO_2(s)$	−260.2	−218.4	115.9	*Titanium*			
$NaOH(s)$	−425.6	−379.5	64.5	Ti(s)	0	0	30.6
$NaOH(aq)$	−470.1	−419.2	48.2	$Ti(g)$	473.0	428.4	180.2
$Na_2CO_3(s)$	−1130.7	−1044.5	135.0	$TiCl_4(l)$	−804.2	−737.2	252.3
$NaHCO_3(s)$	−950.8	−851.0	102	$TiCl_4(g)$	−763.2	−726.3	353.2
$NaNO_3(s)$	−467.9	−367.0	116.5	$TiO_2(s)$	−944.0	−888.8	50.6
$NaNO_3(aq)$	−447.5	−373.2	205.4	*Tungsten*			
$Na_2SO_4(s)$	−1387.1	−1270.2	149.6	W(s)	0	0	32.6
Sulfur				$W(g)$	849.4	807.1	174.0
S(s, rhombic)	0	0	31.8	$WO_3(s)$	−842.9	−764.0	75.9
S(s, monoclinic)	0.3			*Zinc*			
$S(g)$	277.2	236.7	167.7	Zn(s)	0	0	41.6
$S_2(g)$	128.6	79.7	228.2	$Zn(g)$	130.4	94.8	160.9
$H_2S(g)$	−20.6	−33.6	205.7	$Zn^{2+}(aq)$	−153.9	−147.1	−112.1
$H_2S(aq)$	−39.7	−27.9	121	$ZnCl_2(s)$	−415.1	−369.4	111.5
$HS^-(aq)$	−17.6	12.1	62.8	$ZnO(s)$	−350.5	−320.5	43.7
$SO_2(g)$	−296.8	−300.2	248.1	$ZnS(s)$	−206.0	−201.3	57.7
$SO_3(g)$	−395.7	−371.1	256.6	$ZnSO_4(s)$	−982.8	−871.5	110.5
$H_2SO_4(l)$	−814.0	−690.1	156.9				
$H_2SO_4(aq)$	−909.3	−744.6	20				
$HSO_4^-(aq)$	−887.3	−756.0	132				
$SO_4^{2-}(aq)$	−909.3	−744.6	20				

TABLE B.2   Organic Substances

Substance and State	Formula	$\Delta H°_f$ (kJ/mol)	$\Delta G°_f$ (kJ/mol)	$S°$ [J/(K · mol)]
Acetaldehyde(g)	CH_3CHO	−166.2	−133.0	263.8
Acetic acid(l)	CH_3CO_2H	−484.5	−390	160
Acetylene(g)	C_2H_2	227.4	209.9	200.8
Benzene(l)	C_6H_6	49.1	124.5	173.4
Butane(g)	C_4H_{10}	−126	−17	310
Carbon tetrachloride(l)	CCl_4	−135.4	−65.3	216.4
Dichloroethane(l)	CH_2ClCH_2Cl	−165.2	−79.6	208.5
Ethane(g)	C_2H_6	−84.0	−32.0	229.1
Ethanol(l)	C_2H_5OH	−277.7	−174.9	161
Ethanol(g)	C_2H_5OH	−234.8	−167.9	281.5
Ethylene(g)	C_2H_4	52.3	68.1	219.5
Ethylene oxide(g)	C_2H_4O	−52.6	−13.1	242.4
Formaldehyde(g)	$HCHO$	−108.6	−102.5	218.8
Formic acid(l)	HCO_2H	−424.7	−361.4	129.0
Glucose(s)	$C_6H_{12}O_6$	−1273.3	−910	209.2
Methane(g)	CH_4	74.8	−50.8	186.2
Methanol(l)	CH_3OH	−239.2	−166.6	127
Methanol(g)	CH_3OH	−201.0	−162.3	239.8
Propane(g)	C_3H_8	−103.8	−23.4	270.2
Vinyl chloride(g)	$CH_2{=}CHCl$	35	51.9	263.9

Equilibrium Constants at 25 °C

TABLE C.1   Acid-Dissociation Constants at 25 °C

Acid	Formula	K_{a1}	K_{a2}	K_{a3}
Acetic	CH_3CO_2H	1.8×10^{-5}		
Acetylsalicylic	$C_9H_8O_4$	3.0×10^{-4}		
Arsenic	H_3AsO_4	5.6×10^{-3}	1.7×10^{-7}	4.0×10^{-12}
Arsenious	H_3AsO_3	6×10^{-10}		
Ascorbic	$C_6H_8O_6$	8.0×10^{-5}		
Benzoic	$C_6H_5CO_2H$	6.5×10^{-5}		
Boric	H_3BO_3	5.8×10^{-10}		
Carbonic	H_2CO_3	4.3×10^{-7}	5.6×10^{-11}	
Chloroacetic	CH_2ClCO_2H	1.4×10^{-3}		
Citric	$C_6H_8O_7$	7.1×10^{-4}	1.7×10^{-5}	4.1×10^{-7}
Formic	HCO_2H	1.8×10^{-4}		
Hydrazoic	HN_3	1.9×10^{-5}		
Hydrocyanic	HCN	4.9×10^{-10}		
Hydrofluoric	HF	3.5×10^{-4}		
Hydrogen peroxide	H_2O_2	2.4×10^{-12}		
Hydrosulfuric	H_2S	1.0×10^{-7}	$\sim 10^{-19}$	
Hypobromous	$HOBr$	2.0×10^{-9}		
Hypochlorous	$HOCl$	3.5×10^{-8}		
Hypoiodous	HOI	2.3×10^{-11}		
Iodic	HIO_3	1.7×10^{-1}		
Lactic	$HC_3H_5O_3$	1.4×10^{-4}		
Nitrous	HNO_2	4.5×10^{-4}		
Oxalic	$H_2C_2O_4$	5.9×10^{-2}	6.4×10^{-5}	
Phenol	C_6H_5OH	1.3×10^{-10}		
Phosphoric	H_3PO_4	7.5×10^{-3}	6.2×10^{-8}	4.8×10^{-13}
Phosphorous	H_3PO_3	1.0×10^{-2}	2.6×10^{-7}	
Saccharin	$C_7H_5NO_3S$	2.1×10^{-12}		
Selenic	H_2SeO_4	Very large	1.2×10^{-2}	
Selenious	H_2SeO_3	3.5×10^{-2}	5×10^{-8}	
Sulfuric	H_2SO_4	Very large	1.2×10^{-2}	
Sulfurous	H_2SO_3	1.5×10^{-2}	6.3×10^{-8}	
Tartaric	$C_4H_6O_6$	1.0×10^{-3}	4.6×10^{-5}	
Water	H_2O	1.8×10^{-16}		

TABLE C.2 Acid-Dissociation Constants at 25 °C for Hydrated Metal Cations

Cation	K_a	Cation	K_a
$Fe^{2+}(aq)$	3.2×10^{-10}	$Be^{2+}(aq)$	3×10^{-7}
$Co^{2+}(aq)$	1.3×10^{-9}	$Al^{3+}(aq)$	1.4×10^{-5}
$Ni^{2+}(aq)$	2.5×10^{-11}	$Cr^{3+}(aq)$	1.6×10^{-4}
$Zn^{2+}(aq)$	2.5×10^{-10}	$Fe^{3+}(aq)$	6.3×10^{-3}

Note: As an example, K_a for $Fe^{2+}(aq)$ is the equilibrium constant for the reaction

$$Fe(H_2O)_6^{2+}(aq) + H_2O(l) \rightleftharpoons H_3O^+(aq) + Fe(H_2O)_5(OH)^+(aq)$$

TABLE C.3 Base-Dissociation Constants at 25 °C

Base	Formula	K_b
Ammonia	NH_3	1.8×10^{-5}
Aniline	$C_6H_5NH_2$	4.3×10^{-10}
Codeine	$C_{18}H_{21}NO_3$	1.6×10^{-6}
Dimethylamine	$(CH_3)_2NH$	5.4×10^{-4}
Ethylamine	$C_2H_5NH_2$	6.4×10^{-4}
Hydrazine	N_2H_4	8.9×10^{-7}
Hydroxylamine	NH_2OH	9.1×10^{-9}
Methylamine	CH_3NH_2	3.7×10^{-4}
Morphine	$C_{17}H_{19}NO_3$	1.6×10^{-6}
Piperidine	$C_5H_{11}N$	1.3×10^{-3}
Propylamine	$C_3H_7NH_2$	5.1×10^{-4}
Pyridine	C_5H_5N	1.8×10^{-9}
Strychnine	$C_{21}H_{22}N_2O_2$	1.8×10^{-6}
Trimethylamine	$(CH_3)_3N$	6.5×10^{-5}

TABLE C.4 Solubility Product Constants at 25 °C

Compound	Formula	K_{sp}
Aluminum hydroxide	$Al(OH)_3$	1.9×10^{-33}
Barium carbonate	$BaCO_3$	2.6×10^{-9}
Barium chromate	$BaCrO_4$	1.2×10^{-10}
Barium fluoride	BaF_2	1.8×10^{-7}
Barium hydroxide	$Ba(OH)_2$	5.0×10^{-3}
Barium sulfate	$BaSO_4$	1.1×10^{-10}
Cadmium carbonate	$CdCO_3$	1.0×10^{-12}
Cadmium hydroxide	$Cd(OH)_2$	5.3×10^{-15}
Calcium carbonate	$CaCO_3$	5.0×10^{-9}
Calcium fluoride	CaF_2	3.5×10^{-11}
Calcium hydroxide	$Ca(OH)_2$	4.7×10^{-6}
Calcium phosphate	$Ca_3(PO_4)_2$	2.1×10^{-33}
Calcium sulfate	$CaSO_4$	7.1×10^{-5}
Chromium(III) hydroxide	$Cr(OH)_3$	6.7×10^{-31}
Cobalt(II) hydroxide	$Co(OH)_2$	5.9×10^{-15}
Copper(I) bromide	$CuBr$	6.3×10^{-9}
Copper(I) chloride	$CuCl$	1.7×10^{-7}
Copper(II) carbonate	$CuCO_3$	2.5×10^{-10}
Copper(II) hydroxide	$Cu(OH)_2$	1.6×10^{-19}
Copper(II) phosphate	$Cu_3(PO_4)_2$	1.4×10^{-37}
Iron(II) hydroxide	$Fe(OH)_2$	4.9×10^{-17}
Iron(III) hydroxide	$Fe(OH)_3$	2.6×10^{-39}
Lead(II) bromide	$PbBr_2$	6.6×10^{-6}
Lead(II) chloride	$PbCl_2$	1.2×10^{-5}
Lead(II) chromate	$PbCrO_4$	2.8×10^{-13}
Lead(II) iodide	PbI_2	8.5×10^{-9}
Lead(II) sulfate	$PbSO_4$	1.8×10^{-8}
Magnesium carbonate	$MgCO_3$	6.8×10^{-6}
Magnesium fluoride	MgF_2	7.4×10^{-11}
Magnesium hydroxide	$Mg(OH)_2$	5.6×10^{-12}
Manganese(II) carbonate	$MnCO_3$	2.2×10^{-11}
Manganese(II) hydroxide	$Mn(OH)_2$	2.1×10^{-13}
Mercury(I) bromide	Hg_2Br_2	6.4×10^{-23}
Mercury(I) chloride	Hg_2Cl_2	1.4×10^{-18}
Mercury(I) iodide	Hg_2I_2	5.3×10^{-29}
Mercury(II) hydroxide	$Hg(OH)_2$	3.1×10^{-26}
Nickel(II) hydroxide	$Ni(OH)_2$	5.5×10^{-16}
Silver bromide	$AgBr$	5.4×10^{-13}
Silver carbonate	Ag_2CO_3	8.4×10^{-12}
Silver chloride	$AgCl$	1.8×10^{-10}
Silver chromate	Ag_2CrO_4	1.1×10^{-12}
Silver cyanide	$AgCN$	6.0×10^{-17}
Silver iodide	AgI	8.5×10^{-17}
Silver sulfate	Ag_2SO_4	1.2×10^{-5}
Silver sulfite	Ag_2SO_3	1.5×10^{-14}
Strontium carbonate	$SrCO_3$	5.6×10^{-10}
Tin(II) hydroxide	$Sn(OH)_2$	5.4×10^{-27}
Zinc carbonate	$ZnCO_3$	1.2×10^{-10}
Zinc hydroxide	$Zn(OH)_2$	4.1×10^{-17}

TABLE C.5 Solubility Products in Acid (K_{spa}) at 25 °C

Compound	Formula	K_{spa}
Cadmium sulfide	CdS	8×10^{-7}
Cobalt(II) sulfide	CoS	3
Copper(II) sulfide	CuS	6×10^{-16}
Iron(II) sulfide	FeS	6×10^2
Lead(II) sulfide	PbS	3×10^{-7}
Manganese(II) sulfide	MnS	3×10^7
Mercury(II) sulfide	HgS	2×10^{-32}
Nickel(II) sulfide	NiS	8×10^{-1}
Silver sulfide	Ag_2S	6×10^{-30}
Tin(II) sulfide	SnS	1×10^{-5}
Zinc sulfide	ZnS	3×10^{-2}

Note: K_{spa} for MS is the equilibrium constant for the reaction

$$MS(s) + 2\,H_3O^+(aq) \rightleftharpoons M^{2+}(aq) + H_2S(aq) + 2\,H_2O(l)$$

We use K_{spa} for metal sulfides rather than K_{sp} because the traditional values of K_{sp} are now known to be incorrect since they are based on a K_{a2} value for H_2S that is greatly in error (see R. J. Myers, *J. Chem. Educ.*, **1986**, 63, 687–690).

TABLE C.6 Formation Constants for Complex Ions at 25 °C

Complex Ion	K_f	Complex Ion	K_f
$Ag(CN)_2^-$	3.0×10^{20}	$Ga(OH)_4^-$	3×10^{39}
$Ag(NH_3)_2^+$	1.7×10^7	$Ni(CN)_4^{2-}$	1.7×10^{30}
$Ag(S_2O_3)_2^{3-}$	4.7×10^{13}	$Ni(NH_3)_6^{2+}$	2.0×10^8
$Al(OH)_4^-$	3×10^{33}	$Ni(en)_3^{2+}$	4×10^{17}
$Be(OH)_4^{2-}$	4×10^{18}	$Pb(OH)_3^-$	8×10^{13}
$Cr(OH)_4^-$	8×10^{29}	$Sn(OH)_3^-$	3×10^{25}
$Cu(NH_3)_4^{2+}$	5.6×10^{11}	$Zn(CN)_4^{2-}$	4.7×10^{19}
$Fe(CN)_6^{4-}$	3×10^{35}	$Zn(NH_3)_4^{2+}$	7.8×10^8
$Fe(CN)_6^{3-}$	4×10^{43}	$Zn(OH)_4^{2-}$	3×10^{15}

APPENDIX D

Standard Reduction Potentials at 25 °C

Half-Reaction	$E°$ (V)
$F_2(g) + 2\,e^- \longrightarrow 2\,F^-(aq)$	2.87
$O_3(g) + 2\,H^+(aq) + 2\,e^- \longrightarrow O_2(g) + H_2O(l)$	2.08
$S_2O_8{}^{2-}(aq) + 2\,e^- \longrightarrow 2\,SO_4{}^{2-}(aq)$	2.01
$Co^{3+}(aq) + e^- \longrightarrow Co^{2+}(aq)$	1.81
$H_2O_2(aq) + 2\,H^+(aq) + 2\,e^- \longrightarrow 2\,H_2O(l)$	1.78
$Ce^{4+}(aq) + e^- \longrightarrow Ce^{3+}(aq)$	1.72
$MnO_4{}^-(aq) + 4\,H^+(aq) + 3\,e^- \longrightarrow MnO_2(s) + 2\,H_2O(l)$	1.68
$PbO_2(s) + 3\,H^+(aq) + HSO_4{}^-(aq) + 2\,e^- \longrightarrow PbSO_4(s) + 2\,H_2O(l)$	1.628
$2\,HClO\,(aq) + 2\,H^+(aq) + 2\,e^- \longrightarrow Cl_2(g) + 2\,H_2O(l)$	1.61
$Mn^{3+}(aq) + e^- \longrightarrow Mn^{2+}(aq)$	1.54
$MnO_4{}^-(aq) + 8\,H^+(aq) + 5\,e^- \longrightarrow Mn^{2+}(aq) + 4\,H_2O(l)$	1.51
$2\,BrO_3{}^-(aq) + 12\,H^+(aq) + 10\,e^- \longrightarrow Br_2(l) + 6\,H_2O(l)$	1.48
$ClO_3{}^-(aq) + 6\,H^+(aq) + 5\,e^- \longrightarrow 1/2\,Cl_2(g) + 3\,H_2O(l)$	1.47
$Au^{3+}(aq) + 2\,e^- \longrightarrow Au^+(aq)$	1.40
$Cl_2(g) + 2\,e^- \longrightarrow 2\,Cl^-(aq)$	1.36
$Cr_2O_7{}^{2-}(aq) + 14\,H^+(aq) + 6\,e^- \longrightarrow 2\,Cr^{3+}(aq) + 7\,H_2O(l)$	1.36
$O_2(g) + 4\,H^+(aq) + 4\,e^- \longrightarrow 2\,H_2O(l)$	1.23
$MnO_2(s) + 4\,H^+(aq) + 2\,e^- \longrightarrow Mn^{2+}(aq) + 2\,H_2O(l)$	1.22
$2\,IO_3{}^-(aq) + 12\,H^+(aq) + 10\,e^- \longrightarrow I_2(s) + 6\,H_2O(l)$	1.20
$Br_2(l) + 2\,e^- \longrightarrow 2\,Br^-(aq)$	1.09
$HNO_2(aq) + H^+(aq) + e^- \longrightarrow NO(g) + H_2O(l)$	0.98
$NO_3{}^-(aq) + 4\,H^+(aq) + 3\,e^- \longrightarrow NO(g) + 2\,H_2O(l)$	0.96
$2\,Hg^{2+}(aq) + 2\,e^- \longrightarrow Hg_2{}^{2+}(aq)$	0.92
$HO_2{}^-(aq) + H_2O(l) + 2\,e^- \longrightarrow 3\,OH^-(aq)$	0.88
$Hg^{2+}(aq) + 2\,e^- \longrightarrow Hg(l)$	0.85
$ClO^-(aq) + H_2O(l) + 2\,e^- \longrightarrow Cl^-(aq) + 2\,OH^-(aq)$	0.84
$Ag^+(aq) + e^- \longrightarrow Ag(s)$	0.80
$Hg_2{}^{2+}(aq) + 2\,e^- \longrightarrow 2\,Hg(l)$	0.80
$NO_3{}^-(aq) + 2\,H^+(aq) + e^- \longrightarrow NO_2(g) + H_2O(l)$	0.79
$Fe^{3+}(aq) + e^- \longrightarrow Fe^{2+}(aq)$	0.77
$O_2(g) + 2\,H^+(aq) + 2\,e^- \longrightarrow H_2O_2(aq)$	0.70
$MnO_4{}^-(aq) + e^- \longrightarrow MnO_4{}^{2-}(aq)$	0.56
$H_3AsO_4(aq) + 2\,H^+(aq) + 2\,e^- \longrightarrow H_3AsO_3(aq) + H_2O(l)$	0.56
$I_2(s) + 2\,e^- \longrightarrow 2\,I^-(aq)$	0.54
$Cu^+(aq) + e^- \longrightarrow Cu(s)$	0.52
$H_2SO_3(aq) + 4\,H^+(aq) + 4\,e^- \longrightarrow S(s) + 3\,H_2O(l)$	0.45
$O_2(g) + 2\,H_2O(l) + 4\,e^- \longrightarrow 4\,OH^-(aq)$	0.40
$Cu^{2+}(aq) + 2\,e^- \longrightarrow Cu(s)$	0.34
$BiO^+(aq) + 2\,H^+(aq) + 3\,e^- \longrightarrow Bi(s) + H_2O(l)$	0.32

Half-Reaction	$E°$ (V)
$Hg_2Cl_2(s) + 2 e^- \longrightarrow 2 Hg(l) + 2 Cl^-(aq)$	0.28
$AgCl(s) + e^- \longrightarrow Ag(s) + Cl^-(aq)$	0.22
$SO_4^{2-}(aq) + 4 H^+(aq) + 2 e^- \longrightarrow H_2SO_3(aq) + H_2O(l)$	0.17
$Cu^{2+}(aq) + e^- \longrightarrow Cu^+(aq)$	0.15
$Sn^{4+}(aq) + 2 e^- \longrightarrow Sn^{2+}(aq)$	0.15
$S(s) + 2 H^+(aq) + 2 e^- \longrightarrow H_2S(aq)$	0.14
$AgBr(s) + e^- \longrightarrow Ag(s) + Br^-(aq)$	0.07
$2 H^+(aq) + 2 e^- \longrightarrow H_2(g)$	0
$Fe^{3+}(aq) + 3 e^- \longrightarrow Fe(s)$	−0.04
$Pb^{2+}(aq) + 2 e^- \longrightarrow Pb(s)$	−0.13
$CrO_4^{2-}(aq) + 4 H_2O(l) + 3 e^- \longrightarrow Cr(OH)_3(s) + 5 OH^-(aq)$	−0.13
$Sn^{2+}(aq) + 2 e^- \longrightarrow Sn(s)$	−0.14
$AgI(s) + e^- \longrightarrow Ag(s) + I^-(aq)$	−0.15
$Ni^{2+}(aq) + 2 e^- \longrightarrow Ni(s)$	−0.26
$Co^{2+}(aq) + 2 e^- \longrightarrow Co(s)$	−0.28
$PbSO_4(s) + H^+(aq) + 2 e^- \longrightarrow Pb(s) + HSO_4^-(aq)$	−0.296
$Tl^+(aq) + e^- \longrightarrow Tl(s)$	−0.34
$Se(s) + 2 H^+(aq) + 2 e^- \longrightarrow H_2Se(aq)$	−0.40
$Cd^{2+}(aq) + 2 e^- \longrightarrow Cd(s)$	−0.40
$Cr^{3+}(aq) + e^- \longrightarrow Cr^{2+}(aq)$	−0.41
$Fe^{2+}(aq) + 2 e^- \longrightarrow Fe(s)$	−0.45
$2 CO_2(g) + 2 H^+(aq) + 2 e^- \longrightarrow H_2C_2O_4(aq)$	−0.49
$Ga^{3+}(aq) + 3 e^- \longrightarrow Ga(s)$	−0.55
$Cr^{3+}(aq) + 3 e^- \longrightarrow Cr(s)$	−0.74
$Zn^{2+}(aq) + 2 e^- \longrightarrow Zn(s)$	−0.76
$2 H_2O(l) + 2 e^- \longrightarrow H_2(g) + 2 OH^-(aq)$	−0.83
$Cr^{2+}(aq) + 2 e^- \longrightarrow Cr(s)$	−0.91
$Mn^{2+}(aq) + 2 e^- \longrightarrow Mn(s)$	−1.18
$Al^{3+}(aq) + 3 e^- \longrightarrow Al(s)$	−1.66
$Mg^{2+}(aq) + 2 e^- \longrightarrow Mg(s)$	−2.37
$Na^+(aq) + e^- \longrightarrow Na(s)$	−2.71
$Ca^{2+}(aq) + 2 e^- \longrightarrow Ca(s)$	−2.87
$Ba^{2+}(aq) + 2 e^- \longrightarrow Ba(s)$	−2.91
$K^+(aq) + e^- \longrightarrow K(s)$	−2.93
$Li^+(aq) + e^- \longrightarrow Li(s)$	−3.04

APPENDIX E

Properties of Water

Normal melting point   0 °C = 273.15 K

Normal boiling point   100 °C = 373.15 K

Heat of fusion   6.01 kJ/mol at 0 °C

Heat of vaporization   44.94 kJ/mol at 0 °C

                                        44.02 kJ/mol at 25 °C

                                        40.67 kJ/mol at 100 °C

Specific heat   4.179 J/(g · °C) at 25 °C

Ion-product constant, K_w 1.15×10^{-15} at 0 °C

                                        1.01×10^{-14} at 25 °C

                                        5.43×10^{-13} at 100 °C

TABLE E.1   Vapor Pressure of Water at Various Temperatures

Temp (°C)	P_{vap} (mm Hg)	Temp (°C)	P_{vap} (mm Hg)
0	4.58	60	149.4
10	9.21	70	233.7
20	17.5	80	355.1
30	31.8	90	525.9
40	55.3	100	760.0
50	92.5	105	906.0

Answers to Selected Problems

Chapter 1

1.1 (a) Cd; (b) Sb; (c) Am **1.2** (a) silver; (b) rhodium; (c) rhenium; (d) cesium; (e) argon; (f) arsenic **1.3** (a) Ti, metal; (b) Te, semimetal; (c) Se, nonmetal; (d) Sc, metal; (e) At, semimetal; (f) Ar, nonmetal **1.4** copper (Cu), silver (Ag), and gold (Au) **1.5** (a) 3.72×10^{-10} m; (b) 1.5×10^{11} m **1.6** (a) microgram; (b) decimeter; (c) picosecond; (d) kiloampere; (e) millimole **1.7** 37.0 °C; 310.2 K **1.8** (a) 195 K; (b) 316 °F; (c) 215 °F **1.9** 2.212 g/cm^3 **1.10** 6.32 mL **1.11** 428 kJ **1.12** (a) 2300 kJ; (b) 6.3 h **1.13** The results are both precise and accurate. **1.14** (a) 5 significant figures; (b) 6 significant figures; (c) 1, 2, 3, or 4 significant figures; (d) 3 significant figures; (e) 18 students is an exact number; (f) 1 significant figure; (g) 4 significant figures; (h) 3 or 4 significant figures **1.15** (a) 3.774 L; (b) 255 K; (c) 55.26 kg; (d) 906.40 kJ **1.16** (a) 24.612 g; (b) 1.26×10^3 g/L; (c) 41.1 mL **1.17** 32.6 °C (3 significant figures) **1.18** (a) 1947 °F; (b) 6×10^{-11} cm^3 **1.19** 8.88 g; 0.313 ounces **1.20** 2.52 cm^3; 4.45×10^{23} C atoms. **1.21** 300 g

Conceptual Problems

1.22

1.24 red—gas; blue—42; green—lithium, sodium, potassium or rubidium are possible answers **1.26** (a) good precision, poor accuracy; (b) good precision, good accuracy; (c) poor precision, poor accuracy **1.28** The 5 mL graduated cylinder will give more accurate measurements. *Section Problems* **1.30** 118 elements are presently known. About 90 elements occur naturally. **1.32** There are 18 groups in the periodic table. They are labeled as follows: 1A, 2A, 3B, 4B, 5B, 6B, 7B, 8B (3 groups), 1B, 2B, 3A, 4A, 5A, 6A, 7A, 8A.

1.34

1.36

1.38 Li, Na, K, Rb, and Cs **1.40** F, Cl, Br, and I **1.42** a metal **1.44** All match in groups 2A and 7A. **1.46** (a) Gd; (b) Ge; (c) Tc; (d) As **1.48** (a) tellurium; (b) rhenium; (c) beryllium; (d) argon; (e) plutonium **1.50** (a) Tin is Sn, Ti is titanium; (b) Manganese is Mn, Mg is magnesium; (c) Potassium is K, Po is polonium; (d) The symbol for helium is He. **1.52** Mass measures the amount of matter in an object, whereas weight measures the pull of gravity on an object by the earth or other celestial body. **1.54** (a) kilogram, kg; (b) meter, m; (c) kelvin, K; (d) cubic meter, m^3; (e) joule, $(kg \cdot m^2)/s^2$; (f) kg/m^3 or g/cm^3 **1.56** A Celsius degree is larger than a Fahrenheit degree by a factor of 9/5. **1.58** The volume of a cubic decimeter (dm^3) and a liter (L) are the same. **1.60** (a) and (b) **1.62** cL is centiliter $(10^{-2}$ L) **1.64** (a) 6.02×10^1 km; (b) 46 μs; (c) 200,098 g **1.66** 1×10^9 pg/mg; 3.5×10^4 pg/35 ng **1.68** (a) 5 pm $= 5 \times 10^{-10}$ cm $= 5 \times 10^{-3}$ nm; (b) 8.5 $cm^3 = 8.5 \times 10^{-6}$ $m^3 = 8.5 \times 10^3$ mm^3; (c) 65.2 mg $= 0.0652$ g $= 6.52 \times 10^{10}$ pg **1.70** (a) 6 significant figures; (b) 6 significant figures; (c) 4 significant figures; (d) 3 significant figures; (e) 2, 3, 4, or 5 significant figures; (f) 5 significant figures **1.72** 3.6665×10^6 m^3. **1.74** (a) 4.5332×10^2 mg; (b) 4.21×10^{-5} mL; (c) 6.67×10^5 g **1.76** (a) 3.567×10^4 m (4 significant figures); 35,670.1 m (6 significant figures); (b) 69 g (2 significant figures); 68.5 g (3 significant figures); (c) 4.99×10^3 cm (3 significant figures); (d) 2.3098×10^{-4} kg (5 significant figures) **1.78** (a) 10.0; (b) 26; (c) 0.039; (d) 5526; (e) 87.6; (f) 13 **1.80** 11.394 mi/hr **1.82** (a) 110 g; (b) 443.2 m; (c) 7.6181×10^{12} m^2 **1.84** (a) 43,560 ft^3; (b) 3.92×10^8 acre-ft **1.86** (a) 2000 mg/L; (b) 2000 μg/mL; (c) 2 g/L; (d) 2000 ng/μL; (e) 10 g **1.88** 0.61 cm/shake **1.90** 103.8 °F; 72.0 °F **1.92** 3422 °C; 3695 K **1.94** (a) 1.021 °E/°C; (b) 0.5675 °E/°F; (c) H_2O melting point $= 119.8$ °E; H_2O boiling point $= 222.0$ °E; (d) 157.6 °E; (e) Because the outside temperature is 50.0 °F, I would wear a sweater or light jacket. **1.96** 2500 kg **1.98** 0.18 cm^3; 162,000 cm^3 **1.100** 11 g/cm^3 **1.102** Car: 7.1×10^5 J; Truck: 6.7×10^5 J **1.104** 169 kcal *Chapter Problems* **1.106** 2.33 g/cm^3 **1.108** mp $= 801$ °C $= 1474$ °F; bp $= 1413$ °C $= 2575$ °F **1.110** 75.85 mL **1.112** (a) 0.958 61 g/mL; (b) 4047 m^2; (c) 1400 kg; (d) 140 kg; (e) 792 Cal from fat **1.114** (a) 200 kisses; (b) 3.3 mL; (c) 26 Cal/kiss; (d) 51% **1.116** The Celsius and Fahrenheit scales "cross" at -40 °C (-40 °F). **1.118** 5 tablets **1.120** 34.1 °C **1.122** 45.9 g **1.124** (a) metal; (b) indium; (c) 5.904 g/cm^3; (d) 355 °G

Chapter 2

2.1 3/2 **2.2** 2×10^4 Au atoms **2.3** 40 times **2.4** 34 p, 34 e^-, 41 n **2.5** $^{35}_{17}$Cl has 18 n; $^{37}_{17}$Cl has 20 n **2.6** $^{109}_{47}$Ag **2.7** 63.55 amu **2.8** 2.04×10^{22} Cu atoms **2.9** (a) 72.04 g Ti; (b) 7.75 g Na; (c) 614.8 g U

2.10 (a) 0.2405 mol Ti; (b) 1.2670 mol Na; (c) 6.205 mol U
2.11 (a) $^{106}_{44}Ru \rightarrow ^{0}_{-1}e + ^{106}_{45}Rh$; (b) $^{189}_{83}Bi \rightarrow ^{4}_{2}He + ^{185}_{81}Tl$;
(c) $^{204}_{84}Po + ^{0}_{-1}e \rightarrow ^{204}_{83}Bi$ **2.12** $^{4}_{2}He$ **2.13** $^{148}_{69}Tm$ decays to $^{148}_{68}Er$ by either
positron emission or electron capture. **2.14** (a) ^{199}Au decays by beta
emission. ^{173}Au decays by alpha emission; (b) ^{196}Pb decays by
positron emission. ^{206}Pb is nonradioactive.

2.15

2.16 $C_5H_{11}NO_2S$ **2.17** Figure (b) **2.18** $C_9H_{13}NO_3$ **2.19** (a) ionic;
(b) molecular; (c) molecular; (d) ionic **2.20** (a) ionic; (b) molecular
2.21 (a) cesium fluoride; (b) potassium oxide; (c) copper(II) oxide;
(d) barium sulfide; (e) beryllium bromide **2.22** (a) VCl_3; (b) MnO_2;
(c) CuS; (d) Al_2O_3 **2.23** red—potassium sulfide, K_2S;
green—strontium iodide, SrI_2; blue—gallium oxide, Ga_2O_3
2.24 (a) nitrogen trichloride; (b) tetraphosphorus hexoxide;
(c) disulfur difluoride; (d) selenium dioxide **2.25** (a) S_2Cl_2; (b) ICl;
(c) NI_3 **2.26** (a) phosphorus pentachloride; (b) dinitrogen monoxide
2.27 (a) calcium hypochlorite; (b) silver thiosulfate; (c) sodium
dihydrogen phosphate; (d) tin(II) nitrate; (e) lead(IV) acetate;
(f) ammonium sulfate **2.28** (a) Li_3PO_4; (b) $Mg(HSO_4)_2$;
(c) $Mn(NO_3)_2$; (d) $Cr_2(SO_4)_3$ **2.29** Drawing 1 $CaCl_2$; Drawing 2 LiBr
and $NaNO_2$ **2.30** H and He *Conceptual Problems* **2.32** Drawing
(a) represents a collection of SO_2 units. **2.34** Figures (b) and (d)
2.36 (a) $C_3H_7NO_2$; (b) $C_2H_6O_2$; (c) $C_2H_4O_2$ *Section Problems* **2.38**
The law of mass conservation in terms of Dalton's atomic theory
states that chemical reactions only rearrange the way that atoms are
combined; the atoms themselves are not changed. The law of
definite proportions in terms of Dalton's atomic theory states that
the chemical combination of elements to make different substances
occurs when atoms join together in small, whole-number ratios.
2.40 3.7 g

2.42

$$\frac{C:H \text{ mass ratio in benzene}}{C:H \text{ mass ratio in ethane}} = \frac{12}{4.00} = \frac{3}{1}$$

$$\frac{C:H \text{ mass ratio in benzene}}{C:H \text{ mass ratio in ethylene}} = \frac{12}{6.0} = \frac{2}{1}$$

$$\frac{C:H \text{ mass ratio in ethylene}}{C:H \text{ mass ratio in ethane}} = \frac{6.0}{4.00} = \frac{3}{2}$$

2.44 (a) benzene, CH; ethane, CH_3; ethylene, CH_2; (b) These
ratios are consistent with their modern formulas. **2.46** X g
2.48 5.27×10^{-4} x g **2.50** 1 Zn:1 S **2.52** The "other" compound
is not methane

$$\frac{C:H \text{ mass ratio in "other"}}{C:H \text{ mass ratio in methane}} = \frac{4}{3}$$

2.54 The atomic number is equal to the number of protons. The
mass number is equal to the sum of the number of protons and
the number of neutrons. **2.56** The subscript giving the atomic
number of an atom is often left off of an isotope symbol because
one can readily look up the atomic number in the periodic table.
2.58 ^{63}Cu **2.60** (a) carbon, C; (b) argon, Ar; (c) vanadium, V **2.62** (a)
$^{220}_{86}Rn$; (b) $^{210}_{84}Po$; (c) $^{197}_{79}Au$ **2.64** (a) 7 p, 7 e⁻, 8 n; (b) 27 p, 27 e⁻, 33 n;
(c) 53 p, 53 e⁻, 78 n; (d) 58 p, 58 e⁻, 84 n **2.66** (a) $^{24}_{12}Mg$, magnesium;
(b) $^{58}_{28}Ni$, nickel; (c) $^{104}_{46}Pd$, palladium; (d) $^{183}_{74}W$, tungsten **2.68** $^{12}_{6}C$;
$^{33}_{35}Br$; $^{11}_{5}Bo$ **2.70** 10.8 amu **2.72** 25.982 amu for ^{26}Mg;
2.74 Positron emission is the conversion of a proton in the nucleus
into a neutron plus an ejected positron. Electron capture is the
process in which a proton in the nucleus captures an inner-shell

electron and is thereby converted into a neutron. **2.76** In beta
emission a neutron is converted to a proton and the atomic number
increases. In positron emission a proton is converted to a neutron
and the atomic number decreases. **2.78** (a) $^{126}_{50}Sn \rightarrow ^{0}_{-1}e + ^{126}_{51}Sb$;
(b) $^{210}_{88}Ra \rightarrow ^{4}_{2}He + ^{206}_{86}Rn$; (c) $^{77}_{37}Rb \rightarrow ^{0}_{1}e + ^{77}_{36}Kr$;
(d) $^{76}_{36}Kr + ^{0}_{-1}e \rightarrow ^{76}_{35}Br$ **2.80** (a) $^{0}_{1}e$; (b) $^{4}_{2}He$; (c) $^{0}_{-1}e$
2.82 (a) $^{162}_{75}Re \rightarrow ^{158}_{73}Ta + ^{4}_{2}He$; (b) $^{138}_{62}Sm + ^{0}_{-1}e \rightarrow ^{138}_{61}Pm$;
(c) $^{188}_{74}W \rightarrow ^{188}_{75}Re + ^{0}_{-1}e$; (d) $^{165}_{73}Ta \rightarrow ^{165}_{72}Hf + ^{0}_{1}e$ **2.84** ^{160}W is neutron
poor and decays by alpha emission. ^{185}W is neutron rich and
decays by beta emission. **2.86** $^{237}_{93}Np$, $^{233}_{91}Pa$, $^{233}_{92}U$, $^{229}_{90}Th$, $^{225}_{88}Ra$, $^{225}_{89}Ac$,
$^{221}_{87}Fr$, $^{217}_{85}At$, $^{213}_{83}Bi$, $^{213}_{84}Po$, $^{209}_{82}Pb$, $^{209}_{83}Bi$ **2.88** 6 α, 4 β **2.90** A covalent
bond results when two atoms share several (usually two) of their
electrons. An ionic bond results from a complete transfer of one or
more electrons from one atom to another. The C—H bonds in
methane (CH_4) are covalent bonds. The bond in NaCl (Na^+Cl^-)
is an ionic bond. **2.92** Element symbols are composed of one or
two letters. If the element symbol is two letters, the first letter
is uppercase and the second is lowercase. CO stands for carbon
and oxygen in carbon monoxide. **2.94** (a) Be^{2+}, 4 p, 2 e⁻; (b) Rb^+,
37 p, 36 e⁻; (c) Se^{2-}, 34 p, 36 e⁻; (d) Au^{3+} 79 p, 76 e⁻ **2.96** C_3H_8O

2.98

2.100

2.102 (a) KCl; (b) $SnBr_2$; (c) CaO; (d) $BaCl_2$; (e) AlH_3
2.104 (a) barium ion; (b) cesium ion; (c) vanadium(III) ion;
(d) hydrogen carbonate ion; (e) ammonium ion; (f) nickel(II) ion;
(g) nitrite ion; (h) chlorite ion; (i) manganese(II) ion; (j) perchlorate
ion **2.106** (a) $CaBr_2$; (b) $CaSO_4$; (c) $Al_2(SO_4)_3$ **2.108** (a) $CaCl_2$; (b) CaO;
(c) CaS **2.110** (a) SO_3^{2-}; (b) PO_4^{3-}; (c) Zr^{4+}; (d) CrO_4^{2-};
(e) $CH_3CO_2^-$; (f) $S_2O_3^{2-}$ **2.112** (a) NO, nitrogen monoxide; (b) N_2O,
dinitrogen monoxide; (c) NO_2, nitrogen dioxide; (d) N_2O_4,
dinitrogen tetroxide; (e) N_2O_5, dinitrogen pentoxide
2.114 (a) Na_2SO_4; (b) $Ba_3(PO_4)_2$; (c) $Ga_2(SO_4)_3$ *Chapter Problems*
2.116 72.6 amu **2.118** For NH_3, 0.505 g H; For N_2H_4, 0.337 g H
2.120 (a) I; (b) Kr **2.122** 12.0005 amu **2.124** 151.165 amu
2.126 $^{100}_{43}Tc \rightarrow ^{0}_{1}e + ^{100}_{42}Mo$ (positron emission); $^{100}_{43}Tc + ^{0}_{-1}e \rightarrow ^{100}_{42}Mo$
(electron capture)

2.128

Chapter 3

3.1 $2 NaClO_3 \rightarrow 2 NaCl + 3 O_2$ **3.2** (a) $C_6H_{12}O_6 \rightarrow 2 C_2H_6O +$
$2 CO_2$; (b) $6 CO_2 + 6 H_2O \rightarrow C_6H_{12}O_6 + 6 O_2$; (c) $4 NH_3 + Cl_2 \rightarrow$
$N_2H_4 + 2 NH_4Cl$ **3.3** $3 A_2 + 2 B \rightarrow 2 BA_3$ **3.4** (a) 159.7 amu;
(b) 98.1 amu; (c) 192.1 amu; (d) 334.4 amu **3.5** 2.77×10^{-3} mol;
1.67×10^{21} molecules **3.6** (a) 3.33 g $C_4H_6O_3$; (b) 5.87 g $C_9H_8O_4$;

(c) 1.96 g CH_3CO_2H **3.7** 63% **3.8** 4220 g **3.9** Li_2O is the limiting reactant; 41 kg H_2O **3.10** 921 g CO_2 **3.11** (a) $A + B_2 \rightarrow AB_2$; A is the limiting reactant; (b) 1.0 mol of AB_2 **3.12** (a) 0.025 mol; (b) 1.62 mol **3.13** (a) 25.0 g; (b) 67.6 g **3.14** 690 mL **3.15** 1 g **3.16** 0.656 M **3.17** Dilute 6.94 mL of 18.0 M H_2SO_4 with enough water to make 250.0 mL of solution. **3.18** 10.0 mL **3.19** 5.47×10^{-2} M **3.20** 0.758 M **3.21** Because the two volumes are equal and the concentrations are proportional to the number of solute ions, $[OH^-] = 0.67$ M. **3.22** CH_4N; 39.9% C, 13.4% H, 46.6% N **3.23** $MgCO_3$ **3.24** 37.5% C, 4.21% H, 58.3% O **3.25** $C_{10}H_{20}O$ **3.26** $C_5H_{10}O_5$ **3.27** (a) B_2H_6; (b) $C_3H_6O_3$ **3.28** The assumptions that (i) the oil molecules are tiny cubes; (ii) the oil layer is one molecule thick; (iii) the molecular mass of 900 amu for the oil **3.29** 1.0×10^{24} molecules/mole *Conceptual Problems* **3.30** box (b) **3.32** 0.004 mol CO_2; 0.0025 mol H_2O **3.34** 309.36 amu **3.36** (a) $A_2 + 3 B_2 \rightarrow 2 AB_3$; B_2 is the limiting reactant; (b) 2/3 mol AB_3 *Section Problems* **3.38** Equation (b) is balanced, (a) is not balanced. **3.40** (a) $Mg + 2 HNO_3 \rightarrow H_2 + Mg(NO_3)_2$; (b) $CaC_2 + 2 H_2O \rightarrow Ca(OH)_2 + C_2H_2$; (c) $2 S + 3 O_2 \rightarrow 2 SO_3$; (d) $UO_2 + 4 HF \rightarrow UF_4 + 2 H_2O$ **3.42** (a) $SiCl_4 + 2 H_2O \rightarrow SiO_2 + 4 HCl$; (b) $P_4O_{10} + 6 H_2O \rightarrow 4 H_3PO_4$; (c) $CaCN_2 + 3 H_2O \rightarrow CaCO_3 + 2 NH_3$; (d) $3 NO_2 + H_2O \rightarrow 2 HNO_3 + NO$ **3.44** (a) Hg_2Cl_2: 472.1 amu; (b) $C_4H_8O_2$: 88.1 amu; (c) CF_2Cl_2: 120.9 amu **3.46** (a) 558.7 amu; (b) 444.5 amu; (c) 321.8 amu **3.48** (a) 47.87 g; (b) 159.81 g; (c) 200.59 g; (d) 18.02 g **3.50** 0.867 mol **3.52** 119 amu **3.54** 1.97×10^{-3} mol $FeSO_4$; 1.19×10^{21} Fe(II) atoms **3.56** 6.44×10^{-4} mol; 3.88×10^{20} molecules **3.58** Ne **3.60** 166.8 kg **3.62** (a) $2 Fe_2O_3 + 3 C \rightarrow 4 Fe + 3 CO_2$; (b) 4.93 mol C; (c) 59.2 g C **3.64** (a) $2 Mg + O_2 \rightarrow 2 MgO$; (b) 16.5 g O_2, 41.5 g MgO; (c) 38.0 g Mg, 63.0 g MgO **3.66** (a) $2 HgO \rightarrow 2 Hg + O_2$; (b) 42.1 g Hg, 3.36 g O_2; (c) 451 g HgO **3.68** AgCl **3.70** (a) 581 g I_2; (b) 1847 g HI **3.72** 15.8 g NH_3, 83.3 g N_2 left over **3.74** 5.22 g $C_2H_4Cl_2$ **3.76** (a) 12.0 g H_2SO_4; (b) 14.9 g $NiSO_4$ **3.78** 0.526 L CO_2, $CaCO_3$ is the limiting reactant. **3.80** 3.2 g **3.82** 86.8% **3.84** (a) 0.0420 mol; (b) 0.12 mol **3.86** 160 mL **3.88** 0.0685 M **3.90** 0.958 M **3.92** 1.71 M **3.94** 15.5 g **3.96** 57.2 mL **3.98** 20.0% C, 6.72% H, 46.6% N, 26.6% O **3.100** C_7H_7Cl **3.102** SnF_2 **3.104** C_7H_8 **3.106** 13,000 amu **3.108** Disilane is Si_2H_6 **3.110** C_4H_6O **3.112** $C_{12}Br_{10}O$ *Chapter Problems* **3.114** Na^+, 0.147 M; Ca^{2+}, 0.002 98 M; K^+, 0.004 02 M; Cl^-, 0.157 M **3.116** (a) 5.1×10^{-11} mol/L; (b) 1.3×10^{13} g Au **3.118** (a) 39.99% C; 6.713% H; 53.27% O; (h) 2.055% H; 32.70% S; 65.25% O; (c) 24.75% K; 34.77% Mn; 40.51% O; (d) 45.89% C; 2.751% H; 7.647% N; 26.20% O; 17.51% S **3.120** (a) $6 WCl_6 + 8 Bi \rightarrow W_6Cl_{12} + 8 BiCl_3$; (b) 105.4 g Bi; (c) 146 g W_6Cl_{12} **3.122** $C_{10}H_{10}Fe$ **3.124** Na^+, 0.295 M; Li^+, 0.0406 M; SO_4^{2-}, 0.0590 M; PO_4^{3-}, 0.0725 M **3.126** High resolution mass spectrometry is capable of measuring the mass of molecules with a particular isotopic composition. **3.128** 18.1 lb **3.130** $C_3H_{12}N_2Cl_2$ **3.132** The empirical formula is $C_7H_6O_3$; the molecular formula is $C_7H_6O_3$. **3.134** 0.63 g of benzoic acid and 0.37 g of gallic acid **3.136** 4.4 g Fe_2O_3; 5.6 g FeO **3.138** $C_6H_{12}O_6 + 6 O_2 \rightarrow 6 CO_2 + 6 H_2O$; 97.2 g CO_2, 56.1 L CO_2 **3.140** (a) 79.91% Cu, 20.1% S; (b) Cu_2S; (c) 4.2×10^{22} Cu^+ ions/cm^3 **3.142** 5.32 g PCl_3, 4.68 g PCl_5 **3.144** The mass ratio of NH_4NO_3 to $(NH_4)_2HPO_4$ in the mixture is 2 to 1. **3.146** (a) 80 amu; Br; (b) 64 amu; Cu **3.148** (a) (i) $M_2O_3(s) + 3 C(s) + 3 Cl_2(g) \rightarrow 2 MCl_3(l) + 3 CO(g)$; (ii) $2 MCl_3(l) + 3 H_2(g) \rightarrow 2 M(s) + 6 HCl(g)$; (b) 10.8 amu; B; (c) 0.265 g

Chapter 4

4.1 (a) precipitation; (b) redox; (c) acid–base neutralization **4.2** 0.675 M **4.3** A_2Y is the strongest electrolyte because it is completely dissociated into ions. A_2X is the weakest electrolyte because it is the least dissociated. **4.4** (a) $2 Ag^+(aq) + CrO_4^{2-}(aq) \rightarrow Ag_2CrO_4(s)$;

(b) $2 H^+(aq) + MgCO_3(s) \rightarrow H_2O(l) + CO_2(g) + Mg^{2+}(aq)$; (c) $Hg^{2+}(aq) + 2 I^-(aq) \rightarrow HgI_2(s)$ **4.5** (a) $CdCO_3$, insoluble; (b) MgO, insoluble; (c) Na_2S, soluble; (d) $PbSO_4$, insoluble; (e) $(NH_4)_3PO_4$, soluble; (f) $HgCl_2$, soluble **4.6** (a) $Ni^{2+}(aq) + S^{2-}(aq) \rightarrow NiS(s)$; (b) $Pb^{2+}(aq) + CrO_4^{2-}(aq) \rightarrow PbCrO_4(s)$; (c) $Ag^+(aq) + Br^-(aq) \rightarrow AgBr(s)$; (d) $Zn^{2+}(aq) + CO_3^{2-}(aq) \rightarrow ZnCO_3(s)$ **4.7** $3 CaCl_2(aq) + 2 Na_3PO_4(aq) \rightarrow Ca_3(PO_4)_2(s) + 6 NaCl(aq)$; $3 Ca^{2+}(aq) + 2 PO_4^{3-}(aq) \rightarrow Ca_3(PO_4)_2(s)$ **4.8** The precipitate is either $Mg_3(PO_4)_2$ or $Zn_3(PO_4)_2$. **4.9** (a) periodic acid; (b) bromous acid; (c) chromic acid **4.10** (a) H_3PO_3; (b) H_2Se **4.11** (a) $2 Cs^+(aq) + 2 OH^-(aq) + 2 H^+(aq) + SO_4^{2-}(aq) \rightarrow 2 Cs^+(aq) + SO_4^{2-}(aq) + 2 H_2O(l)$; $H^+(aq) + OH^-(aq) \rightarrow H_2O(l)$; (b) $Ca^{2+}(aq) + 2 OH^-(aq) + 2 CH_3CO_2H(aq) \rightarrow Ca^{2+}(aq) + 2 CH_3CO_2^-(aq) + 2 H_2O(l)$; $CH_3CO_2H(aq) + OH^-(aq) \rightarrow CH_3CO_2^-(aq) + H_2O(l)$ **4.12** HY is the strongest acid; HX is the weakest acid. **4.13** (a) Cl -1, Sn $+4$; (b) O -2, Cr $+6$; (c) O -2, Cl -1, V $+5$; (d) O -2, V $+3$; (e) O -2, H $+1$, N $+5$; (f) O -2, S $+6$, Fe $+2$ **4.14** $2 Cu^{2+}(aq) + 4 I^-(aq) \rightarrow 2 CuI(s) + I_2(aq)$; Cu^{2+} $+2$; I^- -1; CuI: Cu $+1$, I -1; I_2: 0; oxidizing agent, Cu^{2+}; reducing agent, I^- **4.15** (a) C is oxidized. C is the reducing agent. The Sn in SnO_2 is reduced. SnO_2 is the oxidizing agent. (b) Sn^{2+} is oxidized. Sn^{2+} is the reducing agent. Fe^{3+} is reduced. Fe^{3+} is the oxidizing agent. (c) The N in NH_3 is oxidized. NH_3 is the reducing agent. Each O in O_2 is reduced. O_2 is the oxidizing agent. **4.16** (a) N. R.; (b) N. R. **4.17** Because B will reduce A^+, B is above A in the activity series. Because B will not reduce C^+, C is above B in the activity series. Therefore C must be above A in the activity series and C will reduce A^+. **4.18** $A > D > B > C$ **4.19** (a) $MnO_4^-(aq) \rightarrow MnO_2(s)$; $IO_3^-(aq) \rightarrow IO_4^-(aq)$; (b) $NO_3^-(aq) \rightarrow NO_2(g)$; $SO_2(aq) \rightarrow SO_4^{2-}(aq)$ **4.20** $2 NO_3^-(aq) + 8 H^+(aq) + 3 Cu(s) \rightarrow 3 Cu^{2+}(aq) + 2 NO(g) + 4 H_2O(l)$ **4.21** $4 Fe(OH)_2(s) + 2 H_2O(l) + O_2(g) \rightarrow 4 Fe(OH)_3(s)$ **4.22** 1.98 M **4.23** $Pb(s) + PbO_2(s) + 2 HSO_4^-(aq) + 2 H^+(aq) \rightarrow 2 PbSO_4(s) + 2 H_2O(l)$ **4.24** For a green process look for a solvent that is safe, non-toxic, non-polluting, and renewable. H_2O would be an excellent green solvent. *Conceptual Problems* **4.26** In the precipitate there are two cations (blue) for each anion (red), so the anion must have a -2 charge and the cation a $+1$ charge for charge neutrality of the precipitate. The cation must be Ag^+ because all Na^+ salts are soluble. Ag_2CrO_4 and Ag_2CO_3 are insoluble and consistent with the observed result. **4.28** The NaOCl concentration is 0.040 M. 67% of the I^- solution from the buret must be added to the flask to react with all of the OCl^-. **4.30** (a) No reaction. (b) Reaction would occur. (c) Reaction would occur. *Section Problems* **4.32** (a) precipitation; (b) redox; (c) acid–base neutralization **4.34** (a) $Hg^{2+}(aq) + 2 I^-(aq) \rightarrow HgI_2(s)$; (b) $2 HgO(s) \xrightarrow{\text{Heat}} 2 Hg(l) + O_2(g)$; (c) $H_3PO_4(aq) + 3 OH^-(aq) \rightarrow PO_4^{3-}(aq) + 3 H_2O(l)$ **4.36** (a) bright; (b) dark; (c) dim **4.38** $Ba(OH)_2$ is soluble in aqueous solution, dissociates into $Ba^{2+}(aq)$ and $2 OH^-(aq)$, and conducts electricity. H_2SO_4 dissociates into $H^+(aq)$ and $HSO_4^-(aq)$. H_2SO_4 solutions conduct electricity. When equal molar solutions of $Ba(OH)_2$ and H_2SO_4 are mixed, the insoluble $BaSO_4$ is formed along with two H_2O. In water, $BaSO_4$ does not produce any appreciable amount of ions and the mixture does not conduct electricity. **4.40** (a) strong; (b) weak; (c) strong; (d) strong; (e) weak; (f) nonelectrolyte **4.42** (a) 2.25 M; (b) 1.42 M **4.44** (a) insoluble; (b) soluble; (c) insoluble; (d) insoluble **4.46** (a) No precipitate will form; (b) $Fe(OH)_2(s)$ will precipitate; (c) No precipitate; (d) No precipitate. **4.48** (a) no precipitate; (b) $BaSO_4(s)$ will precipitate; (c) $AgCl(s)$ will precipitate. **4.50** (a) $Pb(NO_3)_2(aq) + Na_2SO_4(aq) \rightarrow PbSO_4(s) + 2 NaNO_3(aq)$; (b) $3 MgCl_2(aq) + 2 K_3PO_4(aq) \rightarrow Mg_3(PO_4)_2(s) + 6 KCl(aq)$;

(c) $ZnSO_4(aq) + Na_2CrO_4(aq) \rightarrow ZnCrO_4(s) + Na_2SO_4(aq)$
4.52 Add $HCl(aq)$; it will selectively precipitate $AgCl(s)$.
4.54 Cs^+ and/or NH_4^+ **4.56** Add the solution to an active metal, such as magnesium. Bubbles of H_2 gas indicate the presence of an acid. **4.58** (a) $2 H^+(aq) + 2 ClO_4^-(aq) + Ca^{2+}(aq) + 2 OH^-(aq) \rightarrow Ca^{2+}(aq) + 2 ClO_4^-(aq) + 2 H_2O(l)$; (b) $CH_3CO_2H(aq) + Na^+(aq) + OH^-(aq) \rightarrow CH_3CO_2^-(aq) + Na^+(aq) + H_2O(l)$
4.60 (a) $H^+(aq) + OH^-(aq) \rightarrow H_2O(l)$; (b) $H^+(aq) + OH^-(aq) \rightarrow H_2O(l)$ **4.62** (a) basic because there is an excess of KOH; (b) basic because there is an excess of $Ba(OH)_2$. **4.64** (a) 9.0 mL; (b) 11.0 mL
4.66 best reducing agents, the bottom left; best oxidizing agents, top right; (excluding the noble gases) **4.68** (a) gains electrons; (b) loses electrons; (c) loses electrons; (d) gains electrons
4.70 (a) NO_2: O -2, N $+4$; (b) SO_3: O -2, S $+6$; (c) $COCl_2$: O -2, Cl -1, C $+4$; (d) CH_2Cl_2: Cl -1, H $+1$, C 0; (e) $KClO_3$: O -2, K $+1$, Cl $+5$; (f) HNO_3: O -2, H $+1$, N $+5$ **4.72** (a) ClO_3^-: O -2, Cl $+5$; (b) SO_3^{2-}: O -2, S $+4$; (c) $C_2O_4^{2-}$: O -2, C $+3$; (d) NO_2^-: O -2, N $+3$; (e) BrO^-: O -2, Br $+1$; (f) AsO_4^{3-}: O -2, As $+5$ **4.74** (a) $Ca(s)$ is oxidized; $Sn^{2+}(aq)$ is reduced; (b) not a redox reaction **4.76** (a) N. R.; (b) N. R.; (c) N. R.; (d) $Au^{3+}(aq) + 3 Ag(s) \rightarrow 3 Ag^+(aq) + Au(s)$ **4.78** (a) A > B > C > D; (b) (1) N. R.; (2) N. R. **4.80** (a) reduction; (b) oxidation; (c) oxidation; (d) reduction **4.82** (a) $3 e^- + 4 H^+(aq) + NO_3^-(aq) \rightarrow NO(g) + 2 H_2O(l)$; (b) $Zn(s) \rightarrow Zn^{2+}(aq) + 2 e^-$; (c) $Ti^{3+}(aq) + 2 H_2O(l) \rightarrow TiO_2(s) + 4 H^+(aq) + e^-$; (d) $Sn^{4+}(aq) + 2 e^- \rightarrow Sn^{2+}(aq)$ **4.84** (a) oxidation: $Te(s) \rightarrow TeO_2(s)$; reduction: $NO_3^-(aq) \rightarrow NO(g)$; (b) oxidation: $Fe^{2+}(aq) \rightarrow Fe^{3+}(aq)$; reduction: $H_2O_2(aq) \rightarrow H_2O(l)$ **4.86** (a) $14 H^+(aq) + Cr_2O_7^{2-}(aq) + 6 e^- \rightarrow 2 Cr^{3+}(aq) + 7 H_2O(l)$; (b) $4 H_2O(l) + CrO_4^{2-}(aq) + 3 e^- \rightarrow Cr(OH)_4^-(aq) + 4 OH^-(aq)$; (c) $Bi^{3+}(aq) + 6 OH^-(aq) \rightarrow BiO_3^-(aq) + 3 H_2O(l) + 2 e^-$; (d) $H_2O(l) + ClO^-(aq) + 2 e^- \rightarrow Cl^-(aq) + 2 OH^-(aq)$
4.88 (a) $H_2O(l) + 2 MnO_4^-(aq) + 3 IO_3^-(aq) \rightarrow 2 MnO_2(s) + 3 IO_4^-(aq) + 2 OH^-(aq)$; (b) $2 Cu(OH)_2(s) + N_2H_4(aq) \rightarrow 2 Cu(s) + 4 H_2O(l) + N_2(g)$; (c) $3 Fe(OH)_2(s) + 4 H_2O(l) + CrO_4^{2-}(aq) \rightarrow 3 Fe(OH)_3(s) + Cr(OH)_4^-(aq) + OH^-(aq)$; (d) $ClO_4^-(aq) + 2 H_2O_2(aq) \rightarrow ClO_2^-(aq) + 2 H_2O(l) + 2 O_2(g)$
4.90 (a) $Zn(s) + 2 VO^{2+}(aq) + 4 H^+(aq) \rightarrow Zn^{2+}(aq) + 2 V^{3+}(aq) + 2 H_2O(l)$; (b) $2 H^+(aq) + Ag(s) + NO_3^-(aq) \rightarrow Ag^+(aq) + NO_2(g) + H_2O(l)$; (c) $3 Mg(s) + 16 H^+(aq) + 2 VO_4^{3-}(aq) \rightarrow 3 Mg^{2+}(aq) + 2 V^{2+}(aq) + 8 H_2O(l)$; (d) $6 H^+(aq) + IO_3^-(aq) + 8 I^-(aq) \rightarrow 3 I_3^-(aq) + 3 H_2O(l)$
4.92 0.670 g I_2 **4.94** 1.130 M **4.96** 0.134 M **4.98** 80.32% **4.100** 0.101%
***Chapter Problems* 4.102** (a) $4[Fe(CN)_6]^{3-}(aq) + N_2H_4(aq) + 4 OH^-(aq) \rightarrow 4[Fe(CN)_6]^{4-}(aq) + N_2(g) + 4 H_2O(l)$; (b) $SeO_3^{2-}(aq) + Cl_2(g) + 2 OH^-(aq) \rightarrow SeO_4^{2-}(aq) + 2 Cl^-(aq) + H_2O(l)$; (c) $2 Co^{2+}(aq) + H_2O(l) + HO_2^-(aq) + 3 OH^-(aq) \rightarrow 2 Co(OH)_3(s)$ **4.104** (a) C_2H_6: H $+1$, C -3; (b) $Na_2B_4O_7$: O -2, Na $+1$, B $+3$; (c) Mg_2SiO_4: O -2, Mg $+2$, Si $+4$
4.106 (a) C > A > D > B; (b) (1) The reaction, $A^+ + C \rightarrow A + C^+$, will occur; (2) $A^+ + B \rightarrow A + B^+$, will not occur. **4.108** 0.4450% Cu
4.110 $K_{sp} = [Mg^{2+}][F^-]^2 = 7.0 \times 10^{-11}$ **4.112** (a) $Hg_2^{2+}(aq) + 2 Cl^-(aq) \rightarrow Hg_2Cl_2(s)$; (b) $Pb^{2+}(aq) + SO_4^{2-}(aq) \rightarrow PbSO_4(s)$; (c) $Ca^{2+}(aq) + CO_3^{2-}(aq) \rightarrow CaCO_3(s)$; (d) $Ba^{2+}(aq) + SO_4^{2-}(aq) \rightarrow BaSO_4(s)$ **4.114** (a) $2 Mn(OH)_2(s) + H_2O_2(aq) \rightarrow 2 Mn(OH)_3(s)$; (b) $4 H^+(aq) + 3 MnO_4^{2-}(aq) \rightarrow MnO_2(s) + 2 MnO_4^-(aq) + 2 H_2O(l)$; (c) $8 I^-(aq) + IO_3^-(aq) + 6 H^+(aq) \rightarrow 3 I_3^-(aq) + 3 H_2O(l)$; (d) $2 H_2O(l) + 2 P(s) + 3 PO_4^{3-}(aq) + OH^-(aq) \rightarrow 5 HPO_3^{2-}(aq)$ **4.116** (a) $20 H^+(aq) + S_4O_6^{2-}(aq) + 6 Al(s) \rightarrow 4 H_2S(aq) + 6 Al^{3+}(aq) + 6 H_2O(l)$; (b) $14 H^+(aq) + 6 S_2O_3^{2-}(aq) + Cr_2O_7^{2-}(aq) \rightarrow 3 S_4O_6^{2-}(aq) + 2 Cr^{3+}(aq) + 7 H_2O(l)$; (c) $18 H_2O(l) + 14 ClO_3^-(aq) + 3 As_2S_3(s) \rightarrow 14 Cl^-(aq) + 6 H_2AsO_4^-(aq) + 9 HSO_4^-(aq) + 15 H^+(aq)$; (d) $3 H_2O(l) +$

$7 IO_3^-(aq) + 6 Re(s) \rightarrow 7 I^-(aq) + 6 ReO_4^-(aq) + 6 H^+(aq)$; (e) $26 H^+(aq) + 30 HSO_4^-(aq) + As_4(s) + 10 Pb_3O_4(s) \rightarrow 4 H_2AsO_4^-(aq) + 30 PbSO_4(s) + 24 H_2O(l)$; (f) $3 HNO_2(aq) \rightarrow NO_3^-(aq) + 2 NO(g) + H_2O(l) + H^+(aq)$ **4.118** 3.06 g Cu_2O; 7.44 g CuO **4.120** Al **4.122** (a) $2 H^+ + 2 Cl^- + H_2O_2 \rightarrow Cl_2 + 2 H_2O$, H_2O_2 reduced; (b) $6 H^+ + 2 MnO_4^- + 5 H_2O_2 \rightarrow 2 Mn^{2+} + 5 O_2 + 8 H_2O$, H_2O_2 oxidized; (c) $H_2O_2 + Cl_2 \rightarrow 2 H^+ + 2 Cl^- + O_2$, H_2O_2 oxidized. **4.124** 63.68% ***Multiconcept Problems***
4.126 6.5 g $Ba(OH)_2$; 3.5 g NaOH **4.128** (a) $BaSO_4(s)$ and $AgCl(s)$; (b) 150 g $BaCl_2$, 50 g NaCl, 50 g KNO_3 **4.130** (a) $14 H^+(aq) + Cr_2O_7^{2-}(aq) + 6 Cr^{2+}(aq) \rightarrow 8 Cr^{3+}(aq) + 7 H_2O(l)$; (b) K^+, 0.0833 M; NO_3^-, 0.617 M; H^+, 0.183 M; $Cr_2O_7^{2-}$, 0.0250 M; Cr^{3+}, 0.133 M
4.132 (a) (1) $3 Cu(s) + 8 H^+(aq) + 2 NO_3^-(aq) \rightarrow 3 Cu^{2+}(aq) + 2 NO(g) + 4 H_2O(l)$; (2) $2 Cu^{2+}(aq) + 2 SCN^-(aq) + H_2O(l) + HSO_3^-(aq) \rightarrow 2 CuSCN(s) + HSO_4^-(aq) + 2 H^+(aq)$; (3) $10 Cu^+(aq) + 12 H^+(aq) + 2 IO_3^-(aq) \rightarrow 10 Cu^{2+}(aq) + I_2(aq) + 6 H_2O(l)$; (4) $I_2(aq) + 2 S_2O_3^{2-}(aq) \rightarrow 2 I^-(aq) + S_4O_6^{2-}(aq)$; (5) $2 ZnNH_4PO_4 \rightarrow Zn_2P_2O_7 + H_2O + 2 NH_3$; (b) 77.1% Cu; (c) 19.5% Zn **4.134** (a) $5 H_3MO_3(aq) + 2 MnO_4^-(aq) + 6 H^+(aq) \rightarrow 5 H_3MO_4(aq) + 2 Mn^{2+}(aq) + 3 H_2O(l)$; (b) 1.34×10^{-3} mol M_2O_3; 2.68×10^{-3} mol M (c) As.

Chapter 5

5.1 gamma ray, 8.43×10^{18} Hz; radar wave, 2.91×10^9 Hz
5.2 2.93 m; 3.14×10^{-10} m **5.3** (b) has the higher frequency. (b) represents the more intense beam of light. (b) represents blue light. (a) represents red light. **5.4** 397.0 nm **5.5** 1875 nm
5.6 820.4 nm **5.7** 1310 kJ/mol **5.8** IR, 77.2 kJ/mol; UV, 479 kJ/mol; X ray, 2.18×10^4 kJ/mol **5.9** 2.34×10^{-38} m

5.10

n	l	m_l	Orbital	No. of Orbitals
5	0	0	$5s$	1
	1	$-1, 0, +1$	$5p$	3
	2	$-2, -1, 0, +1, +2$	$5d$	5
	3	$-3, -2, -1, 0, +1, +2, +3$	$5f$	7
	4	$-4, -3, -2, -1, 0, +1, +2, +3, +4$	$5g$	9

There are 25 possible orbitals in the fifth shell.
5.11 (a) $2p$; (b) $4f$; (c) $3d$ **5.12** (a) $n = 3$, $l = 0$, $m_l = 0$; (b) $n = 2$, $l = 1$, $m_l = -1, 0, +1$; (c) $n = 4$, $l = 2$, $m_l = -2, -1, 0, +1, +2$
5.13 four nodal planes. **5.14** $n = 4$ and $l = 2$ **5.15** 1.31×10^3 kJ/mol
5.16 Cr, Cu, Nb, Mo, Ru, Rh, Pd, Ag, La, Ce, Gd, Pt, Au, Ac, Th, Pa, U, Np, Cm, Ds, Rg **5.17** (a) Ti, $1s^2 2s^2 2p^6 3s^2 3p^6 4s^2 3d^2$ or [Ar] $4s^2 3d^2$;

$$[Ar]\;\underset{4s}{\upharpoonleft\!\downharpoonright}\quad \underset{3d}{\uparrow\;\uparrow\;\rule{0.4cm}{0.4pt}\;\rule{0.4cm}{0.4pt}\;\rule{0.4cm}{0.4pt}}$$

(b) Zn, $1s^2 2s^2 2p^6 3s^2 3p^6 4s^2 3d^{10}$ or [Ar] $4s^2 3d^{10}$;

$$[Ar]\;\underset{4s}{\upharpoonleft\!\downharpoonright}\quad \underset{3d}{\upharpoonleft\!\downharpoonright\;\upharpoonleft\!\downharpoonright\;\upharpoonleft\!\downharpoonright\;\upharpoonleft\!\downharpoonright\;\upharpoonleft\!\downharpoonright}$$

(c) Sn, $1s^2 2s^2 2p^6 3s^2 3p^6 4s^2 3d^{10} 4p^6 5s^2 4d^{10} 5p^2$ or [Kr] $5s^2 4d^{10} 5p^2$;

$$[Kr]\;\underset{5s}{\upharpoonleft\!\downharpoonright}\quad \underset{4d}{\upharpoonleft\!\downharpoonright\;\upharpoonleft\!\downharpoonright\;\upharpoonleft\!\downharpoonright\;\upharpoonleft\!\downharpoonright\;\upharpoonleft\!\downharpoonright}\quad \underset{5p}{\uparrow\;\uparrow\;\rule{0.4cm}{0.4pt}}$$

(d) Pb, [Xe] $6s^2 4f^{14} 5d^{10} 6p^2$
5.18 Na^+, $1s^2 2s^2 2p^6$; Cl^-, $1s^2 2s^2 2p^6 3s^2 3p^6$ **5.19** Ni **5.20** (a) Ba; (b) Hf; (c) Sn; (d) Lu **5.21** Excited mercury atoms in a fluorescent bulb emit photons, some in the visible but most in the ultraviolet region. Visible photons contribute to light we can see; ultraviolet

photons are invisible to our eyes. To utilize this ultraviolet energy, fluorescent bulbs are coated on the inside with a phosphor that absorbs ultraviolet photons and re-emits the energy as visible light. *Conceptual Problems*

5.22

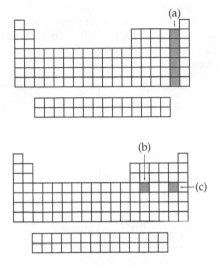

5.24 The green element, molybdenum, has an anomalous electron configuration. Its predicted configuration is $[Ar]\ 5s^2\ 4d^4$. Its anomalous configuration is $[Ar]\ 5s^1\ 4d^5$ because of the resulting half-filled d-orbitals. **5.26** Ga **5.28** Sr (215 pm) > Ca (197 pm) > Br (114 pm) *Section Problems* **5.30** Violet has the higher frequency and energy. Red has the higher wavelength. **5.32** visible; completely within this range; ultraviolet and infrared; partially in this range. **5.34** 5.5×10^{-8} m **5.36** (a) $\nu = 99.5$ MHz, $E = 3.97 \times 10^{-5}$ kJ/mol, $\nu = 1150$ kHz, $E = 4.589 \times 10^{-7}$ kJ/mol. The FM radio wave (99.5 MHz) has the higher energy. (b) $\lambda = 3.44 \times 10^{-9}$ m, $E = 3.48 \times 10^4$ kJ/mol, $\lambda = 6.71 \times 10^{-2}$ m, $E = 1.78 \times 10^{-3}$ kJ/mol. The X ray ($\lambda = 3.44 \times 10^{-9}$ m) has the higher energy. **5.38** (a) 36.4 cm; (b) 34.3 cm **5.40** (a) 1320 nm, near IR; (b) 0.149 m, radio wave; (c) 65.4 nm, UV **5.42** (a) 779 nm, 2.55×10^{-19} J; (b) 649 nm, 3.06×10^{-19} J; (c) 405 nm, 4.91×10^{-19} J **5.44** For $n = 3$, $E = 182.3$ kJ/mol; For $n = 4$, $E = 246.1$ kJ/mol; For $n = 5$, $E = 275.6$ kJ/mol **5.46** 2.45×10^{-12} m, γ ray **5.48** 1.06×10^{-34} m **5.50** 9.14×10^{-24} m/s **5.52** 8×10^{-31} m **5.54** n is the principal quantum number. The size and energy level of an orbital depends on n. l is the angular-momentum quantum number. l defines the three-dimensional shape of an orbital. m_l is the magnetic quantum number. m_l defines the spatial orientation of an orbital. m_s is the spin quantum number. m_s indicates the spin of the electron and can have either of two values, $+1/2$ or $-1/2$. **5.56** The probability of finding the electron drops off rapidly as distance from the nucleus increases, although it never drops to zero, even at large distances. As a result, there is no definite boundary or size for an orbital. However, we usually imagine the boundary surface of an orbital enclosing the volume where an electron spends 95% of its time. **5.58** Part of the electron–nucleus attraction is canceled by the electron–electron repulsion, an effect we describe by saying that the electrons are shielded from the nucleus by the other electrons. The net nuclear charge actually felt by an electron is called the effective nuclear charge, Z_{eff}, and is often substantially lower than the actual nuclear charge, Z_{actual}. $Z_{eff} = Z_{actual} -$ electron shielding **5.60** (a) $4s$: $n = 4$; $l = 0$; $m_l = 0$; $m_s = \pm 1/2$; (b) $3p$: $n = 3$; $l = 1$; $m_l = -1, 0, +1$; $m_s = \pm 1/2$; (c) $5f$: $n = 5$; $l = 3$; $m_l = -3, -2, -1, 0, +1, +2, +3$; $m_s = \pm 1/2$; (d) $5d$: $n = 5$; $l = 2$; $m_l = -2, -1, 0, +1, +2$; $m_s = \pm 1/2$ **5.62** (a) not allowed because for $l = 0$, $m_l = 0$ only; (b) allowed; (c) not allowed

because for $n = 4$, $l = 0, 1, 2,$ or 3 only **5.64** The maximum number of electrons will occur when the 5g orbital is filled: $[Rn]\ 7s^2\ 5f^{14}\ 6d^{10}\ 7p^6\ 8s^2\ 5g^{18} = 138$ electrons **5.66** $E = 328.1$ kJ/mol **5.68** 363 kJ/mol **5.70** The principal quantum number n increases by 1 from one period to the next. As the principal quantum number increases, the number of orbitals in a shell increases. The progression of elements parallels the number of electrons in a particular shell. **5.72** (a) $5d$; (b) $4s$; (c) $6s$ **5.74** (a) $3d$; (b) $4p$; (c) $6d$; (d) $6s$ **5.76** (a) $1s^2\ 2s^2\ 2p^6\ 3s^2\ 3p^6\ 4s^2\ 3d^2$; (b) $1s^2\ 2s^2\ 2p^6\ 3s^2\ 3p^6\ 4s^2\ 3d^{10}\ 4p^6\ 5s^2\ 4d^6$; (c) $1s^2\ 2s^2\ 2p^6\ 3s^2\ 3p^6\ 4s^2\ 3d^{10}\ 4p^6\ 5s^2\ 4d^{10}\ 5p^2$; (d) $1s^2\ 2s^2\ 2p^6\ 3s^2\ 3p^6\ 4s^2\ 3d^{10}\ 4p^6\ 5s^2$; (e) $1s^2\ 2s^2\ 2p^6\ 3s^2\ 3p^6\ 4s^2\ 3d^{10}\ 4p^4$

5.78

(a) Rb, $[Kr]\ \underset{5s}{\uparrow}$

(b) W, $[Xe]\ \underset{6s}{\uparrow\downarrow}\quad \underset{4f}{\uparrow\downarrow\ \uparrow\downarrow\ \uparrow\downarrow\ \uparrow\downarrow\ \uparrow\downarrow\ \uparrow\downarrow\ \uparrow\downarrow}\quad \underset{5d}{\uparrow\ \uparrow\ \uparrow\ \uparrow\ \_}$

(c) Ge, $[Ar]\ \underset{4s}{\uparrow\downarrow}\quad \underset{3d}{\uparrow\downarrow\ \uparrow\downarrow\ \uparrow\downarrow\ \uparrow\downarrow\ \uparrow\downarrow}\quad \underset{4p}{\uparrow\ \uparrow\ \_}$

(d) Zr, $[Kr]\ \underset{5s}{\uparrow\downarrow}\quad \underset{4d}{\uparrow\ \uparrow\ \_\ \_\ \_}$

5.80 $4s > 4d > 4f$ **5.82** (a) 2; (b) 2; (c) 1; (d) 3 **5.84** $Z = 121$ **5.86** Atomic radii increase down a group because the electron shells are farther away from the nucleus. **5.88** F < O < S **5.90** Mg has a higher ionization energy than Na because Mg has a higher Z_{eff} and a smaller size. **5.92** $[Rn]\ 7s^2\ 5f^{14}\ 6d^{10}\ 7p^4$ *Chapter Problems* **5.94** 164 nm **5.96** $\lambda = 410.2$ nm; $E = 291.6$ kJ/mol **5.98** 2279 nm **5.100** (a) 0.151 kJ/mol; (b) 2.17×10^{-8} kJ/mol; (c) 2.91 kJ/mol

5.102

(a) Ra, $[Rn]\ 7s^2$ $[Rn]\ \underset{7s}{\uparrow\downarrow}$

(b) Sc, $[Ar]\ 4s^2\ 3d^1$ $[Ar]\ \underset{4s}{\uparrow\downarrow}\quad \underset{3d}{\uparrow\ \_\ \_\ \_\ \_}$

(c) Lr, $[Rn]\ 7s^2\ 5f^{14}\ 6d^1$

$[Rn]\ \underset{7s}{\uparrow\downarrow}\quad \underset{5f}{\uparrow\downarrow\ \uparrow\downarrow\ \uparrow\downarrow\ \uparrow\downarrow\ \uparrow\downarrow\ \uparrow\downarrow\ \uparrow\downarrow}\quad \underset{6d}{\uparrow\ \_\ \_\ \_\ \_}$

(d) B, $[He]\ 2s^2\ 2p^1$ $[He]\ \underset{2s}{\uparrow\downarrow}\quad \underset{2p}{\uparrow\ \_\ \_}$

(e) Te, $[Kr]\ 5s^2\ 4d^{10}\ 5p^4$

$[Kr]\ \underset{5s}{\uparrow\downarrow}\quad \underset{4d}{\uparrow\downarrow\ \uparrow\downarrow\ \uparrow\downarrow\ \uparrow\downarrow\ \uparrow\downarrow}\quad \underset{5p}{\uparrow\downarrow\ \uparrow\ \uparrow}$

5.104 580 nm

5.106

(a) Sr, $[Kr]\ \underset{5s}{\uparrow\downarrow}$

(b) Cd, $[Kr]\ \underset{5s}{\uparrow\downarrow}\quad \underset{4d}{\uparrow\downarrow\ \uparrow\downarrow\ \uparrow\downarrow\ \uparrow\downarrow\ \uparrow\downarrow}$

(c) Ti, $[Ar]\ \underset{4s}{\uparrow\downarrow}\quad \underset{3d}{\uparrow\ \uparrow\ \_\ \_\ \_}$

(d) Se, $[Ar]\ \underset{4s}{\uparrow\downarrow}\quad \underset{3d}{\uparrow\downarrow\ \uparrow\downarrow\ \uparrow\downarrow\ \uparrow\downarrow\ \uparrow\downarrow}\quad \underset{4p}{\uparrow\downarrow\ \uparrow\ \uparrow}$

5.108 (a) 1.0×10^{-10} m; (b) 1.2×10^6 kJ/mol; (c) X rays **5.110** K, $Z_{eff} = 2.26$; Kr, $Z_{eff} = 4.06$ **5.112** 8.3×10^{28} photons **5.114** 940 kJ/mol

5.116

$$\Delta E = \frac{Z^2 e^2}{2a_0}\left[\frac{1}{n_1{}^2} - \frac{1}{n_2{}^2}\right]$$

This equation shows that ΔE is proportional to

$$\left[\frac{1}{n_1{}^2} - \frac{1}{n_2{}^2}\right]$$

where n_1 and n_2 are integers with $n_2 > n_1$. This is similar to the Balmer–Rydberg equation where $1/\lambda$ or ν is proportional to

$$\left[\frac{1}{m^2} - \frac{1}{n^2}\right]$$

where m and n are integers with $n > m$. **5.118** (a) $3d$, n = 3, l = 2; (b) $2p$, n = 2, l = 1, m_l = −1, 0, +1; $3p$, n = 3, l = 1, m_l = −1, 0, +1; $3d$, n = 3, l = 2, m_l = −2, −1, 0, +1, +2; (c) N, $1s^2\,2s^2\,2p^3$ so the $3s$, $3p$, and $3d$ orbitals are empty; (d) C, $1s^2\,2s^2\,2p^2$ so the $1s$ and $2s$ orbitals are filled; (e) Be, $1s^2\,2s^2$ so the $2s$ orbital contains the outermost electrons; (f) $2p$ and $3p$ (↑ ↑ __) and $3d$ (↑ ↑ __ __ __). **5.120** (a) $1.09 \times 10^{15}\ \text{s}^{-1}$; (b) 1.8 nm

Multiconcept Problems **5.122** (a) $5f$ subshell: $n = 5$, $l = 3$, m_l = −3, −2, −1, 0, +1, +2, +3; $3d$ subshell: $n = 3$, $l = 2$, m_l = −2, −1, 0, +1, +2; (b) 1282 nm; (c) 146 kJ/mol

Chapter 6

6.1 [Rn]; (b) [Kr]; (c) [Ar]; (d) [Ne] **6.2** Zn^{2+} **6.3** (a) O^{2-}; (b) S; (c) Fe; (d) H^- **6.4** K^+, r = 133 pm; Cl^-, r = 184 pm; K, r = 227 pm **6.5** (a) Br; (b) S; (c) Se; (d) Ne **6.6** (a) Be; (b) Ga **6.7** (b) Cl has the highest E_{i1} and smallest E_{i4}. **6.8** Al < Kr < Ca **6.9** Cr can accept an electron into a $4s$ orbital. Both Mn and Fe accept the added electron into a $3d$ orbital that contains an electron, but Mn has a lower value of Z_{eff}. **6.10** The least favorable E_{ea} is for Kr. The most favorable E_{ea} is for Ge. **6.11** (a) [Kr]; (b) [Xe]; (c) [Ar]-like configuration (note that Ga^{3+} has ten $3d$ electrons in addition to the two $3s$ and six $3p$ electrons); (d) [Ne] **6.12** gain 2 electrons **6.13** −562 kJ/mol **6.14** (a) KCl; (b) CaF_2; (c) CaO **6.15** (b) MgO has the larger lattice energy. **6.16** (a) O^{2-}; (b) $O_2{}^{2-}$; (c) $O_2{}^-$ **6.17** (a) $2\,Cs(s) + 2\,H_2O(l) \rightarrow 2\,Cs^+(aq) + 2\,OH^-(aq) + H_2(g)$; (b) $Rb(s) + O_2(g) \rightarrow RbO_2(s)$; (c) $2\,K(s) + 2\,NH_3(g) \rightarrow 2\,KNH_2(s) + H_2(g)$; **6.18** (a) $Be(s) + Br_2(l) \rightarrow BeBr_2(s)$; (b) $Sr(s) + 2\,H_2O(l) \rightarrow Sr(OH)_2(aq) + H_2(g)$; (c) $2\,Mg(s) + O_2(g) \rightarrow 2\,MgO(s)$ **6.19** MgS(s); −2 **6.20** evaporation of seawater; mining deposits of *halite*, or *rock salt* *Conceptual Problems* **6.22** (a) ionic compound; (b) covalent compound

6.24

(a) Al^{3+}; (b) Cr^{3+}; (c) Sn^{2+}; (d) Ag^+ **6.26** (a) I_2; (b) Na; (c) NaCl; (d) Cl_2 **6.28** Green, CBr_4; Blue, SrF_2; Red, PbS or PbS_2

Section Problems **6.30** A covalent bond results when two atoms share several (usually two) of their electrons. An ionic bond results from a complete transfer of one or more electrons from one atom to another. The C—H bonds in methane (CH_4) are covalent bonds. The bond in NaCl (Na^+Cl^-) is an ionic bond. **6.32** (a) 4 p, 2 e$^-$, (b) 37 p, 36 e$^-$; (c) 34 p, 36 e$^-$; (d) 79 p, 76 e$^-$ **6.34** (a) La^{3+}, [Xe]; (b) Ag^+, [Kr] $4d^{10}$; (c) Sn^{2+}, [Kr] $5s^2\,4d^{10}$ **6.36** Ca^{2+}, [Ar]; Ti^{2+}, [Ar] $3d^2$ **6.38** Cr^{2+}; Fe^{2+} **6.40** Largest E_{i1} in group 8A because of the largest values of Z_{eff}; smallest E_{i1} in group 1A because of the

smallest values of Z_{eff}. **6.42** (a) Ca; (b) Ca **6.44** Ar has the highest E_{i2} and the lowest E_{i7}. **6.46** boron **6.48** (a) lowest: K; highest: Li; (b) lowest: B; highest: Cl; (c) lowest: Ca; highest: Cl **6.50** They have the same magnitude but opposite signs. **6.52** Na^+ has a more negative electron affinity than either Na or Cl. **6.54** because of the positive Z_{eff}. **6.56** The electron–electron repulsion is large and Z_{eff} is low. **6.58** $MgCl_2$ > LiCl > KCl > KBr **6.60** +195 kJ/mol **6.62** −325 kJ/mol **6.64** 808 kJ/mol **6.66** −537 kJ/mol **6.68** −176 kJ/mol

6.70

6.72 (a) solid; (b) likely to react with Na, NaAt **6.74** Down each group, the valence electrons are farther from the nucleus and more easily removed. **6.76** (a) $2\,K(s) + 2\,H_2O(l) \rightarrow 2\,K^+(aq) + 2\,OH^-(aq) + H_2(g)$; (b) $2\,K(s) + 2\,NH_3(g) \rightarrow 2\,KNH_2(s) + H_2(g)$; (c) $2\,K(s) + Br_2(l) \rightarrow 2\,KBr(s)$; (d) $K(s) + O_2(g) \rightarrow KO_2(s)$ **6.78** (a) $Cl_2(g) + H_2(g) \rightarrow 2\,HCl(g)$; (b) $Cl_2(g) + Ar(g) \rightarrow$ N. R.; (c) $Cl_2(g) + 2\,Rb(s) \rightarrow 2\,RbCl(s)$ **6.80** $MnO_2(s) + 2\,Br^-(aq) + 4\,H^+(aq) \rightarrow Mn^{2+}(aq) + 2\,H_2O(l) + Br_2(aq)$ **6.82** $2\,Al_2O_3(soln) \rightarrow 4\,Al(l) + 3\,O_2(g)$ **6.84** (a) $TiCl_4$, titanium tetrachloride (b) $Ti(s) + 2\,Cl_2(g) \rightarrow TiCl_4(g)$; (c) $TiCl_4 + 2\,Mg(s) \rightarrow Ti(s) + 2\,MgCl_2(s)$ *Chapter Problems* **6.86** Cu^{2+} has fewer electrons and a larger effective nuclear charge. **6.88** MgF, −294 kJ/mol; MgF_2, −1114 kJ/mol; MgF_2 will form because the overall energy for the formation of MgF_2 is much more negative than for the formation of MgF. **6.90** Cl^+Na^-, +640 kJ/mol. Formation of Cl^+Na^- from its elements is not favored because the net energy change is positive whereas it is negative for the formation of Na^+Cl^-. **6.92** (a) $2\,Li(s) + 2\,H_2O(l) \rightarrow 2\,Li^+(aq) + 2\,OH^-(aq) + H_2(g)$; (b) $2\,Li(s) + 2\,NH_3(g) \rightarrow 2\,LiNH_2(s) + H_2(g)$; (c) $2\,Li(s) + Br_2(l) \rightarrow 2\,LiBr(s)$; (d) $6\,Li(s) + N_2(g) \rightarrow 2\,Li_3N(s)$; (e) $4\,Li(s) + O_2(g) \rightarrow 2\,Li_2O(s)$ **6.94** (a) $MgCl_2$, magnesium chloride; (b) CaO, calcium oxide; (c) Li_3N, lithium nitride; (d) Al_2O_3, aluminum oxide **6.96** When moving diagonally down and right on the periodic table, the increase in atomic radius caused by going to a larger shell is offset by a decrease caused by a higher Z_{eff}. **6.98** E_{ea2} = +744 kJ/mol. O^{2-} is not stable in the gas phase. It is stable in MgO because of the large lattice energy that results from the +2 and −2 charge of the ions and their small size. **6.100** (a) F; (b) Se^{2-} **6.102** 5295 kJ/mol *Multiconcept Problems* **6.104** (a) Fe: [Ar] $4s^2\,3d^6$; Fe^{2+}: [Ar] $3d^6$; Fe^{3+}: [Ar] $3d^5$; (b) $n = 3$, $l = 2$. (c) 40.6 nm; (d) The electron removed from Ru to go from Ru^{2+} to Ru^{3+} is a $4d$ electron. The electron with the higher principal quantum number, $n = 4$, is farther from the nucleus, less tightly held, and requires less energy to remove.

Chapter 7

7.1 (a) polar covalent; (b) ionic; (c) polar covalent; (d) polar covalent **7.2** $CCl_4 \sim ClO_2 < TiCl_3 < BaCl_2$ **7.3** H is positively polarized (blue). O is negatively polarized (red). This is consistent with the electronegativity values for O (3.5) and H (2.1).

7.4

(a) H:S̈:H   (b) structure: H top, :Cl:C:Cl: with :Cl: below

7.5

H:Ö:H + H⁺ ⟶ [H:Ö:H with H on top]⁺

Hydronium ion

7.6

(a) propane; (b) H—Ö—Ö—H; (c) H—C—N̈—H (methylamine);
(d) H—C=C—H (ethene); (e) H—C≡C—H; (f) :Cl:Cl̈—C=Ö:

7.7

structure: H—C—C—Ö—H   and   H—C—Ö—C—H

7.8 $C_4H_5N_3O$

structure of cytosine

7.9 :C≡O:

7.10

(a) :Cl̈—Al—Cl̈: with :Cl̈: below   (b) :Cl̈—Ï—Cl̈: with :Cl̈: below

(c) Xe with :Ö:, :F̈:, :F̈:, :F̈:, :F̈:   (d) :B̈r—Ö—H

7.11

(a) [:Ö—H]⁻   (b) [H—S̈—H with H below]⁺   (c) [:Ö: C—Ö—H with :O: below]⁻

(d) [:Ö: over :Ö—Cl—Ö: with :O: below]⁻

7.12 :N̈=N=Ö: ⟷ :N≡N—Ö:

7.13

7.14

structures (benzene ring resonance)

7.15 nitrogen +1; singly bound oxygen −1; doubly bound oxygen 0
7.16 (a) nitrogen −1; carbon 0; oxygen 0; (b) left oxygen −1; central oxygen +1; right oxygen 0 **7.17** (a) bent; (b) trigonal pyramidal; (c) linear; (d) octahedral;(e) square pyramidal; (f) tetrahedral; (g) tetrahedral; (h) tetrahedral; (i) square planar; (j) trigonal planar

7.18

7.19 (a) tetrahedral; (b) seesaw **7.20** Each C is sp^3 hybridized. The C—C bond is formed by the overlap of one singly occupied sp^3 hybrid orbital from each C. The C—H bonds are formed by the overlap of one singly occupied sp^3 orbital on C with a singly occupied H 1s orbital.

7.21 The carbon in formaldehyde is sp^2 hybridized.

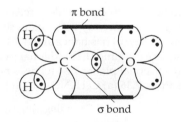

π bond / σ bond

7.22 In HCN the carbon is sp hybridized.

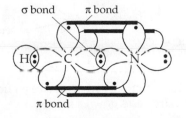

σ bond   π bond   π bond

7.23 In CO_2 the carbon is *sp* hybridized.

7.24 In Cl_2CO the carbon is sp^2 hybridized.

7.25 (a) sp^2 (b) *sp* (c) sp^3

7.26

For He_2^+ σ^*_{1s} ↑

σ_{1s} ↑↓

He_2^+ should be stable with a bond order of 1/2.

7.27

For B_2 σ^*_{2p} —

π^*_{2p} — —

σ_{2p} —

π_{2p} ↑ ↑

σ^*_{2s} ↑↓

σ_{2s} ↑↓

B_2 Bond order = 1; paramagnetic

For C_2 σ^*_{2p} —

π^*_{2p} — —

σ_{2p} —

π_{2p} ↑↓ ↑↓

σ^*_{2s} ↑↓

σ_{2s} ↑↓

C_2 Bond order = 2; diamagnetic

7.28

7.29 because a biologically active molecule is recognized and fits in a receptor molecule in the same way that a hand fits in a glove. **7.30** (a) has no handedness; (b) has handedness. *Conceptual Problems* **7.32** (a) square pyramidal; (b) trigonal pyramidal; (c) square planar; (d) trigonal planar **7.34** (c) does not have a tetrahedral central atom. **7.36** (a) $C_8H_9NO_2$; (b), (c), and (d)

All C's in ring, sp^2, trigonal planar

sp^3, tetrahedral

sp^2, trigonal planar

Section Problems **7.38** Electronegativity increases from left to right across a period and decreases down a group.

7.40 K < Li < Mg < Pb < C < Br **7.42** (a) polar covalent; (b) polar covalent; (c) polar covalent; (d) polar covalent; (e) Na^+–OH^- is ionic; OH^- is polar covalent; (f) polar covalent.

7.44

(a) $\overset{\delta-}{C}$–$\overset{\delta+}{H}$ $\overset{\delta+}{C}$–$\overset{\delta-}{Cl}$ (b) $\overset{\delta-}{Si}$–$\overset{\delta+}{Li}$ $\overset{\delta+}{Si}$–$\overset{\delta-}{Cl}$

(c) $\overset{\delta-}{N}$–$\overset{\delta+}{Cl}$ $\overset{\delta-}{N}$–$\overset{\delta+}{Mg}$

7.46 (a) MgO, $BaCl_2$, LiBr; (b) P_4; (c) $CdBr_2$, BrF_3, NF_3, $POCl_3$
7.48 (a) $MgBr_2$; (b) PBr_3 **7.50** N_2H_2 **7.52** (a) Phosphorus trichloride; (b) Dinitrogen trioxide; (c) Tetraphosphorus heptoxide; (d) Bromine trifluoride; (e) Nitrogen trichloride; (f) Tetraphosphorus hexoxide; (g) Disulfur difluoride; (h) Selenium dioxide **7.54** The transition metals are characterized by partially filled *d* orbitals that can be used to expand their valence shell beyond the normal octet of electrons.

7.56

(a) :Br—C—Br: (b) :Cl—N—Cl: (c) H H
     with :Br: above and below C   :Cl: H—C—C—Cl:
                                                     H H

(d) [:F—B—F:]⁻ with :F: above and below B   (e) [:O—O:]²⁻   (f) [:N≡O:]⁺

7.58

(a) H—N≡N—N̈: ⟷ H—N̈=N=N̈: ⟷ H—N̈—N≡N:

(b) structures with S bonded to three O (sulfite resonance)

(c) [:N≡C—S̈:]⁻ ⟷ [:N̈=C=S̈:]⁻ ⟷ [:N̈—C≡S:]⁻

7.60

$$\text{H—O—C—C—O—H with two =O groups}$$

7.62 (a) yes; (b) yes; (c) yes; (d) yes **7.64** (a) A1; (b) P

7.66

(a)   :Cl—C—O—C—H with =O on first C and H's   (b) H—C—C≡C—H with H's

7.68 :C≡O: carbon −1; oxygen +1;

7.70

:Ö—C̈l—Ö: ⟷ :Ö—C̈l=O

7.72

(a)   C=N=N: (with H's on C)   (b)   C—N=N: (with H's on C)

Structure (a) is more important because of the octet of electrons around carbon.

7.74

7.76 (a) trigonal planar; (b) trigonal bipyramidal; (c) linear;
(d) octahedral **7.78** (a) tetrahedral, 4; (b) octahedral, 6; (c) bent, 3 or 4;
(d) linear, 2 or 5; (e) square pyramidal, 6; (f) trigonal pyramidal, 4
7.80 (a) bent; (b) tetrahedral; (c) bent; (d) trigonal planar
7.82 (a) trigonal bipyramidal; (b) see saw; (c) trigonal pyramidal;
(d) tetrahedral **7.84** (a) tetrahedral; (b) tetrahedral; (c) tetrahedral;
(d) trigonal pyramidal; (e) tetrahedral; (f) linear
7.86 (a) approximately 109°; (b) approximately 120°; (c) 90°;
(d) approximately 120°

7.88

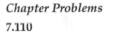

$H-C_a-H$, ~120°, C_b-C_c N, 180°; $H-C_a-H_b$, ~120°;
C_a-C_b-H, ~120°; $C_a-C_b-C_c$, ~120°; $H-C_b-C_c$, ~120°

7.90

109.5° around carbon and 90° around S.

7.92 The geometry about each carbon is tetrahedral with a
$C-C-C$ bond angle of approximately 109°. Because the
geometry about each carbon is tetrahedral, the cyclohexane ring
cannot be flat. **7.94** In a π bond, the shared electrons occupy a
region above and below a line connecting the two nuclei. A σ bond
has its shared electrons located along the axis between the two
nuclei. **7.96** (a) sp (b) sp^2 (c) sp^3 **7.98** (a) sp^2 (b) sp^2 (c) sp^3 (d) sp^2

7.100

$$H-O-\underset{a}{C}-\underset{b}{C}-\underset{c}{C}-\underset{d}{C}-O-H$$

Carbon a, b, and d are sp^2 hybridized and carbon c is sp^3
hybridized. The bond angles around carbons a, b, and d are ~120°.
The bond angles around carbon c are ~109°. The terminal
$H-O-C$ bond angles are ~109°.

7.102

σ^*_{2p}	—		—		—	
π^*_{2p}	↑		↑	↑	↑↓	↑
π_{2p}	↑↓	↑↓	↑↓	↑↓	↑↓	↑↓
σ_{2p}	↑↓		↑↓		↑↓	
σ^*_{2s}	↑↓		↑↓		↑↓	
σ_{2s}	↑↓		↑↓		↑↓	
	O_2^+		O_2		O_2^-	

Bond order: O_2^+, 2.5; O_2, 2; O_2^-, 1.5. All are stable. All have
unpaired electrons. **7.104** (a) C_2 bond order = 2;
(b) Add one electron; (c) C_2^- bond order = 2.5

7.106 (a) diamagnetic; (b) paramagnetic; (c) paramagnetic;
(d) diamagnetic; (e) paramagnetic

7.108

p orbitals in allyl cation

allyl cation showing only
the σ bonds (each C is
sp^2 hybridized)

delocalized MO model for
π bonding in the allyl cation

Chapter Problems

7.110

7.112

All carbons except the two indicated are sp^2.
7.114 Every carbon is sp^2 hybridized. There are 18 σ bonds and
5 π bonds.

7.116

7.118 (a) reactants: boron 0; oxygen 0; product: boron −1; oxygen
+1; (b) Reactants: B, sp^2, trigonal planar; O, sp^3, bent. Product: B,
sp^3, tetrahedral; O, sp^3, trigonal pyramidal. **7.120** The triply bonded
carbon atoms are sp hybridized. The theoretical bond angle for
$C-C\equiv C$ is 180°. Benzyne is so reactive because the $C-C\equiv C$
bond angle is closer to 120° and is very strained.

7.122

7.124

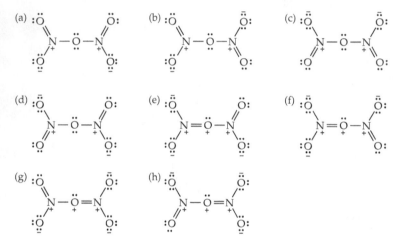

bond order = 3 **7.126** −109 kJ

7.128

Structures (a)–(d) make more important contributions to the resonance hybrid because of only −1 and 0 formal charges on the oxygens.

7.130

21 σ bonds
5 π bonds

Each C with a double bond is *sp²* hybridized. The —CH₃ is *sp³* hybridized.

7.132

(a) σ*₃ₚ   — —   — —

π*₃ₚ   ↑ ↑   ↑↓ ↑↓

π₃ₚ   ↑↓ ↑↓   ↑↓ ↑↓

σ₃ₚ   ↑↓   ↑↓

σ*₃ₛ   ↑↓   ↑↓

σ₃ₛ   ↑↓   ↑↓
       S₂   S₂²⁻

(b) paramagnetic; (c) 2; (d) The two added electrons go into the antibonding π^*_{3p} MOs, and the bond length in S_2^{2-} should be longer.

7.134

(a)

left S: seesaw; right S: bent

(b)

left C: tetrahedral; right C: trigonal planar; central two C's: linear.

Multiconcept Problems

7.136 $\left[:\ddot{O}-H\right]^-$ $:\ddot{O}-H$

(b) The oxygen in OH has a half-filled $2p$ orbital that can accept the additional electron. $n = 2$ and $l = 1$; (c) When OH gains an additional electron, it achieves an octet configuration.

7.138
(a)

(b) Each Cr atom has 6 pairs of electrons around it. The likely geometry about each Cr atom is tetrahedral because each Cr has 4 charge clouds.

7.140 (a) Each carbon is sp^2 hybridized; (b) & (c);

antibonding   —

antibonding   — —

nonbonding   ↑↓ ↑↓

bonding   ↑↓ ↑↓

bonding   ↑↓

(d) The cyclooctatetraene dianion has only paired electrons and is diamagnetic.

Chapter 8

8.1 (a) and (b) are state functions; (c) is not. **8.2** $+1.9 \times 10^4$ J flows into the system **8.3** −0.25 kJ; The expanding system loses work energy and does work on the surroundings. **8.4** (a) $P\Delta V$ is negative for this reaction because the system volume is decreased at constant pressure. (b) ΔH is negative. Its value is slightly more negative than ΔE. **8.5** $w = 0.57$ kJ; $\Delta E = -120$ kJ **8.6** −45.2 kJ **8.7** (a) 780 kJ evolved; (b) 1.24 kJ absorbed **8.8** 1.000×10^3 kJ **8.9** $q = -32$ kJ **8.10** 0.130 J/(g·°C) **8.11** -1.1×10^2 kJ **8.12** −202 kJ **8.13** (a) A + 2 B → D; $\Delta H° = -150$ kJ; (b) red arrow: step 1; green arrow: step 2; blue arrow: overall reaction; (c) top energy level represents A + 2 B, middle energy level represents C + B, bottom energy level represents D

8.14

Reactants $CH_4 + 2 Cl_2$

$\Delta H° = -202$ kJ

$\Delta H° = -98.3$ kJ

$CH_3Cl + HCl + Cl_2$

$\Delta H° = -104$ kJ

Products $CH_2Cl_2 + 2 HCl$

8.15 −901.2 kJ **8.16** +2803 kJ **8.17** +78 kJ **8.18** −81 kJ
8.19 −2635.5 kJ/mol; −45.35 kJ/g **8.20** $\Delta S°$ is negative because
the reaction decreases the number of moles of gaseous molecules.
8.21 The reaction proceeds from a solid and a gas (reactants) to
all gas (product). Randomness increases, so $\Delta S°$ is positive.
8.22 (a) spontaneous; (b) nonspontaneous
8.23 $\Delta G° = -32.9$ kJ; reaction is spontaneous; $T = 190$ °C
8.24 (a) $2 A_2 + B_2 \rightarrow 2 A_2B$; (b) ΔH is negative; ΔS is negative;
(c) low temperatures only **8.25** $C_2H_6O + 3 O_2 \rightarrow 2 CO_2 + 3 H_2O$;
$2 C_{19}H_{38}O_2 + 55 O_2 \rightarrow 38 CO_2 + 38 H_2O$ **8.26** Because the
standard heat of formation of $CO_2(g)$ (−393.5 kJ/mol) is more
negative than that of $H_2O(g)$ (−241.8 kJ/mol), formation of CO_2
releases more heat than formation of H_2O. According to the
balanced equations, combustion of ethanol yields a 2:3 ratio of CO_2
to H_2O, whereas combustion of biodiesel yields a 1:1 ratio. Thus
biodiesel has a more favorable (more negative) combustion
enthalpy per gram *Conceptual Problems* **8.28** (a) yes; $w < 0$;
(b) yes; $\Delta H < 0$; exothermic
8.30

Reactants

Step 1

Net reaction

Step 2

$H°$

Products

8.32 The volume decreases from 5 L to 3 L.

1 atm

$V = 3.00$ L

8.34 $\Delta G < 0$; $\Delta H > 0$; $\Delta S > 0$ *Section Problems* **8.36** Heat is the
energy transferred from one object to another as the result of a
temperature difference between them. Temperature is a measure of
the kinetic energy of molecular motion. Energy is the capacity to do
work or supply heat. Work is defined as the distance moved times
the force that opposes the motion ($w = d \times F$). Kinetic energy is
the energy of motion. Potential energy is stored energy.
8.38 Car: 7.1×10^5 J; truck: 6.7×10^5 J **8.40** −70 J. The energy
change is negative. **8.42** (a) 35 min; (b) 150 min **8.44** (a) −593 J;
(b) 26.4 cm **8.46** $\Delta E = q_v$ is the heat of a reaction at constant
volume. $\Delta H = q_p$ is the heat of a reaction at constant pressure.
8.48 ΔH and ΔE are nearly equal when there are no gases involved
in a chemical reaction, or, if gases are involved, $\Delta V = 0$.
8.50 −0.30 kJ **8.52** 45.4 kJ **8.54** $\Delta E = -314$ kJ **8.56** 25.5 kJ **8.58** 131 kJ
8.60 0.388 kJ is evolved; exothermic. **8.62** Heat capacity is the
amount of heat required to raise the temperature of a substance a
given amount. Specific heat is the amount of heat necessary to raise
the temperature of exactly 1 g of a substance by exactly 1 °C.
8.64 1.23 J/(g·°C) **8.66** −83.7 kJ **8.68** $\Delta H = -56$ kJ/mol; same

temperature increase because NaOH is still the limiting reactant.
8.70 The standard state of an element is its most stable form at
1 atm and 25 °C. **8.72** The overall enthalpy change for a reaction is
equal to the sum of the enthalpy changes for the individual
steps in the reaction. Hess's Law works because of the law of
conservation of energy. **8.74** (a) gas; (b) liquid; (c) gas; (d) solid
8.76 (a) $2 Fe(s) + 3/2 O_2(g) \rightarrow Fe_2O_3(s)$;
(b) $12 C(s) + 11 H_2(g) + 11/2 O_2(g) \rightarrow C_{12}H_{22}O_{11}(s)$;
(c) $U(s) + 3 F_2(g) \rightarrow UF_6(s)$ **8.78** −395.7 kJ/mol **8.80** −909.3 kJ
8.82 = +104 kJ/mol **8.84** −16.9 kJ/mol **8.86** +179.2 kJ
8.88 −6 kJ **8.90** −2645 kJ **8.92** Entropy is a measure of molecular
randomness. **8.94** A reaction can be spontaneous yet endothermic
if ΔS is positive (more randomness) and the $T\Delta S$ term is
larger than ΔH. **8.96** (a) positive; (b) negative **8.98** (a) zero;
(b) zero; (c) negative **8.100** ΔS is positive. The reaction increases
the total number of molecules. **8.102** (a) spontaneous; exothermic.
(b) nonspontaneous; exothermic. (c) spontaneous; endothermic.
(d) nonspontaneous; endothermic. **8.104** 570 K
8.106 (a) spontaneous at all temperatures; (b) has a crossover
temperature; (c) has a crossover temperature; (d) nonspontaneous
at all temperatures **8.108** 31.6 J/(K·mol) *Chapter Problems*
8.110 −468 kJ **8.112** −171.5 kJ **8.114** 279 K **8.116** (a) +34 kJ;
(b) −451 kJ; (c) −87 kJ **8.118** (a) $2 C_8H_{18}(l) + 25 O_2(g) \rightarrow$
$16 CO_2(g) + 18 H_2O(l)$; (b) −259 kJ/mol **8.120** (a) $\Delta G = -T\Delta S_{total}$;
(b) $\Delta S_{surr} = -9399$ J/(K·mol) **8.122** $\Delta H° = +201.9$ kJ **8.124** 311 g
8.126 −56 kJ **8.128** −1198.4 kJ *Multiconcept Problems*

8.130 (a)

$:\ddot{O}$
‖
C
$:\ddot{Cl}$ $\ddot{C}l:$

(b) −183 kJ/mol. The calculation of $\Delta H°_f$ from bond energies
is only an estimate because the bond energies are average
values derived from many different compounds.
8.132 (a) $2 K(s) + 2 H_2O(l) \rightarrow 2 KOH(aq) + H_2(g)$;
(b) −393.2 kJ; (c) 47.7 °C; (d) 0.483 M; 174 mL of 0.554 M H_2SO_4
8.134 (a) Y is ClF_3 and X is ClF;

(b) T-shaped $:\ddot{F}-\ddot{C}l-\ddot{F}:$
$|$
$:\ddot{F}:$

(c) −139.2 kJ/mol ClF_3; (d) 55.9 kJ is released.

Chapter 9

9.1 1.00 atm = 14.7 psi; 1.00 mm Hg = 1.93×10^{-2} psi
9.2 10.3 m **9.3** 0.650 atm **9.4** 1000 mm Hg
9.5   (a)   (b)

9.6 4.461×10^3 mol; 7.155×10^4 g **9.7** 5.0 atm **9.8** 267 mol **9.9** 28 °C
9.10 (a) The volume should increase by about 10%.

(b) the volume should decrease by half;

(c) the volume is unchanged.

9.11 14.8 g; 7.55 L **9.12** 190 L **9.13** 34.1 amu; H_2S, hydrogen sulfide **9.14** $X_{H_2} = 0.7281$; $X_{N_2} = 0.2554$; $X_{NH_3} = 0.0165$ **9.15** $P_{total} = 25.27$ atm; $P_{H_2} = 18.4$ atm; $P_{N_2} = 6.45$ atm; $P_{NH_3} = 0.417$ atm **9.16** 0.0280 atm **9.17** $P_{red} = 300$ mm Hg; $P_{yellow} = 100$ mm Hg; $P_{green} = 200$ mm Hg **9.18** at 37 °C, 525 m/s; at −25 °C, 470 m/s **9.19** −187.0 °C **9.20** (a) O_2, 1.62; (b) C_2H_2, 1.04 **9.21** $^{20}Ne(1.05) > {}^{21}Ne(1.02) > {}^{22}Ne(1.00)$ **9.22** ideal gas law: 20.5 atm; van der Waals equation: 20.3 atm **9.23** 3.8×10^{-5} m **9.24** 2.0% **9.25** (a) 5.9 mm Hg; (b) 0.41 g *Conceptual Problems* **9.26** The picture on the right will be the same as that on the left, apart from random scrambling of the He and Ar atoms. **9.28** (a) the volume will increase by a factor of 1.5; (b) the volume will decrease by a factor of 2; (c) there is no change in volume.

(a) (b) (c)

9.30 (c). **9.32** The gas pressure in the bulb in mm Hg is equal to the difference in the height of the Hg in the two arms of the manometer. **9.34** (a) yellow; (b) 36 amu *Section Problems* **9.36** Temperature is a measure of the average kinetic energy of gas particles. **9.38** 0.632 atm; 6.40×10^4 Pa **9.40** 930 mm Hg **9.42** 1.046×10^5 Pa **9.44** 28.96 amu **9.46** (a) P would triple; (b) P would be 1/3 the initial pressure. (c) P would increase by 1.8 times; (d) P would be 0.17 times the initial pressure. **9.48** They all contain the same number of gas molecules. **9.50** 7210 L; 51.5 L **9.52** 2.1×10^4 mm Hg **9.54** 1×10^{-17} mm Hg **9.56** 1.23×10^4 g **9.58** ice **9.60** Weigh the containers. The heavier container contains O_2. **9.62** 1.5×10^4 g O_2 **9.64** (a) 0.716 g/L; (b) 1.96 g/L; (c) 1.43 g/L **9.66** 34.0 amu **9.68** 0.5469 L **9.70** (a) 9.44 L; (b) 6.05 g Zn **9.72** (a) 380 g; (b) 5.4 days **9.74** $P_{N_2} = 0.7808$ atm; $P_{O_2} = 0.2095$ atm; $P_{Ar} = 0.0093$ atm; $P_{CO_2} = 0.000\,38$ atm **9.76** $P_{O_2} = 0.970$ atm; $P_{CO_2} = 0.007\,11$ atm; **9.78** $X_{HCl} = 0.026$; $X_{H_2} = 0.094$; $X_{Ne} = 0.88$ **9.80** (a) 1.68 atm; (b) 0.219 atm. **9.82** $P_{H_2} = 723$ mm Hg; 3.36 g Mg **9.84** See list in text Section 9.6. **9.86** Heat is the energy transferred from one object to another as the result of a temperature difference between them. Temperature is a measure of the kinetic energy of molecular motion. **9.88** $u = 443$ m/s **9.90** For H_2, $u = 1360$ m/s. For He, $u = 2010$ m/s. **9.92** 17.2 amu **9.94** Relative rates of diffusion are HCl (1.05) > F_2 (1.02) > Ar (1.00). **9.96** −272.83 °C *Chapter Problems* **9.98** (a) ozone depletion; (b) acid rain; (c) global warming; (d) air pollution **9.100** Relative rates of diffusion are $^{35}Cl_2$ (1.03) > $^{35}Cl^{37}Cl$ (1.01) > $^{37}Cl_2$ (1.00). **9.102** 1.1 L **9.104** (a) ideal gas law: 1.79 atm; (b) van der Waals equation: 1.74 atm **9.106** (a) Kr < O_2; (b) O_2 < Kr; (c) Kr < O_2; (d) Both are the same. **9.108** (a) 372 mm Hg; (b) 222 mm Hg; (c) 46.5 mm Hg **9.110** 504.3 g **9.112** (a) Bulb A contains $CO_2(g)$ and $N_2(g)$; B contains $CO_2(g)$, $N_2(g)$, and $H_2O(s)$; (b) $n = 0.0013$ mol H_2O; (c) A contains $N_2(g)$; B contains $N_2(g)$ and $H_2O(s)$; C contains $N_2(g)$ and $CO_2(s)$; (d) 0.010 92 mol N_2; (e) 0.0181 mol CO_2 **9.114** ideal gas law: $P = 59.1$ atm at 0 °C; 70.0 atm at 50 °C; 80.8 atm at 100 °C. van der Waals equation: $P = 36.5$ atm at 0 °C; 48.5 atm at 50 °C; 60.5 atm at 100 °C **9.116** 816 atm **9.118** (a) 0.901 mol; (b) 1.44 atm; (c) $P_{CH_4} = 1.32$ atm; $P_{C_2H_6} = 0.12$ atm; (d) Heat liberated = −843 kJ **9.120** (a) 196 g/mol; XeO_4; (b) $P_{Xe} = 0.313$ atm; $P_{O_2} = 0.626$ atm; $P_{total} = 0.939$ atm **9.122** 1.43 atm **9.124** 12.7% **9.126** $X_{NO_2} = 0.380$;

$X_{N_2O_4} = 0.620$ *Multiconcept Problems* **9.128** (a) 3.75 g; (b) 310 °C; (c) 1.02 atm **9.130** (a) $2\,C_8H_{18}(l) + 25\,O_2(g) \rightarrow 16\,CO_2(g) + 18\,H_2O(g)$; (b) 1.1×10^{11} kg; (c) 5.7×10^{13} L; (d) 59.5 mol, 1.33×10^3 L **9.132** (a) 0.0290 mol; (b) 0.0100 mol A; A = H_2O; (c) 0.0120 mol B; B = CO_2; (d) 0.001 00 mol C; C = O_2; 0.006 00 mol D; 28.0 g/mol; D = N_2; (e) $4\,C_3H_5N_3O_9(l) \rightarrow 10\,H_2O(g) + 12\,CO_2(g) + O_2(g) + 6\,N_2(g)$

Chapter 10

10.1 41%; HF has more ionic character than HCl. **10.2** (a) SF_6 is symmetrical (octahedral) and has no dipole moment; (b) $H_2C{=}CH_2$ is symmetrical; no dipole moment.

(c)

The C–Cl bonds in $CHCl_3$ are polar covalent bonds, and the molecule is polar.

(d)

The C–Cl bonds in CH_2Cl_2 are polar covalent bonds, and the molecule is polar.

10.3
 Net

10.4 The N atom is electron rich (red) because of its high electronegativity. The C and H atoms are electron poor (blue) because they are less electronegative. **10.5** (a) HNO_3; (b) HNO_3; (c) Ar **10.6** H_2S, dipole–dipole, dispersion; CH_3OH, hydrogen bonding, dipole–dipole, dispersion; C_2H_6, dispersion; Ar, dispersion; Ar < C_2H_6 < H_2S < CH_3OH **10.7** (a) positive; (b) negative; (c) positive **10.8** 334 K **10.9** 47 °C **10.10** 31.4 kJ/mol **10.11** (a) 2 atoms; (b) 4 atoms **10.12** 167 pm **10.13** 9.31 g/cm³ **10.14** There are several possibilities. Here's one.

10.15 For CuCl: 4 minuses, 4 pluses. For $BaCl_2$: 8 pluses, 8 minuses **10.16** (a) 1 Re atom, 3 O atoms; (b) ReO_3; (c) +6; (d) linear; (e) octahedral **10.17** The triple point pressure of 5.11 atm **10.18** (a) $CO_2(s) \rightarrow CO_2(g)$; (b) $CO_2(l) \rightarrow CO_2(g)$; (c) $CO_2(g) \rightarrow CO_2(l) \rightarrow$ supercritical CO_2

10.19
(a)

(b) two; (c) Increasing the pressure favors the liquid phase, giving the solid/liquid boundary a negative slope. At 1 atm pressure the liquid phase is more dense than the solid phase. **10.20** As the name implies, the constituent particles in an ionic liquid are cations and anions rather than molecules. **10.21** In ionic liquids the cation has an irregular shape and one or both of the ions are large and bulky to disperse charges over a large volume. Both factors minimize the crystal lattice energy, making the solid less stable and favoring the liquid. *Conceptual Problems* **10.22** The electronegative O atoms are electron rich (red), while the rest of the molecule is electron poor (blue). **10.24** (a) cubic closest-packed; (b) 4 S^{2-}; 4 Zn^{2+} **10.26** (a) normal boiling point $\approx$ 300 K, normal melting point $\approx$ 180 K; (b) (i) solid, (ii) gas, (iii) supercritical fluid

10.28 Here are two possibilities.

10.30

Section Problems **10.32** If a molecule has polar covalent bonds, the molecular shape (and location of lone pairs of electrons) determines whether the bond dipoles cancel and thus whether the molecule has a dipole moment. **10.34** (a) Dipole–dipole forces; dispersion forces are also present; (b) dispersion forces; (c) dispersion forces; (d) dipole–dipole forces and hydrogen bonding; dispersion forces are also present. **10.36** For CH_3OH and CH_4, dispersion forces are small. CH_3OH can hydrogen bond; CH_4 cannot. This accounts for the large difference in boiling points. For 1-decanol and decane, dispersion forces are comparable and relatively large along the C—H chain. 1-decanol can hydrogen bond; decane cannot. This accounts for the 57 °C higher boiling point for 1-decanol.

10.38

10.40 5.05%

10.42

SO_2 is bent and the individual bond dipole moments add to give a net dipole moment. CO_2 is linear and the individual bond dipole moments cancel.

10.44 (a)

10.46

Hydrogen bond

10.48 surface tension **10.50** ΔH_{vap} is usually larger than ΔH_{fusion} because ΔH_{vap} is the heat required to overcome all intermolecular forces. **10.52** (a) $Hg(l) \rightarrow Hg(g)$; (b) no change of state, Hg remains a liquid; (c) $Hg(g) \rightarrow Hg(l) \rightarrow Hg(s)$ **10.54** As the pressure is lowered, more of the liquid H_2O is converted to H_2O vapor. This conversion is an endothermic process and the temperature decreases. The decrease in pressure and temperature takes the system across the liquid/solid boundary in the phase diagram so the H_2O that remains turns to ice. **10.56** 2.40 kJ **10.58** 3.73 kJ

10.60

Molar Heating Curve for Ethanol

10.62 88.2 J/(K·mol) **10.64** 28.0 kJ/mol **10.66** 294 mm Hg

10.68

T(K)	P_{vap}(mm Hg)	ln P_{vap}	$1/T$
263	80.1	4.383	0.003 802
273	133.6	4.8949	0.003 663
283	213.3	5.3627	0.003 534
293	329.6	5.7979	0.003 413
303	495.4	6.2054	0.003 300
313	724.4	6.5853	0.003 195

10.70 ΔH_{vap} = 30.1 kJ/mol **10.72** 30.1 kJ/mol. The calculated ΔH_{vap} and that obtained from the plot in Problem 10.68 are the same. **10.74** molecular solid, CO_2, I_2; metallic solid, any metallic element; covalent network solid, diamond; ionic solid, NaCl **10.76** (a) rubber; (b) Na_3PO_4; (c) CBr_4; (d) quartz; (e) Au **10.78** covalent network **10.80** 201 pm **10.82** The unit cell is the smallest repeating unit in a crystal. **10.84** 128 pm; 8.90 g/cm³ **10.86** 404.9 pm **10.88** 137 pm **10.90** face-centered cubic **10.92** Six Na^+ ions touch each H^- ion, and six H^- ions touch each Na^+ ion. **10.94** 244 pm **10.96** (a) gas; (b) liquid; (c) solid

10.98

10.100 (a) $Br_2(s)$; (b) $Br_2(l)$ **10.102** Solid O_2 does not melt when pressure is applied because the solid is denser than the liquid, and the solid/liquid boundary in the phase diagram slopes to the right. **10.104** The starting phase is benzene as a solid, and the final phase is benzene as a gas.

10.106 solid → liquid → supercritical fluid → liquid → solid → gas
Chapter Problems **10.108** Because chlorine is larger than fluorine, the charge separation is larger in CH_3Cl compared to CH_3F, resulting in CH_3Cl having a slightly larger dipole moment.

10.110 0.192 kJ **10.112** 0.837 atm **10.114** 60% **10.116** 650°C **10.118** −30.7 °C **10.120** 23.3 kJ/mol **10.122** Kr cannot be liquified at room temperature because room temperature is above $T_c(-63 \, °C)$.

10.124 68% **10.126** 6.01×10^{23} atoms/mol **10.128** (a) 556 pm; (b) 2.26 g/cm³ **10.130** Al_2O_3, ionic (greater lattice energy than NaCl because of higher ion charges); F_2, dispersion; H_2O, H–bonding, dipole–dipole; Br_2, dispersion (larger and more polarizable than F_2), ICl, dipole–dipole, NaCl, ionic; $F_2 < Br_2 < ICl < H_2O < NaCl < Al_2O_3$

10.132 (a)

(b) (i) solid, (ii) gas, (iii) liquid, (iv) liquid, (v) solid
Multiconcept Problems **10.134** (a) 1.926 g; (b) Fe_3O_4; (c) 24 Fe atoms; 32 O atoms **10.136** (a) 231 pm; (b) K; (c) density of solid = 0.857 g/cm³; density of vapor = 7.29×10^{-6} g/cm³

Chapter 11

11.1 toluene $< Br_2 <$ KBr **11.2** (a) Na^+ because the Na^+ ion is smaller than the Cs^+ ion; (b) Ba^{2+} because of its higher charge. **11.3** 5.52 mass % **11.4** 4.6×10^{-5} g **11.5** 0.614 M **11.6** molality = 0.0249 m; $X_{C_{27}H_{46}O} = 2.96 \times 10^{-3}$ **11.7** 312 g **11.8** 0.251 M **11.9** 0.513 m **11.10** 0.621 m **11.11** 3.2×10^{-2} mol/(L·atm) **11.12** (a) 0.080 M; (b) 1.3×10^{-5} M **11.13** 98.6 mm Hg **11.14** 17.6 g **11.15** upper curve: pure solvent; lower curve: solution **11.16** (a) 27.1 mm Hg; (b) 46.6 mm Hg **11.17** (a) lower boiling point; (b)

11.18 62.1 °C **11.19** −3.55 °C **11.20** 0.793 m **11.21** 1.9 **11.22** (a) 62 °C; (b) 2 m **11.23** 9.54 atm **11.24** 0.156 M **11.25** 128 g/mol **11.26** 342 g/mol

11.27 (a) and (c)

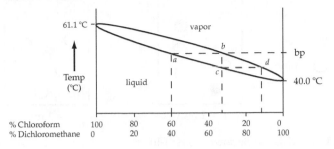

(b) ~50 °C; (d) 90% dichloromethane and 10% chloroform
11.28 Both solvent molecules and small solute particles can pass through a semipermeable dialysis membrane. Only large colloidal particles such as proteins can't pass through. Only solvent molecules can pass through a semipermeable membrane used for osmosis. *Conceptual Problems* **11.30** (a) < (b) < (c)

11.32

Assume that only the blue (open) spheres (solvent) can pass through the semipermeable membrane. There will be a net transfer of solvent from the right compartment (pure solvent) to the left compartment (solution) to achieve equilibrium. **11.34** (b)
11.36 (a) Solution B (i = 3): red line; Solution A (i = 1): blue line; (b) 15.5 °C; (c) Both the solutions are 0.50 m. *Section Problems*
11.38 The larger the surface area, the more solid-solvent interactions, and the more rapidly the solid will dissolve. Powdered NaCl has a much larger surface area than a large block of NaCl.
11.40 Energy is required to overcome intermolecular forces holding solute particles together in the crystal. For an ionic solid, this is the lattice energy. **11.42** Ethyl alcohol and water are both polar with small dispersion forces. They both can hydrogen bond, and are miscible. Pentyl alcohol is slightly polar and can hydrogen bond. It has, however, a relatively large dispersion force because of its size, which limits its water solubility. **11.44** 42.5 °C **11.46** (a) 0.049 ppb; (b) 1.9 × 10⁻⁹ mol/L **11.48** (a) Dissolve 0.150 mol of glucose in water; dilute to 1.00 L; (b) Dissolve 1.135 mol of KBr in 1.00 kg of H_2O; (c) Mix together 0.15 mol of CH_3OH with 0.85 mol of H_2O.
11.50 Dissolve 4.42 × 10⁻³ mol (0.540 g) of $C_7H_6O_2$ in enough $CHCl_3$ to make 165 mL of solution. **11.52** (a) 0.500 M KCl; (b) 1.75 M glucose **11.54** (a) 11.2 mass %; (b) 0.002 70 mass %; (c) 3.65 mass % **11.56** 0.20 ppm **11.58** (a) 0.196 m; (b) $X_{C_{10}H_{14}N_2}$ = 0.0145; $X_{CH_2Cl_2}$ = 0.985 **11.60** 1.81 M **11.62** 10.7 m **11.64** 3.7 g
11.66 (a) 0.0187; (b) 16.0%; (c) 1.06 m **11.68** (a) NH_4Cl; (b) CH_3CO_2Na **11.70** 0.068 M **11.72** 0.06 atm **11.74** 4.8 × 10⁻⁴ mol/L
11.76 NaCl is nonvolatile. Methyl alcohol is volatile. When NaCl is added to water, the vapor pressure of the solution is decreased, which means that the boiling point of the solution will increase. When methyl alcohol is added to water, the vapor pressure of the solution is increased, which means that the boiling point of the solution will decrease.

11.78

11.80 (a) 70.5 mm Hg; (b) 68.0 mm Hg **11.82** (a) 100.57 °C; (b) 101.6 °C **11.84** 2.3 **11.86** 0.514 **11.88** 219 mm Hg **11.90** In the liquid, $X_{acetone}$ = 0.602 and $X_{ethyl\ acetate}$ = 0.398. In the vapor, $X_{acetone}$ = 0.785; $X_{ethyl\ acetate}$ = 0.215 **11.92** 3.6 °C · kg/mol **11.94** 0.573 m **11.96** (a) 13.0 atm; (b) 65.2 atm **11.98** 0.197 M
11.100 K_f for snow (H_2O) is 1.86 °C · kg/mol. Reasonable amounts of salt are capable of lowering the freezing point (ΔT_f) of the snow below −2 °C but are not capable of causing a ΔT_f of more than −30 °C. **11.102** 342.5 amu **11.104** HCl is a strong electrolyte in H_2O and completely dissociates into two solute particles per each HCl. HF is a weak electrolyte in H_2O. Only a few percent of the HF molecules dissociates into ions. **11.106** molecular mass = 538 amu; molecular formula is $C_{40}H_{56}$ *Chapter Problems*
11.108 2.60 × 10³ g $C_2H_6O_2$ **11.110** When solid $CaCl_2$ is added to liquid water, the temperature rises because ΔH_{soln} for $CaCl_2$ is exothermic. When solid $CaCl_2$ is added to ice at 0 °C, some of the ice will melt (an endothermic process) and the temperature will fall because the $CaCl_2$ lowers the freezing point of an ice/water mixture. **11.112** 0.442 **11.114** 1.3 g **11.116** fp = −2.3 °C; bp = 100.63 °C **11.118** (a) 11.7 g of rubbing alcohol; (b) 0.75 mol C_3H_8O **11.120** 2.45% **11.122** 0.51 mm Hg **11.124** molecular mass = 271 amu; molecular formula is $C_{18}H_{24}O_2$ **11.126** (a) 24.07 g $BaSO_4$; (b) More precipitate will form because of the excess $BaCl_2$ in the solution. **11.128** 10% LiCl; 41% H_2O; 49% CH_3OH **11.130** 334 g/mol **11.132** (a) 103.3 °C; (b) 21.3 mm Hg **11.134** (a) 1.31 m; (b) −4.87 °C; (c) 83% **11.136** 89.9 g of $C_{12}H_{22}O_{11}$; 10.2 g of NaCl *Multiconcept Problems* **11.138** (a) C_2H_3; (b) 108 amu; (c) C_8H_{12} **11.140** 5.75 g LiCl; 3.15 g $CaCl_2$

Chapter 12

12.1 (a) 1.6 × 10⁻⁴ M/s; (b) 3.2 × 10⁻⁴ M/s **12.2** Rate of decomposition of N_2O_5 = 2.2 × 10⁻⁵ M/s; Rate of formation of O_2 = 1.1 × 10⁻⁵ M/s **12.3** Rate = $k[BrO_3^-][Br^-][H^+]^2$; 1st order in Br^-, 2nd order in H^+, 4th order overall; Rate = $k[H_2][I_2]$, 1st order in H_2, 1st order in I_2, 2nd order overall **12.4** (a) Rate = $k[H_2O_2][I^-]$; (b) 1.15 × 10⁻²/(M · s); (c) 1.38 × 10⁻³ M/s **12.5** 1/s; 1/s; 1/(M^3 · s); 1/(M · s) **12.6** (a) Zeroth order in A; second order in B; second order overall; (b) rate = $k[B]^2$ **12.7** (a) 0.080 M; (b) 61 h **12.8** A plot of ln[cyclopropane] versus time is linear, indicating that the data fit the equation for a first-order reaction. k = 6.6 × 10⁻⁴/s (0.040/min) **12.9** (a) 11 h; (b) 0.019 M; (c) 22 h **12.10** (a) 5 min;

(b)

○ red   ● blue

12.11 64.2 h **12.12** 1.21 × 10⁻⁴ y⁻¹ **12.13** 14.0% **12.14** 44.5 d
12.15 (a) A plot of 1/[HI] versus time is linear. The reaction is second order. (b) 0.0308/(M · min); (c) 260 min; (d) 81.2 min

12.16 (a) $2 NO_2(g) + F_2(g) \rightarrow 2 NO_2F(g)$; $F(g)$ is a reaction intermediate. (b) each elementary reaction is bimolecular.
12.17 (a) Rate = $k[O_3][O]$; (b) Rate = $k[Br]^2[Ar]$;
(c) Rate = $k[Co(CN)_5(H_2O)^{2-}]$

12.18

$$Co(CN)_5(H_2O)^{2-}(aq) \rightarrow Co(CN)_5^{2-}(aq) + H_2O(l) \quad \text{(slow)}$$

$$Co(CN)_5^{2-}(aq) + I^-(aq) \rightarrow Co(CN)_5I^{3-}(aq) \quad \text{(fast)}$$

Overall reaction $Co(CN)_5(H_2O)^{2-}(aq) + I^-(aq) \rightarrow$
$$Co(CN)_5I^{3-}(aq) + H_2O(l)$$

The rate law for the first (slow) elementary reaction:
Rate = $k[Co(CN)_5(H_2O)^{2-}]$ **12.19** (a) $2 NO(g) + O_2(g) \rightarrow 2 NO_2(g)$;
(b) Rate$_{forward}$ = $k_1[NO][O_2]$ and Rate$_{reverse}$ = $k_{-1}[NO_3]$. Because of the equilibrium, Rate$_{forward}$ = Rate$_{reverse}$, and $k_1[NO][O_2]$ = $k_{-1}[NO_3]$.

$$[NO_3] = \frac{k_1}{k_{-1}}[NO][O_2]$$

The rate law for the rate determining step is Rate = $k_2[NO_3][NO]$. Because 2 NO disappear in the overall reaction for every NO that reacts in the second step, the rate law for the overall reaction is Rate = $-\Delta[NO]/\Delta t = 2 k_2[NO_3][NO]$. In this rate law substitute for $[NO_3]$.

Rate = $2 k_2 \dfrac{k_1}{k_{-1}}[NO]^2[O_2]$, which is consistent with the experimen-

tal rate law; (c) $k = \dfrac{2 k_2 k_1}{k_{-1}}$ **12.20** (a) 80 kJ/mol; (b) endothermic;

(c)

12.21 (a) 104 kJ/mol; (b) 1.4×10^{-4}/s **12.22** (a) zero-order in A, first-order in C_2, first-order in B. (b) Rate = $k[B][C_2]$;

(c)
$$B + C_2 \rightarrow BC_2 \qquad \text{(slow)}$$
$$A + BC_2 \rightarrow AC + BC$$
$$\underline{A + BC \rightarrow AC + B}$$
$$2 A + C_2 \rightarrow 2 AC \qquad \text{(overall)}$$

(d) B is a catalyst. BC_2 and BC are intermediates

12.23

Conceptual Problems **12.24** (a) 2:1:4:2; (b) the k's are all the same

12.26 (a)

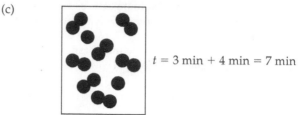

= red
= blue

$t = 2$ min $t = 3$ min

(b) 1 min **12.28** (a) Because the half-life is inversely proportional to the concentration of A molecules, the reaction is second order in A. (b) Rate = $k[A]^2$;

(c)

$t = 3$ min + 4 min = 7 min

12.30 (a) zeroth-order in B; second-order in A. (b) Rate = $k[A]^2$.

(c)
$$2 A \rightarrow A_2 \qquad \text{(slow)}$$
$$\underline{A_2 + B \rightarrow AB + A}$$
$$A + B \rightarrow AB \qquad \text{(overall)}$$
(d) A_2

12.32 (a) $BC + D \rightarrow B + CD$; (b) 1. B–C + D (reactants), A (catalyst); 2. B–C–A (transition state), D (reactant); 3. A–C (intermediate), B (product), D (reactant); 4. A–C–D (transition state), B (product); 5. A (catalyst), C–D + B (products); (c) first step; Rate = $k[A][BC]$; (d) Endothermic *Section Problems*
12.34 (a) 4.0×10^{-5} M/s; (b) 3.9×10^{-5} M/s; (c) 3.8×10^{-5} M/s; (d) 3.7×10^{-5} M/s Rate (d) because it is determined from measurements taken over the smallest time interval.
12.36 (a) 2.4×10^{-5} M/s; (b) 3.1×10^{-5} M/s **12.38** (a) 3 times faster; (b) 2 times faster. **12.40** (a) -2.4×10^{-6} M/s; (b) 9.6×10^{-6} M/s
12.42 Rate = $k[H_2][ICl]$; $1/(M \cdot s)$ **12.44** (a) Rate = $k[CH_3Br][OH^-]$; (b) The rate will decrease by a factor of 5; (c) The rate will increase by a factor of 4. **12.46** (a) Rate = $k[Cu(C_{10}H_8N_2)_2^+]^2[O_2]$; (b) Overall reaction order = 3; (c) The rate will decrease by a factor of 16.
12.48 (a) Rate = $k[NH_4^+][NO_2^-]$; (b) $3.0 \times 10^{-4}/(M \cdot s)$; (c) 6.1×10^{-6} M/s **12.50** (a) 0.015 M; (b) 40 min; (c) 7.2 min
12.52 $t_{1/2}$ = 17 min; t = 69 min **12.54** (a) 5.2×10^{-3} M; (b) 3.1 h
12.56 $t_{1/2}$ = 21 min; t = 42 min **12.58** A plot of $\ln[N_2O]$ versus time is linear. The reaction is first order in N_2O. $k = 3.92 \times 10^{-5}$/s
12.60 2.79×10^{-3}/s **12.62** (a) zeroth-order; (b) 0.031 M; (c) 22 min
12.64 0.247 d^{-1} **12.66** 23.0% **12.68** 621 α particles **12.70** 1.1×10^6 y
12.72 34.6 d **12.74** There is no relationship between the coefficients in a balanced chemical equation for an overall reaction and the exponents in the rate law unless the overall reaction occurs in a single elementary step, in which case the coefficients in the balanced equation are the exponents in the rate; law.
12.76 (a) $H_2(g) + 2 ICl(g) \rightarrow I_2(g) + 2 HCl(g)$; (b) HI(g); (c) Each elementary reaction is bimolecular. **12.78** (a) bimolecular, Rate = $k[O_3][Cl]$; (b) unimolecular, Rate = $k[NO_2]$; (c) bimolecular, Rate = $k[ClO][O]$; (d) termolecular, Rate = $k[Cl]^2[N_2]$
12.80 (a) $2 NO_2Cl(g) \rightarrow 2 NO_2(g) + Cl_2(g)$; (b) 1. unimolecular; 2. bimolecular; (c) Rate = $k[NO_2Cl]$ **12.82** $NO_2(g) + F_2(g) \rightarrow$ $NO_2F(g) + F(g)$ (slow); $F(g) + NO_2(g) \rightarrow NO_2F(g)$ (fast)
12.84 (a) $2 NO(g) + O_2(g) \rightarrow 2 NO_2(g)$; (b) Rate$_{forward}$ = $k_1[NO]^2$ and Rate$_{reverse}$ = $k_{-1}[N_2O_2]$ Because of the equilibrium,

$\text{Rate}_{\text{forward}} = \text{Rate}_{\text{reverse}}$, and $k_1[\text{NO}]^2 = k_{-1}[\text{N}_2\text{O}_2]$.

$$[\text{N}_2\text{O}_2] = \frac{k_1}{k_{-1}}[\text{NO}]^2$$

The rate law for the rate determining step is $\text{Rate} = -\Delta[\text{NO}]/\Delta t = 2k_2[\text{N}_2\text{O}_2][\text{O}_2]$ because two NO molecules are consumed in the overall reaction for every $[\text{N}_2\text{O}_2]$ that reacts in the second step. In this rate law substitute for $[\text{N}_2\text{O}_2]$.

$$\text{Rate} = 2k_2 \frac{k_1}{k_{-1}}[\text{NO}]^2[\text{O}_2]$$

(c) $k = \dfrac{2k_2k_1}{k_{-1}}$ **12.86** Very few collisions involve a collision energy greater than or equal to the activation energy, and only a fraction of those have the proper orientation for reaction.
12.88 104 kJ/mol

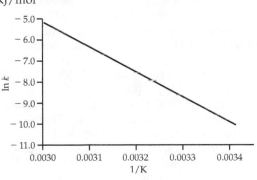

12.90 (a) 134 kJ/mol; (b) 6.0/(M·s) **12.92** 87 kJ/mol
12.94

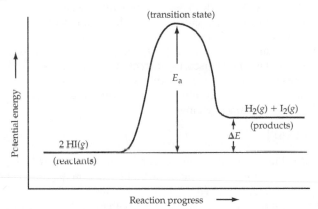

12.96 A catalyst does participate in the reaction, but it is not consumed because it reacts in one step of the reaction and is regenerated in a subsequent step. **12.98** (a) $\text{O}_3(g) + \text{O}(g) \rightarrow 2\,\text{O}_2(g)$; (b) Cl acts as a catalyst; (c) ClO is a reaction intermediate; (d) A catalyst reacts in one step and is regenerated in a subsequent step. A reaction intermediate is produced in one step and consumed in another. **12.100** (a) $\text{NH}_2\text{NO}_2(aq) \rightarrow \text{N}_2\text{O}(g) + \text{H}_2\text{O}(l)$; (b) OH^- acts as a catalyst; NHNO_2^- is a reaction intermediate; (c) The rate will decrease because added acid decreases the concentration of OH^-, which appears in the rate law since it is a catalyst. *Chapter Problems* **12.102** (a) Measure the change in the concentration of AB_2 as a function of time. (b) and (c) If a plot of $[\text{AB}_2]$ versus time is linear, the reaction is zeroth-order and $k = -\text{slope}$. If a plot of $\ln[\text{AB}_2]$ versus time is linear, the reaction is first-order and $k = -\text{slope}$. If a plot of $1/[\text{AB}_2]$ versus time is linear, the reaction is second-order and $k = \text{slope}$. **12.104** (a) $\text{Rate} = k[\text{B}_2][\text{C}]$; (b) $\text{B}_2 + \text{C} \rightarrow \text{CB} + \text{B}$ (slow); $\text{CB} + \text{A} \rightarrow \text{AB} + \text{C}$ (fast); (c) C is a catalyst. C does not appear in the chemical

equation because it is consumed in the first step and regenerated in the second step. **12.106** The first maximum represents the potential energy of the transition state for the first step. The second maximum represents the potential energy of the transition state for the second step. The saddle point between the two maxima represents the potential energy of the intermediate products. **12.108** (a) increase; (b) decrease; (c) increase; (d) no change **12.110** (a) $\text{Rate} = k[\text{C}_2\text{H}_4\text{Br}_2][\text{I}^-]$; (b) $4.98 \times 10^{-3}/(\text{M·s})$; (c) 1.12×10^{-4} M/s **12.112** (a) 2.81×10^{-3} M; (b) 470 min; (c) 63 h **12.114** For $E_a = 50$ kJ/mol, $f = 2.0 \times 10^{-9}$. For $E_a = 100$ kJ/mol, $f = 3.9 \times 10^{-18}$ **12.116** $[\text{A}] = -kt + [\text{A}]_0$; $[\text{A}]_0/2 = -kt_{1/2} + [\text{A}]_0$; $t_{1/2} = [\text{A}]_0/2\,k$. For a zeroth-order reaction, each half-life is half of the previous one. For a first-order reaction, each half-life is the same as the previous one. For a second-order reaction, each half-life is twice the previous one. **12.118** (a) $\text{Rate}_f = k_f[\text{A}]$ and $\text{Rate}_r = k_r[\text{B}]$;

(b)

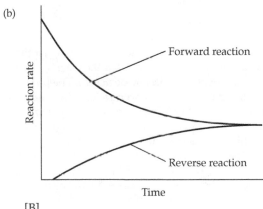

(c) $\dfrac{[\text{B}]}{[\text{A}]} = 3$

12.120 1.6×10^4 y **12.122** 49 °C **12.124** (a) 7.7×10^{-7} s; (b) the speed of mixing **12.126** 2.7×10^2 s **12.128** 15 s **12.130** 5.9×10^9 y **12.132** 1.6×10^{12} **12.134** (a) 238 kJ/mol; (b) 330 s *Multiconcept Problems* **12.136** (a) 8.7×10^{19} molecules/min; (b) 1.2 atm **12.138** (a) 0.71 atm; (b) 2.4 J/s; (c) 0.89 kJ **12.140** -122 J

Chapter 13

13.1 (a) $K_c = \dfrac{[\text{SO}_3]^2}{[\text{SO}_2]^2[\text{O}_2]}$; (b) $K_c = \dfrac{[\text{SO}_2]^2[\text{O}_2]}{[\text{SO}_3]^2}$ **13.2** (a) 7.9×10^4;

(b) 1.3×10^{-5} **13.3** (a) $K_c = \dfrac{[\text{H}^+][\text{C}_3\text{H}_5\text{O}_3^-]}{[\text{C}_3\text{H}_6\text{O}_3]}$; (b) 1.38×10^{-4}

13.4 Mixture (2) and (4) because $K_c = 1$, as for mixture (1).
13.5 9.48 **13.6** at 500 K: $K_p = 1.7 \times 10^4$; at 1000 K: $K_c = 1.1$

13.7 (a) $K_c = \dfrac{[\text{H}_2]^3}{[\text{H}_2\text{O}]^3}$, $K_p = \dfrac{(P_{\text{H}_2})^3}{(P_{\text{H}_2\text{O}})^3}$, $K_p = K_c$

(b) $K_c = [\text{H}_2]^2[\text{O}_2]$, $K_p = (P_{\text{H}_2})^2(P_{\text{O}_2})$, $K_p = K_c(RT)^3$

(c) $K_c = \dfrac{[\text{HCl}]^4}{[\text{SiCl}_4][\text{H}_2]^2}$, $K_p = \dfrac{(P_{\text{HCl}})^4}{(P_{\text{SiCl}_4})(P_{\text{H}_2})^2}$, $K_c(RT)$

(d) $K_c = \dfrac{1}{[\text{Hg}_2^{2+}][\text{Cl}^-]^2}$

13.8 $K_c = 1.2 \times 10^{-42}$. Because K_c is very small, the equilibrium mixture contains mostly H_2 molecules. H is in periodic group 1A. A very small value of K_c is consistent with strong bonding between 2 H atoms, each with one valence electron. **13.9** (a) Because $Q_c < K_c$, the reaction is not at equilibrium. The reaction will proceed to the right to reach equilibrium. (b) Because $Q_c > K_c$, the reaction is not at equilibrium. The reaction will proceed to the left to reach equilibrium. **13.10** (a) (2); (b) (1), reverse; (3), forward

13.11 (a) 3.5×10^{-22} M; (b) 210 H atoms, 6.0×10^{22} H_2 molecules
13.12 $[CO_2] = [H_2] = 0.101$ M; $[CO] = [H_2O] = 0.049$ M
13.13 $[N_2O_4] = 0.0429$ M; $[NO_2] = 0.0141$ M
13.14 $[N_2O_4] = 0.0292$ M; $[NO_2] = 0.0116$ M **13.15** $P_{H_2O} = 0.90$ atm;
$P_{CO} = 1.30$ atm; $P_{H_2} = 1.70$ atm **13.16** (a) increases; (b) decreases;
(c) decreases; (d) increases; At equilibrium,

$$Q_c = K_c = \frac{[CO_2][H_2]}{[CO][H_2O]}$$

If some CO_2 is removed from the equilibrium mixture, the
numerator in Q_c is decreased, which means that $Q_c < K_c$ and the
reaction will shift to the right, increasing the H_2 concentration.
13.17 (a) remains the same; (b) increases; (c) decreases
13.18

13.19 The equilibrium mixture will contain more NO, the higher the
temperature. **13.20** As the temperature is increased the reaction shifts
from right to left. The amount of ethyl acetate decreases. The product
concentrations increase, and the reactant concentrations decrease. This
corresponds to an increase in K_c. **13.21** There are more AB(g) molecules
at the higher temperature. The equilibrium shifted to the right at the
higher temperature, which means the reaction is endothermic.
13.22 (a) remains the same; (b) increases; (c) decreases; (d) remains the
same; (e) decreases **13.23** (a) k_f; (b) 2.5×10^{-28} M^{-1} s^{-1}; (c) k_r decreases
more than k_f decreases, and therefore K_c increases. **13.24** The reaction
will shift to the left. This will decrease the effectiveness of Hb for
carrying O_2. **13.25** 2.58×10^{21} O_2 molecules *Conceptual Problems*
13.26 (a) (1) and (3); (b) $K_c = 1.5$; (c) Because the same number of
molecules appear on both sides of the equation, the volume terms
in K_c all cancel. Therefore, we can calculate K_c without including
the volume. **13.28** (a) (3); (b) reaction (1): reverse direction; reaction
(2): forward direction **13.30** When the stopcock is opened, the
reaction will go in the reverse direction because there will be
initially an excess of AB molecules. **13.32** (a) AB → A + B; (b) The
reaction is endothermic because a stress of added heat (higher
temperature) shifts the AB ⇌ A + B equilibrium to the right.
(c) If the volume is increased, the pressure is decreased.
The stress of decreased pressure will be relieved by a shift in the
equilibrium from left to right, thus increasing the number of A atoms.
13.34

(a) (b) (c)

13.36 (a) A → 2 B; (b) (1) increase, (2) increase, (3) remain the same,
(4) remain the same *Section Problems* **13.38** forward direction
13.40 (a) $K_c = \dfrac{[CO][H_2]^3}{[CH_4][H_2O]}$; (b) $K_c = \dfrac{[ClF_3]^2}{[F_2]^3[Cl_2]}$; (c) $K_c = \dfrac{[HF]^2}{[H_2][F_2]}$

13.42 (a) $K_p = \dfrac{(P_{CO})(P_{H_2})^3}{(P_{CH_4})(P_{H_2O})}$, $\Delta n = 2$ and $K_p = K_c(RT)^2$

(b) $K_p = \dfrac{(P_{ClF_3})^2}{(P_{F_2})^3(P_{Cl_2})}$, $\Delta n = -2$ and $K_p = K_c(RT)^{-2}$

(c) $K_p = \dfrac{(P_{HF})^2}{(P_{H_2})(P_{F_2})}$, $\Delta n = 0$ and $K_p = K_c$

13.44 $K_c = \dfrac{[C_2H_5OC_2H_5][H_2O]}{[C_2H_5OH]^2}$ **13.46** 1.3×10^8 **13.48** 0.058

13.50 29.0 **13.52** (a) $K_c = \dfrac{[CH_3CO_2C_2H_5][H_2O]}{[CH_3CO_2H][C_2H_5OH]}$

(b) $K_c = 3.4$. Because there are the same number of molecules on
both sides of the equation, the volume terms in K_c cancel.
Therefore, we can calculate K_c without including the volume.
13.54 9.0×10^3 **13.56** $K_p = 0.0313$; $K_c = 1.28 \times 10^{-3}$

13.58 (a) $K_c = \dfrac{[CO_2]^3}{[CO]^3}$, $K_p = \dfrac{(P_{CO_2})^3}{(P_{CO})^3}$; (b) $K_c = \dfrac{1}{[O_2]^3}$, $K_p = \dfrac{1}{(P_{O_2})^3}$

(c) $K_c = [SO_3]$, $K_p = P_{SO_3}$; (d) $K_c = [Ba^{2+}][SO_4{}^{2-}]$
13.60 (a) mostly product; (b) mostly reactants **13.62** $K_c = 1.2 \times 10^{82}$
is very large. When equilibrium is reached, very little if any ethanol
will remain because the reaction goes to completion. **13.64** The
reaction is not at equilibrium because $Q_c > K_c$. The reaction will
proceed in the reverse direction to attain equilibrium. **13.66** $Q_p = 178$;
forward direction **13.68** (a) $Q_p = 36.2$; the reaction will
proceed in the reverse direction; (b) $P_{In} = 0.1193$ atm;
$P_{H_2} = 0.0943$ atm; $P_{InH_2} = 0.0167$ atm **13.70** 5.9×10^{-3} M
13.72 $[NO] = 0.056$ M; $[N_2] = [O_2] = 1.37$ M
13.74 $[L\text{-}\alpha\text{-lysine}] = 0.000\,37$ M; $[L\text{-}\beta\text{-lysine}] = 0.002\,63$ M
13.76 (a) 6.8 moles; (b) 0.03 mol CH_3CO_2H; 9.03 mol C_2H_5OH
13.78 $P_{ClF} = P_{F_2} = 0.389$ atm; $P_{ClF_3} = 1.08$ atm **13.80** (a) increases;
(b) increases; (c) decreases; (d) decreases. Disturbing the equilibrium
by decreasing $[Cl^-]$ increases Q_c ($Q_c = 1/[Ag^+]_t[Cl^-]_t$) to a value
greater than K_c. To reach a new state of equilibrium, Q_c must
decrease, which means that the denominator must increase; that is,
the reaction must go from right to left, thus decreasing the amount
of solid AgCl. **13.82** (a) decreases; (b) remains the same;
(c) increases **13.84** $[H_2]$ decreases when the temperature is
increased. As the temperature is decreased, the reaction shifts to the
right. $[CO_2]$ and $[H_2]$ increase, $[CO]$ and $[H_2O]$ decrease, and K_c
increases. **13.86** (a) increases; (b) increases; (c) decreases;
(d) increases **13.88** (a) decreases; (b) increases; (c) no change;
(d) increases **13.90** (a) no shift; (b) toward reactants; (c) toward
products; (d) toward reactants

13.92 $k_f[A][B] = k_r[C]$; $\dfrac{k_f}{k_r} = \dfrac{[C]}{[A][B]} = K_c$

13.94 210 **13.96** k_r increases more than k_f, this means that E_a
(reverse) is greater than E_a (forward). The reaction is exothermic
when E_a (reverse) $> E_a$ (forward).
Chapter Problems **13.98** $[H_2] = [I_2] = 0.045$ M; $[HI] = 0.31$ M
13.100 $[CO] = [H_2] = 0.18$ M; $[H_2O] = 1.02$ M **13.102** A decrease in
volume (a) and the addition of reactants (c) will affect the composition
of the equilibrium mixture, but leave the value of K_c unchanged.
A change in temperature (b) affects the value of K_c. Addition of a
catalyst (d) or an inert gas (e) affects neither the composition of the
equilibrium mixture nor the value of K_c. **13.104** (a) 1.4×10^{-8};
(b) 5.2×10^{15}; (c) 2.7×10^{-24} **13.106** (a) $K_c = 0.573$; $K_p = 23.5$;
(b) The reaction proceeds to the right to reach equilibrium.
$[PCl_5] = 0.365$ M; $[PCl_3] = 0.285$ M; $[Cl_2] = 0.735$ M;

13.108 (a) $K_c = \dfrac{[C_2H_6][C_2H_4]}{[C_4H_{10}]}$ $K_p = \dfrac{(P_{C_2H_6})(P_{C_2H_4})}{P_{C_4H_{10}}}$

(b) 0.19; (c) 38%; $P_{total} = 69$ atm; (d) A decrease in volume
would decrease the % conversion of C_4H_{10}. **13.110** (a) 0.0840;
(b) $[(CH_3)_2C{=}CCH_2] = [HCl] = 0.094$ M;
$[(CH_3)_3CCl] = 0.106$ M; (c) $P_{t\text{-butyl chloride}} = 0.055$ atm;

$P_{\text{isobutylene}} = 0.345$ atm; $P_{\text{HCl}} = 0.545$ atm **13.112** The activation energy (E_a) is positive, and for an exothermic reaction, $E_{a,r} > E_{a,f}$.

$$K_c = \frac{k_f}{k_r} = \frac{A_f e^{-E_{a,f}/RT}}{A_r e^{-E_{a,r}/RT}} = \frac{A_f}{A_r} e^{(E_{a,r}-E_{a,f})/RT}$$

$(E_{a,r} - E_{a,f})$ is positive, so the exponent is always positive. As the temperature increases, the exponent, $(E_{a,r} - E_{a,f})/RT$, decreases and the value for K_c decreases as well. **13.114** (a) $K_c = 1.6 \times 10^{-3}$; (b) $K_p = 0.039$ **13.116** (a) 1.0×10^{-6} atm; (b) exothermic; (c) At 2800 K, $Q_p = 100$, $Q_p > K_p$ so the reaction will go from products to reactants **13.118** $P_{\text{NO}_2} = 0.359$ atm; $P_{\text{N}_2\text{O}_4} = 1.14$ atm **13.120** (a) $P_{\text{NO}} = 0.46$ atm; $P_{\text{NO}_2} = 0.79$ atm; $P_{\text{N}_2\text{O}_3} = 0.20$ atm; (b) 74 L **13.122** 0.826 mol **13.124** (a) 0.002 44; (b) $K_p = 0.140$; (c) $[\text{ClF}_3] = 0.191$ M, $[\text{ClF}] = [\text{F}_2] = 0.0216$ M **13.126** [Fumarate] $= 8.9 \times 10^{-4}$ M; [L-Malate] $= 2.94 \times 10^{-3}$ M *Multiconcept Problems* **13.128 (a)** $K_c = 1.51$; $K_p = 49.6$;

(b)

13.130 (a) 2.5; (b) 0.0034; (c) K_c for the water solution is so much smaller than K_c for the benzene solution because H_2O can hydrogen bond with acetic acid, thus preventing acetic acid dimer formation. Benzene cannot hydrogen bond with acetic acid. **13.132** (a) 1.47; (b) 10.3; (c) In agreement with Le Châtelier's principle, the reaction is endothermic because K_p increases with increasing temperature. **13.134** (a) 1.52; (b) 6.65 kJ **13.136** 6.0×10^2 O_3 molecules **13.138** (a) Because K_p is larger at the higher temperature, the reaction is endothermic. Because the reaction involves breaking two P—Cl bonds and forming just one Cl—Cl bond, it should be endothermic. (b) 99.97%; 1.38 atm

(c)

$$:\ddot{\text{Cl}}\!:$$
$$|$$
$$:\ddot{\text{Cl}}\!-\!\text{P}\!-\!\ddot{\text{Cl}}\!:$$
$$/\quad\backslash$$
$$:\ddot{\text{Cl}}\quad\ddot{\text{Cl}}\!:$$

PCl_5 has no dipole moment because of a symmetrical distribution of Cl's around the central P.

$$:\ddot{\text{Cl}}\!-\!\ddot{\text{P}}\!-\!\ddot{\text{Cl}}\!:$$
$$|$$
$$:\ddot{\text{Cl}}\!:$$

PCl_3 has a dipole moment because the geometry is trigonal pyramidal.

Chapter 14

14.1 (a) $H_2SO_4(aq) + H_2O(l) \rightleftharpoons H_3O^+(aq) + HSO_4^-(aq)$
conjugate base
(b) $HSO_4^-(aq) + H_2O(l) \rightleftharpoons H_3O^+(aq) + SO_4^{2-}(aq)$
conjugate base
(c) $H_3O^+(aq) + H_2O(l) \rightleftharpoons H_3O^+(aq) + H_2O(l)$
conjugate base
(d) $NH_4^+(aq) + H_2O(l) \rightleftharpoons H_3O^+(aq) + NH_3(aq)$
conjugate base

14.2 (a) H_2CO_3; (b) HCO_3^-; (c) H_2O; (d) H_3PO_4

14.3

$$HCl(aq) + NH_3(aq) \rightleftharpoons NH_4^+(aq) + Cl^-(aq)$$
$$\text{Acid}\qquad\text{Base}\qquad\qquad\text{Acid}\qquad\text{Base}$$

Conjugate acid–base pairs

14.4 (a) from right to left; (b) from left to right **14.5** (a) HY; (b) X⁻; (c) to the left. **14.6** (a) $H_9O_4^+$, $H_{19}O_9^+$, $H_{43}O_{21}^+$; (b) $H_9O_4^+$ (4 H_2O), $H_{19}O_9^+$ (9 H_2O), $H_{43}O_{21}^+$ (21 H_2O) **14.7** $[OH^-] = 7.1 \times 10^{-11}$ M, acidic. **14.8** $[H_3O^+] = 5.0 \times 10^{-9}$ M, basic. **14.9** 2.3×10^{-7} M **14.10** (a) 8.20; (b) 4.22 **14.11** (a) $[H_3O^+] = 4.0 \times 10^{-8}$ M; $[OH^-] = 2.5 \times 10^{-7}$ M; (b) $[H_3O^+] = 2 \times 10^{-3}$ M; $[OH^-] = 5 \times 10^{-12}$ M **14.12** (a) 1.30; (b) -0.78; (c) 14.60; (d) 12.30 **14.13** 11.81 **14.14** $K_a = 3.5 \times 10^{-8}$. This value of K_a agrees with the value in Table 14.2. **14.15** (a) HY < HX < HZ; (b) HZ; (c) HY has the highest pH; HX has the lowest pH **14.16** (a) pH = 2.38; $[H_3O^+] = [CH_3CO_2^-] = 4.2 \times 10^{-3}$ M; $[CH_3CO_2H] = 1.00$ M; $[OH^-] = 2.4 \times 10^{-12}$ M; (b) pH = 3.38; $[H_3O^+] = [CH_3CO_2^-] = 4.2 \times 10^{-4}$ M; $[CH_3CO_2H] = 0.0096$ M; $[OH^-] = 2.4 \times 10^{-11}$ M **14.17** pH = 3.20 **14.18** (a) 8.0%; (b) 2.6% **14.19** $[H_3O^+] = [HSO_3^-] = 0.032$ M; $[H_2SO_3] = 0.07$ M; $[SO_3^{2-}] = 6.3 \times 10^{-8}$ M; $[OH^-] = 3.1 \times 10^{-13}$ M; pH = 1.49 **14.20** $[H_2SeO_4] = 0$ M; $[HSeO_4^-] = 0.49$ M; $[SeO_4^{2-}] = 0.011$ M; $[H_3O^+] = 0.51$ M; pH = 0.29; $[OH^-] = 2.0 \times 10^{-14}$ M **14.21** $[NH_4^+] = [OH^-] = 2.7 \times 10^{-3}$ M; $[NH_3] = 0.40$ M; $[H_3O^+] = 3.7 \times 10^{-12}$ M; pH = 11.43 **14.22** pH = 9.45 **14.23** (a) 7.7×10^{-12}; (b) 2.9×10^{-7} (c) 10.26 **14.24** (a) acidic, pH = 4.92; (b) acidic, pH = 5.00 **14.25** pH = 8.32 **14.26** $K_a = 5.6 \times 10^{-10}$; $K_b = 2.0 \times 10^{-5}$; Because $K_b > K_a$, the solution is basic. **14.27** (a) neutral; (b) basic; (c) acidic; (d) acidic; (e) acidic **14.28** (a) H_2Se; (b) HI; (c) HNO_3; (d) H_2SO_3 **14.29** (a) Lewis acid, $AlCl_3$; Lewis base, Cl^-; (b) Lewis acid, Ag^+; Lewis base, NH_3; (c) Lewis acid, SO_2; Lewis base, OH^-; (d) Lewis acid, Cr^{3+}; Lewis base, H_2O

14.30

$$:\ddot{\text{Cl}}\!-\!\text{Be}\!-\!\ddot{\text{Cl}}\!: \;+\; 2\;:\ddot{\text{Cl}}\!:^- \longrightarrow \left[\begin{array}{c} :\ddot{\text{Cl}}\!: \\ | \\ :\ddot{\text{Cl}}\!-\!\text{Be}\!-\!\ddot{\text{Cl}}\!: \\ | \\ :\ddot{\text{Cl}}\!: \end{array} \right]^{2-}$$

14.31 The O^{2-} from CaO is the Lewis base and SO_2 is the Lewis acid.

$$:\ddot{\text{O}}\!-\!\ddot{\text{S}}\!-\!\ddot{\text{O}}\!: \;+\; :\ddot{\text{O}}\!:^{2-} \longrightarrow :SO_3^{2-}$$

14.32 4.101 *Conceptual Problems* **14.34** (a) X^-, Y^-, Z^-; (b) HX < HZ < HY; (c) HY; (d) HX; (e) 20% **14.36** (b) **14.38** (a) $Y^- < Z^- < X^-$; (b) Y^-; (c) X^- (d) the reaction of A^- with water has a 1:1 stoichiometry: $A^- + H_2O \rightleftharpoons HA + OH^-$

14.40

																S	Cl
																Se	Br

(a) H_2S, weakest; HBr, strongest. Acid strength for H_nX increases with increasing polarity of the H—X bond and with increasing size of X. (b) H_2SeO_3, weakest; $HClO_3$, strongest. Acid strength for H_nYO_3 increases with increasing electronegativity of Y. **14.42** (a) $H_3BO_3(aq) + H_2O(l) \rightleftharpoons H_3O^+(aq) + H_2BO_3^-(aq)$ (b) $H_3BO_3(aq) + 2 H_2O(l) \rightleftharpoons H_3O^+(aq) + B(OH)_4^-(aq)$ *Section Problems* **14.44** NH_3, CN^-, and NO_2^- **14.46** (a) SO_4^{2-}; (b) HSO_3^-; (c) HPO_4^{2-}; (d) NH_3; (e) OH^-; (f) NH_2^-

14.48

(a) $CH_3CO_2H(aq) + NH_3(aq) \rightleftharpoons NH_4^+(aq) + CH_3CO_2^-(aq)$
  Acid   Base   Acid   Base

(b) $CO_3^{2-}(aq) + H_3O^+(aq) \rightleftharpoons H_2O(l) + HCO_3^-(aq)$
  Base   Acid   Base   Acid

(c) $HSO_3^-(aq) + H_2O(l) \rightleftharpoons H_3O^+(aq) + SO_3^{2-}(aq)$
  Acid   Base   Acid   Base

(d) $HSO_3^-(aq) + H_2O(l) \rightleftharpoons H_2SO_3(aq) + OH^-(aq)$
  Base   Acid   Acid   Base

14.50 Strong acids: HNO_3 and H_2SO_4; Strong bases: H^- and O^{2-}
14.52 HCl, Cl$^-$ **14.54** (a) $[OH^-] = 2.9 \times 10^{-6}$ M, basic; (b) $[H_3O^+] =$
1.0×10^{-12} M, basic; (c) $[H_3O^+] = 1.0 \times 10^{-4}$ M, acidic;
(d) $[OH^-] = 1.0 \times 10^{-7}$ M, neutral; (e) $[OH^-] = 1.2 \times 10^{-10}$ M,
acidic **14.56** $[H_3O^+] = [OH^-] = 3.9 \times 10^{-6}$ M, neutral
14.58 (a) 4.70; (b) 11.6; (c) 8.449; (d) 3; (e) 15.08 **14.60** (a) 8×10^{-5} M;
(b) 1.5×10^{-11} M; (c) 1.0 M; (d) 5.6×10^{-15} M; (e) 10 M;
(f) 5.78×10^{-6} M **14.62** (a) chlorphenol red; (b) thymol blue;
(c) methyl orange **14.64** 0.0089 g CaO **14.66** (a) 13.90; (b) 1.19;
(c) 2.30; (d) 2.92 **14.68** (a) $C_6H_5OH < HOCl < CH_3CO_2H <$
HNO_3; (b) $HNO_3 > CH_3CO_2H > HOCl > C_6H_5OH$;
1 M HNO_3, $[H_3O^+] = 1$ M; 1 M CH_3CO_2H, $[H_3O^+] = 4 \times 10^{-3}$ M;
1 M HOCl, $[H_3O^+] = 2 \times 10^{-4}$ M; 1 M C_6H_5OH, $[H_3O^+] = 1 \times 10^{-5}$ M
14.70 $K_a = 2.0 \times 10^{-9}$ **14.72** $[H_3O^+] = [C_3H_3O_2^-] = 0.0029$ M;
$[HC_3H_3O_2] = 0.147$ M; pH = 2.54; $[OH^-] = 3.4 \times 10^{-12}$ M;
(b) 3.3% **14.74** pH = 1.59; % dissociation = 1.7%
14.76 $H_2SeO_4(aq) + H_2O(l) \rightleftharpoons H_3O^+(aq) + HSeO_4^-(aq)$;

$$K_{a1} = \frac{[H_3O^+][HSeO_4^-]}{[H_2SeO_4]}$$

$HSeO_4^-(aq) + H_2O(l) \rightleftharpoons H_3O^+(aq) + SeO_4^{2-}(aq)$;

$$K_{a2} = \frac{[H_3O^+][SeO_4^{2-}]}{[HSeO_4^-]}$$

14.78 $[H_3O^+] = [HCO_3^-] = 6.6 \times 10^{-5}$ M; $[H_2CO_3] = 0.010$ M;
$[CO_3^{2-}] = 5.6 \times 10^{-11}$ M; $[OH^-] = 1.5 \times 10^{-10}$ M; pH = 4.18
14.80 pH = 1.08; $[C_2O_4^{2-}] = 6.4 \times 10^{-5}$ M
14.82 (a) $(CH_3)_2NH(aq) + H_2O(l) \rightleftharpoons (CH_3)_2NH_2^+(aq) + OH^-(aq)$;

$$K_b = \frac{[(CH_3)_2NH_2^+][OH^-]}{[(CH_3)_2NH]}$$

(b) $C_6H_5NH_2(aq) + H_2O(l) \rightleftharpoons C_6H_5NH_3^+(aq) + OH^-(aq)$;

$$K_b = \frac{[C_6H_5NH_3^+][OH^-]}{[C_6H_5NH_2]}$$

(c) $CN^-(aq) + H_2O(l) \rightleftharpoons HCN(aq) + OH^-(aq)$;

$$K_b = \frac{[HCN][OH^-]}{[CN^-]}$$

14.84 $K_b = 1 \times 10^{-6}$; $pK_b = 5.8$ **14.86** $[OH^-] = [HC_{18}H_{21}NO_4^+] =$
9.0×10^{-5} M; $[C_{18}H_{21}NO_4] = 0.002\ 41$ M; $[H_3O^+] = 1.1 \times 10^{-10}$ M;
pH = 9.96 **14.88** (a) 2.0×10^{-11}; (b) 1.1×10^{-6}; (c) 2.3×10^{-5};
(d) 5.6×10^{-6}

14.90

(a) $CH_3NH_3^+(aq) + H_2O(l) \rightleftharpoons H_3O^+(aq) + CH_3NH_2(aq)$
  Acid   Base   Acid   Base

(b) $Cr(H_2O)_6^{3+}(aq) + H_2O(l) \rightleftharpoons H_3O^+(aq) + Cr(H_2O)_5OH^{2+}(aq)$
  Acid   Base   Acid   Base

(c) $CH_3CO_2^-(aq) + H_2O(l) \rightleftharpoons OH^-(aq) + CH_3CO_2H(aq)$
  Base   Acid   Base   Acid

(d) $PO_4^{3-}(aq) + H_2O(l) \rightleftharpoons OH^-(aq) + HPO_4^{2-}(aq)$
  Base   Acid   Base   Acid

14.92 (a) basic; (b) neutral; (c) acidic; (d) neutral; (e) basic; (f) acidic
14.94 (a) $[H_3O^+] = [C_2H_5NH_2] = 1.2 \times 10^{-6}$ M; pH = 5.90;
$[C_2H_5NH_3^+] = 0.10$ M; $[NO_3^-] = 0.10$ M; $[OH^-] = 8.0 \times 10^{-9}$ M;
(b) $[CH_3CO_2H] = [OH^-] = 7.5 \times 10^{-6}$ M;
$[CH_3CO_2^-] = 0.10$ M; $[Na^+] = 0.10$ M; $[H_3O^+] = 1.3 \times 10^{-9}$ M;
pH = 8.89; (c) $[Na^+] = [NO_3^-] = 0.10$ M; $[H_3O^+] = [OH^-] =$
1.0×10^{-7} M; pH = 7.00 **14.96** (a) $PH_3 < H_2S < HCl$; electronegativity increases from P to Cl; (b) $NH_3 < PH_3 < AsH_3$;
X—H bond strength decreases from N to As (down a group);
(c) $HBrO < HBrO_2 < HBrO_3$; acid strength increases with the
number of O atoms **14.98** (a) HCl; The strength of a binary acid
H_nA increases as A moves from left to right and from top to bottom
in the periodic table. (b) $HClO_3$; The strength of an oxoacid
increases with increasing electronegativity and increasing oxidation
state of the central atom. (c) HBr; The strength of a binary acid H_nA
increases as A moves from left to right and from top to bottom in
the periodic table. **14.100** (a) H_2Te, weaker X—H bond; (b) H_3PO_4,
P has higher electronegativity; (c) $H_2PO_4^-$, lower negative charge;
(d) NH_4^+, higher positive charge and N is more electronegative
than C **14.102** (a) Lewis acid, SiF_4; Lewis base, F^-; (b) Lewis acid,
Zn^{2+}; Lewis base, NH_3; (c) Lewis acid, $HgCl_2$; Lewis base, Cl^-;
(d) Lewis acid, CO_2; Lewis base, H_2O
14.104

(a) $2\ :\ddot{\underset{..}{F}}:^- + SiF_4 \longrightarrow SiF_6^{2-}$

(b) $4\ \ddot{N}H_3 + Zn^{2+} \longrightarrow Zn(NH_3)_4^{2+}$

(c) $2\ :\ddot{\underset{..}{Cl}}:^- + HgCl_2 \longrightarrow HgCl_4^{2-}$

(d) $H_2\ddot{O}: + CO_2 \longrightarrow H_2CO_3$

14.106 (a) CN^-, Lewis base; (b) H^+, Lewis acid; (c) H_2O, Lewis
base; (d) Fe^{3+}, Lewis acid; (e) OH^-, Lewis base; (f) CO_2, Lewis
acid; (g) $P(CH_3)_3$, Lewis base; (h) $B(CH_3)_3$, Lewis acid
Chapter Problems **14.108** H_2S, acid only. HS^-, acid and a
base. S^{2-}, base only. H_2O, acid and a base. H_3O^+, acid only.
OH^-, base only. **14.110** $HCO_3^-(aq) + Al(H_2O)_6^{3+}(aq) \rightarrow$
$H_2O(l) + CO_2(g) + Al(H_2O)_5(OH)^{2+}(aq)$
14.112 fraction dissociated = 6.09×10^{-10};

% dissociation = 6.09×10^{-8}% **14.114** $K_a = 3.9 \times 10^{-5}$; $pK_a = 4.41$
14.116 $K_{a1} = 1.0 \times 10^{-8}$; $K_{a2} = 7.7 \times 10^{-4}$
14.118 (a) $A^-(aq) + H_2O(l) \rightleftharpoons HA(aq) + OH^-(aq)$; basic;
(b) $M(H_2O)_6{}^{3+}(aq) + H_2O(l) \rightleftharpoons H_3O^+(aq) + M(H_2O)_5(OH)^{2+}(aq)$;
acidic; (c) $2\,H_2O(l) \rightleftharpoons H_3O^+(aq) + OH^-(aq)$; neutral;
(d) $M(H_2O)_6{}^{3+}(aq) + A^-(aq) \rightleftharpoons HA(aq) + M(H_2O)_5(OH)^{2+}(aq)$;
acidic because K_a for $M(H_2O)_6{}^{3+}$ (10^{-4}) is greater than K_b
for A^- (10^{-9}). **14.120** $[H_3O^+] = 0.040$ M; pH = 1.39;
$[HIO_3] = 0.010$ M; $[IO_3{}^-] = 0.040$ M; $[OH^-] = 2.5 \times 10^{-13}$ M
14.122 $[H_3O^+] = [HC_8H_4O_4{}^-] = 0.0051$ M; $[H_2C_8H_4O_4] = 0.020$ M;
$[C_8H_4O_4{}^{2-}] = 3.1 \times 10^{-6}$ M; $[OH^-] = 2.0 \times 10^{-12}$ M; pH = 2.29
14.124 (a) acidic; (b) basic
14.126

Fraction dissociated $= \dfrac{[HA]_{diss}}{[HA]_{initial}}$

For a weak acid, $[HA]_{diss} = [H_3O^+] = [A^-]$

$K_a = \dfrac{[H_3O^+][A^-]}{[HA]} = \dfrac{[H_3O^+]^2}{[HA]}$; $[H_3O^+] = \sqrt{K_a[HA]}$

Fraction dissociated $= \dfrac{[HA]_{diss}}{[HA]} = \dfrac{[H_3O^+]}{[HA]}$

$= \dfrac{\sqrt{K_a[HA]}}{[HA]} = \sqrt{\dfrac{K_a}{[HA]}}$

When the concentration of HA that dissociates is negligible
compared with its initial concentration, the equilibrium
concentration, [HA], equals the initial concentration, $[HA]_{initial}$.

$$\% \text{ dissociation} = \sqrt{\dfrac{K_a}{[HA]_{initial}}} \times 100\%$$

14.128 pH = 2.54 **14.130** $[H_3O^+] = 0.0254$ M; pH = 1.59;
$[OH^-] = 3.9 \times 10^{-13}$ M; $[NO_3{}^-] = 0.0250$ M; $[HNO_2] = 0.0246$ M;
$[NO_2{}^-] = 4.3 \times 10^{-4}$ M *Multiconcept Problems*
14.132 $[H_3PO_4] = 0.67$ M; $[H_2PO_4{}^-] = 0.071$ M; $[HPO_4{}^{2-}] =$
6.2×10^{-8} M; $[PO_4{}^{3-}] = 4.2 \times 10^{-19}$ M; $[H_3O^+] = 0.071$ M;
$[OH^-] = 1.4 \times 10^{-13}$ M; pH = 1.15 **14.134** 0.25 m, $-0.93\ ^\circ$C
14.136 $H_3O^+(aq) + PO_4{}^{3-}(aq) \rightleftharpoons HPO_4{}^{2-}(aq) + H_2O(l)$;
$H_3O^+(aq) + HPO_4{}^{2-}(aq) \rightleftharpoons H_2PO_4{}^-(aq) + H_2O(l)$;
$H_3O^+(aq) + H_2PO_4{}^-(aq) \rightleftharpoons H_3PO_4(aq) + H_2O(l)$; pH = 2.02
14.138 (a) pH = 1.88; (b) 0.48 L. The result in Problem 14.126 can't
be used here because the concentration of HF that dissociates can't
be neglected compared with the initial HF concentration.
14.140 (a) Rate $= k\dfrac{[OCl^-][NH_3]}{[OH^-]}$; $k = 17\ s^{-1}$;

(b) $k_2 = 5.9 \times 10^7\ M^{-1}\,s^{-1}$

Chapter 15

15.1 (a) $HNO_2(aq) + OH^-(aq) \rightleftharpoons NO_2{}^-(aq) + H_2O(l)$;
$NO_2{}^-$ (basic anion), pH > 7.00;
(b) $H_3O^+(aq) + NH_3(aq) \rightleftharpoons NH_4{}^+(aq) + H_2O(l)$;
$NH_4{}^+$(acidic cation), pH < 7.00;
(c) $OH^-(aq) + H_3O^+(aq) \rightleftharpoons 2\,H_2O(l)$; pH = 7.00
15.2 (a) $HF(aq) + OH^-(aq) \rightleftharpoons H_2O(l) + F^-(aq)$; $K_n = 3.5 \times 10^{10}$;
(b) $H_3O^+(aq) + OH^-(aq) \rightleftharpoons 2\,H_2O(l)$; $K_n = 1.0 \times 10^{14}$;
(c) $HF(aq) + NH_3(aq) \rightleftharpoons NH_4{}^+(aq) + F^-(aq)$; $K_n = 6.3 \times 10^5$
15.3 $[H_3O^+] = 1.2 \times 10^{-9}$ M, pH = 8.91; $[OH^-] = 8.2 \times 10^{-6}$ M;
$[Na^+] = [CN^-] = 0.010$ M; $[HCN] = 0.025$ M;

% dissociation = 4.9×10^{-6} % **15.4** pH = 9.55 **15.5** Solution (2) has
the largest percent dissociation. Solution (1) has the lowest pH.
15.6 (a) (1) and (3); (b) (3) **15.7** For the buffer, pH = 3.76;
(a) pH = 3.71; (b) pH = 3.87 **15.8** This solution has less buffering
capacity than the solution in Problem 15.7 because it contains less
HF and F^- per 100 mL. Note that the change in pH is greater than
that in Problem 15.7. **15.9** pH = 9.95 **15.10** Make the Na_2CO_3
concentration 1.4 times the concentration of $NaHCO_3$. **15.11** HOCl
($K_a = 3.5 \times 10^{-8}$) and NaOCl. **15.12** (a) 9.44; (b) 7.87 **15.13** (a) 2.17;
(b) 11.77. The results are consistent with the pH data in Table 15.1
15.14 (a) 12.00; (b) 4.08; (c) 2.15 **15.15** (a) (3); (b) (1); (c) (4); (d) (2)
15.16 40 mL of 0.0400 M NaOH is required to reach the equivalence
point. (a) 6.98; (b) 7.46; (c) 9.75 **15.17** Use thymolphthalein
(pH 9.4–10.6). Bromthymol blue is unacceptable because it changes
color halfway to the equivalence point. **15.18** (a) 4.51; (b) 7.20;
(c) 7.68 **15.19** (a) 5.97; (b) 9.62; (c) 10.91 **15.20** (a) $K_{sp} = [Ag^+][Cl^-]$;
(b) $K_{sp} = [Pb^{2+}][I^-]^2$; (c) $K_{sp} = [Ca^{2+}]^3[PO_4{}^{3-}]^2$; (d) $K_{sp} =$
$[Cr^{3+}][OH^-]^3$ **15.21** 2.1×10^{-33} **15.22** 1.10×10^{-10} **15.23** (a) AgCl,
solubility = 1.3×10^{-5} mol/L (0.0019 g/L); (b) Ag_2CrO_4,
solubility = 6.5×10^{-5} mol/L (0.022 g/L); Ag_2CrO_4 has both the
higher molar and gram solubility, despite its smaller value
of K_{sp}. **15.24** (a) AgZ; (b) AgY **15.25** 1.4×10^{-5} M **15.26** AgCN,
$Al(OH)_3$, and ZnS **15.27** 1.1×10^{-12} M **15.28** $K = 25.4$; 0.045 mol/L
15.29 (a) IP > K_{sp}; a precipitate of $BaCO_3$ will form. (b) IP < K_{sp};
no precipitate will form. **15.30** For $Mn(OH)_2$, IP < K_{sp}; no
precipitate will form. For $Fe(OH)_2$, IP > K_{sp}; a precipitate of
$Fe(OH)_2$ will form. **15.31** $Q_c > K_{spa}$ for CdS; CdS will precipitate.
$Q_c < K_{spa}$ for ZnS; Zn^{2+} will remain in solution. **15.32** 5.3×10^{-5} M
15.33 7.2 *Conceptual Problems* **15.34** (a) (1), (3), and (4); (b) (4)
15.36 (4) **15.38** (a) (1) corresponds to (iii); (2) to (i); (3) to (ii); and (4)
to (iv)

(b)

15.40 (2) is supersaturated; (3) is unsaturated; (4) is unsaturated.
15.42 (a) The lower curve represents the titration of a strong acid;
the upper curve represents the titration of a weak acid. (b) pH = 7
for titration of the strong acid; pH = 10 for titration of the
weak acid. (c) $pK_a \sim 6.3$. *Section Problems* **15.44** (a) pH = 7.00;
(b) pH > 7.00; (c) pH < 7.00; (d) pH > 7.00. **15.46** Solution (a)
15.48 $K_n = 2.3 \times 10^{-5}$; K_n is small so the neutralization reaction
does not proceed very far to completion. **15.50** 1.5×10^{-14}
15.52 (a) pH increases; (b) no change; (c) pH decreases
15.54 3.06 **15.56** 0.022 M **15.58** For 0.10 M HN_3:
% dissociation = 1.4%. For 0.10 M HN_3 in 0.10 M HCl:
% dissociation = 0.019%. The % dissociation is less because
of the common ion (H_3O^+) effect. **15.60** Solutions (a), (c),
and (d) **15.62** Solution (a) **15.64** pH = 9.09. The pH of a buffer
solution will not change on dilution because the acid and base
concentrations will change by the same amount and their ratio
will remain the same. **15.66** pH = 3.67; (a) pH = 3.72;
(b) pH = 3.61 **15.68** 4.04 **15.70** The volume of the 1.0 M NH_3
solution should be 3.5 times the volume of the 1.0 M NH_4Cl
solution **15.72** $H_2PO_4{}^- - HPO_4{}^{2-}$ because the pK_a for $H_2PO_4{}^-$
(7.21) is closest to 7.00. **15.74** 1.8×10^{-10}

15.76 (a) 9.00 mmol; (b) 20.0 mL; (c) 7.00;
(d)

Volume 0.450 M NaOH

15.78 (a) 0.996; (b) 1.60; (c) 12.57 **15.80** 50.0 mL (a) 2.85; (b) 3.46;
(c) 8.25; (d) 12.70 **15.82** (a) 1.74; (b) 2.34; (c) 6.02; (d) 9.70; (e) 11.11
15.84 (a) C; (b) A **15.86** (a) pH = 8.04, phenol red; (b) pH = 7.00,
bromthymol blue or phenol red (Any indicator that changes
color in the pH range 4–10 is satisfactory for a strong acid–strong
base titration.); (c) pH = 5.92, chlorphenol red
15.88 (a) $Ag_2CO_3(s) \rightleftharpoons 2\ Ag^+(aq) + CO_3^{2-}(aq)$;
$K_{sp} = [Ag^+]^2[CO_3^{2-}]$; (b) $PbCrO_4(s) \rightleftharpoons Pb^{2+}(aq) + CrO_4^{2-}(aq)$;
$K_{sp} = [Pb^{2+}][CrO_4^{2-}]$; (c) $Al(OH)_3(s) \rightleftharpoons Al^{3+}(aq) + 3\ OH^-(aq)$;
$K_{sp} = [Al^{3+}][OH^-]^3$; (d) $Hg_2Cl_2(s) \rightleftharpoons Hg_2^{2+}(aq) + 2\ Cl^-(aq)$;
$K_{sp} = [Hg_2^{2+}][Cl^-]^2$ **15.90** (a) 8.4×10^{-9}; (b) 5.8×10^{-3} M;
(c) 0.13 M **15.92** 8.39×10^{-12} **15.94** (a) 4.37×10^{-9}; (b) 1.10×10^{-12};
(c) 7.0×10^{-7}; (d) 3.00×10^{-16} **15.96** (a) 1.1×10^{-5} M;
(b) 1.1×10^{-4} M; (c) 1.6×10^{-5} M **15.98** (a) $AgNO_3$, source of Ag^+;
equilibrium shifts left; (b) HNO_3, source of H_3O^+, removes CO_3^{2-};
equilibrium shifts right; (c) Na_2CO_3, source of CO_3^{2-}; equilibrium
shifts left; (d) NH_3, forms $Ag(NH_3)_2^+$; removes Ag^+; equilibrium
shifts right **15.100** (a) 5.3×10^{-7} M; (b) 2.8×10^{-10} M
15.102 (b), (c), and (d) are more soluble in acidic solution.
(a) $AgBr(s) \rightleftharpoons Ag^+(aq) + Br^-(aq)$;
(b) $CaCO_3(s) + H_3O^+(aq) \rightleftharpoons Ca^{2+}(aq) + HCO_3^-(aq) + H_2O(l)$;
(c) $Ni(OH)_2(s) + 2\ H_3O^+(aq) \rightleftharpoons Ni^{2+}(aq) + 4\ H_2O(l)$;
(d) $Ca_3(PO_4)_2(s) + 2\ H_3O^+(aq) \rightleftharpoons 3\ Ca^{2+}(aq) + 2\ HPO_4^{2-}(aq) +$
$2\ H_2O(l)$ **15.104** (a) more soluble, $Zn(OH)_2(s) + 2\ H_3O^+(aq) \rightleftharpoons$
$Zn^{2+}(aq) + 4\ H_2O(l)$; (b) more soluble, $Zn(OH)_2(s) + 2\ OH^-(aq) \rightleftharpoons$
$Zn(OH)_4^{2-}(aq)$; (c) more soluble, $Zn(OH)_2(s) + 4\ CN^-(aq) \rightleftharpoons$
$Zn(CN)_4^{2-}(aq) + 2\ OH^-(aq)$ **15.106** 3.5×10^{-22} M
15.108 (a) $AgI(s) + 2\ CN^-(aq) \rightleftharpoons Ag(CN)_2^-(aq) + I^-(aq)$;
$K = 2.6 \times 10^4$; (b) $Al(OH)_3(s) + OH^-(aq) \rightleftharpoons Al(OH)_4^-(aq)$;
$K = 6$; (c) $Zn(OH)_2(s) + 4\ NH_3(aq) \rightleftharpoons Zn(NH_3)_4^{2+} + 2\ OH^-(aq)$;
$K = 3.2 \times 10^{-8}$ **15.110** (a) 9.2×10^{-9} M; (b) 0.050 M **15.112** For
$BaSO_4$, $IP = 4.8 \times 10^{-11}$; $IP < K_{sp}$; $BaSO_4$ will not precipitate. For
$Fe(OH)_3$, $IP = 1.6 \times 10^{-20}$; $IP > K_{sp}$; $Fe(OH)_3(s)$ will precipitate.
15.114 $IP = 9.6 \times 10^{-11}$; $IP > K_{sp}$; $Mg(OH)_2(s)$ will precipitate.
15.116 Yes. $Q_c = 1.1 \times 10^{-2}$. For FeS, $Q_c < K_{spa}$, and FeS will not
precipitate. For SnS, $Q_c > K_{spa}$, and SnS will precipitate.
15.118 (i) $Q_c < K_{spa}$; FeS will not precipitate (ii) $Q_c > K_{spa}$; FeS(s)
will precipitate. **15.120** (a) Add Cl^- to precipitate AgCl; (b) Add
CO_3^{2-} to precipitate $CaCO_3$; (c) Add H_2S to precipitate MnS;
(d) Add NH_3 and NH_4Cl to precipitate $Cr(OH)_3$. (Need buffer
to control $[OH^-]$; excess OH^- produces the soluble $Cr(OH)_4^-$.)
***Chapter Problems* 15.122** Prepare aqueous solutions of the three
salts. Add a solution of $(NH_4)_2HPO_4$. If a white precipitate forms,
the solution contains Mg^{2+}. Perform flame tests on the other two
solutions. A yellow flame test indicates Na^+. A violet flame test
indicates K^+.

15.124 (a)

Volume 0.010 M NaOH

(b) 50 mL; (c) pH > 7.00; (d) pH = pK_a = 4.00 **15.126** 5.3×10^{-12}
15.128 $[NH_4^+]$ = 0.50 M; $[NH_3]$ = 1.0 M; pH = 9.55
15.130 molar solubility = 3.5×10^{-11} M; solubility = 3×10^{-9} g/L
15.132 7.51 **15.134** 10.7 mL of 0.10 M CH_3CO_2H and 9.3 mL of
0.15 M CH_3CO_2Na **15.136** (a) pH = 1.00; (b) pH = 1.84;
(c) pH = 5.31; (d) pH = 8.83 **15.138** (a) 2.2×10^{-6} M; (b) 8.64;
(c) 1.2×10^{-3} M ***Multiconcept Problems***
15.140 (a) $HA^-(aq) + H_2O(l) \rightleftharpoons H_3O^+(aq) + A^{2-}(aq)$ $K_{a2} = 10^{-10}$

$HA^-(aq) + H_2O(l) \rightleftharpoons H_2A(aq) + OH^-(aq)$ $K_b = \dfrac{K_w}{K_{a1}} = 10^{-10}$

$2\ HA^-(aq) \rightleftharpoons H_2A(aq) + A^{2-}(aq)$ $K = \dfrac{K_{a2}}{K_{a1}} = 10^{-6}$

$2\ H_2O(l) \rightleftharpoons H_3O^+(aq) + OH^-(aq)$ $K_w = 1.0 \times 10^{-14}$

The principal reaction is the one with the largest K, and that is the
third reaction.

(b) $K_{a1} = \dfrac{[H_3O^+][HA^-]}{[H_2A]}$ and $K_{a2} = \dfrac{[H_3O^+][A^{2-}]}{[HA^-]}$

$[H_3O^+] = \dfrac{K_{a1}[H_2A]}{[HA^-]}$ and $[H_3O^+] = \dfrac{K_{a2}[HA^-]}{[A^{2-}]}$

$\dfrac{K_{a1}[H_2A]}{[HA^-]} \times \dfrac{K_{a2}[HA^-]}{[A^{2-}]} = [H_3O^+]^2$; $\dfrac{K_{a1}K_{a2}[H_2A]}{[A^{2-}]} = [H_3O^+]^2$

Because the principal reaction is
$2\ HA^-(aq) \rightleftharpoons H_2A(aq) + A^{2-}(aq)$
$[H_2A] = [A^{2-}]$; $K_{a1}K_{a2} = [H_3O^+]^2$
$\log K_{a1} + \log K_{a2} = 2\ \log[H_3O^+]$
$\dfrac{\log K_{a1} + \log K_{a2}}{2} = \log\ [H_3O^+]$;
$\dfrac{-\log K_{a1} + (-\log K_{a2})}{2} = -\log\ [H_3O^+]$; $\dfrac{pK_{a1} + pK_{a2}}{2} = pH$;

(c) 3×10^{19} A^{2-} ions **15.142** (a) 2.2×10^{-5} M; (b) [HCl] = 0.124 M;
$[H_3PO_4]$ = 0.0960 M; (c) 100%; (d) 0.89;
(e)

buffer regions

X = equivalence points

mL 0.100 M NaOH

(f) Bromcresol green or methyl orange for the first equivalence point. Thymolphthalein for the second equivalence point.
15.144 4.00×10^{-6}
15.146 (a)

| NH$_4^+$ | CO$_3^{2-}$ | H$_2$O |
| acid | base | acid or base |

$NH_4^+(aq) + CO_3^{2-}(aq) \rightleftharpoons HCO_3^-(aq) + NH_3(aq)$;
(b) $[NH_4^+] = 0.095$ M; $[NH_3] = 0.22$ M; $[CO_3^{2-}] = 0.015$ M; $[HCO_3^-] = 0.065$ M; pH = 9.62; $[H_3O^+] = 2.4 \times 10^{-10}$ M; $[OH^-] = 4.2 \times 10^{-5}$ M; $[H_2CO_3] = 3.6 \times 10^{-4}$ M; (c) For MCO$_3$, IP = 1.5×10^{-4}; IP > $10^3 K_{sp}$ for CaCO$_3$ and BaCO$_3$, but IP < $10^3 K_{sp}$ for MgCO$_3$ so the $[CO_3^{2-}]$ is large enough to give observable precipitation of CaCO$_3$ and BaCO$_3$, but not MgCO$_3$. (d) For M(OH)$_2$, IP = 1.7×10^{-11}; IP < $10^3 K_{sp}$ for all three M(OH)$_2$. None precipitate. (e) In 0.08 M Na$_2$CO$_3$, $[OH^-] = 3.7 \times 10^{-3}$ M. Ca^{2+} and Ba^{2+} cannot be separated from Mg^{2+} using 0.08 M Na$_2$CO$_3$. Na$_2$CO$_3$ is more basic than (NH$_4$)$_2$CO$_3$, and Mg(OH)$_2$ would precipitate along with CaCO$_3$ and BaCO$_3$. **15.148** (a) 1.3 mg; (b) 1.4×10^2 washings; (c) The number of washings seems too high considering that frequent dye application is recommended. If the PbS is located mainly on the surface of the hair, solid particles of PbS can be lost by abrasion during shampooing.

Chapter 16

16.1 (a) spontaneous; (b), (c), and (d) nonspontaneous
16.2 (a) negative; (b) positive; (c) positive; (d) negative
16.3 (a) A$_2$ + AB$_3 \rightarrow$ 3 AB; (b) positive **16.4** (a) disordered N$_2$O (more randomness); (b) quartz glass (amorphous solid, more randomness); (c) 1 mole N$_2$ at STP (larger volume, more randomness); (d) 1 mole N$_2$ at 273 K and 0.25 atm (larger volume, more randomness)
16.5 +160.0 J/K **16.6** ΔS_{total} = −441 J/K. Because ΔS_{total} is negative, the reaction is not spontaneous under standard-state conditions at 25 °C. **16.7** (a) nonspontaneous at 25 °C; (b) 42 °C **16.8** (a) no; (b) 356 °C **16.9** $\Delta H < 0$; $\Delta S < 0$; $\Delta G < 0$ **16.10** (a) +131.5 kJ; (b) Because $\Delta G > 0$, the reaction is nonspontaneous at 25°C (c) 847 °C **16.11** (a) $\Delta S°$ is positive; (b) at high temperature **16.12** (a) −148.4 kJ; (b) No because $\Delta G°_f(C_2H_2) > 0$. **16.13** ΔG = +39.6 kJ mol. Because $\Delta G > 0$, the reaction is spontaneous in the reverse direction. **16.14** (a) (3) has the largest ΔG; (2) has the smallest ΔG; (b) 15 kJ **16.15** 9×10^{-24} **16.16** 0.03 atm **16.17** 80 kJ **16.18** No, because the decrease in entropy of the growing person is more than compensated for by an increase in entropy of the surroundings. **16.19** Yes. You might see an explosion run backwards, which is impossible because it would decrease the entropy of the universe.
Conceptual Problems **16.20** (a)

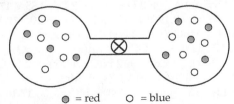

● = red   ○ = blue

(b) $\Delta H = 0$ (no heat is gained or lost in the mixing of ideal gases); $\Delta S > 0$ (the mixture of the two gases has more randomness); $\Delta G < 0$ (the mixing of the two gases is spontaneous); (c) For an isolated system, $\Delta S_{surr} = 0$ and $\Delta S_{sys} = \Delta S_{Total} > 0$ for the spontaneous

process; (d) $\Delta G > 0$ and the process is nonspontaneous.
16.22 $\Delta H < 0$ (heat is lost during condensation); $\Delta S < 0$ (liquid has less randomness than vapor); $\Delta G < 0$ (the reaction is spontaneous) **16.24** (a) 2 A$_2$ + B$_2 \rightarrow$ 2 A$_2$B; (b) $\Delta H < 0$ (because ΔS is negative, ΔH must also be negative in order for ΔG to be negative); $\Delta S < 0$ (the mixture becomes less random going from reactants [3 molecules] to products [2 molecules]); $\Delta G < 0$ (the reaction is spontaneous) **16.26** (a) $\Delta H° > 0$, $\Delta S° > 0$; (b) $\Delta S°$ is for the complete conversion of 1 mole of A$_2$ in its standard state to 2 moles of A in its standard state; (c) There is not enough information to say anything about the sign of $\Delta G°$. $\Delta G°$ decreases (becomes less positive or more negative) as the temperature increases; (d) K_p increases as the temperature increases. As the temperature increases there will be more A and less A$_2$. (e) $\Delta G = 0$ at equilibrium.
16.28 (1) $\Delta G° = 0$; (2) negative; (3) positive
Section Problems **16.30** (a) and (d) nonspontaneous; (b) and (c) spontaneous **16.32** (b) and (d) spontaneous (because of the large positive K_p's) **16.34** Molecular randomness is called entropy. $H_2O(s) \rightarrow H_2O(l)$ at 25 °C. **16.36** (a) +; (b) −; (c) −; (d) + **16.38** (a) −; (b) −; (c) +; (d) −; **16.40** (a) 2.30×10^{-22} J/K; (b) 2.30×10^{-21} J/K; (c) 11.5 J/K **16.42** 9.53×10^{-21} J/K **16.44** 1.17, 1.06 **16.46** (a) H$_2$ at 25 °C in 50 L; (b) O$_2$ at 25 °C, 1 atm; (c) H$_2$ at 100 °C, 1 atm; (d) CO$_2$ at 100 °C, 0.1 atm **16.48** 0.14 J/K **16.50** (a) C$_2$H$_6$(g); (b) CO$_2$(g); (c) I$_2$(g); (d) CH$_3$OH(g) **16.52** −173.0 J/K **16.54** (a) +125 J/K (+, because moles of gas increase); (b) −181.2 J/K (−, because moles of gas decrease); (c) +137.4 J/K (+, because moles of gas increase); (d) −626.4 J/K (−, because moles of gas decrease) **16.56** In any spontaneous process, the total entropy of a system and its surroundings always increases. **16.58** $\Delta S_{surr} = \dfrac{-\Delta H}{T}$; (a) positive; (b) negative.

16.60 (a) +879.3 J/K; (b) There is no temperature at which the reaction is not spontaneous. **16.62** ΔS_{total} = −1097 J/K; Because $\Delta S_{total} < 0$, the reaction is not spontaneous under standard-state conditions at 25 °C. **16.64** ΔS_{sys} = +216.4 J/K; ΔS_{surr} = −609.4 J/K; ΔS_{total} = −393.0 J/K; Because $\Delta S_{total} < 0$, the reaction is not spontaneous under standard-state conditions at 25 °C. (b) 839.2 K **16.66** (a) ΔS_{surr} = −89.5 J/(K · mol); ΔS_{total} = −2.5 J/(K · mol); (b) ΔS_{surr} = −87.0 J/(K · mol); ΔS_{total} = 0; (c) ΔS_{surr} = −84.6 J/(K · mol); ΔS_{total} = +2.4 J/(K · mol). Benzene does not boil at 70 °C (343 K) because ΔS_{total} is negative. The normal boiling point for benzene is 80 °C (353 K), where $\Delta S_{total} = 0$.

16.68

ΔH	ΔS	$\Delta G = \Delta H - T\Delta S$	Reaction Spontaneity
−	+	−	Spontaneous at all temperatures
−	−	− or +	Spontaneous at low temperatures where $|\Delta H| > |T\Delta S|$
			Nonspontaneous at high temperatures where $|\Delta H| < |T\Delta S|$
+	−	+	Nonspontaneous at all temperatures
+	+	− or +	Spontaneous at high temperatures where $T\Delta S > \Delta H$
			Nonspontaneous at low temperature where $T\Delta S < \Delta H$

16.70 (a) $\Delta H > 0$, $\Delta S > 0$, $\Delta G > 0$; (b) $\Delta H > 0$, $\Delta S > 0$, $\Delta G < 0$
16.72 (a) $\Delta G_{vap} = +0.9$ kJ/mol, benzene does not boil;
(b) $\Delta G_{vap} = 0$, 80 °C is the boiling point; (c) $\Delta G_{vap} = -0.9$ kJ/mol,
benzene boils **16.74** 122.4 °C **16.76** (a) $\Delta G°$ is the change in free
energy that occurs when reactants in their standard states are
converted to products in their standard states. (b) $\Delta G°_f$ is the free-
energy change for formation of one mole of a substance in its
standard state from the most stable form of the constituent
elements in their standard states. **16.78** (a) $\Delta H° = 66.4$ kJ;
$\Delta S° = -121.5$ J/K; $\Delta G° = +102.6$ kJ. Because $\Delta G°$ is positive, the
reaction is nonspontaneous under standard-state conditions at
25 °C. (b) $\Delta H° = -77.6$ kJ; $\Delta S° = 494.0$ J/K; $\Delta G° = -224.8$ kJ.
Because $\Delta G°$ is negative, the reaction is spontaneous under
standard-state conditions at 25 °C. (c) $\Delta H° = -492.6$ kJ;
$\Delta S° = -136.1$ J/K; $\Delta G° = -452.0$ kJ; the reaction is spontaneous
16.80 (a) +102.6 kJ; (b) −224.4 kJ; (c) −452 kJ; **16.82** (a) stable;
(b) stable; (c) unstable; (d) unstable **16.84** $\Delta G° = -147.7$ kJ.
Because $\Delta G° < 0$, dichloroethane can be synthesized from
gaseous C_2H_4 and Cl_2, each at 25 °C and 1 atm pressure.
16.86 $\Delta G = +11.8$ kJ/mol; reverse direction. **16.88** $\Delta G° = -6.1$ kJ.
The reaction becomes nonspontaneous at high temperatures
because $\Delta S°$ is negative. The reaction becomes nonspontaneous at
72 °C. **16.90** $\Delta G° = -505.2$ kJ. Because $\Delta G°$ is negative, the reaction
is possible. Look for a catalyst. Because $\Delta G°_f$ for benzene is positive
(+124.5 kJ/mol), the synthesis of benzene from graphite and
gaseous H_2 at 25 °C and 1 atm pressure is not possible.
16.92 $\Delta G = \Delta G° + RT \ln Q$ **16.94** (a) −176.0 kJ;
(b) −133.8 kJ; (c) −141.8 kJ **16.96** (a) If $K > 1$, $\Delta G°$ is negative. (b) If
$K = 1$, $\Delta G° = 0$. (c) If $K < 1$, $\Delta G°$ is positive. **16.98** $K_p = 7.2 \times 10^{24}$
16.100 0.059 atm **16.102** 0.28 atm **16.104** 2.9×10^{28} *Chapter
Problems* **16.106** −0.401 J/K **16.108** (a) Spontaneous does not mean
fast, just possible. (b) For a spontaneous reaction, $\Delta S_{total} > 0$. ΔS_{sys}
can be positive or negative. (c) An endothermic reaction can be
spontaneous if $\Delta S_{sys} > 0$. (d) This statement is true because the
sign of ΔG changes when the direction of a reaction is reversed.

16.110

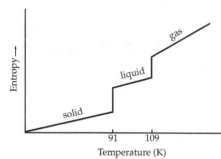

16.112 78 °C **16.114** (a) endothermic; (b) 33.6 kJ **16.116** (a)
$\Delta H° = -1203.4$ kJ; $\Delta S° = -216.6$ J/K; $\Delta G° = -1138.8$ kJ;
spontaneous. $\Delta G°$ becomes less negative as the temperature is
raised. (b) $\Delta H° = +101$ kJ; $\Delta S° = 174.8$ J/K; $\Delta G° = +49$ kJ; not
spontaneous. $\Delta G°$ becomes less positive as the temperature is
raised. (c) $\Delta H° = -852$ kJ; $\Delta S° = -38.5$ J/K; $\Delta G° = -840$ kJ;
spontaneous. $\Delta G°$ becomes less negative as the temperature is
raised. (d) $\Delta H° = +135.6$ kJ; $\Delta S° = +333$ J/K; $\Delta G° = +36.4$ kJ; not
spontaneous. $\Delta G°$ becomes less positive as the temperature is
raised. **16.118** −55.6 kJ/mol **16.120** (a) −252.6 J/(K · mol);
(b) −376 J/(K · mol); (c) −345 J/(K · mol) **16.122** $\Delta S° = -82.0$ J/K;
$\Delta H° = +2.71$ kJ **16.124** (a) $\Delta G° = +70.2$ kJ; (b) $K_{sp} = 5 \times 10^{-13}$;
(c) $\Delta G = 13.2$ kJ/mol. A positive value of ΔG means that the
reverse reaction is spontaneous, which is consistent with the fact
that $Q > K_{sp}$. **16.126** 26 °C **16.128** 1.3×10^7 **16.130** 5.7 mm Hg

16.132 (a) 46 °C; (b) 32 °C *Multiconcept Problems*
16.134 $[N_2] = 0.078$ M; $[H_2] = 0.235$ M; $[NH_3] = 0.043$ M
16.136 (a) −371.4 kJ; (b) −350.1 kJ **16.138** $K_b = 1.6 \times 10^{-5}$;
pH = 11.05 **16.140** $P_{N_2O_4} = 0.24$ atm; $P_{NO_2} = 2.52$ atm

Chapter 17

17.1

$Ni(s) \rightarrow Ni^{2+}(aq) + 2\,e^-$ $Ag^+(aq) + e^- \rightarrow Ag(s)$

17.2 $Pb(s) + Br_2(l) \rightarrow Pb^{2+}(aq) + 2\,Br^-(aq)$. There is a Pb anode in
an aqueous solution of Pb^{2+}. The cathode is a Pt wire that dips into
a pool of liquid Br_2 and an aqueous solution that is saturated with
Br_2. A salt bridge connects the anode and cathode compartment.
The electrodes are connected through an external circuit.
17.3 $Fe(s) \mid Fe^{2+}(aq) \parallel Sn^{2+}(aq) \mid Sn(s)$

17.4 (a) and (b)

(c) $2\,Al(s) + 3\,Co^{2+}(aq) \rightarrow 2\,Al^{3+}(aq) + 3\,Co(s)$;
(d) $Al(s) \mid Al^{3+}(aq) \parallel Co^{2+}(aq) \mid Co(s)$ **17.5** −270 kJ **17.6** −0.74 V
17.7 Cl_2 is the stronger oxidizing agent. Mg is the stronger reducing
agent. **17.8** (a) $E° = 0.23$ V; reaction can occur; (b) $E° = -1.40$ V;
reaction cannot occur **17.9** (a) D is the strongest reducing agent. A^{3+}
is the strongest oxidizing agent. (b) B^{2+} can oxidize C and D. C can
reduce A^{3+} and B^{2+}. (c) $A^{3+} + 2\,D \rightarrow A^+ + 2\,D^+$; 2.85 V **17.10** 0.25 V
17.11 (a) +0.059 V; (b) −0.19 V **17.12** 6.9 **17.13** $K = 10^{31}$ **17.14** −0.140 V
17.15 (a) $Zn(s) + 2\,MnO_2(s) + 2\,NH_4^+(aq) \rightarrow Zn^{2+}(aq) +$
$Mn_2O_3(s) + 2\,NH_3(aq) + H_2O(l)$; (b) $Zn(s) + 2\,MnO_2(s) \rightarrow$
$ZnO(s) + Mn_2O_3(s)$; (c) $Cd(s) + 2\,NiO(OH)(s) + 2\,H_2O(l) \rightarrow$
$Cd(OH)_2(s) + 2\,Ni(OH)_2(s)$; (d) $x\,Li(s) + MnO_2(s) \rightarrow Li_xMnO_2(s)$;
(e) $Li_xC_6(s) + Li_{1-x}CoO_2(s) \rightarrow 6\,C(s) + LiCoO_2(s)$ **17.16** A fuel cell
and a battery are both galvanic cells that convert chemical energy
into electrical energy utilizing a spontaneous redox reacton. A fuel
cell differs from a battery in that the reactants are not contained
within the cell but instead are continuously supplied from an
external reservoir. **17.17** (a) 1.23 V; (b) 1.23 V

17.18 (a)

$[Mg(s) \rightarrow Mg^{2+}(aq) + 2\,e^-] \times 2$

$O_2(g) + 4\,H^+(aq) + 4\,e^- \rightarrow 2\,H_2O(l)$

$2\,Mg(s) + O_2(g) + 4\,H^+(aq) \rightarrow 2\,Mg^{2+}(aq) + 2\,H_2O(l)$

(b)

$[Fe(s) \rightarrow Fe^{2+}(aq) + 2\,e^-] \times 4$

$[O_2(g) + 4\,H^+(aq) + 4\,e^- \rightarrow 2\,H_2O(l)] \times 2$

$4\,Fe^{2+}(aq) + O_2(g) + 4\,H^+(aq) \rightarrow 4\,Fe^{3+}(aq) + 2\,H_2O(l)$

$[2\,Fe^{3+}(aq) + 4\,H_2O(l) \rightarrow Fe_2O_3 \cdot H_2O(s) + 6\,H^+(aq)] \times 2$

$4\,Fe(s) + 3\,O_2(g) + 2\,H_2O(l) \rightarrow 2\,Fe_2O_3 \cdot H_2O(s)$

17.19 (a)

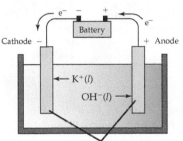

(b) anode $\quad 4\,OH^-(l) \rightarrow O_2(g) + 2\,H_2O(l) + 4\,e^-$

cathode $\quad 4\,K^+(l) + 4\,e^- \rightarrow 4\,K(l)$

overall $\quad 4\,K^+(l) + 4\,OH^-(l) \rightarrow$

$\qquad\qquad 4\,K(l) + O_2(g) + 2\,H_2O(l)$

17.20 (a)

anode $\quad 2\,Cl^-(aq) \rightarrow Cl_2(g) + 2\,e^-$

cathode $\quad 2\,H_2O(l) + 2\,e^- \rightarrow H_2(g) + 2\,OH^-(aq)$

overall $\quad 2\,Cl^-(aq) + 2\,H_2O(l) \rightarrow$

$\qquad\qquad Cl_2(g) + H_2(g) + 2\,OH^-(aq)$

(b) anode $\quad 2\,H_2O(l) \rightarrow O_2(g) + 4\,H^+(aq) + 4\,e^-$

cathode $\quad 2\,Cu^{2+}(aq) + 4\,e^- \rightarrow 2\,Cu(s)$

overall $\quad 2\,Cu^{2+}(aq) + 2\,H_2O(l) \rightarrow$

$\qquad\qquad 2\,Cu(s) + O_2(g) + 4\,H^+(aq)$

(c) anode $\quad 2\,H_2O(l) \rightarrow O_2(g) + 4\,H^+(aq) + 4\,e^-$

cathode $\quad 4\,H_2O(l) + 4\,e^- \rightarrow 2\,H_2(g) + 4\,OH^-(aq)$

overall $\quad 2\,H_2O(l) \rightarrow 2\,H_2(g) + O_2(g)$

17.21

anode $\quad Ag(s) \rightarrow Ag^+(aq) + e^-$

cathode $\quad Ag^+(aq) + e^- \rightarrow Ag(s)$

The overall reaction is transfer of silver metal from the silver anode to the spoon. **17.22** 268 kg **17.23** 7.45 h

17.24 $Ti(s) + 2\,H_2O(l) \rightarrow TiO_2(s) + 2\,H_2(g) \quad E° = 1.066\ V$

17.25 62.6 min

Conceptual Problems

17.26 (a)–(d)

$Zn(s) \rightarrow Zn^{2+}(aq) + 2\,e^- \quad Pb^{2+}(aq) + 2\,e^- \rightarrow Pb(s)$

(e)

anode $\quad Zn(s) \rightarrow Zn^{2+}(aq) + 2\,e^-$

cathode $\quad Pb^{2+}(aq) + 2\,e^- \rightarrow Pb(s)$

overall $\quad Zn(s) + Pb^{2+}(aq) \rightarrow Zn^{2+}(aq) + Pb(s)$

17.28 (a) The three cell reactions are the same except for cation concentrations. $Cu(s) + 2\,Fe^{3+}(aq) \rightarrow Cu^{2+}(aq) + 2\,Fe^{2+}(aq)$;

(b)

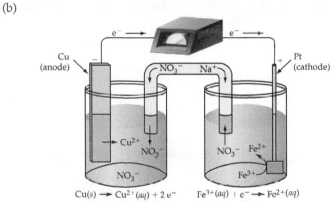

$Cu(s) \rightarrow Cu^{2+}(aq) + 2\,e^- \quad Fe^{3+}(aq) + e^- \rightarrow Fe^{2+}(aq)$

(c) (1) $E = 0.43\ V$, (2) $E = 0.39\ V$; (3) $E = 0.46\ V$. Cell (3) has the largest potential, while cell (2) has the smallest as calculated from the Nernst equation.

17.30 (a) electrolytic

(b)

(c)

anode $\quad 2\,H_2O(l) \rightarrow O_2(g) + 4\,H^+(aq) + 4\,e^-$

cathode $\quad Ni^{2+}(aq) + 2\,e^- \rightarrow Ni(s)$

overall $\quad 2\,Ni^{2+}(aq) + 2\,H_2O(l) \rightarrow$

$\qquad\qquad 2\,Ni(s) + O_2(g) + 4\,H^+(aq)$

17.32 (a) increase; (b) decrease; (c) decrease; (d) no change

17.34 (a), (b) & (c)

(d)

anode	$2 H_2(g) \rightarrow 4 H^+(aq) + 4 e^-$	$E° = 0.00$ V
cathode	$O_2(g) + 4 H^+(aq) + 4 e^- \rightarrow 2 H_2O(l)$	$E° = 1.23$ V
overall	$2 H_2(g) + O_2(g) \rightarrow 2 H_2O(l)$	$E° = 1.23$ V

Section Problems

17.36 The cathode of a galvanic cell is considered to be the positive electrode because electrons flow through the external circuit toward the positive electrode (the cathode).

17.38 (a)

$Cd(s) \rightarrow Cd^{2+}(aq) + 2 e^-$ $Sn^{2+}(aq) + 2 e^- \rightarrow Sn(s)$

(b)

$Al(s) \rightarrow Al^{3+}(aq) + 3 e^-$ $Cd^{2+}(aq) + 2 e^- \rightarrow Cd(s)$

(c)

$Fe^{2+}(aq) \rightarrow Fe^{3+}(aq) + e^-$ $Cr_2O_7{}^{2-}(aq) +$
$14 H^+(aq) + 6 e^- \rightarrow$
$2 Cr^{3+}(aq) + 7 H_2O$

17.40

(a) $Cd(s) | Cd^{2+}(aq) \| Sn^{2+}(aq) | Sn(s)$;

(b) $Al(s) | Al^{3+}(aq) \| Cd^{2+}(aq) | Cd(s)$;

(c) $Pt(s) | Fe^{2+}(aq), Fe^{3+}(aq) \| Cr_2O_7{}^{2-}(aq), Cr^{3+}(aq) | Pt(s)$

17.42 $2 Br^-(aq) + Cl_2(g) \rightarrow Br_2(l) + 2 Cl^-(aq)$

Inert electrodes are required because none of the reactants or products is an electrical conductor.

17.44 (a)

$H_2(g) \rightarrow 2 H^+(aq) + 2 e^-$ $Ag^+(aq) + e^- \rightarrow Ag(s)$

(b)

anode	$H_2(g) \rightarrow 2 H^+(aq) + 2 e^-$
cathode	$2 Ag^+(aq) + 2 e^- \rightarrow 2 Ag(s)$
overall	$H_2(g) + 2 Ag^+(aq) \rightarrow 2 H^+(aq) + 2 Ag(s)$

(c) $Pt(s) | H_2(g) | H^+(aq) \| Ag^+(aq) | Ag(s)$

17.46 (a)

anode	$Co(s) \rightarrow Co^{2+}(aq) + 2 e^-$
cathode	$Cu^{2+}(aq) + 2 e^- \rightarrow Cu(s)$
overall	$Co(s) + Cu^{2+}(aq) \rightarrow Co^{2+}(aq) + Cu(s)$

17.90 (a)

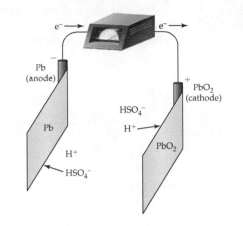

(b)

anode	$2\,Fe(s) \rightarrow 2\,Fe^{2+}(aq) + 4\,e^-$
cathode	$O_2(g) + 4\,H^+(aq) + 4\,e^- \rightarrow 2\,H_2O(l)$

overall	$2\,Fe(s) + O_2(g) + 4\,H^+(aq) \rightarrow 2\,Fe^{2+}(aq) + 2\,H_2O(l)$

(b)

anode	$Pb(s) + HSO_4^-(aq) \rightarrow PbSO_4(s) + H^+(aq) + 2\,e^-$
cathode	$PbO_2(s) + 3\,H^+(aq) + HSO_4^-(aq) + 2\,e^- \rightarrow$ $PbSO_4(s) + 2\,H_2O(l)$

overall	$Pb(s) + PbO_2(s) + 2\,H^+(aq) + 2\,HSO_4^-(aq) \rightarrow$ $2\,PbSO_4(s) + 2\,H_2O(l)$

(c) $K = 1 \times 10^{65}$; (d) cell voltage = 0 **17.92** $E° = 1.23$ V; $\Delta G° = -475$ kJ; $K = 1 \times 10^{83}$; $E = 1.29$ V **17.94** Rust is a hydrated form of iron(III) oxide ($Fe_2O_3 \cdot H_2O$). Rust forms from the oxidation of Fe in the presence of O_2 and H_2O. Rust can be prevented by coating Fe with Zn (galvanizing). **17.96** Cathodic protection is the attachment of a more easily oxidized metal to the metal you want to protect. This forces the metal you want to protect to be the cathode, hence the name, cathodic protection. Zn and Al can offer cathodic protection to Fe (Ni and Sn cannot).

17.48 E is the standard cell potential ($E°$) when all reactants and products are in their standard states—solutes at 1 M concentrations, gases at a partial pressure of 1 atm, solids and liquids in pure form, all at 25 °C. **17.50** −309 kJ **17.52** $x = 3$ **17.54** +1.23 V **17.56** −0.36 V **17.58** $Sn^{4+}(aq) < Br_2(aq) < MnO_4^-(aq)$ **17.60** $Cr_2O_7^{2-}(aq)$ strongest; $Fe^{2+}(aq)$ weakest **17.62** $I_2(s) + Co(s) \rightarrow Co^{2+}(aq) + 2\,I^-(aq)$ $E° = 0.82$ V, $\Delta G° = -1.6 \times 10^2$ kJ **17.64** (a) $E° = 0.26$ V, $\Delta G° = -50$ kJ; (b) $E° = 1.26$ V, $\Delta G° = -730$ kJ; (c) $E° = 0.59$ V, $\Delta G° = -342$ kJ **17.66** (a) $E° = -0.90$ V, nonspontaneous; (b) $E° = 2.11$ V, spontaneous **17.68** (a) $E° = +0.94$ V, $Sn^{2+}(aq)$ can be oxidized by $Br_2(aq)$; (b) $E° = -0.41$ V, $Ni^{2+}(aq)$ cannot be reduced by $Sn^{2+}(aq)$; (c) $E° = -0.93$ V, $Ag(s)$ cannot be oxidized by $Pb^{2+}(aq)$; (d) $E° = +0.37$ V, $I_2(s)$ can be reduced by H_2SO_3 **17.70** (a) no reaction; (b) $Pb(s) + 2\,Ag^+(aq) \rightarrow Pb^{2+}(aq) + 2\,Ag(s)$; (c) $Cl_2(g) + H_2C_2O_4(aq) \rightarrow 2\,Cl^-(aq) + 2\,CO_2(g) + 2\,H^+(aq)$; (d) $Ni(s) + 2\,HClO(aq) + 2\,H^+(aq) \rightarrow Ni^{2+}(aq) + Cl_2(g) + H_2O(l)$ **17.72** 0.87 V **17.74** $E = 0.35$ V, $[Cu^{2+}] = 1 \times 10^{-16}$ M **17.76** 10 **17.78** (a) 0.64 V; (b) 0.77 V; (c) −0.23 V; (d) −1.08 V **17.80** 9.0 **17.82** $\Delta G° = -nFE°$. Because n and F are always positive, $\Delta G°$ is negative when $E°$ is positive because of the negative sign in the equation.

$$E° = \frac{0.0592\ \text{V}}{n} \log K; \quad \log K = \frac{nE°}{0.0592\ \text{V}}; \quad K = 10^{\frac{nE°}{0.0592}}$$

If $E°$ is positive, the exponent is positive (because n is positive), and K is greater than 1. **17.84** 6×10^{35} **17.86** (a) 6×10^8; (b) 10^{128}; (c) 10^{60} **17.88** 9×10^{-3}

17.98 (a)

(b)

anode	$2\,Cl^-(l) \rightarrow Cl_2(g) + 2\,e^-$
cathode	$Mg^{2+}(l) + 2\,e^- \rightarrow Mg(l)$

overall	$Mg^{2+}(l) + 2\,Cl^-(l) \rightarrow Mg(l) + Cl_2(g)$

17.100 Possible anode reactions:

$$2\,Cl^-(aq) \rightarrow Cl_2(g) + 2\,e^-$$
$$2\,H_2O(l) \rightarrow O_2(g) + 4\,H^+(aq) + 4\,e^-$$

Possible cathode reactions:

$$2\,H_2O(l) + 2\,e^- \rightarrow H_2(g) + 2\,OH^-(aq)$$
$$Mg^{2+}(aq) + 2\,e^- \rightarrow Mg(s)$$

Actual reactions:

anode	$2\,Cl^-(aq) \rightarrow Cl_2(g) + 2\,e^-$
cathode	$2\,H_2O(l) + 2\,e^- \rightarrow H_2(g) + 2\,OH^-(aq)$

This anode reaction takes place instead of $2 H_2O(l) \rightarrow$ $O_2(g) + 4 H^+(aq) + 4 e^-$ because of a high overvoltage for formation of gaseous O_2. This cathode reaction takes place instead of $Mg^{2+}(aq) + 2 e^- \rightarrow Mg(s)$ because H_2O is easier to reduce than Mg^{2+}.

17.102 (a) NaBr

anode	$2 Br^-(aq) \rightarrow Br_2(l) + 2 e^-$
cathode	$2 H_2O(l) + 2 e^- \rightarrow H_2(g) + 2 OH^-(aq)$
overall	$2 H_2O(l) + 2 Br^-(aq) \rightarrow$
	$Br_2(l) + H_2(g) + 2 OH^-(aq)$

(b) $CuCl_2$

anode	$2 Cl^-(aq) \rightarrow Cl_2(g) + 2 e^-$
cathode	$Cu^{2+}(aq) + 2 e^- \rightarrow Cu(s)$
overall	$Cu^{2+}(aq) + 2 Cl^-(aq) \rightarrow Cu(s) + Cl_2(g)$

(c) LiOH

anode	$4 OH^-(aq) \rightarrow O_2(g) + 2 H_2O(l) + 4 e^-$
cathode	$4 H_2O(l) + 4 e^- \rightarrow 2 H_2(g) + 4 OH^-(aq)$
overall	$2 H_2O(l) \rightarrow O_2(g) + 2 H_2(g)$

17.104 3.22 g **17.106** Time = 38.9 h; 4.87×10^5 L Cl_2 **17.108** Mn^{2+}

***Chapter Problems* 17.110** (a) $2 MnO_4^-(aq) + 16 H^+(aq) + 5 Sn^{2+}(aq) \rightarrow 2 Mn^{2+}(aq) + 5 Sn^{4+}(aq) + 8 H_2O(l)$; (b) MnO_4^- is the oxidizing agent; Sn^{2+} is the reducing agent; (c) 1.36 V **17.112** (a) Ag^+ is the strongest oxidizing agent; Pb is the strongest reducing agent.

(b)

(c) $Pb(s) + 2 Ag^+(aq) \rightarrow Pb^{2+}(aq) + 2 Ag(s)$; $E° = 0.93$ V; (d) 0.87 V

17.114 (a)

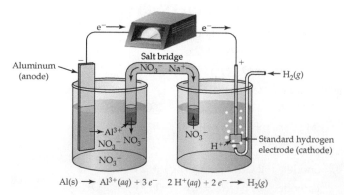

(b) $2 Al(s) + 6 H^+(aq) \rightarrow 2 Al^{3+}(aq) + 3 H_2(g)$; $E° = 1.66$ V;

(c) 1.59 V; (d) $K = 10^{168}$; (e) 1.40 g **17.116** (a) $10 Cl^-(aq) + 2 MnO_4^-(aq) + 16 H^+(aq) \rightarrow 5 Cl_2(g) + 2 Mn^{2+}(aq) + 8 H_2O(l)$; (b) $E° = 0.15$ V, $\Delta G° = -1.4 \times 10^2$ kJ; (c) 69 L **17.118** (a) oxidizing agents: PbO_2, H^+, $Cr_2O_7^{2-}$; reducing agents: Al, Fe, Ag; (b) PbO_2 is the strongest oxidizing agent. H^+ is the weakest oxidizing agent. (c) Al is the strongest reducing agent. Ag is the weakest reducing agent. (d) oxidized by Cu^{2+}: Fe and Al; reduced by H_2O_2: PbO_2 and $Cr_2O_7^{2-}$ **17.120** (a) 1.30 V; (b) 0.98 V **17.122** 1.7×10^{-10} **17.124** $E° = 0.46$ V; $E = 0.04$ V. Because E is positive, the reaction is spontaneous. **17.126** 6×10^{-23}

17.128 (a)

anode	$4[Al(s) \rightarrow Al^{3+}(aq) + 3 e^-]$
cathode	$3[O_2(g) + 4 H^+(aq) + 4 e^- \rightarrow 2 H_2O(l)]$
overall	$4 Al(s) + 3 O_2(g) + 12 H^+(aq) \rightarrow$
	$4 Al^{3+}(aq) + 6 H_2O(l)$

(b) $E = E° - \dfrac{2.303RT}{nF} \log \dfrac{[Al^{3+}]^4}{(P_{O_2})^3[H^+]^{12}}$ where $T = 310$ K

(c) 2.63 V ***Multiconcept Problems* 17.130** (a) $4 CH_2{=}CHCN + 2 H_2O \rightarrow 2 NC(CH_2)_4CN + O_2$; (b) 60.5 kg; (c) 7030 L
17.132 $E° = -2.91$ V **17.134** (a) $Cr_2O_7^{2-}(aq) + 6 Fe^{2+}(aq) + 14 H^+(aq) \rightarrow 2 Cr^{3+}(aq) + 6 Fe^{3+}(aq) + 7 H_2O(l)$; (b) 1.05 V
17.136 (a) $Zn(s) + 2 Ag^+(aq) + H_2O(l) \rightarrow ZnO(s) + 2 Ag(s) + 2 H^+(aq)$; $\Delta H° = -275.9$ kJ; $\Delta S° = -128.0$ J/K; $\Delta G° = -237.8$ kJ; (b) 1.232 V; $K = 4 \times 10^{41}$; (c) decreases; 0.694 V; (d) IP $= 1.6 \times 10^{-11}$; IP $< K_{sp}$, AgCl will not precipitate. IP $= 1.6 \times 10^{-11}$; IP $> K_{sp}$, AgBr will precipitate. **17.138** (a) $2 C_4H_{10}(g) + 13 O_2(g) \rightarrow 8 CO_2(g) + 10 H_2O(l)$; (b) $E° = 1.09$ V; $K = 7 \times 10^{962}$; decrease because $\Delta H° < 0$; (c) 7.00 g; 2.69 L
17.140 (a) $4 Au(s) + 8 CN^-(aq) + O_2(g) + 2 H_2O(l) \rightarrow 4 Au(CN)_2^-(aq) + 4 OH^-(aq)$; (b) -387.0 kJ

Chapter 18

18.1 $d_{H_2} = 8.24 \times 10^{-5}$ g/cm^3. Air is 14 times more dense than H_2.
18.2 (a) 18.2% D; (b) 24.3% ^{13}C (c) 15.0 pounds.

18.3 (a) $H_2O(g) + C(s) \xrightarrow{1000\,°C} CO(g) + H_2(g)$;
(b) $C_3H_8(g) + 3 H_2O(g) \rightarrow 7 H_2(g) + 3 CO(g)$
18.4 (a) SiH_4, covalent; (b) KH, ionic; (c) H_2Se, covalent
18.5 (a) $SrH_2(s) + 2 H_2O(l) \rightarrow 2 H_2(g) + Sr^{2+}(aq) + 2 OH^-(aq)$; (b) $KH(s) + H_2O(l) \rightarrow H_2(g) + K^+(aq) + OH^-(aq)$
18.6 1.7×10^2 kg CaH_2 **18.7** (a) (1) ZrH_x, interstitial, (2) PH_3, covalent, (3) HBr, covalent, (4) LiH, ionic; (b) (1) and (4) solids, (2) and (3) gases; (c) LiH **18.8** $PdH_{0.74}$; $d_H = 0.0841$ g/cm^3; $M_H = 83.4$ M **18.9** 15.5 mL **18.10** (a) Li_2O, Ga_2O_3, CO_2; (b) Li_2O is the most ionic. CO_2 is the most covalent. (c) CO_2 is the most acidic. Li_2O is the most basic. (d) Ga_2O_3
18.11 (a) $Li_2O(s) + H_2O(l) \rightarrow 2 Li^+(aq) + 2 OH^-(aq)$; (b) $SO_3(l) + H_2O(l) \rightarrow H^+(aq) + HSO_4^-(aq)$; (c) $Cr_2O_3(s) + 6 H^+(aq) \rightarrow 2 Cr^{3+}(aq) + 3 H_2O(l)$; (d) $Cr_2O_3(s) + 2 OH^-(aq) + 3 H_2O(l) \rightarrow 2 Cr(OH)_4^-(aq)$
18.12 (a) -1, peroxide; (b) -2, oxide; (c) $-1/2$, superoxide; (d) -1, peroxide; (e) -2, oxide
18.13 (a) $Rb_2O_2(s) + H_2O(l) \rightarrow 2 Rb^+(aq) + HO_2^-(aq) + OH^-(aq)$; (b) $CaO(s) + H_2O(l) \rightarrow Ca^{2+}(aq) + 2 OH^-(aq)$; (c) $2 CsO_2(s) + H_2O(l) \rightarrow O_2(g) + 2 Cs^+(aq) + HO_2^-(aq) + OH^-(aq)$; (d) $SrO_2(s) + H_2O(l) \rightarrow Sr^{2+}(aq) + HO_2^-(aq) + OH^-(aq)$; (e) $CO_2(g) + H_2O(l) \rightleftharpoons H^+(aq) + HCO_3^-(aq)$

18.14

σ^*_{2p}	—	
π^*_{2p}	⇅	↑
π_{2p}	⇅	⇅
σ_{2p}	⇅	
σ^*_{2s}	⇅	
σ_{2s}	⇅	

O_2^-

O_2^- is paramagnetic with one unpaired electron. O_2^- bond order = $(8 - 5)/2 = 1.5$

18.15 H—Ö—Ö—H

The electron dot structure indicates a single bond which is consistent with an O—O bond length of 148 pm. **18.16** $PbS(s) + 4 H_2O_2(aq) \rightarrow PbSO_4(s) + 4 H_2O(l)$ **18.17** $NiSO_4 \cdot 7 H_2O$ **18.18** Hydrogen can be stored as a solid in the form of solid interstitial hydrides or in the recently discovered tube-shaped molecules called carbon nanotubes. **18.19** 1.5×10^{10} kJ; 1.0×10^6 kg O_2 *Conceptual Problems* **18.20** (a) (1) covalent, (2) ionic, (3) covalent, (4) interstitial; (b) (1) H, +1; other element, −3, (2) H, −1; other element, +1, (3) H, +1; other element, −2 **18.22** (a) a superoxide KO_2; (b) attracted; (c) The O—O bond length in O_2^- is longer and the bond energy is smaller than in O_2; (d) basic because of the reaction $2 KO_2(s) + H_2O(l) \rightarrow O_2(g) + 2 K^+(aq) + HO_2^-(aq) + OH^-(aq)$ **18.24** (a) (1) −2, +2; (2) −2, +1; (3) −2, +5; (b) (1) three-dimensional; (2) molecular; (3) molecular; (c) (1) solid; (2) gas or liquid; (3) gas or liquid; (d) (2) hydrogen; (3) nitrogen **18.26** (a) (4); (b) (3); (c) (1) and (4) **18.28** (a) A, KH; B, MgH_2; C, H_2O; D, HCl; (b) HCl; (c) $KH(s) + H_2O(l) \rightarrow H_2(g) + K^+(aq) + OH^-(aq)$ $MgH_2(s) + 2 H_2O(l) \rightarrow 2 H_2(g) + Mg^{2+}(aq) + 2 OH^-(aq)$; (d) HCl reacts with water to give an acidic solution. KH and MgH_2 react with water to give a basic solution.

Section Problems **18.30** Quantitative differences in properties that arise from the differences in the masses of the isotopes are known as isotope effects. Examples: H_2 and D_2 have different melting and boiling points. H_2O and D_2O have different dissociation constants. **18.32** 99.85%, 49.74%, the differences in properties will be larger for H_2O and D_2O rather than for D_2O and T_2O because of the larger relative difference in mass for H and D versus D and T. This is supported by the data in Table 18.1. **18.34** $[D^+] = 4.42 \times 10^{-8}$ M **18.36** 18

$H_2^{16}O$	$H_2^{17}O$	$H_2^{18}O$
$D_2^{16}O$	$D_2^{17}O$	$D_2^{18}O$
$T_2^{16}O$	$T_2^{17}O$	$T_2^{18}O$
$HD^{16}O$	$HD^{17}O$	$HD^{18}O$
$HT^{16}O$	$HT^{17}O$	$HT^{18}O$
$DT^{16}O$	$DT^{17}O$	$DT^{18}O$

18.38 (a) $Zn(s) + 2 H^+(aq) \rightarrow H_2(g) + Zn^{2+}(aq)$; (b) $H_2O(g) + C(s) \rightarrow CO(g) + H_2(g)$; (c) $H_2O(g) + CH_4(g) \rightarrow CO(g) + 3 H_2(g)$; (d) (b) and (c) above; also electrolysis: $2 H_2O(l) \rightarrow 2 H_2(g) + O_2(g)$ **18.40** The steam–hydrocarbon reforming process

$$CH_4(g) + H_2O(g) \xrightarrow[\text{Ni catalyst}]{1100\,°C} CO(g) + 3 H_2(g)$$

$$CO(g) + H_2O(g) \xrightarrow{400\,°C} CO_2(g) + H_2(g)$$

$$CO_2(g) + 2 OH^-(aq) \longrightarrow CO_3^{2-}(aq) + H_2O(l)$$

18.42 (a) LiH; (b) 12.9 kg **18.44** (a) MgH_2, H^-; (b) PH_3, covalent; (c) KH, H^-; (d) HBr, covalent **18.46** H_2S: covalent hydride, gas, weak acid in H_2O; NaH: ionic hydride, solid (salt like), reacts with H_2O to produce H_2; PdH_x: metallic (interstitial) hydride, solid, stores hydrogen **18.48** (a) CH_4, covalent bonding; (b) NaH, ionic bonding **18.50** (a) H—S̈e—H bent; (b) H—Äs—H trigonal pyramidal (with H below As);

(c) H—Si—H tetrahedral (with H above and below Si)

18.52 A nonstoichiometric compound is a compound whose atomic composition cannot be expressed as a ratio of small whole numbers. An example is PdH_x. The lack of stoichiometry results from the hydrogen occupying holes in the solid state structure. **18.54** (a) $d_H = 0.15$ g/cm^3; the density of H in TiH_2 is about 2.1 times the density of liquid H_2. (b) 1.7×10^3 cm^3 **18.56** (a) O_2 is obtained in industry by the fractional distillation of liquid air; (b) In the laboratory, O_2 is prepared by the thermal decomposition of $KClO_3(s)$. $2 KClO_3(s) \xrightarrow[\text{MnO}_2]{\text{Heat}} 2 KCl(s) + 3 O_2(g)$ **18.58** 7.34 L

18.60 (a) $4 Li(s) + O_2(g) \rightarrow 2 Li_2O(s)$; (b) $P_4(s) + 5 O_2(g) \rightarrow P_4O_{10}(s)$; (c) $4 Al(s) + 3 O_2(g) \rightarrow 2 Al_2O_3(s)$; (d) $Si(s) + O_2(g) \rightarrow SiO_2(s)$

18.62 :Ö::Ö:

The electron dot structure shows an O=O double bond. It also shows all electrons paired. This is not consistent with the fact that O_2 is paramagnetic. **18.64** covalent hydride. **18.66** $Li_2O < BeO < B_2O_3 < CO_2 < N_2O_5$ **18.68** $N_2O_5 < Al_2O_3 < K_2O < Cs_2O$ **18.70** (a) CrO_3; (b) N_2O_5; (c) SO_3 **18.72** (a) $Cl_2O_7(l) + H_2O(l) \rightarrow 2 H^+(aq) + 2 ClO_4^-(aq)$; (b) $K_2O(s) + H_2O(l) \rightarrow 2 K^+(aq) + 2 OH^-(aq)$; (c) $SO_3(l) + H_2O(l) \rightarrow H^+(aq) + HSO_4^-(aq)$ **18.74** (a) $ZnO(s) + 2 H^+(aq) \rightarrow Zn^{2+}(aq) + H_2O(l)$; (b) $ZnO(s) + 2 OH^-(aq) + H_2O(l) \rightarrow Zn(OH)_4^{2-}(aq)$ **18.76** A peroxide has oxygen in the −1 oxidation state, for example, H_2O_2. A superoxide has oxygen in the −1/2 oxidation state, for example, KO_2. **18.78** (a) BaO_2; (b) CaO; (c) CsO_2; (d) Li_2O; (e) Na_2O_2

18.80

	O_2		O_2^-		O_2^{2-}	
σ^*_{2p}	—		—		—	
π^*_{2p}	↑	↑	⇅	↑	⇅	⇅
π_{2p}	⇅	⇅	⇅	⇅	⇅	⇅
σ_{2p}	⇅		⇅		⇅	

Bond order = 2   Bond order = 1.5   Bond order = 1

(a) The O—O bond length increases because the bond order decreases. The bond order decreases because of the increased occupancy of antibonding orbitals. (b) O_2^- has 1 unpaired electron and is paramagnetic. O_2^{2-} has no unpaired electrons and is diamagnetic. **18.82** (a) $H_2O_2(aq) + 2 H^+(aq) + 2 I^-(aq) \rightarrow I_2(aq) + 2 H_2O(l)$; (b) $3 H_2O_2(aq) + 8 H^+(aq) + Cr_2O_7^{2-}(aq) \rightarrow 2 Cr^{3+}(aq) + 3 O_2(g) + 7 H_2O(l)$

18.84

:O═Ö–Ö: ⟷ :Ö–Ö═O:

18.86 $3 O_2(g) \xrightarrow[\text{discharge}]{\text{Electric}} 2 O_3(g)$ **18.88** 1.5×10^{11} kg

18.90 $AlCl_3 \cdot 6\, H_2O$

$$\left[\begin{array}{c} OH_2 \\ H_2O\cdots \underset{\underset{OH_2}{|}}{\overset{\overset{|}{Al}}{\Big|}} \cdots OH_2 \\ H_2O \nearrow \qquad \searrow OH_2 \end{array}\right]^{3+}$$

18.92 6.21% **18.94** The mineral gypsum $CaSO_4 \cdot 2\, H_2O$; $x = 2$
Chapter Problems **18.96** a reducing agent; Ca or Al
18.98 2.2×10^3 L **18.100** (a) B_2O_3, diboron trioxide; (b) H_2O_2, hydrogen peroxide; (c) SrH_2, strontium hydride; (d) CsO_2, cesium superoxide; (e) $HClO_4$, perchloric acid (f) BaO_2, barium peroxide
18.102 (a) 6; $^{16}O_2$, $^{17}O_2$, $^{18}O_2$, $^{16}O^{17}O$, $^{16}O^{18}O$, $^{17}O^{18}O$; (b) 18

$^{16}O_3$	$^{16}O_2{}^{17}O$	$^{18}O_3$
$^{17}O_2{}^{16}O$	$^{17}O_3$	$^{16}O_2{}^{18}O$
$^{18}O_2{}^{16}O$	$^{18}O_2{}^{17}O$	$^{17}O_2{}^{18}O$
$^{16}O^{17}O^{16}O$	$^{17}O^{18}O^{17}O$	$^{16}O^{17}O^{18}O$
$^{16}O^{18}O^{16}O$	$^{17}O^{16}O^{17}O$	$^{18}O^{16}O^{18}O$
$^{17}O^{18}O^{16}O$	$^{18}O^{16}O^{17}O$	$^{18}O^{17}O^{18}O$

18.104 (a) $2\, H_2(g) + O_2(g) \rightarrow 2\, H_2O(l)$;
(b) $O_3(g) + 2\, I^-(aq) + H_2O(l) \rightarrow O_2(g) + I_2(aq) + 2\, OH^-(aq)$;
(c) $H_2O_2(aq) + 2\, H^+(aq) + 2\, Br^-(aq) \rightarrow 2\, H_2O(l) + Br_2(aq)$;
(d) $2\, Na(l) + H_2(g) \rightarrow 2\, NaH(s)$;
(e) $2\, Na(s) + 2\, H_2O(l) \rightarrow H_2(g) + 2\, Na^+(aq) + 2\, OH^-(aq)$
18.106 (a) -128.7 kJ; (b) -41.2 kJ; (c) -77.6 kJ; (d) 2802.5 kJ
18.108 80.7 L **18.110** $x = 4$ **18.112** $CaSO_4 \cdot 2\, H_2O$ **18.114** NaO_2 superoxide. **18.116** Ge_3H_8 *Multiconcept Problems* **18.118** 496 J
18.120 M = Sr; SrH_2 **18.122** (a) $PH_3(g) + 2\, O_2(g) \rightarrow H_3PO_4(s)$;
(b) pH = 1.69 **18.124** 7.7×10^{-4} mol/(L·atm)
18.126 (a) 0.58 mm Hg; (b) 9.4×10^{18} HD molecules;
(c) 7.3×10^{14} D_2 molecules **18.128** 150 °C

Chapter 19

19.1 (a) B; (b) Br; (c) Se; (d) Cl
19.2 (a)

Nitrogen can form very strong $p\pi$–$p\pi$ bonds. Phosphorus forms weaker $p\pi$–$p\pi$ bonds, so it tends to form more single bonds.
(b) The larger S atom can accommodate six bond pairs in its valence shell, but the smaller O atom is limited to two bond pairs and two lone pairs. **19.3** Carbon forms strong π bonds with oxygen. Silicon does not form strong π bonds with oxygen, and what results are chains of alternating silicon and oxygen singly bonded to each other. **19.4** An ethane-like structure would require 14 valence electrons and diborane only has 12. **19.5** H—C≡N: The carbon is *sp* hybridized. **19.6** $Hb\text{–}O_2 + CO \rightleftharpoons Hb\text{–}CO + O_2$. Mild cases of carbon monoxide poisoning can be treated with O_2. Le Châtelier's principle says that adding a product (O_2) will cause the reaction to proceed in the reverse direction, back to $Hb\text{–}O_2$. **19.7** (a) $Si_8O_{24}{}^{16-}$; (b) $Si_2O_5{}^{2-}$

19.8

Nitrous oxide, N_2O

:N≡N—Ö: ⟷ :N̈=N=Ö: ⟷ :N̈—N≡O:
(0 +1 −1)   (−1 +1 0)   (−2 +1 +1)

The first structure is most important.

Nitric oxide, NO

:N̈=Ö: ⟷ :N̈=Ö: paramagnetic
(0   0)   (−1 +1)

The first structure is more important.

Nitrous acid, HNO_2

H—Ö—N̈=Ö: ⟷ H—Ö=N̈—Ö:
(0 0 0)   (+1 0 −1)

The first structure is more important.

Nitrogen dioxide, NO_2

:Ö—N̈=Ö: ⟷ :Ö=N̈—Ö: paramagnetic
(−1 +1 0)   (0 +1 −1)

Both structures are of equal importance.

Nitric acid, HNO_3

H—Ö—N=Ö: ⟷ H—Ö—N—Ö: ⟷ H—Ö=N—Ö:
(0 +1 0)   (0 +1 −1)   (+1 +1 −1)
    | ‖ |
   :Ö: Ö: :Ö:
   (−1)   (0)   (−1)

The first two structures are of equal importance. Both are more important than the third structure **19.9** Both P_4O_6 and P_4O_{10} are molecular compounds and have structures with a tetrahedral array of P atoms, as in white phosphorus. One O atom bridges each of the six edges of the P_4 tetrahedron, and an additional, terminal O atom is bonded to each P atom in P_4O_{10}. **19.10** (a) $SO_3{}^{2-}$, $HSO_3{}^-$, $SO_4{}^{2-}$, $HSO_4{}^-$; (b) $HSO_4{}^-$; (c) $SO_3{}^{2-}$; (d) $HSO_4{}^-$

19.11

(a) H—S̈—H bent

(b) :Ö—S̈=Ö: ⟷ :Ö=S̈—Ö: bent

(c) :Ö—S̈=Ö: ⟷ :Ö=S̈—Ö: ⟷ :Ö—S̈=Ö:
         | | ‖
        :Ö: :Ö: Ö:
    trigonal planar

19.12 Because copper is always conducting, a laser printer drum coated with copper would not hold any charge so no document image would adhere to the drum for printing.

Conceptual Problems

19.14

19.16 (a) PF_5 and SF_6; (b) CH_4 and $NH_4{}^+$; (c) CO and NO_2; (d) P_4O_{10}
19.18 (a) OF_2, NF_3, CF_4 and SiF_4, PF_5, SF_6; (b) The small N atom is limited to three nearest neighbors in NF_3, whereas the larger P atom can accommodate five nearest neighbors in PF_5. N uses its three

unpaired electrons in bonding to three F atoms and has one lone pair, whereas P uses all five valence electrons in bonding to five F atoms. Both C and Si have four valence electrons and use sp^3 hybrid orbitals to bond to four F atoms. **19.20** (a) H_2O, CH_4, HF, B_2H_6, NH_3;
(b)

There is a problem in drawing an electron-dot structure for B_2H_6 because this molecule is electron deficient and has two three-center, two-electron bonds. *Section Problems* **19.22** (a) Cl; (b) Si; (c) O **19.24** (a) Al; (b) P; (c) Pb **19.26** (a) I; (b) N; (c) F **19.28** (a) Sn; (b) Ge; (c) Bi **19.30** (a) CaH_2; (b) Ga_2O_3; (c) KCl; (d) $AlCl_3$ **19.32** Molecular: (a) B_2H_6; (c) SO_3; (d) $GeCl_4$. Extended three-dimensional structure: (b) $KAlSi_3O_8$ **19.34** (a) P_4O_{10}; (b) B_2O_3; (c) SO_2; (d) N_2O_3 **19.36** (a) Sn; (b) Cl; (c) Sn; (d) Se; (e) B **19.38** The smaller B atom can bond to a maximum of four nearest neighbors, whereas the larger Al atom can accommodate more than four nearest neighbors. **19.40** In O_2 a π bond is formed by $2p$ orbitals on each O. S does not form strong π bonds with its $3p$ orbitals, which leads to the S_8 ring structure with single bonds. **19.42** +3 for B, Al, Ga and In; +1 for Tl **19.44** Boron is a hard semiconductor with a high melting point. Boron forms only molecular compounds and does not form an aqueous B^{3+} ion. $B(OH)_3$ is an acid. **19.46** $2\ BBr_3(g)\ +\ 3\ H_2(g)\ \xrightarrow[1200\,°C]{Ta\ wire}$ $2\ B(s)\ +\ 6\ HBr(g)$ **19.48** (a) An electron deficient molecule is a molecule that doesn't have enough electrons to form a two-center, two-electron bond between each pair of bonded atoms. B_2H_6 is an electron deficient molecule. (b) A three-center, two-electron bond has three atoms bonded together using just two electrons. The B—H—B bridging bond in B_2H_6 is a three-center two-electron bond. **19.50** (a) Al; (b) Tl; (c) B; (d) B **19.52** (a) Pb; (b) C; (c) Si; (d) C **19.54** (a) tetrahedral, sp^3 (b) linear, sp; (c) trigonal planar, sp^2; (d) trigonal pyramidal, sp^3 **19.56** Diamond is a very hard, high melting solid. It is an electrical insulator. Diamond has a covalent network structure in which each C atom uses sp^3 hybrid orbitals to form a tetrahedral array of σ bonds. The interlocking, three-dimensional network of strong bonds makes diamond the hardest natural substance with the highest melting point for an element. Because the valence electrons are localized in the σ bonds, diamond is an electrical insulator. **19.58** Graphene is a two-dimensional array of hexagonally arranged carbon atoms just one atom thick, essentially one layer of graphite. Graphene is extremely strong and flexible, and is a superb conductor of electricity. **19.60** (a) carbon tetrachloride, CCl_4; (b) carbon monoxide, CO; (c) methane, CH_4 **19.62** (1) To provide the "bite" in soft drinks; $CO_2(aq)\ +\ H_2O(l) \rightleftharpoons H_2CO_3(aq)$. (2) CO_2 in fire extinguishers; CO_2 is nonflammable and 1.5 times more dense than air. (3) Refrigerant; dry ice, sublimes at −78 °C.
19.64

$$SiO_2(l)\ +\ 2\ C(s) \longrightarrow Si(l)\ +\ 2\ CO(g)$$
(Sand)

Purification of silicon for semiconductor devices:
$Si(s)\ +\ 2\ Cl_2(g) \rightarrow SiCl_4(l)$, $SiCl_4$ is purified by distillation.

$SiCl_4(g)\ +\ 2\ H_2(g) \xrightarrow{Heat} Si(s)\ +\ 4\ HCl(g)$; Si is purified by zone refining.

19.66

(a) $SiO_4{}^{4-}$ (b) $Si_4O_{13}{}^{10-}$

The charge on the anion is equal to the number of terminal O atoms. **19.68** (a) $Si_3O_{10}{}^{8-}$; (b) $Ca_2Cu_2Si_3O_{10} \cdot 2\ H_2O$ **19.70** (a) P; (b) Sb and Bi; (c) N; (d) Bi **19.72** (a) N_2O, +1; (b) N_2H_4, −2; (c) Ca_3P_2, −3; (d) H_3PO_3, +3; (e) H_3AsO_4, +5 **19.74** :N≡N:; N_2 is unreactive because of the large amount of energy necessary to break the N≡N triple bond. **19.76** (a) bent; (b) trigonal pyramidal; (c) trigonal bipyramidal; (d) tetrahedral **19.78** White phosphorus contains tetrahedral P_4 molecules with 60° bond angles. Red phosphorus is polymeric. White phosphorus is reactive due to the considerable strain in the P_4 molecule. **19.80** (a) The structure for phosphorous acid is

Only the two hydrogens bonded to oxygen are acidic. (b) Nitrogen forms strong π bonds, and in N_2 the nitrogen atoms are triple bonded to each other. Phosphorus does not form strong $p\pi-p\pi$ bonds, and so the P atoms are single bonded to each other in P_4. **19.82** (a) $2\ NO(g)\ +\ O_2(g) \rightarrow 2\ NO_2(g)$; (b) $4\ HNO_3(aq) \rightarrow 4\ NO_2(aq)\ +\ O_2(g)\ +\ 2\ H_2O(l)$; (c) $3\ Ag(s)\ +\ 4\ H^+(aq)\ +\ NO_3{}^-(aq) \rightarrow 3\ Ag^+(aq)\ +\ NO(g)\ +\ 2\ H_2O(l)$; (d) $N_2H_4(aq)\ +\ 2\ I_2(aq) \rightarrow N_2(g)\ +\ 4\ H^+(aq)\ +\ 4\ I^-(aq)$ **19.84** (a) O; (b) Te; (c) Po; (d) O **19.86** (a) crown-shaped S_8 rings; (b) S_8 rings pack differently; (c) disordered, tangled S_n chains; (d) long polymer chains (S_n, $n > 200,000$) **19.88** (a) hydrogen sulfide, H_2S; lead(II) sulfide, PbS; (b) sulfur dioxide, SO_2; sulfurous acid, H_2SO_3; (c) sulfur trioxide, SO_3; sulfur hexafluoride, SF_6 **19.90** a three-step reaction sequence in which (1) sulfur burns in air to give SO_2; (2) SO_2 is oxidized to SO_3 in the presence of a vanadium(V) oxide catalyst, and; (3) SO_3 reacts with water to give H_2SO_4.

(1) $S(s)\ +\ O_2(g) \rightarrow SO_2(g)$

(2) $2\ SO_2(g)\ +\ O_2(g) \xrightarrow[V_2O_5\ catalyst]{Heat} 2\ SO_3(g)$

(3) $SO_3(g)\ +\ H_2O$ (in conc H_2SO_4) $\rightarrow H_2SO_4(l)$

19.92 (a) $Zn(s)\ +\ 2\ H_3O^+(aq) \rightarrow Zn^{2+}(aq)\ +\ H_2(g)\ +\ 2\ H_2O(l)$; (b) $BaSO_3(s)\ +\ 2\ H_3O^+(aq) \rightarrow H_2SO_3(aq)\ +\ Ba^{2+}(aq)\ +\ 2\ H_2O(l)$; (c) $Cu(s)\ +\ 2\ H_2SO_4(l) \rightarrow Cu^{2+}(aq)\ +\ SO_4{}^{2-}(aq)\ +\ SO_2(g)\ +\ 2\ H_2O(l)$; (d) $H_2S(aq)\ +\ I_2(aq) \rightarrow S(s)\ +\ 2\ H^+(aq)\ +\ 2\ I^-(aq)$ **19.94** (a) Acid strength increases as the number of O atoms increases. (b) In comparison with S, O is much too electronegative to form compounds of O in the +4 oxidation state. Also, an S atom is large enough to accommodate four bond pairs and a lone pair in its valence shell, but an O atom is too small to do so. (c) Each S is sp^3 hybridized with two lone pairs of electrons. The bond angles are therefore 109.5 °. A planar ring would require bond angles of 135°.

19.96 (a) $HBrO_3$, +5; (b) HIO, +1; (c) $NaClO_2$, +3; (d) $NaIO_4$, +7
19.98 (a) iodic acid; (b) chlorous acid; (c) sodium hypobromite; (d) lithium perchlorate
19.100

(a) Trigonal pyramidal

(b) Bent

(c) Bent

(d) Octahedral

19.102 Oxygen atoms are highly electronegative. Increasing the number of oxygen atoms increases the polarity of the O—H bond and increases the acid strength. **19.104** (a) $Br_2(l)$ + $2\,OH^-(aq) \rightarrow OBr^-(aq) + Br^-(aq) + H_2O(l)$;
(b) $Cl_2(g) + H_2O(l) \rightarrow HOCl(aq) + H^+(aq) + Cl^-(aq)$;
(c) $3\,Cl_2(g) + 6\,OH^-(aq) \rightarrow ClO_3^-(aq) + 5\,Cl^-(aq) + 3\,H_2O(l)$
Chapter Problems **19.106** $Mg(s) + 2\,H_2SO_4(l) \rightarrow Mg^{2+}(aq) +$
$SO_4^{2-}(aq) + SO_2(g) + 2\,H_2O(l)$ **19.108** single-stranded silicate chains with an $Si_2O_6^{4-}$ repeating unit **19.110** $N_2H_4(aq) + O_2(aq) \rightarrow$
$N_2(aq) + 2\,H_2O(l)$ **19.112** (a) LiCl; (b) SiO_2; (c) P_4O_{10} **19.114** A portion of the extended graphene

19.116 Earth's crust: O, Si, Al, Fe; Human body: O, C, H, N **19.118** C, Si, Ge and Sn have allotropes with the diamond structure. Sn and Pb have metallic allotropes. C (nonmetal), Si (semimetal), Ge (semimetal), Sn (semimetal and metal), Pb (metal)
19.120 (a) $H_3PO_4(aq) + H_2O(l) \rightleftharpoons H_3O^+(aq) + H_2PO_4^-(aq)$;
H_3PO_4 is a Brønsted–Lowry acid. (b) $B(OH)_3(aq) + 2\,H_2O(l) \rightleftharpoons$
$B(OH)_4^-(aq) + H_3O^+(aq)$; $B(OH)_3$ is a Lewis acid. **19.122** (a) In diamond each C is covalently bonded to four additional C atoms in a rigid three-dimensional network solid. Graphite is a two-dimensional covalent network solid of carbon sheets that can slide over each other. Both are high melting because melting requires the breaking of C—C bonds. (b) Chlorine does not form perhalic acids of the type H_5XO_6 because its smaller size favors a tetrahedral structure over an octahedral one. **19.124** Cl—S—S—Cl
19.126 NH_3

19.128

19.130 P_4O_{10}, H_3PO_4, 0.93 g P_4 **19.132** The angle required by P_4 is 60°. The strain would not be reduced by using sp^3 hybrid orbitals because their angle is ~109°.

Multiconcept Problems
19.134 (a)

$$\cdot \ddot{N}=\ddot{O}: \quad \left[:\ddot{O}-\ddot{O}\cdot\right]^- \longleftrightarrow \left[\cdot\ddot{O}-\ddot{O}:\right]^- \quad \left[:\ddot{O}=\ddot{N}-\ddot{O}-\ddot{O}:\right]^-$$

The O—N—O bond angle should be ~120°.

(b)

σ^*_{2p}	—	
π^*_{2p}	↑	—
σ_{2p}	⇅	
π_{2p}	⇅	⇅
σ^*_{2s}	⇅	
σ_{2s}	⇅	

The bond order is 2 1/2 with one unpaired electron.
19.136 $E° = 0.30\,V$; $\Delta G° = -58\,kJ$; disproportionation of In^+ is spontaneous. $E° = -1.59\,V$; $\Delta G° = +307\,kJ$; disproportionation of Tl^+ is nonspontaneous. **19.138** (a) 8.62% $(NH_4)_2HPO_4$; 91.38%; NH_4NO_3; (b) 7.50 **19.140** (a) $2\,NO_2(aq) + 2\,H_2O(l) \rightarrow$
$HNO_2(aq) + H_3O^+(aq) + NO_3^-(aq)$; (b) $[NO_2^-] = 4.4 \times 10^{-4}\,M$;
pH = 1.15; (c) 5.12 atm; (d) 0.976 g

Chapter 20

20.1 (a) $[Ar]\,3d^3\,4s^2$; (b) $[Ar]\,3d^7$; (c) $[Ar]\,3d^3$; (d) $[Ar]\,3d^9$
20.2 (a) Mn; (b) Ni^{2+}; (c) Ag; (d) Mo^{3+}

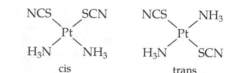

20.3 Z_{eff} increases from left to right. (a) Ti strongest, Zn weakest;
(b) FeO_4^{2-} strongest, VO_4^{3-} weakest **20.4** (a) $Cr_2O_7^{2-}$; (b) Cr^{3+};
(c) Cr^{2+}; (d) Fe^{2+}; (e) Cu^{2+} **20.5** (a) $Cr(OH)_2$; (b) $Cr(OH)_4^-$;
(c) CrO_4^{2-}; (d) $Fe(OH)_2$; (e) $Fe(OH)_3$ **20.6** $[Cr(NH_3)_2(SCN)_4]^-$ **20.7** +2
20.8 (a)

Chelate rings

Chelate ring

(b) Cr^{3+}, glycinate ligand, N and O; the chelate rings are identified in the drawing; (c) 6, octahedral, +3 **20.9** (a) tetraamminecopper(II) sulfate; (b) sodium tetrahydroxochromate(III);
(c) triglycinatocobalt(III); (d) pentaaquaisothiocyanatoiron(III) ion
20.10 (a) $[Zn(NH_3)_4](NO_3)_2$; (b) $Ni(CO)_4$; (c) $K[Pt(NH_3)Cl_3]$;
(d) $[Au(CN)_2]^-$ **20.11** (a) Two

NCS, SCN, H_3N, NH_3 — cis
NCS, NH_3, H_3N, SCN — trans

(b) No isomers; (c) Two

(d) No isomers; (e) Two

trans   cis

(f) None

20.12 (1) and (2) are the same. (3) and (4) are the same. (1) and (2) are different from (3) and (4). **20.13** (b) foot; (d) corkscrew

20.14 (a) (2) and (3) are chiral, and (1) and (4) are achiral;

(b)

Br   N
Br...Rh—N   N...Rh—N
Cl   N   Cl   N
Cl   Br

20.15 (a) $[Fe(C_2O_4)_3]^{3-}$

(c) $[Co(NH_3)_2(en)_2]^{3+}$

20.16 (a) blue; (b) 3.18×10^{-19} J

20.17

(a) Fe^{3+}

[Ar] ↑ ↑ ↑ ↑ ↑   __   __ __ __
      3d   4s   4p

$[Fe(CN)_6]^{3-}$

[Ar] ⇅ ⇅ ↑ | ⇅ ⇅ | ⇅ | ⇅ ⇅ ⇅ |
      3d   4s   4p

      d^2sp^3 1 unpaired e^-

(b) Co^{2+}

[Ar] ⇅ ⇅ ↑ ↑ ↑   __   __ __ __
      3d   4s   4p

$[Co(H_2O)_6]^{2+}$

[Ar] ⇅ ⇅ ↑ ↑ ↑
      3d

| ⇅ | ⇅ ⇅ ⇅ | ⇅ ⇅ | __ __ __ |
| 4s | 4p | 4d | |

      sp^3d^2 3 unpaired e^-

(c) V^{3+}

[Ar] ↑ ↑ __ __ __   __   __ __ __
      3d   4s   4p

$[VCl_4]^-$

[Ar] ↑ ↑ __ __ __ | ⇅ | ⇅ ⇅ ⇅ |
      3d   4s   4p

      sp^3 2 unpaired e^-

(d) Pt^{2+}

[Xe] ⇅ ⇅ ⇅ ↑ ↑   __   __ __ __
      5d   6s   6p

$[PtCl_4]^{2-}$

[Xe] ⇅ ⇅ ⇅ ⇅ | ⇅ | ⇅ | ⇅ ⇅ | __ |
      5d   6s   6p

      dsp^2 no unpaired e^-

20.18

(a) $[Fe(H_2O)_6]^{2+}$ 4 unpaired e^-

(b) $[Fe(CN)_6]^{4-}$ no unpaired e^-

(c) $[VF_6]^{3-}$ 2 unpaired e^-

(d) $[Ni(en)_3]^{2+}$ 2 unpaired e^-

20.19

(a) $[NiCl_4]^{2-}$ (tetrahedral)   (b) $[Ni(CN)_4]^{2-}$ (square planar)

$x^2 - y^2$ __

xy   ⇅

⇅ ↑ ↑ z^2 ⇅
xy xz yz

⇅ ⇅   xz yz   ⇅ ⇅
z^2 x^2-y^2

2 unpaired electrons   no unpaired electrons

20.20 $\Delta G^{\circ}_1 = 243.8$ kJ; $\Delta G^{\circ}_2 = -84.5$ kJ; $\Delta G^{\circ}_3 = -192.3$ kJ; The third step is the most favorable

20.21

$N=N$ $\overset{H}{\underset{H}{}}$ $N=N$

***Conceptual Problems* 20.22** (a) Co; (b) Cr; (c) Zr; (d) Pr

20.24 (a) The atomic radii decrease, at first markedly and then more gradually. Toward the end of the series, the radii increase again. The decrease in atomic radii is a result of an increase in Z_{eff}. The increase is due to electron–electron repulsions in doubly occupied d orbitals. (b) The densities of the transition metals are inversely related to their atomic radii. The densities initially increase from left to right and then decrease toward the end of the series. (c) Ionization energies generally increase from left to right across the series. The general trend correlates with an increase in Z_{eff} and a decrease in atomic radii. (d) The standard oxidation potentials generally decrease from left to right across the first transition series. This correlates with the general trend in ionization energies.
20.26 (1) dichloroethylenediamineplatinum(II); (2) *trans*-diammine-aquachloroplatinate(II) ion; (3) amminepentachloroplatinate(IV) ion; (4) *cis*-diaquabis(ethylenediamine)platinum(IV) ion
20.28 (a) (1) cis; (2) trans; (3) trans; (4) cis; (b) (1) and (4) are the same. (2) and (3) are the same. (c) None of the isomers exist as enantiomers because their mirror images are identical.
20.30

Section Problems 20.32 (a) [Ar] $3d^5\,4s^1$; (b) [Kr] $4d^2\,5s^2$; (c) [Ar] $3d^7$; (d) [Ar] $3d^5$; (e) [Kr] $4d^3$; (f) [Ar] $3d^0$ **20.34** (a) 1; (b) 2; (c) 0; (d) 3
20.36 Ti is harder than K and Ca largely because the sharing of d, as well as s, electrons results in stronger metallic bonding.
20.38 (a) The decrease in radii with increasing atomic number is expected because the added d electrons only partially shield the added nuclear charge. As a result, Z_{eff} increases. With increasing Z_{eff}, the electrons are more strongly attracted to the nucleus, and atomic size decreases. (b) The densities of the transition metals are inversely related to their atomic radii. **20.40** The lanthanide contraction is the general decrease in atomic radii of the f-block lanthanide elements. It is due to the increase in Z_{eff} as the $4f$ subshell is filled.

20.42

Element	$E_{i1} + E_{i2}$ (kJ/mol)
Sc	1866
Ti	1969
V	2061
Cr	2224
Mn	2226
Fe	2324
Co	2408
Ni	2490
Cu	2703
Zn	2639

The general trend is due to the increase in Z_{eff} with increasing atomic number. Higher than expected values for the sum of the first two ionization energies are observed for Cr and Cu because of their anomalous electron configurations (Cr: $3d^5\,4s^1$; Cu: $3d^{10}\,4s^1$). An increasing Z_{eff} affects $3d$ orbitals more than the $4s$ orbital and the second ionization energy for an electron from the $3d$ orbital is higher than expected. **20.44** (a) Cr(s) + 2 H$^+$(aq) →
Cr^{2+}(aq) + H$_2$(g); (b) Zn(s) + 2 H$^+$(aq) → Zn^{2+}(aq) + H$_2$(g);
(c) N.R.; (d) Fe(s) + 2 H$^+$(aq) → Fe^{2+}(aq) + H$_2$(g) **20.46** (b) Mn;
(d) Cu **20.48** Sc(III), Ti(IV), V(V), Cr(VI), Mn(VII), Fe(VI), Co(III), Ni(II), Cu(II), Zn(II) **20.50** Cu^{2+} is a stronger oxidizing agent than Cr^{2+} because of a higher Z_{eff}. **20.52** a reducing agent, because early transition metal atoms have a relatively low effective nuclear charge and are easily oxidized to higher oxidation states.
20.54 Mn^{2+} < MnO$_2$ < MnO$_4^-$ because of increasing oxidation state of Mn. **20.56** (a) Cr$_2$O$_3$(s) + 2 Al(s) → 2 Cr(s) + Al$_2$O$_3$(s);
(b) Cu$_2$S(l) + O$_2$(g) → 2 Cu(l) + SO$_2$(g)
20.58 Cr(OH)$_3$(s) + OH$^-$(aq) → Cr(OH)$_4^-$(aq),
+3 oxidation state. deep green. **20.60** (c) Cr(OH)$_3$ **20.62** (a) Add excess KOH(aq) and Fe^{3+} will precipitate as Fe(OH)$_3$(s). Na$^+$(aq) will remain in solution. (b) Add excess NaOH(aq) and Fe^{3+} will precipitate as Fe(OH)$_3$(s). Cr(OH)$_4^-$(aq) will remain in solution. (c) Add excess NH$_3$(aq) and Fe^{3+} will precipitate as Fe(OH)$_3$(s). Cu(NH$_3$)$_4^{2+}$(aq) will remain in solution.
20.64 (a) Cr$_2$O$_7^{2-}$(aq) + 6 Fe^{2+}(aq) + 14 H$^+$(aq) → 2 Cr^{3+}(aq) + 6 Fe^{3+}(aq) + 7 H$_2$O(l); (b) 4 Fe^{2+}(aq) + O$_2$(g) + 4 H$^+$(aq) → 4 Fe^{3+}(aq) + 2 H$_2$O(l); (c) Cu$_2$O(s) + 2 H$^+$(aq) →
Cu(s) + Cu^{2+}(aq) + H$_2$O(l); (d) Fe(s) + 2 H$^+$(aq) →
Fe^{2+}(aq) + H$_2$(g) **20.66** (a) 2 CrO$_4^{2-}$(aq) + 2 H$_3$O$^+$(aq) →
Cr$_2$O$_7^{2-}$(aq) + 3 H$_2$O(l); (b) [Fe(H$_2$O)$_6$]$^{3+}$(aq) + SCN$^-$(aq) →
[Fe(H$_2$O)$_5$(SCN)]$^{2+}$(aq) + H$_2$O(l); (c) 3 Cu(s) + 2 NO$_3^-$(aq) +
8 H$^+$(aq) → 3 Cu^{2+}(aq) + 2 NO(g) + 4 H$_2$O(l); (d) Cr(OH)$_3$(s) +
OH$^-$(aq) → Cr(OH)$_4^-$(aq); 2 Cr(OH)$_4^-$(aq) + 3 HO$_2^-$(aq) →
2 CrO$_4^{2-}$(aq) + 5 H$_2$O(l) + OH$^-$(aq) **20.68** Ni^{2+} accepts six pairs of electrons, two each from the three ethylenediamine ligands. Ni^{2+} is an electron pair acceptor, a Lewis acid. The two nitrogens in each ethylenediamine donate a pair of electrons to the Ni^{2+}. The ethylenediamine is an electron pair donor, a Lewis base.
20.70 (a) [Ag(NH$_3$)$_2$]$^+$; (b) [Ni(CN)$_4$]$^{2-}$; (c) [Cr(H$_2$O)$_6$]$^{3+}$
20.72 (a) +1; (b) +3; (c) +2; (d) +4; (e) +3 **20.74** (a) Ni(CO)$_4$;
(b) [Ag(NH$_3$)$_2$]$^+$; (c) [Fe(CN)$_6$]$^{3-}$; (d) [Ni(CN)$_4$]$^{2-}$
20.76

The iron is in the +3 oxidation state, and the coordination number is six. The geometry about the Fe is octahedral. There are three chelate rings, one formed by each oxalate ligand. **20.78** (a) +3; (b) +1; (c) +3; (d) +1 **20.80** (a) tetrachloromanganate(II); (b) hexaamminenickel(II); (c) tricarbonatocobaltate(III); (d) bis(ethylenediamine)dithiocyanatoplatinum(IV) **20.82** (a) cesium tetrachloroferrate(III); (b) hexaaquavanadium(III) nitrate; (c) tetraamminedibromocobalt(III) bromide; (d) diglycinatocopper(II) **20.84** (a) [Pt(NH$_3$)$_4$]Cl$_2$; (b) Na$_3$[Fe(CN)$_6$]; (c) [Pt(en)$_3$](SO$_4$)$_2$; (d) Rh(NH$_3$)$_3$(SCN)$_3$

20.86

[Ru(NH₃)₅(NO₂)]Cl   [Ru(NH₃)₅(ONO)]Cl

[Ru(NH₃)₅Cl]NO₂

[Ru(NH₃)₅(NO₂)]Cl and [Ru(NH₃)₅(ONO)]Cl are linkage isomers. [Ru(NH₃)₅Cl]NO₂ is an ionization isomer of both [Ru(NH₃)₅(NO₂)]Cl and [Ru(NH₃)₅(ONO)]Cl.
20.88 (a) [Cr(NH₃)₂Cl₄]⁻ can exist as cis and trans diastereoisomers. (d) [PtCl₂Br₂]²⁻ (square planar) can exist as cis and trans diastereoisomers. **20.90** (c) cis-[Cr(en)₂(H₂O)₂]³⁺; (d) [Cr(C₂O₄)₃]³⁻

20.92

20.94 Plane-polarized light is light in which the electric vibrations of the light wave are restricted to a single plane. The following chromium complex can rotate the plane of plane-polarized light.

[Cr(en)₃]³⁺

20.96 The measure of the amount of light absorbed by a substance is called the absorbance, and a graph of absorbance versus wavelength is called an absorption spectrum; orange

20.98

(a) [Ti(H₂O)₆]³⁺

20.100 (a) +3, M = Cr or Ni; (b)

(c) [Cr(OH)₄]⁻
20.102 [Ti(H₂O)₆]³⁺, Ti³⁺, 3d¹

Ti(H₂O)₆]³⁺ is colored because it can absorb light in the visible region, exciting the electron to the higher-energy set of orbitals.
20.104 Δ = 220 kJ/mol; NCS⁻ is a weaker-field ligand than H₂O; [Ti(NCS)₆]³⁻ color should be red

20.106

(a) $[CrF_6]^{3-}$ (b) $[V(H_2O)_6]^{3+}$ (c) $[Fe(CN)_6]^{3-}$

3 unpaired e⁻

2 unpaired e⁻

1 unpaired e⁻

20.108

Ni²⁺(aq)   Zn²⁺(aq)

Ni²⁺(aq) is green because the Ni²⁺ ion can absorb light, which promotes electrons from the filled d orbitals to the higher energy half-filled d orbitals. Zn²⁺(aq) is colorless because the d orbitals are completely filled and no electrons can be promoted, so no light is absorbed. **20.110** Weak-field ligands produce a small Δ. Strong-field ligands produce a large Δ. For a metal complex with weak-field ligands, $\Delta < P$, where P is the pairing energy, and it is easier to place an electron in either d_{z^2} or $d_{x^2-y^2}$ than to pair up electrons; high-spin complexes result. For a metal complex with strong-field ligands, $\Delta > P$ and it is easier to pair up electrons than to place them in either d_{z^2} or $d_{x^2-y^2}$; low-spin complexes result.

20.112

— x^2-y^2

⇅ xy

⇅ z^2

⇅ ⇅ xz, yz

Square planar geometry is most common for metal ions with d^8 configurations because this configuration favors low-spin complexes in which all four lower energy d orbitals are filled and the higher energy $d_{x^2-y^2}$ orbital is vacant.
Chapter Problems **20.114** (a) $[Mn(CN)_6]^{3-}$; (d) $[FeF_6]^{4-}$
20.116 (a) $4\ Co^{3+}(aq) + 2\ H_2O(l) \rightarrow 4\ Co^{2+}(aq) + O_2(g) + 4\ H^+(aq)$;
(b) $4\ Cr^{2+}(aq) + O_2(g) + 4\ H^+(aq) \rightarrow 4\ Cr^{3+}(aq) + 2\ H_2O(l)$;
(c) $3\ Cu(s) + Cr_2O_7^{2-}(aq) + 14\ H^+(aq) \rightarrow 3\ Cu^{2+}(aq) + 2\ Cr^{3+}(aq) + 7\ H_2O(l)$; (d) $2\ CrO_4^{2-}(aq) + 2\ H^+(aq) \rightarrow Cr_2O_7^{2-}(aq) + H_2O(l)$ **20.118** EDTA⁴⁻ in mayonnaise will complex any metal cations that are present in trace amounts. Free metal ions can catalyze the oxidation of oils, causing the mayonnaise to become rancid. The bidentate ligand $H_2NCH_2CO_2^-$ will not bind to metal ions as strongly as does the hexadentate EDTA⁴⁻ and so would not be an effective substitute for EDTA⁴⁻.

20.120 (a)

square planar nickel(II)   tetrahedral nickel(II)

(b) $NiCl_2L_2$ is tetrahedral, $Ni(NCS)_2L_2$ is square planar.

(c) Square planar cis-$Ni(NCS)_2L_2$ and tetrahedral $NiCl_2L_2$ have a dipole moment. **20.122** Cl⁻ is a weak-field ligand, whereas CN⁻ is a strong-field ligand. Δ for $[Fe(CN)_6]^{3-}$ is larger than the pairing energy P; Δ for $[FeCl_6]^{3-}$ is smaller than P. Fe³⁺ has a $3d^5$ electron configuration.

$[FeCl_6]^{3-}$ $[Fe(CN)_6]^{3-}$
(high spin)   (low spin)

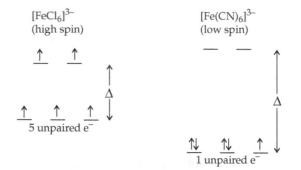

5 unpaired e⁻

1 unpaired e⁻

Because of the difference in Δ, $[FeCl_6]^{3-}$ is high-spin with five unpaired electrons, whereas $[Fe(CN)_6]^{3-}$ is low-spin with only one unpaired electron. **20.124** For d^1–d^3 and d^8–d^{10} complexes, only one ground-state electron configuration is possible. In d^1–d^3 complexes, all the electrons occupy the lower-energy d orbitals, independent of the value of Δ. In d^8–d^{10} complexes, the lower-energy set of d orbitals is filled with three pairs of electrons, while the higher-energy set contains two, three, or four electrons, again independent of the value of Δ. **20.126** $[CoCl_4]^{2-}$ is tetrahedral. $[Co(H_2O)_6]^{2+}$ is octahedral. Because $\Delta_{tet} < \Delta_{oct}$, these complexes have different colors. $[CoCl_4]^{2-}$ has absorption bands at longer wavelengths.

20.128

20.130

1 can exist as enantiomers.

20.132

	Weak-field ligands	Strong-field ligands
Ti^{2+}	2.83	2.83
V^{2+}	3.87	3.87
Cr^{2+}	4.90	2.83
Mn^{2+}	5.92	1.73
Fe^{2+}	4.90	0
Co^{2+}	3.87	1.73
Ni^{2+}	2.83	2.83
Cu^{2+}	1.73	1.73
Zn^{2+}	0	0

The magnetic moment can distinguish between high-spin and low-spin configurations for d^4–d^7.

20.134 (a)

(b) Isomer **2** would give rise to the desired product because it has two trans NO_2 groups. **20.136 (a)** $(NH_4)[Cr(H_2O)_6](SO_4)_2$, ammonium hexaaquachromium(III) sulfate

Cr^{3+} — —

↑ ↑ ↑
3 unpaired e⁻

(b) $Mo(CO)_6$, hexacarbonylmolybdenum(0)

Mo^0 — —

⇅ ⇅ ⇅
low-spin, no unpaired e⁻

(c) $[Ni(NH_3)_4(H_2O)_2](NO_3)_2$, tetramminediaquanickel(II) nitrate

Ni^{2+} ↑ ↑

⇅ ⇅ ⇅
2 unpaired e⁻

(d) $K_4[Os(CN)_6]$, potassium hexacyanoosmate(II)

Os^{2+} — —

⇅ ⇅ ⇅
low-spin, no unpaired e⁻

(e) $[Pt(NH_3)_4](ClO_4)_2$, tetraammineplatinum(II) perchlorate

Pt^{2+}
⇅
⇅
⇅ ⇅
low-spin, no unpaired e⁻

(f) $Na_2[Fe(CO)_4]$, sodium tetracarbonylferrate(–II)

Fe^{2-} ⇅ ⇅ ⇅

⇅ ⇅
no unpaired e⁻

20.138 $Cl^- <$ urea $<$ acetate $< H_2O <$ acac $< NH_3$
Multiconcept Problems **20.140 (a)** Reaction (2) should have the larger entropy change because three bidentate en ligands displace six water molecules. **(b)** $\Delta G° = \Delta H° - T\Delta S°$. Because $\Delta H°_1$ and $\Delta H°_2$ are almost the same, the difference in $\Delta G°$ is determined by the difference in $\Delta S°$. Because $\Delta S°_2$ is larger than $\Delta S°_1$, $\Delta G°_2$ is more negative than $\Delta G°_1$, which is consistent with the greater stability of $Ni(en)_3^{2+}$; **(c)** 180 J/(K • mol)
20.142 (a) $Cr(s) + 2 H^+(aq) \rightarrow Cr^{2+}(aq) + H_2(g)$; **(b)** 1.26 L; **(c)** 2.23; **(d)**

Valence bond orbital diagram

$Cr(H_2O)_6^{2+}$ [Ar] ↑ ↑ ↑ ↑ __
3d

⇅ | ⇅ ⇅ ⇅ | ⇅ ⇅ __ — —
4s   4p   4d
sp^3d^2 4 unpaired e⁻

(e) The addition of excess KCN converts $Cr(H_2O)_6^{2+}(aq)$ to $Cr(CN)_6^{4-}(aq)$. CN^- is a strong field ligand and increases Δ changing the chromium complex from high spin, with 4 unpaired electrons, to low spin, with only 2 unpaired electrons.
20.144 (a) $CrCl_3(H_2O)_6$;
(b)

(c) H_2O is a stronger field ligand than Cl^-. Compound **A** is likely to be violet absorbing in the yellow. Compounds **B** and **C** have weaker field ligands and would appear blue or green absorbing in the orange or red, respectively. (d) **A**, $-1.86\,°C$; **B**, $-1.39\,°C$; **C**, $-0.93\,°C$

20.146 (a) $K = \dfrac{[Cr_2O_7^{2-}]}{[CrO_4^{2-}]^2[H^+]^2} = 1.00 \times 10^{14}$

$[Cr_2O_7^{2-}]/[CrO_4^{2-}]^2 = 1.00 \times 10^{14}\,[H^+]^2$ In neutral solution, $[H^+] = 1.0 \times 10^{-7}$ and $[Cr_2O_7^{2-}]/[CrO_4^{2-}]^2 = 1$, so $[Cr_2O_7^{2-}]$ and $[CrO_4^{2-}]$ are comparable. In basic solution, $[H^+] < 1.0 \times 10^{-7}$ and $[Cr_2O_7^{2-}]/[CrO_4^{2-}]^2 < 1$, so $[CrO_4^{2-}]$ predominates. In acidic solution, $[H^+] > 1.0 \times 10^{-7}$ and $[Cr_2O_7^{2-}]/[CrO_4^{2-}]^2 > 1$, so $[Cr_2O_7^{2-}]$ predominates. (b) $[CrO_4^{2-}] = 2.23 \times 10^{-4}\,M$, $[Cr_2O_7^{2-}] = 4.99 \times 10^{-2}\,M$; (c) $[CrO_4^{2-}] = 2.24 \times 10^{-6}\,M$, $[Cr_2O_7^{2-}] = 5.00 \times 10^{-2}\,M$.

Chapter 21

21.1 The most common oxidation state for the 3B transition metals (Sc, Y, and La) is 3+. The 3+ oxidation state of the cations conveniently matches the 3− charge of the phosphate ion, resulting in a large lattice energy and corresponding insolubility for MPO_4 compounds. **21.2** (a) $Cr_2O_3(s) + 2\,Al(s) \rightarrow 2\,Cr(s) + Al_2O_3(s)$; (b) $Cu_2S(s) + O_2(g) \rightarrow 2\,Cu(s) + SO_2(g)$; (c) $PbO(s) + C(s) \rightarrow Pb(s) + CO(g)$; (d) $2\,K^+(l) + 2\,Cl^-(l) \xrightarrow{\text{electrolysis}} 2\,K(l) + Cl_2(g)$ **21.3** $CaO(s) + SiO_2(s) \rightarrow CaSiO_3(l)$ (slag). The O^{2-} in CaO behaves as a Lewis base and SiO_2 is the Lewis acid. **21.4** The electron configuration for Hg is $[Xe]\,4f^{14}\,5d^{10}\,6s^2$. Assuming the 5d and 6s bands overlap, the composite band can accommodate 12 valence electrons per metal atom. Weak bonding and a low melting point are expected for Hg because both the bonding and antibonding MOs are occupied. **21.5** (a) The composite s–d band can accommodate 12 valence electrons per metal atom. (1) is 1/4 filled, Hf $[Xe]\,(6s^2\,4f^{14}\,5d^2)$. (2) is 5/6 filled, Pt $[Xe]\,6s^2\,4f^{14}\,5d^8$. (3) is 7/12 filled, Re $[Xe]\,6s^2\,4f^{14}\,5d^5$. (b) Re has an excess of 5 bonding electrons and it has the highest melting point and is the hardest; (c) Pt has an excess of only 2 bonding electrons and it has the lowest melting point and is the softest **21.6** Ge doped with As is an n-type semiconductor because As has an additional valence electron. The extra electrons are in the conduction band. The number of electrons in the conduction band of the doped Ge is much higher than for pure Ge, and the conductivity of the doped semiconductor is higher. **21.7** (a) (1), silicon; (2), white tin; (3), diamond; (4), silicon doped with aluminum; (b) (3) < (1) < (4) < (2). Diamond (3) is an insulator with a large band gap. Silicon (1) is a semiconductor with a band gap smaller than diamond. Silicon doped with aluminum (4) is a p-type semiconductor that has vacancies (positive holes) in the valence band. White tin (2) has a partially filled s–p composite band and is a metallic conductor. **21.8** 539 nm

21.9

8 Cu at corners	$8 \times 1/8$	$= 1\,Cu$
8 Cu on edges	$8 \times 1/4$	$= 2\,Cu$
	Total	$= 3\,Cu$
12 O on edges	$12 \times 1/4$	$= 3\,O$
8 O on faces	$8 \times 1/2$	$= 4\,O$
	Total	$= 7\,O$

21.10 $Si(OCH_3)_4 + 4\,H_2O \rightarrow Si(OH)_4 + 4\,HOCH_3$
21.11 $Ba[OCH(CH_3)_2]_2 + Ti[OCH(CH_3)_2]_4 + 6\,H_2O \rightarrow BaTi(OH)_6(s) + 6\,HOCH(CH_3)_2$
$$BaTi(OH)_6(s) \xrightarrow{\text{Heat}} BaTiO_3(s) + 3\,H_2O(g)$$
21.12 (a) ceramic–metal; (b) ceramic–ceramic; (c) ceramic–polymer; (d) ceramic–metal **21.13** The smaller the particle, the larger the band gap and the greater the shift in the color of the emitted light from the red to the violet. The yellow quantum dot is larger because yellow is closer to the red than is the blue. **21.14** (a) 27%; (b) 14% *Conceptual Problem*s **21.16** (a) electrolysis; (b) roasting a metal sulfide; (c) A = Li, electrolysis, B = Hg, roasting of the metal sulfide, C = Mn, reduction of the metal oxide, D = Ca, reduction of the metal oxide. **21.18** (a) (2), bonding MO's are filled. (b) (3), bonding and antibonding MO's are filled. (c) (3) < (1) < (2). Hardness increases with increasing MO bond order.

21.20

Section Problems 21.22 TiO_2, MnO_2, and Fe_2O_3 **21.24** (a) sulfide; (b) oxide; (c) uncombined; (d) sulfide **21.26** The less electronegative early transition metals tend to form ionic compounds by losing electrons to highly electronegative nonmetals such as oxygen. The more electronegative late transition metals tend to form compounds with more covalent character by bonding to the less electronegative nonmetals such as sulfur. **21.28** (a) hematite; (b) galena; (c) rutile; (d) chalcopyrite **21.30** The flotation process exploits the differences in the ability of water and oil to wet the surfaces of the mineral and the gangue. The gangue, which contains ionic silicates, is moistened by the polar water molecules and sinks to the bottom of the tank. The mineral particles, which contain the less polar metal sulfide, are coated by the oil and become attached to the soapy air bubbles created by the detergent. The metal sulfide particles are carried to the surface in the soapy froth, which is skimmed off at the top of the tank. This process would not work well for a metal oxide because it is too polar and will be wet by the water and sink with the gangue. **21.32** Because $E° < 0$ for Zn^{2+}, the reduction of Zn^{2+} is not favored. Because $E° > 0$ for Hg^{2+}, the reduction of Hg^{2+} is favored. The roasting of CdS should yield CdO because, like Zn^{2+}, $E° < 0$ for the reduction of Cd^{2+}. **21.34** (a) $V_2O_5(s) + 5\,Ca(s) \rightarrow 2\,V(s) + 5\,CaO(s)$; (b) $2\,PbS(s) + 3\,O_2(g) \rightarrow 2\,PbO(s) + 2\,SO_2(g)$; (c) $MoO_3(s) + 3\,H_2(g) \rightarrow Mo(s) + 3\,H_2O(g)$; (d) $3\,MnO_2(s) + 4\,Al(s) \rightarrow$

$3\,Mn(s) + 2\,Al_2O_3(s)$; (e) $MgCl_2(l) \xrightarrow{\text{Electrolysis}} Mg(l) + Cl_2(g)$
21.36 $\Delta H° = -882.6\,kJ; \Delta G° = -838.8\,kJ$. $\Delta H°$ and $\Delta G°$ are different because of the entropy change associated with the reaction. The minus sign for $(\Delta H° - \Delta G°)$ indicates that the entropy is negative, which is consistent with a decrease in the number of moles of gas from 3 mol to 2 mol. **21.38** (a) 110 kg;

(b) 1.06×10^5 L **21.40** 0.460 kg **21.42** $Fe_2O_3(s) + 3\,CO(g) \rightarrow 2\,Fe(l)$ $+ 3\,CO_2(g)$. Fe_2O_3 is the oxidizing agent. CO is the reducing agent. **21.44** Slag is a byproduct of iron production, consisting mainly of $CaSiO_3$. It is produced from the gangue in iron ore. **21.46** Molten iron from a blast furnace is exposed to a jet of pure oxygen gas for about 20 minutes. The impurities are oxidized to yield a molten slag that can be poured off. $P_4(l) + 5\,O_2(g) \rightarrow P_4O_{10}(l)$; $6\,CaO(s) + P_4O_{10}(l) \rightarrow 2\,Ca_3(PO_4)_2(l)$ (slag); $2\,Mn(l) + O_2(g) \rightarrow$ $2\,MnO(s)$; $MnO(s) + SiO_2(s) \rightarrow MnSiO_3(l)$ (slag) **21.48** $SiO_2(s) +$ $2\,C(s) \rightarrow Si(s) + 2\,CO(g)$; $Si(s) + O_2(g) \rightarrow SiO_2(s)$; $CaO(s) +$ $SiO_2(s) \rightarrow CaSiO_3(l)$ (slag) **21.50** No. In a blast furnace tungsten carbide (WC) would be formed.

21.52

Each K has a single valence electron and has eight nearest neighbor K atoms. The valence electrons can't be localized in an electron-pair bond between any particular pair of K atoms. **21.54** Malleability and ductility of metals follow from the fact that the delocalized bonding extends in all directions. When a metallic crystal is deformed, no localized bonds are broken. Instead, the electron sea simply adjusts to the new distribution of cations, and the energy of the deformed structure is similar to that of the original. Thus, the energy required to deform a metal is relatively small. **21.56** The energy required to deform a transition metal like W is greater than that for Cs because W has more valence electrons and hence more electrostatic "glue". **21.58** The difference in energy between successive MOs in a metal decreases as the number of metal atoms increases so that the MOs merge into an almost continuous band of energy levels. Consequently, MO theory for metals is often called band theory. **21.60** The energy levels within a band occur in degenerate pairs; one set of energy levels applies to electrons moving to the right, and the other set applies to electrons moving to the left. In the absence of an electrical potential, the two sets of levels are equally populated. As a result there is no net electric current. In the presence of an electrical potential those electrons moving to the right are accelerated, those moving to the left are slowed down, and some change direction. Thus, the two sets of energy levels are now unequally populated. The number of electrons moving to the right is now greater than the number moving to the left, and so there is a net electric current.

21.62

Diagram (b) shows the $2s$ and $2p$ bands overlapping in energy. The resulting composite band is only partially filled. Thus, Be is a good electrical conductor. **21.64** Transition metals have a d band that can

overlap the s band to give a composite band consisting of six MOs per metal atom. Half of the MOs are bonding and half are antibonding, and thus one expects maximum bonding for metals that have six valence electrons per metal atom. Accordingly, the melting points of the transition metals go through a maximum at or near group 6B. **21.66** A semiconductor is a material that has an electrical conductivity intermediate between that of a metal and that of an insulator. Si, Ge, and Sn (gray) are semiconductors.

21.68

The MOs of a semiconductor are similar to those of an insulator, but the band gap in a semiconductor is smaller. As a result, a few electrons have enough energy to jump the gap and occupy the higher-energy, conduction band. The conduction band is thus partially filled, and the valence band is partially empty. When an electrical potential is applied to a semiconductor, it conducts a small amount of current because the potential can accelerate the electrons in the partially filled bands. **21.70** As the band gap increases, the number of electrons able to jump the gap and occupy the higher-energy conduction band decreases, and thus the conductivity decreases. **21.72** An n-type semiconductor is a semiconductor doped with a substance with more valence electrons than the semiconductor itself. Si doped with P is an example.

21.74 In the MO picture, the extra electrons occupy the conduction band. The number of electrons in the conduction band of the doped Ge is much greater than for pure Ge, and the conductivity of the doped semiconductor is correspondingly higher. **21.76** (a) p-type; (b) n-type; (c) n-type **21.78** $Cd(CH_3)_2(g) + H_2Se(g) \rightarrow$ $CdSe(s) + 2\,CH_4(g)$ **21.80** $Al_2O_3 <$ Ge $<$ Ge doped with In $<$ Fe $<$ Cu **21.82** In a diode, current flows only when the junction is under a forward bias. A p–n junction that is part of a circuit and subjected to an alternating potential acts as a rectifier, allowing current to flow in only one direction, thereby converting alternating current to direct current. **21.84** Both an LED and a photovoltaic cell contain p–n junctions, but the two devices involve opposite processes. An LED converts electrical energy to light; a photovoltaic, or solar, cell converts light to electricity. **21.86** 620 nm, orange **21.88** (1) A superconductor is able to levitate a magnet. (2) In a superconductor, once an electric current is started, it flows indefinitely without loss of energy. A superconductor has no electrical resistance. **21.90** Some K^+ ions are surrounded

octahedrally by six $C_{60}{}^{3-}$ ions; others are surrounded tetrahedrally by four $C_{60}{}^{3-}$ ions. **21.92** Ceramics are inorganic, nonmetallic, nonmolecular solids, including both crystalline and amorphous materials. Ceramics have higher melting points, and they are stiffer, harder, and more resistant to wear and corrosion than are metals. **21.94** Ceramics have higher melting points, and they are stiffer, harder, and more wear resistant than metals because they have stronger bonding. They maintain much of their strength at high temperatures, where metals either melt or corrode because of oxidation. **21.96** The brittleness of ceramics is due to strong chemical bonding. In silicon nitride each Si atom is bonded to four N atoms and each N atom is bonded to three Si atoms. The strong, highly directional covalent bonds prevent the planes of atoms from sliding over one another when the solid is subjected to a stress. As a result, the solid can't deform to relieve the stress. It maintains its shape up to a point, but then the bonds give way suddenly and the material fails catastrophically when the stress exceeds a certain threshold value. By contrast, metals are able to deform under stress because their planes of metal cations can slide easily in the electron sea. **21.98** Ceramic processing is the series of steps that leads from raw material to the finished ceramic object.
21.100 $Zr[OCH(CH_3)_2]_4 + 4 H_2O \rightarrow Zr(OH)_4 + 4 HOCH(CH_3)_2$
21.102 $(HO)_3Si-O-H + H-O-Si(OH)_3 \rightarrow (HO)_3Si-O-Si(OH)_3 + H_2O$. Further reactions of this sort give a three-dimensional network of Si–O–Si bridges. On heating, SiO_2 is obtained.
21.104 $2 Ti(BH_4)_3(soln) \rightarrow 2 TiB_2(s) + B_2H_6(g) + 9 H_2(g)$
21.106 $3 SiCl_4(g) + 4 NH_3(g) \rightarrow Si_3N_4(s) + 12 HCl(g)$
21.108 Graphite/epoxy composites are good materials for making tennis rackets and golf clubs because of their high strength-to-weight ratios. *Chapter Problems* **21.110** 119°C
21.112 $2 Eu^{3+}(aq) + Zn(s) \rightarrow 2 Eu^{2+}(aq) + Zn^{2+}(aq)$
$Eu^{2+}(aq) + SO_4{}^{2-}(aq) \rightarrow EuSO_4(s)$ **21.114** The chemical composition of the alkaline earth minerals is that of metal sulfates and sulfites, MSO_4 and MSO_3. **21.116** Band theory better explains how the number of valence electrons affects properties such as melting point and hardness. **21.118** Transition metals have a d band that can overlap the s band to give a composite band consisting of six MOs per metal atom. Half of the MOs are bonding and half are antibonding. Strong bonding and a high enthalpy of vaporization are expected for V because almost all of the bonding MOs are occupied and all of the antibonding MOs are empty. Weak bonding and a low enthalpy of vaporization are expected for Zn because both the bonding and the antibonding MOs are occupied.
21.120 With a band gap of 130 kJ/mol, GaAs is a semiconductor. Because Ge lies between Ga and As in the periodic table, GaAs is isoelectronic with Ge.

GaAs semiconductor

21.122 36.7 g $Y(OCH_2CH_3)_3$; 74.4 g $Ba(OCH_2CH_3)_2$; 109 g $YBa_2Cu_3O_7$
21.124 (a) $6 Al(OCH_2CH_3)_3 + 2 Si(OCH_2CH_3)_4 + 26 H_2O \rightarrow$
$6 Al(OH)_3(s) + 2 Si(OH)_4(s) + 26 HOCH_2CH_3$;

sol

(b) H_2O is eliminated from the sol through a series of reactions

linking the sol particles together through a three-dimensional network of O bridges to form the gel. $(HO)_2Al-O-H + H-O-Si(OH)_3 \rightarrow (HO)_2Al-O-Si(OH)_3 + H_2O$;
(c) The remaining H_2O and solvent are removed from the gel by heating to produce the ceramic, $3 Al_2O_3 \cdot 2 SiO_2$.

21.126

$H_2C=CH + H_2C=CH \longrightarrow -CH_2-CH-CH_2-CH-$
with CN groups below

21.128
(a)

1s

This material is an insulator because all MOs are filled, preventing the movement of electrons.

(b)

Neutral hydrogen atoms have only 1 valence electron, compared with 2 in H^-. Partially empty antibonding MOs will allow the movement of electrons, so the doped material will be a conductor. (c) The missing electrons in the doped material are positive "holes"; p-type *Multiconcept Problems* **21.130** (a) 2.47×10^{-3} cm; (b) 6.11×10^4 unit cells thick **21.132** 74.36% Fe **21.134** (a) 0.954; (b) 2.096 (c) 9.6%; (d) 14.3°; (e) The presence of Fe^{3+} in the semiconductor leads to missing electrons ("positive holes"). This type of doped material is a p-type semiconductor. **21.136** (a) $\Delta G° = +12.6$ kJ; $K_p = 0.028$; (b) $\Delta G° = +45.4$ kJ; $K_p = 1.9 \times 10^{-5}$; (c) $\Delta S°$ is large and negative because as the reaction proceeds in the forward direction, the number of moles of gas decreases from four to one. Because $\Delta S°$ is negative, $-T\Delta S°$ is positive, and as T increases, $\Delta G°$ becomes more positive because $\Delta G° = \Delta H° - T\Delta S°$; (d) The reaction is exothermic because $\Delta H°$ is negative. $Ni(s) + 4 CO(g) \rightleftharpoons Ni(CO)_4(g) +$ heat. Heat is added as the temperature is raised and the reaction proceeds in the reverse direction to relieve this stress, as predicted by Le Châtelier's principle. As the reverse reaction proceeds, the partial pressure of CO increases and the partial pressure of $Ni(CO)_4$ decreases. K_p decreases as calculated because $K_p = P_{Ni(CO)_4}/(P_{CO})^4$. **21.138** (a) $(NH_4)_2Zn(CrO_4)_2(s) \rightarrow ZnCr_2O_4(s) + N_2(g) + 4 H_2O(g)$; (b) 7.251 g; (c) 7.35 L; (d) 1/8 of the tetrahedral holes and 1/2 of the octahedral holes are filled.

(e)

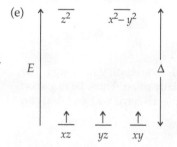

Octahedral Cr^{3+} has three unpaired electrons in the lower-energy d orbitals (xy, xz, yz). Cr^{3+} can absorb visible light to promote one of these d electrons to one of the higher-energy d orbitals making this compound colored. All of the d orbitals in Zn^{2+} are filled and no d electrons can be promoted; consequently the Zn^{2+} ion does not contribute to the color. **21.140** 1.3×10^8

Chapter 22

22.1 (a) Mass defect = 2.2748×10^{-25} g, 0.136 99 g/mol
Binding energy = 8.00 MeV/nucleon = 1.233×10^{10} kJ/mol
22.2 -9.11×10^{-9} g **22.3** 1.79×10^{10} kJ/mol **22.4** 5.31×10^8 kJ/mol
22.5 $^{40}_{18}Ar + ^{1}_{1}p \rightarrow ^{40}_{19}K + ^{1}_{0}n$ **22.6** $^{238}_{92}U + ^{2}_{1}H \rightarrow ^{238}_{93}Np + 2\,^{1}_{0}n$
22.7 1.53×10^4 y *Section Problems* **22.8** The lost mass is converted into the binding energy that is used to hold the nucleons together.

22.10 0.000 828 nm **22.12** (a) 0.480 59 g/mol; (b) 0.854 99 g/mol
22.14 (a) 8.76 MeV/nucleon ; (b) 8.74 MeV/nucleon
22.16 5.42×10^8 kJ/mol **22.18** 1.02×10^{-9} g **22.20** 9.87×10^7 kJ/mol
22.22 (a) $^{113}_{49}In$; (b) $^{13}_{7}N$ **22.24** $^{209}_{83}Bi + ^{58}_{26}Fe \rightarrow ^{266}_{109}Mt + ^{1}_{0}n$ **22.26** $^{12}_{6}C$
Chapter Problems **22.28** 220 W **22.30** 4.12×10^9 kJ/mol
22.32 (a) 0.467 00 g/mol; 8.72 MeV/nucleon; (b) 0.600 15 g/mol;
8.76 MeV/nucleon; ^{64}Zn is more stable. **22.34** 1.77×10^9 kJ/mol
22.36 $^{238}_{92}U + ^{1}_{0}n \rightarrow ^{239}_{94}Pu + 2\,^{0}_{-1}e$ **22.38** 7.80×10^{-14} J
22.40 (a) $^{100}_{43}Tc \rightarrow ^{0}_{1}e + ^{100}_{42}Mo$ (positron emission);
$^{100}_{43}Tc + ^{0}_{-1}e \rightarrow ^{100}_{42}Mo$ (electron capture); (b) positron emission,
-8.3×10^7 kJ/mol; electron capture, 1.6×10^7 kJ/mol. Only electron capture is observed because only this process involves a mass decrease and a release of energy. *Multiconcept Problems*
22.42 11,000 y **22.44** 5.73 L

Chapter 23

23.1

23.2

23.3 Structures (a) and (c) are identical.

23.4

C_7H_{16} $CH_3CH_2CH_2CCH_3$ with CH_3 above and CH_3 below

23.5

(a) carboxylic acid / alcohol — $CH_3-C-C-OH$ with H and O, OH
(b) aromatic ring / alkene — $CH=CH_2$

23.6 (a) O ‖ CH_3CH (b) O ‖ CH_3CH_2COH

(c) O ‖ $CH_3COCH_2CH_3$ $CH_3CH_2COCH_3$

23.7 (a) pentane; 2-methylbutane; 2,2-dimethylpropane;
(b) 3,4-dimethylhexane; (c) 2,4-dimethylpentane;
(d) 2,2,5-trimethylheptane

23.8
(a) $CH_3CH_2CHCHCH_2CH_2CH_2CH_2CH_3$ with CH_3 above and CH_3 below

(b) $CH_3CH_2CH-CCH_2CH_2CH_3$ with CH_3 above, CH_2 and CH_3 below, CH_3

(c) $CH_3CCH_2CHCH_2CH_2CH_2CH_3$ with CH_3, $CH_2CH_2CH_3$ above and CH_3 below

(d) $CH_3CCH_2CHCH_3$ with CH_3, CH_3 above and CH_3 below

23.9 2,3-dimethylhexane **23.10** (a) 3-methyl-1-butene;
(b) 4-methyl-3-heptene; (c) 3-ethyl-1-hexyne;

23.11

23.12 (a) CH₃CH₂CH₂CH₃   (b)

23.13 (a)

23.14 (a) 1,4-dimethylcyclohexane; (b) 1-ethyl-3-methylcyclopentane;
(c) isopropylcyclobutane

23.15

(a)

23.16

(a)   (b)   (c)

23.17

(a)   (b)

23.18

23.19

23.20

23.21

23.22

23.23 Amino acids that contain an aromatic ring: phenylalanine, tryptophan, tyrosine. Amino acids that contain sulfur: methionine, cysteine. Amino acids that are alcohols: serine, threonine, tyrosine. Amino acids that have alkyl-group side chains: alanine, valine, isoleucine, leucine.

23.24   Val-Cys   Cys-Val

23.25 Val-Tyr-Gly; Val-Gly-Tyr; Tyr-Gly-Val; Tyr-Val-Gly; Gly-Tyr-Val; Gly-Val-Tyr **23.26** (a) aldopentose; (b) ketotriose; (c) aldotetrose

23.27

23.28 Original: G–G–C–C–C–G–T–A–A–T
Complement: C–C–G–G–G–C–A–T–T–A

23.29 C–G–T–G–A–T–T–A–C–A   (DNA)
G–C–A–C–U–A–A–U–G–U   (RNA)

23.30 U–G–C–A–U–C–G–A–G–U   (RNA)
A–C–G–T–A–G–C–T–C–A   (DNA)

23.31 (a) adenine (DNA, RNA); (b) thymine (DNA)

23.32

Conceptual Problems **23.34** (a) alkene, ketone, ether; (b) alkene, amine, carboxylic acid **23.36** (a) serine; (b) methionine **23.38** Ser-Val
Section Problems **23.40** A functional group is a part of a larger molecule and is composed of an atom or group of atoms that has a characteristic chemical behavior. They are important because their chemistry controls the chemistry in molecules that contain them.

23.42 (a)

23.44

CH₃CH₂CH₂OH   CH₃CHCH₃   CH₃CH₂OCH₃

23.46 In a straight-chain alkane, all the carbons are connected in a row. In a branched-chain alkane, there are branching connections of carbons along the carbon chain. **23.48** C₃H₉ contains one more H than needed for an alkane. **23.50** (a) 4-ethyl-3-methyloctane; (b) 4-isopropyl-2-methylheptane; (c) 2,2,6-trimethylheptane; (d) 4-ethyl-4-methyloctane

23.52 (a)

CH₃CH₂CHCH₂CH₂CH₃ with CH₂CH₃ branch

(b) CH₃C—CHCH₂CH₃ with CH₃ CH₃ and CH₃

(c) CH₃CH₂C—CHCH₂CH₂CH₃ with CH₂CH₃ and CH₃ CH₃

(d) CH₃CHCH₂CH₂CHCH₂CH₂CH₃ with CH₃ and CHCH₃/CH₃

23.54 Today the term "aromatic" refers to the class of compounds containing a six-membered ring with three double bonds, not to the fragrance of a compound.
23.56 (a) CH₃CH=CHCH₂CH₃; (b) HC≡CCH₂CH₃;

(c)

23.58 (a) 4-methyl-2-pentene; (b) 3-methyl-1-pentene; (c) 1,2-dichlorobenzene, or o-dichlorobenzene; (d) 2-methyl-2-butene; (e) 7-methyl-3-octyne **23.60** (b); (c)

23.62
(a)

(b)

(c)

23.64

(a)

23.66 An aldehyde has a terminal carbonyl group. A ketone has the carbonyl group located between two carbon atoms. **23.68** (a) ketone; (b) aldehyde; (c) ketone; (d) amide; (e) ester **23.70**

23.72 amine, aromatic ring, and ester

carboxylic acid   alcohol

23.74 (a) serine; (b) threonine; (c) proline; (d) phenylalanine; (e) cysteine **23.76** Val-Ser-Phe-Met-Thr-Ala **23.78** Met-Ile-Lys, Met-Lys-Ile, Ile-Met-Lys, Ile-Lys-Met, Lys-Met-Ile, Lys-Ile-Met

23.80 An aldose contains the aldehyde functional group while a ketose contains the ketone functional group.

23.82

23.84 Long-chain carboxylic acids are called fatty acids.

23.86

23.88

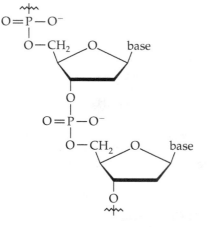

The two fat molecules differ from each other depending on where the palmitic acid chain is located. **23.90** A phosphate group, an aldopentose sugar, and an amine base. **23.92**

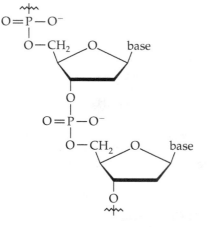

23.94 Original: T–A–C–C–G–A
Complement: A–T–G–G–C–T

23.96 It takes three nucleotides to code for a specific amino acid. In insulin the 21 amino acid chain would require 63 nucleotides and the 30 amino acid chain would require 90 nucleotides.

Chapter Problems **23.98**

(a)   CH₃
|
CH₃CHCH₂CH₂CH₂CH₂CH₃

(b)   CH₃   CH₂CH₃
| |
CH₃CHCH₂CHCH₂CH₃

(c)   CH₃   CH₂CH₃
| |
CH₃CH₂CH—CCH₂CH₂CH₂CH₃
|
CH₃

(d)   CH₃   CH₃
| |
CH₃CHCH₂CCH₂CH₂CH₃
|
CH₃

(e) CH₃   CH₃

(f) CH₃CH₂CHCHCH₂CH₂CH₃
|
H₃C   CHCH₃
|
CH₃

23.100

CH₃(CH₂)₁₈CO(CH₂)₃₁CH₃

23.102

(a)

(b)

23.104 Original: A–G–T–T–C–A–T–C–G
Complement: T–C–A–A–G–T–A–G–C

23.106 (a) Amine, ester, and arene;

(b)

        and CH₃OH

Multiconcept Problems **23.108** (a) CHO; (b) 116 amu;

(c)

(d)

HO—C—C=C—C—OH

23.110 (a) 1.27 g I₂; (b) grams excess I₂ = 1.04 g, grams I₂ reacted = 0.23 g; (c) 46; (d) 1.4

Glossary

Absorption spectrum a plot of the amount of light absorbed versus wavelength (*Section 20.10*)

Accuracy how close to the true value a given measurement is (*Section 1.12*)

Achiral lacking handedness (*Section 20.9*)

Acid a substance that provides H^+ ions when dissolved in water (*Section 4.5*)

Acid–base indicator a substance that changes color in a specific pH range (*Section 14.6*)

Acid–base neutralization reaction a process in which an acid reacts with a base to yield water plus an ionic compound called a salt (*Sections 4.5, 15.1*)

Acid-dissociation constant (K_a) the equilibrium constant for the dissociation of an acid in water (*Section 14.8*)

Actinide one of the 14 inner-transition metals starting with actinium in the periodic table (*Section 1.3*)

Activation energy (E_a) the height of the energy barrier between reactants and products (*Section 12.12*)

Active site a small three-dimensional region of an enzyme with the specific shape necessary to bind the substrate and catalyze the appropriate reaction (*Chapter 12 Inquiry*)

Activity series a list of elements in order of their reducing ability in aqueous solution (*Section 4.8*)

Acyclic an open-chain compound; not containing a ring (*Section 23.5*)

Addition reaction an organic reaction in which a reagent adds to the multiple bond of the unsaturated reactant to yield a saturated product (*Section 23.4*)

Adenosine triphosphate (ATP) a molecule that is formed as the final result of food catabolism and plays a pivotal role in the production of biological energy (*Section 23.9*)

Advanced ceramic a ceramic material that has high-tech engineering, electronic, or biomedical applications (*Section 21.8*)

Alcohol an organic molecule that contains an —OH group (*Section 23.7*)

Aldehyde an organic molecule that contains one alkyl group and one hydrogen bonded to a $C{=}O$ carbon (*Section 23.8*)

Alkali metal an element in group 1A of the periodic table (*Sections 1.4, 6.9*)

Alkaline earth metal an element in group 2A of the periodic table (*Sections 1.4, 6.10*)

Alkane a compound that contains only carbon and hydrogen and has only single bonds (*Section 23.1*)

Alkene a hydrocarbon that has a carbon–carbon double bond (*Section 23.4*)

Alkyl group the part of an alkane that remains when a hydrogen is removed (*Section 23.3*)

Alkyne a hydrocarbon that has a carbon–carbon triple bond (*Section 23.4*)

Allotropes different structural forms of an element (*Section 10.10*)

Alloy a solid solution of two or more metals (*Section 21.2*)

Alpha (α) radiation a type of radioactive emission; a helium nucleus (*Section 2.8*)

Aluminosilicate a silicate mineral in which partial substitution of Si^{4+} by Al^{3+} has occurred (*Section 19.8*)

Amide an organic molecule that contains one alkyl group and one nitrogen bonded to a $C{=}O$ carbon (*Section 23.8*)

Amine an organic derivative of ammonia (*Section 23.7*)

Amino acid a molecule that contains both a basic amine group (—NH_2) and an acidic carboxyl group (CO_2H); the building block from which proteins are made (*Section 23.10*)

Amorphous solid a solid whose constituent particles are randomly arranged and have no ordered, long-range structure (*Section 10.6*)

Amphoteric exhibiting both acidic and basic properties (*Sections 15.12, 18.9*)

Amplitude a wave's height measured from the midpoint between peak and trough (*Section 5.2*)

Anabolism metabolic reaction sequences that put building blocks together to assemble larger molecules (*Section 23.9*)

Angular-momentum quantum number (*l*) a variable in the solutions to the Schrödinger wave equation that gives the three-dimensional shape of an orbital (*Section 5.6*)

Anion a negatively charged atom or group of atoms (*Section 2.11*)

Anode the electrode at which oxidation takes place (*Section 17.1*)

Anodizing the oxidation of a metal anode to yield a protective metal oxide coat (*Chapter 17 Inquiry*)

Antibonding molecular orbital a molecular orbital that is higher in energy than the atomic orbitals it is derived from (*Section 7.13*)

Aqueous solution a solution with water as solvent (*Chapter 4 Introduction*)

Aromatic compound the class of compounds related to benzene (*Section 23.6*)

Arrhenius acid a substance that provides H^+ ions when dissolved in water (*Sections 4.5, 14.1*)

Arrhenius base a substance that provides OH^- ions when dissolved in water (*Sections 4.5, 14.1*)

Arrhenius equation an equation relating reaction rate constant, temperature, and activation energy; $k = Ae^{-E_a/RT}$ (*Section 12.12*)

Atmosphere (atm) a common unit of pressure measurement; standard atmospheric pressure at sea level is defined as exactly 760 mm Hg (*Section 9.1*)

Atom the smallest particle that retains the chemical properties of an element (*Section 2.2*)

Atomic mass the weighted average mass of an element's naturally occurring atoms (*Section 2.6*)

Atomic mass unit (amu) a convenient unit of mass; 1/12th the mass of a $^{12}_{6}C$ atom (*Section 2.6*)

Atomic number (Z) the number of protons in an atom's nucleus (*Section 2.5*)

Aufbau principle a set of rules that guides the electron filling order of orbitals in atoms (*Section 5.11*)

Avogadro's law The volume of a gas at a fixed pressure and temperature is proportional to its molar amount (*Section 9.2*).

Avogadro's number (N_A) the number of units in a mole; 6.022×10^{23} (*Section 2.6*)

Balanced a chemical equation in which the numbers and kinds of atoms are the same on both sides of the reaction arrow (*Section 3.1*)

Balmer–Rydberg equation an equation that accounts for the lines in the hydrogen spectrum (*Section 5.2*)

$$\frac{1}{\lambda} = R_\infty \left[\frac{1}{m^2} - \frac{1}{n^2} \right] \text{ or } \nu = R_\infty \cdot c \left[\frac{1}{m^2} - \frac{1}{n^2} \right]$$

Band gap the energy difference between the bonding MOs in the valence band and the antibonding MOs in the conduction band of a semiconductor (*Section 21.5*)

Band theory the molecular orbital theory for metals (*Section 21.4*)

Base a substance that provides OH^- ions when dissolved in water (*Sections 4.5, 14.1*)

Base-dissociation constant (K_b) the equilibrium constant for the reaction of a base with water (*Section 14.12*)

Basic oxygen process a method for purifying iron and converting it to steel (*Section 21.3*)

Battery *see* Galvanic cell (*Sections 17.1, 17.9*)

Bayer process purification of Al_2O_3 by treating bauxite with hot aqueous NaOH (*Sections 18.9, 21.2*)

Beta (β) radiation a type of radioactive emission consisting of electrons (*Section 2.8*)

Bidentate ligand a ligand that bonds to a metal using electron pairs on two donor atoms (*Section 20.6*)

Bimolecular reaction an elementary reaction that results from a collision between two reactant molecules (*Section 12.9*)

Binary hydride a compound that contains hydrogen and one other element (*Section 18.5*)

Binding energy the energy that holds nucleons together in the nucleus of an atom (*Section 22.1*)

Biochemistry the chemistry of living organisms (*Chapter 23 Introduction*)

Biofuel a fuel such as biodiesel, made from a renewable plant source (*Chapter 8 Inquiry*)

Blast furnace a huge reactor in which iron is produced by reduction of iron ore with carbon monoxide (*Section 21.3*)

Bleaching decolorizing a colored material (*Section 4.11*)

Body-centered cubic packing a packing arrangement of spheres into a body-centered cubic unit cell (*Section 10.8*)

Body-centered cubic unit cell a cubic unit cell with an atom at each of its eight corners and an additional atom in the center of the cube (*Section 10.8*)

Boiling point the temperature at which liquid and vapor coexist in equilibrium (*Section 10.4*)

Bond angle the angle at which two adjacent bonds intersect (*Section 7.9*)

Bond dissociation energy (*D*) the amount of energy necessary to break a chemical bond in an isolated molecule in the gaseous state (*Section 7.2*)

Bond length the minimum-energy distance between nuclei in a covalent bond (*Section 7.1*)

Bond order the number of electron pairs shared between two bonded atoms (*Section 7.5*)

Bonding electron pair a pair of valence electrons in a covalent bond (*Section 7.5*)

Bonding molecular orbital a molecular orbital that is lower in energy than the atomic orbitals it is derived from (*Section 7.13*)

Borane any compound of boron and hydrogen (*Section 19.4*)

Born–Haber cycle a pictorial way of viewing the energy changes in the various steps during formation of an ionic solid from its elements (*Section 6.7*)

Boyle's law The volume of a fixed amount of gas at a constant temperature varies inversely with its pressure (*Section 9.2*).

Bragg equation an equation used in X-ray crystallography for calculating the distance between atoms in a crystal (*Section 10.7*)

Branched-chain alkane an alkane with a branching connection of carbons (*Section 23.1*)

Brønsted–Lowry acid a substance that can transfer H^+ to a base in an acid–base reaction (*Section 14.1*)

Brønsted–Lowry base a substance that can accept H^+ from an acid in an acid–base reaction (*Section 14.1*)

Buffer capacity a measure of the amount of acid or base that a buffer can absorb without a significant change in pH (*Section 15.3*)

Buffer solution a solution of a weak acid and its conjugate base that resists drastic changes in pH (*Section 15.3*)

C-Terminal amino acid the amino acid with a free $-CO_2H$ group on the end of a protein chain (*Section 23.10*)

Carbide a carbon compound in which the carbon atom has a negative oxidation state (*Section 19.7*)

Carbohydrate a large class of organic molecules commonly called sugars and related to glucose (*Section 23.11*)

Carbonyl group the $C=O$ group (*Section 23.8*)

Carboxylate anion the anion $-CO_2^-$ that results from deprotonation of a carboxylic acid (*Section 23.8*)

Carboxylic acid an organic molecule that contains the $-CO_2H$ group (*Section 23.8*)

Catabolism metabolic reaction sequences that break molecules apart (*Section 23.9*)

Catalyst a substance that increases the rate of a reaction without itself being consumed (*Section 12.14*)

Cathode the electrode at which reduction takes place (*Section 17.1*)

Cathode ray the visible glow emitted when an electric potential is applied across two electrodes in an evacuated chamber (*Section 2.3*)

Cathodic protection a technique for protecting a metal from corrosion by connecting it to a second metal that is more easily oxidized (*Section 17.11*)

Cation a positively charged atom or group of atoms (*Section 2.11*)

Cell potential (*E*) *see* Electromotive force (*Section 17.3*)

Cell voltage *see* Electromotive force (*Section 17.3*)

Celsius degree (°C) a common unit of temperature; 0 °C = 273.15 K (*Section 1.8*)

Centimeter (cm) a common unit of length; 1 cm = 0.01 m (*Section 1.7*)

Ceramic an inorganic, nonmetallic, nonmolecular solid (*Section 21.8*)

Ceramic composite a hybrid material made of two ceramics (*Section 21.9*)

Ceramic–metal composite a hybrid material made of a metal reinforced with a ceramic (*Section 21.9*)

Ceramic–polymer composite a hybrid material made of a polymer reinforced with a ceramic (*Section 21.9*)

Chain reaction a self-sustaining reaction whose product initiates further reaction (*Section 22.2*)

Change of state *see* Phase change (*Section 10.4*)

Charles's law The volume of a fixed amount of gas at a constant pressure varies directly with its absolute temperature (*Section 9.2*).

Chelate the cyclic complex formed by a metal atom and a polydentate ligand (*Section 20.6*)

Chelating agent a polydentate ligand (*Section 20.6*)

Chemical bond the force that holds atoms together in chemical compounds (*Section 2.10*)

Chemical compound a chemical substance composed of atoms of more than one element (*Section 2.1*)

Chemical energy potential energy stored in chemical bonds (*Section 8.1*)

Chemical equation a format for writing a chemical reaction, listing reactants on the left, products on the right, and an arrow between them (*Section 2.1*)

Chemical equilibrium the state reached when the concentrations of reactants and products remain constant in time (*Section 13.1*)

Chemical formula a format for listing the number and kind of constituent elements in a compound (*Section 2.1*)

Chemical kinetics the area of chemistry concerned with reaction rates and the sequence of steps by which reactions occur (*Chapter 12*)

Chemical property a characteristic that results in a change in the chemical makeup of a sample (*Section 1.4*)

Chemical reaction the transformation of one substance into another (*Section 2.1*)

Chemistry the study of the composition, properties, and transformations of matter (*Chapter 1*)

Chiral having handedness (*Section 20.9*)

Chlor-alkali industry the commercial method of production for Cl_2 and NaOH by electrolysis of aqueous sodium chloride (*Section 17.13*)

Chromosome a threadlike strand of DNA in the nucleus of cells (*Section 23.13*)

Cis isomer the isomer of a metal complex or alkene in which identical ligands or groups are adjacent rather than opposite (*Sections 20.8, 23.4*)

Clausius–Clapeyron equation a mathematical relationship between vapor pressure and heat of vaporization for a substance (*Section 10.5*)

Coefficient a number placed before a formula in a chemical equation to indicate how many formula units are required to balance the equation (*Section 3.1*)

Colligative property a property that depends only on the amount of dissolved solute rather than on the chemical identity of the solute (*Section 11.5*)

Collision theory a model by which bi-molecular reactions occur when two properly oriented reactant molecules come together in a sufficiently energetic collision (*Section 12.12*)

Colloid a homogeneous mixture containing particles with diameters in the range 2–500 nm (*Section 11.1*)

Combustion a chemical reaction that sustains a flame (*Sections 4.11, 8.7*)

Common-ion effect the shift in the position of an equilibrium on addition of a substance that provides an ion in common with one of the ions already involved in the equilibrium (*Section 15.2*)

Complex ion an ion that contains a metal cation bonded to one or more small molecules or ions (*Section 15.12*)

Condensation the change of a gas to a liquid (*Section 10.4*)

Condensed structure a shorthand method for drawing organic structures in which C—H and C—C single bonds are "understood" rather than shown (*Section 23.1*)

Conduction band the antibonding molecular orbitals in a semiconductor (*Section 21.5*)

Conjugate acid the species HA formed by addition of H^+ to a base A^- (*Section 14.1*)

Conjugate acid–base pair chemical species whose formulas differ only by one proton (*Section 14.1*)

Conjugate base the species A^- formed by loss of H^+ from an acid HA (*Section 14.1*)

Constitutional isomers isomers that have different connections among their constituent atoms (*Section 20.8*)

Contact process the commercial process for making sulfuric acid from sulfur (*Section 19.13*)

Conversion factor an expression that describes the relationship between different units (*Section 1.14*)

Coordinate covalent bond a bond formed when one atom donates two electrons to another atom that has a vacant valence orbital (*Section 7.5*)

Coordination compound a compound in which a central metal ion is attached to a group of surrounding molecules or ions by coordinate covalent bonds (*Section 20.5*)

Coordination number the number of nearest-neighbor atoms in a crystal (*Section 10.8*) or the number of ligand donor atoms that surround a central metal ion in a complex (*Section 20.5*)

Core electrons inner-shell electrons (*Section 6.3*)

Corrosion the oxidative deterioration of a metal, such as the conversion of iron to rust (*Sections 4.11, 17.11*)

Cosmic ray a stream of energetic particles, primarily protons, coming from interstellar space (*Section 22.4*)

Coulomb's law The force resulting from the interaction of two electric charges is equal to a constant k times the magnitude of the charges divided by the square of the distance between them (*Section 6.8*).

Covalent bond a bond that occurs when two atoms share several (usually two) electrons (*Section 2.10; Chapter 7*)

Covalent hydride a compound in which hydrogen is attached to another element by a covalent bond (*Section 18.5*)

Covalent network solid a solid whose atoms are linked together by covalent bonds into a giant three-dimensional array (*Sections 10.6, 10.10*)

Critical mass the amount of material necessary for a nuclear chain reaction to become self-sustaining (*Section 22.2*)

Critical point a combination of temperature and pressure beyond which a gas cannot be liquefied (*Section 10.11*)

Crystal field splitting the energy splitting between two sets of d orbitals in a metal complex (*Section 20.12*)

Crystal field theory a model that views the bonding in metal complexes as arising from electrostatic interactions and considers the effect of the ligand charges on the energies of the metal ion d orbitals (*Section 20.12*)

Crystalline solid a solid whose atoms, ions, or molecules have an ordered arrangement extending over a long range (*Section 10.6*)

Cubic centimeter (cm^3) a common unit of volume, equal in size to the milliliter; $1 \text{ cm}^3 = 10^{-6} \text{ m}^3$ (*Section 1.9*)

Cubic closest-packed a packing arrangement of spheres into a face-centered cubic unit cell with three alternating layers (*Section 10.8*)

Cubic meter (m^3) the SI unit of volume (*Section 1.9*)

Cycloalkane an alkane that contains a ring of carbon atoms (*Section 23.5*)

d-Block element a transition metal element in which d orbitals are filled (*Section 5.13; Chapter 20*)

Dalton (Da) an alternative name for the atomic mass unit, amu (*Section 2.6*)

Dalton's law of partial pressures The total pressure exerted by a mixture of gases in a container at constant V and T is equal to the sum of the pressures exerted by each individual gas in the container (*Section 9.5*).

de Broglie equation an equation that relates mass, wavelength, and velocity, $m = h/\lambda v$ (*Section 5.4*)

Decay constant the first-order rate constant for radioactive decay (*Section 12.6*)

Degenerate having the same energy level (*Section 5.11*)

Density an intensive physical property that relates the mass of an object to its volume (*Section 1.10*)

Deoxyribonucleic acid (DNA) an immense biological molecule, made up of deoxyribonucleotide units and containing an organism's genetic information (*Section 23.13*)

Deposition the change of a gas directly to a solid (*Section 10.4*)

Diamagnetic a substance that has no unpaired electrons and is weakly repelled by a magnetic field (*Section 7.14*)

Diastereoisomers non-mirror-image stereoisomers (*Section 20.8*)

Diffraction scattering of a light beam by an object containing regularly spaced lines or points (*Section 10.7*)

Diffusion the mixing of different gases by random molecular motion with frequent collisions (*Section 9.7*)

Dimensional-analysis a method of problem solving whereby problems are set up so that unwanted units cancel (*Section 1.14*)

Diode a semiconductor device that permits electric current to flow in one direction but is highly resistant to current flow in the opposite direction (*Section 21.6*)

Dipole a pair of separated electrical charges (*Section 10.1*)

Dipole–dipole force an intermolecular force resulting from electrical interactions among dipoles on neighboring molecules (*Section 10.2*)

Dipole moment (μ) the measure of net molecular polarity; $\mu = Q \times r$ (*Section 10.1*)

Diprotic acid an acid that has two dissociable protons (*Section 4.5*)

Disproportionation reaction a reaction in which a substance is both oxidized and reduced (*Section 18.10*)

Dissociate splitting apart to give ions when dissolved in water (*Section 4.2*)

Donor atom the atom attached directly to a metal in a coordination compound (*Section 20.6*)

Doping the addition of a small amount of an impurity to increase the conductivity of a semiconductor (*Section 21.5*)

Double bond a covalent bond formed by sharing four electrons between atoms (*Section 7.5*)

Effective nuclear charge (Z_{eff}) the net nuclear charge actually felt by an electron (*Sections 5.10, 5.14*)

Effusion the escape of gas molecules through a tiny hole in a membrane without molecular collisions (*Section 9.7*)

Electrochemical cell a device for interconverting chemical and electrical energy (*Section 17.1*)

Electrochemistry the area of chemistry concerned with the interconversion of chemical and electrical energy (*Chapter 17*)

Electrode a conductor through which electrical current enters or leaves a cell (*Section 17.1*)

Electrolysis the process of using an electric current to bring about chemical change (*Section 17.12*)

Electrolyte a substance that dissolves in water to produce ions (*Section 4.2*)

Electrolytic cell an electrochemical cell in which an electric current drives a nonspontaneous reaction (*Section 17.12*)

Electromagnetic radiation radiant energy (*Section 5.1*)

Electromagnetic spectrum the range of different kinds of electromagnetic radiation (*Section 5.1*)

Electromotive force (emf) the electrical potential that pushes electrons away from the anode and pulls them toward the cathode (*Section 17.3*)

Electron a negatively charged, fundamental atomic particle (*Section 2.3*)

Electron affinity (E_{ea}) the energy change that occurs when an electron is added to an isolated atom in the gaseous state (*Section 6.5*)

Electron capture a nuclear reaction in which a proton in the nucleus captures an inner-shell electron and is thereby converted into a neutron (*Section 2.8*)

Electron configuration a description of which orbitals in an atom are occupied by electrons (*Section 5.11*)

Electron-dot structure a representation of a molecule that shows valence electrons as dots; also called a Lewis structure (*Section 7.5*)

Electron-sea model a model that visualizes metals as a three-dimensional array of metal cations immersed in a sea of delocalized electrons that are free to move about (*Section 21.4*)

Electronegativity (EN) the ability of an atom in a molecule to attract the shared electrons in a covalent bond (*Section 7.4*)

Electroplating the coating of one metal on the surface of another using electrolysis (*Section 17.13*)

Electrorefining the purification of a metal by means of electrolysis (*Section 17.13*)

Element a fundamental substance that can't be chemically changed or broken down into anything simpler (*Section 1.2*)

Elemental analysis a technique for determining the identities and amounts of elements in a compound (*Section 3.11*)

Elementary reaction a single chemical step in a reaction mechanism (*Section 12.9*)

Elementary step *see* Elementary reaction (*Section 12.9*)

Empirical formula a formula that gives the ratios of atoms in a chemical compound but not necessarily the exact values (*Section 3.10*)

Enantiomers stereoisomers that are non-identical mirror images of each other (*Section 20.9*)

End point the point in a titration at which stoichiometrically equivalent quantities of reactants have been mixed together (*Sections 4.10, 15.5*)

Endothermic a reaction in which heat is absorbed and the temperature of the surroundings falls (*Section 8.6*)

Energy the capacity to do work or supply heat (*Sections 1.11, 8.1*)

Enthalpy (H) the quantity $E + PV$ (*Section 8.4*)

Enthalpy change (ΔH) the heat change in a reaction or process at constant pressure; $\Delta H = \Delta E + P\Delta V$ (*Section 8.4*)

Entropy (S) the amount of molecular randomness in a system (*Sections 8.12, 16.3*)

Entropy of solution (ΔS_{soln}) the entropy change during formation of a solution (*Section 11.2*)

Enzyme a large protein that acts as a catalyst for a biological reaction (*Chapter 12 Inquiry*)

Equilibrium constant (K_c) the constant in the equilibrium equation (*Section 13.2*)

Equilibrium constant (K_p) the equilibrium constant for reaction of gases, defined using partial pressures (*Section 13.3*)

Equilibrium equation an equation that relates the concentrations in an equilibrium mixture (*Section 13.2*)

Equilibrium mixture a mixture of reactants and products at equilibrium (*Section 13.1*)

Equivalence point the point in a titration at which stoichiometrically equivalent quantities of reactants have been mixed together (*Section 15.5*)

Ester an organic molecule that contains the —CO_2R group (*Section 23.8*)

Ether an organic molecule that contains two alkyl groups bonded to the same oxygen atom (*Section 23.7*)

Exothermic a reaction in which heat is evolved and the temperature of the surroundings rises (*Section 8.6*)

Extensive property a property whose value depends on the sample size (*Section 1.4*)

f-Block element a lanthanide or actinide element, in which f orbitals are filled (*Section 5.13*)

Face-centered cubic unit cell a cubic unit cell with an atom at each of its eight corners and an additional atom on each of its six faces (*Section 10.8*)

Faraday the electrical charge on 1 mol of electrons (96,485 C/mol e$^-$) (*Section 17.3*)

Fatty acid a long-chain carboxylic acid found as a constituent of fats and oils (*Section 23.12*)

First law of thermodynamics The total internal energy of an isolated system is constant (*Sections 8.1, 8.2*).

First-order reaction a reaction whose rate depends on the concentration of a single reactant raised to the first power (*Section 12.4*)

Flotation a metallurgical process that exploits differences in the ability of water and oil to wet the surfaces of mineral and gangue (*Section 21.2*)

Formal charge an electron bookkeeping device that tells whether an atom in a molecule has gained or lost electrons compared to an isolated atom (*Section 7.8*)

Formation constant (K_f) the equilibrium constant for formation of a complex ion (*Section 15.12*)

Formula mass the sum of atomic masses of all atoms in one formula unit of a substance (*Section 3.3*)

Formula unit one unit (atom, ion, or molecule) corresponding to a given formula (*Section 3.1*)

Fractional distillation the separation of volatile liquids on the basis of boiling point (*Section 11.10*)

Free-energy change (ΔG) $\Delta G = \Delta H - T\Delta S$ (*Sections 8.13, 16.7*)

Freezing the change of a liquid to a solid (*Section 10.4*)

Frequency (ν) the number of wave maxima that pass by a fixed point per unit time (*Section 5.1*)

Frequency factor the parameter A ($= pZ$) in the Arrhenius equation (*Section 12.12*)

Fuel cell a galvanic cell in which one of the reactants is a traditional fuel such as methane or hydrogen (*Section 17.10*)

Functional group a part of a larger molecule; composed of an atom or group of atoms that has characteristic chemical behavior (*Section 23.2*)

Fusion melting, or the change of a solid to a liquid (*Section 10.4*); also, the joining together of two nuclei in a nuclear reaction, accompanied by release of an enormous amount of energy (*Section 22.2*)

Galvanic cell an electrochemical cell in which a spontaneous chemical reaction generates an electric current (*Section 17.1*)

Galvanizing a process for protecting steel from corrosion by coating it with zinc (*Section 17.11*)

Gamma (γ) radiation a type of radioactive emission consisting of a stream of high-energy photons (*Section 2.8*)

Gangue the economically worthless material consisting of sand, clay, and other impurities that accompanies an ore (*Section 21.2*)

Gas constant (R) the constant in the ideal gas law $PV = nRT$ (*Section 9.3*)

Gas laws relationships among the variables P, V, n, and T for a gas sample (*Section 9.2*)

Gene a segment of a DNA chain that contains the instructions necessary to make a specific protein (*Section 23.13*)

Geometric isomers *see* Diastereoisomers (*Section 20.8*)

Gibbs free-energy change (ΔG) $\Delta G = \Delta H - T\Delta S$ (*Sections 8.13, 16.7*)

Graham's law The rate of effusion of a gas is inversely proportional to the square root of its molar mass (*Section 9.7*).

Gram (g) a common unit of mass; 1 g = 0.001 kg (*Section 1.6*)

Green chemistry a set of guidelines describing environmentally benign chemical reactions and practices (*Chapter 4 Inquiry*)

Ground-state electron configuration the lowest-energy electron configuration of an atom (*Section 5.11*)

Group a column of elements in the periodic table (*Section 1.3*)

Half-life ($t_{1/2}$) the time required for a reactant concentration to drop to one-half its initial value (*Section 12.5*)

Half-reaction the oxidation or reduction part of a redox reaction (*Sections 4.9, 17.1*)

Half-reaction method a method for balancing redox equations (*Section 4.9*)

Hall–Heroult process the commercial method for producing aluminum by electrolysis of a molten mixture of aluminum oxide and cryolite (*Section 17.13*)

Halogen an element in group 7A of the periodic table (*Sections 1.4, 6.11*)

Hard water water that contains appreciable concentrations of Ca^{2+}, Mg^{2+}, or Fe^{2+} cations (*Section 18.13*)

Heat the energy transferred from one object to another as the result of a temperature difference between them (*Section 8.1*)

Heat capacity (C) the amount of heat required to raise the temperature of an object or substance a given amount (*Section 8.7*)

Heat of combustion the amount of energy released on burning a substance (*Section 8.11*)

Heat of formation ($\Delta H°_f$) *see* Standard heat of formation (*Section 8.9*)

Heat of fusion (ΔH_{fusion}) the amount of heat required for melting a solid to a liquid (*Section 10.4*)

Heat of reaction (ΔH) the enthalpy change for a reaction (*Section 8.4*)

Heat of solution (ΔH_{soln}) the enthalpy change during formation of a solution (*Section 11.2*)

Heat of sublimation (ΔH_{subl}) the amount of heat required for sublimation of a solid to a gas (*Section 8.6*)

Heat of vaporization (ΔH_{vap}) the amount of heat required for vaporization of a liquid to a gas (*Section 10.4*)

Heisenberg uncertainty principle The position and the velocity of an electron can never both be known beyond a certain level of precision (*Section 5.5*).

Henderson–Hasselbalch equation an equation relating the pH of a solution to the pK_a of the weak acid; pH = pK_a + log ([base]/[acid]) (*Section 15.4*)

Henry's law The solubility of a gas in a liquid at a given temperature is directly proportional to the partial pressure of the gas over the solution (*Section 11.4*).

Hertz (Hz) a unit of frequency; 1 Hz = 1 s^{-1} (*Section 5.1*)

Hess's law The overall enthalpy change for a reaction is equal to the sum of the enthalpy changes for the individual steps in the reaction (*Section 8.8*).

Heterogeneous catalyst a catalyst that exists in a different phase than the reactants (*Section 12.15*)

Heterogeneous equilibria equilibria in which reactants and products are present in more than one phase (*Section 13.4*)

Hexadentate ligand a ligand with six donor atoms that bonds to a metal (*Section 20.6*)

Hexagonal closest-packed a packing arrangement of spheres into a noncubic unit cell with two alternating layers (*Section 10.8*)

High-spin complex a metal complex in which the *d* electrons are arranged to give the maximum number of unpaired electrons (*Section 20.11*)

Homogeneous catalyst a catalyst that exists in the same phase as the reactants (*Section 12.15*)

Homogeneous equilibria equilibria in which all reactants and products are in a single phase, usually either gaseous or solution (*Section 13.4*)

Hund's rule If two or more degenerate orbitals are available, one electron goes in each until all are half full (*Section 5.11*).

Hybrid atomic orbital a wave function derived by combination of atomic wave functions (*Section 7.11*)

Hydrate a solid compound that contains water molecules (*Section 18.14*)

Hydration the addition of water to an alkene (*Section 23.4*)

Hydrocarbon a compound that contains only carbon and hydrogen (*Section 23.1*)

Hydrogen bond an attractive intermolecular force between a hydrogen atom bonded to an electronegative O, N, or F atom and an unshared electron pair on a nearby electronegative atom (*Section 10.2*)

Hydrogenation the addition of H_2 to an alkene to yield an alkane (*Section 23.4*)

Hydronium ion the protonated water molecule, H_3O^+ (*Sections 4.5, 14.3*)

Hygroscopic absorbing water from the air (*Section 18.14*)

Ideal gas a gas whose behavior exactly follows the ideal gas law (*Section 9.2*)

Ideal gas law a description of how the volume of a gas is affected by changes in pressure, temperature, and amount; $PV = nRT$ (*Section 9.3*)

Infrared radiation electromagnetic radiation with wavelengths in the range 750 nm to 0.1 mm (*Section 5.1*)

Initial rate the instantaneous rate at the beginning of a reaction (*Section 12.1*)

Inner transition metal element an element in the 14 groups shown separately at the bottom of the periodic table (*Section 1.3*)

Instantaneous rate the rate of a reaction at a particular time (*Section 12.1*)

Integrated rate law the integrated form of a rate law (*Section 12.4*)

Intensive property a property whose value does not depend on the sample size (*Section 1.4*)

Intermolecular force an attractive interaction between molecules (*Section 10.2*)

Internal energy (*E*) the sum of kinetic and potential energies for each particle in a system (*Section 8.2*)

International System of Units (SI) the seven base units, along with others derived from them, used for all scientific measurements (*Section 1.5*)

Interstitial hydride a metallic hydride that consists of a crystal lattice of metal atoms with the smaller hydrogen atoms occupying holes between the larger metal atoms (*Section 18.5*)

Ion a charged atom or group of atoms (*Section 2.11*)

Ion–dipole force an intermolecular force resulting from electrical interactions between an ion and the partial charges on a polar molecule (*Section 10.2*)

Ion exchange a process for softening hard water in which the Ca^{2+} and Mg^{2+} ions are replaced by Na^+ (*Section 18.13*)

Ion product (IP) a number defined in the same way as K_{sp}, except that the concentrations in the expression for IP are not necessarily equilibrium values (*Section 15.13*)

Ion-product constant for water (K_w) $[H_3O^+][OH^-] = 1.0 \times 10^{-14}$ (*Section 14.4*)

Ionic bond a bond that results from a transfer of one or more electrons between atoms (*Sections 2.11, 6.7*)

Ionic equation a chemical equation written so that ions are explicitly shown (*Section 4.3*)

Ionic hydride a saltlike, high-melting, white, crystalline compound formed by the alkali metals and the heavier alkaline earth metals (*Section 18.5*)

Ionic liquid a liquid whose constituent particles are ions rather than molecules (*Chapter 10 Inquiry*)

Ionic solid a solid whose constituent particles are ions ordered into a regular three–dimensional arrangement held together by ionic bonds (*Sections 2.11, 6.7*)

Ionization energy (E_i) the amount of energy necessary to remove the outermost electron from an isolated neutral atom in the gaseous state (*Section 6.3*)

Ionization isomers isomers that differ in the anion bonded to the metal ion (*Section 20.8*)

Isomers compounds that have the same formula but a different bonding arrangement of their constituent atoms (*Section 20.8*)

Isotope effect differences in properties that arise from differences in isotopic mass (*Section 18.2*)

Isotopes atoms with identical atomic numbers but different mass numbers (*Section 2.5*)

Joule (J) the SI unit of energy, equal to 1 $(kg \cdot m^2)/s^2$ (*Section 1.11*)

K_a acid-dissociation constant; the equilibrium constant for dissociation of an acid in water (*Section 14.8*)

K_b base-dissociation constant; the equilibrium constant for the reaction of a base with water (*Section 14.12*)

K_b molal boiling-point-elevation constant; the amount by which the boiling point of a solvent is raised by dissolved substances (*Section 11.7*)

K_c equilibrium constant; the constant in the equilibrium equation (*Section 13.2*)

K_f formation constant; the equilibrium constant for formation of a complex ion (*Section 15.12*)

K_f molal freezing-point-depression constant; the amount by which the melting point of a solvent is lowered by dissolved substances (*Section 11.7*)

K_p equilibrium constant; the equilibrium constant for reaction of gases, defined using partial pressures (*Section 13.3*)

K_{sp} solubility-product constant; the equilibrium constant for a dissolution reaction (*Section 15.10*)

K_{spa} solubility-product constant in acid; the equilibrium constant for a dissolution reaction in acid (*Section 15.14*)

K_w ion-product constant for water; $[H_3O^+][OH^-] = 1.0 \times 10^{-14}$ (*Section 14.4*)

Kelvin (K) the SI unit of temperature; $0\ K$ = absolute zero (*Section 1.8*)

Ketone an organic molecule that contains two alkyl groups bonded to a $C\!=\!O$ carbon (*Section 23.8*)

kilogram (kg) the SI unit of mass; $1\ kg = 2.205$ U.S. lb (*Section 1.6*)

Kinetic energy (E_K) the energy of motion; $E_K = (1/2)mv^2$ (*Section 1.11*)

Kinetic–molecular theory a theory describing the quantitative behavior of gases (*Section 9.6*)

Lanthanide one of the 14 inner transition metals starting with lanthanum in the periodic table (*Section 1.3*)

Lanthanide contraction the decrease in atomic radii across the *f*-block lanthanide elements (*Section 20.2*)

Lattice energy (*U*) the sum of the electrostatic interactions between ions in a solid that must be overcome to break a crystal into individual ions (*Section 6.8*)

Law of conservation of energy Energy can be neither created nor destroyed (*Section 8.1*).

Law of definite proportions Different samples of a pure chemical substance always contain the same proportion of elements by mass (*Section 2.1*).

Law of mass conservation Mass is neither created nor destroyed in chemical reactions (*Section 2.1*).

Law of multiple proportions When two elements combine in different ways to form different substances, the mass ratios are small, whole-number multiples of one another (*Section 2.2*).

LD$_{50}$ the amount of a substance that is lethal to 50% of test animals (*Chapter 1 Inquiry*)

Le Châtelier's principle If a stress is applied to a reaction mixture at equilibrium, reaction occurs in the direction that relieves the stress (*Section 13.6*).

Lewis acid an electron-pair acceptor (*Section 14.16*)

Lewis base an electron-pair donor (*Section 14.16*)

Lewis structure an electron-dot structure, or representation of a molecule that shows valence electrons as dots (*Section 7.5*)

Ligand a molecule or ion that bonds to the central metal ion in a complex (*Sections 20.5, 20.6*)

Ligand donor atom an atom attached directly to the metal ion in a metal complex (*Section 20.5*)

Light-emitting diode (LED) a semiconductor device that converts electrical energy into light (*Section 21.6*)

Limiting reactant the reactant present in limiting amount that controls the extent to which a reaction occurs (*Section 3.5*)

Line spectrum the wavelengths of light emitted by an energetically excited atom (*Section 5.2*)

Linkage isomers isomers that arise when a ligand bonds to a metal through either of two different donor atoms (*Section 20.8*)

Lipid a naturally occurring organic molecule that dissolves in nonpolar organic solvents when a sample of plant or animal tissue is crushed or ground (*Section 23.12*)

Liter (L) a common unit of volume; $1\ L = 10^{-3}\ m^3$ (*Section 1.9*)

Lock-and-key model a model that pictures an enzyme as a large, irregularly shaped molecule with a cleft into which substrate can fit (*Chapter 12 Inquiry*)

London dispersion force an intermolecular force resulting from the presence of temporary dipoles in atoms or molecules (*Section 10.2*)

Lone pair electrons a pair of valence electrons not used for bonding (*Section 7.5*)

Low-spin complex a metal complex in which the *d* electrons are paired up to give a maximum number of doubly occupied *d* orbitals and a minimum number of unpaired electrons (*Section 20.11*)

Magnetic quantum number (m_l) a variable in the solutions to the Schrödinger wave equation that defines the spatial orientation of an orbital (*Section 5.6*)

Main-group element an element in the two groups on the left and the six groups on the right of the periodic table (*Section 1.3; Chapters 6, 19*)

Manometer a simple instrument for measuring gas pressure; similar in principle to the mercury barometer (*Section 9.1*)

Mass the amount of matter in an object (*Section 1.6*)

Mass defect the loss in mass that occurs when protons and neutrons combine to form a nucleus (*Section 22.1*)

Mass number (*A*) the total number of protons and neutrons in an atom (*Section 2.5*)

Mass percent a unit of concentration; the mass of one component divided by the total mass of the solution times 100% (*Section 11.3*)

Mass spectrometry a technique for determining molecular mass by passing ionized molecules through a magnetic field (*Section 3.12*)

Matter a term used to describe anything that has mass (*Section 1.6*)

Melting point the temperature at which solid and liquid coexist in equilibrium (*Section 10.4*)

Mesosphere the region of the atmosphere from 50–85 km above the Earth's surface (*Section 9.9*)

Metabolism the sum of the many organic reactions that go on in cells (*Section 23.9*)

Metal complex *see* Coordination compound (*Section 20.5*)

Metal an element on the left side of the periodic table, bounded on the right by a zigzag line running from boron to astatine (*Section 1.4; Chapter 21*)

Metallic hydride a compound formed by reaction of lanthanide, actinide, or some *d*-block transition metals with variable amounts of hydrogen (*Section 18.5*)

Metallic solid a solid consisting of metal atoms, whose crystals have metallic properties such as electrical conductivity (*Section 10.6*)

Metalloid *see* Semimetal (*Section 1.4*)

Metallurgy the science and technology of extracting metals from their ores (*Section 21.2*)

Meter (m) the SI unit of length (*Section 1.7*)

Microgram (μg) a common unit of mass; $1\ \mu g = 0.001\ mg = 10^{-6}\ g$ (*Section 1.6*)

Micrometer (μm) a common unit of length; $1\ \mu m = 0.001\ mm = 10^{-6}\ m$ (*Section 1.7*)

Milligram (mg) a common unit of mass; $1\ mg = 0.001\ g = 10^{-6}\ kg$ (*Section 1.6*)

Milliliter (mL) a common unit of volume; $1\ mL = 1\ cm^3$ (*Section 1.9*)

Millimeter (mm) a common unit of length; 1 mm = 0.001 m (*Section 1.7*)

Millimeter of mercury (mm Hg) a common unit of pressure; the millimeter of mercury, also called a *torr*, is based on atmospheric pressure measurements using a mercury barometer (*Section 9.1*)

Mineral a crystalline, inorganic constituent of the rocks that make up the Earth's crust (*Section 21.1*)

Miscible mutually soluble in all proportions (*Section 11.4*)

Mixture a blend of two or more substances in some arbitrary proportion (*Section 2.10*)

Molal boiling-point-elevation constant (K_b) the amount by which the boiling point of a solvent is raised by dissolved substances (*Section 11.7*)

Molal freezing-point-depression constant (K_f) the amount by which the melting point of a solvent is lowered by dissolved substances (*Section 11.7*)

Molality (m) a unit of concentration; the number of moles of solute per kilogram of solvent (mol/kg) (*Section 11.3*)

Molar heat capacity (C_m) the amount of heat necessary to raise the temperature of 1 mol of a substance 1 °C (*Section 8.7*)

Molar mass the mass of 1 mol of substance; equal to the molecular or formula mass of the substance in grams (*Section 2.6*)

Molarity (M) a common unit of concentration; the number of moles of solute per liter of solution (*Sections 3.6, 11.3*)

Mole (mol) the SI unit for amount of substance; the quantity of a substance that contains as many molecules or formula units as there are atoms in exactly 12 g of carbon-12 (*Section 2.6*)

Mole fraction (X) a unit of concentration; the number of moles of a component divided by the total number of moles in the mixture (*Sections 9.5, 11.3*)

Molecular equation a chemical equation written using the complete formulas of reactants and products (*Section 4.3*)

Molecular formula a formula that tells the identity and numbers of atoms in a molecule (*Section 3.10*)

Molecular mass the sum of atomic masses of the atoms in a molecule (*Section 3.3*)

Molecular orbital theory a quantum mechanical description of bonding in which electrons occupy molecular orbitals that belong to the entire molecule rather than to an individual atom (*Section 7.13*)

Molecular solid a solid whose constituent particles are molecules held together by intermolecular forces (*Section 10.6*)

Molecularity the number of molecules on the reactant side of the chemical equation for an elementary reaction (*Section 12.9*)

Molecule the unit of matter that results when two or more atoms are joined by covalent bonds (*Section 2.10*)

Mond process a chemical method for purification of nickel from its ore (*Section 21.2*)

Monodentate ligand a ligand that bonds to a metal using the electron pair of a single donor atom (*Section 20.6*)

Monoprotic acid an acid that has a single dissociable proton (*Section 4.5*)

Monosaccharide a carbohydrate such as glucose that can't be broken down into smaller molecules by hydrolysis (*Section 23.11*)

N-Terminal amino acid the amino acid with a free —NH_2 group on the end of a protein chain (*Section 23.10*)

n-Type semiconductor a semiconductor doped with an impurity that has more electrons than necessary for bonding (*Section 21.5*)

Nanometer (nm) a common unit of length; 1 nm = 10^{-9} m (*Section 1.7*)

Nanotechnology the study and production of materials and structures that have at least one dimension between 1 nm and 100 nm (*Chapter 21 Inquiry*)

Nernst equation an equation for calculating cell potentials under non-standard-state conditions; $E = E° - (RT \ln Q)/(nF)$ (*Section 17.6*)

Net ionic equation a chemical equation written so that spectator ions are removed (*Section 4.3*)

Neutralization reaction *see* Acid–base neutralization reaction (*Sections 4.5, 15.1*)

Neutron a neutral, fundamental atomic particle in the nucleus of atoms (*Section 2.4*)

Newton (N) the SI unit for force (*Section 9.1*)

Noble gas an element in group 8A of the periodic table (*Sections 1.4, 6.12*)

Node a region where a wave has zero amplitude (*Section 5.7*)

Nonelectrolyte a substance that does not produce ions when dissolved in water (*Section 4.2*)

Nonmetal hydrogen plus elements on the right side of the periodic table, bounded on the left by a zigzag line running from boron to astatine (*Section 1.4*)

Nonspontaneous process a process that requires a continuous input of energy to proceed (*Section 8.13*)

Nonstoichiometric compound a compound whose atomic composition can't be expressed as a ratio of small whole numbers (*Section 18.5*)

Normal boiling point the temperature at which boiling occurs when there is exactly 1 atm of external pressure (*Sections 10.5, 10.11*)

Normal melting point the temperature at which melting occurs when there is exactly 1 atm of external pressure (*Section 10.11*)

Nuclear chemistry the study of the properties and reactions of atomic nuclei (*Section 2.7*)

Nuclear equation an equation for a nuclear reaction in which the sums of the nucleons are the same on both sides and the sums of the charges on the nuclei and any elementary particles are the same on both sides (*Section 2.7*)

Nuclear fission the fragmenting of heavy nuclei (*Section 22.2*)

Nuclear fusion the joining together of light nuclei (*Section 22.2*)

Nuclear reaction a reaction that changes an atomic nucleus (*Section 2.7*)

Nuclear transmutation the change of one element into another by a nuclear reaction (*Section 22.3*)

Nucleic acid a biological molecule made up of nucleotide units linked together to form a long chain (*Section 23.13*)

Nucleon a general term for nuclear particles, both protons and neutrons (*Section 2.8*)

Nucleoside a constituent of nucleotides; composed of an aldopentose sugar plus an amine base (*Section 23.13*)

Nucleotide a building block from which nucleic acids are made; composed of a nucleoside plus phosphoric acid (*Section 23.13*)

Nucleus the central core of an atom consisting of protons and neutrons (*Section 2.4*)

Octet rule the statement that main-group elements tend to undergo reactions that leave them with eight valence electrons (*Section 6.6*)

Orbital a solution to the Schrödinger wave equation, describing a region of space where an electron is likely to be found (*Section 5.6*)

Ore a mineral deposit from which a metal can be produced economically (*Section 21.1*)

Organic chemistry the study of carbon compounds (*Chapter 23*)

Osmosis the passage of solvent through a membrane from the less concentrated side to the more concentrated side (*Section 11.8*)

Osmotic pressure the amount of pressure necessary to cause osmosis to stop (*Section 11.8*)

Ostwald process the commercial process for making nitric acid from ammonia (*Section 19.10*)

Overvoltage the additional voltage required above that calculated for an electrolysis reaction (*Section 17.12*)

Oxidation the loss of one or more electrons by a substance (*Section 4.6*)

Oxidation number a value that measures whether an atom in a compound is neutral, electron-rich, or electron-poor compared to an isolated atom (*Section 4.6*)

Oxidation–reduction (redox) reaction a process in which one or more electrons are transferred between reaction partners (*Section 4.6*)

Oxide a binary compound with oxygen in the −2 oxidation state (*Section 18.9*)

Oxidizing agent a substance that causes an oxidation by accepting an electron (*Section 4.7*)

Oxoacid an acid that contains oxygen in addition to hydrogen and another element (*Section 4.5*)

Oxoanion an anion of an oxoacid (*Section 2.12*)

Ozone layer an atmospheric band stretching from about 20 to 40 km above the Earth's surface (*Section 9.9*)

p-Block element an element in groups 3A–8A, in which p orbitals are filled (*Section 5.13*)

p-Type semiconductor a semiconductor doped with an impurity that has fewer electrons than necessary for bonding (*Section 21.5*)

Paramagnetic a substance that contains unpaired electrons and is attracted by a magnetic field (*Section 7.14*)

Parts per billion (ppb) a concentration unit for very dilute solutions; a concentration of 1 ppb means that each kilogram of solution contains 1 μg of solute (*Section 11.3*)

Parts per million (ppm) a concentration unit for very dilute solutions; a concentration of 1 ppm means that each kilogram of solution contains 1 mg of solute (*Section 11.3*)

Pascal (Pa) the SI unit for pressure (*Section 9.1*)

Pauli exclusion principle No two electrons in an atom can have the same four quantum numbers (*Section 5.9*).

Peptide bond the amide bond linking two amino acids in a protein (*Section 23.10*)

Percent composition a list of elements present in a compound and the mass percent of each (*Section 3.10*)

Percent dissociation the concentration of the acid that dissociates divided by the initial concentration of the acid times 100% (*Section 14.10*)

Percent yield the amount of product actually formed in a reaction divided by the amount theoretically possible and multiplied by 100% (*Section 3.4*)

Period a row of elements in the periodic table (*Section 1.3*)

Periodic table a chart of the elements arranged by increasing atomic number so that elements in a given group have similar chemical properties (*Section 1.3*)

Peroxide a binary compound with oxygen in the −1 oxidation state (*Section 18.10*)

Petroleum a complex mixture of organic substances, primarily hydrocarbons (*Section 8.11*)

pH the negative base-10 logarithm of the molar hydronium ion concentration (*Section 14.5*)

pH titration curve a plot of the pH of a solution as a function of the volume of added base or acid (*Section 15.5*)

Phase a state of matter (*Section 10.4*)

Phase change a process in which the physical form but not the chemical identity of a substance changes (*Section 10.4*)

Phase diagram a plot showing the effects of pressure and temperature on the physical state of a substance (*Section 10.11*)

Photoelectric effect the ejection of electrons from a metal on exposure to radiant energy (*Section 5.3*)

Photon the smallest possible amount of radiant energy; a quantum (*Section 5.3*)

Photovoltaic cell a semiconductor device that converts light into electrical energy (*Section 21.6*)

Physical property a characteristic that can be determined without changing the chemical makeup of a sample (*Section 1.4*)

Pi (π) bond a covalent bond formed by sideways overlap of orbitals in which shared electrons occupy a region above and below a line connecting the two nuclei (*Section 7.12*)

Picometer (pm) a common unit of length; 1 pm = 10^{-12} m (*Section 1.7*)

Planck's constant (h) 6.626×10^{-34} J · s; a fundamental physical constant that relates energy and frequency, $E = h\nu$ (*Section 5.3*)

Polar covalent bond a bond in which the bonding electrons are attracted somewhat more strongly by one atom than by the other (*Section 7.4*)

Polarizability the ease with which a molecule's electron cloud can be distorted by a nearby electric field (*Section 10.2*)

Polyatomic ion a charged, covalently bonded group of atoms (*Section 2.11*)

Polydentate ligand a ligand that bonds to a metal through electron pairs on more than one donor atom (*Section 20.6*)

Polyprotic acid an acid that contains more than one dissociable proton (*Section 14.11*)

Polysaccharide a compound such as cellulose that is made of many simple sugars linked together (*Section 23.11*)

Positron emission a nuclear reaction that converts a proton into a neutron plus an ejected positron (*Section 2.8*)

Potential energy (E_P) energy that is stored, either in an object because of its position or in a molecule because of its chemical composition (*Section 1.11*)

Precipitation reaction a reaction in which an insoluble solid precipitate forms and drops out of solution (*Section 4.4*)

Precision how well a number of independent measurements agree with one another (*Section 1.12*)

Primitive-cubic unit cell a cubic unit cell with an atom at each of its eight corners (*Section 10.8*)

Principal quantum number (n) a variable in the solutions to the Schrödinger wave equation on which the size and energy level of an orbital primarily depends (*Section 5.6*)

Principal reaction the proton-transfer reaction that proceeds farther to the right when calculating equilibrium concentrations in solutions of weak acids (*Section 14.9*)

Property any characteristic that can be used to describe or identify matter (*Section 1.4*)

Protein   a biological molecule made up of many amino acids linked together to form a long chain (*Section 23.10*)

Proton   a positively charged, fundamental atomic particle in the nucleus of atoms (*Section 2.4*)

Pseudohalide   an ion such as cyanide ion that behaves chemically like a halide ion (*Section 19.7*)

Qualitative analysis   a procedure for identifying the ions present in an unknown solution (*Section 15.15*)

Quantized   changing only in discrete amounts (*Section 5.3*)

Quantum   the smallest possible amount of radiant energy (*Section 5.3*)

Quantum mechanical model   a model of atomic structure that concentrates on an electron's wavelike properties (*Section 5.5*)

Quantum number   a variable in solutions to the Schrödinger wave equation that describes the energy level and position in space where an electron is most likely to be found (*Section 5.6*)

Racemic mixture   a 1:1 mixture of enantiomers (*Section 20.9*)

Radioactivity   the spontaneous emission of radiation accompanying a nuclear reaction (*Section 2.8*)

Radiocarbon dating   a technique for dating archaeological artifacts by measuring the amount of ^{14}C in the sample (*Section 22.5*)

Radioisotope   a radioactive isotope (*Section 2.8*)

Raoult's law   The vapor pressure of a solution containing a nonvolatile solute is equal to the vapor pressure of pure solvent times the mole fraction of the solvent (*Section 11.6*).

Rate constant   the proportionality constant in a rate law (*Section 12.2*)

Rate-determining step   the slowest step in a reaction mechanism (*Section 12.11*)

Rate law   an equation that tells how reaction rate depends on the concentration of each reactant (*Section 12.2*)

Reaction intermediate   a species that is formed in one step of a reaction mechanism and consumed in a subsequent step (*Section 12.9*)

Reaction mechanism   the sequence of molecular events that defines the pathway from reactants to products (*Section 12.9*)

Reaction order   the value of the exponents of concentration terms in the rate law (*Section 12.2*)

Reaction quotient (Q_c)   similar to the equilibrium constant K_c except that the concentrations in the equilibrium constant expression are not necessarily equilibrium values (*Section 13.5*)

Reaction rate   the increase in the concentration of a product per unit time or the decrease in the concentration of a reactant per unit time (*Section 12.1*)

Redox reaction   an oxidation–reduction reaction (*Section 4.6*)

Redox titration   a procedure for determining the concentration of a redox agent (*Section 4.10*)

Reducing agent   a substance that causes a reduction by donating an electron (*Section 4.7*)

Reduction   the gain of one or more electrons by a substance (*Section 4.6*)

Replication   the process by which identical copies of DNA are made (*Section 23.13*)

Resonance hybrid   an average of several valid electron-dot structures for a molecule (*Section 7.7*)

Respiration   the process of breathing and using oxygen for biological redox reactions (*Section 4.11*)

Reverse osmosis   the passage of solvent through a membrane from the more concentrated side to the less concentrated side (*Section 11.9*)

Ribonucleic acid (RNA)   a biological polymer of ribonucleotide units that serves to transcribe the genetic information in DNA and uses that information to direct the synthesis of proteins (*Section 23.13*)

Roasting   a metallurgical process that involves heating a mineral in air (*Section 21.2*)

Rounding off   deleting digits to keep only the correct number of significant figures in a calculation (*Section 1.13*)

s-Block element   an element in groups 1A or 2A, in which s orbitals are filled (*Section 5.13*)

Sacrificial anode   an easily oxidized metal that corrodes instead of a less reactive metal to which it is connected (*Section 17.11*)

Salt   an ionic compound formed in an acid–base neutralization reaction (*Section 4.1*)

Salt bridge   a tube that contains a gel permeated with a solution of an inert electrolyte connecting the two sides of an electrochemical cell (*Section 17.1*)

Saponification   the base-catalyzed hydrolysis of an ester to yield a carboxylic acid and an alcohol (*Section 23.8*)

Saturated hydrocarbon   a hydrocarbon that contains only single bonds (*Section 23.4*)

Saturated solution   a solution containing the maximum possible amount of dissolved solute at equilibrium (*Section 11.4*)

Schrödinger wave equation   an equation describing the behavior of an electron in an atom (*Section 5.6*)

Scientific notation   a system in which a large or small number is written as a number between 1 and 10 times a power of 10 (*Section 1.5*)

Second Law of thermodynamics   In any spontaneous process, the total entropy of a system and its surroundings always increases (*Section 16.6*).

Second-order reaction   a reaction whose rate depends on the concentration of a single reactant raised to the second power or on the concentrations of two different reactants, each raised to the first power (*Section 12.7*)

Semiconductor   a material that has an electrical conductivity intermediate between that of a metal and that of an insulator (*Section 21.5*)

Semimetal   an element adjacent to the zigzag boundary between metals and nonmetals (*Section 1.4*)

Semipermeable membrane   a membrane that allows passage of water or other small molecules but not the passage of large solute molecules or ions (*Section 11.8*)

Shell   a grouping of orbitals according to principal quantum number (*Section 5.6*)

Side chain   the group attached to the α carbon of an amino acid (*Section 23.10*)

Sigma (σ) bond   a covalent bond formed by head-on overlap of orbitals in which the shared electrons are centered about the axis between the two nuclei (*Section 7.10*)

Significant figures   the total number of digits in a measurement (*Section 1.12*)

Silicate   an ionic compound that contains silicon oxoanions along with cations, such as Na^+, K^+, Mg^{2+}, or Ca^{2+} (*Section 19.8*)

Simple cubic packing   a packing arrangement of spheres into a primitive-cubic unit cell (*Section 10.8*)

Single bond   a covalent bond formed by sharing two electrons between atoms (*Section 7.5*)

Sintering   a process in which the particles of a powder are "welded" together without completely melting (*Section 21.8*)

Slag a byproduct of iron production, consisting mainly of calcium silicate (*Section 21.3*)

Solubility the amount of a substance that dissolves in a given volume of solvent at a given temperature (*Sections 4.4, 11.4*)

Solubility product (K_{sp}) the equilibrium constant for a dissolution reaction (*Section 15.10*)

Solute the dissolved substance in a solution (*Section 11.1*)

Solution a homogeneous mixture containing particles the size of a typical ion or covalent molecule (*Section 11.1*)

Solvent the major component in a solution (*Section 11.1*)

Sol–gel method a method of preparing ceramics, involving synthesis of a metal oxide powder from a metal alkoxide (*Section 21.8*)

sp Hybrid orbital a hybrid orbital formed by combination of one atomic s orbital with one p orbital (*Section 7.12*)

sp^2 Hybrid orbital a hybrid orbital formed by combination of one s and two p atomic orbitals (*Section 7.12*)

sp^3 Hybrid orbital a hybrid orbital formed by combination of one s and three p atomic orbitals (*Section 7.11*)

sp^3d^2 Hybrid orbital a hybrid orbital formed by combination of one s, three p, and two d atomic orbitals (*Section 20.11*)

Specific heat the amount of heat necessary to raise the temperature of 1 gram of a substance 1 °C (*Section 8.7*)

Spectator ion an ion that appears on both sides of the reaction arrow (*Section 4.3*)

Spectrochemical series an ordered list of ligands in which crystal field splitting increases (*Section 20.12*)

Spin quantum number (m_s) a variable that describes the spin of an electron, either +1/2 or −1/2 (*Section 5.9*)

Spontaneous process one that proceeds on its own without any continuous external influence (*Section 8.13*)

Standard cell potential ($E°$) the cell potential when both reactants and products are in their standard states (*Section 17.3*)

Standard electrode potential *see* Standard reduction potential (*Section 17.4*)

Standard enthalpy of reaction ($\Delta H°$) enthalpy change under standard-state conditions (*Section 8.6*)

Standard entropy of reaction ($\Delta S°$) the entropy change for a chemical reaction under standard-state conditions (*Section 16.5*)

Standard free-energy change ($\Delta G°$) the free-energy change that occurs when reactants in their standard states are converted to products in their standard states (*Section 16.8*)

Standard free energy of formation ($\Delta G°_f$) the free-energy change for formation of 1 mol of a substance in its standard state from the most stable form of the constituent elements in their standard states (*Section 16.9*)

Standard heat of formation ($\Delta H°_f$) the enthalpy change $\Delta H°_f$ for the hypothetical formation of 1 mol of a substance in its standard state from the most stable forms of its constituent elements in their standard states (*Section 8.9*)

Standard hydrogen electrode (S.H.E.) a reference half-cell consisting of a platinum electrode in contact with H_2 gas and aqueous H^+ ions at standard-state conditions (*Section 17.4*)

Standard molar entropy ($S°$) the entropy of 1 mol of a pure substance at 1 atm pressure and a specified temperature, usually 25 °C (*Section 16.5*)

Standard molar volume the volume of 1 mol of a gas at 0 °C and 1 atm pressure; 22.414 L (*Section 9.2*)

Standard reduction potential the standard potential for a reduction half-cell (*Section 17.4*)

Standard temperature and pressure (STP) $T = 273.15$ K; $P = 1$ atm (*Section 9.3*)

State function a function or property whose value depends only on the present condition of the system, not on the path used to arrive at that condition (*Section 8.2*)

Steam–hydrocarbon re-forming process an important industrial method for producing hydrogen from methane (*Section 18.3*)

Stereoisomers isomers that have the same connections among atoms but have a different arrangement of the atoms in space (*Section 20.8*)

Steric factor the fraction of collisions with the proper orientation for converting reactants to products (*Section 12.12*)

Stoichiometry mole/mass relationships between reactants and products (*Section 3.3*)

Straight-chain alkane an alkane that has all its carbons connected in a row (*Section 23.1*)

Stratosphere the region of the atmosphere from 20–50 km above the Earth's surface (*Section 9.9*)

Strong acid an acid that dissociates completely in water to give H^+ ions and is a strong electrolyte (*Sections 4.5, 14.2*)

Strong base a base that dissociates or reacts completely with water to give OH^- ions and is a strong electrolyte (*Sections 4.5, 14.2*)

Strong electrolyte a compound that dissociates completely into ions when dissolved in water (*Section 4.2*)

Strong-field ligand a ligand that has a large crystal field splitting (*Section 20.12*)

Structural formula a representation that shows the specific connections between atoms in a molecule (*Section 2.10*)

Sublimation the direct conversion of a solid to a vapor without going through a liquid state (*Sections 8.6, 10.4*)

Subshell a grouping of orbitals by angular-momentum quantum number (*Section 5.6*)

Subsidiary reaction any proton-transfer process other than the principal one in an acid–base reaction (*Section 14.9*)

Substitution reaction an organic reaction in which one group substitutes for another, particularly on aromatic rings (*Section 23.6*)

Substrate the compound acted on by an enzyme (*Chapter 12 Inquiry*)

Superconducting transition temperature (T_c) the temperature below which a superconductor loses all electrical resistance (*Section 21.7*)

Superconductor a material that loses all electrical resistance below a certain temperature (*Section 21.7*)

Supercritical fluid a state of matter beyond the critical point that is neither liquid nor gas (*Section 10.11*)

Superoxide a binary compound with oxygen in the −1/2 oxidation state (*Section 18.10*)

Supersaturated solution a solution containing a greater-than-equilibrium amount of solute (*Section 11.4*)

Surface tension the resistance of a liquid to spreading out and increasing its surface area (*Section 10.3*)

Suspension a homogeneous mixture containing particles greater than about 1000 nm in diameter that are visible with a low-power microscope (*Section 11.1*)

Symmetry plane a plane that cuts through an object so that one half of the object is a mirror image of the other half (*Section 20.9*)

Temperature a measure of the kinetic energy of molecular motion (*Section 8.1*)

Termolecular reaction an elementary reaction that results from collisions between three reactant molecules (*Section 12.9*)

Theory a consistent explanation of known observations (*Section 1.1*)

Thermochemistry a study of the heat changes that take place during reactions (*Chapter 8*)

Thermodynamic standard state conditions under which thermodynamic measurements are reported; 298.15 K (25 °C), 1 atm pressure for each gas, 1 M concentration for solutions (*Section 8.5*)

Thermodynamics the study of the interconversion of heat and other forms of energy (*Chapter 16*)

Thermosphere the region of the atmosphere from 85–120 km above the Earth's surface (*Section 9.9*)

Third law of thermodynamics The entropy of a perfectly ordered crystalline substance at 0 K is zero (*Section 16.4*).

Three-center, two-electron bond a covalent bond in which three atoms share two electrons (*Section 19.4*)

Titration a procedure for determining the concentration of a solution (*Section 3.9*)

Torr an alternative name for the pressure unit, millimeter of mercury (*Section 9.1*)

Trans isomer the isomer of a metal complex or alkene in which identical ligands or groups are opposite one another rather than adjacent (*Sections 20.8, 23.4*)

Transcription the process by which information in DNA is transferred to and decoded by RNA (*Section 23.13*)

Transistor a semiconductor device that controls and amplifies electrical signals (*Section 21.6*)

Transition metal element an element in the 10 groups in the middle of the periodic table (*Section 1.3; Chapter 20*)

Transition state the configuration of atoms at the maximum in the potential energy profile for a reaction (*Section 12.12*)

Translation the process by which RNA builds proteins (*Section 23.13*)

Transuranium elements the 26 artificially produced elements beyond uranium in the periodic table (*Section 22.3*)

Triacylglycerol a triester of glycerol (1,2,3-propanetriol) with three long-chain carboxylic acids (*Section 23.12*)

Triple bond a covalent bond formed by sharing six electrons between atoms (*Section 7.5*)

Triple point a unique combination of pressure and temperature at which gas, liquid, and solid phases coexist in equilibrium (*Section 10.11*)

Triprotic acid an acid that can provide three H^+ ions (*Section 4.5*)

Troposphere the region of the atmosphere from 0–20 km above the Earth's surface (*Section 9.9*)

Turnover number the number of substrate molecules acted on by one molecule of enzyme per unit time (*Chapter 12 Inquiry*)

Ultraviolet radiation electromagnetic radiation with wavelengths in the range 10–400 nm (*Section 5.1*)

Unimolecular reaction an elementary reaction that involves a single reactant molecule (*Section 12.9*)

Unit cell a small repeating unit that makes up a crystal (*Section 10.8*)

Unsaturated an organic molecule that contains a double or triple bond (*Section 23.4*)

Valence band the bonding molecular orbitals in a semiconductor (*Section 21.5*)

Valence bond theory a quantum mechanical description of bonding that pictures covalent bond formation as the overlap of two singly occupied atomic orbitals (*Section 7.10*)

Valence shell the outermost electron shell (*Section 5.13*)

Valence-shell electron-pair repulsion (VSEPR) model a model for predicting the approximate shape of a molecule (*Section 7.9*)

van der Waals equation a modification of the ideal gas law that introduces correction factors to account for the behavior of real gases (*Section 9.8*)

van der Waals forces an alternative name for intermolecular forces (*Section 10.2*)

van't Hoff factor (*i*) a measure of the extent of dissociation of a substance, used in interpreting colligative property measurements (*Section 11.6*)

Vapor pressure (P_{vap}) the partial pressure of a gas in equilibrium with liquid (*Section 10.5*)

Vaporization the change of a liquid to a gas (*Section 10.4*)

Viscosity the measure of a liquid's resistance to flow (*Section 10.3*)

Visible light electromagnetic radiation with wavelengths in the range 400–780 nm (*Section 5.1*)

Voltaic cell *see* Galvanic cell (*Section 17.1*)

Volume the amount of space occupied by an object (*Section 1.9*)

Water-gas shift reaction a method for the industrial preparation of H_2 by reaction of CO with H_2O (*Section 18.3*)

Watson–Crick model a model of DNA structure, consisting of two polynucleotide strands coiled around each other in a double helix (*Section 23.13*)

Wave function a solution to the Schrödinger wave equation (*Section 5.6*)

Wavelength (λ) the length of a wave from one maximum to the next (*Section 5.1*)

Weak acid an acid that dissociates incompletely in water and is a weak electrolyte (*Sections 4.5, 14.2*)

Weak base a base that dissociates or reacts incompletely with water and is a weak electrolyte (*Sections 4.5, 14.2*)

Weak electrolyte a compound that dissociates incompletely when dissolved in water (*Section 4.2*)

Weak-field ligand a ligand that has a small crystal field splitting (*Section 20.12*)

Work (*w*) the distance (*d*) moved times the force (*F*) that opposes the motion (*Section 8.3*)

X ray electromagnetic radiation with wavelengths in the range 0.01–10 nm (*Section 5.1*)

X-ray crystallography a technique for determining molecular structure by analysis of the diffraction pattern produced when a crystal is struck by X rays (*Section 10.7*)

Yield the amount of product formed in a reaction (*Section 3.4*)

Zeroth-order reaction one whose rate remains constant, independent of reactant concentrations (*Section 12.8*)

Zone refining a purification technique in which a heater melts a narrow zone at the top of a rod of some material and then sweeps slowly down the rod bringing impurities with it (*Section 19.8*)

Index

Photo Credits

(T) = (top); (C) = (center); (L) = (left); (R) = (right); (B) = (bottom)

Chapter 1: 1, Austin Evan, used under a Creative Commons license. *http://www.flickr.com/photos/austinevan/3316195479/;* **1 (T),** US Department of Energy Joint Genome Institute; **1 (L),** Sylvain Grandadam/AGE Fotostock; **1 (R),** Holger Mette/iStockphoto; **2,** McCracken Photographer, Pearson Education; **4,** Sciencephotos/Alamy; **5 (L-R),** Richard Megna/Fundamental Photographs; **7,** McCracken Photographers, Pearson Education; **8 (L-R),** Richard Megna/Fundamental Photographs; **9 (TL),** McCracken Photographers, Pearson Education; **9 (TR),** REUTERS/China Newsphoto HAN/JJ; **9 (BL-BR),** Richard Megna/Fundamental Photographs; **11,** Tom Krueger/iStockphoto; **12 (L),** Mettler Toledo; **12 (R),** OHAUS Corporation.; **12 (B),** Dr. Tony Brain/Science Photo Library/Photo Researchers, Inc.; **14,** Richard Megna/Fundamental Photographs; **15 (L-R),** McCracken Photographers, Pearson Education; **16 (T),** Richard Megna/Fundamental Photographs; **16 (B),** Christian Wilkinson /Shutterstock; **17,** iStockphoto; **18,** Dex Images/Corbis; **19,** McCracken Photographers, Pearson Education; **21,** Texas Instruments Inc.; **22,** Andy Lyons / Getty Images; **23,** Susumu Nishinaga/Photo Researchers, Inc.; **24,** Jeff Richt/Koenigsegg; **26,** Cephalon Corp.

Chapter 2: 34, Armand Photo CGI/Alamy; **35,** Richard Megna/Fundamental Photographs; **36 (L-R),** Richard Megna/Fundamental Photographs; **37,** Richard Megna/Fundamental Photographs; **38 (T-B),** Richard Megna/Fundamental Photographs; **39 (L-R),** Richard Megna/Fundamental Photographs; **42,** James Montgomery/JAI/AGE Fotostock; **45,** Vladimir Chistyakov/AP Wide World Photos; **47,** Richard Megna/Fundamental Photographs; **51,** National Cancer Institute; **55 (T),** Tom Till/Alamy; **55 (B),** Bettmann/Corbis; **59 (T),** Richard Megna/Fundamental Photographs; **59 (B),** Eric Schrader, Pearson Science; **60,** Karel Gallas/Shutterstock; **62,** Richard Megna/Fundamental Photographs; **67 (T),** NASA/Marshall Space Flight Center; **67 (B),** NASA/Space Telescope Science Institute/ESA.

Chapter 3: 74, John Gillmoure/Corbis; **76,** Gregg Adams Photography; **77,** Corbis Royalty Free; **79,** AP Photo/Anja Niedringhaus; **82,** Sergio Piumatti; **88 (L-R),** Richard Megna/Fundamental Photographs; **90,** Paul Silverman/Fundamental Photographs; **91 (L-R),** Richard Megna/Fundamental Photographs; **92,** Paul Silverman/Fundamental Photographs; **93 (L-R),** Richard Megna/Fundamental Photographs; **102 (T),** Library of Congress; **102 (B),** Science Photo Library/Photo Researchers, Inc.

Chapter 4: 112, Bildagentur RM/Tips Italia/Photolibrary; **113,** McCracken Photographers, Pearson Education; **114 (L-R),** Richard Megna/Fundamental Photographs; **117,** Richard Megna/Fundamental Photographs; **118,** McCracken Photographers, Pearson Education; **121,** McCracken Photographers, Pearson Education; **124 (L),** McCracken Photographers, Pearson Education; **124 (C),** Richard Megna/Fundamental Photographs; **124 (R),** McCracken Photographers, Pearson Education; **127,** Picture Desk, Inc./Kobal Collection; **129 (L-R),** McCracken Photographers, Pearson Education; **131 (L-R),** Kip Peticolas & Richard Megna/Fundamental Photographs; **133 (L-R),** Richard Megna/Fundamental Photographs; **137 (L-R),** McCracken Photographers, Pearson Education; **138,** Paul Silverman/Fundamental Photographs; **139,** Jeff Gentner/Stringer/Getty Images; **141,** iStockphoto.

Chapter 5: 150, Pfeiffer; J/ARCO/AGE Fotostock; **152,** Phillip Long/Getty Images - Stone Allstock; **153,** Richard Cummins/Corbis; **154 (CL),** Pictor/ImageState Media Partners Limited; **154 (CR),** Karin Lau/Shutterstock; **154 (BL-BR),** Debra Crowe; **157,** Jens Johnson; **158,** iStockphoto; **161,** Alan Sailer/Flickr RM/Getty Images; **165,** Richard Megna/Fundamental Photographs; **179 (T),** Andre Thijssen/Photolibrary; **179 (B),** General Electric Corporate Research & Development Center.

Chapter 6: 186, Travel Ink/Getty Images; **203,** Richard Megna/Fundamental Photographs; **204 (L-R),** Richard Megna/Fundamental Photographs; **205 (L-R),** Richard Megna/Fundamental Photographs; **206,** Richard Megna/Fundamental Photographs; **207,** iStockphoto; **208,** Llinos Mair Pritchard/Alamy; **209,** AP Photo/Sakchai Lalit.

Chapter 7: 216, FA/COLOR CHINA PHOTO/SIPA Press; **219,** McCracken Photographers, Pearson Education; **253,** McCracken Photographers, Pearson Education; **256,** Jaimie D. Travis/iStockphoto; **257 (L),** iStockphoto; **257 (R),** pixelman/Shutterstock.

Chapter 8: 266, Frank Lane Picture Agency; **270,** iStockphoto; **270,** Dorian Hanner; **273,** mtr/Shutterstock; **276 (T),** Mikko Pitkanen/Shutterstock; **276 (C),** luchschen/Shutterstock; **276 (B),** Ezio Geneletti/Stone/Getty Images; **277,** Richard Megna/Fundamental Photographs; **280,** John McMurry; **281,** McCracken Photographers, Pearson Education; **285,** Fred Lyon/Fred Lyon Pictures; **287,** iStockphoto; **289,** Rob Belknap/iStockphoto; **290,** iStockphoto; **291,** World Pictures/Alamy; **292 (L),** Mikko Pitkanen/Shutterstock; **292 (C),** luchschen/Shutterstock; **292 (R),** Ezio Geneletti/Stone/Getty Images; **294 (L-R),** iStockphoto; **297,** iStockphoto.

Chapter 9: 308, Chuck Pelfley/Photolibrary; **309,** Shutterstock; **310,** NASA; **312,** Pichugin Dmitry/Shutterstock; **314,** Leapingllamas via Flickr, used under a Creative Commons license *http://creativecommons.org/licenses/by/2.0/deed.en;* **316,** iStockphoto; **320,** Paulo Resende/Shutterstock; **321,** Donald Johnston/Getty Images - Stone Allstock; **323,** Eric Schrader, Pearson Science; **325,** David D. Fleetman/SeaPics.com; **330,** U.S. Department of Energy/Photo Researchers, Inc.; **333 (T),** Niilo Tippler/iStockphoto; **333 (B),** Richard Megna/Fundamental Photographs; **334 (B),** NASA; **336,** Charlotte Zeepvat.

Chapter 10: 346, Jeff Foott/Discovery Channel Images/Getty Images; **351,** David Taylor/Science Photo Library/Photo Researchers, Inc.; **355,** Bronwyn Photo/Shutterstock; **357 (R),** Alexel Zaycev/iStockphoto; **357 (L),** Harry Taylor, © Dorling Kindersley, Natural History Museum, London; **359,** Alamy Images Royalty Free; **360,** AP Photo; **362,** Richard Megna/Fundamental Photographs; **364,** Richard Megna/Fundamental Photographs; **366 (L),** Jeffrey A. Scovil Photography; **366 (R),** Ryan McVay/Getty Images - Photodisc./Royalty Free; **368,** Pearson Education/PH College; **371,** Yenwen Lu/iStockphoto; **372,** iStockphoto; **378,** General Electric Corporate Research & Development Center; **380 (T),** Linda Whitwam, © Dorling Kindersley; **380 (B),** Richard Megna/Fundamental Photographs; **382,** Paul Silverman/Fundamental Photographs; **383,** BASF/Fundamental Photographs.

Chapter 11: 392, Kevin Schafer/Corbis; **393,** © Judith Miller/Dorling Kindersley/Lyon and Turnbull Ltd.; **394,** Frontpage/Shutterstock; **396 (L-R),** Richard Megna/Fundamental Photographs; **399,** Invisible/Shutterstock; **403 (L-R),** Charles D. Winters/Photo Researchers, Inc.; **405,** US Navy; **418 (L),** Janice Carr/Centers for Disease Control; **418 (R),** Custom Medical Stock Photography; **419,** Jaime Reina/Agence France Presse/Getty Images; **421,** GSPhotography /Shutterstock; **424,** AJPhoto/Photo Researchers, Inc.

Chapter 12: 432, Richard Carson/Reuters; **433 (L),** Richard Megna/Fundamental Photographs; **433 (R),** Tom Meyers/Photo Researchers, Inc.; **439 (L-R),** McCracken Photographers, Pearson Education; **443 (L-R),** McCracken Photographers, Pearson Education; **447,** Richard Megna/Fundamental Photographs; **449,** Library of Congress; **451,** Nagy Melinda/Shutterstock; **458,** iStockphoto; **461,** DPAphotos/NewsCom; **466,** McCracken Photographers, Pearson Education; **472,** Richard Megna/Fundamental Photographs; **473 (L-R),** McCracken Photographers, Pearson Education.

Chapter 13: 492, Stefan Wermuth/Reuters; **493 (T),** Richard Megna/Fundamental Photographs; **493 (C-B),** AP Photo; **495,** AP Photo/The Oklahoman, Michael Downes; **498,** Eric Schrader, Pearson Science; **502,** Dirk Wiersma/Photo Researchers, Inc.; **510,** Keith Dannemiller/Corbis; **515 (B),** Shutterstock; **515 (L-R),** Richard Megna/Fundamental Photographs; **519,** Charles D. Winters/Photo Researchers, Inc.; **520,** Renn Sminkey, Pearson Science; **524,** Supersonic Aerospace International; **526,** Jon Burbank/The Image Works; **532,** Richard Megna/Fundamental Photographs.

Chapter 14: 538, Stuart Pearce/AGE Fotostock; **550 (T),** Richard Megna/Fundamental Photographs; **550 (B),** Charles D. Winters/Photo Researchers; **553,** Richard Megna/Fundamental Photographs; **559,** Paul Sakuma/AP Photo; **561,** NASA; **562,** Eric Schrader, Pearson Science; **566,** Richard Megna/Fundamental Photographs; **574,** Richard Megna/Fundamental Photographs; **576 (T),** Ben Osborne/Getty Images - Stone Allstock; **576 (B),** Getty Images.

Chapter 15: 586, Vlad61/Shutterstock; **588,** Richard Megna/Fundamental Photographs; **589,** Richard Megna/Fundamental Photographs; **591,** Richard Megna/Fundamental Photographs; **597 (L-R),** Richard Megna/Fundamental

Photographs; **599,** Donald Clegg and Roxy Wilson, Pearson Education; **601,** Richard Megna/Fundamental Photographs; **611,** CMSP/NewsCom; **612,** Richard Megna/Fundamental Photographs; **614,** Richard Megna/Fundamental Photographs; **615,** Photo Researchers, Inc.; **618,** Michael J. Thompson/Shutterstock; **619 (L-R),** Richard Megna/Fundamental Photographs; **622 (L-R),** Richard Megna/Fundamental Photographs; **624,** Richard Megna/Fundamental Photographs; **625,** Richard Megna/Fundamental Photographs; **626,** Richard Megna/Fundamental Photographs; **627 (L-R),** Richard Megna/Fundamental Photographs; **628 (T),** Mediscan; **628 (C),** Mark Miller/Photo Researchers, Inc.

Chapter 16: 640, Gail Shumway/Photographer's Choice/Getty Images; **642,** iStockphoto; **643,** Tatiana Popova/Shutterstock; **646,** Paul Silverman/Fundamental Photographs; **654 (T),** James H. Karales/Photolibrary/Peter Arnold; **654 (B),** Taiga/Shutterstock; **667,** Richard Megna/Fundamental Photographs; **669,** NASA/NOAO/ESA/the Hubble SM4 ERO Team.

Chapter 17: 680, Drive Images/NewsCom; **682 (T-B),** Richard Megna/Fundamental Photographs; **683,** Richard Megna/Fundamental Photographs; **684,** Eric Schrader, Pearson Science; **703 (T),** Liz Strenk/SuperStock; **703 (B),** Tony Freeman/PhotoEdit; **704,** Photos.com; **707,** Porter Gifford; **708 (T),** Courtesy of Seven Cycles, www.sevencycles.com; **708 (B),** Tobias Helbig/iStockphoto; **715 (C),** Photos.com; **715 (T),** Axel Seidemann/AP Photo; **718 (T),** Radius Images/Alamy Images Royalty Free; **718 (B),** Chis DeRuggiero, Anodic Process Tech.; **722,** Eric Schrader, Pearson Science; **724,** Amy Walters/Shutterstock; **725,** iStockphoto.

Chapter 18: 728, Biophoto Associates/Photo Researchers, Inc.; **729,** National Optical Astronomy Observatory/Association of Universities for Research in Astronomy/National Science Foundation (NOAO/AURA/NSF); **731,** Charles Winters/Photo Researchers, Inc.; **733,** SuperStock; **734,** Richard Megna/Fundamental Photographs; **738,** Richard Megna/Fundamental Photographs; **739,** Shutterstock; **741 (L),** McCracken Photographers, Pearson Education; **741 (C),** Richard Megna/Fundamental Photographs; **741 (R),** McCracken Photographers, Pearson Education; **743,** Joanne Harris and Daniel Bubnich/Shutterstock; **745,** Richard Megna/Fundamental Photographs; **747 (TL-TR),** Richard Megna/Fundamental Photographs; **747 (BL-BR),** Richard Megna/Fundamental Photographs; **748,** Paul Silverman/Fundamental Photographs; **750,** Sheila Terry/Photo Researchers, Inc.; **751,** Richard Megna/Fundamental Photographs; **752,** Honda Media/American Honda Motor Co.

Chapter 19: 760, Richard Megna/Fundamental Photographs; **766,** Richard Megna/Fundamental Photographs; **767,** U.S. Borax Inc.; **769,** Richard Megna/Fundamental Photographs; **770 (C),** Russell Lappa/Photo Researchers, Inc.; **770 (R),** Charles D. Winters/Photo Researchers, Inc.; **770 (L),** Richard Megna/Fundamental Photographs; **771,** Michael J. Bronikowski, California Institute of Technology/Jet Propulsion Laboratory; **772,** Martyn F. Chillmaid/Photo Researchers, Inc.; **773,** Robert Semeniuk; **774,** Texas Instruments Inc.; **775 (T-B),** Jeffrey A. Scovil Photography; **776 (T),** Gontar/Shutterstock; **776 (B),** ephotocorp/Alamy Images Royalty Free; **776 (L),** Charles D. Winters/Photo Researchers, Inc.; **776 (R),** Charles D. Winters/Photo Researchers, Inc.; **778 (T),** Harry Taylor, © Dorling Kindersley; **778 (B),** Russ Lappa/Science Source/Photo Researchers, Inc.; **778 (R),** Paul Silverman/Fundamental Photographs; **781 (L),** Donald Clegg and Roxy

Wilson, Pearson Education; **781 (C),** Donald Clegg and Roxy Wilson, Pearson Education; **781 (R),** Richard Megna/Fundamental Photographs; **782,** Kristen Brochmann/Fundamental Photographs; **783,** Tom Bochsler, Pearson Education; **784 (L-R),** Richard Megna/Fundamental Photographs; **785,** Richard Megna/Fundamental Photographs; **786 (L),** Charles D. Winters/Photo Researchers, Inc.; **786 (R),** Russ Lappa/Photo Researchers, Inc.; **787 (T),** Jan Greune/Getty Images - Look; **787 (C),** Marvin Dembinsky Photo Associates/Alamy; **787 (B),** iStockphoto; **788 (L-R),** Richard Megna/Fundamental Photographs.

Chapter 20: 802, Chip Clark, Smithsonian Institute; **806,** iStockphoto; **810,** Richard Megna/Fundamental Photographs; **811,** Jason Seley (1919–1983), Herakles in Ithaka I, 1980-81. Sculpture, welded steel, 342.9 cm. Gift of the Artist, the Herbert F. Johnson Museum of Art, Cornell University. Photo by Robert Barker, Director, Cornell University Photography; **812,** Donald Clegg and Roxy Wilson, Pearson Education; **813 (L-R),** Richard Megna/Fundamental Photographs; **814 (L-R),** Richard Megna/Fundamental Photographs; **815 (B),** Allison Cornford-Matheson/iStockphoto; **815 (T),** Richard Megna/Fundamental Photographs; **816,** Paul Silverman/Fundamental Photographs; **822,** Richard Megna/Fundamental Photographs; **823,** Richard Megna/Fundamental Photographs; **825 (L-R),** Richard Megna/Fundamental Photographs; **832,** Richard Megna/Fundamental Photographs; **833 (T-B),** Richard Megna/Fundamental Photographs; **843,** Howard Ande/AGE Fotostock; **848,** Richard Megna/Fundamental Photographs; **849,** Richard Megna/Fundamental Photographs.

Chapter 21: 852, ImageChina/AP Photo; **853,** Philippe Psaila/SPL/Photo Researchers, Inc.; **854 (L),** Linda Burgess, © Dorling Kindersley; **854 (C-R),** Paul Silverman/Fundamental Photographs; **855,** Photos.com; **857 (T),** Erich Hartmann/Magnum Photos; **857 (B),** ThePropShoppe/iStockphoto; **859,** Courtesy Bethlehem Steel/AFP Photo/NewsCom; **860,** Peter Poulides/Getty Images - Stone Allstock; **870,** PhotoLink/Getty Images - Photodisc-Royalty Free; **871,** Intel Corporation; **872,** Chemical Design Ltd./SPL/Photo Researchers, Inc.; **873 (T),** Richard Megna/Fundamental Photographs; **873 (B),** AP Photo; **875,** Hua-Tay Lin/Oak Ridge National Laboratory; **876 (L-R),** Corning Incorporated; **878,** Northrop Grumman/Military Aircraft Systems Division; **879,** Photos.com; **879 (T),** Mathias Brust; **879 (B),** From S. Asokan, K.M. Krueger, A. Alkhawaldeh, A.R. Carreon, Z. Mu, V.L. Colvin, N.V. Mantzaris, and M.S. Wong, "The Use of Heat Transfer Fluids in the Synthesis of Highquality CdSe Quantum Dots, Core/Shell Quantum Dots, and Quantum Rods," Nanotechnology 16, 2000-2011 (2005). Subashini Asokan and Michael Wong/Rice University.; **880,** Raoul Kopelman.

Chapter 22: 888, David Howells/Corbis; **894,** Los Alamos National Laboratory; **896,** Shutterstock; **898,** Fermilab Visual Media Services; **899,** Thinkstock; **901,** C Gascoigne/Robert Harding World Imagery; **902 (T),** Peter Buckley, Pearson Education; **902 (B),** Keith Brofsky/Getty Images - PhotoDisc; **903 (T),** Martin Dohrn/Science Photo Library/Photo Researchers, Inc.; **903 (L),** Australian Nuclear Science and Technology Organisation; **903 (R),** Roger Tully/Getty Images - Stone Allstock; **904,** Nagra Corp.

Chapter 23: 908, Ron Koeberer /Getty Images - Aurora; **923,** Jill Chen/iStockphoto; **924,** Shutterstock; **927,** Grant Faith/Photographers Choice/Getty Images; **930,** Richard Weiss/Silver Burdett Ginn; **934,** George D. Lepp/Corbis; **936,** Shutterstock; **947,** Laura Clay-Ballard/iStockphoto.

Useful Conversion Factors and Relationships

Length
SI unit: meter (m)

$1 \text{ km} = 10^3 \text{ m} = 0.621\,37 \text{ mi}$

$1 \text{ mi} = 5280 \text{ ft} = 1760 \text{ yd} = 1.6093 \text{ km}$

$1 \text{ m} = 10^2 \text{ cm} = 1.0936 \text{ yd}$

$1 \text{ in.} = 2.54 \text{ cm (exactly)}$

$1 \text{ cm} = 0.393\,70 \text{ in.}$

$1 \text{ Å} = 10^{-10} \text{ m} = 100 \text{ pm}$

Mass
SI unit: kilogram (kg)

$1 \text{ kg} = 10^3 \text{ g} = 2.2046 \text{ lb}$

$1 \text{ lb} = 16 \text{ oz} = 453.59 \text{ g}$

$1 \text{ oz} = 28.35 \text{ g}$

$1 \text{ ton} = 2000 \text{ lb} = 907.185 \text{ kg}$

$1 \text{ metric ton} = 10^3 \text{ kg} = 1.102 \text{ tons}$

$1 \text{ amu} = 1.660\,54 \times 10^{-27} \text{ kg}$

Temperature
SI unit: kelvin (K)

$0 \text{ K} = -273.15 \text{ °C} = -459.67 \text{ °F}$

$\text{K} = \text{°C} + 273.15$

$\text{°C} = \dfrac{5}{9}(\text{°F} - 32)$

$\text{°F} = \dfrac{9}{5}(\text{°C}) + 32$

Energy (derived)
SI unit: joule (J)

$1 \text{ J} = 1 \text{ (kg} \cdot \text{m}^2)/\text{s}^2 = 0.239\,01 \text{ cal}$

$\quad = 1 \text{ C} \times 1 \text{ V}$

$1 \text{ cal} = 4.184 \text{ J (exactly)}$

$1 \text{ eV} = 1.602\,176 \times 10^{-19} \text{ J}$

$1 \text{ MeV} = 1.602\,176 \times 10^{-13} \text{ J}$

$1 \text{ kWh} = 3.600 \times 10^6 \text{ J}$

$1 \text{ Btu} = 1055 \text{ J}$

Pressure (derived)
SI unit: pascal (Pa)

$1 \text{ Pa} = 1 \text{ N/m}^2 = 1 \text{ kg}/(\text{m} \cdot \text{s}^2)$

$1 \text{ atm} = 101{,}325 \text{ Pa} = 1.013\,25 \text{ bar}$

$\quad = 760 \text{ mm Hg (torr)}$

$\quad = 14.70 \text{ lb/in.}^2$

$1 \text{ bar} = 10^5 \text{ Pa}$

Volume (derived)
SI unit: cubic meter (m³)

$1 \text{ L} = 10^{-3} \text{ m}^3 = 1 \text{ dm}^3 = 10^3 \text{ cm}^3$

$\quad = 1.0567 \text{ qt}$

$1 \text{ gal} = 4 \text{ qt} = 3.7854 \text{ L}$

$1 \text{ cm}^3 = 1 \text{ mL}$

$1 \text{ in.}^3 = 16.4 \text{ cm}^3$

Fundamental Constants

Atomic mass unit	1 amu	$= 1.660\,539 \times 10^{-27} \text{ kg}$
	1 g	$= 6.022\,142 \times 10^{23} \text{ amu}$
Avogadro's number	N_A	$= 6.022\,142 \times 10^{23}/\text{mol}$
Boltzmann's constant	k	$= 1.380\,650 \times 10^{-23} \text{ J/K}$
Electron charge	$-e$	$= -1.602\,176 \times 10^{-19} \text{ C}$
Electron charge-to-mass ratio	$-e/m_e$	$= -1.758\,820 \times 10^{11} \text{ C/kg}$
Electron mass	m_e	$= 5.485\,799 \times 10^{-4} \text{ amu}$
		$= 9.109\,382 \times 10^{-31} \text{ kg}$
Elementary charge	e	$= 1.602\,176 \times 10^{-19} \text{ C}$
Faraday's constant	F	$= 9.648\,534 \times 10^4 \text{ C/mol}$
Gas constant	R	$= 8.314\,472 \text{ J/(mol} \cdot \text{K)}$
		$= 0.082\,0582 \text{ (L} \cdot \text{atm)/(mol} \cdot \text{K)}$
Neutron mass	m_n	$= 1.008\,665 \text{ amu}$
		$= 1.674\,927 \times 10^{-27} \text{ kg}$
Pi	π	$= 3.141\,592\,6536$
Planck's constant	h	$= 6.626\,069 \times 10^{-34} \text{ J} \cdot \text{s}$
Proton mass	m_p	$= 1.007\,276 \text{ amu}$
		$= 1.672\,622 \times 10^{-27} \text{ kg}$
Rydberg constant	R_∞	$= 1.097\,373 \times 10^7/\text{m}$
Speed of light	c	$= 2.997\,924\,58 \times 10^8 \text{ m/s}$